PACIFIC
NORTHWEST
CAMPING

PACIFIC
NORTHWEST
CAMPING

SEVENTH EDITION

Tom Stienstra

FOGHORN ✺ OUTDOORS

PACIFIC NORTHWEST CAMPING
SEVENTH Edition

Printing History
1st edition—1988
7th edition—June 2000

5 4 3 2 1 0

Editors: Jean-Vi Lenthe, Carolyn Perkins
Design and Production: Carey Wilson
Cartography: Chris Alvarez, Mike Morgenfeld
Index: Sondra Nation

ISBN: 1-57354-080-3
ISSN: 1078-9588

Published by
Avalon Travel Publishing, Inc.
5855 Beaudry St.
Emeryville, CA 94608 USA

Printed in the United States of America

Please send all comments, corrections,
additions, amendments, and critiques to:

PACIFIC NORTHWEST CAMPING
Seventh Edition
Foghorn Outdoors
Avalon Travel Publishing
5855 Beaudry St.
Emeryville, CA 94608 USA
e-mail: info@travelmatters.com
website: www.travelmatters.com

TABLE OF CONTENTS

Special Topics

WASHINGTON CAMPGROUNDS

OREGON CAMPGROUNDS

MAPS

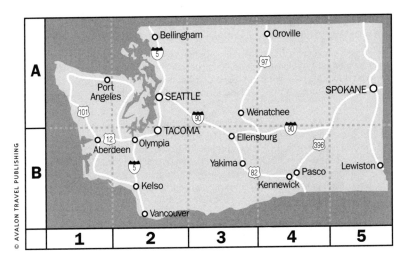

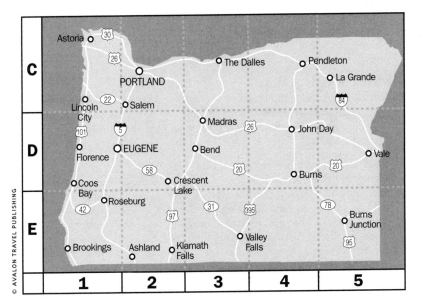

HOW TO USE THIS BOOK

Finding a Campground

You can search for your ideal campground in two ways:

1. If you know the name of the campground you'd like to visit or the nearest town or geographical feature (national or state forest, national or state park or recreation area, wildlife area, lake, river, mountain), look it up in the index beginning on page 809 to locate it and turn to the corresponding page.

2. If you'd like to stay in a particular part of Washington or Oregon and want to find out what campgrounds are available there, turn to the state maps on the previous page or in the back of this book. Find the area where you'd like to camp, such as A3 for North Cascades National Park, and turn to the corresponding chapter. Each chapter opens with a map that clearly numbers every campground in that area. Locate individual camping destinations on the map and then turn to those numbered sites in the chapter for detailed descriptions.

Washington, pages 101-435 (maps A1-B5)

Oregon, pages 436-808 (maps C1-E5)

About the Maps

The maps in this book are designed to show the general location of each campground. Readers are advised to purchase a detailed state map before heading out to any campground, particularly when venturing into remote areas.

What the Ratings Mean

Every campground in this book has been rated on a scale of 1-10. The ratings are based on the scenic beauty of the area only and do not reflect quality control issues such as the cleanliness of the campground or the temperament of the management.

What the Symbols Mean

Listings in this book feature activity symbols that represent the recreational offerings at or very near the campground. Other symbols identify whether there are sites for RVs or tents, or any wheelchair-accessible facilities. Wheelchair accessibility has been indicated when it is mentioned by campground managers, and concerned persons should call the contact number to ensure that their specific needs will be met.

Note to RV and Tent Campers

Those of you with recreational vehicles or tents will find *Pacific Northwest Camping* easy to use. Every camp listing that has RV and/or tent camping sites also has an easy-to-spot RV and/or tent camping symbol. Just flip the pages of the book and look for these symbols: 🚐 or 🏕️ . Occasionally you'll find a campground listing that mentions RV sites but doesn't feature the RV symbol. This occurs in listings in which the access routes may not be safe for RVs.

CREDITS

Senior Research Editor .... Stephani Cruickshank
Research Editor .... Janet Connaughton
Research Editor .... Marilyn Brown-Burnell
Research Editor .... Elizabeth Rodgers

ACKNOWLEDGMENTS

The following state and federal resource experts provided critical information regarding changes in reservations, fees, and recreational services:

Michael Dombeck, Chief, U.S. Forest Service

Linda Feldman and Dick Patterson, U.S. Forest Service
Headquarters, Washington, D.C.

Matt Mathes, U.S. Forest Service, Pacific Region Headquarters,
San Francisco, California

Kathy Burdett, National Park Service, Washington, D.C.

WASHINGTON
National Park Service
Michael Smithson, Olympic National Park

Joyce Brown, North Cascades National Park

Donna Rahier, Mt. Rainier National Park

U.S. Forest Service
Teresa Newton, Gifford Pinchot National Forest,
Mount St. Helens National Volcanic Monument

Pete Erben, Olympic National Forest, Quinalt Ranger District

Susan Graham, Olympic National Forest, Hood Canal Ranger District

Mike Ames, Wenatchee National Forest, Cle Elum Ranger District

Betty Cooney, Wenatchee National Forest, Naches Ranger District

Keith Cornell, Wenatchee National Forest, Leavenworth Ranger District

Margi Gromer, Wenatchee National Forest, Chelan Ranger District

Susan Peterson, Wenatchee National Forest, Lake Wenatchee Ranger District

April McConnaughy, Mt. Baker-Snoqualmie National Forest,
Darrington Ranger District

George McNicholl, Colville National Forest, Kettle Falls Ranger District

Nan Berger, Colville National Forest, Newport Ranger District

Doris Ensor, Colville National Forest, Colville Ranger District

Jack Thorne, Gifford Pinchot National Forest, Cowlitz Ranger District

Linda Turner, Gifford Pinchot National Forest, Mount Adams Ranger District

Eli Warren, Mt. Baker-Snoqualmie National Forest, Mt. Baker Ranger District

Pam Young, Mt. Baker-Snoqualmie National Forest, Skykomish Ranger District

Department of Natural Resources
David Becker, Southwest Region
Dick Dunton, Northeast Region
Jim Monroe, Southeast Region
Shirley Shuttle, South Puget Sound
Sarah Thirtyacre, Central Region

OREGON
U.S. Forest Service
Vicki Ramming, Deschutes National Forest, Bend-Fort Rock Ranger District
Marv Lang, Deschutes National Forest, Bend-Fort Rock Ranger District
Janet Kirsch and Teri Coy, Deschutes National Forest, Crescent Ranger District
Bob Henning, Deschutes National Forest, Sisters Ranger District
Catherine Callaghan, Fremont National Forest, Lakeview Ranger District
Shannon Winegar, Malheur National Forest, Long Creek and
   Bear Valley Ranger Districts
Carole Holly, Malheur National Forest, Prairie City Ranger District
Dennis Beechler, Mount Hood National Forest, Barlow Ranger District
Larry Reed, Mount Hood National Forest, Clackamas River Ranger District
Kevin Flagle, Mount Hood National Forest, Hood River Ranger District
Fran Lanagan, Mount Hood National Forest, Zigzag Ranger District
Barbara Smith, Ochoco National Forest, Prineville Ranger District
John McKelligott, Rogue River National Forest, Applegate Ranger District
Bryce Leppek, Rogue River National Forest, Ashland Ranger District
Scott Beemer, Rogue River National Forest, Butte Falls and
   Prospect Ranger Districts
Harvey Timeus, Siskiyou National Forest, Chetco Ranger District
Cheri Lyda, Siskiyou National Forest, Galice Ranger District
Mary Stansell, Siskiyou National Forest, Gold Beach Ranger District
Don McLennan, Siskiyou National Forest, Illinois Valley Ranger District
Rennay Stinson, Siskiyou National Forest, Powers Ranger District
Mike Harvey, Siuslaw National Forest
Monica Jones, Umatilla National Forest, Heppner Ranger District
Karen Kendall, Umatilla National Forest, North Fork
   John Day Ranger District
Jeff Bloom, Umatilla National Forest, Walla Walla Ranger District
Bonnie Conway, Umpqua National Forest
Cindy Pack, Umpqua National Forest, Cottage Grove Ranger District
Terry Klingenberg, Umpqua National Forest, Diamond Lake Ranger District
Ron Murphy, Umpqua National Forest, North Umpqua Ranger District
Lori Depew, Umpqua National Forest, Tiller Ranger District
Faith Kenney, Wallowa-Whitman National Forest
Denise Mercer, Willamette National Forest, Blue River Ranger District
Abe Quihuis, Willamette National Forest, Detroit Ranger District
Joyce Day, Willamette National Forest, Detroit Ranger District
Dave Graham Willamette National Forest, McKenzie Ranger District
Jan Dowling, Willamette National Forest, Middle Fork Ranger District

Lupe Wilson, Willamette National Forest, Sweet Home Ranger District
Jeanie Sheehan, Winema National Forest

U.S. Army Corps of Engineers
Dustin Bengston, Cottage Grove District
Tom Thomsen, Portland District

Bureau of Land Management
Ken White, Oregon State Office
Fred McDonald, Burns District
Nancy Zepf, Coos Bay District
Doug Huntington, Eugene District
Scott Senter, Lakeview District
Karen Kuralt, Medford District
Roy Tidwell, Prineville District
Chuck White, Roseburg District
Tina Tyler, Salem District
Tom Christensen and Tom Dabbs, Vale District

National Parks
Kent Taylor, Crater Lake National Park
Jean Carter and Bonita Perrigo, Oregon Dunes National Recreation Area

Oregon State Parks
Richard Wilde and Frank Howard

Oregon State Forest
Randy Peterson, Tillamook State Forest, Forest Grove District
Clyde Zeller, Tillamook State Forest, Tillamook District

Technical Review
Michael Hodgson, author of *Facing the Extreme* (with Ruth Anne Kocour), reviewed all the equipment and technical information for this edition.

Dear Campers,

Warning: Do not use any other camping book or even a previous edition of this book. If you plan to enjoy the Pacific Northwest's vast great outdoors, this is the only outdoor guidebook available in the Pacific Northwest that is ready for the 21st century.

Because of significant storm damage to roads across the Pacific Northwest in the late 1990s, many roads, bridges, and campgrounds were closed, and in some cases new routes were made available to reach many campgrounds. That is why all the directions in this book were rewritten, incorporating hundreds of changes, and simplified with a new, easy-to-follow style. Many of the most beautiful places on earth are in Washington and Oregon, and the editorial researchers and I have made it our mission to put the best of the great outdoors right in the palms of your hands—and make it easy for you to enjoy it.

In cross-checks with other books, we discovered that these changes had simply not been made by other publishers, along with directions that were as easy to decipher as Egyptian hieroglyphics. Go ahead and compare: We wouldn't be surprised if the authors had copies of this book sitting on their dashboards!

But that's only a start.

In our mission to make *Pacific Northwest Camping* the best outdoor guidebook ever produced for Washington and Oregon, we estimate that more than 10,000 updates and upgrades have been completed to make this book the most accurate, easy-to-use, and comprehensive resource guidebook for campers ever produced in this region. In addition to deleting closed campgrounds, we have included 75 new campgrounds in this edition.

Also new to this edition are scenic ratings for every campground, icons highlighting recreation options, and all area code changes for phone contacts. We also note parks that accept credit cards and have listed websites where applicable. Every listing was reviewed and often reworked by several resource experts. In addition, our four research editors faxed every listing on every page to the campground owners and public service officials in charge for final checks. In the process, hundreds of people were involved in polishing the final product.

And I'll tell you something else: I'd never dream of roaming about the Pacific Northwest without this book. It's the best guarantee that you will never get stuck for the night without a campsite. The ultimate nightmare? The sun is going down and you don't know where to camp. This book is designed to provide the solution.

The truth is this: When my family, cousins, and friends heard of my mission to write about the best of Washington and Oregon, they all hated me! They figured all of their favorite spots would be revealed to all. But after reviewing the manuscript, they've decided they don't hate me anymore, that is, except for one cousin. That's because they have discovered, as I have, that the Pacific Northwest is filled with beautiful, little-used campgrounds that are perfect jump-off points for adventures—hundreds of outstanding destinations in addition to their sprinkling of favorites.

Despite our efforts, road conditions, fees, and the moods of rangers and campground owners are beyond our control. So if you have a specific need or concern, it's always a good idea to call the campground ahead of time, especially if you have a grumpy dog and need further details on pet regulations, are traveling strictly by credit card (campground owners have been known to refuse plastic without notice), or are expecting to camp in the winter and need specifics on road and trail conditions.

We have incorporated dozens of suggestions inspired by requests from readers, and your comments are always welcome. Write to us at:

Pacific Northwest Camping, 7th edition
Avalon Travel Publishing
5885 Beaudry St.
Emeryville, CA 94608

See you out there.
—Tom Stienstra

ACTIVITY SYMBOLS

= biking

= boating

= fishing

=golf

= hiking

= historical site

= hunting

= horseback riding

= hot springs

= PWC riding

= motorboating

= rafting/canoeing

= rock climbing

= sea kayaking

= snowmobiling

= snowshoeing

= snow skiing

= swimming

= tennis

= waterskiing

= wheelchair access

= RV sites

= tent sites

5% = Five Percent Club

Introduction

Going on a camping trip can be like trying to put hiking boots on an octopus. You've tried it too, eh? Instead of the relaxing, exciting sojourn that was intended, the trip turns into a scenario called You Against the World. You might as well try to fight a volcano.

But it doesn't have to be that way, and that's what this book is all about. If you give it a chance, it can put the mystery, excitement, and fun back into your camping vacations—and remove the fear of snarls, confusion, and occasional temper explosions of volcanic proportions that keep people at home, locked away from the action.

Mystery? There are hundreds of hidden, rarely used campgrounds listed and mapped in this book that you have never dreamed of. *Excitement?* At many of them you'll find the sizzle with the steak, the hike to a great lookout, the big fish at the end of the line. *Fun?* The how-to section of this book can help you take the futility out of your trips and put the fun back in. Add it up, put it in your cash register, and you can turn a camping trip into the satisfying adventure it's meant to be, whether it's just an overnight quicky or a month-long expedition.

It has been documented that 95% of American vacationers use only 5% of the available recreation areas. With this book you can leave the herd, wander and be free, and join the inner circle, the Five Percenters who know the great hidden areas used by so few people. To join the Five Percent Club, you should take a hard look at the maps for the areas you wish to visit and the corresponding listings of campgrounds. As you study the camps, you'll start to feel a sense of excitement building, a feeling that you are about to unlock a door and venture into a world that is rarely viewed. When you feel that excitement, act on it. Parlay that energy into a great trip.

The campground maps and listings can serve in two ways: 1) If you're on the road late in the day and you're stuck for a spot for the night, you can likely find one nearby; or 2) if you are planning a trip, you can tailor a vacation to fit exactly into your plans rather than heading off and hoping—maybe praying—it turns out all right.

For the latter you may wish to obtain additional maps, particularly if you are venturing into areas governed by the U.S. Forest Service or Bureau of Land Management. Both are federal agencies that offer low-cost maps detailing all hiking trails, lakes, streams, and backcountry camps reached via logging roads. How to obtain these and other maps is described in the Resource Guide on pages 96 to 100.

Backcountry camps listed in this book are often in primitive and rugged settings but provide the sense of isolation that you may want from a trip. They also provide good jump-off points for backpacking trips, if that's your calling. These camps are often free, and we have listed hundreds of them.

At the other end of the spectrum are the developed parks for RVs. They offer a home away from home, with everything from full hookups to a grocery store and laundry room. These spots are just as important as the remote camps with no facilities. Instead of isolation, an RV park provides a place to shower and get outfitted for food and clean clothes. For RV cruisers, it's a place to stay in high style while touring the area. RV parks range in price from $12-25 per night, depending on location, and an advance deposit may be necessary in summer months.

Somewhere between the two extremes—the remote, unimproved camps and the lavish RV parks—are hundreds and hundreds of campgrounds that provide a compromise: beautiful settings and some facilities, with a small overnight fee. Piped water, vault toilets, and picnic tables tend to come with the territory, along with a fee that usually ranges from $6-15, with the higher-priced sites located near population centers. Because they offer a bit of both worlds, they are in high demand. Reservations are usually advised, and at state parks, particularly during the summer season, you can expect company. This doesn't mean you need to abandon them in hopes of a less confined environment. For one thing, most state parks have set up quotas so that you don't feel as if you've been squeezed in with a shoehorn, and for another, the same parks are often uncrowded during the off-season or on weekdays.

Prior to your trip you'll want to get organized, and that's where you must start putting socks on that giant octopus. The trick to organization for any task is breaking it down to its key components, then solving each element independent of the others. Remember the octopus. Grab a moving leg, jam on a boot, and make sure it's on tight before reaching for another leg. Do one thing at a time, in order, and all will get done quickly and efficiently.

In the stories that follow, we have isolated the different elements of camping, and you should do the same when planning for your trip. There are separate stories on each of the primary ingredients for a successful trip: 1) Food and cooking gear; 2) Clothing and weather protection; 3) Hiking and foot care and how to choose the right boots and socks; 4) Sleeping gear; 5) Combating bugs and some common sense first-aid; 6) Catching fish, avoiding bears, and camp fun; 7) Outdoors with kids; 8) Weather prediction; and 9) How to beat the time trap. We've also included sections on boat-in and desert camping, and ethics in the outdoors, as well as a camping gear checklist.

Now you can become completely organized for your trip in just one week, spending just a little time each evening. Getting organized is an unnatural act for many. By splitting up the tasks, you take the pressure out of planning and put the fun back in.

As a full-time outdoors writer, the question I am asked more than any other is: "Where are you going this week?" All of the answers are in this book.

CAMPING TIPS

Food and Cooking Gear

It was a warm, crystal clear day, the kind of day when if you had ever wanted to go skydiving, you would go skydiving. That was exactly the case for my old pal Foonsky, who had never before tried the sport. But a funny thing happened after he jumped out of the plane and pulled on the rip cord: His parachute didn't open.

In total free fall, Foonsky watched the earth below getting closer and closer. Not one to panic, he calmly pulled the rip cord on the emergency parachute. Again nothing happened. No parachute, no nothing.

The ground was getting ever closer, and as he tried to search for a soft place to land, Foonsky detected a small object shooting up toward him, growing larger as it approached. It looked like a camper.

Figuring this was his last chance, Foonsky shouted as they passed in midair, "Hey, do you know anything about parachutes?"

The other fellow just yelled back as he headed off into space, "Do you know anything about lighting camping stoves?"

Well, Foonsky got lucky and his parachute opened. As for the other guy, well, he's probably in orbit like a NASA weather satellite. If you've ever had a mishap while lighting a camping stove, you know exactly what I'm talking about.

When it comes to camping, all gear is not created equal. Nothing is more important than lighting your stove easily and having it reach full heat without feeling as if you're playing with a short fuse to a miniature bomb. If your stove does not work right, your trip can turn into a disaster, regardless of how well you have planned the other elements. In addition, a bad stove will add an underlying sense of foreboding to your day. You will constantly have the inner suspicion that your darn stove is going to foul up again.

Camping Stoves

If you are buying a camping stove, remember this one critical rule: Do not leave the store with a new stove unless you have been shown exactly how to use it.

Keep It Wild

"Enjoy America's country and leave no trace." That's the motto of the Leave No Trace program, and we strongly support it. Promoting responsible outdoor recreation through education, research, and partnerships is its mission. Look for the **Keep It Wild Tips,** developed from the policies of Leave No Trace, sprinkled throughout the introduction. For a free pocket-sized, weatherproof card printed with these policies, as well as information that details how to minimize human impact on wild areas, contact Leave No Trace at P.O. Box 997, Boulder CO, 80306; tel. (800) 332-4100; website: www.lnt.org.

Know what you are getting. Many stores that specialize in outdoor recreation equipment now provide experienced campers/employees who will demonstrate the use of every stove they sell and while they're at it, describe their respective strengths and weaknesses.

An innovation by Peak 1 is a two-burner backpacking stove that allows you to boil water and heat a pot of food simultaneously. While that has long been standard for car campers using Coleman's legendary camp stove, it was previously unheard of for wilderness campers in high-elevation areas. Another recent invention is the flameless stove (no kidding) that allows campers to cook in a tent safely for the first time.

A stove that has developed a cult-like following is the little Sierra, which burns small twigs and pinecones, then uses a tiny battery-driven fan to develop increased heat and cooking ability. It's an excellent alternative for long-distance backpacking trips, as it solves the problem of carrying a fuel bottle, especially on expeditions for which large quantities of fuel would otherwise be needed. Some tinkering with the flame (a very hot one) is required, and they are legal and functional only in the alpine zone where dry wood is available. Also note that in years with high fire danger, the U.S. Forest Service will enact rules prohibiting open flames, and fires are also often prohibited above an elevation of 10,000 feet.

I prefer a small, lightweight stove that uses white gas so I can closely gauge fuel consumption. My pal Foonsky uses one with a butane bottle because it lights so easily. We have contests to see who can boil a pot of water faster, and the difference is usually negligible. Thus, other factors are important when choosing a stove.

Stoves are available in many styles and burn a variety of fuels. These are three typical examples. Top: **White gas** stoves are the most popular because they are inexpensive and easy to find; they do require priming and can be explosive. Middle: **Gas canister** stoves burn propane, butane, isobutane, and mixtures of the three. These are the easiest to use but have two disadvantages: 1) Because the fuel is bottled, determining how much fuel is left can be difficult. 2) The fuel is limited to above-freezing conditions. Bottom: **Liquid fuel** stoves burn Coleman Fuel, denatured alcohol, kerosene, and even gasoline; these fuels are economical and have a high heat output, but most must be primed.

Food and Cooking Gear 21

Of these, ease of cleaning the burner is the most important. If you camp often, especially with a smaller stove, the burner holes will eventually become clogged. Some stoves have a built-in cleaning needle; a quick twist of the knob and you're in business. Others require disassembly and a protracted session using special cleaning tools. If a stove is difficult to clean, you will tend to put off doing it, and your stove will sputter and pant while you feel humiliated watching the cold pot of water sitting there.

Before making a purchase, have the salesperson show you how to clean the burner head. Except in the case of large, multiburner family camping stoves, which rarely require cleaning, this test can do more to determine the long-term value of a stove than any other factor.

Fuels for Camping Stoves

White gas and butane have long been the most popular camp fuels, but a newly developed fuel could dramatically change that.

LPG (liquid petroleum gas) comes in cartridges for easy attachment to a stove or lantern. At room temperature, LPG is delivered in a combustible gaseous form. When you shake the cartridge, the contents sound liquid; that is because the gas liquefies under pressure, which is why it is so easy to use. Large amounts of fuel are compressed into small canisters.

While convenience has always been the calling card for LPG, recent innovations have allowed it to become a suitable choice for winter and high-altitude mountaineering expeditions, coming close to matching white gas performance specs. For several years now, MSR, Epi (Coleman), Coleman, Primus, Camping Gaz, Markill, and other makers have been mixing propane, butane, and isobutane to improve performance capabilities.

Two important hurdles that stood in the way of LPG's popularity were recently leaped. Coleman, working in cooperation with the U.S. Postal Service, has developed a program in which three-packs of 170-gram Coleman Max fuel cartridges can be shipped by mail to any address or post office in the 50 states and Puerto Rico. Also, each Coleman Max fuel cartridge is now made of aluminum and comes with a special device that allows the consumer to puncture the cartridge safely once the fuel is gone and then toss it into any aluminum recycling container.

The following details the benefits and drawbacks of other available fuels:

White gas: White gas is the most popular camp fuel because it can be purchased at most outdoor recreation stores and many supermarkets and is inexpensive and effective. It burns hot, has virtually no smell, and evaporates quickly when spilled. If you are caught in wet, miserable weather and can't get a fire going, you can use white gas as an emergency fire starter; however, if you do so, use it sparingly and never on an open flame.

White gas is a popular fuel both for car campers, who use the large, two-burner stoves equipped with a fuel tank and a pump, and for hikers who carry a lightweight backpacking stove. On the latter, lighting can require priming with a gel called priming paste, which some people dislike. Another problem with white gas is that it can be extremely explosive.

As an example, I once almost burned my beard completely off in a mini-explosion while lighting one of the larger stoves designed for car camping. I was in the middle of cooking dinner when the flame suddenly shut down. Sure enough, the fuel tank was empty, and after refilling it, I pumped the tank 50 or 60 times to regain pressure. When I lit a match, the sucker ignited from three feet away. The resulting explosion was like a stick of dynamite going off, and immediately the smell of burning beard was in the air. In a flash, my once thick, dark beard had been reduced to a mass of little yellow burned curlicues.

My error? After filling the tank, I forgot to shut the fuel cock off while pumping up the pressure in the tank. As a result, the stove burners were slowly producing the gas/air mixture as I pumped the tank, filling the air above the stove. Then strike a match from even a few feet away and ka-boom!

Butane: The explosive problem can be solved by using stoves that burn bottled butane fuel. Butane requires no pouring, pumping, or priming, and butane stoves are the easiest to light. Just turn a knob and light—that's it. On the minus side, because it comes in bottles, you never know precisely how much fuel you have left. And when a bottle is empty, you have a potential piece of litter. (Never litter. Ever.)

The other problem with butane is that it just plain does not work well in cold weather or when there is little fuel left in the cartridge. Since you cannot predict mountain weather in spring or fall, you can wind up using more fuel than originally projected. That can be frustrating, particularly if your stove starts wheezing when there are still several days left to go. In addition, with most butane cartridges, if there is any chance of the temperature falling below freezing, you often have to sleep with the cartridge to keep it warm or forget about using it come morning.

Coleman Max Performance Fuel: This new fuel offers a unique approach to solving the consistent burn challenge facing all pressurized gas cartridges: operating at temperatures at or below 0 degrees Fahrenheit. Using a standard propane/butane blend for high-octane performance, Coleman gets around the drop-off in performance other cartridges experience by utilizing a version of fuel injection. A hose inside the cartridge pulls liquid fuel into the stove, where it vaporizes—a switch from the standard approach of pulling only a gaseous form of the fuel into a stove. By drawing liquid out of the cartridge, Coleman gets around the tendency of propane to burn off first and allows each cartridge to deliver a consistent mix of propane and butane to the stove's burners throughout the cartridge's life.

Butane/Propane: This blend offers higher octane performance than butane alone, solving the cold temperature doldrums somewhat. However, propane burns off before butane, so there will be a performance drop as the fuel level in the cartridge lowers.

Propane: Now available for single-burner stoves using larger, heavier cartridges to accommodate higher pressures, propane offers the very best performance of any of the pressurized gas canister fuels.

Primus Tri-Blend: This blend is made up of 20% propane, 70% butane, and 10% isobutane and is designed to burn with more consistent heat and efficiency than standard propane/butane mixes.

Denatured alcohol: Though this fuel burns cleanly and quietly and is virtually explosion proof, it generates much less heat than pressurized or liquid gas fuels.

Kerosene: Never buy a stove that uses kerosene for fuel. Kerosene is smelly and messy, generates low heat, needs priming, and is virtually obsolete as a camp fuel in the United States. As a test I once tried using a kerosene stove. I could scarcely boil a pot of water. In addition, some kerosene leaked out when the stove was packed, ruining everything it touched. The smell of kerosene never did go away. Kerosene remains popular in Europe only because most campers there haven't yet heard much about white gas. When they do, they will demand it.

> During high fire danger the U.S. Forest Service will enact rules prohibiting open flames. Fires are also often prohibited above an elevation of 10,000 feet.

Building Fires

One summer expedition took me to the Canadian wilderness in British Columbia for a 75-mile canoe trip on the Bowron Lake Circuit, a chain of 13 lakes, six rivers, and seven portages. It is one of the truly great canoe trips in the world, a loop that ends just a few hundred feet from its starting point. But at the first camp at Kibbee Lake, my stove developed a fuel leak at the base of the burner, and the nuclear-like blast that followed just about turned Canada into a giant crater.

As a result, the final 70 miles of the trip had to be completed without a stove, cooking on open fires each night. The problem was compounded by the weather. It rained eight of the 10 days. Rain? In Canada, raindrops the size of silver dollars fall so hard they actually bounce on the lake surface. We had to stop paddling a few times in order to empty the rainwater out of the canoe. At the end of the day we'd make camp and then face the test: either make a fire or go to bed cold and hungry.

With an ax, at least we had a chance for success. As soaked as all the downed wood was, I was able to make my own fire-starting tinder from the chips of split logs; no matter how hard it rains, the inside of a log is always dry.

Keep It Wild Tip 1: Campfires

1. Fire use can scar the backcountry. If a fire ring is not available, use a lightweight stove for cooking.
2. Where fires are permitted, use existing fire rings away from large rocks or overhangs.
3. Don't char rocks by building new rings.
4. Gather sticks from the ground that are no larger than the diameter of your wrist.
5. Don't snap branches of live, dead, or downed trees, which can cause personal injury and also scar the natural setting.
6. Put the fire "dead out" and make sure it's cold before departing. Remove all trash from the fire ring and sprinkle dirt over the site.
7. Remember that some forest fires can be started by a campfire that appears to be out. Hot embers burning deep in the pit can cause tree roots to catch fire and burn underground. If you ever see smoke rising from the ground, seemingly from nowhere, dig down and put the fire out.

In miserable weather, matches don't stay lit long enough to get the tinder started. Instead we used either a candle or the little waxlike fire-starter cubes that remain lit for several minutes. From those we could get the tinder going. Then we added small, slender strips of wood that had been axed from the interior of the logs. When the flame reached a foot high, we added the logs, their dry interior facing in. By the time the inside of the logs had caught fire, the outside would be drying from the heat. It wasn't long before a royal blaze was brightening the rainy night.

That's a worst-case scenario, and hopefully you will never face anything like it. Nevertheless, being able to build a good fire and cook on it can be one of the more satisfying elements of a camping trip. At times just looking into the flames can provide a special satisfaction at the end of a good day.

However, never expect to build a fire for every meal or in some cases even to build one at all. Many state and federal campgrounds have been picked clean of downed wood, or forest fire danger forces rangers to prohibit fires altogether during the fire season. In either case you must use your camp stove or go hungry.

But when you can build a fire and the resources for doing so are available, it will enhance the quality of your camping experience. Of the campgrounds listed in this book, those where you are permitted to build fires will usually have fire rings. In primitive areas where you can make your own fire, you should dig a ring eight inches deep, line the edges with rock, and clear all the needles and twigs in a five-foot radius. The next day, when the fire is dead, you can discard the rocks, fill over the black charcoal with dirt, and then scatter pine needles and twigs over it. Nobody will even know you camped there. That's the best way I know to keep a secret spot a real secret.

When you start to build a campfire, the first thing you will notice is that no matter how good your intentions, your fellow campers will not be able to resist moving the wood around. Watch. You'll be getting ready to add a key piece of wood at just the right spot, and your companion will stick his mitts in, confidently believing he has a better idea. He'll shift the fire around and undermine your best-thought-out plans.

So I enforce a rule on camping trips: One person makes the fire while everybody else stands clear or is involved with other camp tasks such as gathering wood, getting water, putting up tents, or planning dinner. Once the fire is going strong, then it's fair game; anyone adds logs at his or her discretion. But in the early, delicate stages of the campfire, it's best to leave the work to one person.

Before a match is ever struck, you should gather a complete pile of firewood. Then start small, with the tiniest twigs you can find, and slowly add larger twigs as you go, crisscrossing them like a miniature tepee. Eventually you will get to the big chunks that will produce high heat. The key is to get one piece of wood burning into another, which then burns into another, setting off what I call the chain of flame. Conversely, single pieces of wood set apart from each other will not burn.

On a dry summer evening at a campsite where plenty of wood is available, about the only way you can blow the deal is to get impatient and try to add the big pieces too quickly. Do that and you'll get smoke, not flames, and it won't be long before every one of your fellow campers is poking at your fire. It will drive you crazy, but they just won't be able to help it.

Cooking Gear

I like traveling light, and I've found that all I need for cooking is a pot, small frying pan, metal pot grabber, fork, knife, cup, and matches. If you want to keep the price of food low and also cook customized dinners each night, a small pressure cooker can be just the ticket. (See "Keeping the Price Down" on page 28.) I store all my gear in one small bag that fits into my pack. If I'm camping out of my four-wheel-drive rig, the little bag of cooking gear is easy to keep track of. Going simple, not complicated, is the key to keeping a camping trip on the right track.

You can get more elaborate by purchasing complete kits with plates, a coffeepot, large pots, and other cookware, but what really counts is having a single pot that makes you happy. It needs to be just the right size, not too big or small, and stable enough so it won't tip over, even if it is at a slight angle on a fire, full of water at a full boil. Mine is just six inches wide and four-and-a-half inches deep. It holds better than a quart of water and has served me well for several hundred camp dinners.

The rest of your cook kit is easy to complete. The frying pan should be small, light-gauge aluminum, and Teflon-coated, with a fold-in handle so it's no hassle to store. A pot grabber is a great addition. It's a little aluminum gadget that clamps to the edge of pots and allows you to lift them and pour water with total control without burning your fingers. For cleanup take a plastic scrubber and a small bottle filled with dish cleaner, and you're in business.

A sierra cup, a wide aluminum cup with a wire handle, is an ideal item to carry because you can eat out of it as well as use it for drinking. This means no plates to scrub after dinner, so cleanup is quick and easy. In addition, if you go for a hike, you can clip it to your belt with its handle.

If you want a more formal setup complete with plates, glasses, silverware, and the like, you can end up spending more time preparing and cleaning up from meals than you do enjoying the country you are exploring. In addition, the more equipment you bring, the more loose ends you will have to deal with, and loose ends can cause plenty of frustration. If you have a choice, go simple.

And remember what Thoreau said: "A man is rich in proportion to what he can do without."

Food and Cooking Tricks

On a trip to the Bob Marshall Wilderness in western Montana, I woke up one morning, yawned, and said, "What've we got for breakfast?"

The silence was ominous. "Well," finally came the response, "we don't have any food left."

"What!?"

"Well, I figured we'd catch trout for meals every other night."

On the return trip, we ended up eating wild berries, buds, and, yes, even roots (not too tasty). When we finally landed the next day at a suburban pizza parlor, we nearly ate the wooden tables.

Running out of food on a camping trip can do more to turn reasonable people into violent grumps than any other event. There's no excuse for it, not when a system for figuring meals can be outlined with precision and little effort. You should not go out and buy a bunch of food, throw it in your rig, and head off for yonder. That leaves too much to chance. And if you've ever been in the woods and real hungry, you'll know it's worth taking a little effort to make sure a day or two of starvation will not occur. Here's a three-step solution:

1. Draw up a general meal-by-meal plan and make sure your companions like what's on it.

2. Tell your companions to buy any specialty items (like a special brand of coffee) on their own and not to expect you to take care of everything.

3. Put all the food on your living room floor and literally plan out every day of your trip, meal by meal, putting the food in plastic bags as you go. That way you will know exact food quotas and will not go hungry.

Fish for your dinner? There's one guarantee as far as that goes: If you expect to catch fish for meals, you will most certainly get skunked. If you don't expect to catch fish for meals, you will probably catch so many they'll be coming out of your ears. I've seen it a hundred times.

Keeping the Price Down

"There must be some mistake," I said with a laugh. "Whoever paid $750 for camp food?"

But the amount was as clear as the digital numbers on the cash register: $753.27.

"How is this possible?" I asked the clerk.

"Just add it up," she responded, irritated.

Then I started figuring. The freeze-dried backpack dinners cost $6 apiece. A small pack of beef jerky went for $2, the beef sticks for 75 cents, granola bars for 50 cents. Multiply it all by four hungry men, including Foonsky, for 21 days. This food was to sustain us on a major expedition—four guys hiking 250 miles over three weeks from Mount Whitney to Yosemite Valley.

The dinners alone cost close to $500. Add in the usual goodies—jerky, granola bars, soup, dried fruit, oatmeal, Tang, candy, and coffee—and I felt as if an earthquake had struck when I saw the tab.

A lot of campers have received similar shocks. In preparation for their trips, campers shop with enthusiasm. Then they pay the bill in horror.

Well, there are solutions, lots of them. You can eat gourmet style in the outback without having your wallet cleaned out. But it requires do-it-yourself cooking, more planning, and careful shopping. It also means transcending the push-button I-want-it-now attitude that so many people can't leave behind when they go to the mountains.

The secret is to bring along a small pressure cooker. A reader in San Francisco, Mike Bettinger, passed this tip on to me. Little pressure cookers weigh about two pounds, which may sound like a lot to backpackers and backcountry campers. But when three or four people are on a trip, it actually saves weight.

The key is that it allows campers to bring items that are difficult to cook at high altitudes, such as brown and white rice; red, black, pinto, and lima beans; and lentils. You pick one or more for a basic staple and then add a variety of freeze-dried ingredients to make a complete dish. Available are packets of meat, vegetables, onions, shallots, and garlic. Sun-dried tomatoes, for instance, reconstitute wonderfully in a pressure cooker. Add herbs, spices, and maybe a few rainbow trout and you will be eating better out of a backpack than most people do at home.

How to Make Beef Jerky in Your Own Kitchen

Start with a couple pieces of meat: lean top round, sirloin, or tri-tip. Cut it into 3/16-inch strips across the grain, trimming out the membrane, gristle, and fat. Marinate the strips for 24 hours in a glass dish. The fun begins in picking a marinade. Try two-thirds teriyaki sauce, one-third Worcestershire sauce. You can customize the recipe by adding pepper, ground mustard, bay leaf, red wine vinegar, garlic, and, for the brave, Tabasco sauce.

After a day or so, squeeze out each strip of meat with a rolling pin, lay them in rows on a cooling rack over a cookie sheet, and dry them in the oven at 125 degrees for 12 hours. Thicker pieces can take as long as 18 to 24 hours.

That's it. The hardest part is cleaning the cookie sheet when you're done. The easiest part is eating your own homemade jerky while sitting at a lookout on a mountain ridge. The do-it-yourself method for jerky may take a day or so, but it is cheaper and can taste better than any store-bought jerky.

"In the morning, I have used the pressure cooker to turn dried apricots into apricot sauce to put on the pancakes we made with sourdough starter," Bettinger said. "The pressure cooker is also big enough for washing out cups and utensils. The days when backpacking meant eating terrible freeze-dried food are over. It doesn't take a gourmet cook to prepare these meals, only some thought beforehand."

Now when Foonsky, Mr. Furnai, Rambob, and I sit down to eat such a meal, we don't call it "eating." We call it "hodgepacking" or "time to pack your hodge." After a particularly long day on the trail, you can do some serious hodgepacking.

If your trip is a shorter one, say for a weekend, you can bring more fresh food to add some sizzle to the hodge. You can design a hot soup/stew mix that is good enough to eat at home.

Start by bringing a pot of water to a full boil, then adding pasta, ramen noodles, or macaroni. While it simmers, cut in a potato, carrot, onion, and garlic clove, and cook for about 10 minutes. When the vegetables have softened, add in a soup mix or two, maybe some cheese, and you are just about in business. But you can still ruin it and turn your hodge into slodge. Make sure you read the directions on the soup mix to determine cooking time. It can vary widely. In addition, make sure you stir the whole thing up; otherwise you will get these hidden dry clumps of soup mix that taste like garlic sawdust.

How do I know? Well, it was up near Kearsage Pass in the Sierra Nevada, where, feeling half-starved, I dug into our nightly hodge. I will never forget that first bite—I damn near gagged to death. Foonsky laughed at me, until he took his first bite (a nice big one) and then turned green.

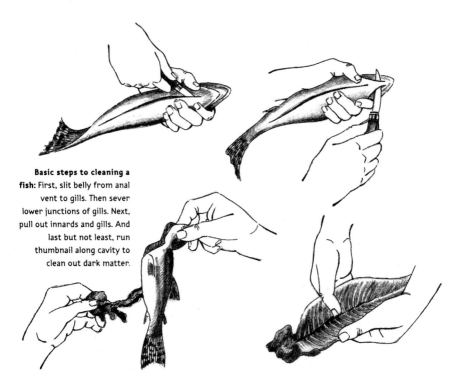

Basic steps to cleaning a fish: First, slit belly from anal vent to gills. Then sever lower junctions of gills. Next, pull out innards and gills. And last but not least, run thumbnail along cavity to clean out dark matter.

Another way to trim food costs is to make your own beef jerky, the trademark staple of campers for more than 200 years. A tiny packet of beef jerky costs $2, and for that 250-mile expedition, I spent $150 on jerky alone. Never again. Now we make our own and get big strips of jerky that taste better than anything you can buy.

If all this still doesn't sound like your idea of a gourmet but low-cost camping meal, well, you are forgetting the main course: rainbow trout. Remember: If you don't plan on catching them for dinner, you'll probably snag more than you can finish in one night's hodgepacking.

Some campers go to great difficulties to cook their trout, bringing along frying pans, butter, grills, tinfoil, and more, but all you need is some seasoned salt and a campfire.

Rinse the gutted trout, and while it's still wet, sprinkle on a good dose of seasoned salt, both inside and out. Clear any burning logs to the side of the campfire, then lay the trout right on the coals, turning it once so both sides are cooked. Sound ridiculous? Sound like you are throwing the fish away? Sound like the fish will burn up? Sound like you will have to eat the campfire ash? Wrong on all counts. The fish cooks perfectly, the ash doesn't stick, and after cooking trout this way, you may never fry trout again.

But if you can't convince your buddies, who may insist the trout should be fried, then make sure you have butter to fry them in, not oil. Also make sure you cook them all the way through, so the meat strips off the backbone in two nice, clean fillets. The fish should end up looking like one that Sylvester the Cat just drew out of his mouth—only the head, tail, and a perfect skeleton.

You can supplement your eats with sweets, nuts, freeze-dried fruits, and drink mixes. In any case, make sure you keep the dinner menu varied. If you and your buddies look into your dinner cups and groan, "Ugh, not this again," you will soon start dreaming of cheeseburgers and french fries instead of hiking, fishing, and finding beautiful campsites.

If you are car camping and have a big ice chest, you can bring virtually anything to eat and drink. If you are on the trail and don't mind paying the price, the newest freeze-dried dinners provide another option.

Some of the biggest advances in the outdoors industry have come in the freeze-dried dinners now available to campers. Some of them are almost good enough to serve in restaurants. Sweet-and-sour pork over rice, tostadas, Burgundy chicken—it sure beats the poopy goop we used to eat, like the old soupy chili-mac dinners that tasted bad and looked so unlike food that consumption was near impossible, even for my dog, Rebel. Foonsky usually managed to get it down, but just barely.

To provide an idea of how to plan a menu, consider what my companions and I ate while hiking 250 miles on California's John Muir Trail:

- Breakfast: instant soup, oatmeal (never get plain), one beef or jerky stick, coffee or hot chocolate.

- Lunch: one beef stick, two jerky sticks, one granola bar, dried fruit, half cup of pistachio nuts, Tang, one small bag of M&Ms.

- Dinner: instant soup, one freeze-dried dinner, one milk bar, rainbow trout.

What was that last item? Rainbow trout? Right! Unless you plan on it, you can catch them every night.

Clothing and Weather Protection

What started as an innocent pursuit of a perfect campground evolved into one heck of a predicament for Foonsky and me.

We had parked at the end of a logging road and then bushwhacked our way down a canyon to a pristine trout stream. On my first cast—a little flip into the plunge pool of a waterfall—I caught a 16-inch rainbow trout, a real beauty that jumped three times. Magic stuff.

Then just across the stream, we saw it: The Perfect Camping Spot. On a sandbar on the edge of the forest, there lay a flat spot, high and dry above the river. Nearby was plenty of downed wood collected by past winter storms that we could use for firewood. And, of course, this beautiful trout stream was bubbling along just 40 yards from the site.

But nothing is perfect, right? To reach it, we had to wade across the river, although it didn't appear to be too difficult. The cold water tingled a bit, and the river came up surprisingly high, just above the belt. But it would be worth it to camp at The Perfect Spot.

Once across the river, we put on some dry clothes, set up camp, explored the woods, and fished the stream, catching several nice trout for dinner. But late that afternoon, it started raining. What? Rain in the summertime? Nature makes its own rules. By the next morning, it was still raining, pouring like a Yosemite waterfall from a solid gray sky.

That's when we noticed The Perfect Spot wasn't so perfect. The rain had raised the river level too high for us to wade back across. We were marooned, wet, and hungry.

"Now we're in a heck of a predicament," said Foonsky, the water streaming off him.

Getting cold and wet on a camping trip with no way to warm up is not only unnecessary and uncomfortable, it can be a fast ticket to hypothermia, the number one killer of campers in the woods. By definition, hypothermia is a condition in which body temperature is lowered to the point that it causes illness. It is particularly dangerous because the afflicted are usually unaware it is setting in. The first sign is a sense of apathy, then a state of confusion, which can lead eventually to collapse (or what appears to be sleep), then death.

You must always have a way to get warm and dry in short order, regardless of any conditions you may face. If you have no way of getting dry, then you must take emergency steps to prevent hypothermia. Those steps are detailed in the first-aid section on page 50.

But you should never reach that point. For starters, always have spare sets of clothing tucked away so no matter how cold and wet you might get, you have something dry to put on. On hiking trips I always carry a second set of clothes, sealed to stay dry, in a plastic garbage bag. I keep a third set waiting back at the truck.

If you are car camping, your vehicle can cause an illusory sense of security. But with an extra set of dry clothes stashed safely away, there is no illusion. The security is real. And remember, no matter how hot the weather is when you start your trip, always be prepared for the worst. Foonsky and I learned the hard way.

So both of us were soaking wet on that sandbar, and with no other choice we tried holing up in the tent for the night. A sleeping bag with Quallofil or another polyester fiberfill can retain warmth even when wet, because the fill is hollow and retains its loft. So as miserable as it was, we made it through the night.

The rain stopped the next day and the river dropped a bit, but it was still rolling big and angry. Using a stick as a wading staff, Foonsky crossed about 80% of the stream before he was dumped, but he made a jump for it and managed to scramble to the riverbank. He waved for me to follow. "No problem," I thought.

It took me 20 minutes to reach nearly the same spot where Foonsky had been dumped. The heavy river current was above my belt and pushing hard. Then in the flash of an instant, my wading staff slipped on a rock. I teetered in the river current and was knocked over like a bowling pin. I became completely submerged. I went tumbling down the river, heading right toward the waterfall. While underwater I looked up at the surface, and I can remember how close it seemed yet how out of control I was. Right then this giant hand appeared, and I grabbed it. It was Foonsky. If it weren't for that hand, I would have sailed right over the waterfall.

My momentum drew Foonsky right into the river, and we scrambled in the current, but I suddenly sensed the river bottom under my knees. On all fours, the two of us clambered ashore. We were safe.

"Thanks ol' buddy," I said.

"Man, we're wet," he responded. "Let's get to the rig and get some dry clothes on."

The Art of Layering

The most important element in enjoying the outdoor experience in any condition is to stay dry and warm. There is no substitute. You must stay dry and you must stay warm.

Thus comes the theory behind layering, which suggests that as your body temperature fluctuates or the weather shifts, you simply peel off or add available layers as needed—and have a waterproof shell available in case of rain.

The introduction of a new era of outdoor clothing has made it possible for campers to turn choosing clothes into an art form. Like art, it comes much more expensive than throwing on a pair of blue jeans, a T-shirt, and some flannel, but for many it is worth the price.

In putting together your ideal layering system, there are some general considerations. What you need to do is create a system that effectively combines elements of breathability, wicking, rapid drying, insulation, durability, wind resistance, and water repellence while still being lightweight and offering the necessary freedom of movement, all with just a few garments.

The basic intent of a base layer is to manage moisture. Your base layer will be the first article of clothing you put on and the last to come off. Since your own skin will be churning out the perspiration, the goal of this second skin is to manage the moisture and move it away from you without trapping your body's heat. The only time that cotton should become a part of your base layer is if you wish to keep cool, not warm, such as in a hot desert climate where evaporative cooling becomes your friend, not your enemy.

That is why the best base layer available is from bicomponent knits, that is, blends of polyester and cotton, which work to provide wicking and insulating properties in one layer. The way it works is that the side facing your skin is water hating, while the side away from your skin is water loving; thus it pulls or "wicks" moisture through. You'll stay dry and happy, even with only one layer on, something not possible with old single-function weaves. The best include Thermax, Capilene, Driclime, Lifa, and Polartec 100.

Stretch fleece and microdenier pile also provide a good base layer, though they can be used as a second layer as well. Microdenier pile can be worn alone or layered under or over other pieces, and it has excellent wicking capability as well as more windproof potential.

The next layer should be a light cotton shirt or a long-sleeved cotton/wool shirt, or both, depending on the coolness of the day. For pants, many just wear blue jeans when camping, but blue jeans can be hot and tight, and once wet, they tend to stay that way. Putting on wet blue jeans on a cold morning is a torturous way to start the day. (I tell you this from experience, since I have suffered that fate a number of times.) A better choice is pants made from a cotton/canvas mix, which are available at outdoors stores. They are light, have a lot of give, and dry quickly. If the weather is quite warm, shorts that have some room to them can be the best choice.

Finally, you'll top the entire ensemble off with a thin windproof, water-resistant layer. You want this layer to breathe like crazy, yet not be so porous that rain runs through it like floodwaters through a leaking dike. Patagonia's Velocity shell is one of the best. Its outer fabric is DWR (durable water-repellent) treated, and the coating is by Gore. Patagonia calls it Pneumatic (Gore now calls it Activent, while Marmot, Moonstone, and North Face all offer their own versions). Though condensation will still build up inside, it manages to get rid of enough moisture.

It is critical to know the difference between "water-resistant" and "waterproof." This is covered later in the chapter under the "Rain Gear" section.

But hey, why does anybody need all this fancy stuff just to go camping? Fair question. Like the introduction of Gore-Tex years ago, all this fabric and fiber mumbo jumbo has its skeptics, including me. You don't have to opt for this aerobic-function fashion statement; it is unnecessary on many camping trips. But the fact is you must be ready for anything when you venture into the outdoors. And the truth is that the new era of outdoor clothing works, and it works better than anything that has come before.

Regardless of what you choose, weather should never be a nuisance or cause discomfort, regardless of what you experience. Instead it should provide a welcome change of pace.

About Hats

One final word of advice: Always pack along a warm hat for those times when you need to seal in warmth. You lose a large percentage of heat through your head. I almost always wear a wide-brimmed hat, something like the legendary outlaws wore 150 years ago. There's actually logic behind it: My hat is made out of kangaroo skin (waterproof), is rigged with a lariat (it can be cinched down when it's windy), and has a wide brim that keeps the tops of my ears from being sunburned (years ago they once were burned to a red crisp on a trip where I was wearing a baseball hat). But to be honest, I like how it looks, kind of like my pal Waylon Jennings.

Vests and Parkas

In cold weather you should take the layer system one step further with a warm vest and a parka jacket. Vests are especially useful because they provide warmth without the bulkiness of a parka. The warmest vests and parkas are either filled with down or Quallofil, or are made with a cotton/wool mix. Each has its respective merits and problems. Down fill provides the most warmth for the amount of weight, but becomes useless when wet, closely resembling a wet dishrag. Quallofil keeps much of its heat-retaining quality even when wet, but is expensive. Vests made of cotton/wool mixes are the most attractive and also are quite warm, but they can be as heavy as a ship's anchor when wet.

Sometimes the answer is combining the two. One of my best camping companions wears a good-looking cotton/wool vest and a parka filled with Quallofil. The vest never gets wet, so weight is not a factor.

Rain Gear

One of the most miserable nights I ever spent in my life was on a camping trip where I didn't bring my rain gear or a tent. Hey, it was early August, the temperature had been in the 90s for weeks, and if anybody had said it was going to rain, I would have told him to consult a brain doctor. But rain it did. And as I got wetter and wetter, I kept saying to myself, "Hey, it's summer, it's not supposed to rain." Then I remembered one of the ten commandments of camping: Forget your rain gear and you can guarantee it will rain.

To stay dry, you need some form of water-repellent shell. It can be as simple as a $5 poncho made out of plastic or as elaborate as a Gore-Tex rain jacket-and-pants set that costs $300. What counts is not how much you spend, but how dry you stay.

The most important thing to realize is that waterproof and water-resistant are completely different things. In addition, there is no such thing as rain gear that is both waterproof and breathable. The more waterproof a jacket is, the less it breathes. Conversely, the more breathable a jacket is, the less waterproof it becomes.

If you wear water-resistant rain gear in a downpour, you'll get soaked. Water-resistant rain gear is appealing because it breathes and will keep you dry in the light stuff, such as mist, fog, even a little splash from a canoe paddle. But in rain? Forget it.

So what is the solution?

Waterproof: impervious to water. Though rain won't penetrate waterproof material, if you're at all mobile, you'll soon find yourself wet from perspiration that can't evaporate.

I've decided that the best approach is a set of fairly light but 100%-waterproof rain gear. I recently bought a hooded jacket and pants from Coleman, and my assessment is that it is the most cost-efficient rain gear I've ever had. All I can say is, hey, it works: I stay dry, it doesn't weigh much, and it didn't cost a fortune.

Water-resistant: resistant but not impervious to water. You'll stay dry using water-resistant material only if it isn't pouring.

You can also stay dry with any of the waterproof plastics and even heavy-duty rubber-coated outfits made for commercial fishermen. But these are uncomfortable during anything but a heavy rain. Because they are heavy and don't breathe, you'll likely get soaked anyway (that is, from your own sweat), even if it isn't raining hard.

On backpacking trips, I still stash a super lightweight water-repellent slicker for day hikes, and a poncho, which I throw over my pack at night to keep it dry. But otherwise I never go anywhere—*anywhere*—without my rain gear.

Some do just fine with a cheap poncho, and note that ponchos can serve other uses in addition to a raincoat. Ponchos can be used as a ground tarp, as a rain cover for supplies or a backpack, or can be roped up to trees in a pinch to provide a quick storm ceiling if you don't have a tent. The problem with ponchos is that in a hard rain, you just don't stay dry. First your legs get wet, then they get soaked. Then your arms follow the same pattern. If you're wearing cotton, you'll find that once part of the garment gets wet, the water will spread until, alas, you are dripping wet, poncho and all. Before long you start to feel like a walking refrigerator.

One high-cost option is buying a Gore-Tex rain jacket and pants. Gore-Tex is actually not a fabric as is commonly believed, but a laminated film that coats a breathable fabric. The result is lightweight, water-repellent, breathable jackets and pants. They are perfect for campers, but they cost a fortune.

Some hiking buddies of mine have complained that the older Gore-Tex rain gear loses its water-repellent quality over time. However, manufacturers insist that this is the result of water seeping through seams, not leaks in the jacket. At each seam, tiny needles have pierced the fabric, and as tiny as the holes are, water will find a way through. An application of Seam Lock, especially at major seams around the shoulders of a jacket, can usually fix the problem.

If you don't want to spend the big bucks for Gore-Tex rain gear but want more rain protection than a poncho affords, a coated nylon jacket is the compromise that many choose. They are inexpensive, have the highest water-repellency of any rain gear, and are warm, providing a good outer shell for your layers of clothing. But they are not without fault. These jackets don't breathe at all, and if you zip them up tight, you can sweat a river.

My brother Rambob gave me a nylon jacket prior to a mountain climbing expedition. I wore that $20 special all the way to the top with no complaints; it's warm and 100% waterproof. The one problem with nylon is when temperatures drop below freezing. It gets so stiff that it feels as if you are wearing a straitjacket. But at $20, it seems like a treasure, especially compared to a $180 Gore-Tex jacket.

There's one more jacket-construction term to know: DWR, or durable water-repellent finish. All of the top-quality jackets these days are DWR treated. The DWR causes water to bead up on the shell. When the DWR wears off, even a once-waterproof jacket will feel like a wet dishrag.

Also note that ventilation is the key to coolness. The only ventilation on most shells is often the zipper. But waterproof jackets need additional openings. Look for mesh-backed pockets and underarm zippers, as well as cuffs, waists, and hems that can be adjusted to open wide. Storm flaps (the baffle over the zipper) that close with hook-and-loop material or snaps let you leave the zipper open for airflow into the jacket.

Other Gear—and a Few Tips

What are the three items most commonly forgotten on a camping trip? A hat, sunglasses, and lip balm.

A hat is crucial, especially when you are visiting high elevations. Without one you are constantly exposed to everything nature can give you. The sun will dehydrate you, sap your energy, sunburn your head, and in worst cases, cause sunstroke. Start with a comfortable hat. Then finish with sunglasses, lip balm, and sunscreen for additional protection. They will help protect you from extreme heat.

To guard against extreme cold, it's a good idea to keep a pair of thin ski gloves stashed away with your emergency clothes, along with a wool ski cap. The gloves should be thick enough to keep your fingers from stiffening up, but pliable enough to allow full movement so you don't have to take them off to complete simple tasks, like lighting a stove. An alternative to gloves is glovelets, which look like gloves with no fingers. In any case, just because the weather turns cold doesn't mean that your hands have to.

And if you fall into a river as Foonsky and I did—well, I hope you have a set of dry clothes waiting back at your rig. Oh, and a hand reaching out to you.

Hiking and Foot Care

We had set up a nice little camp in the woods, and my buddy, Foonsky, was strapping on his hiking boots, sitting against a big Douglas fir.

"New boots," he said with a grin. "But they seem pretty stiff."

We decided to hoof it down the trail for a few hours, exploring the mountain wildlands that are said to hide Bigfoot and other strange creatures. After just a short while on the trail, a sense of peace and calm seemed to settle in. The forest provides the chance to be purified with clean air and the smell of trees, freeing you from all troubles.

But it wasn't long before a look of trouble was on Foonsky's face. And no, it wasn't from seeing Bigfoot.

"Got a hot spot on a toe," he said.

Immediately we stopped. He pulled off his right boot, then his socks, and inspected the left side of his big toe. Sure enough, a blister had bubbled up, filled with fluid, but hadn't popped. From his medical kit, Foonsky cut a small piece of moleskin to fit over the blister and taped it to hold it in place. In a few minutes we were back on the trail.

A half hour later, there was still no sign of Bigfoot. But Foonsky stopped again and pulled off his other boot. "Another hot spot." On the little toe of his left foot was another small blister, over which he taped a Band-Aid to keep it from further chafing against the inside of his new boot.

In just a few days, ol' Foonsky, a strong, 6-foot-5, 200-plus-pound guy, was walking around like a sore-hoofed horse that had been loaded with a month's worth of supplies and ridden over sharp rocks. Well, it wasn't the distance that had done Foonsky in; it was those blisters. He had them on eight of his 10 toes and was going through Band-Aids, moleskin, and tape like a walking emergency ward. If he used any more tape, he would've looked like a mummy from an Egyptian tomb.

If you've ever been in a similar predicament, you know the frustration of wanting to have a good time, wanting to hike and explore the area where you have set up a secluded camp, only to be turned gimplegged by several blisters. No one is immune—all are created equal before the blister god. You can be forced to bow to it unless you get your act together.

That means wearing the right style boots for what you have in mind and then protecting your feet with carefully selected socks. If you are still so unfortunate as to get a blister or two, it means knowing how to treat them fast so they don't turn your walk into a sore-footed endurance test.

What causes blisters? In almost all cases, it is the simple rubbing of a foot against the rugged interior of a boot. That can be worsened by several factors:

1. A very stiff boot or one in which your foot moves inside as you walk, instead of the boot flexing as if it were another layer of skin.

2. Thin, ragged, or dirty socks. This is the fastest route to blisters. Thin socks will allow your feet to move inside of your boots, ragged socks will allow your skin to chafe directly against the boot's interior, and dirty socks will wrinkle and fold, also rubbing against your feet instead of cushioning them.

3. Soft feet. By themselves, soft feet will not cause blisters, but in combination with a stiff boot or thin socks, they can cause terrible problems. The best way to toughen up your feet is to go barefoot. In fact, some of the biggest, toughest-looking guys you'll ever see, from Hell's Angels to pro football players, have feet that are as soft as a baby's butt. Why? Because they never go barefoot and don't hike much.

One summer I hiked 400 miles, including 250 miles in three weeks, along the crest of California's Sierra Nevada, and another 150 miles over several months in an earlier general training program. In that span I got just one blister, suffered on the fourth day of the 250-miler. I treated it immediately and suffered no more. One key is wearing the right boot, and for me, that means a boot that acts as a thick layer of skin that is flexible and pliable to my foot. I want my feet to fit snugly in them, with no interior movement.

Selecting the Right Boots

There are three kinds of boots: mountaineering boots, hiking (or backpacking) boots, and canvas walking shoes. Select the right one for you or pay the consequences.

Mountaineering boots

The stiffest of the lot is the mountaineering boot. These boots are often identified by mid-range tops, laces that extend almost as far as the toe area, and ankle areas that are as stiff as a board. The lack of "give" is what endears them to mountaineers. Their stiffness is preferred when rock climbing, walking off-trail on craggy surfaces, or hiking down the edge of streambeds where walking across small rocks can cause you to turn your ankle. Because these boots don't give on rugged, craggy terrain, they reduce ankle injuries and provide better traction.

The drawback to stiff boots is that if you don't have the proper socks and your foot starts slipping around in the boot, you will get a set of blisters that would raise even Foonsky's eyebrows. But if you just want to go for a walk or a good tromp with a backpack, then hiking shoes or backpacking boots will serve you better.

Canvas walking shoes

Canvas walking shoes are the lightest of all boots, designed for day walks or short backpacking trips. Some of the newer models are like rugged tennis shoes, designed with a canvas top for lightness and a lug sole for traction. These are perfect for people who like to walk but rarely carry a backpack. Because they are flexible, they are easy to break in, and with fresh socks they rarely cause blister problems. Because they are light, general hiking fatigue is greatly reduced.

On the negative side, because canvas shoes have shallow lug soles, traction can be far from good on slippery surfaces. In addition, they provide less than ideal ankle support, which can be a problem in rocky areas, such as along a stream where you might want to go trout fishing. Turn your ankle and your trip can be ruined.

Backpacking boots

My preference is for a premium backpacking boot, the perfect medium between the stiff mountaineering boot and the soft canvas walking shoe. The deep lug bottom provides traction, the high ankle coverage provides support, yet the soft, waterproof leather body gives each foot a snug fit. Add it up and that means no blisters. On the negative side, they can be quite hot, weigh a ton, and if they get wet, take days to dry.

There are a zillion styles, brands, and price ranges to choose from. If you wander about comparing all their many features, you will get as confused as a kid in a toy store. Instead, go into the store with your mind clear about what you want, find it, and buy it. If you want the best, expect to spend $85-110 for canvas walking shoes, from $130-180 and sometimes more for hiking or mountaineering boots. I have spent as much as $250 for hiking boots that I have worn for close to 2,000 miles. Yet another time I spent $185, thinking I was getting stellar quality, but they turned out to be miserable blister makers, and even after a year of trying to get my money's worth, they never worked right on the trail and now occupy a dark place deep in my closet.

This is one area where you don't want to scrimp, so try not to yelp about the high cost. Instead, walk out of the store believing you deserve the best, and that's exactly what you just paid for. Another trick I have learned is to bring several pairs of different style hiking boots on adventures, then change them constantly according to the terrain. Use heavy boots for steep trails with loose footing, lightweight models for flat routes with a hard surface. This works wonders to

---

Keep It Wild Tip 2: Travel Lightly

1. Visit the backcountry in small groups.
2. Below tree line, always stay on designated trails.
3. Don't cut across switchbacks.
4. When traveling cross-country where no trails are available, follow animal trails or spread out with your group so no new routes are created.
5. Read your map and orient yourself with landmarks, a compass, and an altimeter. Avoid marking trails with rock cairns, tree scars, or ribbons.

avoid blisters and muscle soreness because you are constantly changing what I call "the point of attack."

If you plan on using the advice of a shoe salesperson, first look at what kind of boots he or she is wearing. If he or she isn't even wearing boots, then any advice the salesperson might tender may not be worth a plugged nickel. Most people I know who own quality boots, including salespeople, will wear them almost daily if their job allows, since boots are the best footwear available. However, even these well-meaning folks can offer sketchy advice. Every hiker I've ever met will tell you he wears the world's greatest boot.

Instead, enter the store with a precise use and style in mind. Rather than fish for suggestions, tell the salesperson exactly what you want, try two or three brands of the same style, and always try on both boots in a pair simultaneously so you know exactly how they'll feel. If possible, walk up and down stairs with them. Are they too stiff? Are your feet snug yet comfortable, or do they slip? Do they have that "right" kind of feel when you walk?

If you get the right answers to those questions, then you're on your way to blister-free, pleasure-filled days of walking.

Socks

The poor gent was scratching his feet as if ants were crawling over them. I looked closer. Huge yellow calluses covered the bottoms of his feet, and at the ball and heel, the calluses were about a quarter inch thick, cracking and sore.

"I don't understand it," he said. "I'm on my feet a lot, so I bought a real good pair of hiking boots. But look what they've done to my feet. My feet itch so much I'm going crazy."

People can spend so much energy selecting the right kind of boot that they virtually overlook wearing the right kind of socks. One goes with the other.

Your socks should be thick enough to cushion your feet as well as fit snugly. Without good socks you might try to get the bootlaces too tight—and that's like putting a tourniquet on your feet. You should have plenty of clean socks on hand, or plan on washing what you have on your trip. As socks are worn, they become compressed, dirty, and damp. Any one of those factors can cause problems.

My camping companions believe I go overboard when it comes to socks, that I bring too many and wear too many. But it works, so that's where the complaints stop. So how many do I wear? Well, it varies. On day hikes, I have found a sock called a SmartWool that makes my size 13s feel as if I'm walking on pillows. But on long expeditions, the 200-milers, I sometimes wear three socks on each foot, believe it or not. It may sound like overkill, but each has its purpose, and like I said, it works.

The interior sock is thin, lightweight, and made of polypropylene or silk synthetic materials designed to transport moisture away from your skin. With a poly interior sock, your foot stays dry when it sweats. Without a poly sock, your foot can get damp and mix with dirt, which can cause a hot spot to start on your foot. Eventually you get blisters, lots of them.

The second sock is for comfort and can be cotton, but a thin wool-based composite is ideal. Some made of the latter can wick moisture away from the skin, much like polypropylene does. If wool itches your feet, a thick cotton sock can be suitable, though cotton collects moisture and compacts more quickly than other socks. If you're on a short hike though, cotton will do just fine.

The exterior sock should be made of high-quality, thick wool—at least 80% wool. It will cushion your feet, provide that just right snug fit in your boot, and give you some additional warmth and insulation in cold weather. It is critical to keep the wool sock clean. If you wear a dirty wool sock over and over again, it will compact and lose its cushion and start wrinkling while you hike, then your feet will catch on fire from the blisters that start popping up. Of course, when wearing multiple socks, especially a wool composite, you will likely need to go up a boot size so they fit comfortably.

A Few More Tips If you are like most folks—that is, the bottoms of your feet are rarely exposed and quite soft—you can take additional steps in their care. The best tip is keeping a fresh foot pad made of sponge rubber in your boot. Another cure for soft feet is to get out and walk or jog on a regular basis prior to your camping trip.

If you plan to use a foot pad and wear three socks, you will need to use these items when sizing boots. It is an unforgiving error to wear thin cotton socks when buying boots and later try to squeeze all this stuff, plus your feet, into them. There just won't be enough room.

The key to treating blisters is fast work at the first sign of a hot spot. But before you remove your socks, check to see if the sock has a wrinkle in it, a likely cause of the problem. If so, either change socks or pull them tight, removing the tiny folds, after taking care of the blister. Cut a piece of moleskin to cover the offending toe, securing the moleskin with white medical tape. If moleskin is not available, small Band-Aids can do the job, but these have to be replaced daily, and sometimes with even more frequency. At night, clean your feet and sleep without socks.

Two other items that can help your walking is an Ace bandage and a pair of gaiters.

For sprained ankles and twisted knees, an Ace bandage can be like an insurance policy to get you back on the trail and out of trouble. Over the years I have had serious ankle problems and have relied on a good wrap with a four-inch bandage to get me home. The newer bandages come with the clips permanently attached, so you don't have to worry about losing them.

Gaiters are leggings made of plastic, nylon, or Gore-Tex that fit from just below your knees, over your calves, and attach under your boots. They are of particular help when walking in damp areas or in places where rain is common. As your legs brush against ferns or low-lying plants, gaiters will deflect the moisture. Without them, your pants will be soaking wet in short order.

Should your boots become wet, a good tip is never to try to force dry them. Some well-meaning folks will try to dry them quickly at the edge of a campfire or actually put the boots in an oven. While this may dry the boots, it can also loosen the glue that holds them together, ultimately weakening them until one day they fall apart in a heap.

A better bet is to treat the leather so the boots become water repellent. Silicone-based liquids are the easiest to use and least greasy of the treatments available.

A final tip is to have another pair of lightweight shoes or moccasins that you can wear around camp and in the process give your feet the rest they deserve.

Sleeping Gear

One mountain night in the pines on an eve long ago, my dad, brother, and I had rolled out our sleeping bags and were bedded down for the night. After the pre-trip excitement, a long drive, an evening of trout fishing, and a barbecue, we were like three tired doggies who had played too much.

But as I looked up at the stars, I was suddenly wide awake. This kid was still wired. A half hour later? No change—wide awake.

And as little kids can do, I had to wake up ol' dad to tell him about it. "Hey, Dad, I can't sleep."

"This is what you do," he said. "Watch the sky for a shooting star and tell yourself that you cannot go to sleep until you see at least one. As you wait and watch, you will start getting tired, and it will be difficult to keep your eyes open. But tell yourself you must keep watching. Then you'll start to really feel tired. When you finally see a shooting star, you'll go to sleep so fast you won't know what hit you."

Well, I tried it that night and I don't even remember seeing a shooting star, I went to sleep so fast.

It's a good trick, and along with having a good sleeping bag, ground insulation, maybe a tent, or a few tricks for bedding down in a pick-up truck or motor home, you can get a good night's sleep on every camping trip.

More than 20 years after that camping episode with my dad and brother, we made a trip to the planetarium at the Academy of Sciences in San Francisco to see a show on Halley's Comet. The lights dimmed, and the ceiling turned into a night sky, filled with stars and a setting moon. A scientist began explaining phenomena of the heavens.

After a few minutes, I began to feel drowsy. Just then, a shooting star zipped across the planetarium ceiling. I went into a deep sleep so fast it was like I was in a coma. I didn't wake up until the show was over, the lights were turned back on, and the people were leaving.

Feeling drowsy, I turned to see if ol' Dad had liked the show. Oh yeah? Not only had he gone to sleep too, but he apparently had no intention of waking up, no matter what. Just like a camping trip.

Sleeping Bags

Question: What could be worse than trying to sleep in a cold, wet sleeping bag on a rainy night without a tent in the mountains?

Answer: Trying to sleep in a cold, wet sleeping bag on a rainy night without a tent in the mountains when your sleeping bag is filled with down.

Water will turn a down-filled sleeping bag into a mushy heap. Many campers do not like a high-tech approach, but the state-of-the-art polyfiber sleeping bags can keep you warm even when wet. That factor, along with temperature rating and weight, is key when selecting a sleeping bag.

A sleeping bag is a shell filled with heat-retaining insulation. By itself it is not warm. Your body provides the heat, and the sleeping bag's ability to retain that heat is what makes it warm or cold.

The old-style canvas bags are heavy, bulky, cold, and when wet, useless. With other options available, their use is limited. Anybody who sleeps outdoors or backpacks should choose otherwise. Buy and use a sleeping bag filled with down or one of the quality poly-fills. Down is light, warm, and aesthetically pleasing to those who don't think camping and technology mix. If you choose a down bag, be sure to keep it double wrapped in plastic garbage bags on your trip in order to keep it dry. Once wet, you'll spend your nights howling at the moon.

The polyfiber-filled bags are not necessarily better than those filled with down, but they can be. Their one key advantage is that even when wet, some poly-fills can retain up to 85% of your body heat. This

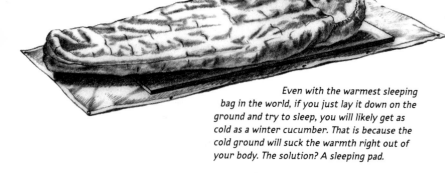

Even with the warmest sleeping bag in the world, if you just lay it down on the ground and try to sleep, you will likely get as cold as a winter cucumber. That is because the cold ground will suck the warmth right out of your body. The solution? A sleeping pad.

allows you to sleep and get valuable rest even in miserable conditions. And my camping experience is that no matter how lucky you may be, there comes a time when you will get caught in an unexpected, violent storm and everything you've got will get wet, including your sleeping bag. That's when a poly-fill bag becomes priceless. You either have one and can sleep, or you don't have one and suffer. It is that simple. Of the synthetic fills, Quallofil made by Dupont is the industry leader.

But just because a sleeping bag uses a high-tech poly-fill doesn't necessarily make it a better bag. There are other factors.

The most important are a bag's temperature rating and weight. The temperature rating of a sleeping bag refers to how cold it can get before you start actually feeling cold. Many campers make the mistake of thinking, "I only camp in the summer, so a bag rated at 30 or 40 degrees should be fine." Later they find out it isn't so fine, and all it takes is one cold night to convince them of that. When selecting the right temperature rating, visualize the coldest weather you might ever confront, and then get a bag rated for even colder weather.

For instance, if you are a summer camper, you may rarely experience a night in the low 30s or high 20s. A sleeping bag rated at 20 degrees would be appropriate, keeping you snug, warm, and asleep. For most campers, I advise bags rated at zero or 10 degrees.

If you buy a poly-filled sleeping bag, never leave it squished in your stuff sack between camping trips. Instead, keep it on a hanger in a closet or use it as a blanket. One thing that can reduce a poly-filled bag's heat-retaining qualities is if you lose the loft out of the tiny hollow fibers that make up the fill. You can avoid this with proper storage.

The weight of a sleeping bag can also be a key factor, especially for backpackers. When you have to carry your gear on your back, every ounce becomes important. Sleeping bags that weigh just three pounds are available, although they are expensive. But if you hike much, it's worth the price to keep your weight to a minimum. For an overnighter, you can get away with a four- or four-and-a-half-pound bag without much stress. However, bags weighing five pounds and up should be left back at the car.

I have two sleeping bags: a seven-pounder that feels like a giant sponge, and a little three-pounder. The heavy-duty model is for pickup truck camping in cold weather and doubles as a blanket at home. The lightweight bag is for hikes. Between the two, I'm set.

Insulation Pads

Even with the warmest sleeping bag in the world, if you just lay it down on the ground and try to sleep, you will likely get as cold as a winter cucumber. That is because the cold ground will suck the warmth right out of your body. The solution is to have a layer of insulation between you and the ground. For this you can use a thin Insulite pad, a lightweight Therm-a-Rest inflatable pad, a foam pad or mattress, air bed, or a cot. Here is a capsule summary of all three:

- **Insulite pads:** They are light, inexpensive, roll up quick for transport, and can double as a seat pad at your camp. The negative side is that in one night, they will compress, making you feel that you are sleeping on granite.

- **Therm-a-Rest pads:** These are a real luxury because they do everything an Insulite pad does, but also provide a cushion. The negative side is that they are expensive by comparison, and if they get a hole in them, they become worthless without a patch kit.

- **Air beds, foam mattresses, and cots:** These are excellent for car campers. The new line of air beds available are outstanding, especially the thicker ones, and inflate quickly with an electric motor inflator that plugs into a power plug or cigarette lighter in your vehicle. Foam mattresses are also excellent, in fact, the most comfortable of all, but their size precludes many from considering them. I've found that cots work great, too. I finally wore out an old wood one just before this book went to press; replaced it immediately with one of the new high-tech and light metal ones. For camping in the back of a pick-up truck with a camper shell, the cots with three-inch legs are best, of course.

A Few Tricks

When surveying a camp area, the most important consideration should be to select a good spot to sleep. Everything else is secondary. Ideally, you want a flat spot that is wind sheltered and on ground soft enough to drive stakes into. Yeah, and I want to win the lottery, too.

Sometimes that ground will have a slight slope to it. In that case, always sleep with your head on the uphill side. If you sleep parallel to the slope, every time you roll over, you'll find yourself rolling down the hill. If you sleep with your head on the downhill side, you'll get a headache that feels as if an ax is embedded in your brain.

When you've found a good spot, clear it of all branches, twigs, and rocks, of course. A good tip is to dig a slight indentation in the ground where your hip will fit. Since your body is not flat, but has curves and edges, it will not feel comfortable on flat ground. Some people even get severely bruised on the sides of their hips when sleeping on flat, hard ground. For that reason alone they learn to hate camping. What a shame, especially when solved so easily with a Therm-a-Rest pad, foam insulation, air bed or a cot.

After the ground is prepared, throw a ground cloth over the spot, which will keep much of the morning dew off you. In some areas, particularly where fog is a problem, morning dew can be heavy and get the outside of your sleeping bag quite wet. In that case, you need overhead protection, such as a tent or some kind of roof, like a poncho or tarp with its ends tied to trees.

Tents and Weather Protection

All it takes is to get caught in the rain once without a tent and you will never go anywhere without one again. A tent provides protection from rain, wind, and mosquito attacks. In exchange, you can lose a starry night's view, though some tents now even provide moon roofs.

A tent can be as complex as a four-season, tubular-jointed dome with a rain fly or as simple as two ponchos snapped together and roped up to a tree. They can be as cheap as a $10 tube tent, which is nothing more than a hollow piece of plastic, or as expensive as a $500 five-person deluxe expedition dome model. They vary greatly in size, price, and put-up time. If you plan on getting a good one, plan on doing plenty of shopping and asking lots of questions. With a little bit of homework, you can get the right answers to these questions:

Will it keep me dry?

On many one-person and two-person tents, the rain fly does not extend far enough to keep water off the bottom sidewalls of the tent. In a driving rain, water can also drip from the rain fly and to the bottom sidewalls of the tent. Eventually the water can leak through to the inside, particularly through the seams where the tent has been sewn together.

A-frame style **tents** have gone the way of the dinosaur. With the world going high-tech, tents of today vary greatly in complexity, size, price, and put-up time. And they wouldn't be fit for the new millennium without offering options such as moon roofs, rain flies, and tent wings. Be sure to purchase the one that's right for your needs.

You must be able to stake out your rain fly so it completely covers all of the tent. If you are tent shopping and this does not appear possible, then don't buy the tent. To prevent potential leaks, use a seam waterproofer such as Seam Lock, a gluelike substance, to close potential leak areas on tent seams. For large umbrella tents, keep a patch kit handy.

Another way to keep water out of your tent is to store all wet garments outside the tent, under a poncho. Moisture from wet clothes stashed in the tent will condense on the interior tent walls. If you bring enough wet clothes into the tent, by the next morning you can feel as if you're camping in a duck blind.

How hard is it to put up?

If a tent is difficult to erect in full sunlight, you can just about forget it at night. Some tents can go up in just a few minutes, without requiring help from another camper. This might be the kind of tent you want.

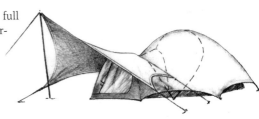

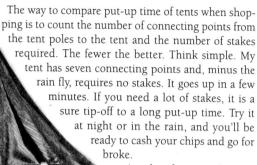

The way to compare put-up time of tents when shopping is to count the number of connecting points from the tent poles to the tent and the number of stakes required. The fewer the better. Think simple. My tent has seven connecting points and, minus the rain fly, requires no stakes. It goes up in a few minutes. If you need a lot of stakes, it is a sure tip-off to a long put-up time. Try it at night or in the rain, and you'll be ready to cash your chips and go for broke.

Another factor is the tent poles themselves. Some small tents have poles that are broken into small sections that are connected by bungee cords. It takes only an instant to convert them to a complete pole.

Some outdoor shops have tents on display on their showroom floor. Before buying the tent, have the salesperson take the tent down and put it back up. If it takes him more than five minutes, or he says he doesn't have time, then keep looking.

Is it roomy enough?
Don't judge the size of a tent on floor space alone. Some tents small on floor space can give the illusion of roominess with a high ceiling. You can be quite comfortable in them and snug.

But remember that a one-person or two-person tent is just that. A two-person tent has room for two people plus gear. That's it. Don't buy a tent expecting it to hold more than it is intended to.

How much does it weigh?
If you're a hiker, this becomes the preeminent question. If it's much more than six or seven pounds, forget it. A 12-pound tent is bad enough, but get it wet and it's like carrying a piano on your back. On the other hand, weight is scarcely a factor if you camp only where you can take your car. My dad, for instance, used to have this giant canvas umbrella tent that folded down to a neat little pack that weighed about 500 pounds.

Family Tents It is always worth spending the time and money to purchase a tent you and your family will be happy with.

Though many good family tents are available for $125-175, particularly from Coleman, Cabela's, and Remington, here is a synopsis of two of the best tents available anywhere, without regard to cost, generally ranging from $350-600:

Sierra Designs Mondo 5CD

tel. (800) 736-8551

10.14 pounds

82 square feet / 20-square-foot covered entry / Inside peak height: five feet, five inches

If you've got a family that likes to head for distant camps, then this is your tent. It's light enough to pack along, yet big enough to accommodate a family of four. Using speed clips, this tent is by far the easiest and quickest to set up of any family tent I've used. A generous rain fly and covered entry area (new adjustment features allow various awning configurations) mean more than adequate protection from the elements, no matter how hard they are pelting down.

Kelty Domolite 6

tel. (800) 423-2320

16.4 pounds

81.5 square feet / Inside peak height: five feet, seven inches

Using three 18-foot-long fiberglass poles, the Domolite boasts a sleek, low profile that slips the wind very nicely. Each pole slides easily through continuous pole sleeves, thanks to rubber-tipped ends, making set-up a snap. Kelty has an optional covered entry area, since without it, the tent is barely adequate shelter should you have to weather a deluge in cramped quarters. Floor seams are taped for added waterproofness. A great package.

Bivouac Bags

If you like going solo and choose not to own a tent at all, a bivy bag, short for bivouac bag, can provide the weather protection you require. A bivy bag is a water-repellent shell in which your sleeping bag fits. It is light and tough, and for some is the perfect alternative to a heavy tent. My own bivy weighs 31 ounces and cost me $240, made by OR (Outdoor Research), and I just plain love the thing on expeditions. On the downside, however, it can be a bit difficult getting settled just right in it, and some say they feel claustrophobic at the close quarters. My biggest fear was the idea of riding out a storm. You can hear the rain hitting you, and sometimes even feel the pounding of the

---

Keep It Wild Tip 3: Camp with Care

1. Choose an existing, legal site. Restrict activities to areas where vegetation is compacted or absent.
2. Camp at least 75 steps (200 feet) from lakes, streams, and trails.
3. Always choose sites that won't be damaged by your stay.
4. Preserve the feeling of solitude by selecting camps that are out of view when possible.
5. Don't dig trenches or build structures or furniture.

---

drops through the bivy bag. For some, it can be unsettling to try and sleep under such circumstances. On the other hand, I've always looked forward to it. In cold weather, it also helps to keep you warm.

Pickup Truck Campers

If you own a pickup truck with a camper shell, you can turn it into a self-contained campground with a little work. This can be an ideal way to go: it's fast, portable, and you are guaranteed a dry environment.

But that does not necessarily mean it is a warm environment. In fact, without insulation from the metal truck bed, it can be like trying to sleep on an iceberg. That is because the metal truck bed will get as cold as the air temperature, which is often much colder than the ground temperature. Without insulation, it can be much colder in your camper shell than it would be on the open ground.

When I camp in my rig, I use a large piece of foam for a mattress and insulation. The foam measures four inches thick, 48 inches wide, and 76 inches long. It makes for a bed as comfortable as anything one might ask for. In fact, during the winter, if I don't go camping for a few weeks because of writing obligations, I sometimes will throw the foam on the floor, lie down the old sleeping bag, light a fire, and camp right in my living room. It's in my blood, I tell you. Air beds and cots are also extremely comfortable and I've used both many times. Whatever you choose, just make sure you have a comfortable sleeping unit. Good sleep makes for great camping trips.

RVs

The problems RVers encounter come from two primary sources: lack of privacy and light intrusion.

The lack of privacy stems from the natural restrictions of where a land yacht can go. Without careful use of the guide portion of this book, motor home owners can find themselves in parking lot settings, jammed in with plenty of neighbors. Because RVs often have large picture windows, you lose your privacy, causing some late nights; then, come daybreak, light intrusion forces an early wake up. The result is you get shorted on your sleep.

The answer is to carry inserts to fit over the inside of your windows. This closes off the outside and retains your privacy. And if you don't want to wake up with the sun at daybreak, you don't have to. It will still be dark.

First Aid and Insect Protection

The mountain night could not have been more perfect, I thought as I lay in my sleeping bag.

The sky looked like a mass of jewels and the air tasted sweet and smelled of pines. A shooting star fireballed across the sky, and I remember thinking, "It just doesn't get any better."

Just then, as I was drifting into sleep, a mysterious buzz appeared from nowhere and deposited itself inside my left ear. Suddenly awake,

I whacked my ear with the palm of my hand, hard enough to cause a minor concussion. The buzz disappeared. I pulled out my flashlight and shined it on my palm, and there, lit in the blackness of night, lay the squished intruder: a mosquito, dead amid a stain of blood.

Satisfied, I turned off the light, closed my eyes, and thought of the fishing trip planned for the next day. Then I heard them. It was a squadron of mosquitoes flying landing patterns around my head. I tried to grab them with an open hand, but they dodged the assault and flew off. Just 30 seconds later another landed in my left ear. I promptly dispatched the invader with a rip of the palm.

Now I was completely awake, so I got out of my sleeping bag to retrieve some mosquito repellent. But en route, several of the buggers swarmed and nailed me in the back and arms. After I applied the repellent and settled snugly again in my sleeping bag, the mosquitoes would buzz a few inches from my ear. After getting a whiff of the poison, they would fly off. It was like sleeping in a sawmill.

The next day, drowsy from little sleep, I set out to fish. I'd walked but 15 minutes when I brushed against a bush and felt this stinging sensation on the inside of my arm, just above the wrist. I looked down: A tick had his clamps in me. I ripped it out before he could embed his head into my skin.

After catching a few fish, I sat down against a tree to eat lunch and just watch the water go by. My dog, Rebel, sat down next to me and stared at the beef jerky I was munching as if it were a T-bone steak. I finished eating, gave him a small piece, patted him on the head, and said, "Good dog." Right then, I noticed an itch on my arm where a mosquito had drilled me. I unconsciously scratched it. Two days later, in that exact spot, some nasty red splotches started popping up. Poison oak. By petting my dog and then scratching my arm, I had transferred the oil residue of the poison oak leaves from Rebel's fur to my arm.

When I returned home, Foonsky asked me about the trip.

"Great," I said. "Mosquitoes, ticks, poison oak. Can hardly wait to go back."

"Sorry I missed out," he answered.

Mosquitoes, No-See-Ums, Gnats, and Horseflies

On a trip to Canada, Foonsky and I were fishing a small lake from the shore when suddenly a black horde of mosquitoes could be seen moving across the lake toward us. It was like when the French army looked across the Rhine and saw the Wehrmacht coming. There was a buzz in the air. We fought them off for a few minutes, then made a fast retreat to the truck and jumped in, content the buggers had been fooled. But somehow still unknown to us, the mosquitoes gained entry to the truck. In 10 minutes, we squished 15 of them as they attempted to plant their oil drills into our skin. Just outside the truck, the black horde waited for us to make a tactical error like rolling down a window. It finally took a miraculous hailstorm to foil the attack.

When it comes to mosquitoes, no-see-ums, gnats, and horseflies, there are times when there is nothing you can do. However, in most situations you can muster a defense to repel the attack.

The first key with mosquitoes is to wear clothing too heavy for them to drill through. Expose a minimum of skin, wear a hat, and tie a bandanna around your neck, preferably one that has been sprayed with repellent. If you try to get by with just a cotton T-shirt, you will be declared a federal mosquito sanctuary.

So first your skin must be well covered, exposing only your hands and face. Second, you should have your companion spray your clothes with repellent. Third, you should dab liquid repellent directly on your skin.

At night, the easiest way to get a good sleep without mosquitoes buzzing in your ear is to sleep in a bug-proof tent. If the nights are warm and you want to see the stars, new tent models are available that have a skylight covered with mosquito netting. If you don't like tents on summer evenings, mosquito netting rigged with an air space at your head can solve the problem. Otherwise prepare to get bitten, even with the use of mosquito repellent.

If your problems are with no-see-ums or biting horseflies, then you need a slightly different approach.

No-see-ums are tiny black insects that look like nothing more than a sliver of dirt on your skin. Then you notice something stinging, and when you rub the area, you scratch up a little no-see-um. The results are similar to mosquito bites, making your skin itch, splotch, and when you get them bad, swell. In addition to using the techniques described to repel mosquitoes, you should go one step further.

The problem is that no-see-ums are tricky little devils. Somehow they can actually get under your socks and around your ankles where they will bite to their hearts' content all night long while you sleep, itch, sleep, and itch some more. The best solution is to apply a liquid repellent to your ankles, then wear clean socks.

Horseflies are another story. They are rarely a problem, but when they get their dander up, they can cause trouble you'll never forget.

One such episode occurred when Foonsky and I were paddling a canoe along the shoreline of a large lake. This giant horsefly, about the size of a fingertip, started dive-bombing the canoe. After 20 minutes, it landed on Foonsky's thigh. He immediately slammed it with an open hand, then let out a blood-curdling "Yeeeee-ow!" that practically sent ripples across the lake. When Foonsky whacked it, the horsefly had somehow turned around and bit him on the hand, leaving a huge red welt.

Mosquito Repellent: Taking vitamin B1 and eating garlic are reputed to act as natural insect repellents, but I've met a lot of mosquitoes that are not convinced. A better bet is to examine the label of the repellent in question for **N,N diethyl-m-toluamide,** commonly known as DEET. That is a poison, and the percentage of it in the container must be listed and will indicate that brand's effectiveness. Inert ingredients are mainly fluids used to fill the bottles.

In the next 10 minutes, that big fly strafed the canoe on more dive-bomb runs. I finally got my canoe paddle, swung it as if it were a baseball bat, and nailed that horsefly as if I'd hit a home run. It landed about 15 feet from the boat, still alive and buzzing in the water. While I was trying to figure what it would take to kill this bugger, a large rainbow trout surfaced and snatched it out of the water, finally avenging the assault.

If you have horsefly or yellow jacket problems, you'd best just leave the area. One, two, or a few can be dealt with. More than that and your fun camping trip will be about as fun as being roped to a tree and stung by an electric shock rod.

On most trips, you will spend time doing everything possible to keep from getting bitten by mosquitoes or no-see-ums. When that fails, you must know what to do next, and fast, if you are among those ill-fated campers who get big red lumps from a bite inflicted from even a microscopic mosquito.

A fluid called After Bite or a dab of ammonia should be applied immediately to the bite. To start the healing process, apply a first-aid gel (not a liquid), such as the one made by Campho-Phenique.

DEET Versus "Natural" Repellents

What is DEET? You're not likely to find the word DEET on any repellent label. That's because DEET stands for N,N diethyl-m-toluamide. If the label contains this scientific name, the repellent contains DEET. Despite fears of DEET-associated health risks and the increased attention given natural alternatives, DEET-based repellents are still acknowledged as by far the best option when serious insect protection is required.

What are the health risks associated with using DEET? A number of deaths and a number of medical problems have been attributed in the press to DEET in recent years—events that those in the DEET community vehemently deny as being specifically DEET related, pointing to reams of scientific documentation as evidence. It does seem logical to assume that if DEET can peel paint, melt nylon, destroy plastic, wreck wood finishes, and damage fishing line, then it must be hell on the skin—perhaps worse.

On one trip, I had a small bottle of mosquito repellent in the same pocket as a Swiss army knife. Guess what happened? The mosquito repellent leaked a bit and literally melted the insignia right off the knife. DEET will also melt synthetic clothes. That is why in bad mosquito country, I'll expose a minimum of skin, just hands and face (with full beard), and apply the repellent only to my cheeks and the back of my hands, perhaps wear a bandanna sprinkled with a few drops as well. That does the trick, with a minimum of exposure to the repellent.

Although nothing definitive has been published, there is a belief among a growing number in the scientific community that repeated applications of products containing low percentages of DEET can be potentially dangerous. It is theorized that this actually puts consumers at a greater risk for absorbing high levels of DEET into the body than if they had just used one application of a 30 to 50% DEET product with an efficacy of four to six hours. Also being studied is the possibility that low levels of DEET, which might not otherwise be of toxicological concern, may become hazardous if they are formulated with solvents or dilutents (considered inert ingredients) that may enhance the absorption rate.

Are natural alternatives a safer choice? To imply that essential oils are completely safe because they are a natural product is not altogether accurate. Essential oils, while derived from plants that grow naturally, are chemicals too. Some are potentially hazardous if ingested, and most are downright painful if they find their way into the eyes or onto mucus membranes. For example, pennyroyal is perhaps the most toxic of the essential oils used to repel insects and can be deadly if taken internally. Other oils used include citronella (perhaps the most common, it's extracted from an aromatic grass indigenous to Southern Asia), eucalyptus, cedarwood, and peppermint.

Three citronella-based products, Buzz Away (manufactured by Quantum), Avon's Skin-So-Soft, and Natrapel (manufactured by Tender), have received EPA registration and approval for sale as repellents for use in controlling mosquitoes, flies, gnats, and midges.

How effective are natural repellents? While there are numerous studies cited by those on the DEET and citronella sides of the fence, the average effective repelling time of a citronella product appears to range from 1.5 to two hours. Tests conducted at Cambridge University, England, comparing Natrapel to DEET-based Skintastic (a low-percentage DEET product) found citronella to be just as effective in repelling mosquitoes. The key here is effectiveness and the amount of time until reapplication.

Citronella products work for up to two hours and then require reapplication (the same holds true for other natural formulations). Products using a low-percentage level of DEET also require reapplication every two hours to remain effective. So if you're going outside for only a short period in an environment where insect bites are more an irritant than a hazard, you would do just as well to go natural.

What other chemical alternatives are there? Another line of defense against insects is the chemical permethrin, used on clothing, not on skin. Permethrin-based products are designed to repel and kill arthropods or crawling insects, making them a preferred repellent for ticks. The currently available products will remain effective, repelling and killing mosquitoes, ticks, and chiggers, for two weeks and through two launderings.

Ticks are nasty little vermin that will wait in ambush, jump on un- **_Ticks_**
suspecting prey, and then crawl to a prime location before filling
their bodies with their victim's blood.

I call them Dracula bugs, but by any name they can be a terrible
camp pest. Ticks rest on grass and low plants and attach themselves
to those who brush against the vegetation (dogs are particularly vulnerable). Typically they are no more than 18 inches above ground, and
if you stay on the trails, you can usually avoid them.

There are two common species of ticks. The common coastal tick
is larger, brownish in color, and prefers to crawl around prior to
putting its clamps on you. The latter habit can be creepy, but when you
feel it crawling, you can just pick it off and dispatch it. The coastal
tick's preferred destination is usually the back of your neck, just
where the hairline starts. The other species, the wood tick, is small and
black, and when he puts his clamps in, it's immediately painful.
When a wood tick gets into a dog for a few days, it can cause a large
red welt. In either case, ticks should be removed as soon as possible.

If you have hiked in areas infested with ticks, it is advisable to
shower as soon as possible, washing your clothes immediately. If you
just leave your clothes in a heap, a tick can crawl out and invade
your home. They like warmth, and one way or another, they can

---

Keep It Wild Tip 4: Sanitation

If no refuse facility is available:

1. Deposit human waste in "cat holes" dug six to eight inches deep.
   Cover and disguise the cat hole when finished.
2. Deposit human waste at least 75 paces (200 feet) from any water
   source or camp.
3. Use toilet paper sparingly. When finished, carefully burn it in the
   cat hole, then bury it.
4. If no appropriate burial locations are available, such as in popular
   wilderness camps above tree line in granite settings, then all
   human refuse should be double-bagged and packed out.
5. At boat-in campsites, chemical toilets are required. Chemical toilets can also solve the problem of larger groups camping for long
   stays at one location where no facilities are available.
6. To wash dishes or your body, carry water away from the source
   and use small amounts of biodegradable soap. Scatter dishwater
   after all food particles have been removed.
7. Scour your campsites for even the tiniest piece of trash and any
   other evidence of your stay. Pack out all the trash you can, even if
   it's not yours. Finding cigarette butts, for instance, provides special
   irritation for most campers. Pick them up and discard them prop-
   erly.
8. Never litter. Never. Or you become the enemy of all others.

end up in your bed. Waking up in the middle of the night with a tick crawling across your chest can really give you the creeps.

Once a tick has its clampers on you, you must decide how long it has been there. If it has been a short time, the most painless and effective method for removal is to take a pair of sharp tweezers and grasp the little devil, making certain to isolate the mouth area, then pull him out. Reader Johvin Perry sent in the suggestion to coat the tick with Vaseline, which will cut off its oxygen supply, after which it may voluntarily give up the hunt.

If the tick has been in longer, you may wish to have a doctor extract it. Some people will burn a tick with a cigarette, or poison it with lighter fluid, but this is not advisable. No matter how you do it, you must take care to remove all of it, especially its clawlike mouth.

The wound, however small, should then be cleansed and dressed. This is done by applying liquid peroxide, which cleans and sterilizes, and then applying a dressing coated with a first-aid gel such as First-Aid Cream, Campho-Phenique, or Neosporin.

Lyme disease, which can be transmitted by the bite of the deer tick, is rare but common enough to warrant some attention. To prevent tick bites, some people tuck their pant legs into their hiking socks and spray tick repellent, called Permamone, on their pants.

The first symptom of Lyme disease is that the bite area will develop a bright red, splotchy rash. Other possible early symptoms include headache, nausea, fever, and/or a stiff neck. If this happens, or if you have any doubts, you should see your doctor immediately. If you do get Lyme disease, don't panic. Doctors say it is easily treated in the early stages with simple antibiotics. If you are nervous about getting Lyme disease, carry a small plastic bag with you when you hike. If a tick manages to get his clampers into you, put it in the plastic bag after you pull it out. Then give it to your doctor for analysis to see if the tick is a carrier of the disease.

During the course of my hiking and camping career, I have removed ticks from my skin hundreds of times without any problems. However, if you are worried about ticks, you can purchase a tick removal kit from any outdoors store. These kits allow you to remove ticks in such a way that their toxins are guaranteed not to enter your bloodstream.

If you are particularly wary of ticks or perhaps even have nightmares of them, wear long pants that are tucked into the socks, as well as a long-sleeved shirt tucked securely into the pants and held with a belt. Clothing should be light in color, making it easier to see ticks, and tightly woven so ticks have trouble hanging on. On one hike with my mom, Eleanor, I brushed more than 100 ticks off my blue jeans in less than an hour, while she did not pick up a single one on her polyester pants.

Perform tick checks regularly, especially on the back of the neck. The combination of DEET insect repellents applied to the skin and permethrin repellents applied directly to clothing is considered to be the most effective line of defense against ticks.

Poison Oak

After a nice afternoon hike, about a five-miler, I was concerned about possible exposure to poison oak, so I immediately showered and put on clean clothes. Then I settled into a chair with my favorite foamy elixir to watch the end of a baseball game. The game went 18 innings; meanwhile, my dog, tired from the hike, went to sleep on my bare ankles.

A few days later I had a case of poison oak. My feet looked as though they had been on fire and put out with an ice pick. The lesson? Don't always trust your dog, give him a bath as well, and beware of extra-inning ball games.

You can get poison oak only from direct contact with the oil residue from the leaves. It can be passed in a variety of ways, as direct as skin-to-leaf contact or as indirect as leaf to dog, dog to sofa, sofa to skin. Once you have it, there is little you can do but itch yourself to death. Applying Caladryl lotion or its equivalent can help because it contains antihistamines, which attack and dry the itch.

A tip that may sound crazy but seems to work is advised by my pal Furniss. You should expose the afflicted area to the hottest water you can stand, then suddenly immerse it in cold water. The hot water opens the skin pores and gets the "itch" out, and the cold water then quickly seals the pores.

In any case, you're a lot better off if you don't get poison oak to begin with. Remember that poison oak can disguise itself. In the spring, it is green; then it gradually turns reddish in the summer. By fall, it becomes a bloody, ugly-looking red. In the winter, it loses its leaves altogether and appears to be nothing more than barren, brown sticks of a small plant. However, at any time and in any form, its contact with skin can quickly lead to infection.

Some people are more easily afflicted than others, but if you are one of the lucky few who aren't, don't cheer too loudly. While some people can be exposed to the oil residue of poison oak with little or no effect, the body's resistance can gradually be worn down with repeated exposure. At one time I could practically play in the stuff and the only symptom would be a few little bumps on the inside of my wrist. Now, over 15 years later, my resistance has broken down. If I merely rub against poison oak now, in a few days the exposed area can look as if it were used for a track meet.

Avoiding Poison Oak Remember the old Boy Scout saying: "Leaves of three, let them be."

So regardless of whether you consider yourself vulnerable or not, you should take heed to reduce your exposure. That can be done by staying on trails when you hike and making sure your dog does the same. Remember, the worst stands of poison oak are usually brush-infested areas just off the trail. Protect yourself also by dressing so your skin is completely covered, wearing long-sleeved shirts, long pants, and boots. If you suspect you've been exposed, immediately wash your clothes and then wash yourself with aloe vera, rinsing with a cool shower.

And don't forget to give your dog a bath as well.

Sunburn

The most common injury suffered on camping trips is sunburn, yet some people wear it as a badge of honor, believing that it somehow enhances their virility. Well, it doesn't. Neither do suntans. And too much sun can lead to serious burns or sunstroke.

It is easy enough to avoid. Use a high-level sunscreen on your skin, apply lip balm with sunscreen, and wear sunglasses and a hat. If any area gets burned, apply first-aid cream, which will soothe and provide moisture for your parched, burned skin.

The best advice is not to get even a suntan. Those who do are involved in a practice that can be eventually ruinous to their skin and possibly lead to cancer.

A Word about Giardia and Cryptosporidium

You have just hiked in to your backwoods spot, you're thirsty and a bit tired, but you smile as you consider the prospects. Everything seems perfect—there's not a stranger in sight, and you have nothing to do but relax with your pals.

You toss down your gear, grab your cup, dip it into the stream, and take a long drink of that ice-cold mountain water. It seems crystal pure and sweeter than anything you've ever tasted. It's not till later that you find out it can be just like drinking a cup of poison.

Whether you camp in the wilderness or not, if you hike, you're going to get thirsty. And if your canteen runs dry, you'll start eyeing any water source. Stop! Do not pass Go. Do not drink.

By drinking what appears to be pure mountain water without first treating it, you can ingest a microscopic protozoan called *Giardia lamblia*. The pain of the ensuing abdominal cramps can make you feel that your stomach and intestinal tract are in a knot, ready to explode. With that comes long-term diarrhea that is worse than even a bear could imagine.

Doctors call the disease *giardiasis*, or giardia for short, but it is difficult to diagnose. One friend of mine who contracted giardia was told he might have stomach cancer before the proper diagnosis was made.

Drinking directly from a stream or lake does not mean you will get giardia, but you are taking a giant chance. There is no reason to assume such a risk, potentially ruining your trip and enduring weeks of misery.

A lot of people are taking that risk. I made a personal survey of campers in the Yosemite National Park wilderness, and found that roughly only one in 20 was equipped with some kind of water-purification system. The result, according to the Public Health Service, is that an average of 4% of all backpackers and campers suffer giardiasis. According to the Parasitic Diseases Division of the Center for Infectious Diseases, the rates range from 1% to 20% across the country.

But if you get giardia, you are not going to care about the statistics. "When I got giardia, I just about wanted to die," said Henry McCarthy, a California camper. "For about 10 days, it was the most terrible thing I have ever experienced. And through the whole thing, I kept thinking, 'I shouldn't have drunk that water, but it seemed all right at the time.'"

That is the mistake most campers make. The stream might be running free, gurgling over boulders in the high country, tumbling into deep, oxygenated pools. It looks pure. Then in a few days, the problems suddenly start. Drinking untreated water from mountain streams is a lot like playing Russian roulette. Sooner or later the gun goes off.

Treating Your Water Means Avoiding Diarrhea: The only sure way to beat giardia and other water-borne diseases is to filter or boil your water before drinking, eating, or brushing your teeth. And the best way to prevent the spread of giardia is to bury your waste products at least eight inches deep and 100 feet away from natural waters.

Filters

There's really no excuse for going without a water filter: Handheld filters are getting more compact, lighter, easier to use, and often less expensive. Having to boil water or endure chemicals that leave a bad taste in the mouth has been all but eliminated.

With a filter, you just pump and drink. Filtering strains out microscopic contaminants, rendering the water clear and somewhat pure. How pure? That depends on the size of the filter's pores—what manufacturers call pore-size efficiency. A filter with a pore-size efficiency of one micron or smaller will remove protozoa like *Giardia lamblia,* and cryptosporidium, as well as parasitic eggs and larva, but it takes a pore-size efficiency of less than 0.4 microns to remove bacteria. All but one of the filters recommended here do that.

A good backcountry water filter weighs less than 20 ounces, is easy to grasp, simple to use, and a snap to clean and maintain. At the very least, buy one that will remove protozoa and bacteria. (A number of cheap, pocket-size filters remove only *Giardia lamblia,* and cryptosporidium. That, in my book, is risking your health to save money.) Consider the flow rate, too: A liter per minute is good.

All filters will eventually clog—it's a sign that they've been doing their job. If you force water through a filter that's becoming difficult to pump, you risk injecting a load of microbial nasties into your bottle. Some models can be backwashed, brushed, or, as with ceramic elements, scrubbed to extend their useful lives. And if the filter has a prefilter to screen out the big stuff, use it: It will give your filter a boost in mileage, which can then top out at about 100 gallons per disposable element. Any of the filters reviewed here will serve well on an outing into the wilds, providing you always play by the manufacturer's rules. They cost about $35-75, up to over $200, depending on the volume of water they are constructed to filter.

- **First Need Deluxe:** The 15-ounce First Need Deluxe from General Ecology does something no other handheld filter will do: It removes protozoa, bacteria, and viruses without using chemicals. Such effectiveness is the result of a fancy three-stage matrix system. Unfortunately, if you drop the filter and unknowingly crack the cartridge, all the little nasties can get through. General Ecology's solution is to include a bottle of blue dye that indicates breaks. The issue hasn't scared off too many folks, though: the First Need has been around since 1982. Additional cartridges cost $30. A final note: The filter pumps smoothly and puts out more than a liter per minute. A favorite of mine.

- **PentaPure Oasis:** The PentaPure Oasis Water Purification System from WTC/Ecomaster offers drinkable water with a twist: You squeeze and sip instead of pumping. Weighing 6.5 ounces, the system packages a three-stage filter inside a 21-ounce-capacity sport bottle with an angled and sealing drinking nozzle, ideal for mountain bikers. The filter removes and/or kills protozoa, bacteria, and viruses, so it's also suitable for world travel. It's certainly convenient: just fill the bottle with untreated water, screw on the cap, give it a firm squeeze (don't expect the easy flow of a normal sport bottle; there's more work being done), and sip. The Oasis only runs into trouble if the water source is shallow; you'll need a cup for scooping.

- **Basic Designs Ceramic:** The Basic Designs Ceramic Filter Pump weighs eight ounces and is as stripped-down a filter as you'll find. The pump is simple, easy to use, and quite reliable. The ceramic filter effectively removes protozoa and bacteria, making it ideal and cost effective for backpacking—but it won't protect against viruses. Also, the filter element is too bulbous to work directly from a shallow water source; like the PentaPure, you'll have to decontaminate a pot, cup, or bottle to transfer your unfiltered water. It's a great buy, though, for anyone worried only about *Giardia lamblia* and cryptosporidium.

- **SweetWater WalkAbout:** The WalkAbout is perfect for the day hiker or backpacker who obsesses on lightening the load. The filter weighs just 8.5 ounces, is easily cleaned in the field, and removes both protozoa and bacteria: a genuine bargain. There are some trade-offs, however, for its diminutiveness. Water delivery is a tad slow at just under a liter per minute, but redesigned filter cartridges ($12.50) are now good for up to 100 gallons.

- **MSR MiniWorks:** Like the WalkAbout, the bargain-priced Mini-Works has a bigger and more expensive water-filtering brother. But in this case the differences are harder to discern: The new 14.3-ounce MiniWorks looks similar to the $140 WaterWorks II, and like the

WaterWorks is fully field-maintainable, while guarding against protozoa, bacteria, and chemicals. But the Mini is the best-executed, easiest-to-use ceramic filter on the market, and it attaches directly to a standard one-quart Nalgene water bottle. Too bad it takes 90 seconds to filter that quart.

- PUR Explorer: The Explorer offers protection from all the bad guys—viruses as well as protozoa and bacteria—by incorporating an iodine matrix into the filtration process. An optional carbon cartridge ($20) neutralizes the iodine's noxious taste. The Explorer is also considered a trusty veteran among water filters because of its smooth pumping action and nifty back-washing feature: With a quick twist, the device switches from filtering mode to self-cleaning mode. It may be on the heavy side (20 ounces) and somewhat pricey, but the Explorer works very well on iffy water anywhere.

- Katadyn U.S.A. Mini Filter: The Mini Filter is a much more compact version of Katadyn's venerable Pocket Filter. This one weighs just eight ounces, ideal for the minimalist backcountry traveler, and it effectively removes protozoa and bacteria. A palm-of-the-hand-size filter, however, makes it challenging to put any kind of power behind the pump's tiny handle, and the filtered water comes through at a paltry half-liter per minute. It also requires more cleaning than most filters—though the good news is that the element is made of long-lasting ceramic. Ironically, one option lets you purchase the Mini Filter with a carbon element instead of the ceramic. The pumping is easier, the flow rate is better, and the price is way down ($99), but I'd only go that route if you'll be pumping from clear mountain streams.

- MSR WaterWorks II Ceramic: At 17.4 ounces the Water-Works II isn't light, but for the same price as the Katadyn you get a better flow rate (90 seconds per liter), an easy pumping action, and—like the original Mini Filter—a long-lasting ceramic cartridge. This filter is a good match for the person who encounters a lot of dirty water—its three-stage filter weeds out protozoa, bacteria, and chemicals—and is mechanically inclined. The MSR can be completely disassembled afield for troubleshooting and cleaning. (If you're not so endowed, take the filter apart at home only, as the potential for confusion is somewhat high.) By the way, the company has corrected the clogging problem that plagued a previous version of the WaterWorks.

Water filters are a wise investment since all wilderness water should be considered contaminated. Make sure the filter can be easily cleaned or has a replaceable cartridge. The filter pores must be .04 microns or less to remove bacteria.

The big drawback with filters is that if you pump water from a mucky lake, the filter can clog in a few days. Therein lies the weakness. Once plugged up, it is useless, and you have to replace it or take your chances.

One trick to extend the filter life is to fill your cook pot with water, let the sediment settle, then pump from there. As an insurance policy, always have a spare filter canister on hand.

Boiling water

Except for water filtration, this is the only treatment that you can use with complete confidence. According to the federal Parasitic Diseases Division, it takes a few minutes at a rolling boil to be certain you've killed *Giardia lamblia*. At high elevations, boil for three to five minutes. A side benefit is that you'll also kill other dangerous bacteria that live undetected in natural waters.

But to be honest, boiling water is a thorn for most people on backcountry trips. For one thing, if you boil water on an open fire, what should taste like crystal-pure mountain water tastes instead like a mouthful of warm ashes. If you don't have a campfire, it wastes stove fuel. And if you are thirsty *now,* forget it. The water takes hours to cool.

The only time boiling always makes sense, however, is when you are preparing dinner. The ash taste will disappear in whatever freeze-dried dinner, soup, or hot drink you make.

Water-purification pills

Pills are the preference for most backcountry campers, and this can get them in trouble. At just $3-8 per bottle, which can figure up to just a few cents per canteen, they do come cheap. In addition, they kill most of the bacteria, regardless of whether you use iodine crystals or potable aqua iodine tablets.

The problem is they just don't always kill *Giardia lamblia,* and that is the one critter worth worrying about on your trip. That makes water-treatment pills unreliable and dangerous.

Another key element is the time factor. Depending on the water's temperature, organic content, and pH level, these pills can take a long time to do the job. A minimum wait of 20 minutes is advised. Most people don't like waiting that long, especially when they're hot and thirsty after a hike and thinking, "What the heck, the water looks fine."

And then there is the taste. On one trip, my water filter clogged and we had to use the iodine pills instead. It doesn't take long to get tired of the iodine-tinged taste of the water. Mountain water should be one of the greatest tasting beverages of the world, but the iodine kills that.

No treatment

This is your last resort and, using extreme care, can be executed with success. One of my best hiking buddies, Michael Furniss, is a nationally renowned hydrologist, and on wilderness trips he has showed me the difference between safe and dangerous water sources.

Long ago, people believed that just finding water running over a rock was a guarantee of its purity. Imagine that. What we've learned is that the safe water sources are almost always small springs located in high, craggy mountain areas. The key is making sure no one has been upstream from where you drink.

Furniss mentioned that another potential problem in bypassing water treatment is that even in settings free of *Giardia lamblia,* you can still ingest other bacteria that cause stomach problems.

No matter how well planned your trip might be, a sudden change in weather can turn it into a puzzle for which there are few answers. Bad weather or an accident can set in motion a dangerous chain of events.

Hypothermia

Such a chain of episodes occurred for my brother Rambob and me on a fishing trip one fall day just below the snow line. The weather had suddenly turned very cold, and ice was forming along the shore of the lake. Suddenly, the canoe became terribly imbalanced, and just that quick it flipped. The little life vest seat cushions were useless, and using the canoe as a paddleboard, we tried to kick our way back to shore where my dad was going crazy at the thought of his two sons drowning before his eyes.

It took 17 minutes in that 38-degree water, but we finally made it to shore. When they pulled me out of the water, my legs were dead, not strong enough even to hold up my weight. In fact, I didn't feel so much cold as tired, and I just wanted to lie down and go to sleep.

I closed my eyes, and my brother-in-law, Lloyd Angal, slapped me in the face several times, then got me on my feet and pushed and pulled me about.

In the celebration over our making it to shore, only Lloyd had realized that hypothermia was setting in. Hypothermia is the condition in which the temperature of the body is lowered to the point that it causes poor reasoning, apathy, and collapse. It can look like the afflicted person is just tired and needs to sleep, but that sleep can be the first step toward a coma.

Ultimately my brother and I shared what little dry clothing remained. Then we began hiking around to get muscle movement, creating internal warmth. We ate whatever munchies were available because the body produces heat by digestion. But most important, we got our heads as dry as possible. More body heat is lost through wet hair than any other single factor.

A few hours later, we were in a pizza parlor replaying the incident, talking about how only a life vest can do the job of a life vest. We decided never again to rely on those little flotation seat cushions that disappear when the boat flips.

Almost by instinct we had done everything right to prevent hypothermia: Don't go to sleep, start a physical activity, induce shivering, put dry clothes on, dry your head, and eat something. That's how you fight hypothermia. In a dangerous situation, whether you fall in a lake or a stream or get caught unprepared in a storm, that's how you can stay alive.

After being in that ice-bordered lake for almost 20 minutes and then finally pulling ourselves to the shoreline, we discovered a strange thing. My canoe was flipped right-side up and almost all of its contents were lost: tackle box, flotation cushions, and cooler. But remaining were one paddle and one fishing rod, the trout rod my grandfather had given me for my 12th birthday.

Lloyd gave me a smile. "This means that you are meant to paddle and fish again," he said with a laugh.

Getting Unlost

You could not have been more lost. But there I was, a guy who is supposed to know about these things, transfixed by confusion, snow, and hoofprints from a big deer.

I discovered it is actually quite easy to get lost. If you don't get your bearings, getting found is the difficult part. This occurred on a wilderness trip where I'd hiked in to a remote lake and then set up a base camp for a deer hunt.

"There are some giant bucks up on that rim," confided Mr. Furnai, who lives near the area. "But it takes a mountain man to even get close to them."

That was a challenge I answered. After four-wheeling it to the trailhead, I tromped off with pack and rifle, gut-thumped it up 100 switchbacks over the rim, then followed a creek drainage up to a small but beautiful lake. The area was stark and nearly tree-less, with bald granite broken only by large boulders. To keep from getting lost, I marked my route with piles of small rocks to act as directional signs for the return trip.

To keep from getting lost, mark your route with **trail ducks**, small piles of rock that act as directional signs for the return trip.

But at daybreak the next day, I stuck my head out of my tent and found eight inches of snow on the ground. I looked up into a gray sky filled by huge, cascading snow-lakes. Visibility was about 50 yards, with fog on the mountain rim. "I better get out of here and get back to my truck," I said to myself. "If my truck gets buried at the trail-head, I'll never get out."

After packing quickly, I started down the mountain. But after 20 minutes, I began to get disorient-ed. You see, all the little piles of rocks I'd stacked to mark the way were now buried in snow, and I had only a smooth white blanket of snow to guide me. Everything

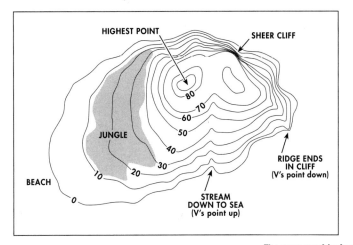

HIGHEST POINT

SHEER CLIFF

80
70
60
50
40
30
20
10

0

JUNGLE

BEACH

**RIDGE ENDS
IN CLIFF
(V's point down)**

**STREAM
DOWN TO SEA
(V's point up)**

looked the same, and it was snowing even harder now.

Five minutes later I started chewing on some jerky to keep warm, then suddenly stopped. Where was I? Where was the creek drainage? Isn't this where I was supposed to cross over a creek and start the switchbacks down the mountain?

Right then I looked down and saw the tracks of a huge deer, the kind Mr. Furnai had talked about. What a predicament: I was lost and snowed in and seeing big hoofprints in the snow. Part of me wanted to abandon all safety and go after that deer, but a little voice in the back of my head won out. "Treat this as an emergency," it said.

The **topographical map** is easier to read than you think. Lines close together mean steep gradients; lines farther apart mean gentle gradients; V-shaped sets of lines pointing to higher elevations mean gulleys or streambeds; V-shaped sets of lines pointing to lower elevations mean ridges.

The first step in any predicament is to secure your present situation, that is, to make sure it does not get any worse. I unloaded my rifle (too easy to slip, fall, and have a misfire), took stock of my food (three days' worth), camp fuel (plenty), and clothes (rain gear keeping me dry). Then I wondered, "Where the hell am I?"

I took out my map, compass, and altimeter, then opened the map and laid it on the snow. It immediately began collecting snowflakes. I set the compass atop the map and oriented it to north. Because of the fog, there was no way to spot landmarks, such as prominent mountaintops, to verify my position. Then I checked the altimeter, which read 4,900 feet. Well, the elevation at my lake was 5,320 feet. That was critical information.

I scanned the elevation lines on the map and was able to trace the approximate area of my position, somewhere downstream from the lake, yet close to a 4,900-foot elevation. "Right here," I said, pointing to a spot on the map with a finger. "I should pick up the switchback trail down the mountain somewhere off to the left, maybe just 40 or 50 yards away."

Slowly and deliberately, I pushed through the light, powdered snow. In five minutes, I suddenly stopped. To the left, across a 10-foot depression in the snow, appeared a flat spot that veered off to the right. "That's it! That's the crossing."

In minutes, I was working down the switchbacks, on my way, no longer lost. I thought of the hoofprints I had seen, and now that I knew my position, I wanted to head back and spend the day hunting. Then I looked up at the sky, saw it filled with falling snowflakes, and envisioned my truck buried deep in snow. Alas, this time logic won out over dreams.

In a few hours, now trudging through more than a foot of snow, I was at my truck at a spot called Doe Flat, and next to it was a giant, all-terrain U.S. Forest Service vehicle and two rangers.

"Need any help?" I asked them.

They just laughed. "We're here to help you," one answered. "It's a good thing you filed a trip plan with our district office in Gasquet. We wouldn't have known you were out here."

"Winter has arrived," said the other. "If we don't get your truck out now, it will be stuck here until next spring. If we hadn't found you, you might have been here until the end of time."

They connected a chain from the rear axle of their giant rig to the front axle of my truck and started towing me out, back to civilization. On the way to pavement, I figured I had gotten some of the more important lessons of my life. Always file a trip plan and have plenty of food, fuel, and a camp stove you can rely on. Make sure your clothes, weather gear, sleeping bag, and tent will keep you dry and warm. Always carry a compass, altimeter, and map with elevation lines, and know how to use them, practicing in good weather to get the feel of it.

And if you get lost and see the hoofprints of a giant deer, well, there are times when it is best to pass them by.

Catching Fish,
Avoiding Bears, and Having Fun

Feet tired and hot, stomachs hungry, we stopped our hike for lunch beside a beautiful little river pool that was catching the flows from a long but gentle waterfall. My brother Rambob passed me a piece of jerky. I took my boots off, then slowly dunked my feet into the cool, foaming water.

I was gazing at a towering peak across a canyon when suddenly, Wham! There was a quick jolt at the heel of my right foot. I pulled my foot out of the water to find that, incredibly, a trout had bitten it.

My brother looked at me as if I had antlers growing out of my head. "Wow!" he exclaimed. "That trout almost caught himself an outdoors writer!"

It's true that in remote areas trout sometimes bite on almost anything, even feet. On one high-country trip I caught limits of trout using nothing but a bare hook. The only problem is that the fish will often hit the splitshot sinker instead of the hook. Of course, fishing isn't usually that easy. But it gives you an idea of what is possible.

Why We Fish: Fishing can give you a sense of exhilaration, like taking a hot shower after being coated with dust. On your walk back to camp, the steps come easy. You suddenly understand what John Muir meant when he talked of developing a oneness with nature, because you have it. That's what fishing can provide.

America's wildlands are home to a remarkable abundance of fish and wildlife. Deer browse with little fear of man, bears keep an eye out for your food, and little critters like squirrels and chipmunks are daily companions. Add in the fishing, and you've got yourself a camping trip.

Your camping adventures will evolve into premium outdoor experiences if you can work in a few good fishing trips, avoid bear problems, and occasionally add a little offbeat fun with some camp games.

He creeps up on the stream as quiet as an Indian scout, keeping his shadow off the water. With his little spinning rod he'll zip his lure within an inch or two of its desired mark, probing along rocks, the edges of riffles, pocket water, or wherever he can find a change in river habitat. Rambob is trout fishing, and he's a master at it.

Trout and Bass

In most cases he'll catch a trout on his first or second cast. After that it's time to move up the river, giving no spot much more than five minutes' due. Stick and move, stick and move, stalking the stream like a bobcat zeroing in on an unsuspecting rabbit. He might keep a few trout for dinner, but mostly he releases what he catches. Rambob doesn't necessarily fish for food. It's the feeling that comes with it.

You don't need a million dollars' worth of fancy gear to catch fish. What you need is the right outlook, and that can be learned. That goes regardless of whether you are fishing for trout or bass, the two most

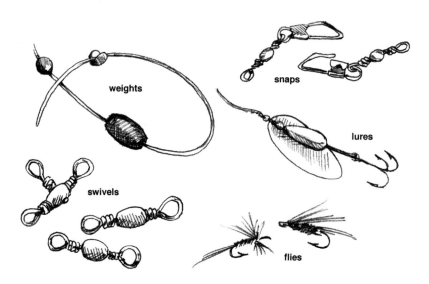

weights

snaps

lures

swivels

flies

popular fisheries in the United States. Your fishing tackle selection should be as simple and clutter free as possible.

At home I've got every piece of fishing tackle you might imagine, more than 30 rods and many tackle boxes, racks and cabinets filled with all kinds of stuff. I've got one lure that looks like a chipmunk and another that resembles a miniature can of beer with hooks. If I hear of something new, I want to try it and usually do. It's a result of my lifelong fascination with the sport.

But if you just want to catch fish, there's an easier way to go. And when I go fishing, I take that path. I don't try to bring everything. It would be impossible. Instead I bring a relatively small amount of gear. At home I will scan my tackle boxes for equipment and lures, make my selections, and bring just the essentials. Rod, reel, and tackle will fit into a side pocket of my backpack or a small carrying bag.

So what kind of rod should be used on an outdoor trip? For most camper/anglers, I suggest the use of a light, multipiece spinning rod that will break down to a small size. The lowest-priced, quality six-piece rod on the market is the Daiwa 6.5-foot pack rod, No. 6752, which is made of a graphite/glass composite that gives it the quality of a much more expensive model. And it comes in a hard plastic carrying tube for protection. Other major rod manufacturers, such as Fenwick, offer similar premium rods. It's tough to miss with any of them.

The use of graphite/glass composites in fishing rods has made them lighter and more sensitive, yet stronger. The only downside to graphite as a rod material is that it can be brittle. If you rap your rod against something, it can crack or cause a weak spot. That weak spot can eventually snap under even light pressure, like setting a hook or casting. Of course, a bit of care will prevent that from ever occurring.

If you haven't bought a fishing reel in some time, you will be surprised at the quality and price of micro spinning reels on the market. The reels come tiny and strong, with rear-control drag systems. Sigma, Shimano, Cardinal, Abu, and others all make premium reels. They're worth it. With your purchase, you've just bought a reel that will last for years and years.

The one downside to spinning reels is that after long-term use, the bail spring will weaken. The result is that after casting and beginning to reel, the bail will sometimes not flip over and allow the reel to retrieve the line. Then you have to do it by hand. This can be incredibly frustrating, particularly when stream fishing, where instant line pickup is essential. The solution is to have a new bail spring installed every few years. This is a cheap, quick operation for a tackle expert.

You might own a giant tackle box filled with lures, but on your fishing trip you are better off to fit just the essentials into a small container. One of the best ways to do that is to use the Plano Micro-Magnum 3414, a tiny two-sided tackle box for trout anglers that fits into a shirt pocket. In mine, I can fit 20 lures in one side of the box and 20 flies, splitshot, and snap swivels in the other. For bass lures, which are bigger, you need a slightly larger box, but the same principle applies.

There are more fishing lures on the market than you can imagine, but a few special ones can do the job. I make sure these are in my box on every trip. For trout, I carry a small black Panther Martin spinner with yellow spots, a small gold Kastmaster, a yellow Roostertail, a gold Z-Ray with red spots, a Super Duper, and a Mepps Lightning spinner.

You can take it a step further using insider's wisdom. My old pal Ed "the Dunk" showed me his trick of taking a tiny Dardevle spoon, spray painting it flat black, and dabbing five tiny red dots on it. It's a real killer, particularly in tiny streams where the trout are spooky.

The best trout catcher I've ever used on rivers is a small metal lure called a Met-L Fly. On days when nothing else works, it can be like going to a shooting gallery. The problem is that the lure is nearly impossible to find. Rambob and I consider the few we have remaining so valuable that if the lure is snagged on a rock, a cold swim is deemed mandatory for its retrieval. These lures are as hard to find in tackle shops as trout can be to catch without one.

For bass, you can also fit all you need into a small plastic tackle box. I have fished with many bass pros, and all of them actually use just a few lures: a white spinner bait, a small jig called a Gits-It, a surface plug called a Zara Spook, and plastic worms. At times, as when the bass move into shoreline areas during the spring, shad minnow imitations like those made by Rebel or Rapala can be dynamite. My favorite is the one-inch, blue-silver Rapala. Every spring as the lakes begin to warm and the fish snap out of their winter doldrums, I like to float and paddle around in my small raft. I'll cast that little Rapala along the shoreline and catch and release hundreds of bass, bluegill, and sunfish. The fish are usually sitting close to the shoreline, awaiting my offering.

Fishing Tips

There's an old angler's joke about how you need to think like a fish. But if you're the one getting zilched, you may not think it's so funny.

The irony is that it is your mental approach, what you see and what you miss, that often determines your fishing luck. Some people will spend a lot of money on tackle, lures, and fishing clothes, and that done, just saunter up to a stream or lake, cast out, and wonder why they are not catching fish. The answer is their mental outlook. They are not attuning themselves to their surroundings.

You must live on nature's level, not your own. Try this and you will become aware of things you never believed even existed. Soon you will see things that will allow you to catch fish. You can get a head start by reading about fishing, but to get your degree in fishing, you must attend the University of Nature.

On every fishing trip, regardless what you fish for, try to follow three hard-and-fast rules:

1. Always approach the fishing spot so you will be undetected.

2. Present your lure, fly, or bait in a manner so it appears completely natural, as if no line was attached.

3. Stick and move, hitting one spot, working it the best you can, then move to the next.

Approach

No one can just walk up to a stream or lake, cast out, and start catching fish as if someone had waved a magic wand. Instead, give the fish credit for being smart. After all, they live there.

Your approach must be completely undetected by the fish. Fish can sense your presence through sight and sound, though this is misinterpreted by most people. By sight, this rarely means the fish actually see you; more likely they will see your shadow on the water or the movement of your arm or rod while casting. By sound, it doesn't mean they hear you talking, but that they will detect the vibrations of your footsteps along the shore, kicking a rock, or the unnatural plunking sound of a heavy cast hitting the water. Any of these elements can spook them off the bite. In order to fish undetected, you must walk softly, keep your shadow off the water, and keep your casting motion low. All of these keys become easier at sunrise or sunset, when shadows are on the water. At midday a high sun causes a high level of light penetration in the water, which can make the fish skittish to any foreign presence.

Like hunting, you must stalk the spots. When my brother Rambob sneaks up on a fishing spot, he is like a burglar sneaking through an unlocked window.

Presentation

Your lure, fly, or bait must appear in the water as if no line were attached, so it looks as natural as possible. My pal Mo Furniss has skin-dived in rivers to watch what the fish see when somebody is fishing.

"You wouldn't believe it," he said. "When the lure hits the water, every trout within 40 feet, like 15, 20 trout, will do a little zigzag. They all see the lure and are aware something is going on. Meanwhile, onshore the guy casting doesn't get a bite and thinks there aren't any fish in the river."

If your offering is aimed at fooling a fish into striking, it must appear as part of its natural habitat, like an insect just hatched or a small fish looking for a spot to hide. That's where you come in.

After you have sneaked up on a fishing spot, you should zip your cast upstream and start your retrieval as soon as it hits the water. If you let the lure sink to the bottom and then start the retrieval, you have no chance. A minnow, for instance, does not sink to the bottom, then start swimming. On rivers, the retrieval should be more of a drift, as if the "minnow" is in trouble and the current is sweeping it downstream.

When fishing on trout streams, always hike and cast upriver and retrieve as the offering drifts downstream in the current. This is effective because trout will sit almost motionless, pointed upstream, finning against the current. This way they can see anything coming their direction, and if a potential food morsel arrives, all they need to do is move over a few inches, open their mouths, and they've got an easy lunch. Thus you must cast upstream.

Conversely, if you cast downstream, your retrieval will bring the lure from behind the fish, where he cannot see it approaching. And I've never seen a trout that had eyes in its tail. In addition, when retrieving a downstream lure, the river current will tend to sweep your lure inshore to the rocks.

Finding Spots

A lot of anglers don't catch fish, and a lot of hikers never see any wildlife. The key is where they are looking.

The rule of the wild is that fish and wildlife will congregate wherever there is a distinct change in the habitat. This is where you should begin your search. To find deer, for instance, forget probing a thick forest, but look for where it breaks into a meadow or a clear-cut has splayed a stand of trees. That's where the deer will be.

The rule of the wild is that wildlife will congregate wherever there is a distinct change in habitat. To find **where fish are hiding**, look where a riffle pours into a small pond, where a rapid plunges into a deep hole and flattens, and around submerged trees, rock piles, and boulders in the middle of a long riffle.

In a river, it can be where a riffle pours into a small pool, a rapid that plunges into a deep hole and flattens, a big boulder in the middle of a long riffle, a shoreline point, a rock pile, a submerged tree. Look for the changes. Conversely, long, straight stretches of shoreline will not hold fish—the habitat is lousy.

On rivers, the most productive areas are often where short riffles tumble into small oxygenated pools. After sneaking up from the downstream side and staying low, you should zip your cast so the lure plops gently into the white water just above the pool. Start your retrieval instantly; the lure will drift downstream and plunk into the pool. Bang! That's where the trout will hit. Take a few more casts and then head upstream to the next spot.

With a careful approach and lure presentation and by fishing in the right spots, you have the ticket to many exciting days on the water.

The first time you come nose-to-nose with a bear can make your skin quiver.

Of Bears and Food

Even the sight of mild-mannered black bears, the most common bear in America, can send shock waves through your body. They weigh 250-400 pounds and have large claws and teeth that are made to scare campers. When they bound, the muscles on their shoulders roll like ocean breakers.

Bears in camping areas are accustomed to sharing the mountains with hikers and campers. They have become specialists in the food-raiding business. As a result, you must be able to make a bear-proof food hang or be able to scare the fellow off. Many campgrounds provide bear- and raccoon-proof food lockers. You can also stash your food in your vehicle, but that limits the range of your trip.

If you are staying at one of the easy backpack sites listed in this book, there will be no food lockers available. Your car will not be there, either. The solution is to make a bear-proof food hang, suspending all of your food wrapped in a plastic garbage bag from a rope in midair, 10 feet from the trunk of a tree and 20 feet off the ground. (Counterbalancing two bags with a rope thrown over a tree limb is very effective, but finding an appropriate limb can be difficult.)

This is accomplished by tying a rock to a rope, then throwing it over a high but sturdy tree limb. Next, tie your food bag to the rope and hoist it in the air. When you are satisfied with the position of the food bag, tie off the end of the rope to another tree. In an area frequented by bears, a good food bag is a necessity—nothing else will do.

I've been there. On one trip my pal Foonsky and my brother Rambob left to fish, and I was stoking up an evening campfire when I felt the eyes of an intruder on my back. I turned around and saw a big bear heading straight for our camp. In the next half hour I scared the bear off twice, but then he got a whiff of something sweet in my brother's pack.

minimum 10 feet

maximum diameter
1 inch

minimum diameter
4 inch

heavy stick

minimum 22 feet to ground

minimum 20 feet to food bags

food wrapped in
plastic bags

In an area frequented by bears, a good **bear-proof food hang** is a must. Food should be stored in a plastic bag 10 feet from the trunk of the tree and at least 20 feet from the ground.

The bear rolled into camp like a truck, grabbed the pack, ripped it open, and plucked out the Tang and the Swiss Miss. The 350-pounder then sat astride a nearby log and lapped at the goodies like a thirsty dog drinking water.

Once a bear gets his mitts on your gear, he considers it his. I took two steps toward the pack, and that bear jumped off the log and galloped across the camp right at me. Scientists say a man can't outrun a bear, but they've never seen how fast I can go up a granite block with a bear on my tail.

Shortly thereafter, Foonsky returned to find me perched on top of the rock and demanded to know how I could let a bear get our Tang. It took all three of us, Foonsky, Rambob, and me, charging at once and shouting like madmen, to clear the bear out of camp and send him off over the ridge. We learned never to let food sit unattended.

When it comes to grizzlies, well, my friends, you need what we call an attitude adjustment. Or that big ol' bear may just decide to adjust your attitude for you, making your stay at the park a short one.

The Grizzly

Grizzlies are nothing like black bears. They are bigger, stronger, have little fear, and take what they want. Some people believe there are many different species of this critter, like Alaskan brown, silvertip, cinnamon, and Kodiak, but the truth is they are all grizzlies. Any difference in appearance has to do with diet, habitat, and life habits, not speciation. By any name, they all come big.

The first thing you must do is determine if there are grizzlies in the area where you are camping. That can usually be done by asking local rangers. If you are heading into Yellowstone or Glacier National Park, or the Bob Marshall Wilderness of Montana, well, you don't have to ask. They're out there, and they're the biggest and potentially most dangerous critters you could run into.

One general way to figure the size of a bear is from his footprint. Take the width of the footprint in inches, add one to it, and you'll have an estimated length of the bear in feet. For instance, a nine-inch footprint equals a 10-foot bear. Any

Grizzly bears are distinguished from **black bears** by a pronounced shoulder hump and a concave facial profile. Grizzlies are generally brown and average 10 to 11 feet in length, while black bears (which can also be brown) maintain lengths of five to seven feet.

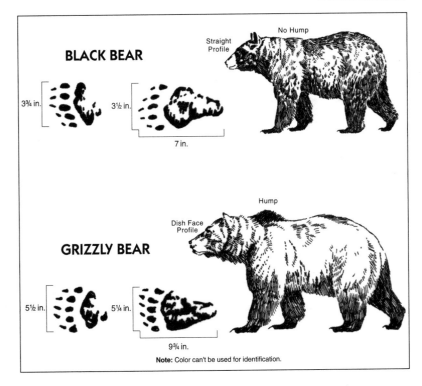

BLACK BEAR

Straight Profile

No Hump

3¾ in.

3½ in.

7 in.

GRIZZLY BEAR

Dish Face Profile

Hump

5½ in.

5¼ in.

9¾ in.

Note: Color can't be used for identification.

bear that big is a grizzly, my friends. In fact, most grizzly footprints average about nine to 10 inches across, and black bears (though they may be brown in color) tend to have footprints only four and a half to six inches across.

Most encounters with grizzlies occur when hikers fall into a silent march in the wilderness with the wind in their faces, and they walk around a corner and right into a big, unsuspecting grizzly. If you do this and see a big hump just behind its neck, well, don't think twice. It's a grizzly.

And then what should you do? Get up a tree, that's what. Grizzlies are so big that their claws cannot support their immense weight, and thus they cannot climb trees. And although their young can climb, they rarely want to get their mitts on you.

If you do get grabbed, every instinct in your body will tell you to fight back. Don't believe it. Play dead. Go limp. Let the bear throw you around a little, because after awhile you become unexciting play material and the bear will get bored. My grandmother was grabbed by a grizzly in Glacier National Park and after a few tosses and hugs, was finally left alone to escape.

Some say it's a good idea to tuck your head under his chin, since that way the bear will be unable to bite your head. I'll take a pass on that one. If you are taking action, any action, it's a signal that you are a force to be reckoned with, and he'll likely respond with more aggression. And bears don't lose many wrestling matches.

What grizzlies really like to do, believe it or not, is to pile a lot of sticks and leaves on you. Just let them, and keep perfectly still. Don't fight them; don't run. And when you have a 100% chance (not 98 or 99) to dash up a nearby tree, that's when you let fly. Once safely in a tree, you can hurl down insults and let your aggression out.

Bear Territory

If you are hiking in a wilderness area that may have grizzlies, it becomes a necessity to wear bells on your pack. That way the bear will hear you coming and likely get out of your way. Keep talking, singing, or maybe even debating the country's foreign policy, but do not fall into a silent hiking vigil. And if a breeze is blowing in your face, you must make even more noise (a good excuse to rant and rave about the government's domestic affairs). Noise is important, because your smell will not be carried in the direction you are hiking. As a result the bear will not smell you coming.

If a bear can hear you and smell you, it will tend to get out of the way and let you pass without your knowing it was even close by. The exceptions are if you are carrying fish or lots of sweets in your pack or if you are wearing heavy, sweet deodorants or makeup. All of these are bear attractants.

In a wilderness camp there are special precautions you should take. Always hang your food at least 100 yards downwind of camp and get it high, 30 feet is reasonable. In addition, circle your camp with rope and hang the bells from your pack on it. Thus, if a bear walks into your camp, he'll run into the rope, the bells will ring, and everybody will have a chance to get up a tree before ol' griz figures out what's going on. Often the unexpected ringing of bells is enough to send him off in search of a quieter environment.

You see, more often than not, grizzlies tend to clear the way for campers and hikers. So be smart, don't act like bear bait, and always have a plan if you are confronted by one.

My pal Foonsky had such a plan during a wilderness expedition in Montana's northern Rockies. On our second day of hiking, we started seeing scratch marks on the trees 13 to 14 feet off the ground.

"Mr. Griz made those," Foonsky said. "With spring here, the grizzlies are coming out of hibernation and using the trees like a cat uses a scratch board to stretch the muscles."

The next day, I noticed Foonsky had a pair of track shoes tied to the back of his pack. I just laughed.

"You're not going to outrun a griz," I said. "In fact, there's hardly any animal out here in the wilderness that man can outrun."

Foonsky just smiled.

"I don't have to outrun a griz," he said. "I just have to outrun you!"

"Now what are we supposed to do?" the young boy asked his dad.

Fun and Games

"Yeah, Dad, think of something," said another son.

Well, Dad thought hard. This was one of the first camping trips he'd taken with his sons and one of the first lessons he received was that kids don't appreciate the philosophic release of mountain quiet. They want action and lots of it. With a glint in his eye, Dad searched around the camp and picked up 15 twigs, breaking them so each was four inches long. He laid them in three separate rows, three twigs in one row, five twigs in another, and seven in the other.

"OK, this game is called 3-5-7," said Dad. "You each take turns picking up sticks. You are allowed to remove all or as few as one twig from a row, but here's the catch: You can pick only from one row per turn. Whoever picks up the last stick left is the loser."

I remember this episode well because those two little boys were my brother Bobby, as in Rambobby, and me. And to this day, we still play 3-5-7 on campouts, with the winner getting to watch the loser clean the dishes. What I have learned in the span of time since that original episode is that it does not matter what your age is: campers need options for camp fun.

Some evenings, after a long hike or ride, you are likely to feel too worn-out to take on a serious romp downstream to fish, or a climb up to a ridge for a view. That is especially true if you have been in the outback for a week or more. At that point a lot of campers will spend their time resting and gazing at a map of the area, dreaming of the next day's adventure, or just take a seat against a rock, watching the colors of the sky and mountain panorama change minute by minute. But kids in the push-button video era, and a lot of adults too, want more. After all, "I'm on vacation; I want some fun."

There are several options, like the 3-5-7 twig game, and they should be just as much a part of your trip planning as arranging your gear.

For kids, plan on games, the more physically challenging the competition, the better. One of the best games is to throw a chunk of wood into a lake and challenge the kids to hit it by throwing rocks. It wreaks havoc on the fishing, but it can keep kids totally absorbed for some time. Target practice with a wrist-rocket slingshot is also all consuming for kids, firing rocks away at small targets like pinecones set on a log.

You can also set kids off on little missions near camp, such as looking for the footprints of wildlife, searching out good places to have a "snipe hunt," picking up twigs to get the evening fire started, or having them take the water purifier to a stream to pump some drinking water into a canteen. The latter is an easy, fun, yet important task that will allow kids to feel a sense of equality they often don't get at home.

For adults, the appeal should be more to the intellect. A good example is star and planet identification, and while you are staring into space, you're bound to spot a few asteroids or shooting stars. A star chart can make it easy to locate and identify many distinctive stars and constellations, such as Pleiades (the Seven Sisters), Orion, and others from the zodiac, depending on the time of year. With a little research, this can add a unique perspective to your trip. You could point to Polaris, one of the most easily identified of all stars, and note that navigators in the 1400s used it to find their way. Polaris, of course, is the North Star and is at the end of the handle of the Little Dipper. Pinpointing Polaris is quite easy. First find the Big Dipper and then locate the outside stars of the ladle of the Big Dipper. They are called the "pointer stars" because they point right at Polaris.

A tree identification book can teach you a few things about your surroundings. It is also a good idea for one member of the party to research the history of the area you have chosen and another to research the geology. With shared knowledge, you end up with a deeper love of wild places.

Another way to add some recreation into your trip is to bring a board game, a number of which have been miniaturized for campers. The most popular are chess, checkers, and cribbage. The latter comes with an equally miniature set of playing cards. And if you bring those little cards, that opens a vast set of other possibilities. With kids along, for instance, just take three queens out of the deck and you can play Old Maid.

But there are more serious card games, and they come with high stakes. Such occurred on one high country trip where Foonsky, Rambob, and I sat down for a late afternoon game of poker. In a game of seven-card stud, I caught a straight on the sixth card and felt like a dog licking on a T-bone. Already I had bet several Skittles and peanut M&Ms on this promising hand.

Then I examined the cards Foonsky had face up. He was showing three sevens, and acting as happy as a grizzly with a pork chop—or a full house. He matched my bet of two peanut M&Ms, then raised me three SweetTarts, one Starburst, and one sour apple Jolly Rancher. Rambob folded, but I matched Foonsky's bet and hoped for the best as the seventh and final card was dealt.

Just after Foonsky glanced at that last card, I saw him sneak a look at my grape stick and beef jerky stash.

"I raise you a grape stick," he said.

Rambob and I both gasped. It was the highest bet ever made, equivalent to a million dollars laid down in Las Vegas. Cannons were going off in my chest. I looked hard at my cards. They looked good, but were they good enough?

Even with a great hand like I had, a grape stick was too much to gamble, my last one with 10 days of trail ahead of us. I shook my head and folded my cards. Foonsky smiled at his victory.

But I still had my grape stick.

Old Tricks Don't Always Work

Most people are born honest, but after a few camping trips, they usually get over it.

I remember some advice I got from Rambob, normally an honest soul, on one camping trip. A giant mosquito had landed on my arm and he alerted me to some expert advice.

"Flex your arm muscles," he commanded, watching the mosquito fill with my blood. "He'll get stuck in your arm, then he'll explode."

For some reason, I believed him. We both proceeded to watch the mosquito drill countless holes in my arm.

Keep It Wild Tip 5: Keep the Wilderness Wild

1. Let nature's sound prevail. Avoid loud voices and noises.
2. Leave radios and tape players at home. At drive-in camping sites, never open car doors with music playing.
3. Careful guidance is necessary when choosing any games to bring for children. Most toys, especially any kind of gun toys with which children simulate shooting at each other, shouldn't be allowed on a camping trip.
4. Control pets at all times or leave them with a sitter at home.
5. Treat natural heritage with respect. Leave plants, rocks, and historical artifacts where you find them.

Alas, the unknowing face sabotage from their most trusted companions on camping trips. It can arise at any time, usually in the form of advice from a friendly, honest-looking face, as if to say, "What? How can you doubt me?" After that mosquito episode, I was a little more skeptical of my dear old brother. Then the next day, when another mosquito was nailing me in the back of the neck, out came this gem:

"Hold your breath," he commanded. I instinctively obeyed. "That will freeze the mosquito," he said, "then you can squish him."

But in the time I wasted holding my breath, the little bugger was able to fly off without my having the satisfaction of squishing him. When he got home, he probably told his family, "What a dummy I got to drill today!"

Over the years, I have been duped numerous times with dubious advice:

On a grizzly bear attack: "If he grabs you, tuck your head under the grizzly's chin; then he won't be able to bite you in the head." This made sense to me until the first time I came face-to-face with a nine-foot grizzly 40 yards away. In seconds, I was at the top of a tree, which suddenly seemed to make the most sense.

On coping with animal bites: "If a bear bites you in the arm, don't try to jerk it away. That will just rip up your arm. Instead force your arm deeper into his mouth. He'll lose his grip and will have to open it to get a firmer hold, and right then you can get away." I was told this in the Boy Scouts, and when I was 14, I had a chance to try it out when a friend's dog bit me as I tried to pet it. What happened? When I shoved my arm deeper into his mouth, he bit me three more times.

On cooking breakfast: "The bacon will curl up every time in a camp frying pan. So make sure you have a bacon stretcher to keep it flat." As a 12-year-old Tenderfoot, I spent two hours looking for the bacon stretcher until I figured out the camp leader had forgotten it. It wasn't for several years until I learned that there is no such thing.

On preventing sore muscles: "If you haven't hiked for a long time and you are facing a rough climb, you can keep from getting sore muscles in your legs, back, and shoulders by practicing the 'Dead Man's Walk.' Simply let your entire body go slack, and then take slow, wobbling steps. This will clear your muscles of lactic acid, which causes them to be so sore after a rough hike." Foonsky pulled this one on me. Rambob and I both bought it and tried it while we were hiking up Mount Whitney, which requires a 6,000-foot elevation gain in six miles. In one 45-minute period, about 30 other hikers passed us and looked at us as if we were suffering from some rare form of mental aberration.

Fish won't bite? No problem: "If the fish are not feeding or will not bite, persistent anglers can still catch dinner with little problem. Keep casting across the current, and eventually, as they hover in the stream, the line will feed across their open mouths. Keep reeling and you will hook the fish right in the side of the mouth. This technique is called 'lining.' Never worry if the fish will not bite, because you can always line 'em." Of course, heh, heh, heh, that explains why so many fish get hooked in the side of the mouth.

How to keep bears away: "To keep bears away, urinate around the borders of your campground. If there are a lot of bears in the area, it is advisable to go right on your sleeping bag." Yeah, surrrrrre.

What to do with trash: "Don't worry about packing out trash. Just bury it. It will regenerate into the earth and add valuable minerals." Bears, raccoons, skunks, and other critters will dig up your trash as soon as you depart, leaving one huge mess for the next camper. Always pack out everything.

Often the advice comes without warning. That was the case after a fishing trip with a female companion, when she outcaught me two to one, the third such trip in a row. I explained this to a shopkeeper, and he nodded, then explained why.

"The male fish are able to detect the female scent on the lure, and thus become aroused into striking."

Of course! That explains everything!

I was just a lad when Foonsky pulled the old snipe-hunt trick on me. It took nearly 30 years to get revenge.

Getting Revenge

You probably know about snipe hunting. That is where the victim is led out at night in the woods by a group, then is left holding a bag.

"Stay perfectly still and quiet," Foonsky explained. "You don't want to scare the snipe. The rest of us will go back to camp and let the woods settle down. Then when the snipe are least expecting it, we'll form a line and charge through the forest with sticks, beating bushes and trees, and we'll flush the snipe out right to you. Be ready with the bag. When we flush the snipe out, bag it. But until we start our charge, make sure you don't move or make a sound or you will spook the snipe and ruin everything."

I sat out there in the woods with my bag for hours, waiting for the charge. I waited, waited, and waited. Nothing happened. No charge, no snipe. It wasn't until well past midnight that I figured something was wrong. When I finally returned to camp, everybody was sleeping.

Well, I tell ya, don't get mad at your pals for the tricks they pull on you. Get revenge. Some 25 years later, on the last day of a camping trip, the time finally came.

"Let's break camp early," Foonsky suggested to Mr. Furnai and me. "Get up before dawn, eat breakfast, pack up, and be on the ridge to watch the sun come up. It will be a fantastic way to end the trip."

"Sounds great to me," I replied. But when Foonsky wasn't looking, I turned his alarm clock ahead three hours. So when the alarm sounded at the appointed 4:30 a.m. wake-up time, Mr. Furnai and I knew it was actually only 1:30 a.m.

Foonsky clambered out of his sleeping bag and whistled with a grin. "Time to break camp."

"You go ahead," I answered. "I'll skip breakfast so I can get a little more sleep. At the first sign of dawn, wake me up, and I'll break camp."

"Me, too," said Mr. Furnai.

Foonsky then proceeded to make some coffee, cook a breakfast, and eat it, sitting on a log in the black darkness of the forest, waiting for the sun to come up. An hour later, with still no sign of dawn, he checked his clock. It now read 5:30 a.m. "Any minute now we should start seeing some light," he said.

He made another cup of coffee, packed his gear, and sat there in the middle of the night, looking up at the stars, waiting for dawn. "Anytime now," he said. He ended up sitting there all night long.

Revenge is sweet. Prior to a fishing trip at a lake, I took Foonsky aside and explained that the third member of the party, Jimbobo, was hard of hearing and very sensitive about it. "Don't mention it to him," I advised. "Just talk real loud."

Meanwhile, I had already told Jimbobo the same thing. "Foonsky just can't hear very good."

We had fished less than 20 minutes when Foonsky got a nibble.

"GET A BITE?" shouted Jimbobo.

"YEAH!" yelled back Foonsky, smiling. "BUT I DIDN'T HOOK HIM!"

"MAYBE NEXT TIME!" shouted Jimbobo with a friendly grin.

Well, they spent the entire day yelling at each other from the distance of a few feet. They never did figure it out. Heh, heh, heh.

That is, I thought so, until we made a trip salmon fishing. I got a strike that almost knocked my fishing rod out of the boat. When I grabbed the rod, it felt as if Moby Dick were on the other end. "At least a 25-pounder," I said. "Maybe bigger."

The fish dove, ripped off line, and then bulldogged. "It's acting like a 40-pounder," I announced, "Huge, just huge. It's going deep. That's how the big ones fight."

Some 15 minutes later, I finally got the "salmon" to the surface. It turned out to be a coffee can that Foonsky had clipped on the line with a snap swivel. By maneuvering the boat, he made the coffee can fight like a big fish.

This all started with a little old snipe hunt years ago. You never know what your pals will try next. Don't get mad. Get revenge.

Camping Options

Boat-in Seclusion
Most campers would never think of trading in their car, pickup truck, or RV for a boat, but people who go by boat on a camping trip enjoy virtually guaranteed seclusion and top-quality outdoor experiences.

food cache (hang downwind)

escape tree

minimum 100 feet

minimum 100 feet

minimum 200 feet

6-8 inch "cat hole" for depositing human waste

minimum 200 feet

Camping with a boat is a do-it-yourself venture in living under primitive circumstances. Yet at the same time you can bring along any luxury item you wish, from giant coolers, stoves, and lanterns to portable gasoline generators. Weight is almost never an issue.

Many outstanding boat-in campgrounds in beautiful surroundings are available in the Pacific Northwest. The best are on the shores of lakes accessible by canoe or skiff, and at offshore islands reached by saltwater cruisers. Several boat-in camps are detailed in this book.

If you want to take the adventure a step further and create your own boat-in camp, perhaps near a special fishing spot, this is a go-for-it deal that provides the best way possible to establish your own secret campsite. But most people who set out freelance style forget three critical items for boat-in camping: a shovel, a sunshade, and an ax. Here is why these items can make a key difference in your trip:

Shovel: Many lakes and virtually all reservoirs have steep, sloping banks. At reservoirs subject to drawdowns, what was lake bottom in the spring can be a campsite in late summer. If you want a flat area for a tent site, the only answer is to dig one out yourself. A shovel gives you that option.

Sunshade: The flattest spots to camp along lakes often have a tendency to support only sparse tree growth. As a result, a natural shield

In setting up camp, always be mindful of potential ecological disturbances. Pitch tents and dispose of human waste at least 200 feet from the water's edge. In grizzly bear territory, increase the distance between your tent and your cooking area, food-hang, and the water's edge threefold. In other words, if you're in grizzly country, do all your cooking 100 yards (not feet) downwind of your sleeping area. If you can establish an escape tree nearby, all the better.

from sun and rain is rarely available. What? Rain in the summer? Oh yeah, don't get me started. A light tarp, set up with poles and staked ropes, solves the problem.

Ax: Unless you bring your own firewood, which is necessary at some sparsely wooded reservoirs, there is no substitute for a good, sharp ax. With an ax, you can almost always find dry firewood, since the interior of an otherwise wet log will be dry. When the weather turns bad is precisely when you will most want a fire. You may need an ax to get one going.

In the search to create your own personal boat-in campsite, you will find that the flattest areas are usually the tips of peninsulas and points, while the protected back ends of coves are often steeply sloped. At reservoirs, the flattest areas are usually near the mouths of the feeder streams and the points are quite steep. On rivers, there are usually sandbars on the inside of tight bends that make for ideal campsites.

Almost all boat-in campsites developed by government agencies are free of charge, but you are on your own. Only in extremely rare cases is piped water available.

Any way you go, by canoe, skiff, or power cruiser, you end up with a one-in-a-million campsite you can call your own.

Desert Outings

It was a cold, snowy day in Missouri when 10-year-old Rusty Ballinger started dreaming about the vast deserts of the West.

"My dad was reading aloud from a Zane Grey book called *Riders of the Purple Sage*," Ballinger said. "He would get animated when he got to the passages about the desert. It wasn't long before I started to have the same feelings."

That was in 1947. Ballinger, now in his 60s, has spent a good part of his life exploring the West, camping along the way. "The deserts are the best part. There's something about the uniqueness of each little area you see," Ballinger said. "You're constantly surprised. Just the time of day and the way the sun casts a different color. It's like the lady you care about. One time she smiles, the next time she's pensive. The desert is like that. If you love nature, you can love the desert. After awhile, you can't help but love it."

A desert adventure is not just an antidote for a case of cabin fever in the winter. Whether you go by RV, pickup truck, car, or on foot, it provides its own special qualities.

If you go camping in the desert, your approach has to be as unique as the setting. For starters, don't plan on any campfires, but bring a camp stove instead. And unlike in the mountains, do not camp near a water hole. That's because an animal such as a badger, coyote, or desert bighorn might be desperate for water, and if you set up camp in the animal's way, you may be forcing a confrontation.

In some areas, there is a danger of flash floods. An intense rain can fall in one area, collect in a pool, then suddenly burst through a narrow canyon. If you are in its path, you could be injured or drowned. The lesson? Never camp in a gully.

"Some people might wonder, 'What good is this place?'" Ballinger said. "The answer is that it is good for looking at. It is one of the world's unique places."

Camp Ethics and Politics

The perfect place to set up a base camp turned out to be not so perfect. In fact, according to Doug Williams of California, it did not even exist.

Williams and his son, James, had driven deep into Angeles National Forest, prepared to set up camp and then explore the surrounding area on foot. But when they reached their destination, no campground existed.

"I wanted a primitive camp in a national forest where I could teach my son some basics," said the senior Williams. "But when we got there, there wasn't much left of the camp, and it had been closed. It was obvious that the area had been vandalized."

It turned out not to be an isolated incident. A lack of outdoor ethics practiced by a few people using the unsupervised campgrounds available on national forestland has caused the U.S. Forest Service to close a few of them and make extensive repairs to others.

"There have been sites closed, especially in Angeles and San Bernardino national forests in Southern California," said David Flohr,

---

Keep It Wild Tip 6: Respect Other Users

1. Horseback riders have priority over hikers. Step to the downhill side of the trail and talk softly when encountering horseback riders.

2. Hikers and horseback riders have priority over mountain bikers. When mountain bikers encounter other users even on wide trails, they should pass at an extremely slow speed. On very narrow trails they should dismount and get off to the side so hikers or horseback riders can pass without having their trip disrupted.

3. Mountain bikes aren't permitted on most single-track trails and are expressly prohibited in designated wilderness areas and all sections of the Pacific Crest Trail. Mountain bikers breaking these rules should be confronted and told to dismount and walk their bikes until they reach a legal area.

4. It's illegal for horseback riders to break off branches that may be in the path of wilderness trails.

5. Horseback riders on overnight trips are prohibited from camping in many areas and are usually required to keep stock animals in specific areas where they can do no damage to the landscape.

---

regional campground coordinator for the U.S. Forest Service. "It's an urban type of thing, affecting forests near urban areas, and not just Los Angeles. They get a lot of urban users and they bring with them a lot of the same ethics they have in the city. They get drinking and they're not afraid to do things. They vandalize and run. Of course, it is a public facility, so they think nobody is getting hurt."

But somebody is getting hurt, starting with the next person who wants to use the campground. And if the ranger district budget doesn't have enough money to pay for repairs, the campground is then closed for the next arrivals. Just ask Doug and James Williams.

In an era of considerable fiscal restraint for the U.S. Forest Service, vandalized campgrounds could face closure instead of repair in the next few years. Williams had just a taste of it, but Flohr, as camping co-ordinator, gets a steady diet.

"It starts with behavior," Flohr said. "General rowdiness, drinking, partying, and then vandalism. It goes all the way from the felt tip pen things (graffiti) to total destruction, blowing up toilet buildings with dynamite. I've seen toilets destroyed totally with shotguns. They burn up tables, burn barriers. They'll burn up signs for firewood, even the shingles right off the roofs of the bathrooms. They'll shoot anything, garbage cans, signs. It can get a little hairy. A favorite is to remove the stool out of a toilet building. We've had people fall in the open hole."

The National Park Service had a similar problem some years back, especially with rampant littering. Park Director Bill Mott responded by creating an interpretive program that attempts to teach visitors the wise use of natural areas, and to have all park workers set examples by picking up litter and reminding others to do the same.

The U.S. Forest Service has responded with a similar program, making brochures available that detail the wise use of national forests. The four most popular brochures are titled: "Rules for Visitors to the National Forest," "Recreation in the National Forests," "Is the Water Safe?" and "Backcountry Safety Tips." These include details on camp-fires, drinking water from lakes or streams, hypothermia, safety, and outdoor ethics. They are available for free by writing to Public Affairs, U.S. Forest Service, 630 Sansome Street, San Francisco, CA 94111.

Flohr said even experienced campers sometimes cross over the ethics line unintentionally. The most common example, he said, is when campers toss garbage into the outhouse toilet, rather than packing it out in a plastic garbage bag.

"They throw it in the vault toilet bowls, which just fills them up," Flohr said. "That creates an extremely high cost to pump it. You know why? Because some poor guy has to pick that stuff out piece by piece. It can't be pumped."

At most backcountry sites, the U.S. Forest Service has implemented a program called "Pack it in, pack it out," even posting signs that remind all visitors to do so. But a lot of people don't do it, and others may even uproot the sign and burn it for firewood.

On a trip to a secluded lake near Carson Pass in the Sierra Nevada, I arrived at a small, little-known camp where the picnic table had been spray painted and garbage had been strewn about. A pristine place, the true temple of God, had been defiled.

Getting Along with Fellow Campers

The most important thing about a camping, fishing, or hunting trip is not where you go, how many fish you catch, or how many shots you fire. It often has little to do with how beautiful the view is, how easy the campfire lights, or how sunny the days are.

Oh yeah? Then what is the most important factor? The answer: The people you are with. It is that simple.

Who would you rather camp with? Your enemy at work or your dream mate in a good mood? Heh, heh. You get the idea. A camping trip is a fairly close-knit experience, and you can make lifetime friends or lifelong enemies in the process. That is why your choice of companions is so important. Your own behavior is equally consequential.

Two Dogs: "There are two dogs inside of you," my dad once said, "a good one, and a bad one. The one you feed is the one that will grow. Always try to feed the good dog."

Yet most people spend more time putting together their camping gear than considering why they enjoy or hate the company of their chosen companions. Here are 10 rules of behavior for good camping mates:

1. No whining: Nothing is more irritating than being around a whiner. It goes right to the heart of adventure, since often the only difference between a hardship and an escapade is simply whether or not an individual has the spirit for it. The people who do can turn a rugged day in the outdoors into a cherished memory. Those who don't can ruin it with their incessant sniveling.

2. Activities must be agreed upon: Always have a meeting of the minds with your companions over the general game plan. Then everybody will possess an equal stake in the outcome of the trip. This is absolutely critical. Otherwise they will feel like merely an addendum to your trip, not an equal participant, and a whiner will be born (see No. 1).

3. Nobody's in charge: It is impossible to be genuine friends if one person is always telling another what to do, especially if the orders involve simple camp tasks. You need to share the space on the same emotional plane, and the only way to do that is to have a semblance of equality, regardless of differences in experience. Just try ordering your mate around at home for a few days. You'll quickly see the results, and they aren't pretty.

4. Equal chances at the fun stuff: It's fun to build the fire, fun to get the first cast at the best fishing spot, and fun to hoist the bagged food for a bear-proof food hang. It is not fun to clean the dishes, collect firewood, or cook every night. So obviously there must be an equal distribution of the fun stuff and the not-fun stuff, and everybody on the trip must get a shot at the good and the bad.

5. **No heroes:** No awards are bestowed for achievement in the outdoors, yet some guys treat mountain peaks, big fish, and big game as if they are prizes in a trophy competition. Actually, nobody cares how wonderful you are, which is always a surprise to trophy chasers. What people care about is the heart of the adventure, the gut-level stuff.

6. **Agree on a wake-up time:** It is a good idea to agree on a general wake-up time before closing your eyes for the night, and that goes regardless of whether you want to sleep in late or get up at dawn. Then you can proceed on course regardless of what time you crawl out of your sleeping bag in the morning, without the risk of whining (see No. 1).

7. **Think of the other guy:** Be self-aware instead of self-absorbed. A good test is to count the number of times you say, "What do you think?" A lot of potential problems can be solved quickly by actually listening to the answer.

8. **Solo responsibilities:** There are a number of essential camp duties on all trips, and while they should be shared equally, most should be completed solo. That means that when it's time for you to cook, you don't have to worry about me changing the recipe on you. It means that when it's my turn to make the fire, you keep your mitts out of it.

9. **Don't let money get in the way:** Of course everybody should share equally in trip expenses, such as the cost of food, and it should be split up before you head out yonder. Don't let somebody pay extra, because that person will likely try to control the trip. Conversely, don't let somebody weasel out of paying a fair share.

10. **Accordance on the food plan:** Always have complete agreement on what you plan to eat each day. Don't figure that just because you like Steamboat's Sludge, everybody else will, too, especially youngsters. Always, always, always check for food allergies such as nuts, onions, or cheese, and make sure each person brings his or her own personal coffee brand. Some people drink only decaffeinated; others might gag on anything but Burma monkey beans.

Obviously, it is difficult to find companions who will agree on all of these elements. This is why many campers say that the best camping buddy they'll ever have is their mate, someone who knows all about them and likes them anyway.

Outdoors with Kids

How do you get a boy or girl excited about the outdoors? How do you compete with the television and remote control? How do you prove to a kid that success comes from persistence, spirit, and logic, which the outdoors teaches, and not from pushing buttons?

The answer is in the **Ten Camping Commandments for Kids.** These are lessons that will get youngsters excited about the outdoors, and will make sure adults help the process along, not kill it. I've put this list together with the help of my own kids, Jeremy and Kris, and their mother, Stephani. Some of the commandments are obvious, some are not, but all are important:

1. Take children to places where there is a guarantee of action. A good example is camping in a park where large numbers of wildlife can be viewed, such as squirrels, chipmunks, deer, and even bears. Other good choices are fishing at a small pond loaded with bluegill, or hunting in a spot where a kid can shoot a .22 at pinecones all day. Boys and girls want action, not solitude.

2. Enthusiasm is contagious. If you aren't excited about an adventure, you can't expect a child to be. Show a genuine zest for life in the outdoors, and point out everything as if it is the first time you have ever seen it.

3. Always, always, always be seated when talking to someone small. This allows the adult and child to be on the same level. That is why fishing in a small boat is perfect for adults and kids. Nothing is worse for youngsters than having a big person look down at them and give them orders. What fun is that?

4. Always *show* how to do something, whether it is gathering sticks for a campfire, cleaning a trout, or tying a knot. Never tell—always show. A button usually clicks to "off" when a kid is lectured. But kids can learn behavior patterns and outdoor skills by watching adults, even when the adults are not aware they are being watched.

5. Let kids be kids. Let the adventure happen, rather than trying to force it within some preconceived plan. If they get sidetracked watching pollywogs, chasing butterflies, or sneaking up on chipmunks, let them be. A youngster can have more fun turning over rocks and looking at different kinds of bugs than sitting in one spot, waiting for a fish to bite.

6. Expect short attention spans. Instead of getting frustrated about it, use it to your advantage. How? By bringing along a bag of candy and snacks. Where there is a lull in the camp activity, out comes the bag. Don't let them know what goodies await, so each one becomes a surprise.

7. Make absolutely certain the child's sleeping bag is clean, dry, and warm. Nothing is worse than discomfort when trying to sleep, but a refreshing sleep makes for a positive attitude the next day. In addition, kids can become quite scared of animals at night. A parent should not wait for any signs of this, but always play the part of the outdoor guardian, the one who will take care of everything.

8. Kids quickly relate to outdoor ethics. They will enjoy eating everything they kill, building a safe campfire, and picking up all their litter, and they will develop a sense of pride that goes with it. A good idea is to bring extra plastic garbage bags to pick up any trash you come across. Kids long remember when they do something right that somebody else has done wrong.

9. If you want youngsters hooked on the outdoors for life, take a close-up photograph of them holding up fish they have caught, blowing on the campfire, or completing other camp tasks. Young children can forget how much fun they had, but they never forget if they have a picture of it.

10. The least important word you can ever say to a kid is "I." Keep track of how often you are saying "Thank you" and "What do you think?" If you don't say them very often, you'll lose out. Finally, the most important words of all are: "I am proud of you."

Predicting Weather

Foonsky climbed out of his sleeping bag, glanced at the nearby meadow, and scowled hard.

"It doesn't look good," he said. "Doesn't look good at all."

I looked at my adventure companion of 20 years, noting his discontent. Then I looked at the meadow and immediately understood why: *"When the grass is dry at morning light, look for rain before the night."*

"How bad you figure?" I asked him.

"We'll know soon enough, I reckon," Foonsky answered. "Short notice, soon to pass. Long notice, long it will last."

When you are out in the wild, spending your days fishing and your nights camping, you learn to rely on yourself to predict the weather. It can make or break you. If a storm hits the unprepared, it can quash the trip and possibly endanger the participants. But if you are ready, a potential hardship can be an adventure.

You can't rely on TV weather forecasters, people who don't even know that when all the cows on a hill are facing north, it will rain that night for sure. God forbid if the cows are all sitting. But what do you expect from TV's talking heads?

Foonsky made a campfire, started boiling some water for coffee and soup, and we started to plan the day. In the process, I noticed the smoke of the campfire: It was sluggish, drifting and hovering.

"You notice the smoke?" I asked, chewing on a piece of homemade jerky.

"Not good," Foonsky said. "Not good." He knew that sluggish, hovering smoke indicates rain.

"You'd think we'd have been smart enough to know last night that this was coming," Foonsky said. "Did you take a look at the moon or the clouds?"

"I didn't look at either," I answered. "Too busy eating the trout we caught." You see, if the moon is clear and white, the weather will be good the next day. But if there is a ring around the moon, the number of stars you can count inside the ring equals the number of days until the next rain. As for clouds, the high, thin clouds called cirrus indicate a change in the weather.

We were quiet for a while, planning our strategy, but as we did so, some terrible things happened: A chipmunk scampered past with his tail high, a small flock of geese flew by very low, and a little sparrow perched on a tree limb quite close to the trunk.

"We're in for trouble," I told Foonsky.

"I know, I know," he answered. "I saw 'em, too. And come to think of it, no crickets were chirping last night either."

"Damn, that's right!"

These are all signs of an approaching storm. Foonsky pointed at the smoke of the campfire and shook his head as if he had just been condemned. Sure enough, now the smoke was blowing toward the north, a sign of a south wind. *"When the wind is from the south, the rain is in its mouth."*

"We'd best stay hunkered down until it passes," Foonsky said.

I nodded. "Let's gather as much firewood now as we can, get our gear covered up, then plan our meals."

"Then we'll get a poker game going."

As we accomplished these camp tasks, the sky clouded up, then darkened. Within an hour we had gathered enough firewood to make a large pile, enough wood to keep a fire going no matter how hard it rained. The day's meals had been separated out of the food bag so it wouldn't have to be retrieved during the storm. We buttoned two ponchos together, staked two of the corners with ropes to the ground, and tied the other two with ropes to different tree limbs to create a slanted roof/shelter.

As the first raindrop fell with that magic sound on our poncho roof, Foonsky was just starting to shuffle the cards.

"Cut for deal," he said.

Just as I did so, it started to rain a bit harder. I pulled out another piece of beef jerky and started chewing on it. It was just another day in paradise.

Weather lore can be valuable. Small signs provided by nature and wildlife can be translated to provide a variety of weather information. Here is the list I have compiled over the years:

When the grass is dry at morning light,
Look for rain before the night.

Short notice, soon to pass.
Long notice, long it will last.

When the wind is from the east,
'Tis fit for neither man nor beast.

When the wind is from the south,
The rain is in its mouth.

When the wind is from the west,
Then it is the very best.

Red sky at night, sailors' delight.
Red sky in the morning, sailors take warning.

When all the cows are pointed north,
Within a day rain will come forth.
Onion skins very thin, mild winter coming in.
Onion skins very tough, winter's going to be very rough.

When your boots make the squeak of snow,
Then very cold temperatures will surely show.

If a goose flies high, fair weather ahead.
If a goose flies low, foul weather will come instead.

A thick coat on a woolly caterpillar means a big, early snow is coming.

Chipmunks will run with their tails up before a rain.

Bees always stay near their hives before a rainstorm.

When the birds are perched on large limbs near tree trunks, an intense but short storm will arrive.

On the coast, if groups of seabirds are flying a mile inland, look for major winds.

If crickets are chirping very loud during the evening, the next day will be clear and warm.

If the smoke of a campfire at night rises in a thin spiral, good weather is assured for the next day.

If the smoke of a campfire at night is sluggish, drifting, and hovering, it will rain the next day.

If there is a ring around the moon, count the number of stars inside the ring, and that is how many days until the next rain.

If the moon is clear and white, the weather will be good the next day.

High, thin clouds, or cirrus, indicate a change in the weather.

Oval-shaped lenticular clouds indicate high winds.

Two levels of clouds moving in different directions indicate changing weather soon.

Huge, dark, billowing clouds, called cumulonimbus, suddenly forming on warm afternoons in the mountains mean that a short but intense thunderstorm with lightning can be expected.

When squirrels are busy gathering food for extended periods, it means good weather is ahead in the short term, but a hard winter is ahead in the long term.

And God forbid if all the cows are sitting down . . . .

Beating the Time Trap

If the great outdoors is so great, then why don't people enjoy it more? The answer is because of the time trap, and I will tell you exactly how to beat it.

For many, the biggest problem is finding the time to go, whether it is camping, hiking, fishing, boating, backpacking, biking, or even just for a good drive in the country. The solution? Well, believe it or not, the answer is to treat your fun just as you treat your work, and I'll tell you how.

Consider how you treat your job: Always on time? Go there every day you are scheduled? Do whatever it takes to get there and get it done? Right? No foolin' that's right. Now imagine if you took the same approach to the outdoors. Suddenly your life would be a heck of a lot better.

The secret is to schedule all of your outdoor activities. For instance, I go fishing every Thursday evening, hiking every Sunday morning, and on an overnight trip every new moon (when stargazing is best). No matter what, I'm going. Just like going to work, I've scheduled it. The same approach works with longer adventures. The only reason I have been able to complete hikes ranging from 200 to 300 miles was that I scheduled the time to do it. The reason I spend 125 to 150 days a year in the field is that I schedule them. In my top year, I had nearly 200 days where at least part of the day was enjoyed taking part in outdoor recreation.

If you get out your calendar and write in the exact dates you are going, then you'll go. If you don't, you won't. Suddenly, with only a minor change in your life plan, you can be living the life you were previously dreaming about.

See you out there.
—Tom Stienstra

CAMPING GEAR CHECKLIST

COOKING GEAR

- Camp fuel
- Camp stove
- Dish soap and scrubber
- Fire-starter cubes or candle
- Itemized food
- Knife, fork
- Matches stored in resealable (such as Ziploc) bags
- Plastic spade
- Pot, pan, cup
- Pot grabber
- Salt, pepper, spices

Optional Cooking Gear
- Ax or hatchet
- Can opener
- Clothespins
- Dustpan
- Grill
- Ice chest
- Spatula
- Tablecloth
- Tinfoil
- Whisk broom
- Wood or charcoal for barbecue

CAMPING CLOTHES

- Cotton/canvas pants
- Cotton shirt
- Hat
- Long-sleeved cotton/wool shirt
- Parka
- Polypropylene underwear
- Rain jacket, pants, or poncho
- Sunglasses
- Vest

Optional Clothing
- Gloves
- Seam Lock
- Shorts
- Ski cap
- Swimsuit

HIKING GEAR

- Backup lightweight shoes
- 80% wool socks
- Gaiters
- Innersole or foot cushion
- Moleskin and medical tape
- Polypropylene socks
- Quality hiking boots
- Strong bootlaces
- Thick cotton socks
- Water-repellent boot treatment

SLEEPING GEAR

- Sleeping bag
- Insulite or Therm-a-Rest pad
- Ground tarp
- Tent

Optional Sleeping Gear
- Air pillow
- Catalytic heater
- Foam pad for truck bed
- Mosquito netting
- RV Windshield light screen

FIRST AID

- Ace bandage
- Adhesive bandages
- After-Bite or ammonia
- Aspirin
- Athletic tape
- Biodegradable soap
- Caladryl or Tecnu
- Campho-Phenique gel
- First-aid cream
- Moleskin
- Mosquito repellent
- Neosporin
- Roller gauze
- Sterile gauze pads
- Sunscreen
- Thermometer
- Towelettes
- Tweezers

Optional First Aid
- Coins for emergency phone calls
- Extra set of matches
- Mirror for signaling
- Water purification system

FISHING/RECREATION GEAR

- Fishing reel with fish-line splitshot, snap swivels
- Fishing rod
- Knife
- Pliers

Optional Recreation Gear
- Backpacking cribbage board
- Deck of cards
- Knapsack for each person
- Stargazing chart
- Tree identification handbook

MISCELLANEOUS

- Camera and film
- Compass
- Feminine hygiene products
- Flashlight
- Handkerchief
- Lantern and fuel
- Lip balm
- Maps
- Nylon rope for food hang
- Plastic garbage bags
- Toilet paper
- Toothbrush and toothpaste
- Watch

Optional Miscellaneous
- Binoculars
- Notebook and pen
- Towel

Resource Guide

U.S. Forest Service, Pacific Northwest Region 6: 333 S.W. First Avenue, Portland, OR 97208-3623; or P.O. Box 3623, Portland, OR 97204; tel. (503) 808-2651, fax (503) 808-2229; website: www.fs.fed.us/r6.

Maps of national forests in Washington and Oregon are available from the district offices listed as a contact for each national forest campground. They are also *available* from an interpretive organization: Nature of the Northwest, 800 Northeast Oregon Street, Room 177, Portland, Or 97232; tel. (503) 872-2750; website: www.naturenw.org.

For further information on individual national forests, write, call, or visit the websites of the following forests:

Washington

- Gifford Pinchot National Forest: 10600 N.E. 51st Circle, Vancouver, WA 98682; tel. (360) 891-5000, fax (360) 750-5045; website: www.fs.fed.us/r6/gpnf

- Olympic National Forest: 1835 Black Lake Boulevard SW, Olympia, WA 98512-5263; tel. (360) 956-2300, fax (360) 956-2330; website: www.fs.fed.us/r6/olympic

- Mount Baker-Snoqualmie National Forest: 21905 64th Avenue West, Mountlake Terrace, WA 98043; tel. (425) 775-9702, (800) 627-0062, fax (425) 744-3255; website: www.fs.fed.us/r6/mbs

- Colville National Forest: 765 S. Main Street, Colville, WA 99114; tel. (509) 684-7000, fax (509) 684-7280.

- Wenatchee National Forest: 215 Melody Lane, Wenatchee, WA 98801-5933; tel. (509) 826-3275, fax (509) 662-4368; website: www.fs.fed.us/r6/wenatchee

- Okanogan National Forest: 1240 S. Second Avenue, Okanogan, WA 98840; tel. (509) 826-3275, fax (509) 422-2014; website: www.fs.fed.us/r6/oka

Oregon

- Deschutes National Forest: 1645 Highway 20 East, Bend, OR 97701; tel. (541) 388-2715, fax (541) 383-5531; website: www.fs.fed.us/r6/deschutes

- Fremont National Forest: HC 10 Box 337, 1300 S. G Street, Lakeview, OR 97630; tel. (541) 947-2151, fax (541) 947-6399; website: www.fs.fed.us/r6/fremont

- Malheur National Forest: 431 Patterson Bridge Road, P.O. Box 909, John Day, OR 97845; tel. (541) 575-3000, fax (541) 575-3001; website: www.fs.fed.us/r6/malheur

- Mount Hood National Forest: 16400 Champion Way, Sandy, OR 97055; tel. (503) 668-1700, fax (503) 668-1794; website: www.fs.fed.us/r6/mthood

- Ochoco National Forest: 3160 N.E. Third Street, Box 490, Prineville, OR 97754; tel. (541) 416-6500, fax (541) 416-6695; website: www.fs.fed.us/r6/ochoco

- Rogue River National Forest: P.O. Box 520, 333 W. Eighth Street, Medford, OR 97501-0209; tel. (541) 858-2200, fax (541) 858-2255; website: www.fs.fed.us/r6/rogue

- Siskiyou National Forest: 200 N.E. Greenfield Road, Box 440, Grants Pass, OR 97526-0242; tel. (541) 471-6500, fax (541) 471-6514; website: www.fs.fed.us/r6/siskiyou

- Siuslaw National Forest: P.O. Box 1148, 4077 S.W. Research Way, Corvallis, OR 97333; tel. (541) 750-7000, fax (541) 750-7234; website: www.fs.fed.us/r6/siuslaw

- Umatilla National Forest: 2517 S.W. Hailey Avenue, Pendleton, OR 97801; tel. (541) 278-3720, fax (541) 278-3730; website: www.fs.fed.us/r6/uma

- Umpqua National Forest: P.O. Box 1008, 2900 N.W. Stewart Parkway, Roseburg, OR 97470; tel. (541) 672-6601, fax (541) 957-3495; website: www.fs.fed.us/r6/umpqua

- Wallowa-Whitman National Forest: P.O. Box 907, 1550 Dewey Avenue, Baker City, OR 97814; tel. (541) 523-1205, fax (541) 523-1315; website: www.fs.fed.us/r6/w-w

- Willamette National Forest: P.O. Box 10607, Eugene, OR 97440 or 211 E. 7th Avenue, Eugene, OR 97401; tel. (541) 465-6521, fax (541) 465-6488; website: www.fs.fed.us/r6/willamette

- Winema National Forest: 2819 Dahlia Street, Klamath Falls, OR 97601; tel. (541) 883-6714, fax (541) 883-6709; website: www.fs.fed.us/r6/winema

State Parks

The Washington and Oregon State Parks systems provide many popular camping spots. Reservations are often a necessity during the summer months. The camps include drive-in numbered sites, tent spaces, and picnic tables, with showers and bathrooms provided nearby. Although some parks are well known, there are still some little-known gems in the state parks systems where campers can get seclusion, even in the summer months.

Washington and Oregon have joined in sponsoring a central reservation system. Reservations can be made for 46 Washington and 26 Oregon state parks through Reservations Northwest at (800) 452-5687. On-line reservations for Oregon State Parks can be made by accessing the website: www.prd.state.or.us. Campgrounds under the system are clearly noted in the "reservations, fees" paragraph of their listings in this book. A nonrefundable reservation fee of $6 and the first night's fee will be required as a deposit, charged to a MasterCard or Visa credit card (debit cards linked to MasterCard or Visa also accepted). Under this system, reservations can be made throughout the year, up to 11 months in advance.

A Washington State Parks central information telephone number is (800) 233-0321. General information regarding Oregon State Parks can be obtained by calling (800) 551-6949.

Washington
Washington Parks and Recreation Commission: 7150 Cleanwater Lane, P.O. Box 42650, Olympia, WA 98504-2650; tel. (800) 233-0321 or (360) 902-8500, fax (360) 753-1594; website: www.parks.wa.gov

National
Parks

Oregon
Oregon Parks and Recreation Department: 1115 Commercial Street NE, Salem, OR 97301-1002; tel. (800) 551-6949, fax (503) 872-5289; website: www.prd.state.or.us

The national parks in Washington and Oregon are natural wonders, ranging from the spectacular Mount Rainier National Park to the lava-strewn Mount St. Helens National Monument to the often fog-bound Olympic National Park.

For information about each of the National Parks in Washington and Oregon, contact the parks directly at the following numbers or addresses:

Washington

- Olympic National Park: 600 East Park Avenue, Port Angeles, WA 98362-6798; tel. (360) 452-4501 or (360) 452-0330, fax (360) 452-0335; website: www.nps.gov/olym

- Mount St. Helens National Volcanic Monument: 42218 NE Yale Bridge Road, Amboy, WA 98601; tel. (360) 247-3900 or (360) 247-3903, fax (360) 247-3901; website: www.fs.fed.us/gpnf

- Mount Rainier National Park: Tahoma Woods, Star Route, Ashford, WA 98304-9751; tel. (360) 569-2211, fax (360) 569-2170; website: www.nps.gov/mora

- North Cascades National Park: Ross Lake and Lake Chelan National Recreation Areas, 2105 State Route 20, Sedro-Woolley, WA 98284; tel. (360) 856-5700, fax (360) 856-1934; website: www.nps.gov/noca

- Lake Roosevelt National Recreation Area: 1008 Crest Drive, Coulee Dam, WA 99116-1259; tel. (509) 633-9441, fax (509) 633-9332; website: www.nps.gov/laro

Oregon

- Crater Lake National Park: P.O. Box 7, Crater Lake, OR 97604; tel. (541) 594-2211, fax (541) 594-2299; website: www.nps.gov/crla

- Columbia River Gorge National Scenic Area: 902 Wasco Avenue, Suite 200, Hood River, OR 97031; tel. (541) 386-2333, fax (541) 386-1916; e-mail: crgnsa@fs.fed.us

- Crooked River National Grassland: 813 S.W. Highway 92, Madras, OR 97741; tel. (541) 416-6640, fax (541) 416-6694; website: www.fs.fed.us/r6/ochoco

- Hells Canyon National Recreation Area: 88401 Highway 82, Enterprise, OR 97828; tel. (541) 426-5546 or (541) 426-4978, fax (541) 426-5520; website: www.fs.fed.us/r6/w-w

- Oregon Dunes National Recreation Area: 855 Highway 101, Reedsport, OR 97467; tel. (541) 271-3611, fax (541) 271-6019.

Department of Natural Resources (DNR)

The Department of Natural Resources manages about five million acres of public land in Washington. All of it is managed under the concept of "multiple use," designed to provide the greatest number of recreational opportunities while still protecting natural resources.

The campgrounds in these areas are among the most primitive, remote, and least known of the camps listed in this book. The campsites are usually free and you are asked to remove all litter and trash from the area, leaving only your footprints behind.

In addition to maps of the area it manages, the Department of Natural Resources also has U.S. Geological Survey maps and U.S. Army Corps of Engineer maps. For information, write or phone the Department of Natural Resources at its state or regional addresses:

- State of Washington: 1111 Washington Street SE, P.O. Box 47000, Olympia, WA 98504-7000; tel. (800) 527-3305 or (360) 902-1000, fax (360) 902-1775; website: www.wa.gov/dnr

- Central Region: 1405 Rush Road, Chehalis, WA 98532-8763; tel. (360) 748-2383, fax (360) 748-2387.

- Northeast Region: 225 S. Silke Road, P.O. Box 190, Colville, WA 99114-0190; tel. (509) 684-7474, fax (509) 684-7484.

- Northwest Region: 919 N. Township Street, Sedro-Woolley, WA 98284-9395; tel. (360) 856-3500, fax (360) 856-2150.

- Olympic Region: 411 Tillicum Lane, Forks, WA 98331-9797; tel. (360) 374-6131, fax (360) 374-5446.

- South Puget Sound Region: 950 Farman Street N., P.O. Box 68, Enumclaw, WA 98022-0068; tel. (360) 825-1631, fax (360) 825-1672.

- Southwest Region: 601 Bond Road, P.O. Box 280, Castle Rock, WA 98611-0280; tel. (360) 577-2025, fax (360) 274-4196.

- Southeast Region: 713 East Bowers Road, Ellensburg, WA 98926-9301; tel. (509) 925-8510, fax (509) 925-8522.

Bureau of Land Management (BLM)

- Oregon/Washington State Office: P.O. Box 2965, Portland, OR 97208; tel. (503) 952-6002, fax (503) 952-6308; website: www.or.blm.gov

- Burns District: HC 74-12533 Highway 20 West, Hines, OR 97738; tel. (541) 573-4400, fax (541) 573-4411.

- Coos Bay District: 1300 Airport Lane, North Bend, OR 97459; tel. (541) 756-0100, fax (541) 751-4303.

- Eugene District: P.O. Box 10226, Eugene, OR 97440; tel. (541) 683-6600, fax (541) 683-6981.

- Lakeview District: HC 10, Box 337, 1300 S. G Street, Lakeview, OR 97630; tel. (541) 947-2177, fax (541) 947-6399.

- Medford District: 3040 Biddle Road, Medford, OR 97504; tel. (541) 770-2200, fax (541) 770-2400.

- Prineville District: P.O. Box 550, Prineville, OR 97754; tel. (541) 416-6700, fax (541) 416-6798.

- Roseburg District: 777 Garden Valley Blvd., Roseburg, OR 97470; tel. (541) 440-4930, fax (541) 440-4948.

- Salem District: 1717 Fabry Road SE, Salem, OR 97306; tel. (503) 375-5646, fax (503) 375-5622.

- Vale District: 100 Oregon Street, Vale, OR 97918-9630; tel. (541) 473-3144, fax (541) 473-6213.

U.S. Army Corps of Engineers

- Portland District: P.O. Box 2946, Portland, OR 97208-2946; tel. (503) 808-5150, fax (503) 808-4515. website: www.nww.usace.army.mil

- Seattle District: P.O. Box 3755, Seattle, WA 98124-3755; tel. (206) 764-3750, (206) 764-6160, fax (206) 764-3769; website: www.nww.usace.army.mil

- Walla Walla District: 201 North 3rd Avenue, Walla Walla, WA 99362-1876; tel. (509) 527-7700, fax (509) 527-7800; website: www.nww.usace.army.mil

Oregon Department of Forestry

- Oregon Department of Forestry: 2600 State Street, Salem, OR 97310; tel. (503) 945-7200, fax (503) 945-7212; website: www.odf.state.or.us

- Tillamook State Forest, Forest Grove District: 801 Gales Creek Road, Forest Grove, OR 97116-1199; tel. (503) 357-2191, fax (503) 357-4548.

- Tillamook State Forest, Tillamook District: 4907 E. 3rd Street, Tillamook, OR 97141-2999; tel. (503) 842-2545, fax (503) 842-3143.

Nature of the Northwest Information Center

- 800 NE Oregon Street, Rm. 177, Portland, OR 97232; tel. (503) 872-2750, fax (503) 731-4066; website: www.naturenw.org

Hoh River Rain Forest

WASHINGTON CAMPGROUNDS

MAP A1

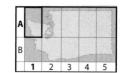

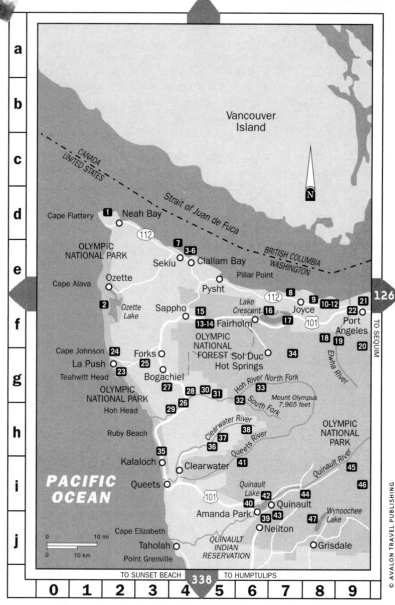

Vancouver Island

CANADA
UNITED STATES

Strait of Juan de Fuca

BRITISH COLUMBIA
WASHINGTON

Cape Flattery **1** Neah Bay

OLYMPIC NATIONAL PARK

7

3-6

Sekiu · Clallam Bay

Cape Alava · Ozette

Pillar Point

2 · Ozette Lake

Pysht

8

9 · Joyce

10-12

21

22

126 · TO SEQUIM

Sappho **15** · Lake Crescent **16**

13-14 · Fairholm

17

Port Angeles

18

19

20

OLYMPIC NATIONAL FOREST · Sol Duc Hot Springs

Cape Johnson **24** · Forks

25

34

Elwha River

La Push **23**

Teahwitt Head · Bogachiel

27

Hoh River North Fork

OLYMPIC NATIONAL PARK

28 **30** **31**

33

Hoh Head

26

32 · South Fork

Mount Olympus 7,965 feet

29

OLYMPIC NATIONAL PARK

Clearwater River

38

Ruby Beach

37

Queets River

36

35

Kalaloch · Clearwater

41

Quinault River

45

46

Queets

PACIFIC OCEAN

Quinault Lake **42**

44

40 · Quinault

Amanda Park **39** **43**

47 · Wynoochee Lake

Cape Elizabeth

Neilton

Taholah

QUINAULT INDIAN RESERVATION

Grisdale

Point Grenville

0   10 mi
0   10 km

TO SUNSET BEACH · 338 · TO HUMPTULIPS

© AVALON TRAVEL PUBLISHING

CHAPTER A1

■ Tyee Motel and RV Park 5

For RVs and trailers only, this private, developed campground is located near the northwestern tip of the Olympic Peninsula. It's a fairly plain-looking park, with two long strips of spaces, but a few sites have views of the Strait of Juan de Fuca. Fishing is excellent in this area. Recreation options include the world-renowned Makah Museum, which details the history of the Makah Indian tribe, and the half-mile hike to Cape Flattery, the northwestern tip of the continental United States. Cape Flattery offers many hiking trails and opportunities for viewing whales, seals, and walrus. Nearby Makah Bay has a beautiful beach and is a popular spot for surfing.

Location: In Neah Bay; map A1, grid d2.

Campsites, facilities: There are 20 pull-through sites for trailers or RVs of any length. Electricity, drinking water, and sewer hookups are provided. Bottled gas, sanitary services, and toilets are available. A store, cafe, ice, and laundry facilities are located within a few blocks. Coin-operated showers, boat docks, launching facilities, and boat rentals are located across the street. Leashed pets and motorbikes are permitted.

Reservations, fees: Reservations accepted. Sites are $16 per night. Major credit cards accepted. Open mid-April through Labor Day weekend.

Directions: From Olympia on Interstate 5, take Exit 104 and drive north on U.S. 101 to the Aberdeen/Highway 8 exit. Turn west on Highway 8 and drive 36 miles to Aberdeen. Continue through Aberdeen four miles to U.S. 101 and turn north and drive 119 miles to Sappho. Turn north on Highway 113 and drive nine miles to a fork with Highway 112. Bear left on Highway 112 and drive 18 miles to the town of Neah Bay. The campground is located just off the highway in the middle of town.

Contact: Phone the park at (360) 645-2223 or write to Tyee Motel and RV Park, P.O. Box 193, Neah Bay, WA 98357.

■ Ozette  6

Many people visit this site set on the shore of Lake Ozette just a few miles from the Pacific Ocean. This is a boater's delight. The camp is remote and private with multiple trailheads and an isolated, mysterious feel to it. The camp is a favorite of backpackers.

Location: On Lake Ozette in Olympic National Park; map A1, grid f2.

Campsites, facilities: There are 13 sites for tents or RVs up to 21 feet long. Drinking water, picnic tables, vault toilets, and fire grills are available. Leashed pets are permitted.

Reservations, fees: No reservations. Sites are $10 per night. Open year-round.

Directions: From Olympia on Interstate 5, take Exit 104 and drive north on U.S. 101 to the Aberdeen/Highway 8 exit. Turn west on Highway 8 and drive 36 miles to Aberdeen. Continue through Aberdeen four miles to U.S. 101, turn north, and drive 119 miles to Sappho. Turn north on Highway 113 and drive nine miles to a fork with Highway 112. Bear left on Highway 112 and drive about nine miles (two miles past Sekiu) to Hoko-Ozette Road. Turn left and drive 21 miles to the ranger station. The camp parking lot is across from the ranger station on the northwest corner of Lake Ozette.

Contact: Olympic National Park, 600 East Park Avenue, Port Angeles, WA 98362; tel. (360) 452-4501, fax (360) 452-0335.

❸ Van Riper's Resort Hotel   7

Part of this campground is on the waterfront and the other part is on a hill overlooking the Strait of Juan de Fuca. Most sites are graveled, many with views of the strait. Other sites are grassy, without views. Hiking, fishing, and boating are among the options here, with salmon fishing being the principal draw. The beaches in the area are a mixture of sand and gravel, and rockhounding for agates and fossils is popular.

Location: On Clallam Bay in Sekiu; map A1, grid e4.

Campsites, facilities: There are 150 sites with full or partial hookups for tents or RVs of any length; 60 are drive-through sites. Electricity, drinking water, and picnic tables are provided. Sanitary services, toilets, showers, and ice are available. A store, cafe, and laundry facilities are located within one mile. Firewood is available for an extra fee. Boat docks, launching facilities, and rentals are available in spring and summer. Leashed pets and motorbikes are permitted.

Reservations, fees: No reservations. Sites are $11-16 per night. Open from April to late September.

Directions: From Olympia on Interstate 5, take Exit 104 and drive north on U.S. 101 to the Aberdeen/Highway 8 exit. Turn west on Highway 8 and drive 36 miles to Aberdeen. Continue through Aberdeen four miles to U.S. 101, turn north, and drive 119 miles to Sappho. Turn north on Highway 113 and drive nine miles to a fork with Highway 112. Bear left on Highway 112 and continue 18 miles to Sekiu. The campground is located off Highway 112, at the north end of Front Street.

Contact: Phone the park at (360) 963-2334 or write to Van Riper's Resort Hotel, P.O. Box 246, Sekiu, WA 98381 or e-mail: vanrip@olypen.com.

❹ Sam's Trailer and RV Park   5

This is an alternative to Van Riper's Resort Hotel, Olson's Resort, Surfside Resort, and Coho Resort and Trailer Park on Clallam Bay. It's a family-oriented park, with grassy sites and many recreation options nearby. Beaches and shopping are within walking distance. Those wanting to visit Cape Flattery, Hoh Rain Forest, or Port Angeles will find this a good central location.

Location: On Clallam Bay; map A1, grid e4.

Campsites, facilities: There are four tent sites and 20 sites for trailers or RVs of any length; 10 are drive-through sites. Electricity, drinking water, sewer hookups, and picnic tables are provided. Sanitary services, toilets, showers, cable TV, and laundry facilities are available. Bottled gas, a store, cafe, and ice are located within one mile. Boat docks, launching facilities, and rentals are located within one mile. Leashed pets and motorbikes are permitted

Reservations, fees: Reservations accepted. Sites are $10-15 per night. Open year-round.

Directions: From Olympia on Interstate 5, take Exit 104 and drive north on U.S. 101 to the Aberdeen/Highway 8 exit. Turn west on Highway 8 and drive 36 miles to Aberdeen. Continue through Aberdeen four miles to U.S. 101, turn north, and drive 119 miles to Sappho. Turn north on Highway 113 and drive nine miles to a fork with Highway 112. Bear left on Highway 112 and drive to Clallam Bay. The campground is on the right just as you come into town.

Contact: Phone the park at (360) 963-2402 or write to Sam's Trailer and RV Park, P.O. Box 45, Clallam Bay, WA 98326 or e-mail: samsrv@hotmail.com.

5 Olson's Resort   5

This full-service camp is large and private. The marina nearby is salmon fishing headquarters. In fact, the resort caters to anglers, offering all-day salmon fishing trips and boat moorage. Chartered trips can be arranged by reservation. A tackle shop, cabins, and a motel are also available. See the description of Van Riper's for details on the Sekiu area.

Location: In Sekiu; map A1, grid e4.

Campsites, facilities: There are 30 tent sites and 100 sites for trailers or RVs of any length, 45 with full hookups and 10 with electricity only. Seven cabins are also available in the summer. Picnic tables, drinking water, sanitary services, flush toilets, showers, a laundry room, store, and ice are available. A cafe, boat docks, launching facilities, and boat rentals are also available on-site. Leashed pets and motorbikes are permitted.

Reservations, fees: No reservations. Sites are $11-15 per night. Cabins are $40-48 per night. Major credit cards accepted. Open year-round.

Directions: From Olympia on Interstate 5, take Exit 104 and drive north on U.S. 101 to the Aberdeen/Highway 8 exit. Turn west on Highway 8 and drive 36 miles to Aberdeen. Continue through Aberdeen four miles to U.S. 101, turn north, and drive 119 miles to Sappho. Turn north on Highway 113 and drive nine miles to a fork with Highway 112. Bear left on Highway 112 and continue to Sekiu. The campground is located off Highway 112, at the north end of Front Street.

Contact: Phone the park at (360) 963-2311 or write to Olson's Resort, P.O. Box 216, Sekiu, WA 98381.

6 Surfside Resort   7

This park is smaller, less crowded, and more secluded than many in the area. Campers can enjoy the park's private beach and panoramic views of the Strait of Juan de Fuca and Vancouver Island to the north. Nearby recreation options include marked hiking and bike trails, beachcombing, a full-service marina, and the finest fishing for miles.

Location: In Sekiu; map A1, grid e4.

Campsites, facilities: There are 10 tent sites and 10 drive-through sites for trailers or RVs of any length. Electricity, drinking water, sewer hookups, and picnic tables are provided. Sanitary services, cable TV, toilets, and showers are available. Bottled gas, a store, a cafe, coin-operated laundry facilities, and ice are located within one mile. Boat docks, launching facilities, and rentals are located within one mile. Leashed pets and motorbikes are permitted.

Reservations, fees: Reservations recommended. Sites are $10-15 per night. Open year-round.

Directions: From Olympia on Interstate 5, take Exit 104 and drive north on U.S. 101 to the Aberdeen/Highway 8 exit. Turn west on Highway 8 and drive 36 miles to Aberdeen. Continue through Aberdeen four miles to U.S. 101 and turn north and drive 119 miles to Sappho. Turn north on Highway 113 and drive nine miles to a fork with Highway 112. Bear left on Highway 112 and continue to Clallam Bay. Continue about one mile west; the campground is located halfway between the towns of Clallam Bay and Sekiu.

Contact: Surfside Resort, P.O. Box 39, Sekiu, WA 98381; tel. (360) 963-2723.

▇ Coho Resort and Trailer Park   5

This is one of several camps in the immediate area. A full-service marina nearby provides boating access. See the descriptions of Van Riper's Resort Hotel, Olson's Resort, and Surfside Resort for information on the area.

Location: Near Sekiu; map A1, grid e4.

Campsites, facilities: There are 100 sites for tents and 108 for tents, trailers, or RVs of any length; 60 are full-hookup sites and the remainder are partial hookups with electricity and water. Cable TV is available. Sanitary services, toilets, coin-operated showers, a cafe, restaurant, laundry facilities, and ice are available. Bottled gas and a store are located within one mile. A full-service marina with docks, launching facilities, gas, and nonmotorized boat rentals is available. Leashed pets and motorbikes are permitted.

Reservations, fees: No reservations. Sites are $12-16 per night. Open from April through September.

Directions: From Olympia on Interstate 5, take Exit 104 and drive north on U.S. 101 to the Aberdeen/Highway 8 exit. Turn west on Highway 8 and drive 36 miles to Aberdeen. Continue through Aberdeen four miles to U.S. 101, turn north, and drive 119 miles to Sappho. Turn north on Highway 113 and drive nine miles to a fork with Highway 112. Bear left on Highway 112 and continue towards Sekiu. The campground is located between Mileposts 15 and 16, about three-quarters of a mile east of Sekiu.

Contact: Coho Resort and Trailer Park, 15572 Highway 112, Sekiu, WA 98381; tel. (360) 963-2333.

▇ Whiskey Creek Beach   7

Located on the beach along the Strait of Juan de Fuca, this campground covers 400 acres and is popular with rock hounds. The setting is rustic, with one mile of beach access and five miles of hiking trails nearby. Five miles away is Olympic National Park, which offers many recreation possibilities. This camp is a good option if the national park camps are full.

Location: On the Strait of Juan de Fuca; map A1, grid e7.

Campsites, facilities: There are 60 tent sites and 11 sites for trailers or RVs of any length, plus six cabins on the beach. Drinking water and picnic tables are provided. Sanitary services and some sewer hookups are available. Launching facilities for small boats are on site. Leashed pets are permitted.

Reservations, fees: Reservations accepted. Sites are $15 per night; cabins are $60 per night. Open from May to late October.

Directions: From Olympia on Interstate 5, take U.S. 101 and drive north 127 miles (five miles past the town of Port Angeles) to a fork with Highway 112. Turn west (right) on Highway 112 and drive 13 miles to Whiskey Creek Beach Road. Turn right and continue 1.5 miles to the campground.

Contact: Whiskey Creek Beach, P.O. Box 130, Joyce, WA 98343; tel. (360) 928-3489, fax (360) 928-3218.

9 Carol's Crescent Beach   6

Set on a half-mile stretch of sandy beach, this campground makes a perfect weekend spot. Popular activities include swimming, fishing, and beachcombing. Numerous attractions and recreation options are available in Port Angeles.

Location: On the Strait of Juan de Fuca; map A1, grid e8.

Campsites, facilities: There are 40 sites for tents, trailers, or RVs with full or partial hookups. Rest rooms, showers, a pay phone, recreation field, and laundry room are available. Leashed pets are permitted.

Reservations, fees: Reservations recommended. Sites are $20-25 per night. The campground is generally open from May to September, but the season may be extended. Call for information.

Directions: From Olympia on Interstate 5, take U.S. 101 and drive north 127 miles (five miles past the town of Port Angeles) to a fork with Highway 112. Turn west (right) on Highway 112 and drive 10 miles to Camp Hayden Road (between Mileposts 53 and 54). Drive northwest on Camp Hayden Road for four miles. The campground is located on the left, on the beach.

Contact: Carol's Crescent Beach, 2860 Crescent Beach Road, Port Angeles, WA 98363; tel. (360) 928-3344.

10 Lyre River   6

This prime spot is one of the rare free campgrounds on the Olympic Peninsula. Though quite primitive, it does offer drinking water and an even more precious commodity in these parts—privacy. The camp is set along the Lyre River and is just a short distance from the ocean.

Location: On the Lyre River; map A1, grid e8.

Campsites, facilities: There are 11 primitive tent sites. Picnic tables, fire grills, tent pads, vault toilets, and drinking water are provided. A roofed group shelter with a fireplace is available. Leashed pets are permitted.

Reservations, fees: No reservations; no fee. Open year-round.

Directions: From Olympia on Interstate 5, take U.S. 101 and drive north 127 miles (five miles past the town of Port Angeles) to a fork with Highway 112. Turn west (right) on Highway 112 and drive to Milepost 46. Look to the right for a paved road between Mileposts 46 and 47; then turn north and drive 0.4 mile to the camp entrance road on the left.

Contact: Department of Natural Resources, Olympic Region, 411 Tillicum Lane, Forks, WA 98331-9797; tel. (360) 374-6131, fax (360) 374-5446.

🔢 Lyre River RV Park   9

This beautiful 80-acre camp is in a wooded area tucked between the Strait of Juan de Fuca and the Lyre River. Freshwater and saltwater beaches are available, giving the park a unique flavor. Kids can give their rods a try in the pond stocked with trout, while adult anglers can head for excellent fishing in the Lyre River and the strait. Tubing down the river is popular here, and bike and hiking trails are available nearby.

Location: Near the Lyre River; map A1, grid e8.

Campsites, facilities: There are 60 sites for tents, trailers, or RVs of any length; 30 are drive-through sites. Electricity, drinking water, sewer hookups, and picnic tables are provided. Bottled gas, sanitary services, toilets, a store, laundry facilities, and ice are available. Showers and firewood are available for an extra fee. Leashed pets and motorbikes are permitted.

Reservations, fees: Reservations accepted. Sites are $14-25 per night for two campers. Group reservations welcome with an advance deposit. Open year-round.

Directions: From Olympia on Interstate 5, take U.S. 101 and drive north 127 miles (five miles past the town of Port Angeles) to a fork with Highway 112. Turn west on Highway 112 and drive 15 miles to West Lyre River Road. Turn right and drive a half mile to the park.

Contact: Lyre River RV Park, 596 West Lyre River Road, Port Angeles, WA 98363; tel. (360) 928-3436.

🔢 Salt Creek Recreation Area   8

Recreation options at this 192-acre park overlooking the Strait of Juan de Fuca include nearby hiking trails, swimming, fishing, horseshoes, and field sports. It's a good layover spot if you're planning to take the ferry out of Port Angeles to Victoria, British Columbia.

Location: Near the Strait of Juan de Fuca; map A1, grid e8.

Campsites, facilities: There are 92 sites for tents, trailers, or RVs of any length. Picnic tables are provided. Sanitary services, toilets, showers, and a playground are available. Firewood is available for an extra fee. Leashed pets are permitted.

Reservations, fees: No reservations. Sites are $8-10 per night for one vehicle; six camper maximum per site. Open year-round.

Directions: From Olympia on Interstate 5, take U.S. 101 and drive north 127 miles (five miles past the town of Port Angeles) to a fork with Highway 112. Turn west (right) on Highway 112 and drive six miles to Camp Hayden Road. Turn north and drive three miles to the campground.

Contact: Salt Creek Recreation Area, 3506 Camp Hayden Road, Port Angeles, WA 98362; tel. (360) 928-3441.

🔢 Bear Creek
Motel and RV Park   7

This quiet little spot is set where Bear Creek empties into the Sol Duc River. It's private and developed, with a choice of sunny or shaded sites in a wooded setting. There are many recreation options in the area, including fishing, hunting, and nature and hiking trails leading to the ocean. Sol Duc Hot Springs is 25 miles north and worth the trip. A restaurant next to the camp serves family-style meals.

Location: On Bear Creek; map A1, grid f5.

Campsites, facilities: There are eight tent sites and 12 drive-through sites for trailers or RVs of any length. Electricity, drinking water, sewer hookups, and picnic tables are provided. Sanitary services, toilets, showers, a cafe, laundry room, and firewood are available. Boat launching facilities are located within a half mile. Leashed pets are permitted.

Reservations, fees: No reservations. Sites are $15 per night. Major credit cards accepted. Open year-round.

Directions: From Olympia on Interstate 5, take Exit 104 and drive north on U.S. 101 to the Aberdeen/Highway 8 exit. Turn west on Highway 8 and drive 36 miles to Aberdeen. Continue through Aberdeen four miles to U.S. 101, turn north, and drive to Forks. Continue past Forks for 15 miles to Milepost 205 (just past Sappho) to the campground.

Contact: Bear Creek Motel and RV Park, P.O. Box 236, Beaver, WA 98305; tel. (360) 327-3660.

14 Bear Creek   8

Fishing and hiking are options here, and while there is no drinking water, there are opportunities for wildlife viewing and photography.

Location: On the Sol Duc River in Hoh Clearwater State Forest; map A1, grid f5.

Campsites, facilities: There are 10 tent sites. Vault toilets and fire pits are available, but there is no drinking water. Some facilities are wheelchair accessible. Leashed pets are permitted.

Reservations, fees: No reservations; no fee. Open year-round.

Directions: From Olympia on Interstate 5, take Exit 104 and drive north on U.S. 101 to the Aberdeen/Highway 8 exit. Turn west on Highway 8 and drive 36 miles to Aberdeen. Continue through Aberdeen four miles to U.S. 101 and turn north and drive to Forks. Continue past Forks for 15 miles to Milepost 206 (two miles past Sappho) to the campground on the right.

Contact: Department of Natural Resources, Olympic Region, 411 Tillicum Lane, Forks, WA 98331-9797; tel. (360) 374-6131, fax (360) 374-5446.

15 Klahowya   8

Klahowya is a good choice if you don't want to venture far from U.S. 101 yet want to retain the feel of Olympic National Forest. Set along the headwaters of the Sol Duc River, this 32-acre camp is pretty and wooded, with hiking trails in the area. Due to its proximity to the highway, this is an extremely popular camp and fills up quickly in the summer.

Location: On the Sol Duc River in Olympic National Forest; map A1, grid f5.

Campsites, facilities: There are 25 tent sites and 30 sites for trailers or RVs up to 30 feet long. Picnic tables are provided. Drinking water, vault and flush toilets, and wheelchair-accessible rest rooms are available. A boat ramp is nearby. Leashed pets are permitted.

Reservations, fees: No reservations. Sites are $7-10 per night. The campground is open from May to mid-October with full service. Limited service is available in the off-season.

Directions: From Interstate 5 at Olympia, turn north on U.S. 101 and drive about 122 miles to Port Angeles. Continue on U.S. 101 for past Port Angeles for about 36 miles (nine miles west of Lake Crescent) to the campground on the right side of the road. (Coming from the other direction on U.S. 101, drive eight miles east of Sappho to the campground.)

Contact: Olympic National Forest, Sol Duc Ranger District, Star Rte. 1, P.O. Box 5750, Forks, WA 98331; tel. (360) 374-6522, fax (360) 374-1250.

16 Fairholm   6

This camp is set on the shore of Lake Crescent, a pretty lake situated within the boundary of Olympic National Park. These campsites are set on the western end of the lake, in a cove with a boat ramp. It's less than a mile off U.S. 101 and gets heavy use during tourist months. A naturalist program may be available in the summer. The elevation is 580 feet.

Location: On Lake Crescent in Olympic National Park; map A1, grid f6.

Campsites, facilities: There are 88 sites for tents, trailers, or RVs up to 21 feet long. Picnic tables and fire grills are provided. A sanitary disposal station, rest rooms, drinking water, and wheelchair-accessible facilities are available. A store and a cafe are within one mile. Boat launching facilities are nearby on Lake Crescent. Leashed pets are permitted.

Reservations, fees: No reservations. Sites are $10 per night. The campground is open year-round, weather permitting.

Directions: From Interstate 5 at Olympia, turn north on U.S. 101 and drive about 122 miles to Port Angeles. Continue on U.S. 101 past Port Angeles for about 26 miles and continue along Lake Crescent to North Shore Road. Turn right and drive one mile to the camp on North Shore Road.

Contact: Olympic National Park, 600 East Park Avenue, Port Angeles, WA 98362; tel. (360) 452-4501, fax (360) 452-0335.

17 Log Cabin Resort   8

This pretty camp along the shore of Lake Crescent is a good spot for boaters, with many sites near the water with excellent views. Fishing and swimming are two options at this family-oriented resort. A marked hiking trail traces the lake's shoreline.

Location: On Lake Crescent in Olympic National Park; map A1, grid f7.

Campsites, facilities: There are 38 sites for trailers or RVs of any length. Electricity, drinking water, sewer hookups, and picnic tables are provided. Sanitary services, toilets, a store, a cafe, laundry facilities, ice, and a playground are available. Showers and firewood are also available for an extra fee. Boat docks, launching facilities, and rentals are located in the resort at Lake Crescent. Leashed pets are permitted.

Reservations, fees: Reservations accepted. Sites are $27 per night. Open from April to September.

Directions: From Interstate 5 at Olympia, turn north on U.S. 101 and drive about 122 miles to Port Angeles. Continue on U.S. 101 for past Port Angeles for about 18 miles and continue along Lake Crescent to East Beach Road. Turn right and drive three miles to the camp at Log Cabin Resort.

Contact: Log Cabin Resort, 3183 East Beach Road, Port Angeles, WA 98363; tel. (360) 928-3325, fax (360) 928-2088. Website: www.logcabinresort.net.

18 Altaire   8

This camp is set on the Elwha River about a mile from Lake Mills, a pretty and well-treed camp with easy highway access. It's a nice layover spot for one night before taking the ferryboat at Port Angeles to Victoria, British Columbia.

Location: On the Elwha River in Olympic National Park; map A1, grid f8.

Campsites, facilities: There are 30 sites for tents, trailers, or RVs up to 21 feet long. Picnic tables and fire grills are provided. Rest rooms and drinking water are available. Some facilities are wheelchair accessible. Leashed pets are permitted.

Reservations, fees: No reservations. Sites are $10 per night. Open June to September.

Directions: From Interstate 5 at Olympia, turn north on U.S. 101 and drive about 122 miles to Port Angeles. Continue on U.S. 101 past Port Angeles for about nine miles (just past Lake Aldwell). Turn left at the signed entrance road and drive four miles south along the Elwha River.

Contact: Olympic National Park, 600 East Park Avenue, Port Angeles, WA 98362; tel. (360) 452-4501, fax (360) 452-0335.

19 Elwha   8

The Elwha River is the backdrop for this popular camp, with excellent hiking trails close by in Olympic National Park; check at one of the visitor centers for maps and backcountry information. Also see the description of neighboring Altaire for more information.

Location: On the Elwha River in Olympic National Park; map A1, grid f8.

Campsites, facilities: There are 41 sites for tents, trailers, or RVs up to 21 feet long. Picnic tables and fire grills are provided. Rest rooms and drinking water are available. Some facilities are wheelchair accessible. Leashed pets are permitted.

Reservations, fees: No reservations. Sites are $10 per night. Open year-round.

Directions: From Interstate 5 at Olympia, turn north on U.S. 101 and drive about 122 miles to Port Angeles. Continue on U.S. 101 for past Port Angeles for about nine miles (just past Lake Aldwell). Turn left at the signed entrance road and drive three miles south along the Elwha River.

Contact: Olympic National Park, 600 East Park Avenue, Port Angeles, WA 98362; tel. (360) 452-4501, fax (360) 452-0335.

20 Heart o' the Hills   10

Heart o' the Hills is nestled on the northern edge of Olympic National Park. You can drive into the park on Hurricane Ridge Road and take one of numerous hiking trails. Little Lake Dawn is less than a half mile to the west. This camp is set at 1,807 feet. Evening naturalist programs are available in the summer.

Location: In Olympic National Park; map A1, grid f9.

Campsites, facilities: There are 105 sites for tents, trailers, or RVs up to 21 feet long. Picnic tables are provided. Rest rooms, drinking water, and wheelchair-accessible facilities are available. Leashed pets are permitted.

Reservations, fees: No reservations. Sites are $10 per night. The campground is open year-round, weather permitting.

Directions: From Interstate 5 at Olympia, turn north on U.S. 101 and drive about 122 miles to Port Angeles to Hurricane Ridge Road. Turn left and drive five miles to the camp on the left. (Access roads can be impassable in severe weather.)

Contact: Olympic National Park, 600 East Park Avenue, Port Angeles, WA 98362; tel. (360) 452-4501, fax (360) 452-0335.

21 Peabody Creek RV Park   5

This three-acre RV park is right in the middle of town but offers a wooded, streamside setting. Nearby recreation options include salmon fishing, an 18-hole golf course, marked biking trails, a full-service marina, and tennis courts. The park is within walking distance of shopping and ferry services.

Location: In Port Angeles; map A1, grid f9.

Campsites, facilities: There are 36 sites for trailers or RVs of any length. Electricity, drinking water, and sewer hookups are provided. Sanitary services, toilets, ice, and laundry facilities are available. A store and a cafe are within one block. Showers are available for an extra fee. Boat docks, launching facilities, and rentals are located within 1.5 miles. Leashed pets are permitted.

Reservations, fees: Reservations accepted. Sites are $21 per night. Open year-round.

Directions: From Interstate 5 at Olympia, turn north on U.S. 101 and drive about 122 miles to Port Angeles to Lincoln. Turn left and drive two blocks to Second Street and the park entrance on the left.

Contact: Peabody Creek RV Park, 127 South Lincoln, Port Angeles, WA 98362; tel. (800) 392-2361 or (360) 457-7092; e-mail: patm@tenforward.com; website: www.members.tripod/peabodyrv.

22 Welcome Inn Trailer and RV Park   5

Welcome Inn is a privately developed campground for RVs and tent campers on an eight-acre site in the woods. Nearby recreation options include an 18-hole golf course, marked hiking trails, a full-service marina, and tennis courts. The park caters to tourists, offering arrangements for fishing charters and Victoria, British Columbia, tours.

Location: Near Port Angeles; map A1, grid f9.

Campsites, facilities: There are 100 sites for tents, trailers, or RVs of any length. Electricity, drinking water, sewer hookups, dump stations, and picnic tables are provided. Bottled gas, sanitary services, toilets, and laundry facilities are available. A store, cafe, and ice are within one mile. Showers are available for an extra fee. Boat docks and launching facilities are located within one mile. Pets and motorbikes are permitted.
Reservations, fees: Reservations accepted. Sites are $14-24 per night. Major credit cards accepted. Open year-round.
Directions: From Interstate 5 at Olympia, turn north on U.S. 101 and drive about 122 miles to Port Angeles. Continue another 1.8 miles west of the ferry terminal to the park (set along the highway).
Contact: Welcome Inn Trailer and RV Park, 1215 Highway 101 West, Port Angeles, WA 98363; tel. (360) 457-1553.

23 Mora   8

At an elevation of 50 feet, this is a good out-of-the-way choice near the Pacific Ocean and the Olympic Coast Marine Sanctuary. The Quillayute River feeds into the ocean near the camp, and upstream is the Bogachiel, a prime steelhead river in winter months. A naturalist program is available during the summer.
Location: Near the Pacific Ocean in Olympic National Park; map A1, grid g2.
Campsites, facilities: There are 94 sites for tents or RVs up to 21 feet long. Picnic tables and fire grills are provided. Drinking water, a sanitary disposal station, rest rooms, and wheelchair-accessible facilities are available. Leashed pets are permitted.
Reservations, fees: No reservations. Sites are $10 per night. Open year-round.
Directions: From Olympia on Interstate 5, take Exit 104 and drive north on U.S. 101 to the Aberdeen/Highway 8 exit. Turn west on Highway 8 and drive 36 miles to Aberdeen. Continue through Aberdeen four miles to U.S. 101, turn north, and drive 108 miles to Forks. Continue past Forks for two miles to La Push Road (Highway 110). Turn west (left) and drive 12 miles to the campground on the left (well signed along route).
Contact: Olympic National Park, 600 East Park Avenue, Port Angeles, WA 98362; tel. (360) 452-4501, fax (360) 452-0335.

24 Lonesome Creek Store and RV Park and Ocean Park Resort   6

This private, developed park is set along the Pacific Ocean and the coastal Dungeness National Wildlife Refuge. It has some of the rare ocean sites available in the area. It offers such recreation options as fishing, beachcombing, boating, whale watching, and sunbathing.
Location: On the Pacific Ocean; map A1, grid g2.
Campsites, facilities: There is a dispersed camping area which can accommodate up to 25 tents and 44 sites for trailers or RVs up to 36 feet. Twenty-two RV sites are on the ocean. Electricity, drinking water, and sewer hookups are provided for RVs. Gasoline and bottled gas, flush toilets, a store with deli, ice, and laundry facili-

ties are available. Showers are available for an extra fee. Boat docks and launching facilities are located within one mile. Leashed pets are permitted.

Reservations, fees: Reservations accepted for RV sites and are recommended for oceanfront sites; phone (800) 487-1267 or access the website: www.lapushwa.com. Sites are $15 per night for tent sites and $20-29 for RV sites. Major credit cards accepted. Open year-round.

Directions: From Olympia on Interstate 5, take Exit 104 and drive north on U.S. 101 to the Aberdeen/Highway 8 exit. Turn west on Highway 8 and drive 36 miles to Aberdeen. Continue through Aberdeen four miles to U.S. 101, turn north, and drive 108 miles to Forks. Continue past Forks for two miles to La Push Road/Highway 110. Turn west (left) and drive 14 miles to the campground on the left.

Contact: Lonesome Creek Store and RV Park and Ocean Park Resort, P.O. Box 67, La Push, WA 98350; tel. (800) 487-1267, (360) 374-5267, (360) 374-4333, fax (360) 374-4153.

25 Three Rivers Resort   6

This small, private camp set on the Quillayute River near its mouth at the Pacific Ocean is a pretty spot with wooded, spacious sites. Beachcombing, hiking, and fishing are options here. The coastal Dungeness National Wildlife Refuge and Pacific Ocean are a short drive to the west. Upstream are the Sol Duc River and Bogachiel River. Hoh Rain Forest, a worthwhile side trip, is about 45 minutes away.

Location: On the Quillayute River; map A1, grid g3.

Campsites, facilities: There are 11 sites for tents, trailers, or RVs of any length, 10 with full or partial hookups, plus five rental cabins. Picnic tables are provided. Bottled gas, flush toilets, a store, a cafe, laundry facilities, and ice are available. Electricity, drinking water, sewer hookups, showers, and firewood are available for an extra fee. Leashed pets are permitted.

Reservations, fees: Reservations accepted. Sites are $8-12 per night; cabins are $35-49 per night. Open year-round.

Directions: From Olympia on Interstate 5, take Exit 104 and drive north on U.S. 101 to the Aberdeen/Highway 8 exit. Turn west on Highway 8 and drive 36 miles to Aberdeen. Continue through Aberdeen four miles to U.S. 101, turn north, and drive 108 miles to Forks. Continue past Forks for two miles to La Push Road/Highway 110. Turn west (left) and drive nine miles to the campground,

Contact: Three Rivers Resort, 7764 La Push Road, Forks, WA 98331; tel. (360) 374-5300.

26 Hoh River Resort   6

This is a nice camp along U.S. 101 with a choice of grassy or graveled shady sites. Marked hiking trails are in the area. It's a pleasant little park, with steelhead and salmon fishing available and elk hunting in season. Horseshoe pits and a recreation field are provided for campers.

Location: On the Hoh River; map A1, grid g4.

Campsites, facilities: There are 23 sites for tents, trailers, or RVs of any length. Electricity, drinking water, sewer hookups, and picnic tables are provided. Flush toilets, a store, gas station, laundry facilities, and ice are available. Showers and firewood are available for an extra fee. Leashed pets and motorbikes are permitted.

Reservations, fees: Reservations accepted. Sites are $10-15 per night. Open year-round.

Directions: From Olympia on Interstate 5, take Exit 104 and drive north on U.S. 101 to the Aberdeen/Highway 8 exit. Turn west on Highway 8 and drive 36 miles to Aberdeen. Continue through Aberdeen four miles to U.S. 101, turn north, and drive 90 miles to the resort (15 miles south of Forks).

Contact: Hoh River Resort, 175443 Highway 101 South, Forks, WA 98331; tel. (360) 374-5566.

27 Bogachiel State Park   6

This is a good base camp for salmon or steelhead fishing trips. The 119-acre park is set on the Bogachiel River, with marked hiking trails in the area. It can be noisy at times—there is a logging mill located directly across the river from the campground. Hunting is popular in the adjacent national forest.

Location: On the Bogachiel River; map A1, grid g4.

Campsites, facilities: There are two primitive tent sites, 34 developed tent sites, and six hookup sites for trailers or RVs up to 35 feet long. Picnic tables and fire grills are provided. A sanitary disposal station, rest rooms, coin-operated showers, and drinking water are available. A store and ice are located within one mile. A boat ramp is nearby. Leashed pets are permitted.

Reservations, fees: No reservations. Sites are $10-15 per night. Open year-round.

Directions: From Olympia on Interstate 5, take Exit 104 and drive north on U.S. 101 to the Aberdeen/Highway 8 exit. Turn west on Highway 8 and drive 36 miles to Aberdeen. Continue through Aberdeen four miles to U.S. 101. Turn north on U.S. 101 and drive 102 miles to the park (six miles south of Forks) on the left (west) side of the road.

Contact: Bogachiel State Park, North Coastal Region, 183983 Highway 101, Forks, WA 98331; tel. (800) 233-0321 or (360) 374-6356.

28 Hoh Oxbow   10

This is the most popular of the five camps on the Hoh River. It's primitive and close to the highway, and the price is right. The adjacent boat launch makes this the camp of choice for anglers.

Location: On the Hoh River; map A1, grid g4.

Campsites, facilities: There are seven sites for tents or small trailers. Picnic tables, fire grills, and tent pads are provided. Vault toilets and a hand boat launch are available, but there is no drinking water. One site is wheelchair accessible. Firearms are prohibited. Leashed pets are permitted.

Reservations, fees: No reservations; no fee. Open year-round.

Directions: From Olympia on Interstate 5, take Exit 104 and drive north on U.S. 101 to the Aberdeen/Highway 8 exit. Turn west on Highway 8 and drive 36 miles to Aberdeen. Continue through Aberdeen four miles to U.S. 101. Turn north on U.S. 101 and drive 90 miles to the resort (15 miles south of Forks). Exit between Mileposts 176 and 177 (the camp is set east of the highway next to the river).

Contact: Department of Natural Resources, Olympic Region, 411 Tillicum Lane, Forks, WA 98331-9797; tel. (360) 374-6131, fax (360) 374-5446.

29 Cottonwood   9

An alternative to Hoh Oxbow, Willoughby Creek, and Minnie Peterson, this primitive camp is also set along the Hoh River. Like Hoh Oxbow, Cottonwood offers the bonus of a boat launch. Its distance from the highway often ensures fewer people.
Location: On the Hoh River; map A1, grid g4.
Campsites, facilities: There are nine sites for tents or small trailers. Picnic tables, fire grills, and tent pads are provided. No drinking water is available. Vault toilets and a boat launch are available. Leashed pets are permitted.
Reservations, fees: No reservations; no fee. Open year-round.
Directions: From Olympia on Interstate 5, take Exit 104 and drive north on U.S. 101 to the Aberdeen/Highway 8 exit. Turn west on Highway 8 and drive 36 miles to Aberdeen. Continue through Aberdeen four miles to U.S. 101. Turn north on U.S. 101 and drive 92 miles to Oil City Road between Mileposts 177 and 178. Turn west on Oil City Road and drive 2.3 miles. Turn left on Road H4060 (gravel) and drive one mile to the camp.
Contact: Department of Natural Resources, Olympic Region, 411 Tillicum Lane, Forks, WA 98331-9797; tel. (360) 374-6131, fax (360) 374-5446.

30 Willoughby Creek   9

This little-known camp along Willoughby Creek and the Hoh River is tiny and rustic, with good fishing nearby. The area gets heavy rainfall. Other campground options in the vicinity are Hoh Oxbow, Cottonwood, and Minnie Peterson.
Location: In Hoh Clearwater State Forest; map A1, grid g5.
Campsites, facilities: There are three campsites for tents or small trailers. Picnic tables, fire grills, and tent pads are provided. Vault toilets are available, but there is no drinking water. Leashed pets are permitted.
Reservations, fees: No reservations; no fee. Open year-round.
Directions: From Olympia on Interstate 5, take Exit 104 and drive north on U.S. 101 to the Aberdeen/Highway 8 exit. Turn west on Highway 8 and drive 36 miles to Aberdeen. Continue through Aberdeen four miles to U.S. 101. Turn north on U.S. 101 and drive about 90 miles. Exit between Mileposts 178 and 179. At Hoh Rain Forest Road/Upper Hoh Valley Road, turn east and drive 3.5 miles to the campground.
Contact: Department of Natural Resources, Olympic Region, 411 Tillicum Lane, Forks, WA 98331-9797; tel. (360) 374-6131, fax (360) 374-5446.

31 Minnie Peterson   9

Not many folks know about this primitive camp, set on the Hoh River on the edge of the Hoh Rain Forest. It's quite pretty and forested, with nice riverside sites. Bring your rain gear.
Location: On the Hoh River; map A1, grid g5.
Campsites, facilities: There are eight campsites for tents or small trailers. Picnic tables, fire grills, and tent pads are provided. Vault toilets and drinking water are

available. Discharging firearms is prohibited. Leashed pets are permitted.

Reservations, fees: No reservations; no fee. Open year-round.

Directions: From Olympia on Interstate 5, take Exit 104 and drive north on U.S. 101 to the Aberdeen/Highway 8 exit. Turn west on Highway 8 and drive 36 miles to Aberdeen. Continue through Aberdeen four miles to U.S. 101. Turn north on U.S. 101 and drive about 90 miles. Exit between Mileposts 178 and 179. At Hoh Rain Forest Road/Upper Hoh Valley Road, turn east and drive 4.5 miles to the campground.

Contact: Department of Natural Resources, Olympic Region, 411 Tillicum Lane, Forks, WA 98331-9797; tel. (360) 374-6131, fax (360) 374-5446.

32 South Fork Hoh   10

This rarely used, beautiful camp set along the cascading South Fork of the Hoh River is way out there. It's tiny and primitive but offers a guarantee of peace and quiet, something many U.S. 101 cruisers would cheerfully give a limb for after a few days of fighting crowds.

Location: In Hoh Clearwater State Forest; map A1, grid g6.

Campsites, facilities: There are three campsites for tents or small trailers. Picnic tables, fire grills, and tent pads are provided. Vault toilets are available. No drinking water. Leashed pets are permitted.

Reservations, fees: No reservations; no fee. Open year-round.

Directions: From Olympia on Interstate 5, take Exit 104 and drive north on U.S. 101 to the Aberdeen/Highway 8 exit. Turn west on Highway 8 and drive 36 miles to Aberdeen. Continue through Aberdeen four miles to U.S. 101. Turn north on U.S. 101 and drive about 94 miles. Exit at Milepost 176. At Hoh Mainline Road turn east and drive 6.5 miles. Turn left on Road H1000 and drive 7.5 miles to the campground on the right. A Department of Natural Resources (DNR) map is advised.

Contact: Department of Natural Resources, Olympic Region, 411 Tillicum Lane, Forks, WA 98331-9797; tel. (360) 374-6131, fax (360) 374-5446.

33 Hoh Rain Forest   10

This camp at a trailhead leading into the interior of Olympic National Park is located in the beautiful heart of a temperate, old-growth rain forest. Hoh Oxbow, Cottonwood, Willoughby Creek, and Minnie Peterson are nearby, set downstream on the Hoh River, outside national park boundaries. In the summer, there are evening naturalist programs, and a visitor center is nearby. This is one of the most popular camps in the park.

Location: In Olympic National Park; map A1, grid g6.

Campsites, facilities: There are 88 sites for tents or RVs up to 21 feet long. Picnic tables and fire grills are provided. A sanitary disposal station, rest rooms, and drinking water are available. Facilities are wheelchair accessible. Leashed pets are permitted.

Reservations, fees: No reservations. Sites are $10 per night. Open year-round.

Directions: From Olympia on Interstate 5, take Exit 104 and drive north on U.S. 101 to the Aberdeen/Highway 8 exit. Turn west on Highway 8 and drive 36 miles to Aberdeen. Continue through Aberdeen four miles to U.S. 101. Turn north on U.S. 101

and drive about 90 miles to Milepost 176. Turn east on Hoh River Road and drive 19 miles to the campground.

Contact: Olympic National Park, 600 East Park Avenue, Port Angeles, WA 98362; tel. (360) 452-4501, fax (360) 452-0335.

34 Sol Duc   10

This site is a nice hideaway, with Sol Duc Hot Springs a highlight. The problem is that it's very popular. The camp fills up quickly on weekends, and a fee is charged to use the hot springs, which have been fully developed since the early 1900s. The camp is set at 1,680 feet along the Sol Duc River. A naturalist program is available in the summer months.

Location: On the Sol Duc River in Olympic National Park; map A1, grid g7.

Campsites, facilities: There are 80 sites for tents or RVs up to 21 feet long. Picnic tables and fire grills are provided. A sanitary disposal station, rest rooms, drinking water, and wheelchair-accessible facilities are available. A store and a cafe are within one mile. Leashed pets are permitted.

Reservations, fees: No reservations. Sites are $10 per night. Open from May to late October, with limited winter facilities.

Directions: From Interstate 5 at Olympia, turn north on U.S. 101 and drive about 122 miles to Port Angeles. Continue on U.S. 101 for past Port Angeles for 27 miles, just past Lake Crescent. Turn left at the Sol Duc turnoff and drive 12 miles to the camp.

Contact: Olympic National Park, 600 East Park Avenue, Port Angeles, WA 98362; tel. (360) 452-4501, fax (360) 452-0335.

35 Kalaloch   10

This camp is located on a bluff above the beach, with some wonderful ocean-view sites. Like other camps set on the coast of the Olympic Peninsula, heavy rain in winter and spring is common, and it's often foggy in the summer. A naturalist program is offered in the summer months. There are several good hiking trails in the park; check out the visitor center for maps and information.

Location: Near the Pacific Ocean in Olympic National Park; map A1, grid h3.

Campsites, facilities: There are 175 sites for tents or RVs up to 21 feet long. Picnic tables and fire grills are provided. Rest rooms, drinking water, wheelchair-accessible facilities, and a sanitary station are available. A store and a restaurant are within one mile. Leashed pets are permitted in the campground.

Reservations, fees: No reservations. Sites are $12 per night. Open year-round.

Directions: From Olympia on Interstate 5, take Exit 104 and drive north on U.S. 101 to the Aberdeen/Highway 8 exit. Turn west on Highway 8 and drive 36 miles to Aberdeen. Continue through Aberdeen four miles to U.S. 101. Turn north on U.S. 101 and drive 83 miles to the campground on the left. It is located near the mouth of the Kalaloch River five miles north of the U.S. 101 bridge over the Queets River.

Contact: Olympic National Park, 600 East Park Avenue, Port Angeles, WA 98362; tel. (360) 452-4501, fax (360) 452-0335.

36 Coppermine Bottom   9

Few tourists ever visit this primitive, hidden campground with river dory launching facilities. It's set on the Clearwater River, a tributary of the Queets River, which runs to the ocean. The boat launch is a bonus and makes this a perfect camp for anglers and river runners who want to avoid the usual U.S. 101 crowds.

Location: On the Clearwater River; map A1, grid h5.

Campsites, facilities: There are nine campsites for tents or small trailers. Picnic tables, fire grills, and tent pads are provided. Vault toilets, a group shelter, and a hand boat launch are available. There is no drinking water available. Leashed pets are permitted.

Reservations, fees: No reservations; no fee. Open year-round.

Directions: From Olympia on Interstate 5, take Exit 104 and drive north on U.S. 101 to the Aberdeen/Highway 8 exit. Turn west on Highway 8 and drive 36 miles to Aberdeen. Continue through Aberdeen four miles to U.S. 101. Turn north on U.S. 101 and drive about 60 miles to Milepost 147. Turn north on Clearwater Mainline Road and drive about 14 miles to C-3000 Road. Turn east on C-3000 Road (a graveled one-lane road) and drive two miles to C-1010 Road. Turn right on C-1010 Road and drive one mile. The camp is on the left. Note: This primary route was washed out in 1999 and is expected to be accessible in October of 2000. Another route is available from U.S. 101 from an unsigned road a quarter mile north of Kalaloch Campground.

Contact: Department of Natural Resources, Olympic Region, 411 Tillicum Lane, Forks, WA 98331-9797; tel. (360) 374-6131, fax (360) 374-5446.

37 Upper Clearwater   8

Upper Clearwater is one of the three primitive camps set along the Clearwater River. This is a great camp—it's very pretty, unused by most tourists, and has a boat ramp and other amenities. Best of all, it's free.

Location: On the Clearwater River; map A1, grid h5.

Campsites, facilities: There are nine sites for tents or small trailers. Picnic tables, fire grills, tent pads, and vault toilets are provided, but there is no drinking water. There are unimproved boat launching facilities for small crafts, such as river dories, rafts, canoes, and kayaks. Leashed pets are permitted.

Reservations, fees: No reservations; no fee. Open year-round.

Directions: From Olympia on Interstate 5, take Exit 104 and drive north on U.S. 101 to the Aberdeen/Highway 8 exit. Turn west on Highway 8 and drive 36 miles to Aberdeen. Continue through Aberdeen four miles to U.S. 101. Turn north on U.S. 101 and drive about 60 miles to Milepost 147. Turn north on Hoh Clearwater Mainline Road and drive about 13 miles to C-3000 Road (a gravel one-lane road). Turn right and drive 3.3 miles. The camp entrance is on the right. Note: The route to Upper Clearwater was washed out in two places in 1999, and there is no reliable date when it will be reopened. Call DNR before planning to visit this site.

Contact: Department of Natural Resources, Olympic Region, 411 Tillicum Lane, Forks, WA 98331-9797; tel. (360) 374-6131, fax (360) 374-5446.

38 Yahoo Lake Walk-In   10

This walk-in camp is located at about 2,000 feet on the edge of tiny Yahoo Lake in an idyllic setting that few people take advantage of. There are hiking trails in the area and fishing in the lake. If you're willing to take a little time to get here, this can be the camper's ideal getaway.

Location: In Hoh Clearwater State Forest; map A1, grid h6.

Campsites, facilities: There are four tent sites at this primitive, hike-in camp. Pit toilets, a group shelter with a fireplace, and a fishing pier are available. There is no drinking water. Leashed pets are permitted.

Reservations, fees: No reservations; no fee. The campground is open year-round, weather and snow level permitting.

Directions: From Olympia on Interstate 5, take Exit 104 and drive north on U.S. 101 to the Aberdeen/Highway 8 exit. Turn west on Highway 8 and drive 36 miles to Aberdeen. Continue through Aberdeen four miles to U.S. 101. Turn north on U.S. 101 and drive about 60 miles to Milepost 147 at Hoh Clearwater Mainline Road. Turn north on Clearwater Mainline Road and drive about 10 miles to C-3000 (a gravel one-lane road). Turn right and drive four miles to C-3100 (a graveled two-lane road). Keep left, and continue on C-3100 another three-quarters of a mile to the trail-head. Hike in 500 feet to the camp. Note: The route to Upper Clearwater was washed out in two places in 1999, and there is no reliable date when it will be reopened. Call DNR before planning to visit this site.

Contact: Department of Natural Resources, Olympic Region, 411 Tillicum Lane, Forks, WA 98331-9797; tel. (360) 374-6131, fax (360) 374-5446.

39 Willaby      8

This pretty, 14-acre wooded camp is set on the shore of Lake Quinault at 200 feet. The Quinault Rain Forest Nature Trail and the Quinault National Recreation Trail System are nearby. Quinault Lake covers about six square miles. This camp is concessionaire operated.

Location: On Lake Quinault in Olympic National Forest; map A1, grid i6.

Campsites, facilities: There are 22 drive-in sites for tents, trailers, or RVs up to 16 feet long. Picnic tables are provided. Drinking water, flush toilets, and electricity in the bathrooms are available. Launching facilities and rentals are available at nearby Quinault Lake. Leashed pets are permitted.

Reservations, fees: No reservations. Sites are $14 per night. Open from mid-April through mid-November, weather permitting.

Directions: From Olympia on Interstate 5, take Exit 104 and drive north on U.S. 101 to the Aberdeen/Highway 8 exit. Turn west on Highway 8 and drive 36 miles to Aberdeen. Continue through Aberdeen four miles to U.S. 101. Turn north on U.S. 101 and drive about 45 miles to the Lake Quinault turnoff and South Shore Road. Turn northeast on South Shore Road and drive 1.5 miles to the camp set on the southern shore of the lake.

Contact: Olympic National Forest, Quinault Ranger District, P.O. Box 9, Quinault, WA 98575; tel. (360) 288-2525.

40 July Creek   7

This primitive camp on the north shore of Quinault Lake is set where July Creek empties into the lake. Full supplies are available on the south shore, where there's a marina. This is a good choice for hikers looking to avoid crowds.

Location: On Quinault Lake in Olympic National Park; map A1, grid i6.

Campsites, facilities: There are 29 walk-in tent sites. Picnic tables and fire grills are provided. Vault toilets and drinking water are available. Leashed pets are permitted.

Reservations, fees: No reservations. Sites are $10 per night. Open year-round.

Directions: From Olympia on Interstate 5, take Exit 104 and drive north on U.S. 101 to the Aberdeen/Highway 8 exit. Turn west on Highway 8 and drive 36 miles to Aberdeen. Continue through Aberdeen four miles to U.S. 101. Turn north on U.S. 101 and drive about 46 miles to Lake Quinault and the town of Amanda Park. Continue two miles north on U.S. 101 to North Shore Road. Turn right and drive two miles along the north shore of Quinault Lake to the camp.

Contact: Olympic National Park, 600 East Park Avenue, Port Angeles, WA 98362; tel. (360) 452-4501, fax (360) 452-0335.

41 Queets   6

This primitive camp on the shore of the Queets River is a gem if you don't mind bringing your own water or purifying river water. Since it's so close to the highway, the camp gets a fair amount of use, so try to arrive as early in the day as possible. A trailhead is available for hikes into the interior of Olympic National Park.

Location: On the Queets River in Olympic National Park; map A1, grid i6.

Campsites, facilities: There are 20 primitive tent sites. Picnic tables and fire grills are provided. Toilets are available, but there is no drinking water. Rest rooms are wheelchair accessible. Leashed pets are permitted.

Reservations, fees: No reservations. Sites are $8 per night. Open year-round.

Directions: From Olympia on Interstate 5, take Exit 104 and drive north on U.S. 101 to the Aberdeen/Highway 8 exit. Turn west on Highway 8 and drive 36 miles to Aberdeen. Continue through Aberdeen four miles to U.S. 101. Turn north on U.S. 101, drive about 45 miles to Lake Quinault, and continue for 19 miles to a signed turnoff for the campground. Turn northeast on an unpaved road and drive 14 miles along the Queets River. The campground is at the end of the road.

Contact: Olympic National Park, 600 East Park Avenue, Port Angeles, WA 98362; tel. (360) 452-4501, fax (360) 452-0335.

42 Gatton Creek   8

This three-acre wooded camp is set on the shore of Lake Quinault (elevation 200 feet) where Gatton Creek empties into it. The Quinault Rain Forest Nature Trail and the Quinault National Recreation Trail System are nearby. Quinault Lake covers about six square miles. This camp, like the others on the lake, is concessionaire operated.

Location: On Lake Quinault in Olympic National Forest; map A1, grid i7.

Campsites, facilities: There are five tent sites and eight overflow RV sites (in a parking area). Picnic tables are provided. Vault toilets, wheelchair-accessible rest rooms, and firewood are available. Leashed pets are permitted.

Reservations, fees: No reservations. Sites are $11 per night. There is no charge for picnicking. Open from May through September, weather permitting.

Directions: From Olympia on Interstate 5, take Exit 104 and drive north on U.S. 101 to the Aberdeen/Highway 8 exit. Turn west on Highway 8 and drive 36 miles to Aberdeen. Continue through Aberdeen four miles to U.S. 101. Turn north on U.S. 101 and drive about 45 miles to the Lake Quinault turnoff and South Shore Road. Turn northeast and drive 3.5 miles to the camp on the southeast shore of Lake Quinault.

Contact: Olympic National Forest, Quinault Ranger District, P.O. Box 9, Quinault, WA 98575; tel. (360) 288-2525.

43 Falls Creek   8

This scenic five-acre wooded camp is set at 200 feet, where Falls Creek empties into Quinault Lake. The Quinault Rain Forest Nature Trail and Quinault National Recreation Trail System are nearby. The camp is located adjacent to the Quinault Ranger Station and historic Lake Quinault Lodge.

Location: On Lake Quinault in Olympic National Forest; map A1, grid i7.

Campsites, facilities: There are 11 tent sites and 20 sites for trailers or RVs up to 16 feet long. Picnic tables are provided. Drinking water, flush toilets, and electricity in the bathrooms are available. Rest rooms are wheelchair accessible. Launching facilities and rentals are available at nearby Quinault Lake. Leashed pets are permitted.

Reservations, fees: No reservations. Sites are $11-14 per night. Open Memorial Day through Labor Day.

Directions: From Olympia on Interstate 5, take Exit 104 and drive north on U.S. 101 to the Aberdeen/Highway 8 exit. Turn west on Highway 8 and drive 36 miles to Aberdeen. Continue through Aberdeen four miles to U.S. 101. Turn north on U.S. 101 and drive about 45 miles to Quinault and South Shore Road. Turn northeast and drive three miles to the camp on the southeast shore of Lake Quinault.

44 Campbell Tree Grove   8

This 14-acre wooded camp (elevation 1,100 feet) is located near trails leading into the Colonel Bob Wilderness; see a U.S. Forest Service map for more information. The West Fork of the Humptulips River runs near the camp. It's a prime base camp for a wilderness expedition. Fishing is an option here as well.

Location: On the Humptulips River in Olympic National Forest; map A1, grid i8.

Campsites, facilities: There are eight tent sites and three sites for trailers or RVs up to 16 feet long. Picnic tables are provided. Vault toilets and drinking water are available. Leashed pets are permitted.

Reservations, fees: No reservations; no fee. The campground is open June through October, weather permitting.

Directions: From Olympia on Interstate 5, take Exit 104 and drive north on U.S. 101 to the Aberdeen/Highway 8 exit. Turn west on Highway 8 and drive 36 miles to Aberdeen. Continue through Aberdeen four miles to U.S. 101. Turn north on U.S. 101 and drive about 20 miles to Humptulips and continue for another four miles to Forest Road 22 (Donkey Creek Road). Turn right and drive about nine miles to Forest Road 2204. Turn left (north) and drive about 14 miles to the campground.

Contact: Olympic National Forest, Quinault Ranger District, P.O. Box 9, Quinault, WA 98575; tel. (360) 288-2525, fax (360) 352-2676.

45 Graves Creek   6

This camp located at an elevation of 540 feet is a short distance from a trailhead leading into the backcountry of Olympic National Park. See an Olympic National Park and U.S. Forest Service map for details. The Upper Quinault River is nearby, and there are lakes in the area.

Location: Near the Quinault River in Olympic National Park; map A1, grid i9.

Campsites, facilities: There are 30 sites for tents or RVs up to 21 feet long. Picnic tables, fire grills, drinking water, and rest rooms are available. The facilities are wheelchair accessible. Leashed pets are permitted.

Reservations, fees: No reservations. There is a $10 per night fee. The campground is open year-round, with limited winter facilities.

Directions: From Olympia on Interstate 5, take Exit 104 and drive north on U.S. 101 to the Aberdeen/Highway 8 exit. Turn west on Highway 8 and drive 36 miles to Aberdeen. Continue through Aberdeen four miles to U.S. 101. Turn north on U.S. 101 and drive about 45 miles to the Lake Quinault turnoff and South Shore Road. Turn east on South Shore Road and drive 15 miles to the campground at road's end. The Graves Creek Ranger Station is located nearby.

Contact: Olympic National Park, 600 East Park Avenue, Port Angeles, WA 98362; tel. (360) 452-4501, fax (360) 452-0335.

46 Staircase   9

This camp is located on the Staircase Rapids of the North Fork of the Skokomish River, about one mile from where it empties into Lake Cushman. A major trailhead at the camp leads to the backcountry of Olympic National Park. See an Olympic National Park and U.S. Forest Service map for details. A beautiful two-mile loop trail runs along the river.

Location: On the North Fork of the Skokomish River in Olympic National Park; map A1, grid i9.

Campsites, facilities: There are 59 sites for tents or RVs up to 21 feet long. Picnic tables and fire grills are provided. Rest rooms, drinking water, and wheelchair-accessible facilities are available. Leashed pets are permitted in camp.

Reservations, fees: No reservations. Sites are $10 per night. Open year-round.

Directions: From Olympia on Interstate 5, take U.S. 101 and drive north about 37 miles to the town of Hoodsport and Lake Cushman Road (County Road 119). Turn west and drive 17 miles to the camp, about a mile above the inlet of Lake Cushman.

Contact: Olympic National Park, 600 East Park Avenue, Port Angeles, WA 98362; tel. (360) 452-4501, fax (360) 452-0335.

This eight-acre camp is set on the shore of Wynoochee Lake at 900 feet. Points of interest include a forest nature trail, Wynoochee Dam Viewpoint, and a 16-mile national recreation trail that goes around the lake. This is one of the most idyllic drive-to settings you could hope to find.

Location: On Wynoochee Lake in Olympic National Forest; map A1, grid j8.

Campsites, facilities: There are 58 sites for tents, trailers, or RVs up to 36 feet long. Picnic tables are provided. Flush toilets, drinking water, and wheelchair-accessible rest rooms are available. There is a dump station nearby. Boat docks and launching facilities are available at Wynoochee Lake. Leashed pets are permitted.

Reservations, fees: No reservations. Sites are $10-12 per night. Open May through September.

Directions: From Olympia on Interstate 5, take Exit 104 and drive north on U.S. 101 to the Aberdeen/Highway 8 exit. Turn west on Highway 8 and drive 36 miles (it becomes Highway 12 at Elma) to Montesano. Continue two miles on Highway 12 to Wynoochee Valley Road. Turn north on Wynoochee Valley Road and drive 12 miles to Forest Road 22. Continue north on Forest Road 22 to Wynoochee Lake. Just south of the lake, bear left and drive on Forest Road 2294 (which runs along the lake's northwest shore), to the camp on the west shore of Wynoochee Lake. A U.S. Forest Service map is helpful.

Contact: Olympic National Forest, Hood Canal Ranger District, P.O. Box 68, Hoodsport, WA 98548; tel. (360) 877-5254.

MAP A2

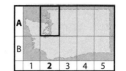

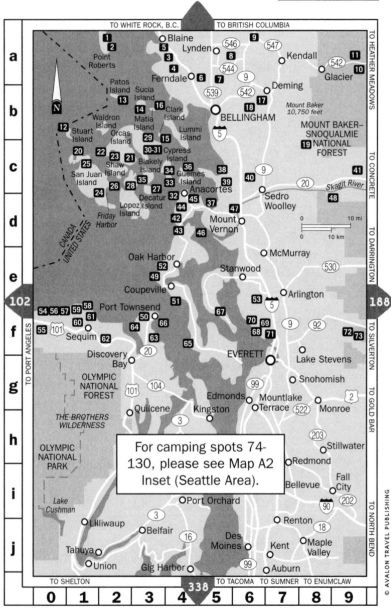

MAP A2 INSET
(SEATTLE AREA)

OLYMPIC
NATIONAL
PARK

OLYMPIC
NATIONAL
FOREST

THE BROTHERS
WILDERNESS

DOSEWALLIPS
STATE PARK

Discovery Bay

Quilcene

Seal Rock

Lake Cushman

Hood Canal

Lilliwaup

Tahuya

Union

Belfair

Bremerton

Port Orchard

Gig Harbor

Gig Harbor

Poulsbo

Kingston

Edmonds

Bainbridge Island

Puget Sound

SEATTLE

Des Moines

Kent

Auburn

Renton

Bellevue

Redmond

EVERETT

Snohomish

Monroe

Duvall

Stillwater

Fall City

Maple Valley

N

© AVALON TRAVEL PUBLISHING

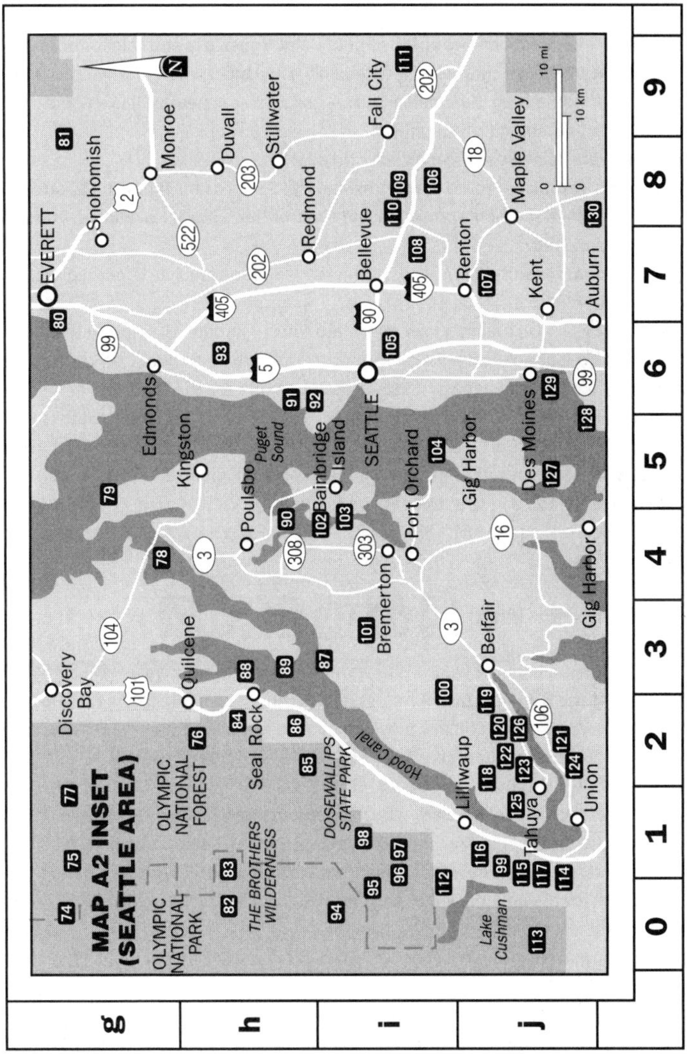

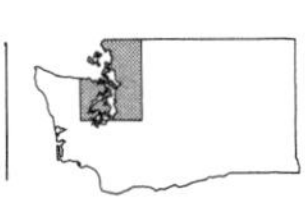

CHAPTER A2

■ Sunny Point Resort   7

This pretty camp set on beautiful, remote Point Roberts is suitable for both trailers and tents. The campground is located only a few blocks from the Pacific Ocean and just half a mile from Lighthouse Park. A golf course is nearby. It is a popular layover for folks catching the early ferry.

Location: On Point Roberts; map A2, grid a2.

Campsites, facilities: There are approximately 25 spaces for tents and 50 sites for trailers or RVs. Rest rooms, showers and a recreation field are available. Leashed pets are permitted.

Reservations, fees: Reservations recommended. Sites are $10-17 per night. Open year-round.

Directions: From Bellingham take Interstate 5 north through Blaine and the border customs Into Canada to Highway 99 North. Continue northeast on Highway 99 North for 19 miles to Highway 17 (look for the signs for the Victoria Ferry). Turn south on Highway 17 and drive 13 miles to Tsawwassen. Continue south across the U.S./Canada border (where Highway 17 becomes Tyee Road); you will have to pass U.S. Customs. Continue south on Tyee Road to Gulf Road. Turn right on Gulf Road and drive half a mile to the park on the right.

Contact: Sunny Point Resort, 1408 Gulf Road, Point Roberts, WA 98281; tel. (360) 945-1986.

■ Whalen's RV Park   6

This little spot, a mix of woods and water, is known to relatively few, especially compared to the RV parks on the Interstate 5 corridor. The park has grassy sites and lots of trees. A recreation field is provided for campers. Nearby recreational options include an 18-hole golf course, a full-service marina, and tennis courts.

Location: On Point Roberts; map A2, grid a2.

Campsites, facilities: There are 100 sites for tents and 50 sites for trailers or RVs of any length. Electricity, drinking water, and picnic tables are provided. Flush toilets, sanitary services, firewood, and showers are available. A store, a cafe, a coin laundry, and ice are located within one mile. Boat docks and launching facilities are nearby. Pets are permitted.

Reservations, fees: Reservations accepted. Sites are $18-20 per night. Open from May to late October.

Directions: From Bellingham take Interstate 5 north through Blaine and the border customs into Canada to Highway 99 North. Continue northeast on Highway BC 99N for 11 miles to BC 10. Turn west and drive to Benson Road. Turn left on Benson Road and drive to Boundary Bay Road. Turn left and drive to Bay View Road. Turn left again and drive half a mile to the park on the left.

Contact: Whalen's RV Park, P.O. Box 985, Point Roberts, WA 98281; tel. (360) 945-2874, fax (360) 945-0934.

3 Birch Bay Resort   5

Good ocean access with a private beach on Birch Bay is a highlight of this private campground, which is actually a large mobile home park with a few spaces for campers. Nearby recreational options include a full-service marina and tennis courts.
Location: On Birch Bay; map A2, grid a4.
Campsites, facilities: There are 64 drive-through sites for trailers or RVs of any length; 40 are full-hookup sites. Electricity, drinking water, sewer hookups, cable TV, and picnic tables are provided. Flush toilets, sanitary services, showers, a recreation hall, satellite TV, and a laundry room are available. A store, a cafe, ice, and boat launching facilities are located within one mile. Leashed pets and motorbikes are permitted.
Reservations, fees: Reservations accepted. Sites are $22 per night. Open year-round.
Directions: From Bellingham drive north on Interstate 5 to Exit 270. Take Exit 270 to Birch Bay-Lynden Road and drive west four miles to Harbor View Road. Turn south on Harbor View and drive 300 feet to the park.
Contact: Birch Bay Resort, 8080 Harbor View, Blaine, WA 98230; tel. (360) 371-7922

4 Birch Bay State Park   8

Birch Bay State Park covers 193 acres and includes a mile-long beach. More than 100 different species of birds, many of which are migrating on the Pacific flyway, can be seen here. Recreation options include the Terrell Marsh Interpretive Trail, one of the few remaining saltwater/freshwater estuaries in northern Puget Sound. Bald eagles and great blue heron feed along the banks of Terrell Creek. Several 18-hole golf courses are located nearby.
Location: On Birch Bay; map A2, grid a4.
Campsites, facilities: There are 146 sites for tents or self-contained RVs and 18 full-hookup sites for trailers or RVs of any length. Picnic tables and fire grills are provided. Flush toilets, coin showers, firewood, and a sanitary disposal station are available. A store, restaurant, coin laundry, and ice are located within one mile. Leashed pets are permitted.
Reservations, fees: Reservations accepted; phone (800) 452-5687 ($6 reservation fee). Sites are $10-16 per night, plus $5 for each extra vehicle per night. Major credit cards accepted. Open year-round.
Directions: From Bellingham drive north on Interstate 5 to Exit 266. At Exit 266 take Grandview west and continue eight miles to Jackson Road. Turn right on Jackson Road, drive a quarter mile to Helwig Road, and turn left. The park will be on your left (route is well signed).
Contact: Birch Bay State Park, 5105 Helwig Road, Blaine, WA 98230; tel. (800) 233-0321 or (360) 371-2800, fax (360) 371-0455.

5 Beachside RV Park   8

Surrounded by evergreens and bay views, this pretty park comes with the opportunity to view a pair of nesting eagles. Hiking, fishing, mountain biking, and nearby golf are also options.

Location: On Birch Bay; map A2, grid a4.

Campsites, facilities: The park has a total of 86 sites, 12 for tents and 74 for trailers or RVs with full hookups. Drinking water, rest rooms, coin laundry facilities, and a group fire pit are available. A grocery store and mini-mart are located within one-half mile. Leashed pets are permitted.

Reservations, fees: Reservations required; phone (360) 371-5962. Sites are $13-20 per night. Major credit cards accepted. Open year-round.

Directions: From Bellingham drive north on Interstate 5 to Exit 270. Turn west on Birch Bay-Lynden Road and drive five miles to Birch Bay Drive. Turn left and drive one mile to the park.

Contact: Beachside RV Park, 7630 Birch Bay Drive, Birch Bay, WA 98230; tel. (360) 371-5962.

6 The Cedars RV Resort   5

An alternative to Windmill Inn and KOA Lynden, this campground provides more direct access from Interstate 5. It's a nice, clean camp with spacious sites and trees. Horseshoe pits, a game room, and a recreation field provide possible activities for campers. Several golf courses are nearby.

Location: In Ferndale; map A2, grid a5.

Campsites, facilities: There are 117 sites for tents, trailers, or RVs of any length. Electricity, drinking water, and cable and sewer hookups are provided. Modem-friendly telephone service is available at some sites. Flush toilets, showers, laundry facilities, a playground, a pool, a small store, and ice are available. Small pets are permitted.

Reservations, fees: Reservations accepted. Sites are $17-26 per night. Major credit cards accepted. Open year-round.

Directions: From Bellingham on Interstate 5, drive north to Ferndale and Exit 263. Take Exit 263 and turn north on Portal Way. Drive less than one mile north to the campground.

Contact: The Cedars RV Resort, 6335 Portal Way, Ferndale, WA 98248; tel. (360) 384-2622, fax (360) 380-6365.

7 Windmill Inn   7

This nice little spot is set near the Nooksack River and Wiser Lake and is within 15 minutes of the Puget Sound. Since it's the last stop before the border, the camp is used primarily as a layover for people heading up to Canada. The setting is quiet and pretty, with lots of trees and flowers. Area attractions include Mount Baker, the quaint little shops of Lynden, and the nearby Birch Bay area, which offers many recreation options.

Location: Near the Nooksack River; map A2, grid a5.

Campsites, facilities: There are eight sites for trailers or RVs of any length. Electricity, drinking water, sewer, cable TV, and phone hookups, a park, and picnic tables are provided. Flush toilets, showers, bottled gas, a store, a cafe, coin laundry facilities, and ice are available within one mile. Boat launching facilities are located within 1.5 miles. Pets are permitted.

Reservations, fees: Reservations accepted. Sites are $18 per night. Major credit cards accepted. Open year-round.

Directions: In Bellingham on Interstate 5, take Exit 256 for Highway 539 (called Meridian Street in Bellingham). Turn north on Highway 539 and drive 10 miles to Lynden. The campground is on the right side of the road as you enter Lynden.

Contact: Windmill Inn, 8022 Guide Meridian Road, Lynden, WA 98264; tel. (360) 354-3424, fax (360) 354-8138.

8 KOA Lynden   9

A holdover spot for vacationers heading north to Canada via Highway 539 and Highway 546, this campground is exceptionally clean and in a lovely setting, with pretty, grassy sites and lots of trees. There is a pond where campers can fish for trout. Tackle and boat rentals are available. Nearby recreational options include an 18-hole golf course and tennis courts.

Location: In Lynden; map A2, grid a5.

Campsites, facilities: There are 80 tent sites and 100 sites for trailers or RVs of any length; 25 are drive-through. There are also 12 cabins. Electricity, drinking water, sewer hookups, and picnic tables are provided. Flush toilets, bottled gas, sanitary services, showers, firewood, a recreation hall, a store, a cafe, laundry facilities, ice, a playground, miniature golf, and a swimming pool are available. Paddle boat rentals are available. Pets are permitted.

Reservations, fees: Reservations accepted. Sites are $22.50-28 per night for two campers, $4 for each additional person. Cabins are $38 per night. Major credit cards accepted. Call the park for group rates. Open year-round.

Directions: From Interstate 5 at Bellingham, take Exit 256 to Highway 539. Turn north on Highway 539 and drive 12 miles to Highway 546. Turn east on Highway 546 (Badger Road) and drive three miles to Line Road. Turn south on Line Road and drive one block to the campground.

Contact: KOA Lynden, 8717 Line Road, Lynden, WA 98264; tel. (360) 354-4772, fax (360) 354-7050.

9 Sumas RV Park   5

Located near the U.S./Canada border, this campground is a holdover spot to spend American dollars before heading into British Columbia. Set in the grassy flatlands, it has graveled sites and a few trees. Nearby recreation options include an 18-hole golf course and tennis courts.

Location: In Sumas; map A2, grid a6.

Campsites, facilities: There are 24 tent sites and 40 sites for trailers or RVs of any length; 12 are drive-through. Electricity, drinking water, and picnic tables are provided. Flush toilets, sanitary services, showers, firewood, and a ballpark are available. A store, a cafe, a coin laundry, and ice are located within one mile. Pets and motorbikes are permitted.

Reservations, fees: Reservations accepted. Sites are $8-17 per night. Open year-round.

Directions: From Interstate 5 at Bellingham, take Exit 256 to Highway 539. Turn north on Highway 539 and drive 12 miles to Highway 546. Turn east on Highway 546 (Badger Road) and drive 14 miles (the road becomes Highway 9) to Sumas and look for Cherry Street. Turn south at Cherry Street and drive two blocks to the park on the left.

Contact: Sumas RV Park, 9600 Easterbrook Road, Sumas, WA 98295; tel. (360) 988-8875.

🔟 Excelsior Group Camp   6

This campground is set near the Nooksack River less than a mile from Nooksack Falls and 1.5 miles from the site of the Excelsior Mine. There are numerous hiking trails available in the Mount Baker Wilderness, located to the east and south. Remember to bring your own water.

Location: Near the Nooksack River in Mount Baker-Snoqualmie National Forest; map A2, grid a9.

Campsites, facilities: There is one group site. Picnic tables, vault toilets, and fire grills are provided, but there is no drinking water. Leashed pets are permitted.

Reservations, fees: Reservations required ($8.65 reservation fee); phone (877) 444-6777 or access the website: www.reserveusa.com. The group site fee is $50-150 per night. Open May through September.

Directions: From Bellingham on Interstate 5, take the Highway 542 exit and drive 37.5 miles (6.5 miles east of Glacier) to the camp on the right.

Contact: Mount Baker-Snoqualmie National Forest, Mount Baker Ranger District, 2105 State Rte. 20, Sedro-Woolley, WA 98284; tel. (360) 856-5700, fax (360) 856-1934.

1️⃣1️⃣ Douglas Fir   10

Set along the Nooksack River, this camp is an alternative to Excelsior Group Camp. Fishing is available on the river, and there are hiking trails in the area. See the descriptions of the above camps for more information on the area.

Location: On the Nooksack River in Mount Baker-Snoqualmie National Forest; map A2, grid a9.

Campsites, facilities: There are 30 sites for tents, trailers, or RVs up to 31 feet long. Picnic tables and fire grills are provided. Drinking water and vault toilets are available. A store, a cafe, a coin laundry, and ice are located within five miles. Leashed pets are permitted.

Reservations, fees: Reservations required ($8.65 reservation fee); phone (877) 444-6777 or access the website: www.reserveusa.com. Sites are $12 per night. Open May through September, with self-service access the remainder of the year.

Directions: From Bellingham on Interstate 5, take the Highway 542 exit and drive 31 miles to Glacier. Continue two miles northeast on Highway 542 to the campground on the left.

Contact: Mount Baker-Snoqualmie National Forest, Mount Baker Ranger District, 2105 State Route 20, Sedro-Woolley, WA 98284; tel. (360) 856-5700, fax (360) 856-1934.

12 Stuart Island
Marine State Park Boat-In   9

This is really stalking the unknown. Stuart Island is a remote little spot on the edge of Canadian waters that covers 153 acres and has excellent harbors for mooring. It's the westernmost of the marine parks, making it a jump-off point for Limekiln, Sucia Island, Orcas Island, and San Juan Island parks. There is good fishing at nearby Reed and Provost Harbors. This park is quiet and primitive, receiving little use even in the summer months.

Location: Northwest of San Juan Island; map A2, grid b1.

Campsites, facilities: There are 19 primitive boat-in campsites. Picnic tables and drinking water are provided. Pit toilets are available. Twenty-two buoys and floats are available for overnight moorage.

Reservations, fees: No reservations. Sites are $5-11 per night. Open May 1 through Labor Day.

Directions: The park is on the north side of Stuart Island and is accessible only by boat. Stuart Island is located northwest of San Juan Island.

Contact: San Juan Marine Area, Star Route, Box 177, Olga, WA 98279; tel. Phone (800) 233-0321, (360) 378-2044.

13 Patos Island State Park Boat-In   9

If you're going to get stranded on an island, this is not a bad choice, provided you like your companion. There are good hiking trails and excellent fishing and clam digging opportunities here. It's tiny, primitive, and used by few.

Location: Near Sucia Island; map A2, b2.

Campsites, facilities: There are seven primitive boat-in campsites. Vault and pit toilets are available, but there is no drinking water. Boat buoys are available for overnight moorage.

Reservations, fees: No reservations. Sites are $5 per night. Open year-round.

Directions: The park is on the east side of Patos Island, which is 2.5 miles northwest of Sucia Island and five miles northwest of Orcas Island. It's accessible only by boat and is the northernmost of the coastal islands.

Contact: San Juan Marine Area, Star Route, Box 177, Olga, WA 98279; tel. (800) 233-0321, (360) 378-2044.

14 Sucia Island
Marine State Park Boat-In   9

Here's a classic spot, with rocky outcrops for lookout points and good beach and fishing areas. Sucia Island covers 562 acres and provides opportunities for hiking, clamming, crabbing, canoeing, and scuba diving. Though primitive, the campground is beautiful and well worth the trip.

Location: Near Orcas Island; map A2, grid b3.

Campsites, facilities: There are 55 primitive boat-in campsites. Picnic tables and vault and composting toilets are available. Campers are asked to pack out their garbage. Boat buoys and floats are available for overnight moorage.

Reservations, fees: No reservations. Sites are $5-11 per night. Open May 1 through September.

Directions: The park is on the north side of Sucia Island, which is located 2.5 miles north of Orcas Island. It's accessible only by boat.

Contact: San Juan Marine Area, Star Route, Box 177, Olga, WA 98279; tel. (800) 233-0321, (360) 378-2044.

15 Clark Island State Park Boat-In   9

Clark Island State Park offers beautiful beaches with opportunities for scuba diving. Beachcombing and sunbathing are two other popular options. It is a short boat trip from nearby Orcas Island. You can pretend you're on a deserted Caribbean island. Well, almost. From the campground there are excellent views of the other nearby islands.

Location: Northeast of Orcas Island; map A2, grid c3.

Campsites, facilities: There are eight primitive boat-in campsites. Vault toilets are available, but there is no drinking water. Boat buoys are available for overnight moorage. No trash services are provided, so you must pack out your garbage.

Reservations, fees: No reservations. Sites are $5-11 per night. Open year-round.

Directions: The campground, accessible only by boat, is on tiny Clark Island, located northeast of Orcas Island. Look for the moorage floats set just offshore the campsites.

Contact: San Juan Marine Area, Star Route, Box 177, Olga, WA 98279; tel. (800) 233-0321, (360) 378-2044.

16 Matia Island State Park Boat-In   9

Campsites here are located just a short walk from the docking facilities, a big plus since many of the other island campgrounds don't have docks. Good fishing and beachcombing are among the highlights. Scuba diving is also popular.

Location: Near Orcas Island; map A2, grid b3.

Campsites, facilities: There are six primitive boat-in campsites. Composting toilets are provided. There is a boat dock, and buoys and floats are available for overnight moorage.

Reservations, fees: No reservations. Sites are $5-11 per night. Open May 1 through September.

Directions: The campground is located on the northeast side of Matia Island, which is 2.5 miles northeast of Orcas Island (located between Clark Island to the southeast, Sucia Island to the northwest, Orcas Island to the south). It's accessible only by boat.

Contact: San Juan Marine Area, Star Route, Box 177, Olga, WA 98279; tel. (800) 233-0321, (360) 378-2044.

17 Lily Lake Hike-In   6

This tiny, remote hike-in campground is one of those that few people ever go to or even know about. Set on little Lily Lake, it's completely secluded and very primitive; you'll have to pack in everything you need and pack out everything that's left. This is a prime area for hiking, and the nearby trails are used by hikers and horse packers alike.

Location: Near Bellingham; map A2, grid b6.

Campsites, facilities: There are six primitive hike-in tent sites. Leashed pets are allowed.

Reservations, fees: No reservations; no fee. Open year-round.

Directions: From Bellingham on Interstate 5, drive south to Exit 240. On Samish Lake Road drive one-half mile north to Barrel Springs Road. Turn left and drive one mile to Road SW-C-1000. Turn right and drive 1.5 miles to the Blanchard Hill Trailhead. Hike 3.2 miles, bear left, and continue one-half mile to the campground. A map is advisable.

Contact: Department of Natural Resources, Northwest Region, 919 North Township Street, Sedro-Woolley, WA 98284-9395; tel. (360) 856-3500.

18 Lizard Lake Hike-In   6

Located just 0.2 mile down the trail from Lily Lake, this hike-in camp is even smaller and more isolated. It's set on Lizard Lake in a pretty, forested area. See the description of Lily Lake for more information.

Location: Near Bellingham; map A2, grid b6.

Campsites, facilities: There are three primitive hike-in tent sites. Picnic tables, tent pads, fire grills, and vault toilets are available, but there is no drinking water. Leashed pets are permitted.

Reservations, fees: No reservations; no fee. Open year-round.

Directions: From Bellingham on Interstate 5, drive south to Exit 240 to Samish Lake Road and drive one-half mile north to Barrel Springs Road. Turn left and drive one mile to Road SW-C-1000. Turn right and drive 1.5 miles to the Blanchard Hill Trailhead. Hike 3.2 miles, bear left, and continue three-quarters of a mile (just past Lily Lake) to the campground. A map is advisable.

Contact: Department of Natural Resources, Northwest Region, 919 North Township Street, Sedro-Woolley, WA 98284-9395; tel. (360) 856-3500.

19 Hutchinson Creek   9

This campground is set in the forest along Hutchinson Creek near the South Fork of the Nooksack River. Managed by the Department of Natural Resources, it's rustic, beautiful, primitive, and unknown to out-of-towners.

Location: Near the South Fork of the Nooksack River; map A2, grid b8.

Campsites, facilities: There are 11 sites for tents or small trailers. Picnic tables, fire grills, vault toilets, and tent pads are provided, but there is no drinking water. A store is located within three miles. Leashed pets are permitted.

Reservations, fees: No reservations; no fee. Open year-round.

Directions: From Seattle drive north on Interstate 5 to Burlington and Highway 20. Turn east on Highway 20 and drive seven miles to Highway 9. Turn north and drive 16 miles to Acme and Mosquito Lake Road (just north of the Nooksack River Bridge). Turn east on Mosquito Lake Road, drive 2.5 miles, and look for a gravel road on the right. Turn right on the gravel road and continue for one-half mile to the campground.

Contact: Department of Natural Resources, Northwest Region, 919 North Township Street, Sedro-Woolley, WA 98284-9395; tel. (360) 856-3500.

20 Posey Island State Park Boat-In   9

If you want a beautiful little spot all to yourself, this is it—the smallest campground in Washington. It's difficult to get here, however. The best way is by skiff, just a short cruise from San Juan Island out of Roche Harbor. This is not only the smallest designated campground in the Pacific Northwest, but one of the most idyllic and beautiful to reach by small boat. There's not much here, and that's exactly why it is so well loved. Everything becomes simplified and it's as if you have the entire world to yourself. And on Posey Island, you do.

Location: Near Roche Harbor; map A2, grid c1.

Campsites, facilities: There is one primitive boat-in campsite. Fire rings and composting toilets are provided.

Reservations, fees: No reservations. The site is $5 per night. Open year-round.

Directions: This little island is just north of Roche Harbor (on San Juan Island) and is accessible only by small boat. From Roche Harbor, you head out Wescott Bay, turn right through Mosquito Pass, and cruise about two miles to Posey Island.

Contact: San Juan Marine Area, Star Route, Box 177, Olga, WA 98279; tel. (800) 233-0321, (360) 378-2044.

21 West Beach Resort Ferry-In

 9

Right on the beach, this resort offers salmon fishing, boating, swimming and an apple orchard. It's an excellent alternative to Moran State Park, which is often full, and offers the same recreation opportunities. The beaches at Orcas Island are prime spots for whale watching and beautiful views, especially at sunrise and sunset.

Location: On Orcas Island; map A2, grid c2.

Campsites, facilities: There are 62 sites for tents, trailers, or RVs. There are also 16 cabins. Rest rooms, showers (from April through October only), a sanitary dump, a public phone, a store, a playground, laundry facilities, ice, bottled gas, and firewood are available. A hot tub is available for a fee. Also on site are a boat ramp, dock, marina, and rentals. Leashed pets are permitted.

Reservations, fees: Reservations recommended. Sites are $20-30 per night; an additional $4 is charged for each pet. Major credit cards accepted. Open year-round.

Directions: From Seattle on Interstate 5, drive north to Burlington and Highway 20. Turn west on Highway 20 and drive 12 miles to the Highway 20 North spur, following signs to the San Juan Islands Ferry Terminal in Anacortes. Take the ferry to Orcas Island. From the ferry landing, turn left and drive for 11 miles on Horseshoe Highway to the entrance of town. A green sign directs you left toward Moran State Park. Turn left and drive one-half mile to Enchanted Forest Road. Turn left again and drive to the end of Enchanted Forest Road and the resort.

Contact: West Beach Resort, 190 Waterfront Way, Eastsound, WA 98245; tel. (360) 376-2240, fax (360) 376-4746; e-mail: vacation@westbeachresort.com. Website: www.westbeach.com.

22 Jones Island
Marine State Park Boat-In   9

This small island is another hidden spot that gets little use, yet is an easy boat ride out of Doe Harbor at Orcas. The campground is near the beach, so you don't have to carry your gear very far. The area offers good fishing and scuba diving. A note of caution: Raccoons have become pests and campers are advised to keep food well contained. Sunsets often provide breathtaking beauty from this island. In addition, it is set amid a national wildlife and migratory bird refuge.

Location: Near Orcas Island; map A2, grid c2.

Campsites, facilities: There are 21 primitive boat-in campsites. Picnic tables and vault, composting, and pit toilets are provided. Boat buoys and floats are available for overnight moorage.

Reservations, fees: No reservations. Sites are $5-11 per night. Open May through September.

Directions: The campground is on tiny Jones Island, located less than one mile off the southwest tip of Orcas Island. This camp is accessible only by boat. Look for the boat buoys just offshore the campsites.

Contact: San Juan Marine Area, Star Route, Box 177, Olga, WA 98279; tel. (800) 233-0321, (360) 378-2044.

23 Blind Island State Park Boat-In   9

This island has few trees and is known for its rocky shoreline. It's dangerous and ill advised to try beaching cruiser-style boats. Moor your boat and bring a life raft to paddle ashore. Blind Island State Park is a designated natural area and is committed to conserving a natural environment in a minimally developed state. This is not a place for large groups to throw big barbecues, but a quiet place in its natural state.

Location: Near Shaw Island; map A2, grid c2.

Campsites, facilities: There are four primitive boat-in campsites. Composting and pit toilets are provided, but there is no drinking water. Boat buoys are available for overnight moorage.

Reservations, fees: No reservations. Sites are $5 per night. Open year-round.

Directions: The campground is located just west of the Shaw Island ferry landing on little Blind Island in Blind Bay. The nearest boat ramps are at Obstruction Pass on Orcas Island or Odlin County Park on Lopez Island.

Contact: San Juan Marine Area, Star Route, Box 177, Olga, WA 98279; tel. (800) 233-0321, (360) 378-2044.

24 Griffin Bay Boat-In   9

How would you like a campground all to yourself? This could be the place. This tiny, remote camp receives almost no use at all, yet it's located on one of the prettiest islands in the area. If you're one of the smart few who are willing to take the time to travel here, you're practically guaranteed a beautiful little spot all to yourself. This ties with Posey Island as the smallest official campground in the Pacific Northwest.

Location: On San Juan Island; map A2, grid c2.

Campsites, facilities: There are three picnic sites and one primitive boat-in campsite. Drinking water, picnic tables, and pit toilets are provided. Two boat buoys are available for overnight moorage.

Reservations, fees: No reservations; no fee. Open year-round.

Directions: Griffin Bay is on the southeast side of San Juan Island (south of Friday Harbor), somewhat protected by Low Point. It's accessible only by boat.

Contact: Department of Natural Resources, Northwest Region, 919 North Township Street, Sedro-Woolley, WA 98284-9395; tel. (360) 856-3500.

25 Lakedale
Campground Ferry-In   6

This is a nice spot for visitors who want the solitude of an island camp, yet all the amenities of a privately run campground. Fishing, swimming, and boating are available at the Lakedale Lakes. A sand volleyball court, a half-court basketball area, and a grassy sports field are also on site. Roche Harbor and Wescott Bay are nearby to the north, and Friday Harbor and its restaurants are nearby to the south.

Location: On San Juan Island; map A2, grid c1.

Campsites, facilities: There are 70 tent sites and 25 sites for trailers or RVs up to 40 feet long; 12 are drive-through, and 19 have partial hookups. There are also six group sites, three tent cabins, and six log cabins. Electricity, drinking water, and picnic tables are provided. Electricity, drinking water, showers, and firewood are available for a fee. Toilets, a store, and ice are available. Boat docks, three swimming beaches, and boat, bike, camping, and fishing gear rentals can be found on site. Leashed pets and motorbikes are permitted.

Reservations, fees: Reservations accepted. Sites are $17-22 per night for tent and RV campers. Power and water are an additional $4 per site. There is a $9.75-11.75 fee for an additional vehicle. Hike-in/bike-in sites are $6-8, and log cabins are $125-190 per night. Major credit cards accepted. Open mid-March to mid-October.

Directions: From Seattle on Interstate 5, drive north to Burlington and Highway 20. Turn west on Highway 20 and drive 12 miles to the Highway 20 North spur, following signs to the San Juan Islands Ferry Terminal in Anacortes. Take the ferry to Friday Harbor on San Juan Island. From the ferry landing at Friday Harbor, drive two blocks on Spring Street to 2nd Street. Turn right (northwest) on 2nd Street and drive one-half mile to Tucker Avenue (Roche Harbor Road). Turn right (north) and continue 4.5 miles to the campground on the left.

Contact: Lakedale Campground, 4313 Roche Harbor Road, Friday Harbor, WA 98250; tel. (800) 617-CAMP (800-617-2267) or (360) 378-2350, fax (360) 378-0944; website: www.lakedale.com.

26 Turn Island State Park Boat-In   10

This is one of about 30 campgrounds in the area that can be reached only by boat. This island is very small, yet just a long hop from San Juan Island off its southern tip. Quiet, primitive, and beautiful, this spot offers good trails for tromping around and year-round angling for rockfish. There are pretty beaches for shell collectors. No cars are allowed unless they float. The island is set within the San Juan Islands National Wildlife Refuge.

Location: Near Friday Harbor; map A2, grid c2.

Campsites, facilities: There are 12 primitive boat-in campsites. Picnic tables are provided, and vault and pit toilets are available. There is no drinking water. Boat buoys are available for overnight moorage.

Reservations, fees: No reservations. Sites are $5 per night. Open year-round.

Directions: Turn Island is located off of the northeast tip of San Juan Island (in the San Juan Channel). It's accessible only by boat.

Contact: San Juan Marine Area, Star Route, Box 177, Olga, WA 98279; tel. (800) 233-0321, (360) 378-2044.

27 James Island State Park Boat-In   9

Small, hidden James Island provides good opportunities for hiking, fishing, and scuba diving. It's quiet and primitive, with lots of trees and a pretty beach for walking or sunbathing.

Location: Near Decatur Island; map A2, grid c3.

Campsites, facilities: There are 13 primitive boat-in campsites. Pit toilets are available. Boat floats and buoys are available for moorage off the east side of the island. A moorage dock on the west side of the island is open from May through September.

Reservations, fees: No reservations. Sites are $5-11 per night. Open year-round.

Directions: This island is east of Decatur Island on Rosario Strait and is only accessible by boat. The campground is on the east side of the island.

Contact: San Juan Marine Area, Star Route, Box 177, Olga, WA 98279; tel. (800) 233-0321, (360) 378-2044.

28 Spencer Spit State Park Ferry-In   9

Spencer Spit State Park offers one of the few island campgrounds accessible to cars via ferry. A long sliver of sand extends far into the water and provides good access to prime clamming areas. Picnicking, beachcombing, and sunbathing are some pleasant activities for campers looking for relaxation.

Location: On Lopez Island; map A2, grid c3.

Campsites, facilities: There are nine walk-in sites and 34 sites for tents or self-contained RVs up to 20 feet long. There are no hookups. Picnic tables and fire grills are provided. A sanitary disposal station and flush toilets are available. Boat docks are nearby. Some facilities are wheelchair accessible. Leashed pets are permitted.

Reservations, fees: Reservations accepted; phone (800) 452-5687 ($6 reservation fee). Sites are $7-11 per night. Open March through October.

Directions: From Seattle on Interstate 5, drive north to Burlington and Highway 20. Turn west on Highway 20 and drive 12 miles to the Highway 20 North spur, following signs to the San Juan Islands Ferry Terminal in Anacortes. Take the ferry to Lopez Island. The park is within walking distance of the ferry terminal.

Contact: Spencer Spit State Park Ferry-In, Route 2, P.O. Box 3600, Lopez, WA 98261; tel. (800) 233-0321, (360) 902-8563, or (360) 378-2044.

29 Moran State Park

Ferry-In  10

This 5,175-acre park offers hiking trails and lake fishing. There are actually four separate campgrounds plus a primitive area. If you drive to the top of Mount Constitution, you'll have a view of Vancouver, Mount Baker, and the San Juan Islands. No RVs are allowed on this winding road. Nearby recreation options include a nine-hole golf course.

Location: On Orcas Island; map A2, grid c3.

Campsites, facilities: There are 15 primitive hike-in/bike-in tent sites and 136 developed sites for tents or RVs up to 45 feet long. No hookups are available. Picnic tables and fire grills are provided. Flush toilets, showers, and firewood are available. Boat docks, fishing supplies, launching facilities, and boat rentals are located at the concession stand in the park. Some facilities are wheelchair accessible. Leashed pets are permitted.

Reservations, fees: Reservations accepted; phone (800) 452-5687 ($6 reservation fee). Sites are $5-11 per night. Major credit cards accepted. Open year-round.

Directions: From Seattle on Interstate 5, drive north to Burlington and Highway 20. Turn west on Highway 20 and drive 12 miles to the Highway 20 North spur, following signs to the San Juan Islands Ferry Terminal in Anacortes. Take the ferry to Orcas Island. From the ferry landing, turn left on Horseshoe Highway and drive 13 miles to Moran State Park. Stop at the campground registration booth for directions to your site.

Contact: Moran State Park Ferry-In, Star Route, Box 22, Eastsound, WA 98245; tel. (800) 233-0321.

30 Doe Island State Park Boat-In 9

Doe Island has a rocky shoreline, which makes an ideal fish habitat, and the scuba diving and fishing are exceptional. Doe Island State Park is a tiny, primitive park that receives little use.

Location: Near Orcas Island; map A2, grid c3.

Campsites, facilities: There are five primitive boat-in campsites. Vault toilets are provided. Boat floats are available for moorage.

Reservations, fees: No reservations. Sites are $5-11 per night. Open year-round.

Directions: This small, secluded island is just off the southeastern shore of Orcas Island off Doe Bay. It's accessible only by boat.

Contact: San Juan Marine Area, Star Route, Box 177, Olga, WA 98279; tel. (800) 233-0321, (360) 378-2044.

31 Obstruction Pass Hike-In 8

It takes a ferryboat ride, a tricky drive, and a half-mile walk to reach this campground, but that helps set it apart from others—you'll find a unique, primitive spot set in a forested area near the shore of Orcas Island with good hiking. Moran State Park is a more developed alternative on this island, with many recreation options.

Location: On Orcas Island; map A2, grid c3.

Campsites, facilities: There are nine primitive, hike-in campsites. Picnic tables are provided and vault toilets are available. There is no drinking water. Two boat buoys are available for overnight moorage.

Reservations, fees: No reservations; no fee. Open year-round.

Directions: From Seattle on Interstate 5, drive north to Burlington and Highway 20. Turn west on Highway 20 and drive 12 miles to the Highway 20 North spur, following signs to the San Juan Islands Ferry Terminal in Anacortes. Take the ferry to Orcas Island. Then drive on the Horseshoe Highway past Moran State Park and continue to the town of Olga and Doe Bay Road. Drive east on Doe Bay Road for one-half mile to Obstruction Pass Road. Turn right and drive two-thirds of a mile. Bear right and proceed straight for less than a mile to the parking area. Hike one-half mile to the campground.

Contact: Department of Natural Resources, Northwest Region, 919 North Township Street, Sedro-Woolley, WA 98284-9395; tel. (360) 856-3500.

32 Pioneer Trails Campground   9

This site offers resort camping in the beautiful San Juan Islands. Tall trees, breathtaking views, cascading waterfalls, and country hospitality can all be found here. Side trips include nearby Deception Pass State Park (eight minutes away) and ferries to Victoria, British Columbia. Horseshoes, an 18-hole golf course, relaxing spas, and lake fishing are among the available activities.

Location: On Fidalgo Island, in the San Juan Islands; map A2, grid d4.

Campsites, facilities: There are 91 sites for tents or RVs, plus 24 covered wagons. Cable TV, rest rooms, showers, a public phone, and laundry facilities are provided. A recreation hall, a playground, and a sports field are available. If RV camping, pets are permitted.

Reservations, fees: Reservations recommended. There is a three-night holiday minimum. Sites are $18-34 per night. Open year-round.

Directions: From Seattle on Interstate 5, drive north to Burlington and take Exit 230 for Highway 20 West. Drive west on Highway 20 for 12 miles. At the traffic signal, turn left (still Highway 20) and drive a half mile to Miller Road. Turn west on Miller Road, drive a quarter of a mile, and look for the park on the right side of the road.

Contact: Pioneer Trails Campground, 7337 Miller Road, Anacortes, WA 98221; tel. (360) 293-5355 or (888) 777-5355.

33 Cypress Head Boat-In   9

Cypress Head is an alternative to Pelican Beach. Primitive but pretty, this camp is in a forested setting right on Puget Sound.

Location: On Cypress Island; map A2, grid c4.

Campsites, facilities: There are five primitive, boat-in campsites. Picnic tables and vault toilets are available. There is no drinking water. Five boat buoys are available for overnight moorage.

Reservations, fees: No reservations; no fee. Open year-round.

Directions: This camp is set on the east shore of Cypress Island and is accessible only by boat. Cypress Island can be accessed by boat from Anacortes. Cruise west through Guemes Channel to Bellingham Channel (located between Cypress Island and Guemes Island). Turn north in Bellingham Channel and cruise to the campground on the southeast side of Cypress Island in Deepwater Bay (just south of Pelican Beach Campground).

Contact: Department of Natural Resources, Northwest Region, 919 North Township Street, Sedro-Woolley, WA 98284-9395; tel. (360) 856-3500, fax (360) 856-2150.

34 Pelican Beach Boat-In   9

This forested island campground offers a group shelter, beach access, and hiking trails. The 1.2-mile trail to Eagle Cliff is a must. Like Cypress Head, this scenic camp is set on the oceanfront in a well-treed area.

Location: On Cypress Island; map A2, grid c4.

Campsites, facilities: There are four primitive boat-in campsites, plus picnic tables, a group shelter, and vault toilets. There is no drinking water. Six buoys are available for overnight moorage.

Reservations, fees: No reservations; no fee. Open year-round.

Directions: This camp is set on the east shore of Cypress Island and is accessible only by boat. Cypress Island can be accessed by boat from Anacortes. Cruise west through Guemes Channel to Bellingham Channel (located between Cypress Island and Guemes Island). Turn north in Bellingham Channel and cruise to the campground on the southeast side of Cypress Island just north of Cypress Head.

Contact: Department of Natural Resources, Northwest Region, 919 North Township Street, Sedro-Woolley, WA 98284-9395; tel. (360) 856-3500, fax (360) 856-2150.

35 Strawberry Island Boat-In   9

This campground is rarely used because of the hazards of landing here (see the directions below). If you can manage to land, however, you'll be rewarded with a pretty, forested camp and complete privacy.

Location: Near Cypress Island; map A2, grid c3.

Campsites, facilities: There are three primitive boat-in campsites. Picnic tables are provided and vault toilets are available. There is no drinking water.

Reservations, fees: No reservations; no fee. Open year-round.

Directions: This island is off the west coast of Cypress Island and is accessible only by small boat. From Anacortes, cruise by boat west through Guemes Channel, continue around the southern end of Cypress Island (Reef Point), and cruise north one mile to Strawberry Bay. Strawberry Island is located in Strawberry Bay. Cypress Island is just east of Strawberry Island. Note: The Department of Natural Resources cautions that strong currents and submerged rocks can make landing difficult. It recommends anchoring your boat and proceeding in a skiff or kayak.

Contact: Department of Natural Resources, Northwest Region, 919 North Township Street, Sedro-Woolley, WA 98284-9395; tel. (360) 856-3500, fax (360) 856-2150.

36 Saddlebag Island State Park Boat-In    9

Saddlebag Island State Park is a good cruise from Anacortes. The island is quiet and primitive, with a nice beach nearby for beachcombing and fine crabbing in the bay. Wildflowers are in bloom from April through June.

Location: Near Guemes Island; map A2, grid c4.

Campsites, facilities: There are five primitive boat-in campsites. Vault and pit toilets are available, but there is no drinking water.

Reservations, fees: No reservations. Sites are $5 per night. Open year-round.

Directions: From Seattle on Interstate 5, drive north to Burlington and Highway 20. Turn west on Highway 20 and drive 12 miles to the Highway 20 North spur, following signs to the San Juan Islands Ferry Terminal in Anacortes. Launch your boat and cruise northeast around the southeast tip of Guemes Island. As you approach, Hat Island will be to your right, Huckleberry Island to your left, and Saddlebag Island to your center in Padilla Bay. Continue to Saddlebag Island. The camp is accessible only by boat.

Contact: San Juan Marine Area, Star Route, Box 177, Olga, WA 98279; tel. (800) 233-0321, (360) 378-2044.

37 Bay View State Park   8

This campground set on Padilla Bay has a large, grassy area for kids, making it a good choice for families. A nice day trip is to take the ferry at Anacortes to Lopez Island (there are several campgrounds there as well).

Location: On Padilla Bay; map A2, grid d5.

Campsites, facilities: There are three primitive sites, 67 sites for tents or self-contained RVs, and nine sites with full hookups for RVs up to 40 feet long. There is also one group tent camp for a maximum of 64 people. Picnic tables are provided. Flush toilets, drinking water, a dump station, and coin showers are available. A store and a coin laundry are eight miles away in Burlington. Leashed pets are permitted.

Reservations, fees: Reservations accepted for family camping; phone (800) 452-5687 ($6 reservation fee). Sites are $10-11 per night. Reservations required for the group camp; $25 reservation fee, plus $1 per person per night. Major credit cards accepted. Open year-round.

Directions: From Seattle on Interstate 5, drive north to Burlington and Highway 20. Turn west on Highway 20 and drive seven miles west (toward Anacortes) to Bay View-Edison Road. Turn right (north) on Bay View-Edison Road and drive four miles to the park.

Contact: Bay View State Park, 1093 Bay View-Edison Road, Brighton, WA 98273; tel. (800) 233-0321, (360) 757-0227.

38 Larrabee State Park   9

This 2,683-acre state park is on Samish Bay in Puget Sound and was the first Washington State Park, dating from 1915. Highlights include tide pools and nine miles of hiking trails, two routes going to small lakes. The park lies on a beautiful stretch of coastline and offers prime spots for wildlife viewing. A relatively short drive south will take you to Anacortes, where you can catch a ferry to Lopez Island.

Location: On Samish Bay; map A2, grid c5.

Campsites, facilities: There are eight primitive tent sites, 53 developed tent sites, and 26 sites for trailers or RVs up to 60 feet long. Picnic tables and fire grills are provided. Flush toilets, a sanitary disposal station, drinking water, sewer hookups, coin showers, and firewood are available. Boat launching facilities can be found nearby. Leashed pets are permitted.

Reservations, fees: Reservations accepted; phone (800) 452-5687 ($6 reservation fee). Sites are $7-16 per night. Major credit cards accepted. Open year-round.

Directions: From South Bellingham on Interstate 5, take the Highway 11 exit and head south. Continue south on Highway 11 (Chuckanut Drive) for seven miles to the park (one mile south of Chuckanut) on the right.

Contact: Larrabee State Park, 245 Chuckanut, Bellingham, WA 98225; tel. (800) 233-0321 or (360) 676-2093.

39 Timberline RV Park   7

This rural RV park is just far enough off the main highway to be overlooked by most tourists. It is clean and has large sites and tall trees. Nearby attractions include Larrabee and Bay View State Parks. Both provide beach access and hiking opportunities.

Location: Near Larrabee and Bay View State Parks; map A2, grid c5.

Campsites, facilities: There are 30 tent sites and 39 sites with full hookups and cable TV for trailers or RVs. Rest rooms, showers, a private phone, laundry room, store, ice, LP gas bottles, and a barbecue are available. There are also horseshoe pits, a recreation hall, a playground, and a sports field. Facilities are wheelchair accessible. Leashed pets are permitted.

Reservations, fees: Reservations necessary. Sites are $10-18 per night. Open year-round.

Directions: From Seattle on Interstate 5, drive north to Exit 232 (Cook Road). Take the exit up and over the highway to the flashing light and Cook Road. Turn left on Cook Road and drive four miles to the light at Highway 20. Turn left at Highway 20 and drive 19 miles (a winding road) to Russell Road. Turn left on Russell Road, look for the campground sign (just past Milepost 82), and continue a quarter of a mile up the hill to the park on the left.

Contact: Timberline RV Park, tel. (360) 826-3131.

40 Burlington KOA   5

This is a fine KOA campground, complete with all the amenities. The sites are spacious and comfortable. Possible side trips include tours of the Boeing plant, Victoria, Vancouver Island, and the San Juan Islands.

Location: In Burlington; map A2, grid c6.

Campsites, facilities: There are 120 sites for tents, trailers, or RVs, plus six cabins. Rest rooms, showers, a sanitary dump, water, electricity, cable TV, and sewer hookups, a public phone, a laundry room, limited groceries, ice, LP gas, and a barbecue are available. There are also an indoor heated pool, a spa with sauna, a recreation hall, game room, playground, mini-golf, horseshoes, and sports field. Leashed pets are permitted.

Reservations, fees: Reservations recommended in the summer. Sites are $19.50-25.50 per night. Major credit cards accepted. Open year-round.

Directions: From Seattle on Interstate 5, drive north to Exit 232 in Burlington. Take the exit up and over the highway to the flashing light and Cook Road. Turn left on Cook Road and drive to Old Highway 99. Turn left and drive 3.5 miles to the campground on the right.

Contact: Burlington KOA, 6397 North Green Road, Burlington, WA 98233; tel. (360) 724-5511.

41 Creekside Campground   6

This pretty, wooded campground is centrally located to nearby recreational opportunities at Baker Lake and the Skagit River. Trout fishing is excellent here. Tackle is available nearby. Horseshoe pits and a recreation hall are also available.

Location: Near the Skagit River; map A2, grid c9.

Campsites, facilities: There are 29 sites for tents, trailers, or RVs up to 40 feet long. Electricity, drinking water, sewer hookups, and picnic tables are provided. Flush toilets, sanitary services, a store, a laundry room, a playground, ice, and showers are available. A cafe is located within one mile. Leashed pets and motorbikes are permitted.

Reservations, fees: Reservations recommended. Sites are $10-22 per night. Open year-round.

Directions: From Seattle on Interstate 5, drive north to Exit 232 (Cook Road). Take the exit up and over the highway to the flashing light and Cook Road. Turn left on Cook Road (Highway 20) and drive four miles to the light at Highway 20. Turn left at Highway 20 and drive 17 miles to Baker Lake Road (near Grasmere/Concrete). Turn left on Baker Lake Road and drive a quarter mile to the camp.

Contact: Phone (360) 826-3566 39602 Baker Lake Road, Concrete, WA 98237.

42 Anacortes RV Park   4

Covering six acres near the bay shoreline, this small, wooded park is not particularly scenic, but it is close to numerous recreation attractions, including a bordering golf course. Tourists planning on taking the ferry to San Juan Island will find this a decent layover spot.

Location: In Anacortes; map A2, grid d4.

Campsites, facilities: There are 14 sites for tents and 16 sites for trailers or RVs of any length. Electricity, drinking water, sewer hookups, and picnic tables are provided. Flush toilets, showers, a clothes dryer, and a playground are available. A store and a cafe are located across the road. Motorbikes and small, leashed pets are permitted.

Reservations, fees: Reservations accepted. Sites are $15-20 per night, with discounted rates available for extended stays. Open year-round.

Directions: From Seattle on Interstate 5, drive north to Burlington and Highway 20. Turn west on Highway 20 and drive 12 miles to the Whidbey Island junction. Continue on Highway 20 for about 100 yards south past the Oak Harbor turnoff for the park on the left.

Contact: Phone (360) 293-3700 7648 Highway 20, Anacortes, WA 98221.

43 Deception Pass State Park   10

This state park is located at beautiful Deception Pass on the west side of Whidbey Island. Recreation options include fishing and swimming at Pass Lake, a freshwater lake within the park. Fly-fishing for trout is a unique bonus for anglers. Scuba diving is also popular. There are several historic Civilian Conservation Corps buildings near the campground.

Location: On Whidbey Island; map A2, grid d4.

Campsites, facilities: There are five primitive tent sites and 246 developed sites for tents, trailers, or self-contained RVs up to 50 feet long. Picnic tables, fire pits, drinking water, showers, flush toilets, and a sanitary disposal station are provided. A concession stand, a boat launch, boat rentals, buoys, and floats are available. The facilities are wheelchair accessible. Leashed pets are permitted.

Reservations, fees: Reservations accepted; phone (800) 452-5687 ($6 reservation fee). Sites are $5-11 per night. Major credit cards accepted. Open year-round, with limited winter services.

Directions: From Seattle on Interstate 5, drive north to Burlington and Highway 20. Turn west on Highway 20 and drive 12 miles. Turn south on Highway 20 South and drive six miles, across the bridge at Deception Pass, to the park on the right.

Contact: Phone (800) 233-0321, call the park at (360) 675-2417 5175 North State Highway 20, Oak Harbor, WA 98277.

44 Washington Park   6

Set in the woods, this city park has many hiking trails in addition to a 2.3-mile paved trail for hikers and bicyclists. Picnic areas are also provided. The Washington State Ferry terminals are located half a mile away, providing access to the San Juan Islands. This is a very popular camp, and it's a good idea to arrive early to claim your spot.

Location: In Washington Park; map A2, grid d4.

Campsites, facilities: There are 70 sites for tents and RVs, 46 with full or partial hookups, and one group site that can accommodate 30 people. Drinking water, rest rooms, showers, a public phone, a playground, a recreation field, a dump station, and a laundry room are available. A day-use area is provided. A boat launch is also available. Leashed pets are permitted.

Reservations, fees: Reservations accepted for residents of Anacortes only. Sites are $12-15 per night; the group site is $50 per night. Open year-round.

Directions: From Seattle on Interstate 5, drive north to Burlington and Highway 20. Turn west on Highway 20 and drive to Anacortes and Commercial Avenue. Turn right and drive to 12th Street. Turn left and drive about four miles, west of the Washington State Ferry Landing. (Note: 12th Street changes names several times, but keep following it).

Contact: Phone the City of Anacortes at (360) 293-1927 P.O. Box 547, Anacortes, WA 98221.

45 Fidalgo Bay Resort   4

This park is five minutes from Anacortes and right on Fidalgo Bay for boating, fishing and swimming, and there's a golf course two miles away.

Location: On Fidalgo Bay; map A2, grid d4.

Campsites, facilities: There are a few tent sites and 187 sites with full hookups for trailers or RVs. Some sites with phone service are available and there is modem access in the clubhouse. Drinking water, flush toilets, showers, one large fire pit, a small boat launch, a grocery store, a dog run, and coin laundry facilities are available. Leashed pets are permitted.

Reservations, fees: Reservations recommended; phone (800) 727-5478, fax (360) 299-3010, or access the website: www.fidalgobay.com. Sites are $22-35 per night. Open year-round.

Directions: From Seattle on Interstate 5, drive north to Burlington and Highway 20. Turn west on Highway 20 and drive about 14 miles to Fidalgo Bay Road. Turn right on Fidalgo Bay Road and drive one mile to the resort.

Contact: Phone (360) 293-5353, fax (360) 299-3010, 1107 Fidalgo Bay Road, Anacortes, WA 982321.

46 Hope Island State Park Boat-In   8

This site on the north side of Hope Island is a primitive alternative to the nearby and more developed drive-to sites. The only catch is you must have a boat to reach it. Solitude is your reward, but the island has little to offer in the way of recreation besides beach access, where campers can sunbathe, walk, or scout for shells.

Location: In Skagit Bay; map A2, grid d5.

Campsites, facilities: There are five primitive, boat-in campsites, plus one pit toilet and one mooring buoy. No drinking water is available.

Reservations, fees: No reservations. Sites are $5 per night. Open year-round.

Directions: Hope Island is in Skagit Bay, directly between the Swinomish Indian Reservation on Fidalgo Island to the east and Whidbey Island to the west. After launching from the harbor at Cornet on Whidbey Island, cruise east out of Cornet Bay and turn south (Skagit Island will be on your left). Continue one mile to Hope Island. The boating access is on the north side of the island. It's accessible only by private boat.

Contact: Phone (800) 233-0321 or (360) 675-2417 41229 State Route 20, Oak Harbor, WA 98277-7924.

47 Riverbend Park   5

Riverbend Park is a pleasant layover spot for Interstate 5 travelers. While not particularly scenic, it's clean and spacious. Access to the Skagit River here is a high point. Nearby recreational options include a casino, an 18-hole golf course, marked bike trails, and tennis courts.

Location: On the Skagit River; map A2, grid d6.

Campsites, facilities: There are 25 tent sites and 95 drive-through sites for trailers or RVs of any length. Electricity, drinking water, sewer and cable TV hookups, and picnic tables are provided. Flush toilets, sanitary services, showers, a laundry room, and a playground are available. A store, a cafe, ice, and a swimming pool are located within one mile. Pets are permitted.

Reservations, fees: Reservations accepted. Sites are $8-20 per night. Major credit cards accepted. Open year-round.

Directions: From Seattle on Interstate 5, drive north to Mount Vernon and the College Way exit. Take the College Way exit and drive one block west to Freeway Drive; then turn north and drive a half mile to the park.

Contact: Phone (360) 428-4044 305 West Stewart Road, Mount Vernon, WA 98273.

48 Rasar State Park   8

This all-season park is the newest in the state park system. At an elevation of 4,000 feet, its 168 acres border North Cascade National Park and is near 10,778-foot Mount Baker and the Baker River watershed. Fishing and hiking are the attractions here.

Location: On the Skagit River; map A2, grid d8.

Campsites, facilities: There are 39 sites for tents, trailers, and RVs, 22 with full hookups. There are also three hiker/biker sites and 10 walk-in sites where there are three four-person Adirondack shelters available. Drinking water, rest rooms, coin showers, fire rings, a reservable kitchen shelter, and garbage service are available. Firewood gathering is prohibited. Leashed pets are permitted.

Reservations, fees: No reservations. Sites are $11-16 per night, $5 for an additional vehicle.

Directions: From Seattle on Interstate 5, drive north to Burlington and the Highway 20 exit. Turn east on Highway 20/North Cascade Highway and drive 20 miles to Lusk Road. Turn right on Lusk Road and drive three-quarters of a mile to Cape Horn Road. Turn left on Cape Horn Road and drive two miles to the park entrance.

Contact: Rasar State Park, 38730 Cape Horn Road, Concrete, WA 98237; phone (360) 826-3942, fax (360) 826-4045, or access the website: www.parks.wa.gov.

49 Fort Ebey State Park   9

This park on the west side of Whidbey Island at Point Partridge covers 228 acres and has access to a rocky beach that is good for hiking. Other options here include fishing and wildlife viewing. Fort Ebey is the site of a historic World War II bunker. There is also a freshwater lake nearby.

Location: On Whidbey Island; map A2, grid e3.

Campsites, facilities: There are three primitive tent sites and 50 developed campsites for tents or self-contained RVs up to 70 feet long. Picnic tables and fire grills are provided. Sanitary disposal service, flush toilets, and coin showers are available. Some facilities are wheelchair accessible. Leashed pets are permitted.

Reservations, fees: Reservations accepted; phone (800) 452-5687 ($6 reservation fee). Sites are $5-10 per night. Major credit cards accepted. Open April through September.

Directions: From Seattle on Interstate 5, drive north to Burlington and Highway 20. Turn west on Highway 20 and drive 23 miles (Whidbey Island) to Libbey Road (near Coveland). Turn right and drive two miles to the park entrance road.

Contact: Phone (800) 233-0321 or (360) 678-4636 395 North Fort Ebey Road, Coupeville, WA 98239.

50 Fort Worden State Park   9

This park is set on the northeastern tip of the Olympic Peninsula, at the northern end of Port Townsend. Highlights here include great lookouts and two miles of trails over the Strait of Juan de Fuca as it feeds into Puget Sound. This 433-acre park is at historic Fort Worden and includes buildings from the turn of the century. Nearby recreation options include marked hiking and biking trails and tennis courts. A ferry at Port Townsend will take you across the strait to Whidbey Island.

Location: Near Puget Sound; map A2, grid f3.

Campsites, facilities: There are three primitive, hike-in/bike-in tent sites and 80 sites for trailers or RVs up to 50 feet long. Picnic tables and fire grills are provided. Toilets, a laundry room, a store, a dinner restaurant, and conference facilities are available. Electricity, drinking water, sewer hookups, showers, and firewood are available for an extra fee. Boat docks, buoys, floats, and launching facilities are nearby. Wheelchair-accessible facilities are available. Leashed pets are permitted.

Reservations, fees: Contact Fort Worden State Park for reservations; phone (360) 385-4730. Sites are $5-16 per night. Open year-round.

Directions: From Olympia, turn north on U.S. 101 and drive 86 miles to Highway 20 (Port Townsend turnoff). Turn north on Highway 20 and drive 13 miles to Port Townsend. Continue through Port Townsend to Battery Drive (well signed along route). Turn at Battery Drive and continue into the park entrance.

Contact: Phone (800) 233-0321 or (360) 385-4730 200 Battery Way, Port Townsend, WA 98638.

51 Fort Casey State Park   10

Fort Casey State Park is a good spot to set up a base camp for a fishing trip, with excellent rock fishing year-round and good salmon and steelhead fishing in season. This park covers 137 acres and is the site of a historic U.S. defense post. Another highlight is an underwater park for divers. You can also take a ferry from here to Port Townsend on the Olympic Peninsula.

Location: On Whidbey Island; map A2, grid e4.

Campsites, facilities: There are three primitive tent sites and 35 developed campsites for tents or self-contained RVs up to 40 feet long. Picnic tables and fire grills are provided. Flush toilets and coin showers are available. Some facilities are wheelchair accessible. Boat launching facilities are located in the park. Pets are permitted.

Reservations, fees: No reservations. Sites are $5-10 per night. Open year-round.

Directions: From Seattle on Interstate 5, drive north to Burlington and Highway 20. Turn west on Highway 20 and drive 35 miles to Coupeville. Continue south on Highway 20 (adjacent to Whidbey Island Naval Air Station) and then turn right (still Highway 20, passing Crockett Lake) to the park entrance.

Contact: Phone (800) 233-0321 or (360) 678-4519 1280 Fort Casey, Coupeville, WA 98239.

52 Oak Harbor City Beach Park 4

Fishing, swimming, boating, and sunbathing are all options at Oak Harbor City Beach Park. Nearby you'll find an 18-hole golf course, a full-service marina, and tennis courts. Fort Ebey and Fort Casey State Parks are both within a short drive and are excellent side trips.

Location: In Oak Harbor; map A2, grid e4.

Campsites, facilities: There are 56 sites for trailers or RVs of any length. Electricity, sewer, drinking water, and picnic tables are provided. Sanitary services, toilets, coin showers, and a playground are available. Bottled gas, a store, a cafe, a coin laundry, and ice are located within one mile. Boat launching facilities are available at Oak Harbor. Leashed pets are permitted.

Reservations, fees: No reservations. Sites are $15 per night. Open year-round.

Directions: From Seattle on Interstate 5, drive north to Burlington and Highway 20. Turn west on Highway 20 and drive 28 miles to the intersection of Highway 20 and Pioneer Way in the town of Oak Harbor on Whidbey Island. Continue straight through the intersection onto Beecksma Drive and drive about one block to the park on the left.

Contact: Phone (360) 679-5551 865 S.E. Berrington Drive, Oak Harbor, WA 98277.

53 Cedar Grove Shores 5

This wooded resort is set on the shore of Lake Goodwin near Wenberg State Park. Trout fishing and swimming are the highlights. Tent campers should try Lake Goodwin Resort. An 18-hole golf course is nearby.

Location: On Lake Goodwin; map A2, grid e6.

Campsites, facilities: There are 48 sites for trailers or RVs. No tents are allowed. Electricity, drinking water, and sewer hookups are provided. Flush toilets, showers, a laundry room, and firewood are available. Bottled gas, sanitary services, a store, a cafe, and ice are located within one mile. Boat docks and launching facilities are available within 1,000 feet on Lake Goodwin. Small pets are permitted.

Reservations, fees: Reservations accepted. Sites are $20-27 per night. Major credit cards accepted. Open year-round.

Directions: From Seattle on Interstate 5, drive north to Exit 206 (10 miles north of Everett). Take Exit 206/Smokey Point and drive west for five miles to Westlake Goodwin Road. Turn (the park is signed) and drive a half mile to the park.

Contact: Phone (360) 652-7083 16529 West Lake Goodwin Road, Stanwood, WA 98292.

54 KOA Port Angeles-Sequim
 5

This private, developed camp covering 41 acres in a country setting is a pleasant park, a typical KOA complete with pool, recreation hall, and playground. Horseshoe pits and a sports field are also available. Mini-golf, two 18-hole golf courses, marked hiking trails, and tennis courts are recreation options.

Location: Near Port Angeles; map A2, grid f0.

Campsites, facilities: There are 90 sites for tents, trailers, or RVs of any length; 45 are drive-through. Picnic tables are provided. There are also 12 cabins. Bottled gas, sanitary services, toilets, showers, a store, laundry facilities, ice, a playground, recreation room, and swimming pool are available. A cafe is located within two miles. Electricity, drinking water, sewer hookups, and firewood are available for an extra fee. Some facilities are wheelchair accessible. Leashed pets and motorbikes are permitted.

Reservations, fees: Reservations accepted. Sites are $22-28 per night; cabins are $40-46 per night. Major credit cards accepted. Open April through October.

Directions: From Interstate 5 at Olympia, turn north on U.S. 101 and drive 116 miles to O'Brien Road, six miles southeast of Port Angeles. Turn left on O'Brien Road and drive half a block to the campground on the right.

Contact: KOA Port Angeles-Sequim, 80 O'Brien Road, Port Angeles, WA 98362; tel. (360) 457-5916, fax (360) 417-0759.

55 Elmer's Travel Trailer Park   4

Located at about 1,000 feet, this 10-acre camp is near the ocean, yet in an urban setting. It's hardly scenic, but will do as a layover for U.S. 101 travelers. Nearby recreation options include an 18-hole golf course, marked hiking trails, and a full-service marina.

Location: Near the Pacific Ocean; map A2, grid f0.

Campsites, facilities: There are 12 sites for trailers or RVs up to 31 feet long. Electricity, drinking water, and sewer hookups are provided. Sanitary services and flush toilets are available. Bottled gas, a store, a cafe, and ice are within one mile.

Reservations, fees: No reservations. Sites are $16 per night. Open year-round.

Directions: From Interstate 5 at Olympia, turn north on U.S. 101 and drive 120 miles (signed for Port Angeles) to the park along the highway (located two miles east of Port Angeles).

Contact: Phone (360) 457-4392 2442 East Highway 101, Port Angeles, WA 98362.

56 Al's RV Trailer Park

          8

This adult-oriented campground is a good choice for motor home owners. The campground is set in the country at about 1,000 feet, yet is centrally located and not far from the Strait of Juan de Fuca. Nearby recreation options include an 18-hole golf course and a full-service marina. Olympic National Park and the Victoria ferry are a short drive away.

Location: Near Port Angeles; map A2, grid f0.

Campsites, facilities: There are 20 sites for tents and 31 for trailers or RVs up to 40 feet long. No fires are allowed. Electricity, drinking water, and hookups for sewer and cable TV are provided. Bottled gas, flush toilets, showers, a clubhouse, and laundry facilities are available. Telephone service is available for most sites. A store, a cafe, and ice are within one mile. Boat docks and launching facilities are located within two miles.

Reservations, fees: Reservations accepted; phone (800) 357-1553. Sites are $14-21 per night. Major credit cards accepted. Open year-round.

Directions: From Olympia on Interstate 5, turn north on U.S. 101 and drive 122 miles to Port Angeles. Continue two miles west on U.S. 101 to North Brook Avenue. Turn right (north) on North Brook Avenue, then left (almost immediately) on Lees Creek Road, and drive a half mile to park.

Contact: Al's RV Trailer Park, 521 North Lees Creek Road, Port Angeles, WA 98362; tel. (360) 457-9844.

57 Dungeness Recreation Area   5

This park overlooks the Strait of Juan de Fuca and is set near the Dungeness National Wildlife Refuge. Nearby recreation options include marked hiking trails, fishing, and golfing. The toll ferry at Port Angeles can take you to Victoria, British Columbia.

Location: Near the Strait of Juan de Fuca; map A2, grid f1.

Campsites, facilities: There are 66 sites for tents, trailers, or RVs of any length; five are pull-through. Picnic tables are provided. Sanitary services, toilets, and a playground are available. Showers and firewood are available for an extra fee. Leashed pets are permitted.

Reservations, fees: No reservations. Sites are $8-10 per night. Open February to October, with facilities limited to day use in the winter. Entrance gates close at dusk year-round.

Directions: From Olympia on Interstate 5, turn north on U.S. 101 and drive 105 miles to Sequim. Continue on U.S. 101 for four miles to Kitchen Dick Road. Turn right on Kitchen Dick Road and drive four miles to the park.

Contact: Dungeness Recreation Area, 554 Voice of America Road, Sequim, WA 98382; tel. (360) 683-5847.

58 Rainbow's End   6

Of the several camps on Sequim Bay, Rainbow's End is one of the nicest. The park is pretty and clean, with a rainbow trout pond and a creek running through the campground. There is a weekly potluck in the summer, with free hamburgers and hot dogs, and a special landscaped area available for reunions, weddings, and other gatherings. Recreation seekers will find an 18-hole golf course, marked bike trails, a full-service marina, and tennis courts nearby.

Location: On Sequim Bay; map A2, grid f1.

Campsites, facilities: There are 10 tent sites and 39 sites for trailers or RVs of any length. Electricity, drinking water, sewer hookups, and cable TV are provided. Telephone hookups at most sites. Sanitary services, toilets, showers, bottled gas, laundry facilities, and a clubhouse are available. A store, a cafe, and ice are located within one mile. Firewood is available for an extra fee. Leashed pets and motorbikes are permitted.

Reservations, fees: Reservations accepted. Weekly and monthly rates are available. Sites are $15-21 per night. Major credit cards accepted. Open year-round.

Directions: From Olympia on Interstate 5, turn north on U.S. 101 and drive 105 miles to Sequim. Continue on U.S. 101 one mile past the River Road exit to the park on the right (along the highway).

Contact: Rainbow's End, 261831 Highway 101, Sequim, WA 98382; tel. (360) 683-3863 or (360) 681-3282 (after 5 p.m.) or fax (360) 592-9371. E-mail: rainborv@olypen.com.

59 Sunshine RV Park   5

This six-acre private camp is set at about 1,000 feet in a wooded area outside of Sequim. Though primarily an RV park, tents are permitted. It has paved, shaded sites, horseshoe pits, and a recreation hall, and is close to an 18-hole golf course and a full-service marina at Sequim Bay.

Location: Near Sequim; map A2, grid f1.

Campsites, facilities: There are 20 sites for tents and 44 for trailers or RVs of any length. Electricity, drinking water, picnic tables, and hookups for sewer and cable TV are provided. Toilets, showers, a recreation hall, and laundry facilities are available. Sanitary services, a store, and a cafe are located within one mile. Pets are permitted.

Reservations, fees: Reservations accepted. Sites are $15-20 per night. Major credit cards accepted. Open year-round.

Directions: From Olympia on Interstate 5, turn north on U.S. 101 and drive 105 miles to Sequim. Continue on U.S. 101 past Sequim for four miles to the park (along the highway).

Contact: Sunshine RV Park, 259790 Highway 101, Sequim, WA 98382; tel. (888) 383-4769 or (360) 683-4769.

60 Sequim West RV Park   5

This two-acre camp is near the Dungeness River and within 10 miles of Dungeness Spit State Park. It's a pleasant spot, with full facilities and an urban setting. An 18-hole golf course and a full-service marina at Sequim Bay are close by.

Location: Near the Dungeness River; map A2, grid f1.

Campsites, facilities: There are 27 drive-through sites with full hookups for trailers or RVs of any length. No tents are allowed. Electricity, drinking water, cable TV, sewer hookups, and picnic tables are provided. Toilets, showers, laundry facilities, a pay phone, and ice are available. Bottled gas, sanitary services, a store, and a cafe are located within one mile. Leashed pets are permitted.

Reservations, fees: Reservations accepted. Sites are $20 per night. Major credit cards accepted. Open year-round.

Directions: From Olympia on Interstate 5, turn north on U.S. 101 and drive 105 miles to Sequim and the Sequim Avenue exit. Take the Sequim Avenue exit and turn left (west) onto Washington Avenue. Drive west about three-quarters of a mile and look for the park on the right.

Directions: From Interstate 5 at Olympia, turn north on U.S. 101 and drive 105 miles to Sequim. Continue on U.S. 101 past Sequim Avenue to Washington Avenue. Turn west to the park entrance.

Contact: Sequim West RV Park, 740 West Washington Avenue, Sequim, WA 98382; tel. (360) 683-4144 or (800) 528-4527, fax (360) 683-6452.

61 Sequim Bay Resort   5

This is Sequim Bay headquarters for salmon anglers. The camp is set in a wooded, hilly area, close to many activity centers, and with an 18-hole golf course nearby.

Location: On Sequim Bay; map A2, grid f1.

Campsites, facilities: There are 43 sites for trailers or RVs of any length; 34 are pull-through. Electricity, drinking water, and sewer and cable TV hookups are provided. Flush toilets and laundry facilities are available. Showers are available for an extra fee. Boat docks and launching facilities are located across the street from the resort. Leashed pets are permitted.

Reservations, fees: No reservations. Sites are $16 per night. Open year-round.

Directions: From Olympia on Interstate 5, turn north on U.S. 101 and drive about 100 miles (near Sequim) to Whitefeather Way (located between Mileposts 267 and 268, 2.5 miles east of Sequim). Turn north on Whitefeather Way and drive one-half mile to West Sequim Bay Road. Turn west and drive one block to the park on the left.

Contact: Sequim Bay Resort, 2634 West Sequim Bay Road, Sequim, WA 98382; tel. (360) 681-3853.

62 Sequim Bay State Park   8

Marked hiking trails, tennis courts, and an underwater park for scuba divers are highlights of this 90-acre camp on Sequim Bay. Because of its unique location, the area gets far less rain than other spots on the Olympic Peninsula, which makes it popular with campers.

Location: On Sequim Bay; map A2, grid f2.

Campsites, facilities: There are three primitive tent sites, 60 developed sites for tents or self-contained RVs, and 26 sites with full hookups for trailers or RVs up to 30 feet long. Picnic tables and fire grills are provided. A sanitary disposal station, toilets, drinking water, showers, and a playground are available. Boat docks, launching facilities, and moorage camping are available. Facilities are wheelchair accessible. Leashed pets are permitted.

Reservations, fees: Reservations accepted; phone (800) 452-5687 ($6 reservation fee). Sites are $5-15 per night. Major credit cards accepted. Open year-round.

Directions: From Olympia on Interstate 5, turn north on U.S. 101 and drive 100 miles (near Sequim) to the park entrance on the right (along the highway). The park is located four miles southeast of the town of Sequim.

Contact: Sequim Bay State Park, 269035 Highway 101, Sequim, WA 98382; tel. (800) 233-0321, (360) 683-4235.

63 Old Fort Townsend State Park   10

Built in 1859, this historic fort is one of the oldest remaining in the state. The scenic campground has access to a good clamming beach, and visitors can also take a self-guided walking tour. Hiking and fishing are among other recreation options here.

Location: Near Quilcene; map A2, grid f3.

Campsites, facilities: There are three primitive tent sites and 40 sites for tents or

RVs up to 40 feet long. Picnic tables and fire grills are provided. Flush toilets, coin showers, a playground, and boat buoys are available. Firewood and showers are available for an extra fee. Leashed pets are permitted.

Reservations, fees: No reservations accepted. Sites are $5-10 per night. Open April through August.

Directions: From Olympia on Interstate 5, turn north on U.S. 101 and drive 85 miles to Highway 20 (Port Townsend turnoff). Turn north on Highway 20 and drive 10 miles to the park entrance road on the right (three miles south of Port Townsend.) Turn right and drive three miles to the park.

Contact: Old Fort Townsend State Park, Route 1, Port Townsend, WA 98368; tel. (800) 233-0321 or (360) 385-3595.

64 Point Hudson Resort   5

Point Hudson Resort is located on the site of an old Coast Guard station in a wooded, hilly part of Port Townsend, a town known for its Victorian architecture. Fishing and boating are popular here, and nearby recreation possibilities include an 18-hole municipal golf course, a full-service marina, Old Fort Townsend State Park, Fort Flagler State Park, and Fort Worden State Park.

Location: In Port Townsend; map A2, grid f3.

Campsites, facilities: There are 60 sites for trailers or RVs of any length (most are drive-through with full hookups). No tents are allowed. Flush toilets, a store, a cafe, three restaurants, laundry facilities, and ice are available. Showers are available for an extra fee. A 100-plus slip marina is on site.

Reservations, fees: Reservations encouraged. Sites are $15-20 per night. Major credit cards accepted. Open year-round.

Directions: From Olympia on Interstate 5, turn north on U.S. 101 and drive 85 miles to Highway 20 (Port Townsend exit). Turn north on Highway 20 and drive 13 miles to Port Townsend and Water Street. Turn north on Water Street and drive one-half mile to Monroe Street. Turn west on Monroe Street and drive two blocks to Jefferson Street. Turn north on Jefferson Street and drive two blocks to the campground on the right.

Contact: Point Hudson Resort, 103 Hudson Street, Port Townsend, WA 98368; tel. (360) 385-2828.

65 South Whidbey State Park   10

Located on the southwest end of Whidbey Island, this wooded park covers 85 acres and provides opportunities for hiking, scuba diving, picnicking, and beachcombing along a sandy beach. There are spectacular views of Puget Sound and the Olympic Mountains.

Location: On Whidbey Island; map A2, grid f4.

Campsites, facilities: There are six primitive tent sites and 54 developed campsites for tents or self-contained RVs up to 45 feet long. Picnic tables and fire grills are provided. Sanitary disposal services, coin showers, and toilets are available. Firewood can be obtained for an extra fee. Some facilities are wheelchair accessible. Leashed pets are permitted.

Reservations, fees: Reservations accepted; phone (800) 452-5687 ($6 reservation fee). Sites are $5-10 per night. Major credit cards accepted. Open February 24 through October.

Directions: From Seattle on Interstate 5, drive north to Burlington and the Highway 20 exit. Take Highway 20 west and drive 28 miles (past Coupeville on Whidbey Island) to the Highway 525 cutoff. Turn south on Highway 525 and drive to Bush Point Road. Turn right (west) and drive to the park access road (well signed). The park can also be reached easily with a ferry ride from Mulkilteo (located southeast of Everett) to Clinton (this also makes a great bike trip to the state park).

Contact: South Whidbey State Park, 4128 Smugglers Cove Road, Freeland, WA 98429; tel. (800) 233-0321 or (360) 321-4559.

66 Fort Flagler State Park

       10

Historic Fort Flagler is a pretty, unique state park, set on Marrowstone Island east of Port Townsend. The RV sites are right on the beach. Anglers like this spot for year-round rockfish and salmon fishing, and crabbing and clamming are good in season. The park offers an underwater park and is popular with scuba divers. Tours of Fort Flagler, which was built in 1898, are available. There is a youth hostel in the park.

Location: Near Port Townsend; map A2, grid f4.

Campsites, facilities: There are 102 tent sites and 14 partial hookup (water and electric) sites for trailers or RVs up to 50 feet long. Picnic tables and fire grills are provided. Flush toilets, coin showers, a sanitary dump station, a store, a cafe, boat buoys, floats, and a launch are available. Facilities are wheelchair accessible. Leashed pets are permitted.

Reservations, fees: Reservations accepted; phone (800) 452-5687 ($6 reservation fee). Sites are $10-16 per night. Major credit cards accepted. Open February through September, weather permitting.

Directions: From Olympia on Interstate 5, turn north on U.S. 101 and drive 80 miles (toward Port Townsend) to the Anderson Lake Road (to Hadlock) exit. Turn right and drive east for three miles to Highway 19. Turn left and drive a half mile to the Hadlock cutoff. Turn right and drive one mile to Oak Bay Road (just south of Hadlock). Turn right and drive one mile to Highway 116 (Ness to Flagler Road). Turn left (east) and drive 14 (over the bridge to Marrowstone Island) to the park at the end of the road.

Contact: Fort Flagler State Park, 10541 Flagler Road, Nordland, WA 98358; tel. (800) 233-0321, (360) 385-1259.

67 Camano Island State Park   9

This camp is set at a southwest point at Camano Island, near Lowell Point and Elger Bay along the Saratoga Passage. The campsites are quiet and private in this wooded park. Good inshore angling for rockfish is available year-round, ad salmon fishing is also good in season. Clamming is excellent during low tides in June. An underwater park is provided for divers. There is also a self-guided nature trail.

Location: On Camano Island; map A2, grid f5.

Campsites, facilities: There is one primitive tent site and 87 developed camp-sites for tents or self-contained RVs up to 30 feet long. There is also one group camp for a maximum of 200 people. Picnic tables and fire grills are provided. Sanitary disposal service, flush toilets, coin showers, and a playground are available. Firewood can be obtained or an extra fee. Boat launching facilities are located in the park. Leashed pets are permitted.

Reservations, fees: No reservations accepted for family camping; sites are $5-10 per night, plus $5 per extra vehicle per night. Reservations required for the group camp; phone (360) 387-3031. The group camp base fee is $25, plus $1 per person per night. Open year-round.

Directions: From Seattle on Interstate 5, drive north (17 miles north of Everett) to Exit 212. Take Exit 212 to Highway 532. Drive west on Highway 532 to Stanwood and continue six miles (to Camano Island) to a fork. Bear left at the fork and continue south on East Camano Drive for nine miles to the park entrance on the right.

Contact: Camano Island State Park, 2269 South Lowell Point Road, Stanwood, WA 98292; tel. (800) 233-0321 or (360) 387-3031.

68 Wenberg State Park   8

This state park is set along the east shore of Lake Goodwin, where the trout fishing can be great. Power boats are allowed, and a seasonal concession stand provides food and fishing supplies. Lifeguards are on duty in the summer.

Location: On Lake Goodwin; map A2, grid f6.

Campsites, facilities: There are 65 developed tent sites, and 10 sites for trailers or RVs up to 50 feet long. Picnic tables are provided. A sanitary disposal station, flush toilets, drinking water, coin showers, a store, and a playground are available. Boat launching facilities are located on Lake Goodwin. Leashed pets are permitted.

Reservations, fees: Reservations accepted, phone (800) 452-5687 ($6 reservation fee). Sites are $11-16 per night. Major credit cards accepted. Open year-round.

Directions: From Seattle on Interstate 5, drive north to Exit 206 (10 miles north of Everett). Take Exit 206/Smokey Point, turn west and drive two miles to Highway 531. Bear right on Highway 531 and drive seven miles to the park entrance on the right (well signed).

Contact: Wenberg State Park, 15430 East Lake Goodwin Road, Stanwood, WA 98292; tel. (800) 233-0321, (360) 652-7417.

69 Lake Goodwin Resort   5

This private campground is set on Lake Goodwin, which is known for good trout fishing. Motorboats are permitted on the lake, and an 18-hole golf course is located nearby. Other activities include swimming in the lake, horseshoe pits, shuffleboard, and a recreation field.

Location: On Lake Goodwin; map A2, grid f6.

Campsites, facilities: There are 20 tent sites and 85 sites for trailers or RVs of any length; eight are drive-through. There is also one fully equipped cabin available. Electricity, drinking water, sewer hookups, and picnic tables are provided. Flush toilets, bottled gas, sanitary services, recreation equipment, a store, a laundry room, ice, a playground, showers, and firewood are available. Boat moorage, a fishing pier, and boat rentals are located nearby on Lake Goodwin.

Reservations, fees: Reservations accepted; phone (800) 242-8169. Sites are $16-25 per night; cabins are $60-75 per night. Major credit cards accepted. Open year-round.

Directions: From Seattle on Interstate 5, drive north to Exit 206 (10 miles north of Everett). Take Exit 206/Smokey Point, turn west, and drive two miles to Highway 531. Bear right on Highway 531 and drive to a stop sign at Lakewood Road. Turn right at Lakewood and drive 3.5 miles to the park.

Contact: Lake Goodwin Resort, 4726 Lakewood Road, Stanwood, WA 98292; tel. (360) 652-8169, fax (360) 652-4025.

70 Kayak Point County Park   5

This large, wooded county park is set on the shore of Puget Sound, with an 18-hole golf course nearby.

Location: On Puget Sound; map A2, grid f6.

Campsites, facilities: There are 32 sites with partial hookups, nine of them tent sites and 23 drive-through for trailers or RVs up to 25 feet long. Drinking water and picnic tables are provided. Flush toilets and firewood are available. Boat docks and launching facilities are located in the park. Leashed pets are permitted.

Reservations, fees: No reservations. Sites are $15 per night. Major credit cards accepted. Open year-round.

Directions: From Seattle on Interstate 5, drive north past Everett to Exit 199 (Tulalip) at Marysville. Take Exit 199, bear left on Tulalip Road, and drive west for 13 miles through the Tulalip Indian Reservation to the park entrance road on the left (signed for Kayak Point). Turn left and drive a half mile to the park.

Contact: Kayak Point County Park, 15422 Marine Drive, Stanwood, WA 98292; tel. (425) 388-6600.

71 Smokey Point RV Park   5

Smokey Point RV Park is an ideal layover for RV cruisers heading up Interstate 5 and looking for a place to spend the night. It's located just off the freeway and is only five miles from the state park and resorts on Lake Goodwin. The park is pleasant and clean, wit full facilities and spacious, shady sites. Marked bike trails are available nearby and use of an athletic club with swimming pool, sauna, and Jacuzzi is available to park guests for a small charge.

Location: Near Lake Goodwin; map A2, grid f7

Campsites, facilities: There are 104 sites for trailers or RVs of any length with full hookups; 38 are drive-through. Electricity, sewer, drinking water, garbage service, cable TV, and picnic tables are provided. Flush toilets, showers, a recreation hall, a laundry room, a playground, and bottled gas are available. Firewood, a store, ice, and a cafe are located within 1,000 feet. Leashed pets are permitted.

Reservations, fees: Reservations recommended. Sites are $18-25 per night, with discounts available for selected club memberships. Major credit cards accepted. Open year-round.

Directions: From Seattle on Interstate 5, drive north past Everett to Exit 206

(Smokey Point). Take Exit 206 and turn left (west) on 172nd Street for a half block, over the freeway. Drive in the left lane and turn left into the gas station. The park is straight ahead.

Contact: Smokey Point RV Park, 17019 28th Drive NE, Arlington, WA 98223; tel. (360) 652-7300 or fax (360) 652-0731.

72 Turlo   8

Set at 900 feet along the South Fork of the Stillaguamish River, Turlo is the westernmost camp located on this stretch of Highway 92. A U.S. Forest Service Public Information Center is nearby. Riverside campsites are available, and the fishing can be good here. A few hiking trails can be found in the area; see a U.S. Forest Service map or consult the nearby information center for trail locations.

Location: On the South Fork of the Stillaguamish River in Mount Baker-Snoqualmie National Forest; map A2, grid f9.

Campsites, facilities: There are 19 sites for tents or RVs up to 31 feet long. Picnic tables are provided. Vault toilets, drinking water, and firewood are available. Some facilities are wheelchair accessible. A store, a cafe, and ice are located one mile away in Robe. Leashed pets are permitted.

Reservations, fees: Reservations accepted; phone (877) 444-6777 ($8.65 reservation fee). Sites are $12 per night, $6 for each additional vehicle. Open mid-May to late September.

Directions: From Seattle on Interstate 5, drive north to Everett and U.S. 2. Turn east on U.S. 2 and drive five miles to Highway 9. Turn north and drive four miles to Highway 92. Turn east on Highway 92 and drive approximately 15 miles to the town of Granite Falls. Continue another 11 miles east on Highway 92 to the campground entrance on the right.

Contact: Mount Baker-Snoqualmie National Forest, Darrington Ranger District, 1405 Emmens Street, Darrington, WA 98241; tel. (360) 436-1155.

73 Verlot   9

This pretty campground is set along the South Fork of the Stillaguamish River, a short distance from the Lake Twenty-Two Research Natural Area and the Maid of the Woods Trail. A U.S. Forest Service map details back roads and hiking trails. Fishing is another recreation option. Campsites with river views are available.

Location: On the South Fork of the Stillaguamish River in Mount Baker-Snoqualmie National Forest; map A2, grid f9.

Campsites, facilities: There are 26 sites for tents, trailers, or RVs up to 31 feet long. Picnic tables are provided. Flush toilets, firewood, and drinking water are available. A store, a cafe, and ice are located within one mile. Leashed pets are permitted.

Reservations, fees: Reservations accepted; phone (877) 444-6777 or access the website: www.reserveusa.com ($8.65 reservation fee). Sites are $12 per night, $6 for each additional vehicle. Open mid-May to late September.

Directions: From Seattle on Interstate 5, drive north to Everett and U.S. 2. Turn east on U.S. 2 and drive five miles to Highway 9. Turn north and drive four miles to Highway 92. Turn east on Highway 92 and drive approximately 15 miles to the town of

Granite Falls, and continue another 11.6 miles east on Highway 92 to the campground entrance on the right.

Contact: Mount Baker-Snoqualmie National Forest, Darrington Ranger District, 1405 Emmens Street, Darrington, WA 98241; tel. (360) 436-1155.

74 Deer Park   9

This camp is set in the Olympic Peninsula's high country at 5,400 feet, just below 6,000-foot Blue Mountain. There are numerous trails in the area, including a major trailhead into the backcountry of Olympic National Park and the Buckhorn Wilderness.

Location: Near Blue Mountain in Olympic National Park; map A2, grid g0.

Campsites, facilities: There are 14 tent sites. Picnic tables and fire grills are provided. Rest rooms and drinking water are available. Leashed pets are permitted.

Reservations, fees: No reservations. Sites are $8 per night. Open mid-June to late September, with limited winter facilities.

Directions: From Olympia on Interstate 5, turn north on U.S. 101 and drive 115 miles to Deer Park Road (about three miles southeast of Port Angeles). Turn left on Deer Park Road and drive 18 miles south to the campground at the end of the road (the last six miles are gravel and is often closed in winter).

Contact: Olympic National Park, 600 East Park Avenue, Port Angeles, WA 98362; tel. (360) 452-4501, fax (360) 452-0335.

75 Dungeness Forks   7

This pretty, wooded spot is nestled at the confluence of the Dungeness and Gray Wolf Rivers. It offers seclusion, yet easy access from the highway. If you want quiet, you'll find it here.

Location: On the Dungeness and Gray Wolf Rivers in Olympic National Forest; map A2, grid g1.

Campsites, facilities: There are 10 tent sites. Picnic tables are provided. Drinking water and vault toilets are available. Leashed pets are permitted.

Reservations, fees: No reservations. Sites are $10 per night. Open May through September.

Directions: From Olympia on Interstate 5 at, turn north on U.S. 101 and drive approximately 100 miles to Palo Alto Road, located 1.5 miles north of Sequim Bay State Park and three miles southeast of Sequim. Turn south (left) on Palo Alto Road and drive about seven miles to Forest Road 2880. Turn west and drive one mile to the campground. A U.S. Forest Service map is advised.

Contact: Olympic National Forest, Quilcene Ranger District, P.O. Box 280, Quilcene, WA 98376; tel. (360) 765-3368, fax (360) 765-2202.

76 Falls View   8

In spite of the rustic setting, this spot on the edge of the Olympic National Forest has a host of facilities and is very popular.

Location: On the Big Quilcene River in Olympic National Forest; map A2, grid h2.

Campsites, facilities: There are 30 sites for tents, trailers, or RVs up to 21 feet long. Picnic tables are provided. Drinking water, flush toilets, and wheelchair-accessible rest rooms are available. Leashed pets are permitted.

Reservations, fees: No reservations. Sites are $10 per night. Open mid-May to mid-September.

Directions: From Olympia on Interstate 5, turn north on U.S. 101 and drive approximately 70 miles to the campground entrance on the left (located about four miles south of Quilcene).

Contact: Olympic National Forest, Quilcene Ranger District, P.O. Box 280, Quilcene, WA 98376; tel. (360) 765-3368, fax (360) 765-2202.

77 East Crossing   6

An alternative to Dungeness Forks, this seven-acre camp is set at about 1,200 feet and offers some improvements, but it's still for individuals seeking an out-of-the-way spot.

Location: In Olympic National Forest; map A2, grid g2.

Campsites, facilities: There are 10 sites for tents only. Picnic tables are provided. Drinking water and vault toilets are available. Leashed pets are permitted.

Reservations, fees: No reservations. Sites are $8 per night. Open May through September.

Directions: From Olympia, turn north on U.S. 101 and drive approximately 100 miles to Palo Alto Road (located 1.5 miles north of Sequim Bay State Park and three miles southeast of Sequim). Turn south (left) on Palo Alto Road and drive eight miles to Forest Road 2860. Turn south on Forest Service 2860 and drive two miles the campground. A U.S. Forest Service map is advised.

Contact: Olympic National Forest, Quilcene Ranger District, P.O. Box 280, Quilcene, WA 98376; tel. (360) 765-3368, fax (360) 765-2202.

78 Kitsap Memorial State Park
       10

Kitsap Memorial State Park is a nice spot for tent campers along the Hood Canal. An 18-hole golf course and swimming, fishing, and hiking at nearby Anderson Lake Recreation Area are among the activities available. A short drive north will take you to historic Old Fort Townsend, an excellent day trip.

Location: On the Hood Canal; map A2, grid g4.

Campsites, facilities: There are 51 sites for tents or self-contained RVs up to 30 feet long. Picnic tables and fire grills are provided. A sanitary disposal service, toilets, and a playground are available. Showers and firewood can be obtained for an extra fee. Boat buoys are available. Leashed pets are permitted.

Reservations, fees: No reservations. Sites are $10 per night. Open year-round.

Directions: From Tacoma on Interstate 5, turn north on Highway 16 and drive 44 miles (Highway 16 turns into Highway 3). Continue north on Highway 3 and drive eight miles to the park entrance on the left. Well signed, the park is located three miles south of the Hood Canal Bridge, four miles north of Poulsbo.

Contact: Kitsap Memorial State Park, 202 N.E. Park Street, Poulsbo, WA 98370; tel. (800) 233-0321 or (360) 779-3205.

79 Captain's Landing   5

Grassy, open sites make this a choice for campers wanting an in-town location. An 18-hole golf course and a full-service marina are close by.

Location: In Hansville; map A2, grid g5.

Campsites, facilities: There are 22 drive-through sites for trailers or RVs of any length. Electricity, drinking water, and sewer hookups are provided. Flush toilets, showers, a store, and ice are available. Boat docks, launching facilities, and boat rentals are located within one mile. Leashed pets are permitted.

Reservations, fees: Reservations accepted. Sites are $18-20 per night. Open year-round.

Directions: From Tacoma on Interstate 5, turn north on Highway 16 and drive 44 miles (Highway 16 turns into Highway 3). Continue north on Highway 3 for 11 miles to Port Gamble, and then bear southeast toward Kingston (still on Highway 3) to Hansville Road (at George's Corner). Turn left on Hansville Road and drive eight miles. The park is on the right side, on the bottom of the hill.

Contact: Captain's Landing, P.O. Box 113, Hansville, WA 98340; tel. (360) 638-2257, fax (360) 638-2258.

80 Lakeside RV Park   8

This camp is landscaped with annuals, roses, other perennials, and shrubs, which provide privacy and gardens for each site. There's a man-made pond stocked with trout year-round.

Location: In the town of Everett; map A2, grid g7

Campsites, facilities: There are nine tent sites and 155 RV sites with full hookups. Drinking water, rest rooms, coin showers and laundry facilities, fire pits, propane gas, phones, and cable TV are available. Some facilities are wheelchair accessible. Leashed pets are permitted.

Reservations, fees: Reservations required; phone (800) 468-7275. Sites are $15.70-32.23 per night. Major credit cards accepted. Open year-round.

Directions: From Seattle on Interstate 5, drive north to Everett and Exit 186. Take Exit 186 and turn west on 128th Street and drive about two miles to Old Highway 99. Turn left (south) on Old Highway 99 and drive one-quarter mile to the park on the left.

Contact: Lakeside RV Park, 12321 Highway 99 South, Everett, WA 98204; tel. (800) 468-7275, fax (206) 347-9052.

81 Flowing Lake County Park   6

This campground has a little something for everyone, including swimming, power boating, waterskiing, and good fishing on Flowing Lake.

Location: Near Snohomish; map A2, grid g8.

Campsites, facilities: There are 10 tent sites and 32 drive-through sites for trailers or RVs up to 25 feet long. Electricity, drinking water, sewer hookups, and picnic tables are provided. Flush toilets, sanitary services, firewood, a playground, boat docks, and launching facilities are available. Leashed pets are permitted.

Reservations, fees: No reservations. Sites are $10-15 per night. Open year-round for self-contained RVs, and from mid-May to late September for other campers.

Directions: From Seattle on Interstate 5, drive north to Everett and U.S. 2. Turn east on U.S. 2 and drive to Milepost 10 and look for 100 Street SE (Westwick Road). Turn left and drive five miles (the road becomes 171st Street SE) to 48th Street Southeast. Turn right and drive about one-half mile into the park at the end of the road.

Contact: Flowing Lake County Park, 3000 Rockefeller Avenue, Everett, WA 98201; (360) 339-1208.

82 Dosewallips   7

Dosewallips is a more remote option to Elkhorn and Collins. Set on the Dosewallips River at 1,540 feet, the camp provides a major trailhead into the backcountry of Olympic National Park. The trail follows the Dosewallips River over Anderson Pass, proceeds along the Quinault River, and ultimately reaches Quinault Lake.

Location: On the Dosewallips River in Olympic National Park; map A2, grid h0.

Campsites, facilities: There are 30 tent sites. Picnic tables and fire grills are provided. Rest rooms, drinking water, and wheelchair-accessible facilities are available. Leashed pets are permitted.

Reservations, fees: No reservations. Sites are $10 per night. Open mid-May to late September.

Directions: From Olympia on Interstate 5, drive north on U.S. 101 for 60 miles to a signed turnoff near Brinnon (located about one mile north of Dosewallips State Park) for Forest Road 2610 (County Road 2500). Turn west and drive 15 miles along the Dosewallips River to the camp at the end of the road.

Contact: Olympic National Park, 600 East Park Avenue, Port Angeles, WA 98362; tel. (360) 452-4501, fax (360) 452-0335.

83 Elkhorn   8

This eight-acre, wooded camp is set on the Dosewallips River at 600 feet, with river and fishing access. It's not far from Olympic National Park, a good side trip.

Location: On the Dosewallips River in Olympic National Forest; map A2, grid h1.

Campsites, facilities: There are 20 sites for tents, trailers, or RVs up to 21 feet long. Picnic tables are provided. Drinking water and vault toilets are available. Leashed pets are permitted.

Reservations, fees: No reservations. Sites are $10 per night. Open mid-May through September.

Directions: From Olympia on Interstate 5, drive north on U.S. 101 for 60 miles to a signed turnoff near Brinnon (about one mile north of Dosewallips State Park) for Forest Road 2610 (County Road 2500). Turn west and drive 10 miles along the Dosewallips River. Look for the camp on the left.

Contact: Olympic National Forest, Quilcene Ranger District, P.O. Box 280, Quilcene, WA 98376; tel. (360) 765-3368, fax (360) 765-2202.

84 Rainbow Group Camp   7

Rainbow Group Camp is in a rugged, primitive setting on the edge of Olympic National Forest, with backcountry access provided on forest roads (a U.S. Forest Service map is advisable). This is an excellent layover spot for U.S. 101 cruisers. Olympic National Park is just a short drive away.

Location: Near Quilcene in Olympic National Forest; map A2, grid h2.

Campsites, facilities: There are group tent sites only. Picnic tables and fire grills are provided. There is no drinking water. Vault toilets are available. A store, a cafe, a coin laundry, and ice are within five miles. Leashed pets are permitted.

Reservations, fees: For reservation and fee information, phone (360) 765-2200. Sites are $50 per night.

Directions: From Interstate 5 at Olympia, go north on U.S. 101 and drive approximately 69 miles to the campground (about six miles past Dosewallips State Park) on the left (near Walker Pass).

Contact: Olympic National Forest, Quilcene Ranger District, P.O. Box 280, Quilcene, WA 98376; tel. (360) 765-3368, fax (360) 765-2202.

85 Collins   7

Most tourists cruising U.S. 101 don't have a clue about this spot, yet it's not far from the highway. This four-acre camp is set on the Duckabush River at 200 feet. It has small, shaded sites, river access nearby, and plenty of fishing and hiking. Dosewallips State Park and Olympic National Park provide two side trips within easy driving distance.

Location: On the Duckabush River in Olympic National Forest; map A2, grid h2.

Campsites, facilities: There are six tent sites and 10 sites for trailers or RVs up to 21 feet long. Picnic tables are provided. Drinking water and vault toilets are available. Leashed pets are permitted.

Reservations, fees: No reservations. Sites are $10 per night. Open mid-May through September.

Directions: From Olympia on Interstate 5, drive north on U.S. 101 for 59 miles to Forest Road 2510 (near Duckabush). Turn left on Forest Road 2510 and drive five miles west. The camp is on the left.

Contact: Olympic National Forest, Hood Canal Ranger District, P.O. Box 68, Hoodsport, WA 98548; tel. (360) 877-5254.

86 Dosewallips State Park   8

This 425-acre park is set on the shore of the Hood Canal at the mouth of Dosewallips River, which gets a fair run of steelhead in winter months. In Hood Canal, fishing for salmon and rockfish is popular. Beachcombers might consider clamming, but check with the Department of Health prior to harvesting any shellfish, due to seasonal and local conditions. This is a popular camp because it's set right off a major highway, so try to arrive early to insure a space.

Location: On Dosewallips Creek; map A2, grid h2.

Campsites, facilities: There are 88 sites for tents, trailers, or RVs up to 60 feet long; 40 are full hook-ups. There are also three wall tents. Fire grills are provided. Coin showers, flush toilets, picnic tables, stoves, and drinking water are available. A recreation hall, a store, a cafe, and laundry facilities are within one mile. Electricity and sewer hookups are available for an extra fee. Facilities are wheelchair accessible. Leashed pets are permitted.

Reservations, fees: Reservations accepted; phone (800) 452-5687 ($6 reservation fee). Sites are $5-16 per night; wall tent sites are $35 per night. Major credit cards accepted. Open year-round.

Directions: From Olympia on Interstate 5, drive north on U.S. 101 for 61 miles (one mile south of Brinnon) to the state park entrance on the right.

Contact: Dosewallips State Park, to P.O. Drawer K, Brinnon, WA 98320; tel. (800) 233-0321 or (360) 796-4415.

87 Scenic Beach State Park   10

Scenic Beach is an exceptionally beautiful state park, with beach access and superb views of the Olympic Mountains. Beachcombing, oyster hunting, and salmon fishing are among your options. A public boat launch can be found one mile north at Misery Point. Wheelchair-accessible nature trails are available at the park.

Location: On the Hood Canal; map A2, grid h3.

Campsites, facilities: There are two primitive tent sites and 50 sites for tents, trailers, or self-contained RVs up to 40 feet long. Picnic tables, drinking water, fire grills, coin showers, a sanitary disposal station, and flush toilets are provided. The facilities are wheelchair accessible. Leashed pets are permitted.

Reservations, fees: Reservations accepted; phone (800) 452-5687 ($6 reservation fee). Sites are $5-11 per night. Open April to mid-November.

Directions: From Tacoma at Interstate 5, turn north on Highway 16 and drive 30 miles to Bremerton to the junction with Highway 3. Turn north on Highway 3 and drive about nine miles and take the first Silverdale exit (Newberry Hill Road.). Turn left and drive approximately three miles to the end of the road. Turn right on Seabeck Highway and follow it to Seabeck. Once in town take the only road that follows the bay west and then turn right at Stavis Bay Road after the grade school. Continue 1.5 miles on the winding road to the park.

Contact: Scenic Beach State Park, P.O. Box 7, Seabeck, WA 98380; tel. (800) 233-0321 or (360) 830-5079.

88 Cove Trailer Park   5

This five-acre private camp is in a rural setting, yet it's fully developed with the shore of Dabob Bay nearby. Sites are grassy and graveled with a few trees. Dosewallips State Park is a short drive away and a possible side trip.

Location: Near Dabob Bay; map A2, grid h3.

Campsites, facilities: There are six tent sites and 32 sites with full hookups (including cable TV) for trailers or RVs up to 38 feet long. Electricity, drinking water, sewer hookups, and picnic tables are provided. Bottled gas, sanitary services, toilets, a store, laundry facilities, and ice are available. Showers are available for an extra fee.

Boat docks and launching facilities are on the Hood Canal within three miles of the park. Leashed pets are permitted.

Reservations, fees: Reservations accepted. Sites are $18.50 per night. Major credit cards accepted. Open year-round.

Directions: From Olympia on Interstate 5, drive north on U.S. 101 for 60 miles to Brinnon (located about one mile north of Dosewallips State Park). Continue three miles north on U.S. 101. The camp is located before Milepost 303.

Contact: Cove Trailer Park, 303075 Highway 101, Brinnon, WA 98320; tel. (360) 796-4723; fax (360) 796-3452; e-mail: covepark@jupitercity.com.

89 Seal Rock 9

Seal Rock is a 30-acre camp set along the shore near the mouth of Dabob Bay. The modern, developed setting provides a good spot for boat owners. This camp gets extremely crowded in the summer months, so reserve your site early.

Location: On Dabob Bay in Olympic National Forest; map A2, grid h3.

Campsites, facilities: There are 40 sites for tents, trailers, or RVs up to 21 feet long. Picnic tables are provided. Drinking water, flush toilets, and wheelchair-accessible facilities are available. Boat docks and launching facilities are nearby on the Hood Canal and in Dabob Bay. Leashed pets are permitted.

Reservations, fees: No reservations. Sites are $10-12 per night. Open mid-April through September.

Directions: From Olympia on Interstate 5, drive north on U.S. 101 for 60 miles to Brinnon (located about one mile north of Dosewallips State Park). Continue two miles north on U.S. 101. The camp is on the shore at Seal Rock.

Contact: Olympic National Forest, Quilcene Ranger District, P.O. Box 280, Quilcene, WA 98376; tel. (360) 765-3368, fax (360) 765-2202.

90 Fay Bainbridge State Park
 10

Set on the edge of Puget Sound, this camp provides all the recreation possibilities of a typical beach park. The primitive walk-in sites are heavily wooded, and the developed sites have great views of the sound. Clamming, diving, picnicking, beachcombing, and kite flying are popular pastimes here. On clear days campers can enjoys views of Mount Rainier and Mount Baker to the east, and at night the park provides beautiful vistas of the lights of Seattle. In the winter months there is excellent salmon fishing just offshore of the park.

Location: On Bainbridge Island; map A2, grid h4.

Campsites, facilities: There are 10 primitive tent sites and 26 sites for tents or self-contained RVs up to 30 feet long. Picnic tables and fire grills are provided. Sanitary disposal service, drinking water, coin showers, toilets, and a playground are available. A store and a cafe are located within one mile. Firewood can be obtained for an extra fee. Some facilities are wheelchair accessible. Boat docks and launching facilities are nearby. Leashed pets are permitted.

Reservations, fees: No reservations. Sites are $11 per night. Open April through August.

Directions: From Tacoma at Interstate 5, turn north on Highway 16 and drive 30 miles to Bremerton to the junction with Highway 3. Turn north on Highway 3 and drive 18 miles to Highway 305. Turn south on Highway 305 and drive over the bridge to Bainbridge Island and continue three miles to Phelps Road Northeast. Turn left (northeast), drive two miles to Port Madison, and continue east one mile to the park entrance (well signed). Note: From Seattle this camp can be more easily accessed by taking Bainbridge Island ferry and then Highway 305 north to the northeast end of the island).

Contact: Fay Bainbridge State Park, 15546 Sunrise, Bainbridge Island, WA 98110; tel. (800) 233-0321 or (206) 842-3931.

91 Orchard Trailer Park   4

Orchard Trailer Park is the smallest and most intimate of the motor home parks in the Seattle area. It's in an urban setting and makes a decent layover spot. An 18-hole golf course is nearby.

Location: In Seattle; map A2, grid h6.

Campsites, facilities: There are 10 sites for trailers or RVs of any length. Electricity, drinking water, and sewer hookups are provided. A laundry room is available. Bottled gas, a store, a cafe, and ice are located within one mile. Pets are not permitted.

Reservations, fees: No reservations. Sites are $19 per night, $114 per week. Open year-round.

Directions: From Interstate 5 in Seattle, take Exit 154 and turn west on Interstate 405/Highway 518 and drive one mile to Highway 99. Turn north on Highway 99 and drive a half mile to South 146th Street. Turn right (east) and drive a short distance to the trailer park on the right.

Contact: Orchard Trailer Park, 4011 South 146th Street, Seattle, WA 98168; tel. (206) 243-1210.

92 Holiday Park Resort   5

Be sure to reserve in advance; this camp is usually full. The downtown sights of Seattle are just a short drive away. Nearby recreation options include an 18-hole golf course, marked bike trails, and tennis courts.

Location: In Seattle; map A2, grid i6.

Campsites, facilities: There are 22 sites for trailers or RVs up to 32 feet long. Electricity, drinking water, and sewer hookups are provided. Flush toilets, showers, a cafe, and a laundry room are available. Bottled gas, sanitary services, a store, and ice are located within one mile.

Reservations, fees: Reservations recommended. Sites are $21 per night. Open year-round.

Directions: In Seattle on Interstate 5, take the 176th Avenue exit. Turn west on 176th Avenue and drive to Aurora Avenue. Turn north and drive to 19250 Aurora Avenue North.

Contact: Holiday Park Resort, 19250 Aurora Avenue North, Seattle, WA 98133; tel. (206) 542-2760.

93 Lake Pleasant RV Park   6

Set on Lake Pleasant, this large, developed camp is geared primarily toward RVers. The setting is pretty, with lakeside sites and plenty of trees. Just off the highway, it's a very popular camp, so expect lots of company, especially in the summer. This is a good spot for a little trout fishing.

Location: On Lake Pleasant; map A2, grid h6.

Campsites, facilities: There are 196 sites for trailers or RVs. Cable TV, modem access, rest rooms, showers, a sanitary dump, a public phone, a laundry room, a playground, and LP gas are available. Facilities are wheelchair accessible. Leashed pets are permitted.

Reservations, fees: Reservations recommended. Sites are $25 per night. Open year-round.

Directions: From the junction of Interstate 5 and Interstate 405 (just south of Seattle), take Interstate 405 and drive to Exit 26. Take that exit to the Bothell/Everett Highway over the freeway and drive south for about a mile and look for the park on the left side. It's marked by a large sign.

Contact: Lake Pleasant RV Park, 24025 Bothell/Everett Highway, Bothell, WA 98021; tel. (425) 487-1785 or (800) 742-0386.

94 Lena Lake Hike-In   8

You can't beat the price of this 135-acre camp set on Lena Lake. The hike in from Lena Creek to the campground is suitable for the entire family, an outstanding way to turn youngsters on to backpacking. The majority of weekend campers would rather not deal with the hike, so this spot is rarely crowded. It's a lovely setting, too, with a pleasantly mild climate in summer.

Location: Near the Hamma Hamma River in Olympic National Forest; map A2, grid i0.

Campsites, facilities: There are 29 primitive sites at this hike-in campground. There is no drinking water. Vault toilets are available. Leashed pets are permitted.

Reservations, fees: No reservations. There is no fee for camping, but you must obtain a $25 annual Trail Park Pass or pay $3 a day to park at the trailhead. Open year-round, weather permitting.

Directions: From Olympia on Interstate 5, turn north on U.S. 101 and drive about 37 miles to Hoodsport. Continue north on U.S. 101 from 14 miles to Forest Road 25. Turn west on Forest Road 25 and drive eight miles to the Lena Creek Camp and the trailhead. Hike 3.2 miles north to Lena Lake. Campsites are scattered around the lake.

Contact: Olympic National Forest, Hood Canal Ranger District, P.O. Box 68, Hoodsport, WA 98548; tel. (360) 877-5254, fax (360) 352-2569.

95 Lena Creek   7

This seven-acre camp is set where Lena Creek empties into the Hamma Hamma River. A trail from the camp leads three miles to Lena Lake and seven miles to Upper Lena Lake. A map of Olympic National Forest details the trail and road system. The camp is rustic with some improvements; primarily a trailhead camp.

Location: On the Hamma Hamma River in Olympic National Forest; map A2, grid i0.

Campsites, facilities: There are 14 sites for tents, trailers, or RVs up to 21 feet long. Picnic tables are provided. Drinking water and vault toilets are available. Wheelchair-accessible rest rooms are available. Leashed pets are permitted.

Reservations, fees: No reservations. Sites are $10 per night. Open mid-May through September.

Directions: From Olympia on Interstate 5, turn north on U.S. 101 and drive about 37 miles to Hoodsport. Continue north on U.S. 101 from 14 miles to Forest Road 25. Turn west on Forest Road 25 and drive eight miles to the camp on the left.

Contact: Olympic National Forest, Hood Canal Ranger District, P.O. Box 68, Hoodsport, WA 98548; tel. (360) 877-5254, fax (360) 352-2569.

96 Lilliwaup Creek   7

This camp is set along Lilliwaup Creek, a quiet and primitive setting, yet has drinking water available. Lilliwaup Creek makes for a nice backdrop, and anglers will enjoy the fishing.

Location: On Lilliwaup Creek in Bert Cole State Forest; map A2, grid i1.

Campsites, facilities: There are 13 sites for tents or small trailers. Picnic tables, fire grills, and tent pads are provided. Vault toilets and drinking water are available. Leashed pets are permitted.

Reservations, fees: No reservations; no fee. Open year-round.

Directions: From Olympia on Interstate 5, turn north on U.S. 101 and drive 41 miles to Lilliwaup (four miles north of Hoodsport). Continue north on U.S. 101 for seven miles to Jorsted Creek Road (Forest Road 24). Turn left and drive 1.5 miles to a fork. Bear left at the fork (still Forest Road 24) and drive five miles to the camp.

Contact: Department of Natural Resources, South Puget Sound Region, P.O. Box 68, Enumclaw, WA 98022-0068; tel. (360) 825-1631, fax (360) 825-1672.

97 Melbourne   7

This primitive camp is on Melbourne Lake at about 1,000 feet in a little-known, rustic setting. Melbourne Lake is not a big well-known reservoir, but a small, lesser-known lake on the southeast flank of the Olympic Mountains. If you want quiet, and don't mind a lack of facilities, this is a good drive-to option. Nearby Lilliwaup Creek has drinking water.

Location: On Melbourne Lake in Hoh Clearwater State Forest; map A2, grid i1.

Campsites, facilities: There are five sites for tents or small trailers. Picnic tables, fire grills, and tent pads are provided. Vault toilets are available. There is no drinking water, so bring your own. Firearms are prohibited. Leashed pets are permitted.

Reservations, fees: No reservations; no fee. Open year-round.

Directions: From Olympia on Interstate 5, turn north on U.S. 101 and drive 41 miles to Lilliwaup (four miles north of Hoodsport). Continue north on U.S. 101 for seven miles to Jorsted Creek Road (Forest Road 24). Turn left and drive 1.5 miles to a fork. Bear left at the fork (still Forest Road 24) and drive four miles to a gravel road. Turn left on the gravel and drive 1.7 miles to a T, turn left, and drive a mile to the camp at Melbourne Lake.

Contact: Department of Natural Resources, South Puget Sound Region, P.O. Box 68, Enumclaw, WA 98022-0068; tel. (360) 825-1631, fax (360) 825-1672.

98 Hamma Hamma   7

A good holdover for vacationers cruising U.S. 101, this camp is set on the Hamma Hamma River at about 600 feet. It's small and primitive, but can be preferable to the expensive developed camps on the U.S. 101 circuit. The Civilian Conservation Corps is memorialized in a wheelchair-accessible interpretive trail that begins in the campground and winds one-quarter mile along the river.

Location: On the Hamma Hamma River in Olympic National Forest; map A2, grid i1.

Campsites, facilities: There are three tent sites and 12 sites for trailers or RVs up to 21 feet long. Picnic tables are provided. Hand-pumped water and vault toilets are available. Some facilities are wheelchair accessible. Leashed pets are permitted.

Reservations, fees: No reservations. Sites are $10 per night. Open May through September.

Directions: From Olympia on Interstate 5, turn north on U.S. 101 and drive 37 miles to Hoodsport. Continue on U.S. 101 for 14 miles north to Forest Road 25. Turn left on Forest Road 25 and drive 6.5 miles to the camp on the left side of the road.

Contact: Olympic National Forest, Hood Canal Ranger District, P.O. Box 68, Hoodsport, WA 98548; tel. (360) 877-5254, fax (360) 352-2569.

99 Minerva Beach
Mobile Village and RV Resort   5

Located on the ocean, this is a perfect layover spot if you're cruising up or down U.S. 101. Recreational opportunities at this park include swimming and salmon fishing. Oysters, crabs, and clams are also available here. A good side trip is nearby Potlatch State Park.

Location: On the Hood Canal; map A2, grid j1.

Campsites, facilities: There are 20 tent sites and 23 sites for trailers or RVs. Cable TV, rest rooms, a public phone, a laundry room, limited groceries, ice, RV supplies, and LP gas are available. There are also horseshoe pits and a gift shop. Leashed pets are permitted.

Reservations, fees: Reservations recommended. Sites are $15-20 per night. Major credit cards accepted. Open year-round.

Directions: From Olympia on Interstate 5, take Exit 104 and drive north on U.S. 101 to the Aberdeen/Highway 8 exit. Turn west on Highway 8 and drive 36 miles to Aberdeen. Continue through Aberdeen four miles to U.S. 101. Turn north on U.S. 101 and drive about 20 miles to Potlatch State Park. Just past Potlatch State Park, look for Minerva Beach Mobile Village and RV Resort, with access to the resort office via the driveway on the left.

Contact: Minerva Beach Mobile Village and RV Resort, 21110 Highway 101 North, Shelton, WA 98584; tel. (360) 877-5145.

100 Toonerville   7

Primitive and rustic, this campground is managed by the Department of Natural Resources and has trails for use by hikers, horses, and motorbikes. It's a pretty, forested, and well-used spot. Be sure to bring your own water, because there is none to be found near here.

Location: In Tahuya State Forest; map A2, grid i2.

Campsites, facilities: There are four sites for tents or small trailers. Picnic tables, fire grills, and tent pads are provided. Vault toilets are available, but there is no drinking water. Leashed pets and motorbikes are permitted.

Reservations, fees: No reservations; no fee. Call for an update on seasonal closures. A map and brochure are available for $2; see the contact information below.

Directions: From Tacoma on Interstate 5, turn north on Highway 16 and drive 30 miles to Bremerton and Highway 3. Turn south on Highway 3 and drive nine miles southwest to Belfair and Highway 300. Turn west on Highway 300 and drive one-third of a mile, then bear left and continue for another 3.3 miles to Belfair-Tahuya Road. Turn right and drive one-half mile to Elfendahl Pass Road. Turn right and drive 2.5 miles (past the Tahuya four-wheel-drive trailhead). At Goat Ranch Road, continue straight through the intersection and drive 3.3 miles to the camp on the left.

Contact: Department of Natural Resources, South Puget Sound Region, P.O. Box 68, Enumclaw, WA 98022-0068; tel. (360) 825-1631, fax (360) 825-1672.

101 Green Mountain Camp Hike-In   7

This is a prime spot, primitive but with hand-pumped water provided. The campground is operated by the Department of Natural Resources and is located in Tahuya State Forest. There are facilities for horses, as well as trails for motor biking, hiking, and horseback riding. The status changes, though; it's a good idea to call first.

Location: In Tahuya State Forest; map A2, grid i3.

Campsites, facilities: There are 13 hike-in sites for tents only. Picnic tables, fire grills, and tent pads are provided. Vault toilets, hand-pumped water, and facilities for horses are available.

Reservations, fees: No reservations; no fee. A gate limits vehicular access to weekends during the months of June through August, from 9 a.m. to dusk. A free map and brochure are available.

Directions: From Tacoma on Interstate 5, turn north on Highway 16 and drive 30 miles to Bremerton and the junction with Highway 3. Turn north on Highway 3 and drive a short distance to the Seabeck Highway. Turn left and drive three miles to Holly Road. Turn left on Holly Road and drive four miles to Tahuya Lake Road. Turn left and drive one mile to Green Mountain Road and the DNR parking lot and trailhead. Hike four miles.

Contact: Department of Natural Resources, South Puget Sound Region, P.O. Box 68, Enumclaw, WA 98022-0068; tel. (360) 825-1631, fax (360) 825-1672.

102 Illahee State Park   9

This 75-acre park is just three miles from civilization in Bremerton, yet virtually unknown to out-of-towners touring the area. The campsites are set in a pretty, forested area, and some are grassy. The park has a ball field, a playground, and beach access. The shoreline is fairly rocky, set on the shore of Port Orchard, though there is a small sandy area for sunbathers. Clamming is popular here. A fishing pier and a moorage float are available for anglers.

Location: Near Bremerton; map A2, grid i4.

Campsites, facilities: There are eight primitive tent sites and 25 sites for tents or self-contained RVs up to 30 feet long. Picnic tables and fire grills are provided. A sanitary disposal service, toilets, and a playground are available. Showers and firewood can be obtained for an extra fee. A coin laundry and ice are located within one mile. Some facilities are wheelchair accessible. Boat docks and launching facilities are available. Leashed pets are permitted.

Reservations, fees: No reservations. Sites are $5-10 per night. Open year-round.

Directions: From Tacoma on Interstate 5, turn north on Highway 16 and drive 30 miles to Bremerton and the junction with Highway 310. Turn east on Highway 310 and drive through Bremerton to Highway 303. Turn north and drive (on the bridge over Port Washington Narrows) and drive to Sylvan Way. Turn right and drive three miles east to the park entrance on the left.

Contact: Illahee State Park, 3540 Bahia Vista, Bremerton, WA 98310; tel. (800) 233-0321, (360) 478-6460.

103 Manchester State Park   9

Set on the edge of Point Orchard, this campground has excellent lookouts across Puget Sound. Manchester State Park has many good hiking trails, along with places for fishing and clamming. The camp gets relatively little use, especially in the off-season, so you're almost always guaranteed a spot. Group and day-use reservations available.

Location: On Puget Sound; map A2, grid i4.

Campsites, facilities: There are 53 sites for tents or self-contained RVs up to 42 feet long. Picnic tables and fire grills are provided. Drinking water, a sanitary disposal station, and toilets are available. Showers and firewood can be obtained for an extra fee. Some facilities are wheelchair accessible. Leashed pets are permitted.

Reservations, fees: Reservations accepted, phone (800) 452-5687 ($6 reservation fee). Sites are $5-10 per night. Major credit cards accepted. Open year-round, with limited winter facilities.

Directions: From Tacoma on Interstate 5, turn north on Highway 16 and drive through Bethel and continue to the Sedgwick Road exit and Highway 160. Turn right (east) and drive one mile to Highway 166. Turn left and drive six miles on Highway 166 to Colby. Turn left and drive along the shore through Manchester and continue for two miles to the park. The last part of the trip is well signed.

Contact: Manchester State Park, P.O. Box 36, Manchester, WA 98353; tel. (800) 233-0321 or (360) 871-4065.

104 Blake Island Boat-In State Park   10

Located on a small island right in the middle of the massive Seattle metropolitan area, this camp offers a combination of primitive setting and developed facilities, including Tillicum Village, a restaurant serving Northwest Indian fare. Good bottom fishing can be found off the reef. A three-quarter-mile nature trail and 15 miles of hiking trails are available.

Location: Near Seattle; map A2, grid i5.

Campsites, facilities: There are 54 primitive, boat-in tent sites. Picnic tables and fire grills are provided. Drinking water, portable toilets, showers, firewood, and a restaurant are available. Some facilities are wheelchair accessible. Boat buoys and floats are available. Leashed pets are permitted.

Reservations, fees: No reservations. Sites are $5-10 per night. Open year-round.

Directions: This island is best reach by launching from Bremerton, Port Orchard, or Manchester. From Manchester it is a two-mile cruise east to the island (three miles west of Seattle). Then trace the shore around to the buoy floats. There are four main camping areas, a take-your-pick deal.

Contact: Blake Island Boat-In State Park, P.O. Box 277, Manchester, WA 98353; tel.(800) 233-0321 or (360) 731-0770.

105 Seattle Tacoma KOA   5

This is a popular urban campground, not far from the highway yet in a pleasant setting. The sites are spacious, with several pull-through to accommodate large RVs. A public golf course is located nearby. During the summer, a tour of Seattle can be taken from the campground.

Location: In Kent; map A2, grid i6.

Campsites, facilities: There are 18 tent sites and 134 sites for trailers or RVs; 103 are full hookups. Rest rooms, showers, water, electricity and sewer hookups, a sanitary dump, a public phone, a laundry room, limited groceries, ice, and RV supplies are available. A large playground, a game room, a heated swimming pool, and a recreation hall are also available. Facilities are wheelchair accessible. Leashed pets are permitted.

Reservations, fees: Reservations recommended. Sites are $25-35 per night. Major credit cards accepted. Open year-round.

Directions: On Interstate 5 in Seattle, take Exit 152 to 188th Street. Drive east (the road name becomes Orillia, then 212th Street) for 2.5 miles to the campground on the right.

Contact: Seattle Tacoma KOA, 5801 South 212th Street, Kent, WA 98032; tel.(800) 562-1892 or (253) 872-8652.

106 Blue Sky RV Park   5

Blue Sky RV Park is in an urban setting just outside of Seattle. It's a good off-the-beaten-path alternative to the crowded camps in the metro area, yet still only a short drive from the main attractions in the city. Nearby Lake Sammamish State Park provides more rustic recreation opportunities, including hiking and fishing.

Location: Near Lake Sammamish State Park; map A2, grid i8.

Campsites, facilities: There are 51 sites for trailers or RVs. Electricity, satellite TV, sewer hookups, and drinking water are provided. Rest rooms, showers, and a laundry room are available. Leashed pets are permitted.

Reservations, fees: Reservations recommended. Call for current rates. Open year-round.

Directions: From Seattle on Interstate 5, drive to the junction with Highway 90. Turn east on Highway 90 and drive 22 miles to Exit 22 (Preston/Falls City exit). Take that exit to S.E. 82nd Street. Turn right on S.E. 82nd Street and drive to 302nd Avenue SE. Turn left and drive a short distance to the campground entrance at the end of the road.

Contact: Blue Sky RV Park, 9002 302nd Avenue SE, Issaquah, WA 98027; tel. (425) 222-7910.

107 Aqua Barn Ranch   4

This large park with spacious sites (grassy for tent campers) is an ideal layover spot for campers who want to avoid the metro-area crowds. You'll find all the amenities, including a pool and hot tub. Numerous recreation options are available in the Seattle area, just 20 minutes north.

Location: South of Seattle; map A2, grid j7.

Campsites, facilities: There are approximately 40 tent sites and 200 sites for trailers or RVs; 90 are full hookups. Electricity and drinking water are provided. Rest rooms, showers, a sanitary dump, a public phone, a laundry room, ice, a restaurant, some picnic tables, and LP gas are available. Recreational facilities include horseshoe pits, a game room, an indoor heated swimming pool, and a playground. Some facilities are wheelchair accessible. Leashed pets are permitted.

Reservations, fees: Reservations recommended. Sites are $17-25 per night. Major credit cards accepted.

Directions: From the junction of Interstate 5 and Interstate 405 south of Seattle, turn east on Interstate 405 and drive to the Enumclaw/Maple Valley exit (Exit 4). Take that exit and turn right (there are no other options) and drive about three miles to the campground on the right.

Contact: Aqua Barn Ranch, 15227 S.E. Renton-Maple Valley Highway, Renton, WA 98058; tel. (425) 255-4618.

108 Trailer Inns RV Park and Recreation Center
 5

This park with all the amenities is a haven for RV travelers, and it's close to Lake Sammamish State Park as well. Nearby recreation options include an 18-hole golf course, hiking trails, marked bike trails, and tennis courts.

Location: Near Lake Sammamish State Park; map A2, grid i7.

Campsites, facilities: There are 104 sites for trailers or RVs of any length. Electricity, satellite TV, drinking water, sewer hookups, and picnic tables are provided.

Flush toilets, bottled gas, showers, a recreation hall, a swimming pool, a laundry room, ice, and a playground are available. Sanitary services, a store, and a cafe are available within one mile. Leashed pets and motorbikes are permitted.

Reservations, fees: Reservations accepted. Sites are $17-32 per night. Open year-round.

Directions: At the junction of Interstate 405 and Interstate 90 south of Seattle, turn east on Interstate 90 and drive 1.5 miles to Exit 11A. Take Exit 11A and continue south on the frontage road to the park.

Contact: Trailer Inns RV Park and Recreation Center, 15531 Southeast 37th Avenue, Bellevue, WA 98006; tel. (425) 747-9181, (509) 248-1142.

109 Issaquah Village RV Park   9

Though Issaquah Village RV Park doesn't allow tents, it's set in a beautiful environment ringed by the Cascade Mountains, making it a more scenic alternative to Blue Sky RV Park. Lake Sammamish State Park is just a few miles north.

Location: In Issaquah; map A2, grid i8.

Campsites, facilities: There are 112 sites for trailers or RVs of any length. No tents are allowed. Cable TV, water, electricity, and sewer hookups, rest rooms, showers, a sanitary dump, a public phone, a laundry room, and LP gas are available. Picnic areas, a playground, and a recreation field are also provided. The facilities are wheelchair accessible. Leashed pets are permitted.

Reservations, fees: Reservations recommended. Sites are $26-29 per night. Major credit cards accepted. Open year-round.

Directions: From Seattle on Interstate 506 (preferred) or Interstate 5, drive to the junction of Interstate 90. Take Interstate 90 east and drive 17 miles to Issaquah and Exit 17. Take Exit 17 and turn left, drive under the freeway and look for the first right. Take the first right for a very short distance and keep bearing right on the frontage road that parallels the freeway. Drive a quarter of a mile to the park on the left.

Contact: Issaquah Village RV Park, 650 First Avenue NE, Issaquah, WA 98027; tel. (800) 258-9233 or (425) 392-9233.

110 Vasa Park Resort   5

I was giving a seminar in Bellevue one evening when a distraught-looking couple walked in and pleaded, "Where can we camp tonight?" I answered, "Just look in the book," and this camp is where they ended up. It was the easiest sale ever made. This is the most rustic of the parks in the immediate Seattle area. The resort is on Lake Sammamish, and the state park is at the south end of the lake. An 18-hole golf course, hiking trails, and marked bike trails are close by.

Location: On Lake Sammamish; map A2, grid i8.

Campsites, facilities: There are 16 tent sites with partial hookups and six sites for trailers or RVs of any length with full hookups. Drinking water and picnic tables are provided. Flush toilets, sanitary services, a playground, showers, and a boat launching facility are available. Bottled gas, firewood, a store, and a cafe are located within one mile. Leashed pets are permitted within the campsites only.

Reservations, fees: Reservations accepted. Sites are $15-20 per night. Open mid-May to mid-October.

Directions: In Bellevue drive east on Interstate 90 to Exit 13. Take Exit 13 to West Lake Sammamish Parkway SE and drive north for one mile to Lake Sammamish. The campground is on the west side of Lake Sammamish.

Contact: Vasa Park Resort, 3560 West Lake Sammamish Parkway SE, Bellevue, WA 98008; tel. (425) 746-3260.

Snoqualmie River Campground

 7

If you're in the Seattle area and stuck for a place for the night, this pretty 10-acre park set along the Snoqualmie River may be a welcome option. Activities include fishing, swimming, road biking, and rafting. Nearby recreation options include several nine-hole golf courses. A worthwhile side trip is beautiful Snoqualmie Falls, 3.5 miles away in the famed *Twin Peaks* country.

Location: On the Snoqualmie River; map A2, grid i9.

Campsites, facilities: There are about 50 tent sites and 50 sites for trailers or RVs of any length. Drinking water and picnic tables are provided. Flush toilets, sanitary services, showers, and a playground are available. Electricity and firewood can be obtained for an extra fee. Bottled gas, a store, a cafe, and ice are located within two miles. Boat launching facilities are located within one-half mile. Leashed pets are permitted.

Reservations, fees: Reservations accepted. Sites are $20-23 per night. Open April to late October, as well as some off-season weekends (call ahead first to verify).

Directions: From the junction of Interstate 5 and Interstate 90 south of Seattle, turn east on Interstate 90. Drive east for 26 miles to Exit 22 (Preston-Fall City). Take that exit and turn north on Preston-Fall City Road and drive 4.5 miles to S.E. 44th Place. Turn east and drive one mile to the campground at the end of the road.

Contact: Snoqualmie River Campground, P.O. Box 16, Fall City, WA 98024; tel. (425) 222-5545.

Lake Cushman State Park

 9

Beach access and good trout fishing are highlights of this 603-acre camp on the shore of Lake Cushman. The 10-mile-long lake is surrounded by the Olympic Mountains, and an 18-hole golf course and marked hiking trails are nearby.

Location: On Lake Cushman; map A2, grid i0.

Campsites, facilities: There are 50 tent sites, 30 sites with full hookups for trailers or RVs up to 60 feet long, and two primitive sites. Picnic tables and fire grills are provided. Sanitary disposal services, drinking water, rest rooms, showers, and wheelchair-accessible facilities are available. A store, a restaurant, and ice can be found within one mile. Firewood is available for an extra fee. Boat docks and launching facilities are located at nearby Lake Cushman. Leashed pets are permitted.

Reservations, fees: Reservations accepted; phone (800) 452-5687 ($6 reservation fee). Sites are $10-15 per night. Major credit cards accepted. Open April through October.

Directions: From Olympia on Interstate 5, take the U.S. 101 exit and drive north 37 miles to Hoodsport and Highway 119 (Lake Cushman Road). Turn west (left) on Lake Cushman Road and drive seven miles to the park on the left.

Contact: Lake Cushman State Park, P.O. Box 128, Hoodsport, WA 98548; tel. (800) 233-0321, (360) 877-5491.

113 Brown Creek   9

Virtually unknown to outsiders, this camp is accessible to two-wheel-drive vehicles, but the road connects to a network of primitive, backcountry forest roads. The small campground (just six acres) is within the vast Olympic National Forest, which offers a plethora of opportunities for outdoors enthusiasts. The wheelchair-accessible Brown Creek Nature Trail begins at the hand pump and makes a one-mile loop around the camp. Obtain a U.S. Forest Service map to expand your trip.

Location: On Brown Creek in Olympic National Forest; map A2 grid j0.

Campsites, facilities: There are seven tent sites and 12 sites for trailers or RVs up to 25 feet long. Picnic tables are provided. Drinking water and vault toilets are available. Leashed pets are permitted.

Reservations, fees: No reservations. Sites are $5-10 per night. Open year-round, with limited winter facilities.

Directions: From Olympia on Interstate 5, take Exit 104 for U.S. 101/Highway 8. Drive north on U.S. 101 for 31 miles (about six miles past Shelton) to Skokomish Valley Road. Turn left and drive five miles (the road becomes Forest Road 23). Continue on Forest Road 23 for nine miles (it becomes Forest Road 2353) to Forest Road 2340. Turn at the campground sign and drive three-quarters of a mile to the camp. A U.S. Forest Service map is advisable.

Contact: Olympic National Forest, Hood Canal Ranger District, P.O. Box 68, Hoodsport, WA 94548; tel. (360) 877-5254, fax (360) 352-2569.

114 Potlatch State Park   8

Vacationers towing boats should consider this camp with spacious drive-through sites. The 57-acre park is set along the Hood Canal, where fishing, clamming, crabbing, and scuba diving should keep visitors busy. Marked hiking trails are located nearby.

Location: On the Hood Canal; map A2, grid j1.

Campsites, facilities: There are two primitive tent sites, 17 developed tent sites, and 18 drive-through sites with full hookups for trailers or RVs up to 60 feet long. Picnic tables, fire grills, and drinking water are provided. Sanitary disposal services and rest rooms with showers are available. Firewood is available for an extra fee. A boat launch is located at the park, and boat docks can be found nearby at the Hood Canal. Leashed pets are permitted.

Reservations, fees: No reservations. Sites are $5-16 per night. Open late March through October.

Directions: From Olympia on Interstate 5, take Exit 104 for U.S. 101/Highway 8. Drive north on U.S. 101 for 22 miles to Shelton. Continue north on U.S. 101 for 12 miles to the park on the right (located along the shoreline of Annas Bay in the Hood Canal).

Contact: Potlatch State Park, P.O. Box D, Hoodsport, WA 98548; tel. (800) 233-0321 or (360) 877-5361.

115 Rest-a-While   5

This seven-acre park, located at sea level on the Hood Canal, offers waterfront sites and a private beach for clamming and oyster gathering, not to mention plenty of opportunities to fish, boat, and scuba dive. It's an alternative to Potlatch State Park and Glen Ayr RV Park.

Location: On the Hood Canal; map A2, grid j1.

Campsites, facilities: There are two tent sites and 80 sites for trailers or RVs of any length; 30 are pull-through. Electricity, drinking water, and sewer and cable TV hookups are provided. Bottled gas, toilets, showers, firewood, a clubhouse, a store, seafood market, hamburger drive-in, laundry facilities, and ice are available. A cafe is within walking distance. Boat docks, launching facilities, scuba diving shop, seasonal boat and kayak rentals, and a private clamming beach are also available. Leashed pets and motorbikes are permitted.

Reservations, fees: Reservations accepted. Sites are $20-22 per night. Open year-round.

Directions: From Olympia on Interstate 5, take Exit 104 for U.S. 101/Highway 8. Drive north on U.S. 101 for 37 miles to Hoodsport. Continue one-half mile north on U.S. 101 to the camp located at Milepost 329.

Contact: Rest-a-While, North 27001 Highway 101, Hoodsport, WA 98548; tel. (360) 877-9474.

116 Big Creek   7

Big Creek is a good alternative to Staircase on the North Fork Skokomish River and Lake Cushman State Park on Lake Cushman, both of which get heavier use. The sites here are large and well spaced over 30 acres.

Location: Near Lake Cushman in Olympic National Forest; map A2, grid j1.

Campsites, facilities: There are 23 sites for tents or RVs up to 30 feet long. Sheltered picnic tables are provided. Drinking water, firewood (summer months), vault toilets, and wheelchair-accessible rest rooms are available. A boat dock and ramp are located at nearby Lake Cushman. Leashed pets are permitted.

Reservations, fees: No reservations. Sites are $10 per night. Open May through September.

Directions: From Olympia on Interstate 5, take Exit 104 for U.S. 101/Highway 8. Drive north on U.S. 101 for 37 miles to Hoodsport and Lake Cushman Road (Highway 119). Turn left on Lake Cushman Road and drive nine miles (two miles north of Lake Cushman State Park) to the T intersection. Turn left and the campground is on the right.

Contact: Olympic National Forest, Hood Canal Ranger District, P.O. Box 68, Hoodsport, WA 94548; tel. (360) 877-5254, fax (360) 352-2569.

117 Glen Ayr RV Park   5

This adults-only, fully developed, nine-acre park is located at sea level on the Hood Canal, where there are opportunities to fish and scuba dive. Salmon fishing is especially excellent. Swimming and boating are two other options. The park has a spa, moorage, horseshoe pits, a recreation field, and a hotel.

Location: On the Hood Canal; map A2, rid j1.

Campsites, facilities: There are 45 sites for trailers or RVs of up to 40 feet in length; nine are pull-through. Electricity, drinking water, cable TV, sewer hookups, and picnic tables are provided. Bottled gas, toilets, showers, a spa, a recreation hall and field, horseshoe pits and laundry facilities are available. A store, a cafe, and ice are within one mile. A boat dock is located across the street from the park. Leashed pets are permitted.

Reservations, fees: Campers must be 18 years of age or older. Reservations accepted. Sites are $23.50 per night for two people. Major credit cards accepted. Open year-round.

Directions: From Olympia on Interstate 5, take Exit 104 for U.S. 101/Highway 8. Drive north on U.S. 101 for 37 miles to Hoodsport. Continue one mile north on U.S. 101 to the park on the left.

Contact: Glen Ayr RV Park, 25381 North U.S. 101, Hoodsport, WA 98548. www.publiconline.com/glenayrcanal.

118 Aldrich Lake   7

This campground on Aldrich Lake is managed by the Department of Natural Resources. Robbins Lake is nearby and has day-use facilities and a hand launch for small boats. To reach Robbins Lake, follow the directions above, except after turning left on Hobaj Lane and driving one-half mile, make another left and drive one mile to the lake.

Location: On Aldrich Lake in Tahuya State Forest; map A2, grid j2.

Campsites, facilities: There are four primitive campsites for tents or small trailers. Picnic tables, fire grills, and tent pads are provided. Vault toilets and drinking water are available. A hand launch for small boats is located at the lake. Leashed pets are permitted.

Reservations, fees: Call the park for an update on seasonal closures and any gate information. There is no fee. A free map and brochure are available; see the contact information below.

Directions: From Tacoma on Interstate 5, drive to the junction with Highway 16. Turn north on Highway 16 and drive 30 miles to Bremerton and Highway 3. Turn west on Highway 3 and drive nine miles to Belfair and Highway 300. Turn west on Highway 300 and drive 12 miles to the town of Tahuya and Belfair-Tahuya Road. Turn north on Belfair-Tahuya Road and drive four miles to Dewatto Road. Turn left on Dewatto Road and drive two miles to Hobaj Lane. Turn left again on Hobaj Lane and drive one-half mile. Then turn right and drive two-thirds of a mile. Turn right again and drive 200 yards to the campground.

Contact: Department of Natural Resources, South Puget Sound Region, P.O. Box 68, Enumclaw, WA 98022-0068; tel. (360) 825-1631, fax (360) 825-1672.

This is a good holdover spot for RV campers preparing to head north. It's a pleasant park, with ocean access and spacious sites. Fishing, swimming, an 18-hole golf course, and marked bike trails provide recreation options.

Location: Near Belfair; map A2, j3.

Campsites, facilities: There are 36 sites for trailers or RVs of any length; 12 are drive-through. Electricity and drinking water are provided. Bottled gas, toilets, showers, picnic tables and a recreation hall are available. A store, a cafe, a coin laundry, and ice are located within one mile. Boat docks and launching facilities are nearby. Phone the park for pet policy.

Reservations, fees: Reservations accepted. Sites are $20 per night. Open year-round.

Directions: From Olympia on Interstate 5, take Exit 104 for U.S. 101/Highway 8. Drive north on U.S. 101 for 22 miles to Shelton and Highway 3. Turn north on Highway 3 and drive approximately 24 miles to the town of Belfair and Highway 300. Turn left on Highway 300 and drive about four miles northeast to Gladwin Beach Road (located between Mileposts 1 and 2). Turn left and drive west about one-half mile to the campground on the right.

Contact: Snooze Junction RV Park, P.O. Box 880, Belfair, WA 98528; tel. (360) 275-2381.

120 Belfair State Park   8

Tent campers will consider this a good alternative to Snooze Junction RV Park. Set along the edge of the Hood Canal, this park offers an unguarded saltwater swimming area, a sports area, and a few wooded campsites. Nearby recreation options include the town of Shelton, which boasts the Forest Festival in May and the Oysterfest in October, and the Puget Sound Naval Shipyard in Bremerton. Big Mission Creek and Little Mission Creek, both located in the park, are habitat for chum salmon during spawning season in the fall.

Location: On the Hood Canal; map A2, rid j2.

Campsites, facilities: There are 137 sites for tents and 47 full-hookup sites for trailers or RVs up to 75 feet long. Picnic tables and fire grills are provided. A sanitary disposal station, flush toilets, coin showers, a swimming area, and a playground are available. A store and a restaurant are located within one mile. Electricity, drinking water, and sewer hookups can be obtained for an extra fee. Some facilities are wheelchair accessible. Leashed pets are permitted.

Reservations, fees: Reservations accepted; phone (800) 452-5687 ($6 reservation fee). Sites are $10-16 per night. Major credit cards accepted. Open year-round.

Directions: From Tacoma on Interstate 5, drive to the Highway 16 exit. Take the Highway 16 northwest and drive about 30 miles to Bremerton and Highway 3. Turn south on Highway 3 and continue nine miles to Belfair and Highway 300. Turn west on Highway 300 and drive three miles to the park on the left.

Contact: Belfair State Park, N.E. 410 Beck Road, Belfair, WA 98528; tel. (800) 233-0321 or (360) 275-0668.

121 Twanoh State Park

 8

If you're cruising U.S. 101, this camp is only a short drive east off Highway 106. Often bypassed by visitors touring Washington, it's a prime recreation area, with opportunities for swimming, waterskiing, fishing, and boating on the beautiful Hood Canal. The water here is warmer because it's saltwater from the sound. Other amenities include a tennis court, horseshoe pits, and a concession stand.

Location: Near Union; map A2, grid j2.

Campsites, facilities: There are 17 tent sites and nine sites for trailers or RVs up to 35 feet long; 13 with full and nine with partial hookups. Picnic tables and fire grills are provided. Flush toilets, a store, and a playground are available. Electricity, drinking water, sewer hookups, showers, and firewood can be obtained for an extra fee. Some facilities are wheelchair accessible. Leashed pets are permitted.

Reservations, fees: No reservations. Sites are $5-16 per night. Open April through October.

Directions: From Olympia on Interstate 5, take Exit 104 for U.S. 101/Highway 8. Drive north on U.S. 101 for 32 miles (about eight miles past Shelton) to Highway 106. Turn east on Highway 106 and drive 10 miles (through the town of Union) to the park on Hood Canal.

Contact: Twanoh State Park, P.O. Box 2520, Belfair, WA 98528; tel. (800) 233-0321, (360) 275-2222.

122 Tahuya River Horse Camp   7

Set along the Tahuya River, Tahuya River Horse Camp is good base for trips into Tahuya State Forest. The nearby trails can be used by hikers, horses, or motorbikes. Fishing is another recreation option here.

Location: On the Tahuya River in Tahuya State Forest; map A2, grid j2.

Campsites, facilities: There are nine primitive campsites for tents or small trailers. Picnic tables, fire grills, and tent pads are provided. Vault toilets, drinking water, and equestrian facilities are available. Leashed pets and motorbikes are permitted.

Reservations, fees: Call the park for an update on seasonal closures and any gate information. There is no fee. A free map and brochure are available; see the contact information below.

Directions: From Tacoma on Interstate 5, drive to the junction with Highway 16. Turn north on Highway 16 and drive about 30 miles to Bremerton and Highway 3. Turn south on Highway 3 and drive eight miles southwest to the town of Belfair and Highway 300. Turn west on Highway 300 west and drive one-third of a mile. Bear left and continue for 3.3 miles to Belfair-Tahuya Road. Turn right on Belfair-Tahuya Road and drive 1.7 miles to Spillman Road. Turn right on Spillman Road and drive two miles, and then turn left and drive three-quarters of a mile to the campground.

Contact: Department of Natural Resources, South Puget Sound Region, P.O. Box 68, Enumclaw, WA 98022-0068; tel. (360) 825-1631, fax (360) 825-1672.

123 Howell Lake   8

Nestled along Lake Howell, this pretty spot managed by the Department of Natural Resources doesn't get a lot of use. But it's a great deal, with water, scenery, and a boat launch, plus trails for hikers, horses, and motorbikes-and very few people.
Location: In Tahuya State Forest; map A2, grid j2.
Campsites, facilities: There are six campsites for tents or small trailers. Picnic tables, fire grills, and tent pads are provided. Vault toilets and drinking water are available. A boat launch for small craft is located at Howell Lake. Leashed pets and motorbikes are permitted.
Reservations, fees: Call the park for an update on seasonal closures and any gate information. There is no fee. A free map and brochure are available; see the contact information below.
Directions: From Tacoma on Interstate 5, drive to the junction with Highway 16. Turn north on Highway 16 and drive about 30 miles to Bremerton and Highway 3. Turn south on Highway 3 and drive eight miles southwest to the town of Belfair and Highway 300. Turn west on Highway 300 west and drive one-third of a mile. Then bear left and continue for 3.3 miles to Belfair-Tahuya Road. Turn right on Belfair-Tahuya Road and drive 4.5 miles to the campground.
Contact: Department of Natural Resources, South Puget Sound Region, P.O. Box 68, Enumclaw, WA 98022-0068; tel. (360) 825-1631, fax (360) 825-1672.

124 Robin Hood Village   5

This wooded park, an option near Toonerville Multiple Use Area and Howell Lake, has access to the Hood Canal. Nearby recreation options include an 18-hole golf course.
Location: Near the Hood Canal; map A2, grid j2.
Campsites, facilities: There are four tent sites and 16 sites for trailers or RVs of any length. Electricity, drinking water, sewer and cable TV hookups, and picnic tables are provided. Toilets, showers, a restaurant, an espresso stand, a liquor store, massage therapist, and laundry room are available. Bottled gas, sanitary services, a store and ice can be found within one mile. Boat docks and launching facilities are located in the park. Leashed pets are permitted.
Reservations, fees: Reservations accepted. Sites are $18-22 per night. Open year-round.
Directions: From Tacoma drive northeast on Highway 16 for about 30 miles to Bremerton and Highway 3. Turn south on Highway 3 and drive eight miles southwest to the town of Belfair and Highway 106. Bear southeast on Highway 106 and drive 13 miles to the campground at East 6780 Highway 106 along Hood Canal.
Contact: Robin Hood Village, East 6780 Highway 106, Union, WA 98592; tel. (360) 898-2163, fax (360) 898-2164.

125 Twin Lakes   7

Free and quiet, this wooded campground is in Tahuya State Forest and managed by the Department of Natural Resources. The fishing can be decent, and other highlights include privacy, shady sites, lake views, and even a boat ramp. Don't forget to bring water.

Location: In Tahuya State Forest; map A2, grid j1.

Campsites, facilities: There are six primitive campsites for tents or small trailers. Picnic tables, fire grills, and tent pads are provided. Vault toilets are available, but there is no drinking water. A hand launch for small boats can be found at the lake. Leashed pets are permitted.

Reservations, fees: Call the park for an update on seasonal closures and any gate information. There is no fee. A free map and brochure are available; see the contact information below.

Directions: From Tacoma on Interstate 5, drive to the junction with Highway 16. Turn north on Highway 16 and drive about 30 miles to Bremerton and Highway 3. Turn south on Highway 3 and drive eight miles southwest to the town of Belfair and Highway 300. Turn west on Highway 300 west and drive one-third of a mile, then bear left and continue for 3.3 miles to Belfair-Tahuya Road. Turn right on Belfair-Tahuya Road and drive one-half mile to Elfendahl Pass Road. Turn right on Elfendahl Pass Road and drive 2.5 miles to Twin Lakes Road. Turn left on Twin Lakes Road and drive 1.7 miles. Then turn right and drive one-half mile to the camp.

Contact: Department of Natural Resources, South Puget Sound Region, P.O. Box 68, Enumclaw, WA 98022-0068; tel. (360) 825-1631, fax (360) 825-1672.

126 Camp Spillman   7

Camp Spillman is one of four campgrounds (along with Tahuya River Horse Camp, Howell Lake, and Twin Lakes) set in the immediate vicinity of Tahuya State Forest. This one sits along the Tahuya River, with wooded riverside sites and trails for hikers, horses, and motorbikes.

Location: On the Tahuya River in Tahuya State Forest; map A2, grid j2.

Campsites, facilities: There are six primitive campsites for tents or small trailers. Picnic tables, fire grills, and tent pads are provided. Vault toilets and drinking water are available. Leashed pets and motorbikes are permitted.

Reservations, fees: Call the park for an update on seasonal closures and any gate information. There is no fee. A free map and brochure are available; see the contact information below.

Directions: From Tacoma on Interstate 5, drive to the junction with Highway 16. Turn north on Highway 16 and drive about 30 miles to Bremerton and Highway 3. Turn south on Highway 3 and drive eight miles southwest to the town of Belfair and Highway 300. Turn west on Highway 300 and drive one-third of a mile. Then bear left and continue for 3.3 miles to Belfair-Tahuya Road. Turn right on Belfair-Tahuya Road and drive one-half mile to Elfendahl Pass Road. Turn right on Elfendahl Pass

Road and drive 2.5 miles to Twin Lakes Road. Turn left and drive two-thirds of a mile to the camp.

Contact: Department of Natural Resources, South Puget Sound Region, P.O. Box 68, Enumclaw, WA 98022-0068; tel. (360) 825-1631, fax (360) 825-1672.

127 Gig Harbor RV Resort   7

This is a popular layover spot for folks heading up to Bremerton. Just a short jaunt off the highway, it's pleasant, clean, and friendly. An 18-hole golf course, a full-service marina, and tennis courts are located nearby. Look for the great view of Mount Rainier from the end of the harbor.

Location: Near Tacoma; map A2, grid j5.

Campsites, facilities: There are 100 sites for trailers or RVs of any length; 28 are pull-through sites. Electricity, drinking water, cable TV and sewer hookups are provided. Bottled gas, sanitary services, toilets, showers, a clubroom, a store, a laundry room, ice, a playground, a sports field, and a heated swimming pool are available. Leashed pets are permitted.

Reservations, fees: Reservations recommended in the summer. Sites are $28-31 per night. Major credit cards accepted. Open year-round.

Directions: From Tacoma drive northwest on Highway 16 for 12 miles northwest to Burnham Drive/North Rosedale exit. Take that exit and continue to the stop sign at Burnham Drive. Turn right on Burnham Drive and drive one mile to the campground on the left.

Contact: Gig Harbor RV Resort, 9515 Burnham Drive NW, Gig Harbor, WA 98332; tel. (800) 526-8311, (253) 858-8138; fax (253) 858-8399.

128 Dash Point State Park   8

This urban state park has beach access, plus an 18-hole golf course and marked hiking trails nearby. Tacoma offers a variety of activities and attractions, including the Tacoma Art Museum (with a children's gallery); the Washington State Historical Society Museum; the Seymour Botanical Conservatory at Wrights Park; Point Defiance Park, Zoo, and Aquarium; the Western Washington Forest Industries Museum; and the Fort Lewis Military Museum. The Old Town area along the waterfront has been renovated, and there are two public fishing piers there.

Location: Near Tacoma; map A2, grid j5.

Campsites, facilities: There are 110 tent sites and 28 sites for trailers or RVs up to 35 feet long. Water and electrical hookups are available. Picnic tables are provided. Flush toilets, a sanitary disposal station, a playground, electricity, drinking water, showers, and firewood are available. Leashed pets are permitted.

Reservations, fees: Reservations accepted; phone (800) 452-5687 ($6 reservation fee). Sites are $5-15 per night. Open year-round.

Directions: At the junction of Highway 99 and Highway 509 in Federal Way (between Seattle and Tacoma), turn west on Highway 509. Drive west for five miles to the park on the right.

Contact: Dash Point State Park, 5700 West Dash Point Road, Federal Way, WA 98003; tel. (800) 233-0321, (253) 593-2206.

129 Saltwater State Park   10

Set on the edge of Seattle and beautiful Puget Sound, Saltwater is a nice state park for tent or RV campers. There are beautiful views of Maury and Vashon Islands and of the Olympic Mountains. Beaches offer clamming and picnic facilities, and scuba diving is a popular pastime. There are also foot trails that lead through Kent Smith Canyon. Sorely Creek runs through the park.

Location: Near Seattle; map A2, grid j6.

Campsites, facilities: There are 52 sites for tents or self-contained RVs up to 50 feet long. Picnic tables and fire grills are provided. Flush toilets, a sanitary disposal station, showers, a playground, and firewood are available. A store, a restaurant, and ice are located within one mile. Some facilities are wheelchair accessible. Boat buoys are nearby on Puget Sound. Leashed pets are permitted.

Reservaions, fees: No reservations. Sites are $10 per night. Open late March through early September.

Directions: From the junction of Interstate 5 and Highway 516 (located between Seattle and Tacoma three miles south of SeaTac International Airport), take Highway 516 and drive west for two miles to Highway 509. Turn left and drive one mile to the park access road on the right. Turn right (well signed) and drive a half mile to the park on the shore of Puget Sound.

Contact: Saltwater State Park, 25205 Eighth Place South, Des Moines, WA 98198; tel. (800) 233-0321, (206) 764-4128.

130 Game Farm Wilderness Park   6

The Game Farm Wilderness Park is just minutes from downtown Auburn. Located along the scenic Stuck River, it was designed with group outings in mind. Mount Rainier, the Seattle waterfront, and the Cascade Mountains are all only a short drive away.

Location: On the Stuck River in Auburn; map A2, grid j8.

Campsites, facilities: There are six group campsites for tents, trailers, and RVs, each with water and power hookups, a fire ring, and a picnic table. There are four sleeping units per site. Campers also have access to an open-air shelter during their stay. A dump station and rest rooms are located on site. Leashed pets are permitted.

Reservations, fees: Reservations required. Group sites are $25 per night for city residents and $35 for nonresidents. Open the first working day in January for residents, the first working day of February for nonresidents. The park closes at the end of October.

Directions: On Interstate 5 drive to Exit 142 and Highway 18. Turn east on Highway 18 and drive to the Auburn/Enumclaw exit. Take that exit and drive to the light at Auburn Way. Turn left on Auburn Way South and drive one mile to Howard Road. Exit to the right on Howard Road and drive to the stop sign at R Street. Turn right on R Street and drive 1.5 miles to Stuck River Drive SE (just over the river). Turn left and drive one-quarter mile upriver to the park on the left at 2401 Stuck River Drive.

Contact: City of Auburn Parks and Recreation Department, 25 West Main Street, Auburn, WA 98001; tel. (253) 931-3043.

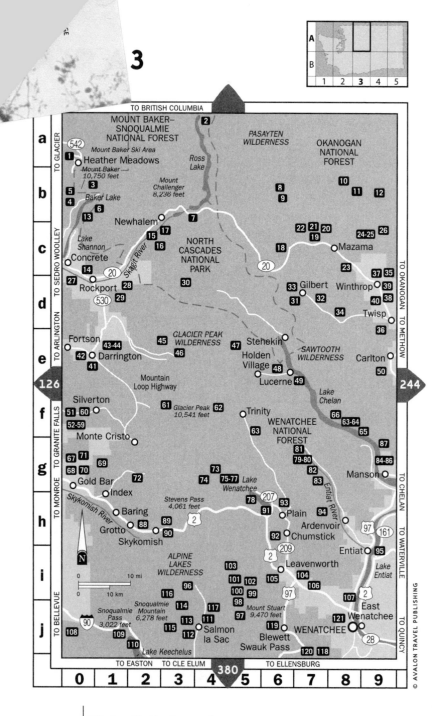

3

TO BRITISH COLUMBIA

MOUNT BAKER–
SNOQUALMIE
NATIONAL FOREST

PASAYTEN
WILDERNESS

OKANOGAN
NATIONAL
FOREST

a

TO GLACIER

542

Mount Baker Ski Area

1 Heather Meadows

Mount Baker
10,750 feet

3

Ross
Lake

Mount
Challenger
8,236 feet

2

10

b

5

4

Baker Lake

6

8

9

11   12

13

Newhalem

7

c

TO SEDRO WOOLLEY

Lake
Shannon

15   17

16

Skagit River

NORTH
CASCADES
NATIONAL
PARK

18

22 21 20
    19

24-25   26

Mazama

Concrete

14

20

23

37 35
39

d

TO ARLINGTON

27

Rockport   28

530   29

30

33 Gilbert
31   32

34

Winthrop

40   38

Twisp

36

e

Fortson

43-44

42 Darrington
41

GLACIER PEAK
WILDERNESS

45

46

47 Stehekin

Holden
Village

48

Lucerne 49

SAWTOOTH
WILDERNESS

Carlton

50

126

Mountain
Loop Highway

Lake
Chelan

244

f

TO GRANITE FALLS

Silverton

51 60
52-59

61 Glacier Peak
   10,541 feet

62

Monte Cristo

Trinity

63

WENATCHEE
NATIONAL
FOREST

66

63-64
65

87

84-86

g

TO MONROE

67 71
68 70

69

72

Gold Bar

73

74

75-77 Lake
Wenatchee

81
79-80

82

83

Manson

TO CHELAN

h

Skykomish River

Index

Baring

Grotto   88   89

Skykomish   90

Stevens Pass
4,061 feet

2

78

207

91

93

Plain

Ardenvoir
Chumstick

94

Entiat River

97   161

TO WATERVILLE

N

0   10 mi
0   10 km

ALPINE
LAKES
WILDERNESS

103

101 102

116   96

114

117

113 111

115 112

100 99
98

97

Mount Stuart
9,470 feet

92

2   209

Leavenworth

105

104

106

97

107

Entiat   95

Lake
Entiat

2 East
   Wenatchee

© AVALON TRAVEL PUBLISHING

i

TO BELLEVUE

90   Snoqualmie
     Pass
     3,022 feet

108

109

110 Lake Keechelus

Snoqualmie
Mountain
6,278 feet

Salmon
la Sac

119 121

WENATCHEE

120 118

TO QUINCY

j

Blewett
Swauk Pass

28

380

TO EASTON   TO CLE ELUM   TO ELLENSBURG

| 0 | 1 | 2 | 3 | 4 | 5 | 6 | 7 | 8 | 9 |

CHAPTER A3

1 Silver Fir 9

This campground is set on the North Fork of the Nooksack River just a short distance from the North Fork Nooksack Research Natural Area. Fishing is available nearby, and in the winter the area becomes a cross-country ski area. You're strongly advised to obtain a U.S. Forest Service map in order to take maximum advantage of the recreational opportunities in the area.

Location: On the North Fork of the Nooksack River in Mount Baker-Snoqualmie National Forest; map A3, grid a0.

Campsites, facilities: There are 20 sites for tents, trailers, or RVs up to 21 feet long. Picnic tables and barbecue grills are provided. Drinking water, vault toilets, and a group picnic shelter are available. Leashed pets are permitted.

Reservations, fees: Reservations accepted; phone (877) 444-6777 or access the website: www.reserveusa.com ($8.65 reservation fee). Sites are $12 per night. Open May through September.

Directions: From Interstate 5 at Bellingham, turn east on Highway 542 and drive 31 miles to Glacier. Continue east on Highway 542 for 12.5 miles to the campground on the right.

Contact: Mount Baker-Snoqualmie National Forest, Mount Baker Ranger District, 2105 Highway 20, Sedro-Woolley, WA 98284; tel. (360) 856-5700; fax (360) 856-1934.

2 Hozomeen 9

Hozomeen campground is just inside the U.S./Canada border at the north end of Ross Lake, at 1,600 feet elevation. It takes quite an effort to get here, which tends to weed out all but the most stalwart campers. This is good news for those few, for they will find a quiet, uncrowded camp in a beautiful setting.

Location: On Ross Lake in Ross Lake National Recreation Area; map A3, grid a4.

Campsites, facilities: There are 122 sites for tents or RVs up to 22 feet long. Picnic tables and fireplaces are provided. No garbage service; pack out refuse. Pit toilets, drinking water, and a boat launch on Ross Lake are available. Leashed pets are permitted.

Reservations, fees: No reservations; no fee. Open late May through October.

Directions: This campground is accessible only through Canada. From the town of Hope, B.C., turn south on Silver-Skagit Road. Drive south for 39 miles to the campground at the north end of Ross Lake. It is a narrow dirt/gravel road, often rough.

Contact: North Cascades National Park Headquarters, 2105 Highway 20, Sedro-Woolley, WA 98284; tel. (360) 856-5700.

3 Park Creek 6

This pretty camp, set at 800 feet amid a heavily wooded area, is on Park Creek a short distance from the north shore of Baker Lake. It's primitive and small but gets its fair share of use.

Location: Near Baker Lake in Mount Baker-Snoqualmie National Forest; map A3, grid b0.

Campsites, facilities: There are 12 sites for tents or small RVs. Picnic tables are provided. Vault toilets are available, but there is no drinking water. Boat docks, launching facilities, and rentals are nearby on Baker Lake. Leashed pets are permitted.

Reservations, fees: Reservations required; phone (877) 444-6777 or access the website: www.reserveusa.com ($8.65 reservation fee). Sites are $7 per night. Open mid-May to early September.

Directions: From Interstate 5 at Burlington, turn east on Highway 20 and drive approximately 24 miles to Milepost 82 and Baker Lake Highway (Forest Road 11). Turn north on Baker Lake Highway and drive about 19.5 miles to Forest Road 1144. Turn northwest and drive about 200 yards to the campground. A U.S. Forest Service map is helpful.

Contact: Mount Baker-Snoqualmie National Forest, Mount Baker Ranger District, 2105 Highway 20, Sedro-Woolley, WA 98284; tel. (360) 856-5700; fax (360) 856-1934.

4 Panorama Point   9

Panorama Point is a well-maintained campground on the northwest shore of Baker Lake. The reservoir is one of the better fishing lakes in the area. The camp is true to its name, with incredible scenic views. Hiking trails are nearby.

Location: On Baker Lake in Mount Baker-Snoqualmie National Forest; map A3, grid b0.

Campsites, facilities: There are 16 sites for tents, trailers, or RVs up to 21 feet long. Picnic tables are provided. Well water and vault toilets are available. A store and ice are located within one mile. A boat ramp is adjacent to the camp. Boat docks and rentals are nearby. Leashed pets are permitted.

Reservations, fees: Reservations accepted for some sites; phone (877) 444-6777 or access the website: www.reserveusa.com ($8.65 reservation fee). Sites are $12 per night. Open May to mid-September.

Directions: From Interstate 5 at Burlington, turn east on Highway 20 and drive approximately 24 miles to Milepost 82 and Baker Lake Highway (Forest Road 11). Turn north on Baker Lake Highway and drive 18.7 miles to the campground entrance on the right on the shore of Baker.

Contact: Mount Baker-Snoqualmie National Forest, Mount Baker Ranger District, 2105 Highway 20, Sedro-Woolley, WA 98284; tel. (360) 856-5700; fax (360) 856-1934.

5 Boulder Creek   8

An alternative to Horseshoe Cove, this campground is set on Boulder Creek about one mile from the shore of Baker Lake. A boat launch is located at Panorama Point. Wild berries can be found in the area in season. The campground offers prime views of Mount Baker.

Location: Near Baker Lake in Mount Baker-Snoqualmie National Forest; map A3, grid b0.

Campsites, facilities: There are eight tent sites and two group sites. Picnic tables and fire grills are provided. Pit toilets are available, but there is no drinking water. Boat docks and launching facilities are nearby on Baker Lake. Leashed pets are permitted.

Reservations, fees: Reservations required for group sites and are available for some family sites; phone (877) 444-6777 or access the website: www.reserveusa.com ($8.65 reservation fee). Family sites are $7 per night; group sites are $55 per night. Open mid-May to early September.

Directions: From Interstate 5 at Burlington, turn east on Highway 20 and drive approximately 24 miles to Milepost 82 and Baker Lake Highway (Forest Road 11). Turn north on Baker Lake Highway and drive 17.4 miles to the campground on the right.

Contact: Mount Baker-Snoqualmie National Forest, Mount Baker Ranger District, 2105 Highway 20, Sedro-Woolley, WA 98284; tel. (360) 856-5700; fax (360) 856-1934.

6 Maple Grove Hike-In, Boat-In   9

Looking for a quiet spot on the edge of a lake? Except on summer weekends when there is a lot of water sports activity, here it is. This rustic campground is on the shore of Baker Lake and is hike-in or boat-in only. Privacy and great mountain views are your reward for the extra effort, and it's all free.

Location: On Baker Lake in Mount Baker-Snoqualmie National Forest; map A3, grid b1.

Campsites, facilities: There are five primitive tent sites that are only accessible by boat or on foot. Picnic tables are provided. There is no drinking water. Boat launching facilities are located nearby on Baker Lake. Leashed pets are permitted.

Reservations, fees: No reservations; no fee. Open year-round.

Directions: From Interstate 5 at Burlington, turn east on Highway 20 and drive approximately 24 miles to Milepost 82 and Baker Lake Highway (Forest Road 11). Turn north on Baker Lake Highway and drive 13.3 miles to Forest Road 1106. Turn east (right) on Forest Road 1106 and drive across Baker Dam to Forest Road 1107. Turn left and drive one-half mile to the parking area and the trailhead on the left. To reach the camp by boat, launch at one of the campgrounds on the west side of the lake (Horseshoe Cove is the closest) or take Trail 610 (Baker Lake Trail) and walk in four miles to the camp. A U.S. Forest Service map is recommended.

Contact: Mount Baker-Snoqualmie National Forest, Mount Baker Ranger District, 2105 Highway 20, Sedro-Woolley, WA 98284; tel. (360) 856-5700; fax (360) 856-1934.

7 Colonial Creek Campground   7

Colonial Creek Campground (elevation 1,200 feet) sits along the shore of Diablo Lake in the Ross Lake National Recreation Area. The five-mile-long lake offers many hiking and fishing possibilities. A naturalist program and guided walks are available during the summer months.

Location: On Diablo Lake in Ross Lake National Recreation Area; map A3, grid b3.

Campsites, facilities: There are 164 campsites for tents or trailers, including a few walk-in tent sites. Eighteen lakefront sites remain open through the winter, but no services are available. Picnic tables and fireplaces are provided. Flush toilets, drinking water, a dump station, three boat docks, and a boat ramp are available. Some facilities are wheelchair accessible. Leashed pets are permitted.

Reservations, fees: No reservations accepted. Sites are $10 per night. Open mid-April to mid-October; 18 lakefront sites are open through the winter (no services).

Directions: From Interstate 5 at Burlington, take Exit 230 and drive east to Highway 20. Turn east on Highway 20, drive 46 miles to Marblemount, and continue east on Highway 20 for 24 miles to the campground entrance.

Contact: North Cascades National Park Headquarters, 2105 Highway 20, Sedro-Woolley, WA 98284; tel. (360) 856-5700.

8 Harts Pass  10

This pretty little campground is near the Pasayten Wilderness, which offers 500 miles of trails leading to alpine meadows and glacier-fed lakes and streams, and along ridges to spectacular mountain heights. Slate Peak, just above Harts Pass, is the highest point above sea level in Washington State. Contact the district ranger for details. The Pacific Crest Trail passes near the camp and offers a great view of the northern Cascade Range.

Location: Near the Pasayten Wilderness in Okanogan National Forest; map A3, grid b6.

Campsites, facilities: There are five walk-in tent sites. Picnic tables and fire grills are provided. Vault toilets are available, but there is no drinking water or garbage service; pack out refuse. Leashed pets are permitted.

Reservations, fees: No reservations accepted. Overnight parking requires a $25 annual pass or $5 per night ($10 for three nights). Open mid-July to late September.

Directions: From Burlington drive east on Highway 20 and for 120 miles to Mazama Road. Turn left on Mazama Road and drive one-quarter mile to County Road 9140. Turn left and drive northwest for seven miles to Lost River, where the pavement ends and the road soon becomes Forest Road 5400. Continue on Forest Road 5400 for 12.5 miles northwest to the campground. Note: The road to Harts Pass beyond Ballard Campground is rough and closed to trailers.

Contact: Okanogan National Forest, Methow Valley Visitor Center, P.O. Box 579, Winthrop, WA 98862; tel. (509) 996-4000; fax (509) 997-9770.

9 Meadows 9

This campground is about one mile from Harts Pass and offers the same opportunities. It is set adjacent to the Pacific Crest Trail. In summer, the camp is beautiful, set in an area of spruce and subalpine fir, with lots of wildflowers in the spring.

Location: Near the Pacific Crest Trail in Okanogan National Forest; map A3, grid b6.

Campsites, facilities: There are 14 tent sites. Picnic tables and fire grills are provided. Vault toilets are available, but there is no drinking water or garbage service; pack out refuse. Leashed pets are permitted.

Reservations, fees: No reservations accepted. Overnight parking requires a $25 annual pass or $5 per night ($10 for three nights). Open mid-July to late September.

Directions: From Burlington drive east on Highway 20 and for 120 miles to Mazama Road. Turn left on Mazama Road and drive one-quarter mile to County Road 9140. Turn left and drive northwest for seven miles to Lost River, where the pavement ends and the road soon becomes Forest Road 5400. Continue on Forest Road 5400 for 12.5 miles Forest Road 5400-500. Turn south (left) and drive one mile to the campground.

Contact: Okanogan National Forest, Methow Valley Visitor Center, P.O. Box 579, Winthrop, WA 98862; tel. (509) 996-4000; fax (509) 997-9770.

10 Honeymoon   8

This campground is set at 3,300 feet along Eightmile Creek. If you continue north seven miles to the end of Forest Road 5130, you'll reach a trailhead providing access to the Pasayten Wilderness. See a U.S. Forest Service map for details. Why is it named Honeymoon? Well, seems a forest ranger and his bride chose this very quiet and secluded spot along the creek to spend their wedding night.

Location: On Eightmile Creek in Okanogan National Forest; map A3, grid b8.

Campsites, facilities: There are six sites for tents, trailers, or small RVs up to 18 feet long. Picnic tables and fire grills are provided. Vault toilets are available, but there is no drinking water or garbage service; pack out refuse. Leashed pets are permitted.

Reservations, fees: No reservations accepted. Overnight parking requires a $25 annual pass or $5 per night ($10 for three nights). Open June to late September.

Directions: From Burlington drive east on Highway 20 and for 134 miles to Winthrop and County Road 1213/West Chewuch Road. Turn north on County Road 1213/West Chewuch Road and drive 6.5 miles (where it merges with Forest Road 5130. Continue north on Forest Road 5130 for 10 miles to the campground on the right.

Contact: Okanogan National Forest, Methow Valley Visitor Center, P.O. Box 579, Winthrop, WA 98862; tel. (509) 996-4000; fax (509) 997-9770.

11 Chewuch    6

Set along the Chewuch River, this campground is a more primitive alternative to nearby Falls Creek. Fishing is a highlight, and by traveling north, you can access trailheads that lead into the Pasayten Wilderness. See a U.S. Forest Service map for specific locations.

Location: On the Chewuch River in Okanogan National Forest; map A3, grid b8.

Campsites, facilities: There are two tent sites and two sites for trailers up to 16 feet long. Fire grills are provided. Vault toilets are available. There is no drinking water or garbage service; pack out refuse. Leashed pets are permitted.

Reservations, fees: No reservations. Overnight parking requires a $25 annual pass or $5 per night ($10 for three nights). Open June to late September.

Directions: From Burlington drive east on Highway 20 for 134 miles to Winthrop and County Road 1213/West Chewuch Road. Turn north on County Road 1213/West Chewuch Road and drive 6.5 miles (where it merges with Forest Road 51. Continue north on Forest Road 51 for seven miles to the campground on the right.

Contact: Okanogan National Forest, Methow Valley Visitor Center, P.O. Box 579, Winthrop, WA 98862; tel. (509) 996-4000; fax (509) 997-9770.

12 Camp 4    6

Camp 4 is the smallest and most primitive of the three camps along the Chewuch River (the others are Chewuch and Falls Creek). There are three trailheads five miles north of camp: two at Lake Creek and another at Andrews Creek. They all have corrals, hitching rails, truck docks, and water for the stock at the trailheads, but no live stock are permitted in the campground itself. Trails leading into the Pasayten

Wilderness leave from both locations. Contact the U.S. Forest Service for details.

Location: On the Chewuch River in Okanogan National Forest; map A3, grid b9.

Campsites, facilities: There are five tent sites. Fire grills are provided. Vault toilets are available, but there is no drinking water or garbage service; pack out refuse. Leashed pets are permitted, but no livestock are permitted in camp.

Reservations, fees: No reservations. Overnight parking requires a $25 annual pass or $5 per night ($10 for three nights). Open June to late September.

Directions: From Burlington drive east on Highway 20 for 134 miles to Winthrop and County Road 1213/West Chewuch Road. Turn north on County Road 1213/West Chewuch Road and drive 6.5 miles (where it merges with Forest Road 51. Continue north on Forest Road 51 for 11 miles to the campground on the right.

Contact: Okanogan National Forest, Methow Valley Visitor Center, P.O. Box 579, Winthrop, WA 98862; tel. (509) 996-4000; fax (509) 997-9770.

13 Horseshoe Cove   9

Anglers will find good fishing at this campground set on the shore of 5,000-acre Baker Lake, where rainbow trout, kokanee salmon, cutthroat trout, and Dolly Varden trout await. Other highlights are swimming access from the campground and a boat ramp. Some hiking trails can be found nearby.

Location: On Baker Lake in Mount Baker-Snoqualmie National Forest; map A3, grid b0.

Campsites, facilities: There are eight sites for tents only and 34 sites for tents, trailers, or RVs up to 25 feet long. Picnic tables are provided. Drinking water and flush toilets are available. A boat ramp is adjacent to camp. Leashed pets are permitted.

Reservations, fees: Reservations accepted for some sites, phone (877) 444-6777 or access the website: www.reserveusa.com ($8.65 reservation fee). Sites are $10 per night. Open May through September; one loop remains open through the off-season on a no service, no fee basis.

Directions: From Interstate 5 at Burlington, turn east on Highway 20 and drive approximately 24 miles to Milepost 82 and the Baker Lake Highway (Forest Road 11). Turn north on Baker Lake Highway and drive about 14.8 miles to Forest Road 1118. Turn east on Forest Road 1118 and drive two miles to the campground. A U.S. Forest Service map is recommended.

Contact: Mount Baker-Snoqualmie National Forest, Mount Baker Ranger District, 2105 Highway 20, Sedro-Woolley, WA 98284; tel. (360) 856-5700; fax (360) 856-1934.

14 Rockport State Park   8

This state park covers 457 acres and offers five miles of hiking trails and four Adirondack (three-sided, roofed) shelters. The campground is set among old-growth Douglas firs and is near the Skagit River, a good steelhead stream.

Location: Near the Skagit River; map A3, grid c0.

Campsites, facilities: There are three primitive tent sites, eight developed, walk-in tent sites, and 50 sites with full hookups for trailers or RVs up to 60 feet long. There is also one group tent site. Picnic tables and fire grills are provided. Flush toilets, a sanitary disposal station, and drinking water are available. Showers and firewood are available for a fee. Some facilities are wheelchair accessible. A store, gas, and ice are located within one mile. Leashed pets are permitted.

Reservations, fees: Reservations required for the group site only, phone (360) 853-8461. Sites are $5-15 per night. The group site is $25, plus $1 per person per night. Open April to late October.

Directions: From Interstate 5 at Burlington, turn east on Highway 20 and drive 33 miles to Concrete. Continue east on Highway 20 for seven miles to the park (one mile west of Rockport).

Contact: Rockport State Park, 5051 Highway 20, Concrete, WA 98237; tel. (360) 853-8461.

15 Goodell Creek Campground   7

Goodell Creek Campground is an alternative to the nearby and larger Newhalem Creek Campground. This one is set at 500 feet elevation where Goodell Creek pours into the Skagit River in the Ross Lake National Recreation Area. It's a popular put-in site for raft trips downriver.

Location: On Goodell Creek and the Skagit River in Ross Lake National Recreation Area; map A3, grid c2.

Campsites, facilities: There are 21 campsites for tents or RVs up to 22 feet long and two group sites (Upper and Lower Goodell). Picnic tables and fire rings are provided. Pit toilets are available. Drinking water is available in the family sites, but not in the group sites. Leashed pets are permitted.

Reservations, fees: Reservations required for group sites only; phone (360) 873-4590, extension 16, for group reservations and fee information. No reservations accepted for family sites. Family sites are $10 per night. Open year-round, but there are no services (and also no fees) in the winter.

Directions: On Interstate 5 drive to Exit 230/Highway 20 at Burlington. Turn east on Highway 20, and drive 46 miles to Marblemount. Continue on Highway 20 for 13 miles east to the campground entrance.

Contact: North Cascades National Park Headquarters, 2105 Highway 20, Sedro-Woolley, WA 98284; tel. (360) 856-5700.

16 Marble Creek   7

This primitive campground is set on Marble Creek. Continuing on Forest Road 1530 will take you up to Bush Lake. A trailhead to Hidden Lake just inside the boundary of North Cascades National Park can be found about five miles from camp at the end of Forest Road 1540. See a U.S. Forest Service map for details.

Location: On Marble Creek in Mount Baker-Snoqualmie National Forest; map A3, grid c2.

Campsites, facilities: There are 24 sites for tents, trailers, or RVs up to 22 feet long. Picnic tables and fire grills are provided. Vault toilets are available, but there is no drinking water. Leashed pets are permitted.

Reservations, fees: No reservations; no fee. Open mid-May to mid-September.

Directions: From Interstate 5 drive to Exit 230/Highway 20 at Burlington. Turn east on Highway 20, and drive 46 miles to Marblemount and Forest Road 15 (Cascade River Road). Cross the bridge, turn east on Cascade River Road, and drive eight miles to Forest Road 1530. Turn south on Forest Road 1530 and drive one mile to the campground. A U.S. Forest Service map is advised.

Contact: Mount Baker-Snoqualmie National Forest, Mount Baker Ranger District, 2105 Highway 20, Sedro-Woolley, WA 98284; tel. (360) 856-5700; fax (360) 856-1934.

🔳 Newhalem Creek Campground   7

This spot is set along the Skagit River west of Newhalem at 500 feet elevation. Good hiking possibilities abound in the immediate area, and naturalist programs are available. Be sure to visit the North Cascades Visitor Center at the top of the hill from the campground. If full, try Goodell Creek Campground, located just one mile west on Highway 20.

Location: Near the Skagit River in Ross Lake National Recreation Area; map A3, grid c3.

Campsites, facilities: There are 129 sites for tents or RVs up to 32 feet long. Picnic tables and fireplaces are provided. Flush toilets, drinking water, and a sanitary dump station are available. Some facilities are wheelchair accessible. Leashed pets are permitted.

Reservations, fees: No reservations. Sites are $12 per night. Open mid-May to mid-October.

Directions: On Interstate 5 drive to Exit 230/Highway 20 at Burlington. Turn east on Highway 20, and drive 46 miles to Marblemount. Continue 14 miles east on Highway 20 to the camp.

Contact: North Cascades National Park Headquarters, 2105 Highway 20, Sedro-Woolley, WA 98284; tel. (360) 856-5700.

🔳 Lone Fir   9

Lone Fir is set at 3,800 feet along the banks of Early Winters Creek. To the west is Washington Pass Overlook, which offers a spectacular view. Anglers can fish in the creek, and many hiking trails crisscross the area. A U.S. Forest Service map will provide details. A loop trail through the campground woods is wheelchair accessible for four-tenths of a mile. See the description of Early Winters for more information.

Location: On Early Winters Creek in Okanogan National Forest; map A3, grid c6.

Campsites, facilities: There are 27 sites for tents, trailers, or RVs up to 21 feet long. Drinking water, fire grills, garbage service, and picnic tables are provided. Vault toilets are available. Leashed pets are permitted.

Reservations, fees: No reservations; no camping fee. Overnight parking requires a $25 annual pass or $5 daily fee per vehicle. Open June to late September.

Directions: From Burlington drive east on Highway 20 for 107 miles to the campground (11 miles west of Mazama).

Contact: Okanogan National Forest, Methow Valley Visitor Center, P.O. Box 579, Winthrop, WA 98862; tel. (509) 996-4000; fax (509) 997-9770.

19 Early Winters   6

The confluence of Early Winters Creek and the Methow River mark the site of this campground. Several hiking trails can be found in the area, including one that leads south to Cedar Creek Falls. Other possible side trips are Goat Wall to the north and the town of Winthrop to the south, which boasts a historical museum, a state fish hatchery, and Pearrygin Lake State Park. Early Winters Information Center is adjacent to the camp and can provide detailed information.

Location: On Early Winters Creek in Okanogan National Forest; map A3, grid c7.

Campsites, facilities: There are seven tent sites and six sites for tents, trailers, or RVs up to 24 feet long. Drinking water, fire grills, garbage service, and picnic tables are provided. Vault toilets are available. There is a small store and snack bar in Mazama, about two miles away. Leashed pets are permitted.

Reservations, fees: No reservations; no camping fee. Overnight parking requires a $25 annual pass or $5 daily fee per vehicle. Open June through October, weather permitting.

Directions: From Burlington drive east on Highway 20 for 116 miles to the campground (if you reach County Road 1163 near Mazama, you have gone two miles too far).

Contact: Okanogan National Forest, Methow Valley Visitor Center, P.O. Box 579, Winthrop, WA 98862; tel. (509) 996-4000; fax (509) 997-9770.

20 Ballard   6

Ballard is located at an elevation of 2,600 feet, about half a mile from River Bend. A hitching rail and stock truck dock are available at the Robinson Creek Trailhead near the campground, where there are several primitive sites. Stock are not permitted in the campground, however. Numerous hiking trails can be found in the area, including one that heads west and eventually hooks up with the Pacific Crest Trail. See the description of Early Winters Campground for area information.

Location: Near the Methow River in Okanogan National Forest; map A3, grid c7.

Campsites, facilities: There are seven tent sites. Picnic tables and fire grills are provided. Vault toilets are available, but there is no drinking water or garbage service; pack out refuse. Leashed pets are permitted. No livestock is permitted in camp.

Reservations, fees: No reservations; no camping fee. Overnight parking requires a $25 annual pass or $5 daily fee per vehicle. Open June through October, weather permitting.

Directions: From Burlington drive east on Highway 20 for 120 miles to Mazama Road. Turn left on Mazama Road and drive one-quarter mile to County Road 9140. Turn left and drive northwest for seven miles to Lost River, where the pavement ends and the road soon becomes Forest Road 5400. Continue northwest on Forest Road 5400 for two miles to the campground on the left.

Contact: Okanogan National Forest, Methow Valley Visitor Center, P.O. Box 579, Winthrop, WA 98862; tel. (509) 996-4000; fax (509) 997-9770.

21 River Bend   6

This campground is located along the Methow River about two miles from the boundary of the Pasayten Wilderness. Several trails near the camp provide access to the wilderness, and another trail follows the Methow River west for about eight miles before hooking up with the Pacific Crest Trail near Azurite Peak; a U.S. Forest Service map will show you the options.

Location: On the Methow River in Okanogan National Forest; map A3, grid c7.

Campsites, facilities: There are five sites for tents, trailers, or RVs. Picnic tables and fire grills are provided, but there is no drinking water. Vault toilets are available. Leashed pets are permitted.

Reservations, fees: No reservations; no camping fee. Overnight parking requires a $25 annual pass or $5 daily fee per vehicle. Open June to late September.

Directions: From Burlington drive east on Highway 20 for 120 miles to Mazama Road. Turn left on Mazama Road and drive one-quarter mile to County Road 9140. Turn left and drive northwest for seven miles to Lost River, where the pavement ends and the road soon becomes Forest Road 5400. Continue northwest on Forest Road 5400 for two miles to Forest Road 5400-600. Turn west on Forest Road 5400-600 and drive one-half mile to the campground.

Contact: Okanogan National Forest, Methow Valley Visitor Center, P.O. Box 579, Winthrop, WA 98862; tel. (509) 996-4000; fax (509) 997-9770.

22 Klipchuck   6

Located at an elevation of 3,000 feet along Early Winters Creek, Klipchuck provides hiking aplenty. A short loop trail from the camp leads about five miles up and over Delancy Ridge to Driveway Butte and down to the creek. Another trail starts nearby on Forest Road 200 (Sandy Butte-Cedar Creek Road) and goes two miles up Cedar Creek to lovely Cedar Creek Falls. Still another option is a two-mile trail along Early Winters Creek from the campground. See the description of Early Winters for more information.

Location: On Early Winters Creek in Okanogan National Forest; map A3, grid c7.

Campsites, facilities: There are six tent sites and 40 sites for tents, trailers, or RVs up to 32 feet long. Drinking water and picnic tables are provided. Flush and vault toilets are available. Leashed pets are permitted.

Reservations, fees: No reservations; no camping fee. Overnight parking requires a $25 annual pass or $5 daily fee per vehicle. Open June to late September.

Directions: From Burlington drive east on Highway 20 for 115 miles to Forest Road 300. (If you reach the Methow River Valley, you have gone four miles past the turnoff.) Turn left (signed) and drive northwest one mile.

Contact: Okanogan National Forest, Methow Valley Visitor Center, P.O. Box 579, Winthrop, WA 98862; tel. (509) 996-4000; fax (509) 997-9770.

23 Rocking Horse Ranch   7

This ranch is set in the lovely Methow River Valley, which is flanked on both sides by national forest. There are numerous trails nearby and a horse stable at the ranch. Owen Wister, who wrote the novel, *The Virginian,* lived in the nearby town of Winthrop at the turn of the century. Portions of the novel were based on his experiences in this area.

Location: In the Methow River Valley; map A3, grid c8.

Campsites, facilities: There are 25 tent sites and 10 drive-through sites for trailers or RVs of any length. Electricity, drinking water, sewer hookups, and picnic tables are provided. Flush toilets, sanitary services, showers, a horse stable, corrals, and firewood are available. Some facilities are wheelchair accessible. Leashed pets and motorbikes are permitted.

Reservations, fees: Reservations accepted. Sites are $12-15 per night. Open April to late October.

Directions: From Burlington drive east on Highway 20 for 123 miles to the campground located nine miles northwest of Winthrop.

Contact: Rocking Horse Ranch, Star Route, 18381 Highway 20, Winthrop, WA 98862; tel. (509) 996-2768.

Nice   6

Nice (pronounced like "ice") is along Eightmile Creek about four miles from Buck Lake. A trail leading into the Pasayten Wilderness can be found at the end of Forest Road 5130. Pearrygin Lake State Park is just a few miles to the south, near Winthrop.

Location: On Eightmile Creek in Okanogan National Forest; map A3, grid c9.

Campsites, facilities: There are four tent sites. Picnic tables and fire grills are provided. Vault toilets are available, but there is no drinking water or garbage service; pack out refuse. Leashed pets are permitted.

Reservations, fees: No reservations; no camping fee. Overnight parking requires a $25 annual pass or $5 daily fee per vehicle. Open June to late September.

Directions: From Burlington drive east on Highway 20 for 134 miles to Winthrop and County Road 1213 (W. Chewuch Road). Turn north on West Chewuch Road and drive 6.5 miles (the road becomes Forest Road 51.) Continue on Forest Road 51 and drive three miles to Forest Road 5130 (Eightmile Creek Road). Turn left (northwest) and drive four miles to the campground.

Contact: Okanogan National Forest, Methow Valley Visitor Center, P.O. Box 579, Winthrop, WA 98862; tel. (509) 996-4000; fax (509) 997-9770.

Flat   6

This campground is set along Eightmile Creek two miles from where it empties into the Chewuch River. Buck Lake is about three miles away. This is the closest of six camps to County Road 1213. Other options are Honeymoon, Nice, and Falls Creek.

Location: On Eightmile Creek in Okanogan National Forest; map A3, grid c9.

Campsites, facilities: There are 12 sites for tents, trailers, or RVs up to 15 feet long. Picnic tables and fire grills are provided, but there is no drinking water. Vault toilets are available. Leashed pets are permitted.

Reservations, fees: No reservations; no camping fee. Overnight parking requires a $25 annual pass or $5 daily fee per vehicle. Open June to late September.

Directions: From Burlington drive east on Highway 20 for 134 miles to Winthrop and County Road 1213 (W. Chewuch Road). Turn north on West Chewuch Road and drive 6.5 miles (the road becomes Forest Road 51.) Continue on Forest Road 51 and drive three miles to Forest Road 5130 (Eightmile Creek Road). Turn left (northwest) and drive two miles to the campground on the left.

Contact: Okanogan National Forest, Methow Valley Visitor Center, P.O. Box 579, Winthrop, WA 98862; tel. (509) 996-4000; fax (509) 997-9770.

26 Falls Creek   7

Falls Creek is a quiet and pretty campground located at the confluence of its namesake, Falls Creek, and the Chewuch River, about a 20-minute drive out of Winthrop. Highlights include fishing access and a wheelchair-accessible, 200-foot trail to a waterfall starting across the road from the campground.

Location: On the Chewuch River in Okanogan National Forest; map A3, grid c9.

Campsites, facilities: There are seven sites for tents, trailers, or RVs up to 18 feet long. Picnic tables are provided, but there is no drinking water. There is a wheelchair-accessible trail by the camp. Vault toilets are available. Leashed pets are permitted.

Reservations, fees: No reservations; no camping fee Overnight parking requires a $25 annual pass or $5 daily fee per vehicle. Open June to late September.

Directions: From Burlington drive east on Highway 20 for 134 miles to Winthrop and County Road 1213 (W. Chewuch Road). Turn north on West Chewuch Road and drive 6.5 miles (the road becomes Forest Road 51.) Continue on Forest Road 51 and drive 5.2 miles to the campground. A U.S. Forest Service map is advised.

Contact: Okanogan National Forest, Methow Valley Visitor Center, P.O. Box 579, Winthrop, WA 98862; tel. (509) 996-4000; fax (509) 997-9770.

27 Howard Miller Steelhead Park   5

This grassy county park has access to the Skagit River, which has been designated a Wild and Scenic River. True to its name, the steelhead fishing here is good in season. Campsites at this pretty spot are sunny and spacious. A bald eagle sanctuary is located at the east end of the park; December through February is the best time to observe them.

Location: On the Skagit River; map A3, grid d0.

Campsites, facilities: There are seven sites for tents and 49 sites for tents, trailers, or RVs of any length; 15 sites have electrical and water hookups, and 29 sites have electrical hookups. Some sites can accommodate group camps. Electricity, drinking water, fire pits, and picnic tables are provided. Flush toilets, garbage service, sanitary disposal station, showers, a clubhouse, a picnic shelter, Adirondacks (three-sided, roofed shelters), and a playground are available. A store and ice are located within one mile. Boat launching facilities are located on the Skagit River. Some facilities and sites are wheelchair accessible. Leashed pets and motorbikes are permitted.

Reservations, fees: Reservations recommended ($2 reservation fee). Sites are $12-16 per night. Major credit cards accepted. Open year-round.

Directions: On Interstate 5 drive to Exit 230/Highway 20 at Burlington. Turn east on Highway 20, and drive 44 miles to Rockport and Rockport-Darrington Road (Highway 530). Turn south and drive three blocks to the camp.

Contact: Howard Miller Steelhead Park, P.O. Box 127, Rockport, WA 98283; tel. (360) 853-8808; fax (360) 853-7315.

28 Wilderness Village and RV Park

Located near the Skagit River, this park is cool and wooded, with nice, gr[ass] and nearby access to the river and fishing. Horseshoe pits and a sports f[ield] recreation alternatives. Rockport State Park and hiking trails are nearby.

Location: Near the Skagit River; map A3, grid d1.

Campsites, facilities: There are 20 tent sites and 32 drive-through sites for trailers or RVs of any length. Electricity, cable TV, drinking water, sewer hookups, and picnic tables are provided. Flush toilets, sanitary services, showers, a recreation hall, and a laundry room are available. A cafe and ice are located within two miles. Leashed pets are permitted.

Reservations, fees: Reservations accepted. Sites are $11-16 per night. Open year-round.

Directions: From Burlington drive east on Highway 20 for 44 miles to Rockport. Continue east on Highway 20 for five miles to the park. The park is between Mileposts 102 and 103 on the right.

Contact: Wilderness Village and RV Park, 57588 Highway 20, Rockport, WA 98283; tel. (360) 873-2571.

29 Clark's Skagit River RV Park   9

This beautiful camp is nestled in the trees along the Skagit River, where trout fishing and river walks keep visitors happy. Side trips include hiking trails among the glaciers and waterfalls close to the campground. There are also three hydroelectric plants nearby that offer tours. Recreational facilities include horseshoes and a sports field for volleyball, croquet, and badminton.

Location: On the Skagit River; map A3, grid d1.

Campsites, facilities: There are 48 sites for tents, trailers, and RVs, plus 34 cabins. Rest rooms, showers, a sanitary dump, a public phone, a laundry room, horseshoe pits, a sports field for volleyball, croquet and badminton, and a restaurant are available. Leashed pets are permitted.

Reservations, fees: Reservations recommended. Sites are $10-20 per night. Cabins are $59-129. Major credit cards accepted. There is an added charge for pets in the cabins. Open year-round.

Directions: From Burlington drive east on Highway 20 for 44 miles to Rockport. Continue east on Highway 20 for six miles to the campground on the left (between Mileposts 103 and 104).

Contact: Clark's Skagit River RV Park, 58468 Clark Cabin Road, Rockport, WA 98283; tel. (800) 273-2606, (360) 873-2250; fax (360) 873-4077; website: www.north-cascades.com.

30 Mineral Park   6

Here's another classic, primitive camping area that can provide a jump-off for many adventures. This rustic site is set on the Cascade River and is near numerous trails leading into the Glacier Peak Wilderness. Fishing in the river can be quite good at times.

Location: On the Cascade River in Mount Baker-Snoqualmie National Forest; map A3, grid d3.

Campsites, facilities: There are six tent sites. Picnic tables, fire rings, and vault toilets are provided, but there is no drinking water. Leashed pets are permitted.

Reservations, fees: No reservations; no fee. Open mid-May to mid-September, weather permitting.

Directions: From Burlington drive east on Highway 20 for 47 miles to Marblemount and Cascade River Road (Forest Road 15). Cross the bridge and continue east on Cascade River Road and drive 16 miles to the campground.

Contact: Mount Baker-Snoqualmie National Forest, Mount Baker Ranger District, 2105 Highway 20, Sedro-Woolley, WA 98284; tel. (360) 856-5700; fax (360) 856-1934.

31 South Creek   6

Though small, quiet, and little known, South Creek Campground packs a wallop with good recreation options. It's set at the confluence of the Twisp River and South Creek at a major trailhead that accesses the Lake Chelan-Sawtooth Wilderness. See a U.S. Forest Service map for details.

Location: On the Twisp River in Okanogan National Forest; map A3, grid d7.

Campsites, facilities: There are four sites for tents or small trailers, plus a few sites with parking for RVs up to 30 feet in length. No drinking water is available. Picnic tables and fire grills are provided. A vault toilet is available. No garbage service; pack out refuse. Leashed pets are permitted.

Reservations, fees: No reservations; no camping fee Overnight parking requires a $25 annual pass or $5 daily fee per vehicle. Open late May to early September.

Directions: From Burlington drive east on Highway 20 for 145 miles to Twisp and County Road 9114. Turn west on County Road 9114 and drive 22 miles (the road becomes Forest Road 44). Continue west (the road becomes Forest Road 44, then Forest Road 4440) to the campground on the left.

Contact: Okanogan National Forest, Methow Valley Visitor Center, P.O. Box 579, Winthrop, WA 98862; tel. (509) 996-4000; fax (509) 997-9770.

32 Poplar Flat   7

This campground is set at 2,900 feet along the Twisp River. Many trails in the area follow streams, some of them providing access to the Lake Chelan-Sawtooth Wilderness. Twisp River Horse Camp, across the river from the campground, has facilities for horses.

Location: On the Twisp River in Okanogan National Forest; map A3, grid d7.

Campsites, facilities: There are 16 sites for tents, trailers, or RVs up to 21 feet long. Drinking water, fire grills, and picnic tables are provided. Vault toilets are available. Some facilities are wheelchair accessible. Leashed pets are permitted.

Reservations, fees: No reservations; no camping fee. Overnight parking requires a $25 annual pass or $5 daily fee per vehicle. Open May to September.

Directions: From Burlington drive east on Highway 20 for 145 miles to Twisp and County Road 9114. Turn west on County Road 9114 and drive 11 miles (the road becomes Forest Road 44). Continue west for 9.5 miles to the campground on the left.

Contact: Okanogan National Forest, Methow Valley Visitor Center, P.O. Box 579, Winthrop, WA 98862; tel. (509) 996-4000; fax (509) 997-9770.

33 Roads End   8

Roads End is set along the Twisp River at a major trailhead that provides access to mountain views and the Lake Chelan-Sawtooth Wilderness. The trail intersects with the Pacific Crest Trail about nine miles from the camp. A U.S. Forest Service map is essential.

Location: On the Twisp River in Okanogan National Forest; map A3, grid d7.

Campsites, facilities: There are four sites for tents or small trailers. Vault toilets and firewood are available, but there is no drinking water. Picnic tables and fire grills are provided. There is no garbage service; pack out refuse. Leashed pets are permitted.

Reservations, fees: No reservations; no camping fee. Overnight parking requires a $25 annual pass or $5 daily fee per vehicle. Open late May to early September.

Directions: On Interstate 5 drive to Exit 230/Highway 20 at Burlington. Turn east on Highway 20, and drive 145 miles to Twisp and County Road 9114. Turn west on County Road 9114 and drive 11 miles (the road becomes Forest Road 44). Continue west for 13.5 miles to the campground. A U.S. Forest Service map is advisable.

Contact: Okanogan National Forest, Methow Valley Visitor Center, P.O. Box 579, Winthrop, WA 98862; tel. (509) 996-4000; fax (509) 997-9770.

34 War Creek  6

This campground is set along the Twisp River near the trailhead for Trail 408, which provides access to the Lake Chelan-Sawtooth Wilderness. Backpackers can take this path down into the Lake Chelan National Recreation Area, finishing the trip at the shore of Lake Chelan and the National Park Service outpost. It's a 15-mile trek, so contact the U.S. Forest Service for details.

Location: On the Twisp River in Okanogan National Forest; map A3, grid d8.

Campsites, facilities: There are 11 sites for tents, trailers, or RVs up to 21 feet long. Drinking water, fire grills, and picnic tables are provided. Vault toilets and firewood are available. Leashed pets are permitted.

Reservations, fees: No reservations; no camping fee. Overnight parking requires a $25 annual pass or $5 daily fee per vehicle. Open May to September.

Directions: On Interstate 5 drive to Exit 230/Highway 20 at Burlington. Turn east on Highway 20, and drive 145 miles to Twisp and County Road 9114. Turn west on County Road 9114 and drive 11 miles (the road becomes Forest Road 44). Continue west on Forest Road 44 for 3.5 miles to the campground.

Contact: Okanogan National Forest, Methow Valley Visitor Center, P.O. Box 579, Winthrop, WA 98862; tel. (509) 996-4000; fax (509) 997-9770.

35 Pearrygin Lake State Park

 8

This 578-acre park is located in the beautiful Methow Valley, ringed by the North Cascade Mountains. The area is ideal for wildflower and wildlife viewing in the spring. The campground has access to a sandy beach and facilities for swimming, boating, fishing, and hiking. The sites are set close together and don't offer much privacy, but they are spacious, and a variety of recreation options make it worth the crunch. In the winter there are opportunities for snowmobiling, cross-country skiing, and ice fishing. A nine-hole golf course is nearby.

Location: On Pearrygin Lake; map A3, grid d9.

Campsites, facilities: There are 53 tent sites and 30 sites for tents or RVs up to 60 feet in length; 30 have full hookups. Picnic tables and fire grills are provided. Flush toilets, sanitary services, and drinking water are available. Showers and firewood are available for a fee. A store, a cafe, and ice are located within one mile. Some facilities are wheelchair accessible. Boat launching facilities are available. Leashed pets are permitted.

Reservations, fees: Reservations accepted, phone (800) 452-5687 ($6 reservation fee). Sites are $11-16 per night. Major credit cards accepted. Open April through October.

Directions: On Interstate 5 drive to Exit 230/Highway 20 at Burlington. Turn east on Highway 20, and drive 134 miles to Winthrop and County Road 1631 (E. Chewuch Road). Turn north on County Road 1631 and drive about four miles to the park on the right.

Contact: Pearrygin Lake State Park, Route 1, P.O. Box 300, Winthrop, WA 98862; tel. (800) 233-0321, (509) 996-2370.

36 River Bend Trailer Park 6

The shore of the Methow River skirts this campground. Trout fishing, river rafting, and swimming are popular here, and there is a nice separate area for tent campers set right along the river. U.S. 101 North access is nearby and convenient for campers heading that way. The description of KOA Methow River detail the recreation possibilities available within 10 miles.

Location: Near the Methow River; map A3, grid d9.

Campsites, facilities: There are 35 tent and 69 sites accommodating RVs and trailers of any length; 30 are pull through and 31 are on the riverfront. Picnic tables are provided. Flush toilets, sanitary services, firewood, a store, a laundry room, ice, a playground, electricity (30 and 50 watt), modem access, drinking water, sewer hookups, and showers are available. Leashed pets and motorbikes are permitted.

Reservations, fees: Reservations accepted. Sites are $14-18 per night; call for weekly rates. Major credit cards accepted. Open year-round.

Directions: On Interstate 5 drive to Exit 230/Highway 20 at Burlington. Turn east on Highway 20, and drive 143 miles to the campground. It is located two miles west of Twisp.

Contact: River Bend Trailer Park, 19961 Highway 20, Twisp, WA 98856; tel. (509) 997-3500, (800) 686-4498; website: www. riverbenrv.com.

37 Derry's Resort   7

Pearrygin Lake is the backdrop for this exceptionally clean and pretty lakeshore campground with comfortable, shady sites. Fishing, swimming, and boating access is a short distance away. Other nearby recreation options include an 18-hole golf course, hiking trails, and a riding stable. See the description of KOA Methow River for more details on the area.

Location: On Pearrygin Lake; map A3, grid d9.

Campsites, facilities: There are 90 tent sites and 64 drive-through sites for trailers or RVs of any length. There are also two cabins. Electricity, drinking water, sewer hookups, and picnic tables are provided. Flush toilets, showers, firewood, sanitary services, a store, a laundry room, ice, and a playground are available. A cafe and go-cart track are located within one-quarter mile. Boat docks, launching facilities, boat rentals and a swimming area with a waterslide are available on Pearrygin Lake. Leashed pets and motorbikes are permitted.

Reservations, fees: Reservations accepted. Sites are $16-20 per night; cabins are $60 per night. Major credit cards accepted. Open mid-April to November.

Directions: On Interstate 5 drive to Exit 230/Highway 20 at Burlington. Turn east on Highway 20, and drive 134 miles to Winthrop and Riverside Avenue. Turn north on Riverside Avenue and drive 0.1 mile to Bluff Street. Turn northeast on Bluff Street and drive 1.5 miles to Pearrygin Lake Road. Turn east on Pearrygin Lake Road and continue one mile to the resort on the right.

Contact: Derry's Resort, Route 1, Box 307, Winthrop, WA 98862; tel. (509) 996-2322.

38 KOA Methow River-Winthrop

          7

Here's another campground set along the Methow River, which offers opportunities for fishing, boating, swimming, and rafting. The park has a free shuttle into Winthrop, an interesting town with many restored, turn-of-the-century buildings lining the main street, including the Shafer Museum, which displays lots of period items. If you would like to observe wildlife, take a short, two-mile drive southeast out of Winthrop on County Road 9129 on the east side of the Methow River. Turn east on County Road 1631 into Davis Lake, and follow the signs to the Methow River Habitat Management Area Headquarters. Depending upon the time of year, you may see mule deer, porcupine, bobcat, mountain lion, snowshoe hare, black bear, red squirrel, and many species of birds. However, if you're looking for something tamer, other nearby recreation options include an 18-hole golf course and tennis courts.

Location: On the Methow River; map A3, grid d9.

Campsites, facilities: There are 90 sites for tents, trailers, or RVs of any length; some drive-through sites are available. There are also 17 one- or two-room cabins. Drinking water and picnic tables are provided. Flush toilets, electricity, firewood, sewer hookups, sanitary services, showers, a recreation hall, bike and video rentals, a store, a laundry room, ice, a playground, and a swimming pool are available. Bottled gas and a cafe are located within one mile. There is a courtesy shuttle to and from Winthrop. Leashed pets and motorbikes are permitted.

Reservations, fees: Reservations accepted, phone (800) 562-2158. Sites are $20-25 per night; cabins are $35-47 per night. Major credit cards accepted. Open mid-April to November.

Directions: On Interstate 5 drive to Exit 230/Highway 20 at Burlington. Turn east on Highway 20, and drive 134 miles to Winthrop. Continue on Highway 20 one mile east. The camp is between Mileposts 194 and 195, on the left.

Contact: KOA Methow River-Winthrop, P.O. Box 305, Winthrop, WA 98862; tel. (509) 996-2258; fax (509) 996-3848.

39 Pine-Near Trailer Park   9

Not far from the Methow River, this camp is an adequate layover spot for Highway 20 cruisers and a good alternative camp to the more crowded sites at Pearrygin Lake. See the description of KOA Methow River for information on the various activities available in the Winthrop area.

Location: On the Methow River; map A3, grid d9.

Campsites, facilities: There are 40 tent sites and 28 sites for trailers or RVs of any length; 14 are drive-through. Electricity, drinking water, sewer hookups, and picnic tables are provided. Flush toilets, sanitary services, showers, and a laundry room are available. A store and a cafe are located within one mile. Leashed pets and motorbikes are permitted.

Reservations, fees: Reservations accepted. Sites are $8-14 per night. Major credit cards accepted. Open year-round.

Directions: On Interstate 5 drive to Exit 230/Highway 20 at Burlington. Turn east on Highway 20, and drive 134 miles to Winthrop. Continue on Highway 20 one block north of Riverside Drive to Castle Avenue. Turn east and drive three blocks to the park on the left.

Contact: Pine-Near Trailer Park, Route 1, P.O. Box 400-32, Winthrop, WA 98862; tel. (509) 996-2391.

40 Big Twin Lake Campground

        5

As the name implies, this campground is set along the shore of Twin Lakes. See the description of KOA Methow River for information on the various activities available in the Winthrop area.

Location: On Twin Lakes; map A3, grid d9.

Campsites, facilities: There are 35 tent sites and 68 sites for trailers or RVs of any length; 18 are drive-through. Electricity, drinking water, sewer hookups, and picnic tables are provided. Flush toilets, sanitary services, showers, firewood, ice, and a playground are available. Boat docks, launching facilities, and rentals can be obtained on Big Twin Lake. Leashed pets and motorbikes are permitted.

Reservations, fees: Reservations accepted. Sites are $12-20 per night. Open April to late October.

Directions: On Interstate 5 drive to Exit 230/Highway 20 at Burlington. Turn east on Highway 20, and drive 134 miles to Winthrop. Continue on Highway 20 for three miles to Twin Lakes Road. Turn west on Twin Lakes Road and drive two miles to the campground.

Contact: Big Twin Lake Campground, Route 2, Box 795, Winthrop, WA 98862; tel.(509) 996-2650; website: www.methownet.com/bigtwin.

41 Clear Creek   8

This nice, secluded spot is set in old-growth fir on the water, but doesn't get heavy use. It's set at the confluence of Clear Creek and the Sauk River, a designated Wild and Scenic River. A trail from camp leads about a mile up to Frog Lake.

Location: On Clear Creek and the Sauk River in Mount Baker-Snoqualmie National Forest; map A3, grid e0.

Campsites, facilities: There are 12 sites for tents, trailers, or RVs up to 21 feet long. Picnic tables and fire grills are provided. Vault toilets and firewood are available. There is no drinking water. Some facilities are wheelchair accessible. A store, a cafe, a coin laundry, and ice are located within four miles. Leashed pets are permitted.

Reservations, fees: No reservations; sites are $7 per night. Open late May to early September.

Directions: From Seattle on Interstate 5, drive north to Exit 208 and the junction with Highway 530. Turn east on Highway 530 and drive 32 miles to Darrington and Forest Road 20 (Mountain Loop Highway). Turn south on Forest Road 20 and drive 3.3 miles to the campground entrance on the left.

Contact: Mount Baker-Snoqualmie National Forest, Darrington Ranger District, 1405 Emmens Street, Darrington, WA 98241; tel. (360) 436-1155; fax (360) 436-1309.

42 Squire Creek County Park   7

This wooded, low-cost RV park near the outback along Squire Creek is about three miles from the boundaries of the Boulder River Wilderness.

Location: On Squire Creek; map A3, grid e0.

Campsites, facilities: There are 30 drive-through sites for trailers or RVs up to 25 feet long, and two sites that can accommodate trailers up to 70 feet long. Drinking water, fire rings and picnic tables are provided. Flush toilets, sanitary services, and firewood are available. A store is located three miles east in Darrington. Leashed pets are permitted.

Reservations, fees: No reservations accepted. Sites are $10-15 per night. Open year-round.

Directions: From Seattle on Interstate 5, drive north to Exit 208 and the junction with Highway 530. Turn east on Highway 530 and drive 26 miles to the park on the left.

Contact: Squire Creek County Park, 9629 32nd Street SE, Everett, WA 98205; tel. (425) 388-6600; fax (425) 377-9509.

43 Cascade Kamloops Trout Farm/RV Park

 5

Campers will find a little bit of both worlds at this campground-a rustic quietness with all facilities available. A bonus is a trout pond, stocked year-round. No boats are allowed. Nearby recreation options include marked hiking trails, snowmobiling, cross-country skiing, river rafting, and tennis courts.

Location: In Darrington; map A3, grid e1.

Campsites, facilities: There are two tent sites and 32 sites for trailers or RVs of any length. Electricity, drinking water, sewer hookups, and picnic tables are provided. Flush toilets, sanitary services, showers, firewood, a laundry room, a trout pond, and a recreation hall are available. Bottled gas, a store, a cafe, and ice are located within one mile. Pets and motorbikes are permitted.

Reservations, fees: Reservations accepted. Sites are $14-16 per night. Open year-round.

Directions: From Seattle on Interstate 5, drive north to Exit 208 and the junction with Highway 530. Turn east on Highway 530 and drive 32 miles to Darrington and Madison Street. Turn right on Madison Street and drive about four blocks to Darrington Street. Turn right and drive two blocks to the park.

Contact: Cascade Kamloops Trout Farm/ RV Park, P.O. Box 1205, Darrington, WA 98241; tel.(360) 436-1003; website: www.websnw.com/kamloops.

44 William C. Dearinger   7

This secluded campground is on the Sauk River and is managed by the Department of Natural Resources. It may be a little difficult to reach, but that's why you'll probably be the only one here. It's pretty, with lots of trees and sites overlooking the river.

Location: On the Sauk River; map A3, grid e1.

Campsites, facilities: There are 12 sites for tents or small trailers. Picnic tables, fire grills, and tent pads are provided. Vault toilets and firewood are available, but there is no drinking water. Leashed pets are permitted.

Reservations, fees: No reservations; no fee. Open year-round.

Directions: From Seattle on Interstate 5, drive north to Exit 208 and the junction with Highway 530. Turn east on Highway 530 and drive 32 miles to Darrington. Continue on Highway 530 one-third mile to Mountain Loop Road. Turn east on Mountain Loop Road and drive one-half mile; then continue straight for five miles to East Sauk Prairie Road. Turn left and drive two-thirds of a mile to Road SWD 5000. Bear right on Road SWD 5000 and drive 2.7 miles. Bear left for one mile to Road SWD 5400. Turn left on SWD 5400 and drive a quarter-mile to the campground.

Contact: Department of Natural Resources, Northwest Region, 411 Tillicum Lane, Forks, WA 98331-9797; tel. (360) 856-3500.

45 Buck Creek   9

Quiet and remote, this primitive campground is set along Buck Creek near its confluence with the Suiattle River in the Glacier Peak Wilderness. There's a large

(18 feet by 18 feet) Adirondack shelter by the creek and stands of old-growth timber. A zigzagging trail routed into the Glacier Peak Wilderness is accessible about one mile west of camp. See a U.S. Forest Service map for specifics.

Location: Near the Suiattle River in Mount Baker-Snoqualmie National Forest; map A3, grid e2.

Campsites, facilities: There are 26 sites for tents, trailers, or RVs up to 30 feet long. Picnic tables are provided. Vault toilets and firewood are available, but there is no drinking water. Leashed pets are permitted.

Reservations, fees: No reservations; sites are $7 per night. Open June to through September.

Directions: From Seattle on Interstate 5, drive north to Exit 208 and the junction with Highway 530. Turn east on Highway 530 and drive 32 miles to Darrington. Continue 7.5 miles on Highway 530 to Forest Road 26 (Suiattle River Road). Turn right (southeast) on Forest Road 26 and drive 15.2 miles to the campground. A U.S. Forest Service map is essential. Note: In the past, Forest Road 26 has been closed due to flooding; it is advisable to phone ahead for current conditions.

Contact: Mount Baker-Snoqualmie National Forest, Darrington Ranger District, 1405 Emmens Street, Darrington, WA 98241; tel. (360) 436-1155; fax (360) 436-1309.

46 Sulphur Creek   8

Fishing access to the river across the road is a highlight of this campground set along the Suiattle River near the border of the Glacier Peak Wilderness. It's a good base camp for a wilderness expedition, with a trailhead leading deep into the backcountry located about a quarter-mile south of the campground. The trail hooks up with the Pacific Crest Trail.

Location: On the Suiattle River in Mount Baker-Snoqualmie National Forest; map A3, grid e3.

Campsites, facilities: There are 20 sites for tents, trailers, or RVs up to 15 feet long. Picnic tables and fire grills are provided. Downed wood can be gathered and used for firewood. Vault toilets are available. There is no drinking water. Leashed pets are permitted.

Reservations, fees: No reservations; sites are $7 per night. Open June through September.

Directions: From Seattle on Interstate 5, drive north to Exit 208 and the junction with Highway 530. Turn east on Highway 530 and drive 32 miles to Darrington. Continue 7.5 miles to Forest Road 26 (Suiattle River Road), turn right, and drive 22 miles southeast on Forest Road 26 to the campground on the right. A U.S. Forest Service map is advisable. Note: Forest Road 26 is subject to flooding; phone ahead for current conditions.

Contact: Mount Baker-Snoqualmie National Forest, Darrington Ranger District, 1405 Emmens Street, Darrington, WA 98241; tel. (360) 436-1155; fax (360) 436-1309.

47 Holden Ballpark
Ferry-In, Bus-In   7

Getting here is half the fun, with ferryboat rides provided by the Lake Chelan Boat Company that emphasize fun and education along with transportation. Several trails to lakes in the Glacier Peak Wilderness are accessible from a trail next to the campground, which is set along Railroad Creek. Since this area is on the eastern slope of the Cascade Range, it's drier than the western slopes and not as heavily forested. However, there is no shortage of glacier-fed streams and lakes in the area. See a U.S. Forest Service map for details. Less than a mile from the campground is the Holden Mine site, which was Washington's largest copper and zinc mine until it closed in 1957. Many of the buildings from the mining town have been preserved, and Holden Village offers housing and meals for travelers as space allows.

Location: Near the Glacier Peak Wilderness in Wenatchee National Forest; map A3, grid e5.

Campsites, facilities: There are two primitive tent sites that are accessible only by boat or ferry, followed by a 12-mile hike or bus trip via Holden Village up the Railroad Creek Valley. Picnic tables and fire rings are provided. One Wallowa (nonenclosed, platform) pit toilet is available, but there is no drinking water. Be prepared to protect food from bears.

Reservations, fees: No reservations; no fee. Open May through September.

Directions: From Wenatchee drive north on U.S. 97 and drive about 40 miles to Chelan and the ferry. Take the ferry and proceed to Lucerne, 41 miles northwest of the town of Chelan. (This spectacular voyage costs about $22 round-trip. For more information call (509) 682-2224.) From Lucerne, take the bus 12 miles west to Holden Village. The campground is at the end of the road.

Contact: Wenatchee National Forest, Chelan Ranger District, 428 West Woodin Avenue, Chelan, WA 98816; tel. (509) 682-2576; fax (509) 682-9004.

48 Domke Lake Ferry-In, Hike-In   9

Little known and little used, this is a perfect jump-off for a wilderness backpacking trip. Domke Lake is about one mile long and one-half mile wide and offers good fishing by boat. Trails continue past the lake into the Glacier Peak Wilderness. See a U.S. Forest Service map for details.

Location: Near the Glacier Peak Wilderness in Wenatchee National Forest; map A3, grid e6.

Campsites, facilities: There are eight tent sites accessible only by boat, ferry, or float plane. Picnic tables are provided. Pit toilets and boat docking are available, but there is no drinking water. Boat rentals are available at Domke Lake Resort. Be prepared to protect food from bears.

Reservations, fees: No reservations; no camping fee; $5 per day docking charge. Open May to late October.

Directions: From Wenatchee drive north on U.S. 97 for 40 miles to Chelan and the ferry. Take the ferry and proceed to Lucerne, 41 miles northwest of the town of Chelan. (This spectacular voyage costs about $22 round-trip. For more information call (509) 682-2224.) From Lucerne, hike, bike, or motorbike on Trail 1280 for 2.5 miles to Domke Lake and the campground. The campground is also directly accessible by float plane. (Call Chelan Airways at (509) 682-5555 for more information.)

Contact: Wenatchee National Forest, Chelan Ranger District, 428 West Woodin Avenue, Chelan, WA 98816; tel. (509) 682-2576; fax (509) 682-9004.

49 Lucerne   10

This campground is set along the shore of 55-mile-long Lake Chelan, the second deepest lake in North America, with a depth of 1,500 feet. Mountains reaching to 8,000 feet flank each side of the lake. This is the only national forest camp in the vicinity that offers drinking water. Fishing, hiking, and boating are among your options here. See the description of Holden for information on the Holden Mine and Village, which is nearby.

Location: On Lake Chelan in Wenatchee National Forest; map A3, grid e7.

Campsites, facilities: There are two tent sites accessible only by boat, ferry, or float plane. Drinking water, fire grills, and picnic tables are provided. Pit toilets and boat docks are available.

Reservations, fees: No reservations; no camping fee; $5 per day docking charge. Open April through October.

Directions: From Wenatchee drive north on U.S. 97 for 40 miles to Chelan and the ferry. Take the ferry and proceed to Lucerne, 41 miles northwest of the town of Chelan on the west shore of Lake Chelan. (This spectacular voyage costs about $22 round-trip. For more information call (509) 682-2224.)

Contact: Wenatchee National Forest, Chelan Ranger District, 428 West Woodin Avenue, Chelan, WA 98816; tel. (509) 682-2576; fax (509) 682-9004.

50 Foggy Dew   6

This private, remote campground is set at the confluence of Foggy Dew Creek and the North Fork of Old Creek. There are several trails nearby that provide access to various backcountry lakes and streams. To get to the trailheads, just follow the forest roads near camp. Bicycles and motorbikes are allowed on Trails 417, 429, and 431. In the winter the area is open for both cross-country skiing and snowmobiling. See a U.S. Forest Service map for options.

Location: On Foggy Dew Creek in Okanogan National Forest; map A3, grid e9.

Campsites, facilities: There are 13 sites for tents, trailers, or RVs. Picnic tables and fire grills are provided. Vault toilets and drinking water are available, but not garbage service; pack out refuse. Leashed pets are permitted.

Reservations, fees: No reservations; no camping fee. Overnight parking requires a $25 annual pass or $5 daily fee per vehicle. Open late May to early September.

Directions: From Burlington drive east on Highway 20 for 145 miles to Twisp. Continue east on Highway 20 for three miles to Highway 153. Turn south on Highway 153 and drive 12 miles to County Road 1029 (Gold Creek Road). Turn south and drive one mile to Forest Road 4340. Turn west and drive four miles to the campground.

Contact: Okanogan National Forest, Methow Valley Visitor Center, P.O. Box 579, Winthrop, WA 98862; tel. (509) 996-4000; fax (509) 997-9770.

51 Gold Basin   9

This is the largest campground in Mount Baker-Snoqualmie National Forest, and since it's loaded with facilities, it's a favorite with RVers. The campground is set at 1,100 feet along the South Fork of the Stillaguamish River, with riverside sites, easy access, and a wheelchair-accessible interpretive trail. Fishing, rafting and hiking are options.

Location: On the South Fork of the Stillaguamish River in Mount Baker-Snoqualmie National Forest; map A3, grid f0.

Campsites, facilities: There are 10 tent sites and 83 sites for tents, trailers, or RVs up to 60 feet long. There is an overflow area available for group camping accommodating a maximum of 25 people. Picnic tables are provided. Vault toilets, drinking water, showers, and firewood are available. A store, a cafe, and ice are located within 2.5 miles. Some facilities are wheelchair accessible. Leashed pets are permitted.

Reservations, fees: Some sites can be reserved; phone (877) 444-6777 or access the website: www.reserveusa.com ($8.65 reservation fee). Sites are $14 per night; the group site is $100 per night. Open mid-May to early September.

Directions: From Seattle drive on Interstate 5 north to Everett and Highway 92. Turn east on Highway 92 and drive about 15 miles to the town of Granite Falls and Mountain Loop Highway (Forest Road 7). Continue east on Mountain Loop Highway for 13.5 miles to the campground entrance on the left.

Contact: Mount Baker-Snoqualmie National Forest, Darrington Ranger District, 1405 Emmens Street, Darrington, WA 98241; tel. (360) 436-1155; fax (360) 436-1309.

52 Beaver Plant Lake Hike-In   8

This campground is on Beaver Plant Lake, one of four campgrounds detailed in the area (the others are Upper Ashland Lake, Lower Ashland Lake, and Twin Falls Lake). Excellent hiking trails are a highlight of the region.

Location: On Beaver Plant Lake; map A3, grid f0.

Campsites, facilities: There is a dispersed camping area at this primitive, hike-in campground. A backcountry (Wallowa) toilet and firewood are available. There is no drinking water. Leashed pets are permitted.

Reservations, fees: No reservations; no fee. Open mid-June through October.

Directions: From Seattle drive north on Interstate 5 to Everett and Highway 92. Turn east on Highway 92 and drive about 15 miles to the town of Granite Falls and Mountain Loop Highway (Forest Road 7). Continue east on Mountain Loop Highway for 15 miles to Forest Road 4020. Turn right (south) on Forest Road 4020 and drive 2.5 miles to Forest Road 4021. Turn right on Forest Road 4021 and drive two miles to the Ashland Lakes Trailhead. From the trailhead, hike 2.1 miles to the campground.

Contact: Department of Natural Resources, Northwest Region, 919 North Township Street, Sedro-Woolley, WA 98284-9395; tel. (360) 856-3500.

53 Upper Ashland Lake Hike-In   9

Reaching this primitive and very beautiful camp requires a short hike that's well worth the effort. The site is little known, so you can expect quiet and privacy. Several good hiking trails can be found near camp. A map available from the Department of Natural Resources is helpful.

Location: Near Upper Ashland Lake; map A3, grid f0.

Campsites, facilities: There is a dispersed camping area at this primitive, hike-in campground. A backcountry (Wallowa) toilet and firewood are available, but there is no drinking water. Leashed pets are permitted.

Reservations, fees: No reservations; no fee. Open mid-June through October.

Directions: From Seattle drive on Interstate 5 north to Everett and Highway 92. Turn east on Highway 92 and drive about 15 miles to the town of Granite Falls and Mountain Loop Highway. Turn north on Mountain Loop Highway and drive 15 miles to Forest Road 4020. Turn right (south) on Forest Road 4020 and drive 2.5 miles to Forest Road 4021. Turn right on Forest Road 4021 and drive 2.6 miles to the Ashland Lakes Trailhead. From the trailhead, hike two miles to the campground.

Contact: Department of Natural Resources, Northwest Region, 919 North Township Street, Sedro-Woolley, WA 98284-9395; tel. (360) 856-3500.

54 Lower Ashland Lake Hike-In   8

This campground is on Lower Ashland Lake, set adjacent to Upper Ashland Lake; see the description of Upper Ashland Lake for details.

Location: On Lower Ashland Lake; map A3, grid f0.

Campsites, facilities: There is a dispersed camping area at this primitive, hike-in campground. A backcountry (Wallowa) toilet and firewood are available, but there is no drinking water. Leashed pets are permitted.

Reservations, fees: No reservations; no fee. Open mid-June through October.

Directions: From Seattle drive on Interstate 5 north to Everett and Highway 92. Turn east on Highway 92 and drive about 15 miles to the town of Granite Falls and Mountain Loop Highway. Turn north on Mountain Loop Highway and drive 15 miles to Forest Road 4020. Turn right (south) on Forest Road 4020 and drive 2.5 miles to Forest Road 4021. Turn right on Forest Road 4021 and drive two miles to the Ashland Lakes Trailhead. From the trailhead, hike three miles to the campground.

Contact: Department of Natural Resources, Northwest Region, 919 North Township Street, Sedro-Woolley, WA 98284-9395; tel. (360) 856-3500.

55 Esswine Group Camp   6

This small, quiet camp is a great place for a restful group getaway. The lack of drinking water is the only drawback. Esswine is one of the few U.S. Forest Service campgrounds in the area that require (or even accept) reservations; get yours in early. Fishing access is available nearby. The Boulder River Wilderness is located to the north; see a U.S. Forest Service map for trailhead locations.

Location: In Mount Baker-Snoqualmie National Forest; map A3, grid f0.

Campsites, facilities: This is a specially designated group campground with four tent sites. Picnic tables are provided. Vault toilets and firewood are available, but there is no drinking water. A store, a cafe, and ice are located within four miles. Leashed pets are permitted.

Reservations, fees: Reservations required; phone (877) 444-6777 or access the website: www.reserveusa.com. The fee is $40-60 per night. Open mid-May to early September.

Directions: From Seattle drive on Interstate 5 north to Everett and Highway 92. Turn east on Highway 92 and drive about 15 miles to the town of Granite Falls and Mountain Loop Highway (Forest Road 7). Continue northeast on Mountain Loop Highway for 16 miles to the campground entrance on the left.

Contact: Mount Baker-Snoqualmie National Forest, Darrington Ranger District, 1405 Emmens Street, Darrington, WA 98241; tel. (360) 436-1155; fax (360) 436-1309.

56 Boardman Creek   7

Roomy sites and river access highlight this pretty riverside camp. The fishing is can be excellent near here. Forest roads in the area will take you to several backcountry lakes, including Boardman Lake, Lake Evan, and Ashland Lakes. Get a U.S. Forest Service map, set up your camp, and go for it.

Location: On the South Fork of the Stillaguamish River in Mount Baker-Snoqualmie National Forest; map A3, grid f0.

Campsites, facilities: There are eight tent sites and two sites for tents, trailers, or RVs of any length. Picnic tables are provided. Vault toilets and firewood are available, but there is no drinking water. Leashed pets are permitted.

Reservations, fees: No reservations; sites are $7 per night.

Directions: From Seattle drive on Interstate 5 north to Everett and Highway 92. Turn east on Highway 92 and drive about 15 miles to the town of Granite Falls and Mountain Loop Highway (Forest Road 7). Continue northeast on Mountain Loop Highway for 16.5 miles to the campground entrance on the left.

Contact: Mount Baker-Snoqualmie National Forest, Darrington Ranger District, 1405 Emmens Street, Darrington, WA 98241; tel. (360) 436-1155; fax (360) 436-1309.

57 Coal Creek Bar Group Camp   8

A U.S. Forest Service map will unlock the beautiful country around this campground set along the South Fork of the Stillaguamish River near Coal Creek. Fishing access is available, and nearby forest roads lead to Coal Lake and a trailhead that takes you to other backcountry lakes.

Location: On the South Fork of the Stillaguamish River in Mount Baker-Snoqualmie National Forest; map A3, grid f0.

Campsites, facilities: There are two tent sites and two trailer sites. Picnic tables and fire grills are provided. Vault toilets and firewood are available. There is no drinking water. Leashed pets are permitted.

Reservations, fees: Reservations required, phone (360) 436-1155. Sites are $60 per night for the entire camp. Open mid-May to late September.

Directions: From Seattle drive on Interstate 5 north to Everett and Highway 92. Turn east on Highway 92 and drive about 15 miles to the town of Granite Falls and Mountain Loop Highway (Forest Road 7). Continue northeast on Mountain Loop Highway for 23.5 miles to the campground entrance on the left.

Contact: Mount Baker-Snoqualmie National Forest, Darrington Ranger District, 1405 Emmens Street, Darrington, WA 98241; tel. (360) 436-1155; fax (360) 436-1309.

58 Tulalip Millsite Group Camp   7

This campground is set along the South Fork of the Stillaguamish River, nearby to several other camps: Turlo, Verlot, Gold Basin, Esswine, Boardman Creek, Coal Creek Bar, and Red Bridge. A trailhead about one mile east of camp leads north into the Boulder River Wilderness. There are numerous creeks and streams that crisscross this area, providing good fishing prospects.

Location: On the South Fork of the Stillaguamish River in Mount Baker-Snoqualmie National Forest; map A3, grid f0.

Campsites, facilities: This is a specially designated group camp that will accommodate up to 60 people. Picnic tables and fire grills are provided. Vault toilets are available, but there is no drinking water. Leashed pets are permitted.

Reservations, fees: Reservations required, phone (360) 436-1155. Sites are $75 per night. Open mid-May to late September.

Directions: From Seattle drive on Interstate 5 north to Everett and Highway 92. Turn east on Highway 92 and drive about 15 miles to the town of Granite Falls and Mountain Loop Highway (Forest Road 7). Continue northeast on Mountain Loop Highway for 18.5 miles to the campground entrance on the right.

Contact: Mount Baker-Snoqualmie National Forest, Darrington Ranger District, 1405 Emmens Street, Darrington, WA 98241; tel. (360) 436-1155; fax (360) 436-1309.

59 Red Bridge   9

Red Bridge is another classic spot, one of several in the vicinity, and a good base camp for a backpacking expedition. The campground is set at 1,300 feet on the South Fork of the Stillaguamish River near Mallardy Creek. It has pretty, riverside sites with old-growth fir. A trailhead two miles east of camp leads to Granite Pass in the Boulder River Wilderness.

Location: On the South Fork of Stillaguamish River in Mount Baker-Snoqualmie National Forest; map A3, grid f0.

Campsites, facilities: There are two tent sites and 14 sites for tents, trailers, or RVs up to 31 feet long. Picnic tables are provided. Vault toilets are available, but there is no drinking water. Some facilities are wheelchair accessible. Leashed pets are permitted.

Reservations, fees: No reservations; sites are $7 per night. Open late May to early September.

Directions: From Seattle drive on Interstate 5 north to Everett and Highway 92. Turn east on Highway 92 and drive about 15 miles to the town of Granite Falls and Mountain Loop Highway (Forest Road 7). Continue northeast on Mountain Loop Highway for 18 miles to the campground entrance on the right.

Contact: Mount Baker-Snoqualmie National Forest, Darrington Ranger District, 1405 Emmens Street, Darrington, WA 98241; tel. (360) 436-1155; fax (360) 436-1309.

60 Twin Falls Lake Hike-In   9

People willing to grunt a little will find good hiking, backpacking, and trout fishing at this site. It's a beautiful and secluded area, yet it's not a long drive from Seattle.

Location: On Twin Falls Lake; map A3, grid f0.

Campsites, facilities: There is a dispersed camping area at this primitive, hike-in campground. A backcountry (Wallowa) toilet and firewood are available, but there is no drinking water. Leashed pets are permitted.

Reservations, fees: No reservations; no fee. Open mid-June through October.

Directions: From Seattle drive on Interstate 5 north to Everett and Highway 92. Turn east on Highway 92 and drive about 15 miles to the town of Granite Falls and Mountain Loop Highway (Forest Road 20). Continue on Mountain Loop Highway for 15 miles to Forest Road 4020. Turn south on Forest Road 4020 and drive 2.5 miles to Forest Road 4021. Turn right on Forest Road 4021 and drive two miles to the Ashland Lakes Trailhead. Hike in 4.5 miles from the trailhead.

Contact: Department of Natural Resources, Northwest Region, 919 North Township Street, Sedro-Woolley, WA 98284-9395; tel. (360) 856-3500.

61 Bedal 9

This campground, set at the confluence of the North and South Forks of the Sauk River, offers shaded sites, river views, and good fishing. It's a bit primitive, but you can't beat the price. North Fork Falls is about a mile up the North Fork of the Sauk from camp and worth the trip.

Location: On the Sauk River in Mount Baker-Snoqualmie National Forest; map A3, grid f3.

Campsites, facilities: There are 19 sites for tents, trailers, or RVs up to 21 feet long. Picnic tables and a picnic shelter are provided. Vault toilets are available, but there is no drinking water. Some facilities are wheelchair accessible. A U.S. Forest Service district office is 17 miles from the campground, in Darrington.

Reservations, fees: No reservations; sites are $7 per night. Open May to early September.

Directions: From Seattle on Interstate 5 drive north to Exit 208 and the junction with Highway 530. Turn east on Highway 530 and drive 32 miles to Darrington and Forest Road 20 (Mountain Loop Highway). Turn right (south) on Forest Road 20 and drive 17 miles to the campground on the right. A U.S. Forest Service map is advised.

Contact: Mount Baker-Snoqualmie National Forest, Darrington Ranger District, 1405 Emmens Street, Darrington, WA 98241; tel. (360) 436-1155; fax (360) 436-1309.

62 Phelps Creek 7

This campground is set at the confluence of Phelps Creek and the Chiwawa River. There's a key trailhead for backpackers and horseback riders nearby that provides access to the Glacier Peak Wilderness and Spider Meadows. It's advisable to obtain a U.S. Forest Service map.

Location: On the Chiwawa River in Wenatchee National Forest; map A3, grid f4.

Campsites, facilities: There are seven sites for tents or trailers less than 30 feet long. Picnic tables and fire grills are provided. Pit toilets are available, but there is no drinking water. Horse facilities are nearby. Leashed pets are permitted.

Reservations, fees: No reservations. Sites are $5 per night. Open mid-June to mid-October.

Directions: From Seattle on Interstate 5 drive north to Everett and U.S. 2. Turn east on U.S. 2 and drive 87 miles to Highway 207. Turn north on Highway 207 and drive four miles to Chiwawa Loop Road. Turn east on Chiwawa Loop Road and drive 1.4 miles to Chiwawa Valley Road (Forest Road 6200). Bear left (north) and continue for 23.6 miles to the campground.

Contact: Wenatchee National Forest, Lake Wenatchee Ranger District, 22976 Highway 207, Leavenworth, WA 98826; tel. (509) 763-3103; fax (509) 763-3211.

63 Deer Point Ferry-In   9

Here's another little-known spot set along the shore of Lake Chelan. If you want to camp on the remote east shore, this is one of three camps. The others are Prince Creek and Mitchell Creek. This is a good camp for anglers, because there isn't much to do but relax and wait for the fish to bite.

Location: On Lake Chelan in Wenatchee National Forest; map A3, grid f8.

Campsites, facilities: There are five tent sites accessible only by boat, ferry, or float plane. Picnic tables and fire rings are provided. Pit toilets are available, but there is no drinking water. A floating dock can accommodate about eight boats. Be prepared to protect food from bears.

Reservations, fees: No reservations, no camping fee; $5 per day docking fee. Open May through October.

Directions: From Wenatchee drive north on U.S. 97 and drive about 40 miles to Chelan and the ferry. Take the ferry and proceed to Deer Point, 22 miles from Chelan. (This voyage costs about $22 round-trip. For more information call (509) 682-2224.)

Contact: Wenatchee National Forest, Chelan Ranger District, 428 West Woodin Avenue, Chelan, WA 98816; tel. (509) 682-2576; fax (509) 682-9004.

64 Twenty-Five Mile Creek State Park   8

This campground is located on Twenty-Five Mile Creek near where it empties into Lake Chelan. Fishing access is close by, and fishing supplies, a dock, and boat moorage are available. There is also a small wading area for kids. Forest Road 5900, which heads west from the park, accesses several trailheads leading into the U.S. Forest Service lands of the Chelan Mountains. Obtain a U.S. Forest Service map of Wenatchee National Forest for details.

Location: Near Lake Chelan; map A3, grid f8.

Campsites, facilities: There are 63 standard campsites and 23 utility sites for trailers or RVs up to 30 feet long. Picnic tables are provided. A boat dock, fishing piers, marina, boat ramp, gasoline, grocery store, rest rooms, drinking water, electricity, and sewer hookups are available.

Reservations, fees: Reservations accepted, phone (800) 452-5687 ($6 reservation fee). Sites are $11-16 per night. Major credit cards accepted. Open early April to late October.

Directions: From Wenatchee drive north on U.S. 97 for 27 miles to Chelan and Highway 972 (Navarre Coulee Road). Turn left (north) and drive 16 miles to South Lakeshore Road. Turn left (northwest) and drive 12 miles to the park.

Contact: Twenty-Five Mile Creek State Park; Route 1, P.O. Box 142A, Chelan, WA 98816; tel. (800) 233-0321, (509) 687-3710.

65 Graham Harbor   **10**

This campground is set along Lake Chelan at the mouth of Graham Harbor Creek. It's one of the more remote and primitive campgrounds on giant Chelan. Fishing and boating are the main recreation attractions here.

Location: On Lake Chelan in Wenatchee National Forest; map A3, grid f8.

Campsites, facilities: There are five tent sites accessible only by boat, ferry, or float plane. Picnic tables and fire rings are provided. Pit toilets are available, but there is no drinking water. A floating dock can accommodate about 10 boats. Be prepared to protect food from bears.

Reservations, fees: No reservations, no camping fee; $5 per day docking fee. Open year-round.

Directions: From Wenatchee drive on U.S. 97 and drive about 40 miles to Chelan and the ferry. Take the ferry and proceed to Graham Harbor Creek, 31 miles from Chelan. (This voyage costs about $22 round-trip. For more information call (509) 682-2224.) The campground is also directly accessible by float plane. (Call Chelan Airways at (509) 682-5555 for more information.)

Contact: Wenatchee National Forest, Chelan Ranger District, 428 West Woodin Avenue, Chelan, WA 98816; tel. (509) 682-2576; fax (509) 682-9004.

66 Prince Creek   **10**

This camp is set along the shore of Lake Chelan at the mouth of Prince Creek. A trail from camp follows Prince Creek into the Lake Chelan-Sawtooth Wilderness, and then connects to a network of other trails—all of which lead to various lakes and streams. A U.S. Forest Service map shows details.

Location: On Lake Chelan in Wenatchee National Forest; map A3, grid f8.

Campsites, facilities: There are six tent sites accessible only by boat, ferry, or float plane. Picnic tables and fire rings are provided. Pit toilets are available, but there is no drinking water. A floating dock can accommodate about three boats. Be prepared to protect food from bears.

Reservations, fees: No reservations, no fee; $5 per day docking fee. Open May to mid-November.

Directions: From Wenatchee drive on U.S. 97 and drive about 40 miles to Chelan and the ferry. Take the ferry and proceed to Prince Creek, 35 miles from Chelan. (This voyage costs about $22 round-trip. For more information call (509) 682-2224.) The campground is also directly accessible by float plane. (Call Chelan Airways at (509) 682-5555 for more information.)

Contact: Wenatchee National Forest, Chelan Ranger District, 428 West Woodin Avenue, Chelan, WA 98816; tel. (509) 682-2576; fax (509) 682-9004.

67 Wallace Falls State Park Walk-In   8

Seattle is loaded with people, but very few of them know of this tiny jewel nestled in the forest near the scenic Wallace Falls. The campground is located in a heavily treed area at the trailhead to the falls. The trail leads along the Wallace River and is a lovely hike.

Location: Near Gold Bar; map A3, grid g0.

Campsites, facilities: There are walk-in six tent sites. Picnic tables and fire grills are provided. Flush toilets and drinking water are available. Some facilities are wheelchair accessible. Leashed pets are permitted.

Reservations, fees: No reservations accepted. Sites are $10 per night, plus $5 per extra vehicle each night. Open February through October.

Directions: From Seattle on Interstate 5, drive north to Everett and U.S. 2. Turn east on U.S. 2 and drive 28 miles to the town of Gold Bar and look for the sign for Wallace Falls State Park. Turn northeast at the sign and drive two miles to the park.

Contact: Wallace Falls State Park, P.O. Box 106, Gold Bar, WA 98251; tel. (800) 233-0321, (360) 793-0420.

68 Cutthroat Lakes Hike-In 9

Reaching this spot requires following difficult directions, but it's worth the effort. You'll find beautiful lakeside camps, trout fishing, hiking, and few other campers. The "lakes" are actually small ponds, but they're very pretty.

Location: On Bald Mountain; map A3, grid g0.

Campsites, facilities: There are 10 tent sites at this primitive, hike-in campground. Picnic tables, fire grills, and tent pads are provided. Portable vault toilets are available, but there is no drinking water. Leashed pets are permitted.

Reservations, fees: No reservations; no fee. Open mid-June through October.

Directions: From Seattle drive on Interstate 5 north to Everett and Highway 92. Turn east on Highway 92 and drive about 15 miles to the town of Granite Falls and Mountain Loop Highway (Forest Road 7). Continue northeast on Mountain Loop for 18 miles to Forest Road 4030 (at the bridge). Turn south and drive for three miles to Forest Road 4032 (follow the Mallard Ridge signs). Follow Road 4032 for one mile to the end where the trailhead begins. Hike 4.5 miles to Cutthroat Lakes.

Contact: Department of Natural Resources, Northwest Region, 919 North Township Street, Sedro-Woolley, WA 98284-9395; tel. (360) 856-3500.

69 Big Greider Lake Hike-In 8

This primitive campground on Big Greider Lake is an alternative to Little Greider Lake Campground, adjacent to Little Greider Lake. Hiking trails can be found nearby.

Location: On Big Greider Lake; map A3, grid g1.

Campsites, facilities: There are five tent sites at this primitive, hike-in campground. Picnic tables, fire grills, and tent pads are provided. Portable vault toilets and firewood are available, but there is no drinking water. Leashed pets are permitted.

Reservations, fees: No reservations; no fee. Open mid-June through October.

Directions: From Seattle on Interstate 5, drive north to Everett and U.S. 2. Turn east on U.S. 2 and drive 24 miles to Sultan. Continue one-half mile east to Sultan Basin Road. Turn north on Sultan Basin Road and drive 13.6 miles to a fork. Take the middle road (Road SLS 4000) and drive 8.5 miles to the Greider Lake Trailhead. From the trailhead, hike 2.5 miles to the campground.

Contact: Department of Natural Resources, Northwest Region, 919 North Township Street, Sedro-Woolley, WA 98284-9395; tel. (360) 856-3500.

70 Little Greider Lake Hike-In   8

This is prime country for hiking, backpacking, and trout fishing. The primitive, wooded campground is on Little Greider Lake.

Location: On Little Greider Lake; map A3, grid g1.

Campsites, facilities: There are nine tent sites at this primitive, hike-in campground. Picnic tables, fire grills, and tent pads are provided. Portable vault toilets and firewood are available. There is no drinking water. Leashed pets are permitted.

Reservations, fees: No reservations; no fee. Open mid-June through October.

Directions: From Seattle on Interstate 5, drive north to Everett and U.S. 2. Turn east on U.S. 2 and drive 24 miles to Sultan. Continue one-half mile east to Sultan Basin Road. Turn north on Sultan Basin Road and drive 13.6 miles to a fork. Take the middle road (Road SLS 4000) and drive 8.5 miles to the Greider Lake Trailhead. From the trailhead, hike 2.5 miles to the campground.

Contact: Department of Natural Resources, Northwest Region, 919 North Township Street, Sedro-Woolley, WA 98284-9395; tel. (360) 856-3500.

71 Boulder Lake Hike-In   9

This primitive, hike-in campground is on Boulder Lake. It's one of three hike-in camps in the immediate area: Little Greider Lake and Big Greider Lake are the other two. Hiking and fishing are two options.

Location: On Boulder Lake; map A3, grid g1.

Campsites, facilities: There are nine sites for tents at this primitive, hike-in campground. Picnic tables, fire grills, and tent pads are provided. Portable vault toilets and firewood are available. There is no drinking water. Leashed pets are permitted.

Reservations, fees: No reservations; no fee. Open mid-June through October.

Directions: From Seattle on Interstate 5, drive north to Everett and U.S. 2. Turn east on U.S. 2 and drive 24 miles to Sultan. Continue one-half mile east to Sultan Basin Road. Turn north on Sultan Basin Road and drive 13.6 miles to a fork. Take the middle road (Road SLS 4000) and drive 8.5 miles to the Greider Lake Trailhead. Bear right on Road SLS 7000 and drive one mile to the Boulder Lake Trailhead. From the Boulder Lake Trailhead hike 3.8 miles to the campground.

Contact: Department of Natural Resources, Northwest Region, 919 North Township Street, Sedro-Woolley, WA 98284-9395; tel. (360) 856-3500.

72 Troublesome Creek   8

Here's another one I bet you've never heard of. This campground is set along the North Fork of the Skykomish River among old-growth pine and fir. Highlights include a nature trail adjacent to the camp and rafting and good fishing in the river.

Location: On the North Fork of the Skykomish River in Mount Baker-Snoqualmie National Forest; map A3, grid g2.

Campsites, facilities: There are 24 sites for tents, trailers, or RVs up to 21 feet long and six walk-in tent sites. Picnic tables are provided. Drinking water and vault toilets are available. Some facilities are wheelchair accessible. Leashed pets are permitted.

Reservations, fees: Some sites, including three that are wheelchair accessible, may be reserved; phone (877) 444-6777 or access the website: www.reserveusa.com ($8.65 reservation fee). Sites are $6.50-10 per night. Open Memorial Day through Labor Day.

Directions: From Seattle on Interstate 5, drive north to Everett and U.S. 2. Turn east on U.S. 2 and drive 36 miles to the town of Index and Forest Road 63 (Index-Galena Road). Turn northeast on Forest Road 63 and drive 12 miles to the campground on the right.

Contact: Mount Baker-Snoqualmie National Forest, Skykomish Ranger District, P.O. Box 305, Skykomish, WA 98288; tel. (360) 677-2414.

73 Soda Springs   7

This campground along Wenatchee River Road is a small, quiet, closer-to-civilization alternative to Tumwater, without drinking water and with no trailer turnaround. It's off the beaten path in a pleasant wooded area. There are some excellent hiking trails nearby.

Location: On the Little Wenatchee River in Wenatchee National Forest; map A3, grid g4.

Campsites, facilities: There are five tent sites. Picnic tables and fire grills are provided. Pit toilets are available, but there is no drinking water. Leashed pets are permitted.

Reservations, fees: No reservations; no fee. Open May to late October, weather permitting.

Directions: From Seattle on Interstate 5, drive north to Everett and U.S. 2. Turn east on U.S. 2 and drive 87 miles to Highway 207. Turn north on Highway 207 and drive nine miles to Forest Road 6500. Continue west on Forest Road 6500 for seven miles to the campground.

Contact: Wenatchee National Forest, Lake Wenatchee Ranger District, 22976 Highway 207, Leavenworth, WA 98826; tel. (509) 763-3103; fax (509) 763-3211.

74 Lake Creek   6

Fishing can be excellent at this camp set in a remote and primitive spot along the Little Wenatchee River. Berry picking is a bonus in late summer.

Location: On the Little Wenatchee River in Wenatchee National Forest; map A3, grid g4.

Campsites, facilities: There are eight sites for tents, trailers or RVs. Picnic tables and fire grills are provided, but there is no drinking water. Pit toilets are available. Leashed pets are permitted.

Reservations, fees: No reservations; no fee. Open May to early November, weather permitting.

Directions: From Seattle on Interstate 5, drive north to Everett and U.S. 2. Turn east on U.S. 2 and drive 87 miles to Highway 207. Turn north on Highway 207 and drive nine miles to Forest Road 6500. Turn west on Forest Road 6500 and drive nine miles to the campground.

Contact: Wenatchee National Forest, Lake Wenatchee Ranger District, 22976 Highway 207, Leavenworth, WA 98826; tel. (509) 763-3103; fax (509) 763-3211.

75 Napeequa Crossing   8

Fishing access is nearby and a trail from this camp on the White River heads east for about 3.5 miles to Twin Lakes in the Glacier Peak Wilderness. It's definitely worth the hike, with scenic views and wildlife observation as your reward.

Location: On the White and Napequa Rivers in Wenatchee National Forest; map A3, grid g5.

Campsites, facilities: There are five sites for tents, trailers, or RVs up to 30 feet long. Picnic tables and fire grills are provided. Pit toilets are available, but there is no drinking water. Leashed pets are permitted.

Reservations, fees: No reservations; no fee. Open year-round, weather and snow level permitting.

Directions: From Seattle on Interstate 5, drive north to Everett and U.S. 2. Turn east on U.S. 2 and drive 87 miles to Highway 207. Turn north on Highway 207 and drive four miles to Chiwawa Loop Road. Turn right (east) and drive 0.9 mile to Forest Road 6400 (White River Road). Turn left (northwest) and drive 5.9 miles to the campground.

Contact: Wenatchee National Forest, Lake Wenatchee Ranger District, 22976 Highway 207, Leavenworth, WA 98826; tel. (509) 763-3103; fax (509) 763-3211.

76 White River Falls   9

Though very primitive, this quiet and beautiful campground is a perfect spot for those seeking solitude in the wilderness. It's next to White River Falls on the White River, and close to a major trailhead that connects to a network of hiking trails into the Glacier Peak Wilderness.

Location: On the White River in Wenatchee National Forest; map A3, grid g5.

Campsites, facilities: There are five tent sites. Picnic tables and fire grills are provided. Pit toilets are available, but there is no drinking water. Leashed pets are permitted.

Reservations, fees: No reservations; no fee. Open June to mid-October.

Directions: From Seattle on Interstate 5, drive north to Everett and U.S. 2. Turn east on U.S. 2 and drive 87 miles to Highway 207. Turn north on Highway 207 and drive four miles to Chiwawa Loop Road. Turn right (east) and drive 0.9 mile to Forest Road 6400 (White River Road). Turn left (northwest) and drive 9.9 miles to the campground.

Contact: Wenatchee National Forest, Lake Wenatchee Ranger District, 22976 Highway 207, Leavenworth, WA 98826; tel. (509) 763-3103 or fax 509) 763-3211.

77 Lake Wenatchee State Park

 8

Thanks to a nice location and drive-in sites that are spaced just right, you can expect plenty of company at this campground. The secluded campsites are set at the southeast end of Lake Wenatchee, which offers plenty of recreation opportunities, with a boat ramp nearby. In winter, there are groomed cross-country ski trails.

Location: On Lake Wenatchee; map A3, grid g5.

Campsites, facilities: There are two primitive tent sites and 197 developed sites for tents or self-contained RVs. Drinking water, fire grills, and picnic tables are provided. Flush toilets, a sanitary disposal station, a store, ice, showers, firewood, a restaurant, a playground, and horse rentals are available. Some facilities are wheelchair accessible. Boat docks, launching facilities, and rentals are nearby. Leashed pets are permitted.

Reservations, fees: Reservations accepted, phone (800) 452-5687 ($6 fee). Sites are $5-10 per night. Open April through September, weather permitting.

Directions: From Seattle on Interstate 5, drive north to Everett and U.S. 2. Turn east on U.S. 2 and drive 84 miles to Coles Corner and Highway 207. Turn north (left) on Highway 207 and drive three miles to the park entrance.

Contact: Lake Wenatchee State Park, Highway 207, Leavenworth, WA 98826; tel. (800) 233-0321 or (509) 763-3101.

78 Glacier View   9

This campground on the southwestern shore of Lake Wenatchee, near the head of the lake, and is one of the quieter camps on the lake. It's a popular spot for boating, swimming, fishing, and waterskiing. There are also some good hiking trails in the area and a golf course within a 10 minute drive.

Location: On Lake Wenatchee in Wenatchee National Forest; map A3, grid h5.

Campsites, facilities: There are 16 tent sites and four sites for very small RVs. Trailers are not recommended. Drinking water, fire grills, and picnic tables are provided. Pit toilets and a boat launch for very small boats are available. Leashed pets are permitted.

Reservations, fees: No reservations. $10 per night. Open June through September, weather permitting.

Directions: From Seattle on Interstate 5, drive north to Everett and U.S. 2. Turn east on U.S. 2 and drive 100 miles to Leavenworth and Highway 207. Turn north on Highway 207 and drive 3.5 miles to Cedar Brae Road. Turn west and drive four miles to Forest Road 290. Continue west on Forest Road 290 for 1.5 miles to the campground.

Contact: Wenatchee National Forest, Lake Wenatchee Ranger District, 22976 Highway 207, Leavenworth, WA 98826; tel. (509) 763-3103 or fax 509) 763-3211.

79 Silver Falls   10

This campground, an enchanted spot, is set at the confluence of Silver Creek and the Entiat River. A trail from camp leads one-half mile to the base of beautiful Silver Falls. Another 1.5 barrier-free trail overlooks the river.

Location: On the Entiat River in Wenatchee National Forest; map A3, grid g7.

Campsites, facilities: There are 30 sites for tents, trailers, or RVs up to 21 feet long, plus one group site. Drinking water, fire grills, and picnic tables are provided. Vault toilets are available. Some facilities are wheelchair accessible. Pets are permitted.

Reservations, fees: Reservations required for groups only, phone (877) 444-6777 or access the website: www.reserveusa.com ($8.65 reservations fee). Family sites are $9 per vehicle per night; the group site is $60 a night. Open mid-May to mid-October.

Directions: From Seattle on Interstate 5, drive north to Everett and U.S. 2. Turn east on U.S. 2 and drive 120 miles to U.S. 97-A. Turn north on U.S. 97-A and drive 18.5 miles to Entiat River Road. Turn northwest and drive 30 miles to the campground on the left.

Contact: Wenatchee National Forest, Entiat Ranger District, P.O. Box 476, Entiat, WA 98822; tel. (509) 784-1511.

🔟 Cottonwood   8

At 3,100 feet, this campground along the Entiat River is at a major trailhead leading into the Glacier Peak Wilderness and is a favorite with serious hikers. A U.S. Forest Service map details the backcountry. A bonus is good berry picking in season. Fishing is another alternative.

Location: On the Entiat River in Wenatchee National Forest; map A3, grid g7.

Campsites, facilities: There are 25 sites for tents or small RVs. Drinking water, fire grills, and picnic tables are provided. Pit toilets are available. Leashed pets are permitted.

Reservations, fees: No reservations accepted. Sites are $8 per vehicle per night. Open late June to mid-October.

Directions: From Seattle on Interstate 5, drive north to Everett and U.S. 2. Turn east on U.S. 2 and drive 120 miles to U.S. 97-A. Turn north on U.S. 97-A and drive 18.5 miles to Entiat River Road. Turn northwest and drive 38 miles to the campground on the left.

Contact: Wenatchee National Forest, Entiat Ranger District, P.O. Box 476, Entiat, WA 98822; tel. (509) 784-1511.

81 North Fork   8

One of seven campgrounds nestled along the Entiat River, North Fork is near the confluence of the Entiat and the North Fork of the Entiat River. Highlights of this pretty and shaded camp include river fishing access and Entiat Falls, which are nearby.

Location: On the Entiat River in Wenatchee National Forest; map A3, grid g7.

Campsites, facilities: There are eight tent sites and one site for a small RV. Drinking water, fire grills, and picnic tables are provided. Pit toilets are available. Leashed pets are permitted.

Reservations, fees: No reservations. Sites are $7 per vehicle per night. Open mid-June to mid-October.

Directions: From Seattle on Interstate 5, drive north to Everett and U.S. 2. Turn east on U.S. 2 and drive 120 miles to U.S. 97-A. Turn north on U.S. 97-A and drive 18.5 miles to Entiat River Road. Turn northwest and drive 33 miles to the campground on the left.

Contact: Wenatchee National Forest, Entiat Ranger District, P.O. Box 476, Entiat, WA 98822; tel. (509) 784-1511.

82 Lake Creek   7

This camp is located at the confluence of Lake Creek and the Entiat River, at a trail crossroads. One trail heads northeast up to Lake Creek Basin in the Chelan Mountains, and several others head south and west into the Entiat Mountains. Consult a U.S. Forest Service map for more details on backcountry routes.

Location: On the Entiat River in Wenatchee National Forest; map A3, grid g7.

Campsites, facilities: There are 18 tent sites. Drinking water, picnic tables, and fire grills are provided. Vault toilets are available. Leashed pets are permitted.

Reservations, fees: No reservations. Sites are $8 per night per vehicle. Open May to mid-October.

Directions: From Seattle on Interstate 5, drive north to Everett and U.S. 2. Turn east on U.S. 2 and drive 120 miles to U.S. 97-A. Turn north on U.S. 97-A and drive 18.5 miles to Entiat River Road. Turn northwest and drive 28 miles to the campground on the left.

Contact: Wenatchee National Forest, Entiat Ranger District, P.O. Box 476, Entiat, WA 98822; tel. (509) 784-1511.

83 Fox Creek   7

Fishing access is a draw at this camp along the Entiat River near Fox Creek. During the winter, some of the snow-covered logging roads in the area are open for use by snowmobiles and cross-country skiers. Contact the U.S. Forest Service for details.

Location: On the Entiat River in Wenatchee National Forest; map A3, grid g7.

Campsites, facilities: There are 16 tent sites. Drinking water, fire grills, and picnic tables are provided. Vault toilets are available. Leashed pets are permitted.

Reservations, fees: No reservations. Sites are $8 per night per vehicle. Open May to mid-October.

Directions: From Seattle on Interstate 5, drive north to Everett and U.S. 2. Turn east on U.S. 2 and drive 120 miles to U.S. 97-A. Turn north on U.S. 97-A and drive 18.5 miles to Entiat River Road. Turn northwest and drive 27 miles to the campground on the left.

Contact: Wenatchee National Forest, Entiat Ranger District, P.O. Box 476, Entiat, WA 98822; tel. (509) 784-1511.

84 Lake Chelan State Park
 10

This is the recreation headquarters for Lake Chelan. The park provides boat docks and concession stands on the shore of the 55-mile lake. See the descriptions of Holden Ballpark, Domke Lake, Lucerne, Deer Point, Graham Harbor, and Prince Creek for some of the recreation options available. Water sports include fishing, swimming, scuba diving, and waterskiing.

Location: On Lake Chelan; map A3, grid g9.

Campsites, facilities: There are two primitive tent sites, 127 developed tent sites, and 17 sites with full hookups for trailers or RVs up to 30 feet. Picnic tables are provided. Flush toilets, a sanitary disposal station, a store, a restaurant, ice, a playground, electricity, drinking water, sewer hookups, showers, a beach area, a boat dock, and launching facilities are available. Some facilities are wheelchair accessible.

Reservations, fees: Reservations accepted, phone (800) 452-5687 ($6 reservation fee). Sites are $11-16 per night. Major credit cards accepted. Open April through October.

Directions: From Wenatchee drive north on U.S. 97-A for 27 miles to Highway 9761 (Navarre Coulee Road). Turn left (north) and drive 16 miles to the park and South Lakeshore Road (well signed).

Contact: Lake Chelan State Park, Route 1, P.O. Box 90, Chelan, WA 98816; tel. (800) 233-0321 or (509) 687-3710.

85 Kamei Resort   6

This resort is on Lake Wapato, about two miles from Lake Chelan. Note that this is a seasonal lake that closes midsummer. If you have an extra day, take the ferryboat ride on Lake Chelan, which is detailed in the trip note for Holden. It's an adventure in itself.

Location: On Lake Wapato; map A3, grid g9.

Campsites, facilities: There are 50 sites for tents, trailers, or RVs of any length. Electricity, drinking water, some sewer hookups, and picnic tables are provided. Flush toilets, showers, and ice are available. Boat docks, launching facilities, and rentals are nearby. Leashed pets and motorbikes are permitted.

Reservations, fees: Reservations accepted beginning in January. Sites are $15 per night. Open late April through July.

Directions: From Wenatchee drive north on U.S. 97-A and drive 40 miles to the town of Chelan and Highway 150. Turn west on Highway 150 and drive seven miles to Wapato Lake Road. Turn north on Wapato Lake Road and drive three miles to the resort at 5000 Wapato Lake Road.

Contact: Kamei Resort, 2300 Wapato Lake Road Route 1, P.O. Box 238, Manson, WA 98831; tel. (509) 687-3690.

86 Lakeview Park   6

This developed park for RVs and trailers is set along the shore of Lake Chelan. It's a more commercial alternative to the primitive U.S. Forest Service campgrounds scattered around the lake. This resort has an interesting quirk: they'll accept tent campers, but only families with children—no couples or singles. Their reason? To discourage noise and parties, they say. No such restrictions for RVers, though.

Location: On Lake Chelan; map A3, grid g9.

Campsites, facilities: There are 30 sites for trailers or RVs of any length. The sites will also accommodate tents, but only families are permitted to tent camp. Electricity, drinking water, and sewer hookups are provided. Flush toilets, sanitary services, and showers are available. Boat docks and launching facilities are located within one mile. Leashed pets are permitted.

Reservations, fees: Reservations accepted. Sites are $10-15 per night. Open April to November.

Directions: From Wenatchee drive north on U.S. 97-A for 40 miles to the town of Chelan and Highway 150. Turn west on Highway 150 and drive 5.2 miles northwest to the park on the right.

Contact: Lakeview Park, P.O. Box 324, Manson, WA 98831; (509) 687-3612.

87 Mitchell Creek Ferry-In   8

Primitive and remote, Mitchell Creek Campground is nestled along the shore of Lake Chelan, where fishing, swimming, boating, hiking, and waterskiing keep visitors busy.

Location: On Lake Chelan in Wenatchee National Forest; map A3, grid g9.

Campsites, facilities: There are six tent sites accessible only by boat, ferry, or float plane. Picnic tables and fire rings are provided. Pit toilets and a group shelter are available, but there is no drinking water. An on-site floating dock has a 17-boat capacity.

Reservations, fees: No reservations, no camping fee; $5 per day docking fee. Open May to late October.

Directions: From Wenatchee drive north on U.S. 97-A for 40 miles to the town of Chelan. Take the ferry to Mitchell Creek, 15 miles from Chelan. (This voyage costs about $22 round-trip. For more information call (509) 682-2224.) The campground is also directly accessible by float plane. (Call Chelan Airways at (509) 682-5555.)

Contact: Wenatchee National Forest, Chelan Ranger District, 428 West Woodin Avenue, Chelan, WA 98816; tel. (509) 682-2576; fax (509) 682-9004.

88 Money Creek Campground   5

Money Creek Campground is on the Skykomish River in an old-growth stand, with hiking trails a moderate driving distance away. Railroad buffs will be interested in the fact that the Burlington Northern rail runs along the western boundary of the campground.

Location: On the Skykomish River in Mount Baker-Snoqualmie National Forest; Map A3, grid h2.

Campsites, facilities: There are 24 sites for tents, trailers, or RVs up to 21 feet long. Picnic tables are provided. Vault toilets and drinking water are available. A store, a cafe, and ice are located within 3.5 miles. Some sites are wheelchair accessible. Leashed pets are permitted.

Reservations, fees: Some sites can be reserved; phone (877) 444-6777 or access the website: www.reserveusa.com ($8.65 reservation fee). Sites are $12 per night, plus $6.50 for each additional vehicle. Open Memorial Day through Labor Day.

Directions: From Seattle on Interstate 5, drive north to Everett and U.S. 2. Turn east on U.S. 2 and drive 46 miles to Old Cascade Highway, 11 miles east of Index. Turn south on Old Cascade Highway and drive across the bridge to the campground.

Contact: Mount Baker-Snoqualmie National Forest, Skykomish Ranger District, P.O. Box 305, Skykomish, WA 98288; tel. (360) 677-2414; fax (425) 744-3265.

89 Beckler River   7

Located on the Beckler River at an elevation of 900 feet, this camp has scenic river-side sites in old-growth timber and good fishing prospects. The Skykomish Ranger Station is just a couple of miles away; the rangers will be happy to provide you with maps and answer any questions.

Location: On the Beckler River in Mount Baker-Snoqualmie National Forest; map A3, grid h3.

Campsites, facilities: There are 27 sites for tents, trailers, or RVs up to 21 feet long. Picnic tables and fire grills are provided. Vault toilets and drinking water are available. A store, a cafe, and ice are located within two miles. Some sites and facilities are wheelchair accessible. Leashed pets are permitted.

Reservations, fees: Some sites can be reserved; phone (877) 444-6777 or access the website: www.reserveusa.com ($8.65 reservation fee). Sites are $10 per night. Open Memorial Day through Labor Day.

Directions: From Seattle on Interstate 5, drive north to Everett and U.S. 2. Turn east on U.S. 2 and drive 49 miles to Skykomish. Continue east on U.S. 2 for one-half mile to Forest Road 65. Turn north (left) on Forest Road 65 and drive 1.6 miles to the camp on the left.

Contact: Mount Baker-Snoqualmie National Forest, Skykomish Ranger District, P.O. Box 305, Skykomish, WA 98288; tel. (360) 677-2414; fax (425) 744-3265.

90 Miller River Group Camp   8

This campground, located along the Miller River a short distance from the boundary of the Alpine Lakes Wilderness, is in prime mountain territory. If you continue another seven miles on Forest Road 6410, you'll get to a trailhead leading to Lake Dorothy and many other backcountry lakes. Be aware that there is a group limit of 12 people in wilderness areas. A U.S. Forest Service map is essential.

Location: Near the Alpine Lakes Wilderness in Mount Baker-Snoqualmie National Forest; map A3, grid h3.

Campsites, facilities: This is a group camp with 18 sites for tents, trailers, or RVs. Picnic tables and fire grills are provided. Vault toilets, drinking water, a group barbecue, and a 24-foot group table are available. A store, a cafe, and ice are within five miles. Leashed pets are permitted.

Reservations, fees: Reservations required, phone (877) 444-6777 or access the website: www.reserveusa.com ($8.65 reservation fee). Sites are $50 for the first 50 people, $125 for 51-75, and $150 for 76-100 campers. Open mid-May to mid-September.

Directions: From Seattle on Interstate 5, drive north to Everett and U.S. 2. Turn east on U.S. 2 and drive 46 miles to Old Cascade Highway, 11 miles east of Index. Turn south on Old Cascade Highway and drive one mile (across the bridge) to Forest Road 6410. Turn right (south) and drive two miles to the campground on the left.

Contact: Mount Baker-Snoqualmie National Forest, Skykomish Ranger District, P.O. Box 305, Skykomish, WA 98288; tel. (360) 677-2414; fax (425) 744-3265.

91 Nason Creek

This campground is on Nason Creek near Lake Wenatchee. Recreat ties include swimming, fishing, and waterskiing. Boat rentals, horseback golfing are nearby.

Location: Near Lake Wenatchee in Wenatchee National Forest; map A3, grid h6.

Campsites, facilities: There are 29 tent sites and 41 sites for tents, trailers, or RVs up to 31 feet long. Drinking water, fire grills, picnic tables, and flush toilets are provided. Boat launching facilities are nearby.

Reservations, fees: No reservations. Sites are $10 per night. Open May to late October.

Directions: From Seattle on Interstate 5, drive north to Everett and U.S. 2. Turn east on U.S. 2 and drive 87 miles to Highway 207, one mile west of Winton. Turn north on Highway 207 and drive 3.5 miles to Cedar Brae Road (County Road 413). Turn west and drive 100 yards to the campground.

Contact: Wenatchee National Forest, Lake Wenatchee Ranger District, 22976 Highway 207, Leavenworth, WA 98826; tel. (509) 763-3103; fax (509) 763-3211.

92 Tumwater      7

This large, popular camp provides a little bit of both worlds. It's a good layover for campers cruising U.S. 2. But there are also two forest roads nearby, each less than a mile long, which end at trailheads that provide access to the Alpine Lakes Wilderness. If you don't like to hike, no problem. The camp is on the Wenatchee River in Tumwater Canyon.

Location: Near the Alpine Lakes Wilderness in Wenatchee National Forest; map A3, grid h6.

Campsites, facilities: There are 84 sites for tents, trailers, or RVs up to 30 feet long, and one group site for up to 75 people. Drinking water, fire grills, and picnic tables are provided. Flush toilets are available. Some facilities are wheelchair accessible. Leashed pets are permitted.

Reservations, fees: Reservations required for the group site only, phone (800) 274-6104. Rates are $11 per night for single sites, and $60 for group sites. Open May to mid-October.

Directions: From Seattle on Interstate 5, drive north to Everett and U.S. 2. Turn east on U.S. 2 and drive 93 miles to the campground, 10 miles west of Leavenworth.

Contact: Wenatchee National Forest, Leavenworth Ranger District, 600 Sherbourne, Leavenworth, WA 98826; tel. (509) 548-6977; fax (509) 548-5817.

93 Midway Village Grocery and RV Park
5

This private campground is along the Wenatchee River a short distance from Lake Wenatchee State Park and Fish Lake, noted for great fishing year-round. Nearby recreation options include waterskiing, swimming, boating, fishing, hiking, and bike riding. The average annual snowfall is 12 feet; winter options include snowmobiling, cross-country skiing, dogsledding, and ice fishing.

Location: On the Wenatchee River; map A3, grid h6.

Campsites, facilities: There are 18 sites for trailers or RVs of any length. Electricity (20 and 30 amp), drinking water, sewer hookups, and picnic tables are provided. A store, showers, firewood, a cafe, a laundry room, ice, bottled gas, and a playground are available. Boat docks, launching facilities, and rentals are nearby. Leashed pets and motorbikes are permitted.

Reservations, fees: Reservations accepted. Sites are $9-15 per night. Major credit cards accepted. Open year-round.

Directions: From Seattle on Interstate 5, drive north to Everett and U.S. 2. Turn east on U.S. 2 and drive 88 miles over Steven's Pass to Coles Corner at Highway 207. Turn left (north) on Highway 207 and drive four miles, crossing the bridge over the Wenatchee River to a Y. Turn right at the Y and drive one-quarter mile to the park on the right.

Contact: Midway Village Grocery and RV Park, 14193 Chiwawa Loop Road, Leavenworth, WA 98826; tel. (509) 763-3344.

94 Pine Flat 5

This camp has ready access to the Mad River ORV (off-road vehicles) area and is popular with bikers and ORV enthusiasts.

Location: Near Entiat River, in Wenatchee National Forest; map A3, grid h8.

Campsites, facilities: There are seven tent sites and one group site, which can accommodate up to 50 campers. Drinking water, garbage service, vault toilets, and fire grills are available.

Reservations, fees: Reservations required for group site only; phone (877) 444-6777 or access the website: www.reserveusa.com ($8.65 reservation fee). Sites are $5 per night; the group site is $60 per night. Open late May through October, weather permitting.

Directions: From Wenatchee drive north on U.S. 97-A for 18.5 miles to Entiat River Road. Turn (left) northwest on County Road 371/Entiat River Road and drive nine miles to Forest Road 5700. Continue northwest on Forest Road 5700 for one mile to the campground.

Contact: Wenatchee National Forest, Entiat Ranger District, P.O. Box 476, Entiat, WA 98822; tel. (509) 784-1511; fax (509) 784-1150.

95 Entiat City Park 8

Lake Entiat is actually a dammed portion of the Columbia River. Rocky Reach Dam, located 10 miles south, is the closest to this campground. Access to nearby launching facilities makes this a good camping spot for boaters.

Location: On the Columbia River; map A3, grid h9.

Campsites, facilities: There are 50 tent sites and 31 sites for trailers or RVs. Electricity, drinking water, and picnic tables are provided. Flush toilets, sanitary services, showers, a playground, bottled gas, a store, a cafe, a laundry room, and ice are available. Boat docks and launching facilities are nearby. Motorbikes are permitted. No open fires, dogs or alcohol are permitted.

Reservations, fees: Phone for reservation information. Sites are $13-16 per night. Open April to mid-September.

Directions: From Wenatchee drive north on U.S. 97-A for 16 miles to Entiat and the park entrance on the right (Shearson Street is adjacent on the left). Turn right and drive to the park along the shore of Lake Entiat.

Contact: Entiat City Park, P.O. Box 228, Entiat, WA 98822; tel. (800) 736-8428, (509) 784-1500.

96 Fish Lake   10

This campground is way out there, and just a short jaunt to the Alpine Lakes Wilderness. There are numerous opportunities to access trails into the backcountry. The camp is nestled along the shore of tiny Tucquala Lake, a jewel near the headwaters of the Cle Elum River.

Location: On Tucquala Lake in Wenatchee National Forest; map A3, grid i3.

Campsites, facilities: There are 15 tent sites. Picnic tables and fire grills are provided. Vault toilets are available, but there is no drinking water. Leashed pets are permitted.

Reservations, fees: No reservations; no fee. Open July through September.

Directions: In Seattle on Interstate 5, turn east on Interstate 90 and drive 78 miles to Exit 80 (two miles before Cle Elum). Take Exit 80 and turn north on Bullfrog Road and drive four miles to Highway 903. Continue north on Highway 903 for 19 miles to Forest Road 4330. Turn northeast and drive 11 miles to the campground. The access road is rough; no trailers are permitted.

Contact: Wenatchee National Forest, Cle Elum Ranger District, West Second Street, Cle Elum, WA 98922; tel. (509) 674-4411; fax (509) 674-4794.

97 Eightmile   8

Trailheads for backpackers providing access to many lakes and streams in the Alpine Lakes Wilderness are located within two miles of the campground set along Icicle and Eightmile Creeks. Horseback riding opportunities are within four miles and golf within five miles.

Location: Near the Alpine Lakes Wilderness in Wenatchee National Forest; map A3, grid i5.

Campsites, facilities: There are 45 sites for tents, trailers, or RVs up to 21 feet long. Drinking water, fire grills, and picnic tables are provided. Vault toilets are available. Leashed pets are permitted.

Reservations, fees: Reservations required for group sites only; phone (800) 274-6104 ($16 reservation fee). Rates are $9 per night for single sites, and $60 per night for group sites. Open mid-April to late October.

Directions: From Seattle on Interstate 5, drive north to Everett and U.S. 2. Turn east on U.S. 2 and drive 103 miles to Leavenworth and County Road 76 (Icicle River Road). Turn south and drive eight miles to the campground.

Contact: Wenatchee National Forest, Leavenworth Ranger District, 600 Sherbourne, Leavenworth, WA 98826; tel. (509) 548-6977; fax (509) 548-5817.

98 Bridge Creek   8

This is a small, quiet spot along Icicle and Bridge Creeks. About two miles south of the camp at Eightmile Creek is a trail that accesses the Alpine Lakes Wilderness. See a U.S. Forest Service map for details. Horseback riding opportunities are within four miles and golf within five miles.

Location: On Icicle Creek in Wenatchee National Forest; map A3, grid i5.

Campsites, facilities: There are six tent sites. Drinking water, fire grills, and picnic tables are provided. Vault toilets are available. Leashed pets are permitted.

Reservations, fees: Reservations required for groups only; phone (800) 274-6104. Single sites are $8 per night, and group sites are $60 per night. Open mid-April to late October.

Directions: From Seattle on Interstate 5, drive north to Everett and U.S. 2. Turn east on U.S. 2 and drive 103 miles to Leavenworth and County Road 76 (Icicle River Road). Turn south and drive 9.4 miles to the campground.

Contact: Wenatchee National Forest, Leavenworth Ranger District, 600 Sherbourne, Leavenworth, WA 98826; tel. (509) 548-6977; fax (509) 548-5817.

99 Johnny Creek   8

This campground is set along Icicle and Johnny Creeks. See Bridge Creek Camp for area information.

Location: On Icicle Creek in Wenatchee National Forest; map A3, grid i5.

Campsites, facilities: There are 65 sites for tents, trailers, or RVs up to 30 feet long. Drinking water, fire grills, and picnic tables are provided. Vault toilets are available. Some facilities are wheelchair accessible. Leashed pets are permitted.

Reservations, fees: No reservations. Sites are $8-9 per night. Open May to late October.

Directions: From Seattle on Interstate 5, drive north to Everett and U.S. 2. Turn east on U.S. 2 and drive 103 miles to Leavenworth and County Road 76 (Icicle River Road). Turn south and drive 12.4 miles to the campground.

Contact: Wenatchee National Forest, Leavenworth Ranger District, 600 Sherbourne, Leavenworth, WA 98826; tel. (509) 548-6977; fax (509) 548-5817.

100 Chatter Creek   8

Icicle and Chatter Creeks are the backdrop for this creekside campground. Trails lead out in several directions from the camp into the Alpine Lakes Wilderness.

Location: Near the Alpine Lakes Wilderness in Wenatchee National Forest; map A3, grid i5.

Campsites, facilities: There are nine tent sites and three sites for tents, trailers, or RVs up to 21 feet long. Drinking water, fire grills, and picnic tables are provided. Vault toilets are available. Leashed pets are permitted.

Reservations, fees: Reservations required for group sites only, phone (800) 274-6104 ($16 reservation fee). Rates are $8 per night for single sites, and $60 per night for group sites. Open May to late October.

Directions: From Seattle on Interstate 5, drive north to Everett and U.S. 2. Turn east on U.S. 2 and drive 103 miles to Leavenworth and County Road 76 (Icicle River Road). Turn south and drive 16.1 miles to the campground.

Contact: Wenatchee National Forest, Leavenworth Ranger District, 600 Sherbourne, Leavenworth, WA 98826; tel. (509) 548-6977; fax (509) 548-5817.

101 Rock Island 8

Rock Island is one of several campgrounds in the immediate area along Icicle Creek about a mile from the trailhead that takes hikers into the Alpine Lakes Wilderness. This is a pretty spot, with good fishing access.

Location: Near the Alpine Lakes Wilderness in Wenatchee National Forest; map A3, grid i5.

Campsites, facilities: There are 12 tent sites and 10 sites for tents, trailers, or RVs up to 21 feet long. Drinking water, fire grills, and picnic tables are provided. Vault toilets are available. Leashed pets are permitted.

Reservations, fees: No reservations accepted. Sites are $8 per night. Open May to late October.

Directions: From Seattle on Interstate 5, drive north to Everett and U.S. 2. Turn east on U.S. 2 and drive 103 miles to Leavenworth and County Road 76 (Icicle River Road). Turn south and drive 17.7 miles to the campground.

Contact: Wenatchee National Forest, Leavenworth Ranger District, 600 Sherbourne, Leavenworth, WA 98826; tel. (509) 548-6977; fax (509) 548-5817.

102 Ida Creek 8

This campground is one of several small, quiet camps along Icicle and Ida Creeks, with recreation options similar to Chatter Creek and Rock Island campgrounds.

Location: On Icicle Creek in Wenatchee National Forest; map A3, grid i5.

Campsites, facilities: There are five tent sites and five sites for tents, trailers, or RVs up to 21 feet long. Drinking water, fire grills, and picnic tables are provided. Vault toilets are available. Leashed pets are permitted.

Reservations, fees: No reservations. Sites are $8 per night. Open May to late October.

Directions: From Seattle on Interstate 5, drive north to Everett and U.S. 2. Turn east on U.S. 2 and drive 103 miles to Leavenworth and County Road 76 (Icicle River Road). Turn south and drive 14.2 miles to the campground.

Contact: Wenatchee National Forest, Leavenworth Ranger District, 600 Sherbourne, Leavenworth, WA 98826; tel. (509) 548-6977; fax (509) 548-5817.

103 Blackpine Creek Horse Camp
 8

Blackpine Creek Horse Camp is set on Black Pine Creek near Icicle Creek, at a major trailhead leading into the Alpine Lakes Wilderness. It's one of seven rustic camps on the creek, with the distinction of being the only one with facilities for horses. For that reason, it's often used as a base camp for horse pack trips.

Location: Near the Alpine Lakes Wilderness in Wenatchee National Forest; map A3, grid i5.

Campsites, facilities: There are 10 sites for tents, trailers, or RVs up to 21 feet long. Drinking water, fire grills, and picnic tables are provided. Vault toilets, firewood, and riding facilities are available. Leashed pets are permitted.

Reservations, fees: No reservations. Sites are $7 per night. Open mid-May to late October.

Directions: From Seattle on Interstate 5, drive north to Everett and U.S. 2. Turn east on U.S. 2 and drive 103 miles to Leavenworth and County Road 76 (Icicle River Road). Turn south and drive 19.2 miles to the campground.

Contact: Wenatchee National Forest, Leavenworth Ranger District, 600 Sherbourne, Leavenworth, WA 98826; tel. (509) 548-6977; fax (509) 548-5817.

104 Pine Village Resort/KOA Leavenworth

      8

This lovely resort is near the quaint "Bavarian village" of Leavenworth, to which the park provides a free shuttle in the summer. The spectacularly scenic area is surrounded by the Cascade Mountains and set among ponderosa pines. The camp has access to the Wenatchee River, not to mention many luxurious extras, including a hot tub and heated pool. The park allows campfires and has firewood available. Nearby recreation options include an 18-hole golf course and hiking trails. Make a point to spend a day in Leavenworth if possible; it offers authentic German food and architecture along with music and art shows in the summer.

Location: Near the Wenatchee River; map A3, grid i7.

Campsites, facilities: There are 40 tent sites and 60 sites for trailers or RVs of any length; 22 are drive-through. Picnic tables are provided. Flush toilets, sanitary services, showers, firewood, a recreation hall, cable TV, a store, a laundry room, ice, a playground, a spa, a heated swimming pool, electricity, drinking water, and sewer hookups are available. Bottled gas and a cafe are located within one mile. Pets and motorbikes are permitted.

Reservations, fees: Reservations accepted. Sites are $24-32 per night. Open April to November.

Directions: From Seattle on Interstate 5, drive north to Everett and U.S. 2. Turn east on U.S. 2 and drive 103 miles to Leavenworth. Continue east on U.S. 2 for one-quarter mile to River Bend Drive. Turn north and drive one-half mile to the campground on the right.

Contact: Pine Village Resort/KOA Leavenworth, 11401 River Bend Drive, Leavenworth, WA 98826; tel. (509) 548-7709; fax (509) 548-7709; website: www.koa.com.

105 Icicle River RV Park   9

Icicle River RV Park is one of three campgrounds in the immediate area. The others are Pine Village Resort and Chalet Trailer Park. This pretty, wooded spot is set along the Icicle River, where fishing and swimming are available. The park is exceptionally clean and scenic, and even has its own putting green. An 18-hole golf course and hiking trails are nearby.

Location: On Icicle River; map A3, grid i6.

Campsites, facilities: There are 100 sites for trailers or RVs of any length; 14 are drive-through. Electricity, drinking water, sewer hookups, and picnic tables are provided. Flush toilets, cable TV, modem access, a hot tub and bottled gas are available. Showers and firewood are available for an extra fee. Pets are permitted.

Reservations, fees: Reservations accepted. Sites are $22-26 per night. Open year-round.

Directions: From Seattle on Interstate 5, drive north to Everett and U.S. 2. Turn east on U.S. 2 and drive 103 miles to Leavenworth and County Road 76 (Icicle River Road). Turn south and drive three miles to the park on the left.

Contact: Icicle River RV Park, 7305 Icicle Road, Leavenworth, WA 98826; tel.(509) 548-5420; fax (509) 548-6207.

106 Chalet Trailer Park   5

This park along the Wenatchee River near Leavenworth is within walking distance of quaint Bavarian Village shops and restaurants. A pleasant grassy area is provided for tents. Nearby recreation options include an 18-hole golf course and fishing hiking, biking, and swimming opportunities.

Location: On the Wenatchee River; map A3, grid i7.

Campsites, facilities: There are 29 sites for trailers or RVs of any length, and a grassy area for tents. Electricity, drinking water, sewer and cable TV hookups, and picnic tables are provided. Flush toilets, sanitary services, propane, and showers are available. Bottled gas, a store, a cafe, a coin-laundry, and ice can be found within one mile. Leashed pets and motorbikes are permitted.

Reservations, fees: No reservations. Sites are $22-24 per night. Open early May through early October.

Directions: From Seattle on Interstate 5, drive north to Everett and U.S. 2. Turn east on U.S. 2 and drive 103 miles to Leavenworth and Duncan Road. Turn south and drive 150 feet to the campground on the right.

Contact: Chalet Trailer Park, P.O. Box 288, Leavenworth, WA 98826; tel. (509) 548-4578.

107 Lincoln Rock State Park   5

An alternative to nearby Entiat City Park, this place is ideal for families with RVs or trailers. It's adjacent to the Rocky Reach Dam along the shore of Lake Entiat. Water sports include swimming, boating, and waterskiing.

Location: On Lake Entiat; map A3, grid i8.

Campsites, facilities: There are 27 sites for tents or self-contained RVs, and 67 sites with full hookups for trailers or RVs up to 65 feet long. Picnic tables and fire grills are provided. Flush toilets, a sanitary disposal station, a playground, athletic fields, horseshoe pits, swimming beach, amphitheater, three picnic shelters, showers, and firewood are available. Some facilities are wheelchair accessible. Boat docks and launching facilities are located on Lake Entiat. Leashed pets are permitted.

Reservations, fees: Reservations accepted, phone (800) 452-5687 ($6 reservation fee). Sites are $5-14 per night. Open March through September.

Directions: From Wenatchee drive northeast on U.S. 2 for seven miles to the park on the left.

Contact: Lincoln Rock State Park, Route 3, P.O. Box 3137, East Wenatchee, WA 98801; tel. (800) 233-0321 or (509) 884-8702.

108 Tinkham   9

Travelers heading west to Seattle will find this campground along the Snoqualmie River a good layover for the night. Not far north is the Alpine Lakes Wilderness, a spectacularly beautiful area. See a U.S. Forest Service map for trail locations. There are several ski areas to the east. Franklin Falls, a side trip worth taking, is also nearby.

Location: On the Snoqualmie River in Mount Baker-Snoqualmie National Forest; map A3, grid j0.

Campsites, facilities: There are 48 sites for tents, trailers, or RVs up to 35 feet long. Picnic tables are provided. Vault toilets, garbage bins, and drinking water are available. Firewood is available for purchase. Some facilities are wheelchair accessible. Leashed pets are permitted.

Reservations, fees: Some sites can be reserved; phone (877) 444-6777 or access the website: www.reserveusa.com ($8.65 reservation fee). Sites are $12 per night. Open mid-May to mid-September.

Directions: In Seattle on Interstate 5, turn east on Interstate 90. Drive east on Interstate 90 to Exit 42. Take that exit and turn right on Tinkham Road (Forest Road 55) and drive southeast 1.5 miles to the campground on the left. A U.S. Forest Service map is advisable.

Contact: Mount Baker-Snoqualmie National Forest, North Bend Ranger District, 42404 SE North Bend Way, North Bend, WA 98045; tel. (425) 888-1421.

109 Denny Creek   8

This site, along with the others nearby, is very near the water. The campground is secluded in an area of Douglas fir, hemlock, and cedar, with hiking trails available in addition to swimming and rafting opportunities. Golf is nearby.

Location: On Denny Creek; map A3, grid j1.

Campsites, facilities: There are 33 sites for tents or trailers up to 35 feet long and one group site which can accommodate up to 35 campers. Picnic tables and drinking water is provided. Electricity is available at some sites for an extra charge. Vault and flush toilets, fire pits and a dump station are available. Firewood is available for purchase. Leashed pets are permitted.

Reservations, fees: Reservations accepted for family sites and required for the group site; phone (877) 444-6777 or access the website: www.reserveusa.com ($8.65 reservation fee). Sites are $12-14 per night with an additional $7 per additional vehicle. The group site is $75 per night. Open late May to mid-October, weather permitting.

Directions: In Seattle on Interstate 5, turn east on Interstate 90. Drive east on Interstate 90 to Exit 47. Take that exit, cross the freeway, and at the T intersection turn right and drive one quarter mile to Denny Creek Road (Forest Road 58). Turn left on Denny Creek Road and drive two miles to the campground on the left.

Contact: Mt. Baker-Snoqualmie National Forest, North Bend Ranger District, 42404 SE North Bend Way, North Bend, WA 98045; tel. (425) 888-1421; fax (425) 888-1910.

110 Crystal Springs   6

This campground is just off Interstate 90, but with old-growth trees and a short drive to Kachess and Keechelus Lakes. Both lakes have boat ramps. For winter sports, there are also several sno-parks in the area. The Pacific West Ski Area is at the north end of Keechelus Lake.

Location: Near Kachess and Keechelus Lakes in Wenatchee National Forest; map A3, grid j2.

Campsites, facilities: There are 20 tent sites and six sites for tents, trailers, or RVs up to 21 feet long. Drinking water, fire grills, and picnic tables are provided. Pit toilets and firewood are available. Leashed pets are permitted.

Reservations, fees: No reservations. Sites are $12 per night for the first vehicle, $10 per night for the second vehicle. Open mid-May to mid-September.

Directions: In Seattle on Interstate 5, turn east on Interstate 90. Drive east on Interstate 90 for 60 miles to Exit 62. Take that exit to Forest Road 212. Turn northwest on Forest Road 212 and drive one-half mile to the campground.

Contact: Wenatchee National Forest, Cle Elum Ranger District, West Second Street, Cle Elum, WA 98922; tel. (509) 674-4411; fax (509) 674-4794.

111 Cayuse Horse Camp   6

It's located along the Cle Elum River at major trailheads for horses and hikers and marked trails for bikers. See Salmon La Sac Campground for further information.

Location: On the Cle Elum River in Wenatchee National Forest; map A3, grid j4.

Campsites, facilities: There 21 sites for tents, trailers, or RVs, with some sites 25 feet and some up to 40 feet long. Picnic tables are provided. Drinking water, fire pits, vault toilets, and garbage bins are available. Available stock facilities include corrals, troughs and hitching posts. Bring your own stock feed. Leashed pets are permitted.

Reservations, fees: No reservations. Sites are $12 per night for the first vehicle, $10 per night for each additional vehicle. Open from mid-May to mid-September, depending on weather.

Directions: In Seattle on Interstate 5, turn east on Interstate 90. Drive east on Interstate 90 for 78 miles to Exit 80 (two miles before Cle Elum). Take that exit and turn north on Bullfrog Road and drive four miles to Highway 903. Continue north on Highway 903 for 18 miles to the campground on the right.

Contact: Wenatchee National Forest, Cle Elum Ranger District, West Second Street, Cle Elum, WA 98922; tel. (509) 674-4411; fax (509) 674-4794.

112 Wish Poosh   7

The shore of Cle Elum Lake is the site of this camp, where waterskiing, sailing, fishing, and swimming are among recreation possibilities.

Location: On Cle Elum Lake in Wenatchee National Forest; map A3, grid j3.

Campsites, facilities: There are 17 tent sites and 22 sites for tents, trailers, or RVs up to 21 feet long. Drinking water, fire grills, and picnic tables are provided. Flush toilets, firewood, a restaurant, and ice are available. Boat docks and launching facilities are located on Cle Elum Lake. Leashed pets are permitted.

Reservations, fees: No reservations. Sites are $12 per night for the first vehicle, $10 per night for the second vehicle. Open mid-May to mid-September.

Directions: In Seattle on Interstate 5, turn east on Interstate 90. Drive east on Interstate 90 for 78 miles to Exit 80 (two miles before Cle Elum). Take that exit, turn north on Bullfrog Road, and drive four miles to Highway 903. Continue north on Highway 903 for nine miles to the campground.

Contact: Wenatchee National Forest, Cle Elum Ranger District, West Second Street, Cle Elum, WA 98922; tel. (509) 674-4411; fax (509) 674-4794.

113 Red Mountain   6

This alternative to nearby Wish Poosh has two big differences: there is no drinking water, and it's not on Cle Elum Lake. The camp is along the Cle Elum River a mile from the lake, just above where the river feeds into it. It has the same wintertime options as Wish Poosh.

Location: On the Cle Elum River in Wenatchee National Forest; map A3, grid j3.

Campsites, facilities: There are 11 sites for tents. Picnic tables and fire grills are provided. Pit toilets and firewood are available, but there is no drinking water. Leashed pets are permitted.

Reservations, fees: No reservations. Sites are $7 per vehicle per night, with a two-vehicle maximum. Open mid-May to mid-November.

Directions: In Seattle on Interstate 5, turn east on Interstate 90. Drive east on Interstate 90 for 78 miles to Exit 80 (two miles before Cle Elum). Take that exit and turn north on Bullfrog Road and drive four miles to Highway 903. Continue north on Highway 903 for 19 miles to the campground.

Contact: Wenatchee National Forest, Cle Elum Ranger District, West Second Street, Cle Elum, WA 98922; tel. (509) 674-4411; fax (509) 674-4794.

114 Salmon La Sac   6

One of the most developed camps in the area, this is an ideal base camp for backpackers and day hikers and is popular with kayakers. It's located along the Cle Elum River at a major trailhead, and hikers can follow creeks heading off in several directions, including into the Alpine Lakes Wilderness. Campground hosts will answer all your questions.

Location: On the Cle Elum River in Wenatchee National Forest; map A3, grid j3.

Campsites, facilities: There are 30 tent sites and 96 sites for tents, trailers, or RVs up to 21 feet long, plus one group site. A horse-use camp is also available. Drinking water, fire grills, and picnic tables are provided. Flush toilets are available. Some facilities are wheelchair accessible. Leashed pets are permitted.

Reservations, fees: Some sites can be reserved; phone (877) 444-6777 or access the website: www.reserveusa.com ($8.65 reservation fee). Sites are $12 per night for the first vehicle, $10 per night for the second vehicle. The group fee is $60 a night. Open late May to late September.

Directions: In Seattle on Interstate 5, turn east on Interstate 90. Drive east on Interstate 90 for 78 miles to Exit 80 (two miles before Cle Elum). Take that exit, turn north on Bullfrog Road, and drive four miles to Highway 903. Continue north on Highway 903 for 21 miles to the campground.

Contact: Wenatchee National Forest, Cle Elum Ranger District, West Second Street, Cle Elum, WA 98922; tel. (509) 674-4411; fax (509) 674-4794.

115 Kachess   8

This is the only campground on the shore of Kachess Lake, a reservoir with the potential for low water lines in the summer, but it's a winner. Recreation opportunities include waterskiing, fishing, hiking, and bicycling. A trail from camp heads north into the Alpine Lakes Wilderness; see a U.S. Forest Service map for details. A self-guided interpretive trail is also available. The Kachess Sno-Park is about a mile south of the campground and provides parking and access to forest roads, and open areas are ideal for snowmobiling and cross-country skiing.

Location: On Kachess Lake in Wenatchee National Forest; map A3, grid j3.

Campsites, facilities: There are 133 tent sites and 50 sites for trailers or RVs up to 32 feet long. A group site is also available. Drinking water, fire grills, and picnic tables are provided. Rest rooms and sanitary disposal stations are located at Kachess Lake. Some facilities are wheelchair accessible. Leashed pets are permitted but aren't allowed in swimming areas.

Reservations, fees: Some sites can be reserved; phone (877) 444-6777 or access the website: www.reserveusa.com ($8.65 reservation fee). Sites are $12 per night for the first vehicle, $10 per night for the second vehicle. The group fee is $60 per night. Open late May to mid-September.

Directions: In Seattle on Interstate 5, turn east on Interstate 90. Drive east on Interstate 90 for 59 miles to Exit 62. Take that exit to Forest Road 49 and turn northeast and drive 5.5 miles to the campground.

Contact: Wenatchee National Forest, Cle Elum Ranger District, West Second Street, Cle Elum, WA 98922; tel. (509) 674-4411; fax (509) 674-4794.

116 Owhi Walk-In   8

This spot has everything. Well, everything but drinking water. It's located on the shore of Cooper Lake, near the boundary of the Alpine Lakes Wilderness. A nearby trailhead provides access to several lakes in the wilderness and extends to the Pacific Crest Trail; see a U.S. Forest Service map for details. Fishing, swimming, and canoeing are all popular at Cooper Lake.

Location: On Cooper Lake in Wenatchee National Forest; map A3, grid j3.

Campsites, facilities: There are 28 walk-in tent sites. Picnic tables and fire grills are provided. Pit toilets are available, but there is no drinking water. Boat docks and launching facilities are nearby. Leashed pets are permitted.

Reservations, fees: No reservations. Sites are $7 per vehicle per night, with a two-vehicle maximum. Open mid-June to mid-October.

Directions: In Seattle on Interstate 5, turn east on Interstate 90. Drive east on Interstate 90 for 78 miles to Exit 80 (two miles before Cle Elum). Turn north on Bull-frog Road and drive four miles to Highway 903. Turn north on Highway 903 and drive 19 miles to Forest Road 46. Turn west on Forest Road 46 and drive five miles to Forest Road 4616. Bear north for less than a quarter-mile to the campground. Campsites are located 100 to 300 feet from the parking lot.

Contact: Wenatchee National Forest, Cle Elum Ranger District, West Second Street, Cle Elum, WA 98922; tel. (509) 674-4411; fax (509) 674-4794.

117 Beverly   6

This primitive campground on the North Fork of the Teanaway River has good fishing, though it's primarily a hiker's camp, with several trails leading up nearby creeks and into the Alpine Lakes Wilderness. Self-issued permits are required for wilderness hiking.

Location: On the North Fork of the Teanaway River in Wenatchee National Forest; map A3, grid j4.

Campsites, facilities: There are 13 tent sites and three sites for trailers or RVs up to 21 feet long. Picnic tables and fire grills are provided. Pit toilets are available, but there is no drinking water. Leashed pets are permitted.

Reservations, fees: No reservations; no fee. Open June to mid-November.

Directions: In Seattle on Interstate 5, turn east on Interstate 90. Drive east on Interstate 90 for 80 miles to Cle Elum and Exit 86. Take Exit 86 to Highway 970. Turn east on Highway 970 and drive eight miles to Teanaway Road (County Road 970). Turn north on Teanaway Road and drive 13 miles to the end of the paved road. Continue north on Forest Road 9737 and drive four miles to campground.

Contact: Wenatchee National Forest, Cle Elum Ranger District, West Second Street, Cle Elum, WA 98922; tel. (509) 674-4411; fax (509) 674-4794.

118 Ken Wilcox Horse Camp   8

The last couple of miles of road are pretty rough, suitable only for high-clearance vehicles or pickups. This scenic camp near Haney Meadows has been adopted by a local horsemen's association that helps maintain the horse trails. Hikers also use the camp.

Location: Near Swauk Creek at Haney Meadows in Wenatchee National Forest: map A3, grid j7.

Campsites, facilities: There are 25 sites for tents, trailers, or RVs up to 25 feet. No drinking water, but vault toilets and fire pits are available. Available stock facilities include hitching equipment (rails and rings for suspending a high line).

Reservations, fees: No reservations; no fee. Open year-round, weather permitting.

Directions: In Seattle on Interstate 5, turn east on Interstate 90. Drive east on Interstate 90 for 80 miles to Cle Elum and Exit 86. Take Exit 86 to County Road 970. Turn east on County Road 970 and drive 12 miles to U.S. 97. Turn north on U.S. 97 and drive 15 miles to the summit of Swauk Pass and Forest Road 9716. Turn right on Forest Road 9716 (gravel) and drive about four miles to Forest Road 9712. Turn left on Forest Road 9712 and drive about five miles to the camp on the left.

Contact: Wenatchee National Forest, Cle Elum Ranger District, West Second Street, Cle Elum, WA 98922; tel. (509) 674-4411; fax (509) 674-4794.

119 Blu Shastin RV Park   6

This park is set in a mountainous area near Penshastin Creek. Gold panning in the river is a popular activity here, and rumor has it that the Penshastin is the best-producing river in the state. The camp has sites on the river bank and plenty of shade trees. A heated pool, a recreation field, and horseshoe pits provide possible activities in the park. Hiking trails and marked bike trails are nearby.

Location: Near Penshastin Creek; map A3, grid j6.

Campsites, facilities: There are 86 sites for tents, trailers, or RVs of any length; seven are drive-through. Electricity, drinking water, sewer hookups, fire rings, and picnic tables are provided. Flush toilets, sanitary services, showers, a recreation hall, firewood, a laundry room, ice, a playground, horseshoes, badminton, volleyball, and a heated swimming pool are available. Bottled gas, a store, and a cafe are located within one mile. Leashed pets and motorbikes are permitted.

Reservations, fees: Reservations recommended. Sites are $17-22 per night. Major credit cards accepted. Open year-round.

Directions: From Leavenworth drive south on U.S. 2 for four miles to U.S. 97. Turn south on U.S. 97 and drive seven miles to the park on the right.

Contact: Blu Shastin RV Park, 3300 Highway 97, Leavenworth, WA 98826; tel. (509) 548-4184 or (888) 548-4184.

120 Swauk   7

Good fishing and some decent hiking trails can be found at this campground along Swauk Creek. It's a prime spot, particularly during the winter months. About three miles east of the campground is Swauk Sno-Park, which provides a parking area and access to forest roads and open areas for snowmobiling and cross-country skiing. Also near the sno-park on Forest Road 9716 is the Swauk Forest Discovery Trail. This interpretive trail is three miles long and explains some of the effects of logging and U.S. Forest Service management of the forest habitat.

Location: On Swauk Creek in Wenatchee National Forest; map A3, grid j7.

Campsites, facilities: There are 23 sites for tents, trailers, or RVs. Fire grills and picnic tables are provided. Pit toilets and firewood are available, but no drinking water. Leashed pets are permitted.

Reservations, fees: No reservations. Sites are $10 per vehicle per night, with a two-vehicle maximum. Open mid-April to late September.

Directions: In Seattle on Interstate 5, turn east on Interstate 90. Drive east on Interstate 90 for 80 miles to Cle Elum and Exit 86. Take Exit 86 to County Road 970. Turn east on County Road 970 and drive 12 miles to U.S. 97. Turn north on U.S. 97 and drive 10 miles to the campground on the right (near Swauk Pass).

Contact: Wenatchee National Forest, Cle Elum Ranger District, West Second Street, Cle Elum, WA 98922; tel. (509) 674-4411; fax (509) 674-4794.

121 Wenatchee Confluence State Park

 10

This state park just outside of Wenatchee on the Columbia River provides a relaxing atmosphere and many activities. Recreation possibilities include fishing, swimming, boating, and waterskiing. Interpretive hiking trails are also available. Sports enthusiasts are provided with playing fields and tennis and basketball courts. Daroga State Park and Lake Chelan to the north offer side trip possibilities.

Location: On the Columbia River; map A3, grid j8.

Campsites, facilities: There are eight developed tent sites and 51 hookup sites for trailers or RVs up to 65 feet long. Picnic tables, stoves, drinking water, showers, flush toilets, a swimming beach, two picnic shelters, athletic fields, an interpretive nature trail, and a sanitary disposal station are provided. A boat launch is available. The facilities are wheelchair accessible. Leashed pets are permitted.

Reservations, fees: Reservations accepted, phone (800) 452-5687 ($6 reservation fee). Sites are $11-16 per night. Open year-round.

Directions: From Seattle on Interstate 5. drive north to Everett and U.S. 2. Turn east on U.S. 2 and drive 121 miles to Wenatchee. The park is located at the north end of Wenatchee on Olds Station Road.

Contact: Wenatchee Confluence State Park, 333 Olds Station Road, Wenatchee, WA 98801; tel. (800) 233-0321, (509) 664-6373.

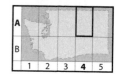

MAP A4

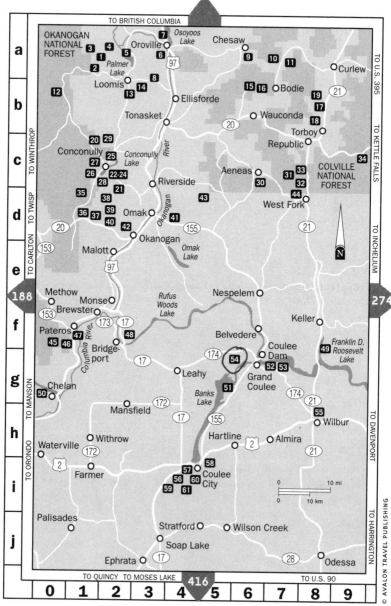

CHAPTER A4

1 Toats Coulee   6

One of three little-known camps in the vicinity, this wooded spot is set along Toats Coulee Creek. Some moose are in the area. A road for snowmobile use follows the South Fork of Toats Coulee Creek, swinging south and then heading east along Cecil Creek. Contact the Department of Natural Resources for details.

Location: On Toats Coulee Creek; map A4, grid a1.

Campsites, facilities: There are nine sites for tents or small trailers. Picnic tables, fire grills, and tent pads are provided. Vault toilets are available. There is no drinking water. Leashed pets are permitted.

Reservations, fees: No reservations; no fee. Open year-round.

Directions: From Wenatchee drive north on U.S. 97 for 120 miles to Tonasket and Forest Street. Turn left and drive 0.2 mile (crossing the Okanogan River) to Highway 7. Turn right (north) on Highway 7 (Loomis-Oroville Highway) and drive five miles. At the fork continue on Loomis-Oroville Highway for about 12 miles to Toats Coulee Road, 2.1 miles north of Loomis. Turn left and drive 5.5 miles to the lower site. Continue 0.1 mile to the upper site, located at the junction of Road OM-T-2000 and Road OM-T-1000).

Contact: Department of Natural Resources, Northeast Region, P.O. Box 190, Colville, WA 99114-0190; tel. (360) 902-1234, (509) 684-7474, or fax (509) 684-7484.

2 Cold Springs   8

It's quite a drive to get here, but you'll be happy you made the effort to reach this pretty and forested camp, with sites near a small stream. Trails for horseback riding, hiking, and snowmobiling run through the area. Because the camp is little known and remote, it's advisable to obtain a map of the area from the Department of Natural Resources. Don't be surprised if you see moose tromping around these parts.

Location: Near Cold Creek; map A4, grid a1.

Campsites, facilities: There are nine campsites for tents or small trailers. Picnic tables, fire grills, and tent pads are provided. Vault toilets and drinking water are available. Leashed pets are permitted.

Reservations, fees: No reservations; no fee. Open year-round.

Directions: From Wenatchee drive north on U.S. 97 for 120 miles to Tonasket and Forest Street. Turn left and drive 0.2 mile (crossing the Okanogan River) to Highway 7. Turn right (north) on Highway 7 (Loomis-Oroville Highway) and drive five miles. At the fork continue on Loomis-Oroville Highway for about 12 miles to Toats Coulee Road, 2.1 miles north of Loomis. Turn left and drive 5.5 miles to the Touts Coulee Lower Site camp. Continue 0.1 mile to the upper site at the junction of roads. Take Road OM-T-1000 for 2.1 miles to Cold Creek Road. Turn right (gravel road) and drive 0.4 mile. Bear right and continue 1.8 miles. Bear left and drive 2.7 miles to the camp, past the picnic area.

Contact: Department of Natural Resources, Northeast Region, P.O. Box 190, Colville, WA 99114-0190; tel. (360) 902-1234, (509) 684-7474, or fax (509) 684-7484.

3 North Fork Nine Mile   6

Northwestern moose frequent this campground in the forest along the North Fork of Toats Coulee Creek and Nine Mile Creek. It's advisable to obtain a map that details the area from the Department of Natural Resources.

Location: On the North Fork of Toats Coulee Creek; map A4, grid a1.

Campsites, facilities: There are 11 campsites for tents or small trailers. Picnic tables, fire grills, and tent pads are provided. Vault toilets and drinking water are available. Leashed pets are permitted.

Reservations, fees: No reservations; no fee. Open year-round.

Directions: From Wenatchee drive north on U.S. 97 for 120 miles to Tonasket and Forest Street. Turn left and drive 0.2 mile (crossing the Okanogan River) to Highway 7. Turn right (north) on Highway 7 (Loomis-Oroville Highway) and drive five miles. At the fork continue on Loomis-Oroville Highway for about 12 miles to Toats Coulee Road, 2.1 miles north of Loomis. Turn left and drive 5.5 miles to the Touts Coulee Lower Site camp. Continue 0.1 mile to the upper site at the junction of roads. Take Road OM-T-1000 for 2.5 miles to the campground.

Contact: Department of Natural Resources, Northeast Region, P.O. Box 190, Colville, WA 99114-0190; tel. (360) 902-1234, (509) 684-7474, or fax (509) 684-7484.

4 Chopaka Lake   8

This campground provides a classic setting for the expert angler. It's nestled along the western shore of Chopaka Lake, which is stocked with Atlantic salmon. Only catch-and-release fly-fishing with barbless hooks is allowed.

Location: On Chopaka Lake; map A4, grid a2.

Campsites, facilities: There are 15 campsites for tents or small trailers. Picnic tables, fire grills, and tent pads are provided. Vault toilets, drinking water, and boat launching facilities are available. Some facilities are wheelchair accessible. Leashed pets are permitted.

Reservations, fees: No reservations; no fee. Open year-round.

Directions: From Wenatchee drive north on U.S. 97 for 120 miles to Tonasket and Forest Street. Turn left and drive 0.2 mile (crossing the Okanogan River) to Highway 7. Turn right (north) on Highway 7 (Loomis-Oroville Highway) and drive five miles. At the fork continue on Loomis-Oroville Highway for about 12 miles to Toats Coulee Road, 2.1 miles north of Loomis. Turn left and drive 1.5 miles. Turn right onto a steep, one-lane road and drive 3.4 miles. Bear left, drive 1.7 miles, turn right, and drive two miles to the campground.

Contact: Department of Natural Resources, Northeast Region, P.O. Box 190, Colville, WA 99114-0190; tel. (360) 902-1234, (509) 684-7474, or fax (509) 684-7484.

5 Palmer Lake   8

This shorefront camp is the only one at Palmer Lake. An array of Washington wildlife call the area home. The winter range of the deer is in the Sinlahekin Valley to the south of Palmer Lake. There are numerous migration routes in the region. Wildlife (not for hunting) include the endangered bighorn sheep, cougar, bald and golden eagles, black and brown bear, and grouse. See the description of Chopaka Lake for information on fishing for Atlantic salmon in nearby Chopaka Lake.

Location: On Palmer Lake; map A4, grid a2.

Campsites, facilities: There are six campsites for tents or small trailers. Picnic tables, fire grills, and tent pads are provided. Vault toilets and a fishing pier are available, but there is no drinking water. Leashed pets are permitted.

Reservations, fees: No reservations; no fee. Open year-round, weather permitting.

Directions: From Wenatchee drive north on U.S. 97 for 120 miles to Tonasket and Forest Street. Turn left and drive 0.2 mile, crossing the Okanogan River, to Highway 7. Turn right (north) on Highway 7 (Loomis-Oroville Highway) and drive 18.5 miles, 8.5 miles past Loomis. Stay to the right and drive to the camp at the north end of the lake.

Contact: Department of Natural Resources, Northeast Region, P.O. Box 190, Colville, WA 99114-0190; tel. (360) 902-1234, (509) 684-7474, or fax (509) 684-7484.

6 Sun Cove Resort   9

This beautiful resort, surrounded by trees and hills and set along the shore of Wannacut Lake, is a nice little spot that doesn't get much traffic. Fishing, swimming, boating, and hiking are all summertime options. The park provides full facilities, including a heated pool, a playground and recreation hall for kids. For the horsy set, guided trail and overnight rides are available next door to the resort.

Location: On Wannacut Lake; map A4, grid a3.

Campsites, facilities: There are 22 tent sites and 26 drive-through sites for trailers or RVs of any length and two sites up to 38 feet long. Electricity, drinking water, sewer hookups, and picnic tables are provided. Flush toilets, sanitary services, a recreation hall, a store, a cafe, a laundry room, ice, a playground, and a swimming pool are available, as are showers for an extra fee. Boat docks, launching facilities, and rentals are also available. Leashed pets are permitted.

Reservations, fees: Reservations accepted. Sites are $16-20 per night. Open late April through October.

Directions: From Oroville (on U.S. 97 just south of the Canadian border), drive west on Ellemehan Mountain Road for about six miles to Wannacut Lake Road. Turn left (south) and drive five miles to the resort at the end of the road.

Contact: Sun Cove Resort, 93 East Wannacut Lane, Oroville, WA 98844; tel. (509) 476-2223; fax (509) 476-2223.

■ Osoyoos Lake State Park

 9

The park is located along the shore of Osoyoos Lake, where swimming, waterskiing, and fishing for trout and spiny rays are all possibilities. This is a beautiful park near the Canadian border. Many years ago the area was the site of the annual Okanogan (which means "rendezvous") of the Washington and British Columbia Indians. They would gather and share supplies of fish and game for the year. Osoyoos Lake is a winter nesting area for geese. An 18-hole golf course is nearby. Fishing gear and concessions are available at the park.

Location: On Osoyoos Lake; map A4, grid a3.

Campsites, facilities: There are six primitive tent sites and 80 sites for tents or self-contained RVs up to 45 feet long. Picnic tables and fire grills are provided. Flush toilets, drinking water, sanitary services, a store, a cafe, showers, firewood, and a playground are available. A coin-operated laundry facility and ice are located within one mile. Boat launching facilities are nearby. Leashed pets are permitted.

Reservations, fees: Reservations accepted; phone (800) 452-5687 ($6 reservation fee). Sites are $5-11 per night. Major credit cards accepted. Open year-round.

Directions: From Oroville, on U.S. 97 just south of the Canadian border, drive north on U.S. 97 for one mile to the park entrance on the right.

Contact: Osoyoos Lake State Park, Route 1, P.O. Box 102 A, Oroville, WA 98844; tel. (800) 233-0321 or (509) 476-3321.

■ Spectacle Lake Resort   7

This pleasant resort on the shore of long, narrow Spectacle Lake has grassy, shaded sites. Recreation options include swimming, fishing and hunting.

Location: On Spectacle Lake; map A4, grid a3.

Campsites, facilities: There are 40 sites for tents, trailers, or RVs of any length. Electricity, drinking water, sewer hookups, and picnic tables are provided. Flush toilets, bottled gas, sanitary services, showers, a store, a laundry room, ice, a playground, recreation hall, exercise room, and a swimming pool are available. Boat docks, launching facilities, and rentals are also available. Leashed pets and motorbikes are permitted.

Reservations, fees: Reservations accepted. Sites are $14-15 per night. Open mid-April to late October.

Directions: From East Wenatchee drive north on U.S. 97 for 199 miles to Tonasket. At 4th Street, turn left, cross the bridge, and drive to Highway 7. Turn right on Highway 7 and drive about 12 miles to Holmes Road. Turn left (south) on Holmes Road and drive one-half mile to McCammon Road. Turn west and drive one block to the park at the end of the road.

Contact: Spectacle Lake Resort, 10 McCammon Road, Tonasket, WA 98855; (509) 223-3433.

9 Beth Lake   7

This campground can be found along little Beth Lake, which is adjacent to Beaver Lake. Side trip options in the area include Lost Lake, Bonaparte Lake, and several hiking trails, one of which leads up to the Mount Bonaparte Lookout.

Location: On Beth Lake in Okanogan National Forest; map A4, grid a6.

Campsites, facilities: There are 17 sites for tents, trailers, or RVs up to 31 feet long, plus one multiple site. Drinking water and picnic tables are provided. Vault toilets, a picnic area, and boat launching facilities are available. Leashed pets are permitted.

Reservations, fees: No reservations accepted. Sites are $5 per vehicle per night. Open mid-May to mid-September.

Directions: From East Wenatchee drive north on U.S. 97 for 199 miles to Tonasket and Highway 20. Turn east on Highway 20 and drive 20 miles to Bonaparte Lake Road (County Road 4953). Turn left (north) and drive six miles Bonaparte Lake and Forest Road 32. Turn right (north) and drive six miles to County Road 9480. Turn left (northwest) and drive one mile to the campground.

Contact: Okanogan National Forest, Tonasket Ranger District, 1 West Winesap Avenue, Tonasket, WA 98855; tel. (509) 486-2186; fax (509) 486-5161.

10 Lost Lake   7

This camp on the shore of Lost Lake keeps visitors happy with fishing, swimming, hiking, hunting, and horseback riding. The Big Tree Botanical Area is about a mile away.

Location: On Lost Lake in Okanogan National Forest; map A4, grid a6.

Campsites, facilities: There are 12 single and six multiple sites for tents, trailers, or RVs up to 31 feet long. There is also one group unit available only by reservation. Drinking water and picnic tables are provided. Vault toilets are available. Boat docks and launching facilities are nearby. Leashed pets are permitted.

Reservations, fees: Reservations required for the group site; phone (509) 486-2186. Single and multiple sites are $6 per vehicle per night; group rates are $40 for up to 25 people, $60 for 26 to 50 people, and $80 for 51 to 100 people. Open mid-May to mid-September.

Directions: From East Wenatchee drive north on U.S. 97 for 199 miles to Tonasket and Highway 20. Turn east on Highway 20 and drive 20 miles to Bonaparte Lake Road (County Road 4953). Turn left (north) and drive six miles to Forest Road 32. Turn right (north) and drive three miles to Forest Road 33. Turn northwest and drive four miles to the campground.

Contact: Okanogan National Forest, Tonasket Ranger District, 1 West Winesap Avenue, Tonasket, WA 98855; tel. (509) 486-2186; fax (509) 486-5161.

11 Beaver Lake   7

The southeastern shore of long, narrow Beaver Lake, one of several lakes in this area, is the home of this camp. Fishing, swimming, hunting, and hiking are all possibilities here. See the descriptions of Lost Lake and Bonaparte Lake for information on the other lakes.

Location: On Beaver Lake in Okanogan National Forest; map A4, grid a7.

Campsites, facilities: There are nine single and two multiple sites for tents, trailers, or RVs up to 21 feet long. Drinking water and picnic tables are provided. Vault toilets are available. Boat launching facilities are located within 100 yards of the campground. No boats with gas engines are permitted. Leashed pets are permitted.

Reservations, fees: No reservations. Sites are $5 per vehicle per night. Open mid-May to mid-September.

Directions: From East Wenatchee drive north on U.S. 97 for 199 miles to Tonasket and Highway 20. Turn east on Highway 20 and drive 20 miles to Bonaparte Lake Road (County Road 4953). Turn left (north) and drive six miles to Bonaparte Lake and Forest Road 32. Turn right (north) and drive six miles to the campground.

Contact: Okanogan National Forest, Tonasket Ranger District, 1 West Winesap Avenue, Tonasket, WA 98855; tel. (509) 486-2186; fax (509) 486-5161.

🔢12 Tiffany Spring   7

Located at an elevation of 6,800 feet, this camp is less than a mile hike from Tiffany Lake. Tiffany Mountain rises 8,200 feet in the distance. There are some good hiking trails in the area. No other campgrounds are in the vicinity, and it's advisable to obtain a U.S. Forest Service map of the area.

Location: Near Tiffany Lake in Okanogan National Forest; map A4, grid b0.

Campsites, facilities: There are six tent sites for trailers or RVs up to 15 feet long. Picnic tables are provided. Vault toilets are available, but there is no drinking water. No garbage service is provided, so trash must be packed out. Leashed pets are permitted.

Reservations, fees: No reservations; no fee. Open July to late September.

Directions: From East Wenatchee drive north on U.S. 97 for 88 miles to Okanogan and County Road 9229. Turn north and drive 17.5 miles northwest to Conconully and County Road 2017. Turn left on County Road 2017 and drive 1.5 miles to Forest Road 37. Turn right (northwest) and drive 21 miles to Forest Road 39. Turn right (northeast) on Forest Road 39 and proceed 7.5 miles to the campground.

Contact: Okanogan National Forest, Tonasket Ranger District, 1 West Winesap Avenue, Tonasket, WA 98855; tel. (509) 486-2186; fax (509) 486-5161.

🔢13 Rainbow Resort   7

This resort on Spectacle Lake is an alternative to Spectacle Lake Resort, with pretty lake views and full facilities. Nearby activities include swimming, fishing, hunting, tennis, and horseback riding, including overnight trail rides.

Location: On Spectacle Lake; map A4, grid b2.

Campsites, facilities: There are 14 tent sites and 40 sites for trailers or RVs of any length; 21 are drive-through. Electricity, drinking water, sewer hookups, and picnic tables are provided. Flush toilets, showers, firewood, ice, boat docks, boat rentals, and launching facilities are available. Leashed pets and motorbikes are permitted.

Reservations, fees: Reservations accepted. Sites are $16 per night. Major credit cards accepted. Open April through October.

Directions: From East Wenatchee drive north on U.S. 97 for 132 miles to Ellisford and Loomis Highway. Turn west on Loomis Highway and drive 9.5 miles to the resort on the left.

Contact: Rainbow Resort, 761 Loomis Highway, Tonasket, WA 98855; tel.(800)) 347-4375, (509) 223-3700.

14 Spectacle Falls Resort

      8

Spectacle Falls Resort, on the shore of Spectacle Lake, is open only as long as fishing is allowed, which means an early closing in July. Be sure to phone ahead of time to verify whether it's open. Recreation options include hiking, swimming, fishing, tennis, and horseback riding, including guided trails and overnight rides.
Location: On Spectacle Lake; map A4, grid b3.
Campsites, facilities: There are 10 tent sites and 28 drive-through sites for trailers or RVs of any length. Electricity, drinking water, sewer hookups, and picnic tables are provided. Flush toilets, sanitary services, showers, ice, boat docks, launching facilities, and boat rentals are available. Leashed pets and motorbikes are permitted.
Reservations, fees: Reservations accepted. Sites are $16 per night. Open mid-April to late July.
Directions: From East Wenatchee drive north on U.S. 97 for 119 miles to Tonasket and Loomis Highway. Turn northwest on Loomis Highway and drive 15 miles to the resort.
Contact: Spectacle Falls Resort, 879 Loomis Highway, Tonasket, WA 98855; tel. (509) 223-4141; e-mail: jwalsh@nvinet.com.

15 Bonaparte Lake

       7

This campground is located on the southern shore of Bonaparte Lake. See the description of Bonaparte Lake Resort for lake recreation information. There are several trails nearby that provide access to Mount Bonaparte Lookout. Consult a U.S. Forest Service map for details.
Location: On Bonaparte Lake in Okanogan National Forest; map A4, grid b6.
Campsites, facilities: There are 15 single and 10 multiple sites for tents, trailers, or RVs up to 31 feet long, plus three bike-in/hike-in sites and one group site which can accommodate up to 30 people. Drinking water, vault toilets, fire grills, and picnic tables are provided. Sanitary services, a store, a cafe, and ice can be found within one mile. Boat docks (including a wheelchair-accessible fishing dock) and launching facilities are also available. Leashed pets are permitted.
Reservations, fees: No reservations accepted. For fee information, phone (509) 486-2186. Open mid-May to mid-September.
Directions: From East Wenatchee drive north on U.S. 97 for 199 miles to Tonasket and Highway 20. Turn east on Highway 20 and drive 20 miles to Bonaparte Lake Road (County Road 4953). Turn left (north) and drive six miles to Bonaparte Lake and Forest Road 32 and the campground on the left.
Contact: Okanogan National Forest, Tonasket Ranger District, 1 West Winesap Avenue, Tonasket, WA 98855; tel. (509) 486-2186; fax (509) 486-5161.

16 Bonaparte Lake Resort

 6

Fishing is popular at this resort on the southeast shore of Bonaparte Lake. Other recreational activities include hiking and hunting in the nearby U.S. Forest Service lands and snowmobiling and cross-country skiing in the winter.

Location: On Bonaparte Lake; map A4, grid b6.

Campsites, facilities: There are 10 tent sites and 35 sites for trailers or RVs of any length; some are drive-through. Ten cabins are also available. Electricity, drinking water, sewer hookups, and picnic tables are provided. Flush toilets, bottled gas, sanitary services, showers, firewood, a recreation hall, a store, a restaurant, a laundry room, ice, a playground, boat docks, launching facilities, and boat rentals are available. Leashed pets and motorbikes (licensed drivers only) are permitted.

Reservations, fees: Reservations accepted. Sites are $8-14 per night; cabins are $30-45 per night. Open April through October.

Directions: From East Wenatchee drive north on U.S. 97 for 199 miles to Tonasket and Highway 20. Turn east on Highway 20 and drive 20 miles to Bonaparte Lake Road (County Road 4953). Turn left (north) and drive six miles to Bonaparte Lake and the resort on the left.

Contact: Bonaparte Lake Resort, 615 Bonaparte Road, Tonasket, WA 98855; tel. (509) 486-2828; fax (509) 486-1987.

17 Curlew Lake State Park

 8

Boredom is banned at this park on the eastern shore of Curlew Lake. Beach access, swimming, waterskiing, hiking, and excellent fishing for trout and bass are just some of the activities. Nearby recreation options include an 18-hole golf course, and in the winter, snowmobiling. The park is located in the heart of a historic gold-mining district, so you may want to bring along a pan and give it a whirl.

Location: On Curlew Lake; map A4, grid b8.

Campsites, facilities: There are five primitive tent sites, 57 developed tent sites, and 25 sites for trailers or RVs up to 30 feet long. Picnic tables are provided. Flush toilets, sanitary services, electricity, drinking water, sewer hookups, showers, firewood, and boat launching facilities are available. Leashed pets are permitted.

Reservations, fees: No reservations accepted. Sites are $10-16 per night. Open April to late October.

Directions: From Spokane on Interstate 90, turn north on U.S. 395 and drive 87 miles to Colville and Highway 20. Turn west on Highway 20 and continue 34 miles to Highway 21 (two miles east of Republic). Turn north and drive 6.5 miles to the park entrance on the left.

Contact: Curlew Lake State Park, 974 Curlew Lake Street, Republic, WA 99166; tel. (800) 233-0321, (509) 775-3592.

18 Tiffany's Resort   7

Tiffany's Resort is in a pretty, wooded setting along the western shore of Curlew Lake. Highlights include spacious sites, lake access, and good fishing. This is a smaller, more private alternative to Black's Beach Resort.

Location: On Curlew Lake; map A4, grid b8.

Campsites, facilities: There are four tent sites and 15 sites for trailers or RVs of any length. Electricity, drinking water, sewer hookups, and picnic tables are provided. Flush toilets, showers, firewood, a store, a laundry room, ice, and a playground are available. Boat docks, launching facilities, and rentals are nearby. Pets and motorbikes are permitted.

Reservations, fees: Reservations accepted. Sites are $17 per night. Major credit cards accepted. Open April to late October.

Directions: From Spokane on Interstate 90, turn north on U.S. 395 and drive 87 miles to Colville and Highway 20. Turn west on Highway 20 and drive 36 miles into the town of Republic and Klondike Road. Turn right on Klondike Road and drive 10.2 miles (Klondike Road will turn into West Curlew Lake Road). Continue on West Curlew Road about five miles to the resort.

Contact: Tiffany's Resort, 58 Tiffany Road, Republic, WA 99166; tel. (509) 775-3152; website: www.tiffanysresort.com.

19 Black's Beach Resort   7

Here's another resort along Curlew Lake. This one is much larger, with beautiful waterfront sites and full facilities. Waterskiing, swimming, and fishing are all options.

Location: On Curlew Lake; map A4, grid b8.

Campsites, facilities: There are 120 sites for trailers or RVs of any length; 60 are drive-through. Electricity, drinking water, sewer hookups, and picnic tables are provided. Flush toilets, sanitary services, showers, a store, a laundry room, ice, and a playground are available. Boat docks, launching facilities, and rentals are located at the resort. Leashed pets and motorbikes are permitted.

Reservations, fees: Reservations accepted. Sites are $16-18 per night. Open April through October; three winterized sites are open year-round.

Directions: From Spokane on Interstate 90, turn north on U.S. 395 and drive 87 miles to Colville Highway 20. Turn west on Highway 20 and continue 34 miles to Highway 21 (two miles east of Republic). Turn north and drive 10 miles to West Curlew Lake Road. Turn north on West Curlew Lake Road and continue to the resort on the lake.

Contact: Black's Beach Resort, 80 Black Beach Road, Republic, WA 99166; tel. (509) 775-3989.

20 Kerr   6

This camp is located at 3,100 feet along Salmon Creek, about four miles north of Conconully Lake, and is one of many campgrounds near the lake. Fishing prospects can be decent here, and there are numerous recreation options available at Conconully Lake.

Location: On Salmon Creek in Okanogan National Forest; map A4, grid c1.

Campsites, facilities: There are 13 sites for tents, trailers, or RVs up to 21 feet long. Picnic tables and fire grills are provided. Vault toilets are available, but there is no drinking water. No garbage service is provided, so trash must be packed out. Leashed pets are permitted.

Reservations, fees: No reservations; no fee. Open mid-May to mid-September.

Directions: From East Wenatchee drive north on U.S. 97 for 88 miles to Okanogan and County Road 9229. Turn left (north) on County Road 9229 and drive 17.5 miles to Conconully and County Road 2361. Turn northwest on County Road 2361 and drive four miles (the road becomes Forest Road 38) to the campground on the left.

Contact: Okanogan National Forest, Tonasket Ranger District, 1 West Winesap Avenue, Tonasket, WA 98855; tel. (509) 486-2186; fax (509) 486-5161.

21 Jack's RV Park and Motel

       5

This park is in the town of Conconully, not far from Conconully Lake. Horseshoe pits can be found in the park, and nearby recreation options include hiking trails, fishing, hunting, snowmobiling, and water sports at the lake.

Location: Near Conconully Lake; map A4, grid c2.

Campsites, facilities: There are 57 sites for trailers or RVs of any length; 20 are drive-through. Electricity, drinking water, cable TV, sewer hookups, and picnic tables are provided. Flush toilets, propane gas, showers, firewood, and a laundry room are available. A store, a cafe, and ice are located within two blocks. Boat docks, launching facilities, and rentals are nearby. Pets and motorbikes are permitted.

Reservations, fees: Reservations accepted. Sites are $16 per night. Major credit cards accepted. Open mid-April through October, weather permitting.

Directions: From East Wenatchee drive north on U.S. 97 for 88 miles to Okanogan and Pine Street/Conconully Highway. Turn left and drive 17.5 miles northwest to Conconully and Broadway Street. Turn east and drive one block to A Avenue. Turn north on A Avenue and drive less than one block to the park on the right.

Contact: Jack's RV Park and Motel, P.O. Box 98, Conconully, WA 98819; tel. (800) 893-5668, (509) 826-0132; fax (509) 826-2086.

22 Lazy Days RV Park   5

This park is in downtown Conconully, a short distance from the lake. The park is geared specifically toward RVs, with shaded grassy sites. Nearby recreational opportunities include hiking, fishing, swimming, boating—and in the winter, snowmobiling.

Location: Near Conconully Lake; map A4, grid c2.

Campsites, facilities: There are 43 drive-through sites for trailers or RVs of any length. Electricity, drinking water, sewer hookups, and picnic tables are provided. Flush toilets, firewood, showers, a laundry room, cable TV, and ice are available. Bottled gas, sanitary services, a store, a cafe, and ice are located within two blocks. Boat docks, launching facilities, and rentals are nearby. Leashed pets are permitted.

Reservations, fees: Reservations accepted. Sites are $15 per night. Open April through October, weather permitting.

Directions: From East Wenatchee drive north on U.S. 97 for 88 miles to Okanogan and Pine Street/Conconully Highway. Turn left and drive 17.5 miles northwest to Conconully and Broadway Street. Turn east and drive one block to A Avenue. Turn south on A Avenue and drive about half a block to the park on the right.

Contact: Lazy Days RV Park, P.O. Box 67, Conconully, WA 98819; tel. (509) 826-0326.

23 Maple Flats RV Park and Resort

 9

This campground near Conconully Lake is in a beautiful setting, in a valley between two lakes. Nearby recreation options include hiking and biking on the many nature trails in the area, an 18-hole golf course (15 miles away), trout fishing in the well-stocked Upper and Lower Conconully Lakes, and, in the winter, snowmobiling and cross-country skiing.

Location: Near Conconully Lake; map A4, grid c2.

Campsites, facilities: There is room for six tents in a dispersed camping area and 25 drive-through sites for trailers or RVs of any length with full hookups, including 30-amp electrical and cable TV; 12 sites are drive-through. Furnished cabins are also available. Electricity, drinking water, sewer hookups, and picnic tables are provided. Flush toilets, showers, a laundry room, and a covered gazebo with electricity are available. Groceries, dining, dancing, propane, and boat, snowmobile, and jet ski rentals are located within two blocks. Boat docks and launching facilities are also nearby. Leashed pets and motorbikes are permitted.

Reservations, fees: Reservations accepted. Sites are $10-15 per night. Open April through October.

Directions: From East Wenatchee drive north on U.S. 97 for 88 miles to Okanogan and Pine Street/Conconully Highway. Turn left and drive 17.5 miles northwest to Conconully and Silver Street. Turn east and drive one block to A Avenue. Turn north on A Avenue and drive to the park on the right.

Contact: Maple Flats RV Park and Resort, P.O. Box 126, Conconully, WA 98819; tel. (800) 683-1180, (509) 826-4231.

24 Kozy Kabins and RV Park 7

This quiet and private park is in Conconully, with a small creek running through it and plenty of greenery. A full-service marina is located close by. If you continue northeast of town on County Road 4015, the road will get a bit narrow for awhile, but will widen again when you enter the Sinlahekin Habitat Management Area, which is managed by the Department of Fish and Game. There are some primitive campsites in this valley, especially along the shores of the lakes in the area.

Location: Near Conconully Lake; map A4, grid c2.

Campsites, facilities: There are six tent sites, 14 drive-through for trailers or RVs, six of which can accommodate a length of 20 feet, and seven cabins. Electricity, drinking water, sewer hookups, and picnic tables are provided. Flush toilets, showers, and firewood are available. Bottled gas, sanitary services, a store, a cafe, a coin-operated laundry facilities, and ice are located within one mile. Cabin rentals, boat docks, launching facilities, and boat rentals are nearby. Pets and motorbikes are permitted.

Reservations, fees: Reservations accepted. Sites are $8-12 per night; cabins are $35 per night. Open year-round.

Directions: From East Wenatchee drive north on U.S. 97 for 88 miles to Okanogan and Pine Street/Conconully Highway. Turn left and drive 17.5 miles northwest to Conconully and Broadway Street. Turn east and drive one block to A Avenue. The park is at the junction of A Avenue and Broadway.

Contact: Kozy Kabins and RV Park, P.O. Box 82, Conconully, WA 98819; tel. (509) 826-6780.

25 Conconully Lake Resort   6

This resort is one of several in Conconully, set along the shore of Conconully Lake. Tents are permitted, but this is a prime vacation destination for RVers. Trout fishing, swimming, and boating are all options here.

Location: On Upper Conconully Lake; map A4, grid c2.

Campsites, facilities: There are 11 sites for trailers or RVs of any length with full hookups, plus some cabins. Electricity, drinking water, sewer hookups, fire rings and picnic tables are provided. Flush toilets, showers, and ice are available. Bottled gas, sanitary services, a store with tackle, a cafe, and coin-operated laundry facilities are located within one mile. Boat docks, launching facilities, and a variety of boat rentals are available. Leashed pets and motorbikes are permitted.

Reservations, fees: Reservations accepted. Sites are $19 per night; call for cabin fees. Open late April to late October.

Directions: From East Wenatchee drive north on U.S. 97 for 88 miles to Okanogan and Pine Street/Conconully Highway. Turn left and drive 17.5 miles northwest to Conconully and Lake Street. Turn right on Lake Street and drive one mile to the park on the right.

Contact: Conconully Lake Resort, P.O. Box 131, Conconully, WA 98819; tel. (509) 826-0813, (800) 850-0813, or fax (509) 826-1292; e-mail: janie46@juno.com or leight@televar.com.

26 Liar's Cove Resort   6

Roomy sites for RVs can be found at this camp on the shore of Conconully Lake. Tents are allowed, too. Fishing, swimming, boating, and hiking opportunities are located nearby.

Location: On Conconully Lake; map A4, grid c1.

Campsites, facilities: There are 30 sites for tents, trailers, or RVs up to 50 feet long; 20 are drive-through. Electricity, drinking water, sewer hookups, and picnic tables are provided. Flush toilets, showers, cable TV, and ice are available. Bottled gas, sanitary services, a store, and a cafe are located within one mile. Boat docks, launching facilities, and boat rentals are available. Leashed pets and motorbikes are permitted.

Reservations, fees: Reservations accepted. Sites are $18-19 per night. Open April to early November.

Directions: From East Wenatchee drive north on U.S. 97 for 88 miles to Okanogan and Pine Street/Conconully Highway. Turn left and drive 16.5 miles northwest to Conconully and look for the park on the left. It's located one-quarter of a mile south of Conconully.

Contact: Liar's Cove Resort, P.O. Box 72, Conconully, WA 98819; tel. (800) 830-1288 or (509) 826-1288.

27 Shady Pines Resort   6

This camp on Conconully Lake near Conconully State Park is an option if the state park campground is full, which occurs often in the summertime. See the descriptions of Kozy Kabins and RV Park and Conconully State Park for area information.

Location: On Conconully Reservoir; map A4, grid c2.

Campsites, facilities: There are 22 sites for trailers or RVs of any length; 21 sites have full hookups. Electricity, drinking water, sewer hookups, and picnic tables are provided. Flush toilets, ice, showers, and firewood are available. Bottled gas, sanitary services, a store, a cafe, and a coin-operated laundry facility are located within one mile. Boat launching facilities and boat rentals are available. Leashed pets and motorbikes are permitted.

Reservations, fees: Reservations accepted. Sites are $18-19 per night. Open mid-April to late October.

Directions: From East Wenatchee drive north on U.S. 97 for 88 miles to Okanogan and Pine Street/Conconully Highway. Turn left and drive 16.5 miles northwest to Conconully and Broadway Street. Turn west and drive one mile. The park is on the west shore of the lake.

Contact: Shady Pines Resort, P.O. Box 44, Conconully, WA 98819; tel. (800) 552-2287 or (509) 826-2287.

28 Conconully State Park   7

Conconully State Park is set along Conconully Lake, where a boat launch, beach access, swimming, and fishing provide all sorts of water sports possibilities. Visitors can also explore a nice half-mile nature trail or take a trip to the Sinlahekin Habitat Management Area, which is accessible via County Road 4015. This route heads northeast along the shore of Conconully Lake on the other side of U.S. 97. The road is narrow at first, but then becomes wider as it enters the Habitat Management Area.

Location: On Conconully Lake; map A4, grid c2.

Campsites, facilities: There are six primitive tent sites and 75 sites for tents or self-contained RVs up to 60 feet long. Drinking water, fire grills, and picnic tables are provided. Flush toilets, a dump station, showers, firewood, and a playground are available. A store, a cafe, a coin-operated laundry facility, and ice are located within one mile. Boat launching facilities are nearby. Leashed pets are permitted.

Reservations, fees: No reservations accepted. Sites are $5-16 per night. Open April through September.

Directions: From East Wenatchee drive north on U.S. 97 for 97 miles to Omak and take the North Omak exit. At the base of the hill, turn right and drive two miles until you reach Conconully Road. Turn right and drive 19 miles north to the park entrance.

Contact: Conconully State Park, P.O. Box 95, Conconully, WA 98819; tel. (800) 233-0321, (509) 826-7408.

29 Sugarloaf   6

At 2,400 feet this campground on the shore of Sugarloaf Lake is the smallest and most private of the camps on the lake, and one of the least used. Conconully State Park and Information Center are nearby.

Location: On Sugarloaf Lake in Okanogan National Forest; map A4, grid c2.

Campsites, facilities: There are four tent sites and one site for a tent, trailer, or RV up to 21 feet long. Picnic tables are provided, but there is no drinking water. No garbage service is provided, so trash must be packed out. Vault toilets and firewood are available. Boat launching facilities are available nearby. No boats with gas motors are permitted. Leashed pets are permitted.

Reservations, fees: No reservations; no fee. Open mid-May to mid-September.

Directions: From East Wenatchee drive north on U.S. 97 for 88 miles to Okanogan and County Road 9229. Turn north and drive about 17.5 miles northwest to Conconully and County Road 4015. Turn right (northwest) on County Road 4015 and drive 4.5 miles to the campground on the left.

Contact: Okanogan National Forest, Tonasket Ranger District, 1 West Winesap Avenue, Tonasket, WA 98855; tel. (509) 486-2186; fax (509) 486-5161.

30 Lyman Lake   5

Little known and little used, this campground along the shore of Lyman Lake is an idyllic setting for those wanting solitude and quiet. The lake is quite small, but fishing is an option for patient anglers.

Location: On Lyman Lake in Okanogan National Forest; map A4, grid c6.

Campsites, facilities: There are four sites for tents, trailers, or RVs up to 31 feet long. Picnic tables and fire grills are provided. Vault toilets are available, but there is no drinking water. No garbage service is provided, so trash must be packed out. Leashed pets are permitted.

Reservations, fees: No reservations; no fee. Open mid-May to mid-September.

Directions: From East Wenatchee drive north on U.S. 97 for 119 miles to Tonasket and Highway 20. Turn east on Highway 20 and drive 12.5 miles to County Road 9455. Turn right (southeast) on County Road 9455 and drive 13 miles to County Road 3785. Turn right (south) on County Road 3785 and drive 2.5 miles to the campground entrance.

Contact: Okanogan National Forest, Tonasket Ranger District, 1 West Winesap Avenue, Tonasket, WA 98855; tel. (509) 486-2186; fax (509) 486-5161.

31 Swan Lake   8

Scenic views greet visitors on the drive to and at this campground on the shore of Swan Lake, elevation 3,700 feet. A beautiful hiking trail circles the lake, and swimming, boating, fishing, mountain biking, and hiking are some of the possibilities here. It's a good out-of-the-way spot for RV cruisers seeking a rustic setting.

Location: On Swan Lake in Colville National Forest; map A4, grid c7.

Campsites, facilities: There are 25 sites for tents, trailers, or RVs up to 31 feet long. Drinking water, fire grills, and picnic tables are provided. Vault toilets, firewood, boat docks, and launching facilities are available. Gas motors are prohibited on the lake. Leashed pets are permitted.

Reservations, fees: No reservations accepted. Sites are $8 per night. Open May through September.

Directions: From Spokane on Interstate 90, turn north on U.S. 395 and drive 87 miles to Highway 20. Turn west on Highway 20 and drive 36 miles to the town of Republic and Highway 21. Turn south on Highway 21 and drive seven miles to Forest Road 53 (Scatter Creek Road). Turn right (southwest) on Forest Road 53 and drive eight miles to the campground.

Contact: Colville National Forest, Republic Ranger District, Republic, WA 99166; tel. (509) 775-3305; fax (509) 775-7401.

32 Long Lake   9

Long Lake is the third and smallest of the three lakes in this area (the others are Swan Lake and Ferry Lake). Expert fly fishermen can get a quality experience here angling for the cutthroat trout. A nice hiking trail circles the lake. The drive on Highway 21 south of Republic is particularly beautiful, with views of the Sanpoil River.

Location: On Long Lake in Colville National Forest; map A4, grid c7.

Campsites, facilities: There are 12 sites for tents, trailers, or RVs up to 21 feet long. Drinking water, fire grills, and picnic tables are provided. Vault toilets and firewood are available. Launching facilities are nearby. No gas motors are allowed on the lake, and fishing is restricted (fly-fishing only). Leashed pets are permitted.

Reservations, fees: No reservations. Sites are $8 per night. Open May through September.

Directions: From Spokane on Interstate 90, turn north on U.S. 395 and drive 87 miles to Highway 20. Turn west on Highway 20 and drive 36 miles to the town of Republic and Highway 21. Turn south on Highway 21 and drive seven miles to Forest Road 53 (Scatter Creek Road). Turn right (southwest) on Forest Road 53 and drive eight miles to Forest Road 400. Turn south and drive 1.5 miles to the camp.

Contact: Colville National Forest, Republic Ranger District, Republic, WA 99166; tel. (509) 775-3305; fax (509) 775-7401.

33 Ferry Lake   7

This is one of three fishing lakes within a four-square-mile area. The others are Swan Lake and Long Lake. For more information, see the descriptions of the preceding two campgrounds.

Location: On Ferry Lake in Colville National Forest; map A4, grid c7.

Campsites, facilities: There are nine sites for tents, trailers, or RVs up to 20 feet long. There is no drinking water. Fire grills and picnic tables are provided. Vault toilets and firewood are available. Launching facilities are nearby. Gas motors are prohibited on the lake. Leashed pets are permitted.

Reservations, fees: No reservations; no fee. Open May through September, weather permitting.

Directions: From Spokane on Interstate 90, turn north on U.S. 395 and drive 87 miles to Highway 20. Turn west on Highway 20 and drive 36 miles to the town of Republic and Highway 21. Turn south on Highway 21 and drive seven miles to Forest Road 53 (Scatter Creek Road). Turn right (southwest) on Forest Road 53 and drive six miles to Forest Road 5330. Turn right (north) on Forest Road 5330 and drive one mile to Forest Road 100. Turn right (north) and drive 500 yards to the campground.

Contact: Colville National Forest, Republic Ranger District, Republic, WA 99166; tel. (509) 775-3305; fax (509) 775-7401.

34 Sherman Pass Overlook   6

This roadside campground is located near Sherman Pass (5,575 feet), the highest pass in the state of Washington. Sherman Pass Scenic Byway is routed by there. Several trails passing through camp provide access to various peaks and vistas in the area. No other campgrounds are in the immediate vicinity.

Location: At Sherman Pass in Colville National Forest; map A4, grid c9.

Campsites, facilities: There are nine sites for tents, trailers, or RVs up to 24 feet long. There is no drinking water. Fire grills and picnic tables are provided. Vault toilets are available. Leashed pets are permitted.

Reservations, fees: No reservations; no fee. Open mid-May to late September.

Directions: From Spokane on Interstate 90, turn north on U.S. 395 and drive 87 miles to Highway 20. Turn west on Highway 20 and drive 19.5 miles to the campground.

Contact: Colville National Forest, Kettle Falls Ranger District, 255 West 11th Street, Kettle Falls, WA 99141; tel. (509) 738-6111; fax (509) 738-7701.

35 Loup Loup   6

At 4,200 feet, this campground is set next to the Loup Loup Ski Area, which has facilities for both downhill and cross-country skiing. It's just far enough off Highway 20 to be missed by many out-of-towners.

Location: Near Loup Loup Ski Area in Okanogan National Forest; map A4, grid d1.

Campsites, facilities: There are 32 sites for tents, trailers, or RVs up to 21 feet long. Drinking water and picnic tables are provided. Vault toilets and a dump station are available. Leashed pets are permitted.

Reservations, fees: No reservations. An annual pass ($25) or $5 daily fee per parked vehicle is required. Open May through September, weather permitting.

Directions: From East Wenatchee drive north on U.S. 97 for 88 miles to Okanogan and Highway 20. Turn west and drive 21 miles to Forest Road 42. Turn north on Forest Road 42 and drive one mile to the campground.

Contact: Okanogan National Forest, Methow Valley Visitor Center, P.O. Box 579, Winthrop, WA 98862; tel. (509) 997-4000; fax (509) 997-9770; e-mail: fsinfor@methow.com.

36 J. R.    7

This camp can be found along Frazier Creek near the Loup Loup summit and ski area. Some of the recreation possibilities in the surrounding area include fishing, hunting, cross-country skiing, snowmobiling, hiking, and bicycling. This is a good layover for travelers looking for a spot on Highway 20.

Location: On Frazier Creek in Okanogan National Forest; map A4, grid d1.

Campsites, facilities: There are six sites for tents, trailers, or RVs up to 25 feet long. Drinking water and picnic tables are provided. Vault toilets and a dump station are available. Leashed pets are permitted.

Reservations, fees: No reservations; no camping fee. An annual pass ($25) or $5 daily fee per parked vehicle is required. Open late May to early September.

Directions: From East Wenatchee drive north on U.S. 97 for 88 miles to Okanogan and Highway 20. Turn west and drive 22 miles to the campground.

Contact: Okanogan National Forest, Methow Valley Visitor Center, P.O. Box 579, Winthrop, WA 98862; tel. (509) 997-4000; fax (509) 997-9770; e-mail: fsinfor@methow.com.

37 Sportsman's Camp   6

This is a popular camp with hunters in season, who may bring horses, which are allowed in the camp although there are no stock facilities. This camp is shady and grassy with a small stream. There are some roads in the area that can be used by hikers and bikers. Highway 20 east of Interstate 5 is a designated scenic route.

Location: On Sweat Creek, in Lower Loomis State Forest; map A4, grid d2.

Campsites, facilities: There are six pull-through sites for tents, trailers, or RVs, up to 30 feet, and a small, dispersed area for tents. Picnic tables and fire pits are provided. Vault toilets are available, but there is no drinking water. A gazebo shelter is also available. Leashed pets are permitted.

Reservations, fees: No reservations; no fee. Open year-round, weather permitting.

Directions: From East Wenatchee drive north on U.S. 97 for 88 miles to Okanogan and Highway 20. Turn west and drive 15 miles to Sweat Creek Road. Turn left on Sweat Creek Road and drive one mile to the campground on the right.

Contact: Department of Natural Resources, Northeast Region, P.O. Box 190, Colville, WA 99114-0190; tel. (509) 684-7474; fax (509) 684-7484.

38 Rock Lakes   8

Trout fishing can be good at this scenic campground set in a forested area along the shore of Rock Lake. There are some roads in the area used by hikers and bikers. A good bet is to combine a trip here with nearby Leader Lake. Highway 20 east of Interstate 5 is a designated scenic route.

Location: On Rock Lake; map A4, grid d2.

Campsites, facilities: There are eight sites for tents or small trailers. Picnic tables and fire pits are provided. Vault toilets are available, but there is no drinking water. Leashed pets are permitted.

Reservations, fees: No reservations; no fee. Open year-round.

Directions: From East Wenatchee drive north on U.S. 97 for 88 miles to Okanogan and Highway 20. Turn west and drive 10 miles to Loup Loup Canyon Road. Turn left on Loup Loup Canyon Road and drive 4.8 miles to Rock Lakes Road. Turn left on Rock Lakes Road and drive 5.8 miles to the campground entrance. Turn left and drive a quarter mile to the campground.

Contact: Department of Natural Resources, Northeast Region, P.O. Box 190, Colville, WA 99114-0190; tel. (509) 684-7474; fax (509) 684-7484.

39 Rock Creek   6

This wooded campground is at the confluence of Rock and Loup Loup Creeks. A group shelter is available. It's advisable to obtain a map detailing the area from the Department of Natural Resources.

Location: On Rock Creek and Loup Loup Creek; map A4, grid d2.

Campsites, facilities: There are six sites for tents, small trailers, or RVs up to 30 feet. Picnic tables and fire pits are provided. Vault toilets, a picnic area and drinking water are available. Leashed pets are permitted.

Reservations, fees: No reservations; no fee. Open year-round.

Directions: From East Wenatchee drive north on U.S. 97 for 88 miles to Okanogan and Highway 20. Turn west and drive 10 miles to Loup Loup Canyon Road. Turn left on Loup Loup Canyon Road and drive 3.9 miles to the camp on the left.

Contact: Department of Natural Resources, Northeast Region, P.O. Box 190, Colville, WA 99114-0190; tel. (509) 684-7474; fax (509) 684-7484.

40 Leader Lake   7

This primitive but pretty camp set along the shore of Leader Lake is just far enough off the beaten path to get missed by many travelers. The boat ramp is a bonus, and trout fishing can be good in season.

Location: On Leader Lake; map A4, grid d2.

Campsites, facilities: There are 16 sites for tents or small trailers. Picnic tables and fire pits are provided. Vault toilets, a boat ramp, and a fishing pier are available, but there is no drinking water. Boat launching facilities are nearby. Leashed pets are permitted.

Reservations, fees: No reservations; no fee. Open year-round.

Directions: From East Wenatchee drive north on U.S. 97 for 88 miles to Okanogan and Highway 20. Turn west and drive eight miles to Leader Lake Road. Turn left and drive 0.4 mile to the campground.

Contact: Department of Natural Resources, Northeast Region, P.O. Box 190, Colville, WA 99114-0190; tel. (509) 684-7474; fax (509) 684-7484.

41 Eastside Park and Campground

   6

This city park is in the town of Omak, along the shore of the Okanogan River. Trout fishing is excellent here, and there is a boat ramp near the campground. Nearby recreation options include an 18-hole golf course, a pool, and a sports field.

Location: On the Okanogan River; map A4, grid d4.

Campsites, facilities: There are 50 tent sites and 76 drive-through sites for trailers or RVs of any length. Electricity, drinking water, sewer hookups, and picnic tables are provided. Flush toilets, sanitary services, showers, a swimming pool, and a playground are available. A store, a cafe, a coin-laundry, and ice are located within one mile. Boat launching facilities are nearby. Leashed pets are permitted.

Reservations, fees: No reservations. Sites are $10-12 per night. Open April through September, weather permitting.

Directions: From East Wenatchee drive north on U.S. 97 for 94 miles to Omak and Highway 155. Turn right (east) on Highway 155 and drive 0.3 mile to the campground on the left.

Contact: City of Omak, P.O. Box 72, Omak, WA 98841; tel. (509) 826-1170; fax (509) 826-6531.

42 American Legion Park   6

This city park is located along the shore of the Okanogan River in an urban setting. The sites are graveled and sunny. Anglers may want to try their hand at the excellent bass fishing here. There is a historical museum at the park.

Location: On the Okanogan River; map A4, grid d3.

Campsites, facilities: There are 35 sites for trailers or RVs of any length. Drinking water and picnic tables are provided. Flush toilets and showers are available. A store, a cafe, a coin-laundry, and ice are located within one mile.

Reservations, fees: No reservations accepted. Sites are $3-5 per night. Open year-round.

Directions: From East Wenatchee drive north on U.S. 97 for 88 miles to Okanogan and Highway 215. Turn left (north) on Highway 215 and drive about three miles to the campground on the right.

Contact: Okanogan City Hall, P.O. Box 752, Okanogan, WA 98840; tel. (509) 422-3600.

43 Crawfish Lake   8

This pretty, remote, and primitive camp is set at 4,500 feet along the shore of Crawfish Lake. Fishing and crawdad hunting are popular. For the latter, just put a small piece of chicken on a hook and wait 'til the little critters get their pinchers on it.

Location: On Crawfish Lake in Okanogan National Forest; map A4, grid d5.

Campsites, facilities: There are 19 sites for tents, trailers, or RVs up to 31 feet long. Picnic tables and fire grills are provided. Vault toilets are available, but there is no drinking water. No garbage service is provided, so trash must be packed out. Boat launching facilities are located on the lake. Leashed pets are permitted.

Reservations, fees: No reservations; no fee. Open mid-May to mid-September.

Directions: From East Wenatchee drive north on U.S. 97 for 102 miles to Riverside and County Road 9320. Turn right (east) on County Road 9320 and drive 20 miles (County Road 9320 becomes Forest Road 30) to Forest Road 30-100. Turn right and drive a half mile to the campground.

Contact: Okanogan National Forest, Tonasket Ranger District, 1 West Winesap Avenue, Tonasket, WA 98855; tel. (509) 486-2186; fax (509) 486-5161.

44 Ten Mile   7

Located about nine miles from Swan Lake, Ferry Lake, and Long Lake, this campground along the Sanpoil River is a good choice for a multi-day trip, visiting each of the lakes. There is fishing in the Sanpoil River, and a hiking trail leads west from camp for about 2.5 miles.

Location: On the Sanpoil River in Colville National Forest; map A4, grid d7.

Campsites, facilities: There are nine sites for tents, trailers, or RVs up to 21 feet long. Picnic tables, vault toilets, and firewood are available. There is no drinking water. Leashed pets are permitted.

Reservations, fees: No reservations; no fee. Open mid-May to mid-October.

Directions: From Spokane on Interstate 90, turn north on U.S. 395 and drive 87 miles to Highway 20. Turn west on Highway 20 and drive 40 miles to Republic and Highway 21. Turn south on Highway 21 for 10 miles to the campground entrance on the left.

Contact: Colville National Forest, Republic Ranger District, Republic, WA 99166; tel. (509) 775-3305; fax (509) 775-7401.

45 Whistlin' Pine Resort

         8

This camp nestled in a valley on the shores of 200-acre Alta Lake offers horseback riding and a nearby 18-hole golf course. See the description of Alta Lake State Park (campground number 46) for additional activities.

Location: On Alta Lake; map A4, grid f0.

Campsites, facilities: There are 30 tent sites and nine sites for trailers or RVs up to 30 feet long. Cabins are also available for rental. Electricity, drinking water, and picnic tables are provided. Flush toilets, showers, firewood, and ice are available. Sanitary services can be found within one mile. Boat docks, launching facilities, and rentals are available. Pets (cats only) and motorbikes are permitted.

Reservations, fees: Reservations accepted. Sites are $15-20 per night; cabins are $30-40 per night. Open April through Labor Day weekend.

Directions: From East Wenatchee drive north on U.S. 97 for 64 miles to Highway 153, just south of Pateros. Turn left (northwest) on Highway 153 and drive two miles to Alta Lake Road. Turn southwest and drive three miles to the resort at the end of the road.

Contact: Whistlin' Pine Resort, P.O. Box 284, Pateros, WA 98846; tel. (509) 923-2548.

46 Alta Lake State Park

          8

This state park is nestled among the pines along the shore of Alta Lake, where a half-mile-long swimming beach and boat launch are available. An 18-hole golf course and a riding stable are close by, and a nice one-mile hiking trail leads up to a scenic lookout.

Location: On Alta Lake; map A4, grid f0.

Campsites, facilities: There are 11 primitive tent sites, 158 developed tent sites, and 31 sites for trailers or RVs up to 40 feet long. Picnic tables and fireplaces are provided. Flush toilets, drinking water, showers, electricity, firewood, and sanitary services are available. A store, a cafe, and ice can be found within one mile. Some facilities are wheelchair accessible. Boat launching facilities are nearby. Leashed pets are permitted.

Reservations, fees: No reservations. Sites are $5-16 per night. Open April through September.

Directions: From East Wenatchee drive north on U.S. 97 for 64 miles to Highway 153 (just south of Pateros). Turn left (northwest) on Highway 153 and drive two miles to Alta Lake Road. Turn left (southwest) and drive three miles to the park at the end of the road.

Contact: Alta Lake State Park, Star Route 40, Pateros, WA 98846; tel. (800) 233-0321 or (509) 923-2473.

47 Superstop RV Park and Marina

 6

This shorefront park and marina on the Columbia River is close to an 18-hole golf course, hiking trails, a riding stable, and tennis courts. Special note for RV campers: A full hookup gets you 10% off anything in the restaurant.

Location: On the Columbia River; map A4, grid f1.

Campsites, facilities: There are three tent sites and 12 sites for trailers or RVs of any length. Electricity, drinking water, and sewer hookups are provided. Flush toilets, bottled gas, sanitary services, a store, a restaurant, and ice are available. Boat docks and launching facilities are nearby. Leashed pets and motorbikes are permitted.

Reservations, fees: Reservations accepted; phone (509) 923-2200, extension 181. Sites are $8-16 per night. Open year-round.

Directions: From East Wenatchee drive north on U.S. 97 for 66 miles to Pateros. Look for the park at the south end of town along the highway.

Contact: Superstop RV Park and Marina, P.O. Box 147, Pateros, WA 98846; tel. (509) 923-2200; fax (509) 923-2726.

48 Bridgeport State Park   8

Bridgeport State Park is located along the shore of Rufus Woods Lake, a reservoir on the Columbia River above Chief Joseph Dam. Highlights include beach access and a boat launch. There are also hiking trails, but the parks department warns that rattlesnakes might be lurking in certain areas. Nearby recreation options include an 18-hole golf course.

Location: On Rufus Woods Lake; map A4, grid f2.

Campsites, facilities: There are 14 sites for tents or self-contained RVs, and 20 sites with water and electrical hookups for trailers or RVs up to 45 feet long. Eight group campsites are also available. Drinking water, fire grills, and picnic tables are provided. Flush toilets, showers, firewood, and a dump station are available. A store, a cafe, and ice are located within one mile. Boat docks and launching facilities are nearby on both the upper and lower portions of the reservoir. Leashed pets are permitted.

Reservations, fees: No reservations. Sites are $10-16 per night. Open April to late October.

Directions: From East Wenatchee drive north on U.S. 97 for 71 miles to Highway 17. Turn south on Highway 17 and drive eight miles southeast to the park entrance.

Contact: Bridgeport State Park, P.O. Box 846, Bridgeport, WA 98813; tel. (800) 233-0321, (509) 686-7231.

49 Keller Ferry   7

This camp can be found along the shore of Franklin Roosevelt Lake, a large reservoir created by Grand Coulee Dam, about 15 miles west of camp. Waterskiing, fishing, and swimming are all options here.

Location: On Franklin Roosevelt Lake in Lake Roosevelt National Recreation Area; map A4, grid f8.

Campsites, facilities: There are 50 sites for tents, trailers, or RVs up to 16 feet long. Drinking water, fire grills, and picnic tables are provided. Flush toilets, sanitary services, ice, and a playground are available. A cafe is located within one mile. Boat docks, launching facilities, fuel, and a marine dump station are also available. Leashed pets are permitted.

Reservations, fees: No reservations. Sites are $5-10 per night; there is a $6 launch fee. Open year-round, weather permitting.

Directions: From Spokane on U.S. 90, turn west on U.S. 2 and drive 71 miles to Wilbur and Highway 21. Turn north and drive 14 miles to the campground.

Contact: Lake Roosevelt National Recreation Area, 1008 Crest Drive, Coulee Dam, WA 99116; tel. (509) 633-9441.

50 Lakeshore RV Park and Marina

 7

This municipal park and marina on Lake Chelan serves all members of the family, with fishing, swimming, boating, and hiking among the available activities. An 18-hole championship golf course and putting green, lighted tennis courts, and a visitor center are nearby. A trip worth taking is the ferry ride to one of several landings on the lake.

Location: On Lake Chelan; map A4, grid g0.

Campsites, facilities: There are 160 sites for trailers or RVs of any length. Electricity, drinking water, sewer hookups, and picnic tables are provided. Flush toilets, sanitary services, and showers are available. A store, a cafe, a coin-operated laundry facility, ice, a playground, and bottled gas can be found within one mile. Boat docks and launching facilities are nearby.

Reservations, fees: Reservations accepted beginning December 15. Sites are $11-27 per night. Open year-round.

Directions: From East Wenatchee drive north U.S. 2 for 40 miles to Chelan (after crossing the Dan Gordon Bridge, the road name changes to Saunders Street). Continue for 0.1 mile to Johnson Street. Turn left and drive 0.2 mile (the road becomes Highway 150/Manson Highway) to the campground on the left.

Contact: City of Chelan, P.O. Box 1669, Chelan, WA 98816; tel. (509) 682-8024; fax (509) 682-8248,.

51 Steamboat Rock State Park

      10

Steamboat Rock State Park is set along the shores of Banks Lake, a reservoir a few miles up from the Grand Coulee Dam. The park has a swimming beach, and fishing and waterskiing are popular. Horse trails are available in nearby Northrup Canyon. During the winter, the park is used by snowmobilers, cross-country skiers, and ice anglers.

Location: On Banks Lake; map A4, grid g5.

Campsites, facilities: There are two primitive tent sites, five sites for tents or self-contained RVs, 100 sites with full hookups for trailers or RVs up to 60 feet long, and 13 boat-in campsites. Picnic tables and fire grills are provided. Flush toilets, a cafe, and a playground are available. Some facilities are wheelchair accessible. Boat launching facilities are nearby. Leashed pets are permitted.

Reservations, fees: Reservations accepted, phone (800) 452-5687 ($6 reservation fee). Sites are $5-16 per night. Major credit cards accepted. Open year-round, with limited winter facilities.

Directions: From East Wenatchee drive north U.S. 2 for 70 miles to Highway 155 (five miles east of Coulee City). Turn north and drive 18 miles to the park on the left.

Contact: Steamboat Rock State Park, P.O. Box 352, Electric City, WA 99123; tel. (800) 233-0321 or (509) 633-1304.

52 Spring Canyon

        6

This large, developed campground is a popular vacation destination. Fishing for bass, walleye, trout, and sunfish are popular at the Franklin Roosevelt Lake. And if you don't like to fish, try waterskiing. The campground is not far from Grand Coulee Dam. Lake Roosevelt National Recreation Area offers numerous recreation options, such as programs conducted by rangers that include guided canoe trips, historical tours, campfire talks, and guided hikes. All programs are free of charge. This lake is known as a prime location to view bald eagles, especially in the winter months. Side trip options include visiting the Colville Tribal Museum in the town of Coulee Dam and touring the Grand Coulee Dam Visitor Center.

Location: On Franklin Roosevelt Lake in Lake Roosevelt National Recreation Area; map A4, grid g6.

Campsites, facilities: There are 87 sites for tents, trailers, or self-contained RVs up to 26 feet long. Drinking water, fire grills, and picnic tables are provided. Flush toilets, sanitary services, a cafe, and a playground are available. Some facilities are wheelchair accessible. Boat docks and launching facilities are available. Leashed pets are permitted.

Reservations, fees: No reservations accepted. Sites are $5-10 per night; there is a $6 launch fee. Open year-round, weather permitting.

Directions: From the junction of Interstate 90 and Highway 17 (just south of Moses Lake), drive north on Highway 17 for 45 miles to U.S. 2. Turn east on U.S. 2 and drive five miles to Highway 155. Turn left (north) and drive 26 miles to Grand Coulee and Highway 174. Turn right (east) on Highway 174 and drive three miles to the campground entrance.

Contact: Lake Roosevelt National Recreation Area, 1008 Crest Drive, Coulee Dam, WA 99116; tel. (509) 633-9441.

53 Lakeview Terrace Mobile Park

 6

This pleasant resort is near Franklin Roosevelt Lake, which was created by Grand Coulee Dam. It's a slightly less crowded option to the national park camps in the vicinity. See the description of Spring Canyon (campground number 51) for water recreation options. A full-service marina and tennis courts are nearby.

Location: Near Franklin Roosevelt Lake; map A4, grid g7.

Campsites, facilities: There are 20 tent sites and 15 drive-through sites for trailers or RVs of any length. Electricity, drinking water, sewer hookups, and picnic tables are provided. Flush toilets, showers, a laundry room, and a playground are available. Boat docks, launching facilities, and rentals are nearby. Leashed pets are permitted.

Reservations, fees: Reservations accepted. Sites are $15 per night. Open year-round.

Directions: From the junction of Interstate 90 and Highway 17 (just south of Moses Lake), drive north on Highway 17 for 45 miles to U.S. 2. Turn east on U.S. 2 and drive five miles to Highway 155. Turn left (north) and drive 26 miles to Grand Coulee and Highway 174. Turn right (east) on Highway 174 and drive 3.5 miles east to the park entrance.

Contact: Lakeview Terrace Mobile Park, Highway 174, Grand Coulee, WA 99133; tel. (509) 633-2169.

54 Coulee Playland Resort and RV Park

 7

This park on North Banks Lake, south of the Grand Coulee Dam, is pretty and well treed, with spacious sites for both tents and RVs. The Grand Coulee Laser Light Show is just two miles away and well worth a visit. Hiking trails, marked bike trails, a full-service marina, and tennis courts are close by.

Location: Near the Grand Coulee Dam; map A4, grid g5.

Campsites, facilities: There are 65 sites for tents, trailers, or RVs of any length. One yurt, which sleeps five, is also available. Electricity, drinking water, sewer hookups, and picnic tables are provided. Flush toilets, sanitary services, a store, a laundry room, showers, firewood, ice, a playground, boat docks, launching facilities, boat rentals, gas, and a bait and tackle shop are available. Bottled gas and a cafe are located within one mile. Pets and motorbikes are permitted.

Reservations, fees: Reservations accepted. Sites are $17-19 per night. Major credit cards accepted. Open year-round, with limited winter facilities.

Directions: From the junction of Interstate 90 and Highway 17 (just south of Moses Lake), drive north on Highway 17 for 45 miles to U.S. 2. Turn east on U.S. 2 and drive five miles to Highway 155. Turn left (north) and drive 26 miles to Grand Coulee and Electric City. The campground is just off the highway.

Contact: Coulee Playland Resort and RV Park, P.O. Box 457, Electric City, WA 99123; tel. (509) 633-2671.

55 River Rue RV Park   7

This camp is located in high desert terrain, but it is surrounded by lots of trees. Several hiking trails leave from the campground. You can fish, swim, water ski, or rent a houseboat at Lake Roosevelt, which is a mile away. Another nearby side trip is the Grand Coulee Dam.

Location: Near the Columbia River; map A4, grid h8.

Campsites, facilities: There are 86 sites for tents, trailers, or RVs. Rest rooms, showers, a sanitary dump, a pay phone, limited groceries, ice, snack bar, RV supplies, fishing tackle, and LP gas are available. Recreational facilities include a playground, a sports field, and horseshoe pits. The facilities are wheelchair accessible. Leashed pets are permitted.

Reservations, fees: Reservations recommended. Sites are $14-19 per night. Open April through October.

Directions: From Spokane drive west on U.S. 2 for about 66 miles (one mile past Wilbur) to Highway 174. Turn north on Highway 174 and drive one-quarter of a mile to Highway 21. Turn north on Highway 21 and drive 13 miles to the park on the right.

Contact: River Rue RV Park, 44892 State Route 21 North, Wilbur, WA 99185; tel.(509) 647-2647.

56 Blue Lake Resort   6

Blue Lake Resort is in a desert-like area along the shore of Blue Lake between Sun Lakes State Park and Lake Lenore Caves State Park. Both are excellent side trips. Activities at Blue Lake include trout fishing, swimming, and boating. Tackle and boat rentals are available at the resort.

Location: On Blue Lake; map A4, grid i4.

Campsites, facilities: There are 30 tent sites and 56 sites for trailers or RVs of any length with full or partial hookups; six are drive-through. There are also 10 cabins that sleep up to four people. Electricity, drinking water, sewer hookups, and picnic tables are provided. Flush toilets, sanitary services, firewood, showers, a store, ice, a roped swimming area, volleyball, a playground, boat docks, launching facilities, and boat rentals are available. Leashed pets and motorbikes are permitted.

Reservations, fees: Reservations accepted. Sites are $14.50 per night; cabins are $34-69 per night. Major credit cards accepted. Open April through September.

Directions: From the junction of Interstate 90 and Highway 17 (just south of Moses Lake), drive north on Highway 17 for 36 miles to the park on the right.

Contact: Blue Lake Resort, 31199 Highway 17 North, Coulee City, WA 99115; tel. (509) 632-5364; fax (509) 632-5388.

57 Sun Lakes State Park
         10

Sun Lakes State Park is on the shore of Park Lake, which is used primarily by boaters and water-skiers. The Lake Lenore Caves can be reached by a trail at the north end of the lake. Dry Falls and the interpretive center are also within the park boundaries. Nearby recreation possibilities include an 18-hole golf course, hiking trails, and a riding stable.

Location: On Park Lake; map A4, grid i4.

Campsites, facilities: There are 174 sites for tents or self-contained RVs, 10 group campsites, and 18 sites with full hookups for trailers or RVs up to 50 feet long. Picnic tables are provided. Flush toilets, a dump station, a cafe, a laundry room, ice, a swimming pool, electricity, drinking water, sewer hookups, showers, and firewood are available. A store is located within one mile. Some facilities are wheelchair accessible. Boat docks, launching facilities, and rentals are nearby. Leashed pets are permitted.

Reservations, fees: Reservations accepted; phone (800) 452-5687 ($6 reservation fee). Sites are $11-16 per night. Major credit cards accepted. Open year-round.

Directions: From the junction of Interstate 90 and Highway 17 (just south of Moses Lake), drive north on Highway 17 for 36 miles to the park on the right.

Contact: Sun Lakes State Park, Star Route 1, P.O. Box 136, Coulee City, WA 99115; tel. (800) 233-0321, (509) 632-5583.

58 Coulee City Park   6

Coulee City Park is a well-maintained park located in shade trees on the south shore of 30-mile-long Banks Lake, where boating, fishing, and waterskiing are popular. An 18-hole golf course is close by.

Location: On Banks Lake; map A4, grid i5.

Campsites, facilities: There are 100 tent sites and 60 sites for trailers or RVs up to 35 feet long; 32 are drive-through sites will full hookups. Electricity, drinking water, sewer hookups, and picnic tables are provided. Flush toilets, sanitary services, showers, and a playground are available. Bottled gas, firewood, a store, a restaurant, a cafe, a coin-laundry, and ice are located within one mile. Boat docks and launching facilities are nearby.

Reservations, fees: No reservations accepted. Sites are $10-15 per night. Open mid-April through September, weather permitting.

Directions: From East Wenatchee drive north on U.S. 2 for 60 miles to Coulee City and the junction with Highway 17. Continue east on U.S. 2 for two miles to the park.

Contact: Coulee City Park, P.O. Box 398, Coulee City, WA 99115; tel. (509) 632-5331.

59 Sun Village Resort   6

Like Blue Lake Resort, this campground is along the shore of Blue Lake. The setting is hot desert, perfect for swimming and fishing. See the description of Sun Lakes State Park for information on the nearby state parks and other recreation options.

Location: On Blue Lake; map A4, grid i4.

Campsites, facilities: There are four tent sites and 95 sites for trailers or RVs of any length; 40 are drive-through. Electricity, drinking water, sewer hookups, and picnic tables are provided. Flush toilets, bottled gas, sanitary services, a store, a cafe, a laundry room, ice, a playground, boat docks, launching facilities, and boat rentals are available. Showers and firewood available for an extra fee. Leashed pets and motorbikes are permitted.

Reservations, fees: Reservations accepted. Sites are $12-16 per night. Major credit cards accepted. Open mid-April to October.

Directions: From the junction of Interstate 90 and Highway 17 (just south of Moses Lake), drive north on Highway 17 for 36 miles to Blue Lake and Park Lake Road. Turn east on Park Lake Road (the south entrance) and drive one-half mile to the resort on the right.

Contact: Sun Village Resort, 33575 Park Lake Road NE, Coulee City, WA 99115; tel. (509) 632-5664; fax (509) 632-5360.

Laurent's

60 Sun Lakes Park Resort   6

This camp is run by the concessionaire that operates within Sun Lakes State Park. It offers full facilities and is a slightly more developed alternative to the state campground. See the description of Sun Lakes State Park.

Location: Sun Lakes State Park; map A4, grid i4.

Campsites, facilities: There are 110 sites for trailers or RVs of any length; 64 are drive-through. Electricity, drinking water, sewer hookups, and picnic tables are provided. Flush toilets, bottled gas, sanitary services, a store, showers, firewood, a snack bar, a laundry room, ice, a playground, boat rentals and a swimming pool are available. Boat docks and launching facilities are nearby. Leashed pets are permitted.

Reservations, fees: Reservations accepted. Sites are $21-23 per night. Open mid-April to mid-October, weather permitting.

Directions: From the junction of Interstate 90 and Highway 17 (just south of Moses Lake), drive north on Highway 17 for 38 miles to the park on the right (within Sun Lakes State Park, well signed).

Contact: Sun Lakes Park Resort, 34228 Park Lake Road NE, Coulee City, WA 99115; tel. (509) 632-5291.

61 Coulee Lodge Resort

 8

One of five camps in the general area and one of three in the immediate vicinity, Blue Lake offers plenty of summertime recreation options. See the description of Sun Lakes State Park for details.

Location: On Blue Lake; map A4, grid i4.

Campsites, facilities: There are 14 tent sites and 28 sites for trailers or RVs up to 35 feet long; seven are drive-through sites. Electricity, drinking water, sewer hookups, and picnic tables are provided. Flush toilets, bottled gas, sanitary services, a store, showers, firewood, a laundry room, boat docks, boat and jet ski rentals, launching facilities, and ice are available. A cafe is located within five miles. Some facilities are wheelchair accessible. Leashed pets and motorbikes are permitted.

Reservations, fees: Reservations accepted. Sites are $14-17 per night. Major credit cards accepted. Open mid-April to October.

Directions: From the junction of Interstate 90 and Highway 17 (just south of Moses Lake), drive north on Highway 17 for 39 miles to the north end of Blue Lake.

Contact: Coulee Lodge Resort, 33017 Park Lake Road NE, Coulee City, WA; tel. (509) 632-5565; fax (509) 632-8607.

A GROVE OF ASPEN

MAP A5

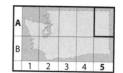

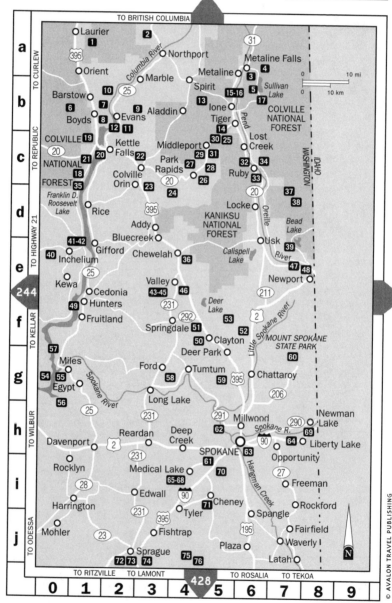

TO BRITISH COLUMBIA

a — Laurier **1** — **2** — Northport — Metaline Falls — **4**
Orient — Marble — Metaline — **3** — **31**

b — Barstow — **10** — Spirit — **15-16** — Sullivan Lake — **5**
6 — **7** — Aladdin — **13** — Ione — **17** — COLVILLE NATIONAL FOREST
Boyds — **8** — Evans — **9** — Tiger — **14**
12 **11**

c — COLVILLE **19** — Kettle Falls — **22** — Middleport — **30** **25** — Lost Creek
20 — Park Rapids — **29** **31** — **32** — **34**
21 **20** — **27** **28** — Ruby — **33**
NATIONAL — **18** — Colville Orin — **23** — **26**
FOREST **35** — **24** — Locke — **20** — **37** **38**

d — Franklin D. Roosevelt Lake — Rice — **395** — KANIKSU NATIONAL FOREST — Bead Lake — **39**
Addy — Usk
Bluecreek — Calispell Lake

e — **41-42** — Gifford — Chewelah — **36** — Oreille River — **47** **48**
40 — Inchelium — Newport
Kewa — **25** — Valley — **46** — **211**
Cedonia — **43-45** — Deer Lake

f — **49** — Hunters — **231** — **53** — **2**
Fruitland — **292** — **52** — MOUNT SPOKANE STATE PARK
Springdale — **51** — **50** — Clayton — **60**
Deer Park

g — **57** — Ford — **58** — Tumtum — **59** — **395** — Chattaroy
54 **55** — Miles — **206**
Egypt
56 — **25** — Long Lake

h — **231** — Millwood — Newman Lake — **290**
Davenport — Reardan — Deep Creek — **291** — Spokane R. — **69**
2 — **62** — **90** — **64** — Liberty Lake
231 — SPOKANE — **63** — Opportunity

i — Rocklyn — **28** — Medical Lake — **61** — **27** — Freeman
65-68 — **70** — Rockford
Harrington — Edwall — **90** — Cheney — Spangle
231 — **71** — Tyler — **195**

j — Mohler — **23** — Fishtrap — Plaza — Fairfield — Waverly
Sprague — **75** — Latah
72 **73** **74** — **76**

TO RITZVILLE — TO LAMONT — **428** — TO ROSALIA — TO TEKOA

TO CURLEW — TO REPUBLIC — TO HIGHWAY 21 — **244** — TO KELLAR — TO WILBUR — TO ODESSA

0 10 mi
0 10 km

Columbia River
Pend Oreille
WASHINGTON / IDAHO
Little Spokane River
Spokane River
Hangman Creek

N

0 1 2 3 4 5 6 7 8 9

© AVALON TRAVEL PUBLISHING

CHAPTER A5

1 Pierre Lake   8

Pierre Lake, a quiet, little-known jewel near the Canadian border, is the setting. It's only a short drive from U.S. 395, yet the campground gets relatively little use. The camp is set on the west shore of the lake. Boating, fishing, and hiking are some of the recreation possibilities here.

Location: On Pierre Lake in Colville National Forest; map A5, grid a1.

Campsites, facilities: There are 15 sites for tents, trailers, or RVs up to 24 feet long. Fire grills and picnic tables are provided. Drinking water, vault toilets, boat docks, and launching facilities are available on site. A convenience store and ice are located nearby (within seven miles). Leashed pets are permitted.

Reservations, fees: No reservations; no fee. Open mid-April to mid-October.

Directions: From Spokane drive north on U.S. 395 for 74 miles to Colville. Continue north on U.S. 395 for about 25 miles to Barstow and County Road 4013. Turn right (north) on County Road 4013 and drive nine miles to the campground on the west side of Pierre Lake.

Contact: Colville National Forest, Kettle Falls Ranger District, Kettle Falls, WA 99141; tel. (509) 738-6111; fax (509) 738-7701.

2 Sheep Creek   8

This campground is in a forested area along Sheep Creek, about four miles from the Columbia River and very close to the Canadian border. It's a primitive camp, yet it has drinking water and is crowded with locals on the Fourth of July weekend. The fishing can be good nearby.

Location: On Sheep Creek; map A5, grid a3.

Campsites, facilities: There are 11 sites for tents or small trailers. Picnic tables, fire grills, and tent pads are provided. Vault toilets, drinking water, a fishing pier, and a group shelter are available. Restaurants and stores are located within five miles. Some facilities are wheelchair accessible. Leashed pets are permitted.

Reservations, fees: No reservations; no fee. Open mid-April through November, weather permitting.

Directions: From Spokane drive north on U.S. 395 for 84 miles to Kettle Falls and Highway 25. Turn north on Highway 25 and drive 33 miles to Northport. Continue north on Highway 25 for three-quarters of a mile to Sheep Creek Road (across the Columbia River Bridge). Turn left on Sheep Creek Road and drive 4.3 miles (on a gravel road) to the campground entrance on the right.

Contact: Department of Natural Resources, Northeast Region, P.O. Box 190, Colville, WA 99114-0190; tel. (509) 684-7474; fax (509) 684-7484.

3 Mill Pond   6

Mill Pond Campground, located along the shore of a small reservoir just north of Sullivan Lake, is a good base camp for backpackers. A trail starts across the road and takes off into the backcountry. A wheelchair-accessible historical interpretive trail is located at the opposite end of the lake. There is also a pretty waterfall with a great view. All amenities are a short drive away in Metaline Falls. See the descriptions of East and West Sullivan Lakes for other information about the area.

Location: Near Sullivan Lake in Colville National Forest; map A5, grid a6.

Campsites, facilities: There are 10 sites for tents, trailers, or RVs up to 21 feet long. Hand-pumped water, fire rings, and picnic tables are provided. Vault toilets and garbage bins are available. A trailer dump station is located within one mile. A small boat launch is available; only electric motors are permitted. Leashed pets are permitted.

Reservations, fees: No reservations. Sites are $10 per night, $5 per night extra vehicle fee. Open late May to early September.

Directions: From Spokane drive north on U.S. 395 for six miles to U.S. 2. Turn northeast on U.S. 2 and drive 30 miles to the Metaline turnoff and Highway 211 West. Turn northwest on Highway 211 West and drive 15 miles to Usk and Highway 20. Turn northwest (left) and drive 34 miles to Tiger and Highway 31. Turn north on Highway 31 and drive 15 miles to the town of Metaline Falls and Sullivan Lake Road (County Road 9345). Turn east on Sullivan Lake Road and drive 7.5 miles to the campground on the east end of Mill Pond.

Contact: Colville National Forest, Sullivan Lake Ranger District, 12641 Sullivan Lake Road, Metaline Falls, WA 99153; tel. (509) 446-7500; fax (509) 446-7580.

4 East Sullivan   7

This campground along the north shore of Sullivan Lake is a popular vacation destination, with boating, fishing, swimming, sailing, waterskiing, and hiking trails among the activities available. The beautiful Salmo-Priest Wilderness is located just three miles to the east. It gets light use, which means quiet, private trails. This is a prime place to view wildlife, including the rare Woodland caribou and Rocky Mountain bighorn sheep. A nearby grass airstrip provides an opportunity for fly-in camping.

Location: On Sullivan Lake in Colville National Forest; map A5, grid a6.

Campsites, facilities: There are 38 sites for tents, trailers, or RVs up to 55 feet long. Drinking water, fire grills, and picnic tables are provided. Vault toilets, garbage service and a trailer dump station are available. Some facilities are wheelchair accessible. A boat dock and launching facilities are nearby. Leashed pets are permitted.

Reservations, fees: Reservations accepted; phone (877) 444-6777 or access the website: www.reserveusa.com ($8.65 reservation fee). Sites are $10 per night, $5 per night extra vehicle fee. Some double sites are available for $18 per night. Open late May through August.

Directions: From Spokane drive north on U.S. 395 for six miles to U.S. 2. Turn northeast on U.S. 2 and drive 30 miles to the Metaline turnoff and Highway 211 West. Turn northwest on Highway 211 West and drive 15 miles to Usk and Highway 20. Turn northwest (left) and drive 34 miles to Tiger and Highway 31. Turn north on Highway 31 and drive 15 miles to the town of Metaline Falls and Sullivan Lake Road (County Road 9345). Turn east on Sullivan Lake Road and drive eight miles to Sullivan Creek Road. Turn left (east) and drive a quarter mile to the campground on the right.

Contact: Colville National Forest, Sullivan Lake Ranger District, 12641 Sullivan Lake Road, Metaline Falls, WA 99153; tel. (509) 446-7500; fax (509) 446-7580.

5 West Sullivan   7

This campground is set along the northwestern shore of Sullivan Lake and is a popular destination for boating, fishing, swimming, sailing, waterskiing, and hiking. A nearby grass airstrip provides the opportunity for fly-in camping.

Location: On Sullivan Lake in Colville National Forest; map A5, grid b6.

Campsites, facilities: There are six sites for tents, trailers, or RVs up to 30 feet long. Drinking water, fire rings, and picnic tables are provided. Flush and vault toilets, a dump station, garbage bins, a boat launch, developed swimming beach, and floating swim platform are available. Some facilities are wheelchair accessible. Leashed pets are permitted.

Reservations, fees: Reservations accepted; phone (877) 444-6777 or access the website: www.reserveusa.com ($8.65 reservation fee). Sites are $10 per night, $5 per night extra vehicle fee. Open late May through August.

Directions: From Spokane drive north on U.S. 395 for six miles to U.S. 2. Turn northeast on U.S. 2 and drive 30 miles to the Metaline turnoff and Highway 211 West. Turn northwest on Highway 211 West and drive 15 miles to Usk and Highway 20. Turn northwest (left) and drive 34 miles to Tiger and Highway 31. Turn north on Highway 31 and drive 15 miles to the town of Metaline Falls and Sullivan Lake Road (County Road 9345). Turn east on Sullivan Lake Road and drive 8.1 miles to the campground on the left (set at the foot of Sullivan Lake, just across the road from the Sullivan Lake Ranger Station).

Contact: Colville National Forest, Sullivan Lake Ranger District, 12641 Sullivan Lake Road, Metaline Falls, WA 99153; tel. (509) 446-7500; fax (509) 446-7580.

6 Davis Lake   8

This campground is set at 4,600 feet elevation. It is a scenic spot and the fishing is often very good. Only small boats are permitted on the small, shallow lake. A one-mile trail loops the lake.

Location: On Davis Lake, in Colville National Forest; map A5, grid b1.

Campsites, facilities: There are four sites for tents or small trailers. Picnic tables and fire pits are provided. There is no drinking water or garbage service, but a vault toilet is available. Leashed pets are permitted.

Reservations, fees: No reservations; no fee. Open April through November, weather permitting.

Directions: From Spokane drive north on U.S. 395 for 84 miles to Kettle Falls. Continue north on U.S. 395 for nine miles to Deadman Creek Road. Turn west on Deadman Creek Road and drive about three miles to County Road 465 (Jack Knife cutoff). Turn right and drive 2.5 miles. Bear right and drive about one-half mile to County Road 480. Turn left and drive about three miles to County Road 080. Turn right and drive about three miles to Davis Lake. Note: The access road is very rough, high-clearance vehicles recommended.

Contact: Colville National Forest, Kettle Falls Ranger District, Kettle Falls, WA 99141; tel. (509) 738-6111; fax (509) 738-7701.

7 Whispering Pines RV Park

 7

This campground is a good layover for U.S. 395 RV cruisers. Located along the shore of the Franklin Roosevelt Lake, it has wild turkeys and deer, basketball and volleyball courts, horseshoes and croquet. It's close to marked bike trails, a full-service marina, and tennis courts. Riding stables are available 20 miles away, and a golf course is within 15 miles. A good side trip is to Colville National Forest East Portal Interpretive Area, 10 miles away and worth a side trip. (Drive south to the junction of Highway 20 and continue southwest for about six miles). Highlights include a nature trail and the Bangs Mountain auto tour, a five-mile drive that takes you through old-growth forest to Bangs Mountain Vista overlooking the Roosevelt Lake-Kettle Falls area.

Location: On Franklin Roosevelt Lake; map A5, grid b1.

Campsites, facilities: There are 15 tent sites and 42 sites for trailers or RVs of any length; 40 are drive-through sites. Some cabins are also available. Electricity, drinking water, sewer hookups, and picnic tables are provided. Flush toilets, sanitary services, a laundry room, a playground, a store, showers, and firewood are available. Lake swimming and fishing are on site. Leashed pets are permitted.

Reservations, fees: Reservations accepted. Sites are $11-15 per night. Weekly and monthly rates are available. Call for cabin rates. Open year-round.

Directions: From Spokane turn north on U.S. 395 and drive 84 miles to the town of Kettle Falls. Continue north on U.S. 395 for 6.5 miles to the campground entrance road on the right. Turn east at the sign for the campground and drive 300 yards to the camp.

Contact: Whispering Pines RV Park, P.O. Box 778, Kettle Falls, WA 99141; tel. (800) 597-4423 or (509) 738-2593.

8 Kamloops Island 10

This is one of the more primitive campgrounds located along Franklin Roosevelt Lake. It's located at Kamloops Island, an optimum area for waterskiing and fishing, and there are unbelievably beautiful views of water and mountains.

Location: On Franklin Roosevelt Lake in Lake Roosevelt National Recreation Area; map A5, grid b1.

Campsites, facilities: There are 17 tent sites. Picnic tables and fire grills are provided. Vault toilets are available, but there is no drinking water. Boat docks are nearby. Leashed pets are permitted.

Reservations, fees: No reservations. Sites are $5-10 per night. Open year-round, weather permitting.

Directions: From Spokane turn north on U.S. 395 and drive 84 miles to the town of Kettle Falls. Continue north on U.S. 395 (crossing the Columbia River) for seven miles to the Hedlund Bridge turnoff. Turn right and cross Hedlund Bridge and drive to the campground on the left.

Contact: Lake Roosevelt National Recreation Area, 1008 Crest Drive, Coulee Dam, WA 99116; tel. (509) 633-9441; fax (509) 633-9332.

9 Williams Lake   7

With a plethora of camps on nearby Franklin Roosevelt Lake, this secluded spot in a pretty, forested setting provides a less crowded alternative. It's set along the shore of Williams Lake, where the ice fishing, the only kind permitted, can be good. A developed swimming area is located half a mile away.

Location: On Williams Lake; map A5, grid b2.

Campsites, facilities: There are eight sites for tents or small trailers. Picnic tables, fire grills, and tent pads are provided. Vault toilets, drinking water, and a boat launch are available. Some facilities are wheelchair accessible. Leashed pets are permitted.

Reservations, fees: No reservations; no fee. Open mid-April through November.

Directions: From Spokane drive north for 74 miles to Colville. Continue north on U.S. 395 for two miles to Williams Lake Road. Turn north on Williams Lake Road and drive 13.7 miles to the campground entrance road on the left.

Contact: Department of Natural Resources, Northeast Region, P.O. Box 190, Colville, WA 99114-0190; tel. (509) 684-7474; fax (509) 684-7484.

10 North Gorge   7

This is the first of many campgrounds we discovered along the shore of 130-mile-long Franklin Roosevelt Lake, which was formed by damming the Columbia River at Coulee. Recreation options include waterskiing and swimming, plus fishing for walleye, trout, bass, and sunfish. During the winter, the lake level is drawn down, and a unique trip is to walk along the lake's barren edge. See the description of Kamloops Island for more recreation information.

Location: On Franklin Roosevelt Lake in Lake Roosevelt National Recreation Area; map A5, grid b2.

Campsites, facilities: There are 10 sites for tents, trailers, or RVs. Drinking water, fire grills, and picnic tables are provided. Vault toilets, boat docks, and launching facilities are available. Leashed pets are permitted.

Reservations, fees: No reservations. Sites are $5-10 per night; there is a $6 launch fee. Open year-round.

Directions: From Spokane on Interstate 90, drive north on U.S. 395 for 84 miles to the town of Kettle Falls and Highway 25. Turn north (right) on Highway 25 and drive 20 miles to the campground entrance.

Contact: Lake Roosevelt National Recreation Area, 1008 Crest Drive, Coulee Dam, WA 99116; tel. (509) 633-9441; fax (509) 633-9332.

11 Evans   9

Like North Gorge, this campground is set along the shore of Franklin Roosevelt Lake. Fishing, swimming, and waterskiing are among the activities here. See the description of Kamloops Island for more information.

Location: On Franklin Roosevelt Lake in Lake Roosevelt National Recreation Area; map A5, grid b2.

Campsites, facilities: There are 46 sites for tents, trailers, or RVs up to 26 feet long. Drinking water, fire grills, and picnic tables are provided. Flush toilets, a dump station, a store, boat docks, launching facilities, and a playground are available. Some facilities are wheelchair accessible. Leashed pets are permitted.

Reservations, fees: No reservations. Sites are $5-10 per night; there is a $6 launch fee. Open year-round, with limited facilities in the winter.

Directions: From Spokane on Interstate 90, drive north on U.S. 395 for 84 miles to the town of Kettle Falls and Highway 25. Turn north (right) on Highway 25 and drive eight miles to the campground entrance.

Contact: Lake Roosevelt National Recreation Area, 1008 Crest Drive, Coulee Dam, WA 99116; tel. (509) 633-9441; fax (509) 633-9332.

12 Marcus Island   8

This campground just south of Evans is quite similar to that camp, including a location nestled along the edge of Franklin Roosevelt Lake. Waterskiing, fishing, and swimming are the primary recreation options. See the description of Kamloops Island for information about the park and side trip options in the area.

Location: On Franklin Roosevelt Lake in Lake Roosevelt National Recreation Area; map A5, grid b2.

Campsites, facilities: There are 20 sites for tents, trailers, or RVs up to 20 feet long. Drinking water, fire grills, and picnic tables are provided. Vault toilets and a boat dock are available. A store is located within one mile. Leashed pets are permitted.

Reservations, fees: No reservations. Sites are $5-10 per night. Open year-round, weather permitting.

Directions: From Spokane on Interstate 90, drive north on U.S. 395 for 84 miles to the town of Kettle Falls and Highway 25. Turn north (right) on Highway 25 and drive four miles to the campground entrance.

Contact: Lake Roosevelt National Recreation Area, 1008 Crest Drive, Coulee Dam, WA 99116; tel. (509) 633-9441; fax (509) 633-9332.

13 Big Meadow Lake   8

Big Meadow Lake is at 3,400 feet with 71 surface acres. The camp, located in a pretty scenic area, is quiet, remote, and relatively unknown. The U.S. Forest Service has provided a wildlife viewing platform, where osprey, ducks, geese, moose, elk, and even cougar may be spotted, and an environmental education lab is near the campground.

Location: On Big Meadow Lake in Colville National Forest; map A5, grid b4.

Campsites, facilities: There are 16 sites for tents, trailers, or RVs up to 32 feet long.

Fire grills, picnic tables, and vault toilets are provided, but there is no drinking water. A boat launch, rest rooms, and a wheelchair-accessible nature trail and fishing pier are available. Leashed pets are permitted.

Reservations, fees: No reservations; no fee. Open May through November, weather permitting.

Directions: From Spokane drive north on U.S. 395 for 74 miles to Colville and Highway 20. Turn east on Highway 20 and drive one mile to Colville-Aladdin Northpoint Road (County Road 9435). Turn north and drive 20 miles to Meadow Creek Road. Turn east and travel six miles to the campground on the right. Note: The surface of the access road changes dramatically depending on the season.

Contact: Colville National Forest, Colville Ranger District, 755 South Main Street, Colville, WA 99114; tel. (509) 684-7010; fax (509) 684-7280.

14 Lake Leo   6

Lake Leo is the northernmost and quietest camp on the chain of lakes in the immediate vicinity. Frater and Nile Lakes, both pretty small, are a mile north. In winter, there is a Nordic ski trail that starts adjacent to the camp. Fishing and boating are two recreation options here.

Location: On Lake Leo in Colville National Forest; map A5, grid b5.

Campsites, facilities: There are eight sites for tents, trailers, or RVs up to 15 feet long. Picnic tables are provided, but there is no drinking water. Pit toilets and firewood are available. A boat ramp is available and launching facilities are nearby. Leashed pets are permitted.

Reservations, fees: No reservations. Sites are $8 per night. Open mid-May to mid-September.

Directions: From Spokane on Interstate 90, drive north on U.S. 395 for 74 miles to Colville and Highway 20. Turn east on Highway 20 and drive 23 miles to the campground. The entrance is on the south (right) side of the road.

Contact: Colville National Forest, Colville Ranger District, 755 South Main Street, Colville, WA 99114; tel. (509) 684-7010; fax (509) 684-7280.

15 Ione RV Park and Motel   8

This is a good layover for campers with RVs or trailers who want to stay in town. The park is on the shore of the Pend Oreille River, which offers fishing, swimming, several bike trails, and boating. Bighorn sheep may be spotted in the winter.

Location: On the Pend Oreille River; map A5, grid b5.

Campsites, facilities: There are seven tent sites and 19 sites for trailers or RVs of any length. Electricity, drinking water, sewer hookups, and picnic tables are provided. Flush toilets, sanitary services, showers, and a laundry room are available. A store, a cafe, and ice are located within one mile. Boat docks, launching facilities, and a playground are nearby. Leashed pets and motorbikes are permitted.

Reservations, fees: Reservations accepted. Sites are $10-18 per night. Major credit cards accepted. Open year-round.

Directions: From Spokane drive north on U.S. 2 for 48 miles to the junction with Highway 20 at the Washington/Idaho border. Turn west on Highway 20 and drive 48 miles northwest to Tiger and Highway 31. Turn north on Highway 31 and drive four miles to Ione. Cross a spillway (it looks like a bridge) on Highway 31 and to the campground on the right.

Contact: Ione RV Park and Motel, P.O. Box 730, Ione, WA 99139; tel. (509) 442-3213; fax (509) 442-3503; e-mail: clarkd@ iomet.com.

16 Edgewater   6

Edgewater can be found on the shore of the Pend Oreille River about two miles upstream from the Box Canyon Dam. The camp is not far out of Ione, yet it has a primitive feel to it. Fishing is popular here.

Location: On the Pend Oreille River in Colville National Forest; map A5, grid b5.

Campsites, facilities: There are 23 sites for tents, trailers, or RVs up to 20 feet long. Drinking water, fire grills, garbage collection, and picnic tables are provided. Vault toilets are available. A boat launch is nearby. Leashed pets are permitted.

Reservations, fees: No reservations. Sites are $10 per night, $5 extra vehicle fee. Open late May to early September.

Directions: From Spokane drive north on U.S. 395 for six miles to U.S. 2. Turn northeast on U.S. 2 and drive 30 miles to the Metaline turnoff and Highway 211 West. Turn northwest on Highway 211 West and drive 15 miles to Usk and Highway 20. Turn northwest (left) and drive 34 miles to Tiger and Highway 31. Turn north on Highway 31 and drive 15 miles to the town of Metaline Falls and Sullivan Lake Road (County Road 9345). Turn east (right) on Sullivan Lake Road and drive a quarter mile to County Road 3669. Turn north (left) on County Road 3669 and drive two miles to the campground entrance road on the left. Turn left and drive a quarter mile to the campground.

Contact: Colville National Forest, Sullivan Lake Ranger District, 12641 Sullivan Lake Road, Metaline Falls, WA 99153; tel. (509) 446-7500; fax (509) 446-7580.

17 Noisy Creek   7

This campground is in an idyllic setting adjacent to where Noisy Creek pours into Sullivan Lake. Waterskiing is allowed on the 3.5-mile-long lake. A trail near camp heads east along Noisy Creek and then north up to Hall Mountain (elevation 6,323 feet), which is bighorn sheep country.

Location: On Sullivan Lake in Colville National Forest; map A5, grid b6.

Campsites, facilities: There are 19 sites for trailers or RVs up to 35 feet long. Drinking water, fire rings, and picnic tables are provided. Vault toilets are available. Boat launching facilities are nearby. Leashed pets are permitted.

Reservations, fees: Reservations accepted; phone (877) 444-6777 or access the website: www.reserveusa.com ($8.65 reservation fee). Sites are $10 per night, $5 extra vehicle fee. Open late May to early September.

Directions: From Spokane drive north on U.S. 395 for six miles to U.S. 2. Turn northeast on U.S. 2 and drive 30 miles to the Metaline turnoff and Highway 211 West. Turn northwest on Highway 211 West and drive 15 miles to Usk and Highway 20. Turn northwest (left) and drive 34 miles to Tiger and Highway 31. Turn north on Highway 31 and drive 15 miles to the town of Metaline Falls and Sullivan Lake

Road (County Road 9345). Turn east (right) on Sullivan Lake Road and drive eight miles to the campground on the right (on the south end of Sullivan Lake).

Contact: Colville National Forest, Sullivan Lake Ranger District, 12641 Sullivan Lake Road, Metaline Falls, WA 99153; tel. (509) 446-7500; fax (509) 446-7580.

18 Lake Ellen    7

Fishing and swimming are permitted on this good-sized lake, located about three miles west of the Columbia River and the Lake Roosevelt National Recreation Area. See a U.S. Forest Service map for details.

Location: On Lake Ellen in Colville National Forest; map A5, grid c1.

Campsites, facilities: There are 11 sites for tents, trailers, or RVs up to 22 feet long. Picnic tables are provided, but there is no drinking water. Vault toilets and boat docks are available. Some facilities are wheelchair accessible. Leashed pets are permitted.

Reservations, fees: No reservations; no fee. Open mid-April to mid-October.

Directions: From Spokane drive north on U.S. 395 for 87 miles to Colville and Highway 20. Turn west on Highway 20 and drive 14 miles (crossing the Columbia River) to County Road 3. Turn left and drive south for 4.5 miles to County Road 412. Turn right on County Road 412 and drive five miles to the campground.

Contact: Colville National Forest, Kettle Falls Ranger District, Kettle Falls, WA 99141; tel. (509) 738-6111; fax (509) 738-7701.

19 Trout Lake   8

At elevation 3,100 feet this pristine mountain lake has great fishing. The nearby, five-mile-long Hoodoo Canyon Trail offers spectacular views.

Location: On Trout Lake in Colville National Forest; map A5, grid c1.

Campsites, facilities: There are four tent sites. No drinking water; fire pits are provided. No garbage service; pack it out. A vault toilet is available. Leashed pets are permitted.

Reservations, fees: No reservations; no fee. Open April through November, weather permitting.

Directions: From Spokane turn north on U.S. 395 and drive 87 miles to Colveille and Highway 20. Turn west on Highway 20 and drive 15 miles (crossing the Columbia River) to Trout Lake Road (County Road 020). Turn right on Trout Lake Road and drive five miles to the campground.

Contact: Colville National Forest, Kettle Falls Ranger District, Kettle Falls, WA 99141; tel. (509) 738-6111; fax (509) 738-7701.

20 Kettle Falls   10

This is a modern, developed campground that attracts fairly heavy use in the summer months. It's located along the shore of Franklin Roosevelt Lake, where waterskiing, swimming, and fishing are all options. In the summer the rangers offer campfire programs in the evenings.

Location: On Franklin Roosevelt Lake in Lake Roosevelt National Recreation Area; map A5, grid c1.

Campsites, facilities: There are 77 sites for tents, trailers, or RVs up to 26 feet long. Drinking water, fire grills, and picnic tables are provided. Flush toilets, a dump station, firewood, a cafe, and a playground are available. A store is located within one mile. Some facilities are wheelchair accessible. Boat docks, fuel, and launching facilities are available. Leashed pets are permitted.

Reservations, fees: No reservations. Sites are $5-10 per night; there is a $6 launch fee. Major credit cards accepted. Open year-round, with limited facilities in the winter.

Directions: From Spokane drive north on U.S. 395 for 84 miles to the town of Kettle Falls. Continue on U.S. 395 for three miles to Kettle Park Road on the left. Turn left and drive two miles to the campground on the right.

Contact: Lake Roosevelt National Recreation Area, 1008 Crest Drive, Coulee Dam, WA 99116; tel. (509) 633-9441; fax (509) 633-9332.

21 Canyon Creek   6

This roadside campground is located near the Bangs Mountain Auto Tour and within hiking distance of the East Portal Historical Site. It's a very pretty area not far from the Columbia River, which offers a myriad of recreation options.

Location: Near the East Portal Historical Site in Colville National Forest; map A5, grid c1.

Campsites, facilities: There are 12 sites for tents, trailers, or RVs up to 30 feet long. Fire grills, and picnic tables are provided, but there is no drinking water. Vault toilets are available. Some facilities are wheelchair accessible. Pets are permitted.

Reservations, fees: No reservations; no fee. Open mid-April to late October.

Directions: From Spokane drive north on U.S. 395 for 87 miles to Highway 20. Turn west on Highway 20 and drive 18 miles (crossing the Columbia River) to Forest Road 136. Turn left and drive south for one-third of a mile to the campground on the left.

Contact: Colville National Forest, Kettle Falls Ranger District, Kettle Falls, WA 99141; tel. (509) 738-6111; fax (509) 738-7701.

22 Douglas Falls   8

This campground in a wooded area along Mill Creek which includes Douglas Falls, is just outside of town and is one of the best deals in the state. A great camp for families or groups, it has drinking water, a beautiful setting, easy access, a swinging bridge, a waterfall nearby, and even a baseball field, all for free.

Location: On Mill Creek; map A5, grid c2.

Campsites, facilities: Ten sites for tents or small trailers. Picnic tables, fire grills, and tent pads are provided. Vault toilets and drinking water are available. A barrier-free vault toilet, trails, and picnic areas are also available. A baseball field is nearby. Leashed pets are permitted.

Reservations, fees: No reservations; no fee. Open Memorial Day weekend through November.

Directions: From Spokane drive north on U.S. 395 for 74 miles to Colville and Highway 20. Turn east on Highway 20 and drive 1.1 miles to Aladdin Road. Turn north and drive two miles to Douglas Falls Road. Turn left and drive three miles to the campground on the left.

Contact: Department of Natural Resources, Northeast Region, P.O. Box 190, Colville, WA 99114-0190; tel. (509) 684-7474; fax (509) 684-7484.

23 Rocky Lake   6

This isn't exactly paradise, but remarkable recreational diversity is just down the road. The campground is set on Rocky Lake, a shallow, weedy pond lined with a lot of rocks. But if you backtrack a bit on Rocky Lake Road, you'll see the entrance signs for the nearby Little Pend Oreille Habitat Management Area, a premium area for hiking, fishing, hunting, and photographing wildlife.

Location: On Rocky Lake; map A5, grid d3.

Campsites, facilities: There are seven sites for tents or small trailers. Picnic tables, fire grills, and tent pads are provided. Vault toilets, drinking water, and a boat launch are available. Leashed pets are permitted.

Reservations, fees: No reservations; no fee. Open to overnight camping from mid-April through May and from Labor Day weekend through November. The interim period, June to early September, is open to day-use only.

Directions: From Spokane drive north on U.S. 395 for drive 74 miles to Colville and Highway 20. Turn east on Highway 20 and drive six miles to Artman-Gibson Road. Turn right on Artman-Gibson Road and drive 3.2 miles to a one-lane gravel road. Turn right on the one-lane gravel road (unnamed) and drive about one-half mile. Bear left and continue another two miles to the campground.

Contact: Department of Natural Resources, Northeast Region, P.O. Box 190, Colville, WA 99114-0190; tel. (509) 684-7474; fax (509) 684-7484.

24 Starvation Lake   8

Starvation Lake is only 15 feet deep and has a weed problem, OK for fishing but not for swimming. Osprey and bald eagles frequent the area. It's advisable to obtain a detailed map of the area. The camp is used extensively by locals during the early fishing season (end of April to early June), but is uncrowded thereafter, though the fishing is then catch-and-release. Boats must not exceed 16 feet.

Location: On Starvation Lake; map A5, grid d4.

Campsites, facilities: There are eight sites for tents, small trailers, or RVs; six are pull-through sites. Picnic tables and fire grills are provided. Vault toilets, including one barrier-free; drinking water, and a barrier-free fishing dock are available. Leashed pets are permitted.

Reservations, fees: No reservations; no fee. Open mid-April through November, weather permitting.

Directions: From Spokane drive north on U.S. 395 for 74 miles to Colville and Highway 20. Turn east on Highway 20 and drive 10.5 miles to a gravel road. Turn right on a gravel road and drive one-third mile to an intersection. Turn left and drive one-half mile to the campground on the right.

Contact: Department of Natural Resources, Northeast Region, P.O. Box 190, Colville, WA 99114-0190; tel. (509) 684-7474; fax (509) 684-7484.

25 Sherry Creek   6

An old fire camp, this camp is near the ORV trail network of the Pend Orielle Lake system, but it is basically a fishing camp. It's advisable to obtain a detailed map of the area. Biking and hiking on the ORV trails is an option.

Location: Near Sherry Lake; map A5, grid c5.

Campsites, facilities: There are three sites for tents and small trailers. Picnic tables and fire pits are provided. Vault toilets are available, but there is no drinking water or garbage service. Leashed pets are permitted.

Reservations, fees: No reservations; no fee. Open May through November, weather permitting.

Directions: From Spokane drive north on U.S. 395 for 74 miles to Colville and Highway 20. Turn east on Highway 20 and drive 23.8 miles to a gravel road. Turn right and drive about one-half mile to the campground.

Contact: Department of Natural Resources, Northeast Region, P.O. Box 190, Colville, WA 99114-0190; tel. (509) 684-7474; fax (509) 684-7484.

26 Flodelle Creek   8

This campground is set where hiking, hunting, and fishing are quite good. It's advisable to obtain a detailed map of the area. Off-road vehicle trails are available at this camp, and they are often in use, so don't count on a particularly quiet camping experience.

Location: On Flodelle Creek; map A5, grid c4.

Campsites, facilities: There are eight sites for tents or small trailers. Picnic tables, fire grills, and tent pads are provided. Vault toilets and drinking water are available. Leashed pets and motorbikes are permitted.

Reservations, fees: No reservations. Sites are $8 per night. Open May through November, weather permitting.

Directions: From Spokane drive north on U.S. 395 for drive 74 miles to Colville and Highway 20. Turn east on Highway 20 and drive 19.4 miles to an unnamed two-lane gravel road on the right. Turn right on that road and drive one-quarter mile to the campground entrance road on the left.

Contact: Department of Natural Resources, Northeast Region, P.O. Box 190, Colville, WA 99114-0190; tel. (509) 684-7474; fax (509) 684-7484.

27 Little Twin Lakes   6

Sites at this pretty, wooded campground on the shore of Little Twin Lakes have lake views and an unbeatable price. It's rare to find such a nice spot on the water for free. See the description of North Gorge for more information.

Location: On Little Twin Lakes in Colville National Forest; map A5, grid c4.

Campsites, facilities: There are 20 sites for tents, trailers, or RVs up to 16 feet long. Fire grills and picnic tables are provided. There is no drinking water. Pit toilets and firewood are available. Boat docks and launching facilities are located nearby. Leashed pets are permitted.

Reservations, fees: No reservations; no fee. Open May to mid-Nove
er permitting.

Directions: From Spokane drive north on U.S. 395 for 74 miles to Col
way 20. Turn east on Highway 20 and drive 12.5 miles to County R
northeast and drive 1.5 miles to Forest Road 4939. Turn right (nortl
miles to the campground.

Contact: Colville National Forest, Colville Ranger District, 755 South Main Street,
Colville, WA 99114; tel. (509) 684-7010; fax (509) 684-7280.

28 Lake Gillette   8

This pretty and popular camp is right on the shore of Lake Gillette. Like neighboring East Gillette Campground, it fills up fast in the summer. The camp is popular with off-road vehicle users.

Location: On Lake Gillette in Colville National Forest; map A5, grid c5.

Campsites, facilities: There are 14 sites for tents, trailers, or RVs up to 31 feet long. Drinking water, fire grills, and picnic tables are provided. Vault toilets, sanitary services and an amphitheater are available. A store and ice are located within one mile. Some facilities are wheelchair accessible. Boat docks, launching facilities, and rentals are nearby. Leashed pets are permitted.

Reservations, fees: No reservations. Sites are $8-14 per night. Open mid-May to late September.

Directions: From Spokane drive north on U.S. 395 for 74 miles to Colville and Highway 20. Turn east on Highway 20 and drive 20 miles to County Road 4987 (Lake Gillette Road). Turn right (east) on Lake Gillette Road and drive one-half mile to the campground on the right.

Contact: Colville National Forest, Colville Ranger District, 755 South Main Street, Colville, WA 99114; tel. (509) 684-7010; fax (509) 684-7280.

29 Gillette   6

This beautiful-and extremely popular-campground is near Lake Gillette, just south of Beaver Lodge Resort and Lake Thomas, one in a chain of seven lakes. There are a few hiking trails in the area. See the description of Beaver Lodge Resort for other recreation information. Be sure to make reservations early.

Location: Near Lake Gillette in Colville National Forest; map A5, grid c4.

Campsites, facilities: There are 30 sites for tents, trailers, or RVs up to 31 feet long. Drinking water, fire grills, and picnic tables are provided. Vault toilets and sanitary services are available. A store and ice are located within one mile. Some facilities are wheelchair accessible. Boat docks, launching facilities, and rentals are nearby. Leashed pets are permitted.

Reservations, fees: No reservations. Sites are $8 per night. Open mid-May to late September.

Directions: From Spokane drive north on U.S. 395 for 74 miles to Colville and Highway 20. Turn east on Highway 20 and drive 20 miles to County Road 4987 (Lake Gillette Road). Turn right (east) on Lake Gillette Road and drive one-half mile to the campground on the left.

,ntact: Colville National Forest, Colville Ranger District, 755 South Main Street, Colville, WA 99114; tel. (509) 684-7010; fax (509) 684-7280.

30 Lake Thomas 6

This camp on the shore of Lake Thomas is a less crowded alternative to the campgrounds at Lake Gillette. See the descriptions of Lake Gillette, Gillette, and Beaver Lodge Resort for recreation information.

Location: On Lake Thomas in Colville National Forest; map A5, grid c5.

Campsites, facilities: There are 15 tent sites. Drinking water, fire grills, tent pads, and picnic tables are provided. Vault toilets and firewood are available. Sanitary services are located within one mile. Boat docks, launching facilities, and rentals are nearby. Leashed pets are permitted.

Reservations, fees: No reservations. Sites are $8 per night. Open mid-May to late September.

Directions: From Spokane drive north on U.S. 395 for 74 miles to Colville and Highway 20. Turn east on Highway 20 and drive 20 miles to County Road 4987 (Lake Gillette Road). Turn right (east) on Lake Gillette Road and drive one mile to the campground.

Contact: Colville National Forest, Colville Ranger District, 755 South Main Street, Colville, WA 99114; tel. (509) 684-7010; fax (509) 684-7280.

31 Beaver Lodge Resort

 9

This developed camp is along the shore of Lake Gillette, one in a chain of seven lakes. Information is available at Little Pend Oreille at the southern end of the chain. Hiking trails and marked bike trails are close to the camp, and a Nordic ski trail can be found at Lake Leo at the northern end of the lake chain.

Location: On Lake Thomas; map A5, grid c5.

Campsites, facilities: There are 35 sites for trailers or RVs of any length, and seven cabins. Electricity, drinking water, sewer hookups, and picnic tables are provided. Flush toilets, bottled gas, showers, firewood, a recreation hall, a store, a cafe, ice, boat rentals and a playground are available. A dump station is located within one mile. Boat docks and launching facilities are nearby. Leashed pets and motorbikes are permitted.

Reservations, fees: Reservations accepted. Sites are $8-14 per night; cabins are $40-60 per night. Major credit cards accepted. Open year-round.

Directions: From Spokane drive north on U.S. 395 for 74 miles to Colville and Highway 20. Turn east on Highway 20 and drive 25 miles to the lodge on the right.

Contact: Beaver Lodge Resort, 2430 Highway 20 East, Colville, WA 99114; tel. (509) 684-5657.

32 Blueslide Resort 7

Trout fishing is excellent at this resort along the shore of the Pend Oreille River. The resort offers full facilities for anglers, including tackle, boat rentals, and a marina with the only boat gas for 57 miles. The park is lovely, with grassy, shaded sites and is located along the waterfowl migratory path. Nearby recreation options include marked bike trails. The only other campground in the vicinity is the Outpost Resort (see next listing).

Location: On the Pend Oreille River; map A5, grid c6.

Campsites, facilities: There are seven tent sites and 44 sites for trailers or RVs of any length; four are drive-through. There are also four motel units and five cabins. Electricity, drinking water, fire pits, sewer hookups, and picnic tables are provided. Flush toilets, sanitary services, showers, a recreation hall, several sports fields, a store, propane, a laundry room, ice, firewood, a playground, a heated swimming pool, boat docks, launching facilities, and boat fuel are available. Leashed pets and motorbikes are permitted.

Reservations, fees: Reservations recommended. Sites are $12-16 per night. Cabins are $44-59 per night. Major credit cards accepted. Open year-round, but only cabins are available in the winter.

Directions: From Spokane drive north on U.S. 395 for six miles to U.S. 2. Turn north on U.S. 2 and drive 34 miles to Highway 211. Turn left and drive 18 miles to Highway 20. Turn left and drive 22 miles to the park (located on the right at milepost 400).

Contact: Blueslide Resort, 400041 State Route 20, Cusick, WA 99119; tel. (509) 445-1327.

33 Outpost Resort   8

This comfortable campground in a pretty setting along the shore of the Pend Oreille River has fairly spacious sites and views of snowcapped mountains. If you're cruising Highway 20, Blueslide Resort is located about five miles north, the nearest alternative if this camp is full.

Location: On the Pend Oreille River; map A5, grid c6.

Campsites, facilities: There are 12 tent sites and 12 drive-through sites with full hookups for trailers or RVs of any length. There are also four cabins. Picnic tables are provided. Flush toilets, sanitary services, a store, a cafe, ice, electricity, drinking water, sewer hookups, showers, a swimming area, boat rentals, boat docks, and launching facilities are available. Leashed pets and motorbikes are permitted.

Reservations, fees: Reservations accepted. Sites are $10-15 per night; cabins are $40-65 per night. Major credit cards accepted. Open year-round, with limited winter facilities.

Directions: From Spokane drive north on U.S. 395 for six miles to U.S. 2. Turn north on U.S. 2 and drive 34 miles to Highway 211. Turn left and drive 18 miles to Highway 20. Turn left and drive 17 miles to the park (located between mileposts 405 and 406).

Contact: Outpost Resort, 405351 Highway 20, Cusick, WA 99119; tel. (509) 445-1317.

34 Panhandle   9

In the tall trees and with views of the river, here's a scenic spot to set up camp along the shore of the Pend Oreille River. This is a good base for a fishing or waterskiing trip. The campground is located in an area of old-growth trees directly across the river from the Outpost Resort. A network of hiking trails can be accessed by taking Forest Roads to the east. See a U.S. Forest Service map for details.

Location: On the Pend Oreille River in Colville National Forest; map A5, grid c6.

Campsites, facilities: There are 11 sites for tents, trailers, or RVs up to 32 feet long. Drinking water, fire rings and picnic tables are provided. Vault toilets and a small boat launch are available. Leashed pets are permitted.

Reservations, fees: No reservations. Sites are $9 per night, $4.50 per extra vehicle. Open late May to late September.

Directions: From Spokane drive north on U.S. 395 for six miles to U.S. 2. Turn north on U.S. 2 and drive 30 miles to the Metaline turnoff and Highway 211 West. Take Highway 211 West and drive for 15 miles to the junction of Highway 20. Cross Highway 20, driving through the town of Usk. Continue across the Pend Oreille River to Le Clerk Road. Turn left and drive 15 miles north on Le Clerk Road to the campground on the left.

Contact: Colville National Forest, Newport Ranger District, 315 North Warren Avenue, Newport, WA 99156; tel. (509) 447-7300; fax (509) 447-7301.

35 Haag Cove   8

This campground is tucked away in a cove along the shore of Franklin Roosevelt Lake (Columbia River). A good side trip is to the Sherman Creek Habitat Management Area, located just north of camp. It's rugged and steep, but a good place to see and photograph wildlife.

Location: On Franklin Roosevelt Lake in Lake Roosevelt National Recreation Area; map A5, grid d1.

Campsites, facilities: There are 18 sites for tents, trailers, or RVs up to 26 feet long. Drinking water, fire grills, and picnic tables are provided. Vault toilets and boat docks are available. Leashed pets are permitted.

Reservations, fees: No reservations. Sites are $5-10 per night. Open year-round, weather permitting.

Directions: From Spokane drive north on U.S. 395 for 84 miles to the town of Kettle Falls and Highway 20. Continue on Highway 20 and drive 7.5 miles to Kettle Falls Road. Turn left (south) and drive two miles to the campground.

Contact: Lake Roosevelt National Recreation Area, 1008 Crest Drive, Coulee Dam, WA 99116; tel. (509) 633-9441; fax (509) 633-9332.

36 The New 49er Motel and RV Park   6

This is the heart of mining country. The park is in a mountainous setting next to a motel, with grassy sites. Nearby recreation options include an 18-hole golf course, hiking trails, and marked bike trails. This is a good deal for RV cruisers—a rustic setting right in town.

Location: Near Chewelah; map A5, grid e4.

Campsites, facilities: There are 27 drive-through sites with full hookups for trailers or RVs up to 30 feet long. Flush toilets, sanitary services, showers, a spa, a recreation hall, ice, picnic tables, and an indoor, heated swimming pool are available. Bottled gas, a store, a cafe, ice, and coin-operated laundry facilities are located within one mile. Pets are permitted.

Reservations, fees: Reservations accepted. Sites are $16.50 per night. Major credit cards accepted. Open year-round.

Directions: From Spokane drive north on U.S. 395 and drive 44 miles to Chewelah and the park on the right (on U.S. 395 at the south edge of town, well signed).
Contact: The New 49er Motel and RV Park, South 311 Park Street, Chewelah, WA 99109; tel. (509) 935-8613; fax (509) 935-8705.

37 Browns Lake   8

This campground is set along the shore of Browns Lake about five miles from South Skookum Lake. No motorized boats are permitted on the lake, and only fly-fishing is allowed. A hiking trail leaves the campground and ties into a wheelchair-accessible interpretive trail with beautiful views along the way.
Location: On Browns Lake in Colville National Forest; map A5, grid d7.
Campsites, facilities: There are 18 sites for tents, trailers, or RVs up to 21 feet long. Picnic tables are provided, but there is no drinking water. Vault toilets are available. A primitive boat launch is available for small boats such as canoes, row boats, and inflatables. Leashed pets are permitted.
Reservations, fees: No reservations. Sites are $7 per night, $3.50 per extra vehicle. Open late May to late September.
Directions: From Spokane drive north on U.S. 395 for six miles to U.S. 2. Turn north on U.S. 2 and drive 30 miles to the Metaline turnoff and Highway 211 West. Turn northwest on Highway 211 West and drive for 15 miles to Usk and Highway 20. Drive north on Highway 20 a short distance to County Road 3389. Turn right (east) on County Road 3389 and drive (over the Pend Oreille River) for four miles to a fork with Forest Road 5030. Bear north and drive four miles to the campground.
Contact: Colville National Forest, Newport Ranger District, 315 North Warren Avenue, Newport, WA 99156; tel. (509) 447-7300; fax (509) 447-7301.

38 South Skookum Lake   7

The western shore of South Skookum Lake, at the foot of Kings Mountain (elevation 4,383 feet), is the site of this camp. A 1.3-mile-long hiking trail circles the water, and a spur trail has an overlook of the lake and a view of Kings Mountain.
Location: On South Skookum Lake in Colville National Forest; map A5, grid d7.
Campsites, facilities: There are 25 sites for tents, trailers, or RVs up to 30 feet long. Drinking water and picnic tables are provided. Vault toilets, a boat launch for small boats, and a wheelchair-accessible fishing dock are available. Leashed pets are permitted.
Reservations, fees: No reservations. Sites are $9 per night, $4.50 per extra vehicle. Open late May to late September.
Directions: From Spokane drive north on U.S. 395 for six miles to U.S. 2. Turn north on U.S. 2 and drive 30 miles to the Metaline turnoff and Highway 211 West. Turn northwest on Highway 211 West and drive for 15 miles to Usk and Highway 20. Drive north on Highway 20 a short distance to County Road 3389. Turn right (east) on County Road 3389 and drive (over the Pend Oreille River) for 6.5 miles to the campground.
Contact: Colville National Forest, Newport Ranger District, 315 North Warren Avenue, Newport, WA 99156; tel. (509) 447-7300; fax (509) 858-2402.

39 Skookum Creek   5

This campground is in a wooded area along Skookum Creek, about 1.5 miles from where it empties into the Pend Oreille River. It's a good canoeing spot, has drinking water, and gets little attention. And you can't beat the price of admission.

Location: Near the Pend Oreille River; map A5, grid e7.

Campsites, facilities: There are 10 sites for tents or small trailers. Picnic tables, fire grills, and tent pads are provided. Vault toilets and drinking water are available. Leashed pets are permitted.

Reservations, fees: No reservations; no fee. Open mid-April through October, weather permitting.

Directions: From Spokane drive north on U.S. 395 for six miles to U.S. 2. Turn north on U.S. 2 and drive 48 miles to Newport and Highway 20. Turn west on Highway 20 and drive 16 miles northwest to the town of Usk. Continue east across the bridge for 0.9 mile to Le Clerc Road. Turn right on Le Clerc Road and drive 2.2 miles to a one-lane gravel road. Turn left and drive a very short distance to another gravel road. Turn left and drive a quarter mile to the campground.

Contact: Department of Natural Resources, Northeast Region, P.O. Box 190, Colville, WA 99114-0190; tel. (509) 684-7474; fax (509) 684-7484.

40 Rainbow Beach Resort   8

This quality resort is set along the shore of Twin Lakes Reservoir in the Colville Indian Reservation. Nearby recreation options include hiking trails, marked bike trails, a full-service marina, and tennis courts.

Location: On Twin Lakes Reservoir; map A5, grid e0.

Campsites, facilities: There are three tent sites and 14 sites for trailers or RVs of any length; five are drive-through. In the winter, eight cabins are available. Electricity, drinking water, sewer hookups, and picnic tables are provided. Flush toilets, bottled gas, sanitary services, a shower, firewood, a recreation hall, a store, a laundry room, ice, boat rentals, docks and launching facilities, and a playground are available. Leashed pets are permitted.

Reservations, fees: Reservations required. Sites are $9.50-16 per night. Cabins are $45-50 per night. There is a small pet fee. Campsites are available April through October; cabins are available November through February.

Directions: From Spokane drive north on U.S. 395 for 84 miles to the town of Kettle Falls and Highway 20. Turn east on Highway 20 and drive five miles to the turnoff for Inchelium. Turn south and drive about 20 miles to Inchelium and Bridge Creek-Twin Lakes County Road. Turn west and drive two miles to Stranger Creek Road. Turn left and drive one-quarter of a mile to the resort on the right.

Contact: Rainbow Beach Resort, 18 North Twin Lakes Road, Inchelium, WA 99138; tel. (509) 722-5901; fax (509) 722-7080.

41 Clover Leaf   8

This camp is small and quite primitive. In this particular area of Roosevelt Lake,

waterskiing is not advised, but fishing is fine. See the descripti~~
land and North Gorge for recreation details.

Location: On Franklin Roosevelt Lake in Lake Roosevelt Natic~~
map A5, grid e1.

Campsites, facilities: There are eight tent sites. Drinking wa~~
nic tables are provided. Vault toilets are available. Boat la~~
nearby. Leashed pets are permitted.

Reservations, fees: No reservations. Sites are $5-10 per night; ther~~ ..
fee. Open year-round, with limited winter facilities.

Directions: From Spokane on Interstate 90, drive west for four miles to U.S. 2.
Turn west on U.S. 2 and drive 34 miles to Highway 25. Turn north (right) on Highway
25 and drive 61 miles to Davenport and the campground (located about two miles
south of Gifford).

Contact: Lake Roosevelt National Recreation Area, 1008 Crest Drive, Coulee Dam,
WA 99116; tel. (509) 633-9441; fax (509) 633-9332.

42 Gifford   7

Fishing and waterskiing are two of the draws at this camp on the shore of Franklin
Roosevelt Lake (Columbia River). For a more detailed description of Roosevelt
Lake, see the descriptions of Kamloops Island and North Gorge.

Location: On Franklin Roosevelt Lake in Lake Roosevelt National Recreation Area;
map A5, grid e1.

Campsites, facilities: There are 47 sites for tents, trailers, or RVs up to 20 feet
long. Drinking water, fire grills, and picnic tables are provided. Vault toilets are available. Boat docks and launching facilities are nearby. Leashed pets are permitted.

Reservations, fees: No reservations. Sites are $5-10 per night; there is a $6 launch
fee. Open year-round, with limited winter facilities.

Directions: From Spokane on Interstate 90, drive west for four miles to U.S. 2.
Turn west on U.S. 2 and drive 34 miles to Davenport and Highway 25. Turn north
(right) on Highway 25 and drive 60 miles to the campground (located about three
miles south of Gifford).

Contact: Lake Roosevelt National Recreation Area, 1008 Crest Drive, Coulee Dam,
WA 99116; tel. (509) 633-9441; fax (509) 633-9332.

43 Winona Beach
Resort and RV Park   9

This beautiful and comfortable resort on the shore of Waitts Lake has spacious
sites and friendly folks. In the spring, the fishing for brown trout and rainbow trout
can be quite good. The trout head to deeper water in the summer, and bluegill and
perch are easier to catch.

Location: On Waitts Lake; map A5, grid e3.

Campsites, facilities: There are 17 tent sites and 38 sites for trailers or RVs of any
length; 20 are lakeside. There are also seven cabins available. Electricity, drinking
water, sewer hookups, and picnic tables are provided. Flush toilets, showers, sanitary services, firewood, a snack bar, a general store, a cafe, an antique store, and ice

..ilable. Boat docks, launching facilities, and rentals are on site. Leashed
. and motorbikes are permitted.

Reservations, fees: Reservations accepted. Sites are $13-19 per night. Cabins
are $49-75 per night. A small pet fee is charged. Major credit cards accepted. Open
April through October.

Directions: From Spokane drive north on U.S. 395 for 42 miles to the Valley-Waitts
Lake exit. Turn west (left) at that exit and drive one mile to Highway 231. Turn right
(north) on Highway 231 and drive 1.5 miles to the town of Valley and Valley-Waitts Lake
Road. Turn left and drive three miles to Winona Beach Road. Turn left and drive one-
quarter mile to the resort.

Contact: Winona Beach Resort and RV Park, 33022 Winona Beach Road, Valley,
WA 99181; tel. (509) 937-2231; fax (509) 937-2215.

44 Silver Beach Resort

 6

Silver Beach Resort offers grassy sites on the shore of Waitts Lake, where fishing
and waterskiing are popular. See the description of Winona Beach Resort and RV
Park for information about the lake.

Location: On Waitts Lake; map A5, grid e3.

Campsites, facilities: There are 53 sites for trailers or RVs of any length; four are
drive-through sites. Electricity, drinking water, sewer hookups, and picnic tables are
provided. Flush toilets, bottled gas, sanitary services, a store, showers, a restaurant,
a laundry room, ice, a playground, boat docks, launching facilities, and boat rentals
are available. Leashed pets are permitted.

Reservations, fees: Reservations accepted. Sites are $18.50 per night. Major
credit cards accepted. Open late April through September.

Directions: From Spokane drive north on U.S. 395 for 42 miles to the Valley-Waitts
Lake exit. Turn west (left) at that exit and drive six miles to Waitts Lake and the
resort on the left-hand side near the shore of the lake.

Contact: Silver Beach Resort, 3323 Waitts Lake Road, Valley, WA 99181; tel. (509) 937-
2811; fax (509) 937-2816.

45 Waitts Lake Resort 6

The shore of Waitts Lake is the home of this clean, comfortable resort, where
lake views are available and ice fishing is popular in the winter. See the description
of Winona Beach Resort and RV Park for information about the lake.

Location: On Waitts Lake; map A5, grid e3.

Campsites, facilities: There are 20 sites for tents, trailers, or RVs of any length; 16
are full-hookup sites on the lake. Drinking water, fire rings and picnic tables are provided. Flush toilets, showers, a store, a year-round restaurant, firewood, boat docks,
boat rentals, launching facilities, and ice are available.

Reservations, fees: Reservations required. Sites are $16.50 per night. Major cred-
it cards accepted. Open early April to late October.

Directions: From Spokane drive north on U.S. 395 for 42 miles to the Valley-Waitts

Lake exit. Turn west (left) at that exit and drive one mile to Highway 231. Turn right (north) on Highway 231 and drive 1.5 miles to the town of Valley and Valley-Waitts Lake Road. Turn left and drive three miles to the resort.

Contact: Waitts Lake Resort, 3365 Waitts Lake Road, Valley, WA 99181; tel. (509) 937-2400.

46 Jump Off Joe Mobile Park and Resort   7

Located on the edge of Jump Off Joe Lake, this wooded campground offers lake views and easy boating access. Recreational activities include boating, fishing, and swimming. Spokane and Grand Coulee Dam are both within a short drive and provide excellent side-trip options.

Location: On Jump Off Joe Lake; map A5, grid e4.

Campsites, facilities: There are 20 sites for tents and 20 sites for trailers or RVs with full hookups. Drinking water, picnic tables, and fire rings are provided. Rest rooms, showers, a pay phone, horseshoe pits, a recreation field, a store, a swimming beach and a barbecue are available. The camp also rents boats and has a boat ramp and dock. The facilities are wheelchair accessible. Leashed pets are permitted.

Reservations, fees: Reservations recommended. Sites are $15-17 per night. A pet fee of $2.50 per night is charged. Open April through October.

Directions: From Spokane drive north on U.S. 395 for about 40 miles (three miles south of the town of Valley) to the Jump Off Joe Road exit (mile marker 198). Take that exit, turn west and drive 1.2 miles to the campground on the right.

Contact: Jump Off Joe Mobile Park and Resort, 3290 East Jump Off Joe Road, Valley, WA 99181; tel. (509) 937-2133.

47 Pioneer Park   6

Pioneer Park Campground is set near the shore of Box Canyon Reservoir on the Pend Oreille River near Newport. The launch and adjoining parking area are suitable for larger boats. Waterskiing and water sports are popular here. There is a wheelchair-accessible interpretive trail with a boardwalk and beautiful views of the river. Signs along the way explain the history of Native Americans who once inhabited the area.

Location: On the Pend Oreille River in Colville National Forest; map A5, grid e7.

Campsites, facilities: There are 14 sites for tents, trailers, or RVs up to 32 feet long. Drinking water and picnic tables are provided. Vault toilets are available. Boat docks, launching facilities, and rentals are nearby. Leashed pets are permitted.

Reservations, fees: No reservations. Sites are $8 per night. Open May to late September, weather permitting. Note: This camp is under reconstruction and is not expected to reopen before May 2001. Call for current status.

Directions: From Spokane drive north on U.S. 395 for six miles to U.S. 2. Turn north on U.S. 2 and drive 41 miles to Newport. Continue across the Pend Oreille River to Le Clerc Road (County Road 9305). Turn left on Le Clerc Road and drive two miles to the campground on the left.

Contact: Colville National Forest, Newport Ranger District, 315 North Warren Avenue, Newport, WA 99156; tel. (509) 447-7300; fax (509) 447-7301.

48 Old American Kampground 5

Old American Kampground is near the Pend Oreille River, right in Newport at the Washington/Idaho border. The intersection of U.S. 2 and Highway 41 is a major junction for this part of the country. The park is pretty, with river frontage and full facilities for boating and fishing. If you want a more secluded spot, Pioneer Park is about a 15-minute drive away on the east side of the river.

Location: Near the Pend Oreille River; map A5, grid e8.

Campsites, facilities: There are three tent sites and 84 sites for trailers or RVs of any length. Electricity, cable TV, drinking water, and sewer hookups are provided. Flush toilets, picnic tables, sanitary services, a laundry room, showers, boat docks, launching facilities, a club house, hot tub, and propane gas are available. Leashed pets and motorbikes are permitted.

Reservations, fees: Reservations preferred. Sites are $10-25 per night. Major credit cards accepted. Open year-round.

Directions: From Spokane drive north on U.S. 395 for six miles to U.S. 2. Turn north on U.S. 2 and drive 48 miles to Newport and Newport Avenue. Turn north on Newport Avenue and drive one block to the campground at the end of the road.

Contact: Old American Kampground, 701 North Newport Avenue, Newport, WA 99156; tel. (509) 447-3663; fax (509) 447-0679; website: www.kmresorts.com.

49 Hunters 8

This campground on a shoreline point along Roosevelt Lake (Columbia River) is a good spot for swimming, fishing, or waterskiing. See the descriptions of Kamloops Island and North Gorge for further information on the area.

Location: On Franklin Roosevelt Lake in Lake Roosevelt National Recreation Area; map A5, grid f1.

Campsites, facilities: There are 42 sites for tents, trailers, or RVs up to 26 feet long. Drinking water, fire grills, and picnic tables are provided. Flush toilets, a store, and ice are available within one mile. Boat docks and launching facilities are nearby. Leashed pets are permitted.

Reservations, fees: No reservations. Sites are $5-10 per night; there is a $6 launch fee. Open year-round, with limited winter facilities.

Directions: From Spokane on Interstate 90, drive west for four miles to U.S. 2. Turn west on U.S. 2 and drive 34 miles to Davenport and Highway 25. Turn north on Highway 25 and drive 47 miles to Hunters and the campground access road on the west side of the road (well signed). Turn left at the access road and drive two miles to the campground.

Contact: Lake Roosevelt National Recreation Area, 1008 Crest Drive, Coulee Dam, WA 99116; tel. (509) 633-9441; fax (509) 633-9332.

50 Shore Acres 8

Located along the shore of Loon Lake at 2400 feet elevation, this family-oriented campground has a long expanse of beach and is an alternative to Granite Point Park across the lake. Note: If you're planning on visiting this park on a weekend, be aware of the policy of full-weekend reservations. You can't stay just a Friday or Saturday night; you have to reserve for the whole weekend. See the description of Granite Point Park for details about the fishing opportunities.

Location: On Loon Lake; map A5, grid f4.

Campsites, facilities: There are 30 sites for trailers or RVs up to 42 feet long and 10 cabins. Electricity, drinking water, sewer hookups, and picnic tables are provided. Flush toilets, sanitary services, a general store, showers, firewood, propane, ice, a playground, a swimming area, boat docks, boat rentals, and launching facilities are available.

Reservations, fees: Reservations recommended. Sites are $20 per night. Cabins are $400-600 per week; call for nightly rates. Open mid-April through September.

Directions: From Spokane drive north on U.S. 395 for 30 miles to Highway 292. Turn west on Highway 292 and drive two miles to Shore Acres Road. Turn left and drive another two miles to the park.

Contact: Shore Acres, 41987 Shore Acres Road, Loon Lake, WA 99148; tel. (800) 900-2474 or (509) 233-2474.

🗀 Granite Point Park   8

This camp is on the shore of Loon Lake, a clear, clean, spring-fed lake with a sandy beach and swimming area. In the spring the Mackinaw trout range from four to 30 pounds and can be taken by deep-water trolling (downriggers suggested). Easier to catch are the kokanee salmon and rainbow trout in the 12- to 14-inch class. A sprinkling of perch, sunfish, and bass come out of their hiding places when the weather heats up.

Location: On Loon Lake; map A5, grid f4.

Campsites, facilities: There are 68 sites for trailers or RVs of any length. Electricity, drinking water, sewer hookups, and picnic tables are provided. Flush toilets, showers, a recreation hall, a store, a cafe, a laundry room, ice, a playground, three swimming areas with two miles of beach, two swimming docks, boat docks, boat rentals, and launching facilities are available. Bottled gas is located within one mile. Pets are not permitted.

Reservations, fees: Reservations accepted. Sites are $18-20 per night for two campers, $3.50 each additional camper. Open mid-April to mid-September.

Directions: From Spokane drive north on U.S. 395 for 26 miles (eight miles past the town of Deer Park) to the campground on the left.

Contact: Granite Point Park, 41000 Granite Point Road, Loon Lake, WA 99148; tel. (509) 233-2100.

🗀 Jerry's Landing   8

The shore of Eloika Lake is home to this camp in a lovely evergreen setting with abundant wildlife. Trout fishing can be excellent as soon as the ice is off the lake in spring. During the hot days of summer, crappie and perch fishing is good.

Location: On Eloika Lake; map A5, grid f6.

Campsites, facilities: There are 24 sites for tents, trailers, or RVs of any length; 20 are full hookups and four of these are drive-through sites. Drinking water, fire rings, and picnic tables are provided. Flush toilets, a dump station, a store, ice, showers, and firewood are available. Bottled gas is available within one mile. Boat docks, launching facilities, and rentals are nearby. Leashed pets are permitted.

Reservations, fees: Reservations accepted. Sites are $14-15 per night. Major credit cards accepted. Open April through September.

Directions: From Spokane drive north on U.S. 395 for six miles to U.S. 2. Turn north on U.S. 2 and drive 23 miles to Oregon Road. Turn west on Oregon Road and drive one mile to the campground on the left.

Contact: Jerry's Landing, North 41114 Lakeshore Drive, Elk, WA 99009; tel. (509) 292-2337.

53 Pend Oreille County Park   6

This is the only campground around, and it's not a bad choice if you're looking for a layover spot. It's a good alternative to the often-crowded Mount Spokane State Park. There are many hiking trails and nature hikes on the grounds, and other nearby activities include fishing and hunting.

Location: Near Newport; map A5, grid f5.

Campsites, facilities: There are 34 sites for tents and two sites for RVs or trailers. Rest rooms, showers, and a barbecue are provided. Leashed pets are permitted.

Reservations, fees: Reservations accepted. Sites are $8 per night. Open Memorial Day to Labor Day.

Directions: From Spokane drive north on U.S. 395 for six miles to U.S. 2. Turn north on U.S. 2 and drive 31 miles to the county park entrance on the left (west side).

Contact: Pend Oreille County Department of Parks and Recreation, P.O. Box 5067, Newport, WA 99156; tel. (509) 447-4821.

54 Seven Bays
Resort and Marina   6

Manicured grassy, lakeside sites among deciduous trees and friendly folks are the highlights of this resort on the shore of Roosevelt Lake. This is an alternative to Fort Spokane and Hawk Creek. A full-service marina sets this spot apart from the others.

Location: On Franklin Roosevelt Lake; map A5, grid g0.

Campsites, facilities: There are 24 tent sites and 48 sites for trailers or RVs of any length; 29 have full hookups and two are drive-through sites. Flush toilets, picnic tables, bottled gas, a dump station, showers, a store, a cafe, a laundry room, and ice are available. Boat docks and launching facilities are located at the resort. Leashed pets are permitted.

Reservations, fees: Reservations accepted. Sites are $10-15 per night. Major credit cards accepted. Open year-round.

Directions: From Spokane on Interstate 90, drive west for four miles to U.S. 2. Turn west on U.S. 2 and drive 34 miles to Highway 25. Turn north on Highway 25 and drive 23 miles to Miles-Creston Road. Turn south and drive five miles to the resort.

Contact: Seven Bays Resort, Route 1, P.O. Box 624, Davenport, WA 99122; tel. (509) 725-1676.

55 Fort Spokane   8

Rangers offer evening campfire programs and guided daytime activities at this modern campground on the shore of Roosevelt Lake. This is one of 16 campgrounds on the 130-mile-long lake.

Location: On Franklin Roosevelt Lake in Lake Roosevelt National Recreation Area; map A5, grid g0.

Campsites, facilities: There are 67 sites for tents, trailers, or RVs up to 26 feet long. Drinking water, picnic tables, and fire grills are provided. Flush toilets, sanitary services, and a playground are available. A store and ice are located within one mile. Some facilities are wheelchair accessible. Boat docks, launching facilities, and a marine dump station are nearby. Leashed pets are permitted.

Reservations, fees: No reservations. Sites are $5-10 per night; there is a $6 launch fee. Open year-round, with limited winter facilities.

Directions: From Spokane on Interstate 90, drive west for four miles to U.S. 2. Turn west on U.S. 2 and drive 34 miles to Davenport and Highway 25. Turn north (right) on Highway 25 and drive 22 miles to the campground entrance.

Contact: Lake Roosevelt National Recreation Area, 1008 Crest Drive, Coulee Dam, WA 99116; tel. (509) 633-9441; fax (509) 633-9332.

56 Hawk Creek   8

This is a pleasant camping spot along the shore of Roosevelt Lake (Columbia River), adjacent to the mouth of Hawk Creek. The bay is a popular fishing area.

Location: On Franklin Roosevelt Lake in Lake Roosevelt National Recreation Area; map A5, grid g0.

Campsites, facilities: There are 20 sites for tents, trailers, or RVs up to 16 feet long. Picnic tables, fire grills, and drinking water are provided. Vault toilets are available. Boat docks and launching facilities are nearby. Leashed pets are permitted.

Reservations, fees: No reservations. Sites are $5-10 per night; there is a $6 launch fee. Open year-round, with limited winter facilities.

Directions: From Spokane on Interstate 90, drive west for four miles to U.S. 2. Turn west on U.S. 2 and drive 34 miles to Davenport and Highway 25. Turn north (right) on Highway 25 and drive 23 miles to Miles-Creston Road. Turn northwest (left) and drive 10 miles to the campground at the mouth of Hawk Creek.

Contact: Lake Roosevelt National Recreation Area, 1008 Crest Drive, Coulee Dam, WA 99116; tel. (509) 633-9441; fax (509) 633-9332.

57 Porcupine Bay   8

This is a good spot for campers with boats because of its proximity to a nearby dock and launch. A swimming beach is adjacent to the campground.

Location: On Franklin Roosevelt Lake in Lake Roosevelt National Recreation Area; map A5, grid g0.

Campsites, facilities: There are 31 sites for tents, trailers, or RVs up to 20 feet long. Drinking water, picnic tables, and fire grills are provided. Flush toilets and a playground are available. Boat docks and launching facilities are nearby. Some facilities are wheelchair accessible. Leashed pets are permitted.

Reservations, fees: No reservations. Sites are $5-10 per night; there is a $6 launch fee. Open year-round, weather permitting.

Directions: From Spokane on Interstate 90, drive west for four miles to U.S. 2. Turn west on U.S. 2 and drive 34 miles to Davenport and Highway 25. Turn north (right) on Highway 25 and drive 19 miles to Porcupine Bay Road. Turn right (east) and drive 4.3 miles to the campground.

Contact: Lake Roosevelt National Recreation Area, 1008 Crest Drive, Coulee Dam, WA 99116; tel. (509) 633-9441; fax (509) 633-9332.

58 Long Lake
Camp and Picnic Area   8

This campground is located about 45 minutes from Spokane. Most of the facilities, including the swim area, are wheelchair accessible. Amenities include picnic areas, drinking water, and a scenic river view—and you can't beat the price. It's slightly more well known than many of the Department of Natural Resources camps.

Location: On the Spokane River; map A5, grid g3.

Campsites, facilities: There are 12 sites for tents or small trailers. Picnic tables, fire grills, and tent pads are provided. Vault toilets and drinking water are available. Most of the facilities are wheelchair accessible.

Reservations, fees: No reservations; no fee. Open April through September.

Directions: From Spokane on Interstate 90, drive west for four miles to U.S. 2. Turn west on U.S. 2 and drive 21 miles to Reardan and Highway 231. Turn north on Highway 231 and drive 14.2 miles to Long Lake Dam Road (Highway 291). Turn right and drive 4.7 miles to the campground entrance on the right.

Contact: Department of Natural Resources, Northeast Region, P.O. Box 190, Colville, WA 99114-0190; tel. (509) 684-7474; fax (509) 684-7484.

59 Dragoon Creek   5

This spot is not far from U.S. 395, but it's quiet, rustic, and set along Dragoon Creek, a tributary to the Little Spokane River. The Department of Natural Resources offers a map that details the region. The area is forested, and the camp has shaded sites.

Location: Near the Little Spokane River; map A5, grid g5.

Campsites, facilities: There are 22 sites for tents or small trailers. Picnic tables, fire grills, and tent pads are provided. Vault toilets and drinking water are available. Leashed pets are permitted.

Reservations, fees: No reservations; no fee. Open April through September.

Directions: From Spokane drive north on U.S. 395 for 10.2 miles to Dragoon Creek Road. Turn left on Dragoon Creek Road and drive 0.4 mile to the campground entrance.

Contact: Department of Natural Resources, Northeast Region, P.O. Box 190, Colville, WA 99114-0190; tel. (509) 684-7474; fax (509) 684-7484.

60 Mount Spokane State Park   8

This is a prime hideaway on the slopes of Mount Spokane (5,878 feet). Its little brother, Mount Kit Carson (5,180 feet), sits alongside. Nearby recreation options include marked hiking trails, an equestrian trail, and tennis courts. In the winter Mount Spokane Ski Resort operates here. Don't miss the fantastic views at the wonderful Vista House restaurant. This is one of the better short trips available out of Spokane.

Location: On Mount Spokane; map A5, grid g7.
Campsites, facilities: There are two primitive tent sites and 12 sites for tents or self-contained RVs up to 30 feet long. Drinking water, fire grills, and picnic tables are provided. Flush toilets and a cafe are available. A coin-operated laundry facility is located within one mile. Leashed pets are permitted.
Reservations, fees: No reservations. Sites are $5-10 per night. Open June through September, weather permitting.
Directions: From Spokane drive north on U.S. 395 for six miles to U.S. 2. Turn north on U.S. 2 and drive six miles to Highway 206. Turn northeast on Highway 206 and drive 19 miles north to the park.
Contact: Mount Spokane State Park, Route 1, P.O. Box 336, Mead, WA 99021; tel. (800) 233-0321, (509) 456-4169.

61 Overland Station   7

This is one of seven campgrounds located in the immediate Spokane area. A number of side trips will clue you in to the history of the area, including the Cheney Cowles Memorial Museum and the Museum of Native American Cultures. Riverfront Park is the site of the 1974 World Exposition, and it now offers a science center and planetarium, an opera house, a Japanese garden, a gondola ride, a carousel, an ice-skating rink, and a five-screen theater. The closest lake with good fishing is Eloika Lake, described in the description of Jerry's Landing.
Location: Near Eloika Lake; map A5, grid i5.
Campsites, facilities: There are 32 sites for tents, trailers or RVs of any length; 18 are drive-through. Electricity, drinking water, sewer hookups, and picnic tables are provided. Flush toilets, showers, a laundry room, and a playground are available. Leashed pets are permitted.
Reservations, fees: Reservations accepted. Sites are $16-24 per night. Weekly and monthly rates are available. Open year-round.
Directions: On Interstate 90 in Spokane, drive about eight miles west and to Exit 272. Take that exit and drive one block east to the park on the right.
Contact: Overland Station, 107 West Geiger Boulevard, Spokane, WA 99205; tel. (509) 747-1703.

62 Riverside State Park   8

This is a good option for people looking for a more rural alternative to the camps set on the outskirts of Spokane. The large state park provides an interpretive center, riding stables, and trails for hiking, horseback riding, and off-road vehicles. Nearby recreation options include an 18-hole golf course. A local point of interest is the unique Bowl and Pitcher Lava Formation in the river.

Location: Near Spokane; map A5, grid h5.

Campsites, facilities: There are two primitive tent sites and 101 sites for tents or self-contained RVs up to 45 feet long. Picnic tables and fire grills are provided. Flush toilets, showers, and firewood are available. A store, a restaurant, and ice are located within three miles. Boat launching facilities are located on the Spokane River about seven miles away at the reservoir. Leashed pets are permitted.

Reservations, fees: No reservations. Sites are $7-11 per night. Open year-round.

Directions: In Spokane on Interstate 90, take the Maple Street North exit, and drive north 1.1 miles to Maxwell Street (the road becomes Aubrey L. White Parkway). Turn west (left) and drive 1.9 miles, bearing left along the Spokane River to the park entrance. From the park entrance continue for 1.5 miles on Aubrey L. White Parkway to the campground.

Contact: Riverside State Park, North 4427 Aubrey L. White Parkway, Spokane, WA 99205; tel. (800) 233-0321 or (509) 456-3964.

63 Trailer Inns RV Park   5

This large RV park is a perfect layover on the way to Idaho. It's as close to a hotel as an RV park can get. Nearby recreation options include an 18-hole golf course, a racquet club, and tennis courts. See the description of Overland Station for information on attractions in Spokane.

Location: In Spokane; map A5, grid h6.

Campsites, facilities: There are 97 sites for trailers or RVs of any length; 30 are drive-through. Electricity, drinking water, sewer hookups, and picnic tables are provided. Flush toilets, bottled gas, showers, TV, a laundry room, ice, and a playground are available. Sanitary services, a store, and a cafe are within one mile. Leashed pets and motorbikes are permitted.

Reservations, fees: Reservations accepted. Sites are $15-21 per night. Major credit cards accepted. Open year-round.

Directions: Note that your route will depend on your heading: In Spokane eastbound on Interstate 90, take Exit 285 (Sprague Avenue/Eastern Road) to Eastern Road. Drive 0.1 mile on Eastern Road to Fourth Avenue. Turn west on Fourth Avenue and drive two blocks to the campground. In Spokane westbound on Interstate 90, take Exit 284 (Havana Street). Drive one block south on Havana Street to Fourth Avenue. Turn east on Fourth Avenue and drive one mile to the park.

Contact: Trailer Inns RV Park, 6021 East Fourth Avenue, Spokane, WA 99212; tel. (800) 659-4864, (509) 535-1811.

64 KOA Spokane

 5

This campground along the shore of the Spokane River is close to an 18-hole golf course and tennis courts. See the description of Overland Station for information on attractions in Spokane.

Location: On the Spokane River; map A5, grid h7.

Campsites, facilities: There are 50 tent sites and 150 sites for trailers or RVs of any length; 109 are drive-through sites. Electricity, cable TV, sewer hookups, and drinking water are provided. Picnic tables, flush toilets, a dump station, showers, a recreation hall, a store, a laundry room, ice, a playground, modem access, and a swimming pool are available. Some facilities are wheelchair accessible. A cafe is located within two miles. Leashed pets are permitted.

Reservations, fees: Reservations accepted. Sites are $20-30 per night. Major credit cards accepted. Open March through November.

Directions: From Spokane drive east on Interstate 90 for 13 miles to Exit 293. Take that exit to Barker Road. Turn north on Barker Road and drive one-half mile to the campground.

Contact: KOA Spokane, 3025 North Barker, Otis Orchards, WA 99027; tel. (800) 562-3309, (509) 924-4722. Website: www.koa.com.

65 Picnic Pines on Silver Lake

 8

This shorefront resort on Silver Lake caters primarily to RVs, though tent campers are welcome. Fishing can be excellent here. Nearby recreation options include marked bike trails, a full-service marina, and tennis courts. See the description of West Medical Lake Resort for further details.

Location: On Silver Lake; map A5, grid i4.

Campsites, facilities: There are 13 tent sites and 18 for trailers or RVs up to 35 feet in length; six with full and 12 with partial hookups. Hookups are available only from mid-March to mid-October. Picnic tables, flush toilets, a store, restaurant, lounge, a bait shop, boat docks, boat rentals, launching facilities, ice, and a swimming beach are available. Bottled gas and a coin-operated laundry facility are located within two miles. Leashed pets and motorbikes are permitted.

Reservations, fees: Reservations accepted. Sites are $15 per night. Major credit cards accepted. Open year-round.

Directions: In Spokane on Interstate 90, drive west to Exit 270 and Medical Lake Road. Take that exit and turn west on Medical Lake Road and drive to Silver Lake Road. Turn left and drive one-half mile to the park.

Contact: Picnic Pines on Silver Lake, South 9212 Silver Lake Road, Medical Lake, WA 99022; tel. (509) 299-3223.

66 West Medical Lake Resort

 7

This family-operated shorefront resort, one of five campgrounds on Medical Lake, is a popular spot for Spokane locals who make the half-hour drive. There are actually two lakes. West Medical is the larger of the two and also has the better fishing, with boat rentals available. Medical Lake is just a quarter-mile wide and a half-mile long, and boating is restricted to rowboats, canoes, kayaks, and sailboats The lakes got their names from the wondrous medical powers once attributed to these waters.

Location: On West Medical Lake; map A5, grid i4.

Campsites, facilities: There are 20 tent sites and 20 sites for trailers or RVs. Picnic tables are provided. Flush toilets, showers, a cafe, and ice are available. Electricity, drinking water, and sewer hookups can be obtained for an extra fee. Boat and fishing docks, launching facilities, and boat and barge rentals are nearby. Leashed pets and motorbikes are permitted.

Reservations, fees: Reservations required. Sites are $12-14 per night. Open late April through September.

Directions: In Spokane on Interstate 90, drive west to Exit 264 and Salnave Road. Take that exit and turn north on Salnave Road and drive six miles to Fancher Road. Turn right (west) and drive 200 yards, bear left on Fancher Road and drive 200 yards to the campground.

Contact: West Medical Lake Resort, P.O. Box 216, Medical Lake, WA 99022; tel. (509) 299-3921.

67 Mallard Bay Resort   7

This resort on the shore of Medical Lake is close to marked bike trails and tennis courts. See the description of West Medical Lake Resort for more details.

Location: On Medical Lake; map A5, grid i4.

Campsites, facilities: There are 50 sites for tents, trailers, or RVs of any length, plus two cabins. Electricity, drinking water, and picnic tables are provided. Flush toilets, bottled gas, sanitary services, showers, a store, a tackle shop, ice, swimming facilities with a diving board, a playground, boat docks, launching facilities, and rentals are available. Leashed pets and motorbikes are permitted.

Reservations, fees: Reservations accepted. Sites are $15 per night; cabins are $39 per night. Open mid-April to late September.

Directions: In Spokane on Interstate 90, drive west to Exit 264 and Salnave Road. Take that exit and turn north on Salnave Road and drive 1.5 miles to a junction signed by Mallard Bay Resort. Turn right at that sign and drive one-half mile on a dirt road to the resort.

Contact: Mallard Bay Resort, 14601 Salnave Road, Cheney, WA 99004; tel. (509) 299-3830.

68 Rainbow Cove Campground

 7

This pretty, wooded resort on the shore of Medical Lake is close to marked bike trails and tennis courts. See the description of West Medical Lake Resort for more details about the lake.

Location: On Clear Lake; map A5, grid i4.

Campsites, facilities: There are four tent sites and 16 sites for trailers or RVs of any length. Electricity, drinking water, and picnic tables are provided. Showers, flush toilets, some sewer hookups, a cafe, ice, boat docks, boat rentals, and launching facilities are available. Leashed pets are permitted.

Reservations, fees: Reservations accepted. Sites are $15 per night. Open mid-April through September.

Directions: In Spokane on Interstate 90, drive west to Exit 264 and Salnave Road. Take that exit and turn north on Salnave Road and drive a very short distance to Clear Lake Road. Turn north on Clear Lake Road and follow the signs to the campground.

Contact: Rainbow Cove Campground, 12514 South Clear Lake Road, Medical Lake, WA 99022; tel. (509) 299-3717.

69 Alpine Motel-RV and Tent Park of Spokane

 7

This urban campground just outside of Spokane is primarily a layover camp, but could be a good base for those planning on visiting the Spokane area. Recreational activities include seasonal swimming.

Location: Near Spokane; map A5, grid h8.

Campsites, facilities: There are 38 sites for tents, trailers, or RVs. Drinking water, electricity, sewer hookups and picnic tables are provided. Rest rooms, showers, a public phone, a coin-operated laundry facility, a heated swimming pool, a fenced dog run, and ice are available. The facilities are wheelchair accessible. Leashed pets are permitted.

Reservations, fees: Reservations recommended. Sites are $20-24 per night. Major credit cards accepted. Open year-round.

Directions: In Spokane on Interstate 90, drive east for 12 miles to Exit 293 and Barker Road/Green Acres. Take that exit and turn north on Barker Road. Drive north one-half block on Barker Road to the campground on the left.

Contact: Alpine Motel-RV and Tent Park of Spokane, P.O. Box 363, Greenacres, WA; tel. (509) 928-2700 99016.

70 Yogi Bear's Camp Resort  6

Located in a wooded, rural area, yet just 10 minutes from downtown Spokane, this park is large, with towering ponderosa pines. Highlights feature an 18-hole golf course next door, and several other courses within 20 minutes of the resort. See the description of Overland Station for details on the Spokane area.

Location: West of Spokane; map A5, grid i5.

Campsites, facilities: There are 168 sites for tents, trailers, or RVs up to 70 feet long, with full hookups, including electricity, water, sewer, cable TV, and modem-friendly phone service; 35 sites are drive-through. There are also cabins and trailer rentals. Flush toilets, sanitary services, showers, propane, a laundry room, an RV wash station, and a playground are available. Amenities include a camp store, an activity center with an indoor pool, a spa, an exercise room, a game room, a snack shack, a dog walk, and various sports facilities (volleyball, basketball, badminton, miniature golf and daily organized recreational activities). Some facilities are wheelchair accessible. Leashed pets and motorbikes are permitted.

Reservations, fees: Reservations accepted. Sites are $21-33 per night; cabins are $80, RV rentals are $60 per night. Open year-round.

Directions: In Spokane on Interstate 90, drive to Exit 272 and Westbow Road. Take that exit and turn east on Westbow Road and drive to Thomas Mallen Road. Turn right (south) on Thomas Mallen Road and drive one-half mile to the campground on the right.

Contact: Yogi Bear's Camp Resort, 7520 South Thomas Mallen Road, Cheney, WA 99004; tel. (800) 494-7275, (509) 747-9415; fax (509) 459-0148. Website: www.jelly-stone-spokane.com.

71 Peaceful Pines RV Park   6

This campground is little-known by most travelers. It's a remote site just a short distance from Turnbull National Wildlife Refuge, an expanse of marsh and pine that is a significant stopover point for migratory birds on the Pacific Flyway. You can pick up a map and bird checklist at the refuge headquarters. This is a prime spot, only a 30-minute drive out of Spokane, yet relatively unknown.

Location: Near Turnbull National Wildlife Refuge; map A5, grid i5.

Campsites, facilities: There are 20 tent sites and 24 sites for trailers or RVs of any length. Electricity, drinking water, sewer hookups, and picnic tables are provided. Flush toilets, sanitary services, and showers are available. A store, a cafe, and ice are located within one mile, and a coin-operated laundry facility is within three miles. Leashed pets and motorbikes are permitted.

Reservations, fees: Reservations accepted. Sites are $11.50-14 per night. Open year-round.

Directions: In Spokane on Interstate 90, drive southwest for 10 miles to the Highway 270/Highway 904 exit. Take that exit and turn south on Highway 904 and drive six miles to Cheney; then continue for one mile to the campground on the left (seven miles from the Interstate 90 turnoff).

Contact: Peaceful Pines RV Park, 1231 West First Street, Cheney, WA 99004; tel. (509) 235-4966.

72 Sprague Lake Resort   5

This developed campground is on the shore of Sprague Lake, about 35 miles from Spokane. It's a pleasant, grassy setting.

Location: On Sprague Lake; map A5, grid j2.

Campsites, facilities: There are 50 tent sites and 30 drive-through sites for trailers or RVs of any length. Electricity, drinking water, sewer hookups, and picnic tables are provided. Flush toilets, sanitary services, a small store, a laundry room, showers, ice, a playground, boat docks, launching facilities, and rentals are available. Leashed pets are permitted.

Reservations, fees: Reservations accepted. Sites are $15-18 per night. Open April through October.

Directions: In Spokane on Interstate 90, drive west to the Sprague Business Center exit. Take that exit and drive two miles to the resort (well signed).

Contact: Sprague Lake Resort, 1999 Sprague Lake Resort Road, Sprague, WA 99032; tel. (509) 257-2864.

73 Four Seasons Campground   7

This campground along the shore of Sprague Lake, one of the top fishing waters in the state, has spacious sites with plenty of vegetation. The fishing for rainbow trout is best in May and June, with some bass in spring and fall. Because there is an abundance of natural feed in the lake, the fish reach larger sizes here than in neighboring lakes. Walleye up to 11 pounds are taken here. Perch, crappie, walleye, blue gill, and catfish are abundant. In late July through August, a fair algae bloom is a turnoff for swimmers and water-skiers.

Location: On Sprague Lake; map A5, grid j2.

Campsites, facilities: There are 25 tent sites, 38 sites for trailers or RVs and four, fully equipped cabins, each of which can sleep six. Electricity, drinking water, sewer hookups, and picnic tables are provided. Flush toilets, sanitary services, showers, firewood, fire pits and grills, ice, a playground, a store with fishing tackle, a fish cleaning station, a small basketball court, and a swimming pool are available. Boat and fishing docks, launching facilities, and rentals are nearby. Leashed pets and motorbikes are permitted.

Reservations, fees: Reservations accepted. Sites are $13-17 per night. Cabins are $60-70 per night. Open March through October, weather permitting.

Directions: From Spokane on Interstate 90, drive west for about 40 miles to Exit 245. Take Exit 245 and drive south to Fourth Street. Turn right and drive one block to B Street. Turn right and drive two blocks to First Street. Turn left (west) and drive one-half mile to a Y intersection. Bear right to Doerschlag Road and drive one mile to Lake Road. Turn left and drive four miles to Bob Lee Road. Turn left and drive one mile to the campground.

Contact: Four Seasons Campground, 2384 North Bob Lee Road, Sprague, WA 99032; tel. (509) 257-2332.

74 Last Roundup Motel RV Park, and Campground

      5

Located just on the outskirts of Sprague, this camp is in a meadow-like, flat area with a rural feel and sunny, grassy sites. Fishing is excellent year-round at nearby Sprague Lake.

Location: Near Sprague Lake; map A5, grid j3.

Campsites, facilities: There are 13 sites for trailers or RVs up to 40 feet long, plus a grass area for tents. Electricity, drinking water, and sewer hookups are provided. Flush toilets, showers, a laundry room, and ice are available. Bottled gas, sanitary services, a gift shop and store, and a cafe are located within one mile. Leashed pets and motorbikes are permitted.

Reservations, fees: Reservations accepted. Sites are $12-16 per night. Major credit cards accepted. Open year-round.

Directions: From Spokane drive west on Interstate 90 for 35 miles to Sprague and Exit 245. Take Exit 245 and drive one-half mile south on Highway 23 to Fourth Street. Turn west and drive one block to B Street. Turn north and drive three blocks to First Street. Turn east on First Street and drive one block to the park on the right.

Contact: Last Roundup Motel, RV Park, and Campground, 312 East First Street, Sprague, WA 99032; tel. (509) 257-2583; fax (509) 257-2615.

75 Williams Lake Resort   6

This resort is on the shore of Williams Lake, which is just under three miles long and is popular for swimming and waterskiing. It's also one of the top fishing lakes in the region for rainbow and cutthroat trout. The lake is bordered in some areas by rocky cliffs. See the description of Peaceful Pines Campground for information on nearby Turnbull National Wildlife Refuge.

Location: On Williams Lake; map A5, grid j4.

Campsites, facilities: There are 15 tent sites and 60 sites for trailers or RVs of any length; one is a drive-through site. Electricity, drinking water, and picnic tables are provided. Sewer hookups, flush toilets, bottled gas, sanitary services, firewood, a store, a cafe, a restaurant, showers, ice, a playground, boat docks, launching facilities, and boat rentals are available. Leashed pets and motorbikes are permitted.

Reservations, fees: Reservations accepted. Sites are $16-19 per night. Major credit cards accepted. Open mid-April to October.

Directions: From Spokane drive west on Interstate 90 for 10 miles to Exit 270 and Highway 904. Turn south on Highway 904, and drive six miles to Cheney and Cheney Plaza Road. Turn south on Cheney Plaza Road and drive 11.2 miles to Williams Lake Road. Turn west and drive 3.5 miles to the campground on the left.

Contact: Williams Lake Resort, 18617 West Williams Lake Road, Cheney, WA 99004; tel. (509) 235-2391.

76 Bunkers Resort   8

This campground is on the shore of Williams Lake. See the description of Williams Lake Resort for information on the lake, and the description of Peaceful Pines Campground for information on nearby Turnbull National Wildlife Refuge

Location: On Williams Lake; map A5, grid j4.

Campsites facilities: There are 10 drive-through sites for trailers or RVs of any length and four fully equipped cabins. Electricity, drinking water, and picnic tables are provided. Flush toilets, bottled gas, sanitary services, recreation hall, a restaurant, a store, a cafe, ice, boat and fishing docks, launching facilities, and rentals are available. Leashed pets are permitted.

Reservations, fees: Reservations accepted. Sites are $12-21.50 per night; cabins are $55-70 per night. Major credit cards accepted. Open mid-April to October.

Directions: From Spokane drive west on Interstate 90 for 10 miles to Exit 270 and Highway 904. Turn south on Highway 904, and drive six miles to Cheney and Mullinex Road. Turn south on Mullinex Road and drive 12 miles to the resort.

Contact: Bunkers Resort, 36402 South Bunker Landing Road, Cheney, WA 99004; tel. (509) 235-5212.

On Long Beach Peninsula

MAP B1

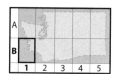

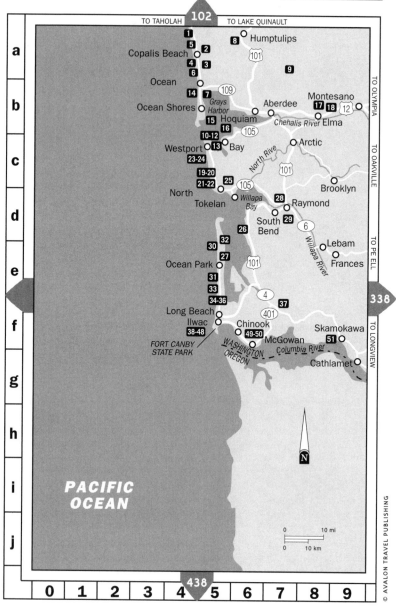

CHAPTER B1

■ Pacific Beach State Park   10

You can thank supply and demand for the popularity of this nine-acre beachfront campground In Pacific Beach. Since there are no other coastal camps in the immediate vicinity, it tends to get crowded. Activities here include clamming, beachcombing, and surf fishing.

Location: On the Pacific Ocean; map B1, grid a4.

Campsites, facilities: There are 33 tent sites and 31 sites for trailers or RVs up to 45 feet long. Picnic tables are provided. A sanitary disposal station, drinking water, coin-operated showers, and toilets are available. Some facilities are wheelchair accessible. Leashed pets are permitted.

Reservations, fees: Reservations accepted; phone (800) 452-5687 ($6 reservation fee). Sites are $10-15 per night. Major credit cards accepted. Open year-round.

Directions: From Olympia on Interstate 5, take Exit 104 to U.S. 101. Drive west on U.S. 101 six miles to Highway 8. Turn west on Highway 8 (which becomes U.S. 12) to Hoquiam and Highway 109. Take Highway 109 and drive 37 miles north to Pacific Beach.

Contact: Pacific Beach State Park, 148 State Route 115, Hoquiam, WA 98550; tel. (800) 233-0321, (360) 289-3553.

■ Tidelands on the Beach   7

This flat wooded campground covering 47 acres has beach access and a great ocean view, and though it's primarily an RV park, the sites are pleasant and grassy. In the spring, azaleas and wildflowers abound. Horseshoe pits and a sports field offer recreation possibilities. This is a more remote option than the other sites in the area.

Location: Near Copalis Beach; map B1, grid a4.

Campsites, facilities: There are 100 tent sites and 55 sites for trailers or RVs of any length; 25 are drive-through sites. There are also three two-bedroom cabins. Electricity, drinking water, sewer hookups, and picnic tables are provided. Sanitary services, toilets, firewood, coin-operated showers, ice, and a playground are available. Boat docks and a cafe are located within one mile. A golf course is located nearby. Leashed pets are permitted.

Reservations, fees: Reservations accepted. Sites are $12-16 per night; cabins are $75 per night. Open year-round.

Directions: From Olympia on Interstate 5, take Exit 104 to U.S. 101. Drive west on U.S. 101 six miles to Highway 8. Turn west on Highway 8 (which becomes U.S. 12) to Hoquiam and Highway 109. Take Highway 109 and drive about 20 miles to the campground between Mileposts 20 and 21. It's located about one mile south of Copalis Beach.

Contact: Tidelands on the Beach, P.O. Box 36, Copalis Beach, WA 98535; tel. (360) 289-8963.

3 Rod's Beach Resort   8

A prime spot for RVers, this well-maintained 10-acre park has large, flat, grassy sites among cedar, spruce, and a beach, plus nice sunsets. Access to the ocean and fishing are highlights.

Location: Near Copalis Beach; map B1, grid a4.

Campsites, facilities: There are 80 sites for trailers or RVs of any length; 25 are drive-through sites. No tents are allowed. Electricity, drinking water, sewer hookups, and cable TV are provided. There is also a motel at the resort. Sanitary services, toilets, showers, a recreation hall, a store, ice, and a playground are available. Bottled gas and a cafe are located within one mile. A seasonal swimming pool is available for an extra fee. Leashed pets are permitted.

Reservations, fees: Reservations accepted. Sites are $12-16 per night. Open March through October.

Directions: From Olympia on Interstate 5, take Exit 104 to U.S. 101. Drive west on U.S. 101 six miles to Highway 8. Turn west on Highway 8 (which becomes U.S. 12) to Hoquiam and Highway 109. Take Highway 109 and drive about 20 miles to the campground. It's located about one mile south of Copalis Beach at milepost 20.

Contact: Rod's Beach Resort, P.O. Box 507, 2961 State Route 109, Copalis Beach, WA 98535; tel. (360) 289-2222.

4 Driftwood Acres Ocean Camp   7

Spreading over some 150 acres, Driftwood Acres Ocean Camp is family friendly, with beach access, spacious RV sites, secluded tent spots, evergreens and marked hiking trails. It is located along a tidal river basin, out of the wind. Additional facilities within five miles include an 18-hole golf course and a riding stable.

Location: In Copalis Beach; map B1, grid a4.

Campsites, facilities: There are 50 tent sites and 25 sites for trailers or RVs of any length. Drinking water, firewood, fire pits, an armload of firewood, and picnic tables are provided. Electricity, sewer hookups, cable TV, showers, dump station, flush toilets, and firewood are available. Bottled gas, a store, a cafe, and ice are located within one mile. Leashed pets are permitted.

Reservations, fees: Reservations accepted; call ahead for fees. Open Memorial Day weekend and from July 4 through Labor Day weekend.

Directions: From Olympia on Interstate 5, take Exit 104 to U.S. 101. Drive west on U.S. 101 six miles to Highway 8. Turn west on Highway 8 (which becomes U.S. 12) to Hoquiam and Highway 109. Take Highway 109 and drive about 21 miles to Copalis Beach. Continue one-half mile north to the camp on the left, between mileposts 21 and 22.

Contact: Driftwood Acres Ocean Camp, P.O. Box 216, Copalis Beach, WA 98535; tel. (360) 289-3484.

5 Copalis Beach Surf and Sand   5

Though not particularly scenic, this five-acre park is a decent layover for an RV vacation and will do the job if you're tired and ready to get off U.S. 101. It does have beach access. The surrounding terrain is flat and grassy.

Location: In Copalis Beach; map B1, grid a4.

Campsites, facilities: There are seven tent sites and 50 sites for trailers or RVs of any length; 20 are drive-through sites. Electricity, drinking water, sewer hookups, cable TV hookups, and picnic tables are provided. Sanitary services, laundry facilities, toilets, showers, a cafe, a lounge, and ice are available. Bottled gas and a store are located within one mile. Leashed pets are permitted.

Reservations, fees: Reservations accepted. Sites are $15-24.50 per night. Major credit cards accepted. Open year-round.

Directions: From Olympia on Interstate 5, take Exit 104 to U.S. 101. Drive west on U.S. 101 six miles to Highway 8. Turn west on Highway 8 (which becomes U.S. 12) to Hoquiam and Highway 109. Take Highway 109 and drive 21 miles to Copalis Beach and Heath Road. Turn west on Heath Road and 0.2 mile to the campground.

Contact: Copalis Beach Surf and Sand, P.O. Box 208, Copalis Beach, WA 98535; tel. (360) 289-2707, fax (360) 289-4083.

6 Riverside RV Resort   8

River access is a bonus at this nice and exceptionally clean three-acre park where most sites have a river view. Salmon fishing is said to be excellent in the Copalis River, and a boat ramp is available nearby for anglers. Swimming and beachcombing are two other options.

Location: Near Copalis Beach; map B1, grid a4.

Campsites, facilities: There are 15 tent sites and 53 sites with full hookups for trailers or RVs of any length; 20 are drive-through sites. Electricity, drinking water, sewer hookups, and picnic tables are provided. Sanitary services, toilets, showers, hot tub, firewood, and a recreation hall are available. A store, a cafe, and ice are located within one mile. Leashed pets and motorbikes are permitted.

Reservations, fees: Reservations accepted. Sites are $14-17 per night. Major credit cards accepted. Open year-round.

Directions: From Olympia on Interstate 5, take Exit 104 to U.S. 101. Drive west on U.S. 101 six miles to Highway 8. Turn west on Highway 8 (which becomes U.S. 12) to Hoquiam and Highway 109. Take Highway 109 and drive 21 miles to Copalis Beach. The park is off the highway on the left.

Contact: Riverside RV Resort, P.O. Box 307, Copalis Beach, WA 98535; tel. (360) 289-2111.

7 Ocean Mist Resort   9

Surf fishing is popular on the nearby Pacific, and there are salmon and canoeing opportunities at the Capellis River, also nearby. There's a golf course within five miles.

Location: On Conners Creek; map B1, grid b5.

Campsites, facilities: There are 120 RV sites, 112 full and eight partial-hookups. There is also a dispersed area that can accommodate a maximum of 20 tents. Drinking water, electricity, sewer, and cable TV are provided. Picnic tables, rest rooms with showers, a dump station, two community fire pits, and coin-operated laundry facilities are available. A grocery store is within one mile in Ocean City. Leashed pets are permitted.

Reservations, fees: Reservations required in the summer; phone (360) 289-3656 or fax (360) 289-2807. Sites are $10-25 per night. Major credit cards accepted. Open year-round.

Directions: From Olympia on Interstate 5, take Exit 104 to U.S. 101. Drive west on U.S. 101 six miles to Highway 8. Turn west on Highway 8 (which becomes U.S. 12) to Hoquiam and Highway 109. Take Highway 109 and drive 19 miles to the campground on the left.

Contact: Ocean Mist Resort, 2781 State Route 109, Ocean City, WA 98569; tel. (360) 289-3656, fax (360) 289-2807.

8 Riverview Recreation Area

 7

This five-acre camp is set at about 1,000 feet along the Humptulips River in a beautiful spot, with boating and fishing access not far from camp. It's a good layover if you're cruising U.S. 101, but it's popular, so plan on arriving early.

Location: On the Humptulips River; map B1, grid a6.

Campsites, facilities: There are eight tent sites and 12 sites for trailers or RVs of any length; six are drive-through sites. Picnic tables are provided. Electricity, drinking water, sewer hookups, flush toilets, showers, and firewood are available. A store, a cafe, and ice are within one mile. Boat launching facilities are located nearby at the Humptulips River. Leashed pets and motorbikes are permitted.

Reservations, fees: No reservations accepted. Sites are $6-15 per night. Open year-round.

Directions: From Olympia on Interstate 5, take Exit 104 to U.S. 101. Drive west on U.S. 101 six miles to Highway 8. Turn west on Highway 8 (which becomes U.S. 12) to Aberdeen and U.S. 101. Turn north on U.S. 101 and drive 22 miles to Humptulips and Kirkpatrick Road. Turn west on Kirkpatrick Road and drive one-quarter of a mile to the park.

Contact: Riverview Recreation Area, P.O. Box 97, Humptulips, WA 98552; tel. (360) 987-2216, fax (360) 987-2216.

9 Schafer State Park   8

This heavily wooded, rural camp covers 119 acres along the East Fork of the Satsop River. There are good canoeing and kayaking spots, some with Class II and Class III rapids, along the Middle and West Forks of the Satsop. At one time this park was the Schafer Logging Company Park and was used by the employees and their families.

Location: On the Satsop River; map B1, grid a7.

Campsites, facilities: There are two primitive tent sites, 47 developed tent sites, and six sites with water and electric hookups for trailers or RVs up to 40 feet long. Picnic tables and fire grills are provided. A sanitary disposal station, toilets, and a playground are available. Water, showers, and firewood are also available for an additional charge. Some facilities are wheelchair accessible. Leashed pets are permitted.

Reservations, fees: No reservations accepted. Sites are $5-15 per night. Open late April through September.

Directions: From Olympia on Interstate 5, take Exit 104 to U.S. 101. Drive west on U.S. 101 six miles to Highway 8. Turn west on Highway 8 to Elma (Highway 8 becomes Highway 12). Continue west on Highway 12 for seven miles to East Satsop Road (four miles east of Montesano). Turn north and drive eight miles to the park.

Contact: Schafer State Park, Route 1, P.O. Box 87, Elma, WA 98541; tel. (800) 233-0321, (360) 482-3852.

10 Jolly Rogers RV Park   7

This camp covering one acre near Westport Harbor is your typical beachside RV park, with concrete sites and nearby beach access. It's a prime spot to watch ocean sunsets, and on a clear day snow-capped Mount Rainier is visible. Westport Light and Westhaven State Parks are nearby and offer day-use facilities along the ocean.

Location: Near Westport Harbor; map B1, grid c5.

Campsites, facilities: There are 25 sites with full hookups for trailers or RVs of any length. Sanitary services, toilets, coin-operated showers, and boat docks are available. Bottled gas, a store, a cafe, and laundry facilities are located within one mile. Leashed pets and motorbikes are permitted.

Reservations, fees: Reservations accepted. Sites are $15 per night. Open year-round.

Directions: From Olympia on Interstate 5, take Exit 104 to U.S. 101. Drive west on U.S. 101 six miles to Highway 8. Turn west on Highway 8 (which becomes U.S. 12) to Aberdeen and Highway 105. Turn south on Highway 105 and drive 22 miles southwest to Westport and Neddie Rose Drive. Turn right (north) and drive a very short distance to the park on the right (Westport Docks).

Contact: Jolly Rogers RV Park, P.O. Box 342, Westport, WA 98595; tel. (360) 268-0265, fax (360) 268-0265.

11 Grizzly Joe's RV Park   9

This landscaped, one-acre park has ocean views on three sides and is graveled and level. Snow-capped Mount Rainier is visible, and the sunsets are spectacular. Westport Light and Westhaven State Parks are nearby with multiple recreational options.

Location: On Point Chehalis; map B1, grid c5.

Campsites, facilities: There are 35 sites with full hookups and pull-through for trailers or RVs of any length. Electricity, drinking water, sewer and cable TV are provided. Sanitary services, flush toilets, showers, patio/picnic area with fire pit, fish cleaning station, outdoor cooking facilities, and boat docks are available. Bottled gas, a store, a cafe, laundry facilities, firewood, and ice are located within one-quarter mile. Leashed pets and permitted.

Reservations, fees: Reservations recommended. Sites are $18 per night. Open year-round.

Directions: From Olympia on Interstate 5, take Exit 104 to U.S. 101. Drive west on U.S. 101 six miles to Highway 8. Turn west on Highway 8 (which becomes U.S. 12) to Aberdeen and Highway 105. Turn south on Highway 105 and drive 22 miles southwest to

Westport and Neddie Rose Drive. Turn north and drive to Point Chehalis. The park is at the end of the road.

Contact: Grizzly Joe's RV Park, P.O. Box 1755, Westport, WA 98595; tel. (360) 268-5555, fax (360) 268-1212.

12 Pacific Aire RV Resort

       7

This 32-acre park has its own hiking and biking trails, and nearby are Westhaven and Westport Light State Parks, popular with hikers, rock hounds, scuba divers, and surf anglers. Swimming, fishing, and crabbing off of the docks are also options.

Location: Near Westport Harbor; map B1, grid c5.

Campsites, facilities: There are 50 tent sites and 120 sites with full hookups for trailers or RVs of any length. Hookups include phone and cable TV. Picnic tables and fire pits, grills, and rings are provided. Drinking water, sanitary services, flush toilets, showers, coin-operated laundry facilities, a grocery store, propane, seasonal heated pool, horseshoe pits, playground, fish cleaning station, and a 2,400-square-foot recreation hall are available. A marina is located three blocks away. Leashed pets are permitted.

Reservations, fees: Reservations recommended during the summer; phone (800) JOY-CAMP/569-2267. Sites are $14-20 per night; $5 per additional vehicle. Major credit cards accepted. Open year-round.

Directions: From Olympia on Interstate 5, take Exit 104 to U.S. 101. Drive west on U.S. 101 six miles to Highway 8. Turn west on Highway 8 (which becomes U.S. 12) to Aberdeen and Highway 105. Turn south on Highway 105 and drive 22 miles southwest to Westport and Montesano Street (the first exit in Westport). Turn right (northeast) on Montesano and drive three miles to the resort on the left.

Contact: Pacific Aire RV Resort, P.O. Box 1878, Westport, WA 98595; tel. (360) 268-0207; e-mail: pacaire@techline.com; website: www.westportwa.com/pacaire/index.html.

13 Coho RV Park, Motel & Charter

      4

This two-acre park is one of 10 camping options in the immediate area. This one has its own tuna-fishing and whale-watching charters. Nearby Westhaven and Westport Light State Parks are popular with rock hounds, scuba divers, and surf anglers. A full-service marina is within five miles of the campground.

Location: Near Westport Harbor; map B1, grid c5.

Campsites, facilities: There are 76 sites with full hookups for trailers or RVs of any length; six are drive-through sites. No tents are permitted. Sanitary services, cable TV, toilets, showers, laundry facilities, a meeting hall, ice, and fishing charters are available. Bottled gas, a store, and a cafe are within one mile. Boat docks and launching facilities are located one block from this park. Leashed pets are permitted.

Reservations, fees: Reservations accepted. Sites are $18-20 per night for two campers, $2 each additional person. Major credit cards accepted. Open year-round.

Directions: From Olympia on Interstate 5, take Exit 104 to U.S. 101. Drive west on U.S. 101 six miles to Highway 8. Turn west on Highway 8 (which becomes U.S. 12) to Aberdeen and Highway 105. Turn south on Highway 105 and drive 22 miles southwest to Westport and Montesano Street (the first exit in Westport). Turn right (northeast) and drive 3.5 miles to Nyhus Street. Turn northwest and drive 2.5 blocks to the campground on the left.

Contact: Coho RV Park, P.O. Box 1087, Westport, WA 98595; tel. (360) 268-0111, fax (360) 268-9425; e-mail: coho@techline.com.

14 Ocean City State Park   9

This 131-acre oceanfront camp is one of the choice spots in the area for tent campers. It's close to many interesting shops and restaurants in town, and a short drive from an 18-hole golf course. Beachcombing, clamming, and fishing are possibilities at this park.

Location: Near Hoquiam; map B1, grid b5.

Campsites, facilities: There are three primitive tent sites, 149 developed tent sites, and 29 sites with full hookups for trailers or RVs up to 55 feet long. Picnic tables are provided, and sanitary services and toilets are available. An extra fee is charged for showers and firewood. Some facilities are wheelchair accessible. Leashed pets are permitted.

Reservations, fees: Reservations accepted; phone (800) 452-5687 ($6 reservation fee). Sites are $10-15 per night. Open year-round.

Directions: From Olympia on Interstate 5, take Exit 104 to U.S. 101. Drive west on U.S. 101 six miles to Highway 8. Turn west on Highway 8 (which becomes U.S. 12) to Aberdeen and continue to Hoquiam and Highway 109. Turn northwest on Highway 109 and drive 20 miles to the park entrance road (south of Ocean City) on the left. Turn left and drive 1.5 miles south to the park.

Contact: Ocean City State Park, 148 State Route 115, Hoquiam, WA 98550; tel. (800) 233-0321, (360) 289-3553.

15 Totem RV and Trailer Park   8

This two-acre park with large, grassy sites is close to Westhaven State Park, which offers day-use facilities. Marked bike trails, a full-service marina, and tennis courts are within five miles of the campground.

Location: In Westport; map B1, grid b5.

Campsites, facilities: There are 76 sites for trailers or RVs of any length; 10 can be used by tents; 46 are full hookups, and 55 are drive-through sites. Electricity, drinking water, sewer hookups, and picnic tables are provided. Sanitary services, toilets, showers, a store, laundry facilities, and ice are available. Bottled gas and a cafe are located next door. A store is located within one-half mile. Boat docks, launching facilities, and fishing charters are nearby. Leashed pets and motorbikes are permitted.

Reservations, fees: Reservations accepted. Sites are $16-18 per night. Open year-round.

Directions: From Olympia on Interstate 5, take Exit 104 to U.S. 101. Drive west on U.S.

101 six miles to Highway 8. Turn west on Highway 8 (which becomes U.S. 12) to Aberdeen and Highway 105. Turn south on Highway 105 and drive 18 miles southwest to the turnoff for Westport. Turn north on the Highway 105 spur and drive four miles to Dock Avenue. Turn east on Dock Avenue and drive one block to Nyhus Street. Turn north on Nyhus Street and drive two blocks to the park on the left.

Contact: Totem RV and Trailer Park, P.O. Box 1166, Westport, WA 98595; tel. (888) TOTEM-RV/868-3678 or (360) 268-0025; e-mail: andrni@techline.com.

🔢 Holand Center   6

This pleasant, 18-acre RV park is one of several in the immediate area. The sites are graveled or grassy with pine trees between, and have ample space. There is no beach access from the park, but full recreational facilities are nearby.

Location: In Westport; map B1, grid b5.

Campsites, facilities: There are 80 sites with full hookups for trailers or RVs up to 40 feet long. Picnic tables are provided. Toilets, laundry facilities, and showers are available. Bottled gas, a store, a cafe, and ice are located within one mile. Boat docks and launching facilities are nearby. Leashed pets are permitted.

Reservations, fees: Reservations accepted. Sites are $16 per night. Open year-round.

Directions: From Olympia on Interstate 5, take Exit 104 to U.S. 101. Drive west on U.S. 101 six miles to Highway 8. Turn west on Highway 8 (which becomes U.S. 12) to Aberdeen and Highway 105. Turn south on Highway 105 and drive 22 miles to Westport. Continue on Highway 105 to Wilson Street. The park is at the corner of Highway 105 and Wilson Street.

Contact: Holand Center, P.O. Box 1752, Westport, WA 98595; tel. (360) 268-9582, fax (360) 532-3818.

🔢 Lake Sylvia State Park   8

A host of marked hiking trails highlight this 234-acre camp on the shore of Lake Sylvia. Additional recreation options include trout fishing and swimming. If Lake Sylvia is full, nearby camps are East Crossing and Rainbow Cove.

Location: On Lake Sylvia; map B1, grid b8.

Campsites, facilities: There are two primitive tent sites and 35 sites for tents or self-contained RVs up to 30 feet long. Picnic tables and fire grills are provided. Drinking water, a sanitary disposal station, toilets, a store, fishing supplies, a cartop boat launch, boat rentals, and a playground are available. An extra fee is charged for showers and firewood. A Laundromat and ice are located within one mile. Some facilities are wheelchair accessible. Leashed pets are permitted.

Reservations, fees: No reservations accepted. Sites are $10-15 per night. Open year-round.

Directions: From Olympia on Interstate 5, take Exit 104 to U.S. 101. Drive west on U.S. 101 six miles to Highway 8. Turn west on Highway 8 and drive 26 miles to Montesano and the last exit, Highway 7. Turn and drive to Pioneer (the only stoplight in town). Turn left on Pioneer and drive three blocks to Third Street. Turn right and drive two miles to the park entrance (route is well signed).

Contact: Lake Sylvia State Park, Montesano, WA 98563; tel. (800) 233-0321, (360) 249-3621, P.O. Box 701.

18 Travel Inn Resort   7

There are five major rivers or lakes within 15 minutes of this camp (Satsop, Chehalis, Wynoochee, Black River, and Lake Sylvia). Nearby Lake Sylvia State Park provides multiple marked hiking trails. Additional recreation options include trout fishing, swimming and golf (three miles away).

Location: On Lake Sylvia; map B1, grid b8.

Campsites, facilities: There are 10 tent sites and 144 sites for RVs; 134 are full and 10 are partial hookups. Cable TV is provided with hookups. Picnic tables and fire grills are provided. Drinking water, a dump station, garbage service, flush toilets, showers, phone service, coin-operated laundry facilities, two community fire pits, a gazebo, a heated swimming pool, hot tubs, game room, and a social hall are available. A grocery store and restaurant are available within one mile. Some facilities are wheelchair accessible. Leashed pets are permitted.

Reservations, fees: Reservations required for major holidays only; phone (800) 871-2888 (from Oregon and Washington only). Sites are $25 per night. Major credit cards accepted. Open year-round.

Directions: From Olympia on Interstate 5, take Exit 104 to U.S. 101. Drive west on U.S. 101 six miles to Highway 8. Turn west on Highway 8 and drive to Elma. Take the first Elma exit and at the stop sign at Highway 12, turn right and drive 200 yards to the end of the highway. Turn right and drive another 200 yards to the resort.

Contact: Travel Inn Resort, 801 East Main Street, Elma, WA 98541; tel. (360) 482-3877, fax (360) 482-5123.

19 Twin Harbors State Park   8

Sprawling over 1,881 acres, this is one of the largest campgrounds on the coast, and therefore quite popular. The sites are very close together and often crammed to capacity in the summer months. Highlights include beach access and marked hiking trails, including the Shifting Sands Nature Trail. Fishing boats can be chartered nearby in Westport.

Location: On the Pacific Ocean; map B1, grid c5.

Campsites, facilities: There are 249 sites for tents, trailers, or RVs up to 35 feet long; 49 have full hookups. Picnic tables and fire grills are provided. Drinking water, a sanitary disposal station, toilets, and a playground are available. A store, a cafe, and ice can be found within one mile. Firewood is available for an extra fee. Some facilities are wheelchair accessible. Leashed pets are permitted.

Reservations, fees: Reservations accepted; phone (800) 452-5687 ($6 reservation fee). Sites are $11-16 per night. Major credit cards accepted. Open February through October.

Directions: From Olympia on Interstate 5, take Exit 104 to U.S. 101. Drive west on U.S. 101 six miles to Highway 8. Turn west on Highway 8 (which becomes U.S. 12) to Aberdeen and Highway 105. Turn south (left) and drive southwest for approximately 20 miles to the park entrance. The park is located three miles south of Westport.

Contact: Twin Harbors State Park, Twin Harbors State Park, Westport, WA 98595; tel. (800) 233-0321 or (360) 268-9717.

20 Pacific Motel and RV Park

     5

This five-acre park has grassy, shaded sites in a wooded setting. It's near Twin Harbors and Westport Light State Parks, both of which have beach access. A full-service marina is located within 2 miles.

Location: Near Twin Harbors; map B1, grid c5.

Campsites, facilities: There are 10 tent sites and 80 sites for trailers or RVs of any length; 32 are drive-through sites. Electricity, drinking water, and sewer hookups are provided. Sanitary services, toilets, a recreation hall with a kitchen, cable TV, a public phone and fax, coin-operated showers and laundry facilities, and a swimming pool are available. Bottled gas, a store, a cafe, and ice are located within one mile. Boat launching and boat docks are nearby in a full-service marina. Leashed pets and motorbikes are permitted.

Reservations, fees: Reservations accepted. Major credit cards accepted. Sites are $13-18 per night. Open year-round.

Directions: From Olympia on Interstate 5, take Exit 104 to U.S. 101. Drive west on U.S. 101 six miles to Highway 8. Turn west on Highway 8 (which becomes U.S. 12) to Aberdeen and Highway 105. Turn south (left) and drive southwest for approximately 18 miles. At the Highway 105 spur road (to Westport), turn north and drive 1.7 miles to the park.

Contact: Pacific Motel and RV Park, 330 South Forrest, Westport, WA 98595; tel. (360) 268-9325.

21 Grayland Beach State Park   8

This 411-acre oceanfront park has nearly 7,449 feet of excellent beach access, including a self-guided interpretive trail. It's one of the best parks in the immediate area and quite popular with out-of-towners, especially during the summer season. Recreation options include fishing, beachcombing, and kite flying. The campsites are relatively spacious for a state park, but they are not especially private.

Location: On the Pacific Ocean; map B1, grid c5.

Campsites, facilities: There are three primitive tent sites and 60 full-hookup sites for trailers or RVs up to 40 feet long. Picnic tables, toilets, and fire grills are provided. Showers are available for an extra fee. Some facilities are wheelchair accessible.

Reservations, fees: Reservations accepted; phone (800) 452-5687 ($6 reservation fee). Sites are $11-16 per night. Open year-round.

Directions: From Olympia on Interstate 5, take Exit 104 to U.S. 101. Drive west on U.S. 101 six miles to Highway 8. Turn west on Highway 8 (which becomes U.S. 12) to Aberdeen and Highway 105. Turn south (left) and drive 22 miles to the park entrance. The park is just south of the town of Grayland on the right (west).

Contact: Grayland Beach State Park, c/o Twin Harbors State Park, Westport, WA 98595; tel. (800) 233-0321 or (360) 268-9717.

22 Ocean Gate Resort

 5

This privately run, seven-acre park with beach access provides an alternative to the publicly run Grayland Beach State Park. Fishing, beach biking, and beach-combing are highlights.

Location: In Grayland; map B1, grid c5.

Campsites, facilities: There are 20 tent sites and 24 sites for trailers or RVs of any length (12 are drive-through), as well as six cabins. Electricity, drinking water, sewer hookups, and picnic tables are provided. Toilets, showers, and a playground are available. Bottled gas, a store, a cafe, laundry facilities, and ice can be found within one mile. Leashed pets and motorbikes are permitted.

Reservations, fees: Reservations accepted. Sites are $13-19 per night; cabins are $45-90 per night for up to eight people. Open year-round.

Directions: From Olympia on Interstate 5, take Exit 104 to U.S. 101. Drive west on U.S. 101 six miles to Highway 8. Turn west on Highway 8 (which becomes U.S. 12) to Aberdeen and Highway 105. Turn south (left) and drive 21 miles to the Y in the road. Take Highway 105 left toward Grayland. The park is in Grayland between mileposts 26 and 27.

Contact: Ocean Gate Resort, P.O. Box 67, Grayland, WA 98547 tel. (800) 473-1956 or (360) 267-1956.

23 Hammond Trailer Park   5

The park covers five acres and has nearby beach access for hiking and biking on the beach. A full-service marina is within five miles.

Location: In Westport; map B1, grid c5.

Campsites, facilities: There are 34 sites with full hookups for tents, trailers, or RVs of any length. Sanitary services, toilets, showers, cable TV, and laundry facilities are available. Bottled gas, a store, a cafe, and ice are within one mile. Boat docks, launching facilities, and boat rentals are nearby. Small leashed pets are permitted.

Reservations, fees: Reservations required. Sites are $12 per night. Open year-round.

Directions: From Olympia on Interstate 5, take Exit 104 to U.S. 101. Drive west on U.S. 101 six miles to Highway 8. Turn west on Highway 8 (which becomes U.S. 12) to Aberdeen and Highway 105. Turn south (left) and drive 22 miles to Westport and Montesano Street. Turn north on Montesano Street and drive one-half mile to the park on the left.

Contact: Hammond Trailer Park, P.O. Box 2134, 1845 South Montesano Street, Westport, WA 98595; tel. (360) 268-9645.

24 Islander RV Park   8

Located on Grays Harbor, which has a full-service marina, this three-acre park isn't far from Westport Light and Westhaven State Parks, which offer oceanfront day-use facilities. On-site amenities at Islander RV Park include a hair salon, a gift shop, a restaurant, a motel, live music, dancing, and even fishing charters.

Location: On Grays Harbor; map B1, grid c5.

Campsites, facilities: There are 60 sites with full hookups for trailers or RVs up to 40 feet long; 30 are drive-through sites. Toilets, showers, a coffee shop, a restaurant, laundry facilities, ice, a swimming pool, boat docks, and fishing charters are available. Bottled gas, sanitary services, and a store are located within one mile. Leashed pets and motorbikes are permitted.

Reservations, fees: Reservations accepted. Sites are $15-20 per night. Major credit cards accepted. Open year-round.

Directions: From Olympia on Interstate 5, take Exit 104 to U.S. 101. Drive west on U.S. 101 six miles to Highway 8. Turn west on Highway 8 (which becomes U.S. 12) to Aberdeen and Highway 105. Turn south (left) and drive 22 miles to Westport and Dock Avenue. Turn east on Dock Avenue and drive three blocks to Westhaven Drive. Turn north and drive one-third mile to Neddie Rose Avenue. Turn east and drive one block to the park.

Contact: Islander RV Park, P.O. Box 488, Westport, WA 98595; tel. (800) 322-1740, (360) 268-9166, fax (360) 268-0902.

25 Best Western Shores Motel and RV Park   4

This is a small, private park designed for families. Beach access and golf are not far, and Twin Harbors and Grayland Beach State Parks are just a few minutes away. This is an excellent layover for tourists who want to get off U.S. 101.

Location: In Grayland; map B1, grid c5.

Campsites, facilities: There are 30 drive-through sites for trailers or RVs of any length. Electricity, drinking water, sewer hookups, basic cable TV, and picnic tables are provided. Flush toilets, showers, ice, propane, a pay phone, snacks, and a playground are available. Sanitary services, firewood, a store, and a cafe are located within one mile. Leashed pets are permitted.

Reservations, fees: Reservations preferred. Sites are $12.50 per night. Major credit cards accepted. Open year-round.

Directions: From Olympia on Interstate 5, take Exit 104 to U.S. 101. Drive west on U.S. 101 six miles to Highway 8. Turn west on Highway 8 (which becomes U.S. 12) to Aberdeen and Highway 105. Turn south (left) and drive 22 miles southwest to Westport. Continue south on Highway 105 to Grayland. The RV park is located in town, right along Highway 105 on the right.

Contact: Best Western Shores Motel and RV Park, P.O. Box 689, Grayland, WA 98547; tel. (360) 267-6115.

26 Happy Trails Bay Center KOA   7

This 11-acre camp on the shore of Willapa Bay has a trail leading to the beach. The campsites are graveled and shady.

Location: On Willapa Bay; map B1, grid d6.

Campsites, facilities: There are 22 tent sites and 55 sites for trailers or RVs of any length, 11 with full and 44 with partial hookups; 15 sites are drive-through sites. There are also two cabins. Drinking water and picnic tables are provided. Bottled gas, sanitary services, toilets, showers, a recreation hall, a store, laundry facilities, and ice are available. Electricity, sewer hookups, and firewood are available There is a cafe nearby. Boat docks and launching facilities are about three miles from camp on Willapa Bay. Leashed pets and motorbikes are permitted.

Reservations, fees: Reservations accepted. Sites are $18.50-24 per night; cabins are $36 per night. Major credit cards accepted. Open mid-March through mid-October.

Directions: From Kelso/Longview on Interstate 5, turn west on Highway 4 and drive 63 miles to U.S. 101. Turn north on U.S. 101 and drive about 10 miles to Bay Center/Dike exit between mileposts 42 and 43 (16 miles south of Raymond). Turn west and drive three miles to the campground.

Contact: Happy Trails-Bay Center KOA, P.O. Box 315, Bay Center, WA 98527; tel. (360) 875-6344.

27 Evergreen Court

 5

This five-acre, wooded campground with beach access is near Leadbetter Point State Park, a day-use park and natural area that adjoins a wildlife refuge. The trails at Leadbetter lead through the dunes and woods and provide opportunities for seeing both marine birds and waterfowl, especially in the spring and fall. At low tide one can bike for 20 miles. There is also a boat launch. Within five miles of the campground are two nine-hole golf courses.

Location: Near Leadbetter Point State Park; map B1, grid e5.

Campsites, facilities: There are eight tent sites and 34 sites for trailers or RVs of any length. Electricity, drinking water, sewer hookups, cable TV, and picnic tables are provided. Sanitary services, toilets, showers, firewood, and a playground are available. A store, a cafe, and laundry facilities are within two miles. Leashed pets and motorbikes are permitted.

Reservations, fees: Reservations accepted. Sites are $12-13 per night. Open year-round.

Directions: From Kelso/Longview on Interstate 5, turn west on Highway 4 and drive 63 miles to U.S. 101. Turn south on U.S. 101 and drive 13 miles to the junction with Highway 103. Turn north on Highway 103 and drive nine miles to the campground.

Contact: Evergreen Court, P.O. Box 1310, Ocean Park, WA 98640; tel. (360) 665-6351.

28 Timberland RV Park 7

The wooded shore of the Willapa River is the setting for this three-acre park, with fishing, hunting, clamming, and golfing among the nearby recreation options. The river is a popular spot during salmon or steelhead runs.

Location: Near the Willapa River; map B1, grid d7.

Campsites, facilities: There is an area for dispersed tent camping and 24 drive-through sites for trailers or RVs of any length. Electricity, drinking water, sewer hookups, cable TV, and picnic tables are provided. Toilets and showers are available.

Bottled gas, sanitary services, a store, a cafe, laundry facilities, and ice are located within one mile. Boat docks can be found nearby where the Willapa River empties into Willapa Bay. Leashed pets and motorbikes are permitted.

Reservations, fees: Reservations accepted. Sites are $9-15 per night. Open year-round.

Directions: From Olympia on Interstate 5, take Exit 104 to U.S. 101. Drive west on U.S. 101 six miles to Highway 8. Turn west on Highway 8 (which becomes U.S. 12) to Aberdeen and Highway 105. Turn southwest on Highway 105 and drive six blocks to Crescent Street. Turn south on Crescent Street and drive two blocks to the end of the street.

Contact: Timberland RV Park, 850 Crescent Street, Raymond, WA 98577; tel. (800) 563-3325, or (360) 942-3325.

29 Southbend
Mobile and RV Park   7

This small, wooded park covering two acres near the Willapa River makes a decent layover for tourists traveling U.S. 101. Additional facilities within five miles of the campground include an 18-hole golf course.

Location: On the Willapa River; map B1, grid d7.

Campsites, facilities: There are two tent sites and six drive-through sites for trailers or RVs of any length. Electricity, drinking water, and sewer hookups are provided. Toilets, showers, a recreation hall, and a laundry room are available. Bottled gas, a store, a cafe, and ice are within one mile. Boat docks and launching facilities can be found nearby where the Willapa River empties into Willapa Bay. Pets and motorbikes are permitted.

Reservations, fees: Reservations accepted. Sites are $15 per night. Open year-round.

Directions: From Kelso/Longview on Interstate 5, turn west on Highway 4 and drive 63 miles to U.S. 101. Bear north on U.S. 101 drive 20 miles to South Bend and Central. Turn south on Central and drive to the campground in town.

Contact: Southbend Mobile and RV Park, P.O. Box 4, South Bend, WA 98586; tel. (360) 875-5165.

30 Ocean Park Resort
        5

This wooded, 10-acre campground with access to the shoreline of Willapa Bay is primarily for RVs. The sites are grassy and shaded. To the north, Leadbetter Point State Park provides a side-trip option.

Location: On Willapa Bay; map B1, grid e5.

Campsites, facilities: There are seven tent sites and 70 sites for trailers or RVs of any length; 34 are drive-through sites. Electricity, drinking water, sewer hookups, and picnic tables are provided. Bottled gas, toilets, a recreation hall, laundry facilities, ice, a playground, firewood, a hot tub, and a swimming pool are available. An extra fee is charged for showers. A store and a cafe can be found within one mile.

Boat docks and launching facilities are located nearby on Willapa Bay. Le
and motorbikes are permitted.

Reservations, fees: Reservations accepted. Sites are $17-21 per night. O₁
round.

Directions: From Kelso/Longview on Interstate 5, turn west on Highway
drive 63 miles to U.S. 101. Turn south on U.S. 101 and drive 13 miles to the junction
with Highway 103. Turn north on Highway 103 and drive 11 miles to the town of
Ocean Park and 259th Street. Turn east on 259th Street and drive two blocks to the
end of the road.

Contact: Ocean Park Resort, P.O. Box 339, Ocean Park, WA 98640; tel. (800) 835-4634
or (360) 665-4585, fax (360) 665-4130.

31 Westgate Motor and Trailer Court

       9

Highlights of this very pretty and clean four-acre camp include beach access,
oceanfront sites, and all the amenities. There are 28 miles of beach that can be
driven on. Additional facilities within five miles of the campground include an 18-
hole golf course.

Location: Near Long Beach; map B1, grid e5.

Campsites, facilities: There are 39 sites for trailers or RVs of any length; 15 are
drive-through sites. There are also six cabins. Electricity, drinking water, cable
TV, and sewer hookups are provided. Rest rooms, showers, a recreation hall, and
ice are available. A store, a cafe, and coin-operated laundry facilities can be found
about four miles away. Boat docks and launching facilities are located nearby on
Willapa Bay. Leashed pets are permitted.

Reservations, fees: Reservations accepted. Sites are $19-20 per night; cabins
are $47.50-65 per night. Major credit cards accepted. Open year-round.

Directions: From Kelso/Longview on Interstate 5, turn west on Highway 4 and
drive 63 miles to U.S. 101. Turn south on U.S. 101 and drive 13 miles to the junction
with Highway 103. Turn north on Highway 103 and drive 7.5 miles to the campground
on the south edge of the town of Ocean Park.

Contact: Westgate Motor and Trailer Court, 20803 Pacific Highway, Ocean Park, WA
98640; tel. (360) 665-4211.

32 Ocean Aire   4

This camp covers two acres and has access to the shoreline of Willapa Bay. Tennis courts and a golf course can be found within five miles. Leadbetter Point State
Park, about eight miles north, is open for day use and provides footpaths for walking through the state-designated natural area and wildlife refuge.

Location: Near Willapa Bay; map B1, grid e5.

Campsites, facilities: There are 46 sites for trailers or RVs of any length, 8 are
drive-through sites. No tents are allowed. Electricity, drinking water, sewer hookups,
and picnic tables are provided. Sanitary services, toilets, showers, laundry facilities,
and ice are available. A store and a cafe can be found next door. Boat rentals are
nearby on Willapa Bay. Leashed pets are permitted.

Reservations, fees: Reservations accepted. Sites are $14-17 per night. Open year-round.

Directions: From Kelso/Longview on Interstate 5, turn west on Highway 4 and drive 63 miles to U.S. 101. Turn south on U.S. 101 and drive 13 miles to the junction with Highway 103. Turn north on Highway 103 and drive 11 miles to the town of Ocean Park and 259th Street. Turn east on 259th Street and drive two blocks to the camp.

Contact: Ocean Aire, P.O. Box 155, Ocean Park, WA 98640; tel. (360) 665-4027.

33 Pegg's RV Park   5

Pan fishing and beachcombing are two possible activities at this wooded three-acre campground with beach access. There is also charter fishing and clamming in season. An 18-hole golf course is located within five miles.

Location: Near Long Beach; map B1, grid e5.

Campsites, facilities: There 30 sites for trailers or RVs up to 40 feet. Electricity, drinking water, cable TV, sewer hookups, and picnic tables are provided. Sanitary services, toilets, showers, a recreation hall, laundry facilities, and ice are available. Bottled gas, a store, and a cafe can be found within one mile. Leashed pets are permitted.

Reservations, fees: Reservations accepted. Sites are $17 per night. Open mid-April through September.

Directions: From Kelso/Longview on Interstate 5, turn west on Highway 4 and drive 63 miles to U.S. 101. Turn south on U.S. 101 and drive 13 miles to the junction with Highway 103. Turn north on Highway 103 and drive 5.5 miles to the campground.

Contact: Pegg's RV Park, 15301 Pacific Highway, Long Beach, WA 98631; tel. (360) 642-2451.

34 Ma and Pa's Pacific RV Park   7

This park on six acres with beach access has spacious grassy sites near the shore. Additional facilities found within five miles of the campground include an 18-hole golf course, marked bike trails, and a riding stable.

Location: Near Long Beach; map B1, grid f5.

Campsites, facilities: There are four acres for tenting and 53 sites for trailers or RVs of any length. Electricity, drinking water, sewer hookups, and picnic tables are provided. Toilets, laundry facilities, and ice are available. An extra fee is charged for showers. Bottled gas, a store, and a cafe can be found within one mile. Leashed pets are permitted.

Reservations, fees: Reservations accepted. Sites are $18.55 per night for two people. Additional persons are $2 per night. Major credit cards accepted. Open year-round.

Directions: From Kelso/Longview on Interstate 5, turn west on Highway 4 and drive 63 miles to U.S. 101. Turn south on U.S. 101 and drive 13 miles to the junction with Highway 103. Turn north on Highway 103 and drive four miles to the campground.

Contact: Ma and Pa's Pacific RV Park, 10515 Pacific Highway, Long Beach, WA 98631; tel. (360) 642-3253, fax (360) 642-5039.

35 Cranberry RV Park 5

This park covers three acres and has beach access. Additional facilities found within five miles of the campground include an 18-hole golf course, marked bike trails, tennis courts, and a riding stable.

Location: Near Long Beach; map B1, grid f5.

Campsites, facilities: There are 20 sites for trailers or RVs of any length in this adult-only campground; nine sites are drive through. No tents are allowed. Electricity, drinking water, cable TV, and sewer hookups are provided. Sanitary services, toilets, showers, and a recreation room are available. Bottled gas, a store, a cafe, and laundry facilities can be found within one mile. Leashed pets are permitted.

Reservations, fees: Reservations accepted. Sites are $12 per night. Open year-round, weather permitting.

Directions: From Kelso/Longview on Interstate 5, turn west on Highway 4 and drive 63 miles to U.S. 101. Turn south on U.S. 101 and drive 13 miles to the junction with Highway 103. Turn north on Highway 103 and drive 4.5 miles to Cranberry Road. Turn east and drive one-quarter mile to the campground.

Contact: Cranberry RV Park, 1801 Cranberry Road, Long Beach, WA 98631; tel. (360) 642-2027.

36 Andersen's RV Park on the Ocean

 7

A path through the dunes will get you to the beach in a flash from this five-acre camp set in a flat, sandy area with graveled sites. Recreation options include beach bonfires, beachcombing, surf fishing, and clamming (seasonal). Additional facilities found within five miles of the campground include marked dune trails, a nine-hole golf course, a riding stable, and tennis courts.

Location: Near Long Beach; map B1, grid f5.

Campsites, facilities: There are 15 tent sites and 59 sites for trailers or RVs of any length. Electricity, drinking water, sewer hookups, cable TV, and picnic tables are provided. Tent sites have water only. Sanitary services, toilets, showers, a hall, laundry facilities, ice, propane, bottled gas, a fax machine, a horseshoe pit, and a playground are available. A store and cafe can be found within two miles. Leashed pets are permitted.

Reservations, fees: Reservations accepted. Sites are $16-20 per night. Open year-round.

Directions: From Kelso/Longview on Interstate 5, turn west on Highway 4 and drive 63 miles to U.S. 101. Turn south on U.S. 101 and drive 13 miles to the junction with Highway 103. Turn north on Highway 103 and drive five miles to the park.

Contact: Andersen's RV Park on the Ocean, 1400 138th Street, Long Beach, WA 98631; tel. (360) 642-2231 or (800) 645-6795, fax (360) 642-2231.

You want quiet and solitude? You found it. This tiny, primitive campground is a jewel set in a wooded area near Western Lakes, just outside of Naselle. It's a prime camp for travelers heading to the coast who want a day or two of privacy before they hit the crowds. There are some good hiking trails nearby.

Location: Near Naselle; map B1, grid f7.

Campsites, facilities: There are three primitive tent sites. Picnic tables, fire grills, tent pads, and vault toilets are provided, but there is no drinking water. Leashed pets are permitted.

Reservations, fees: No reservations; no fee. Open year-round.

Directions: From Kelso/Longview on Interstate 5, turn west on Highway 4 and drive 60 miles to milepost 3 and C-Line Road. Turn north on C-Line Road (two-lane gravel road) uphill and take the left fork at Naselle Youth Camp Entrance and drive 2.9 miles to C-2600 (gravel one-lane road). Turn left on Road C-2600 and drive 0.9 mile to C-2650. Turn right and drive 0.3 mile to the campground.

Contact: Department of Natural Resources, Central Region, 1405 Rush Road, Chehalis, WA 98532-8763; tel. (360) 748-2383.

38 The Beacon-Charters and RV Park

       8

This two-acre park at the Port of Ilwaco docks has riverside access and a view of the Columbia River. Highlights include ocean and river charter fishing during the season (roughly from mid-May through late September), and narrated river tours by a nationally known Lewis and Clark author and historian, leading up to the 100th anniversary of 2004. History buffs from back east are booking ahead. Nearby Fort Canby State Park offers numerous hiking trails and an interpretive center on maritime and military history. Additional facilities within five miles of the campground include an 18-hole golf course and horseback riding (seasonal).

Location: Near Fort Canby State Park; map B1, grid f5.

Campsites, facilities: There are 10 primitive tent sites by the Bay and 60 sites for trailers or RVs of any length. Electricity, drinking water, and sewer hookups are provided. Restrooms, a fish cleaning station, a mini-market, bait, and ice are available. Showers can be obtained for an extra fee. Bottled gas, a store, a cafe, and coin-operated laundry facilities are located within one mile. Boat docks and launching facilities are nearby. Leashed pets are permitted.

Reservations, fees: Reservations accepted. Sites are $10-20 per night. Major credit cards accepted. Open year-round.

Directions: From Kelso/Longview on Interstate 5, turn west on Highway 4 and drive 63 miles to U.S. 101. Turn south on U.S. 101 and drive 13 miles to the junction with Highway 103. Turn north on Highway 103 and drive two miles to Highway 100. Turn south and drive to Ilwaco. The park is on the corner of Howerton and Elizabeth at the east end of the Port of Ilwaco.

Contact: The Beacon-Charters and RV Park, P.O. Box 74, Ilwaco, WA 98624; tel. (877) 642-2138 or (360) 642-2138; website: www.beaconcharters.com

This five-acre park located where the Pacific Ocean and the Columbia River meet has beach and fishing access nearby. Fish and clam cleaning facilities can be found in the park. A maritime museum, hiking trails, a full-service marina, and a riding stable are located within five miles of the park.

Location: Near Fort Canby State Park; map B1, grid f5.

Campsites, facilities: There are some tent sites and 43 sites for trailers or RVs of any length. Electricity, drinking water, sewer, and cable TV hookups are provided. Sanitary services, toilets, coin-operated showers, and a laundry room are available. Bottled gas, a store, and a cafe are located within one mile. Boat docks, launching facilities, and rentals are nearby. Leashed pets are permitted.

Reservations, fees: Reservations accepted. Sites are $10 for tents and $20 for RVs per night. Open year-round.

Directions: From Kelso/Longview on Interstate 5, turn west on Highway 4 and drive 63 miles to U.S. 101. Turn south on U.S. 101 and drive 13 miles to the junction with Highway 103. Turn north on Highway 103 and drive two miles to Highway 100. Turn south and drive to Ilwaco. At the junction of Spruce Street SW and First Street, turn west on Spruce Street and drive one block to Second Avenue SW. Turn south on Second Avenue SW and drive four blocks south to the campground.

Contact: Fisherman's Cove RV Park, P.O. Box 921, Ilwaco, WA 98624; tel. (877) 268-3789, (360) 642-3689.

40 Wildwood RV Park and Campground

 5

This pretty, wooded park, for those age 50 and over, covers five acres and has beach access, pan fishing, and its own little pond. Additional facilities found within five miles of the campground include an 18-hole golf course, a full-service marina, and tennis courts. See the Beacon-Charters RV Park for attractions at nearby Fort Canby State Park.

Location: Near Fort Canby State Park; map B1, grid f5.

Campsites, facilities: There are 25 tent sites and 30 sites for trailers or RVs of any length at this campground for the age-50-and-over crowd. Electricity, drinking water, sewer hookups, and picnic tables are provided. Sanitary services and toilets are available. Showers can be obtained for an extra fee. Bottled gas, firewood, a store, a cafe, laundry facilities, and ice are located within one mile. Leashed pets are permitted.

Reservations, fees: Reservations accepted. Sites are $15-22 per night. Open April through September.

Directions: From Kelso/Longview on Interstate 5, turn west on Highway 4 and drive 63 miles to U.S. 101. Turn south on U.S. 101 and drive 12 miles to Sandridge Road (located one-half mile east of the junction with Highway 103). Turn north and drive three-quarters of a mile to the park.

Contact: Wildwood RV Park and Campground, Route 1, Box 76, Long Beach, WA 98631; tel. (360) 642-2131.

41 KOA Ilwaco   5

This 17-acre camp is about nine miles from the beach. Pan fishing, horseshoe pits, and a recreation room provide possible activities. Additional facilities found within five miles of the campground include a maritime museum, hiking trails, and a nine-hole golf course.

Location: Near Fort Canby State Park; map B1, grid f5.

Campsites, facilities: There are 50 tent sites and 114 drive-through sites for trailers or RVs of any length. Four cabins are also available. Electricity and drinking water are provided. Full hookups with cable TV are available. Bottled gas, sanitary services, toilets, showers, a recreation hall, a store, laundry facilities, ice, and a playground are available. Leashed pets are permitted.

Reservations, fees: Reservations accepted; phone (800) 562-3258. Sites are $22-30 per night; cabins are $45 per night. Major credit cards accepted. Open mid-May to mid-October.

Directions: From Kelso/Longview on Interstate 5, turn west on Highway 4 and drive 63 miles to U.S. 101. Turn south on U.S. 101 and drive 13 miles to the junction with Highway 103. The campground is located at the junction.

Contact: KOA Ilwaco, P.O. Box 549, Ilwaco, WA 98624; tel. (360) 642-3292.

42 Sou'Wester Lodge and Trailer Park
       7

This three-acre camp with beach access is one of the few sites in the immediate area that provide spots for tent camping. Fishing is a recreation option. The area sports the Lewis and Clark Interpretive Center, a light house, museums, fine dining, bicycle and boat rentals, bicycle and hiking trails, and bird sanctuaries. Additional facilities found within five miles of the campground include an 18-hole golf course, a full-service marina, and a riding stable.

Location: In Seaview on the Long Beach Peninsula; map B1, grid f5.

Campsites, facilities: There are 10 tent sites and 60 sites for trailers or RVs of any length; five are drive-through sites. Electricity, drinking water, and sewer hookups are provided. Toilets, showers, cable TV, and laundry facilities are available. Bottled gas, sanitary services, a store, a cafe, and ice are located within one mile. Boat launching facilities are nearby. Leashed pets and motorbikes permitted.

Reservations, fees: Reservations accepted. Sites are $17-26 per night. Major credit cards accepted. Open year-round.

Directions: From Kelso/Longview on Interstate 5, turn west on Highway 4 and drive 63 miles to U.S. 101. Turn south on U.S. 101 and drive 13 miles to the junction with Highway 103. Turn north on Highway 103 and drive to Seaview Beach Access Road (38th Place). Turn left and drive toward the ocean. Look for the campground on the left.

Contact: Sou'Wester Lodge and Trailer Park, P.O. Box 102, Seaview, WA 98644; tel. (360) 642-2542.

43 Fort Canby State Park 10

This 1,881-acre park is the choice spot in the area for tent campers two places to camp: a general camping area and the Lake O'Neil area, sites right on the water. Highlights at the park include hiking trails and opportunities for surf, jetty, and ocean fishing. An interpretive center highlights the Lewis and Clark expedition and maritime and military history.

Location: On the Pacific Ocean; map B1, grid f5.

Campsites, facilities: There are four primitive tent sites, 190 developed tent sites, and 60 sites with full hookups for trailers or RVs up to 45 feet long, cabins and yurts, picnic tables, and fire grills are provided. A sanitary disposal station and toilets are available. Showers can be obtained for an extra fee. A store and a restaurant are located within one mile. Boat launching facilities are nearby. Leashed pets are permitted.

Reservations, fees: Reservations accepted; phone (800) 452-5687 ($6 reservation fee). Sites are $11-16 per night. Cabins and yurts are $35 per night. Major credit cards accepted. Open year-round.

Directions: From Kelso/Longview on Interstate 5, turn west on Highway 4 and drive 63 miles to U.S. 101. Turn south on U.S. 101 and drive 13 miles to the junction with Highway 103 (a flashing light). Turn west and drive two miles to Highway 100 and continue (on Highway 100) to the park.

Contact: Fort Canby State Park, P.O. Box 488, Ilwaco, WA 98624; tel. (800) 233-0321 or (360) 642-3078.

44 Oceanic RV Park 3

This two-acre camp is within five miles of an 18-hole golf course, marked bike trails, and a full-service marina.

Location: In Long Beach; map B1, grid f5.

Campsites, facilities: There are 20 drive-through sites for trailers or RVs of any length. No tents are allowed. Electricity, drinking water, and sewer hookups are provided. Toilets and showers are available. Bottled gas, sanitary services, a store, a cafe, coin-operated laundry facilities, and ice are located within one mile. Boat docks, launching facilities, and rentals are nearby. Leashed pets are permitted.

Reservations, fees: Reservations accepted. Sites are $14-18 per night. Major credit cards accepted. Open year-round.

Directions: From Kelso/Longview on Interstate 5, turn west on Highway 4 and drive 63 miles to U.S. 101. Turn south on U.S. 101 and drive 13 miles to the junction with Highway 103. Turn north on Highway 103 and drive two miles to Long Beach. Continue to the campground at the south junction of Pacific Highway and Fifth Avenue.

Contact: Oceanic RV Park, P.O. Box 242, Long Beach, WA 98631; tel. (360) 642-3836 or e-mail: oceanic@aone.com.

45 Sand-Lo Motel and RV Park 3

This tiny three-acre park with beach access is within five miles of an 18-hole golf course, a full-service marina, and a riding stable.

Location: Near Long Beach; map B1, grid f5.

Campsites, facilities: There are 15 sites for trailers or RVs of any length. Electricity, drinking water, and cable TV and sewer hookups are provided. Sanitary services, toilets, showers, and laundry facilities are available. Bottled gas, a store, a cafe, and ice are located within one mile. Leashed pets and motorbikes are permitted.

Reservations, fees: Reservations accepted. Sites are $17.75 per night. Major credit cards accepted. Open year-round.

Directions: From Kelso/Longview on Interstate 5, turn west on Highway 4 and drive 63 miles to U.S. 101. Turn south on U.S. 101 and drive 13 miles to the junction with Highway 103. Turn north on Highway 103 and drive three miles to the park.

Contact: Sand-Lo Motel and RV Park, P.O. Box 736, Long Beach, WA 98631; tel. (360) 642-2600.

46 Driftwood RV Park   2

This two-acre park has grassy, shaded sites and beach access. Additional facilities within five miles of the campground include an 18-hole golf course and a full-service marina.

Location: Near Long Beach; map B1, grid f5.

Campsites, facilities: There are 56 sites for trailers or RVs of any length; 22 are drive-through sites. Electricity, drinking water, sewer hookups, and picnic tables are provided. Toilets, showers, laundry facilities, and cable TV are available. Bottled gas, a store, and a cafe can be found within one mile. Leashed pets are permitted.

Reservations, fees: Reservations accepted. Sites are $19 per night. Major credit cards accepted. Open March through October.

Directions: From Kelso/Longview on Interstate 5, turn west on Highway 4 and drive 63 miles to U.S. 101. Turn south on U.S. 101 and drive 13 miles to the junction with Highway 103. Turn north on Highway 103 and drive two miles to the park on the right, at 14th North and Pacific.

Contact: Driftwood RV Park, P.O. Box 296, Long Beach, WA 98631; tel. (360) 642-2711; e-mail: driftwood-rvpark.com.

47 Anthony's Home Court RV Park   2

This two-acre park with beach access is an alternative to Driftwood RV Park, which is just down the street. Additional facilities found within five miles of the campground include an 18-hole golf course, marked bike trails, and a riding stable.

Location: In Long Beach; map B1, grid f5.

Campsites, facilities: There are 25 sites for trailers or RVs. Electricity, drinking water, sewer hookups, and picnic tables are provided. Toilets, laundry facilities, ice, and cable TV are available. An extra fee is charged for showers. Bottled gas, sanitary services, a store, and a cafe are located within one mile. Leashed pets are permitted.

Reservations, fees: Reservations accepted. Sites are $15-17 per night. Open year-round.

Directions: From Kelso/Longview on Interstate 5, turn west on Highway 4 and drive 63 miles to U.S. 101. Turn south on U.S. 101 and drive 13 miles to the junction with Highway 103. Turn north on Highway 103 and drive two miles to the park on the right.

Contact: Anthony's Home Court RV Park, P.O. Box 1532, Long Beach, WA 98631; tel. (360) 642-2802; e-mail: djh@aone.com.

48 Sand Castle RV Park   3

This very clean, though not particularly scenic, park covers two acres, has beach access, and is one of several in the immediate area. Additional facilities found within five miles of the campground include an 18-hole golf course, marked bike trails, a full-service marina, and a riding stable.

Location: In Long Beach; map B1, grid f5.

Campsites, facilities: There are 38 sites for trailers or RVs of any length. Tents are permitted with RVs. Electricity, drinking water, sewer, cable TV hookups, and picnic tables are provided. Sanitary services, toilets, laundry facilities, and a pay phone are available. An extra fee is charged for showers. Bottled gas, a store, ice, and a cafe can be found within one mile. Boat docks, launching facilities, and rentals are nearby. Leashed pets and motorbikes are permitted.

Reservations, fees: Reservations accepted. Sites are $18-25 per night. Major credit cards accepted. Open year-round.

Directions: From Kelso/Longview on Interstate 5, turn west on Highway 4 and drive 63 miles to U.S. 101. Turn south on U.S. 101 and drive 13 miles to the junction with Highway 103. Turn north on Highway 103 and drive two miles to the park on the right.

Contact: Sand Castle RV Park, 1100 North Pacific Highway, Long Beach, WA 98631; tel. (360) 642-2174, fax (360) 642-7122.

49 River's End Campground and RV Park   6

This wooded campground spreads over five acres and has riverside access. Salmon fishing is available here. Additional facilities found within five miles of the campground include marked bike trails and a full-service marina. Also nearby is Fort Columbia State Park, which has an interpretive center featuring the history of coastal artillery.

Location: Near Fort Columbia State Park; map B1, grid f6.

Campsites, facilities: There are 24 tent sites and 54 sites for trailers or RVs of any length; 15 are drive-through sites. Electricity, drinking water, sewer hookups, cable TV, and picnic tables are provided. Sanitary services, toilets, a recreation hall, laundry facilities, ice, and a playground are available. Showers and firewood can be obtained for an extra fee. Bottled gas, a store, and a cafe are located within one mile. Boat docks, launching facilities, and rentals are nearby on the Columbia River. Leashed pets and motorbikes permitted.

Reservations, fees: Reservations accepted. Sites are $12-18 per night. Open April to late October.

Directions: From Kelso/Longview on Interstate 5, turn west on Highway 4 and drive 60 miles to Highway 401. Turn south on Highway 401 and drive 14 miles to the park entrance (just south of Chinook).

Contact: River's End Campground and RV Park, P.O. Box 280, Chinook, WA 98614; tel. (360) 777-8317.

50 Mauch's Sundown RV Park, Inc.   5

This adults-only park covers four acres, has riverside access, and is in a wooded, hilly setting with grassy sites. It's near Fort Columbia State Park, which has a newly renovated interpretive center featuring the history of coastal artillery.

Location: Near Fort Columbia State Park; map B1, grid f6.

Campsites, facilities: There are 50 sites for trailers or RVs of any length at this adult-oriented park. Electricity, drinking water, sewer hookups, and picnic tables are provided. Sanitary services, cable TV, toilets, coin-operated showers, firewood, laundry facilities, a store, propane gas, and ice are available. A cafe is located within three miles. Boat docks and launching facilities are nearby on the Columbia River. Small pets and motorbikes are permitted.

Reservations, fees: Reservations accepted. Sites are $8-20 per night. Open year-round.

Directions: From Kelso/Longview on Interstate 5, turn west on Highway 4 and drive 60 miles to Highway 401. Turn south on Highway 401 and drive to U.S. 101. Take U.S. 101 to the right and continue for a half mile (do not go over the bridge) to the park on the right. The address is 158 State Route 101.

Contact: Mauch's Sundown RV Park, Inc., P.O. Box 129, Chinook, WA 98614; tel. (360) 777-8713.

51 Skamokawa Vista Park

   7

This camp covers 30 acres and has access to the Columbia River, where fishing, swimming, and boating are all options. Additional facilities found within five miles of the campground include a full-service marina and additional tennis courts.

Location: Near the Columbia River; map B1, grid f8.

Campsites, facilities: There are four tent sites, nine sites for tents or RVs, and 21 sites for trailers or RVs of any length. Electricity, drinking water, and picnic tables are provided. Ten of the 21 RV sites offer direct water hookups. Flush toilets, a dump station, showers, firewood, tennis and basketball courts, and a playground are available. Bottled gas, a store, a cafe, and ice are located within one mile. Boat docks and launching facilities are nearby. Leashed pets and motorbikes are permitted.

Reservations, fees: Reservations accepted. Sites are $10-17 per night. Open year-round.

Directions: From Kelso/Longview on Interstate 5, turn west on Highway 4 and drive 35 miles to Skamokawa. Continue west on Highway 4 one-half mile to the campground.

Contact: Skamokawa Vista Park, P.O. Box 220, Skamokawa, WA 98647; tel. (360) 795-8605.

MOUNT RAINIER

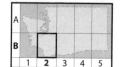

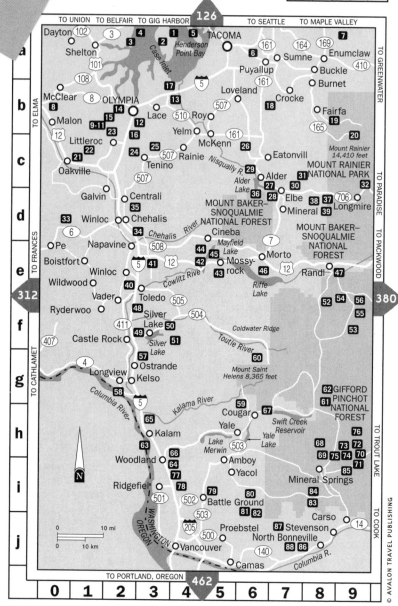

CHAPTER B2

◼ Penrose Point State Park   8

This park on Carr Inlet in Puget Sound, overlooking Lake Bay, has a remote feel, but it's actually not far from Tacoma. Because of the circular driving route needed to get here, a lot of people bypass it. The park is known for its excellent fishing, clamming and oysters.

Location: On Puget Sound; map B2, grid a3.

Campsites, facilities: There are 83 sites developed sites for tents or self-contained RVs up to 35 feet long and one primitive tent site. Picnic tables, drinking water and fire grills are provided. A sanitary disposal station, coin-operated showers, and toilets are available. Some facilities are wheelchair accessible. Boat docks are nearby and can be used for overnight moorage for a fee. Leashed pets are permitted.

Reservations, fees: Reservations accepted; phone (800) 452-5687 ($6 reservation fee). Sites are $5-11 per night. Major credit cards accepted. Open April through August.

Directions: From Tacoma drive north on Highway 16 for about 10 miles to Highway 302. Turn west and drive about five miles to Key Peninsula Highway. Turn south and drive 9.2 miles through the towns of Key Center and Home to Cornwall Road KPS. Turn left and drive 1.25 miles to 158 Avenue KPS and the park entrance.

Contact: Penrose Point State Park, 321-158th Avenue KPS, Lake Bay, WA 98439; tel. (800) 233-0321, (253) 884-2514.

◼ Joemma Beach State Park   8

This beautiful camp set along the shore of the peninsula is a less crowded alternative to Penrose Point State Park. Drinking water and boating facilities make it a winner.

Location: On Puget Sound; map B2, grid a3.

Campsites, facilities: There are three primitive sites and 19 sites for tents, trailers, or RVs up to 35 feet long. Picnic tables, fire grills, and tent pads are provided. Vault toilets, drinking water, boat launching facilities, and a dock are available. Leashed pets are permitted.

Reservations, fees: Reservations accepted. Sites are $10 per night; there is a $3 launch fee. Open Memorial Day through Labor Day.

Directions: From Tacoma on Interstate 5, turn north on Highway 16. Drive 10 miles north to Highway 302. Turn west and drive three miles to Gig Harbor-Longbranch Road. Turn left and drive about 15 miles to the town of Home. In Home at the bridge, turn south on Longbranch Road and drive 1.3 miles to Whiteman Road. Turn right and drive 2.3 miles to Bay Road. Turn right and drive one mile to the camp on the right.

Contact: Joemma Beach State Park, 11101 56th Street NW, Gig Harbor, WA 98332; tel. (800) 233-0321, (253) 265-3606.

3 Jarrell Cove State Park   8

This wooded park is rarely crowded and offers a protected cove for boating and docking facilities. A private marina is nearby. Fishing here is excellent, and there is a nice beach for sunbathing or beachcombing.

Location: On Harstine Island; map B2, a2.

Campsites, facilities: There are 20 sites for tents or self-contained RVs up to 30 feet long. Picnic tables and fire grills are provided. Flush toilets and coin-operated showers are available. Not all of the facilities are wheelchair accessible. Boat docks are available for overnight moorage for a fee. Leashed pets are permitted.

Reservations, fees: Reservations accepted. Sites are $10 per night; there is an $8-11 moorage fee. Open April through October.

Directions: From Olympia on Interstate 5, turn north on U.S. 101 and drive 22 miles to Shelton and Highway 3. Turn east on Highway 3 and drive about eight miles to Pickering Road. Turn right and drive to the Harstine Bridge. Turn left, cross the bridge to Harstine Island, and continue to a stop sign at North Island Drive. Turn left and drive four miles to the park on the left (well signed).

Contact: Jarrell Cove State Park, East 391 Wingert Road, Shelton, WA 98584; tel. (800) 233-0321 or (360) 426-9226.

4 Jarrell Cove Marina   6

The marina and nearby Puget Sound are the big bonus here.

Location: Near Shelton; map B2, grid a3.

Campsites, facilities: There are four sites for trailers or RVs up to 27 feet long. Drinking water, electricity, and picnic tables are provided. Bottled gas, toilets, showers, sanitary services, a store, a laundry room, barbecues, boat docks, and boat rentals are available. Leashed pets are permitted.

Reservations, fees: Reservations accepted. Sites are $25 per night. Open year-round.

Directions: From Olympia on Interstate 5, turn north on U.S. 101 and drive 22 miles to Shelton and Highway 3. Turn east on Highway 3 and drive about eight miles to Pickering Road. Turn right and drive to the Harstine Bridge. Turn left, cross the bridge to Harstine Island, and continue to a stop sign at North Island Drive. Turn left on North Island Drive to Haskell Hill Road. Turn west on Haskell Hill Road and drive one mile to the marina.

Contact: Jarrell Cove Marina, 220 East Wilson Road, Shelton, WA 98584; tel. (360) 426-8823.

5 Kopachuck State Park   8

Located on Henderson Bay on Puget Sound near Tacoma, this is a nice, developed park with full facilities for tent campers. There is a large beach area for clamming or lounging. Fishing access is available by boat only. A boat launch is located not far from camp.

Location: On Puget Sound; map B2, grid a4.

Campsites, facilities: There are two primitive tent sites and 41 developed sites for tents or self-contained RVs up to 35 feet long. Picnic tables, drinking water and fire grills are provided. A sanitary disposal station, coin-operated showers, toilets, and boat buoys are available. Some facilities are wheelchair accessible. Leashed pets are permitted.

Reservations, fees: Reservations accepted. Sites are $7-11 per night. Open March through October.

Directions: From Tacoma on Interstate 5, turn north on Highway 16. Drive seven miles north and look for the sign for Kopachuck State Park. At the sign, turn west and drive five miles to the camp (well signed).

Contact: Kopachuck State Park, 11101 56th Street NW, Gig Harbor, WA 98332; tel. (800) 233-0321 or (253) 265-3606.

6 Majestic Manor RV Park

       7

This clean, pretty park along the Puyallup River with views of Mt. Rainier caters to RVers. Nearby recreation options include an 18-hole golf course, a full-service marina, and tennis courts. For information on the attractions in Tacoma, see the description of Dash Point State Park.

Location: On the Puyallup River; map B2, grid a6.

Campsites, facilities: There are 12 tent sites and 118 sites for trailers or RVs of any length. Electricity, drinking water, and sewer hookups are provided. Flush toilets, bottled gas, sanitary services, showers, a recreation hall, a store, laundry facilities, ice, and a swimming pool are available. A cafe is located within one mile. Leashed pets and motorbikes are permitted.

Reservations, fees: Reservations accepted. Sites are $20-24 per night. Open year-round.

Directions: From near Tacoma on Interstate 5, take Exit 135 to Highway 167. Drive east on Highway 167 (River Road) for four miles to the park on the right.

Contact: Majestic Manor RV Park; fax (253) 841-2248, 7022 River Road, Puyallup, WA 98371; tel. (800) 348-3144 or (253) 845-3144.

7 Kanaskat-Palmer State Park   8

This wooded campground offers private campsites along the Green River. In summer the river is ideal for rafting and kayaking. In winter it attracts a nice run of steelhead. You can explore the area's hiking trails year-round.

Location: On the Green River; map B2, grid a9.

Campsites, facilities: There are 31 tent sites and 19 drive-through sites for trailers or RVs up to 35 feet long. Picnic tables are provided. Electricity, flush toilets, showers, and sanitary services are available. Some facilities are wheelchair accessible. Boat rentals can be found nearby on the Green River. Leashed pets are permitted.

Reservations, fees: Reservations accepted. Sites are $11-16 per night. Major credit cards accepted. Open year-round, with limited facilities in the winter.

Directions: From Puyallup at the junction of Highway 167 and Highway 410, turn southeast on Highway 410 and drive 25 miles to Enumclaw and Farman Road. Turn northeast on Farman Road and drive 11 miles to the park on the left.

Contact: Kanaskat-Palmer State Park, 23700 Flaming Geyser, Auburn, WA 98002; tel. (800) 233-0321 or (360) 886-0148.

8 Porter Creek   7

This primitive, rustic campground less than 20 miles from Olympia in Capitol Forest is managed by the Department of Natural Resources. Set along the shore of Porter Creek, it offers trails for hiking, horseback riding, or motorbiking.

Location: On Porter Creek in Capitol Forest; map B2, grid b0.

Campsites, facilities: There are 16 primitive sites for tents or small trailers. Picnic tables, fire grills, and tent pads are provided. There is no drinking water. Vault toilets and horse-loading ramps are available. Leashed pets and motorbikes are permitted.

Reservations, fees: No reservations; no fee. Open April through October.

Directions: On Interstate 5 drive to Exit 68 (10 miles south of Chehalis) and U.S. 12. Turn west on U.S. 12 and drive 21 miles to Porter and Porter Creek Road. Turn northeast on Porter Creek Road and drive three miles to a junction; then continue straight for another one-half mile to the campground on the left.

Contact: Department of Natural Resources, Central Region, 1405 Rush Road, Chehalis, WA 98532-8763; tel. (360) 748-2383; fax (360) 748-2387.

9 Middle Waddell   7

This wooded campground is nestled along Waddell Creek in Capitol Forest. The trails are used primarily for motorbikes, making for a rather noisy atmosphere. Remember, no drinking water is available here.

Location: On Waddell Creek in Capitol Forest; map B2, grid b1.

Campsites, facilities: There are 24 sites for tents, trailers, or RVs. Picnic tables, fire grills, and tent pads are provided. Vault toilets are available, but there is no drinking water. Leashed pets and motorbikes are permitted.

Reservations, fees: No reservations; no fee. Open April through October.

Directions: From Olympia on Interstate 5, drive south for about 10 miles to Exit 95 and Highway 121. Turn west on Highway 121 and drive four miles to Littlerock. Continue west for one mile to Waddell Creek Road. Turn right and drive three miles and look for the campground entrance road on the left.

Contact: Department of Natural Resources, Central Region, 1405 Rush Road, Chehalis, WA 98532-8763; tel. (360) 748-2383; fax (360) 748-2387.

10 Fall Creek   7

This wooded camp on Fall Creek in Capitol Forest is a good alternative to Middle Waddell, since the trails here are for hikers and horseback riders only. That means no motorbikes and a more peaceful setting.

Location: On Fall Creek in Capitol Forest; map B2, grid b1.

Campsites, facilities: There are eight primitive campsites for tents or small trailers. Picnic tables, fire grills, and tent pads are provided. Vault toilets, drinking water, and a horse-loading ramp are available, but there is no drinking water. Leashed pets are permitted.

Reservations, fees: No reservations; no fee. Open April through October.

Directions: From Olympia on Interstate 5, turn north on U.S. 101 and drive four miles to Mud Bay exit. Take that to Delphi Road and drive south for six miles to Waddell Creek Road (bear right at the junction). Continue straight on Waddell Creek Road for two miles to the Triangle (Waddell Creek Road turns into Sherman Valley Road). Continue straight on Sherman Valley Road for one mile (pavement ends, the road becomes C-Line Road) and continue two miles to Road D-3000. Turn right and drive three miles to the campground on the left.

Contact: Department of Natural Resources, Central Region, 1405 Rush Road, Chehalis, WA 98532-8763; tel. (360) 748-2383; fax (360) 748-2387.

11 Margaret McKenny   7

This camp is used primarily as a trailhead for horseback riders. This cool, scenic, streamside campground in Capitol Forest is managed by the Department of Natural Resources. Nearby trails can be used by hikers as well as horseback riders.

Location: In Capitol Forest; map B2, grid b1.

Campsites, facilities: There are 25 primitive sites for tents or small trailers; seven sites are walk-ins. Picnic tables, fire grills, and tent pads are provided. Pit toilets, a campfire circle, and a horse-loading ramp are available, but there is no drinking water. Leashed pets are permitted.

Reservations, fees: No reservations; no fee. Open April through October.

Directions: From Olympia on Interstate 5, drive south for about 10 miles to Exit 95 and Highway 121. Turn west on Highway 121 and drive four miles to Littlerock. Continue west for one mile to Waddell Creek Road. Turn right and drive 2.5 miles and look for the campground entrance road on the left.

Contact: Department of Natural Resources, Central Region, 1405 Rush Road, Chehalis, WA 98532-8763; tel. (360) 748-2383; fax (360) 748-2387.

12 Olympia Campground   7

This campground in a natural, wooded setting has all the comforts. Nearby recreation options include an 18-hole golf course, hiking trails, marked bike trails, and tennis courts.

Location: Near Olympia; map B2, grid b2.

Campsites, facilities: There are 95 sites for tents, trailers, or RVs of any length; 40 are drive-through, 29 of which are full hookups and 41 with electricity and water. Two cabins are also available. Drinking water and picnic tables are provided. Flush toilets, bottled gas, a gas station, sanitary services, showers, a recreation hall, TV hookups, a store, laundry facilities, ice, a playground, a heated swimming pool in the summer, and firewood are available. A cafe is located within two miles. Leashed pets and motorbikes are permitted.

Reservations, fees: Reservations accepted. Sites are $18-24 per night for two people, plus $4 for each additional person; cabins are $35 per night for two people. Open year-round.

Directions: From Olympia on Interstate 5, take Exit 101 to Airdustrial Way. Bear east for one-quarter mile to Center Street. Turn right on Center Street and drive one mile to 83rd Avenue. Turn right on 83rd Avenue and drive an eighth of a mile to the park on the left.

Contact: Olympia Campground, 1441 83rd Avenue SW, Olympia, WA 98512; tel. (360) 352-2551.

13 Martin Way Mobile Home and RV Park   2

This park, oriented to campers 55 and older, is in urban Olympia. Nearby recreation options include an 18-hole golf course, a full-service marina, tennis courts, and the Nisqually National Wildlife Refuge, home to seven miles of foot trails and a great variety of plant and animal life.

Location: In Olympia; map B2, grid b4.

Campsites, facilities: There are 18 sites for trailers or RVs of any length in this adult-oriented campground; seven sites are drive-through. Electricity, drinking water, and sewer and cable TV hookups are provided. Flush toilets, showers, and a laundry room are available. Bottled gas, sanitary services, a store, a cafe, and ice are located within one mile. No pets are allowed.

Reservations, fees: Reservations accepted. Sites are $13-21 per night. Open year-round.

Directions: From Interstate 5 in Olympia, take Exit 111 to Marvin Road. Drive south for one-quarter mile to Martin Way. Turn right (west) and drive two blocks to the park on the left.

Contact: Martin Way Mobile Home and RV Park, 8103 Martin Way SE, Lacey, WA 98516; tel. (360) 491-6840.

14 Columbus Park   7

This spot in a wooded area along the shore of Black Lake is an option to Salmon Shores Resort. Nearby recreation possibilities include an 18-hole golf course.

Location: On Black Lake; map B2, grid b2.

Campsites, facilities: There are 23 sites for trailers or RVs of any length. Electricity, drinking water, and picnic tables are provided. Flush toilets, sanitary services, a laundry room, ice, showers, firewood, a playground, boat docks, and launching facilities are available. Bottled gas, ice, and a store are within one mile; there is a restaurant within three miles. Leashed pets are permitted.

Reservations, fees: Reservations recommended. Sites are $15 per night. Open year-round.

Directions: From Interstate 5 in Olympia, take the U.S. 101 exit and drive 1.7 miles northwest to Black Lake Boulevard. Turn south on Black Lake Boulevard and drive 3.5 miles to park on the left.

Contact: Columbus Park, 5700 Black Lake Boulevard, Olympia, WA 98502; tel. (360) 786-9460; e-mail: columbusprk@earthnet.com.

15 Salmon Shores Resort

 7

This resort on Black Lake is a large, popular campground that comfortably accommodates tents and RVs alike. Sites are near the lakeshore. An 18-hole golf course, a full-service marina, and a riding stable are nearby. This is one of two camps in the immediate vicinity.

Location: On Black Lake; map B2, grid b2.

Campsites, facilities: There are 20 tent sites and 45 sites for trailers or RVs of any length. Electricity, drinking water, sewer hookups, and picnic tables are provided. Flush toilets, bottled gas, sanitary services, showers, a store, a laundry room, ice, firewood, a café, and a playground are available. Boat docks, launching facilities, and rentals are located four miles away. Leashed pets are permitted.

Reservations, fees: Reservations accepted. Sites are $13-16 per night; call for weekly and monthly rates. Open year-round.

Directions: From Interstate 5 in Olympia take the U.S. 101 exit and drive 1.7 miles northwest to Black Lake Boulevard. Turn south on Black Lake Boulevard and drive 3.5 miles to the resort.

Contact: Salmon Shores Resort, 5446 Black Lake Boulevard, Olympia, WA 98512; tel. (360) 357-8618.

16 American Heritage Campground   6

This spacious, wooded campground just off the highway is near lots of activities, including an 18-hole golf course, hiking trails, marked bike trails, and tennis courts. The park features novelty cycle rentals, free wagon rides, and free nightly movies. It's exceptionally clean and very pretty, making for a pleasant layover on your way up or down Interstate 5.

Location: Near Olympia; map B2, grid b2.

Campsites, facilities: There are 23 tent sites and 72 sites for tents, trailers or RVs of any length. Electricity, sewer hookups, Drinking water and picnic tables are provided. Electrical and sewer hookups, flush toilets, bottled gas, sanitary services, showers, a recreation hall, a group pavilion, recreation programs, a store, a laundry room, ice, a playground, a heated swimming pool, and firewood are available. Leashed pets are permitted.

Reservations, fees: Reservations accepted. Sites are $19-27 per night for two people, plus $4 for each additional person. Major credit cards accepted. Open Memorial Day through Labor Day weekend.

Directions: From Olympia on Interstate 5, drive five miles south to Exit 99. Take that exit and drive one-quarter mile east to Kimmie Street. Turn south on Kimmie Street and drive one-quarter mile to the campground.

Contact: American Heritage Campground, 9610 Kimmie Street SW, Olympia, WA 98512; tel. (360) 943-8778.

17 Nisqually Plaza RV Park

 5

This campground is located on McAlister Creek, where salmon fishing and boating are popular. Nearby recreation opportunities include an 18-hole golf course and the Nisqually National Wildlife Refuge, which offers seven miles of foot trails for viewing a great variety of flora and fauna.

Location: Near McAlister Creek; map B2, grid b3.

Campsites, facilities: There are 51 sites for trailers or RVs of any length; eight are drive-through sites. Electricity, drinking water, sewer hookups, telephone, cable TV, and picnic tables are provided. Flush toilets, bottled gas, sanitary services, a store, a cafe, a laundry room, ice, a playground, and a seasonal swimming pool are available. Some facilities are wheelchair accessible. Boat launching facilities are nearby. Leashed pets are permitted.

Reservations, fees: Reservations accepted. Sites are $10-20 per night. Open year-round.

Directions: In Olympia on Interstate 5, take Exit 114, turn right, and drive a short distance to Martin Way. Turn right and drive a short distance to the first road, a private access road for the park. Turn right and drive to the park.

Contact: Nisqually Plaza RV Park, 10220 Martin Way East, Olympia, WA 98516; tel. (360) 491-3831.

18 Rainbow Resort   8

This wooded park along the shore of Tanwax Lake has spacious, shady sites with views of mountains, forest, and lake. Highlights include good fishing, a seasonal fishpond, and a nearby riding stable.

Location: On Tanwax Lake; map B2, grid b6.

Campsites, facilities: There are about 50 sites for trailers or RVs up to 40 feet long. Electricity, drinking water, sewer hookups, and picnic tables are provided. Flush toilets, bottled gas, firewood, a recreation hall, showers, a store, a laundry room, a hot tub, ice, cable TV, boat docks, boat rentals, launching facilities, and a playground are available. A cafe is located within seven miles. Small leashed pets are permitted.

Reservations, fees: Reservations accepted. Sites are $21 per night. Open year-round.

Directions: From Tacoma on Interstate 5, drive south to Exit 127 and Highway 512. Turn east on Highway 512 and drive to Highway 161. Turn south Highway 161 and drive to Tanwax Drive. Turn east on Tanwax Drive and drive to the resort on Tanwax Lake.

Contact: Rainbow Resort, 34217 Tanwax Lake Court East, Eatonville, WA 98328; tel. (360) 879-5115.

19 Evans Creek   7

This primitive campground is located close to Evans Creek in an off-road-vehicle area near the northwestern corner of Mount Rainier National Park. If you're looking for a quiet, secluded spot, this isn't it. The two nearby roads that lead into the park are secondary or gravel roads and provide access to several other primitive camp-grounds and backcountry trails in the park. A national forest map details the back roads and hiking trails.

Location: On Evans Creek in Mount Baker-Snoqualmie National Forest; map B2, grid b8.

Campsites, facilities: There are 27 tent sites. Picnic tables, hand-pumped water, and fire grills are provided. Vault toilets are available, and downed firewood can be gathered. Leashed pets are permitted.

Reservations, fees: No reservations; no fee. Open mid-June to late September.

Directions: From Tacoma on Interstate 5, turn east on Highway 167 and drive nine miles to Highway 410. Continue 11 miles east on Highway 410 to the town of Buck-ley and Highway 165. Turn south on Highway 165 and drive 11 miles to Forest Road 7920. Turn left and drive 1.5 miles to the campground on the right.

Contact: Mount Baker-Snoqualmie National Forest, White River Ranger District, 450 Roosevelt Avenue East, Enumclaw, WA 98022; tel. (360) 825-6585; fax (360) 825-0660.

20 Ipsut Creek   7

This camp is at the end of Carbon River Road and at the beginning of several trails that lead into the backcountry of Mount Rainier National Park, past lakes, glaciers, waterfalls, and many other wonders. Obtain a map from the National Park Service for details, and get a wilderness permit if you plan to stay overnight in the backcountry.

Location: Near the Carbon River in Mount Rainier National Park; map B2, grid b8.

Campsites, facilities: There are 29 sites for tents and one group camp. Picnic tables are provided. Pit toilets are available, but there is no drinking water. Leashed pets are permitted in camp, but not on wilderness trails.

Reservations, fees: No reservations; no fee. Open Memorial Day to Labor Day.

Directions: From Puyallup drive east on Highway 167 and to Highway 410. Turn east on Highway 410 and drive 11 miles to the town of Buckley and Highway 165. Turn south on Highway 165 and drive to a fork with Carbon River Park Road. Bear left and drive five miles to the campground. Note: Due to flood damage the camp access road is open to high-clearance vehicles only.

Contact: Mount Rainier National Park, Tahoma Woods, Ashford, WA 98304; tel. (360) 569-2211.

21 North Creek   8

This little-known, wooded campground managed by the Department of Natural Resources is set along Cedar Creek. There are trails for hikers only. An option is vis-iting the Chehalis River, a short drive to the west. A canoe launch off U.S. 12 is avail-able north of Oakville.

Location: On Cedar Creek; map B2, grid c1.

Campsites, facilities: There are five primitive sites for tents or small trailers. Fire grills, and tent pads are provided. Vault toilets and drinking water are available. Mountain bikes are permitted on the roads only; trails are reserved for hikers. Leashed pets are permitted.

Reservations, fees: No reservations; no fee. Open April through October.

Directions: From Olympia drive south on Interstate 5 for 16 miles to U.S. 12. Turn west on U.S. 12 and drive 12 miles to Oakville. Continue west on U.S. 12 for 2.5 miles to D-Line Road (Cedar Creek entrance). Turn right (east) and drive 4.5 miles to the camp on the right (paved road all the way).

Contact: Department of Natural Resources, Central Region, 1405 Rush Road, Chehalis, WA 98532-8763; tel. (360) 748-2383; fax (360) 748-2387.

22 Sherman Valley   7

This is one of nine secluded camps located in Capitol Forest and managed by the Department of Natural Resources. Sherman Valley's pleasant, shady campsites are set along the shore of Porter Creek. Hiking trails can be found nearby.

Location: On Cedar Creek in Capitol Forest; map B2, grid c1.

Campsites, facilities: There are seven primitive sites for tents or small trailers and three walk-in sites. Picnic tables, fire grills, and tent pads are provided. Vault toilets and drinking water are available. Mountain bikes are permitted on the roads only; trails are reserved for hikers. Leashed pets are permitted.

Reservations, fees: No reservations; no fee. Open April through October.

Directions: From Olympia drive south on Interstate 5 for 16 miles to U.S. 12. Turn west on U.S. 12 and drive 12 miles to Oakville. Continue west on U.S. 12 for 2.5 miles to D-Line Road (Cedar Creek entrance). Turn right (east) and drive 6.5 miles to the camp on the right (paved road all the way).

Contact: Department of Natural Resources, Central Region, 1405 Rush Road, Chehalis, WA 98532-8763; tel. (360) 748-2383; fax (360) 748-2387.

23 Mima Falls Trailhead   10

A highlight here is the excellent loop trail for hikers and horseback riders that leads to beautiful Mima Falls. The campground is very quiet and pretty, which, when combined with the drinking water and free admission, makes this a first-rate choice. One of the unique qualities of this campground is that it provides facilities for both wheelchair users as well as for horseback riders. That means that wheelchair users with horses can access the wonderful five-mile loop trail to 90-foot Mima Falls. The trail runs across its brink.

Location: Near Mima Falls; map B2, grid c2.

Campsites, facilities: There is a primitive, dispersed camping area for about five tents or small trailers. Picnic tables, fire grills, and tent pads are provided. Vault toilets and a horse-loading ramp are available, but there is no drinking water. Leashed pets are permitted. The campground is wheelchair accessible.

Reservations, fees: No reservations; no fee. Open April through October.

Directions: From Olympia on Interstate 5, drive south for 10 miles to Highway 121. Turn west on Highway 121 and drive four miles west to Littlerock. Continue west for one mile to Mima Road. Turn left on Mima Road and drive 1.5 miles to Bordeaux Road. Turn right on Bordeaux Road and drive one-half mile to Marksman Road. Turn right and drive two-thirds of a mile to the campground access road on the left. Turn left and drive 200 yards to the campground.

Contact: Department of Natural Resources, Central Region, 1405 Rush Road, Chehalis, WA 98532-8763; tel. (360) 748-2383; fax (360) 748-2387.

24 Millersylvania State Park

 8

This popular park not too far from Olympia offers a host of activities, including swimming, trout fishing, hiking, and even a few gut-thumping fitness trails. The park is set along the shore of Deep Lake. Historic highlights are the groves of old-growth trees and the Civilian Conservation Corps buildings.

Location: On Deep Lake; map B2, grid c2.

Campsites, facilities: There are four primitive tent sites, 135 developed tent sites, and 52 sites for trailers or RVs up to 45 feet long. Picnic tables and fire grills are provided. Flush toilets, a sanitary disposal station, a playground, electricity, drinking water, showers, boat docks and launching facilities, and firewood are available. A store, a restaurant, and ice are located within one mile. Some facilities are wheelchair accessible. Leashed pets are permitted.

Reservations, fees: Reservations accepted; phone (800) 452-5687 ($6 reservation fee). Sites are $5-15 per night. Major credit cards accepted. Open year-round.

Directions: From Olympia on Interstate 5, drive south for 10 miles to Exit 95 and Highway 121. Turn east on Maytown Road (Highway 121) and drive to Tilley Road. Turn north and drive one-half mile to the park.

Contact: Millersylvania State Park, 1224 Tilley Road South, Olympia, WA 98502; tel. (800) 233-0321 or (360) 753-1519.

25 Offut Lake RV Resort 8

This lovely wooded campground is on Offut Lake, just enough off the beaten track to provide a bit of seclusion. Fishing, swimming, and boating are favorite activities here. Anglers will find everything they need, including tackle and boat rentals, at the resort.

Location: On Offut Lake; map B2, grid c3.

Campsites, facilities: There are 20 tent sites and 51 sites for trailers or RVs up to 40 feet in length; 35 sites have full hookups and 16 have electricity only. There are also four cabins. Picnic tables are provided. Flush toilets, sanitary services, firewood, a recreation hall, a store, a laundry room, ice, coin-operated showers, and a playground are available. Boat rentals and docks are available; no gas motors permitted. Showers can be obtained for an extra fee. Some facilities are wheelchair accessible. Leashed pets and are permitted.

Reservations, fees: Reservations accepted. Sites are $17-22 per night. Major credit cards accepted. Open year-round.

Directions: From Olympia on Interstate 5, drive south for seven miles to Exit 99. Take that exit and turn east on 93rd Avenue and drive four miles to Old Highway 99. Turn south and drive four miles to Offut Lake Road. Turn east and drive 1.5 miles to the resort.

Contact: Offut Lake RV Resort, 4005 120th Avenue SE, Tenino, WA 98589; tel. (360) 264-2438; website: www.kalama.com/~offutlake.

26 Henley's Silver Lake Resort

 8

This full-facility resort is a perfect family vacation destination. It's one of the rare private campgrounds that cater to tent campers and RV cruisers. Silver Lake is beautiful and stocked with trout. Highlights include a 250-foot boat dock and 50 rental rowboats.

Location: On Silver Lake; map B2, grid c6.

Campsites, facilities: There is a very large area for dispersed tent camping and 30 sites for trailers or RVs; 15 sites have full hookups. There are also six cabins. Rest rooms, a sanitary dump, a public phone, snacks, boat rentals, a boat ramp, and a dock are available. Leashed pets are permitted except in the cabins.

Reservations, fees: Reservations for cabins and full-hookup RV sites are accepted. Sites are $8-12 per night; cabins are $55 a night. Open the first day of the fishing season in April through October, weather permitting.

Directions: From Tacoma on Interstate 5, drive south for five miles to Highway 512. Turn east of Highway 512 and drive two miles to Highway 7. Turn south on Highway 7 and drive about 26 miles (two miles straight beyond the blinking light) to Silver Lake Road on the right (well signed). Turn right and drive one-quarter mile to the resort on the left.

Contact: Henley's Silver Lake Resort, 40718 South Silver Lake Road East, Eatonville, WA 98328; tel. (360) 832-3580.

27 Alder Lake Park   6

This municipal park along the shore of Alder Lake has pretty campsites near the water and lots of trees and shrubbery. It's a very decent spot to spend a weekend, especially if you want to get off the highway and enjoy some peace and quiet. The Mount Rainier Scenic Railroad leaves from Elbe regularly and makes its way through the forests to Mineral Lake. It features open deck cars, live music, and restored passenger cars.

Location: On Alder Lake; map B2, grid c6.

Campsites, facilities: There 16 tent sites and 87 sites for trailers or RVs of any length, 37 are full hookups, 25 have water and electricity only, with flush toilets and showers available. In the boathouse campground there are 24 sites with drinking water and electricity only. Vault and flush toilets and showers are available. Boat docks and launching facilities are on Alder Lake.

Reservations, fees: Reservations accepted. Sites are $12-17 per night. Open year-round, excluding December 20 through January 2.

Directions: From Chehalis drive south on Interstate 5 for 10 miles to U.S. 12. Turn east and drive 31 miles to Morton and Highway 7. Turn north on Highway 7 and drive 17 miles to Elbe. Bear left on Highway 7 and drive to the park entrance road on the left (on the east shore of Alder Lake).

Contact: Alder Lake Park, Tacoma Power at 50324 School Road, Eatonville, WA 98328; tel. (360) 569-2778.

28 Rocky Point Campground   5

On the shores of Alder Lake, this campground serves as overflow for neighboring Alder Lake Park. It is one mile from the Mount Rainier Scenic Railroad, which leaves from Elbe regularly and makes its way through the forests to Mineral Lake. It features open deck cars, live music, and restored passenger cars.

Location: On Alder Lake; map B2, grid c6.

Campsites, facilities: There are 25 sites for RVs or trailers up to 40 feet in length. Drinking water and electricity are provided. Vault toilets and a boat ramp are available. Boat docks and launching facilities are nearby on Alder Lake.

Reservations, fees: No reservations. Sites are $16 per night. Open mid-May through mid-September.

Directions: From Chehalis drive south on Interstate 5 for 10 miles to U.S. 12. Turn east and drive 31 miles to Morton and Highway 7. Turn north on Highway 7 and drive 17 miles to Elbe. Bear left on Highway 7 and drive to the park entrance road on the left (on the east shore of Alder Lake).

Contact: Rocky Point Campground, Tacoma Power at 50324 School Road, Eatonville, WA 98328; tel. (360) 569-2778.

29 Eagle's Nest Motel-Alder Lake
   8

This wooded RV park overlooking Alder Lake is a cozy little spot with all the amenities. It's a smaller, more secluded option for RVs, yet still close to Tacoma. See Alder Lake Park for information on the Mount Rainier Scenic Railroad.

Location: On Alder Lake; map B2, grid c6.

Campsites, facilities: There are 10 sites for trailers or RVs up to 25 feet long. Electricity, drinking water, and sewer hookups are provided. Boat launching facilities are located on Alder Lake. Small, leashed pets are permitted.

Reservations, fees: Reservations accepted. Sites are $15 per night. Major credit cards accepted. Open year-round.

Directions: From Chehalis drive south on Interstate 5 for 10 miles to U.S. 12. Turn east and drive 31 miles to Morton and Highway 7. Turn north on Highway 7 and drive 17 miles to Elbe. Bear left on Highway 7 and drive to the RV park entrance road on the left (well signed).

Contact: Eagle's Nest Motel-Alder Lake, 52120 Mountain Highway East, Eatonville, WA 98328; tel. (360) 569-2533.

30 Sahara Creek Horse Camp   6

This is a pretty camp set near the foot of Mount Rainier with multiple horse trailheads and a host on site.

Location: Near Elbe; map B2, c7.

Campsites, facilities: There are 18 tent sites. Picnic tables and fire pits are provided. A covered pavilion, vault toilets, and corrals are available, but there is no drinking water. Leashed pets are permitted.

Reservations, fees: No reservations; no fee. Open year-round.

Directions: From Chehalis drive south on Interstate 5 for 10 miles to U.S. 12. Turn east and drive 31 miles to Morton and Highway 7. Turn north on Highway 7 and drive 17 miles to Elbe and Highway 706. Turn east (right) and drive five miles to the campground on the left.

Contact: Department of Natural Resources, South Puget Sound Region, P.O. Box 68, Enumclaw, WA 98022-0068; tel. (360) 825-1631; fax (360) 825-1672.

31 Elbe Hills   6

Here's a spot for four-wheel-drive cowboys. The Department of Natural Resources manages this wooded campground and provides eight miles of trails for short-wheelbase four-wheel-drive vehicles. Beware: Trucks often get stuck here or can't make it up the hills when it's wet and slippery, which, of course, they love.

Location: Near Elbe; map B2, grid c7.

Campsites, facilities: There are three primitive campsites for tents or small trailers. Picnic tables, fire grills, and tent pads are provided. Pit toilets and a group shelter are available, but there is no drinking water. Leashed pets are permitted.

Reservations, fees: No reservations; no fee. Open year-round.

Directions: From Chehalis drive south on Interstate 5 for 10 miles to U.S. 12. Turn east and drive 31 miles to Morton and Highway 7. Turn north on Highway 7 and drive 17 miles to Elbe and Highway 706. Turn east (right) and drive six miles to a Department of Natural Resources access road on the left. Turn left and drive three miles. Bear right and continue one-half mile, then turn left and drive about 100 yards to the four-wheel-drive trailhead.

Contact: Department of Natural Resources, South Puget Sound Region, P.O. Box 68, Enumclaw, WA 98022-0068; tel. (360) 825-1631; fax (360) 825-1672.

32 Cougar Rock   9

Located at 3,180 feet at the foot of awesome Mount Rainier, this park provides a recreation program, and trout fishing is allowed without a permit. See Gateway Inn and RV Park for information on the nearby park sights and visitor centers.

Location: In Mount Rainier National Park; map B2, grid c9.

Campsites, facilities: There are 200 sites for tents or RVs up to 30 feet long. A group camp is also available. Picnic tables are provided. Flush toilets, drinking water, a camp store (two miles away), and a sanitary disposal station are available. Some facilities are wheelchair accessible. Leashed pets are permitted.

Reservations, fees: Reservations accepted up to five months in advance for the late June to early September season; phone (800) 365-CAMP (800-365-2267) or access the website: www.reservations.nps.gov. Sites are $12-14 per night. Major credit cards accepted. Open mid-May to mid-October.

Directions: From Tacoma on Interstate 5, drive south for five miles to Highway 512. Turn east of Highway 512 and drive two miles to Highway 7. Turn south on Highway 7 and drive to Elbe and Highway 706. Continue east on Highway 706 and drive 12 miles to the park entrance. Continue 11 miles to the campground entrance on the left (about two miles past the Longmire developed area).

Contact: Mount Rainier National Park, Tahoma Woods, Ashford, WA 98304; tel. (360) 569-2211; fax (360) 569-2170.

33 Rainbow Falls State Park   8

Although this campground is only about 20 minutes from Interstate 5, out-of-towners pass it every time. It's a nice spot, with a swinging bridge (built in 1934) over the Chehalis River, now closed to foot traffic due to flood damage. There is a pool at the base of Rainbow Falls for swimming and trout fishing, plus a playground for kids and 6.5 miles of hiking trails, including a self-guided nature trail through the old-growth forest.

Location: On the Chehalis River; map B2, grid d1.

Campsites, facilities: There are three primitive tent sites and 47 sites for tents or self-contained RVs up to 32 feet long. Picnic tables are provided. Flush toilets, drinking water, a sanitary disposal station, showers, firewood, and a playground are available. Leashed pets are permitted.

Reservations, fees: Reservations accepted. Sites are $5-10 per night. Open April through August.

Directions: From Chehalis on Interstate 5, take Exit 77 to Highway 6. Turn west and drive 17 miles to the park entrance.

Contact: Rainbow Falls State Park, 4008 Highway 6, Chehalis, WA 98532; tel. (800) 233-0321 or (360) 291-3767.

34 Stan Hedwall Park   5

This park along the Chehalis River is a possible layover for Interstate 5 travelers. Recreational opportunities include fishing, hiking, and golf (an 18-hole course and hiking trails are nearby).

Location: On the Chehalis River; map B2, grid d2.

Campsites, facilities: There are 29 sites for trailers or RVs of any length. Electricity, drinking water, and picnic tables are provided. Flush toilets, showers, sanitary services, and a playground are available. Bottled gas, a store, a cafe, and coin-operated laundry facilities are located within one mile. Leashed pets are permitted.

Reservations, fees: Reservations accepted. Sites are $15 per night. Open March through October.

Directions: Near Chehalis on Interstate 5, take Exit 76 to Rice Road. Turn south and drive one-eighth mile to the park.

Contact: Stan Hedwall Park, P.O. Box 871, Chehalis, WA 98532; tel. (360) 748-0271; fax (360) 748-6993.

35 Peppertree West RV Park   5

If you're driving Interstate 5 and looking for a stopover, this spot is a good choice for tent campers or RVers. Surrounded by Chehalis Valley farmland, it's near an 18-hole golf course, hiking trails, and tennis courts.

Location: In Centralia; map B2, grid d2.

Campsites, facilities: There are 20 tent sites and 42 sites for trailers or RVs of any length; 28 are drive-through sites, and 25 of these are full hookups. Electricity, drinking water, and cable TV are provided. Flush toilets, sanitary services, showers, a recreation hall, a laundry room, ice, bottled gas, a store, and a cafe are available. Boat launching facilities are nearby. Leashed pets and motorbikes are permitted.

Reservations, fees: Reservations accepted. Sites are $16-20 per night. Major credit cards accepted. Open year-round.

Directions: From Centralia on Interstate 5, take Exit 81 to Melon Street. Turn west and then take the first left to the park (located in the southeast corner of Centralia).

Contact: Peppertree West RV Park, 1208 Alder Street, Centralia, WA 98531; tel. (360) 736-1124.

36 Alder Lake   7

This campground is on the shore of Alder Lake in an area managed by the Department of Natural Resources. It's a nice, forested camp with good fishing nearby. Another recreation option is the Mount Rainier Scenic Railroad, which travels from Elbe through the forests to Mineral Lake.

Location: On Alder Lake; map B2, grid d6.

Campsites, facilities: There are 27 sites for tents or small trailers and one group site which can accommodate up to 100 campers. Picnic tables, fire grills, and tent pads are provided. Vault toilets, drinking water, a group shelter, and a boat launch are available. Leashed pets are permitted.

Reservations, fees: Reservations required for the group site only; phone (800) 527-3305, extension 111. There is no fee, but there is a limit of two vehicles per family site. Open late May to mid-September.

Directions: From Chehalis drive south on Interstate 5 for 10 miles to U.S. 12. Turn east and drive 31 miles to Morton and Highway 7. Turn north on Highway 7 and drive 15 miles (two miles west of Elbe) to Pleasant Valley Road. Turn left on Pleasant Valley Road and drive four miles to the camp at the end of the road.

Contact: Department of Natural Resources, Central Region, 1405 Rush Road, Chehalis, WA 98532-8763; tel. (360) 748-2383; fax (360) 748-2387.

37 Gateway Inn and RV Park   8

This wooded park is very close to Mount Rainier, one of the most spectacular mountains in the hemisphere. After entering at the Nisqually (southwestern) entrance to Mount Rainier National Park and driving on Nisqually Paradise Road for about five miles, you'll find the Longmire Visitor Center, which offers general park information and exhibits about the plants and geology of the area. Continuing into the park for 10 more miles, you'll arrive at the Paradise Visitor Center, which has more exhibits and an observation deck. This is the only road into the park that's open year-round.

Location: Near Mount Rainier National Park; map B2, grid d8.

Campsites, facilities: There is a dispersed area which can accommodate seven tents and 16 sites for trailers or RVs of any length; eight have full hookups. There are also nine cabins. Electricity, drinking water, and picnic tables are provided. Vault toilets, restaurant, and a mini-mart are available. Leashed pets are permitted.

Reservations, fees: Reservations accepted. Sites are $8-15 per night; cabins are $59 per night for two people, plus $10 for each additional person. Major credit cards accepted. Open April through September.

Directions: From Chehalis drive south on Interstate 5 for 10 miles to U.S. 12. Turn east and drive 31 miles to Morton and Highway 7. Turn north on Highway 7 and drive 17 miles to Elbe and Highway 706. Turn east on Highway 706 and drive 12 miles to the campground on the right. This park is located 100 feet from the south-western entrance to Mount Rainier National Park.

Contact: Gateway Inn and RV Park, 38820 Highway 706 East, Ashford, WA 98304; tel. (360) 569-2506.

38 Mounthaven at Cedar Park   6

A creek runs through this wooded campground within one-half mile of the Nisqually entrance to Mount Rainier National Park. See the description of Gateway Inn and RV Park for information about the national park.

Location: Near Mount Rainier National Park; map B2, grid d8.

Campsites, facilities: There is one tent site, 17 for trailers or RVs of any length, and 11 furnished cabins. Electricity, drinking water, and sewer hookups are provided. Flush toilets, showers, a laundry room, firewood, ice, and a playground are available. A restaurant and a store are within one mile. Leashed pets are permitted.

Reservations, fees: Reservations accepted. Sites are $20 per night; cabins are $65-180 per night. Open year-round.

Directions: From Chehalis drive south on Interstate 5 for 10 miles to U.S. 12. Turn east and drive 31 miles to Morton and Highway 7. Turn north on Highway 7 and drive 17 miles to Elbe and Highway 706. Turn east on Highway 706 and drive to Ashford and continue for 4.5 miles to the campground on the right.

Contact: Mounthaven at Cedar Park, 38210 Highway 706 East, Ashford, WA 98304; tel. (360) 569-2594.

39 Sunshine Point   7

This is one of five campgrounds in Mount Rainier National Park near the Nisqually entrance. Ipsut Creek and Cougar Rock and White River and Ohanapecosh are the others. Sunshine Point is the only one that's open year-round. See the description of Gateway Inn and RV Park for information about nearby sights and facilities.

Location: In Mount Rainier National Park; map B2, grid d8.

Campsites, facilities: There are 18 sites for tents or RVs up to 25 feet long. Picnic tables are provided. Drinking water and pit toilets are available. Some facilities are wheelchair accessible. Leashed pets are permitted in the camp, but not on trails or in the wilderness.

Reservations, fees: Reservations accepted. Sites are $10 per night. Major credit cards accepted. Open year-round.

Directions: From Chehalis drive south on Interstate 5 for 10 miles to U.S. 12. Turn east and drive 31 miles to Morton and Highway 7. Turn north on Highway 7 and drive 17 miles to Elbe and Highway 706. Turn east on Highway 706 and drive 12 miles. The campground is just inside the park entrance.

Contact: Mount Rainier National Park, Tahoma Woods, Ashford, WA 98304; tel. (360) 569-2211; fax (360) 569-2170.

40 River Oaks RV Park    8

This camp is set right on the Cowlitz River, with opportunities for swimming, boating, and fishing. Every spring the river is the site of a big smelt run, and they come thick. Using a dip net, you can fill a five-gallon bucket with just a couple of dips.
Location: On the Cowlitz River; map B2, grid e2.
Campsites, facilities: There are 50 tent sites and 24 sites for trailers or RVs of any length with full hookups. Drinking water is provided. Flush toilets, showers, sanitary services, a laundry room, picnic tables, and ice are available. Bottled gas, a store, and a cafe are located within one mile. Boat launching facilities are nearby. Leashed pets and motorbikes are permitted.
Reservations, fees: Reservations accepted. Sites are $15-22 per night. Open year-round.
Directions: From Castle Rock on Interstate 5, take Exit 59 for Highway 506. Turn west on Highway 506 for one-third of a mile to the park.
Contact: River Oaks RV Park, 491 Highway 506, Toledo, WA 98591; tel. (360) 864-2895.

41 Lewis and Clark State Park   8

The highlight of this state park is an immense old-growth forest that contains some good hiking trails and a 1.5-mile nature trail. There is an interpretive center for Mount St. Helens, plus a kids' fishing pond stocked with trout.
Location: Near Chehalis; map B2, grid e3.
Campsites, facilities: There are 25 sites for tents or self-contained RVs. Picnic tables and fire grills are provided. Flush toilets, drinking water, firewood, and a playground are available. Leashed pets are permitted.
Reservations, fees: No reservations. Sites are $10 per night. Open year-round.
Directions: From Chehalis drive south on Interstate 5 to Exit 68 and U.S. 12. Drive east on U.S. 12 for three miles to Jackson Highway. Turn right and drive two miles to the park entrance on the right.
Contact: Lewis and Clark State Park, 4583 Jackson Highway, Winlock, WA 98596; tel. (800) 233-0321 or (360) 864-2643.

42 Mayfield Lake County Park
      7

This camp has a relaxing atmosphere and comfortable, wooded sites. Recreational activities include waterskiing, fishing, swimming, and boating. A great side trip is touring nearby Mount St. Helens.
Location: On Mayfield Lake; map B2, grid e4.
Campsites, facilities: There are 54 sites for tents, trailers, or self-contained RVs. Rest rooms, showers, a public phone, and a barbecue are available. A sanitary dump station is located within one-half mile. Facilities are wheelchair accessible. Leashed pets are permitted.

Reservations, fees: Reservations recommended. Sites are $11 per night. Open May through September.

Directions: From Longview on Interstate 5, drive north to Exit 68 and U.S. 12. Turn east on U.S. 12 and drive 11 miles. Look for the campground entrance signs on the left.

Contact: Mayfield Lake County Park, 180 Beach Road, Mossyrock, WA 98564; tel. (360) 985-2364.

43 Winston Creek   7

This popular rustic campground has a Douglas fir forest and stream. Activities are fishing or a walk through the woods. It's peaceful with lots of wildlife. If you really like the woods, this is your place.

Location: On Winston Creek; map B2, grid e5.

Campsites, facilities: There are 11 tent sites. Picnic tables and fire pits are provided. Drinking water, a vault toilet, and garbage bins are available. Leashed pets are permitted.

Reservations, fees: No reservations; no fee. There is a seven-day stay limit. Open April through October.

Directions: From Longview on Interstate 5, drive north to Exit 68 and U.S. 12. Turn east on U.S. 12 and drive 15 miles to Winston Creek Road between mileposts 82 and 83. Turn south onto Winston Creek Road and drive about 3.5 miles to Longbell Road. Turn left on Longbell Road and drive one mile to the campground on the right.

Contact: Department of Natural Resources, Central Region, 1405 Rush Road, Chehalis, WA 98532-8763; tel. (360) 748-2383; fax (360) 748-2387.

44 Harmony Lakeside RV Park   6

This park on Mayfield Lake offers numerous recreational activities, including fishing, boating, and a lake view from some sites. Ike Kinswa State Park is a nearby option.

Location: Near Mayfield Lake; map B2, grid e4.

Campsites, facilities: There are 80 sites for trailers or RVs of any length; 48 are full-hookup sites, and the rest have water and electricity only. Flush toilets, sanitary services, ice, a pay phone, boat docks, and launching facilities are available. Showers, firewood, and ice are available for a fee. Leashed pets and motorbikes are permitted.

Reservations, fees: Reservations preferred. Sites are $19-21 per night; call for monthly rates. Open year-round.

Directions: From Longview on Interstate 5, drive north to Exit 68 and U.S. 12. Turn east on U.S. 12 and drive 21 miles to Silver Creek Road (Highway 122). Turn north and drive 2.3 miles to the park.

Contact: Harmony Lakeside RV Park, 563 Highway 122, Silver Creek, WA 98585; tel. (360) 983-3804; e-mail: maynardt@i-link-2.net; website: www.gocampingamerica.com/harmonylakeside.

 8

ground covering 454 acres on the shore of Mayfield Lake is in the midst
...house of recreational possibilities, including hiking trails, driftwood
collecting, swimming, waterskiing, and boating. Fishing for rainbow and silver
trout is a year-round affair here and can be quite good. Two fish hatcheries are located nearby. A spectacular view of Mount St. Helens can be found at a vista point
11 miles east. This is a very popular campground, and space is rarely available on
summer weekends. Be sure to reserve at least a month in advance.

Location: At Mayfield Lake; map B2, grid e5.

Campsites, facilities: There are two primitive tent sites, 60 developed tent sites, and
41 sites for trailers or RVs up to 60 feet long. Picnic tables and fire grills are provided. Flush toilets, a sanitary disposal station, a store, a cafe, a playground, drinking
water, showers, and firewood are available. Some facilities are wheelchair accessible. Boat docks and launching facilities are nearby. Leashed pets are permitted.

Reservations, fees: Reservations accepted; phone (800) 452-5687 ($6 reservation
fee). Sites are $5-16 per night. Major credit cards accepted. Open year-round.

Directions: From Longview on Interstate 5, drive north to Exit 68 and U.S. 12. Turn
east on U.S. 12 and drive 21 miles to Silver Creek Road (Highway 122). Turn north and
drive 3.5 miles to the park entrance.

Contact: Ike Kinswa State Park, 873 Harmony Road, Silver Lake, WA 98585; tel.
(800) 233-0321 or (360) 983-3402.

46 Redmon's RV Park  9

This is a clean, comfortable campground in a beautiful setting. Side trips include
visiting huge Riffe Lake to the southeast or driving up Strawberry Mountain or to the
edge of Mount St. Helens National Volcanic Monument (from Randle, head south on
Highway 26).

Location: Near Riffe Lake; map B2, grid e6.

Campsites, facilities: There are four drive-through sites for trailers or RVs of any
length. Electricity, drinking water, and sewer hookups are provided. Flush toilets,
bottled gas, sanitary services, a store, a nine-hole golf course, and ice are available. Some facilities are wheelchair accessible. Leashed pets are permitted.

Reservations, fees: Reservations accepted. Sites are $20 per night. Open year-round.

Directions: From Longview on Interstate 5, drive north to Exit 68 and U.S. 12. Turn east
on U.S. 12 and drive 50 miles to Glenoma. The park is in town along the highway.

Contact: Redmon's RV Park, 8136 Highway 12, Glenoma, WA 98336; tel. (360) 498-5425.

47 Maple Grove Campground and RV Park

 9

This RV park along the shore of the Cowlitz River offers views of snow-capped Mt.
Helens and is close to hiking trails. For an excellent drive, from the park head
along winding Highway 26, which starts at Randle and goes up to Strawberry Moun-

tain (elevation 5,464 feet). It's a good lookout point toward Mount St. Helens to the west.

Location: On the Cowlitz River; map B2, grid e8.

Campsites, facilities: There are 40 sites for tents, trailers, or RVs and about 54 full-hookup sites for trailers or RVs of any length (44 are drive-through sites). Electricity, drinking water, and picnic tables are provided. Flush toilets, sanitary services, firewood, a recreation hall, a store, a laundry room, showers, bottled gas, ice, and a playground are available. Restaurants are available within three miles. Leashed pets are permitted.

Reservations, fees: Reservations required. Sites are $12-20 per night. Open year-round, with limited winter facilities.

Directions: From Longview on Interstate 5, drive north to Exit 68 and U.S. 12. Turn east on U.S. 12 and drive 48 miles to Randle. The park is in town along the highway.

Contact: Maple Grove Campground and RV Park, P.O. Box 205, Randle, WA 98377; tel. (360) 497-2741.

48 Fox Store and RV Park

 7

This wooded park is about 400 yards from the Toutle River and one-half mile from the Cowlitz River. Take your pick. Seaquest State Park and Silver Lake to the east provide two excellent, activity-filled side-trip options.

Location: Near the Toutle River; map B2, grid f2.

Campsites, facilities: There are 52 sites for trailers or RVs of any length and a large dispersed tent camping area. Electricity, drinking water, sewer hookups, and picnic tables are provided. Flush toilets, showers, propane, coin-operated laundry facilities, a store with video rentals and ice are available. Boat launching facilities are nearby. Leashed pets and motorbikes are permitted.

Reservations, fees: Reservations accepted. Sites are $12-18 per night. Major credit cards accepted. Open year-round.

Directions: From Longview on Interstate 5, drive 10 miles north to Castle Rock and Exit 52. Take Exit 52 and drive 100 yards east to the park.

Contact: Fox Store and RV Park, 112 Burma Road, Castle Rock, WA 98611; tel. (360) 274-6785.

49 Mount St. Helens RV Park

 9

Though this cozy park just outside of Castle Rock is close to the highway, it has a secluded feel. Fishing and boating are available nearby on Silver Lake. A good side trip is touring Mount St. Helens. The park is located only three miles from the Mount St. Helens Visitor Center.

Location: Near Silver Lake; map B2, grid f2.

Campsites, facilities: There are approximately 90 sites for tents, trailers, or RVs with full or partial hookups. Cable TV, rest rooms, showers, propane, coin-operated laundry facilities, a sanitary dump, a public phone, and ice are available. Horseshoes, a recreation hall, and a playground are also provided. The facilities are wheelchair accessible. Leashed pets are permitted.

Reservations, fees: Reservations recommended in the summer; phone (360) 274-8522. Sites are $16-18 per night. Open year-round.

Directions: From Longview on Interstate 5, drive 10 miles north to Castle Rock and Exit 49 and Highway 504. Take Exit 49 and drive east on Highway 504 for two miles to Schaffran Road. Turn left (well signed) and drive to the park at the top of the hill.

Contact: Mount St. Helens RV Park, 167 Schaffran Road, Castle Rock, WA 98611; tel. (360) 274-8522.

50 Seaquest State Park   6

This state park is located across from Silver Lake, which is considered one of western Washington's premier bass, trout, and salmon fishing lakes. Other highlights include eight miles of hiking trails and the Mount St. Helens Interpretive Center, courtesy of the U.S. Forest Service. The park is popular for day use as well as camping; it's advisable to arrive early to claim a spot. This camp is filled nightly because it is set along the paved road to the awesome Johnston Ridge Observatory, the premier lookout of Mount St. Helens.

Location: Near Silver Lake; map B2, grid f3.

Campsites, facilities: There are four primitive tent sites and 92 sites for tents and self-contained RVs; 16 have full hookups. Drinking water and picnic tables are provided. Flush toilets, a playground, six horseshoe pits, a ball field, a sanitary disposal station, showers, and firewood are available. A store is within one mile. Some facilities are wheelchair accessible. Leashed pets are permitted.

Reservations, fees: Reservations accepted; phone (800) 452-5687 ($6 reservation fee). Sites are $5-16 per night. Major credit cards accepted. Open year-round.

Directions: From Longview on Interstate 5, drive 10 miles north to Castle Rock and Exit 49 and Highway 504. Take Exit 49 and drive east on Highway 504 for seven miles to the park.

Contact: Seaquest State Park, P.O. Box 3030, Spirit Lake Highway, Castle Rock, WA 98611; tel. (800) 233-0321 or (360) 274-8633.

51 Silver Lake Motel and Resort   9

This park is set along the shore of Silver Lake, one of Washington's better lakes for largemouth bass, trout, perch, crappie, bluegill, and salmon fishing. It's an excellent alternative to the more crowded campground at Seaquest State Park.

Location: On Silver Lake; map B2, grid f3.

Campsites, facilities: There are 13 tent sites and 22 sites for trailers or RVs of any length. Electricity, drinking water, sewer hookups, and picnic tables are provided. Flush toilets, a store, showers, ice, boat docks, boat rentals, launching facilities, and playground are available. Sanitary services are within one mile and a cafe within four miles. Leashed pets are permitted.

Reservations, fees: Reservations accepted. Sites are $14-20 per night. Major credit cards accepted. Open year-round.

Directions: From Longview on Interstate 5, drive 10 miles north to Castle Rock and

Exit 49 and Highway 504. Take Exit 49 and drive east on Highw[...]
the park on the right.

Contact: Silver Lake Motel and Resort, 3201 Spirit Lake High[...]
98645; tel. (360) 274-6141; fax (360) 274-2183.

52 Iron Creek   7

One of the more popular U.S. Forest Service campgrounds, this [...]
Cispus River near its confluence with Iron Creek. The camp is also located along the
access route that leads to the best viewing areas on the eastern flank for Mount St.
Helens, a breathtaking view of Spirit Lake and the blast zone of the volcano.

Location: On the Cispus River in Gifford Pinchot National Forest; map B2, grid f8.

Campsites, facilities: There are 98 sites for tents, trailers, or RVs. Drinking water
and picnic tables are provided. Vault toilets and firewood are available. Some facilities are wheelchair accessible. Leashed pets are permitted.

Reservations, fees: Some sites can be reserved by calling (877) 444-6777 or access the website: www.reserveusa.com ($8.65 reservation fee). Rates are $10
per night for a single site and $20 per night for a double site, plus $5 for each additional vehicle. Open mid-May to late October.

Directions: From Olympia on Interstate 5, drive south to Exit 68 and U.S. 12. Turn
east on U.S. 12 and drive 48 miles to Randle and Highway 131. Turn south and drive
one mile (it becomes Forest Road 25). Continue south on Forest Road 25 and drive
nine miles to a fork. Bear left at the fork, continue across the bridge, turn left and
drive two miles to the campground entrance on the left (along the south shore of the
Cispus river).

Contact: Gifford Pinchot National Forest, Cowlitz Ranger District, P.O. Box 670,
Randle, WA 98377; tel. (360) 497-1100; fax (360) 497-1102.

53 Green River Horse Camp   8

This camp is in an area of beautiful, old-growth timber. There is access to great
trails into the Mt. St. Helens blast area. Golden Mountain Trail is a loop of about 19
miles, and backcountry camping is another option. The lookout from Windy Ridge of
Spirit Lake with Mount St. Helens is one of the most drop-dead awesome views in
North America, of Spirit Lake, the blast zone and the open crater of Mount St. Helens.

Location: Near Spirit and Ryan Lakes, in Gifford Pinchot National Forest; map
B2, grid f9.

Campsites, facilities: There are eight sites, which can accommodate up to two
trailer rigs or three vehicles each. Camping is permitted in designated sites only.
Drinking water is available five miles north at Norway Pass Trailhead. Vault toilets,
fire rings, and picnic tables are provided. Call for current status of stock facilities.
Leashed pets are permitted.

Reservations, fees: No reservations; no fee. Donations accepted. Open year-
round, weather permitting.

Directions: From Olympia on Interstate 5, drive south to Exit 68 and U.S. 12. Turn
east on U.S. 12 and drive 48 miles to Randle and Highway 131. Turn south and drive
one mile (It becomes Forest Road 25). Turn south and drive 18 miles (it becomes For-

26) to Forest Road 99. Turn west (toward Windy Ridge) and 8.5 miles to For-
Road 26. Turn north and drive five miles to Forest Road 2612 (gravel). Turn west
d drive about two miles to the campground entrance on the left.
Contact: Gifford Pinchot National Forest, Mount St. Helens National Volcanic
Monument, 42218 N.E. Yale Bridge Road, Amboy, WA 98601; tel. (360) 247-3900; fax
(360) 247-3901.

54 Tower Rock   5

This campground along the Cispus River is an option to nearby and North Fork. It has
shaded and sunny sites, with lots of trees and plenty of room. Fishing is popular here.
Location: On the Cispus River in Gifford Pinchot National Forest; map B2, grid f8.
Campsites, facilities: There are 22 sites for tents, trailers, or RVs up to 21 feet long.
Drinking water and picnic tables are provided. Vault toilets and firewood are available.
Leashed pets are permitted.
Reservations, fees: Reservations accepted; phone (877) 444-6777 or access the
website: www.reserveusa.com ($8.65 reservation fee). Sites are $9 per night, plus
$5 for each additional vehicle. Open mid-May to late September.
Directions: From Olympia on Interstate 5, drive south to Exit 68 and U.S. 12. Turn
east on U.S. 12 and drive 48 miles to Randle and Highway 131. Turn south and drive
one mile to Forest Road 23. Turn left on Forest Road 23 and drive eight miles to
the campground entrance road on the right.
Contact: Gifford Pinchot National Forest, Cowlitz Ranger District, P.O. Box 670,
Randle, WA 98377; tel. (360) 497-1100; fax (360) 497-1102.

55 Blue Lake Creek   7

This classic Washington hideaway along Blue Lake Creek is a good base camp for
the 3.5-mile hike to Blue Lake. The trailhead is about one-half mile from the camp.
There are also mountain biking and ORV trails.
Location: Near Blue Lake in Gifford Pinchot National Forest; map B2, grid f9.
Campsites, facilities: There are 11 sites for tents, trailers, or RVs up to 31 feet long.
Picnic tables are provided. A vault toilets and hand-pumped water are available.
Firewood can be gathered outside of the campground area. Leashed pets and mo-
torbikes are permitted.
Reservations, fees: Reservations accepted. Sites are $8 per night, plus $5 for
each additional vehicle. Open mid-May to late October.
Directions: From Olympia on Interstate 5, drive south to Exit 68 and U.S. 12. Turn
east on U.S. 12 and drive 48 miles to Randle and Highway 131. Turn south and drive
one mile to Forest Road 23. Turn south and drive about 10 miles to the campground.
Contact: Gifford Pinchot National Forest, Cowlitz Ranger District, P.O. Box 670,
Randle, WA 98377; tel. (360) 497-1100; fax (360) 497-1102.

56 North Fork   6

This campground along the North Cispus River offers fishing, as well as nature
trails, bike paths, and a scenic viewing area. A national forest map details the backcountry.

Location: On the Cispus River in Gifford Pinchot National Forest; map B2, grid f9.

Campsites, facilities: There are 33 sites for tents, trailers, or RVs up to 31 feet long. Drinking water and picnic tables are provided. Vault toilets and firewood are available. Leashed pets are permitted.

Reservations, fees: Reservations accepted. Sites are $9 per night, plus $5 for each additional vehicle. Open mid-May to late September.

Directions: From Olympia on Interstate 5, drive south to Exit 68 and U.S. 12. Turn east on U.S. 12 and drive 48 miles to Randle and Highway 131. Turn south and drive one mile to Forest Road 23. Turn south and drive 11 miles to the campground.

Contact: Gifford Pinchot National Forest, Cowlitz Ranger District, P.O. Box 670, Randle, WA 98377; tel. (360) 497-1100; fax (360) 497-1102.

57 Cedars RV Park   6

This private park surrounded by cedar forest provides a good stopover for Interstate 5 travelers looking for a spot near Kelso. Campsites are graveled and shady. The nearby Cowlitz River is a highlight, along with the park's natural setting.

Location: Near the Cowlitz River; map B2, grid g3.

Campsites, facilities: There are three tent sites and 25 full-hookup sites for trailers or RVs up to 36 feet in length; two are drive-through sites. Electricity, sewer and cable TV hookups, drinking water, and picnic tables are provided. Flush toilets, showers, sanitary services, and a laundry room are available. There is a mini-mart 1.5 miles away. Leashed pets and motorbikes are permitted.

Reservations, fees: Reservations accepted. Sites are $11-15 per night. Open year-round.

Directions: Near Kelso on Interstate 5, take Exit 46 to Headquarters Road. Drive east for 100 feet to Bond Road. Turn north and drive one-third mile to Beauvais Road. Turn east and drive 50 feet to the park on the right.

Contact: Cedars RV Park, 115 Beauvais Road, Kelso, WA 98626; tel. (360) 274-5136.

58 Oaks Trailer and RV Park   2

This park in an urban area near Kelso/Longview is a good layover spot if you're heading south on Interstate 5 to Oregon or west on Highway 4 to the coast. An 18-hole golf course and a full-service marina are close by.

Location: In Commerce; map B2, grid g2.

Campsites, facilities: There are 62 drive-through sites for trailers or RVs up to 30 feet long. Electricity, drinking water, and sewer hookups are provided. Flush toilets, sanitary services, showers, and a laundry room are available. Bottled gas, a store, and a cafe are located within one mile. Leashed pets are permitted.

Reservations, fees: Reservations accepted. Sites are $14.50 per night. Open year-round.

Directions: Near Longview on Interstate 5, take Exit 36 on Highway 432. Drive west on Highway 432 for 2.5 miles to Third Avenue. Turn left and drive one block to California. Turn right and drive a short distance to the park entrance.

Contact: Oaks Trailer and RV Park, 636 California Way, Longview, WA 98632; tel. (360) 425-2708; fax (360) 575-9987.

59 Lake Merrill   7

This is the best choice in the area for campers seeking a quiet setting. The campground is nestled in old-growth trees on the shore of Lake Merrill, very near Mount St. Helens. It's a free and often less-crowded alternative to the more developed parks in the area, especially along the main access roads to viewing areas of the volcano.
Location: Near Mount St. Helens; map B2, grid g6.
Campsites, facilities: There are 11 tent sites. Picnic tables, fire grills, and tent pads are provided. Vault toilets, a wheelchair-accessible vault toilet and campsite, firewood, and hand-pumped water are available. Boat launching facilities are located on Lake Merrill. Leashed pets are permitted.
Reservations, fees: No reservations; no fee. Open May through November, weather permitting.
Directions: From Woodland on Interstate 5, take Exit 21 for Highway 503. Drive east on Highway 503 for 23 miles to Highway 503 Spur. Drive northeast on Highway 503 Spur to Forest Road 81. Turn left on Forest Road 81 and drive 4.5 miles. Turn left on the access road and continue to the campground.
Contact: Department of Natural Resources, Southwest Region, P.O. Box 280, Castle Rock, WA 98611-0280; tel. (360) 577-2025 or (360) 274-4196.

60 Kalama Horse Camp   8

This is the most popular horse camp in the area with the enthusiastic volunteer support of local equestrians. Weekends are often full; come early. There are at least 56 miles of scenic horse trails. The camp is very near Mount St. Helens.
Location: Near Mount St. Helens; map B2, grid g6.
Campsites, facilities: There are at least 10 sites for tents, trailers, or RVs, six of which will accommodate two vehicles. Fire rings, picnic tables, and 10-foot-by-10-foot corrals are provided. A staging and mounting assist area with stock water, stock loading ramp, hitching rails, vault and composting toilets (one of which is wheelchair accessible) are available, but there is no drinking water. There is also a 24-by-36-foot log cabin shelter with a picnic table, a picnic area with horseshoe pits. Boat launching facilities are located on Lake Merrill. Leashed pets are permitted.
Reservations, fees: No reservations; no fee. Donations accepted. Open year-round, weather permitting.
Directions: From Woodland on Interstate 5, take Exit 21 for Highway 503. Drive east on Highway 503 and drive 23 miles to the Highway 503 spur. Continue northeast on Highway 503 spur to Forest Road 81 (at Yale Lake, one mile south of Cougar). Turn left on Forest Road 81 and drive about eight miles to the camp.
Contact: Gifford Pinchot National Forest, Mount St. Helens National Volcanic Monument, 42218 N.E. Yale Bridge Road, Amboy, WA 98601-0369; tel. (360) 247-3900; fax (360) 247-3901.

61 Lower Falls   10

This is one of the great spots in the Pacific Northwest. The camp is set in the primary viewing area for six major waterfalls on the Lewis River. The spectacular Lewis River Trail is available for hiking or horseback riding, and there is a wheelchair-accessible loop. Several other hiking trails in the area branch off along backcountry streams. See a U.S. Forest Service map for details. The elevation is 1,400 feet.

Location: On the Lewis River in Gifford Pinchot National Forest; map B2, grid g8.

Campsites, facilities: There are 42 sites for tents, trailers, or RVs up to 35 feet long. Composting toilets and drinking water are available. Leashed pets are permitted.

Reservations, fees: Reservations accepted. Rates are $12 per night for single sites, $18 per night for double sites, and $5 for each additional vehicle. Open May through September.

Directions: From Woodland on Interstate 5, take Exit 21 for Highway 503. Drive east on Highway 503 and drive 23 miles to Highway 503 Spur. Drive northeast on Highway 503 Spur for seven miles (the road becomes Forest Road 90). Continue east on Forest Road 90 for 21 miles to the campground along the Lewis River.

Contact: Gifford Pinchot National Forest, Mount St. Helens National Volcanic Monument, 42218 N.E. Yale Bridge Road, Amboy, WA 98601-0369; tel. (360) 247-3900; fax (360) 247-3901.

62 Lewis River Horse Camp   7

During the summer months, Memorial Day through Labor Day, the camp is reserved for equestrians only. The camp is not particularly scenic, but the area around it is. There are six waterfalls nearby on the Lewis River, for example. There are many trails, all of which are open to mountain bikers and some to motorcycles. The spectacular Lewis River Trail is available for hiking or horseback riding, and there is a wheelchair-accessible loop. Several other hiking trails in the area branch off along backcountry streams. See a U.S. Forest Service map for details.

Location: Near the Lewis River and Quartz Creek in Gifford Pinchot National Forest; map B2, grid g8.

Campsites, facilities: There are nine sites for tents, trailers, or RVs. Picnic tables, fire rings and hitching facilities (high lines) are provided. A composting toilet and stock water are available. No drinking water. Leashed pets are permitted.

Reservations, fees: No reservations; no fee. Donations accepted. Open year-round, weather permitting.

Directions: From Woodland on Interstate 5, take Exit 21 for Highway 503. Drive east on Highway 503 and drive 23 miles to Highway 503 Spur. Drive northeast on Highway 503 Spur for seven miles (the road becomes Forest Road 90). Continue east on Forest Road 90 for 21 miles, past the Pine River Information Station, to the campground along the Lewis River.

Contact: Gifford Pinchot National Forest, Mount St. Helens National Volcanic Monument, 42218 N.E. Yale Bridge Road, Amboy, WA 98601-0369; tel. (360) 247-3900; fax (360) 247-3901.

63 Louis Rasmussen RV Park

 7

This park in an urban area along the shore of the Columbia River is a perfect lay-over spot for Interstate 5 cruisers heading for Portland. Nearby recreation options include a full-service marina, day-use marine park, a walking trail and tennis courts.

Location: On the Columbia River; map B2, grid h3.

Campsites, facilities: There are 10 tent sites and 22 sites for trailers or RVs of any length. Electricity, drinking water and sewer hookups are provided in the RV sites. Flush toilets, drinking water, a dump station, and showers are available. Bottled gas, a store, a cafe, coin-operated laundry facilities, and ice are located within one mile. Boat docks and launching facilities are nearby. Some facilities are wheelchair accessible. Leashed pets and motorbikes are permitted.

Reservations, fees: Reservations accepted. Sites are $9-14 per night. Open year-round.

Directions: From Kalama (between Kelso and Woodland) on Interstate 5, take Exit 30, and drive west 100 feet to Hendrickson Drive. Turn south and drive one-half mile to the park.

Contact: Louis Rasmussen RV Park, P.O. Box 70, Kalama, WA 98625; tel. (360) 673-2626.

64 Woodland   7

This is an optimum spot for people who are touring Washington on Interstate 5 but want a quiet setting along the way. The campground is nestled in an area of ever-green and deciduous trees (maple and red alder), so it's private, yet near the main highway. It has playground equipment for the kids. A popular side trip is a visit to the Hulda Klager Lilac Gardens in Woodland.

Location: Near Woodland; map B2, grid i3.

Campsites, facilities: There are 10 sites for tents or small trailers. Picnic tables, fire grills, and tent pads are provided. Vault toilets, drinking water, firewood, horseshoe pits, volleyball and basketball courts, and a children's playground are available. Some facilities are wheelchair accessible. Leashed pets are permitted.

Reservations, fees: No reservations; no fee. Open May to September.

Directions: From Woodland on Interstate 5, take Exit 21 and drive east for 100 yards to East CC Street. Turn right and drive across the Lewis River to just south of the bridge to County Road 1. Turn right on County Road 1 and drive a quarter-mile to 389th Street. Turn left on 389th Street and drive 2.5 miles to the campground on the left.

Contact: Department of Natural Resources, Southwest Region, P.O. Box 280, Castle Rock, WA 98611-0280; tel. (360) 577-2025 or (360) 274-4196.

65 Camp Kalama RV and Campground

 6

This option to Louis Rasmussen RV Park has a rustic setting, with open and wooded areas and some accommodations for tent campers. It's set along the

Kalama River, where salmon and steelhead fishing is popular. A full-service marina is nearby.

Location: On the Kalama River; map B2, grid h3.

Campsites, facilities: There are 30 tent sites and 120 sites for trailers or RVs of any length; 17 are drive-through sites. Electricity, drinking water, sewer and cable TV hookups, and picnic tables are provided. Flush toilets, showers, bottled gas, sanitary services, a store, a cafe, a beauty shop, a recreation room, firewood, a laundry, ice, boat launching facilities, a beach area, and a playground are available. Some facilities are wheelchair accessible. Leashed pets and motorbikes are permitted.

Reservations, fees: Reservations accepted. Sites are $12-21 per night for two campers. Open year-round.

Directions: From near Kalama (between Kelso and Woodland) on Interstate 5, take Exit 32 and drive south on the frontage road for one block to the campground.

Contact: Camp Kalama RV and Campground, 5055 North Meeker Drive, Kalama, WA 98625; tel. (800) 750-2456 or (360) 673-2456; fax (360) 673-2324.

66 Lewis River RV Park   7

This park is along the Lewis River, where the salmon and steelhead can run thick in season. It's a pleasant camp, with a choice of paved or grassy shaded sites. An 18-hole golf course is nearby.

Location: On the Lewis River; map B2, grid h3.

Campsites, facilities: There are 90 sites for tents, trailers, or RVs of any length; five are drive-through sites. Electricity, drinking water, sewer hookups, and picnic tables are provided. Flush toilets, firewood, sanitary services, showers, a store, a laundry room, ice, and a swimming pool are available. Launching facilities are nearby on the Lewis River. Leashed pets are permitted.

Reservations, fees: Reservations accepted. Sites are $16-20 per night. Major credit cards accepted. Open year-round.

Directions: In Woodland on Interstate 5, take Exit 21 for Highway 503. Drive east on Highway 503 (Lewis River Road) for four miles to the park.

Contact: Lewis River RV Park, 3125 Lewis River Road, Woodland, WA 98674; tel. (360) 225-9556.

67 Lone Fir Resort   4

This private campground near Yale Lake (the smallest of four lakes in the area) is designed primarily for motor-home use, with grassy sites and plenty of shade trees. Mount St. Helens is a side trip option. The trailhead for the summit climb is nearby at Climber's Bivouac on the south flank of the volcano. Note: It is the only trailhead available for the summit climb. Summit permits are available at the store in Cougar, along the with a great little burger shop.

Location: Near Yale Lake; map B2, grid h6.

Campsites, facilities: There are eight tent sites and 17 sites for trailers or RVs of any length. Electricity, drinking water, sewer hookups, and picnic tables are provided. Flush toilets, a laundry room, a restaurant, showers, ice, and a swimming pool are available. Bottled gas, a store, and a cafe are within one mile. Boat docks and launching facilities are nearby. Pets and motorbikes are permitted.

Reservations, fees: Reservations accepted. Sites are $13-16 per night. Major credit cards accepted. Open year-round.

Directions: In Woodland on Interstate 5, take Exit 21 for Highway 503. Drive east on Highway 503 for 29 miles to Cougar and the resort turnoff (signed, in town, with the park visible from the road).

Contact: Lone Fir Resort, 16806 Lewis River Road, Cougar, WA 98616; tel. (360) 238-5210.

68 Paradise Creek   9

This alternative to the Beaver site lies deeper in Gifford Pinchot National Forest among old-growth woods at the confluence of Paradise Creek and the Wind River. Lava Butte is a short distance from the camp and is accessible by trail.

Location: On Paradise Creek and the Wind River in Gifford Pinchot National Forest; map B2, grid h8.

Campsites, facilities: There are 42 sites for tents, trailers, or RVs up to 25 feet long. Drinking water, fire grills, and picnic tables are provided. Vault toilets are available. One toilet is wheelchair accessible. Leashed pets are permitted.

Reservations, fees: Reservations accepted; phone (877) 444-6777 or access the website: www.reserveusa ($8.65 reservation fee). Sites are $9-18 per night, plus $5 for each additional vehicle. Open mid-May to mid-November.

Directions: From Vancouver, WA, on Interstate 205, take Highway 14 and drive east for 50 miles to Carson and the Wind River Highway (County Road 30). Turn north on the Wind River Highway and drive 20 miles (the road becomes Forest Road 30) to the camp on the right.

Contact: Gifford Pinchot National Forest, Wind River Ranger Work Center, 1262 Hemlock Road, Carson, WA 98610; tel. (509) 427-3200; fax (509) 427-3215.

69 Falls Creek Horse Camp   5

This camp with multiple horse trails is set along the Race Track Trail adjacent to the western border of Indian Heaven Wilderness. A wilderness trailhead is available right at the camp.

Location: Near the Pacific Crest Trail in Gifford Pinchot National Forest; map B2, grid h8.

Campsites, facilities: There are six sites for tents, trailers, or RVs up to 15 feet long. Picnic tables and fire grills are provided. Pit toilets and a stock loading ramp are available, but there is no drinking water. Leashed pets are permitted.

Reservations, fees: No reservations; no fee. Open mid-June to late September.

Directions: From Vancouver, WA, on Interstate 205, take Highway 14 and drive east for 50 miles to Carson and the Wind River Highway. Turn north on the Wind River Highway and drive six miles to Forest Road 65. Turn north and drive 15 miles to the campground.

Contact: Gifford Pinchot National Forest, Mount Adams Ranger District, 2455 Highway 141, Trout Lake, WA 98650; tel. (509) 395-3400; fax (509) 395-3424.

70 Smokey Creek   7

This primitive, little-used campground in an area of old-growth Douglas fir is set along Smokey Creek. A trail leading into the Indian Heaven Wilderness passes near the camp. Berry picking can be good here in season. See the description of Tillicum and Saddle and Walupt Horse Camp and Morrison Creek for details on the recreation options in the immediate area.

Location: Near the Indian Heaven Wilderness in Gifford Pinchot National Forest; map B2, grid h9.

Campsites, facilities: There are three sites for trailers or RVs up to 22 feet long. Picnic tables are provided. Pit toilets are available, but there is no drinking water. Leashed pets are permitted.

Reservations, fees: No reservations; no fee. Open June to late September.

Directions: From Vancouver, WA, on Interstate 205, take Highway 14 and drive east for 66 miles to Highway 141. Turn north on Highway 141 and drive 25 miles to Trout Lake and County Road 141 (Forest Road 24). Turn left (west) and drive two miles to a fork. Bear left at the fork and drive about 10 miles (the road becomes Forest Road 24) to the campground.

Contact: Gifford Pinchot National Forest, Mount Adams Ranger District, 2455 Highway 141, Trout Lake, WA 98650; tel. (509) 395-3400; fax (509) 395-3424.

71 Goose Lake   9

This beautiful campground is set at an elevation of 3,600 feet along the shore of Goose Lake and is the place for fishing and berry picking in the summer. The northern edge of Big Lava Bed is adjacent to the camp.

Location: On Goose Lake in Gifford Pinchot National Forest; map B2, grid h9.

Campsites, facilities: There are 25 tent sites and one site for trailers or RVs up to 18 feet long. Picnic tables and fire rings are provided. Vault toilets are available, but there is no drinking water. A boat ramp is nearby. Leashed pets are permitted.

Reservations, fees: Reservations accepted; phone (877) 444-6777 or access the website: www.reserveusa.com ($8.65 reservation fee). Sites are $11-13 per night, plus $5 for each additional vehicle. Open mid-June to late September.

Directions: From Vancouver, WA, on Interstate 205, take Highway 14 and drive east for 66 miles to Highway 141. Turn north on Highway 141 and drive 25 miles to Trout Lake and County Road 141 (Forest Road 24). Turn left (west) and drive two miles to a fork. Bear left at the fork and drive about seven miles to a fork with Forest Road 60. Bear left on Forest Road 60 and drive five miles west to the camp.

Contact: Gifford Pinchot National Forest, Mount Adams Ranger District, 2455 Highway 141, Trout Lake, WA 98650; tel. (509) 395-3400; fax (509) 395-3424.

72 Cultus Creek   7

Located at an elevation of 4,000 feet along Cultus Creek on the edge of the Indian Heaven Wilderness, this camp is close to trails that will take you into the backcountry, which has numerous small meadows and lakes among the old-growth stands of fir and pines. Horse trails can be found as well. It is about a two-mile climb to access the Pacific Crest Trail. Evening programs are conducted by the campground hosts, and there are huckleberries in season.

Location: Near the Indian Heaven Wilderness in Gifford Pinchot National Forest; map B2, grid h9.

Campsites, facilities: There are 43 sites for tents, trailers, or RVs up to 32 feet long. Drinking water, picnic tables, and fire rings are provided. Vault toilets and firewood are available. Some facilities are wheelchair accessible. Leashed pets are permitted.

Reservations, fees: Reservations accepted; phone (877) 444-6777 or access the website: www.reserveusa.com ($8.65 reservation fee). Rates are $11-22 per night and $5 for each additional vehicle. Open June through September.

Directions: From Vancouver, WA, on Interstate 205, take Highway 14 and drive east for 66 miles to Highway 141. Turn north on Highway 141 and drive 25 miles to Trout Lake and County Road 141 (Forest Road 24). Turn left (west) and drive two miles to a fork. Bear left at the fork and drive about 15 miles (the road becomes Forest Road 24) to the campground.

Contact: Gifford Pinchot National Forest, Mount Adams Ranger District, 2455 Highway 141, Trout Lake, WA 98650; tel. (509) 395-3400; fax (509) 395-3424.

73 Tillicum   8

This pretty camp is primitive but well forested and within walking distance of a number of recreation options. A trail from the camp leads southwest past little Meadow Lake to Squaw Butte, then over to Big Creek. Give it a try; it's a nice hike, as well as an excellent ride for mountain bikers. This is a premium area for picking huckleberries in August and early September. The Lone Butte Wildlife Habitat Area to the south provides a great side trip.

Location: Near Meadow Lake in Gifford Pinchot National Forest; map B2, grid h9.

Campsites, facilities: There are eight sites for tents only and 37 sites for tents, trailers, or RVs up to 18 feet long. Drinking water, picnic tables, and fire rings are provided. Pit toilets and firewood are available. Leashed pets are permitted.

Reservations, fees: No reservations; no fee. Open mid-June to late September.

Directions: From Vancouver, WA, on Interstate 205, take Highway 14 and drive east for 66 miles to Highway 141. Turn north on Highway 141 and drive 25 miles to Trout Lake and County Road 141 (Forest Road 24). Turn left (west) and drive two miles to a fork. Bear left at the fork and drive 20 miles (the road becomes Forest Road 24) to the campground.

Contact: Gifford Pinchot National Forest, Mount St. Helens National Volcanic Monument, 42218 N.E. Yale Bridge Road, Amboy, WA 98601; tel. (360) 247-3900; fax (360) 247-3901.

74 Little Goose   5

This campground is near Little Goose Creek and the backcountry of the Indian Heaven Wilderness. See the description of Tillicum and Saddle in this chapter, and Walupt Horse Camp and Morrison Creek in Chapter B3 for details of the area. Since this camp has drinking water, it gets heavier use than most of the others in the immediate vicinity, though it's close to the road and sometimes dusty. Huckleberry picking is quite good in August and early September.

Location: On Little Goose Creek in Gifford Pinchot National Forest; map B2, grid h9.

Campsites, facilities: There are 28 sites for tents, trailers, or RVs up to 18 feet long. Drinking water, picnic tables, and fire rings are provided. Pit toilets are available. Leashed pets are permitted.

Reservations, fees: No reservations; no fee. Open June to late September.

Directions: From Vancouver, WA, on Interstate 205, take Highway 14 and drive east for 66 miles to Highway 141. Turn north on Highway 141 and drive 25 miles to Trout Lake and County Road 141 (Forest Road 24). Turn left (west) and drive two miles to a fork. Bear left at the fork (the road becomes Forest Road 24) and drive 11 miles (one mile past Smokey Creek) to the campground.

Contact: Gifford Pinchot National Forest, Mount Adams Ranger District, 2455 Highway 141, Trout Lake, WA 98650; tel. (509) 395-3400; fax (509) 395-3424.

75 Little Goose Horse Camp   7

Vertical clearance can be a problem here due to overhanging trees. Four trails are accessible from the camp; two are for hiking and horses only. There are faucets, but check to see if the water is currently potable; bring your own if in doubt.

Location: Near Little Goose Creek in Gifford Pinchot National Forest; map B2, grid h9.

Campsites, facilities: There are three sites for tents, trailers, or RVs. Stock water is generally available in the creek, but there is no drinking water. Picnic tables and fire rings are provided. A vault toilet is available. Leashed pets are permitted.

Reservations, fees: No reservations; no fee. Open June to late September.

Directions: From Vancouver, WA, on Interstate 205, take Highway 14 and drive east for 66 miles to Highway 141. Turn north on Highway 141 and drive 25 miles to Trout Lake and County Road 141 (Forest Road 24). Turn left (west) and drive two miles to a fork. Bear left at the fork (the road becomes Forest Road 24) and drive 11 miles (one mile past Smokey Creek) to the campground on the left.

Contact: Gifford Pinchot National Forest, Mount Adams Ranger District, 2455 Highway 141, Trout Lake, WA 98650; tel. (509) 395-3400; fax (509) 395-3424.

76 Saddle   5

This rustic site receives relatively little use. There are two lakes nearby, Big and Little Mosquito Lakes, which are fed by Mosquito Creek. So, as long as we're on the subject, mosquito attacks in late spring and early summer can be like squadrons of World War II bombers moving in. The Pacific Crest Trail passes right by camp. The area is known for premium huckleberry picking in August and early September.

Location: Near Mosquito Lakes in Gifford Pinchot National Forest; map B2, grid h9.

Campsites, facilities: There are 12 tent sites. Picnic tables and fire rings are provided. Drinking water, pit toilets, and firewood are available. Leashed pets are permitted.

Reservations, fees: No reservations; no fee. Open mid-June to late September.

Directions: From Vancouver, WA, on Interstate 205, take Highway 14 and drive east for 66 miles to Highway 141. Turn north on Highway 141 and drive 25 miles to

Trout Lake and County Road 141 (Forest Road 24). Turn left (west) and drive two miles to a fork. Bear left at the fork (the road becomes Forest Road 24) and drive 19 miles to Forest Road 2480. Turn right and drive one mile to the campground.

Contact: Gifford Pinchot National Forest, Mount St. Helens National Volcanic Monument, 42218 N.E. Yale Bridge Road, Amboy, WA 98601; tel. (360) 247-3900 or (360) 247-3901.

77 Paradise Point State Park   8

Good fishing is a bonus at this campground on the East Fork of the Lewis River. An 18-hole golf course and a two-mile hiking trail are some of the recreation possibilities. This is a good RV layover for Interstate 5 travelers, but it does fill up quickly, so plan on arriving early in the day.

Location: On the East Fork of the Lewis River; map B2, grid i4.

Campsites, facilities: There are nine primitive tent sites and 70 sites for tents or self-contained RVs up to 45 feet long. Drinking water, fire grills, and picnic tables are provided. Flush toilets, sanitary services, firewood, and showers are available. Boat launching facilities are located nearby on the East Fork of the Lewis River. Leashed pets are permitted.

Reservations, fees: Reservations accepted; phone (800) 452-5687 ($6 reservation fee). Sites are $5-10 per night. Major credit cards accepted. Open year-round.

Directions: From Vancouver, WA, on Interstate 5, drive north on Interstate 5 for 15 miles to Paradise Point State Park exit. Take that exit and follow the signs to the campground.

Contact: Paradise Point State Park, Route 1, P.O. Box 33914, Ridgefield, WA 98642; tel. (800) 233-0321 or (360) 263-2350.

78 Big Fir Campground and RV Park
   6

This campground is in a heavily wooded, rural area not far from Paradise Point State Park. It's nestled among hills with shaded gravel sites and wild berries. See the description of Paradise Point State Park for details on the area.

Location: Near Paradise Point State Park; map B2, grid i4.

Campsites, facilities: There are 33 tent sites and 37 sites for trailers or RVs of any length; three are drive-through sites. Electricity, drinking water, sewer hookups, and picnic tables are provided. Flush toilets, sanitary services, showers, a store, and ice are available. Boat launching facilities are located within 1.5 miles. Leashed pets and motorbikes are permitted.

Reservations, fees: Reservations accepted. Sites are $12-18.50 per night. Open year-round.

Directions: From Vancouver, WA, on Interstate 5, drive north on Interstate 5 to Exit 14 (Ridgefield exit). Take that exit to Highway 269. Drive east on Highway 269 (the road changes names several times) for two miles to 10th Avenue. Turn right and drive to the first intersection at 259th Street. Turn left and drive two miles to the park on the right (route is well signed).

Contact: Big Fir Campground and RV Park, 5515 N.E. 259th Street, Ridgefield, WA 98642; tel. (800) 532-4397 or (360) 887-8970.

79 Battle Ground Lake State Park

      8

This state park has horseback riding trails and some primitive campsites that will accommodate campers with horses. The lake is good for swimming and fishing, and it has a nice beach area; no motorized boats are allowed. If you're traveling on Interstate 5 and looking for a layover, this camp 15 minutes from the highway is ideal. In July and August, there are several local fairs and celebrations. Like many of the easy-access state parks on Interstate 5, it fills up quickly on weekends.

Location: On Battle Ground Lake; map B2, grid i5.

Campsites, facilities: There are 15 primitive tent sites and 35 sites for tents or self-contained RVs up to 50 feet long. Drinking water, fire grills, and picnic tables are provided. Flush toilets, a sanitary disposal station, showers, a store, firewood, a restaurant, and a playground are available. Some facilities are wheelchair accessible. Boat launching facilities and rentals are nearby. Leashed pets are permitted.

Reservations, fees: Reservations accepted; phone (800) 452-5687 ($6 reservation fee). Sites are $5-10 per night. Major credit cards accepted. Open year-round.

Directions: From Vancouver, WA, drive north on Highway 503 for 15 miles to the Battle Ground crossroads and Main Street. Turn right (east) and drive under two miles to N.E. 142nd Avenue. Turn left and drive a half mile to Heisson Road. Turn right and drive three miles to the park entrance on the left (route well signed).

Contact: Battle Ground Lake State Park, 17612 N.E. Palmer Road, Battle Ground, WA 98604; tel. (800) 233-0321 or (360) 687-4621.

80 Sunset

     9

This campground is located at an elevation of 1,000 feet along the East Fork of the Lewis River. Fishing, hiking, huckleberry picking, and mushroom hunting are some of the favored pursuits of visitors. Scenic Sunset Falls is located just upstream of the campground. A barrier-free viewing trail leads to an overlook.

Location: On the East Fork of the Lewis River in Gifford Pinchot National Forest; map B2, grid i6.

Campsites, facilities: There are six walk-in sites and 10 sites for tents, trailers, or RVs up to 22 feet long. Well water and picnic tables are provided. Pit toilets and firewood are available. Leashed pets are permitted.

Reservations, fees: Reservations accepted. Sites are $9 per night, plus $5 for each additional vehicle. Open year-round.

Directions: From Vancouver, WA, drive north on Interstate 5 about seven miles to County Road 502. Turn east on Highway 502 and drive six miles to Highway 503. Turn left and drive north for five miles to Lucia Falls Road. Turn right and drive eight miles to Moulton. Turn right on Old County Road 12 and drive seven miles to the Forest Boundary and the campground entrance on the right.

Contact: Gifford Pinchot National Forest, Wind River Work Center, 1262 Hemlock Road, Carson, WA 98610; tel. (509) 427-3200; fax (509) 427-3215.

81 Cold Creek   6

OK, the directions are complicated. Hey, Waylon once told me that few things worth remembering come easy, right? Well, sometimes. This campground is set in a forested area about 1,000 feet from Cedar Creek, with plenty of trails around for hiking and horseback riding. The camp gets minimal use, although it has drinking water. A large shelter available for groups makes this an ideal destination for families.

Location: On Cedar Creek; map B2, grid i6.

Campsites, facilities: There are six campsites for tents or small trailers. Picnic tables, fire grills, and tent pads are provided. Vault toilets and drinking water are available. Some facilities are wheelchair accessible. Leashed pets are permitted.

Reservations, fees: No reservations; no fee. Open May through September. Note: The camp is undergoing restoration; phone for current information.

Directions: From Vancouver, WA, on Interstate 5, drive on Interstate 5 to Exit 9 and N.E. 179th Street. Turn east and drive 5.5 miles to Highway 503. Turn right and drive 1.5 miles to N.E. 159th Street. Turn left on N.E. 159th Street and drive three miles to 182nd Avenue. Turn right and drive one mile to N.E. 139th (Road L-1400). Turn left and drive eight miles to Road L-1000. Turn left and drive three miles. Turn left at the campground entrance road and drive one mile to the camp.

Contact: Department of Natural Resources, Southwest Region, P.O. Box 280, Castle Rock, WA 98611-0280; tel. (360) 577-2025 or (360) 274-4196.

82 Rock Creek
Campground and Horse Camp   6

Here's an alternative to Cold Creek. Also managed by the Department of Natural Resources, this camp can be found in a wooded area along Rock Creek. Hikers and horseback riders will find plenty of trails nearby. For equestrians, the camp has facilities for horses.

Location: On Rock Creek; map B2, grid i6.

Campsites, facilities: There are 19 campsites for tents or small trailers. Picnic tables, fire grills, and tent pads are provided. Vault toilets, drinking water, a horse-loading ramp and corrals are available. Some facilities are wheelchair accessible. There is a campground host on site. Leashed pets are permitted.

Reservations, fees: No reservations; no fee. Open year-round, weather permitting.

Directions: From Vancouver, WA, on Interstate 5, drive on Interstate 5 to Exit 9 and N.E. 179th Street. Turn east and drive 5.5 miles to Highway 503. Turn right and drive 1.5 miles to N.E. 159th Street. Turn left on N.E. 159th Street and drive three miles to 182nd Avenue. Turn right and drive one mile to N.E. 139th (Road L-1400). Turn left and drive eight miles to Road L-1000. Turn left and drive 3.5 miles (passing Cold Creek Campground after three miles) to Road L-1200. Turn left and drive 200 yards to the campground on your right.

Contact: Department of Natural Resources, Southwest Region, P.O. Box 280, Castle Rock, WA 98611-0280; tel. (360) 577-2025 or (360) 274-4196.

83 Panther Creek   10

This campground along Panther Creek in old-growth forest several miles from the Wind River Ranger Station is a good choice for those who enjoy fishing, hiking, and horseback riding. The Pacific Crest Trail is accessible from neighboring Panther Creek Horse Camp.

Location: On Panther Creek in Gifford Pinchot National Forest; map B2, grid i8.

Campsites, facilities: There are 33 sites for tents, trailers, or RVs up to 25 feet long and one equestrian site, with a stock loading ramp, across from this camp at Panther Creek Horse Camp. Drinking water and picnic tables are provided. Pit toilets are available. Leashed pets are permitted.

Reservations, fees: Reservations accepted; phone (877) 444-6777 or access the website: www.reserveusa.com ($8.65 reservation fee). Sites are $9-18 per night. Open mid-May to mid-October.

Directions: From Vancouver, WA, on Interstate 205, take Highway 14 and drive east for 50 miles to Carson and the Wind River Highway (County Road 30). Turn north and drive nine miles to Forest Road 6517 (just past Stabler). Turn right (east) on Forest Road 6517 and drive 1.5 miles to the campground entrance road on the right.

Contact: Gifford Pinchot National Forest, Wind River Work Center, 1262 Hemlock Road, Carson, WA 98610; tel. (509) 427-3200; fax (509) 427-3215.

84 Beaver    7

This campground along the Wind River is a nice spot, with fishing access and pretty, shaded sites. Though small and remote, it has drinking water, for many the ideal combination.

Location: On the Wind River in Gifford Pinchot National Forest; map B2, grid i8.

Campsites, facilities: There are 26 sites for tents, trailers, or RVs up to 25 feet long and one group site which can accommodate up to 40 campers. Drinking water, fire grills, and picnic tables are provided. Pit toilets are available. Two campsites are wheelchair accessible. Leashed pets permitted.

Reservations, fees: Reservations accepted; phone (877) 444-6777 or access the website: www.reserveusa.com ($8.65 reservation fee). Sites are $11-22 per night; the group sites is $65 per night. Open mid-April to late September.

Directions: From Vancouver, WA, on Interstate 205, take Highway 14 and drive east for 50 miles to Carson and the Wind River Highway. Turn north and drive 12 miles to the campground entrance (three miles past Stabler).

Contact: Gifford Pinchot National Forest, Wind River Work Center, 1262 Hemlock Road, Carson, WA 98610; tel. (509) 427-3200; fax (509) 427-3215.

85 Crest Horse Camp   6

This primitive equestrian campground is set along Falls Creek near the Pacific Crest Trail, adjacent to the western boundary of the Indian Heaven Wilderness. It is an excellent jump-off spot for wilderness treks with horses or other stock animals.

Location: Bordering Big Lava Bed in Gifford Pinchot National Forest; map B2, grid i9.

Campsites, facilities: There are three sites for tents, trailers, or RVs. Fire pits are provided, but there is no drinking water. A stock loading ramp and a vault toilet are available. Leashed pets are permitted.

Reservations, fees: No reservations; no fee. Open mid-May to mid-October, weather permitting.

Directions: From Vancouver, WA, on Interstate 205, take Highway 14 and drive east for 50 miles to Carson and the Wind River Highway. Turn north and drive nine miles to Forest Road 6517. Turn right (east) on Forest Road 6517 and drive 1.5 miles to Forest Road 65. Turn left (north) on Forest Road 65 and drive about 14 miles to the camp on the left.

Contact: Gifford Pinchot National Forest, Wind River Work Center, 1262 Hemlock Road, Carson, WA 98610; tel. (509) 427-3200; fax (509) 427-3215.

86 Beacon Rock State Park

      8

This state park is set along the Columbia River with 14 miles of hiking trails heading inland. One trail leads to Beacon Rock, the second largest monolith in the world, which overlooks the Columbia River Gorge. The only downer: often windy here. If you like to fish, sturgeon are plentiful in the Columbia in June, when the arrival of smelt can inspire feeding frenzies. Remember, there is a six-foot maximum size limit for Mr. Sturgy. When the Outdoor Writers Association of America had its national convention in Portland, this is where we had our breakout day to test new equipment.

Location: On the Columbia River; map B2, grid j7.

Campsites, facilities: There are 33 developed sites for tents or self-contained RVs up to 50 feet long. Picnic tables and fire grills are provided. Flush toilets, a sanitary disposal station, coin-operated showers, firewood to purchase, and a playground are available. Some facilities are wheelchair accessible. Boat docks, launching facilities, and rentals are nearby. Leashed pets are permitted.

Reservations, fees: Reservations accepted. Sites are $10 per night; there is a $4 launch fee. Open year-round, with limited winter facilities.

Directions: From Vancouver, WA, on Interstate 205, take Highway 14 and drive east for 35 miles. The park straddles the highway; follow the signs to the campground.

Contact: Beacon Rock State Park, 34841 Highway 14, Skamania, WA 98648; tel. (800) 233-0321 or (509) 427-8265.

87 Dougan Creek   7

This very popular campground located on Dougan Creek where it empties into the Washougal River is small and remote, but it has drinking water and an on-site host. The camp is heavily forested and has pretty sites with river views.

Location: Near the Washougal River; map B2, grid j7.

Campsites, facilities: There are seven campsites for tents or small trailers. Picnic tables, fire grills, and tent pads are provided. Vault toilets and drinking water are available. Leashed pets are permitted.

Reservations, fees: No reservations; no fee. Open mid-May to mid-September.

Directions: From Vancouver, WA, on Interstate 205, take Highway 14 and drive east for 20 miles to Highway 140. Turn north on Highway 140 and drive five miles to Washougal River Road. Turn right on Washougal River Road and drive about seven miles until you come to the end of the pavement and pass the picnic area on the left. The campground is just beyond the picnic area.

Contact: Department of Natural Resources, Southwest Region, P.O. Box 280, Castle Rock, WA 98611-0280; tel. (360) 577-2025 or (360) 274-4196.

88 Beacon Rock Resort   7

This trailer park is set along the Columbia River, a short distance from Beacon Rock State Park. See the description of the state park for details. Nearby recreation options include a nine-hole golf course four miles away and two 18-hole golf courses, eight and 12 miles away, respectively.

Location: On the Columbia River; map B2, grid j7.

Campsites, facilities: There are 20 sites for trailers or RVs of any length; three are drive-through sites. Electricity, drinking water, sewer hookups, and picnic tables are provided. Flush toilets, bottled gas, showers, firewood, a store, a recreation hall, a laundry room, and ice are available. Boat launching facilities are located within one-quarter mile on the Columbia River. Leashed pets are permitted.

Reservations, fees: Reservations accepted with a deposit. Sites are $11-16 per night. Open year-round.

Directions: From Vancouver, WA, on Interstate 205, take Highway 14 and drive east for 34 miles to Skamania. Look for the park along Highway 14 at the corner of Moorage Road.

Contact: Beacon Rock Resort, 62 Moorage Road, Skamania, WA 98648; tel. (509) 427-8473.

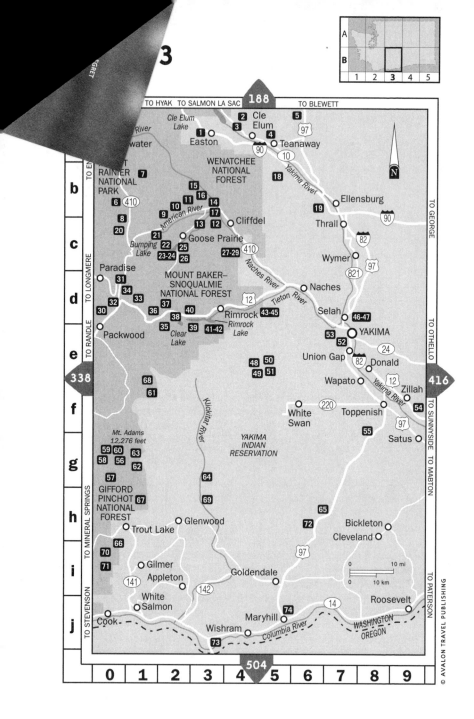

3

188 TO HYAK · TO SALMON LA SAC · TO BLEWETT

Cle Elum Lake

2
3
1 Easton
Cle Elum
4 Teanaway
5
97

10

WENATCHEE NATIONAL FOREST

18 Yakima River

MOUNT RAINIER NATIONAL PARK

7

15
11 16
6 410
9 10
8
20
13 12
21
Bumping Lake
22
25
23-24 26

14
17
Cliffdel

Goose Prairie

27-29 410

19 Ellensburg
Thrall
90

82

Wymer
97

Naches River

821

Paradise
31
34
33
32
30
Packwood

MOUNT BAKER– SNOQUALMIE NATIONAL FOREST

36
37
38 40
35 39
41-42

12

Rimrock
Rimrock Lake
43-45

Tieton River

Naches

Selah
46-47

53
52 Yakima
24
82 Donald

Clear Lake

48 50
49 51

Union Gap
Wapato
12
Zillah
54

68
61

Klickitat River

YAKIMA INDIAN RESERVATION

White Swan
220
Toppenish
55
Satus
97

Mt. Adams 12,276 feet
59 60 63
58 56 62
57
GIFFORD PINCHOT NATIONAL FOREST
67

64

69

65
72

Bickleton
Cleveland

Trout Lake
Glenwood

66
70
71

Gilmer
Appleton
141
142

Goldendale

97

0   10 mi
0   10 km

Cook
White Salmon
Wishram
Maryhill
74
14
Roosevelt

73
Columbia River

WASHINGTON
OREGON

504

0 1 2 3 4 5 6 7 8 9

TO ENUMCLAW · TO GEORGE · TO LONGMIRE · TO OTHELLO · TO RANDLE · TO SUNNYSIDE · TO MABTON · TO MINERAL SPRINGS · TO STEVENSON · TO PATERSON

338
416

© AVALON TRAVEL PUBLISHING

N

CHAPTER B3

◘ Lake Easton State Park

 8

This campground offers a multitude of recreational opportunities. For starters, it's set along the shore of Lake Easton, with Kachess Lake and Keechelus Lake just a short drive away. The park provides opportunities for both summer and winter recreation, including swimming, fishing, boating, cross-country skiing, and snowmobiling. Nearby recreation options include an 18-hole golf course and hiking trails.

Location: On Lake Easton; map B3, grid a3.

Campsites, facilities: There are two primitive tent sites, 92 developed tent sites, and 45 sites for trailers or RVs up to 60 feet long. Picnic tables and fire grills are provided. Flush toilets, a sanitary disposal station, a playground, electricity, drinking water, sewer hookups, showers, and firewood are available. A cafe and ice are located within one mile. Some facilities are wheelchair accessible. Boat launching facilities and floats are located on Lake Easton. Leashed pets are permitted.

Reservations, fees: Reservations accepted; phone (800) 452-5687 ($6 reservation fee). Sites are $7-16 per night. Major credit cards accepted. Open mid-April through mid-October.

Directions: From Seattle drive east on Interstate 90 for 68 miles to the park entrance on the right (it is located one mile west of the town of Easton).

Contact: Lake Easton State Park, P.O. Box 26, Easton, WA 98925; tel. (800) 233-0321, (509) 656-2586.

◙ Indian Horse Camp 6

This campground along the Middle Fork of the Teanaway River is in a very primitive setting, with sunny, open sites along the water. Be sure to bring your own drinking water. Quiet and solitude are highlights of this little-used camp. It's an easy drive from here to trailheads accessing the Mount Stuart Range.

Location: On the Middle Fork of the Teanaway River; map B3, grid a4.

Campsites, facilities: There are 10 campsites for tents or small trailers. Picnic tables, fire grills, and tent pads are provided. Pit toilets are available, but there is no drinking water. Some saddle-stock facilities are available, including hitching posts and corrals. Some facilities are wheelchair accessible. Leashed pets are permitted. Call for pet policy.

Reservations, fees: No reservations; no fee. Open year-round, weather permitting (heavy snows are generally expected from December through March).

Directions: From Seattle drive east on Interstate 90 for 80 miles to Cle Elum and Exit 85 and Highway 970. Turn east on Highway 970 and drive 6.9 miles to Teanaway Road. Turn left on Teanaway Road and drive 7.3 miles to West Fork Teanaway Road. Turn left and drive 0.6 mile to Middle Fork Teanaway Road. Turn right and drive 3.9 miles to the campground on the left.

Contact: Department of Natural Resources, Southeast Region, 713 East Bowers Road, Ellensburg, WA 98926-9341; tel. (509) 925-8510; fax (509) 925-8522.

❸ McKean's Trailer Park   6

Native Americans named the town of Cle Elum for "swift water," and this in-town camp is convenient for taking advantage of the waters of the Yakima River. You can rent rafts and canoes in Cle Elum and enjoy a 16-mile raft trip down the river to Thorp, where the rental company offers to pick you up and bring you back to Cle Elum. The Cle Elum Historical Telephone Museum is also in town. Lake Easton State Park and Trailer Corral are also located near the Yakima River.

Location: Near the Yakima River; map B3, grid a4.

Campsites, facilities: There are 10 sites for trailers or RVs. Electricity, drinking water, sewer hookups, and picnic tables are provided. A cafe is available. Bottled gas, sanitary services, a store, a coin laundry, and ice are located within one mile. Call for pet policy.

Reservations, fees: Reservations recommended. Sites are $15 per night. Open March to late December.

Directions: From Seattle drive east on Interstate 90 for 80 miles to Cle Elum and take the first exit to Highway 903. Continue east on Highway 903 (the road becomes East First Street) for two miles to the park on the left (1011 East First Street).

Contact: McKean's Trailer Park, 327 Lincoln Street, Cle Elum, WA 98922; tel. (509) 674-2254.

❹ Trailer Corral   7

This wooded campground along the Yakima River offers a choice of grassy or graveled sites. See the description of McKean's Trailer Park for river rafting information. Nearby recreation options include an 18-hole golf course, marked hiking trails, and tennis courts.

Location: On the Yakima River; map B3, grid a5.

Campsites, facilities: There are three tent sites and 24 sites for trailers or RVs of any length, plus six cabins. Electricity, drinking water, sewer, cable TV and picnic tables are provided. Flush toilets, sanitary services, showers, firewood, laundry facilities, and ice are available. A store is located within one mile. Boat launching facilities are nearby. Leashed pets are permitted.

Reservations, fees: Reservations accepted. Sites are $13-18 per night. Major credit cards accepted. Open year-round.

Directions: From Seattle drive east on Interstate 90 for 80 miles to Cle Elum and Exit 85 and Highway 970. Turn east on Highway 970 and drive one mile to the park on the left.

Contact: Trailer Corral, 2781 Highway 970, Cle Elum, WA 98922; tel. (509) 674-2433.

❺ Mineral Springs   6

This campground at the confluence of Medicine and Swauk Creeks is one of five campgrounds along U.S. 97. Fishing, berry picking, and hunting are good in season in this area. In the winter, cross-country skiing and snowshoeing are two options.

Location: On Medicine Creek in Wenatchee National Forest; map B3, grid a6.

Campsites, facilities: There are five tent sites and seven sites for tents, trailers, or RVs up to 21 feet long. Drinking water and picnic tables are provided. Vault toilets are available. Leashed pets are permitted.

Reservations, fees: No reservations accepted. Sites are $8 per vehicle per night, with a two-vehicle limit. Open mid-April to late November.

Directions: From Seattle drive east on Interstate 90 for 80 miles to Cle Elum and Exit 85 and Highway 970. Turn northeast on Highway 970 drive 12 miles to U.S. 97. Continue northeast (the road becomes U.S. 97) and drive about seven miles to the campground on the left.

Contact: Wenatchee National Forest, Cle Elum Ranger District, 830 West Second Street, Cle Elum, WA 98922; tel. (509) 674-4411; fax (509) 674-4794.

6 Silver Springs   9

This campground along the White River on the northeastern border of Mount Rainier National Park is a good alternative to the more crowded camps in the park. It's located in a beautiful section of old-growth forest and is very scenic. Hiking is the choice of recreational options. A U.S. Forest Service information center is one mile away from the campground entrance on Highway 410.

Location: In Mount Baker-Snoqualmie National Forest; map B3, grid b0.

Campsites, facilities: There are 16 tent sites and 40 sites for tents, trailers, or RVs up to 21 feet long. Picnic tables and fire grills are provided. Flush toilets, drinking water, and downed firewood for gathering are available. Leashed pets are permitted.

Reservations, fees: Reservations accepted for some sites; phone (877) 444-6777 or access the website: www.reserveusa.com ($8.65 reservation fee). Sites are $12 per night; $6 extra vehicle fee. Open mid-May to late September.

Directions: From Enumclaw drive east on Highway 410 for 31 miles (one mile south of the turnoff of the turnoff for Corral Pass) to the campground entrance on the right.

Contact: Mount Baker-Snoqualmie National Forest, White River Ranger District, 450 Roosevelt Avenue East, Enumclaw, WA 98022; tel. (360) 825-6585; fax (360) 825-0660.

7 Corral Pass   10

This is the most remote of the campgrounds in the area. Set at 5,600 feet, it's primitive, quiet, and an ideal base camp for a hiking trip. Groups of horse-packers heading into the adjacent Norse Peak Wilderness frequent the camp. The best trip is the six-mile backpack up to Hidden Lake and then along a river canyon to Echo Lake. Several trails nearby lead to backcountry fishing lakes and streams. See a U.S. Forest Service map for details. In late summer and fall, visitors can find wild berries in the area.

Location: In Mount Baker-Snoqualmie National Forest; map B3, grid b1.

Campsites, facilities: There are 23 tent sites. Picnic tables and fire grills are provided. Vault toilets and a horse-loading ramp are available, but there is no drinking water. Downed firewood can be gathered. Leashed pets are permitted.

Reservations, fees: No reservations; no fee. Open July to late September.

Directions: From Enumclaw drive east on Highway 410 for 30 miles to Forest Road 7174 (near Silver Springs Camp). Turn east (left) and drive six miles to the camp. It's a curvy dirt road and not suitable for trailers or RVs.

Contact: Mount Baker-Snoqualmie National Forest, White River Ranger District, 450 Roosevelt Avenue East, Enumclaw, WA 98022; tel. (360) 825-6585; fax (360) 825-0660.

8 Dalles   10

This campground along the confluence of Minnehaha Creek and the White River. "Dalles" means "rapids." A nature trail is nearby, and the White River entrance to Mount Rainier National Park is about 14 miles south on Highway 410. The camp sits amid a grove of old-growth trees; a particular point of interest is a huge old Douglas fir that is more than nine feet in diameter and 235 feet tall. This is one of the prettiest camps in the area.

Location: In Mount Baker-Snoqualmie National Forest; map B3, grid b1.

Campsites, facilities: There are 44 sites for tents, trailers, or RVs up to 21 feet long. Picnic tables, fire grills, vault toilets, and drinking water are provided. Firewood is available. There is a large shaded picnic area for day use. Leashed pets are permitted.

Reservations, fees: Reservations accepted for some sites; phone (877) 444-6777 or access the website: www.reserveusa.com ($8.65 reservation fee). Sites are $8-10 per night. Open mid-May to late September.

Directions: From Enumclaw drive east on Highway 410 for 25.5 miles to the campground (three miles inside the forest boundary) on the right.

Contact: Mount Baker-Snoqualmie National Forest, White River Ranger District, 450 Roosevelt Avenue East, Enumclaw, WA 98022; tel. (360) 825-6585; fax (360) 825-0660.

9 Pleasant Valley   7

This campground is a good base camp for a hiking trip. A trail from the camp follows Kettle Creek up to the American Ridge and Kettle Lake in the William O. Douglas Wilderness. It joins another trail that follows the ridge and then drops down to Bumping Lake. A U.S. Forest Service map is essential. In the winter the area is popular with cross-country skiers.

Location: On the American River in Wenatchee National Forest; map B3, grid b2.

Campsites, facilities: There are 16 sites for tents, trailers, or RVs up to 32 feet long. Picnic tables and fire grills are provided. Drinking water, garbage service, and vault toilets are available. Downed firewood may be gathered. Some facilities are wheelchair accessible. Leashed pets are permitted.

Reservations, fees: No reservations accepted. Rates are $10-13 per night for single sites, $17 per night for double sites, and $5 for each additional vehicle. Open mid-June to late November.

Directions: From Yakima drive northwest on U.S. 12 for 18 miles to Highway 410. Bear northwest on Highway 410 and drive 37 miles to the campground on the left.

Contact: Wenatchee National Forest, Naches Ranger District, 10061 Highway 12, Naches, WA 98937; tel. (509) 653-2205; fax (509) 653-2638.

10 Pine Needle Group Camp

 7

This is a reservations-only group campground on the edge of the William O. Douglas Wilderness along the American River. There are trails leading south into the backcountry at nearby camps; see a U.S. Forest Service map. The camp is easy to reach, rustic, and beautiful. Fishing access is available. For a side trip, visit Bumping Lake to the south, where boating, fishing, and swimming are all possible options.

Location: On the American River in Wenatchee National Forest; map B3, grid b2.

Campsites, facilities: There are six group sites for tents, trailers, or RVs up to 21 feet long, with a maximum capacity of 60 campers and eight vehicles. Picnic tables are provided. Pit toilets are available, but there is no drinking water. Downed firewood may be gathered. Leashed pets are permitted.

Reservations, fees: Reservations required. Sites are $20 per night on weekdays and $40 per night on weekends. Discounts are available for three or more consecutive days. Open late April to mid-September.

Directions: From Yakima drive northwest on U.S. 12 for 18 miles to Highway 410. Bear northwest on Highway 410 and drive 30.5 miles to the campground on the left.

Contact: Wenatchee National Forest, Naches Ranger District, 10061 Highway 12, Naches, WA 98937; tel. (509) 653-2205; fax (509) 653-2638.

11 Hells Crossing   7

This campground lies along the American River. A steep trail from the camp leads up to Goat Peak and follows the American Ridge in the William O. Douglas Wilderness. Other trails join the ridgeline trail and connect with lakes and streams. A U.S. Forest Service map details the backcountry.

Location: On the American River in Wenatchee National Forest; map B3, grid b3.

Campsites, facilities: There are 18 sites for tents, trailers, or RVs up to 16 feet long. Drinking water (at the west end of camp) and picnic tables are provided. Vault toilets are available. Downed firewood may be gathered. Leashed pets are permitted.

Reservations, fees: No reservations accepted. Rates are $10-13 per night for single sites, $17 per night for double sites, and $5 for each additional vehicle. Open late May to late November.

Directions: From Yakima drive northwest on U.S. 12 for 18 miles to Highway 410. Bear northwest on Highway 410 and drive 33.5 miles northwest on Highway 410 to the campground on the right.

Contact: Wenatchee National Forest, Naches Ranger District, 10061 Highway 12, Naches, WA 98937; tel. (509) 653-2205; fax (509) 653-2638.

12 Sawmill Flat   7

This campground on the Naches River near Halfway Flat offers fishing access and a hiking trail that leads west from Halfway Flat for several miles into the backcountry. Another trailhead is located at Boulder Cave to the south. See a U.S. Forest Service map for details.

Location: On the Naches River in Wenatchee National Forest; map B3, grid c3.

Campsites, facilities: There are 25 sites for tents, trailers, or RVs up to 24 feet long. Drinking water and picnic tables are provided. Vault toilets, a dump station and an Adirondack group shelter are available. Downed firewood may be gathered. Some facilities are wheelchair accessible, including one campsite. Leashed pets are permitted.

Reservations, fees: No reservations accepted. Rates are $10-13 per night for single sites, $17 per night for double sites, and $5 for each additional vehicle. Open April through November.

Directions: From Yakima drive northwest on U.S. 12 for 18 miles to Highway 410. Bear northwest on Highway 410 and drive 23.5 miles to the campground on the left.

Contact: Wenatchee National Forest, Naches Ranger District, 10061 Highway 12, Naches, WA 98937; tel. (509) 653-2205; fax (509) 653-2638.

⓭ Cedar Springs   6

The Bumping River is the locale of this camp. If you continue driving southwest for 11 miles on Forest Road 1800/Bumping River Road, you'll get to Bumping Lake, where recreation options abound.

Location: On the Bumping River in Wenatchee National Forest; map B3, grid c3.

Campsites, facilities: There are 15 sites for tents, trailers, or RVs up to 22 feet long, including two multi-family sites. Picnic tables are provided. Drinking water, vault toilets and firewood are available. Leashed pets are permitted.

Reservations, fees: No reservations accepted. Rates are $9 per night for single sites, $18 per night for double sites, and $5 for each additional vehicle. Open late May to late November.

Directions: From Yakima drive northwest on U.S. 12 for 18 miles to Highway 410. Bear northwest on Highway 410 and drive 28.5 miles to the campground access Road (Forest Road 1800/Bumping River Road). Turn southwest and drive one-half mile to the campground on the left.

Contact: Wenatchee National Forest, Naches Ranger District, 10061 Highway 12, Naches, WA 98937; tel. (509) 653-2205; fax (509) 653-2638.

⓮ Little Naches   5

This campground on the Little Naches River near the American River, 24 miles from Mount Rainier, is just 0.1 mile off the road, and the easy access is a major attraction for highway cruisers. Fishing access is available from camp.

Location: On the Little Naches River in Wenatchee National Forest; map B3, grid b3.

Campsites, facilities: There are 21 sites for tents, trailers, or RVs up to 20 feet long and two multi-family sites. Drinking water, picnic tables, and fire grills are provided. Vault toilets and garbage service are available. Some facilities are wheelchair accessible. Leashed pets are permitted.

Reservations, fees: No reservations accepted. Rates are $9 per night for single sites, $18 per night for double sites, and $5 for each additional vehicle. Open late May to late November.

Directions: From Yakima drive northwest on U.S. 12 for 18 miles to Highway 410. Bear northwest on Highway 410 and drive 25 miles to the campground access road (Forest Road 1900). Turn left and drive 100 yard to the campground on the left.

Contact: Wenatchee National Forest, Naches Ranger District, 10061 Highway 12, Naches, WA 98937; tel. (509) 653-2205; fax (509) 653-2638.

15 Crow Creek   5

This campground on the Little Naches River is popular with ORVers. A trail heading out from the camp leads into the backcountry and then forks in several directions. One route leads to the American River, another follows West Quartz Creek, and another goes along Fife's Ridge into the Norse Peak Wilderness (where no motorized vehicles are permitted). See a U.S. Forest Service map for details. There is good seasonal hunting and fishing in this area.

Location: On the Little Naches River in Wenatchee National Forest; map B3, grid b3.

Campsites, facilities: There are 15 sites for tents, trailers, or RVs up to 30 feet long. Picnic tables and fire grills are provided. Vault toilets and a dump station are available, but there is no drinking water. Downed firewood may be gathered. Some facilities are wheelchair accessible. Leashed pets are permitted.

Reservations, fees: No reservations accepted. Sites are $5 per night per vehicle. Open mid-April to late November.

Directions: From Yakima drive northwest on U.S. 12 for 18 miles to Highway 410. Bear northwest on Highway 410 and drive 24.5 miles to Forest Road 1900. Turn northwest and drive 2.5 miles to Forest Road 1902. Turn west and drive one-half mile to the campground on the right.

Contact: Wenatchee National Forest, Naches Ranger District, 10061 Highway 12, Naches, WA 98937; tel. (509) 653-2205; fax (509) 653-2638.

16 Kaner Flat   7

This campground near the Little Naches River is on the site of a wagon-train camp on the Old Naches Trail, a route used in the 1800s by wagon trains, Native Americans, and the U.S. Cavalry on their way to west side markets. The Naches Trail is now used by motorcyclists and narrow clearance four-wheel-drive enthusiasts.

Location: Near the Little Naches River in Wenatchee National Forest; map B3, grid b3.

Campsites, facilities: There are 41 sites for tents, trailers, or RVs up to 30 feet long, including two wheelchair accessible sites. Drinking water and picnic tables are provided. Vault, composting, and flush toilets (one of which is barrier-free) and garbage service are available. Leashed pets are permitted.

Reservations, fees: No reservations accepted. Sites are $9-18 per night, $5 for each additional vehicle. Open mid-April to late November.

Directions: From Yakima drive northwest on U.S. 12 for 18 miles to Highway 410. Bear northwest on Highway 410 and drive 25 miles to Forest Road 1900. Turn northwest and drive 2.5 miles to the campground on the right.

Contact: Wenatchee National Forest, Naches Ranger District, 10061 Highway 12, Naches, WA 98937; tel. (509) 653-2205; fax (509) 653-2638.

17 Indian Flat Group Camp   7

This is a reservations-only group campground set along the American River. Fishing access is available. A trail from the camp leads into the backcountry, west along Fife's Ridge, and farther north to the West Quartz Creek drainage. A U.S. Forest Service map details the adventure possibilities.

Location: On the American River in Wenatchee National Forest; map B3, grid b3.

Campsites, facilities: There are group sites for tents, trailers, or RVs up to 30 feet long, with a maximum capacity of 65 campers and 22 vehicles. Drinking water and picnic tables are provided. Vault toilets and firewood are available. Leashed pets are permitted.

Reservations, fees: Reservations required. Sites are $45 per night on week days and $125 per night on weekends. Discounts are available for three or more consecutive days. Open late May to mid-September.

Directions: From Yakima drive northwest on U.S. 12 for 18 miles to Highway 410. Bear northwest on Highway 410 and drive 27 miles to the campground on the left.

Contact: Wenatchee National Forest, Naches Ranger District, 10061 Highway 12, Naches, WA 98937; tel. (509) 653-2205; fax (509) 653-2638.

18 Taneum   7

This rustic spot along Taneum Creek has been getting increased use in recent years due to off-road-vehicle displacement in other areas. Fishing is popular here in the summer, and in the winter months snowshoeing and cross-country skiing trails are available.

Location: On Taneum Creek in Wenatchee National Forest; map B3, grid b5.

Campsites, facilities: There are 14 sites for trailers or RVs up to 21 feet long. Picnic tables are provided. Drinking water and firewood are available. Some facilities are wheelchair accessible. Leashed pets are permitted.

Reservations, fees: No reservations accepted. Rates are $8 per night for single sites, $16 per night for double sites, and $5 for each additional vehicle, with a two-vehicle limit. Open May to late September.

Directions: From Ellensburg drive northeast on U.S. 90 for about 12 miles to Thorp Prairie Road. Turn south on Thorp Prairie Road and drive four miles (crossing back over the freeway) to Taneum Road. Turn right and drive west for three miles (it becomes Forest Road 33). Continue west for three miles to the campground.

Contact: Wenatchee National Forest, Cle Elum Ranger District, 830 West Second Street, Cle Elum, WA 98922; tel. (509) 674-4411; fax (509) 674-4794.

19 KOA Ellensburg   8

This is one of the few campgrounds in a 25-mile radius, and it's exceptionally clean and scenic. It offers well-maintained, shaded campsites along the Yakima River. The Kittitas County Historical Museum is in town at Third and Pine Streets, and then there's the town-sponsored Ellensburg Roundup every weekend during the summer. Nearby recreation options include an 18-hole golf course and tennis courts.

Location: On the Yakima River; map B3, grid b6.

Campsites, facilities: There are 25 tent sites and 100 sites for trailers or RVs of any length; 48 are drive-through sites. Electricity and sewer hookups are available for an added charge. Drinking water and picnic tables are provided. Flush toilets, sanitary services, showers, a recreation hall, a store, laundry facilities, ice, a playground, video rentals, a seasonal wading pool, and a swimming pool are available. Bottled gas and a cafe are located within one mile. Leashed pets and motorbikes are permitted.

Reservations, fees: Reservations accepted. Sites are $18-25 per night. Major credit cards accepted. Open year-round.

Directions: From Seattle drive east on Interstate 90 for 106 miles to Exit 106 (near Ellensburg). Take that exit. The campground will be spotted at the exit.

Contact: KOA Ellensburg, 32 Thorp Highway South, Ellensburg, WA 98926; tel. (800) 562-7610, (509) 925-9319; fax (509) 925-8607.

20 White River   7

This campground is set on the White River at 4,400 feet. A trail near camp leads a short distance (but vertically, it's a rise of 2200 feet) to the Sunrise Visitor Center. Local rangers recommend that trailers be left at White River Campground and the 11-mile road trip to Sunrise be made by car. From there, you can take several trails that lead to backcountry lakes and glaciers. This camp is often used by climbers planning to summit Mount Rainier.

Location: On the White River in Mount Rainier National Park; map B3, grid c0.

Campsites, facilities: There are 117 sites for tents or RVs up to 20 feet long. Picnic tables and fire grills are provided. Flush toilets and drinking water are available. Some facilities are wheelchair accessible. Leashed pets are permitted in camp, but not on trails or in the wilderness.

Reservations, fees: No reservations accepted. Sites are $10 per night. Major credit cards accepted. Open mid-June to mid-September.

Directions: From Enumclaw drive southeast on Highway 410 to the entrance of Mount Rainier National Park and White River Road. Turn right and drive seven miles to the campground.

Contact: Mount Rainier National Park, Tahoma Woods, Ashford, WA 98304; tel. (360) 569-2211; fax (360) 569-2170.

21 Lodgepole   6

This campground is located along the American River about eight miles east of the boundary of Mount Rainier National Park. See the description of Gateway Inn and RV Park for information on Mount Rainier. Fishing access is available nearby.

Location: On the American River in Wenatchee National Forest; map B3, grid c2.

Campsites, facilities: There are 33 sites for tents, trailers, or RVs up to 20 feet long. Drinking water and picnic tables are provided. Vault toilets, garbage service, and firewood are available. Leashed pets are permitted.

Reservations, fees: No reservations accepted. Sites are $9 per night, $5 for each additional vehicle. Open mid-June to mid-September.

Directions: From Yakima drive northwest on U.S. 12 for 18 miles to Highway 410. Bear northwest on Highway 410 and drive 40.5 miles (eight miles east of the national park boundary) to the campground on the right.

Contact: Wenatchee National Forest, Naches Ranger District, 10061 Highway 12, Naches, WA 98937; tel. (509) 653-2205; fax (509) 653-2638.

22 Bumping Crossing   5

This campground is set on the Bumping River about a mile from the boat landing at Bumping Lake. It is a more primitive option to Bumping Lake and Boat Landing. It's a very good spot for a weekend trip, but remember to bring your own drinking water.

Location: On the Bumping River in Wenatchee National Forest; map B3, grid c2.

Campsites, facilities: There are 12 sites for tents, trailers, or RVs up to 15 feet long. Picnic tables are provided. Vault toilets are available, but there is no drinking water. A store, a cafe, and ice are located within one mile. Boat docks, launching facilities, and rentals are nearby on Bumping Lake. Leashed pets are permitted.

Reservations, fees: No reservations; no fee. Open late May to late November.

Directions: From Yakima drive northwest on U.S. 12 for 18 miles to Highway 410. Turn left (northwest) on Highway 410 and drive 28.5 miles to Forest Road 1800. Turn left (southwest) and drive 10 miles (along the Bumping River) to the campground on the right.

Contact: Wenatchee National Forest, Naches Ranger District, 10061 Highway 12, Naches, WA 98937; tel. (509) 653-2205; fax (509) 653-2638.

23 Lower Bumping Lake

       7

A variety of water activities are allowed at Bumping Lake, including waterskiing, fishing (salmon and trout), and swimming. A boat ramp is available nearby the camp. There are also several hiking trails that go into the William O. Douglas Wilderness area surrounding the lake.

Location: On Bumping Lake in Wenatchee National Forest; map B3, grid c2.

Campsites, facilities: There are 23 sites for tents, trailers, or RVs up to 50 feet long, two of which are wheelchair accessible. Drinking water and picnic tables are provided. Rest rooms with showers, fire pits and a dump station are available. Boat launching facilities are located nearby at Bumping Lake Campground. Leashed pets are permitted.

Reservations, fees: No reservations accepted. Sites are $10-13 per night, $5 for each additional vehicle. Open mid-May to late November, weather permitting.

Directions: From Yakima drive northwest on U.S. 12 for 18 miles to Highway 410. Turn left (northwest) on Highway 410 and drive 28.5 miles to Forest Road 1800. Turn left (southwest) and drive 11 miles (along the Bumping River) to the end of the pavement and look for the campground entrance road on the right.

Contact: Wenatchee National Forest, Naches Ranger District, 10061 Highway 12, Naches, WA 98937; tel. (509) 653-2205; fax (509) 653-2638.

24 Bumping Lake and Boat Landing

 7

Woods and water, this spot has them both. A variety of water activities are allowed at Bumping Lake, including waterskiing, fishing (salmon and trout), and swimming. Six campsites are adjacent to the boat facilities. There are also several hiking trails that go into the William O. Douglas Wilderness area surrounding the lake. This is one of the more developed camps in the area, with the added bonus of a boat ramp.

Location: On Bumping Lake in Wenatchee National Forest; map B3, grid c2.

Campsites, facilities: There are 45 sites for tents, trailers, or RVs up to 30 feet long. Drinking water and picnic tables are provided. Vault toilets, garbage service, and firewood are available. Boat docks, launching facilities, and rentals are nearby. Leashed pets are permitted.

Reservations, fees: No reservations accepted. Sites are $10-13 per night, $5 for each additional vehicle. Open mid-May to late November.

Directions: From Yakima drive northwest on U.S. 12 for 18 miles to Highway 410. Turn left (northwest) on Highway 410 and drive 28.5 miles to Forest Road 1800. Turn left (southwest) and drive 11 miles (along the Bumping River) to the end of the pavement and look for the campground entrance road on the right.

Contact: Wenatchee National Forest, Naches Ranger District, 10061 Highway 12, Naches, WA 98937; tel. (509) 653-2205; fax (509) 653-2638.

25 Soda Springs   7

Highlights of this camp along Bumping Creek include natural mineral springs and a nature trail. Fishing access is available. A sheltered picnic area is provided.

Location: On the Bumping River in Wenatchee National Forest; map B3, grid c2.

Campsites, facilities: There are 26 sites for tents, trailers, or RVs up to 30 feet in length. Drinking water and picnic tables are provided. Vault toilets, a dump station, firewood, several picnic shelters with fireplaces, garbage service, and some wheelchair-accessible facilities are available. Leashed pets are permitted.

Reservations, fees: No reservations accepted. Sites are $10-13 per night, $5 for each additional vehicle. Open May to late November.

Directions: From Yakima drive northwest on U.S. 12 for 18 miles to Highway 410. Turn left (northwest) on Highway 410 and drive 28.5 miles to Forest Road 1800. Turn left (southwest) and drive five miles (along the Bumping River) to the campground on the left.

Contact: Wenatchee National Forest, Naches Ranger District, 10061 Highway 12, Naches, WA 98937; tel. (509) 653-2205; fax (509) 653-2638.

26 Cougar Flat   7

One of several camps in the immediate vicinity, this spot along the Bumping River is close to good fishing, and a trail from the camp follows the river and then heads up the tributaries. See the Chapter B3 map for nearby camping options.

)n the Bumping River in Wenatchee National Forest; map B3, grid c2.
, **facilities:** There are 12 sites for tents, trailers, or RVs up to 20 feet long.
ater and picnic tables are provided. Vault toilets and garbage service are
Some facilities are wheelchair accessible. Leashed pets are permitted.
ons, fees: No reservations accepted. Sites are $10-13 per night; $5 for
each additional vehicle. Open late May to mid-September.

Directions: From Yakima drive northwest on U.S. 12 for 18 miles to Highway 410. Turn left (northwest) on Highway 410 and drive 28.5 miles to Forest Road 1800. Turn left (southwest) and drive six miles (along the Bumping River) to the campground on the left.

Contact: Wenatchee National Forest, Naches Ranger District, 10061 Highway 12, Naches, WA 98937; tel. (509) 653-2205; fax (509) 653-2638.

27 Squaw Rock Resort   8

This park in a stand of old-growth fir and pine on the Naches River is close to a host of activities, including trout fishing, hiking trails, marked bike trails, and a riding stable. The park has a pool and hot tub. The nearby town of Naches, located southeast of the campground on Highway 410, offers all services.

Location: On the Naches River; map B3, grid c4.

Campsites, facilities: There are 25 tent sites and 65 sites for trailers or RVs of any length. Electricity, drinking water, and picnic tables are provided. Some sewer hookups, flush toilets, bottled gas, sanitary services, showers, a recreation hall, a store, a cafe, ice, a playground, a hot tub, and a swimming pool are available. Leashed pets are permitted.

Reservations, fees: Reservations accepted. Sites are $20 per night. Major credit cards accepted. Open year-round.

Directions: From Yakima drive northwest on U.S. 12 for 18 miles to Highway 410. Turn left on Highway 410 and drive 15 miles to the campground on the left.

Contact: Squaw Rock Resort, 15070 Highway 410, Naches, WA 98937; tel. (509) 658-2926; fax (509) 658-2927.

28 Cottonwood   7

Pretty, shaded sites and river views are the main draw at this camp along the Naches River. Sawmill Flat, Little Naches, Crow Creek, Kaner Flat, and Halfway Flat provide nearby alternatives.

Location: On the Naches River in Wenatchee National Forest; map B3, grid c4.

Campsites, facilities: There are 16 sites for tents, trailers, or RVs up to 22 feet long. Drinking water is available. Picnic tables are provided. Vault toilets, garbage service, a store, a cafe, and ice are available nearby. Some facilities are wheelchair accessible. Leashed pets are permitted.

Reservations, fees: No reservations accepted. Sites are $10-13 per night, $5 for each additional vehicle. Open April through November.

Directions: From Yakima drive northwest on U.S. 12 for 18 miles to Highway 410. Turn left (northwest) on Highway 410 and drive 17.5 miles to the campground on the left.

Contact: Wenatchee National Forest, Naches Ranger District, 10061 Highway 12, Naches, WA 98937; tel. (509) 653-2205; fax (509) 653-2638.

29 Halfway Flat 7

Fishing, hiking, and ORV opportunities abound at this campground along the Naches River. A trail leads from the campground into the backcountry of the William O. Douglas Wilderness, which can also be reached by car. No motorized vehicles are permitted in the wilderness itself, however. Try hoofing it.

Location: On the Naches River in Wenatchee National Forest; map B3, grid c4.

Campsites, facilities: There are nine sites for tents, trailers, or RVs up to 27 feet long. Picnic tables are provided. Vault toilets, garbage service, and firewood are available, but there is no drinking water. Leashed pets are permitted.

Reservations, fees: No reservations accepted. Sites are $7 per night. Open April to late November.

Directions: From Yakima drive northwest on U.S. 12 for 18 miles to Highway 410. Turn left (northwest) on Highway 410 and drive 17 miles to the campground on the left.

Contact: Wenatchee National Forest, Naches Ranger District, 10061 Highway 12, Naches, WA 98937; tel. (509) 653-2205; fax (509) 653-2638.

30 Packwood Trailer and RV Park 6

This is a pleasant campground, especially in the fall when the maples turn. Groups are welcome. Mount Rainier National Park is just 25 miles north, and this camp is a good alternative if the park is full. Nearby recreation options include a riding stable and tennis courts.

Location: In Packwood; map B3, grid d0.

Campsites, facilities: There are 15 tent sites and 88 sites for trailers or RVs of any length. Electricity, drinking water, sewer hookups, and picnic tables are provided. Flush toilets, sanitary services, showers, a store, and a laundry room are available. A cafe and bottled gas are available within walking distance. Leashed pets and motorbikes are permitted.

Reservations, fees: Reservations accepted. Sites are $11-20 per night. Major credit cards accepted. Open year-round.

Directions: On Interstate 5 drive to Exit 68 (south of Chehalis) and U.S. 12. Turn east on U.S. 12 and drive 65 miles to Packwood. The park is on the north side of the highway in town.

Contact: Packwood Trailer and RV Park, P.O. Box 309, Packwood, WA 98361; tel. (360) 494-5145; fax (360) 494-2841.

31 Ohanapecosh 8

This camp is located at the foot of North America's most beautiful volcano, Mount Rainier. It is also set along the Ohanapecosh River and near a visitor center, with exhibits on the history of the forest, plus visitor information. Note that Highway 706 heading west and Highway 123 heading north are closed by snowfall in winter.

Location: On the Ohanapecosh River in Mount Rainier National Park; map B3, grid d0.

Campsites, facilities: There are 205 sites for tents or RVs up to 30 feet long. Picnic tables are provided. Flush toilets, drinking water, and a sanitary disposal station are available. Some facilities are wheelchair accessible. Leashed pets are permitted in camp, but not on trails or in the wilderness.

Reservations, fees: Reservations accepted up to five months in advance for the late June to early September season; phone (800) 365-CAMP (800-365-2267) or access the website: www.reservations.nps.gov. Sites are $12-14 per night. Major credit cards accepted. Open mid-May through September.

Directions: On Interstate 5 drive to Exit 68 (south of Chehalis) and U.S. 12. Turn east on U.S. 12 and drive 72 miles (seven miles past Packwood) to Highway 123. Turn north and drive five miles to the Ohanapecosh entrance to the park. The camp is next to the visitor center as you enter the park.

Contact: Mount Rainier National Park, Tahoma Woods, Ashford, WA 98304; tel. (360) 569-2211; fax (360) 569-2170.

32 La Wis Wis   7

This camp is ideally located for day trips to Mount Rainier and Mount St. Helens. It's set on the Cowlitz River, near the Ohanapecosh River in an old-growth forest. Hikers can explore the nature trails throughout the area. The entrance to Mount Rainier National Park and the Ohanapecosh Hot Springs is about seven miles south of the camp.

Location: On the Cowlitz River in Gifford Pinchot National Forest; map B3, grid d0.

Campsites, facilities: There are 117 sites for tents, trailers, or RVs up to 24 feet long. Picnic tables are provided. Flush and vault toilets, drinking water, and firewood are available. Leashed pets are permitted.

Reservations, fees: No reservations accepted. Sites are $10-16 per night. The maximum stay is 14 days. Open mid-May to late September.

Directions: On Interstate 5 drive to Exit 68 (south of Chehalis) and U.S. 12. Turn east on U.S. 12 and drive 72 miles (about seven miles past Packwood) to Forest Road 1272. Turn left and drive one-half mile to the campground.

Contact: Gifford Pinchot National Forest, Cowlitz Ranger District, Packwood, WA 98361; tel. (360) 494-0600; fax (360) 494-0602.

33 Soda Springs   6

Set along Summit Creek and the wilderness border, this is a primitive camp which is ideal as a jumping-off base camp for a backpacking expedition or daily hiking trips in the Cascade Range. One trail out of camp is routed three miles up to Jug Lake in the William Douglas Wilderness. There are several trails and lakes to choose as destinations. Obtain a U.S. Forest Service map for details.

Location: On Summit Creek in Gifford Pinchot National Forest; map B3, grid d1.

Campsites, facilities: There are six primitive tent sites. Picnic tables are provided. A vault toilet is available, but there is no drinking water. Leashed pets are permitted.

Reservations, fees: No reservations; no fee. Open mid-June to early September.

Directions: On Interstate 5 drive to Exit 68 (south of Chehalis) and U.S. 12. Turn east on U.S. 12 and drive 75 miles (two miles past the Highway 123 turnoff) to Forest Road 45. Turn left and drive seven miles (the road becomes Forest Road 4510) to the camp.

Contact: Gifford Pinchot National Forest, Cowlitz Ranger District, Packwood, WA 98361; tel. (360) 494-0600; fax (360) 494-0602.

34 Summit Creek   5

This very primitive campground along Summit Creek is another good base camp for trips into the Cascade Range backcountry. See the description of Soda Springs.
Location: On Summit Creek in Gifford Pinchot National Forest; map B3, grid d1.
Campsites, facilities: There are six primitive tent sites. Picnic tables are provided. A vault toilets is available, but there is no drinking water. Leashed pets are permitted.
Reservations, fees: No reservations; no fee. Open mid-June to early September.
Directions: On Interstate 5 drive to Exit 68 (south of Chehalis) and U.S. 12. Turn east on U.S. 12 and drive 75 miles (two miles past the Highway 123 turnoff) to Forest Road 45. Turn left and drive three miles (the road becomes Forest Road 4510) to the campground.
Contact: Gifford Pinchot National Forest, Cowlitz Ranger District, Packwood, WA 98361; tel. (360) 494-0600; fax (360) 494-0602.

35 Clear Lake North   7

This campground hails from an elevation of 3,100 feet along the shore of Clear Lake, which is the forebay for Rimrock Lake. Swimming is allowed and you can fish. This camp is primitive and gets relatively little use.
Location: On Clear Lake in Wenatchee National Forest; map B3, grid d2.
Campsites, facilities: There are 34 sites for tents, trailers, or RVs up to 22 feet long. Picnic tables are provided. Vault toilets and garbage service are available. There are wheelchair-accessible rest rooms. There is no drinking water at Clear Lake North, but there is drinking water at Clear Lake South Campground. Boat docks, launching facilities, and rentals are nearby. Leashed pets are permitted.
Reservations, fees: No reservations accepted. Sites are $9 per night. Open mid-April to late November.
Directions: From Yakima drive northwest on Interstate 12 for 17 miles to the junction with Highway 410. Turn west on U.S. 12 and drive 31 miles to County Road 1200. Turn south and drive one mile to Forest Road 1200. Turn south and drive one mile to Forest Road 1200-840. Continue south for one-half mile to the campground.
Contact: Wenatchee National Forest, Naches Ranger District, 10061 Highway 12, Naches, WA 98937; tel. (509) 653-2205; fax (509) 653-2638.

36 White Pass   7

This campground on the shore of Leech Lake at an elevation of 4,500 feet is near trails leading into the Goat Rocks Wilderness to the south and the William O. Douglas Wilderness to the north. A trailhead for the Pacific Crest Trail is also nearby. Beautiful Leech Lake is popular for fly-fishing (the only type of fishing allowed here). White Pass Ski Area is located across the highway.
Location: On Leech Lake in Wenatchee National Forest; map B3, grid d2.

Campsites, facilities: There are 16 sites for tents, trailers, or RVs up to 20 feet long. Picnic tables are provided. Vault toilets, a dump station, and firewood are available, but there is no drinking water. A store, a cafe, a coin laundry, and ice are located within one mile. Boat docks and launching facilities are nearby. No motorized boats are allowed. Leashed pets are permitted.

Reservations, fees: No reservations accepted. Sites are $7 per night. Open June to late November.

Directions: On Interstate 5 drive to Exit 68 (south of Chehalis) and U.S. 12. Turn east on U.S. 12 and drive 84 miles (three miles past the White Pass Ski Area) to the campground entrance road on the left side. Turn north and drive 200 yards to Leech Lake.

Contact: Wenatchee National Forest, Naches Ranger District, 10061 Highway 12, Naches, WA 98937; tel. (509) 653-2205; fax (509) 653-2638.

37 Dog Lake  5

This campground is on the shore of Dog Lake at 3,400 feet in elevation. Nearby trails lead into the William O. Douglas Wilderness. See a U.S. Forest Service map for details. Boating and fishing are two options here.

Location: On Dog Lake in Wenatchee National Forest; map B3, grid d2.

Campsites, facilities: There are 11 sites for tents, trailers, or RVs up to 20 feet long. Picnic tables are provided. Vault toilets are available, but there is no drinking water. Boat docks and launching facilities are nearby. Leashed pets are permitted, but no horses are allowed in the campground.

Reservations, fees: No reservations accepted. Sites are $5 per night. Open late May to late November.

Directions: On Interstate 5 drive to Exit 68 (south of Chehalis) and U.S. 12. Turn east on U.S. 12 and drive 87 miles (six miles past the White Pass Ski Area) to the campground entrance road on the left side.

Contact: Wenatchee National Forest, Naches Ranger District, 10061 Highway 12, Naches, WA 98937; tel. (509) 653-2205; fax (509) 653-2638.

38 Clear Lake South 7

This campground (elevation 3,100 feet) is located near the east shore of Clear Lake, which is the forebay for Rimrock Lake. Fishing and swimming are options. For winter travelers, several sno-parks in the area offer snowmobiling and cross-country skiing. There are many hiking trails to the north; see a U.S. Forest Service map.

Location: In Wenatchee National Forest; map B3, grid d2.

Campsites, facilities: There are 23 sites for tents, trailers, or RVs up to 22 feet long. Drinking water, picnic tables, garbage service, and vault toilets are available. Downed firewood may be gathered. Boat docks and launching facilities are nearby. Leashed pets are permitted.

Reservations, fees: No reservations accepted. Sites are $9 per night. Open mid-April to late November.

Directions: From Yakima drive northwest on Interstate 82 for 17 miles to the junction with Highway 410. Turn west on U.S. 12 and drive 31 miles (past Rimrock Lake) to County Road 1200. Turn south and drive one mile to Forest Road 1200. Turn south and drive one mile to the campground.

Contact: Wenatchee National Forest, Naches Ranger District, 10061 Highway 12, Naches, WA 98937; tel. (509) 653-2205; fax (509) 653-2638.

39 Silver Beach Resort   8

This resort along the shore of Rimrock Lake is one of several camps in the immediate area. It's very scenic, with beautiful lakefront sites. Hiking trails, marked bike trails, a full-service marina, and a riding stable are close by.

Location: On Rimrock Lake; map B3, grid d3.

Campsites, facilities: There are 65 tent sites and 30 sites for trailers or RVs and three cabins with kitchens. Electricity, drinking water, sewer hookups, and picnic tables are provided. A cafe, store, dump station, bottled gas, propane, ice, a playground, a hot tub, boat docks, launching facilities, and boat and jet ski rentals are available. Pets are permitted.

Reservations, fees: Reservations accepted. Sites are $13-18 per night; cabins are $75 per night. Major credit cards accepted. Open year-round, with limited winter facilities.

Directions: From Yakima drive northwest on Interstate 82 for 17 miles to the junction with Highway 410. Turn west on U.S. 12 and drive 20 miles to Rimrock Lake. Turn left at the resort.

Contact: Silver Beach Resort, 40350 Highway 12, Rimrock, WA 98937; tel. (509) 672-2500.

40 Indian Creek   7

Fishing, swimming, and waterskiing are among the activities at this shorefront campground on Rimrock Lake (elevation 3,000 feet). The camp is adjacent to Rimrock Lake Marina. Many excellent hiking trails to the north are routed into the William O. Douglas Wilderness.

Location: On Rimrock Lake in Wenatchee National Forest; map B3, grid d3.

Campsites, facilities: There are 39 sites for tents, trailers, or RVs up to 32 feet long. Drinking water and picnic tables are provided. Vault toilets, a cafe, a store, garbage service, and ice are available. Downed firewood may be gathered. Boat docks, launching facilities, and rentals are nearby. Leashed pets are permitted.

Reservations, fees: No reservations accepted. Sites are $10-13 per night. Open late May to mid-September.

Directions: From Yakima drive northwest on Interstate 82 for 17 miles to the junction with Highway 410. Turn west on U.S. 12 and drive 20 miles to Rimrock Lake. Turn left at the campground.

Contact: Wenatchee National Forest, Naches Ranger District, 10061 Highway 12, Naches, WA 98937; tel. (509) 653-2205; fax (509) 653-2638.

41 South Fork   8

This campground (at 5,000 feet) along the South Fork of the Tieton River less than a mile from where it empties into Rimrock Lake is often a good spot for trout fishing and swimming. By traveling a bit farther south on Tieton River Road, you can see the huge Blue Slide, an enormous prehistoric rock and earth slide that has a curious blue tinge to it.

Location: On the South Fork of the Tieton River in Wenatchee National Forest; map B3, grid d3.

Campsites, facilities: There are nine sites for tents, trailers, or RVs up to 20 feet long, including three multi-family sites. Picnic tables are provided. Vault toilets and garbage service are available, but there is no drinking water. Boat docks are nearby. Leashed pets are permitted.

Reservations, fees: No reservations accepted. Sites are $7 per night. Open late May to mid-September.

Directions: From Yakima drive northwest on Interstate 82 for 17 miles to the junction with Highway 410. Turn west on U.S. 12 and drive 31 miles to County Road 1000. Turn south and drive four miles to the campground entrance road.

Contact: Wenatchee National Forest, Naches Ranger District, 10061 Highway 12, Naches, WA 98937; tel. (509) 653-2205; fax (509) 653-2638.

42 Peninsula  7

Swimming, fishing, and waterskiing are all allowed at Rimrock Lake (elevation 3,000 feet), where this shorefront camp is located. The nearby vicinity of a boat ramp is a big plus. This is one of several camps on the lake. A nearby sno-park offers wintertime fun, including cross-country skiing and snowmobiling.

Location: On Rimrock Lake in Wenatchee National Forest; map B3, grid d3.

Campsites, facilities: There is a dispersed camping area for tents, trailers, or RVs up to 20 feet long. Vault toilets and picnic tables are available, but there is no drinking water. Boat docks and launching facilities are nearby. Leashed pets are permitted.

Reservations, fees: No reservations accepted. Sites are $5 per night per vehicle. Open mid-April to late November.

Directions: From Yakima drive northwest on Interstate 82 for 17 miles to the junction with Highway 410. Turn west on U.S. 12 and drive 31 miles to County Road 1000. Turn south and drive three miles to Forest Road 711. Turn west and drive one mile (bearing left at the fork for the boat ramp) to the camp.

Contact: Wenatchee National Forest, Naches Ranger District, 10061 Highway 12, Naches, WA 98937; tel. (509) 653-2205; fax (509) 653-2638.

43 Willows  5

This primitive, beautiful, and easily accessible camp can be found on the Tieton River at 2,400 feet elevation. Rimrock Lake to the west provides many recreation options, and hiking trails leading into the William O. Douglas Wilderness are within driving distance.

Location: On the Tieton River in Wenatchee National Forest; map B3, grid d5.

Campsites, facilities: There are 16 sites for tents, trailers, or RVs up to 20 feet long. Picnic tables are provided. Drinking water, vault toilets and garbage service are available. Leashed pets are permitted.

Reservations, fees: No reservations accepted. Sites are $9 per night. Open April to late November.

Directions: From Yakima drive northwest on Interstate 82 for 17 miles to the junction with Highway 410. Turn west on U.S. 12 and drive 16 miles to the campground.

Contact: Wenatchee National Forest, Naches Ranger District, 10061 Highway 12, Naches, WA 98937; tel. (509) 653-2205; fax (509) 653-2638.

44 Hause Creek   7

Several creeks converge at this campground along the Tieton River (elevation 2,500 feet). The Tieton Dam, which creates Rimrock Lake, is just upstream. This is one of the larger, more developed camps in the area. Willows is a primitive alternative.

Location: On the Tieton River in Wenatchee National Forest; map B3, grid d5.

Campsites, facilities: There are 42 sites for tents, trailers, or RVs up to 30 feet long. Drinking water and picnic tables are provided. Flush toilets, a dump station, and firewood are available. Some facilities are wheelchair accessible. Boat docks, launching facilities, and rentals are located on Rimrock Lake. Leashed pets are permitted.

Reservations, fees: Reservations accepted; phone (877) 444-6777 or access the website: www.reserveusa.com ($8.65 reservation fee). Sites are $10-13 per night. Open late May to late November.

Directions: From Yakima drive northwest on Interstate 82 for 17 miles to the junction with Highway 410. Turn west on U.S. 12 and drive 18 miles to the campground.

Contact: Wenatchee National Forest, Naches Ranger District, 10061 Highway 12, Naches, WA 98937; tel. (509) 653-2205; fax (509) 653-2638.

45 Windy Point   5

This campground, located along the Tieton River at an elevation of 2,000 feet, is more isolated than the camps set westward toward Rimrock Lake. Drinking water is a bonus. Fishing access is available.

Location: On the Tieton River in Wenatchee National Forest; map B3, grid d5.

Campsites, facilities: There are 15 sites for tents, trailers, or RVs up to 22 feet long. Drinking water and picnic tables are provided. Vault toilets, garbage service, and firewood are available. Leashed pets are permitted.

Reservations, fees: No reservations accepted. Sites are $10-13 per night. Open April to late November.

Directions: From Yakima drive northwest on Interstate 82 for 17 miles to the junction with Highway 410. Turn west on U.S. 12 and drive nine miles to the campground.

Contact: Wenatchee National Forest, Naches Ranger District, 10061 Highway 12, Naches, WA 98937; tel. (509) 653-2205; fax (509) 653-2638.

46 Yakima Sportsman State Park   8

Kayaking and rafting are possible at this park on the Yakima River. No swimming is allowed. There is also a fishing pond for children (no anglers over age 15 are al-

lowed). Nearby recreation options include an 18-hole golf course and hiking trails. See the description of KOA Yakima for information on other points of interest in Yakima.
Location: On the Yakima River; map B3, grid d7.
Campsites, facilities: There are two primitive tent sites, 28 sites for tents or self-contained RVs, and 37 drive-through sites with full hookups for trailers or RVs up to 60 feet in length. Picnic tables and fire grills are provided. Flush toilets, sanitary services, and a playground are available. Showers and firewood can be obtained for an extra fee. A store and ice are within one mile. Leashed pets are permitted.
Reservations, fees: Reservations accepted; phone (800) 452-5687 ($6 reservation fee). Sites are $7-16 per night. Major credit cards accepted. Open year-round.
Directions: In Yakima (on Interstate 82), turn east on Terrace Heights Road and drive and short distance. Turn right and drive one mile to Normal Road. Turn right and drive west for a one-half mile to park entrance (route is well signed). Park is set on the east shore of the Yakima River.
Contact: Yakima Sportsman State Park, Route 9, P.O. Box 498, Yakima, WA 98901; tel. (800) 233-0321 or (509) 575-2774.

47 KOA Yakima   6

This campground along the Yakima River offers well-maintained, shaded sites and fishing access. Some points of interest in Yakima are the Yakima Valley Museum and the Yakima Trolley Lines, which offer rides on restored trolley cars originally built in 1906. Indian Rock Paintings State Park is five miles west of Yakima on U.S. 12. Nearby recreation options include an 18-hole golf course, hiking trails, marked bike trails, and tennis courts.
Location: On the Yakima River; map B3, grid d7.
Campsites, facilities: There are 50 tent sites and 90 drive-through sites for trailers or RVs of any length. Cabins are also available. Picnic tables are provided. Flush toilets, bottled gas, sanitary services, showers, a recreation hall, a store, laundry facilities, ice, a playground, electricity, drinking water, sewer hookups, firewood, and boat rentals, including paddleboats, are available. A cafe is located within one mile. Leashed pets and motorbikes permitted.
Reservations, fees: Reservations accepted. Sites are $22-27 per night; cabins are $38-44 per night. Major credit cards accepted. Open year-round.
Directions: In Yakima on Interstate 82 drive to the Highway 24 exit. Turn east on Highway 24 and drive one mile to Keyes Road. Turn north on Keyes Road and drive 300 yards to the campground.
Contact: KOA Yakima, 1500 Keyes Road, Yakima, WA 98901; tel. (800) 562-5773 or (509) 248-5882. Website: www.koa.com.

48 Clover Flats   8

This campground is in the subalpine zone on the slope of Darland Mountain, which peaks at 6,982 feet. Trails connect the area with the Goat Rocks Wilderness, six miles to the west. Contact the Department of Natural Resources or Wenatchee National Forest for details. See the description of Ahtanum Camp for information on winter snowmobiling.

Location: Near the Goat Rocks Wilderness; map B3, grid e4.

Campsites, facilities: There are nine campsites for tents or small trailers. Picnic tables, fire grills, and tent pads are provided. Pit toilets and drinking water are available. Leashed pets are permitted.

Reservations, fees: No reservations; no fee. Open year-round, weather permitting (heavy snows are generally expected from December through March).

Directions: From Yakima drive south on Interstate 82 for two miles to Union Gap and Ahtanum Road. Turn right (west) and drive 20 miles to Tampico and Road A-2000 (Middle Fork Road). Turn west and drive 18.7 miles to the camp on the left. Note: The last few miles of Road A-2000 are very steep, with a 12-13% grade. High clearance vehicles only recommended.

Contact: Department of Natural Resources, Southeast Region, 713 East Bowers Road, Ellensburg, WA 98926-9341; tel. (509) 925-8510; fax (509) 925-8522.

49 Tree Phones   7

This forested campground along the Middle Fork of Ahtanum Creek is close to hiking, motorbiking, and horseback riding trails. A shelter with a wood stove is available year-round for picnics. During the summer months, there are beautiful wildflower displays. See the description of Ahtanum Camp for snowmobiling information.

Location: On the Middle Fork of Ahtanum Creek; map B3, grid e4.

Campsites, facilities: There are 14 campsites for tents or small trailers. Picnic tables, fire grills, and tent pads are provided. Drinking water and pit toilets are available. A 20-by-40-foot snow shelter and saddle-stock facilities are also available. Leashed pets and motorbikes are permitted.

Reservations, fees: No reservations; no fee. Open year-round, weather permitting (heavy snows are expected from December through March).

Directions: From Yakima drive south on Interstate 82 for two miles to Union Gap and Ahtanum Road. Turn right (west) and drive 20 miles to Tampico and Road A-2000 (Middle Fork Road). Turn west and drive 15.3 miles to the campground entrance on the left. Note: High clearance vehicles only recommended.

Contact: Department of Natural Resources, Southeast Region, 713 East Bowers Road, Ellensburg, WA 98926-9341; tel. (509) 925-8510; fax (509) 925-8522.

50 Snow Cabin   7

Located in an area of old-growth timber, this place is popular with horse campers, who use it to access old logging roads. There are cutthroat trout in Ahtanum Creek, and fishing is permitted.

Location: On the North Fork of Ahtanum Creek; map B3, grid e5.

Campsites, facilities: There are eight sites for tents or small trailers. Picnic tables, fire grills, and tent pads are provided. Pit toilets are available, but there is no drinking water. Saddle-stock facilities are available. Leashed pets are permitted.

Reservations, fees: No reservations; no fee. Open year-round, weather permitting.

Directions: From Yakima drive south on Interstate 82 for two miles to Union Gap and Ahtanum Road. Turn right (west) and drive 20 miles to Tampico and Road A-2000 (Middle Fork Road). Turn west and drive 9.5 miles to Road !-3000 (North Fork Ahtanum Road). Turn west and drive 5.6 miles (bearing left for the last mile) to the Gray Rock Trailhead. From Gray Rock, continue 1.5 miles to the campground on the left. Note: High clearance vehicles only recommended.

Contact: Department of Natural Resources, Southeast Region, 713 East Bowers Road, Ellensburg, WA 98926-9341; tel. (509) 925-8510; fax (509) 925-8522.

51 Ahtanum Camp   7

This campground on Ahtanum Creek is one of four primitive sites within 10 miles. For a good side trip, continue driving on Road A-2000 for 14 miles, where you'll reach the Darland Mountain viewpoint at 6,900 feet. The road gets very steep near the lookout and is not suitable for RVs or trailers. In the winter, this area offers 60 miles of groomed trails for snowmobilers. A snow shelter is provided at Tree Phones. Contact the Department of Natural Resources for a map.

Location: On Ahtanum Creek; map B3, grid e5.

Campsites, facilities: There are 11 campsites for tents or small trailers. Picnic tables, fire grills, and tent pads are provided. Pit toilets and drinking water are available. Some wheelchair accessible facilities. Leashed pets are permitted.

Reservations, fees: No reservation; no fee. Open year-round, weather permitting.

Directions: From Yakima drive south on Interstate 82 for two miles to Union Gap and Ahtanum Road. Turn right (west) and drive 20 miles to Tampico and Road A-2000 (Middle Fork Road). Turn west and drive 9.5 miles to the campground entrance on the right. Note: High clearance vehicles only recommended.

Contact: Department of Natural Resources, Southeast Region, 713 East Bowers Road, Ellensburg, WA 98926-9341; tel. (509) 925-8510; fax (509) 925-8522.

52 Circle H RV Ranch   8

This pleasant, centrally located, and clean park with a western flavor has comfortable, spacious sites among ornamental trees and roses. Nearby recreation options include an 18-hole golf course, hiking trails, marked bike trails, and a riding stable. See the description of KOA Yakima for information on points of interest in Yakima.

Location: In Yakima; map B3, grid e7.

Campsites, facilities: There are 12 tent sites and 64 sites for trailers or RVs of any length; 16 are drive-through sites. Electricity, drinking water, sewer hookups, and picnic tables are provided. Flush toilets, showers, two recreation halls, laundry facilities, a playground, 18-hole mini-golf course, and a swimming pool are available. Bottled gas, a store, a cafe, and ice are located within one mile. Mini-storage units are available for a fee. Leashed pets and motorbikes are permitted.

Reservations, fees: Reservations accepted. Sites are $15-19 per night. Major credit cards accepted. Open year-round.

Directions: In Yakima on Interstate 82, take Exit 34 and drive one block to South 18th Street. Turn north and drive one-quarter mile to the campground on the right.

Contact: Circle H RV Ranch, 1107 South 18th Street, Yakima, WA 98901; tel. (509) 457-3683; fax (509) 457-3683.

53 Trailer Inn RV Park   7

Like the Trailer Inns RV Park in Spokane, this spot has many of the luxuries you'd find in a hotel, including a pool, a hot tub, a sauna, on-site security, and a large-screen TV. An 18-hole golf course, hiking trails, marked bike trails, and tennis courts are close by. It's especially pretty in the fall when the sycamores turn. See the description of KOA Yakima for information on some of the points of interest in Yakima.

Location: In Yakima; map B3, grid e7.

Campsites, facilities: There are 152 sites for tents, trailers or RVs of any length; 30 are drive-through sites. Electricity, drinking water, sewer hookups, cable TV and picnic tables are provided. Flush toilets, bottled gas, sanitary services, showers, a recreation hall, a laundry room, ice, a swimming pool, a whirlpool, TV room with a 52-inch screen, a dog walk, an enclosed barbecue (no open fires permitted), and a playground are available. A store and a cafe are located within one block. Leashed pets are permitted.

Reservations, fees: Reservations accepted. Sites are $15-24 per night. Major credit cards accepted. Open year-round.

Directions: In Yakima on Interstate 82, take Exit 31 and drive three blocks south on North First Street to the park on the west side of the road.

Contact: Trailer Inn RV Park, 1610 North First Street, Yakima, WA 98901; tel. (509) 452-9561.

54 Granger Mobile Villa   6

This park near the Yakima River has nice, grassy sites with lots of shade. Granger is known as "Washington's Fruit Basket," and tourists can pick their own fruits and vegetables from local farms. Several wineries in the area offer tours. A unique side trip can be made to the Toppenish Wildlife Refuge, which is particularly good for bird-watching. It's 15 miles away, south of Toppenish on U.S. 97. Call (509) 865-2405 for information.

Location: Near the Yakima River; map B3, grid f9.

Campsites, facilities: There are 45 tent sites and 25 drive-through sites for trailers or RVs of any length. Electricity, drinking water, and sewer hookups are provided. Flush toilets, sanitary services, showers, and a laundry room are available. Bottled gas, a store, a cafe, and ice are located within one mile. Leashed pets are permitted.

Reservations, fees: Reservations accepted. Sites are $15 per night. Open year-round.

Directions: In Yakima on Interstate 82, drive south for 25 miles to Granger and Highway 223. Take the Highway 223 exit in Granger and continue to the park on the left.

Contact: Granger Mobile Villa, P.O. Box 695, Granger, WA 98932; tel. (509) 854-1300.

55 Yakama Nation RV Resort   3

The park is set within the Yakama Indian Reservation (the tribe spells its name differently from the river and town), where a casino and movie theater are near the resort. The Toppenish Wildlife Refuge, the No. 1 side trip, is almost always a good spot to see a large variety of birds. Nearby Toppenish, a historic Old West town with a museum, is also worth a side trip.

Location: Near the Yakima River; map B3, grid f8.

Campsites, facilities: There are 10 tent sites, 95 sites for RVs, and 14 tepees which can accommodate up to 10 campers each. Drinking water, picnic tables, and fire pits are provided. Electricity, sewer, cable TV, modem access, and phone hookups, a sanitary disposal station, garbage service, flush toilets, showers, a playground, recreation room, exercise room, jogging track, ball courts, bicycle rentals, a heated pool, and coin-operated laundry facilities are available. A picnic shelter with drinking water, propane, and a sink is available in the tent area. A restaurant and grocery store are located within 1.5 miles. Leashed pets are permitted.

Reservations, fees: Reservations recommended; phone (800) 874-3087. Sites are $12-20 per night. Tepees are $30 per night for five campers, plus $3 each additional person. Major credit cards accepted. Open year-round.

Directions: From Yakima drive south on Interstate 82 for 12 miles to Toppenish and U.S. 97. Turn south on U.S. 97 and drive 1.7 miles to the resort.

Contact: Yakama Nation RV Resort, 280 Buster Road, Toppenish, WA 98948; tel. (800) 874-3087; website: www.yakamanation.com.

56 Horseshoe Lake   8

The shore of Horseshoe Lake is the site of this campground. A trail from the camp goes up nearby Green Mountain (elevation 5,000 feet). Another trail heads up the north flank of Mount Adams. See a U.S. Forest Service map for details. Berry picking is an option in the late summer months and fishing is also an option.

Location: On Horseshoe Lake in Gifford Pinchot National Forest; map B3, grid g0.

Campsites, facilities: There are 11 sites for tents, trailers, or RVs up to 16 feet long. Picnic tables are provided. Pit toilets are available, but there is no drinking water. Firewood may be gathered outside the campground area. Primitive launching facilities are located on the lake, but all gasoline motors are prohibited on the water. Leashed pets are permitted.

Reservations, fees: No reservations; no fee. Open mid-June to late September.

Directions: From Chehalis drive south on Interstate 5 for 10 miles to Exit 68 and U.S. 12. Turn east on U.S. 12 and drive 48 miles to Randle and Woods Creek Road (U.S. 131). Turn south and drive one mile to Forest Road 23. Turn left (southeast) and drive 29 miles to Forest Road 2329. Turn northeast and drive seven miles to Forest Road 078 (bearing right at the junction with Forest Road 5601). Turn left and drive 1.5 miles to the campground.

Contact: Gifford Pinchot National Forest, Randle Ranger District, P.O. Box 670, Randle, WA 98377; tel. (360) 497-1100; fax (360) 497-1102.

57 Takhlakh  9

This campground is along the shore of Takhlakh Lake, one of five lakes in the area, all accessible by car. It's a beautiful place, but alas, mosquitoes abound until late July. A viewing area (Mount Adams is visible across the lake) is available for visitors, while the more ambitious can go berry picking, fishing, and hiking.

Location: On Takhlakh Lake in Gifford Pinchot National Forest; map B3, grid g0.

Campsites, facilities: There are 54 sites for tents, trailers, or RVs up to 21 feet long. Drinking water and picnic tables are provided. Vault toilets are available. Firewood may be gathered outside the campground area. Boat launching facilities are available in the day-use area, but all gasoline motors are prohibited on the lake. Some facilities are wheelchair accessible. Leashed pets are permitted.

Reservations, fees: Reservations accepted; phone (877) 444-6777 or access the website: www.reserveusa.com ($8.65 reservation fee). Sites are $9 per night, $5 for each additional vehicle. Open mid-June to late September.

Directions: From Chehalis drive south on Interstate 5 for 10 miles to Exit 68 and U.S. 12. Turn east on U.S. 12 and drive 48 miles to Randle and Woods Creek Road (U.S. 131). Turn south and drive one mile to Forest Road 23. Turn left (southeast) and drive 29 miles to Forest Road 2329. Turn northeast and drive seven miles to Forest Road 078 (bearing right at the junction with Forest Road 5601). Turn left and drive two miles to the campground.

Contact: Gifford Pinchot National Forest, Randle Ranger District, P.O. Box 670, Randle, WA 98377; tel. (360) 497-1100; fax (360) 497-1102.

58 Olallie Lake 8

This campground is located at 4,000 feet on the shore of Olallie Lake, a small alpine lake that is one of several in the area fed by streams coming off the glaciers on nearby Mount Adams (elevation 12,276 feet). A word to the wise: Mosquitoes can be a problem in the spring and early summer. (See the information on protection against insects in the Camping Tips section at the beginning of this book.)

Location: On Olallie Lake in Gifford Pinchot National Forest; map B3, grid g0.

Campsites, facilities: There are five sites for tents, trailers, or RVs up to 21 feet long. Picnic tables are provided. Pit toilets are available, but there is no drinking water. Firewood may be gathered outside the campground area. Boat launching facilities are nearby, but all gasoline motors are prohibited on the lake. Leashed pets are permitted.

Reservations, fees: No reservations accepted. Sites are $6 per night, and $4 for each additional vehicle. Open July to late September.

Directions: From Chehalis drive south on Interstate 5 for 10 miles to Exit 68 and U.S. 12. Turn east on U.S. 12 and drive 48 miles to Randle and Woods Creek Road (U.S. 131). Turn south and drive one mile to Forest Road 23. Turn left (southeast) and drive 29 miles to Forest Road 2329. Turn left (northeast) and drive one mile to a junction with Forest Road 5601. Turn left and drive one-half mile to the campground.

Contact: Gifford Pinchot National Forest, Randle Ranger District, P.O. Box 670, Randle, WA 98377; tel. (360) 497-1100; fax (360) 497-1102.

59 Adams Fork   7

This campground is set at 2,600 feet along the Upper Cispus River near Adams Creek at the foot of Mount Adams and is popular with ORV enthusiasts. A nearby trail leads north to Blue Lake, about a half-mile walk from the camp.

Location: On the Cispus River in Gifford Pinchot National Forest; map B3, grid g0.

Campsites, facilities: There are 24 sites for tents, trailers, or RVs up to 21 feet long. Drinking water and picnic tables are provided. Vault toilets are available. Firewood may be gathered outside the campground area. Leashed pets are permitted.

Reservations, fees: Reservations accepted; phone (877) 444-6777 or access the website: www.reserveusa.com ($8.65 reservation fee). Sites are $9 per night, group sites are $11-22 per night, and additional vehicles are $5 each. Open May to late October.

Directions: On Interstate 5 drive to Exit 68 (south of Chehalis) and U.S. 12. Turn east on U.S. 12 and drive 48 miles to Randle and Woods Creek Road (U.S. 131). Turn right (south) and drive one mile to Forest Road 23. Turn left (southeast) and drive 18 miles to Forest Road 21. Turn left (southeast) on Forest Road 21 and drive five miles to the campground entrance road (Forest Road 56). Turn east and drive 200 yards to the campground.

Contact: Gifford Pinchot National Forest, Randle Ranger District, P.O. Box 670, Randle, WA 98377; tel. (360) 497-1100; fax (360) 497-1102.

60 Cat Creek   5

This small, rustic camp is set along Cat Creek at its confluence with the Cispus River about 10 miles from the summit of Mount Adams. A trail starts less than a mile from the camp and leads up along Blue Lake Ridge to Blue Lake. See a U.S. Forest Service map for details.

Location: On Cat Creek and the Cispus River in Gifford Pinchot National Forest; map B3, grid g0.

Campsites, facilities: There are five sites for tents, trailers, or RVs up to 15 feet long. Picnic tables and fire grills are provided. Pit toilets and firewood are available, but there is no drinking water. Firewood may be gathered outside the campground area. Leashed pets are permitted.

Reservations, fees: No reservations accepted; no fee. Open mid-May to late October.

Directions: On Interstate 5 drive to Exit 68 (south of Chehalis) and U.S. 12. Turn east on U.S. 12 and drive 48 miles to Randle and Woods Creek Road (U.S. 131). Turn right (south) and drive one mile to Forest Road 23. Turn left (southeast) and drive 18 miles to Forest Road 21. Turn left (east) on Forest Road 21 and drive six miles to the campground.

Contact: Gifford Pinchot National Forest, Randle Ranger District, P.O. Box 670, Randle, WA 98377; tel. (360) 497-1100; fax (360) 497-1102.

61 Walupt Horse Camp   7

Fishing access at Walupt Lake is just a mile from this camp. Several trails lead from the lake into the backcountry of the southern Goat Rocks Wilderness, which has 85 miles of trails that can be used by horses. If you have planned a multi-day horse packing trip, you need to bring in your own feed for the horses. Feed must be pellets or processed grain only. Hay is not permitted in the wilderness.

Location: Near the Goat Rocks Wilderness in Gifford Pinchot National Forest; map B3, grid f1.

Campsites, facilities: There are six sites for equestrians in tents, trailers, or RVs up to 18 feet long. Picnic tables and drinking water are provided. Vault toilets and firewood are available. Leashed pets are permitted.

Reservations, fees: Reservations required; phone (877) 444-6777 or access the website: www.reserveusa.com ($8.65 reservation fee). Sites are $9 per night, $5 for each additional vehicle. Open June through September, weather permitting.

Directions: On Interstate 5 drive to Exit 68 (south of Chehalis) and U.S. 12. Turn east on U.S. 12 and drive 62 miles to Forest Road 21 (2.5 miles southwest of Packwood). Turn right (southeast) and drive 16.5 miles to Forest Road 2160. Turn left (east) and drive 3.5 miles to the campground.

Contact: Gifford Pinchot National Forest, Cowlitz Ranger District, Packwood, WA 98361; tel. (360) 494-0600; fax (360) 494-0602.

62 Killen Creek   7

This campground along Killen Creek at the foot of Mount Adams (elevation 12,276 feet) marks the start of a three-mile trail that leads up the mountain and connects with the Pacific Crest Trail. It's worth the effort. Berry picking is another summertime option.

Location: Near Mount Adams in Gifford Pinchot National Forest; map B3, grid g1.

Campsites, facilities: There are eight sites for tents, trailers, or RVs up to 21 feet long. Picnic tables are provided. Pit toilets are available, but there is no drinking water. Firewood may be gathered outside the campground area. Leashed pets are permitted.

Reservations, fees: No reservations; no fee. Open July to late September.

Directions: On Interstate 5 drive to Exit 68 (south of Chehalis) and U.S. 12. Turn east on U.S. 12 and drive 48 miles to Randle and Woods Creek Road (U.S. 131). Turn right (south) and drive one mile to Forest Road 23. Turn left (southeast) and drive 29 miles to Forest Road 2329. Turn left (northeast) and drive six miles to Forest Road 073. Turn left (west) and drive 200 yards to the campground.

Contact: Gifford Pinchot National Forest, Randle Ranger District, P.O. Box 670, Randle, WA 98377; tel. (360) 497-1100; fax (360) 497-1102.

63 Keene's Horse Camp   7

This campground is set at 4,200 feet along the South Fork of Spring Creek on the northwest flank of Mount Adams (elevation 12,276 feet). The Pacific Crest Trail passes within a couple of miles of the camp. A number of trails lead from here into the backcountry and to several alpine meadows. The meadows are fragile, so walk along their outer edges.

Location: On the South Fork of Spring Creek in Gifford Pinchot National Forest; map B3, grid g1.

Campsites, facilities: There are 12 sites for tents, trailers, or RVs up to 21 feet long. Picnic tables and fire grills are provided. Pit toilets and hitching facilities (high lines) are available, but there is no drinking water. Firewood may be gathered outside the campground area. Leashed pets are permitted.

Reservations, fees: No reservations; no fee. Open July to late September.

Directions: On Interstate 5 drive to Exit 68 (south of Chehalis) and U.S. 12. Turn east on U.S. 12 and drive 48 miles to Randle and Woods Creek Road (U.S. 131). Turn right (south) and drive one mile to Forest Road 23. Turn left (southeast) and drive 29 miles to Forest Road 2329. Turn left and drive eight miles to Forest Road 82 to the campground entrance on the left. A U.S. Forest Service map is advised.

Contact: Gifford Pinchot National Forest, Randle Ranger District, P.O. Box 670, Randle, WA 98377; tel. (360) 497-1100; fax (360) 497-1102.

64 Island Camp   8

This campground in a forested area along Bird Creek is close to lava tubes and blowholes. In the winter, the roads are used for snowmobiling. A snowmobile shelter with a wood stove is available year-round for picnics. See the description of Maryhill State Park for information on the nearby Klickitat Habitat Management Area.

Location: On Bird Creek; map B3, grid g3.

Campsites, facilities: There are six campsites for tents or small trailers. Picnic tables, fire grills, and tent pads are provided. Pit toilets are available, but there is no drinking water. Leashed pets are permitted.

Reservations, fees: No reservations; no fee. Open year-round.

Directions: From Yakima drive south on Interstate 82 for 15 miles to U.S. 97. Turn south and drive 49 miles to Goldendale and Highway 142. Turn right (west) and drive 10 miles to Counts Road. Turn right (northwest) and drive 26 miles to Glenwood, and continue for one-quarter mile to Bird Creek Road. Turn right and drive 0.9 mile to K-3000 Road (still Bird Creek Road). Turn left, drive over the cattle guard, and drive 1.2 miles to Road S-4000. Turn right and drive 1.3 miles to Road K-4000. Turn left and drive 3.4 miles to Road K-4200. Turn left and drive 1.1 miles to the campground entrance on the left. Turn left and drive a quarter-mile to the campground.

Contact: Department of Natural Resources, Southeast Region, 713 East Bowers Road, Ellensburg, WA 98926-9341; tel. (509) 925-8510; fax (509) 925-8522.

65 Brooks Memorial State Park   7

There is only one other campground (Maryhill State Park) within 25 miles of this forested park at an elevation of nearly 3,000 feet. Highlights include several miles of hiking trails, a 1.5-mile-long nature trail, and excellent fishing for trout in the nearby Klickitat River. An unusual side trip is bird-watching at Toppenish National Wildlife Refuge, 28 miles north of the park on U.S. 97; phone the refuge at (509) 865-2405 for details. If you like stargazing, the Goldendale Observatory is located just one mile north of Goldendale. It contains one of the largest telescopes in the world available for public use; phone (509) 773-3141 for hours of operation.

Location: Near the Goldendale Observatory; map B3, grid h7.

Campsites, facilities: There are two primitive tent sites, 22 developed sites for tents or self-contained RVs, and 23 sites with water and electrical hookups for trailers or RVs up to 50 feet long. Picnic tables and fire grills are provided. Flush toilets, sanitary services, and a playground are available. Showers can be obtained for an extra fee. A store is located within one mile. Leashed pets are permitted.

Reservations, fees: No reservations accepted. Sites are $7-16 per night. Open year-round, with limited winter facilities.

Directions: From Yakima drive south on Interstate 82 for 15 miles to U.S. 97. Turn south and drive 37 miles to the park on the right (well signed).

Contact: Brooks Memorial State Park, 2465 Highway 97, Goldendale, WA 98620; tel. (800) 233-0321 or (509) 773-5382.

66 Peterson Prairie   8

Here's a good base camp if you want to have a short ride to town as well as access to the nearby wilderness areas. This is a prime spot for huckleberry picking, too. A sno-park in the area is open for winter recreation, with snowmobiling and cross-country skiing trails.

Location: Near the town of Trout Lake in Gifford Pinchot National Forest; map B3, grid i0.

Campsites, facilities: There are 23 sites for tents, trailers, or RVs up to 32 feet long, and one group site. Drinking water, picnic tables, and fire rings are provided. Vault toilets are available. Some facilities are wheelchair accessible. Leashed pets are permitted.

Reservations, fees: Reservations required for the group site only; phone (877) 444-6777 or access the website: www.reserveusa.com ($8.65 reservation fee). Rates are $11-22 per night for individual sites and $27-59 per night for the group site. Open May to late September.

Directions: From Hood River, OR, drive north on Highway 35 (over the Columbia River) to Highway 14. Turn left and drive two miles to Highway 141. Turn right (north) on Highway 141 and drive 25.5 miles to Forest Road 24 (5.5 miles beyond and southwest of the town of Trout Lake). Bear right (west) and drive 2.5 miles to the campground.

Contact: Gifford Pinchot National Forest, Mount Adams Ranger District, 2455 Highway 141, Trout Lake, WA 98650; tel. (509) 395-3400; fax (509) 395-3424.

67 Morrison Creek   7

Here's a prime yet little-known spot. It's located along Morrison Creek at an elevation of 4,600 feet near the southern slopes of Mount Adams, which at an elevation of 12,276 feet is the second-highest mountain in Washington (Rainier is higher). Nearby trails will take you to the snowfields and alpine meadows of the Mount Adams Wilderness.

Location: On Morrison Creek in Gifford Pinchot National Forest; map B3, grid h1.

Campsites, facilities: There are 12 tent sites. Picnic tables and fire rings are provided in some sites. Vault toilets are available, but there is no drinking water. Leashed pets are permitted.

Reservations, fees: No reservations; no fee. Open July to late September.

Directions: From Hood River, OR, drive north on Highway 35 (over the Columbia River) to Highway 14. Turn left and drive two miles to Highway 141. Turn right (north) on Highway 141 and drive 20 miles to County Road 17 (just 200 yards east of the town of Trout Lake). Turn right (north) and drive two miles to Forest Road 80. Turn right (north) and drive 3.5 miles to Forest Road 8040. Bear left (north) and drive six miles to the campground.

Contact: Gifford Pinchot National Forest, Mount Adams Ranger District, 2455 Highway 141, Trout Lake, WA 98650; tel. (509) 395-3400; fax (509) 395-3424.

68 Walupt Lake 8

This is a good base camp for a multi-day vacation. For starters, the camp is set along the shore of Walupt Lake. In addition, several nearby trails lead into the backcountry and to other smaller alpine lakes. See a U.S. Forest Service map for details.

Location: On Walupt Lake in Gifford Pinchot National Forest; map B3, grid e1.

Campsites, facilities: There are 44 sites for tents, trailers, or RVs up to 22 feet long. Picnic tables are provided. Drinking water and pit and vault toilets are available. There is primitive boat access with a 10 mph speed limit; no waterskiing is allowed. Leashed pets are permitted.

Reservations, fees: Reservations accepted; phone (877) 444-6777 or access the website: www.reserveusa.com ($8.65 reservation fee). Sites are $11.50-23 per night, $5 for each additional vehicle. Open mid-June to early September.

Directions: On Interstate 5 drive to Exit 68 (south of Chehalis) and U.S. 12. Turn east on U.S. 12 and drive 62 miles to Forest Road 21 (2.5 miles southwest of Packwood). Turn right (southeast) and drive 16.5 miles to Forest Road 2160. Turn left (east) and drive 4.5 miles to the campground.

Contact: Gifford Pinchot National Forest, Cowlitz Ranger District, Packwood, WA 98361; tel. (360) 494-0600; fax (360) 494-0602.

69 Bird Creek 7

This campground in a forested area along Bird Creek is one of two camps in the immediate area. (The other, also a primitive site, is Island Camp.) This spot lies just east of the Mount Adams Wilderness and is within three miles of Island Camp, where there are snowmobile trails. See the description of Maryhill State Park for information on the nearby Klickitat Habitat Management Area.

Location: Near the Mount Adams Wilderness; map B3, grid h3.

Campsites, facilities: There are eight campsites for tents or small trailers. Picnic tables, fire grills, and tent pads are provided. Pit toilets are available, but there is no drinking water. Some facilities are wheelchair accessible. Leashed pets are permitted.

Reservations, fees: No reservations; no fee. Open May to mid-October, weather permitting.

Directions: From Yakima drive south on Interstate 82 for 15 miles to U.S. 97. Turn south and drive 49 miles to Goldendale and Highway 142. Turn right (west) and drive 10 miles to Counts Road. Turn right (northwest) and drive 26 miles to Glenwood. From the post office in Glenwood, continue a quarter mile to Bird Creek Road. Turn right and drive 0.9 mile. Turn left (still Bird Creek Road), cross the cattle guard to Road K-3000, and drive 1.2 miles to Road S-4000 (gravel). Turn right and drive 1.3 miles to Road K-4000. Turn left and drive two miles to the campground on the left.

Contact: Department of Natural Resources, Southeast Region, 713 East Bowers Road, Ellensburg, WA 98926-9341; tel. (509) 925-8510; fax (509) 925-8522.

70 Oklahoma   7

This pretty campground is set along Little White Salmon River. Fishing can be excellent in this area. As to why they named the camp "Oklahoma," who knows? If you do, drop me a line.

Location: On the Little White Salmon River in Gifford Pinchot National Forest; map B3, grid i0.

Campsites, facilities: There are 23 sites for tents, trailers, or RVs up to 22 feet long. Drinking water, fire rings, and picnic tables are provided. Vault toilets are available. Some facilities are wheelchair accessible. Pets are permitted.

Reservations, fees: Reservations accepted; phone (877) 444-6777 or access the website: www.reserveusa.com ($8.65 reservation fee). Sites are $11 per night, $5 for each additional vehicle. Open mid-May to mid-October.

Directions: From Hood River, OR, drive north on Highway 35 and for one mile over the Columbia River to Highway 14. Turn left on Highway 14 and drive about five miles to Cook and County Road 1800. Turn right (north) and drive 14 miles (the road becomes Cook-Underwood Road, then Willard Road, then Oklahoma Road) to the campground entrance.

Contact: Gifford Pinchot National Forest, Mount Adams Ranger District, 2455 Highway 141, Trout Lake, WA 98650; tel. (509) 395-3400; fax (509) 395-3424.

71 Moss Creek   7

This campground on the White Salmon River is a short distance from Willard and Big Cedars County Park. Good fishing prospects can be found here, usually with few other people around. You get all the amenities, including nice, shaded sites.

Location: On the Little White Salmon River in Gifford Pinchot National Forest; map B3, grid i0.

Campsites, facilities: There are 18 sites for tents, trailers, or RVs up to 32 feet long. Drinking water, fire rings, and picnic tables are provided. Vault toilets are available. Some facilities are wheelchair accessible. Pets are permitted.

Reservations, fees: Reservations accepted; phone (877) 444-6777 or access the website: www.reserveusa.com ($8.65 reservation fee). Sites are $11 per night; $5 for each additional vehicle. Open mid-May to late September.

Directions: From Hood River, OR, drive north on Highway 35 and for one mile over the Columbia River to Highway 14. Turn left on Highway 14 and drive about five miles to Cook and County Road 1800. Turn right (north) and drive eight miles (the road becomes Cook-Underwood Road, then Willard road, then Oklahoma Road) to the campground entrance.

Contact: Gifford Pinchot National Forest, Mount Adams Ranger District, 2455 Highway 141, Trout Lake, WA 98650; tel. (509) 395-3400; fax (509) 395-3424.

72 Pine Springs Resort   7

This is an alternative to the state campground at Brooks Memorial State Park. It's a small, wooded camp with a stream running close by. Side trips include adjacent Brooks Memorial State Park, Goldendale Observatory State Park, and the Columbia River.

Location: Near Brooks Memorial State Park; map B3, grid h6.

Campsites, facilities: There are 11 tent sites and 21 sites for trailers or RVs. CableTV, water, electricity and sewer hookups, a public phone, limited groceries, ice, snacks, RV supplies, and LP gas are available. Horseshoe pits are also provided. Leashed pets are permitted.

Reservations, fees: Reservations recommended. Sites are $5-12 per night. Open March 1 through mid-November, weather permitting.

Directions: From Portland drive east on Interstate 30 to Biggs and U.S. 97. Turn north and drive 11 miles to Goldendale. Continue north on U.S. 97 for 11.5 miles to the resort on the left. The park is located between Mileposts 24 and 25.

Contact: Pine Springs Resort, 2471 Highway 97, Goldendale, WA 98620; tel. (509) 773-4434.

73 Horsethief Lake State Park   10

This is a good spot to camp if you're driving along the Columbia River Highway. The state park sits along the shore of Horsethief Lake adjacent to the Dalles Dam. There are hiking trails and access to both the lake and the Columbia River. Non-powered boats are allowed, and anglers can try for trout and bass. See the description of Maryhill State Park for information on other recreation options in the region.

Location: Near Dalles Dam; map B3, grid j3.

Campsites, facilities: There are two primitive tent sites and 12 sites for tents or self-contained RVs up to 30 feet long. Drinking water, fire grills, and picnic tables are provided. Flush toilets, firewood, and sanitary services are available. A store and a cafe are located within one mile. Boat launching facilities are located on both the lake and the river. Leashed pets are permitted.

Reservations, fees: No reservations accepted. Sites are $5-10 per night. Open April to late October.

Directions: From Portland drive east on Interstate 30 for 76 miles to The Dalles and Highway 197. Turn north on Highway 197, cross over the Columbia River and drive four miles to Highway 14. Turn right (east) and drive two miles to the park entrance on the left.

Contact: Horsethief Lake State Park, 50 Highway 97, Goldendale, WA 98620; tel. (800) 233-0321 or (509) 767-1159.

⁷⁴ Maryhill State Park

 8

Fishing, waterskiing, and windsurfing are among the possibilities at this park along the Columbia River. The climate here is very pleasant from March through mid-November. Two interesting places can be found near Maryhill: one is a replica of Stonehenge, located on a bluff overlooking the Columbia River, and the other is the Maryhill Museum; call (509) 773-3733 for details. A great side trip 30 miles northwest is the Klickitat Habitat Management Area. It's run by the Department of Fish and Game and has some primitive camping spots and a boat launch along the Klickitat River, where you can enjoy boating, fishing, hunting, or observing wildlife. To get there, drive 11 miles west of Goldendale on Highway 142, continue northwest on Glendale Road for five miles, and look for the headquarters on your left. The public areas beyond the wildlife refuge headquarters are easier to get to. Another treat at the refuge is Stinson Flat, a good steelhead spot.

Location: On the Columbia River; map B3, grid j5.

Campsites, facilities: There are 20 tent sites (three primitive) and 50 sites with full hookups for trailers or RVs up to 50 feet long. Picnic tables are provided. Flush toilets, sanitary services, a store, and a cafe are available. Electricity, drinking water, sewer hookups, and showers are available. Firewood can be obtained for an extra fee. Some facilities are wheelchair accessible. Boat docks and launching facilities are nearby. Leashed pets are permitted.

Reservations, fees: Reservations accepted; phone (800) 452-5687 ($6 reservation fee). Sites are $11-16 per night. Major credit cards accepted. Call for group camping information. Open year-round.

Directions: From Portland drive east on Interstate 30 for 93 miles to Biggs and Highway 97. Turn north on Highway 97, cross over the Columbia River and drive three miles to the junction with Highway 14. Turn right (east) and drive one mile to the park entrance on the right.

Contact: Maryhill State Park, 50 Highway 97, Goldendale, WA 98620; tel. (800) 233-0321 or (509) 773-5007.

MAP B4

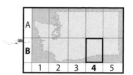

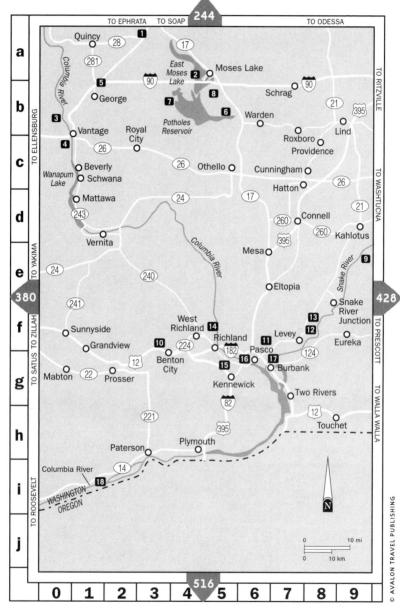

TO EPHRATA   TO SOAP   **244**   TO ODESSA

a

Quincy (28) **1**

(17)

(281)

Columbia River

East Moses Lake

b

(90)

5 George

2 Moses Lake

8

Schrag (90)

(21) (395)

TO RITZVILLE

3

7

6 Warden

TO ELLENSBURG

c

4 Vantage

Royal City

Potholes Reservoir

Roxboro Lind

(26)

(26) Othello

Providence

d

Wanapum Lake

Beverly
Schwana

Cunningham

Hatton (26)

Mattawa

(24)

(17)

(260) Connell

TO WASHTUCNA

(243)

Columbia River

(395) (260)

Kahlotus (21)

Vernita

Mesa

e

TO YAKIMA

(24)

(240)

Eltopia

Snake River

9

380

(241)

Snake River Junction

428

f

TO SATUS TO ZILLAH

Sunnyside

West Richland

14

13

Levey

12

TO PRESCOTT

Grandview

(224)

Richland
(182)

11 Pasco

Eureka

g

Mabton (22) Prosser

(12)

10 Benton City

15

16

17 Burbank

(124)

TO WALLA WALLA

Kennewick

(82)

Two Rivers

h

(221)

(395)

(12)

Touchet

Paterson

Plymouth

N

i

TO ROOSEVELT

Columbia River

(14)

18

WASHINGTON
OREGON

0   10 mi

j

0   10 km

0 1 2 3 4 516 5 6 7 8 9

© AVALON TRAVEL PUBLISHING

CHAPTER B4

◻ Oasis RV Park and Golf   5

This can be an extremely warm, arid area during the summer months, but, fortunately, Oasis Park Resort offers shaded sites. There are two fishing ponds at the resort: one has bass and crappie, while the other is for kids. Nearby recreation options include an 18-hole golf course. Mineral baths are located just a few miles north.

Location: Near Soap Lake; map B4, grid a3.

Campsites, facilities: There are 38 tent sites and 68 sites for trailers or RVs of any length; 10 are drive-through sites. Picnic tables, flush toilets, a miniature nine-hole golf course, bottled gas, sanitary services, a store, propane gas, a laundry room, ice, a swimming pool, and a fishing pond for children are provided. Electricity, drinking water, sewer hookups, and showers are available. A cafe is located within one mile. Leashed pets and motorbikes are permitted.

Reservations, fees: Reservations requested. Sites are $12-18 per night. Open year-round, with limited winter facilities.

Directions: From Spokane drive west on Interstate 90 Exit 151 (near George) to Highway 283/28. Turn northeast and drive 18 miles to the park on the left (just before reaching the town of Ephrata).

Contact: Oasis RV Park and Golf, 2541 Basin Street SW, Ephrata, WA 98823; tel. (877) 754-5102, (509) 754-5102.

◻ Big Sun Resort   5

This park is a short distance from Moses Lake State Park, which is open for day-use only. You'll find shady picnic spots with tables and fire grills, beach access, and moorage floats. Waterskiing is allowed on the lake.

Location: Near Moses Lake State Park; map B4, grid a4.

Campsites, facilities: There are 10 tent sites and 50 sites for trailers or RVs of any length; 15 are drive-through sites. Electricity, drinking water, sewer hookups, and picnic tables are provided. Flush toilets, pay showers, a recreation hall, a laundry room, ice, and a playground are available. Sanitary services, a store, and a cafe are within one mile. Boat docks, launching facilities, and rentals are nearby. Leashed pets and motorbikes are permitted.

Reservations, fees: Reservations accepted. Sites are $13.50-20 per night. Open March through October. Please note: The future of this resort is uncertain; call for current status before planning your trip.

Directions: From Spokane drive west on Interstate 90 to Moses Lake and Exit 176. Take that exit to Broadway and drive one-half mile to Burress Avenue. Turn west on Burress Avenue and drive one block to the park.

Contact: Big Sun Resort, 2300 West Marina, Moses Lake, WA 98837; tel. (509) 765-8294; fax (509) 765-8874.

❸ Vantage Riverstone Resort   6

This campground offers pleasant, grassy sites overlooking the Columbia River a short distance from the state park (see Ginkgo-Wanapum State Park, south of Interstate 90). This is the only campground in the immediate area that provides space for tent camping. The next closest is 12 miles away at Shady Tree RV Park in George.
Location: On the Columbia River; map B4, grid b0.
Campsites, facilities: There are 50+ tent sites and 50 sites for trailers or RVs of any length. Drinking water, picnic tables, electricity, sewer hookups, flush toilets, sanitary services, showers, a recreation hall, a laundry room, ice, a playground, and a swimming pool are available. A store and a cafe are located next to the resort. Boat docks and launching facilities are nearby. Leashed pets and motorbikes are permitted.
Reservations, fees: Reservations accepted. Sites are $19-23 per night. Major credit cards accepted. Open year-round.
Directions: From Spokane drive west on Interstate 90 to Vantage and the Vantage Highway (Exit 136). Take that exit, turn north, and drive north for three blocks to the resort on the left.
Contact: Vantage Riverstone Resort, P.O. Box 1101, Vantage, WA 98950; tel. (509) 856-2230.

❹ Ginkgo-Wanapum State Park   7

There are actually two separate parks here, Ginkgo State Park and Wanapum State Recreation Area. Camping is permitted only at Wanapum, which is seven miles south of the main entrance at Ginkgo. The recreation highlights are at Ginkgo, which is set along Wanapum Lake and the Columbia River. The park is the site of an ancient petrified forest, and there is an interpretive center and trail. Options include hiking, swimming, boating, waterskiing, and fishing. The campground at Wanapum is set up primarily for RVs, with full hookups, rest rooms, and showers.
Location: On the Columbia River and Wanapum Lake; map B4, grid c0.
Campsites, facilities: There are 50 sites with full hookups for trailers or RVs up to 60 feet. Picnic tables, fire grills, and flush toilets are provided. Showers and firewood are available for an extra fee. Boat docks and launching facilities are nearby. Leashed pets are permitted.
Reservations, fees: No reservations accepted. Sites are $16 per night. Open April through October.
Directions: From Spokane drive west on Interstate 90 to Vantage and the Vantage Highway (Exit 136). Take that exit, turn south on Vantage Highway, and drive three miles south to the park on the right.
Contact: Ginkgo-Wanapum State Park, Vantage, WA 98950; tel. (800) 233-0321 or (509) 856-2700.

❺ Shady Tree RV Park   8

This is an oasis in a desert-like area, with shade trees and grassy sites. There is a great natural outdoor amphitheater seating 2,000, scene of major concerts from

June through September, just eight miles away. Another option is Martha Lake, small and public, within one mile of Moses Lake State Park, about 30 miles away.

Location: Near George Washington; map B4, grid b1.

Campsites, facilities: There are 30 tent sites and 41 sites for trailers or RVs of any length; four are drive-through sites. Electricity, drinking water, sewer hookups, garbage service, and picnic tables are provided. Flush toilets, showers, and a laundry room are available. Leashed pets and motorbikes are permitted.

Reservations, fees: No reservations accepted. Sites are $16-18 per night. Open year-round.

Directions: From Spokane drive west on Interstate 90 to Exit 151 (two miles east of George). Take that exit and bear right to the campground right at the corner (just off the highway at the intersection of Highways 281 and 283).

Contact: Shady Tree RV Park, 1099 Highway 283 North, Quincy, WA 98848; tel. (509) 785-2851.

6 Mar-Don Resort   7

This park is located on Potholes Reservoir with opportunities for fishing, swimming, and boating. A marina, tackle, and boat rentals are all available. Hiking trails and marked bike trails are close by. There is also a 26-unit motel at the resort.

Location: Near Potholes Reservoir; map B4, grid b5.

Campsites, facilities: There are 300 sites for tents, trailers, or RVs of any length; seven are drive-through sites. Electricity, drinking water, sewer hookups, and picnic tables are provided. Flush toilets, bottled gas, sanitary services, showers, a game room, a store, a laundry room, ice, a playground, boat moorage, boat rentals, and launching facilities are available. Some facilities are wheelchair accessible. Leashed pets are permitted.

Reservations, fees: Reservations recommended. Sites are $16-19 per night. Major credit cards accepted. Open year-round.

Directions: From Spokane drive west on Interstate 90 to Moses Lake and Exit 179 and Highway 17. Turn south and drive nine miles to Highway 262. Turn west and drive 10 miles to the resort on the southern shore of Potholes Reservoir.

Contact: Mar-Don Resort, 8198 Highway 262 Southeast, Othello, WA 99344; tel. (800) 416-2736 or (509) 346-2651.

7 Potholes State Park   8

This park is on Potholes Reservoir, where fishing is the highlight. Trout, walleye, crappie, and perch are among the species taken here. Waterskiing and hiking are two other options. There is a nice beach near the campground. A side trip to the Columbia Wildlife Refuge is recommended.

Location: On Potholes Reservoir; map B4, grid b4.

Campsites, facilities: There are 126 sites for tents, trailers, or RVs up to 50 feet long; 60 have full hookups. Picnic tables and fire grills are provided. Flush toilets, sanitary services, a store, and a playground are available. Showers and firewood can be obtained for an extra fee. Boat launching facilities and rentals are nearby. Leashed pets are permitted.

Reservations, fees: Reservations accepted; phone (800) 452-5687 ($6 reservation fee). Sites are $5-16 per night. Open April through October.

Directions: From Spokane drive west on Interstate 90 to Moses Lake and Exit 179 and Highway 17. Turn south and drive nine miles to Highway 262. Turn west and drive 11 miles to the resort on the southern shore of Potholes Reservoir (well signed).

Contact: Potholes State Park, 6762 Highway 262 East, Othello, WA 99344; tel. (800) 233-0321 or (509) 765-7271.

8 Willows Trailer Village   5

One of two campgrounds in the area, this one has grassy, shaded sites, horseshoe pits, barbecues, and a recreation field. See the description of Big Sun Resort for information on recreation spots in the vicinity.

Location: Near Moses Lake State Park; map B4, grid b5.

Campsites, facilities: There are 20 tent sites and 65 drive-through sites for trailers or RVs of any length. Electricity, drinking water, sewer hookups, and picnic tables are provided. Flush toilets, bottled gas, showers, a store, a laundry room, and ice are available. There is also a hairdresser and a barber shop on site. Leashed pets are permitted.

Reservations, fees: No reservations accepted. Sites are $12.50-16.50 per night. Open year-round.

Directions: From Spokane drive west on Interstate 90 to Moses Lake and Exit 179 and Highway 17. Turn south and drive 2.5 miles to Road M. Turn west and drive 300 yards to the park.

Contact: Willows Trailer Village, 1347 Road M Southeast, Moses Lake, WA 98837; tel. (509) 765-7531.

9 Windust   6

Windust is the only game in town, with no other campgrounds within a 20-mile radius. The camp is along the shore of Sacajawea Lake near the Lower Monumental Dam on the Snake River. Swimming and fishing are popular.

Location: On Sacajawea Lake; map B4, grid e9.

Campsites, facilities: There is space for 28 tents, trailers, or RVs in open camping areas at both ends of the park. Drinking water, picnic tables, and fire grills are provided. Flush toilets and a playground are available. Some facilities are wheelchair accessible. Boat docks and launching facilities are nearby. Leashed pets are permitted.

Reservations, fees: Reservations accepted; phone (877) 444-6777 or access the website: www.reserveusa.com ($8.65 reservation fee). Sites are $8 per night. Open year-round, with no fee and limited facilities from October through March.

Directions: From Pasco drive east on U.S. 12 for four miles to Pasco/Kaholtus Road. Turn east and drive 28 miles to Burr Canyon Road. Turn right on Burr Canyon Road and drive six miles to the park (from the north, the Burr Canyon Road becomes Highway 263).

Contact: U.S. Army Corps of Engineers, 2339 Ice Harbor Drive, Burbank, WA 99323; tel. (509) 547-7781; fax (509) 543-3201.

🔟 Beach RV Park   8

If it's getting late, you'd best stop here—the only option for a long stretch. This park along the shore of the Yakima River is a pleasant spot, with spacious RV sites and a large grassy area with poplar trees and shrubs providing privacy between sites. Nearby recreation options include an 18-hole golf course, a full-service marina, and tennis courts.

Location: On the Yakima River; map B4, grid f3.

Campsites, facilities: There are 39 sites for trailers or RVs of any length; five are drive-through sites. Electricity, drinking water, sewer hookups, and cable TV are provided. Flush toilets, showers, a laundry room, and ice are available. Bottled gas, sanitary services, a store, and a cafe are located within one mile. Boat launching facilities are nearby. Leashed pets and motorbikes are permitted.

Reservations, fees: Reservations accepted. Sites are $18 per night. Open year-round.

Directions: From Pasco drive west on U.S. 12 past Richland and continue eight miles to the Benton City exit. Take that exit and drive one block north to Abby Avenue. Turn west and drive to the park at 113 Abby Avenue.

Contact: Beach RV Park, 113 Abby Avenue, WA 99320; tel. (509) 588-5959.

1️⃣1️⃣ Arrowhead RV Park   5

This is a decent layover spot in Pasco. Nearby recreation options include an 18-hole golf course, a full-service marina, and tennis courts.

Location: Near the Columbia River; map B4, grid f6.

Campsites, facilities: There are 35 tent sites and 80 sites for trailers or RVs of any length; 33 are drive-through sites. Electricity (50 Amp), drinking water, sewer hookups, and picnic tables are provided. Flush toilets, showers, a pay phone, and a laundry room are available. A store and a cafe are located within walking distance. Small pets and motorbikes are permitted.

Reservations, fees: Reservations accepted. Sites are $18-30 per night for two people. Open year-round.

Directions: In Pasco on U.S. 395, take the Hillsboro Street exit, turn east, and drive a very short distance to Commercial Avenue. Turn south and drive less than one-half mile to the park entry.

Contact: Arrowhead RV Park, 3120 Commercial Avenue, Pasco, WA 99301; tel. (509) 545-8206.

1️⃣2️⃣ Charbonneau Park   6

This shorefront camp along the Snake River just above Ice Harbor Dam is a good spot for fishing, boating, swimming, and waterskiing. The dam's visitor center (open daily from April through October) features exhibits and a view through Lucite glass of a salmon fish ladder.

Location: On the Snake River; map B4, grid f8.

Campsites, facilities: There is a dispersed camping area accommodating about 100 tents and 80 sites for tents, trailers, or RVs of any length, 14 with full hookups. Picnic tables and fire grills are provided. Flush toilets, a dump station, showers, a playground, and a primitive overflow camping area are available. Some facilities are wheelchair accessible. A marina with boat docks, launching facilities, and a marine dump station are nearby. Leashed pets are permitted.

Reservations, fees: Reservations accepted; phone (877) 444-6777 or access the website: www.reserveusa.com ($8.65 reservation fee). Sites are $12-14 per night. Open April through October with full facilities and gate closure from 10 p.m. to 6 a.m.; there are limited facilities the rest of the year.

Directions: In Pasco drive southeast on U.S. 12 for five miles to Highway 124. Turn east and drive eight miles to Sun Harbor Road. Turn north and drive two miles to the park.

Contact: U.S. Army Corps of Engineers, Route 6, Box 693, Pasco, WA 99301-9165; tel. (509) 547-7781.

13 Fishhook Park   6

If you're driving along Highway 124 and you need a spot for the night, make the turn on Fishhook Park Road and check out this wooded camp along the Snake River. Some lawn area is provided, along with places to swim, fish, and water-ski.

Location: On the Snake River; map B4, grid f8.

Campsites, facilities: There are 24 tent-only sites and 41 sites for tents, trailers, or RVs of any length; eight are drive-through sites. Picnic tables and fire grills are provided. Drinking water, electricity, flush toilets, sanitary services, showers, telephone service, and a playground are available. Some facilities are wheelchair accessible. Boat docks and launching facilities are nearby. Leashed pets are permitted.

Reservations, fees: Reservations accepted; phone (877) 444-6777 or access the website: www.reserveusa.com ($8.65 reservation fee). Sites are $10-18 per night. Open May through September. Park gates are locked from 10 p.m. to 6 a.m.

Directions: In Pasco drive southeast on U.S. 12 for five miles to Highway 124. Turn east and drive 16 miles to Fishhook Park Road. Turn left on Fishhook Park Road and drive four miles to the park.

Contact: U.S. Army Corps of Engineers, 2339 Ice Harbor Drive, Burbank, WA 99323; tel. (509) 547-7781; fax (509) 543-3201.

14 Desert Gold RV Park and Motel   6

This is a nice RV park about a mile from the Columbia River. Nearby recreation options include an 18-hole golf course, hiking trails, a full-service marina, and tennis courts. You can also visit the Department of Energy public information center at the Hanford Science Center. The park has a pool and spa if you just want to relax without going anywhere.

Location: Near the Columbia River; map B4, grid f5.

Campsites, facilities: There are 90 sites for trailers or RVs of any length; 15 are drive-through sites. Electricity, drinking water, sewer hookups, cable TV, and picnic tables are provided. Flush toilets, showers, bottled gas, sanitary services, a store, a laundry room, ice, a game/meeting room, video rentals, and a swimming pool are available. A cafe is located within one mile. Boat docks and launching facilities are nearby on the Columbia River. Leashed pets are permitted.

Reservations, fees: Reservations accepted. Sites are $18 per night for two people. Major credit cards accepted. Open year-round.

Directions: In Richland on Interstate 182, take Exit 3 (Queensgate). Turn right and drive to Columbia Park Trail (the first left). Turn left and drive about two miles to the park.

Contact: Desert Gold RV Park and Motel, 611 Columbia Park Trail, Richland, WA 99352; tel. (800) 788-GOLD/4653 or (509) 627-1000.

15 Columbia Park Campground

 6

This campground is in a grassy suburban area on the Columbia River, adjacent to Columbia Park. Nearby activities include waterskiing on the Columbia River, an 18-hole golf course, hiking trails, marked bike trails, and tennis courts. The sun can feel like a branding iron during the summer.

Location: On the Columbia River; map B4, grid g5.

Campsites, facilities: There are 22 tent sites and 100 sites for trailers or RVs; 26 are drive-through sites. Electricity, drinking water, and picnic tables are provided. Flush toilets, sanitary services, ice, and a playground are available. Showers and firewood can be obtained for an extra fee. A store and a cafe are located within one mile. Boat docks and launching facilities are nearby. Leashed pets and motorbikes are permitted.

Reservations, fees: Reservations accepted. Sites are $7-11 per night. Open year-round.

Directions: In Kennewick on U.S. 395/Highway 240 drive toward the Columbia River. Continue to the campground along the highway. The campground is located adjacent to Columbia Park.

Contact: Columbia Park Campground, 6601 S.E. Columbia, Kennewick, WA 99352; tel. (509) 783-3711, (509) 585-4295; fax (509) 586-9022.

16 Greentree RV Park   6

This shady park in urban Pasco is close to an 18-hole golf course, hiking trails, a full-service marina, and tennis courts. The Franklin County Historical Museum, which is located in town, and the Sacajawea State Park Museum and Interpretive Center, located three miles southeast of town, both offer extensive collections of Native American artifacts.

Location: In Pasco; map B4, grid g6.

Campsites, facilities: There are 40 sites for trailers or RVs of any length. Electricity, drinking water, and sewer hookups are provided. A laundry room and showers are available. Bottled gas, a store, a cafe, and ice are located within one mile. Boat docks, launching facilities, and rentals are nearby. Pets and motorbikes are permitted.

Reservations, fees: Reservations accepted. Sites are $18 per night; call for weekly and monthly rates. Open year-round.

Directions: In Pasco on Interstate 182, take Exit 13 to the first intersection. The park is at the southwest corner the intersection.

Contact: Greentree RV Park, 2103 North Fifth Avenue, No. 69, Pasco, WA 99301; tel. (509) 547-6220.

🔳 Hood Park   6

A more developed, nearby alternative to Columbia Park Campground, this park has river access for swimming and boating. Other recreation options include basketball and horseshoes. McNary Wildlife Refuge is right next door, and Sacajawea State Park is within four miles.

Location: On the Snake River; map B4, grid g6.

Campsites, facilities: There are 68 sites for tents, trailers, or RVs of any length. Drinking water, fire grills, and picnic tables are provided. Flush toilets, sanitary services, showers, electricity, a playground, horseshoe pits, basketball court, and a primitive overflow camping area are available. A restaurant and convenience store are located within two miles. Some facilities are wheelchair accessible. Boat docks and launching facilities are nearby. Leashed pets are permitted.

Reservations, fees: Reservations accepted; phone (877) 444-6777 or access the website: www.reserveusa.com ($8.65 reservation fee). Sites are $14-16 per night, and $7 per night in the overflow area. Open April through September. The gates are locked from 10 p.m. to 6 a.m.

Directions: In Pasco drive southeast on U.S. 12 for five miles to the junction with Highway 124. Turn left (east) on Highway 124 and drive an extremely short distance to the park entrance on the right.

Contact: U.S. Army Corps of Engineers, 2339 Ice Harbor Drive, Burbank, WA 99323; tel. (509) 547-7781; fax (509) 543-3201.

🔳 Crow Butte State Park
 8

How would you like to be stranded on a romantic island? Well, this park offers a possibility. This state park is set on an island in the Columbia River and is the only campground in a 25-mile radius. Waterskiing, fishing, swimming, and hiking are among the possibilities here. The Umatilla National Wildlife Refuge is adjacent to the park and allows fishing and hunting in specified areas.

Location: On the Columbia River; map B4, grid i1.

Campsites, facilities: There are two primitive tent sites and 50 sites with full hookups for trailers or RVs up to 60 feet long. Fire grills and picnic tables are provided. Flush toilets, showers, and a sanitary disposal station are available. Some facilities are wheelchair accessible. Boat launching facilities are nearby. Leashed pets are permitted.

Reservations, fees: Reservations accepted; phone (800) 452-5687 ($6 reservation fee). Sites are $5-16 per night. Open year-round, with limited winter facilities.

Directions: From the junction of Interstate 82/U.S. 395 and Highway 20 at Plymouth, just north of the Columbia River, turn west on Highway 14. Drive to Paterson and continue west for 15 miles to the park entrance road on the left. Turn left and drive one mile (across the bridge) to the park on the island.

Contact: Crow Butte State Park, P.O. Box 217, Paterson, WA 99345; tel. (800) 233-0321 or (509) 875-2644.

PALOUSE FALLS STATE PARK

DON PITCHER

MAP B5

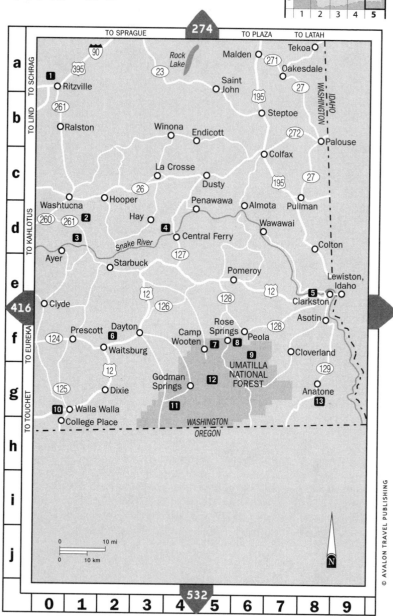

TO SPRAGUE   274   TO PLAZA   TO LATAH

a TO SCHRAG TO LIND   90   395   Rock Lake   23   Malden   271   Tekoa   Oakesdale   27   Saint John   195   WASHINGTON IDAHO
Ritzville ①

b   261   Ralston   Winona   Endicott   Steptoe   272   Palouse

c   La Crosse   Dusty   Colfax   195   27

d TO KAHLOTUS Washtucna   26   Hooper   Hay   ② 261 260   Penawawa   Almota   Pullman   Wawawai   ④ Central Ferry   Snake River   ③ Ayer   Starbuck   127   Colton

e 416 TO EUREKA   Clyde   Pomeroy   12   126   128   12   Lewiston, Idaho   ⑤ Clarkston

f   124   Prescott   Dayton   ⑥   Waitsburg   Camp Wooten   Rose Springs   ⑦ ⑧ Peola   ⑨   128   Asotin   Cloverland

g TO TOUCHET   125   Dixie   Godman Springs   ⑫   ⑪   UMATILLA NATIONAL FOREST   129   Anatone   ⑬   ⑩ Walla Walla   College Place   WASHINGTON   OREGON

h

i

j   0   10 mi   0   10 km   N

0 1 2 3 4   532   5 6 7 8 9

CHAPTER B5

◼ Best Inn and RV and Suites   7

If all you have is a tent, well, this is the only site to stake it within a radius of 25 miles. The nearest fishing is at Sprague Lake, 22 miles north on U.S. 395. Burroughs Historical Museum is a possible side trip in town. An 18-hole golf course and tennis courts are nearby.

Location: In Ritzville; map B5, grid a0.

Campsites, facilities: There are 39 drive-through sites for tents, trailers, or RVs of any length. Electricity, piped water, sewer hookups, cable TV, and picnic tables are provided. Flush toilets, sanitary services, showers, a laundry room, ice, a playground, a hot tub, and a seasonal swimming pool are available. Bottled gas, a store, and a cafe are located within one mile. Leashed pets and motorbikes are permitted.

Reservations, fees: Reservations accepted. Sites are $20-25 per night. Major credit cards accepted. Open mid-April to mid-October.

Directions: From Pasco, take U.S. 395 and drive 85 miles north to Ritzville to Interstate 90. Take Interstate 90 east and drive one-half mile to Exit 221. Take that exit to Highway 261 and bear left (Division Street, not signed) and drive one-half block to a four-way stop at Smitty's Boulevard. Turn right and drive short distance to the hotel/RV check-in on the left.

Contact: Best Inn and RV and Suites, 1513 Smitty's Boulevard, Ritzville, WA 99169; tel. (509) 659-1007; fax (509) 659-1025.

◻ Palouse Falls State Park   10

You have to navigate a roundabout circuit of highways to get here, but this remote state park is well worth the trip. Set at the confluence of the Snake and Palouse Rivers, it's almost unknown and gets relatively little use even in the summer months. Spectacular 190-foot Palouse Falls is a sight not to miss. In recent years a wheelchair-accessible trail has been completed. The park has shaded picnic facilities and an abundance of wildlife.

Location: On the Snake and Palouse Rivers; map B5, grid d1.

Campsites, facilities: There are 10 primitive campsites and 10 sites for tents, self-contained trailers, or RVs up to 40 feet long. Picnic tables and fire grills are provided. Pit toilets are available. Some facilities are wheelchair accessible. Leashed pets are permitted.

Reservations, fees: No reservations accepted. Sites are $7 per night. Open April to late September, weather permitting.

Directions: From Spokane drive south on U.S. 195 for 59 miles to Highway 26. Turn west on Highway 26 and drive 17 miles southwest to Highway 127. Turn south on Highway 127 and drive 28 miles to U.S. 12. Turn west on U.S. 12 and drive nine miles to Highway 261. Turn west and drive 22 miles (crossing the river) to the park entrance (located seven miles northwest of Lyons Ferry). Turn right and drive to the park.

Contact: Palouse Falls State Park, P.O. Box 157, Starbuck, WA 99359; tel. (800) 233-0321 or (509) 646-3252.

3 Lyon's Ferry State Park

 8

This state park at the confluence of the Snake and Palouse Rivers is loaded with activities, including fishing, hiking, swimming, waterskiing, and boating. A good side trip is a visit to beautiful Palouse Falls, located seven miles north.

Location: On the Snake River; map B5, grid d1.

Campsites, facilities: There are two primitive tent sites and 50 sites for tents or self-contained trailers or RVs. Picnic tables and fire grills are provided. Flush toilets, sanitary services, and showers are available. Some facilities are wheelchair accessible. Boat docks and launching facilities are nearby. Leashed pets are permitted.

Reservations, fees: No reservations accepted. Sites are $10 per night. Open April through September.

Directions: From Spokane drive south on U.S. 195 for 59 miles to Highway 26. Turn west on Highway 26 and drive 17 miles southwest to Highway 127. Turn south on Highway 127 and drive 28 miles to U.S. 12. Turn west on U.S. 12 and drive nine miles to Highway 261. Turn west and drive 20 miles (crossing the river) to the park entrance (just north of the river on the right). Turn right and drive to the park.

Contact: Lyon's Ferry State Park, P.O. Box 157, Starbuck, WA 99359; tel. (800) 233-0321 or (509) 646-3252.

4 Central Ferry State Park

 8

This is the only campground within a 20-mile radius. It's located along the shore of the Snake River and has a beach. Waterskiing, sailing, boating, swimming, and fishing for bass and catfish are all options here.

Location: On the Snake River; map B5, grid d4.

Campsites, facilities: There are eight primitive tent sites and 60 sites with full hookups for trailers or RVs up to 45 feet long. There is also one group camp accommodating up to 100 people. Picnic tables and fire grills are provided. Flush toilets, a sanitary service station, electricity, piped water, sewer hookups, a group fire ring, three horseshoe pit areas, and showers are available. A store and a restaurant are within two miles. Some facilities are wheelchair accessible. Boat docks, launching facilities, and a fishing pier are within the park. Leashed pets are permitted.

Reservations, fees: Contact Reservations Northwest at (800) 452-5687 ($6 reservation fee). Sites are $15 per night. For group camp reservations, phone (509) 549-3551; group sites are $25 per night plus $1 per night per camper and $10 per night per RV. Major credit cards accepted. Open mid-March to mid-November.

Directions: From Spokane, drive south on U.S. 195 for 59 miles to Highway 26. Turn west on Highway 26 and drive 17 miles southwest to Highway 127. Turn south on Highway 127 and drive 17 miles to the park entrance on the right (set on the north shore of the Snake River).

Contact: Central Ferry State Park, Route 3, P.O. Box 99, Pomeroy, WA 99347; tel. (800) 233-0321 or (509) 549-3551.

5 Chief Timothy State Park

       8

This unusual state park is set on a bridged island in the Snake River and is accessible to cars. All water sports are offered here, including fishing, swimming, boating, waterskiing, and sailing, plus docks for boating campers, a beach area, and an interpretive center focusing on the Lewis and Clark Expedition. Outfitters in Clarkston will take you sightseeing up the Grand Canyon of the Snake River. Call the Clarkston Chamber of Commerce at (509) 758-7712 or fax (509) 751-8767 for details.

Location: On the Snake River; map B5, grid e8.

Campsites, facilities: There are two primitive tent sites and 60 sites with water and electrical hookups for trailers or RVs of any length. Picnic tables and fire grills are provided. Flush toilets, sanitary services, and a playground are available. Electricity, piped water, sewer hookups, and showers are available. Firewood can be obtained for an extra fee. Some facilities are wheelchair accessible. Boat docks and launching facilities are nearby. Leashed pets are permitted.

Reservations, fees: Reservations accepted; phone (800) 452-5687 ($6 reservation fee). Major credit cards accepted. Sites are $7-16 per night. Open year-round, with limited winter facilities.

Directions: From Clarkston on the Washington/Idaho border, drive west on U.S. 12 for seven miles to the signed park entrance road on the right. Turn north and drive one mile to the park, set on a bridged island in the Snake River.

Contact: Chief Timothy State Park, Highway 12, Clarkston, WA 99403; tel. (800) 233-0321, (509) 758-9580.

6 Lewis and Clark Trail State Park   8

If it's getting late and you need to stop, consider this camp, the only one within 20 miles. It's not a bad choice, since it's set along the original Lewis and Clark Trail. During the summer the rangers offer campfire programs, where they share the details of the site's history. The campground is in a forested, "prairie country" environment.

Location: On the Lewis and Clark Trail; map B5, grid f2.

Campsites, facilities: There are four primitive tent sites and 30 sites for tents or self-enclosed trailers or RVs up to 28 feet long. Picnic tables and fire grills are provided. Flush toilets, showers, firewood, and sanitary services are available. A store, a cafe, and ice are located within one mile. Leashed pets are permitted.

Reservations, fees: No reservations accepted. Sites are $7-16 per night. Open year-round.

Directions: From Walla Walla drive east on U.S. 12 for 22 miles to Waitsburg. Bear right on U.S. 12 and drive east for four miles to the park entrance on the left.

Contact: Lewis and Clark Trail State Park, Route 1, P.O. Box 90, Dayton, WA 99328; tel. (800) 233-0321 or (509) 337-6457.

7 Tucannon 8

For people willing to rough it, this backcountry camp in Umatilla National Forest is the place, with plenty of hiking, fishing, and hunting, all in a rugged setting. The camp is not far from the Tucannon River, which offers a myriad of options for vacationers. Camp Wooten State Park is just a half mile to the south.

Location: In Umatilla National Forest; map B5, grid f5.

Campsites, facilities: There are 13 sites for tents, trailers, or RVs up to 15 feet long. Picnic tables and fire grills are provided. Vault toilets are available, but there is no piped water. Leashed pets are permitted.

Reservations, fees: No reservations; no fee. Open May to late November.

Directions: From Clarkston, drive west on U.S. 12 for 37 miles to Pomeroy. Continue west for five miles to Tatman Mountain Road (signed for Camp Wooten). Turn left (south) and drive 19 miles (the road becomes Forest Road 47). Once inside the national forest boundary, continue southwest on Forest Road 47 for four miles to the campground on the left.

Contact: Umatilla National Forest, Pomeroy Ranger District, 71 West Main Street, Pomeroy, WA 99347; tel. (509) 843-1891; fax (509) 843-4621.

8 Alder Thicket 7

This is probably the first time you've heard of this place. Hardly anybody knows about it, including people who live relatively nearby in Walla Walla. It's a prime base camp for a backcountry hiking adventure in summer or a jumping-off point for a hunting trip in the fall. This is a very primitive camp, but it's great if you're looking for quiet and solitude.

Location: In Umatilla National Forest; map B5, grid f5.

Campsites, facilities: There are four sites for tents, trailers, or RVs up to 15 feet long. Picnic tables and fire grills are provided. Vault toilets are available, but there is no piped water. Leashed pets are permitted.

Reservations, fees: No reservations; no fee. Open mid-May to mid-November.

Directions: From Clarkston, drive west on U.S. 12 for 37 miles to Pomeroy and Highway 128. Turn south and drive seven miles to a fork. At the fork continue straight to Forest Road 40 (15 miles from Pomeroy to the national forest boundary) and continue 3.5 miles to the campground on the right.

Contact: Umatilla National Forest, Pomeroy Ranger District, 71 West Main Street, Pomeroy, WA 99347; tel. (509) 843-1891; fax (509) 843-4621.

9 Big Springs 8

In the fall Big Springs is used primarily by hunters, while come summer this nice, cool site is a possible base camp for a backpacking trip. Though quite primitive with little in the way of activity options, this is a perfect spot to get away from it all. It's advisable to obtain a U.S. Forest Service map.

Location: In Umatilla National Forest; map B5, grid f6.

Campsites, facilities: There are eight tent sites. Picnic tables are provided. Vault toilets are available, but there is no piped water. Leashed pets are permitted.

Reservations, fees: No reservations; no fee. Open mid-May to mid-November.

Directions: From Clarkston drive west on U.S. 12 for 37 miles to Pomeroy and Highway 128. Turn south and drive 25 miles to Forest Road 42 (to the Clearwater Lookout Tower). Turn left and continue on Forest Road 42 for five miles to the campground entrance road (Forest Road 4225). Turn right and drive to the campground on the right.

Contact: Umatilla National Forest, Pomeroy Ranger District, 71 West Main Street, Pomeroy, WA 99347; tel. (509) 843-1891; fax (509) 843-4621.

10 Walla Walla Campground 6

This 300-acre park feels rustic despite its address within Walla Walla city limits. The campground is wooded with grassy sites. The park is divided by Garrison Creek, with the campground on one side and a picnic area, playground, and historical museum on the other. In May the Balloon Stampede, a well-known hot air balloon festival, brings tourists in hordes, as does July's Mountain Man Rendezvous. Also in July the drama department from the city college performs musicals at the park's amphitheater. This is the only campground we've found for miles, and it's a prime choice.

Location: In Fort Walla Walla Park; map B5, grid g0.

Campsites, facilities: There are 49 tent sites and 21 sites with partial hookups for trailers or RVs up to 35 feet. An overflow area is also provided. Rest rooms, showers, water and electricity hookups, a phone, and a sanitary dump station are available. Leashed pets are permitted.

Reservations, fees: Reservations accepted. Sites are $10 (without utilities) and $15 (with utilities) per night. Open year-round, with limited winter services.

Directions: In Walla Walla on U.S. 12, take the Highway 125 exit and drive south for 2.5 miles to Dalles Military Road. Turn right on Dalles Military Road and continue one-half mile to the campground.

Contact: Walla Walla Campground, Dalles Military Road, P.O. Box 1530, Walla Walla, WA 99362; tel. (509) 527-3770.

11 Godman   8

This tiny, little-known spot bordering a wilderness area is primarily used as a base camp for backcountry expeditions. A trailhead provides access to the Wenaha-Tucannon Wilderness for both hikers and horseback riders. Horse facilities are available at the trailhead. In the winter the trails and roads are used for snowmobiling.

Location: Near the Wenaha-Tucannon Wilderness in Umatilla National Forest; map B5, grid g4.

Campsites, facilities: There are eight sites for tents, trailers, or RVs up to 15 feet long, plus one cabin that can accommodate up to eight people. Picnic tables and fire grills are provided. Vault toilets are available, but there is no piped water. Facilities are available for horses, including hitching rails and a spring. Leashed pets are permitted.

Reservations, fees: No reservations accepted. There is no fee for the campsites, but cabins are $25 a night plus $5 per person. Open mid-June to late October; cabins are available year-round.

Directions: From Walla Walla drive northeast on U.S. 12 for 32 miles to Dayton and North Fork Touchet River Road. Turn right on North Fork Touchet River Road and drive 14 miles southeast to the national forest boundary and continue to Kendall Skyline Road. Turn south and drive 11 miles to the campground on the right.

Contact: Umatilla National Forest, Pomeroy Ranger District, 71 West Main Street, Pomeroy, WA 99347; tel. (509) 843-1891; fax (509) 843-4621.

12 Teal Spring   8

The views of the surrounding forest are astonishing from the nearby lookout. Teal Springs Camp is set 5,700 feet and is one of several small, primitive camps in the area. A U.S. Forest Service map details the backcountry roads, trails, and streams. Hunting is popular in the fall, and a snow shelter is available for winter use.

Location: In Umatilla National Forest; map B5, grid g5.

Campsites, facilities: There are eight sites for tents, trailers, or RVs up to 15 feet long. Vault toilets are available, but there is no piped water. Picnic tables and fire grills are provided. Leashed pets are permitted.

Reservations, fees: No reservations; no fee. Open June to mid-November.

Directions: From Clarkston, drive west on U.S. 12 for 37 miles to Pomeroy and Highway 128. Turn south and drive 25 miles to Forest Road 42 (to the Clearwater Lookout Tower). Turn left and continue on Forest Road 42 and drive one mile to the campground entrance road. Turn right and drive 200 yards to the campground.

Contact: Umatilla National Forest, Pomeroy Ranger District, 71 West Main Street, Pomeroy, WA 99347; tel. (509) 843-1891; fax (509) 843-4621.

13 Fields Spring State Park   8

Just about nobody knows about this spot, and it's a good one. Tucked away in the southeast corner of the state, it has a designated environmental learning center. This park is noted for its variety of bird life and wildflowers. A hiking trail leads up to Puffer Butte at 4,500 feet, which offers a panoramic view of the Snake River Canyon, the Wallowa Mountains, and Idaho, Oregon, and Washington. Two day-use areas with boat launches, managed by the Department of Fish and Game, are within about 25 miles of the park. One is the Snake River Access, 22.5 miles south of Asotin on Snake River Road; the other is the Grande Ronde River Access, 24 miles south of Asotin on the same road. During the winter this state park is open for snowmobiling and cross-country skiing.

Location: Near Puffer Butte; map B5, grid g8.

Campsites, facilities: There are two primitive tent sites and 20 sites for tents or self-contained RVs up to 30 feet long. Piped water, picnic tables, and fire grills are provided. Flush toilets, a sanitary disposal station, and a playground are available. Showers and firewood can be obtained for an extra fee. A store, a restaurant, and ice are located within one mile. Some facilities are wheelchair accessible. Leashed pets are permitted.

Reservations, fees: No reservations accepted. Sites are $5-10 per night. Open year-round, with limited winter facilities.

Directions: From Clarkston turn south on Highway 129 and drive 28.5 miles (just south of Rattlesnake Pass) to the park entrance on the east side of the road.

Contact: Fields Spring State Park, P.O. Box 86, Anatone, WA 99401; tel. (800) 233-0321 or (509) 256-3332.

COAST CAMPING SUNSET

OREGON CAMPGROUNDS

MAP C1

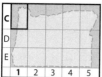

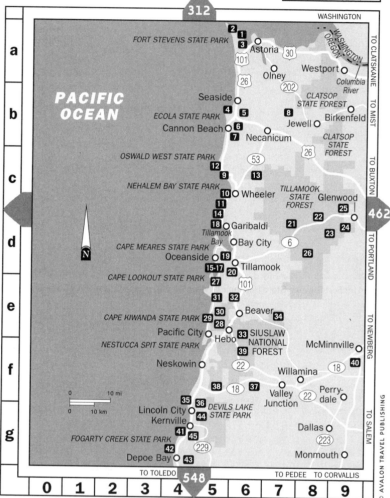

PACIFIC OCEAN

WASHINGTON

312

548

462

TO CLATSKANIE
TO MIST
TO BUXTON
TO PORTLAND
TO NEWBERG
TO SALEM

FORT STEVENS STATE PARK
Astoria
30
101
Olney
26
Westport
202
Columbia River
WASHINGTON
OREGON

Seaside
CLATSOP STATE FOREST
ECOLA STATE PARK
Cannon Beach
Jewell
Birkenfeld
Necanicum
26
CLATSOP STATE FOREST

OSWALD WEST STATE PARK
53
NEHALEM BAY STATE PARK
Wheeler
TILLAMOOK STATE FOREST
Glenwood

Garibaldi
Tillamook Bay
CAPE MEARES STATE PARK
Bay City
6
Oceanside
Tillamook
CAPE LOOKOUT STATE PARK
101

Beaver
CAPE KIWANDA STATE PARK
Pacific City
Hebo
SIUSLAW NATIONAL FOREST
McMinnville
NESTUCCA SPIT STATE PARK
22
Neskowin
Willamina
18

38   18   37
Valley Junction
22
Perry-dale

35   36   DEVILS LAKE STATE PARK
Lincoln City
Kernville   44
41   45
Dallas
223
FOGARTY CREEK STATE PARK
42   229
Depoe Bay   43
Monmouth

0   10 mi
0   10 km

TO TOLEDO   TO PEDEE   TO CORVALLIS

0   1   2   3   4   5   6   7   8   9

© AVALON TRAVEL PUBLISHING

CHAPTER C1

1 Astoria/ Warrenton Seaside KOA

 3

This campground is nestled in a wooded area adjacent to Fort Stevens State Park, and tours of that historical military site can be arranged. This is an excellent option if the state park campground is full. A host of activities are available in the immediate area, including bicycling, hiking, deep-sea fishing, and beachcombing. Horse stables are located within 10 miles. See the description of Fort Stevens State Park for further details about the area.

Location: Near Fort Stevens State Park; map C1, grid a6.

Campsites, facilities: There are 100 sites for tents, trailers, or RVs up to 80 feet. Cable TV, rest rooms, showers, security, a public phone, a laundry room, limited groceries, ice, snacks, RV supplies, LP gas, and a barbecue are available. Recreational facilities include a playground, a game room, a recreation field, horseshoes, a spa, and a heated swimming pool. Some facilities are wheelchair accessible. Leashed pets are permitted.

Reservations, fees: Reservations recommended. Sites are $24-34 per night. Major credit cards accepted. Open year-round.

Directions: From Portland turn west on U.S. 26 and drive 73 miles to the junction with U.S. 101. Turn right (north) on U.S. 101 and drive about 15 miles (about one-quarter mile past the Camp Rilea Army Base). Turn west on Perkins Road/Highway 104 at the sign for Fort Stevens State Park and drive about one mile to Ocean View Cemetery Road. Turn left and drive about 2.5 miles (Ocean View Cemetery Road becomes Ridge Road) to the campground directly across from the state park.

Contact: Astoria/Warrenton Seaside KOA, 1100 Ridge Road, Hammond, OR 97121; tel. (800) 562-8506, (503) 861-2606; fax (503) 861-3209; website: www.koa.com

2 Fort Stevens State Park

 8

This is a classic spot, set at the northern tip of Oregon, right where the Columbia River enters the Pacific Ocean. A historical military area, fresh water lake, swimming, beachcombing, trails, wildlife viewing, and a historic shipwreck site make Fort Stevens a uniquely diversified park. This 3,700-acre park has nine miles of bike trails and six miles of hiking trails, allowing exploration of the park through spruce and hemlock forests, wetlands, dunes, and shore pines. The trailhead for the Oregon Coast Trail is here as well. History buffs will find a museum, tours of the fort and artillery batteries, and the remains of the *Peter Iredale* shipwreck.

Location: At the mouth of the Columbia River; map C1, grid a6.

Campsites, facilities: There are 253 tent sites, 289 sites with full or partial hookups for trailers or RVs up to 50 feet, and a special camping area for hikers and bicyclists. Fifteen yurts and five group tent areas are also available. Picnic tables and fire grills are provided. Drinking water, garbage bins, flush toilets, a sanitary disposal station, showers, firewood, and a playground are available. Some facilities are wheelchair accessible. Boat docks and launching facilities are nearby. Leashed pets are permitted.

Reservations, fees: Reservations accepted; phone (800) 452-5687 ($6 reservation fee). Sites are $13-20 per night, and $4.50 for hikers/bikers. Yurts are $30 per night Open year-round.

Directions: From Portland turn west on U.S. 26 and drive 73 miles to the junction with U.S. 101. Turn right (north) on U.S. 101 and drive about 15 miles (about one-quarter mile past the Camp Rilea Army Base). Turn west on Perkins Road/Highway 104 at the sign for Fort Stevens State Park and drive about one mile to Ocean View Cemetery Road. Turn left and drive about 2.5 miles (Ocean View Cemetery Road becomes Ridge Road) to the park entrance.

Contact: Fort Stevens State Park, Ridge Road, Hammond, OR 97121; tel. (800) 551-6949, (503) 861-1671.

❸ Kampers
West Campground   7

Located just four miles from Fort Stevens State Park, this privately run site offers full RV services. Nearby recreation possibilities include an 18-hole golf course, hiking trails, marked bike trails, and a riding stable.

Location: Near Fort Stevens State Park; map C1, grid a6.

Campsites, facilities: There are 10 tent sites and 210 sites for trailers or RVs of any length. Electricity, drinking water, and picnic tables are provided. Flush toilets, bottled gas, sanitary services, showers, laundry facilities, and ice are available. A store and a cafe are within one mile. Leashed pets and motorbikes are permitted.

Reservations, fees: Reservations accepted. Sites are $17.50-22 per night. Open year-round.

Directions: From Portland turn west on U.S. 30 and drive 105 miles north and west to Astoria and the junction of U.S. 101. Turn south and drive 6.5 miles to the Warrenton/Hammond Junction. Turn west on Warrenton and drive 1.5 miles to the campground on the right.

Contact: Kampers West Campground, 1140 N.W. Warrenton Drive, Warrenton, OR 97146; tel. (503) 861-1814; fax (503) 861-3620.

❹ Venice RV Park   3

This park along the Neawanna River—one of two rivers running through Seaside—is less than a mile from the beach. Seaside offers beautiful ocean beaches for fishing and surfing, moped and bike rentals, shops, and a theater. The city provides swings and volleyball nets on the beach. An 18-hole golf course is located nearby.

Location: On the Neawanna River; map C1, grid b5.

Campsites, facilities: There are 31 sites for trailers or RVs of any length; 13 are pull-through sites. Electricity, drinking water, sewer, cable TV, and picnic tables are provided. Flush toilets, showers, a laundry room, and ice are available. A store and a cafe are located within one mile. Leashed pets are permitted.

Reservations, fees: Reservations preferred. Sites are $22 per night. Open year-round.

Directions: From Portland on Interstate 5, turn west on U.S. 26 and drive 73 miles to the junction with U.S. 101. Turn north on U.S. 101 and drive four miles to Seaside. Continue to the north end of town and turn left (west) on 24th Avenue. The campground is on the corner at 1032 24th Avenue.

Contact: Venice RV Park, 1032 24th Avenue, Seaside, OR 97138; tel. (503) 738-8851.

5 Forest Lake Resort   6

This park is on the shore of the Necanicum River, which attracts a steelhead run every winter. The river is low during the summer but still provides many pools for swimming. Boating is allowed on the river. A small, scenic lake in the campground attracts wildlife. No swimming or boating is allowed on the campground lake, but it's stocked with trout, a practice that began in 1988. Nearby recreation options include an 18-hole golf course, a small amusement park, and a riding stable.

Location: On the Necanicum River; map C1, grid b6.

Campsites, facilities: There are 25 tent sites and 33 sites for trailers or RVs of any length; 14 are drive-through sites. Electricity, drinking water, sewer hookups, fire rings, and picnic tables are provided. Flush toilets, showers, firewood, and laundry facilities are available. Bottled gas, sanitary services, a store, ice, and a cafe are located within one mile. Boat launching facilities are nearby. Leashed pets and motorbikes are permitted.

Reservations, fees: Reservations accepted. Sites are $17-20 per night. Open year-round.

Directions: From Portland on Interstate 5, turn west on U.S. 26 and drive 73 miles to the junction with U.S. 101. Turn north on U.S. 101 and drive just under one mile to the park on the right.

Contact: Forest Lake Resort, HCR 63, Box 255, Seaside, OR 97138; tel. (503) 738-6779.

6 Sea Ranch RV Park

         9

This resort is in a wooded area with nearby access to the beach. Activities at the camp include stream fishing, and you can go horseback riding and swimming on the seashore. A golf course is six miles away, and the historical Lewis and Clark Trail is nearby. Elk hunters camp here in season. The beach and the town of Cannon Beach are within walking distance of the resort.

Location: Near the Pacific Ocean; map C1, grid b6.

Campsites, facilities: There are 71 sites for tents, trailers, and RVs. Rest rooms, showers, a sanitary dump, and a public phone are available. Supplies are available within two miles. Leashed pets are permitted.

Reservations, fees: Reservations recommended. Sites are $19-22 per night. Major credit cards accepted. Open year-round.

Directions: From Portland on Interstate 5, turn west on U.S. 26 and drive 73 miles to the junction with U.S. 101. Turn south on U.S. 101 and drive three miles to the Cannon Beach exit. The park is south 0.3 mile on the left.

Contact: Sea Ranch RV Park, P.O. Box 214, Cannon Beach, OR 97110; tel. (503) 436-2815.

7 RV Resort at Cannon Beach 9

This private resort is located about seven blocks from one of the nicest beaches in the region. From the town of Cannon Beach you can walk for miles in either direction. Ecola State Park is just two miles north. Nearby recreational facilities include marked bike trails, a riding stable, and tennis courts.

Location: Near Ecola State Park; map C1, grid b6.

Campsites, facilities: There are 100 sites for trailers or RVs of any length; 11 are drive-through sites. Electricity, drinking water, sewer hookups, and picnic tables are provided. Flush toilets, bottled gas, showers, firewood, a recreation hall, a store, a spa, a laundry room, ice, a playground, and a swimming pool are available. Leashed pets are permitted.

Reservations, fees: Reservations accepted. Sites are $23-34 per night. Open year-round.

Directions: From Portland on Interstate 5, turn west on U.S. 26 and drive 73 miles to the junction with U.S. 101. Turn south on U.S. 101 and drive four miles to the Cannon Beach exit at Milepost 29.5. Turn left (east) and drive 200 feet to the campground.

Contact: RV Resort at Cannon Beach, P.O. Box 219, Cannon Beach, OR 97110; tel. (503) 436-2231; fax (503) 436-1527.

8 Saddle Mountain State Park 7

This is a good alternative to the many beachfront parks to the south. A 2.5-mile trail climbs to the top of Saddle Mountain, a great lookout on clear days. This park is a real find for the naturalist interested in rare and unusual varieties of plants, many of which have established themselves along the slopes of this isolated mountain.

Location: On Saddle Mountain; map C1, grid b7.

Campsites, facilities: There are 10 primitive tent sites. Drinking water, garbage bins, picnic tables, and fire grills are provided. Flush toilets and firewood are available. Leashed pets are permitted.

Reservations, fees: No reservations accepted. Sites are $7-10 per night, $7 for an additional vehicle. Open March through October.

Directions: From Portland turn west on U.S. 26 and drive about 63 miles to Necanicum Junction and Saddle Mountain Road. Turn north on Saddle Mountain Road and drive eight miles to the park.

Contact: Saddle Mountain State Park, P.O. Box 681, Cannon Beach, OR 97110; tel. (800) 551-6949 or (503) 436-2844.

9 Nehalem Bay State Park 7

This state park located on a sandy point separating the Pacific Ocean and Nehalem Bay offers six miles of beach frontage. Crabbing and fishing on the bay are popular. The neighboring towns of Manzanita and Newhalem offer fine dining and shopping. Oregon Coast Trail passes through the park. A horse camp with corrals and a 7.5-mile equestrian trail are available. There is also a 1.75-mile bike trail. An airport is adjacent to the park.

Location: On the Pacific Ocean; map C1, grid c5.

Campsites, facilities: There are 281 sites for trailers or RVs up to 60 feet long and a special camping area for hikers and bicyclists. There are also 12 yurts and 17 sites with stock corrals. Electricity, drinking water, picnic tables, and fire grills are provided. Flush toilets, a sanitary disposal station, showers, and firewood are available. Some facilities are wheelchair accessible. Boat launching facilities are located nearby on Nehalem Bay, and an airstrip is located adjacent to the park. Leashed pets are permitted.

Reservations, fees: Reservations accepted; phone (800) 452-5687 ($6 reservation fee). Sites are $10-19 per night, and $4 for hikers/bikers. Yurts are $27 per night; horse sites are $10 per night and $1.50 per horse per night. There is a charge of $7 per night for an additional vehicle. Major credit cards accepted. Open year-round.

Directions: From Portland drive west on U.S. 26 for 73 miles to the junction with U.S. 101. Turn south on U.S. 101 and drive 19 miles to Manzanita. Turn right (west) on the park entrance road and drive 1.5 miles to the campground.

Contact: Nehalem Bay State Park, 9500 Sandpiper Lane, Nehalem, OR 97131; tel. (503) 368-5154.

🔟 Jetty Fishery RV Park   7

This small park is located at the base of a mile-long jetty that extends out into Nehalem Bay and the ocean. Fishing and crabbing are good off the jetty, but sometimes the snags bite well, too. The small beach on the bay side of the jetty is a popular spot for kids. For boaters there is an adjacent full-service marina.

Location: On Nehalem Bay; map C1, grid c5.

Campsites, facilities: There are 10 tent sites and 14 sites for trailers or RVs of any length. Electricity, drinking water, and picnic tables are provided. Flush toilets, bottled gas, firewood, a store, showers, a cafe, ice, boat docks, launching facilities, and boat rentals are available. Leashed pets are permitted.

Reservations, fees: Reservations accepted. Sites are $18 per night. Open year-round.

Directions: From Portland on Interstate 5, turn west on U.S. 26 and drive 73 miles to the junction with U.S. 101. Turn south on U.S. 101 and drive 27 miles to the park entrance.

Contact: Jetty Fishery RV Park, 27550 Highway 101 North, Rockaway, OR 97136; tel. (503) 368-5746; fax (503) 568-5748.

🔢 Shorewood Travel Trailer Village   7

This park is on an ideal beach for surf fishing for perch or beachcombing during low tides. The 1.5-mile hike to the Tillamook Bay jetty is a good side trip. An 18-hole golf course is located a short drive from the park.

Location: On the Pacific Ocean; map C1, grid c5.

Campsites, facilities: There are 105 sites for trailers or RVs of any length. No tents are allowed. Electricity, drinking water, and picnic tables are provided. Flush toilets, sanitary services, cable TV, showers, a laundry room, and ice are available. A store and a cafe are located within one mile. Leashed pets are permitted.

Reservations, fees: Reservations accepted. Sites are $21 per night. Open year-round.

Directions: From Portland on Interstate 5, turn west on U.S. 26 and drive 73 miles to the junction with U.S. 101. Turn south on U.S. 101 and drive 30 miles to the town of Rockaway Beach. Continue on U.S. 101 to about one mile south of town to the Shorewood sign; then turn west and drive three blocks to the park.

Contact: Shorewood Travel Trailer Village, 17600 Ocean Boulevard, Rockaway Beach, OR 97136; tel. (503) 355-2278.

🔢 Oswald West State Park   8

This state park is set along a dramatic section of the Oregon coast with rugged cliffs rising high above the ocean. This is not beach-walking territory, but the park does offer 15 miles of hiking trails, including the Oregon Coast Trail and a trail to the point of Cape Falcon, where campers can enjoy scenic views. A small beach attracts windsurfers and boogie boarders and several fishing streams are nearby. The park is in a beautiful rain forest setting, with gigantic spruce and cedar trees.

Location: On the Pacific Ocean; map C1, grid c5.

Campsites, facilities: There are 36 primitive walk-in tent sites. Wheelbarrows are available for campers to transport their supplies. Picnic tables and fire grills are provided. Drinking water, flush toilets, garbage bins, and firewood are available. Leashed pets are permitted.

Reservations, fees: No reservations accepted. Sites are $10-14 per night. Major credit cards accepted. Open March through October.

Directions: From Portland turn west on U.S. 26 and drive 73 miles to the junction with U.S. 101. Turn south on U.S. 101 and drive four miles to Cannon Beach. Continue 10 miles south on U.S. 101 to the parking area. Walk one-quarter mile to the campground.

Contact: Oswald West State Park, 9500 Sandpiper Lane, Nehalem, OR 97131; tel. (800) 452-5687 or (503) 368-5943.

🔢 Nehalem Falls   10

This beautiful campground, among old-growth hemlock and spruce, is within a two-minute walk of lovely Nehalem Falls. A one-half mile loop trail follows along the adjacent Nehalem River, where fishing and swimming are options.

Location: In Tillamook State Forest; map C1, grid c6.

Campsites, facilities: There are 14 sites for tents, trailers or RVs up to 40 feet long, four walk-in tent sites, and one group site. Drinking water, picnic tables, garbage bins, fire grills and vault toilets are available. Some facilities are wheelchair accessible. Leashed pets are permitted.

Reservations, fees: Reservations accepted for the group site only; phone (503) 842-2545. Family sites are $10 per night, walk-in sites are $5 per night, and the group site is $25 per night; $2 per night for an additional vehicle. Open Memorial Day weekend through October.

Directions: From Tillamook on U.S. 101 northbound, drive 22 miles to Highway 53. Turn right (east) and drive 1.3 miles to Miami Foley Road. Turn right (south) and drive one mile to Foss Road (narrow and rough). Turn left and drive seven miles to the campground on the left.

Contact: Tillamook State Forest, Tillamook District, 4907 Third Street, Tillamook, OR 97141; tel. (503) 842-2545; fax (503) 842-3143, or access the website: www.odf.state.or.us.

Barview Jetty County Park

        7

This park covering 160 acres is near the beach, adjacent to Tillamook Bay in a wooded area. The sites are set on grassy hills. Nearby recreation options include an 18-hole golf course, hiking trails, bike trails, surf and scuba fishing, and a full-service marina.

Location: Near Garibaldi; map C1, grid d5.

Campsites, facilities: There are 249 sites for tents or RVs of any length, 60 with full hookups. Electricity, drinking water, sewer hookups, and picnic tables are provided. Flush toilets, a dump station, showers, and a playground are available. Bottled gas, a store, a cafe, and ice are located within one mile. Leashed pets are permitted.

Reservations, fees: Reservations accepted; phone (503) 322-3522. Sites are $14-18 per night, plus $2 for each additional vehicle, a $2 dump station fee, a $1 shower fee, and $5 for firewood. Open year-round.

Directions: From Portland on Interstate 5, turn west on U.S. 26 and drive 24 miles to Highway 6. Turn left on Highway 6 and drive 44 miles to Tillamook. Turn north on U.S. 101 and drive 12 miles to the park on the left (two miles north of the town of Garibaldi).

Contact: Barview Jetty County Park, P.O. Box 633, Garibaldi, OR 97118; tel. (503) 322-3522; fax (503) 842-2721.

Happy Camp Resort   9

The camp is set along the shore of the bay, a short drive from Cape Lookout State Park, Cape Meares State Park, and the national wildlife refuge. Netarts Bay offers sheltered waters, perfect for small boaters to take advantage of the excellent crabbing. Shoreliners can discover good crabbing and fair perch fishing. Crabbing gear, boat rentals, and crab cooking gear are available. Riding stables are nearby.

Location: On Netarts Bay; map C1, grid d5.

Campsites, facilities: There are 30 sites for trailers or RVs of any length; 16 are partial and eight are full hookup. Electricity, drinking water, cable TV, and picnic tables are provided. Flush toilets, sanitary services, showers, and sewer hookups are available. A store, a cafe, a coin-operated laundry facilities, bottled gas, ice, and firewood are located within one mile. Boat docks, launching facilities, and rentals are nearby. Leashed pets are permitted.

Reservations, fees: Reservations required. Sites are $24 per night. Open February through October.

Directions: From Portland turn west on U.S. 26 and drive 24 miles to Highway 6. Turn west on Highway 6 and drive 44 miles to Tillamook and Netarts Highway. Turn west on Netarts Highway and drive seven miles to the campground entrance.

Contact: Happy Camp Resort, P.O. Box 82, Netarts, OR 97143; tel. (503) 842-4012.

16 Big Spruce RV Park   8

This trailer park is one block from the boat launch on Netarts Bay. See the description of Happy Camp Resort for details on the fishing here.

Location: On Netarts Bay; map C1, grid d5.

Campsites, facilities: There are 23 sites for trailers or RVs of any length; seven are drive-through sites. Electricity, drinking water, sewer hookups, and picnic tables are provided. Flush toilets, bottled gas, cable TV, showers, a crab cooker, fish cleaning station, and a laundry room are available. A store, ice, clamming and crabbing gear, a cafe, and ice are located within one mile. Boat docks, launching facilities, and boat rentals are nearby. Leashed pets are permitted.

Reservations, fees: Reservations accepted. Sites are $17.50 per night for two campers and two vehicles, $2 additional for each additional camper or vehicle. Open year-round.

Directions: From Portland turn west on U.S. 26 and drive 24 miles to Highway 6. Turn west on Highway 6 and drive 44 miles to Tillamook and Netarts Highway. Turn west on Netarts Highway and drive 6.5 miles to the campground entrance.

Contact: Big Spruce RV Park, 4850 Netarts Highway West, Tillamook, OR 97141; tel. (503) 842-7443; fax (503) 815-1641.

17 Bay Shore RV Park   8

This is one of three camps on the east shore of Netarts Bay. See the description of Happy Camp Resort for more information about the fishing here. A golf course is located eight miles away. Sunsets and wildlife watching are notable here.

Location: On Netarts Bay; map C1, grid d5.

Campsites, facilities: There are 53 sites for trailers or RVs of any length; 11 are drive-through sites. Electricity, drinking water, sewer hookups, and picnic tables are provided. Flush toilets, bottled gas, coin-operated showers, a meeting room, a laundry room, crab-cooking facilities, crab bait, and ice are available. A store and a cafe are within one mile. Boat docks, launching facilities, and rentals are nearby. Leashed pets are permitted.

Reservations, fees: Reservations recommended. Sites are $20-22 per night. Major credit cards accepted. Open year-round.

Directions: From Portland turn west on U.S. 26 and drive 24 miles to Highway 6. Turn west on Highway 6 and drive 44 miles to Tillamook and Netarts Highway. Turn west on Netarts Highway and drive six miles to the campground entrance.

Contact: Bay Shore RV Park, P.O. Box 218, Netarts, OR 97413; tel. (503) 842-7774.

18 Biak-by-the-Sea RV Park   7

This park along the shore of Tillamook Bay is a prime retreat for deep-sea fishing, crabbing, clamming, surf fishing, scuba diving, and beachcombing. The nearby town of Tillamook is home to a cheese factory and a historical museum. A good side trip is Cape Meares State Park, where you can hike through the national wildlife preserve and see how the seabirds nest along the cliffs. There is also a golf course nearby.

Location: On Tillamook Bay; map C1, grid d5.

Campsites, facilities: There are 45 drive-through sites for trailers or RVs of any length. Electricity, drinking water, sewer hookups, and cable TV are provided. Flush toilets, coin-operated showers, and laundry facilities are available. Bottled gas, a store, a cafe, and ice are located within one mile. Boat docks, launching facilities, and rentals are nearby. Leashed pets and motorbikes are permitted.

Reservations, fees: Reservations recommended. Sites are $16 per night. Major credit cards accepted. Open year-round.

Directions: From Portland turn west on U.S. 26 and drive 24 miles to Highway 6. Turn west on Highway 6 and drive 44 miles to Tillamook and U.S. 101. Turn north and drive 10 miles to 10th Street. Turn left on 10th Street and drive to the park on the left (just over the tracks).

Contact: Biak-by-the-Sea RV Park, P.O. Box 162, Garibaldi, OR 97118; tel. (503) 322-2765.

19 Pacific Campground   6

This campground is located at the southern end of Tillamook Bay, not far from the Wilson River. The Tillamook Cheese Factory—the place for cheese tours, is just south of the park. An 18-hole golf course is also nearby. See the description of Biak-by-the-Sea Trailer Court for more information about the area.

Location: On Tillamook Bay; map C1, grid d5.

Campsites, facilities: There are 20 tent sites and 31 drive-through sites for trailers or RVs of any length. Electricity, drinking water, sewer hookups, and picnic tables are provided. Flush toilets, cable TV, showers, firewood, and ice are available. A store and a cafe are located within one mile. Leashed pets (except in the tent area) and motorbikes are permitted.

Reservations, fees: Reservations accepted. Sites are $12-22 per night for two people, plus $1 for each additional person. Open year-round.

Directions: From Portland turn west on U.S. 26 and drive 24 miles to Highway 6. Turn west on Highway 6 and drive 44 miles to Tillamook. Turn north on U.S. 101 and drive 1.5 miles to the campground entrance across from the Tillamook Cheese Factory.

Contact: Pacific Campground, 1950 Suppress Road North, Tillamook, OR 97141; tel. (503) 842-5201.

20 Pleasant Valley RV Park   8

This campground along the Tillamook River is very clean, with many recreation options in the immediate area.

Location: On the Tillamook River; map C1, grid d5.

Campsites, facilities: There are 10 tent sites and 74 sites for trailers or RVs of any length, plus two cabins. Drinking water and picnic tables are provided. Flush toilets, bottled gas, sanitary services, showers, firewood, a recreation hall, electricity, sewer hookups, cable TV, a store, a laundry room, ice, and a playground are available. Boat launching facilities are nearby. Leashed pets are permitted.

Reservations, fees: Reservations accepted. Sites are $14-19.50 per night; cabins are $25 per night. Open year-round.

Directions: From Portland turn west on U.S. 26 and drive 24 miles to Highway 6. Turn west on Highway 6 and drive 44 miles to Tillamook and U.S. 101. Turn south on U.S. 101 and drive six miles to the campground entrance on the right.

Contact: Pleasant Valley RV Park, 11880 Highway 101 South, Tillamook, OR 97141; tel. (503) 842-4779.

21 Jones Creek   7

Set in a forest of fir, hemlock, spruce and alder, campsites here are spacious and private. The adjacent Wilson River provides opportunities for steelhead and salmon fishing (artificial lures only). There's a scenic 1.5 mile trail along the riverfront. The camp fills up on holiday weekends.

Location: On the Wilson River in Tillamook State Forest; map C1, grid d7.

Campsites, facilities: There are 28 sites for tents, trailers or RVs (27 are 50 feet long and one is 72 feet long and pull-through), nine walk-in tent sites, and one group site. Drinking water, picnic tables, fire grills, vault toilets, garbage bins, a camp host and a horseshoe pit are available. Some facilities are wheelchair accessible. Leashed pets are permitted.

Reservations, fees: Reservations required for the group site only; phone (503) 842-2545. Sites are $10 per night, walk-in sites are $5 per night, and the group site is $25 per night; an additional vehicle is $2 per night. Open Memorial Day weekend through October.

Directions: From Portland turn west on U.S. 26 and drive 24 miles to Highway 6. Turn west on Highway 6 and drive 28 miles to Milepost 22.7 and North Fork Road. Turn right and drive one-quarter mile to the campground on the left.

Contact: Tillamook State Forest, Tillamook District, 4907 Third Street, Tillamook, OR 97141; tel. (503) 842-2545; fax (503) 842-3143, or access the website: www.odf.state.or.us.

22 Elk Creek Walk-In   7

This small campground is set among fir, alder, and maple on Elk Creek and borders the Wilson River, where steelhead and salmon fishing are options (artificials only).

Location: On Elk Creek in Tillamook State Forest; map C1, grid d8.

Campsites, facilities: There are 15 walk-in tent sites. Drinking water, picnic tables, fire grills, and vault toilets are available. Pack out all garbage. Some facilities are wheelchair accessible. Leashed pets are permitted.

Reservations, fees: No reservations accepted. Sites are $5 per night, $2 per night for an additional vehicle. Open Memorial Day weekend through October.

Directions: From Portland turn west on U.S. 26 and drive 24 miles to Highway 6. Turn west on Highway 6 and drive 23 miles to Milepost 28 and the campground entrance road on the right. Turn right on Elk Creek Road and drive one-half mile to the campground on the left.

Contact: Tillamook State Forest, Forest Grove District, 801 Gales Creek Road,

Forest Grove, OR 97116; tel. (503) 357-2191; website: www.odf.state.or.us.

23 Stagecoach Horse Camp   6

This camp is for horse camping only. There's a small seasonal stream through the camp. Two-hour and four-hour loop trails can be accessed as well from the camp.
Location: In Tillamook State Forest; map C1, grid d8.
Campsites, facilities: There are 11 sites for tents, trailers or RVs up to 30 feet long. No drinking water, but picnic tables, fire grills, a picnic shelter with 16 tables, and vault toilets are available. Pack out all garbage. Stock facilities include two corrals at each site and stock water. Some facilities are wheelchair accessible. Leashed pets are permitted.
Reservations, fees: No reservations accepted. Sites are $5 per night, $2 per night for an additional vehicle. Open year-round.
Directions: From Portland turn west on U.S. 26 and drive 24 miles to Highway 6. Turn west on Highway 6 and drive 19 miles to Beaver Dam Road. Turn left (south) and drive one mile to University Falls Road. Turn right and drive 3.5 miles to Rutherford Road. Turn right again and drive a short distance to the first gravel road on the left. Turn left and drive one-half mile to the campground on the left.
Contact: Tillamook State Forest, Forest Grove District, 801 Gales Creek Road, Forest Grove, OR 97116; tel. (503) 357-2191, or access the website: www.odf.state.or.us.

24 Browns ATV Camp   6

This camp is located next to the Devil's Lake Fork of the Wilson River and has sites with and without tree cover. It is surrounded by miles of ATV trails and caters to off-highway vehicle campers. Don't expect peace and quiet. No fishing is allowed here.
Location: In Tillamook State Forest; map C1, grid d9.
Campsites, facilities: There are 29 sites for tents, trailers, or RVs up to 45 feet long. Drinking water, picnic tables, fire grills, garbage bins, and vault toilets are available. Some facilities are wheelchair accessible. Leashed pets are permitted.
Reservations, fees: No reservations accepted. Sites are $10 per night, $2 per night for an additional vehicle. Open March through November.
Directions: From Portland turn west on U.S. 26 and drive 24 miles to Highway 6. Turn west on Highway 6 and drive 19 miles to Beaver Dam Toad. Turn left (south) and drive 2.5 miles to Scoggins Road. Turn left (southeast) and drive one-half mile to the campground.
Contact: Tillamook State Forest, Forest Grove District, 801 Gales Creek Road, Forest Grove, OR 97116; tel. (503) 357-2191, or access the website: www.odf.state.or.us.

25 Gales Creek   7

Gales Creek runs through this heavily forested camp. The Gales Creek Trailhead is accessible from camp, providing hiking and mountain biking opportunities. A day use picnic area is also available.

Location: On Gales Creek in Tillamook State Forest; map C1, grid c9.

Campsites, facilities: There are 19 sites for tents, trailers, or RVs up to 35 feet long, and four walk-in sites. Drinking water, picnic tables, fire grills, garbage bins, and vault toilets are available. Some facilities are wheelchair accessible. Leashed pets are permitted.

Reservations, fees: No reservations accepted. Family sites are $10 per night; walk-in sites are $5 per night; an additional vehicle is $2 per night. Open Memorial Day weekend through October.

Directions: From Portland turn west on U.S. 26 and drive 24 miles to Highway 6. Turn west on Highway 6 and drive 17 miles to the campground entrance road (Rogers Road) on the right at Milepost 35. Turn right on Rogers Road and drive one mile to the campground.

Contact: Tillamook State Forest, Forest Grove District, 801 Gales Creek Road, Forest Grove, OR 97116; tel. (503) 357-2191; website: www.odf.state.or.us.

26 7 Jordan Creek ATV Staging Area   6

This camp is located at the bottom of a scenic, steep canyon next to Jordan Creek. Wooded campsites are clustered around a central parking area, and the park caters to ATV campers. There are almost 40 miles of ATV trails, ranging from moderate to difficult. There's no fishing in Jordan Creek.

Location: Near Jordan Creek in Tillamook State Forest; map C1, grid d8.

Campsites, facilities: There are six sites for tents, trailers, or RVs of any length. No drinking water, but picnic tables, fire grills, garbage bins, and vault toilets are available. Some facilities are wheelchair accessible. Leashed pets are permitted.

Reservations, fees: No reservations accepted. Sites are $5 per night, $2 per night for an additional vehicle. Open March through November.

Directions: From Tillamook on U.S. 101, turn east on Highway 6 and drive 17.9 miles to Jordan Creek Road. Turn right and drive 22 miles to the campground on the right.

Contact: Tillamook State Forest, Tillamook District, 4907 East Third Street, Tillamook, OR 97141; tel. (503) 842-2545; fax (503) 842-3143, or access the website: www.odf.state.or.us.

27 Cape Lookout State Park   8

Located on a sand spit between Netarts Bay and the ocean, Cape Lookout has more than eight miles of hiking and walking trails that wind through old-growth forest. The Cape Lookout Trail follows the headland for more than two miles. Another walk will take you out through a variety of estuarine habitats along the five-mile sand spit that extends between the ocean and Netarts Bay. This is a paradise for bird-watchers, with many species to view. You might also catch the local hang- and paragliders that frequent the park. Fishing is another option here.

Location: Near Netarts Bay; map C1, grid e5.

Campsites, facilities: There are 177 tent sites, 35 sites with full or partial hookups for trailers or RVs up to 60 feet long, and a special tent camping area for hikers and bicyclists. There are also four group tent areas and 10 yurts. Picnic tables and fire grills are provided. Flush toilets, sanitary services, showers, garbage bins, and firewood are available. A restaurant is located within one mile. Some facilities are wheelchair accessible. Leashed pets are permitted.

Reservations, fees: Reservations accepted; phone (800) 452-5687 ($6 reservation fee). Sites are $13-20 per night, $4 per night for hikers/bikers, and yurts are $30 per night; an additional vehicle is $7 per night. Open year-round.

Directions: From Portland turn west on U.S. 26 and drive 24 miles to Highway 6. Turn west on Highway 6 and drive 44 miles to Tillamook. Turn southwest on Netarts Road and drive 11 miles to the park entrance.

Contact: Cape Lookout State Park, 13000 Whiskey Creek Road West, Tillamook, OR 97141; tel. (800) 452-5687 or (503) 842-4981.

28 Webb Park   7

This public campground is an excellent alternative to the more crowded commercial RV parks off U.S. 101. It's not as developed, but offers a quiet, private setting and access to the ocean. Fishing and swimming are among your options here.

Location: Near the Pacific Ocean; map C1, grid e5.

Campsites, facilities: There are 30 sites for tents, trailers, or RVs; six have partial hookups. Drinking water, a dump station, showers, flush toilets, and beach launching are available. Leashed pets are permitted.

Reservations, fees: No reservations accepted. Sites are $14-16 per night. Open year-round.

Directions: From Portland turn west on U.S. 26 and drive 24 miles to Highway 6. Turn west on Highway 6 and drive 44 miles to Tillamook and U.S. 101. Turn south on U.S. 101 and drive about 25 miles to the Pacific City exit and Highway 30. From Pacific City, turn north on Highway 30 and drive one mile to Cape Kiwanda. The camp is located on the right.

Contact: Tillamook County Parks, P.O. Box 1072, Pacific City, OR 97135; tel. (503) 965-5001; fax (503) 842-2721.

29 Cape Kiwanda RV Park   8

This ocean view park is a short distance from Cape Kiwanda State Park, which is open for day-use only. Highlights at the park include a boat launch and hiking trails that lead out to the cape. A recreation option is four miles south at Nestucca Spit, where there is another day-use park. The point extends about three miles and is a good spot for bird-watching.

Location: On the Pacific Ocean; map C1, grid e5.

Campsites, facilities: There are 30 tent sites and 150 sites for trailers or RVs of any length. Electricity, drinking water, sewer hookups, and picnic tables are provided. Flush toilets, sanitary services, showers, firewood, a recreation hall, laundry facilities, propane, a seafood market, a gift shop, an automatic teller machine, and a playground are available. Bottled gas, a store, a cafe, and ice are located within one mile. Boat docks, launching facilities, and rentals are nearby. Leashed pets and motorbikes are permitted.

Reservations, fees: Reservations accepted. Sites are $15-23 per night. Open year-round.

Directions: From Portland, turn west on U.S. 26 and drive 24 miles to Highway 6. Turn west on Highway 6 and drive 44 miles to Tillamook and U.S. 101. Turn south on U.S. 101 and drive 25 miles to the Pacific City exit and Brooten Road. Turn right and drive three miles toward Pacific City and Three Capes Drive. Turn left, cross the bridge, and bear right on Three Capes Drive. Continue one mile north to the park on the right.

Contact: Cape Kiwanda RV Park, P.O. Box 129, Pacific City, OR 97135; tel. (503) 965-6230; fax (503) 965-6235. Website: capekiwanda@oregoncoast.com.

30 Raines
Resort and RV Park   6

This campground is on the Nestucca River, which attracts a king salmon run from late August through Thanksgiving. A full-service marina is close by. This is a good camp for watching wildlife.

Location: On the Nestucca River; map C1, grid e5.

Campsites, facilities: There are 12 sites for tents, trailers or RVs up to 30 feet. Electricity, drinking water, sewer hookups, and picnic tables are provided. Flush toilets, sanitary services, showers, and a laundry room are available. Bottled gas, a cafe, a store, and ice are located within one mile. Boat docks and launching facilities are located at the resort. Leashed dogs are permitted.

Reservations, fees: Reservations accepted. Sites are $15-20 per night, $7-10 per night for tents. Open year-round.

Directions: From Portland, drive west on U.S. 26 for 24 miles to Highway 6. Turn west on Highway 6 and drive 44 miles to Tillamook at U.S. 101. Turn south on U.S. 101 and drive 25 miles to the Pacific City exit. Turn right on Brooten Road and drive six miles to the Woods Bridge. Turn left on Ferry Street and cross Woods Bridge. After crossing the bridge, the park entrance is immediately to the right.

Contact: Raines Resort and RV Park, P.O. Box 777, Pacific City, OR 97135; tel. (503) 965-6371.

31 Sand Beach   5

This area is known for its beach area with large sand dunes, which are popular with off-road vehicle enthusiasts. It's noisy and can be windy. The campground is set along the shore of Sand Lake, which is actually more like an estuary since the ocean is just around the bend. This is the only coastal U.S. Forest Service campground for many miles, and it's quite popular. If you're planning a trip for midsummer, be sure to reserve far in advance. Entry permits are required for three-day holiday weekends.

Location: In Siuslaw National Forest; map C1, grid e5.

Campsites, facilities: There are 101 sites for tents, trailers, or RVs up to 30 feet long. (If filled, the east and west parking lots provide additional sites for trailers or RVs.) Picnic tables and fire pits are provided. Drinking water, garbage bins, and flush toilets are available. Leashed pets are permitted.

Reservations, fees: Reservations accepted; phone (877) 444-6777 or access the website: www.reserveusa.com ($8.65 reservation fee). Sites are $12 per night, $6 for an additional vehicle. Open late April to late September.

Directions: From Tillamook on U.S. 101, drive south for 11 miles to County Road 8. Turn west on County Road 8 and follow the signs to the campground.

Contact: Siuslaw National Forest, Hebo Ranger District, 31525 Highway 22, Hebo, OR 97122; tel. (503) 392-3161; fax (503) 392-4203.

32 Camper Cove
RV Park and Campground   6

This small, wooded campground along Beaver Creek is just far enough off the highway to provide quiet. The park can be used as a base camp for anglers, with steelhead and salmon fishing in season in the nearby Nestucca River. It gets crowded here, especially in the summer months, so be sure to make a reservation whenever possible. Ocean beaches are four miles away.

Location: On Beaver Creek; map C1, grid e6.

Campsites, facilities: There are five tent sites and 17 sites for RVs up to 40 feet long, plus two cabins. Electricity, drinking water, sewer hookups, and picnic tables are provided. Flush toilets, fire pits, a dump station, showers, firewood, a recreation hall, laundry facilities, and ice are available. Leashed pets are permitted.

Reservations, fees: Reservations accepted. Sites are $13.50-17.50 and cabin rentals are $30 per night. Open year-round.

Directions: From Portland, turn west on U.S. 26 and drive 24 miles to Highway 6. Turn west on Highway 6 and drive 44 miles to Tillamook and U.S. 101. Turn south on U.S. 101 and drive 11.5 miles to the park entrance on the right (2.5 miles north of Beaver).

Contact: Camper Cove RV Park and Campground, P.O. Box 42, Beaver, OR 97108; tel. (503) 398-5334.

33 Hebo Lake   7

This U.S. Forest Service campground along the shore of Hebo Lake is a secluded spot with sites nestled under trees. The trailhead for the eight-mile-long Pioneer-Indian Trail is located in the campground. The trail around the lake is barrier free.

Location: On Hebo Lake in Siuslaw National Forest; map C1, grid e6.

Campsites, facilities: There are 15 sites for tents, trailers, or RVs up to 18 feet long. Picnic tables and fire pits are provided. Drinking water, garbage bins, and vault toilets are available. Boats without motors are allowed on the lake. Leashed pets are permitted.

Reservations, fees: No reservations accepted. Sites are $6 per night, $3 for an additional vehicle. Open May to mid-October.

Directions: On U.S. 101 southwest of Portland, drive to the town of Hebo and Highway 22. Turn east on Highway 22 and drive one-quarter mile to Forest Road 14. Turn left (east) and drive five miles to the campground.

Contact: Siuslaw National Forest, Hebo Ranger District, 31525 Highway 22, Hebo, OR 97122; tel. (503) 392-3161; fax (503) 392-4203.

34 Rocky Bend 5

This campground along the Nestucca River is a little-known, secluded spot that provides guaranteed peace and quiet. There isn't much in the way of recreational activities out here, but hiking, fishing, clamming, and swimming are available along the coast, a relatively short drive away.

Location: On the Nestucca River in Siuslaw National Forest; map C1, grid e7.

Campsites, facilities: There are six tent sites. Picnic tables and fire pits are provided, but there is no drinking water. Vault toilets are available. No garbage service is provided, so you must pack out what you bring in. Leashed pets are permitted.

Reservations, fees: No reservations; no fee. Open year-round.

Directions: On U.S. 101 southwest of Portland, drive to the tiny town of Beaver and Blaine Road. Turn east on Blaine Road (keep right; Blaine Road turns into Nestucca River Access Road) and drive 15.5 miles to the campground.

Contact: Siuslaw National Forest, Hebo Ranger District, 31525 Highway 22, Hebo, OR 97122; tel. (503) 392-3161; fax (503) 392-4203.

35 Tree N' Sea Trailer Park   5

This quiet campground on the ocean in Lincoln City is a pleasant RV park that makes an adequate layover spot. Crabbing is a popular activity here. See the descriptions of KOA Lincoln City and Devil's Lake State Park for recreation options.

Location: On the Pacific Ocean; map C1, grid f4.

Campsites, facilities: There are seven sites for trailers or RVs of any length. Electricity, drinking water, cable TV, and sewer hookups are provided. Flush toilets and showers are available. A store, a cafe, and coin-operated laundry facilities are located within one mile. Small, leashed pets are permitted.

Reservations, fees: Reservations recommended. Sites are $16-22 per night. Open year-round.

Directions: From Portland drive south on Highway 99 West to Highway 18. Turn west on Highway 18 and drive 47 miles to U.S. 101. Turn south on U.S. 101 and drive five miles to Lincoln City. Turn west on Southwest 51st Street and drive one block to the park.

Contact: Tree N' Sea Trailer Park, 1015 Southwest 51st Street, Lincoln City, OR 97367; tel. (541) 996-3801.

36 KOA Lincoln City

 7

This area offers opportunities for beachcombing, tide pooling, and fishing along a seven-mile stretch of beach. Two stops to consider if you're going into Lincoln City for supplies: the Premier Market, which has smoked salmon, and the Colonial Bakery, which carries the best pastries west of Paris. Nearby recreation options include an 18-hole golf course and tennis courts.

Location: Near the Pacific Ocean; map C1, grid f5.

Campsites, facilities: There are 15 tent sites and 52 sites for trailers or RVs up to 60 feet long; 13 are drive-through sites. There are also one-room camping cabins. Electricity, drinking water, cable TV, modem access, flush toilets, a dump station, public phones, showers, a store, a cafe, a gift shop, LP gas, ice, RV supplies, video rentals, a game room, coin-operated laundry facilities, and a playground are available. Firewood is available for purchase. Leashed pets are permitted.

Reservations, fees: Reservations accepted. Sites are $19-24 per night, double-occupancy; cabins are $35 per night. Open year-round.

Directions: From Portland drive south on Highway 99 West to Highway 18. Turn west on Highway 18 and drive 47 miles to U.S. 101. Turn south on U.S. 101 and drive 1.5 miles to East Devil's Lake Road. Turn east on East Devil's Lake Road and drive one mile to the park.

Contact: KOA Lincoln City, 5298 N.E. Park Lane, Otis, OR 97368; tel. (541) 994-2961; fax (541) 994-9454.

37 Wandering Spirit RV Park   6

The major draw here is the nearby casino, but there is the added benefit of shaded sites next to the Yamhill River, providing fishing and swimming options. Fishing is good for steelhead and salmon in season. Golf courses and wineries are available within 10 miles.

Location: On the Yamhill River; map C1, grid f6.

Campsites, facilities: There are 79 sites for trailers and RVs up to 45 feet long, and 10 tent sites. Drinking water, electricity, sewer hookups, drinking water, cable TV, telephone service, rest rooms, showers, a sanitary disposal station, laundry facilities, and a mini-mart are available. Propane, a club house, a basketball hoop, an exercise and game room, and horseshoe pits are also on site. A 24-hour free bus shuttles campers to and from the Spirit Mountain Casino, restaurants, and shops less than two miles away. Some facilities are wheelchair accessible. Leashed pets are permitted.

Reservations, fees: Reservations recommended; phone (800) 390-6980. Sites are $10 for tents, $22 for RVs per night. Open year-round.

Directions: From Salem drive west on Highway 22 about 25 miles to Highway 18. Turn west on Highway 18 and drive about nine miles to the park on the left.

Contact: Wandering Spirit RV Park, 28800 Salmon River Highway, Grand Ronde, OR 97347; tel. (800) 390-6980; fax (503) 879-5171.

38 Lee's Evergreen RV Park   4

This wooded camp is set on the Salmon River, with opportunities for trout fishing. Nearby side trip options include H. B. Van Ouzer Forest Wayside and Devil's Lake State Park. Beach access is just a short drive west.

Location: On the Salmon River; map C1, grid f5.

Campsites, facilities: There are six sites for tents and 19 for trailers and RVs. Electricity, sewer hookups, drinking water, cable TV, rest rooms, showers, a sanitary dump, a public phone, horseshoe pits, and LP gas are available. Small leashed pets are permitted.

Reservations, fees: No reservations accepted. Sites are $10 per night. Open year-round.

Directions: From Salem drive west on Highway 22 for 25 miles to Highway 18. Turn west on Highway 18 and drive about 25 miles toward Otis, to Milepost 6. Turn right at Milepost 6 and drive to the park on the right.

Contact: Lee's Evergreen RV Park, 609 Salmon River Highway, Otis, OR 97368; tel. (541) 994-3116.

39 Castle Rock 4

This tiny spot along Three Rivers provides an alternative for tent campers to the large beachfront RV parks popular on the Oregon coast. Fishing can be good here. Though primitive, this camp is along the edge of the highway and can fill up quickly.

Location: On Three Rivers in Siuslaw National Forest; map C1, grid f6.

Campsites, facilities: There are four tent sites. Drinking water, picnic tables, garbage bins, and a vault toilet are provided. Leashed pets are permitted.

Reservations, fees: No reservations; no fee. Open year-round.

Directions: On U.S. 101 southwest of Portland, drive to the town of Hebo and Highway 22. Turn east on Highway 22 and drive five miles to the campground.

Contact: Siuslaw National Forest, Hebo Ranger District, 31525 Highway 22, Hebo, OR 97122; tel. (503) 392-3161; fax (503) 392-4203.

40 Mulkey RV Park 7

If you're in the area and looking for a camping spot, you'd best stop here—there are no other campgrounds within 30 miles. This wooded park is set near the South Yamhill River. Nearby recreation options include an 18-hole golf course, tennis courts, and the Western Deer Park and Arboretum, which has a playground.

Location: Near the South Yamhill River; map C1, grid f9.

Campsites, facilities: There are 70 sites for tents, trailers, or RVs of any length. Electricity, drinking water, sewer hookups, and picnic tables are provided. Flush toilets, showers, a store, bottled gas, and a laundry are available. Leashed pets and motorbikes are permitted.

Reservations, fees: Reservations recommended. Sites are $15-19 per night. Major credit cards accepted. Open year-round.

Directions: From Portland turn south on Highway 99 and drive about 31 miles to McMinnville and Highway 18. Turn southwest on Highway and drive 3.5 miles to the park entrance.

Contact: Mulkey RV Park, 14325 S.W. Highway 18, McMinnville, OR 97128; tel. (877) 472-2475, (503) 472-2475.

41 Sea and Sand RV Park 9

Beachcombing for fossils and agates is popular at this oceanfront park near Gleneden Beach on Siletz Bay. The sites have ocean views and pleasant terraces. The Siletz River and numerous small creeks are in the area.

Location: Near Siletz Bay; map C1, grid g4.

Campsites, facilities: There are 85 sites for trailers or RVs up to 35 feet long. Electricity, drinking water, sewer hookups, cable TV, and picnic tables are provided. Flush toilets, showers, sanitary services, firewood, and a laundry room are available. A store, a cafe, and ice are located within one mile. Leashed pets are permitted.

Reservations, fees: Reservations accepted. Sites are $20-23 per night. Open year-round.

Directions: From Portland turn south on Highway 99 West and drive southwest to Highway 18. Turn west on Highway 18 and drive 47 miles to U.S. 101. Turn south on U.S. 101 and drive five miles to Lincoln City. Continue another nine miles south on U.S. 101 to the campground entrance.

Contact: Sea and Sand RV Park, 4985 Highway 101 North, Depoe Bay, OR 97341; tel. (541) 764-2313; fax (541) 764-2313.

42 Pirates Cove RV Park   9

Perched on rock cliffs with stunning views of the ocean, this park has everything an ocean camper could want. Prime oceanfront sites are available, and this is an excellent spot for whale watching, especially in August, when they migrate north, and in January and February, when they return south. This is a scenic stretch of coastline, and some of the prime side trips include Depoe Bay State Park and Depoe Creek. Nearby recreation options include an 18-hole golf course, tennis courts, and a public aquarium.

Location: Near Depoe Bay State Park; map C1, grid g4.

Campsites, facilities: There are 101 sites for trailers or RVs of any length. Electricity, drinking water, sewer hookups, and picnic tables are provided. Flush toilets, bottled gas, showers, a recreation hall, a store, a laundry room, ice, a playground, and cable TV are available. Leashed pets are permitted.

Reservations, fees: Reservations accepted; phone (800) 452-2104. Sites are $17-29 per night. Open year-round.

Directions: From Portland drive south on Highway 99 West to Highway 18. Turn west on Highway 18 and drive 47 miles to U.S. 101. Turn south on U.S. 101 and drive five miles to Lincoln City. Continue south on U.S. 101 about 13 miles to the park at the edge of the town of Depoe Bay.

Contact: Pirates Cove RV Park, P.O. Box 1278, Depoe Bay, OR 97341 tel. (800) 452-2104, (541) 765-2302; fax (541) 765-2153.

43 Beverly Beach State Park   7

This beautiful campground is in a wooded, grassy area on the east side of U.S. 101. Giant, wind-sculpted trees surround the campsites along Spencer Creek. Like magic, you walk through a tunnel under the roadway and emerge on a beach that extends from Yaguna Head to the headlands of Otter Rock and from which a lighthouse is visible. A one-mile hiking trail is available. Just a mile to the north is a small day-use state park called Devil's Punchbowl, named for an unusual bowl-shaped rock formation with caverns under it where the waves rumble about. For some great ocean views, head north one more mile to the Otter Crest Wayside. The Oregon Coast Aquarium is within a few minutes drive.

Location: On the Pacific Ocean; map C1, grid g4.

Campsites, facilities: There are 129 tent sites, 129 sites with full or partial hookups for trailers or RVs of any length, and a special camping area for hikers and bicyclists, as well as a reserved group area. There is also a village of 21 yurts. Picnic tables and fire grills are provided. Drinking water, flush toilets, showers, garbage bins, and a sanitary disposal station are available. Some facilities are wheelchair accessible. Leashed pets are permitted.

Reservations, fees: Reservations accepted; phone (800) 452-5687 ($6 reservation fee). Sites are $11-21 per night, and $4 for hikers/bikers, yurts are $30 per night; $7 per night for an additional vehicle. Major credit cards accepted. Open year-round.

Directions: From Interstate 5 at Albany, turn west on U.S. 20 and drive 66 miles to Newport and U.S. 101. Turn north on U.S. 101 and drive seven miles to the park entrance.

Contact: Beverly Beach State Park, 198 N.E. 123rd Street, Newport, OR 97365; tel. (800) 551-6949, (503) 265-9278.

44 Devil's Lake State Park

 7

The only coastal camp in Oregon located in the midst of a city, Devil's Lake is a center of summertime activity, a take-your-pick deal. You can boat, canoe, kayak, fish, or water-ski. An alternative is to head west and explore the seven miles of beaches. Lincoln City also has a number of arts and crafts galleries in town. Devil's Lake State Park is two miles east and offers facilities for day use only.

Location: On Devil's Lake; map C1, grid g5.

Campsites, facilities: There are 54 tent sites and 31 sites with full hookups for trailers or RVs up to 60 feet long. There are also 10 yurts and a separate area for hikers and bikers. Picnic tables and fire grills are provided. Drinking water, garbage bins, flush toilets, showers, and firewood are available. Some facilities are wheelchair accessible. Boat docks and launching facilities are nearby. Leashed pets are permitted.

Reservations, fees: Reservations accepted; phone (800) 452-5687 ($6 reservation fee). Sites are $13-20 per night, $4.25 for hikers/bikers, and yurts are $30 per night; an additional vehicle is $7 per night. Major credit cards accepted. Open mid-April to late October.

Directions: From Portland drive south on Highway 99 West to Highway 18. Turn west on Highway 18 and drive 47 miles to U.S. 101. Turn south on U.S. 101 and drive five miles to Lincoln City. Follow the signs to the park in town.

Contact: Devil's Lake State Park, 1452 N.E. Sixth Street, Lincoln City, OR 97367; tel. (503) 994-2002 or (800) 452-5687.

45 Sportsman's Landing RV Park   7

This park lies along the shore of the Siletz River, with full boating facilities and a restaurant that's world famous for its Belgian waffles and crepes. If you head farther east on Highway 229, you'll discover several forest roads that lead into the Siuslaw National Forest and provide access to a number of creeks. See a U.S. Forest Service map for details.

Location: On the Siletz River; map C1, grid g5.

Campsites, facilities: There are 32 sites for trailers or RVs of any length. Electricity, drinking water, cable TV, telephone service, and sewer hookups are provided. Showers, a cafe, a barbecue area, and a laundry room are available. Boat rentals and moorage facilities and a fishing dock are available. Boat launching facilities are nearby. Leashed pets are permitted.

Reservations, fees: Reservations recommended. Sites are $16 per night. Open year-round.

Directions: From Portland drive south on Highway 99 West to Highway 18. Turn west on Highway 18 and drive 47 miles to U.S. 101. Turn south on U.S. 101 and drive five miles to Lincoln City. Continue six miles south on U.S. 101, then drive 3.8 miles east on Highway 229 to the park entrance.

Contact: Sportsman's Landing RV Park, 3804 Siletz Highway, Lincoln City, OR 97367; tel. (541) 996-4225; fax (541) 994-4688.

BOB RACE

MULTNOMAH FALLS

MAP C2

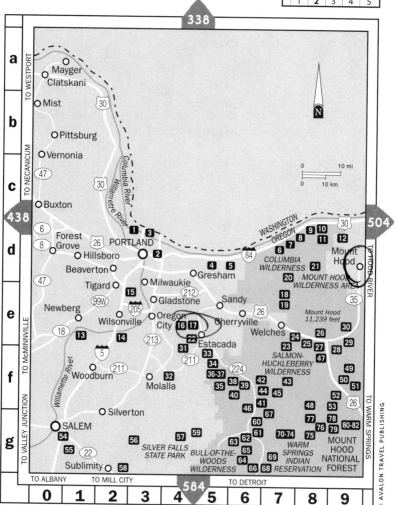

CHAPTER C2

■ Jantzen Beach RV Park   4

This RV campground is located near the banks of the Columbia River on the outskirts of Portland. Options include limited fishing and seasonal swimming. An 18-hole golf course, a riding stable, and tennis courts are close by.

Location: Near the Columbia River; map C2, grid d3.

Campsites, facilities: There are 169 sites for trailers or RVs of any length. Electricity, drinking water, sewer hookups, cable TV, modem access, and picnic tables are provided. Flush toilets, showers, a recreation hall, a laundry room, a playground, and a swimming pool are available. Bottled gas, a store, ice, and a cafe are within one mile. Boat docks, launching facilities, and rentals are nearby. Leashed pets are permitted.

Reservations, fees: Reservations accepted. Sites are $24-26 per night. Major credit cards accepted. Open year-round.

Directions: Form Portland on Interstate 5 drive four miles north to the Jantzen Beach exit (Exit 308) and take Hayden Island Drive. Turn west on Hayden Island Drive and drive one-half mile to the park on the right.

Contact: Jantzen Beach RV Park, 1503 North Hayden Island Drive, Portland, OR 97217; tel. (503) 289-7626; fax (503) 289-9220.

■ Portland Meadows RV Park

   6

From this small, landscaped, and tidy park, many recreation opportunities are available in the Portland area. Numerous marinas on the Willamette and Columbia Rivers offer boat trips and rentals, and the city parks and nearby state parks have hiking, bicycling, and horseback riding possibilities; call (503) 238-7488 for more information. The Columbia River Highway (U.S. 30) is a scenic drive. If golf is your game, Portland has 18 public golf courses. The winter ski areas at Mount Hood are within an hour's drive.

Location: Near the Columbia River; map C2, grid d3.

Campsites, facilities: There are 32 sites with full hookups for trailers or RVs. Electricity, drinking water, and sewer hookups are provided. Flush toilets, bottled gas, sanitary services, showers, a store, a laundry room, cable TV, and ice are available. Leashed pets under 20 pounds are permitted.

Reservations, fees: Reservations accepted. Sites are $17-19 per night. Open year-round.

Directions: From Portland on Interstate 5, take the Columbia Boulevard exit. Drive one-half mile east, turn north on Martin Luther King Boulevard (Union Avenue), and continue another half mile to Gertz Road. Turn east on Gertz Road and continue to the campground.

Contact: Portland Meadows RV Park, 222 Northeast Gertz Road, Portland, OR 97211; tel. (503) 285-1617; fax (503) 285-6041; e-mail: pmrv222aol.com.

3 Fir Grove RV and Trailer Park 7

This park is near the banks of the Columbia River in the outskirts of Portland. See the description of Portland Meadows RV Park for information about the nearby recreation opportunities.

Location: Near the Columbia River; map C2, grid d3.

Campsites, facilities: There six sites for trailers or RVs of any length. Electricity, drinking water, and sewer hookups are provided. Flush toilets, laundry facilities, and showers are available. Bottled gas, sanitary services, a store, a cafe, and a playground are located within one mile. Leashed pets and motorbikes are permitted.

Reservations, fees: Reservations accepted. Sites are $22-25 per night. Open year-round.

Directions: In Portland on Interstate 205, take Exit 23B onto Columbia Boulevard and drive about 400 yards northeast to Northeast Killingsworth. Drive about one mile west on Northeast Killingsworth to the park entrance.

Contact: Fir Grove RV and Trailer Park, 5541 Northeast 72nd Street, Portland, OR 97218; tel. (503) 252-9993.

4 Crown Point RV Park 6

This little park is located near the Columbia River along scenic U.S. 30. Crown Point State Park is nearby and is open during the day. It offers views of the Columbia River Gorge and the historic Vista House, a memorial built in 1918 to honor Oregon's pioneers. Multnomah Falls offers another possible side trip.

Location: Near the Columbia River; map C2, grid d5.

Campsites, facilities: There are 10 tent sites and 21 sites for trailers or RVs of any length. Electricity, drinking water, and picnic tables are provided. Flush toilets, bottled gas, sanitary services, coin-operated showers, a beauty shop, and a laundry room are available. There is a store and ice within one mile. Leashed pets are permitted.

Reservations, fees: Reservations accepted. Sites are $20 per night. Open year-round.

Directions: From Portland on Interstate 84 eastbound, drive to Exit 18/Lewis and Clark State Park exit. Turn southeast on U.S. 30 (Crown Point Highway) and drive 400 yards to the park. (Note: This route includes a 10% grade. To avoid it, take the following route: From Portland drive east on Interstate 84 to Exit 18/Lewis and Clark State Park exit. Drive through the park for 7.3 miles on the Historic Columbia River Highway to the park on the right.)

Contact: Crown Point RV Park, 37000 East Historic Columbia River Highway, Corbett, OR 97019; tel. (503) 695-5207.

5 Oxbow County Campground 7

This 1,000-acre park along the Sandy River, a short distance from the Columbia River Gorge, is a designated natural preservation area. Fishing, swimming, and non-motorized boating are permitted here.

Location: On the Sandy River; map C2, grid d6.

Campsites, facilities: There are 67 sites for tents, trailers, or RVs up to 35 feet long. Picnic tables are provided. Drinking water, flush and vault toilets, coin-operated showers, firewood, barbecues, fire rings, and a playground are available. Boat launching facilities are nearby. Gates lock at sunset and open at 6 a.m. No pets are permitted.

Reservations, fees: No reservations accepted. Sites are $10-15 per night. Open year-round, but subject to periodic closure; call for current status.

Directions: From Portland on Interstate 84, drive to Exit 17. Turn south on Highway 257 and drive three miles to Division Street. Turn left and drive seven miles to the park.

Contact: Oxbow County Campground, 3010 Southeast Oxbow Parkway, Gresham, OR 97080; tel. (503) 663-4708.

6 Ainsworth State Park   8

This state park is set along the scenic Columbia River Gorge, where the world's greatest concentration of high waterfalls, including famous Multnomah Falls, is on view. From the Nesmith Point Trail, there's a great view of St. Peter's Dome. A two-mile section of the Columbia River Gorge Trail connects this park with John Yeon State Park, which is open during the day. Anglers should check out the Bonneville Fish Hatchery, home to an unusual giant sturgeon.

Location: Along the Columbia River Gorge; map C2, grid d7

Campsites, facilities: There are 45 sites with full hookups for trailers or RVs up to 60 feet long, and a hiker/biker site for primitive tent camping. Picnic tables and fire grills are provided. Drinking water, flush toilets, showers, garbage bins, sanitary disposal station, firewood, and a laundry room are available. Leashed pets are permitted.

Reservations, fees: No reservations accepted. Sites are $13-20 per night, $5 per night for hiker/biker sites; $7 per night for an additional vehicle. Major credit cards accepted. Open March through October, weather permitting).

Directions: From Portland on Interstate 84 eastbound, drive 37 miles to Exit 35. Turn southwest and continue a short distance to the park. An alternate route is to take the historic Columbia River Highway, a designated scenic highway, all the way from Portland (37 miles).

Contact: Columbia River Gorge District, P.O. Box 100, Corbett, OR 97019; tel. (800) 551-6949, (503) 695-2301.

7 Eagle Creek   8

This is a good base camp for a hiking trip. The camp is set at 400 feet elevation among old-growth Douglas fir and hemlock. The Eagle Creek Trail leaves the campground and goes 13 miles to Wahtum Lake, where it intersects with the Pacific Crest Trail. There is a primitive campground at the 7.5-mile point. The upper seven miles of the trail pass through the Hatfield Wilderness.

Location: Near the Columbia Wilderness in Mount Hood National Forest; map C2, grid d7.

Campsites, facilities: There are 19 sites for tents, trailers, or RVs up to 20 feet long. Picnic tables and fire grills are provided. Drinking water, garbage bins, and flush toilets are available. Boat docks and launching facilities are nearby on the Columbia River. Leashed pets are permitted.

Reservations, fees: Reservations required for groups. Sites are $10-12 per night, $5 per night for an additional vehicle. Open mid-May to October.

Directions: From Portland drive east on Interstate 84 for 40 miles to Bonneville. Continue east for two miles to the campground.

Contact: Columbia River Gorge National Scenic Area, 902 Wasco Avenue, Suite 200, Hood River, OR 97031; tel. (541) 386-2333; fax (541) 386-1916.

8 Cascade Locks Marine Park

 8

This public riverfront park covers 200 acres and offers a museum and boat rides. The salmon fishing is excellent here. Nearby recreation options include hiking trails and tennis courts.

Location: In Cascade Locks; map C2, grid d8.

Campsites, facilities: There are 35 sites for tents, trailers, and RVs of any length. Picnic tables are provided. Drinking water, flush toilets, sanitary services, showers, boat docks, launching facilities, and a playground are available. Bottled gas, a store, a cafe, a coin laundry, and ice are located within one mile. Leashed pets and motorbikes are permitted.

Reservations, fees: No reservations accepted. Sites are $10 per night. Open year-round, with limited winter facilities.

Directions: From Portland drive east on Interstate 84 for 44 miles to Cascade Locks. Take Exit 44 to Wanapa Street and drive one-half mile to the sign for the park on the left. Turn left and drive to the park (well signed).

Contact: Cascade Locks Marine Park, P.O. Box 307, Cascade Locks, OR 97014; tel. (541) 374-8619; fax (541) 374-8428.

9 Herman Creek Horse Camp   5

This rustic campground with spacious sites is set at 1,000 feet elevation and is located about one-half mile from Herman Creek, not far from the Pacific Crest Trail. This is a particularly beautiful area, separated from Washington by the Columbia River. There are many recreation options here, including biking, hiking, fishing, and boat trips.

Location: Near the Pacific Crest Trail in Mount Hood National Forest; map C2, grid d8.

Campsites, facilities: There are seven sites for tents, trailers, or RVs up to 24 feet long. Drinking water, garbage bins, fire grills, and picnic tables are provided. Stock handling facilities are available. Sanitary services, showers, a store, a cafe, a coin laundry, and ice are nearby. Leashed pets are permitted.

Reservations, fees: No reservations accepted. Sites are $8 per night, $5 per night for an additional vehicle. Open mid-May to October.

Directions: From Portland drive east on Interstate 84 for 44 miles to Cascade Locks and Exit 44. Take that exit and drive straight ahead to the frontage road (Wanapa Street). Continue 1.5 miles (the road becomes Herman Creek Road) to the campground on the right.

Contact: Columbia River Gorge National Scenic Area, 902 Wasco Avenue, Suite 200, Hood River, OR 97031; tel. (541) 386-2333; fax (541) 386-1916.

10 Wyeth   5

This is a good layover spot for Columbia River corridor cruisers. The camp is set at 400 feet elevation along Gordon Creek, near the Columbia. See the description of Herman Horse Camp for recreation details.

Location: On Gordon Creek in Mount Hood National Forest; map C2, grid d8.

Campsites, facilities: There are 17 sites for tents, trailers, or RVs up to 32 feet long. Fire grills and picnic tables are provided. Drinking water and flush toilets are available. Leashed pets are permitted.

Reservations, fees: No reservations accepted. Sites are $10 per night, $5 per night for an additional vehicle. Open mid-May to October.

Directions: From Portland drive east on Interstate 84 for 44 miles to Cascade Locks. Continue east on Interstate 84 for seven miles to Wyeth and Exit 51. Turn right and drive a quarter-mile to the campground entrance.

Contact: Columbia River Gorge National Scenic Area, 902 Wasco Avenue, Suite 200, Hood River, OR 97031; tel. (541) 386-2333; fax (541) 386-1916.

11 KOA Cascade Locks   5

This is a good layover spot for RVers touring the Columbia River corridor. The campground offers level, shaded RV sites and grassy tent sites. Nearby recreation options include bike trails, hiking trails, and tennis courts. The 200-acre Cascade Locks Marine Park is nearby and offers everything from museums to boat trips.

Location: Near the Columbia River; map C2, grid d8.

Campsites, facilities: There are 78 sites for tents, trailers or RVs of any length, plus nine cabins. Electricity, drinking water, sewer hookups, and picnic tables are provided. Flush toilets, bottled gas, sanitary services, showers, firewood, a hot tub, cable TV hookups, modem, a recreation hall, a store, a laundry room, ice, a playground, and a heated swimming pool are available. A cafe is located within one mile. Leashed pets and motorbikes are permitted.

Reservations, fees: Reservations accepted by calling (800) KOA-8698. Sites are $19-24 per night; cabins are $32-38 per night for two people. Open mid-March to mid-October. Major credit cards accepted.

Directions: From Portland drive east on Interstate 84 for 44 miles to Cascade Locks and Exit 44. Turn east on Forest Lane and drive one mile to the campground.

Contact: KOA Cascade Locks, 841 N.W. Forest Lane, Cascade Locks, OR 97014; tel. (541) 374-8668. Website: www.koa.com.

12 Viento State Park   8

(handwritten note: "Next to RR tracks")

This park along the Columbia River Gorge offers scenic hiking trails and some of the best windsurfing in the Gorge. Take the picturesque drive along old U.S. 30, which skirts the Columbia River. Viento has a day-use picnic area right next to a babbling creek. Weekend interpretive programs are offered during the summer. There are three other day-use state parks along Interstate 84 just west of Viento: Wygant, Vinzenz Lausmann, and Seneca Fouts. All are accessible by eastbound traffic only and offer quality hiking trails and scenic views.

Location: Along the Columbia River Gorge; map C2, grid d9.

Campsites, facilities: There are 17 tent sites and 58 sites with water and electrical hookups for trailers or RVs up to 30 feet long. Picnic tables and fire grills are provided. Drinking water, garbage bins, flush toilets, showers, firewood, and a laundry room are available. Leashed pets are permitted.

Reservations, fees: No reservations. Sites are $13-20 per night, $7 per night for an additional vehicle. Major credit cards accepted. Open March through October, weather permitting.

Directions: From Portland drive east on Interstate 84 for 56 miles to Exit 56 (eight miles west of Hood River). Take Exit 56 and drive to the park entrance.

Contact: Columbia River Gorge District, P.O. Box 100, Corbett, OR 97019; tel. (541) 374-8811 or (800) 551-6949.

13 Champoeg State Heritage Area

   7

Situated on the south bank of the Willamette River, this state park has an interpretive center, a botanical garden featuring native plants, and hiking and bike trails. In July a pageant reenacting the early history of the area is staged Thursday through Sunday evenings. There is also a log cabin museum, the historic Newell House, and a visitor center worth a tour. An amphitheater in the park is the site of summer concerts and special events.

Location: On the Willamette River; map C2, grid e1.

Campsites, facilities: There are 46 tent sites and 46 sites for trailers or RVs up to 50 feet with partial hookups. There are also three group areas that accommodate a maximum of 30 tents each, 12 walk-in sites, a hiker/biker camp, an RV group area with 25 sites, and six yurts. Picnic tables and fire grills are provided. Drinking water, garbage bins, flush toilets, a sanitary disposal station, showers, a group recreation hall for up to 55 people, and firewood are available. Some facilities are wheelchair accessible. Boat docking facilities are nearby. Leashed pets are permitted.

Reservations, fees: Reservations accepted; phone (800) 452-5687 ($6 reservation fee). Sites are $13-19 per night, $4 per night for hiker/bikers; yurts are $30 per night; $7 per night for an additional vehicle. Major credit cards accepted. Open year-round, with limited winter facilities.

Directions: From Portland drive south on Interstate 5 to Exit 278, the Donald/Aurora exit. Take that exit and turn west (right) on Ehlen Road and drive three miles to Case Road. Turn north and drive 5.5 miles (road becomes ⊔ poeg Road) to the park on the right.

Contact: Champoeg State Heritage Area, 7679 Champoeg Road NE, Saint Paul, OR 97137; tel. (800) 452-5687, (503) 678-1251, extension 225.

14 Isberg RV Park   7

This RV campground is in a rural area just off the main highway. The setting is very pretty, thanks to lots of evergreen trees that shelter the camp from the highway. Portland and Salem are just 20 minutes away.

Location: Near Aurora; map C2, grid e2.

Campsites, facilities: There are 127 sites for trailers or RVs of any length. Electricity, drinking water, and sewer hookups are provided. Flush toilets, bottled gas, showers, a recreation hall, a store, a swimming pool, a laundry room, and ice are available. Leashed pets are permitted.

Reservations, fees: Reservations accepted. Sites are $21.50-24 per night. Open year-round.

Directions: From Portland drive south on Interstate 5 to Exit 278, the Donald/Aurora exit. Take that exit and turn left (east) on Ehlen Road and drive a quarter mile to the park on the left.

Contact: Isberg RV Park, 21599 Dolores Way NE, Aurora, OR 97002; tel. (503) 678-2646; fax (503) 678-2724.

15 RV Park of Portland

        6

This park just south of Portland in a wooded setting has spacious sites, all with access to lawn areas. See the description of Portland Meadows RV Park for information about recreation possibilities in the area.

Location: In Tualatin; map C2, grid e3.

Campsites, facilities: There are 100 drive-through sites for trailers or RVs of any length. Electricity, drinking water, sewer hookups, and picnic tables are provided. Flush toilets, sanitary services, showers, a laundry room, and a playground are available. Bottled gas, a store, a cafe, and ice are within one mile. Leashed pets and motorbikes are permitted.

Reservations, fees: Reservations accepted. Sites are $22 per night. Open year-round.

Directions: From Portland drive south on Interstate 5 to Tualatin and Exit 289. Take Exit 289, turn east on Highway 212, and drive one-quarter mile to the park.

Contact: RV Park of Portland, 6645 Southwest Nyberg Road, Tualatin, OR 97062; tel. (503) 692-0225; website: www.rvparkofportland.com.

16 Barton Park   6

Getting here may seem a bit of a maze, but the trip is well worth it. This camp on the Clackamas River is surrounded by woods and tall trees. There is a swimming area

.ne nearby Clackamas River provides good salmon fishing.

.he Clackamas River; map C2, grid e4.

.cilities: There are 96 sites for tents, trailers, and RVs. Rest rooms, ,anitary dump, a public phone, and a barbecue are available. Recre- ,lities include horseshoe pits, a playground, volleyball, basketball, and a ,p. Supplies are available within one mile. Leashed pets are permitted.

✓ations, fees: Reservations recommended. Sites are $12-16 per night. ,า May through September.

Directions: From Portland drive south on Interstate 5 to Interstate 205. Turn east and drive about 20 miles to the Clackamas/Estacada exit (Highway 212). Turn east on Highway 212 and drive about five miles to the Carver exit (Highway 224). Turn right on Highway 224 and drive about 6.5 miles to the town of Barton and Baker's Ferry Road. Turn right and drive one-quarter mile to Barton Park Road. Turn left and drive to the park on the left.

Contact: Clackamas County Parks Department, 9101 S.E. Sunnybrook Boulevard, Clackamas, OR 97015; tel. (503) 353-4400.

🔳17 Milo McIver State Park

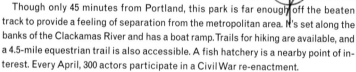 7

Though only 45 minutes from Portland, this park is far enough off the beaten track to provide a feeling of separation from the metropolitan area. It's set along the banks of the Clackamas River and has a boat ramp. Trails for hiking are available, and a 4.5-mile equestrian trail is also accessible. A fish hatchery is a nearby point of interest. Every April, 300 actors participate in a Civil War re-enactment.

Location: On the Clackamas River; map C2, grid e5.

Campsites, facilities: There are nine primitive tent sites and 44 sites with water and electrical hookups for trailers or RVs up to 50 feet long. There are a few hiker/biker sites and three group tent areas. Picnic tables and fire grills are provided. Drinking water, garbage bins, flush toilets, sanitary disposal station, showers, picnic shelters, and firewood are available. Facilities are wheelchair accessible. Boat launching facilities, an 18-hole disc golf course and horse rentals are nearby. Group facilities are available. Leashed pets are permitted.

Reservations, fees: Reservations accepted; phone (800) 452-5687 ($6 reservation fee). Sites are $10-16 per night, $7 per night for an additional vehicle; group sites are $60 per night. Major credit cards accepted. Open mid-March through October.

Directions: From Portland drive east on U.S. 26 from Gresham 11 miles to Sandy and Highway 211. Turn right (south) and drive six miles to a junction. Turn south (still Highway 211) and drive five miles to the park entrance road on the right.

Contact: Milo McIver State Park, 24101 South Entrance Road, Estacada, OR 97023; tel. (503) 630-7150, (800) 551-6949.

🔳18 McNeil 5

This campground is set at an elevation of 2,040 feet in Old Maid Flat, a special geological area along the Clear Fork of the Sandy River. There's a good view of Mount

Hood from the campground entrance. Several trails nearby provide access to the wilderness backcountry. See a U.S. Forest Service map for details.

Location: On the Clear Fork of the Sandy River in Mount Hood National Forest; map C2, grid e7.

Campsites, facilities: There are 34 sites for tents, trailers, or RVs up to 22 feet long. Picnic tables and vault toilets are provided. There is no drinking water. Leashed pets are permitted.

Reservations, fees: Reservations accepted; phone (877) 444-6777 or access the website: www.reserveusa.com ($8.65 reservation fee). Sites are $10 per night, $5 per night for an additional vehicle. Open May to late September.

Directions: From Portland drive 40 miles east on U.S. 26 to Zigzag. Turn left on County Road 18/East Lolo Pass Road and drive 4.5 miles to Forest Road 1825. Turn right on Forest Road 1825, drive less than one mile, bear right onto a bridge to stay on Forest Road 1825, and drive one-quarter mile to the campground on the left.

Contact: Mount Hood National Forest, Zigzag Ranger District, 65000 East Highway 26, Welches, OR 97067; tel. (503) 622-7674; fax (503) 622-3163.

19 Riley Horse Camp 6

Riley Horse Camp is close to McNeil and offers the same opportunities, except Riley provides stock facilities and is reserved for horse camping only on holidays. Secluded in an area of Douglas fir and lodgepole pine at 2,100 feet elevation, this is a popular base camp for horse packing trips.

Location: Near the Clear Fork of the Sandy River in Mount Hood National Forest; map C2, grid e7.

Campsites, facilities: There are 14 sites for tents, trailers, or RVs up to 16 feet long. Drinking water, fire grills, vault toilets, and picnic tables are provided. Facilities for horses are available. Leashed pets are permitted.

Reservations, fees: Reservations accepted for some sites; phone (877) 444-6777 or access the website: reserveusa.com ($8.65 reservation fee). Sites are $12 per night, $6 per night for an additional vehicle. Open May to late September.

Directions: From Portland drive 40 miles east on U.S. 26 to Zigzag. Turn right (northeast) on County Road 18/East Lolo Pass Road and drive four miles to Forest Road 1825. Turn right and drive one-half mile to Forest Road 380. Turn right and drive 100 yards to the camp.

Contact: Mount Hood National Forest, Zigzag Ranger District, 65000 East Highway 26, Welches, OR 97067; tel. (503) 622-7674; fax (503) 622-3163.

20 Lost Lake 9

Only non-motorized boats are allowed on this 240-acre clear lake set against the Cascade Range. This campground is nestled in an old growth forest of cedar, Douglas fir and hemlock trees at 3,200 feet. Many sites have a lake view, and there is a great view of Mt. Hood from the campground. Significant improvements to this campground were completed in late 1999.

Location: On Lost Lake, Mount Hood National Forest, Hood River District; map C2, grid e8.

Campsites, facilities: There are 125 sites for tents, trailers, or RVs up to 32 feet long, and there is one large, separate group site. A horse camp with a corral is also available. Picnic tables and fire rings with grills are provided. Drinking water, vault toilets, garbage containers, a dump station and a covered picnic shelter are available. Cabins, a grocery store, showers, beach picnic areas, a boat launch, and boat rentals are nearby. Many sites are wheelchair accessible, and there is barrier-free boating and fishing, as well as 3.5 miles of barrier-free trails. Leashed pets are permitted.

Reservations, fees: Reservations accepted for group sites only. Call Lost Lake Resort at (541) 386-6366. Major credit cards accepted. Sites are $15-20 per night, with an additional $5 per extra vehicle. Group sites are $40 per night. The campground is open from mid-May to mid-October, depending on weather

Directions: From Portland drive 62 miles east on Interstate 84 to the city of Hood River. Take Exit 62/Westcliff exit to Cascade Road and drive east on Cascade Road to 13th Street. Turn right on 13th Street and drive through Hood River Heights. The road turns into Dee Highway. Continue seven miles, then turn right onto Lost Lake Road (Forest Road 13). Continue seven miles to the campground.

Contact: Mount Hood National Forest, Hood River Ranger District, 6780 Highway 35, Mt. Hood, OR 97041; tel. (541) 352-6002; fax (541) 352-7365.

21 Kinnickkinnick   5

The campground is on a peninsula that juts into the lake. Only non-motorized boats are allowed on this lake. Tree cover is fairly sparse, so campsite privacy varies. More than half of the sites are a short walk in from your vehicle.

Location: On Laurence Lake in Mount Hood National Forest; map C2, grid d8.

Campsites, facilities: There are 20 sites for tents, trailers, or RVs up to 16 feet long. No drinking water is available, but picnic tables and fire rings with fire grills are provided. Vault toilets, garbage bins, and a boat ramp are available. Some sites are wheelchair accessible. Leashed pets are permitted.

Reservations, fees: No reservations accepted. Major credit cards accepted. Sites are $10 per night. Major credit cards accepted. Open May through September, weather permitting.

Directions: From Portland drive 62 miles west on Interstate 84 to the city of Hood River. Take Exit 64 and drive about 14 miles south on Highway 35 to the town of Mt. Hood and Cooper Spur Road. Turn right and drive three miles to Parkdale and Clear Creek Road. Turn left (south) and drive three miles to the Laurence Lake turnoff. Turn right on Forest Road 2840 (Laurence Lake Road) and drive four miles to the campground on the right.

Contact: Mount Hood National Forest, Hood River Ranger District, 6780 Highway 35, Mt. Hood, OR 97041; tel. (541) 352-6002; fax (541) 352-7365.

22 Lost Creek    8

This campground near McNeil and Riley has some of the same opportunities. Set in a cool, lush area on a creek at 2,600 feet elevation, it's barrier free and offers an interpretive nature trail about one-mile long and a wheelchair-accessible fishing pier.

Location: On Lost Creek in Mount Hood National Forest; map C2, grid e5.

Campsites, facilities: There are five walk-in sites for tents and nine sites for trailers or RVs up to 22 feet long. Facilities are wheelchair accessible. Drinking water, garbage service, fire grills, vault toilets, and picnic tables are provided. Leashed pets are permitted.

Reservations, fees: Reservations for some sites accepted; phone (877) 444-6777 or access the website: www.reserveusa.com ($8.65 reservation fee). Sites are $12-14 per night, $6 per night for an additional vehicle. Open May to late September.

Directions: From Portland drive 40 miles east on U.S. 26 to Zigzag. Turn north on County Road 18/East Lolo Pass Road and drive 4.5 miles to Forest Road 1825. Turn right and drive two miles to a fork. Bear right and drive 200 yards to the campground on the right, just past the entrance to Riley Horse Camp.

Contact: Mount Hood National Forest, Zigzag Ranger District, 65000 East Highway 26, Welches, OR 97067; tel. (503) 622-7674; fax (503) 622-3163.

23 Green Canyon   8

Few out-of-towners know about this winner. But the locals do, and they keep the place hopping in the summer. The camp sits at 1,600 feet elevation along the banks of the Salmon River. A long trail cuts through the site and parallels the river, passing through a magnificent old-growth forest. See a U.S. Forest Service map for details.

Location: On the Salmon River in Mount Hood National Forest; map C2, grid e7.

Campsites, facilities: There are 15 sites for tents, trailers, or RVs up to 22 feet long. Picnic tables, garbage service, and fire grills are provided. Pit toilets are available. Drinking water is intermittently available. A store, a cafe, and ice are located within five miles. Some facilities are wheelchair accessible. Leashed pets are permitted.

Reservations, fees: No reservations accepted. Sites are $12-14 per night, $6 per night for an additional vehicle. Open May to late September.

Directions: From Portland drive east on U.S. 26 for 39 miles to Forest Road 2618 (Salmon River Road) near Zigzag. Turn right and drive 4.5 miles to the campground on the right.

Contact: Mount Hood National Forest, Zigzag Ranger District, 65000 East Highway 26, Welches, OR 97067; tel. (503) 622-7674; fax (503) 622-3163.

24 Toll Gate   8

This shady campground along the banks of the Zigzag River near Rhododendron is extremely popular, and finding a site on a summer weekend can be next to impossible. Luckily you can get a reservation. There are numerous hiking trails in the area. The nearest one to this campground leads east for several miles along the river. A historic Civilian Conservation Corps shelter from the 1930s is located in the campground and can be used by campers.

Location: On the Zigzag River in Mount Hood National Forest; map C2, grid e7.

Campsites, facilities: There are 14 tent sites and nine sites for trailers or RVs up to 16 feet long. Picnic tables and fire grills are provided. Drinking water, garbage service, and pit toilets are available. Leashed pets are permitted.

Reservations, fees: Reservations accepted for some sites; phone (877) 444-6777 or access the website: www.reserveusa.com ($8.65 reservation fee). Single sites are $12-14 per night, $5 per night for an additional vehicle. Double sites are $24 per night, $5 per night for an additional vehicle. Open late May to late September.

Directions: From Portland drive east on U.S. 26 and drive 40 miles to Zigzag. Continue 2.5 miles southeast on U.S. 26 to the campground entrance.

Contact: Mount Hood National Forest, Zigzag Ranger District, 65000 East Highway 26, Welches, OR 97067; tel. (503) 622-7674; fax (503) 622-3163.

25 Camp Creek   8

This campground is set at 2,200 feet elevation, along Camp Creek, not far from the Zigzag River and looks similar to Toll Gate, but larger and further from the road. A hiking trail runs through camp and along the river, and another leads south to Still Creek. This campground, along with Toll Gate to the west, is very popular and you'll probably need a reservation.

Location: Near the Zigzag River in Mount Hood National Forest; map C2, grid e8.

Campsites, facilities: There are 24 sites for tents, trailers, or RVs up to 22 feet long. Drinking water, garbage bins, fire grills, and picnic tables are provided. Vault toilets are available. Leashed pets are permitted.

Reservations, fees: Reservations accepted for some sites; phone (877) 444-6777 or access the website: www.reserveusa.com ($8.65 reservation fee). Sites are $12-14 per night, $6 per night for an additional vehicle. Open late May to late September.

Directions: From Portland drive east on U.S. 26 and drive 40 miles to Zigzag. Continue southeast on U.S. 26 for about four miles to the camp on the right.

Contact: Mount Hood National Forest, Zigzag Ranger District, 65000 East Highway 26, Welches, OR 97067; tel. (503) 622-7674; fax (503) 622-3163.

26 Alpine   8

This small campground is one mile from the Timberline Ski Area lodge at 5,400 feet elevation on the south slopes of Mount Hood. It can get quite crowded here on weekends. In spite of some traffic noise, the big trees lend a mountain feel and year-round snow skiing and boarding are less than one mile away. The Pacific Crest Trail can be accessed from the Timberline Lodge. Be sure to come prepared for very cold nights.

Location: Near the Pacific Crest Trail in Mount Hood National Forest; map C2, grid e8.

Campsites, facilities: There are 16 tent sites. Drinking water, fire grills, vault toilets, garbage service, and picnic tables are provided. Leashed pets are permitted.

Reservations, fees: No reservations accepted. Sites are $8 per night, $4 per night for an additional vehicle. Open July to late September.

Directions: From Portland drive east on U.S. 26 and drive 55 miles to the small town of Government Camp. Continue east for one mile to Timberline Road (Forest Road 173). Turn left and drive 4.5 miles to the campground on the left.

Contact: Mount Hood National Forest, Zigzag Ranger District, 65000 East Highway 26, Welches, OR 97067; tel. (503) 622-7674; fax (503) 622-3163.

27 Still Creek   6

This primitive camp at 3,600 feet elevation, shaded primarily by fir and hemlock, is located along Still Creek where it pours off the south slope of Mount Hood. Adjacent to Summit Meadows, site of a pioneer gravesite from Oregon Trail days, it's a great place for views of mountains, sunsets, and wildlife. Anglers should bring along their rods: The fishing in Still Creek can be excellent.

Location: On Still Creek in Mount Hood National Forest; map C2, grid e8.

Campsites, facilities: There are 27 sites for tents or trailers up to 27 feet long. Picnic tables, garbage service, and fire grills are provided. Pit toilets and drinking water are available. Leashed pets are permitted.

Reservations, fees: Reservations accepted for some sites; phone (877) 444-6777 or access the website: www.reserveusa.com ($8.65 reservation fee). Sites are $12 per night, $6 per night for an additional vehicle. Open mid-June to late September.

Directions: From Portland drive 55 miles east on U.S. 26 to Government Camp. Continue east on U.S. 26 for one mile to Forest Road 2650. Turn right and drive south for 500 yards to the campground.

Contact: Mount Hood National Forest, Zigzag Ranger District, 65000 East Highway 26, Welches, OR 97067; tel. (503) 622-7674; fax (503) 622-3163.

28 Grindstone   7

This tiny campground, set at 3,400 feet elevation in a meadow along Barlow Creek, is a little-known and little-used spot. You won't find much out here but wind, water, and trees—but sometimes that's all you need. High-clearance vehicles recommended. This camp was a site first used by the pioneers.

Location: Near Barlow Creek in Mount Hood National Forest; map C2, grid e9.

Campsites, facilities: There are three primitive sites for tents. Picnic tables and fire grills are provided. Vault toilets are available, but there is no drinking water and no garbage service; pack out all garbage. Leashed pets are permitted.

Reservations, fees: No reservations; no fee. Open May through September.

Directions: From Portland turn east on U.S. 26 and drive 57 miles (just past the town of Government Camp) to the junction with Highway 35. Turn right (southeast) on U.S. 26 and drive 4.5 miles to Forest Road 3530. Turn right and drive two miles to the campground on the right.

Contact: Mount Hood National Forest, Hood River Ranger District, 6780 Highway 35, Mount Hood, OR 97041; tel. (541) 352-6002; fax (541) 352-7365.

29 Devil's Half Acre Meadow   8

Used by the pioneers, this campground is set at 3,600 feet elevation a few miles upstream on Barlow Creek from Grindstone Campground. Several hiking trails close to camp, including the Pacific Crest Trail, lead to small lakes in the area. There are many historic points of interest in the vicinity. High-clearance vehicles recommended.

Location: On Barlow Creek in Mount Hood National Forest; map C2, grid e9.

Campsites, facilities: There are five sites for tents, trailers, or RVs up to 16 feet long. Picnic tables and fire grills are provided. Firewood and pit toilets are available, but there is no drinking water and no garbage service; pack out all garbage. Leashed pets are permitted.

Reservations, fees: No reservations; no fee. Open May to October.

Directions: From Portland turn east on U.S. 26 and drive 57 miles (just past the town of Government Camp) to the junction with Highway 35. Turn right (southeast) on U.S. 26 and drive 4.5 miles to Forest Road 3530. Turn southeast and drive one mile to the campground.

Contact: Mount Hood National Forest, Hood River Ranger District, 6780 Highway 35, Mount Hood, OR 97041; tel. (541) 352-6002; fax (541) 352-7365.

30 Robinhood   8

This campground along the East Fork of the Hood River at the base of Mount Hood marks the start of a trail (East Fork Trail) that follows the river north for about four miles, then joins a network of trails that provide access to the Mount Hood Wilderness. Fishing is another option here. The elevation is 3,500 feet.

Location: On the East Fork of the Hood River in Mount Hood National Forest; map C2, grid e9.

Campsites, facilities: There are 24 sites for tents or trailers up to 18 feet long. Drinking water, fire grills, and picnic tables are provided. Garbage containers are available. Leashed pets are permitted.

Reservations, fees: No reservations accepted. Sites are $10-12 per night, $5 per each additional vehicle. Open late May to early September, weather permitting.

Directions: From Portland drive east on Interstate 84 for 65 miles to the town of Hood River and Exit 64 (Highway 35). Turn south on Highway 35 (Mount Hood Highway) and drive 28 miles to the campground on the right.

Contact: Mount Hood National Forest, Hood River Ranger District, 6780 Highway 35, Mount Hood, OR 97041; tel. (541) 352-6002; fax (541) 352-7365.

31 Metzler Park   8

This county campground on a small stream not far from the Clackamas River is a hot spot for fishing, swimming, and picnicking. Be sure to make your reservation early at this very popular park.

Location: On Clear Creek; map C2, grid f4.

Campsites, facilities: There are 70 sites for tents, trailers, and RVs. Electricity, rest rooms, showers, a sanitary dump, a public phone, a playground, and a recreation field are available. Propane, ice, and laundry facilities are located within five miles. Leashed pets are permitted.

Reservations, fees: Reservations recommended; phone (503) 655-8521. Sites are $10-14 per night. Open May through September.

Directions: From Portland drive east on U.S. 26 from Gresham 11 miles to Sandy and Highway 211. Turn right (south) and drive six miles to a junction. Turn south (still Highway 211) and drive over the bridge to South Springwater Road. Turn left on South Springwater Road and drive about one-quarter mile to Metzler Park Road. Turn left on Metzler Park Road and drive three-quarters of a mile to the park on the left.

Contact: Clackamas County Parks Department, S.E. Sunnybrook Boulevard, Clackamas, OR 97015; tel. (503) 345-4414; fax (503) 345-4420.

32 Feyrer Memorial Park   5

Located on the scenic Molalla River, this county park offers swimming and excellent salmon fishing. This is a superb option for weary Interstate 5 cruisers; the park is only 30 minutes off the highway and provides a peaceful, serene environment.

Location: On the Molalla River; map C2, grid f4.

Campsites, facilities: There are 19 sites for trailers and RVs. Electricity, drinking water, rest rooms, showers, a sanitary dump, and a public phone are provided. There is also a playground and recreation field. Some facilities are wheelchair accessible. Supplies are available within three miles. Leashed pets are permitted.

Reservations, fees: Reservations recommended; call (503) 655-8521. Sites are $10-14 per night. Open May through September.

Directions: From Portland drive south on Interstate 5 to Woodburn and Exit 271. Take that exit and drive east on Highway 214 and continue (the road changes to Highway 211 at the crossing with Highway 99E) to Molalla and Feyrer Park Road. Turn right and drive three miles to the park on the left.

Contact: Clackamas County Parks Department, S.E. Sunnybrook Boulevard, Clackamas, OR 97015; tel. (503) 345-4414; fax (503) 345-4420.

33 Promontory   7

This Portland General Electric camp on North Fork Reservoir is part of a large recreation area and park. The water is calm and ideal for boating, and the trout fishing is excellent. This reservoir is actually a dammed-up overflow on the Clackamas River. A trail travels along about one mile of the lake shoreline.

Location: On North Fork Reservoir; map C2, grid f5.

Campsites, facilities: There are 58 sites for tents, trailers, or RVs up to 35 feet long, and one group site that can accommodate up to 35 people. There are no RV hookups. Rest rooms, garbage bins, showers, limited groceries, ice, a playground, horseshoes, covered picnic shelters with sinks and electric stoves, and snacks are available. A fish cleaning station, a fishing pier, a children's fishing pond, a boat ramp, a dock, and boat rentals are also on site. Some facilities are wheelchair accessible, including restrooms, some sites, the boat ramp and the fishing pier. Leashed pets are permitted.

Reservations, fees: Reservations recommended; phone (503) 630-7229. Sites are $14 per night. Open May 15 to November 1.

Directions: From Portland drive east on U.S. 26 from Gresham 11 miles to Sandy and Highway 211. Turn right (south) and drive six miles to a junction. Turn south (still Highway 211) and drive six miles to Estacada. Continue south on Highway

224 and drive seven miles to the campground on the right. The route is well signed.

Contact: Portland General Electric, 121 S.W. Salmon Street, Portland, OR 97204; tel. (503) 464-8515; fax (503) 464-2944; website: www.pge-online.com.

34 Lazy Bend   8

This campground is set at 800 feet elevation along the banks of the Clackamas River near the large North Fork Reservoir. It's far enough off the highway to provide a secluded, primitive feeling, though it fills quickly on weekends and holidays. There's catch-and-release fishing only in the Clackamas.

Location: On the Clackamas River in Mount Hood National Forest; map C2, grid f5.

Campsites, facilities: There are 21 sites for tents, trailers, or RVs up to 16 feet long. Picnic tables, garbage service, and fireplaces are provided. Drinking water and flush toilets are available. Leashed pets are permitted.

Reservations, fees: Reservations accepted for some sites; phone (877) 444-6777 or access the website: www.reserveusa.com ($8.65 reservation fee). Sites are $12 per night, $6 per night for an additional vehicle. Open late April through Labor Day.

Directions: From Portland drive east on U.S. 26 from Gresham 11 miles to Sandy and Highway 211. Turn right (south) and drive six miles to a junction. Turn south (still Highway 211) and drive six miles to Estacada. Continue south on Highway 224 and drive 10.5 miles to the campground on the right.

Contact: Mount Hood National Forest, Estacada Ranger District, 595 N.W. Industrial Way, Estacada, OR 97023; tel. (503) 630-6861; fax (503) 630-2299.

35 Fish Creek   8

This campground is located along the banks of the Clackamas River at an elevation of 900 feet, not far from the Clackamas River Trail and North Fork Reservoir. There's catch-and-release fishing only on the Clackamas River.

Location: On the Clackamas River in Mount Hood National Forest; map C2, grid f5.

Campsites, facilities: There are 24 sites for tents, trailers, or RVs up to 16 feet long. Picnic tables, garbage service, and fire grills are provided. Vault toilets and drinking water are available. Some facilities are wheelchair accessible. Leashed pets are permitted.

Reservations, fees: Reservations accepted for some sites; phone (877) 444-6777 or access the website: www.reserveusa.com ($8.65 reservation fee). Sites are $12 per night, $6 per night for an additional vehicle. Open late May to early September.

Directions: From Portland drive east on U.S. 26 from Gresham 11 miles to Sandy and Highway 211. Turn right (south) and drive six miles to a junction. Turn south (still Highway 211) and drive six miles to Estacada. Continue south on Highway 224 for 15.5 miles to the campground on the right.

Contact: Mount Hood National Forest, Estacada Ranger District, 595 N.W. Industrial Way, Estacada, OR 97023; tel. (503) 630-6861; fax (503) 630-2299.

36 Armstrong 5

This campground is set at an elevation of 900 feet along the banks of the Clackamas River and offers good fishing access. Fishing is catch-and-release only. See Fish Creek Campground, which is about 200 yards away, for more details on the area.

Location: On the Clackamas River in Mount Hood National Forest; map C2, grid f5.

Campsites, facilities: There are 12 sites for tents, trailers, or RVs up to 16 feet long. Picnic tables and fire rings are provided. Vault toilets and drinking water are available. Garbage service is available in the summer only. Some facilities are wheelchair accessible. Leashed pets are permitted.

Reservations, fees: Reservations accepted for some sites; phone (877) 444-6777 or access the website: www.reserveusa.com ($8.65 reservation fee). Sites are $12 per night, $6 per night for an additional vehicle. Open year-round, with limited winter services.

Directions: From Portland drive east on U.S. 26 from Gresham 11 miles to Sandy and Highway 211. Turn right (south) and drive six miles to a junction. Turn south (still Highway 211) and drive six miles to Estacada. Continue south on Highway 224 and drive 15 miles to the campground on the right.

Contact: Mount Hood National Forest, Estacada Ranger District, 595 N.W. Industrial Way, Estacada, OR 97023; tel. (503) 630-6861; fax (503) 630-2299.

37 Carter Bridge 5

This is a small, flat campground popular with anglers. The Clackamas River flows along one end, and the other borders the highway, with the attendant traffic noise. See Fish Creek for more details.

Location: On the Clackamas River in Mount Hood National Forest; map C2, grid f5.

Campsites, facilities: There are 15 sites for tents, trailers, or RVs up to 28 feet long. No drinking water is available, but picnic tables and fire pits are provided. Vault toilets and garbage bins are available. One toilet is wheelchair accessible. Leashed pets are permitted.

Reservations, fees: No reservations accepted. Sites are $10 per night, $5 per night for an additional vehicle. Open late May to early September, weather permitting.

Directions: From Portland drive east on U.S. 26 from Gresham 11 miles to Sandy and Highway 211. Turn right (south) and drive six miles to a junction. Turn south (still Highway 211) and drive six miles to Estacada. Continue south on Highway 224 and drive 15.2 miles to the campground on the left.

Contact: Mount Hood National Forest, Estacada Ranger District, 595 N.W. Industrial Way, Estacada, OR 97023; tel. (503) 630-6861; fax (503) 630-2299.

38 Lockaby 6

This campground is set at an elevation of 900 feet, along the banks of the Clackamas River, next to Fish Creek and Armstrong. Fishing in the Clackamas River is catch-and-release only.

Location: On the Clackamas River in Mount Hood National Forest; map C2, grid f6.

Campsites, facilities: There are 30 sites for tents, trailers, or RVs up to 16 feet long. Picnic tables, fireplaces, drinking water, garbage service, and vault toilets are available. Leashed pets are permitted.

Reservations, fees: Reservations accepted for some sites; phone (877) 444-6777 or access the website: www.reserveusa.com ($8.65 reservation fee). Sites are $12 per night, $6 per night for an additional vehicle. Open late May to early September.

Directions: From Portland drive east on U.S. 26 from Gresham 11 miles to Sandy and Highway 211. Turn right (south) and drive six miles to a junction. Turn south (still Highway 211) and drive six miles to Estacada. Continue south on Highway 224 and drive 15.3 miles to the campground on the left.

Contact: Mount Hood National Forest, Estacada Ranger District, 595 N.W. Industrial Way, Estacada, OR 97023; tel. (503) 630-6861; fax (503) 630-2299.

39 Roaring River   8

This campground, set among old-growth cedars at the confluence of the Roaring and Clackamas Rivers at an elevation of 1,000 feet, has access to the Dry Ridge Trail. The trail starts in camp, and it's a butt-kicker of an uphill climb. Several other trails into the adjacent roadless area are accessible from camp. See a U.S. Forest Service map for details.

Location: On the Roaring River in Mount Hood National Forest; map C2, grid f6.

Campsites, facilities: There are 19 sites for tents, trailers, or RVs up to 16 feet long. Picnic tables, garbage service, fireplaces, drinking water, and vault toilets are available. Leashed pets are permitted.

Reservations, fees: Reservations accepted for some sites; phone (877) 444-6777 or access the website: www.reserveusa.com ($8.65 reservation fee). Sites are $12 per night, $6 per night for an additional vehicle. Open mid-May to mid-September.

Directions: From Portland drive east on U.S. 26 from Gresham 11 miles to Sandy and Highway 211. Turn right (south) and drive six miles to a junction. Turn south (still Highway 211) and drive six miles to Estacada and Highway 224. Bear south on Highway 224 and drive 18 miles to the campground on the left.

Contact: Mount Hood National Forest, Estacada Ranger District, 595 N.W. Industrial Way, Estacada, OR 97023; tel. (503) 630-6861; fax (503) 630-2299.

40 Sunstrip   3

This campground on the banks of the Clackamas River offers fishing and rafting access. One of several camps along the Highway 224 corridor, Sunstrip is a favorite with rafting enthusiasts and can fill up quickly on weekends. For those wanting another kind of experience, however, the fact that the campground is squeezed between the river and the highway, with power lines traversing the site, may be a turn-off.

Location: On the Clackamas River in Mount Hood National Forest; map C2, grid f6.

Campsites, facilities: There are nine sites for tents, trailers, or RVs up to 18 feet long. Picnic tables, garbage service, fireplaces, drinking water, and vault toilets are available. Leashed pets are permitted.

Reservations, fees: Reservations accepted for some sites; phone (877) 444-6777 or access the website: www.reserveusa.com ($8.65 reservation fee). Sites are $12 per night, $6 per night for an additional vehicle. Open year-round, with limited winter services.

Directions: From Portland drive east on U.S. 26 from Gresham 11 miles to Sandy and Highway 211. Turn right (south) and drive six miles to a junction. Turn south (still Highway 211) and drive six miles to Estacada and Highway 224. Bear south on Highway 224 and drive 19 miles to the campground.

Contact: Mount Hood National Forest, Estacada Ranger District, 595 N.W. Industrial Way, Estacada, OR 97023; tel. (503) 630-6861; fax (503) 630-2299.

41 Alder Flat Hike-In   9

This secluded hike-in campground is set along the banks of the Clackamas River in old-growth forest. If you want peace and quiet and don't mind the short walk to get it, this is the spot. Be sure to pack out whatever you bring in and remember that fishing in the Clackamas River is catch-and-release only.

Location: On the Clackamas River in Mount Hood National Forest; map C2, grid f6.

Campsites, facilities: There are six tent sites at this hike-in campground. Picnic tables and fire grills are provided. There is no drinking water, no toilet, and no garbage service; pack out all garbage. Leashed pets are permitted.

Reservations, fees: No reservations; no fee. Open year-round.

Directions: From Portland drive east on U.S. 26 from Gresham 11 miles to Sandy and Highway 211. Turn right (south) and drive six miles to a junction. Turn south (still Highway 211) and drive six miles to Estacada and Highway 224. Bear south on Highway 224 and drive 26 miles to the Ripplebrook Ranger Station. Parking for the camp is about one-half mile west of the ranger station at the Alder Flat Trailhead. Hike one mile to the campground.

Contact: Mount Hood National Forest, Clackamas Ranger District, 61431 East Highway 224, Estacada, OR 97023; tel. (503) 630-4256.

42 Hideaway Lake   9

This is a jewel of a spot—a small, deep lake where non-motorized boats are allowed, but must be carried about 100 yards to the lake. The campsites are separate and scattered around the water. At the north end of the lake, an 8.5-mile loop trail goes past a number of lakes in the Rock Lakes Basin, all of which support populations of rainbow and brook trout. If you don't want to make the whole trip in a day, you can camp overnight at Serene Lake. See a U.S. Forest Service map for information.

Location: Near the Rock Lakes Basin in Mount Hood National Forest; map C2, grid f6.

Campsites, facilities: There are nine sites for tents, small trailers, or camper vans up to 16 feet long. Picnic tables and fire grills are provided. Pit toilets are available. There is no drinking water. Leashed pets are permitted.

Reservations, fees: No reservations accepted. Sites are $10 per night, $5 per night for an additional vehicle. Open mid-June to late September, weather permitting.

Directions: From Portland drive east on U.S. 26 from Gresham 11 miles to Sandy and Highway 211. Turn right (south) and drive six miles to a junction. Turn south (still Highway 211) and drive six miles to Estacada and Highway 224. Bear south on Highway 224 and drive 27 miles to Forest Road 57. Turn east and drive 7.5 miles to Forest Road 58. Turn left and drive three miles north to Forest Road 5830. Turn left (northwest) and drive 5.5 miles to the campground on the left.

Contact: Mount Hood National Forest, Estacada Ranger District, 595 N.W. Industrial Way, Estacada, OR 97023; tel. (503) 630-6861; fax (503) 630-2299.

43 High Rock Springs   7

This small, remote campground is set at 5,200 feet elevation, within two miles of Stet Mountain. A half-mile climb earns a tremendous view of the surrounding area, including Mount Hood. About four miles east of the camp are trails that lead to some of the fishing lakes in the Rock Lakes Basin. In August and September ripe huckleberries are yours for the picking.

Location: Near the Rock Lakes Basin in Mount Hood National Forest; map C2, grid f7.

Campsites, facilities: There are seven tent sites. Picnic tables and fire grills are provided. A pit toilet is available. There is no drinking water and no garbage service; pack out all garbage. Leashed pets are permitted.

Reservations, fees: No reservations; no fee. Open mid-June to late September, weather permitting.

Directions: From Portland drive east on U.S. 26 from Gresham 11 miles to Sandy and Highway 211. Turn right (south) and drive six miles to a junction. Turn south (still Highway 211) and drive six miles to Estacada and Highway 224. Bear south on Highway 224 and drive 27 miles to Forest Road 57. Turn east and drive 7.5 miles to Forest Road 58. Turn left and drive nine miles to Forest Road 58-190. Turn left and drive 1.5 miles to the campground.

Contact: Mount Hood National Forest, Estacada Ranger District, 595 N.W. Industrial Way, Estacada, OR 97023; tel. (503) 630-6861; fax (503) 630-2299.

44 Indian Henry   8

One of the most popular campgrounds in the Estacada Ranger District, Indian Henry is located along the banks of the Clackamas River at an elevation of 1,250 feet and has a wheelchair-accessible trail. Group campsites and an amphitheater are available. The nearby Clackamas River Trail has fishing access.

Location: On the Clackamas River in Mount Hood National Forest; map C2, grid f7.

Campsites, facilities: There are 86 sites for tents, trailers, or RVs up to 22 feet long, and eight group tent sites. Picnic tables, garbage service, and fire grills are provided. Flush toilets, a sanitary dump station, and drinking water are available. Some facilities are wheelchair accessible. Leashed pets are permitted.

Reservations, fees: Reservations accepted for some sites; phone (877) 444-6777 or access the website: www.reserveusa.com ($8.65 reservation fee). Sites are $12 per night, $6 per night for an additional vehicle. Call for group site rates. Open late May to early September.

Directions: From Portland drive east on U.S. 26 from Gresham 11 miles to Sandy and Highway 211. Turn right (south) and drive six miles to a junction. Turn south (still Highway 211) and drive six miles to Estacada and Highway 224. Bear south on Highway 224 and drive 23 miles to Forest Road 4620. Turn right and drive one-half mile southeast to the campground on the left.

Contact: Mount Hood National Forest, Estacada Ranger District, 595 N.W. Industrial Way, Estacada, OR 97023; tel. (503) 630-6861; fax (503) 630-2299.

45 Lake Harriet   5

Formed by a dam on the Oak Grove Fork of the Clackamas River, this little lake is a popular spot during the summer. Rowboats and boats with small motors are permitted, but only non-motorized boats are encouraged. The lake is stocked regularly and can provide good fishing for a variety of trout, including brown, brook, rainbow, and cutthroat. Anglers often stand shoulder-to-shoulder in summer.

Location: On Lake Harriet in Mount Hood National Forest; map C2, grid f7.

Campsites, facilities: There are 10 sites for tents, trailers, or RVs up to 30 feet long. Picnic tables and fire grills are provided. Drinking water and vault toilets are available. Garbage service is provided in the summer. Some facilities are wheelchair accessible. A fishing pier and boat launching facilities are located on the lake. Leashed pets are permitted.

Reservations, fees: Reservations accepted for some sites; phone (877) 444-6777 or access the website: www.reserveusa.com ($8.65 reservation fee). Sites are $12 per night, $6 per night for an additional vehicle. Open year-round, with limited winter services.

Directions: From Portland drive east on U.S. 26 from Gresham 11 miles to Sandy and Highway 211. Turn right (south) and drive six miles to a junction. Turn south (still Highway 211) and drive six miles to Estacada and Highway 224. Bear south on Highway 224 and drive 27 miles to Forest Road 57. Turn east and drive 7.5 miles to Forest Road 58. Turn left and drive 7.5 miles to Forest Road 4630. Turn left and drive two miles to the campground on the left.

Contact: Mount Hood National Forest, Estacada Ranger District, 595 N.W. Industrial Way, Estacada, OR 97023; tel. (503) 630-6861; fax (503) 630-2299.

46 Ripplebrook   7

Shaded sites with river views are a highlight at this campground along the banks of the Oak Grove Fork of the Clackamas River, where fishing is artificial lures and catch-and-release only. Note that the road to this camp was closed for two years in the late 1990s, and only recently have campers begun to return.

Location: On the Oak Grove Fork of the Clackamas River in Mount Hood National Forest; map C2, grid f6.

Campsites, facilities: There are 13 sites for trailers or RVs up to 16 feet long. Picnic tables, garbage service, and fire grills are provided. Vault toilets are available, but there is no drinking water. Leashed pets are permitted; horses are not allowed in the campground.

Reservations, fees: Reservations accepted for some sites; phone (877) 444-6777 or access the website: www.reserveusa.com ($8.65 reservation fee). Sites are $10 per night, $6 per night for an additional vehicle. Open late April to late September.

Directions: From Portland drive east on U.S. 26 from Gresham 11 miles to Sandy and Highway 211. Turn right (south) and drive six miles to a junction. Turn south (still Highway 211) and drive six miles to Estacada and Highway 224. Bear south on Highway 224 and drive 26.5 miles to the campground entrance on the left.

Contact: Mount Hood National Forest, Estacada Ranger District, 595 N.W. Industrial Way, Estacada, OR 97023; tel. (503) 630-6861; fax (503) 630-2299.

47 Trillium Lake   9

This campground is set at 3,600 feet elevation along the shores of Trillium Lake, which is about one-half mile long and one-quarter mile wide. Fishing is good in the evening here, and the nearby boat ramp makes this an ideal camp for anglers. The lake is great for canoes, rafts, and small rowboats. Trillium Lake is an extremely popular vacation destination, so expect plenty of company. Reservations highly recommended.

Location: On Trillium Lake in Mount Hood National Forest; map C2, grid f8.

Campsites, facilities: There are 55 sites for tents, trailers, or RVs up to 40 feet long. Picnic tables and fire grills are provided. Pit toilets and drinking water are available. Some sites are wheelchair accessible. Boat docks and launching facilities are available on the lake, but no motors are allowed. Leashed pets are permitted.

Reservations, fees: Reservations accepted for some sites; phone (877) 444-6777 or access the website: www.reserveusa.com ($8.65 reservation fee). Sites are $12-14 per night, multifamily sites are $24 per night, and an additional vehicle is $6. Open late May to late September.

Directions: From Portland drive east on U.S. 26 and drive 55 miles to the small town of Government Camp. Continue east on U.S. 26 to Forest Road 2656. Turn right and drive 1.3 miles to the campground on the right.

Contact: Mount Hood National Forest, Zigzag Ranger District, 65000 East Highway 26, Welches, OR 97067; tel. (503) 622-7674; fax (503) 622-3163.

48 Meditation
Point Walk-In/Boat-In   9

Accessible only by foot or boat, this remote and rustic camp set at 3,200 feet elevation offers a more secluded location along Timothy Lake than Gone Creek, Hoodview, Oak Fork, and Pine Point. It's the only campground on the north shore of the lake, which means you'll get a quieter, less crowded environment, though you'll have to bring your own water. See the descriptions of Hoodview and Gone Creek for details about the lake. Timothy Lake Trail makes a 14-mile loop around the lake. Bring a shovel for sanitation purposes.

Location: On Timothy Lake in Mount Hood National Forest; map C2, grid f8.

Campsites, facilities: There are four boat-in or walk-in tent sites. Picnic tables and fire grills are provided. No toilets are available. There is no drinking water, and garbage must be packed out. Boat docks and launching facilities are nearby. Leashed pets are permitted.

Reservations, fees: No reservations; no fee. Open late May to mid-September.

Directions: From Portland drive east on U.S. 26 and drive 57 miles to the junction with Highway 35 (two miles past Government Camp). Turn right (southeast) on U.S. 26 for 15 miles to Forest Road 42/Skyline Road. Turn right and drive eight miles south to Forest Road 57. Turn right and drive five miles to Pine Point Campground. Park and hike one mile or take a boat to the north shore of the lake.

Contact: Mount Hood National Forest, Zigzag Ranger District, 65000 East Highway 26, Welches, OR 97067; tel. (503) 622-7674; fax (503) 622-3163.

49 Barlow Creek   7

This campground is set along Barlow Creek at an elevation of 3,100 feet. It is located on Old Barlow Road, which was the wagon trail for early settlers in this area. It is one of several primitive U.S. Forest Service camps in the immediate vicinity. There may not be much to do in these parts, but you sure can't beat the price. If this campground is full, Barlow Crossing Campground is one mile southeast on Forest Road 3530.

Location: On Barlow Creek in Mount Hood National Forest; map C2, grid f9.

Campsites, facilities: There are five sites for tents. Picnic tables and fire grills are provided. Vault toilets are available, but there is no drinking water and no garbage service; pack out all garbage. Leashed pets are permitted.

Reservations, fees: No reservations; no fee. Open May through September.

Directions: From Portland drive east on U.S. 26 and drive 57 miles to the junction with Highway 35 (two miles past Government Camp). Turn right (southeast) on U.S. 26 and drive 12 miles to Forest Road 43. Turn left and drive five miles to Forest Road 3530. Turn north (left) and drive 1.5 miles to the campground on the left.

Contact: Mount Hood National Forest, Hood River Ranger District, 6780 Highway 35, Mount Hood, OR 97041; tel. (541) 352-6002; fax (541) 352-7365.

50 Frog Lake   7

This classic spot in the Cascade Range is on the shore of little Frog Lake (more of a pond than a lake), at an elevation of 3,800 feet, a short distance from the Pacific Crest Trail. Several other trails lead to nearby lakes. A possible day trip is Clear Lake to the south, which offers more recreation options.

Location: Near the Pacific Crest Trail in Mount Hood National Forest; map C2, grid f9.

Campsites, facilities: There are 33 sites for tents, trailers, or RVs up to 22 feet long. Drinking water, garbage bins, and picnic tables are provided. Vault toilets and firewood are available. Boat launching facilities are nearby. No motorized boats are allowed. Leashed pets are permitted. Some barrier-free facilities are available.

Reservations, fees: Reservations accepted for some sites; phone (877) 444-6777 or access the website: www.reserveusa.com ($8.65 reservation fee). Sites are $10-12 per night, $6 per night for an additional vehicle. Open mid-June to mid-September.

Directions: From Portland drive east on U.S. 26 and drive 57 miles to the junction with Highway 35 (two miles past Government Camp). Turn right (southeast) on U.S. 26 and drive seven miles to Forest Road 2610. Turn southeast and drive one mile to Forest Road 230. Turn south and drive about 500 yards to the campground.

Contact: Mount Hood National Forest, Hood River Ranger District, 6780 Highway 35, Mount Hood, OR 97041; tel. (541) 352-6002; fax (541) 352-7365.

51 White River Station   9

This tiny campground is set along the White River at an elevation of 3,000 feet. It is located on Old Barlow Road, an original wagon trail used by early settlers. One of several small, secluded camps in the area, White River Station is quiet and private, but with poor fishing prospects.

Location: On the White River in Mount Hood National Forest; map C2, grid f9.

Campsites, facilities: There are five sites for tents and RVs up to 24 feet long. Picnic tables and fire grills are provided. Vault toilets are available, but there is no drinking water and no garbage service; pack out all garbage. Leashed pets are permitted.

Reservations, fees: No reservations; no fee. Open May through September.

Directions: From Portland drive east on U.S. 26 and drive 57 miles to the junction with Highway 35 (two miles past Government Camp). Turn left on Highway 35 and drive two miles east to Forest Road 48. Turn right (south) and drive nine miles southeast to Forest Road 43. Turn right and drive one-quarter mile to Forest Road 3530. Turn left and drive 1.5 miles to the campground on the left.

Contact: Mount Hood National Forest, Barlow Ranger District, Bear Springs Work Center, 73558 Highway 216, Maupin, OR 97037; tel. (541) 467-5180.

52 Clear Lake   4

This campground is along the shore of Clear Lake, a spot favored by anglers, swimmers, and windsurfers; but it is a reservoir and subject to water level fluctuations. The camp is wooded, with shady sites and is set at 3,600 feet elevation. The camp is sometimes noisy from the revels of the party set. If you want quiet, this camp is probably not for you. A nearby trail heads north from the lake and provides access to the Pacific Crest Trail and Frog Lake, both good recreation options.

Location: Near the Pacific Crest Trail in Mount Hood National Forest; map C2, grid f9.

Campsites, facilities: There are 28 sites for tents, trailers, or RVs up to 32 feet long. Picnic tables, fire grills, drinking water, garbage bins, firewood, and vault toilets are available. Some facilities are wheelchair accessible. Boat launching facilities are nearby and motorboats are allowed, but the speed limit is 10 mph. Leashed pets are permitted.

Reservations, fees: Reservations accepted for some sites; phone (877) 444-6777 or access the website: www.reserveusa.com ($8.65 reservation fee). Sites are $10-12 per night, $6 per night for an additional vehicle. Open late May to early September.

Directions: From Portland drive east on U.S. 26 and drive 57 miles to the junction with Highway 35 (two miles past Government Camp). Turn right (southeast) on U.S. 26 and drive nine miles to Forest Road 2630. Turn south and drive one mile to the campground on the right.

Contact: Mount Hood National Forest, Hood River Ranger District, 6780 Highway 35, Mount Hood, OR 97041; tel. (541) 352-6002; fax (541) 352-7365.

53 Little Crater   5

This camp set at 3,200 feet elevation next to Crater Creek and scenic Little Crater Lake. This camp is popular with hunters in the fall. Both the drinking water and the lake water flow from an artesian well, and the water is numbing cold. The Pacific Crest Trail is set near camp, providing hiking trail access. Fishing is poor at Little Crater lake. It is about a mile to little Timothy Lake, where a 10 mph speed limit is enforced. Bring your mosquito repellent; you'll need it. See the description of Gone Creek for more information about Timothy Lake.

Location: On Little Crater Lake in Mount Hood National Forest; map C2, grid f9.

Campsites, facilities: There are 16 sites for tents, trailers, or RVs up to 22 feet long. Picnic tables, garbage bins, and fire grills are provided. Vault toilets, firewood, and drinking water are available. Leashed pets are permitted.

Reservations, fees: Reservations accepted for some sites; phone (877) 444-6777 or access the website: reserveusa.com ($8.65 reservation fee). Sites are $12 per night, $6 per night for an additional vehicle. Open June to mid-September.

Directions: From Portland drive east on U.S. 26 and drive 57 miles to the junction with Highway 35 (two miles past Government Camp). Turn right (southeast) on U.S. 26 and drive 15 miles to Forest Road 42 (Skyline Road). Turn right and drive about six miles to Forest Road 58. Turn right and drive about 2.5 miles to the campground on the left.

Contact: Mount Hood National Forest, Zigzag Ranger District, 65000 East Highway 26, Welches, OR 97067; tel. (503) 622-7674; fax (503) 622-3163.

54 Forest Glen RV Resort   6

This RV resort is located directly behind Thrill Ville USA, an amusement park with rides, miniature golf, Go-Karts, waterslides, and a snack bar. Thrill Ville is open during the summer months. Another bonus is that the campgrounds has fishing pond with bass and trout available. A winery tour at Willamette Vineyards is available just one mile south via Interstate 5, and a golf course is available one mile to the north. Campsites here are often more private and shaded than many RV parks.

Location: South of Salem; map C2, grid g0.

Campsites, facilities: There are 95 sites for trailers or RVs of any length, some with picnic tables and fire pits. Electricity, drinking water, and sewer hookups are provided. Flush toilets, showers, and a laundry room are available. A clubhouse with exercise equipment and games and a playground are available nearby. A store, a cafe, and ice are located within two miles. Leashed pets are permitted. Some facilities are wheelchair accessible.

Reservations, fees: Reservations accepted. Sites are $18 per night. Open year-round.

Directions: From Salem drive south on Interstate 5 for one mile to Exit 248. Take that exit and turn left on Delaney Road and drive 100 yards to Enchanted Way. Turn right and drive a quarter mile to the park on the left.

Contact: Forest Glen RV Resort, 8372 Enchanted Way, Turner, OR 97392; tel. (503) 363-7616.

55 Salem Campground and RVs

 5

This park with shaded sites is just off Interstate 5 in Salem. A picnic area and a lake for swimming are within walking distance, and a nine-hole golf course, hiking trails, a riding stable, and tennis courts are nearby.

Location: In Salem; map C2, grid g1.

Campsites, facilities: There are 30 tent sites and 190 sites with full hookups for trailers or RVs of any length, most of which are drive-through sites. Picnic tables are provided. Flush toilets, bottled gas, sanitary services, showers, a recreation hall, a store, a laundry room, ice, a playground, electricity, drinking water, and sewer hookups are available. A cafe is located within one mile. Leashed pets and motorbikes are permitted.

Reservations, fees: Reservations accepted. Sites are $13-19 per night. Open year-round.

Directions: From Salem on Interstate 5, take Exit 253 to Highway 22. Turn east and drive east for one-quarter mile to Lancaster Drive. Turn right on Lancaster Drive and drive to Hagers Grove Road. Turn then on Hagers Grove Road and drive to the park.

Contact: Salem Campground and RVs, 3700 Hagers Grove Road SE, Salem, OR 97301; tel. (800) 826-9605 or (503) 581-6736; fax (888) 827-9605.

56 Silver Falls State Park   8

This is Oregon's largest state park, covering more than 8,700 acres. Numerous trails crisscross the area, including a seven-mile jaunt that meanders past 10 majestic waterfalls (some over 100 feet high) in the rain forest of Silver Creek Canyon. Four of these falls have an amphitheater-like surrounding where you can walk behind the falls and feel the misty spray. A horse camp and a 14-mile equestrian trail are available in the park. Fitness-conscious campers can check out the three-mile jogging trail or the four-mile bike trail. There is also a rustic nature lodge and group lodging facilities.

Location: Near Salem; map C2, grid g3.

Campsites, facilities: There are 51 tent sites and 54 sites with water and electrical hookups for trailers or RVs up to 60 feet long. Picnic tables and fire grills are provided. There are also a group site, cabins, and a designated horse camp. Drinking water, garbage bins, flush toilets, sanitary services, showers, firewood, and a playground are available. Some facilities are wheelchair accessible. Leashed pets are permitted.

Reservations, fees: Reservations accepted. Sites are $13-20 per night, the group site is $60 per night, cabins are $35 per night, and horse campsites are $13 per night with a $1.50 fee per horse. There is a $7 per night charge for an additional vehicle. Major credit cards accepted. Open mid-April to late October.

Directions: From Salem on Interstate 5, take Exit 253 to Highway 22. Turn east and drive five miles to Highway 214. Turn left (east) and drive 15 miles to the park.

Contact: Silver Falls State Park, 20024 Silver Falls Highway SE, Sublimity, OR 97385; tel. (503) 873-8681 or (800) 452-5687.

57 Shady Cove   7

This campground is on the Little North Santiam River in the recently designated Opal Creek Scenic Recreation Area. Little North Santiam Trail is adjacent to the campground.

Location: On the North Santiam River in Willamette National Forest; map C2, grid g4.

Campsites, facilities: There are 12 sites for tents or trailers up to 16 feet long. Picnic tables, garbage service (summer only), fire grills, and vault toilets are available. There is no drinking water. Leashed pets are permitted.

Reservations, fees: No reservations accepted. Sites are $5-10 per night, $3 per night for an additional vehicle. Open year-round, weather permitting.

Directions: From Salem on Interstate 5, take Exit 253 to Highway 22. Turn east and drive 23 miles to Mehama and Little North Santiam Road (Forest Road 2209). Turn left and drive 17 miles northeast to the fork. Bear right on Forest Road 2207 and continue for two miles to the campground on the right.

Contact: Willamette National Forest, Detroit Ranger District, HC 73, P.O. Box 320, Mill City, OR 97360; tel. (503) 854-3366; fax (503) 854-4239.

58 Fishermen's Bend   7

Fishermen's Bend is a popular site for anglers of all ages, and the sites are spacious. A barrier-free fishing and river viewing area and a network of trails provide access to more than a mile of river. There's a one-mile, self-guided nature trail, and the nature center has a variety of displays. The amphitheater has films and activities on weekends. The front gate closes at 10 p.m.

Location: On the North Santiam River; map C2, grid g2.

Campsites, facilities: There are 39 sites for tents, trailers, or RVs; 21 are pull through with water hookups, and 18 are tent/camper sites with water spigots nearby. There are also three group sites available for up to 60 people each, and two cabins. Drinking water, picnic tables and fire pits are provided. Restrooms with flush toilets, sinks and hot showers are available, with wheelchair facilities, as well as a dump station and garbage containers. A boat ramp, day-use area with playgrounds, baseball, volleyball, and basketball courts and fields, horseshoe pits, firewood for sale, and a picnic shelter are also available. Leashed pets are permitted.

Reservations, fees: Reservations accepted for group sites only; phone (800) 452-5687 ($6 reservation fee). Sites are $12-18 per night, $5 per night for an additional vehicle. Group sites are $60-90 per night. Cabins are $35 per night. Open mid-May to mid-October.

Directions: From Salem on Interstate 5, take Exit 253 to Highway 22. Turn east and drive 32 miles to the campground on the right.

Contact: Bureau of Land Management, Salem District Office, 1717 Fabry Road SE Salem, OR 97306; tel. (503) 375-5646; fax (503) 375-5622.

59 Elkhorn Valley   7

This pretty campground along the Little North Santiam River, not far from the North Fork of the Santiam River, has easy access, an on-site host, and is only a short drive away from a major metropolitan area. The front gate is locked from 10 p.m. to 7 a.m. daily. This is an alternative to Shady Cove, which is located about 10 miles to the east.

Location: On the Little North Santiam River; map C2, grid g5.

Campsites, facilities: There are 24 sites for tents, trailers, or RVs up to 18 feet long. Picnic tables, garbage bins, fire grills, vault toilets, and drinking water are available. Firewood is available for purchase. Leashed pets are permitted.

Reservations, fees: No reservations accepted. Sites are $10 per night, $5 per night for an additional vehicle. There is a 14-day stay limit. Open mid-May to late September.

Directions: From Salem on Interstate 5, take Exit 253 to Highway 22. Turn east and drive 25 miles to Elkhorn Road. Turn left (northeast) and drive nine miles to the campground on the left.

Contact: Bureau of Land Management, Salem District Office, 1717 Fabry Road SE, Salem, OR 97306; tel. (503) 375-5646; fax (503) 375-5622.

60 Riverside   8

The banks of the Clackamas River are home to this campground set an elevation of 1,400 feet. A trail worth hiking leaves the camp and follows the river for four miles north. Fishing is another option here, and several old forest roads in the vicinity make excellent mountain biking trails.

Location: On the Clackamas River in Mount Hood National Forest; map C2, grid g6.

Campsites, facilities: There are 16 sites for tents, trailers, or RVs up to 22 feet long. Picnic tables, garbage service, and fire grills are provided. Vault toilets and drinking water are available. Leashed pets are permitted; no horses are allowed in the campground.

Reservations, fees: Reservations accepted for some sites; phone (877) 444-6777 or access the website: www.reserveusa.com ($8.65 reservation fee). Sites are $12 per night, $6 per night for an additional vehicle. Open mid-May to late September.

Directions: From Portland drive east on U.S. 26 from Gresham 11 miles to Sandy and Highway 211. Turn right (south) and drive six miles to a junction. Turn south (still Highway 211) and drive six miles to Estacada and Highway 224. Bear south on Highway 224 and drive 27 miles and into national forest (Highway 224 becomes Forest Road 46). Continue 2.5 miles south on Forest Road 46 to the campground on the right.

Contact: Mount Hood National Forest, Estacada Ranger District, 595 N.W. Industrial Way, Estacada, OR 97023; tel. (503) 630-6861; fax (503) 630-2299.

61 Riverford 4

Good fishing is a bonus around this campground at the confluence of the Clackamas and Collawash Rivers, a two-minute walk from the campground. It's small, and the sites provide little privacy. It is set at an elevation of 1,500 feet.

Location: On the Clackamas and Collawash Rivers in Mount Hood National Forest; map C2, grid g6.

Campsites, facilities: There are 10 sites for tents. Picnic tables and fire grills are provided. Vault toilets are available. Garbage service is provided in the summer. There is no drinking water at the campground; water is available at nearby Two Rivers Picnic Area. Leashed pets are permitted.

Reservations, fees: No reservations accepted. Sites are $10 per night, $5 per night for an additional vehicle. Open year-round, with limited winter services.

Directions: From Portland drive east on U.S. 26 from Gresham 11 miles to Sandy and Highway 211. Turn right (south) and drive six miles to a junction. Turn south (still Highway 211) and drive six miles to Estacada and Highway 224. Bear south on Highway 224 and drive 27 miles in national forest (the road becomes Forest Road 46). Continue south on Forest Road 3.5 miles to the campground on the right.

Contact: Mount Hood National Forest, Estacada Ranger District, 595 N.W. Industrial Way, Estacada, OR 97023; tel. (503) 630-6861; fax (503) 630-2299.

62 Raab   7

This camp is set at an elevation of 1,500 feet along the banks of the Collawash River about a mile from its confluence with the Clackamas River. It gets moderate use, but it's usually quiet and has a nice, secluded atmosphere with lots of privacy among the sites.

Location: On the Collawash River in Mount Hood National Forest; map C2, grid g6.

Campsites, facilities: There are 27 sites for tents, trailers, or RVs up to 22 feet long. Picnic tables, garbage service, and fire grills are provided. Vault toilets are available. There is no drinking water in the campground; water is available one mile away at Two Rivers Picnic Area. Leashed pets are permitted.

Reservations, fees: Reservations accepted for some sites; phone (877) 444-6777 or access the website: www.reserveusa.com ($8.65 reservation fee). Sites are $10 per night, $5 per night for an additional vehicle. Open late May to early September.

Directions: From Portland drive east on U.S. 26 from Gresham 11 miles to Sandy and Highway 211. Turn right (south) and drive six miles to a junction. Turn south (still Highway 211) and drive six miles to Estacada and Highway 224. Bear south on Highway 224 and drive 27 miles in national forest (the road becomes Forest Road 46). Continue south on Forest Road 46 for 2.5 miles to Forest Road 63. Turn right and drive 1.5 miles to the campground on the right.

Contact: Mount Hood National Forest, Estacada Ranger District, 595 N.W. Industrial Way, Estacada, OR 97023; tel. (503) 630-6861; fax (503) 630-2299.

63 Kingfisher   7

This pretty campground set at an elevation of 1,250 feet among old-growth forest is situated along the banks of the Hot Springs Fork of the Collawash River, and is about three miles from Bagby Hot Springs, a U.S. Forest Service day-use area. It's an easy 1.5-mile hike to the hot springs from the day-use area. Fishing access is near the camp.

Location: On the Hot Springs Fork of the Collawash River in Mount Hood National Forest; map C2, grid g6.

Campsites, facilities: There are 23 sites for tents, trailers, or RVs up to 16 feet long. Picnic tables and fireplaces are provided. Garbage service is provided during the summer. Vault toilets and drinking water are available. Leashed pets are permitted.

Reservations, fees: Reservations accepted for some sites; phone (877) 444-6777 or access the website: www.reserveusa.com ($8.65 reservation fee). Sites are $12 per night, $6 per night for an additional vehicle. Open year-round, with limited winter facilities.

Directions: From Portland drive east on U.S. 26 from Gresham 11 miles to Sandy and Highway 211. Turn right (south) and drive six miles to a junction. Turn south (still Highway 211) and drive six miles to Estacada and Highway 224. Bear south on Highway 224 and drive 27 miles in national forest (the road becomes Forest Road 46). Continue south on Forest Road 46 for 3.5 miles to Forest Road 63. Turn right and drive three miles to Forest Road 70. Turn right again and drive one mile to the campground on the left.

Contact: Mount Hood National Forest, Estacada Ranger District, 595 N.W. Industrial Way, Estacada, OR 97023; tel. (503) 630-6861; fax (503) 630-2299.

64 Humbug   9

Fishing and hiking are popular at this campground along the banks of the Breitenbush River about four miles from where it empties into Detroit Lake. The lake offers many other recreation opportunities. The Humbug Flat Trailhead is behind Sites 9 and 10, and a scenic stroll through an old-growth forest follows the Breitenbush River. The rhododendrons put on a spectacular show from May through July.

Location: On the Breitenbush River in Willamette National Forest; map C2, grid g6.

Campsites, facilities: There are 21 sites for tents, trailers, or RVs up to 22 feet long. Picnic tables, garbage service (summer only), fire grills, drinking water, and vault toilets are available. Leashed pets are permitted.

Reservations, fees: No reservations accepted. Sites are $8 per night, $5 per night for an additional vehicle. Open year-round, weather permitting, with limited winter facilities.

Directions: From Salem on Interstate 5, take Exit 253, turn east on Highway 22 and drive 52 miles to Detroit. Turn left on Forest Road 46/Breitenbush Road and drive five miles northeast to the campground on the right.

Contact: Willamette National Forest, Detroit Ranger District, HC 73, P.O. Box 320, Mill City, OR 97360; tel. (503) 854-3366; fax (503) 854-4239.

65 Elk Lake   9

This remote and primitive campground is on the shore of Elk Lake, where boating, fishing, and swimming can be quite good in the summer and wildflowers bloom in the meadow. Several nearby trails provide access to the Bull of the Woods Wilderness. There are beautiful views of Battle Ax Mountain. Please pack out your garbage.

Location: Near the Bull of the Woods Wilderness in Willamette National Forest; map C2, grid g6.

Campsites, facilities: There are 14 primitive tent sites. There is no drinking water, and garbage must be packed out. Primitive launching facilities are available. Leashed pets are permitted.

Reservations, fees: No reservations; no fee. Open July to mid-September.

Directions: From Salem on Interstate 5, take Exit 253, turn east on Highway 22 and drive 52 miles to Detroit. Turn left on Forest Road 46/Breitenbush Road and drive 4.5 miles. Turn left on Forest Road 4696/Elk Lake Road and continue north less than one mile. Turn left on Forest Road 4697 and drive 9.5 miles to the campground on the left. The road is extremely rough for the last two miles. High-clearance vehicles are recommended.

Contact: Willamette National Forest, Detroit Ranger District, HC 73, P.O. Box 320, Mill City, OR 97360; tel. (503) 854-3366; fax (503) 854-4239.

66 Breitenbush Lake   9

This lakeside campground is set at 5,500 feet on the western border of the Warm Springs Indian Reservation. Breitenbush is a large lake next to the Mount Jefferson Wilderness. Numerous trails provide access to other lakes in the area, and horses are allowed in areas specified by the U.S. Forest Service. The Pacific Crest Trail skirts the camp to the west on the reservation property, but no other access to the reservation is allowed. Ripe huckleberries can be found in these parts in late August and September.

Location: On Breitenbush Lake in Mount Hood National Forest; map C2, grid g6.

Campsites, facilities: There are 20 sites for tents or trailers. Picnic tables and fire grills are provided. Vault toilets are available. There is no drinking water. A store and ice are located within five miles. Boat docks, launching facilities, and rentals are nearby. Leashed pets are permitted. Pack out all garbage.

Reservations, fees: No reservations; no fee. Open mid-June to late September.

Directions: From Portland drive east on U.S. 26 from Gresham 11 miles to Sandy and Highway 211. Turn right (south) and drive six miles to a junction. Turn south (still Highway 211) and drive six miles to Estacada and Highway 224. Bear south on Highway 224 and drive 27 miles in national forest (the road becomes Forest Road 46). Continue south on Forest Road 46 for 28.5 miles to Forest Road 4220. Turn left and drive 8.5 miles to the lake and the campground on the right. Be aware that the access road to the lake is not maintained and can be rough. Only high-clearance vehicles are recommended. Special note: At time of publication in spring of 2000, Forest Road 4220 was closed because a bridge had been washed out. Another access route is available through Olallie Lake Campground; see that camp listing for directions.

Contact: Mount Hood National Forest, Estacada Ranger District, 595 N.W. Industrial Way, Estacada, OR 97023; tel. (503) 630-6861; fax (503) 630-2299.

67 Rainbow   6

This campground is set at an elevation of 1,400 feet along the banks of the Oak Grove Fork of the Clackamas River, not far from where it empties into the Clackamas River. The camp is located less than a quarter mile from Ripplebrook Campground.
Location: On the Oak Grove Fork of the Clackamas River in Mount Hood National Forest; map C2, grid g7.
Campsites, facilities: There are 17 sites for tents, trailers, or RVs up to 16 feet long. There is no drinking water. Garbage service is provided during the summer. Fire grills and picnic tables are provided. Vault toilets are available. Leashed pets are permitted.
Reservations, fees: Reservations accepted for some sites; phone (877) 444-6777 or access the website: www.reserveusa.com ($8.65 reservation fee). Sites are $10 per night, $5 per night for an additional vehicle. Open year-round, with limited winter services.
Directions: From Portland drive east on U.S. 26 from Gresham 11 miles to Sandy and Highway 211. Turn right (south) and drive six miles to a junction. Turn south (still Highway 211) and drive six miles to Estacada and Highway 224. Bear south on Highway 224 and drive 27 miles in national forest (the road becomes Forest Road 46). Continue south and drive about 100 yards to the campground on the right.
Contact: Mount Hood National Forest, Ranger District, 595 N.W. Industrial Way, Estacada, OR 97023; tel. (503) 630-6861; fax (503) 630-2299.

68 Breitenbush   8

Fishing access is a plus at this campground along the Breitenbush River. The South Breitenbush Gorge National Recreation Trail is three miles away. Breitenbush Hot Springs is just over a mile away. If this campground is crowded, try nearby Cleater Bend.
Location: On the Breitenbush River in Willamette National Forest; map C2, grid g7.
Campsites, facilities: There are 29 sites for tents, trailers, or RVs up to 22 feet long (longer trailers may be difficult to park and turn). Picnic tables, garbage service (summer only), and fire grills are provided. Drinking water and vault toilets are available. Leashed pets are permitted.
Reservations, fees: No reservations accepted. Sites are $8-16 per night, $5 per night for an additional vehicle. Open year-round, weather permitting, with limited winter facilities.
Directions: From Salem on Interstate 5, take Exit 253, turn east on Highway 22, and drive 50 miles to Detroit. Turn left (north) on Forest Road 46/Breitenbush Road and drive 10 miles to the campground on the right.
Contact: Willamette National Forest, Detroit Ranger District, HC 73, Box 320, Mill City, OR 97360; tel. (503) 854-3366; fax (503) 854-4239.

69 Cleater Bend 8

Creek views are a highlight of this camp on the banks of the Breitenbush River with pretty, shaded sites. The camp is one-quarter mile from Breitenbush; see the description of Breitenbush Campground for area details.

Location: Near the Breitenbush River in Willamette National Forest; map C2, grid g7.

Campsites, facilities: There are nine sites for tents, trailers, or RVs up to 16 feet long. Picnic tables, garbage service (summer only), fire grills, drinking water, and vault toilets are available. Leashed pets are permitted.

Reservations, fees: No reservations accepted. Sites are $8 per night, $5 per night for an additional vehicle. Open year-round, weather permitting.

Directions: From Salem on Interstate 5, take Exit 253, turn east on Highway 22, and drive 50 miles to Detroit. Turn left on Forest Road 46/Breitenbush Road and drive nine miles to the campground on the right.

Contact: Willamette National Forest, Detroit Ranger District, HC 73, Box 320, Mill City, OR 97360; tel. (503) 854-3366; fax (503) 854-4239.

70 Camp Ten 9

Here's a camp along the shore of Olallie Lake, a popular area. This one is set at an elevation of 5,000 feet on the western shore in the midst of the Olallie Lake Scenic Area, which is home to a number of pristine mountain lakes and a network of hiking trails. See a U.S. Forest Service map for trail locations. Boats without motors—including canoes, kayaks, and rafts—are permitted on the lake.

Location: On Olallie Lake in Mount Hood National Forest; map C2, grid g7.

Campsites, facilities: There are 10 sites for tents, trailers, or RVs up to 16 feet long. Picnic tables, garbage service, and fire grills are provided. Pit toilets are available. There is no drinking water. Boat docks, launching facilities, boat rentals, and a store that sells fishing tackle and other supplies are nearby. Leashed pets are permitted.

Reservations, fees: No reservations accepted. Sites are $8 per night, $5 per night for an additional vehicle. Open mid-June to late September, weather permitting.

Directions: From Portland drive east on U.S. 26 from Gresham 11 miles to Sandy and Highway 211. Turn right (south) and drive six miles to a junction. Turn south (still Highway 211) and drive six miles to Estacada and Highway 224. Bear south on Highway 224 and drive 27 miles in national forest (the road becomes Forest Road 46). Continue south on Forest Road 46 for 20 miles to Forest Road 4690. Turn left on and drive southeast for 8.2 miles to Forest Road 4220. Turn right (south) and drive about six miles of rough road to the campground.

Contact: Mount Hood National Forest, Estacada Ranger District, 595 N.W. Industrial Way, Estacada, OR 97023; tel. (503) 630-6861; fax (503) 630-2299.

71 Lower Lake 7

This sunny, open campground is set at an elevation of 4,600 feet about three-quarters of a mile from Lower Lake, a small, deep lake that's perfect for fishing and swimming. The camp is less than a mile from Olallie Lake and near a network of trails that provide access to other nearby lakes. We advise you to obtain a U.S. Forest Service map that details the backcountry roads and trails.

Location: Near Olallie Lake in Mount Hood National Forest; map C2, grid g7.

Campsites, facilities: There are nine walk-in tent sites. Picnic tables and fire grills are provided. Pit toilets and garbage service are available. There is no drinking water. Boat docks, launching facilities, and rentals are nearby at Olallie Lake. Leashed pets are permitted.

Reservations, fees: No reservations accepted. Sites are $8 per night, $5 per night for an additional vehicle. Open mid-June to late September.

Directions: From Portland drive east on U.S. 26 from Gresham 11 miles to Sandy and Highway 211. Turn right (south) and drive six miles to a junction. Turn south (still Highway 211) and drive six miles to Estacada and Highway 224. Bear south on Highway 224 and drive 27 miles in national forest (the road becomes Forest Road 46). Continue south on Forest Road 46 for 20 miles to Forest Road 4690. Turn left on and drive southeast for 8.2 miles to Forest Road 4220. Turn right (south) and drive about 4.5 miles of rough road to the campground to the campground on the right.

Contact: Mount Hood National Forest, Estacada Ranger District, 595 N.W. Industrial Way, Estacada, OR 97023; tel. (503) 630-6861; fax (503) 630-2299.

72 Olallie Meadows   7

This campground is set at 4,500 feet along a large and peaceful, alpine meadow about three miles from Olallie Lake. The Pacific Crest Trail passes very close to camp. See the description of Paul Dennis for area details.

Location: Near Olallie Lake in Mount Hood National Forest; map C2, grid g7.

Campsites, facilities: There are seven sites for tents, trailers, or RVs up to 16 feet long. Picnic tables, garbage service, and fire grills are provided. Pit toilets are available. There is no drinking water. Boat docks, launching facilities, and rentals are located about three miles away on Olallie Lake. Leashed pets are permitted.

Reservations, fees: No reservations accepted. Sites are $8 per night, $5 per night for an additional vehicle. Open mid-June to late September.

Directions: From Portland drive east on U.S. 26 from Gresham 11 miles to Sandy and Highway 211. Turn right (south) and drive six miles to a junction. Turn south (still Highway 211) and drive six miles to Estacada and Highway 224. Bear south on Highway 224 and drive 27 miles in national forest (the road becomes Forest Road 46). Continue south on Forest Road 46 for 20 miles to Forest Road 4690. Turn left on and drive southeast for 8.2 miles to Forest Road 4220. Turn right (south) and drive 1.5 miles to the campground on the left.

Contact: Mount Hood National Forest, Estacada Ranger District, 595 N.W. Industrial Way, Estacada, OR 97023; tel. (503) 630-6861; fax (503) 630-2299.

73 Paul Dennis   10

This campground is set at an elevation of 5,000 feet along the north shore of Olallie Lake. From here you can see the reflection of Mount Jefferson (10,497 feet). Boats with motors are not permitted on the lake. A trail from camp leads to Nep-Te-Pa Lake, Monon Lake, and Long Lake, which lies just east of the border of the Warm Springs Indian Reservation. It's advisable to obtain a U.S. Forest Service map.

Location: On Olallie Lake in Mount Hood National Forest; map C2, grid g7.

Campsites, facilities: There are 15 sites for tents or small campers up to 16 feet long (trailers not recommended) and three hike-in tent sites. Picnic tables, garbage service, and fire grills are provided. Pit toilets are available. There is no drinking water. A store and ice are nearby. Boat docks, launching facilities, and rentals are located on Olallie Lake. Leashed pets are permitted.

Reservations, fees: No reservations accepted. Sites are $12 per night. Open mid-June to late September.

Directions: From Portland drive east on U.S. 26 from Gresham 11 miles to Sandy and Highway 211. Turn right (south) and drive six miles to a junction. Turn south (still Highway 211) and drive six miles to Estacada and Highway 224. Bear south on Highway 224 and drive 27 miles in national forest (the road becomes Forest Road 46). Continue south on Forest Road 46 for 20 miles to Forest Road 4690. Turn left on and drive southeast for 8.2 miles to Forest Road 4220. Turn right (south) and drive 6.2 miles to Forest Road 4220-170. Turn left and drive one-eighth mile to the campground.

Contact: Mount Hood National Forest, Estacada Ranger District, 595 N.W. Industrial Way, Estacada, OR 97023; tel. (503) 630-6861; fax (503) 630-2299.

74 Peninsula   10

Peninsula, the largest of several campgrounds along Olallie Lake, is set at an elevation of 4,900 feet on the south shore. The amphitheater is near camp, and during the summer rangers present campfire programs. Boats without motors are permitted on the lake. Numerous smaller lakes in the area can be reached from trails nearby. See the description of Paul Dennis for details.

Location: On Olallie Lake in Mount Hood National Forest; map C2, grid g7.

Campsites, facilities: There are 35 sites for tents, trailers, or RVs up to 24 feet long, and six walk-in tent sites. Picnic tables, garbage service, and fire grills are provided. Vault toilets are available. There is no drinking water. Some facilities are wheelchair accessible. Boat docks, launching facilities, and rentals are nearby. Leashed pets are permitted.

Reservations, fees: No reservations accepted. Sites are $8 per night, $5 per night for an additional vehicle. Open mid-June to late September.

Directions: From Portland drive east on U.S. 26 from Gresham 11 miles to Sandy and Highway 211. Turn right (south) and drive six miles to a junction. Turn south (still Highway 211) and drive six miles to Estacada and Highway 224. Bear south on Highway 224 and drive 27 miles in national forest (the road becomes Forest Road 46). Continue south on Forest Road 46 for 20 miles to Forest Road 4690. Turn left on and drive southeast for 8.2 miles to Forest Road 4220. Turn right (south) and drive 6.5 miles of rough road to the campground.

Contact: Mount Hood National Forest, Estacada Ranger District, 595 N.W. Industrial Way, Estacada, OR 97023; tel. (503) 630-6861; fax (503) 630-2299.

75 Shellrock Creek   6

Used primarily as an overflow area for Lake Harriet campground, this quiet little campground is set at an elevation of 2,200 feet at a nice spot on Shellrock Creek. Small trout can be caught here, but remember that on the Clackamas River it's catch-and-release only. It's advisable to obtain a U.S. Forest Service map that details the backcountry roads and trails.

Location: On Shellrock Creek in Mount Hood National Forest; map C2, grid g8.

Campsites, facilities: There are eight sites for tents, trailers, or RVs up to 16 feet long. Picnic tables and fire grills are provided. Garbage service is provided during the summer. Vault toilets are available. There is no drinking water. Leashed pets are permitted.

Reservations, fees: No reservations accepted. Sites are $10 per night, $5 per night for an additional vehicle. Open year-round, with limited winter services.

Directions: From Portland drive east on U.S. 26 from Gresham 11 miles to Sandy and Highway 211. Turn right (south) and drive six miles to a junction. Turn south (still Highway 211) and drive six miles to Estacada and Highway 224. Bear south on Highway 224 and drive 27 miles in national forest (the road becomes Forest Road 46) to Forest Road 57. Turn left (east) and drive 7.5 miles to Forest Road 58. Turn left and drive north one mile to the campground on the left.

Contact: Mount Hood National Forest, Estacada Ranger District, 595 N.W. Industrial Way, Estacada, OR 97023; tel. (503) 630-6861; fax (503) 630-2299.

76 Oak Fork   8

This forested camp is set in heavy timber and bear grass along the south shore of Timothy Lake, just east of Hoodview and Gone Creek campgrounds. Refer to these camps for more details.

Location: On Timothy Lake in Mount Hood National Forest; map C2, grid g8.

Campsites, facilities: There are 47 sites for tents, trailers, or RVs up to 32 feet long. Picnic tables and fire grills are provided. Drinking water, firewood, and vault toilets are available. A boat ramp and launching facilities are nearby; only non-motorized boats are allowed. Leashed pets are permitted.

Reservations, fees: Reservations accepted for some sites; phone (877) 444-6777 or access the website: www.reserveusa.com ($8.65 reservation fee). Sites are $12-14 per night, $6 per night for an additional vehicle. Open June through mid-September.

Directions: From Portland turn east on U.S. 26 and drive 57 miles (just past the town of Government Camp) to the junction with Highway 35. Turn southeast on U.S. 26 and drive 15 miles to Forest Road 42 (Skyline Road). Turn right and drive eight miles to Forest Road 57. Turn right and drive three miles to the park on the right.

Contact: Mount Hood National Forest, Zigzag Ranger District, 65000 East Highway 26, Welches, OR 97067; tel. (503) 622-7674; fax (503) 622-3163.

77 Pine Point   8

One of five camps on Timothy Lake, this spot is located at an elevation of 3,200 feet on the southwest shore and has lake access and more open vegetation than the other Timothy Lake campgrounds. The trail that leads around the lake and to the Pacific Crest Trail is just outside of the camp. See the description of Gone Creek for boating and fishing details.

Location: On Timothy Lake in Mount Hood National Forest; map C2, grid g8.

Campsites, facilities: There are 25 sites for tents, trailers, or RVs up to 31 feet long (10 single sites, 10 double sites, and five group sites). Picnic tables, garbage service and fire grills are provided. Drinking water, firewood, a wheelchair-accessible fishing pier, and vault toilets are available. A boat ramp and launching facilities are nearby; only non-motorized boats are allowed. Leashed pets are permitted.

Reservations, fees: Reservations accepted for some sites; phone (877) 444-6777 or access the website: www.reserveusa.com ($8.65 reservation fee). Sites are $12-14 per night, group sites are $24-30 per night; $6 per night for an additional vehicle. Open late May to mid-September.

Directions: From Portland turn east on U.S. 26 and drive 57 miles (just past the town of Government Camp) to the junction with Highway 35. Turn southeast on U.S. 26 and drive 15 miles to Forest Road 42 (Skyline Road). Turn right and drive eight miles to Forest Road 57. Turn right and drive four miles to the park on the right.

Contact: Mount Hood National Forest, Zigzag Ranger District, 65000 East Highway 26, Welches, OR 97067; tel. (503) 622-7674; fax (503) 622-3163.

78 Hoodview   9

Here's another camp along the south shore of Timothy Lake; this one is set at 3,200 feet elevation. A trail out of camp branches south for a few miles, and if followed to the east, eventually leads to the Pacific Crest Trail. See the description of Gone Creek for boating and fishing information.

Location: On Timothy Lake in Mount Hood National Forest; map C2, grid g9.

Campsites, facilities: There are 43 sites for tents, trailers, or RVs up to 31 feet long. Picnic tables, garbage service, and fire grills are provided. Drinking water, firewood, and vault toilets are available. A boat ramp is nearby and motorized boats are allowed but are limited to a speed of 10 mph. Leashed pets are permitted.

Reservations, fees: Reservations accepted for some sites; phone (877) 444-6777 or access the website: www.reserveusa.com ($8.65 reservation fee). Sites are $12-14 per night, $6 per night for an additional vehicle. Open mid-May to mid-September.

Directions: From Portland turn east on U.S. 26 and drive 57 miles (just past the town of Government Camp) to the junction with Highway 35. Turn southeast on U.S. 26 and drive 15 miles to Forest Road 42 (Skyline Road). Turn right and drive eight miles to Forest Road 57. Turn right and drive three miles to the campground on the right.

Contact: Mount Hood National Forest, Zigzag Ranger District, 65000 East Highway 26, Welches, OR 97067; tel. (503) 622-7674; fax (503) 622-3163.

79 Summit Lake   6

This is an idyllic setting in a remote area along the western slopes of the Cascade Range at an elevation of 4,200 feet. Located on the shore of little Summit Lake, the camp is primitive but a jewel. It's a perfect alternative to the more crowded camps at Timothy Lake, and you can access all the same recreation options by driving just a short distance north.

Location: On Summit Lake in Mount Hood National Forest; map C2, grid g9.

Campsites, facilities: There are six tent sites. Fire grills, garbage service, and picnic tables are provided. Vault toilets and drinking water are available. There is no drinking water. Non-motorized boats are allowed. Leashed pets are permitted.

Reservations, fees: No reservations accepted. Sites are $8 per night. Open late May through September, weather permitting.

Directions: From Portland turn east on U.S. 26 and drive 57 miles (just past the town of Government Camp) to the junction with Highway 35. Turn southeast on U.S. 26 and drive 15 miles to Forest Road 42 (Skyline Road). Turn right and drive 12 miles south to Forest Road 141 (a dirt road). Turn right and drive west about one mile to the campground on the left.

Contact: Mount Hood National Forest, Clackamas Ranger District, (503) 834-2275. Estacada Ranger Station, 595 N.W. Industrial Way, Estacada, OR 97023.

80 Gone Creek   8

This campground set along the south shore of Timothy Lake at 3,200 feet is one of four camps at the lake. Timothy Lake provides good fishing for brook trout, cutthroat trout, rainbow trout, and kokanee salmon. Boats with motors are allowed, but a 10 mph speed limit keeps it quiet. Several trails in the area—including the Pacific Crest Trail—provide access to several small mountain lakes.

Location: On Timothy Lake in Mount Hood National Forest; map C2, grid g9.

Campsites, facilities: There are 45 sites for tents, trailers, or RVs up to 31 feet long. Drinking water, fire grills, garbage service, and picnic tables are provided. Vault toilets and firewood are available. A boat ramp is nearby. Leashed pets are permitted.

Reservations, fees: Reservations accepted for some sites; phone (877) 444-6777 or access the website: www.reserveusa.com ($8.65 reservation fee). Sites are $12-14 per night, $6 per night for an additional vehicle. Open mid-May to mid-September.

Directions: From Portland turn east on U.S. 26 and drive 57 miles (just past the town of Government Camp) to the junction with Highway 35. Turn southeast on U.S. 26 and drive 15 miles to Forest Road 42 (Skyline Road). Turn right and drive eight miles to Forest Road 57. Turn right and drive one mile west to the campground on the right.

Contact: Mount Hood National Forest, Zigzag Ranger District, 65000 East Highway 26, Welches, OR 97067; tel. (503) 622-7674; fax (503) 622-3163.

81 Joe Graham Horse Camp   8

This campground is named for a forest ranger and is set at 3,250 feet elevation among majestic Douglas fir and hemlock, just north of tiny Clackamas Lake. It's one of two campgrounds in the area that allows horses; see the description of Clackamas Lake for additional information. Timothy Lake (the setting for the Gone Creek, Hoodview, Oak Fork, Pine Point, and Meditation Point sites) provides a nearby alternative to the northwest. The Pacific Crest Trail is located just east of camp.

Location: Near Clackamas Lake in Mount Hood National Forest; map C2, grid g9.

Campsites, facilities: There are 14 sites for tents, trailers, horse trailers, or RVs up to 28 feet long; nine have corrals. Picnic tables, hitching posts, garbage service, and fire grills are provided. Drinking water, vault toilets, and firewood are available. Leashed pets are permitted.

Reservations, fees: Reservations accepted for some sites; phone (877) 444-6777 or access the website: www.reserveusa.com ($8.65 reservation fee). Sites are $12 per night, $6 per night for an additional vehicle. Open mid-May to mid-September.

Directions: From Portland turn east on U.S. 26 and drive 57 miles (just past the town of Government Camp) to the junction with Highway 35. Turn southeast on U.S. 26 and drive 15 miles to Forest Road 42 (Skyline Road). Turn right and drive eight miles to the campground on the left.

Contact: Mount Hood National Forest, Zigzag Ranger District, 65000 East Highway 26, Welches, OR 97067; tel. (503) 622-7674; fax (503) 622-3163.

82 Clackamas Lake   7

This camp set at 3,400 feet elevation is a good place to go to escape the hordes of people at the lakeside sites at neighboring camps. The Pacific Crest Trail passes nearby, and Timothy Lake is little more than a one-mile hike from camp. See the description of Gone Creek for information on Timothy Lake.

Location: Near the Clackamas River in Mount Hood National Forest; map C2, grid g9.

Campsites, facilities: There are 46 sites for tents, trailers, horse trailers, or RVs up to 16 feet long. Some sites have hitch rails. Drinking water, garbage service, fire grills, and picnic tables are provided. Vault toilets and firewood are available. Boat docks and launching facilities are nearby at Timothy Lake, but only non-motorized boats are allowed. Leashed pets are permitted.

Reservations, fees: Reservations accepted for some sites; phone (877) 444-6777 or access the website: www.reserveusa.com ($8.65 reservation fee). Sites are $12 per night, $6 per night for an additional vehicle. Open June to mid-September.

Directions: From Portland turn east on U.S. 26 and drive 57 miles (just past the town of Government Camp) to the junction with Highway 35. Turn southeast on U.S. 26 and drive 15 miles to Forest Road 42 (Skyline Road). Turn right and drive eight miles to Forest Road 57. Continue 500 feet past the Clackamas Lake Historic Ranger Station to Forest Road 4270. Turn left and drive one-half mile to the campground on the left.

Contact: Mount Hood National Forest, Zigzag Ranger District, 65000 East Highway 26, Welches, OR 97067; tel. (503) 622-7674; fax (503) 622-3163.

MAP C3

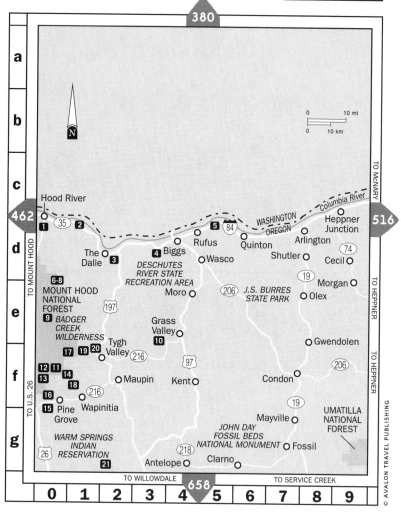

380

a

b

N

0   10 mi

0   10 km

c

Hood River

462

Columbia River

516

WASHINGTON
OREGON

1 35 **2**

5 84

Heppner
Junction

TO McNARY

TO MOUNT HOOD

d

Rufus

Quinton Arlington

74

The
Dalle **3**

4 Biggs

Wasco

Shutler Cecil

DESCHUTES
RIVER STATE
RECREATION AREA

206 J.S. BURRES
STATE PARK

19 Morgan

TO HEPPNER

6-8

MOUNT HOOD
NATIONAL
FOREST

Moro

Olex

e

197

9 BADGER
CREEK
WILDERNESS

Grass
Valley

10

Tygh
Valley 216

17 **19** **20**

97

Gwendolen

TO HEPPNER

206

f

12 **11**

13 **14**

18

216

Maupin

Kent

Condon

TO U.S. 26

16

15 Pine
Grove

Wapinitia

19

Mayville

UMATILLA
NATIONAL
FOREST

g

WARM SPRINGS
INDIAN
RESERVATION

26

JOHN DAY
FOSSIL BEDS
NATIONAL MONUMENT Fossil

218

21

Antelope Clarno

© AVALON TRAVEL PUBLISHING

TO WILLOWDALE **658** TO SERVICE CREEK

0   1   2   3   4   5   6   7   8   9

CHAPTER C3

1 Tucker County Park   6

This county park along the banks of the Hood River is just far enough out of the way to be missed by most of the tourist traffic. Recreation includes trout fishing, rafting, and kayaking.

Location: On the Hood River; map C3, grid d0.

Campsites, facilities: There are 75 tent sites and 13 sites for tents, trailers, or RVs up to 30 feet long. Picnic tables and fire rings are provided. Electricity, drinking water, flush toilets, showers, firewood, and a playground are available. A store, a cafe, coin-operated laundry facilities, and ice are located within two miles. Leashed pets are permitted. Most facilities are wheelchair accessible.

Reservations, fees: No reservations accepted. Sites are $13-14 per night. Open April through October.

Directions: From Portland turn east on Interstate 84 and drive about 65 miles to the town of Hood River to Exit 62. Take the exit and drive east on Cascade Street and continue to 13th Street (first light). Turn right (south) and drive through and out of town. Thirteenth Street becomes Tucker Road and then Dee Highway (Highway 281). Follow the signs to Parkdale. The park is four miles out of town on the right.

Contact: Hood River County Parks, 918 18th Street, Hood River, OR 97031; tel. (541) 387-6889 for fax (541) 386-6325. Website: www.dguesshrcparkbuild@gorge.net.

2 Memaloose State Park   7

This park borrows its name from ancient Native Americans who used nearby Memaloose Island as a sacred burial ground. Set along the hottest part of the scenic Columbia River Gorge, it makes a prime layover spot for campers cruising the Oregon-Washington border. Nature programs and interpretive events are also held here. This popular camp receives a good deal of traffic, so plan on arriving early to claim a spot.

Location: In the Columbia River Gorge; map C3, grid d1.

Campsites, facilities: There are 67 tent sites and 43 sites with full hookups for trailers or RVs up to 60 feet long. Picnic tables and fire grills are provided. Drinking water, garbage bins, flush toilets, sanitary disposal station, showers, and firewood are available. Leashed pets and motorbikes are permitted.

Reservations, fees: Reservations accepted; phone (800) 452-5687 ($6 reservation fee). Sites are $11-19 per night, $7 per night for an additional vehicle. Major credit cards accepted. Open mid-March to late October.

Directions: This park is accessible only to westbound traffic on Interstate 84. From The Dalles drive west on Interstate 84 for 11 miles to the signed turnoff. (The park is located about 75 miles east of Portland.)

Contact: Columbia River Gorge District, P.O. Box 100, Corbett, OR 97019; tel. (541) 478-3008 or (800) 551-6949.

◪ Lone Pine RV Park   7

This private park isn't far from the Columbia River, where fishing, boating, and swimming are options. The area gets hot weather and occasional winds shooting through the river canyon during summer months. Nearby recreation possibilities include an 18-hole golf course and tennis courts.

Location: Near the Columbia River; map C3, grid d2.

Campsites, facilities: There are 22 drive-through sites for trailers or RVs of any length. Electricity, drinking water, and sewer hookups are provided. Flush toilets, showers, a cafe, a laundry room, ice, and a playground are available. Bottled gas and sanitary services are located within one mile. Boat docks and launching facilities are nearby. Leashed pets are permitted.

Reservations, fees: Reservations accepted. Sites are $20-22 per night. Open mid-April through September.

Directions: From Portland turn east on Interstate 84 and drive about 90 miles to The Dalles and Exit 87. Take Exit 87 to U.S. 197 and drive less than a quarter-mile to the park.

Contact: Lone Pine RV Park, 335 U.S. 197, The Dalles, OR 97058; tel. (541) 296-9133.

◪ Deschutes River State Recreation Area
        7

This tree-shaded park in the Deschutes Canyon along the Deschutes River offers bicycling and hiking trails and good steelhead fishing in season. The Atiyeh Deschutes River Trail at river level is a favorite jaunt for hikers; be sure to look for the basketlike nests of the orioles. There's a small day-use state park called Heritage Landing across the river, which has a boat ramp and rest room facilities. The U.S. Army Corps of Engineers offers a free train ride and tour of the dam at The Dalles during the summer. Good rafting is a bonus here. For 25 miles upstream the river is mostly inaccessible by car. Many fishermen launch boats here and then go upstream to the fishing grounds for steelhead. Note that no fishing is allowed from a boat; you must wade into the river or fish from shore.

Location: On the Deschutes River; map C3, grid d3.

Campsites, facilities: There are 35 primitive sites for tents, trailers, or self-contained RVs up to 30 feet long, 34 electric sites, and one covered camper wagon. There is also a group area for RVs and tents. Picnic tables and fire grills are provided. Drinking water, garbage bins, and flush toilets are available. Leashed pets are permitted.

Reservations, fees: Group reservations accepted; phone (800) 452-5682 ($6 reservation fee). Sites are $10-21 per night; the covered wagon fee is $30 per night; an additional vehicle is $5 per night. Major credit cards accepted. Open late April to October.

Directions: From Portland turn east on Interstate 84 and drive about 90 miles to The Dalles. Continue east on Interstate 84 for 12 miles to Exit 97, turn right, and drive 50 feet to Biggs-Rufus Highway. Turn left and drive about one mile, cross the Deschutes River, and turn right to the campground entrance.

Contact: Deschutes River State Recreation Area, 89600 Biggs-Rufus Highway, Wasco, OR 97065; tel. (541) 739-2322 or (800) 452-5687.

5 Le Page Park 6

One half of the campsites are adjacent to the John Day River and the other half are on the other side of the road. The John Day River feeds into the Columbia just one-eighth mile north of the campground. The campground is partially shaded. Fishing includes smallmouth bass and catfish during the summer season. The day-use area has a swimming beach, lawn, a boat launch, and boat docks. There are several other campgrounds nearby.

Location: On the John Day River; map C3, grid d5.

Campsites, facilities: There are five tent sites and 22 partial hookup sites for tents, trailers, or RVs up to 40 feet long. Picnic tables and fire pits are provided. Drinking water and electricity, restrooms with flush toilets, sinks, and hot showers are available, as well as a boat ramp, docks, a dump station, and garbage containers. Food and laundry services are available five miles away in the town of Rufus. Leashed pets are permitted.

Reservations, fees: Reservations recommended, phone (877) 444-6777 or access the website: www.reserveusa.com ($8.65 reservation fee). Sites are $10-16 per night, $3 per night for an additional vehicle. Open April through October.

Directions: From Portland on Interstate 84, drive east 120 miles (30 miles past The Dalles) to Exit 114, the John Day River Recreation Area. The campground is located just off Interstate 84.

Contact: Army Corps of Engineers, Portland District, P.O. Box 2946, Portland, OR 97208-2946; tel. (503) 808-5150; fax (503) 808-4515.

6 Knebal Springs 6

This spot is in a semi-primitive area near Knebal Springs, an ephemeral water source. The Knebal Springs Trailhead is at the campground. A trail from the camp provides access to a network of other trails in the area. A U.S. Forest Service map is advised.

Location: Near Knebal Springs in Mount Hood National Forest; map C3, grid e0.

Campsites, facilities: There are five sites for tents and small trailers or RVs up to 22 feet long. Drinking water, picnic tables and fire grills are provided. Vault toilets and horse loading and tending facilities are available. Leashed pets are permitted. All garbage must be packed out.

Reservations, fees: No reservations accepted. There is no fee. Open June to early October, weather permitting.

Directions: From Portland turn east on Interstate 84 and drive about 90 miles to Exit 87. Take Exit 87 and turn south on U.S. 197 and drive 13 miles to Dufur and Dufur Valley Road. Turn right on Dufur Valley Road and drive west for 12 miles to Forest Road 44. Continue west on Forest Road 44 for four miles to Forest Road 4430. Turn north and drive four miles to Forest Road 1720. Turn southwest and drive one mile to the campground.

Contact: Mount Hood National Forest, Barlow Ranger District, 780 N.E. Court Street, Dufur, OR 97021; tel. (541) 467-2291; fax (541) 467-2291.

7 Eightmile Crossing   7

This campground is set at an elevation of 4,200 feet along Eightmile Creek. It gets relatively little camping pressure. It's pretty and shaded, with sites scattered along the banks of the creek. From the day-use area you can access a nice hiking trail that runs along Eightmile Creek. The fishing can be good here, so bring your gear.

Location: On Eightmile Creek in Mount Hood National Forest; map C3, grid e0.

Campsites, facilities: There are 24 sites for tents, trailers, or RVs up to 30 feet long. No drinking water is available, and all garbage must be packed out. Picnic tables and fire grills are provided. Vault toilets are available. Leashed pets are permitted.

Reservations, fees: No reservations accepted. There is no fee. Open June to mid-October.

Directions: From Portland turn east on Interstate 84 and drive about 90 miles to Exit 87. Take Exit 87 and turn south on U.S. 197 and drive 13 miles to Dufur and Dufur Valley Road. Turn right on Dufur Valley Road and drive west for 12 miles to Forest Road 44. Continue west on Forest Road 44 for four miles to Forest Road 4430. Turn right and drive a short distance to the campground.

Contact: Mount Hood National Forest, Barlow Ranger District, 780 N.E. Court Street, Dufur, OR 97021; tel. (541) 467-2291; fax (541) 467-2291.

8 Pebble Ford   6

This is just a little camping spot by the side of the gravel forest road. Primitive and quiet, it's an alternative to the better-known Eightmile Crossing. There are some quality hiking trails in the area if you're willing to drive two or three miles.

Location: In Mount Hood National Forest; map C3, grid e0.

Campsites, facilities: There are three sites for tents, trailers, or RVs up to 16 feet long. Picnic tables and fire grills are provided. Vault toilets are available. There is no drinking water. Leashed pets are permitted.

Reservations, fees: No reservations accepted. There is no fee. Open July to early October.

Directions: From Portland turn east on Interstate 84 and drive about 90 miles to Exit 87. Take Exit 87 and turn south on U.S. 197 and drive 13 miles to Dufur and Dufur Valley Road. Turn right on Dufur Valley Road and drive west for 12 miles to Forest Road 44. Continue west on Forest Road 44 for five miles to Forest Road 130. Turn left (south) and a short distance to the campground on the left.

Contact: Mount Hood National Forest, Barlow Ranger District, 780 N.E. Court Street, Dufur, OR 97021; tel. (541) 467-2291; fax (541) 467-2271.

9 Badger Lake   8

This campground is set at an elevation of 4,400 feet, along the shore of Badger Lake. Non-motorized boating is permitted if you can manage to get a boat in here over the rough roads. No trailers are allowed on campground roads. The camp is adjacent to the Badger Creek Wilderness, and numerous trails provide access to the backcountry. Badger Creek Trail heads out of camp northeast along Badger Creek for several miles.

Location: On Badger Lake in Mount Hood National Forest; map C3, grid e0.

Campsites, facilities: There are four sites for tents only, accessible only by high-clearance vehicles. Picnic tables and fire grills are provided. Vault toilets are available. There is no drinking water and all garbage must be packed out. Leashed pets are permitted.

Reservations, fees: No reservations accepted. There is no fee. Open July to early October.

Directions: From Portland drive east on Interstate 84 for 65 miles to Hood River, Exit 64 and Highway 35. Turn south and drive 37 miles to Forest Road 48. Turn left and drive 16 miles to Forest Road 4860. Turn left (north) and drive eight miles to Forest Road 140. Bear right and drive four miles to the lake. The last two miles on this primitive road require a high-clearance vehicle.

Contact: Mount Hood National Forest, Barlow Ranger District, 780 N.E. Court Street, Dufur, OR 97021; tel. (541) 467-2291; fax (541) 467-2271.

10 Beavertail   6

This isolated campground is set at an elevation of 2,900 feet along the banks of the Deschutes River, with fishing and rafting options. The Deschutes is one of the classic steelhead streams in the Pacific Northwest. The camp is open with canyon views. This is my favorite put-in spot for a drift boat for fishing float trips on the Deschutes. I've made the trip from Beavertail to the mouth of the Deschutes, ideal in four days, camping at BLM boat-in sites along the river, fly-fishing for steelhead. A boating pass is required to float the river. There are 12 other BLM campgrounds located along upper and lower Deschutes River Road. The hardest part is getting used to the freight trains that rumble through the canyon at night.

Location: On the Deschutes River; map C3, grid e3.

Campsites, facilities: There are 17 sites for tents, trailers, or RVs up to 30 feet long, and two group sites. Picnic tables, garbage bins, and fire grills are provided. Vault toilets are available. There is no drinking water. Some facilities are wheelchair accessible. Boat launching facilities are nearby. Leashed pets are permitted.

Reservations, fees: No reservations accepted. Sites are $5-10 per night, with a 14-day stay limit. Open year-round.

Directions: From Portland drive east on U.S. 84 to The Dalles and Highway 197. Turn south and drive to Maupin. Continue through Maupin, cross the bridge, and within a mile look for Deschutes River Road on your left. Turn left on Deschutes River Road and drive 21 miles northeast to the campground.

Contact: Bureau of Land Management, Prineville District, P.O. Box 550, Prineville, OR 97754; tel. (541) 416-6700; fax (541) 416-6798.

11 Bonney Meadow   9

At 4,800-foot elevation, this primitive campground is located on the east side of the Cascade Range. As a result, there is little water in the area-and also very few people, so you're liable to have the place all to yourself. Bonnie Meadow Trail leaves from the campground and travels 1.5 miles up to a group of small lakes. There are great mountain views from this trail. See a U.S. Forest Service map for details.

Location: In Mount Hood National Forest; map C3, grid f0.

Campsites, facilities: There are eight sites for tents and small trailers or RVs up to 16 feet long. Picnic tables and fire grills are provided. Vault toilets are available. There is no drinking water. Leashed pets are permitted.

Reservations, fees: No reservations accepted. There is no fee. Open July to early October.

Directions: From Portland turn east on Interstate 84 and drive 65 miles to the town of Hood River, Exit 64 and Highway 35. Turn south on Highway 35 and drive 37 miles to Forest Road 48. Turn left and drive 14 miles to Forest Road 4890. Turn left and drive four miles north to Forest Road 4891. Turn right and drive a short distance to the campground.

Contact: Mount Hood National Forest, Barlow Ranger District, 780 N.E. Court Street, Dufur, OR 97021; tel. (541) 467-2291; fax (541) 467-2271.

12 Keeps Mill    9

This small, pretty campground is located at the confluence of Clear Creek and the White River. The elevation is 2,600 feet. Many hiking trails are in the area, some with awesome views of the White River Canyon, but be warned. These are butt-kicking, canyon climbs.

Location: On Clear Creek in Mount Hood National Forest; map C3, grid f0.

Campsites, facilities: There are five sites for tents. The road to the campground is not good for trailers. Picnic tables and fire grills are provided. Vault toilets are available. There is no drinking water. Leashed pets are permitted.

Reservations, fees: No reservations accepted. There is no fee. Open May through September.

Directions: From Portland drive east on U.S. 26 for 55 miles to Government Camp. Continue three miles to a junction and turn right on U.S. 26 and drive south for 12 miles to Highway 216. Turn left (east) on Highway 216 and drive three miles to Forest Road 2120. Turn left (north) on Forest Road 2120 and drive three miles to the campground.

Contact: Mount Hood National Forest, Barlow Ranger District, 780 N.E. Court Street, Dufur, OR 97021; tel. (541) 467-5180; fax (541) 328-6222.

13 Clear Creek Crossing   7

This campground along the banks of Clear Creek is a secluded, little-known spot set at an elevation of 3,600 feet. Clear Creek Trail begins at the campground and is a very pretty walk. Fishing and hiking are two recreation options here.

Location: On Clear Creek in Mount Hood National Forest; map C3, grid f0.

Campsites, facilities: There are seven sites for tents, trailers, or RVs up to 16 feet long. Picnic tables and fire grills are provided. Vault toilets are available. There is no drinking water, and all garbage must be packed out. Leashed pets are permitted.

Reservations, fees: No reservations accepted. There is no fee. Open May through September.

Directions: From Portland drive east on U.S. 26 for 55 miles to Government Camp. Continue three miles to a junction, turn right on U.S. 26, and drive south for 12 miles to Highway 216. Turn left (east) on Highway 216 and drive three miles to Forest Road 2120. Turn left (north) on Forest Road 2120 and drive three miles to the campground.

Contact: Mount Hood National Forest, Barlow Ranger District, Bear Springs Work Center, 73558 Highway 216, Maupin, OR 97037; tel. (541) 467-5180.

14 Rock Creek Reservoir   7

Fishing is excellent, and the environment is perfect for canoes or rafts at this campground along the shore of Rock Creek Reservoir at 2,200 feet elevation. Mount Hood can be seen from the day-use area. No hiking trails are in the immediate vicinity, but there are many old forest roads that are ideal for walking or mountain biking.

Location: On Rock Creek Reservoir in Mount Hood National Forest; map C3, grid f0.

Campsites, facilities: There are 33 sites for tents, trailers, or RVs up to 18 feet long. Picnic tables, garbage service, and fire grills are provided. Vault toilets, drinking water, and firewood are available. Some of the facilities are wheelchair accessible. There are boat docks nearby, but no motorboats are allowed on the reservoir. Leashed pets are permitted.

Reservations, fees: Reservations accepted; phone (877) 444-6777 or access the website: www.reserveusa.com ($8.65 reservation fee). Sites are $10-12 per night, $6 per night for an additional vehicle. Open mid-April to early October.

Directions: From Portland turn east on Interstate 84 and drive 91 miles to The Dalles, Exit 87, and Highway 197. Turn south and drive 31 miles to Tygh Valley and Wamic Market Road. Turn right and drive west for six miles to Forest Road 48. Turn west and drive one mile to Forest Road 4820. Turn west and drive a short distance to the campground.

Contact: Mount Hood National Forest, Barlow Ranger District, 780 N.E. Court Street, Dufur, OR 97021; tel. (541) 467-2291; fax (541) 467-2271.

15 Bear Springs   6

This campground is set along the banks of Indian Creek on the border of the Warm Springs Indian Reservation. The Bear Springs Work Center is near the camp, and rangers will be happy to supply maps and answer your questions about the area. There are both secluded and open sites set in old-growth forest.

Location: On Indian Creek in Mount Hood National Forest; map C3, grid f0.

Campsites, facilities: There are 21 sites for tents, trailers, or RVs up to 32 feet long. Drinking water, fire grills, garbage bins, and picnic tables are provided. Vault toilets and firewood are available. Leashed pets are permitted.

Reservations, fees: Reservations accepted; phone (877) 444-6777 or access the website: www.reserveusa.com ($8.65 reservation fee). Sites are $9 per night, plus $5 for each additional vehicle. Open June through September.

Directions: From Portland drive east on U.S. 26 for 55 miles to Government Camp. Continue three miles to a junction, turn right on U.S. 26, and drive south for 12 miles to Highway 216. Turn left (east) on Highway 216 and drive five miles to Reservation Road. Turn east (right) on Reservation Road and look for the campground on the right.

Contact: Mount Hood National Forest, Barlow Ranger District, Bear Springs Work Center, 73558 Highway 216, Maupin, OR 97037; tel. (541) 467-5180.

16 McCubbins Gulch   5

This is a small, primitive camp along a small creek that offers decent fishing and ATV recreation. Though out of the way, the camp is heavily used, so claim a spot early in the day. To the south is the Warm Springs Indian Reservation. A nearby camping option is Bear Springs.

Location: In Mount Hood National Forest; map C3, grid f0.

Campsites, facilities: There are 18 sites for tents and RVs up to 25 feet long. Picnic tables and fire grills are provided. Vault toilets are available. There is no drinking water and all garbage must be packed out. Leashed pets are permitted.

Reservations, fees: No reservations accepted. There is no fee. Open May through September.

Directions: From Portland drive east on U.S. 26 for 55 miles to Government Camp. Continue three miles to a junction and turn right on U.S. 26 and drive south for 12 miles to Highway 216. Turn left (east) on Highway 216 and drive six miles to Forest Road 2110. Turn a sharp left and drive 1.5 miles to the campground entrance on the right.

Contact: Mount Hood National Forest, Barlow Ranger District, (541) 467-5180, Bear Springs Work Center, 73558 Highway 216, Maupin, OR 97037.

17 Forest Creek   6

The elevation here is 3,000 feet. This very old camp along Forest Creek on the original Barlow Trail was once used by early settlers. Shaded by old-growth Douglas fir and ponderosa pine forest, you'll find solitude here. See a U.S. Forest Service map for specific roads and trails.

Location: On Forest Creek in Mount Hood National Forest; map C3, grid f1.

Campsites, facilities: There are eight sites for tents, trailers, or RVs up to 16 feet long. No drinking water is available. Picnic tables and fire grills are provided. Vault toilets are available. Leashed pets are permitted. Pack out all garbage.

Reservations, fees: No reservations accepted. There is no fee. Open July to early October.

Directions: From Portland turn east on Interstate 84 and drive 91 miles to The Dalles, Exit 87, and Highway 197. Turn south and drive 31 miles to Tygh Valley and Wamic Market Road. Turn right and drive west for six miles to Forest Road 48. Continue west and drive 12.5 miles southwest to Forest Road 4885. Turn left and drive one mile to Forest Road 3530. Turn left to the campground.

Contact: Mount Hood National Forest, Barlow Ranger District, 780 N.E. Court Street, Dufur, OR 97021; tel. (541) 467-2291; fax (541) 467-2271.

18 Bonney Crossing   7

This campground at 2,200 feet elevation along Badger Creek is the trailhead for the Badger Creek Trail, which provides access to the Badger Creek Wilderness. The camp gets fairly light use and is usually very quiet. Fishing is available in the creek and is usually pretty good. Horse campers are welcome here.

Location: On Badger Creek in Mount Hood National Forest; map C3, grid f1.

Campsites, facilities: There are eight sites for tents, trailers, or RVs up to 16 feet long. Picnic tables and fire grills are provided. Vault toilets are available. Stock facilities include horse corrals. There is no drinking water. Leashed pets are permitted. Pack out all garbage.

Reservations, fees: No reservations accepted. Sites are $3 per night. Open mid-April to mid-October.

Directions: From The Dalles drive south on U.S. 197 for 32 miles to Tygh Valley. Take the Tygh Valley exit to Tygh Valley Road. Turn west and drive one-fourth mile to Wamic Market Road (County Road 226). Turn west (right) and drive eight miles to Wamic. Continue through Wamic and drive seven miles to Forest Road 4810. Bear right and drive three miles to Forest Road 4811. Turn right and drive two miles to a junction with Forest Road 2710. Turn right and drive three miles to the campground on the right.

Contact: Mount Hood National Forest, Barlow Ranger District, 780 N.E. Court Street, Dufur, OR 97021; tel. (541) 467-2291; fax (541) 467-2271.

19 Pine Hollow
　　Lakeside Resort   8

This resort on the shore of Pine Hollow Reservoir is the best game in town for RV campers, with shaded lakefront sites and scenic views. Year-round fishing, boating, swimming, and waterskiing are some recreation options here.

Location: On Pine Hollow Reservoir; map C3, grid f1.

Campsites, facilities: There are 35 tent sites and 75 sites for trailers or RVs. Electricity, drinking water, and picnic tables are provided. Flush toilets, bottled gas, sanitary services, showers, firewood, a store, a cafe, a laundry room, and ice are available. Boat docks, launching facilities, and rentals are nearby. Leashed pets are permitted.

Reservations, fees: Reservations accepted. Sites are $15-20 per night. Open mid-March through October.

Directions: From Portland turn east on Interstate 84 and drive 91 miles to The Dalles, Exit 87, and Highway 197. Turn south and drive 31 miles to Tygh Valley and Wamic Market Road. Turn west and drive 4.5 miles to Ross Road. Turn north and drive 3.5 miles to the campground.

Contact: Pine Hollow Lakeside Resort, 34 North Mariposa Drive, Wamic, OR 97063 tel. (541) 544-2271.

20 Wasco County Fairgrounds   6

This county campground is set near the confluence of Badger and Tygh Creeks. Hiking trails, marked bike trails, and tennis courts are close by.

Location: Near Badger Creek; map C3, grid f1.

Campsites, facilities: There are 50 tent sites and 100 drive-through sites for trailers or RVs of any length. Electricity, drinking water, and picnic tables are provided. Flush toilets, a dump station, garbage bins, and coin-operated showers are available. Two community kitchens are available for a fee. A store, a cafe, and ice are located within one mile. Leashed pets are permitted. Some facilities are wheelchair accessible. Horse facilities are available, including stalls and an arena.

Reservations, fees: Reservations accepted. Sites are $10-12 per night. Open May through October.

Directions: From Portland turn east on Interstate 84 and drive 91 miles to The Dalles, Exit 87, and Highway 197. Turn south and drive 31 miles to Tygh Valley and Main Street. Turn right at Main Street and drive two blocks to Fairgrounds Road. Turn right and drive one mile to the fairgrounds on the right.

Contact: Wasco County, 81849 Fairgrounds Road, Tygh Valley, OR 97063; tel. (541) 483-2288.

21 Kah-Nee-Ta Resort   6

This is the only public camp on the east side of the Warm Springs Indian Reservation; there are no other camps within 30 miles. The Warm Springs River runs nearby, with opportunities for fishing. Recreation options in the area include an 18-hole golf course, mini-golf, biking and hiking trails, a riding stable, and tennis courts.

Location: On the Warm Springs Indian Reservation; map C3, grid g2.

Campsites, facilities: There are 50 drive-through sites for trailers or RVs of any length. Electricity, drinking water, cable TV, and sewer hookups are provided. Flush toilets, bottled gas, sanitary services, showers, a cafe, laundry facilities, ice, a playground, a spa with a therapist, mineral and mud baths, and an Olympic-sized, spring-fed swimming pool with a 140-foot water slide are available. Some facilities are wheelchair accessible. Leashed pets and motorbikes are permitted, but some areas are restricted.

Reservations, fees: Reservations accepted. Sites are $32 per night; call for special winter rates. Open year-round.

Directions: From Portland turn east on U.S. 26 and drive about 105 miles to Warm Springs and Agency Hot Springs Road on the left. Turn left and drive 11 miles northeast to Kah-Nee-Ta and the resort on the right.

Contact: Kah-Nee-Ta Resort, P.O. Box K, Warm Springs, OR 97761; tel. (541) 553-1112; fax (541) 302-6622; website: www.kahneetaresort.com.

MAP C4

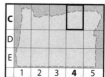

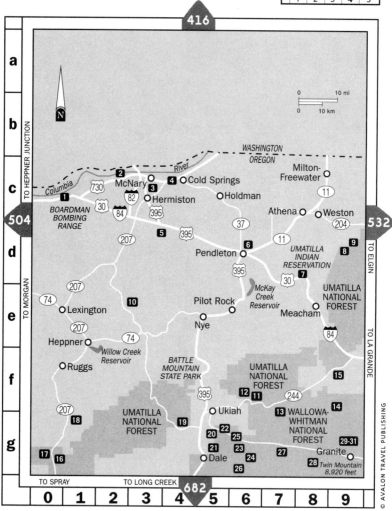

416

TO HEPPNER JUNCTION

504

532
TO ELGIN

TO MORGAN

TO LA GRANDE

© AVALON TRAVEL PUBLISHING

WASHINGTON
OREGON

Columbia   River

2 McNary
1
BOARDMAN
BOMBING
RANGE

730
82
30
84

3 Hermiston
4 Cold Springs
Holdman

Milton-
Freewater

11

Athena   Weston
204

395
5
395

37

6 Pendleton
395

11

9
UMATILLA   **8**
INDIAN
RESERVATION

30   **7**

McKay
Creek
Reservoir

UMATILLA
NATIONAL
FOREST

207

74
207
Lexington

10

Pilot Rock

Nye

Meacham

84

207
74
Heppner
Willow Creek
Reservoir

Ruggs

BATTLE
MOUNTAIN
STATE PARK

395

UMATILLA
NATIONAL
FOREST

12
11

244

15

UMATILLA
NATIONAL
FOREST

207
18

19

Ukiah

20 **22**
25
21 **23**
Dale   **24**
26

13 WALLOWA-
WHITMAN
NATIONAL
FOREST

14

29-31
Granite
27
28 Twin Mountain
8,920 feet

17 **16**

TO SPRAY   TO LONG CREEK

682

0 1 2 3 4 5 6 7 8 9

N

0   10 mi
0   10 km

CHAPTER C4

1 Boardman Marina Park

 7

This campground is near the Columbia River among maple, sycamore, and linden trees. In addition to fishing for bass, walleye, and crappie, nearby recreation options include a golf course, a marina, and tennis courts.

Location: On the Columbia River; map C4, grid c1.

Campsites, facilities: There are 63 sites for tents, trailers, or RVs of any length. Electricity, drinking water, and sewer hookups are available. Flush toilets, showers, fire grills, a sanitary disposal station, garbage bins, coin-operated laundry facilities, a day-use area with picnic shelters, a pay phone, firewood, and a boat dock are available. A boat marina, gasoline, propane, ice, and a grocery store are available within one mile. Leashed pets are permitted.

Reservations, fees: Reservations accepted; phone (888) 481-7217 or fax (541) 481-2828. Sites are $15-18 per night, $2 per night for a third vehicle. Open year-round.

Directions: From Portland on Highway 84 eastbound, drive 164 miles to Boardman and Exit 164. Take that exit and turn north on Main Street and drive one-half mile to the park.

Contact: Boardman Marina Park, P.O. Box 8, Boardman, OR 97818; tel. (541) 481-7217.

2 Shady Rest Mobile Home Park

    7

This campground is along the Columbia River in a grassy area surrounded by old-growth trees. Nearby recreation includes a golf course, a marina, and tennis courts.

Location: On the Columbia River; map C4, grid c2.

Campsites, facilities: There are 26 drive-through sites for trailers or RVs of any length. Electricity, drinking water, cable TV, and sewer hookups are provided. Flush toilets, showers, a laundry room, and a swimming pool are available. A store, a cafe, and ice are located within one mile. Boat docks and launching facilities are nearby. Leashed pets are permitted.

Reservations, fees: Reservations accepted. Sites are $17 per night. Open year-round.

Directions: From Portland, drive east on U.S. 84 for roughly 170 miles past Boardman to the junction of U.S. 84 and U.S. 730. Turn northeast on U.S. 730 and drive 16 miles to Umatilla and the park at 28716 Highway 730.

Contact: Shady Rest Mobile Home Park, 28716 Highway 730, Umatilla, OR 97882; tel. (541) 922-5041.

3 Dun-Rollin Trailer Park

        8

This RV park is not far from the Columbia River and the Cold Springs National Wildlife Refuge. A golf course, bike paths, a marina, and tennis courts are close by.

Location: Near the Columbia River; map C4, grid c3.

Campsites, facilities: There are 15 sites for trailers or RVs of any length. Electricity, drinking water, and sewer hookups are provided. Flush toilets, sanitary disposal services, showers, laundry facilities, and a playground are available. Bottled gas, a store, a cafe, and ice are located within one mile. Leashed pets and motorbikes are permitted.

Reservations, fees: Reservations accepted. Sites are $15 per night. Open year-round.

Directions: From Pendleton, drive west on U.S. 84 for 25 miles to Stanfield. Turn north on U.S. 395 and drive seven miles to Hermiston and Jennie Avenue. Turn right and drive a half mile to the park on the left.

Contact: Dun-Rollin Trailer Park, 445 East Jennie, Hermiston, OR 97838; tel. (541) 567-6918.

◪ Hat Rock Campground   7

This campground is not far from Hat Rock State Park, a day-use area with a boat launch along the banks of the Columbia River. The campground itself is very pretty, with lots of trees and close access to the river and fishing.

Location: Near the Columbia River; map C4, grid c4.

Campsites, facilities: There are eight tent sites and 60 sites for trailers or RVs of any length, 30 with full and 30 with partial hookups. Electricity, drinking water, sewer hookups, and picnic tables are provided. Flush toilets, sanitary disposal services, showers, a store, a cafe, a laundry room, a swimming pool, and ice are available. Boat docks and launching facilities are nearby. Leashed pets are permitted.

Reservations, fees: Reservations accepted. Sites are $14-15 per night. Open year-round.

Directions: From Portland drive east on U.S. 84 for roughly 170 miles past Boardman to the junction of U.S. 84 and U.S. 730. Turn northeast on U.S. 730 and drive 18 miles to the junction with Interstate 82. Continue east on U.S. 730 for one mile to the state park access road. Turn left (north) and drive one-half mile to the park on the left.

Contact: Hat Rock Campground, 82280 Hatrock Road, Hermiston, OR 97838; tel. (541) 567-4188, or the Hat Rock Store, tel. (541) 567-0917.

◫ Fort Henrietta RV Park

 7

The park is located in the historic community of Echo along the Umatilla River. The river provides some good trout fishing. This is a quiet, pleasant layover spot for travelers cruising Interstate 84.

Location: On the Umatilla River; map C4, grid d3.

Campsites, facilities: There are seven sites for trailers or RVs and an area for dispersed tent camping. Drinking water, rest rooms, showers, and a sanitary dump are provided. Some of the facilities are wheelchair accessible. The camp is within walking distance of two restaurants. Licensed, leashed pets are permitted.

Reservations, fees: No reservations accepted. Sites are $15 per night. Open year-round.

Directions: From Pendleton drive west on Interstate 84 to Exit 188 and the Echo Highway. Take the exit and turn southeast and drive one mile; cross the railroad tracks and drive to Dupont Street. Turn south and drive 0.3 mile to Main Street. Turn west and drive one block to the park on the left.

Contact: Echo City Hall, P.O. Box 9, Echo, OR 97826; tel. (541) 376-8411; fax (541) 376-8218.

6 Brook RV Park   5

This pleasant, riverside suburban park in Pendleton is also on the historic Oregon Trail. Waterfowl can be observed at the McKay Creek National Wildlife Refuge seven miles south of Pendleton. The Pendleton Mills and outlet are in town. Other nearby recreation opportunities include a golf course, bike paths, and tennis courts.

Location: Near the McKay Creek National Wildlife Refuge; map C4, grid d6.

Campsites, facilities: There are 43 sites for trailers or RVs. Electricity, drinking water, sewer hookups, and picnic tables are provided. Flush toilets, cable TV, showers, and a laundry room are available. Bottled gas, sanitary disposal services, a store, and a cafe are located within one mile. Small leashed pets are permitted.

Reservations, fees: Reservations accepted. Sites are $17 per night. Open year-round.

Directions: From Pendleton on Interstate 84, drive east for three miles to Exit 213. Take that exit and drive 2.3 miles to Southeast Eighth Street. Turn right and drive two blocks. Cross the bridge at road's end and enter the park.

Contact: Brook RV Park, Northeast Eighth Street, Pendleton, OR 97801; tel. (541) 276-53535.

7 Emigrant Springs State Heritage Area   7

Perched near the summit of the Blue Mountains, Emigrant Springs provides an opportunity to explore a popular pioneer stopover along the Oregon Trail. The park is nestled in an old-growth forest, lush with flora and teeming with native wildlife. You can explore nearby attractions such as the Blue Mountain Crossing Oregon Trail interpretive park or the Pendleton Woolen Mills and underground tours.

Location: Near the Umatilla Indian Reservation; map C4, grid d8.

Campsites, facilities: There are 33 tent sites, 18 sites with full hookups for trailers or RVs up to 60 feet long, a designated horse camp, and eight cabins. Picnic tables and fire grills are provided. Drinking water, garbage bins, flush toilets, showers, firewood, a laundry room, some horse facilities, a community building with a kitchen, a basketball court, an amphitheater, and a playground are available. Leashed pets are permitted.

Reservations, fees: Reservations accepted; phone (800) 452-5687 ($6 reservation fee). Sites are $7-17 per night; cabins are $20-35 per night, and horse campsites are $7 per horse per night and $1.50 per horse; each additional vehicle is $7 per night. Major credit cards accepted. Open year-round.

Directions: From Pendleton drive southeast on Interstate 84 for 26 miles to Exit 234. Take that exit to Old Oregon Trail Road (frontage road) and drive one-half mile to the park on the right.

Contact: Emigrant Springs State Heritage Area, P.O. Box 85, Meacham, OR 97859; tel. (541) 983-2277.

8 Umatilla Forks   3

It can get very hot at this camp located in a canyon between the South and North Forks of the Umatilla River. Set at 2,400 feet elevation, it has some tree cover, but little privacy between sites. Fishing (catch-and-release only) and hiking in the North Fork Umatilla Wilderness are popular activities from early spring to late fall.

Location: Along the Umatilla River in Umatilla National Forest; map C4, grid d9.

Campsites, facilities: There are seven tent sites and eight sites that can accommodate tents, trailers, or RVs. Drinking water, picnic tables, fire grills, and vault toilets are provided. Garbage bins are available in the summer. Leashed pets are permitted.

Reservations, fees: No reservations. Sites are $8 per night, $5 per night for an additional vehicle. Open April to October.

Directions: From Pendleton drive north on Highway 11 and drive about 25 miles to Athena and Pamgrun Road. Turn right on Pamgrun Road and drive five miles to Spring Hollow Road. Turn left on Spring Hollow Road (it becomes Thorn Hollow Road) and drive about 6.5 miles to Bingham Road (River Road). Turn left on Bingham Road (River Road), cross the railroad tracks, and follow signs for about five miles to Gibbon. Cross the railroad tracks at Gibbon and continue on Bingham Road (becomes Forest Road 32) about 11 miles to the campground on the right.

Contact: Umatilla National Forest, Walla Walla Ranger District, 1415 West Rose Street, Walla Walla, WA 99362; tel. (509) 522-6290; fax (509) 522-6000.

9 Woodward   7

Nestled among the trees at an elevation of 4,950 feet, with some privacy screening between campsites, this popular campground has a view of Langdon Lake (though campers do not have access to the private lake). A flat trail circles the camp.

Location: Near Langdon Lake in Umatilla National Forest; map C4, grid d9.

Campsites, facilities: There are 18 sites for tents, trailers, or RVs. Drinking water, picnic tables, garbage bins, fire grills, and wheelchair-accessible vault toilets are provided. A picnic shelter is available by reservation. Leashed pets are permitted.

Reservations, fees: No reservations accepted. Sites are $10 per night, $5 per night for an additional vehicle. Open mid-June to mid-September.

Directions: From Pendleton on Interstate 84, turn north on Highway 11 and drive approximately 27 miles to Weston and Highway 204. Turn east on Highway 204 and drive 17 miles to the campground along the highway (near Langdon Lake).

Contact: Umatilla National Forest, Walla Walla Ranger District, 1415 West Rose Street, Walla Walla, WA 99362; tel. (509) 525-6290; fax (509) 522-6000.

10 Cutsforth County Park   8

Though just a short jaunt from the interstate, this park is secluded and private. It's set beside a small, wheelchair-accessible pond in a quiet, wooded area. Trout fishing is available in the stocked ponds. See the description of Anson Wright County Park for details on the area.

Location: On Willow Creek; map C4, grid e3.

Campsites, facilities: There are 35 sites for tents, trailers, or RVs up to 30 feet. Rest rooms, showers, horseshoes, firewood, ice, and a playground are provided. Some facilities are wheelchair accessible. Supplies are available in Heppner (22 miles away). Leashed pets are permitted.

Reservations, fees: No reservations accepted. Sites are $6-10 per night. Open May 15 to November 20, weather permitting.

Directions: From Pendleton on Interstate 84, drive west for 27 miles to Highway 207 (Heppner Highway). Turn south and drive 30 miles to Lexington and Highway 74. Turn left on Highway 74 and drive 10.5 miles to Willow Creek Road. Turn left on Willow Creek Road and drive for 23 miles to the park.

Contact: Morrow County Public Works, P.O. Box 428, Lexington, OR 97839; tel. (541) 989-9500; fax (541) 989-8352.

11 Lane Creek   4

This campground is set at 3,850 feet along Camas Creek and Lane Creek, just inside the forest boundary, with easy access to all the amenities of town. It's a popular stop for overnighters passing through. Some of the sites are close enough to the highway to get the noise. Highlights include a hot springs (privately owned) and good hunting and fishing. A U.S. Forest Service map details the back roads.

Location: On Camas Creek in Umatilla National Forest; map C4, grid f6.

Campsites, facilities: There are eight sites for tents, trailers, or RVs up to 45 feet long. Drinking water is available in the summer only. Picnic tables, garbage bins, and fire grills are provided. Vault toilets are available. Leashed pets are permitted.

Reservations, fees: No reservations accepted. Sites are $5 per night. Open March through November.

Directions: From Pendleton drive south on U.S. 395 for 50 miles to Ukiah and Highway 244. Turn east on Highway 244 and drive nine miles to the campground.

Contact: Umatilla National Forest, North Fork John Day Ranger District, P.O. Box 158, Ukiah, OR 97880; tel. (541) 427-3231; fax (541) 276-5026.

12 Bear Wallow Creek   5

Set near the confluence of Bear Wallow and Camus Creeks at an elevation of 3,900 feet, this is one of three camps off Highway 244. The others are Lane Creek and Frazier. It's quiet, primitive, and used primarily in the summer months. A three-quarter-mile interpretive trail highlighting steelhead habitat meanders next to Bear Wallow Creek. The trail is wheelchair accessible.

Location: On Bear Wallow Creek in Umatilla National Forest; map C4, grid f6.

Campsites, facilities: There are eight sites for tents, trailers, or RVs up to 30 feet long. No drinking water is available, and garbage bins are provided in the summer only. Picnic tables and fire grills are provided. Vault toilets are available. Some facilities are wheelchair accessible. Leashed pets are permitted.

Reservations, fees: No reservations accepted. Sites are $5 per night with a 14-day stay limit. Open March through November.

Directions: From Pendleton drive south on U.S. 395 for 50 miles to Ukiah and Highway 244. Turn east on Highway 244 and drive 10 miles to the camp.

Contact: Umatilla National Forest, North Fork John Day Ranger District, P.O. Box 158, Ukiah, OR 97880; tel. (541) 427-3231; fax (541) 276-5026.

13 Frazier   5

This campground set at 4,300 feet along the banks of Frazier Creek is a popular hunting area that also has some fishing. It's advisable to obtain a map of Umatilla National Forest. This campground is popular in the summer with the ATV crowd. There are nearly 100 miles of all-terrain-vehicle and motorcycle trails at the nearby Winom-Frazier Off-Highway-Vehicle Complex. On weekends it's not a good spot for the traditional camper looking for quiet and solitude. Lehman Hot Springs, one mile away, provides a side trip option.

Location: On Frazier Creek in Umatilla National Forest; map C4, grid f7.

Campsites, facilities: There are 18 sites for tents, trailers, or RVs up to 30 feet long and some group sites. Picnic tables, fire grills, a picnic shelter, and vault toilets are available. There is no drinking water and no garbage bins except in summer. Some facilities are wheelchair accessible. An all-terrain-vehicle loading ramp is available. Leashed pets are permitted.

Reservations, fees: No reservations accepted. Sites are $5 per night; group sites are $10 per night. There is no fee. Open March through November.

Directions: From Pendleton drive south on U.S. 395 for 50 miles to Ukiah and Highway 244. Turn east on Highway 244 and drive 16 miles to Forest Road 5226. Turn south and drive a half mile to the campground.

Contact: Umatilla National Forest, North Fork John Day Ranger District, P.O. Box 158, Ukiah, OR 97880; tel. (541) 427-3231; fax (541) 276-5026.

14 Spool Cart   6

This campground set at 3,500 feet elevation on the banks of the Grande Ronde River gets its name from the large cable spools that were left on a cart at the site for some years. Hilgard Junction State Park to the north provides numerous recreation options, and the Oregon Trail Interpretive Park is nearby. This camp is popular with hunters in the fall. It's advisable to obtain a map of Wallowa-Whitman National Forest that details the back roads and other side trips.

Location: On the Grande Ronde River in Wallowa-Whitman National Forest; map C4, grid f9.

Campsites, facilities: There are 16 sites for tents, trailers, or RVs up to 22 feet long. Picnic tables and fire grills are provided. Firewood and vault toilets are available. There is no drinking water, and all garbage must be packed out. Leashed pets are permitted.

Reservations, fees: No reservations. Sites are $8 per night. Open late May to late November.

Directions: From Pendleton drive southeast on U.S. 84 for 42 miles to Highway 244. Turn southwest and drive 13 miles to Forest Road 51. Turn south and drive seven miles to the campground on the right.

Contact: Wallowa-Whitman National Forest, LaGrande Ranger District, 3502 Highway 30, LaGrande, OR 97850; tel. (541) 963-7186; fax (541) 962-8580.

15 Birdtrack Springs   7

Set at an elevation of 3,100 feet about a five-minute walk from the Grande Ronde River, this campground has open, spacious sites right off the highway. Surrounding woods are primarily Douglas and white fir.

Location: Near the Grande Ronde River in Wallowa-Whitman National Forest; map C4, grid f9.

Campsites, facilities: There are 16 sites for tents. Picnic tables, garbage service (summer only), and fire rings are provided. Vault toilets are available. There is no drinking water. Leashed pets are permitted.

Reservations, fees: No reservations. Sites are $8 per night. Open mid-May through November, weather permitting.

Directions: From Pendleton drive southeast on U.S. 84 for 42 miles to Highway 244. Turn southwest and drive 13 miles to the campground on the left.

Contact: Wallowa-Whitman National Forest, LaGrande Ranger District, 3502 Highway 30, LaGrande, OR 97850; tel. (541) 963-7186; fax (541) 962-8580.

16 Bull Prairie   8

This campground is set along the shore of Bull Prairie Lake, a 24-acre lake set at 4,000-foot elevation. Boating (no motors permitted), swimming, fishing, and hunting are some of the options here. A hiking trail circles the lake. This spot attracts little attention from out-of-towners, yet offers plenty of recreation opportunities, making it an ideal vacation destination for many.

Location: On Bull Prairie Lake in Umatilla National Forest; map C4, grid g0.

Campsites, facilities: There are 28 sites for tents, trailers, or RVs up to 31 feet long. Picnic tables and fire grills are provided. Drinking water, sanitary disposal services, garbage bins (summer only), firewood, and vault toilets are available. Boat docks, launching facilities, and a wheelchair-accessible boat ramp are on site. Pets are permitted.

Reservations, fees: No reservations accepted. Sites are $12 per night, $5 per night for an additional vehicle. Open May to October.

Directions: From U.S. 84 at Heppner Junction and Exit 147, turn south on Highway 74 and drive 45 miles to Heppner and Highway 207. Turn right on Highway 207 and drive roughly 35 miles to the national forest boundary and continue four miles to Forest Road 2039 (paved). Turn left and drive three miles northeast to the campground on the right.

Contact: Umatilla National Forest, Heppner Ranger District, P.O. Box 7, Heppner, OR 97836; tel. (541) 676-9187; fax (541) 676-2105.

17 Fairview 5

This rugged and primitive campground adjacent to Fairview Springs near Mahogany Butte is a small campsite known by very few people. Located in a remote area at 4,300 feet, it's primarily used as a base camp by hunters. Very easy to miss—and not even marked on maps for the Umatilla National Forest.

Location: Near Bull Prairie Lake in Umatilla National Forest; map C4, grid g0.

Campsites, facilities: There are five sites for trailers or RVs up to 16 feet long. Picnic tables and fire grills are provided. Firewood and vault toilets are available. There is no drinking water and all garbage must be packed out. Boat docks and launching facilities are nearby at Bull Prairie Lake. Leashed pets are permitted.

Reservations, fees: No reservations; no fee. Open May to late October.

Directions: From U.S. 84 at Heppner Junction and Exit 147, turn south on Highway 74 and drive 45 miles to Heppner and Highway 207. Turn right on Highway 207 and drive roughly 35 miles to the national forest boundary. Continue four miles to Forest Road 2039 (the turnoff for Bull Prairie Lake). Continue on Highway 207 for one mile to Forest Road 400 (if you pass through the immediate series of hairpin turns, you have gone too far). Turn west and drive 500 yards to the campground

Contact: Umatilla National Forest, Heppner Ranger District, P.O. Box 7, Heppner, OR 97836; tel. (541) 676-9187; fax (541) 676-2105.

18 Anson Wright County Park 7

Set within wooded hills on a small stream, this county park offers visitors prime trout fishing in several stocked ponds as well as hiking opportunities. There is a wheelchair-accessible fishing pond. Attractions in the area include the Pendleton Mills, Emigrant Springs State Park, Hardman Ghost Town (10 miles away), and the Columbia River. There's also a nearby opal mine.

Location: On Rock Creek; map C4, grid g1.

Campsites, facilities: There are 34 sites for tents, trailers, or RVs up to 30 feet. Rest rooms, showers, a barbecue, firewood, ice, and a playground are provided. Some facilities are wheelchair accessible. Leashed pets are permitted.

Reservations, fees: No reservations accepted. Sites are $6-10 per night. Open May 16 to November 16, weather permitting.

Directions: On U.S. 84 drive to Exit 182 and the junction of Highway 207. Take that exit and drive southwest on Highway 207 and drive 46 miles to the park access road (signed). Turn south and drive 21 miles to the park.

Contact: Morrow County Public Works, P.O. Box 428, Lexington, OR 97839; tel. (541) 989-9500.

19 Divide Well 5

This is a primitive, remote and little-used campground. It is set at 4,700 feet and can serve as a good base camp for a hunting trip. Mule deer and Rocky Mountain elk can be spotted in the surrounding ponderosa pine and fir forest. Potamus Point Scenic Overlook, offering a spectacular view of the John Day River drainage, is 11 miles south of the camp on Forest Road 5316.

Location: In Umatilla National Forest; map C4, grid g4.

Campsites, facilities: There are 11 primitive tent sites and three primitive group sites. Picnic tables and a vault toilet are provided, but there is no drinking water. Pack out all garbage. Leashed pets are permitted.

Reservations, fees: No reservations; no fee. Open March through November.

Directions: From Pendleton drive south on U.S. 395 for 50 miles to Highway 244. Turn east on Highway 244 and drive one mile to Ukiah and Forest Road 52. Turn south on Forest Road 52 and drive 10 miles southeast to Forest Road 5312. Turn left and drive six miles to Forest Road 5320 and drive one mile to Forest Road 5327. Turn right and drive a half mile to the campground. A U.S. Forest Service map is recommended.

Contact: Umatilla National Forest, North Fork John Day Ranger District, P.O. Box 158, Ukiah, OR 97880; tel. (541) 427-3231; fax (541) 276-5026.

20 Ukiah-Dale Forest State Recreation Site   7

Fishing is a prime activity at this campground on Camas Creek, set at an elevation of 3,140 feet near the banks of the North Fork of the John Day River. It's a good layover for visitors cruising U.S. 395 looking for a spot for the night. Emigrant Springs State Park near Pendleton is a possible side trip.

Location: Near the North Fork of the John Day River; map C4, grid g5.

Campsites, facilities: There are 28 primitive sites for tents, trailers, or self-contained RVs up to 50 feet long. Picnic tables and fire pits are provided. Drinking water, firewood, and flush toilets are available. Leashed pets are permitted.

Reservations, fees: No reservations accepted. Sites are $7-11 per night. Open mid-April to late October.

Directions: From Pendleton drive south on U.S. 395 for 50 miles to Highway 244 (near Ukiah). Continue south on U.S. 395 for three miles to the park.

Contact: Ukiah-Dale Forest State Recreation Site, P.O. Box 85, Meacham, OR 97859; tel. (800) 551-6949, (541) 983-2277.

21 Tollbridge   4

This small, secluded campground (elevation 3,800 feet) lies at the confluence of Desolation Creek and the North Fork of the John Day River, and is adjacent to the Bridge Creek Wildlife Area. It can be beautiful or ugly, depending upon which direction you look. It's dusty in the summer, and there's sparse tree cover. Hunting and fishing are two options here. There's a geological interpretive sign in the camp.

Location: On the North Fork of the John Day River in Umatilla National Forest; map C4, grid g5.

Campsites, facilities: There are seven sites for tents, trailers, or RVs up to 31 feet long. Picnic tables and fire grills are provided. Drinking water and a vault toilet are available, but all garbage must be packed out. Leashed pets are permitted.

Reservations, fees: No reservations. Sites are $5 per night, with a 14-day stay limit. Open year-round, with no winter maintenance (November through March).

Directions: From Pendleton drive south on U.S. 395 for 50 miles to the intersection with Highway 244. Continue south on U.S. 395 for 18 miles to Forest Road 55 (one mile north of Dale). Turn left and drive one-half mile southeast to Forest Road 10. Turn and drive a short distance to the campground.

Contact: Umatilla National Forest, North Fork John Day Ranger District, P.O. Box 158, Ukiah, OR 97880; tel. (541) 427-3231; fax (541) 276-5026.

22 Drift Fence   5

Get this: It's not marked on the Umatilla National Forest Map. Hunting is a highlight at this campground set at 4,250 feet, with some elk and deer in the area. The camp is adjacent to Blue Mountain National Forest Scenic Byway. The Bridge Creek Interpretive Trail, located three miles northwest of the campground off Forest Road 52, leads to a beautiful view of open meadow with various wildflowers and wildlife. Elk may be seen roaming in the Bridge Creek area. A number of diseased trees have been cut down here in an attempt to curtail the disease's spread.

Location: Near Ross Springs in Umatilla National Forest; map C4, grid g5.

Campsites, facilities: There are six sites for tents, trailers, or RVs up to 16 feet long. There is no drinking water, and all garbage must be packed out. A vault toilet and picnic tables are available. Leashed pets are permitted.

Reservations, fees: No reservations; no fee. Open March through November.

Directions: From Pendleton drive south on U.S. 395 for 50 miles to Highway 244. Turn east on Highway 244 and drive one mile to Ukiah and Forest Road 52. Turn south on Forest Road 52 and drive eight miles to the campground on the right.

Contact: Umatilla National Forest, North Fork John Day Ranger District, P.O. Box 158, Ukiah, OR 97880; tel. (541) 427-3231; fax (541) 276-5026.

23 Gold Dredge Camp   7

Hunting and fishing are among the possibilities at this campground along the banks of the North Fork of the John Day River, a federally certified Wild and Scenic river. Dredge tailings from old mining activity are visible from the camp. By traveling to the end of Forest Road 5506, you can access a trail that heads into the adjacent North Fork John Day Wilderness.

Location: On the North Fork of the John Day River in Umatilla National Forest; map C4, grid g6.

Campsites, facilities: There are six sites for tents, trailers, or RVs. No drinking water or fire grills are provided, but vault toilets and picnic tables are available. All garbage must be packed out. Leashed pets are permitted.

Reservations, fees: No reservations; no fee. Open March through November.

Directions: From Pendleton drive south on U.S. 395 for 62 miles to Forest Road 55 (one mile north of Dale). Turn left and drive six miles to the crossroads. Continue east on Forest Road 5506 for 2.5 miles to the campground. Note: The last two miles of road are very rough).

Contact: Umatilla National Forest, North Fork John Day Ranger District, P.O. Box 158, Ukiah, OR 97880; tel. (541) 427-3231; fax (541) 276-5026.

24 Oriental Creek   4

This campground is set in a stand of mixed conifer at 3,500 feet along the banks of the North Fork of the John Day River and is popular with horse campers. Evidence of old mining activity is visible here. Nearby trails provide access to the North Fork John Day Wilderness. Hunting and fishing are two possible activities here. No motorbikes are permitted in the wilderness area. Be advised that the road in to this campground is rough and narrow in places.

Location: On the North Fork of the John Day River in Umatilla National Forest; map C4, grid g6.

Campsites, facilities: There are seven primitive tent sites. Pit toilets and picnic tables are available, but there is no drinking water. All garbage must be packed out. One toilet is wheelchair accessible. Leashed pets are permitted.

Reservations, fees: No reservations; no fee. Open March through November.

Directions: From Pendleton drive south on U.S. 395 for 62 miles to Forest Road 55 (one mile north of Dale). Turn left and drive six miles to the crossroads. Continue east on Forest Road 5506 for six miles to the campground. This road is rough and not recommended for trailers.

Contact: Umatilla National Forest, North Fork John Day Ranger District, P.O. Box 158, Ukiah, OR 97880; tel. (541) 427-3231; fax (541) 276-5026.

25 Driftwood   6

This tiny campground with ponderosa pine and Douglas fir cover, is located on the banks of the North Fork of the John Day River at an elevation of 3,855 feet. Recreational opportunities include hunting, fishing, swimming, rafting, and float tubing. It is similar to Gold Dredge Campground.

Location: On the North Fork of the John Day River in Umatilla National Forest; map C4, grid g6.

Campsites, facilities: There are five sites for tents and trailers. A vault toilet and picnic tables are provided, but there is no drinking water. All garbage must be packed out. Leashed pets are permitted.

Reservations, fees: No reservations; no fee. Open March through November.

Directions: From Pendleton drive south on U.S. 395 for 62 miles to Forest Road 55 (one mile north of Dale). Turn left and drive six miles to the crossroads. Continue east on Forest Road 5506 for one mile to the campground. Note: The last two miles of road are very rough.

Contact: Umatilla National Forest, North Fork John Day Ranger District, P.O. Box 158, Ukiah, OR 97880; tel. (541) 427-3231; fax (541) 276-5026.

26 Welch Creek   5

This primitive camp is located on the banks of Desolation Creek. Road noise may be a problem for some, and there's little privacy among sites. There's trail access to the Desolation Area, both for non-motorized and motorized traffic. Hunting and fishing are popular here.

Location: On Desolation Creek in Umatilla National Forest; map C4, grid g6.

Campsites, facilities: There are five primitive tent sites. Picnic tables and a vault toilet are provided, but there is no drinking water. All garbage must be packed out. Leashed pets are permitted.

Reservations, fees: No reservations; no fee. Open March through November.

Directions: From Pendleton drive south on U.S. 395 for 62 miles to Forest Road 55 (one mile north of Dale). Turn left and drive and drive one mile to Forest Road 10. Turn right and drive 13 miles to the campground.

Contact: Umatilla National Forest, North Fork John Day Ranger District, P.O. Box 158, Ukiah, OR 97880; tel. (541) 427-3231; fax (541) 276-5026.

27 Winom Creek   2

This campground has access to the Winom ATV Trail Complex, 140 miles of ATV trails of varying difficulty. It was developed in the late '80s for ATV enthusiasts. Check the campground bulletin boards for detailed maps of the terrain. The camp is also near the John Day North Fork Wilderness. Note that a fire during the 1990s burned a portion of the campground and surrounding area, but with the arrival of the new century, it is beginning to green up again.

Location: On Winom Creek in Umatilla National Forest; map C4, grid g7.

Campsites, facilities: There are five sites for tents, trailers, or RVs, and three group sites. Picnic tables and fire rings are provided. Vault toilets and an ATV loading ramp are available. There is no drinking water, and garbage must be packed out. Two of the group sites have picnic shelters. Some facilities are wheelchair accessible.

Reservations, fees: No reservations; no fee. Open March through November, weather permitting.

Directions: From Pendleton drive south on U.S. 395 for 50 miles to Highway 244. Turn east on Highway 244 and drive one mile to Ukiah and Forest Road 52. Turn south on Forest Road 52 and drive 20 miles to Forest Road 440. Turn right and drive one mile to the campground on the right. The last mile of the access road is narrow and steep.

Contact: Umatilla National Forest, North Fork John Day Ranger District, P.O. Box 158, Ukiah, OR 97880; tel. (541) 427-3231; fax (541) 276-5026.

28 North Fork John Day   6

This campground is located in a conifer stand along the banks of the North Fork of the John Day River and is an ideal base camp for a wilderness backpacking trip. There's a great view of salmon spawning in the river in the fall. A horse-handling area is also available for wilderness users. Trails from camp lead into the North Fork John Day Wilderness. The camp is set at an elevation of 5,200 feet at the intersection of Elkhorn and Blue Mountain National Forest Scenic Byways. No motorbikes are permitted in the wilderness.

Location: On the North Fork of the John Day River in Umatilla National Forest; map C4, grid g8.

Campsites, facilities: There are 15 sites for tents, trailers, or RVs up to 22 feet

long, and two additional tent-only sites. Picnic tables and fire grills are provided. Vault toilets are available. There is no drinking water. All garbage must be packed out. Leashed pets are permitted.

Reservations, fees: No reservations. Sites are $5 per night, with a 14-day stay limit. Open March through November.

Directions: From Pendleton drive south on U.S. 395 for 50 miles to Highway 244. Turn east on Highway 244 and drive one mile to Ukiah and Forest Road 52. Turn south on Forest Road 52 and drive 36 miles to the campground.

Contact: Umatilla National Forest, North Fork John Day Ranger District, P.O. Box 158, Ukiah, OR 97880; tel. (541) 427-3231; fax (541) 276-5026.

29 Anthony Lakes

 10

This campground is set at 7,100 feet elevation, adjacent to Anthony Lake, where boating without motors is permitted. Sites are wooded with good screening between them. Alas, mosquitoes are often in particular abundance. Several smaller lakes within two miles by car or trail are ideal for trout fishing from a raft, float tube, or canoe. Sometimes mountain goats can be seen from the Elkhorn Crest Trail, which begins near here. Weekends and holidays are full.

Location: On Anthony Lake in Wallowa-Whitman National Forest; map C4, grid g9.

Campsites, facilities: There are 37 sites for tents, trailers, or RVs up to 22 feet long. Drinking water, fire grills, garbage bins (summer only), and picnic tables are provided. Vault toilets are available. Some facilities are wheelchair accessible. Boat launching facilities are nearby. Leashed pets are permitted.

Reservations, fees: No reservations. Sites are $8 per night. Open July to late September.

Directions: From Baker City on Interstate 84, turn north on U.S. 30. Drive north for 10 miles to Haines and County Road 1146 (signed for Anthony Lakes Ski Resort). Turn left on County Road 1146 and drive 20 miles (the road becomes Forest Road 73) to the campground on the left.

Contact: Wallowa-Whitman National Forest, Baker Ranger District, 3165 10th Street. Baker City, OR 97814; tel. (541) 523-1932; fax (541) 523-1965.

30 Grande Ronde Lake

 8

This campground is located in Douglas and white fir, set at an elevation of 6,800 feet along the shore of Grande Ronde Lake, a small lake where the trout fishing can be good. Mountain goats are sometimes seen in the area. Several trails are to the south near Anthony Lake. A map of Wallowa-Whitman National Forest details the possibilities.

Location: On Grande Ronde Lake in Wallowa-Whitman National Forest; map C4, grid g9.

Campsites, facilities: There are eight sites for tents, trailers, or RVs up to 16 feet long. Picnic tables and fire grills are provided. Drinking water and vault toilets are available, but garbage must be packed out. Boat docks and launching facilities are nearby. Leashed pets are permitted.

Reservations, fees: No reservations accepted. Sites are $8 per night. Open July to mid-September.

Directions: From Baker City on Interstate 84, turn north on U.S. 30. Drive north for 10 miles to Haines and County Road 1146 (signed for Anthony Lakes Ski Resort). Turn left on County Road 1146 and drive 20 miles (the road becomes Forest Road 73) to the campground on the right.

Contact: Wallowa-Whitman National Forest, Baker Ranger District, 3160 10th Street, Baker City, OR 97814; tel. (541) 523-4476; fax (541) 523-1965.

31 Mud Lake  7

This campground is in fir forest on the shore of small Mud Lake, where the trout fishing can be fairly good. Mud Lack is shallow and more marshy than muddy. The campground is tiny and pleasant, set at an elevation of 7,100 feet, with lots of vegetation and relatively little use. Bring your mosquito repellent.

Location: On Mud Lake in Wallowa-Whitman National Forest; map C4, grid g9.

Campsites, facilities: There are three tent sites and five sites for trailers or RVs up to 16 feet long. Picnic tables and fire grills are provided. Drinking water and vault toilets are available, but all garbage must be packed out. Boat docks and launching facilities are located nearby at Anthony Lake. Leashed pets are permitted.

Reservations, fees: No reservations accepted. Sites are $8 per night. Open July to mid-September.

Directions: From Baker City on Interstate 84, turn north on U.S. 30. Drive north for 10 miles to Haines and County Road 1146 (signed for Anthony Lakes Ski Resort). Turn left on County Road 1146 and drive 21 miles (the road becomes Forest Road 73) to the campground on the left.

Contact: Wallowa-Whitman National Forest, Baker Ranger District, 3165 10th Street, Baker City, OR 97814; tel. (541) 523-1932; fax (541) 523-1965.

CONTEMPLATING A STREAM

MAP C5

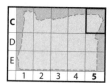

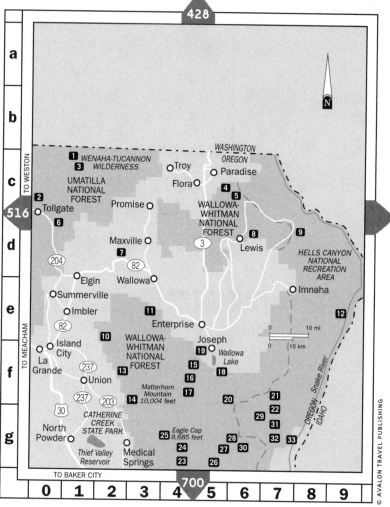

CHAPTER C5

1 Mottet 6

This campground is set at 5,200 feet along a ridgetop in a heavily timbered forest. A trailhead is available that leads down to the South Fork of the Walla Walla River. Located far from the beaten path, it's quite primitive and relatively unknown, so you're almost guaranteed privacy.

Location: Near the South Fork of the Walla Walla River in Umatilla National Forest; map C5, grid c1.

Campsites, facilities: There are seven sites for tents, trailers, or RVs. Picnic tables and fire grills are provided. Spring water and vault toilets are available. Trash must be packed out; no garbage facilities are provided. Leashed pets are permitted.

Reservations, fees: No reservations; no fee. Open late June to mid-October, weather permitting.

Directions: From Pendleton drive north on Highway 11 and drive 16 miles to Highway 204 near Weston. Turn east on Highway 204 and drive 17.5 miles to Forest Road 64. Turn left and drive about 15 miles on Forest Road 64 to Forest Road 6403. Turn left and drive about two miles to the campground on the left. The road is rough for the last 1.5 miles.

Contact: Umatilla National Forest, Walla Walla Ranger District, 1415 West Rose Street, Walla Walla, WA 99362; tel. (509) 522-6290; fax (509) 522-6000.

2 Target Meadows 6

This quiet campground with shady sites and a sunny meadow is set at 4,800 feet, adjacent to the Burnt Cabin Trailhead, which leads to the South Fork of the Walla Walla River. An old military site can be viewed here.

Location: Near the South Fork of the Walla Walla River in Umatilla National Forest; map C5, grid c0.

Campsites, facilities: There are four tent sites and seven for tents, trailers, or RVs. Drinking water, garbage bins, picnic tables, fire grills, and vault toilets are provided. Leashed pets are permitted.

Reservations, fees: No reservations accepted. Sites are $10 per night, $5 per night for an additional vehicle. Open mid-June to mid-September.

Directions: From Pendleton drive north on Highway 11 and drive 16 miles to Highway 204 near Weston. Turn east on Highway 204 and drive 17.5 miles to Forest Road 64. Turn left and drive one-half mile to Forest Road 6401. Turn left (north) and drive two miles to Road 6401-050. Turn north and drive a half mile to the camp.

Contact: Umatilla National Forest, Walla Walla Ranger District, 1415 West Rose Street, Walla Walla, WA 99362; tel. (509) 522-6290; fax (509) 522-6000.

3 Jubilee Lake   8

This campground along the shore of 90-acre Jubilee Lake (elevation 4,800 feet) is a good area for swimming, fishing, and hiking. This is the largest and most popular campground in Umatilla National Forest, and it fills up on weekends and holidays. Non-motorized boats are permitted. A 2.8-mile trail loops around the lake and is designated to provide different levels of handicapped accessibility. Fishing access is available along the trail.

Location: On Jubilee Lake in Umatilla National Forest; map C5, grid c1.

Campsites, facilities: There are 51 sites for tents, trailers, or RVs up to 27 feet long, with some drive-through sites. Picnic tables and fire grills are provided. Drinking water, firewood, four picnic areas, and flush toilets are available. Some facilities are barrier-free. Boat docks and launching facilities are nearby. Leashed pets are permitted. Garbage service is provided during the summer.

Reservations, fees: No reservations accepted. Sites are $14 per night, plus $5 for each additional vehicle. Open mid-June through September.

Directions: From Pendleton drive north on Highway 11 and drive 16 miles to Highway 204 near Weston. Turn east on Highway 204 and drive 17.5 miles to Forest Road 64. Turn left and drive 12 miles northeast to Forest Road 250. Turn south and drive less than a half mile to the camp.

Contact: Umatilla National Forest, Walla Walla Ranger District, 1415 West Rose Street, Walla Walla, WA 99362; tel. (509) 522-6290; fax (509) 522-6000.

4 Coyote   4

This campground set at 4,800 feet adjacent to Coyote Springs is the largest of the three primitive camps in the vicinity, offering open sites and privacy.

Location: Near Coyote Springs in Wallowa-Whitman National Forest; map C5, grid c5.

Campsites, facilities: There are 29 sites for tents, trailers, or RVs up to 22 feet long. Picnic tables and fire grills are provided. Vault toilets are available, but there is no drinking water, and all garbage must be packed out. A spring is located within one-quarter mile. Pets are permitted.

Reservations, fees: No reservations; no fee. Open mid-May to December.

Directions: From LaGrande drive northeast on Highway 82 for 62 miles to Enterprise and Highway 3. Turn north on Highway 3 and drive 15 miles to Forest Road 46. Turn northeast and drive 25 miles to the campground.

Contact: Wallowa-Whitman National Forest, Wallowa Valley Ranger District, Wallowa Mountains Visitor Center, 88401 Highway 82, Enterprise, OR 97828; tel. (541) 426-5546.

5 Dougherty Springs   5

This wooded, primitive campground (elevation 5,100 feet) adjacent to Dougherty Springs is one in a series of remote camps set near natural springs. This camp is located in an open area in sparse Douglas and white fir. Deer, elk, birds and small mammals can be seen in the area. Hells Canyon National Recreation Area to the east provides many recreation options.

Location: Near Dougherty Springs in Wallowa-Whitman National Forest; map C5, grid c6.

Campsites, facilities: There are 12 sites for tents, trailers, or RVs up to 22 feet long. Picnic tables and fire grills are provided. Vault toilets are available, but there is no drinking water, and all garbage must be packed out. Pets are permitted.

Reservations, fees: No reservations; no fee. Open June to late November.

Directions: From LaGrande drive northeast on Highway 82 for 62 miles to Enterprise and Highway 3. Turn north on Highway 3 and drive 15 miles to Forest Road 46. Turn northeast and drive 30 miles to the campground.

Contact: Hells Canyon National Recreation Area, Wallowa Mountains Visitor Center, 88401 Highway 82, Enterprise, OR 97828; tel. (541) 426-5546.

6 Woodland   4

This primitive camp with easy highway access and related road noise can be a perfect spot for Interstate 84 cruisers looking for a short detour. Both shaded and sunny sites are available. It is popular with hunters during the fall. See a U.S. Forest Service map for details about the recreation options within driving distance.

Location: In Umatilla National Forest; map C5, grid d0.

Campsites, facilities: There are six sites for tents, trailers, or RVs. Picnic tables, fire grills, and vault toilets are provided, but there is no drinking water. No garbage facilities are provided, so campers must pack out their own trash. Leashed pets are permitted.

Reservations, fees: No reservations accepted. Sites are $5 per night. Open mid-June to mid-November, weather permitting.

Directions: From Pendleton drive north on Highway 11 and drive 16 miles to Highway 204 near Weston. Turn east on Highway 204 and drive 23 miles. The campground is located just off the highway on the left.

Contact: Umatilla National Forest, Walla Walla Ranger District, 1415 West Rose Street, Walla Walla, WA 99362; tel. (509) 522-6290; fax (509) 522-6000.

7 Minam State Park   7

Located in a remote, steep valley, large pine trees dominate the landscape of this park. The Wallowa River flows through the park and is noted for fishing and rafting, especially for spring and fall steelhead fishing. Wildlife is abundant, including deer, elk, bear, cougar, and occasionally, mountain sheep down river. This is a good launch point to float the wild and scenic Grande Ronde River. The park is small and pretty, and well worth the detour off Interstate 84.

Location: Near the Grande Ronde River; map C5, grid d2.

Campsites, facilities: There are 12 primitive sites for tents, trailers, or self-contained RVs up to 71 feet long. Picnic tables and fire grills are provided. Drinking water, garbage bins, and pit toilets are available. Raft rentals are available nearby. Leashed pets are permitted.

Reservations, fees: No reservations accepted. Sites are $7-10 per night, $7 per night for an additional vehicle. Open year-round.

Directions: From LaGrande drive northeast on Highway 82 for 18 miles to Elgin; then continue 14 miles to the park entrance road. Turn left (north) and drive one-half mile to the park.

Contact: Minam State Park, 72214 Marina Lane, Joseph, OR 97846; tel. (541) 432-8855, (800) 551-6949.

🎱 Vigne   5

This campground, at 3,500 feet elevation along the banks of Chesnimnus Creek, has pretty, shaded riverside sites among Douglas and white fir. Fishing is a recreation possibility here, along with exploring a few of the many hiking trails in the area. See a U.S. Forest Service map for details.

Location: On Chesnimnus Creek in Wallowa-Whitman National Forest; map C5, grid d6.

Campsites, facilities: There are seven sites for tents, trailers, or RVs up to 22 feet long. Picnic tables and fire grills are provided. Vault toilets are available, but there is no drinking water and all garbage must be packed out. Pets are permitted.

Reservations, fees: No reservations; no fee. Open mid-April to late November.

Directions: From LaGrande drive northeast on Highway 82 for 62 miles to Enterprise and Highway 3. Turn north on Highway 3 and drive 15 miles to Forest Road 46. Turn northeast and drive 10 miles to Forest Road 4625. Turn east and drive 10 miles to the campground.

Contact: Wallowa-Whitman National Forest, Wallowa Valley Ranger District; Wallowa Mountains Visitor Center, 88401 Highway 82, Enterprise, OR 97828; tel. (541) 426-5546.

🎱 Buckhorn   8

Set at 5,200 feet elevation, adjacent to Buckhorn Springs, this small, primitive, and obscure camp gets little use. The elevation offers a spectacular view of the Imnaha River drainage.

Location: Near Buckhorn Overlook in Wallowa-Whitman National Forest; map C5, grid d7.

Campsites, facilities: There are six sites for tents or trailers. Picnic tables and fire grills are provided. Vault toilets are available, but there is no drinking water and all garbage must be packed out. Leashed pets are permitted.

Reservations, fees: No reservations; no fee. Open June to late November.

Directions: From LaGrande drive northeast on Highway 82 for 62 miles to Enterprise. Continue east for three miles on Highway 83 to County Road 772. Turn north and drive 32 miles to a junction at Thomason Meadows. Continue straight on Forest Road 46 for 10 miles to Forest Road 780. Turn right and drive one-quarter mile to the campground.

Contact: Hells Canyon National Recreation Area; Wallowa Mountains Visitor Center, 88401 Highway 82, Enterprise, OR 97828; tel. (541) 426-5546.

10 Hot Lake RV Resort

 8

This camp is located on the shore of Hot Lake, where fishing, boating, hunting, and swimming are all possible. It's also on the historic Old Oregon Trail. Attractions in the area include Hilgard Junction State Park and Wallowa-Whitman National Forest.

Location: On Hot Lake; map C5, grid e2.

Campsites, facilities: There are 100 wide sites for tents, trailers, or RVs. Drinking water, rest rooms, showers, laundry facilities, groceries, a sanitary dump station, a public phone, a swimming pool, a hot spa, ice, and RV supplies are available. Some facilities are wheelchair accessible. Leashed pets are permitted.

Reservations, fees: Reservations recommended. Sites are $22 per night. Open year-round.

Directions: At the junction of Interstate 84 and Highway 203 one mile south of La Grande drive southeast on Highway 203 for five miles to Foothill Road. Turn left and drive three-tenths of a mile to the resort.

Contact: Hot Lake RV Resort, 65182 Hot Lake Lane, LaGrande, OR 97850; tel. (541) 963-5253.

11 Boundary   6

This pretty, private campground is set 100 yards from the banks of Bear Creek at 3,600 feet elevation and is heavily wooded with tamarack, Douglas, red, and white fir. Nearby trails provide access to the Eagle Cap Wilderness. This is another in a series of little-known primitive sites in the area.

Location: Near the Eagle Cap Wilderness in Wallowa-Whitman National Forest; map C5, grid e3.

Campsites, facilities: There are eight primitive tent sites. There is no drinking water and all garbage must be packed out. Pets are permitted.

Reservations, fees: No reservations; no fee. Open mid-June to November.

Directions: From LaGrande drive north on Highway 82 for 46 miles to Wallowa and Forest Road 8250. Turn south and drive eight miles to Forest Road 8250-040. Turn south and drive three-quarters of a mile to the camp.

Contact: Wallowa-Whitman National Forest, Eagle Cap Ranger District; Wallowa Mountains Visitor Center, 88401 Highway 82, Enterprise, OR 97828; tel. (541) 426-5546.

12 Saddle Creek   8

This campground is set at 6,800 feet in a wooded environment, on a ridge between two canyons, providing excellent views of the Seven Devil Mountains. Nearby trails provide access to Saddle Creek and Hells Canyon National Recreation Area. Note that a fire here has left its mark on the area.

Location: Near the Hells Canyon Wilderness in Wallowa-Whitman National Forest; map C5, grid e9.

Campsites, facilities: There are seven sites for tents. Picnic tables and fire grills are provided. Vault toilets are available, but there is no drinking water and all garbage must be packed out. Leashed pets are permitted. Note: RVs and trailers are not recommended on the access road.

Reservations, fees: No reservations; no fee. Open July to mid-November.

Directions: From LaGrande turn north on Highway 82 and drive 62 miles to Enterprise and the junction of Highway 3. At the junction bear south on Highway 82 and drive six miles to Joseph and Highway 350. Turn east on Highway 350 and drive 30 miles to the small town of Imnaha Forest Road 4240. Drive straight up the hill on Forest Road 4240 and continue 19 miles to the campground.

Contact: Hells Canyon National Recreation Area; Wallowa Mountains Visitor Center, 88401 Highway 82, Enterprise, OR 97828; tel. (541) 426-5546.

🔲 13 Moss Springs   7

At 5,400 feet, this campground provides good views of the Grande Ronde Valley. A trailhead at this camp provides access to the Eagle Cap Wilderness, a good jump-off point for a multi-day backpacking trip. Obtain a map of Wallowa-Whitman National Forest for detailed trail information. This camp is also a popular spot with horse packers. A loading ramp is provided.

Location: Near the Eagle Cap Wilderness in Wallowa-Whitman National Forest; map C5, grid f2.

Campsites, facilities: There are 11 tent and trailer sites. Picnic tables and fire grills are provided. No drinking water, but horse facilities and vault toilets are available. All garbage must be packed out. Leashed pets are permitted.

Reservations, fees: No reservations. Sites are $8 per night. Open June to mid-October.

Directions: From LaGrande drive east on Highway 237 for 15 miles to Cove and County Road 237. Turn southeast and drive 1.5 miles to Forest Road 6220. Turn east and drive eight miles to the camp entrance.

Contact: Wallowa-Whitman National Forest, LaGrande Ranger District, 3502 Highway 30, LaGrande, OR 97850; tel. (541) 963-7186; fax (541) 962-8580.

🔲 14 North Fork
Catherine Trailhead   5

This campground along the North Fork of Catherine Creek is located near a trailhead that provides access to various lakes and streams in the Eagle Cap Wilderness. The elevation here is 4,400 feet. It's a good starting point for a hiking trip. The camp is popular with hunters in the fall. A national forest map details the possibilities.

Location: Near the Eagle Cap Wilderness in Wallowa-Whitman National Forest; map C5, grid f3.

Campsites, facilities: There are six sites for tents or trailers. Picnic tables and fire grills are provided. Vault toilets are available. There is no drinking water, and all garbage must be packed out. Pets are permitted.

Reservations, fees: No reservations; no fee. Open June to late October.

Directions: From LaGrande drive southeast on Highway 203 for 14 miles to

Union. Continue southeast on Highway 203 for 10 miles to Forest Road 7785. Turn east and drive four miles east on Forest Road 7785 to a fork. Bear left at the fork (still on 7785) and drive 3.5 miles northeast to the camp.
Contact: Wallowa-Whitman National Forest, LaGrande Ranger District, 3502 Highway 30, LaGrande, OR 97850; tel. (541) 963-7186; fax (541) 962-8580.

15 Hurricane Creek   5

This campground along Hurricane Creek at an elevation of 5,000 feet, is on the edge of the Eagle Cap Wilderness and is a good place to begin a backcountry backpacking trip. There is no access for RVs, providing more of a wilderness environment. Obtaining maps of the area from the ranger district is essential.
Location: Near the Eagle Cap Wilderness in Wallowa-Whitman National Forest; map C5, grid f4.
Campsites, facilities: There are eight tent sites. Picnic tables and fire grills are provided. Firewood and vault toilets are available, but there is no drinking water, and all garbage must be packed out. Leashed pets are permitted.
Reservations, fees: No reservations; no fee. Open mid-June to late October.
Directions: From LaGrande turn north on Highway 82 and drive 62 miles to Enterprise and the junction with Highway 3. Continue south on Highway 82 to Joseph and Forest Road 8205. Turn southwest and drive 3.5 miles to the campground.
Contact: Wallowa-Whitman National Forest, Eagle Cap Ranger District,. Wallowa Mountains Visitor Center, 88401 Highway 82, Enterprise, OR 97828.

16 Shady    6

This campground along the banks of the Lostine River at an elevation of 5,400 feet is close to trails that provide access to the Eagle Cap Wilderness, a beautiful and pristine area that's perfect for an extended backpacking trip. The camp has wooded as well as meadow areas. Mountain sheep can sometimes be spotted.
Location: On the Lostine River in Wallowa-Whitman National Forest; map C5, grid f4.
Campsites, facilities: There are 12 sites for tents, trailers, or RVs up to 16 feet long. Vault toilets are available, but there is no drinking water, and all garbage must be packed out. Picnic tables and fire grills are provided. Pets are permitted.
Reservations, fees: No reservations; no fee. Open mid-June to November.
Directions: From LaGrande turn north on Highway 82 and drive 52 miles to Lostine and Forest Road 8210. Turn south and drive 15 miles to the campground.
Contact: Wallowa-Whitman National Forest, Eagle Cap Ranger District; Wallowa Mountains Visitor Center, 88401 Highway 82, Enterprise, OR 97828; tel. (541) 426-5546.

17 Two Pan   6

This campground lies at the end of a Forest Road on the banks of the Lostine River. Adjacent trails provide access to numerous lakes and streams in the Eagle Cap Wilderness. At 5,600 feet, this is a prime jump-off spot for a multi-day wilderness adventure. Another campground option is Williamson, seven miles north on Forest Road 8210, or Shady.

Location: On the Lostine River in Wallowa-Whitman National Forest; map C5, grid f4.

Campsites, facilities: There are eight tent or trailer sites. Vault toilets are available, but there is no drinking water, and all garbage must be packed out. Picnic tables and fire grills are provided. Pets are permitted.

Reservations, fees: No reservations; no fee. Open mid-June to November.

Directions: From LaGrande turn north on Highway 82 and drive 52 miles to Lostine and Forest Road 8210. Turn south and drive 17 miles to the campground.

Contact: Wallowa-Whitman National Forest, Eagle Cap Ranger District; Wallowa Mountains Visitor Center, 88401 Highway 82, Enterprise, OR 97828; tel. (541) 426-5546.

18 Wallowa Lake State Park

 8

Surrounded on three sides by 9,000-foot tall, snow-capped mountains and a large, clear lake, Wallowa Lake, this area is popular for fishing and boating. You can also enjoy hiking, horseback riding, bumper boats, canoeing, miniature golf or a tram ride up 4,000 feet to a mountain top. A nearby artist community makes world-class bronze castings and tours are available. This is also the gateway to Hells Canyon, the deepest gorge in North America. Other highlights include a pretty one-mile nature trail and trailheads that provide access into the Eagle Cap Wilderness. A marina is nearby for boaters and anglers. Picnicking, swimming, and wildlife viewing are a few of the other activities available to visitors.

Location: On Wallowa Lake; map C5, grid f5.

Campsites, facilities: There are 89 tent sites and 121 full-hookup sites for trailers or RVs up to 90 feet long, some hiker/biker sites, three group tent areas, and two yurts. Electricity, drinking water, sewer hookups, and picnic tables are provided. Drinking water, garbage bins, flush toilets, sanitary disposal services, showers, and firewood are available. A store, a cafe, and ice are located within one mile. Some facilities are wheelchair accessible. Boat docks, launching facilities, and rentals are nearby. Leashed pets are permitted.

Reservations, fees: Reservations accepted; phone (800) 551-6949 ($6 reservation fee). Sites are $11-20 per night, hiker/biker sites are $4 per night, group areas are $60 per night, yurts are $29 per night; an additional vehicle is $7 per night. Major credit cards accepted. Open year-round.

Directions: From LaGrande turn north on Highway 82 and drive 62 miles to Enterprise and the junction with Highway 3. Continue south on Highway 82 to Joseph. Continue for six miles to the south shore of the lake and the campground.

Contact: Wallowa Lake State Park, 72214 Marina Lane, Joseph, OR 97846; tel. (800) 551-6949, (541) 432-4185.

19 Mountain View Motel and Trailer Park

 3

This park is not far from Wallowa Lake. There are views of Seven Devil's Mountain Range and of the Eagle Cap Wilderness. Nearby recreational facilities include a golf course, hiking trails, bike paths, and a riding stable.

Location: Near Wallowa Lake; map C5, grid f5.

Campsites, facilities: There are 14 tent sites and 14 sites for trailers or RVs of any length; three are drive-through sites. Electricity, drinking water, sewer hookups, and picnic tables are provided at eight sites. Flush toilets and showers are available. Bottled gas, a store, a cafe, and a coin laundry are located within two miles. Leashed pets are permitted.

Reservations, fees: Reservations accepted. Sites are $10-15 per night. Open year-round.

Directions: From LaGrande turn north on Highway 82 and drive 62 miles to Enterprise and the junction with Highway 3. Continue south on Highway 82 for four miles to the campground (1.5 miles north of Joseph).

Contact: Mountain View Motel and Trailer Park, 83450 Joseph Highway, Joseph, OR 97846; tel. (541) 432-2982.

20 Lick Creek   7

This campground is set at an elevation of 5,400 feet in a parklike setting along the banks of Lick Creek in Hells Canyon National Recreation Area. It is secluded and pretty. Tall Douglas fir, white fir, tamarack and lodgepole pine intersperse the campground, providing habitat for some of the birds and small mammals you might see.

Location: On Lick Creek in Wallowa-Whitman National Forest; map C5, grid f6.

Campsites, facilities: There are seven tent sites and five sites for trailers or RVs up to 30 feet long. Picnic tables and fire grills are provided. Vault toilets are available, but there is no drinking water, and garbage must be packed out. Pets are permitted.

Reservations, fees: No reservations; no fee. Open mid-June to late November.

Directions: From LaGrande turn north on Highway 82 and drive 62 miles to Enterprise and the junction with Highway 3. Continue south on Highway 82 to Joseph and Highway 350. Turn east and drive 7.5 miles to Forest Road 39. Turn south and drive 15 miles to the campground.

Contact: Hells Canyon National Recreation Area, Wallowa Mountains Visitor Center, 88401 Highway 82, Enterprise, OR 97828; tel. (541) 426-5546.

21 Blackhorse   7

This campground along the banks of the Imnaha River in Hells Canyon National Recreation Area is in a secluded section of Wallowa-Whitman National Forest at an elevation of 4,000 feet.

Location: On the Imnaha River in Wallowa-Whitman National Forest; map C5, grid f7.

Campsites, facilities: There are 16 sites for tents, trailers, or RVs up to 30 feet long. Picnic tables and fire grills are provided. Drinking water, firewood, and vault toilets are available, but all garbage must be packed out. Pets are permitted.

Reservations, fees: No reservations. Sites are $5 per night. Open June to late November.

Directions: From Interstate 84 at LaGrande, turn north on Highway 82 and drive 62 miles to Enterprise. Continue six miles south to Joseph and then drive 7.5 miles east on Highway 350. Turn south on Forest Road 39 and drive 29 miles to the campground.

Contact: Hells Canyon National Recreation Area, Wallowa Mountains Visitor Center, 88401 Highway 82, Enterprise, OR 97828; tel. (541) 426-5546.

22 Ollokot 6

This campground on the banks of the Imnaha River in Hells Canyon National Recreation Area at an elevation of 4,000 feet is a primitive alternative to the other camps in the immediate area. It's named for Chief Joseph's brother, a member of the Nez Perce tribe. For those seeking a little more solitude, this could be the spot.

Location: On the Imnaha River in Wallowa-Whitman National Forest; map C5, grid g7.

Campsites, facilities: There are 12 sites for tents, trailers, or RVs up to 30 feet long. Picnic tables and fire grills are provided. Drinking water and vault toilets are available, but all garbage must be packed out. Pets are permitted.

Reservations, fees: No reservations. Sites are $5 per night. Open June to late November.

Directions: From Interstate 84 at LaGrande, turn north on Highway 82 and drive 62 miles to Enterprise. Continue six miles south to Joseph, and then drive 7.5 miles east on Highway 350. Turn south on Forest Road 39 and drive 30 miles to the campground.

Contact: Hells Canyon National Recreation Area; Wallowa Mountains Visitor Center, 88401 Highway 82, Enterprise, OR 97828; (541) 426-5546.

23 Tamarack 5

Located at 4,600 feet on the banks of Eagle Creek in a beautiful area with lush vegetation and abundant wildlife, this camp is a good spot for a fishing and hiking trip in a remote setting.

Location: On Eagle Creek in Wallowa-Whitman National Forest; map C5, grid g4.

Campsites, facilities: There are 12 tent sites and 12 sites for trailers or RVs up to 22 feet long. Picnic tables and fire grills are provided. Drinking water, firewood, and vault toilets are available, but all garbage must be packed out. Pets are permitted.

Reservations, fees: No reservations. Sites are $5 per night. Open June to late October.

Directions: From Baker City drive north on Interstate 84 for six miles to Highway 203. Turn east on Highway 203 and drive 17 miles to Medical Springs and Big Springs Road (Forest Road 67). Turn left and drive 15.5 miles across Eagle Creek to Forest Road 77. Turn left on Forest Road 77 and drive 300 yards to the campground.

Contact: Wallowa-Whitman National Forest, Pine Ranger District, 38470 Pinetown Lane, Halfway, OR 97834; tel. (541) 742-7511; fax (541) 742-6705.

24 Two Color 6

This campground is set at 4,800 feet elevation along the banks of Eagle Creek, about a mile north of Tamarack. Another option for campers is nearby Boulder Park campground, three miles northeast on Forest Road 7755.

Location: On Eagle Creek in Wallowa-Whitman National Forest; map C5, grid g4.

Campsites, facilities: There are 14 sites for tents and six sites for trailers or RVs up to 22 feet long. Picnic tables and fire grills are provided. Drinking water and vault toilets are available, but garbage must be packed out. Pets are permitted.

Reservations, fees: No reservations; no fee. Open mid-June to late October.

Directions: From Baker City drive northeast on Highway 203 for 23 miles to the town of Medical Springs and Forest Road 67. Turn southeast and drive 15.5 miles across Eagle Creek to Forest Road 77. Turn northeast on Forest Road 77 and drive 1.5 miles to Road 7755 (which merges with 77) and the campground entrance on the right.

Contact: Wallowa-Whitman National Forest, LaGrande Ranger District, 3502 Highway 30, LaGrande, OR 97850; tel. (541) 963-7186; fax (541) 962-8580.

25 West Eagle Meadow   7

This campground in a big, open meadow is set at 5,200 feet elevation about a five-minute walk from West Eagle Creek. The Eagle Cap Wilderness is nearby, offering a good opportunity to observe wildlife.

Location: Near West Eagle Creek in Wallowa-Whitman National Forest; map C5, grid g4.

Campsites, facilities: There are 24 sites for tents. Picnic tables, garbage service (summer only), and fire rings are provided. There is no drinking water. Vault toilets are available. Stock facilities include corrals, hitching rails, and a nearby loading ramp. Some facilities are wheelchair accessible. Pets are permitted.

Reservations, fees: No reservations; no fee. Open mid-June to late October.

Directions: From Baker City drive north on Interstate 84 for six miles to Highway 203. Turn east and drive 17 miles to the town of Medical Springs and Forest Road 67. Turn left on Forest Road 67 and drive 15.5 miles (across Eagle Creek) to Forest Road 77. Turn left and drive 20 miles to the campground on the left.

Contact: Wallowa-Whitman National Forest, LaGrande Ranger District, 3502 Highway 30, LaGrande, OR 97850; tel. (541) 963-7186; fax (541) 962-8580.

26 Eagle Forks   6

This campground at 3,000 feet of elevation, is located at the confluence of Little Eagle Creek and Eagle Creek. A trail follows the creek northwest for five miles, making for a prime day hike, though the spot attracts few people. It's quite pretty as well and perfect for a weekend getaway or an extended layover.

Location: On Eagle Creek in Wallowa-Whitman National Forest; map C5, grid g5.

Campsites, facilities: There are seven tent sites and five sites for trailers or RVs up to 21 feet long. Picnic tables and fire grills are provided. Firewood, drinking water, and vault toilets are available, but all garbage must be packed out. Pets are permitted.

Reservations, fees: No reservations; no fee. Open June to late October.

Directions: From Baker City drive east on Highway 86 for 36 miles to Richland. Turn north on Eagle Creek Road and drive to Newbridge; continue on Forest Road 7735 for seven miles to the campground entrance on the left.

Contact: Wallowa-Whitman National Forest, Pine Ranger District, General Delivery, Halfway, OR 97834; tel. (541) 742-7511; fax (541) 742-6705.

27 McBride 6

This campground is set along the banks of Brooks Ditch at an elevation of 4,800 feet. It is little used, primitive, and obscure. Though not particularly scenic, it will work as a quick, free layover spot.
Location: On Brooks Ditch in Wallowa-Whitman National Forest; map C5, grid g5.
Campsites, facilities: There are 11 tent sites and eight sites for trailers or RVs up to 16 feet long. Picnic tables and fire grills are provided. Drinking water and vault toilets are available, but all garbage must be packed out. Leashed pets are permitted.
Reservations, fees: No reservations; no fee. Open mid-May to late October.
Directions: From Baker City drive east on Highway for 52 miles to Halfway. Turn northwest on Highway 413 and drive six miles to Forest Road 7710. Turn west and drive 2.5 miles to the campground.
Contact: Wallowa-Whitman National Forest, Pine Ranger District, 38470 Pinetown Lane, Halfway, OR 97834; tel. (541) 742-7511; fax (541) 742-6705.

28 Twin Lakes 6

This campground is nestled at 6,500 foot elevation, between the little Twin Lakes, both of which offer excellent fishing. Nearby trails provide access to backcountry lakes and streams. See a U.S. Forest Service map for details. Another campground option is Fish Lake, about six miles south on Forest Road 66.
Location: Near Twin Lakes in Wallowa-Whitman National Forest; map C5, grid g6.
Campsites, facilities: There are six tent sites. Picnic tables and fire grills are provided. Firewood and vault toilets are available, but there is no drinking water, and all garbage must be packed out. Leashed pets are permitted.
Reservations, fees: No reservations; no fee. Open July to mid-September.
Directions: From Baker City on Interstate 84, turn east on Highway 86. Drive east on Highway 86 for 52 miles to Halfway and County Road 733. Turn north on County Road 733 and drive five miles north to Fish Lake Road (Forest Road 66). Turn north and drive 24 miles to the campground.
Contact: Hells Canyon National Recreation Area; Wallowa Mountains Visitor Center, 88401 Highway 82, Enterprise, OR 97828; tel. (541) 426-5546.

29 Hidden 5

River views and spacious sites can be found at this campground in an exceptionally pretty spot along the banks of the Imnaha River in the Hells Canyon National Recreation Area. It's essential to obtain a map of Wallowa-Whitman National Forest that details back roads and hiking trails. If full, Coverdale Campground is an option just four miles northeast on Forest Road 3960.
Location: On the Imnaha River in Wallowa-Whitman National Forest; map C5, grid g6.
Campsites, facilities: There are 10 tent sites and three tent or trailer sites. Picnic tables and fire grills are provided. Drinking water, firewood, and vault toilets

are available, but all garbage must be packed out. Leashed pets are permitted.

Reservations, fees: No reservations; no fee. Open June to late November.

Directions: From LaGrande drive east on Highway 82 for 62 miles to Enterprise. Continue six miles south to Joseph and Highway 350. Turn east and drive 7.5 miles to Wallowa Mountain Loop Road (Forest Road 39). Turn south and drive 29 miles to Forest Road 3960. Turn right (southwest) and drive seven miles to the campground.

Contact: Hells Canyon National Recreation Area; Wallowa Mountains Visitor Center, 88401 Highway 82, Enterprise, OR 97828; tel. (541) 426-5546.

30 Fish Lake   6

This pretty, well-forested camp at an elevation of 6,600 feet, with comfortable sites along the shore of Fish Lake, makes a good base for a fishing trip. Side trip options include hiking on nearby trails that lead to mountain streams.

Location: On Fish Lake in Wallowa-Whitman National Forest; map C5, grid g6.

Campsites, facilities: There are 10 tent sites and five sites for trailers or RVs up to 22 feet long. Picnic tables and fire grills are provided. Spring water, firewood, and vault toilets are available. Boat launching facilities are nearby. Leashed pets are permitted. Garbage must be packed out.

Reservations, fees: No reservations. Sites are $5 per night. Open mid-June to late October.

Directions: From Interstate 84 at Baker City, drive four miles north; then turn east on Highway 86 and drive 52 miles to Halfway. From Halfway drive five miles north on County Route 733, then 18.5 miles north on Forest Road 66.

Contact: Wallowa-Whitman National Forest, Pine Ranger District, 38470 Pinetown Lane, Halfway, OR 97834; tel. (541) 742-7511; fax (541) 742-6705.

31 Evergreen   6

This campground can be found along the banks of the Imnaha River in Hells Canyon National Recreation Area. It's one of seven camps in the vicinity. The camp is popular with hunters in the fall.

Location: On the Imnaha River in Wallowa-Whitman National Forest; map C5, grid g7.

Campsites, facilities: This is a group campsite for tents, trailers, or RVs up to 31 feet long. Vault toilets are available, but there is no drinking water, and all garbage must be packed out. Picnic tables and fire grills are provided. Pets are permitted.

Reservations, fees: No reservations; no fee. Open June to late November.

Directions: From LaGrande turn north on Highway 82 and drive 62 miles to Enterprise and the junction with Highway 3. Continue on Highway 82 for six miles to Joseph and Highway 350. Turn east on Highway 350 and drive 7.5 miles to Forest Road 39. Turn south and drive about 30 miles (slow, often twisty) to Forest Road 3960. Turn right and drive seven miles to the campground.

Contact: Hells Canyon National Recreation Area; Wallowa Mountains Visitor Center, 88401 Highway 82, Enterprise, OR 97828; tel. (541) 426-5546.

32 Indian Crossing 6

This campground is set at an elevation of 4,500 feet and is more developed than near-by Evergreen and Hidden Campgrounds. The trailhead for the Eagle Cap Wilderness is near this camp. Obtain a U.S. Forest Service map for side trip possibilities.

Location: On the Imnaha River in Wallowa-Whitman National Forest; map C5, grid g7.

Campsites, facilities: There are 14 sites for tents, trailers, or RVs up to 30 feet long. Drinking water, picnic tables, and fire grills are provided, but all garbage must be packed out. Vault toilets and horse facilities are available. Pets are permitted.

Reservations, fees: No reservations. Sites are $5 per night. Open June to late November.

Directions: From LaGrande turn north on Highway 82 and drive 62 miles to Enterprise and the junction with Highway 3. Continue on Highway 82 for six miles to Joseph and Highway 350. Turn east on Highway 350 and drive 7.5 miles to Forest Road 39. Turn south and drive about 30 miles (slow, often twisty) to Forest Road 3960. Turn right and drive 10 miles to the campground at the end of the road.

Contact: Hells Canyon National Recreation Area; Wallowa Mountains Visitor Center, 88401 Highway 82, Enterprise, OR 97828; tel. (541) 426-5546.

33 Lake Fork 6

This little campground (at 3,200 feet elevation) along the banks of Lake Fork Creek is tucked away off the main road and is an ideal jumping-off point for a back-packing trip. A trail from camp follows the creek west for about 10 miles to Fish Lake, then continues on to several smaller lakes.

Location: On Lake Fork Creek in Wallowa-Whitman National Forest; map C5, grid g7.

Campsites, facilities: There are 10 sites for tents, trailers, or RVs up to 22 feet long. Picnic tables and fire grills are provided. Drinking water and vault toilets are available, but all garbage must be packed out. Pets are permitted.

Reservations, fees: No reservations accepted. Sites are $4 per night. Open June to late November.

Directions: From Baker City drive east on Highway 86 for 82 miles to Forest Road 39. Turn north and drive eight miles to the campground entrance road on the left.

Contact: Hells Canyon National Recreation Area; Wallowa Mountains Visitor Center, 88401 Highway 82, Enterprise, OR 97828; tel. (541) 426-5546.

BOATS AT NEWPORT

BOB RACE

MAP D1

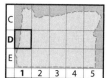

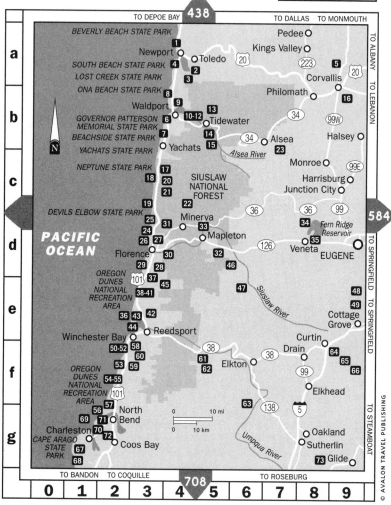

TO DEPOE BAY **438**

TO DALLAS TO MONMOUTH

a

BEVERLY BEACH STATE PARK **1**
Newport
Toledo
SOUTH BEACH STATE PARK **4**
LOST CREEK STATE PARK **2**
3
Pedee
Kings Valley
20
223
5
TO ALBANY
TO LEBANON
Corvallis
20

b

ONA BEACH STATE PARK **8**
9
Waldport
13
GOVERNOR PATTERSON **6** **10-12**
MEMORIAL STATE PARK
BEACHSIDE STATE PARK **7**
14
YACHATS STATE PARK Yachats **15**
Tidewater
34
Alsea
Alsea River **23**
Philomath
16
34
99W
Halsey

c

NEPTUNE STATE PARK **17**
18 **20**
21
SIUSLAW
NATIONAL
FOREST
22
DEVILS ELBOW STATE PARK **19**
Monroe
99E
Harrisburg
Junction City
36
36
99

d

**PACIFIC
OCEAN**
25 **31**
24
26 **27**
Minerva
33
Mapleton
Florence **30**
32
46
126
Veneta
34
Fern Ridge
Reservoir
35
EUGENE
TO SPRINGFIELD

e

29 **28**
OREGON
DUNES
NATIONAL
RECREATION
AREA
101 **37**
38-41 **45**
36 **43** **42**
47
Siuslaw River
48
49
Cottage
Grove
TO SPRINGFIELD

f

Winchester Bay **44** Reedsport
50-52 **58**
60
53 **59**
OREGON
DUNES
NATIONAL
RECREATION
AREA 101
54-55
38
38
61
62 Elkton
Curtin
Drain
64
99 **65**
66
Elkhead

g

57
56
North
69 **71** Bend
Charleston **70**
CAPE ARAGO **72** Coos Bay
STATE **67**
PARK **68**
0   10 mi
0   10 km
63 138
5
Oakland
Sutherlin
73 Glide
TO STEAMBOAT

TO BANDON TO COQUILLE **708** TO ROSEBURG

584

0   1   2   3   4   5   6   7   8   9

© AVALON TRAVEL PUBLISHING

CHAPTER D1

1 Agate Beach RV Park 6

This park is a short distance from Agate Beach Wayside, a small state park with beach access. Agate hunting can be good. Sometimes the agates are covered by a layer of sand, and you have to dig a bit. But other times wave action will clear the sand, unveiling the agates at low tides. Beverly Beach State Park is located 4.5 miles north.
Location: Near the Pacific Ocean; map D1, grid a4.
Campsites, facilities: There are 32 sites for trailers or RVs up to 40 feet long. Electricity, drinking water, sewer hookups, cable TV, and picnic tables are provided. Flush toilets, sanitary services, showers, and a laundry room are available. A store and ice are located within one mile. Leashed pets are permitted.
Reservations, fees: Reservations accepted. Sites are $21.50-22.50 per night. Open year-round.
Directions: From Albany drive west on U.S. 20 for 66 miles to Newport and U.S. 101. Turn north on U.S. 101 and drive three miles to the park on the north end of town.
Contact: Agate Beach RV Park, 6138 North Coast Highway, Newport, OR 97365; tel. (541) 265-7670.

2 Harbor Village RV Park 6

This wooded and landscaped park is near the shore of Yaquina Bay. See the description of Newport Marina and RV Park for information on attractions in Newport. Nearby recreation options include clamming, crabbing, deep-sea fishing, an 18-hole golf course, hiking trails, and a full-service marina.
Location: On Yaquina Bay; map D1, grid a4.
Campsites, facilities: There are 140 sites for trailers or RVs. Electricity, drinking water, sewer hookups, cable TV, and picnic tables are provided. Flush toilets, showers, and a laundry room are available. Bottled gas, a store, and a cafe are within one mile. Boat docks, launching facilities, and rentals are nearby. One leashed pet per site is permitted.
Reservations, fees: Reservations accepted. Sites are $15 for two people per night. Open year-round.
Directions: From Albany drive west on U.S. 20 for 65.5 miles into Newport and John Moore Road. Turn south on John Moore Road and drive one-half mile to the bay and Bay Boulevard. Bear left and drive a short distance to the park entrance on the left.
Contact: Harbor Village RV Park, 923 S.E. Bay Boulevard, Newport, OR 97365; tel. (541) 265-5088; fax (541) 265-5895.

3 Newport Marina and RV Park 7

This park is set along the shore of Yaquina Bay near Newport, a resort town that offers a variety of attractions. Among them are ocean fishing, a museum and aquarium at the nearby Hatfield Marine Science Center, the Undersea Garden, the Waxworks, Ripley's Believe It or Not, and the Lincoln County Historical Society Museum. Nearby recreation options include an 18-hole golf course, hiking trails, a full-service marina, and tennis courts.

Location: On Yaquina Bay; map D1, grid a4.

Campsites, facilities: There are 115 sites for trailers or RVs. Electricity, drinking water, and sewer hookups are provided. Flush toilets, showers, cable TV, a store, a laundry room, and ice are available. A marina with boat docks and launching facilities are available on-site. Leashed pets are permitted.

Reservations, fees: Reservations accepted. Sites are $22.47 per night. Open year-round.

Directions: From Albany drive west on U.S. 20 for 66 miles to Newport and U.S. 101. Turn south on U.S. 101 and travel one-quarter mile to Marine Science Drive. Turn east and drive a half mile to the park entrance on the left.

Contact: Newport Marina and RV Park, 600 S.E. Bay Boulevard, Newport, OR 97365, or to 2301 S.E. O.S.U. Drive, Newport, OR 97365; tel. (541) 867-3321; fax (541) 867-3352.

4 South Beach State Park   7

This park along the beach offers opportunities for beachcombing, fishing, crabbing, windsurfing, boating, and hiking. In fact, the Oregon Coast Trail passes right through the park. A primitive hike-in campground is also available. See the description of Newport Marina and RV Park for information on attractions in Newport.

Location: On the Pacific Ocean; map D1, grid a4.

Campsites, facilities: There are 238 sites for trailers or RVs of any length, and a special primitive camping area for hikers and bicyclists. There are also three group sites and 15 yurts. Electricity, drinking water, fire grills, garbage bins, and picnic tables are provided. Flush toilets, a sanitary disposal station, showers, and firewood are available. Some facilities are wheelchair accessible. Leashed pets are permitted.

Reservations, fees: Reservations accepted; phone (800) 452-5687 ($6 reservation fee). Sites are $13-20 per night; yurts are $27 per night; the group fee is $40-60 per night; and the fee for hikers/bicyclists is $4. Major credit cards accepted. Open year-round.

Directions: From Albany drive west on U.S. 20 for 66 miles to Newport and U.S. 101. Turn south and drive two miles to the park entrance on the right.

Contact: South Beach State Park, 5580 South Coast Highway, South Beach, OR 97366; tel. (541) 867-4715.

5 Corvallis Motorhome Park

       5

This is a decent layover spot on your way to and from the coast. It's in a bucolic setting, across the way from Oregon State University cow and llama grazing land. Nearby recreation options include an 18-hole golf course, hiking trails, and a riding stable.

Location: In Corvallis; map D1, grid a8.

Campsites, facilities: There are 27 sites for trailers or RVs. Electricity, drinking water, and sewer hookups are provided. Flush toilets, showers, a store, a cafe, a laundry room, and ice are available. Bottled gas and sanitary services are located within one mile. Pets are permitted.

Reservations, fees: Reservations accepted. Sites are $15 per night. Open year-round.

Directions: In Corvallis drive west on U.S. 20 for 2.5 miles to 53rd Street. Turn north and drive 1.3 miles to the park on the right.

Contact: Corvallis Motorhome Park, 200 Northwest 53rd Street, Corvallis, OR 97330; tel. (541) 752-2334; fax (541) 757-2390.

6 Beachside State Park   7

This state park offers about nine miles of beach and is not far from Alsea Bay and the Alsea River. Every site is seconds from the beach. This is a popular winter camping park. Within 30 miles in either direction, you'll find visitor centers, tide pools, hiking and driving tours, three lighthouses, crabbing, clamming, fishing, an aquarium, and science centers. See the description of Waldport/Newport KOA for more information on the fishing opportunities in the area.

Location: Near Alsea Bay; map D1, grid b4.

Campsites, facilities: There are 50 sites for tents, 32 sites with water and electrical hookups for trailers or RVs up to 30 feet long, two yurts, and a special camping area for hikers and bicyclists. Picnic tables and fire grills are provided. Drinking water, garbage bins, flush toilets, showers, and firewood are available. Some facilities are wheelchair accessible. Leashed pets are permitted.

Reservations, fees: Reservations accepted; phone (800) 452-5687 ($6 reservation fee). Sites are $13-19 per night and yurts are $30 per night; the fee is $4 per night for hikers/bicyclists and $7 per night for an additional vehicle. Major credit cards accepted. Open mid-March through October, weather permitting.

Directions: From Albany drive west on U.S. 20 for 66 miles to Newport and U.S. 101. Turn south on U.S. 101 and drive 16 miles to Waldport. Continue south on U.S. 101 for four miles to the park entrance.

Contact: Beachside State Park, P.O. Box 693, Waldport, OR 97394; tel. (541) 563-3220.

7 Tillicum Beach   8

Ocean-view campsites are a big draw at this campground along the water just south of Beachside State Park. Nearby Forest Roads provide access to streams in the mountains east of the beach area. A U.S. Forest Service map details the possibilities. Since it's just off the highway, this camp fills up very quickly in the summer, so expect crowds.

Location: On the Pacific Ocean in Siuslaw National Forest; map D1, grid b3.

Campsites, facilities: There are 61 sites for tents, trailers, or RVs up to 40 feet long. Picnic tables and fire grills are provided. Flush toilets, garbage bins, and drinking water are available. Leashed pets are permitted.

Reservations, fees: No reservations accepted. Sites are $12 per night, $6 for an additional vehicle. Open year-round.

Directions: From Albany drive west on U.S. 20 for 66 miles to Newport and U.S. 101. Turn south on U.S. 101 and drive 14 miles to Waldport. Continue south on U.S. 101 for 4.5 miles to the campground entrance on the right.

Contact: Siuslaw National Forest, Waldport Ranger District, P.O. Box 400, Waldport, OR 97394; tel. (541) 563-3211; fax (541) 563-3124; concessionaire, tel. (541) 822-3799.

8 Seal Rock
Trailer and RV Cove 8

This trailer park is on the rugged coastline near Seal Rock State Park (open for day use only), where you may find seals, sea lions, and a variety of birds. The ocean views are stunning.

Location: Near Seal Rock State Park; map D1, grid b4.

Campsites, facilities: There are 26 sites for trailers or RVs of any length; two are drive-through sites. Electricity, drinking water, sewer hookups, and picnic tables are provided. Flush toilets and showers are available. Firewood, a store, a cafe, and ice are located within one mile.

Reservations, fees: Reservations accepted. Sites are $18-28 per night. Open year-round.

Directions: From Albany drive west on U.S. 20 for 66 miles to Newport and U.S. 101. Turn south and drive 10 miles to the town of Seal Rock. Continue south on U.S. 101 for one-quarter mile to the park entrance on the left.

Contact: Seal Rock Trailer and RV Cove, P.O. Box 71, Seal Rock, OR 97376; tel. (541) 563-3955.

9 Waldport/
Newport KOA 8

This pretty park set amid some of the oldest pine trees in Oregon is within walking distance to the beach, the bay, and downtown Waldport—and to top it off, the campsites have beautiful ocean views. Alsea Bay's sandy and rocky shorelines make this area a favorite with anglers. The crabbing and clamming can also be quite good. Ona Beach State Park, about five miles north on U.S. 101, offers more fishing and a boat ramp along Beaver Creek. It's open for day use only. Other nearby recreation options include hiking trails, marked bike trails, the Oregon Coast Aquarium, and a marina.

Location: On Alsea Bay; map D1, grid b4.

Campsites, facilities: There are 12 tent sites and 75 sites for trailers or RVs of any length, plus 15 cabins. Electricity, drinking water, cable TV, and sewer hookups are provided. Flush toilets, showers, and a recreation hall are available. Bottled gas, sanitary services, a store, a cafe, a coin laundry, and ice are located within one mile. Boat docks, launching facilities, and boat rentals are nearby. Leashed pets are permitted.

Reservations, fees: Reservations accepted. Sites are $18-26 per night. Open year-round.

Directions: From Albany drive west on U.S. 20 for 66 miles to Newport and U.S. 101. Turn south and drive to milepost 155 at the north end of the Alsea Bay

Bridge. The park is located on the west side of the bridge.

Contact: Waldport/ Newport KOA, P.O. Box 397, Waldport, OR 97394; tel. (541) 563-2250; fax (541) 563-4098.

10 Drift Creek Landing

        6

This campground is along the shore of the Alsea River in a heavily treed and mountainous area. The Oregon Coast Aquarium is 15 miles away, and an 18-hole golf course is located nearby. For more information on the area, see the description of Waldport/Newport KOA.

Location: On the Alsea River; map D1, grid b4.

Campsites, facilities: There are 60 drive-through sites for trailers or RVs of any length. Electricity, drinking water, and sewer hookups are provided. Flush toilets, private telephone service, cable TV, bottled gas, showers, a recreation hall, a store, a cafe, a laundry room, boat docks, boat rentals, and launching facilities are available. Leashed pets are permitted.

Reservations, fees: Reservations accepted. Sites are $13-18 per night. Open year-round.

Directions: From Albany drive west on U.S. 20 for 66 miles to Newport and U.S. 101. Turn south and drive 14 miles to Waldport and Highway 24. Turn east on Highway 34 and drive 3.5 miles to the campground.

Contact: Drift Creek Landing, 3851 Highway 34, Waldport, OR 97394; tel. (541) 563-3610.

11 Fishin' Hole Trailer Park   6

This is one of several campgrounds along the shore of the Alsea River. For information on the area, see the description of Waldport/Newport KOA.

Location: On the Alsea River; map D1, grid b4.

Campsites, facilities: There are 16 tent sites and 20 sites for trailers or RVs of any length. Electricity, drinking water, sewer hookups (10 sites only), picnic tables, flush toilets, showers, a cafe, a laundry room, boat docks, boat rentals, and launching facilities are available. Leashed pets are permitted.

Reservations, fees: Reservations accepted; call (800) 597-2853. Sites are $13 per night, $1 additional fee for cable TV, $16 addition fee for full-hookup. Open year-round.

Directions: From Albany drive west on U.S. 20 for 66 miles to Newport and U.S. 101. Turn south and drive 14 miles to Waldport and Highway 34. Turn east on Highway 34 and drive four miles to the entrance on the left.

Contact: Fishin' Hole Trailer Park, 3911 Highway 34, Waldport, OR 97394; tel. (541) 563-3401.

12 Chinook Trailer Park   7

This trailer park is along the shore of the Alsea River, about 3.5 miles from the ocean. For more information on the area, see the description of Waldport/Newport KOA.

Location: On the Alsea River; map D1, grid b5.

Campsites, facilities: There are six sites for tents and 22 sites for trailers or RVs of any length; 10 with full and 12 with partial hookups. Electricity, drinking water, cable TV, sewer hookups, flush toilets, showers, and a laundry room are available. Bottled gas, a store, a cafe, and ice are within one mile. Boat docks are nearby. Leashed pets and motorbikes are permitted.

Reservations, fees: Reservations accepted. Sites are $12-16 per night. Open year-round.

Directions: From Albany drive west on U.S. 20 for 66 miles to Newport and U.S. 101. Turn south and drive 14 miles to Waldport and Highway 34. Turn east on Highway 34 and drive 3.5 miles to the park entrance.

Contact: Chinook Trailer Park, 3299 Highway 34, Waldport, OR 97394; tel. (541) 563-3485.

13 Taylor's Landing   7

This campground is along the Alsea River. For more information on the area, see the description of Waldport/Newport KOA.

Location: On the Alsea River; map D1, grid b5.

Campsites, facilities: There are six tent sites and 28 sites for trailers or RVs. Electricity, drinking water, cable TV, sewer hookups, and picnic tables are provided. Flush toilets, bottled gas, showers, a cafe, and a laundry room are available. Boat docks, launching facilities, and rentals are nearby. Leashed pets are permitted.

Reservations, fees: Reservations accepted. Sites are $20 per night. Open year-round.

Directions: From Albany drive west on U.S. 20 for 66 miles to Newport and U.S. 101. Turn south and drive 14 miles to Waldport and Highway 34. Turn east on Highway 34 and drive seven miles to the entrance on the right.

Contact: Taylor's Landing, 7164 Alsea Highway 34, Waldport, OR 97394; tel. (541) 528-3388.

14 Canal Creek   5

This pleasant little campground is just off the beaten path in a large, wooded, open area along Canal Creek. It feels remote, yet has easy access and is close to the coast and all the amenities. The climate here is relatively mild, with 13 degrees Fahrenheit being the coldest winter temperature recorded in recent years. On the other hand, there is the rain—lots of it.

Location: On Canal Creek in Siuslaw National Forest; map D1, grid b5.

Campsites, facilities: There are seven sites for tents only and 10 sites for tents or small RVs, plus a group area. Picnic tables and fire grills are provided. Drinking water, garbage bins, and vault toilets are available. The group site has a picnic shelter and a play area. Leashed pets are permitted.

Reservations, fees: No reservations accepted. Sites are $7 per night, $3.50 for an additional vehicle. Open year-round.

Directions: From Albany drive west on U.S. 20 for 15 miles to Philomath and Highway 34. Turn south on Highway 34 and drive 52 miles to Forest Road 3462. Turn south and drive four miles to the camp.

Contact: Siuslaw National Forest, Waldport Ranger District, P.O. Box 400, Waldport, OR 97394; tel. (541) 563-3211; fax (541) 563-3124.

15 Blackberry   7

This is a good base camp for a fishing trip on the Alsea River. The U.S. Forest Service provides boat launches and picnic areas at several spots along this stretch of river. Often there will be a camp host, who can give you inside information on nearby recreational opportunities. Large fir trees and lawn separate the sites.

Location: On the Alsea River in Siuslaw National Forest; map D1, grid b5.

Campsites, facilities: There are 32 sites for tents, trailers, or RVs. Picnic tables and fire grills are provided. Drinking water, garbage bins, and flush toilets are available. There is no firewood. A boat ramp is on site. Leashed pets are permitted.

Reservations, fees: No reservations accepted. Sites are $7 per night, $3.50 for an additional vehicle. Open May through October. Note: Phone ahead to make sure this campground is open; it may close without notice.

Directions: From Albany drive west on U.S. 20 for 15 miles to Philomath and Highway 34. Turn south on Highway 34 and drive 41 miles to the campground entrance.

Contact: Siuslaw National Forest, Waldport Ranger District, P.O. Box 400, Waldport, OR 97394; tel. (541) 563-3211; fax (541) 563-3124.

16 Willamette City Park   8

This 40-acre city park is on the banks of the Willamette River just outside Corvallis. The camping area is actually a large clearing near the entrance to the park, which has been left in its natural state. There are trails leading down to the river, and the birdwatching is good here.

Location: On the Willamette River; map D1, grid b9.

Campsites, facilities: There are 13 sites for tents, trailers, or RVs of any length. Vault toilets, drinking water, a covered outdoor kitchen area, picnic tables, and a small playground are available. Bottled gas, a store, a cafe, a coin laundry, and ice are within one mile. There is a dump station in the center of town, three miles away. Boat docks and launching facilities are located within one mile. Leashed pets are permitted.

Reservations, fees: No reservations accepted. Sites are $9 per night. Open April to mid-November to self-contained RVs and from March through October to tents, trailers, and RVs.

Directions: On Interstate 5, take Exit 228 (five miles south of Albany) to Highway 34. Turn west and drive nine miles to Corvallis and Highway 99W. Turn south and drive one miles to S.E. Goodnight Road. Turn east and drive a half mile to the park.

Contact: Corvallis Department of Parks and Recreation, P.O. Box 1083, Corvallis, OR 97339; tel. (541) 766-6918.

⅓ Cape Perpetua   8

This U.S. Forest Service campground is set along Cape Creek in the Cape Perpetua Scenic Area. The visitor information center provides hiking and driving maps to guide you through this spectacular region, and you can also watch a movie about the area. Maps highlight the tide-pool and picnic spots. The coastal cliffs are perfect for whale watching from December through March. Neptune State Park is just south and offers additional rugged coastline vistas.

Location: On Cape Creek in Siuslaw National Forest; map D1, grid c4.

Campsites, facilities: There are 37 sites for tents, trailers, or RVs up to 22 feet long, plus one group site that can accommodate 100 campers. Picnic tables and fire grills are provided. Flush toilets, drinking water, and garbage bins are available. Leashed pets are permitted.

Reservations, fees: Reservations required for the group site; phone (541) 822-3799. Individual sites are $12 per night, $6 for an additional vehicle; call for group site rates. Open mid-May to late September.

Directions: From Albany drive west on U.S. 20 for 66 miles to Newport and U.S. 101. Turn south and drive 23 miles to Yachats. Continue three miles south on U.S. 101 to the entrance on the left.

Contact: Concessionaire, (541) 822-3799. Siuslaw National Forest, Waldport Ranger District, P.O. Box 400, Waldport, OR 97394; tel. (541) 563-3211; fax (541) 563-3124; concessionaire, tel. (541) 822-3799.

⅛ Sea Perch   8

Sea Perch is right in the middle of one of the most scenic areas on the Oregon coast. This private camp just south of Cape Perpetua has sites on the beach and lawn areas, plus its own shell museum. For more information on the area, see the description of Cape Perpetua.

Location: Near Cape Perpetua; map D1, grid c3.

Campsites, facilities: There are four tent sites and 14 drive-through sites for tents, trailers, or RVs of any length. Electricity, drinking water, sewer hookups, and picnic tables are provided. Flush toilets, sanitary services, showers, firewood, a recreation hall, a laundry room, ice, and a beach are available. Leashed pets and motorbikes are permitted.

Reservations, fees: Reservations accepted. Sites are $19.50-26.75 per night. Open year-round.

Directions: From Albany drive west on U.S. 20 for 66 miles to Newport and U.S. 101. Turn south and drive 6.5 miles to the campground at milepost 171 on the right.

Contact: Sea Perch, 95480 Highway 101, Yachats, OR 97498; tel. (541) 547-3505.

19 Carl G. Washburne State Park   7

These are spacious campsites with a buffer of native plants between you and the highway. At night you can hear the pounding surf. There is a creek running through the campground, and elk have been known to wander through. Short hikes lead from the campground to a two-mile-long beach, extensive tide pools along the base of the cliffs, and a three-mile trail to Heceta Head Lighthouse. Just three miles south of the park are the Sea Lion Caves, where an elevator takes visitors down into the cavern for an insider's view of the life of a sea lion.

Location: On the Pacific Ocean; map D1, grid c3.

Campsites, facilities: There are seven primitive walk-in sites, 58 sites with full hookups for trailers or RVs up to 45 feet long, and two yurts. A special area is available for hikers and bicyclists. Drinking water, garbage bins, a sanitary disposal station, and picnic tables are provided. Flush toilets, showers, and firewood are available. Leashed pets are permitted.

Reservations, fees: No reservations accepted. Sites are $13-20 per night, $4 per night for hikers/bicyclists; yurts are $30 per night; an additional vehicle is $7 per night. Open year-round.

Directions: From Eugene drive west on Highway 126 for 61 miles to Florence and U.S. 101. Turn north on U.S. 101 and drive 12.5 miles to the park entrance road (well signed, 10 miles south of the town of Yachats). Turn west and drive a quarter mile to the park.

Contact: Carl G. Washburne State Park, 93111 Highway 101 N, Florence, OR 97439; tel. (800) 452-5687 or (541) 547-3416.

20 Rock Creek   7

This little campground is set along Rock Creek just one-quarter mile from the ocean. It's a premium spot for coastal-highway travelers, although it can get packed very quickly. An excellent side trip is Cape Perpetua, a designated scenic area located a few miles up the coast. The cape offers beautiful ocean views and a visitor center that will supply you with information on nature trails, picnic spots, tide pools, and where to find the best viewpoints in the area.

Location: On Rock Creek in Siuslaw National Forest; map D1, grid c4.

Campsites, facilities: There are 16 sites for tents, trailers, or RVs up to 22 feet long. Fire grills and picnic tables are provided. Flush toilets, garbage bins, and drinking water are available. Leashed pets are permitted.

Reservations, fees: No reservations accepted. Sites are $12 per night, $6 for an additional vehicle. Major credit cards accepted. Open late May to mid-September.

Directions: From Albany drive west on U.S. 20 for 66 miles to Newport and U.S. 101. Turn south and drive 23 miles to Yachats. Continue south on U.S. 101 for 10 miles to the campground entrance on the left.

Contact: Siuslaw National Forest, Waldport Ranger District, P.O. Box 400, Waldport, OR 97394; tel. (541) 563-3211; fax (541) 563-3124; concessionaire, tel. (541) 822-3799.

21 Lanham Bike-In Camp   7

This very primitive camp is a good layover spot for cyclists working their way along the coast highway—and you can't beat the price. See the description of Rock Creek for area information.

Location: In Siuslaw National Forest; map D1, grid c4.

Campsites, facilities: There are six primitive hike-in/bike-in tent sites. Picnic tables and fire grills are provided. Garbage bins are available, but there is no drinking water here; it can be obtained at Rock Creek. Leashed pets are permitted.

Reservations, fees: No reservations accepted. There is no fee. Open year-round.

Directions: From Albany drive west on U.S. 20 for 66 miles to Newport and U.S. 101. Turn south and drive 23 miles to Yachats. Continue south on U.S. 101 for 10 miles (just past Rock Creek Campground) to the campground entrance. Hike or bike in from there.

Contact: Siuslaw National Forest, Waldport Ranger District, P.O. Box 400, Waldport, OR 97394; tel. (541) 563-3211; fax (541) 563-3124.

22 North Fork Siuslaw   6

Little known and little used, this wooded camp along the North Fork of the Siuslaw River is the ideal hideaway. A dirt road opposite the camp follows Wilhelm Creek for about two miles. A newly constructed trail through old-growth forest is nearby. See a U.S. Forest Service map for other side trip possibilities.

Location: On the North Fork of the Siuslaw River in Siuslaw National Forest; map D1, grid c4.

Campsites, facilities: There are five tent sites. Picnic tables and fire grills are provided. Pit toilets and garbage bins are available, but there is no drinking water. Leashed pets are permitted.

Reservations, fees: No reservations accepted. There is no fee in winter; sites are $5 per night in summer, $2.50 for an additional vehicle. Open year-round.

Directions: From Eugene drive west on Highway 126 for 50 miles to County Road 5070/North Fork (located one mile east of Florence). Turn right and drive 12 miles northeast to the campground.

Contact: Siuslaw National Forest, Mapleton Ranger District, 4480 Highway 101, Building G, Florence, OR 97439; tel. (541) 902-8526; fax (541) 902-6946.

23 Alsea Falls   8

The beautiful surroundings of Alsea Falls can be enjoyed by exploring the trails that wander through the park and lead to the picnic area down near the falls. Trails to McBee Park and Green Peak Falls can be accessed from the campground along the South Fork of the river. The campsites are situated in a 40-year-old forest of Douglas fir and vine maple. On a warm day Alsea Falls offers cool relief along the river. The area was named after its original inhabitants, the Alsea Indians.

Location: Adjacent to the South Fork of the Alsea River; map D1, grid c7.

Campsites, facilities: There are 22 sites for tents, trailers, or RVs up to 30 feet long. Fire pits are provided. Drinking water, vault toilets, garbage bins, and fireplaces for wood and charcoal are available. Leashed pets are permitted.

Reservations, fees: No reservations accepted. Sites are $6 per night, with an additional charge of $4 per each additional vehicle. Open mid-May to late September.

Directions: From Albany drive west on U.S. 20 for nine miles to Corvallis. Turn south (left) onto Highway 99 and drive 15 miles to County Road 45120. Turn west (right) and drive five miles to Alpine Junction. Continue along the South Fork Alsea Access Road nine miles to the campground on the right.

Contact: Bureau of Land Management, Salem District Office, 1717 Fabry Road SE, Salem, OR 97306; tel. (503) 375-5646; fax (503) 375-5622.

24 Alder Dune   7

This wooded campground is located near four lakes—Alder Lake, Sutton Lake, Dune Lake, and Mercer Lake (the largest). A boat launch is available at Sutton Lake. An option is exploring the expansive sand dunes in the area by foot. There is no off-road-vehicle access here. See the description of Lane County Harbor Vista Park for other information on the area.

Location: Near Alder Lake in Siuslaw National Forest; map D1, grid d3.

Campsites, facilities: There are 39 sites for tents, trailers, or RVs up to 30 feet long. Picnic tables and fire grills are provided. Flush toilets, garbage bins, and drinking water are available. Leashed pets are permitted.

Reservations, fees: No reservations accepted. Sites are $12 per night, $10 for an additional vehicle. Open mid-May through mid-September.

Directions: From Eugene drive west on Highway 126 for 61 miles to Florence and U.S. 101. Turn north on U.S. 101 and drive eight miles to the campground on the left.

Contact: Siuslaw National Forest, Mapleton Ranger District, 4480 Highway 101, Building G, Florence, OR 97439; tel. (541) 902-8526; fax (541) 902-6946.

25 Sutton   7

This campground is located adjacent to Sutton Creek not far from Sutton Lake. Holman Vista on Sutton Beach Road provides a beautiful view of the dunes and ocean, and vegetation provides some privacy between sites. Wading and fishing are both popular. A hiking trail system leads from the camp out to the dunes. There is no off-road-vehicle access here. An alternative camp is Alder Dune to the north.

Location: Near Sutton Lake in Siuslaw National Forest; map D1, grid d3.

Campsites, facilities: There are 80 sites for tents, trailers, or RVs up to 30 feet long, some with partial hookups. There are also group sites. Picnic tables and fire grills are provided. Flush toilets, garbage bins, and drinking water are available. A boat ramp is nearby. Leashed pets are permitted.

Reservations, fees: Reservations necessary for group sites only. Rates are $12-15 per night for single sites, $7 for an additional vehicle; group sites are $40-100 per night. Open year-round.

Directions: From Eugene drive west on Highway 126 for 61 miles to Florence and U.S. 101. Turn north on U.S. 101 and drive six miles to Sutton Beach Road (Forest Road 794). Turn northwest and drive 1.5 miles to the campground entrance.

Contact: Siuslaw National Forest, Mapleton Ranger District, 4480 Highway 101, Building G, Florence, OR 97439; tel. (541) 902-8526; fax (541) 902-6946.

26 Harbor Vista County Park   6

This county park located out among the dunes near the entrance to the harbor offers a great lookout point from the observation deck. A number of side trips are available, including Darlington State Park, Jessie M. Honeyman Memorial State Park (see the description of Jessie M. Honeyman), and the Indian Forest, just four miles north of Florence. Florence also has displays of Native American dwellings and crafts.

Location: Near Florence; map D1, grid d3.

Campsites, facilities: There are 38 sites for tents, trailers, or RVs up to 60 feet long. Picnic tables and garbage bins are provided. Electricity, flush toilets, fire rings, sanitary disposal station, coin-operated showers, drinking water, a pay phone, and a playground are available. Pets and motorbikes are permitted.

Reservations, fees: Reservations accepted. Sites are $11-15 per night, $3 per night for a third vehicle. Open year-round.

Directions: From Eugene drive west on Highway 126 for 61 miles to Florence and U.S. 101. Continue straight (through the lighted intersection) onto 94th Street and drive west to Rhododendron Drive. Turn right and drive two miles to Harbor Vista Road and continue to the campground at 87658 Harbor Vista Road.

Contact: Harbor Vista County Park, Harbor Vista Road, Florence, OR 97439; tel. (541) 997-5987 87658.

27 B & E Wayside Mobile and RV Park   5

This landscaped park is beautifully maintained, clean, and quiet. See the descriptions of Lane County Harbor Vista Park and Port of Siuslaw RV and Marina for side trip ideas. Nearby recreation options include two golf courses and a riding stable (two miles away).

Location: Near Florence; map D1, grid d3.

Campsites, facilities: There are 24 sites for trailers or RVs of any length. Electricity, drinking water, sewer hookups, and picnic tables are provided. Flush toilets, sanitary services, showers, and a laundry room are available. Bottled gas, a store, a cafe, and ice are located within two miles. Boat launching facilities are nearby. Small leashed pets are permitted.

Reservations, fees: Reservations accepted. Sites are $18 per night. Open year-round.

Directions: From Eugene drive west on Highway 126 for 61 miles to Florence and U.S. 101. Turn north on U.S. 101 and drive 1.8 miles to the park on the right.

Contact: B & E Wayside Mobile and RV Park, 3760 Highway 101 North, Florence, OR 97439; tel. (541) 997-6451.

28 Lakeshore RV Park   5

Here's a prime area for vacationers. This park is set along the shore of Woahink Lake, a popular spot to fish for trout, perch, catfish, crappie, bluegill, and bass. It's adjacent to Jessie M. Honeyman Memorial State Park and the Oregon Dunes National Recreation Area. Off-road-vehicle access to the dunes is four miles northeast of the park. Hiking trails through the dunes can be found at Honeyman Memorial State Park. If you set out across the dunes off the trail, note your path. People hiking off-trail commonly get lost here.

Location: On Woahink Lake; map D1, grid d3.

Campsites, facilities: There are 20 sites for trailers or RVs of any length; six are drive-through sites. Electricity, drinking water, cable TV, and sewer hookups are provided. Flush toilets, showers, and a laundry room are available. A cafe is located within three miles. Boat docks are nearby. Leashed pets are permitted.

Reservations, fees: Reservations accepted. Sites are $18 per night. Open year-round.

Directions: From Eugene drive west on Highway 126 for 61 miles to Florence and U.S. 101. Turn south on U.S. 101 and drive four miles to milepost 195 and the park on the left.

Contact: Lakeshore RV Park, 83763 Highway 101, Florence, OR 97439; tel. (541) 997-2741; website: www.lakeshorerv.com.

29 Jessie M. Honeyman Memorial State Park   7

This popular state park is located along the shore of Cleowax Lake and adjacent to the dunes of the Oregon Dunes National Recreation Area. There are two miles of dunes between the park and the ocean. The dunes here are quite impressive, with some reaching to 500 feet. The two lakes in the park offer facilities for boating, fishing, and swimming. A one-mile hiking trail with access to the dunes is available in the park and off-road vehicle trails are located nearby in the sand dunes.

Location: Near Cleowax Lake; map D1, grid d3.

Campsites, facilities: There are 237 sites for tents and 141 sites for trailers or RVs up to 60 feet long (with full or partial hookups), a special camping area for hikers and bicyclists, six group tent areas, and 10 yurts. Picnic tables, garbage bins, and fire grills are provided. Drinking water, flush toilets, sanitary services, showers, playgrounds, evening interpretive programs and events, and firewood are available. Some facilities are wheelchair accessible. Boat docks and launching facilities are nearby. Leashed pets are permitted.

Reservations, fees: Reservations accepted; phone (800) 452-5687 ($6 reservation fee). Sites are $10-16 per night, $4 for hikers/bicyclists; group areas are $60 per night' yurts are $30 per night; an additional vehicle is $7 per night. Open year-round.

Directions: From Eugene drive west on Highway 126 for 61 miles to Florence and U.S. 101. Turn south on U.S. 101 and drive three miles to the park entrance.

Contact: Jessie M. Honeyman Memorial State Park, 84505 Highway 101, Florence, OR 97439; tel. (800) 551-6949, (541) 997-3641.

30 Port of Siuslaw RV and Marina

 8

This public resort can be found along the Siuslaw River in a grassy, urban setting. Anglers with boats will find that the U.S. 101 bridge support pilings make good spots for crabbing and fishing for perch and flounder. A new set of docks with drinking water, electricity, gasoline, and security, and a fish cleaning station are available. The sea lion caves and estuary are a bonus for wildlife lovers, and nearby lakes make swimming and waterskiing a possibility. Golf is within driving distance, and horses can be rented about 9 miles away.

Location: On the Siuslaw River; map D1, grid d4.

Campsites, facilities: There are 84 sites for tents, trailers, or RVs of any length. Electricity, drinking water, sewer hookups, cable TV and picnic tables are provided. Flush toilets, sanitary services, showers, a laundry room, and boat docks are available. A cafe and ice are located within one mile. Leashed pets are permitted.

Reservations, fees: Reservations accepted. Sites are $16-18 per night. Open year-round.

Directions: From Eugene drive west on Highway 126 for 61 miles to Florence and U.S. 101. Turn south on U.S. 101 and drive to Harbor Street. Turn east on Harbor Street and drive about three blocks to the park and marina.

Contact: Port of Siuslaw RV and Marina, P.O. Box 1638, Florence, OR 97439; tel. (541) 997-3040.

31 Mercer Lake Resort   7

This resort is set along the shore of Mercer Lake, one of a number of lakes that have formed among the ancient dunes in this area.

Location: On Mercer Lake; map D1, grid d4.

Campsites, facilities: There are 13 sites for trailers or RVs of any length; four are drive-through sites. Electricity, drinking water, cable TV, sewer hookups, and picnic tables are provided. Flush toilets, sanitary services, showers, a store, a laundry room, and ice are available. Boat docks, launching facilities, and fishing boat rentals are on-site. Leashed pets are permitted.

Reservations, fees: Reservations accepted. Sites are $15-19 per night. Open year-round.

Directions: From Eugene drive west on Highway 126 for 61 miles to Florence and U.S. 101. Turn north on U.S. 101 and drive five miles to Mercer Lake Road. Turn east and drive one mile to Bay Berry Lane. Turn left and drive to the campground.

Contact: Mercer Lake Resort, 88875 Bayberry Lane, Florence, OR 97439; tel. (800) 355-3633, (541) 997-3633; fax (541) 997-5096; e-mail: mlr@presys.com.

32 Archie Knowles

6

This little campground along Knowles Creek about three miles east of Mapleton is rustic with mixed forested and lawn areas, yet offers proximity to the highway. Staff at the ranger station in Mapleton can provide maps and information and answer any questions.

Location: On Knowles Creek in Siuslaw National Forest; map D1, grid d5.

Campsites, facilities: There are nine sites for tents, trailers, or RVs up to 16 feet long. Picnic tables and fire grills are provided. Flush toilets, garbage bins, and drinking water are available. Leashed pets are permitted.

Reservations, fees: No reservations accepted. Sites are $10 per night, $7 for an additional vehicle. Open May to late September.

Directions: From Eugene drive west on Highway 126 44 miles to the campground entrance (three miles east of Mapleton).

Contact: Siuslaw National Forest, Mapleton Ranger District, 4480 Highway 101, Building G, Florence, OR 97439; tel. (541) 902-8526; fax (541) 902-6946.

33 Maple Lane Trailer Park-Marina   5

This park along the shore of the Siuslaw River in Mapleton is close to boat rentals and hiking trails. The general area is surrounded by Siuslaw National Forest land. A U.S. Forest Service map details nearby backcountry side trip options.

Location: On the Siuslaw River; map D1, grid d5.

Campsites, facilities: There are two tent sites and 46 sites with full hookups for trailers or RVs of any length. Electricity, drinking water, and sewer hookups are provided. Flush toilets, bottled gas, sanitary services, and showers are available. A store, a cafe, and ice are located within one mile. A bait and tackle shop is open during the fishing season. Boat docks and launching facilities are on-site. Small pets (under 15 pounds) are permitted.

Reservations, fees: Reservations accepted. Sites are $7-14 per night. Open year-round.

Directions: From Eugene drive west on Highway 126 for 47 miles to Mapleton. Continue on Highway 126 for one-quarter mile past the business district to the park entrance

Contact: Maple Lane Trailer Park-Marina, 10730 Highway 126, Mapleton, OR 97453; tel. (541) 268-4822.

34 Fern Ridge Shores   7

This camp is in a wooded area along the shore of Fern Ridge Reservoir, where swimming, boating, and bass fishing are among the pastimes. You might catch a glimpse of an egret, heron, osprey, deer, or red fox. This is a friendly, family-oriented park that makes a great vacation destination, as well as an excellent layover for travelers cruising Interstate 5.

Location: On Fern Ridge Reservoir; map D1, grid d8.

Campsites, facilities: There are 61 sites for trailers and RVs up to 40 feet long. Rest rooms, showers, a sanitary dump station, security, a public phone, and ice are available. Recreational facilities include horseshoes, a field, a boat ramp, and a dock. Some facilities are wheelchair accessible. Two leashed pets per site are permitted.

Reservations, fees: Reservations recommended. Sites are $20-25 per night. Open year-round.

Directions: From Eugene drive west on Highway 126 for 10 miles to Veneta. Continue west on Highway 126 for 7.6 miles to Ellmaker Road. Turn north on Ellmaker Road and drive 1.1 miles to Jeans Road. Then turn east and drive 1.3 miles to the park on the right.

Contact: Fern Ridge Shores, 29652 Jeans Road, Veneta, OR 97487; tel. (541) 935-2335; fax (541) 935-5417.

35 Richardson Park

 7

This pretty Lane County park is a favorite for sailing and sailboards, as the wind is consistent. Boating and water skiing are also popular. A walking trail around the reservoir doubles as a bike trail, with swimming, fishing, and watching wildlife as optional activities. The Corps of Engineers has wildlife areas nearby. The historic Applegate Trail is featured in a kiosk display in the park. Three sites are wheel-chair accessible, as are the restrooms.

Location: On the Fern Ridge Reservoir; map D1, grid d8.

Campsites, facilities: There are 88 partial hookup sites for tents, trailers, or RVs up to 60 feet long, and seven group sites (maximum 16 people per site). Electricity, drinking water, picnic tables, and fire pits are provided. Restrooms with flush toilets, sinks, and hot showers, a dump station, and garbage bins are available. A part-time attended marina with minimal supplies, including ice, a boat launch and transient boat docks, unsupervised swimming, and a playground are available in the park. There is a small town within 10 miles. Leashed pets are permitted.

Reservations, fees: Reservations accepted. Call (541) 935-2005. Reservations must be made at least two weeks before the date you want, and there is a reservation fee of $10. Sites are $15 per night, with an additional charge of $35 per additional vehicle over two. Call for group site fees. Maximum stay is 14 days in a 30-day period. Open mid-April through mid-October.

Directions: In Eugene on Interstate 5, drive to Exit 195B and Belt Line Road. Turn west on Belt Line Road and drive 6.5 miles to Junction City Airport exit and Highway 99. Turn right on Highway 99 and drive north for two blocks to Clear Lake Road. Turn left and drive 8.5 miles to the campground on the left.

Contact: Richardson Park, 25950 Richardson Park Road, Junction City, OR 97448; tel. (541) 935-2005.

36 Carter Lake 9

This campground is on the north shore of Carter Lake, where you can fish almost right from your campsite. Boating, swimming, and fishing are permitted on this long, narrow lake, which is set among dunes overgrown with vegetation. The nearby Taylor Dunes Trail is an easy half-mile wheelchair-accessible trail to the dunes past Taylor Lake. Hiking is allowed in the dunes, but there is no off-road-vehicle access here. If you want off-road access, head north one mile to Siltcoos Road, turn west, and drive 1.3 miles to Driftwood II.

Location: On Carter Lake in Oregon Dunes National Recreation Area; map D1, grid e3.

Campsites, facilities: There are 23 sites for tents, trailers, or RVs up to 35 feet long. Picnic tables, garbage service, and fire grills are provided. Drinking water and flush toilets are available. Leashed pets are permitted.

Reservations, fees: No reservations accepted. Sites are $13 per night, $7 per night for an additional vehicle. Open mid-May through September.

Directions: From Eugene drive west on Highway 126 for 61 miles to Florence and U.S. 101. Turn south on U.S. 101 and drive 8.5 miles to Forest Road 1084. Turn right on Forest Road 1084 and drive west 200 yards to the camp.

Contact: Oregon Dunes National Recreation Area, 855 Highway 101, Reedsport, OR 97467; tel. (541) 271-3611; fax (541) 750-7244.

37 Woahink Lake RV Resort   7

One of several RV parks in the Florence area, this quiet, clean camp is located on Woahink Lake, where trout fishing is an option. Nearby Oregon Dunes National Recreation Area is a good side trip.

Location: On Woahink Lake; map D1, grid e3.

Campsites, facilities: There are 76 sites for trailers or RVs of any length. No tent camping is allowed. Electricity, drinking water, sewer hookups, rest rooms, showers, cable TV, a public phone, and a laundry room are available. Recreational facilities include horseshoe pits, a recreation hall, a game room, and a boat dock. One large or two small leashed pets per site are permitted.

Reservations, fees: Reservations recommended; phone (800) 659-6454 or e-mail: wohink@presys.com. Sites are $21 per night. Open year-round.

Directions: From Eugene drive west on Highway 126 for 61 miles to Florence and U.S. 101. Turn south on U.S. 101 and drive 5.1 miles to the camp on the right.

Contact: Woahink Lake RV Resort, 83570 Highway 101 South, Florence, OR 97439; tel. (541) 997-6454; fax (541) 902-0481; website: wohink@presys.com.

38 Driftwood II   6

This is primarily a campground for off-road vehicles. It's set near the ocean, but without an ocean view, in Oregon Dunes National Recreation Area and has off-road-vehicle access. Several small lakes, the Siltcoos River, and Siltcoos Lake are nearby. Note that ATV use is prohibited between 10 p.m. and 6 a.m.

Location: Near Siltcoos Lake in Oregon Dunes National Recreation Area; map D1, grid e3.

Campsites, facilities: There are 69 sites for tents, trailers, or RVs up to 50 feet long. Picnic tables, garbage service, and fire grills are provided. Drinking water and flush and vault toilets are available. A sanitary disposal station is located within five miles. Some facilities are wheelchair accessible. Boat docks, launching facilities, and rentals can be found about four miles away on Siltcoos Lake. Leashed pets are permitted.

Reservations, fees: Reservations accepted; phone (877) 444-6777 or access the website: www.reserveusa.com ($8.65 reservation fee). Sites are $13 per night, $7 per night for each additional vehicle. Open year-round.

Directions: From Eugene drive west on Highway 126 for 61 miles to Florence and U.S. 101. Turn south on U.S. 101 and drive seven miles to Siltcoos Beach Road. Turn right and drive 1.5 miles west to the campground.

Contact: Oregon Dunes National Recreation Area, 855 Highway 101, Reedsport, OR 97467; tel. (541) 271-3611; fax (541) 750-7244.

39 Lagoon   9

One of several campgrounds in the area, this one is along the lagoon about one mile from Siltcoos Lake and set one-half mile inland. The Lagoon Trail is a prime spot for wildlife viewing for marine birds and other aquatic species.

Location: Near Siltcoos Lake in Oregon Dunes National Recreation Area; map D1, grid e3.

Campsites, facilities: There are 39 sites for tents, trailers, or RVs up to 35 feet long. Picnic tables, garbage service, and fire grills are provided. Drinking water and flush and vault toilets are available. A telephone and sanitary services are located within five miles. Boat docks, launching facilities, and rentals are nearby on Siltcoos Lake. Leashed pets are permitted.

Reservations, fees: No reservations accepted. Sites are $13 per night, $7 per night for an additional vehicle. Open year-round.

Directions: From Eugene drive west on Highway 126 for 61 miles to Florence and U.S. 101. Turn south on U.S. 101 and drive seven miles to Siltcoos Beach Road. Turn right and drive 1.2 miles inland on Siltcoos Beach Road to the campground.

Contact: Oregon Dunes National Recreation Area, 855 Highway 101, Reedsport, OR 97467; tel. (541) 271-3611; fax (541) 750-7244.

40 Tyee   6

This wooded campground along the shore of the Siltcoos River is an option to Driftwood II and Lagoon. Swimming, fishing, and waterskiing are permitted at the nearby lake, where there is a canoe portage trail and a boat ramp. Off-road-vehicle access to the dunes is available from Driftwood II, and there are hiking trails in the area.

Location: On the Siltcoos River in Oregon Dunes National Recreation Area; map D1, grid e3.

Campsites, facilities: There are 16 sites for tents, trailers, or RVs up to 30 feet long. Picnic tables, garbage service, and fire grills are provided. Drinking water, vault toilets and a day-use area (with horseshoe pits, electricity, and 10 tables) are available. A store, boat docks, launching facilities, and rentals are nearby. Some facilities are wheelchair accessible. Leashed pets are permitted.

Reservations, fees: No reservations accepted. Sites are $13 per night, $7 per night for an additional vehicle. Open year-round.

Directions: From Eugene drive west on Highway 126 for 61 miles to Florence and U.S. 101. Turn south on U.S. 101 and drive six miles to the Westlake turnoff. Turn and you'll see the campground.

Contact: Oregon Dunes National Recreation Area, 855 Highway 101, Reedsport, OR 97467; tel. (541) 271-3611; fax (541) 750-7244.

41 Waxmyrtle   7

One of three camps in the immediate vicinity, Waxmyrtle is adjacent to Lagoon and less than a mile from Driftwood II. The camp is near the Siltcoos River and a couple of miles from Siltcoos Lake, a good-sized lake with boating facilities where you can water-ski, fish, and swim. A pleasant hiking trail is available that meanders through the dunes and along the estuary.

Location: Near Siltcoos Lake in Oregon Dunes National Recreation Area; map D1, grid e3.

Campsites, facilities: There are 54 sites for tents, trailers, or RVs up to 35 feet long. Picnic tables, garbage service, and fire grills are provided. Drinking water and flush toilets are available. Boat docks, launching facilities, and rentals are nearby on Siltcoos Lake. Leashed pets are permitted.

Reservations, fees: No reservations accepted. Sites are $13 per night, $7 per night for an additional vehicle. Open late May to mid-October.

Directions: From Eugene drive west on Highway 126 for 61 miles to Florence and U.S. 101. Turn south on U.S. 101 and drive seven miles to Siltcoos Beach Road. Turn right and drive 1.3 miles west to the campground.

Contact: Oregon Dunes National Recreation Area, 855 Highway 101, Reedsport, OR 97467; tel. (541) 271-3611; fax (541) 750-7244.

42 Tahkenitch Landing   6

This camp overlooking Tahkenitch Lake has easy access for fishing and swimming. Fishing is excellent on Tahkenitch, which means "a lake with many fingers." There is no drinking water here, but water, a boat ramp, and a dock are available nearby at Tahkenitch Lake.

Location: Near Tahkenitch Lake in Oregon Dunes National Recreation Area; map D1, grid e3.

Campsites, facilities: There are 27 sites for tents, trailers, or RVs up to 30 feet long. Picnic tables and garbage service are provided. Vault toilets, boat launching facilities, and a floating dock are available, but there is no drinking water. Leashed pets are permitted.

Reservations, fees: No reservations accepted. Sites are $12 per night, $7 per night for an additional vehicle. Open year-round.

Directions: From Eugene drive west on Highway 126 for 61 miles to Florence and U.S. 101. Turn south on U.S. 101 and drive 14 miles to the campground on the east side of the road.

Contact: Oregon Dunes National Recreation Area, 855 Highway 101, Reedsport, OR 97467; tel. (541) 271-3611; fax (541) 750-7244.

43 Tahkenitch   7

This very pretty campground is located in a wooded area across the highway from Tahkenitch Lake, which has numerous coves and backwater areas for fishing and swimming. A hiking trail close to the camp goes through the dunes out to the beach, as well as to Threemile Lake. If this camp is filled, Tahkenitch Landing provides nearby space.

Location: Near Tahkenitch Lake in Oregon Dunes National Recreation Area; map D1, grid e3.

Campsites, facilities: There are 25 sites for tents, trailers, or RVs up to 30 feet long. Picnic tables, garbage service, and fire grills are provided. Drinking water and flush and vault toilets are available. Boat docks and launching facilities are on the lake across the highway. Leashed pets are permitted.

Reservations, fees: No reservations accepted. Sites are $13 per night, $7 per night for an additional vehicle. Open mid-May through Labor Day weekend.

Directions: From Eugene drive west on Highway 126 for 61 miles to Florence and U.S. 101. Turn south on U.S. 101 and drive 14 miles. The campground entrance is on the right.

Contact: Oregon Dunes National Recreation Area, 855 Highway 101, Reedsport, OR 97467; tel. (541) 271-3611; fax (541) 750-7244.

44 Surfwood
Campground and RV Park   6

Fishing is the focal point at this park located half a mile from the marina at Winchester Bay. Hiking is another option, with trails heading west across the dunes to the ocean and east to lakes in wooded areas. An elk preserve can be found adjacent to Highway 38 some 10 miles to the east. The campground itself has pull-through sites separated by shrubs that create privacy.

Location: On Winchester Bay; map D1, grid e3.

Campsites, facilities: There are 22 tent sites and 141 sites for trailers or RVs; 64 are drive-through sites. Electricity, drinking water, sewer hookups, and picnic tables are provided. Flush toilets, sanitary services, showers, firewood, a store, a laundry room, ice, a playground, modem access, and a seasonal pool are available. Boat docks and launching facilities are within a half mile. Leashed pets and motorbikes are permitted.

Reservations, fees: Reservations accepted. Sites are $12-17 per night. Open year-round.

Directions: From Eugene drive south on Interstate 5 to Exit 162 and Highway 38. Turn west on Highway 38 and drive to Reedsport and U.S. 101. Turn south and 2.5 miles to the park (located one-half mile north of Winchester Bay).

Contact: Surfwood Campground and RV Park, 75381 Highway 101, Reedsport, OR 97467; tel. (541) 271-4020; e-mail: surfwood@harborside.com; website: www.paulspc.com/surfwood.

45 Darlings Resort   7

This park can be found in a rural area along the north shore of Siltcoos Lake, adjacent to the extensive Oregon Dunes National Recreation Area. Sites are right on the lake; fish from your picnic table. An access point to the dunes for hikers and off-road vehicles is just across the highway. The lake has a full-service marina.

Location: On Siltcoos Lake; map D1, grid e4.

Campsites, facilities: There are 42 sites for trailers or RVs of any length; 18 have full hookups. Electricity, cable TV, drinking water, sewer hookups, and picnic tables are provided. Flush toilets, showers, firewood, a store, a tavern, a deli, boat docks, boat rentals, launching facilities, and a laundry room are available. Leashed pets are permitted.

Reservations, fees: Reservations accepted. Sites are $14-18 per night. Open year-round.

Directions: From Eugene drive west on Highway 126 for 61 miles to Florence and U.S. 101. Turn south on U.S. 101 and drive five miles to North Beach Road. Turn east and drive one-half mile to the resort.

Contact: Darlings Resort, 4879 Darling Loop, Florence, OR 97439; tel. (541) 997-2841; e-mail: vambrosi@lycosmail.com; website: www.darlingsresort.com.

46 Whittaker Creek   7

This campground is home to one of the area's premier salmon spawning grounds, where annual runs of chinook, coho salmon, and steelhead can be viewed from the campground. The Old Growth Ridge Trail can be accessed from the campground. This moderately difficult trail ascends 1,000 feet above the Siuslaw River through a stand of old-growth Douglas fir. Fishing is for trout and crayfish.

Location: Near the Siuslaw River; map D1, grid e6.

Campsites, facilities: There are 31 sites for tents, trailers, or RVs up to 35 feet long. Picnic tables and fire pits are provided. Drinking water, vault toilets (wheelchair accessible), garbage bins, boat ramp, camp host, swimming beach, playground and a picnic shelter are available. Leashed pets are permitted. One campsite is wheelchair accessible.

Reservations, fees: No reservations accepted. Sites are $8 per night, with an additional charge of $5 per each additional vehicle. Open mid-May through mid-October, weather permitting.

Directions: From Eugene drive west on Highway 126 for 33 miles to Siuslaw River Road. Turn left (south) and drive two miles to the campground on the right.

Contact: Bureau of Land Management, Eugene District Office, P.O. Box 10226, Eugene, OR 97440-2226; tel. (541) 683-6600; fax (541) 683-6981.

47 Clay Creek   7

Clay Creek Trail, a two-mile loop takes you to a ridge overlooking the river valley and is well worth the walk. Fishing for trout and crayfish is popular. Sites are situated in a forest of cedars, Douglas fir and maple trees. The campground gets a medium amount of use.

Location: Near the Siuslaw River; map D1, grid e6.

Campsites, facilities: There are 21 sites for tents, trailers, or RVs up to 35 feet long. Picnic tables and fire pits are provided. Drinking water, vault toilets (one is wheelchair accessible), garbage bins, a swimming beach with changing rooms, softball field, horseshoe pits, playground, and two group picnic shelters with fireplaces are available. Leashed pets are permitted. One campsite is wheelchair accessible.

Reservations, fees: No reservations accepted. Sites are $8 per night, with an additional charge of $5 per each additional vehicle. Open mid-May through mid-October, depending on the weather.

Directions: From Eugene drive west on Highway 126 for 33 miles to Siuslaw River Road. Turn left (south) and drive 9.7 miles to Siuslaw River Access Road. Bear left and continue six miles to the campground on the right.

Contact: Bureau of Land Management, Eugene District Office, P.O. Box 10226, Eugene, OR 97440-2226; tel. (541) 683-6600; fax (541) 683-6981.

48 KOA Sherwood Forest   5

Located seven miles south of Eugene, this is an easy-to-reach layover for RV travelers heading up and down on Interstate 5. Nearby recreational facilities include a golf course and tennis courts.

Location: Near Eugene; map D1, grid e9.

Campsites, facilities: There are 20 tent sites and 100 sites for trailers or RVs of any length. Electricity, drinking water, sewer hookups, and picnic tables are provided. Flush toilets, sanitary services, showers, a recreation hall, a store, a laundry room, ice, a playground, and a swimming pool are available. Bottled gas and a cafe are within one mile. Pets and motorbikes are permitted.

Reservations, fees: Reservations accepted. Sites are $17-22 per night. Open year-round.

Directions: From Eugene drive south on Interstate 5 for seven miles to the Creswell exit. Take that exit and turn west on Oregon Avenue and drive one-half block to the campground at 298 East Oregon Avenue.

Contact: KOA Sherwood Forest, 298 East Oregon Avenue, Creswell, OR 97426; tel. (541) 895-4110.

49 Taylor's Travel Park   5

An alternative to KOA Sherwood Forest, this small ma-and-pa operation is close to the Coast Fork of the Willamette River. Recreational offerings 15 miles away include a golf course and a full-service marina.

Location: Near the Willamette River; map D1, grid e9.

Campsites, facilities: There are 10 tent sites and 20 sites for trailers or RVs of any length. Electricity, drinking water, sewer hookups, and picnic tables are provided in the summer months. Flush toilets, sanitary services, showers, and a playground are available. Bottled gas, a store, a cafe, a coin laundry, and ice are within one mile. Leashed pets and motorbikes are permitted.

Reservations, fees: Reservations accepted. Sites are $12 per night. Open year-round, with limited winter facilities.

Directions: From Eugene drive south on Interstate 5 for seven miles to the Creswell exit. Take that exit and turn west on Oregon Avenue and drive one-quarter mile to Highway 99. Turn south and drive 1.2 miles to Davisson Road. Turn left and drive south for one-half mile to the park.

Contact: tel. (541) 895-4715 82149 Davisson Road, Creswell, OR 97426.

50 Umpqua Lighthouse State Park   7

This park is near Lake Marie and less than a mile from Salmon Harbor on Winchester Bay. Located near the mouth of the Umpqua River, this unusual area has dunes as high as 500 feet. Hiking trails lead out from the park and into the Oregon Dunes National Recreation Area. The park offers more than two miles of beach access on the ocean and half a mile along the Umpqua River. The adjacent lighthouse is still in operation and tours are available during the summer season.

Location: On the Umpqua River; map D1, grid f2.

Campsites, facilities: There are 42 tent sites, 20 sites with full hookups for trailers or RVs up to 45 feet long, two cabins, and two yurts. Drinking water, garbage bins, and picnic tables are provided. Flush toilets, showers, and firewood are available. Boat docks and launching facilities are on the Umpqua River. Leashed pets are permitted.

Reservations, fees: Reservations accepted; phone (800) 452-5687 ($6 reservation fee). Sites are $10-17 per night, cabins are $35 per night, yurts are $27 per night; an additional vehicle is $7 per night. Major credit cards accepted. Open year-round.

Directions: From Eugene drive south on Interstate 5 to Exit 162 and Highway 38. Turn west on Highway 38 and drive 64 miles to Reedsport and U.S. 101. Turn south on U.S. 101 and drive six miles to the park entrance.

Contact: Umpqua Lighthouse State Park, C/O Sunset Bay State Park, 10965 Cape Arago Highway, Coos Bay, OR 97420; tel. (800) 551-6949 or (541) 271-4118.

51 Discovery Point RV Park

         7

This resort is on the shore of Winchester Bay in a fishing village near the mouth of the Umpqua River. For details on nearby recreation options, see the description of Surfwood Campground and RV Park.

Location: On Winchester Bay; map D1, grid f2.

Campsites, facilities: There are 15 tent sites and 50 sites for trailers or RVs of any length; 14 are drive-through sites. Electricity, drinking water, sewer hookups, and picnic tables are provided. Flush toilets, showers, a store, a laundry room, and ice are available. Sanitary services and bottled gas are located within one mile. Boat docks and launching facilities are nearby. Leashed pets and motorbikes are permitted.

Reservations, fees: Reservations accepted. Sites are $18-20 per night. Open year-round.

Directions: From Eugene drive south on Interstate 5 to Exit 162 and Highway 38. Turn west on Highway 38 and drive 64 miles to Reedsport and U.S. 101. Turn south on U.S. 101 and drive to the Windy Cove exit near Winchester Bay. Take that exit and drive west 1.5 miles to the resort.

Contact: Discovery Point RV Park, HC 81, P.O. Box 242, Reedsport, OR 97467; tel. (541) 271-3443; fax (541) 271-9357.

52 Windy Cove County Park

 7

This county park is actually comprised of two parks, Windy Cove A and B. Set near ocean beaches and sand dunes, both offer other nearby recreational facilities, including an 18-hole golf course, hiking trails, and a lighthouse.

Location: On the Pacific Ocean; map D1, grid f2.

Campsites, facilities: There are 29 tent sites and 40 sites with full hookups for trailers or RVs up to 60 feet long. Electricity, drinking water, sewer hookups, and picnic tables are provided. Flush toilets, showers, and cable TV are available. Bottled gas, sanitary services, a store, a cafe, a coin laundry, and ice are located within one mile. Boat docks, launching facilities, boat charters, and rentals are nearby. Leashed pets are permitted.

Reservations, fees: No reservations accepted. Sites are $12-15 per night. Open year-round.

Directions: From Eugene drive south on Interstate 5 to Exit 162 and Highway 38. Turn west on Highway 38 and drive 64 miles to Reedsport and U.S. 101. Turn south on U.S. 101 and drive to the Windy Cove exit near Winchester Bay. Take that exit and drive west to the park on the left.

Contact: Windy Cove County Park, 684 Salmon Harbor, Reedsport, OR 97467; tel. (541) 271-5634.

53 Osprey Point RV Resort

 7

This is one of Oregon's premier bass fishing lakes and yet only three miles from the ocean. The resort is situated in a large open area adjacent to Tenmile Lake and a half mile from North Lake. Nearby hiking trails are in the Oregon Dunes National Recreation Area, and wooded trails are at the Elliot State Forest. This is a destination resort more than an overnight stop, with weekend barbecues and occasional live entertainment.

Location: on Tenmile Lake; map D1, grid f2.

Campsites, facilities: There are 20 tent sites, and 132 sites for tents, trailers, or RVs of any size. RV sites have electricity, drinking water, sewer, picnic tables, fire pits, phone and cable TV provided. The park is also modem friendly. Drinking water, restrooms with flush toilets and showers, garbage bins, dump station, coin-operated laundry facilities, restaurant, cocktail lounge, grocery store, full service marina with boat docks, launch, fishing pier, fish cleaning station, horseshoe pits, volleyball, tether ball, a recreation hall, video arcade, beauty and barber shops, and pizza parlor are available. Leashed pets are permitted.

Reservations, fees: Reservations accepted; call (541) 759-2801. Sites are $16-28 per night, with an additional charge of $2.50 per each additional vehicle. Major credit cards accepted. Open year-round.

Directions: From Coos Bay drive north on U.S. 101 for 13 miles to the Lakeside exit. Take that exit and turn left (north) on North Lake Road, and drive a half mile to the resort on the right.

Contact: Osprey Point RV Resort, 1505 N. Lake Road, Lakeside, OR 97449; tel. (541) 759-2801; fax (541) 759-3198.

Spinreel  6

This campground, primarily for off-road-vehicle enthusiasts, is several miles inland at the outlet of Tenmile Lake in the Oregon Dunes National Recreation Area. A boat launch is located near the camp. Other recreational opportunities include hiking trails and off-road-vehicle access to the dunes. Off-road-vehicle rentals are available adjacent to the camp.

Location: On Tenmile Creek in Oregon Dunes National Recreation Area; map D1, grid f2.

Campsites, facilities: There are 36 sites for tents, trailers, or RVs up to 40 feet long. Drinking water, garbage service, and flush toilets are available. Picnic tables and fire grills are provided. Firewood, a store, and a Coin laundry are nearby. Boat docks, launching facilities, and rentals are located on Tenmile Lake. Leashed pets are permitted.

Reservations, fees: No reservations accepted. Sites are $13 per night. Open year-round.

Directions: From Coos Bay drive north on U.S. 101 for 10 miles to the campground entrance road (well signed). Turn northwest and drive one mile to the campground.

Contact: Oregon Dunes National Recreation Area, 855 Highway 101, Reedsport, OR 97467; tel. (541) 271-3611; fax (541) 750-7244.

Oregon Dunes KOA 5

This ATV-friendly park has direct access to Oregon Dunes National Recreation Area with miles of ATV trails. It is a fairly open campground with almost no tree cover ore vegetation. A small lake is on the premises, and the ocean is a 15-minute drive away. Mill Casino is about six miles south on US 101. Freshwater and ocean fishing are nearby. A golf course is about 5 miles away.

Location: slx miles north of North Bend, next to the Oregon Dunes National Recreation Area; map D1, grid f2.

Campsites, facilities: There are 85 tent sites, 61 sites for tents, trailers, or RVs of any size, and three cabins. RV sites have electricity, drinking water, sewer, picnic tables, fire pits, and satellite TV provided. There is a data port on-site for computers. Drinking water, restrooms with flush toilets and showers, garbage bins, wheelchair facilities, coin-operated laundry, mini-mart, horseshoe pits, volleyball, and a picnic shelter with electricity, sink, and electric cook tops are available. ORV rentals are nearby. Leashed pets are permitted.

Reservations, fees: Reservations recommended; call (541) 756-4851. Sites are $20-26 per night, with an additional charge of $2 per each additional vehicle. Major credit cards accepted. Open year-round.

Directions: From Coos Bay drive north on U.S. 101 past North Bend for six miles to Milepost 229 and the campground entrance road on the left.

Contact: Oregon Dunes KOA, 4135 Coast Highway, North Bend, OR 97459; tel. (541) 756-4851; fax (541) 756-8838.

56 Wild Mare Horse Camp

 7

This horse camp has paved parking, with single and double corrals. No off-road vehicles are allowed within the campground. Horses can be ridden straight out into the dunes—they cannot be ridden on the developed trails. The heavily treed shoreline gives rise to treed sites, with some bushes.

Location: Oregon Dunes National Recreation Area; map D1, grid g2.

Campsites, facilities: There are 12 horse campsites for tents, trailers, or RVs up to 50 feet long. There is a maximum of two vehicles per site. Picnic tables and fire pits are provided. Drinking water, vault toilets and garbage bins are available. Leashed pets are permitted.

Reservations, fees: Reservations accepted; phone (877) 444-6777 ($8.65 reservation fee). Sites are $12 per night, $7 per each additional vehicle. Major credit cards accepted. Open year-round.

Directions: From Coos Bay drive north on U.S. 101 for 1.5 miles to Horsfall Dunes and Beach Access Road. Turn left and drive west for one mile to the campground access road. Turn and drive three-quarters of a mile to the campground on the left.

Contact: Oregon Dunes National Recreation Area, 855 U.S. Highway 101, Reedsport, OR 97467; (541) 271-3611; fax (541) 750-7244.

57 Bluebill

 6

This campground gets very little camping pressure although there are some good hiking trails available. It's next to little Bluebill Lake, which sometimes dries up during the summer. A one-mile trail goes around the lake bed. The camp is a short distance from Horsfall Lake, which is surrounded by private property. If you continue west on the Forest Road, you'll come to a picnicking and parking area near the beach that has off-road-vehicle access to the dunes at the Horsfall day-use area or Horsfall Beach.

Location: On Bluebill Lake in Oregon Dunes National Recreation Area; map D1, grid g2.

Campsites, facilities: There are 18 sites for tents, trailers, or RVs up to 30 feet long. Picnic tables, garbage service, and fire grills are provided. Flush toilets and drinking water are available. Leashed pets are permitted.

Reservations, fees: No reservations accepted. Sites are $13 per night, and $7 per night for each additional vehicle. Open May through November.

Directions: From Coos Bay drive north on U.S. 101 for 1.5 miles north to Horsfall Dunes and Beach Access Road. Turn west and drive one mile to Horsfall Road. Turn northwest and drive two miles to the campground entrance.

Contact: Oregon Dunes National Recreation Area, 855 Highway 101, Reedsport, OR 97467; tel. (541) 271-3611; fax (541) 750-7244.

58 William M. Tugman State Park

 7

This campground is relatively unknown and set along the shore of Eel Lake, which offers almost five miles of shoreline for swimming, fishing, boating, and sailing. It's perfect for bass fishing. A boat ramp is available, but there is a 10 mph speed limit for boats. Oregon Dunes National Recreation Area is across the highway. Hiking is available just a few miles north at Umpqua Lighthouse State Park. A trail along the south end of the lake allows hikers to get away from the developed areas of the park and explore the lake's many outlets.

Location: On Eel Lake; map D1, grid f3.

Campsites, facilities: There are 112 sites with water and electrical hookups for trailers or RVs up to 50 feet long, a special camping area for hikers, and three yurts. Electricity, drinking water, and picnic tables are provided. Flush toilets, sanitary services, showers, firewood, a picnic shelter, and a laundry room are available. Some facilities are wheelchair accessible. Boat docks and launching facilities are nearby. Leashed pets are permitted.

Reservations, fees: Reservations accepted; phone (800) 452-5687. Sites are $12-15 per night, $4 per night for hikers/bicyclists, yurts are $29 per night; $7 per night for an additional vehicle. Major credit cards accepted. Open year-round.

Directions: From Eugene drive south on Interstate 5 to Exit 162 and Highway 38. Turn west on Highway 38 and drive 64 miles to Reedsport and U.S. 101. Turn south on U.S. 101 and drive eight miles to the park entrance on the left.

Contact: Sunset Bay State Park, 10965 Cape Arago Highway, Coos Bay, OR 97420; tel. (541) 759-3604 or (800) 551-6949.

59 North Lake Resort and Marina   8

This 40-acre resort along the shore of Tenmile Lake is wooded and secluded, with a private beach, a perfect layover spot for U.S. 101 travelers. The lake has a full-service marina, and bass fishing can be good here.

Location: On Tenmile Lake; map D1, grid f3.

Campsites, facilities: There are 100 sites for trailers or RVs of any length. Picnic tables are provided. Flush toilets, sanitary services, showers, firewood, a store, ice, electricity, phone/modem hookups, cable TV, drinking water, coin-operated laundry facilities, horseshoe pits, a volleyball court, and sewer hookups are available. A cafe, boat docks, launching facilities, and rentals are nearby. Leashed pets are permitted.

Reservations, fees: Reservations accepted. Sites are $22 per night. Open March through October.

Directions: From Eugene drive south on Interstate 5 to Exit 162 and Highway 38. Turn west on Highway 38 and drive 64 miles to Reedsport and U.S. 101. Turn south on U.S. 101 and drive 11 miles to Lakeside exit. Take that exit and drive east on North Lake Avenue for three-quarters of a mile, then continue on North Lake Road for one-half mile to the resort on the left.

Contact: North Lake Resort and Marina, 2090 North Lake Avenue, Lakeside, OR 97449; tel. (541) 759-3515; fax (541) 759-3515.

60 Eel Creek   8

This campground along Eel Creek is near both Eel and Tenmile Lakes. Waterskiing is allowed on Tenmile Lake but not at Eel Lake. Nearby trails access the Umpqua Dunes Scenic Area, where you'll find spectacular scenery in an area closed to off-road vehicles. Off-road access is available at Spinreel.

Location: Near Eel Lake in Oregon Dunes National Recreation Area; map D1, grid f3.

Campsites, facilities: There are 52 sites for tents, trailers, or RVs up to 35 feet long. Picnic tables, garbage service, and fire grills are provided. Drinking water and flush and vault toilets are available. Boat docks, launching facilities, and rentals are nearby. Leashed pets are permitted.

Reservations, fees: No reservations accepted. Sites are $13 per night, $7 per night for an additional vehicle. Open year-round.

Directions: From Eugene drive south on Interstate 5 to Exit 162 and Highway 38. Turn west on Highway 38 and drive 64 miles to Reedsport and U.S. 101. Turn south on U.S. 101 and drive 10.5 miles to the park entrance.

Contact: Oregon Dunes National Recreation Area, 855 Highway 101, Reedsport, OR 97467; tel. (541) 271-3611; fax (541) 750-7244.

61 Loon Lake Recreational Area Campground
   8

Loon Lake was created 1400 years ago when a nearby mountain crumbled and slid downhill, damming the creek with house-sized boulders. Today the lake is a half-mile wide, nearly two miles long, covers 260 acres and is over 200 feet deep in places. It is ideally located to provide a warm, wind-sheltered summer climate for various water activities. A nature trail leads to a waterfall about a half mile away. Evening interpretive programs are held during summer weekends.

Location: on Loon Lake; map D1, grid f5.

Campsites, facilities: There are 61 sites for tents, trailers, or RVs of any size. There are also five group sites for up to 15 people per site. Picnic tables and fire pits are provided. Drinking water, restrooms with flush toilets and showers, garbage bins, dump station, a sand beach, restaurant, mini- mart, boat ramp and moorings, amphitheater, and gasoline are available. Leashed pets are permitted.

Reservations, fees: Reservations required for group sites only; call Reservations Northwest at (800) 452-5687 ($6 reservation fee). Family sites are $12-13 per night, with an additional charge of $7 per each additional vehicle. Group sites are $15 per night. Open late May through mid-September, depending on the weather.

Directions: From Eugene drive south on Interstate 5 to Exit 162 and Highway 38. Turn west on Highway 38 and drive 43 miles to Milepost 13.5 and County Road 3 exit. Turn south and drive 7.5 miles to the campground.

Contact: Bureau of Land Management, Coos Bay District Office, 1300 Airport Lane, North Bend, OR 97459; tel. (541) 756-0100; fax (541) 751-4303.

62 Loon Lake Lodge Resort   8

This resort has one mile of lake frontage and is nestled among the tall trees on pretty Loon Lake. It's not a long drive from either U.S. 101 or Interstate 5, making it an ideal layover spot for travelers eager to get off the highway. The lake offers good bass fishing, swimming, boating, and waterskiing.

Location: On Loon Lake; map D1, grid f5.

Campsites, facilities: There are 100 sites for tents, trailers, or RVs up to 32 feet, 50 are partial hookups; group sites and cabins are also available. Electricity, drinking water, a public phone, security, ice, a game room, restaurant, bar, grocery store, ice, gas, and a beach are available. A boat ramp, dock, marina, and rentals are also available. Leashed pets are permitted.

Reservations, fees: Reservations recommended. Sites are $16-19 per night. Cabins are $54-69 per night. Major credit cards accepted. Open year-round.

Directions: From Eugene drive south on Interstate 5 to Exit 162 and Highway 38. Turn west on Highway 38 and drive 43 miles to milepost 13.5 and County Road 3 exit. Turn south and drive 8.2 miles to the resort on the right.

Contact: Loon Lake Lodge Resort, 9011 Loon Lake Road, Reedsport, OR 97467; tel. (541) 599-2244; fax (541) 599-2274.

63 Tyee (BLM)   7

Here's a classic spot, set along the Umpqua River with great steelhead, salmon, and small mouth bass fishing in season, yet very few people know of it. Boat launches are available a few miles upstream and downstream of the campground. The camp isn't far from Interstate 5, and it's the only campground in the immediate vicinity.

Location: On the Umpqua River; ma D1, grid f6.

Campsites, facilities: There are 15 sites for tents, trailers, or RVs up to 25 feet long. Drinking water, garbage service, fire grills, and picnic tables are provided. Vault toilets and a day-use area with horseshoe pits, a pavilion, electricity, and 10 tables are available. A store is located within one mile. Some facilities are wheelchair accessible. Leashed pets are permitted.

Reservations, fees: No reservations accepted. Sites are $7 per night, plus $3 for each additional vehicle. Open year-round.

Directions: From Roseburg drive north on Interstate 5 to Exit 136 and Highway 138. Take that exit and drive west on Highway 138 for 12 miles. Cross Bullock Bridge and continue to County Road 57. Turn right and drive one-half mile to the campground entrance.

Contact: Bureau of Land Management, Roseburg District, 777 Garden Valley Boulevard, Roseburg, OR 97470; tel. (541) 440-4930; fax (541) 440-4948.

64 Pass Creek County Park   7

This decent layover spot for travelers on Interstate 5 can be found in a wooded, hilly area with many shaded sites. View of the mountains give the park scenic value. There is a covered pavilion with a family-sized barbecue grill, for get-togethers. You can find fishing and other water activities 11 miles away, and there is a covered bridge for the history seekers. There are no other campgrounds in the immediate area, so if it's late and you need a place to stay, grab this one.

Location: Near Cottage Grove; map D1, grid f9.

Campsites, facilities: There are 10 tent sites and 30 sites for trailers or RVs up to 30 feet long. Electricity, drinking water, sewer hookups, and picnic tables are provided. Flush toilets, showers, and a playground are available. A store, a café, and ice are within one mile. Leashed pets are permitted.

Reservations, fees: No reservations accepted. Sites are $11-14 per night. Open March through October.

Directions: On Interstate 5 drive to Exit 163 (between Roseburg and Eugene). Take Exit 163 and turn west on Curtain Park Road. Drive west (under the freeway) for a very short distance to the park entrance.

Contact: Pass Creek County Park, P.O. Box 81, Curtin, OR 97428; tel. (541) 942-3281.

65 Pine Meadows   6

This campground is set near the banks of Cottage Grove Reservoir, where boating, fishing, waterskiing, and swimming are among the recreation options. It's an easy hop from Interstate 5, but a lot of campers don't realize it.

Location: On Cottage Grove Reservoir; map D1, grid f9.

Campsites, facilities: There are 92 sites for tents, trailers, or RVs of any length, with some drive-through sites. Drinking water, picnic tables, garbage bins, and fire rings are provided. Flush toilets, sanitary disposal station, showers, children's play area, an amphitheater, interpretive displays, and a swimming area are available. A boat dock, launching facilities, and a mini-market are nearby. Leashed pets and street-legal motorbikes are permitted.

Reservations, fees: Reservations accepted; phone (877) 444-6777 or access the website: www.reserveusa.com ($8.65 reservation fee). Sites are $12 per night, $4 per night for an additional vehicle. Open mid-May to mid-September.

Directions: From Eugene drive south on Interstate 5 past Cottage Grove to Exit 172. Take that exit to London Road and drive south for 4.5 miles to Reservoir Road. Turn left and drive three miles to the camp entrance on the right.

Contact: U.S. Army Corps of Engineers, Recreation Information, Cottage Grove, OR 97424; tel. (541) 942-8657, (541) 942-5631; fax (541) 942-1305; website: www.nwp.usace.army.mil.

66 Primitive Cottage Grove Lake Walk-In   6

This campground on Cottage Grove Reservoir is open to boating, fishing, waterskiing, and swimming. See the description of neighboring Pine Meadows for more information.

Location: On Cottage Grove Reservoir; map D1, grid f9.

Campsites, facilities: There are 15 walk-in sites. Picnic tables, vault toilets, drinking water, garbage bins, sanitary services, and fire rings are available. Boat docks, launching facilities, and a mini-market are nearby. Leashed pets and street-legal motorbikes are permitted.

Reservations, fees: Reservations required; phone (877) 444-6777 or access the website: www.reserveusa.com ($8.65 reservation fee). Sites are $6 per night, $4 per night for an additional vehicle. Open late May to early September.

Directions: From Eugene drive south on Interstate 5 past Cottage Grove to Exit 172. Take that exit to London Road and drive south for 4.5 miles to Reservoir Road. Turn left and drive three miles to the camp entrance.

Contact: U.S. Army Corps of Engineers, Recreation Information, Cottage Grove, OR 97424; tel. (541) 942-8657, (541) 942-5631; fax (541) 942-1305; website: www.nwp.usace.army.mil.

67 Sunset Bay State Park

 8

Situated in one of the most scenic areas on the Oregon Coast, this park features beautiful, sandy beaches protected by towering sea cliffs. A network of hiking trails connects Sunset Bay with nearby Shore Acres and Cape Arago Parks. Swimming, boating, fishing, clamming, and golfing are some of the options here.

Location: Near Sunset Bay; map D1, grid g1.

Campsites facilities: There are 66 sites for tents or self-contained RVs, 34 sites with full hookups for trailers or RVs up to 47 feet long, a separate area for hikers and bicyclists, eight yurts, and one group camp. Drinking water, picnic tables, garbage bins, and fire grills are provided. Flush toilets, showers, a group shelter, a boat ramp, and firewood are available. A restaurant is located within 2.5 miles. Some facilities are wheelchair accessible. Leashed pets are permitted.

Reservations, fees: Reservations accepted; phone (800) 452-5687 ($6 reservation fee). Sites are $13-19 per night, sites for hikers/bicyclists are $4 per night, yurts are $27 per night, the group camp is $60 per night for up to 25 people; $7 per night for an additional vehicle. Major credit cards accepted. Open May through September.

Directions: In Coos Bay, take the Charleston Ocean Beaches exit to Newmark Avenue and drive west for three miles to Cape Arago Highway. Turn left and drive about five miles south to Charleston and cross the South Slough Bridge. Continue on Cape Arago Highway about three miles to the park entrance on the left.

Contact: Sunset Bay State Park, 10965 Cape Arago Highway, Coos Bay, OR 97420; tel. (541) 888-4902.

68 Bastendorff Beach Park

 8

This campground provides access to the ocean and a small lake. Nearby activities include sand-dune buggy riding, clamming, crabbing, fishing, swimming, whale watching, and boating. Horses may be rented near Bandon. A nice side trip is to Shore Acres State Park and Botanical Gardens, about 2.5 miles away.

Location: Near Cape Arago State Park; map D1, grid g1

Campsites, facilities: There are 25 tent sites and 56 sites for trailers or RVs with partial hookups. Drinking water, picnic tables, rest rooms, coin-operated showers, a sanitary dump, a public phone, and a fireplace are provided. A fish cleaning station, horseshoe pits, a playground, basketball courts, and a picnic area with shelter and barbecue are also available. The facilities are wheelchair accessible. Leashed pets are permitted.

Reservations, fees: Reservations accepted for the shelter only. Call (541) 396-3121. Sites are $9-17 per night. Open year-round.

Directions: In Coos Bay, take the Charleston Ocean Beaches exit to Newmark Avenue and drive west for three miles to Cape Arago Highway. Turn left and drive about five miles south to Charleston and cross the South Slough Bridge. Continue on Cape Arago Highway about two miles to the park entrance.

Contact: Coos County Parks, Coos County Courthouse, 250 North Baxter Street, Coquille, OR 97423, or Bastendorff Beach Park, 4250 Bastendorff Beach Road, Coos Bay, OR 97420; tel. (541) 888-5353.

69 Charleston Marina RV Park

      7

This large, developed park and marina is located near Charleston on the Pacific Ocean. Recreational activities in and near the campground include hiking, swimming, clamming, crabbing, boating, huckleberry and blackberry picking, and fishing for tuna, salmon, and halibut.

Location: On Coos Bay; map D1, grid g1.

Campsites, facilities: There are 108 sites for tents, trailers, or RVs up to 50 feet. Drinking water, cable TV, rest rooms, showers, a sanitary dump, a public phone, a laundry room, a playground, and LP gas are available. A marina with a boarding dock and launch ramp are on-site. The facilities are wheelchair accessible. Leashed pets are permitted.

Reservaions, fees: Reservations recommended. Sites are $10-17 per night, $1 per day for an additional vehicle. Open year-round.

Directions: In Coos Bay take the Charleston Ocean Beaches exit to Newmark Avenue and drive west for three miles to Cape Arago Highway. Turn left and drive about five miles south to Charleston and cross the South Slough Bridge; continue to Boat Basin Drive. Turn right and drive one-quarter mile to Kingfisher Drive. Turn right and drive 200 feet to the campground on the left.

Contact: Charleston Marina RV Park, P.O. Box 5409, Charleston, OR 97420-0607; tel. the park at (541) 888-9512; fax (541) 888-6111; website: www.charlestonmarina.com.

70 Oceanside RV Park

       7

This is one of several private, developed parks in the Charleston area. The park is within walking distance of the Pacific Ocean, with opportunities for swimming, fishing, clamming, crabbing, and boating. A marina is 1.5 miles away.

Location: Near the Pacific Ocean; map D1, grid g1.

Campsites, facilities: There are 10 tent sites and 70 full-hookup sites (30 or 50 amp) for trailers or RVs. Rest rooms, showers, a sanitary dump, a public phone, a fish cleaning station, and LP gas are available. There is also some fishing equipment. The facilities are wheelchair accessible. Leashed pets are permitted.

Reservations, fees: Reservations recommended. Sites are $10-20 per night. Open year-round.

Directions: In Coos Bay, take the Charleston Ocean Beaches exit to Newmark Avenue and drive west for three miles to Cape Arago Highway. Turn left and drive about five miles south to Charleston and cross the South Slough Bridge. Continue on Cape Arago Highway for 1.8 miles to the park entrance on the right.

Contact: Oceanside RV Park, 9838 Cape Arago Highway, Charleston, OR 97420; tel. (541) 888-2598, (800) 570-2598; e-mail: oceanside@harborside.com; website: www.harborside.com/home/o/oceanside.

71 Horsfall   4

This campground is actually a nice, large paved area for parking RVs. It's the staging area for off-road-vehicle access into the southern section of Oregon Dunes National Recreation Area. If Horsfall is full, try Horsfall Beach nearby, an overflow area with 34 tent and RV sites.

Location: In Oregon Dunes National Recreation Area; map D1, grid g2.

Campsites, facilities: There are 69 sites for trailers or RVs up to 50 feet in length. Drinking water, garbage service, coin-operated showers, a pay phone, and flush toilets are available. Leashed pets are permitted.

Reservations, fees: Reservations accepted; phone (877) 444-6777 or access the website: www.reserveusa.com ($8.65 reservation fee). Sites are $13 per night, $7 per night for an additional vehicle. Open year-round.

Directions: From Coos Bay drive north on U.S. 101 for 1.5 miles to Horsfall Road. Turn west on Horsfall Road and drive about one mile to the campground access road. Turn on the campground access road and drive one-half mile to the campground.

Contact: Oregon Dunes National Recreation Area, 855 Highway 101, Reedsport, OR 97467; tel. (541) 271-3611; fax (541) 750-7244.

72 Kelley's RV Park   5

This clean, well-maintained RV park is in the town of Coos Bay, well known for its salmon, deep-sea fishing, and lumber. The shaded picnic area overlooks the scenic bay. Nearby recreation options include a full-service marina.

Location: Near Coos Bay; map D1, grid g2.

Campsites, facilities: There are 38 sites for trailers or RVs of any length; three are drive-through sites. Electricity, drinking water, sewer hookups, and picnic tables are provided. Flush toilets and a laundry room are available. Bottled gas, a store, and a cafe are located within one mile. Boat docks and launching facilities are nearby. Leashed pets are permitted.

Reservations, fees: Reservations accepted. Sites are $15-16 per night. Open year-round.

Directions: In Coos Bay on U.S. 101, drive to the Charleston exit. Take the Charleston exit to South Empire Boulevard and drive 4.5 miles to the park at 555 South Empire Boulevard.

Contact: Kelley's RV Park, 555 South Empire Boulevard, Coos Bay, OR 97420; tel. (541) 888-6531; e-mail: kellysrv@gte.net.

73 Whistler's Bend  7

This county park along the banks of the North Umpqua River is an idyllic spot because it's just a 20-minute drive from Interstate 5, yet it gets little pressure from outsiders. Two boat ramps accommodate boaters, and fishing is a plus. A wildlife reserve provides habitat for deer.

Location: On the North Umpqua River; map D1, grid g8.

Campsites, facilities: There are 23 sites for tents, trailers, or RVs up to 35 feet long. Group camping is available. Picnic tables and fire grills are provided. Drinking water, flush toilets, showers, a playground, and launching facilities are available. Leashed pets are permitted.

Reservations, fees: Reservations accepted for group sites only. Call (541) 440-4500. Sites are $10 per night, plus $3 for each additional vehicle; call for group camping fees. Open year-round.

Directions: From Roseburg drive east on Highway 138 for 12 miles to Whistler's Bend Park Road (well signed). Turn left and drive two miles to the end of the road and the park entrance.

Contact: Whistler's Bend, 2828 Whistlers Park Road, Roseburg, OR 97470; tel. (541) 673-4863.

REBEL SWIMMING

MAP D2

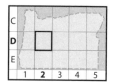

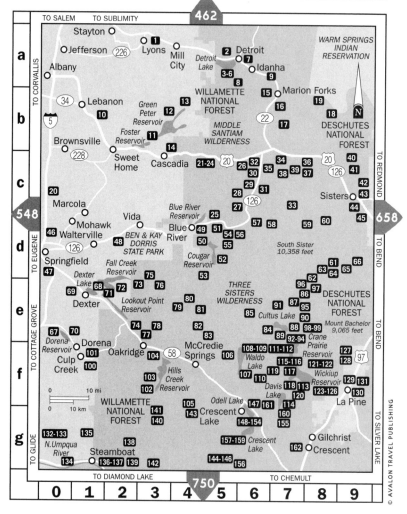

© AVALON TRAVEL PUBLISHING

CHAPTER D2

■ John Neal Memorial Park   6

Set on the banks of the North Santiam River, this camp offers good boating and trout fishing possibilities. Other options include exploring lakes and trails in the adjacent national forest land or visiting Silver Falls State Park.

Location: On the North Santiam River; map D2, grid a3.

Campsites, facilities: There are 40 sites for tents, trailers, and self-contained RVs. Rest rooms, garbage bins, and drinking water are available. Recreational facilities include a boat ramp, a playground, horseshoes, a barbecue, and a recreation field. Ice and a grocery are located within one mile. Leashed pets are permitted.

Reservations, fees: No reservations. Sites are $10 per night. Open May through October, depending on weather.

Directions: From Salem drive east on Highway 22 for about 20 miles to Highway 226. Turn right and drive south for two miles to Lyons and John Neal Park Road. Turn east and drive a short distance to the campground on the left.

Contact: Linn County Parks Department, 3010 Ferry Street SW, Albany, OR 97321; tel. (541) 967-3917; fax (541) 924-0202.

■ Detroit Lake State Park   7

This campground is set at 1,600 feet along the shore of Detroit Lake, which is 400 feet deep, nine miles long, and has more than 32 miles of shoreline. The park offers a fishing dock and a moorage area, and a boat ramp and bathhouse are available nearby at the Mongold Day Use Area. The lake is crowded on the opening day of trout season in late April because it's heavily stocked.

Location: On Detroit Lake; map D2, grid a5.

Campsites, facilities: There are 132 tent sites and 179 sites with full or partial hookups for trailers or RVs up to 60 feet long, and 82 boat slips. Drinking water, garbage bins, fire grills, and picnic tables are provided. Flush toilets, showers, a playground, swimming areas, a store, a visitor center, and firewood are available. Boat docks and launching facilities are nearby. Leashed pets are permitted.

Reservations, fees: Contact Reservations Northwest at (800) 452-5687 ($6 reservation fee). Sites are $13-22 per night, $7 per night for an additional vehicle. Boating moorage is $7 per night. Major credit cards accepted. Open March through November, weather permitting.

Directions: From Salem drive east on Highway 22 for 50 miles to the park entrance on the right (located two miles west of Detroit).

Contact: Detroit Lake State Park, P.O. Box 549, Detroit, OR 97342; tel. (541) 854-3346.

■ Piety Island Boat-In   10

This island gets crowded and has a reputation for sometimes attracting rowdy groups. Other campgrounds along the shore have drinking water. Piety Island Trail is a 1.5-mile climb to the top of the island. You'll find great vistas on this island.

Location: On Detroit Lake in Willamette National Forest; map D2, grid a5.

Campsites, facilities: There are 12 tent sites on this island campground, which is accessible by boat only. Picnic tables and fire grills are provided. Pit toilets are available, but there is no drinking water, and all garbage must be packed out. Boat docks, launching facilities, and rentals are nearby. Leashed pets are permitted.

Reservations, fees: No reservations; no fee. Open May to late September.

Directions: From Salem drive east on Highway 22 for 45 miles to Detroit Lake. Continue east on Highway 22 along the north side of the lake to the boat ramp (a boat ramp is located three miles west of the town of Detroit). Launch your boat and head southeast to the island in the middle of the lake. The campground is located on the east side of the island.

Contact: Willamette National Forest, Detroit Ranger District, HC 73, Box 320, Mill City, OR 97360; tel. (503) 854-3366; fax (503) 854-4239.

4 Southshore   9

This popular camp is along the south shore of Detroit Lake, where fishing, swimming, and waterskiing are some of the recreation options. The Stahlman Point Trailhead is about one-half mile from camp. There's a day-use area for picnicking and swimming. The views of the lake and surrounding mountains are outstanding.

Location: On Detroit Lake in Willamette National Forest; map D2, grid a5.

Campsites, facilities: There are eight walk-in tent sites and 24 sites for tents, trailers, or RVs up to 22 feet long. Fire grills, garbage service, and picnic tables are provided. Vault toilets and drinking water are available. Boat launching facilities are nearby at a day-use area. Leashed pets are permitted.

Reservations, fees: No reservations. Sites are $12-20 per night, $5 per night for an additional vehicle. Open mid-April to late September, with a gate preventing access during the off season.

Directions: From Salem drive east on Highway 22 for 52 miles to Detroit. Continue southeast on Highway 22 for 2.5 miles to Forest Road 10 (Blowout Road). Turn right and drive four miles to the campground on the right.

Contact: Willamette National Forest, Detroit Ranger District, HC 73, Box 320, Mill City, OR 97360; tel. (503) 854-3366; fax (503) 854-4239.

5 Cove Creek   10

See the description of Southshore and Hoover for recreation options.

Location: On Detroit Lake in Willamette National Forest; map D2, grid a5.

Campsites, facilities: There are 63 sites for tents, trailers, or RVs, and one group site. Picnic tables, garbage service, and fire rings are provided. Drinking water, rest rooms with flush toilets and coin-operated showers, garbage bins, and a boat ramp are available. Some facilities are wheelchair accessible. Leashed pets are permitted.

Reservations, fees: Reservations for group site only. Call (877) 444-6777. Sites are $16 per night, $5 per night for an additional vehicle. Group sites are $120 per night. Open late May to late September.

Directions: From Salem drive east on Highway 22 for 52 miles to Detroit. Continue southeast on Highway 22 for 2.5 miles to Forest Road 10 (Blowout Road). Turn right and drive three miles to the campground on the right.

Contact: Willamette National Forest, Detroit Ranger District, HC 73, Box 320, Mill City, OR 97360; tel. (503) 854-3366; fax (503) 854-4239.

⑥ Hoover 9

This campground is along the eastern arm of Detroit Lake, near the mouth of the Santiam River. There is a wheelchair-accessible fishing area and nature trail. You're likely to see osprey fishing during the day, a truly special sight. See the description of Southshore for other recreation options.

Location: On Detroit Lake in Willamette National Forest; map D2, grid a5.

Campsites, facilities: There are 34 sites for tents, trailers, or RVs up to 32 feet long. Picnic tables, garbage service, and fire grills are provided. Flush toilets and drinking water are available. Some facilities are wheelchair accessible. Boat docks and launching facilities are nearby. Leashed pets are permitted.

Reservations, fees: No reservations. Sites are $12-20 per night, $5 per night for an additional vehicle. Open mid-April to late September; a gate prevents access in the off season.

Directions: From Salem drive east on Highway 22 for 52 miles to Detroit. Continue southeast on Highway 22 for 2.5 miles to Forest Road 10 (Blowout Road). Turn right and drive one mile to the campground on the right.

Contact: Willamette National Forest, Detroit Ranger District, HC 73, Box 320, Mill City, OR 97360; tel. (503) 854-3366; fax (503) 854-4239.

⑦ Upper Arm 7

This little campground is set along the shore of the narrow upper arm of Detroit Lake, close to where the Breitenbush River empties into it. It's the smallest and most primitive camp in the area with a large day-use area.

Location: On Detroit Lake in Willamette National Forest; map D2, grid a6.

Campsites, facilities: There are five tent sites. Fire grills and picnic tables are provided. Pit toilets and garbage service (summer only) are available. There is no drinking water. Boat docks, launching facilities, and rentals are nearby. Leashed pets are permitted.

Reservations, fees: No reservations; no fee. Open year-round.

Directions: From Salem drive east on Highway 22 for 52 miles to Detroit and Forest Road 46 (Breitenbush Road). Turn left and drive one mile northeast to the campground on the left.

Contact: Willamette National Forest, Detroit Ranger District, HC 73, Box 320, Mill City, OR 97360; tel. (503) 854-3366; fax (503) 854-4239.

⑧ Hoover Group Camp 9

This is a perfect spot for a family reunion or club trip. Detroit Lake offers a myriad of activities, including hiking, fishing, swimming, and boating, just to name a few. The campground has nice, open sites and direct access to the lake. See trip note for Hoover campground.

Location: On Detroit Lake in Willamette National Forest; map D2, grid a5.

Campsites, facilities: There are nine sites for tents, trailers, or RVs up to 15 feet long. This is a group camp that will accommodate up to 70 people. Drinking water and picnic tables are provided. Vault toilets and a group picnic shelter are available. Boat docks, launching facilities, and rentals are nearby. Leashed pets are permitted.

Reservations, fees: Reservations required; call (877) 444-6777 or access the website: www.reserveusa.com ($8.65 reservation fee). Group sites are $120 per night, with a two-night minimum for weekend reservations. Open mid-April to late September.

Directions: From Salem drive east on Highway 22 for 52 miles to Detroit. Continue southeast on Highway 22 for 2.5 miles to Forest Road 10 (Blowout Road). Turn right and drive one-half mile to the campground on the right.

Contact: Willamette National Forest, Detroit Ranger District, HC 73, Box 320, Mill City, OR 97360; tel. (503) 854-3366; fax (503) 854-4239.

9 Whispering Falls   10

This popular campground is on the banks of the Santiam River where you can fish. If the campsites at Detroit Lake are crowded, this provides a more secluded option, and it's only about a 10-minute drive from the lake. There is a small waterfall right across the river from the campground. Ospreys sometimes nest near the waterfall.

Location: On the Santiam River near Detroit Lake in Willamette National Forest; map D2, grid a6.

Campsites, facilities: There are 16 sites for tents, trailers, or RVs up to 22 feet long. Picnic tables, garbage service, and fire grills are provided. Drinking water and flush toilets are available. Leashed pets are permitted.

Reservations, fees: No reservations. Sites are $10 per night, $5 per night for an additional vehicle. Open mid-April to late September; a gate prevents access in the off season

Directions: From Salem drive east on Highway 22 for 52 miles to Detroit. Continue east on Highway 22 for eight miles to the campground on the right.

Contact: Willamette National Forest, Detroit Ranger District, HC 73, Box 320, Mill City, OR 97360; tel. (503) 854-3366; fax (503) 854-4239.

10 Waterloo County Campground
   8

There is more than a mile of South Santiam River frontage in this campground. Swimming, fishing, picnicking, and field sports are options here. Small boats with trolling motors are the only boats usable here.

Location: On the South Santiam River; map D2, grid b1.

Campsites, facilities: There are 121 sites for tents, trailers, or RVs; 101 have partial hookups. Drinking water, fire pits, and picnic tables are provided. Rest rooms with showers are available. Boat ramps and a playground are located in the surrounding day-use area. A small grocery is located with one mile. Leashed pets are permitted.

Reservations, fees: No reservations accepted. Sites are $12-15 per night; there is a $5 fee for one additional vehicle. Senior discounts are available. Open year-round.

Directions: From Albany drive east on U.S. 20 for about 20 miles through Lebanon to the Waterloo exit. Turn north at the Waterloo exit and drive approximately two miles to the camp on the right. The camp is on the south side of the South Santiam River.

Contact: Linn County Parks Department, 3010 Ferry Street SW, Albany, OR 97321; tel. (541) 967-3917; fax (541) 924-0202.

11 Sunnyside County Park

      8

This is Linn County's most popular park. Recreation options include boating, fishing, waterskiing, and swimming. A golf course is located within 15 miles.

Location: On Foster Reservoir; map D2, grid b3.

Campsites, facilities: There are 165 sites for tents, trailers, or RVs. Electricity and drinking water are available at 133 sites; 27 sites are reserved for groups, who must take a minimum of eight sites, with a maximum of eight people per site. Drinking water, flush toilets, showers, a sanitary dump station, picnic areas, volleyball courts, a boat ramp, and moorage are available. Firewood can be obtained for a fee. Additional facilities are located within two miles. Leashed pets are permitted.

Reservations, fees: Reservations are recommended for groups; phone (541) 967-3917. Sites are $12-26 per night; there is a $5 fee for one additional vehicle. Senior discounts are available. Open April through October.

Directions: From Albany drive east on U.S. 20 for about 35 miles (through Lebanon and Sweet Home) to the Quartzville Road exit (near Foster Reservoir). Turn north on Quartzville Road and drive one mile to the campground on the right. The camp is on the south side of Foster Reservoir.

Contact: Linn County Parks Department, 3010 Ferry Street SW, Albany, OR 97321; tel. (541) 967-3917; fax (541) 924-0202.

12 Whitcomb Creek County Park

       8

This camp is on the north shore of Green Peter Reservoir in a wooded area with lots of ferns, which gives it a rain forest feel. Recreation options include swimming, sailing, hiking, and picnicking. Two boat ramps are located on the reservoir about a mile from camp.

Location: On Green Peter Reservoir; map D2, grid b3.

Campsites, facilities: There are 39 tent, trailer, or RV sites. Picnic tables are provided. Drinking water is available to haul; vault toilets and garbage bins are available. Facilities are within 15 miles. Leashed pets are permitted.

Reservations, fees: Reservations are recommended for groups; phone (541) 967-3917. Sites are $9 per night. Open April through October.

Directions: From Albany drive east on U.S. 20 for about 35 miles (through Lebanon and Sweet Home) to the Quartzville Road exit (near Foster Reservoir). Turn north on Quartzville Road and drive 10 miles to the campground.

Contact: Linn County Parks Department, 3010 Ferry Street SW, Albany, OR 97321; tel. (541) 967-3917; fax (541) 924-0202.

13 Yellowbottom   7

This campground is across the road from Quartzville Creek and is always missed by out-of-town visitors. It's nestled under a canopy of old-growth forest. The Rhododendron Trail, which is just under a mile, provides a challenging hike through forest and patches of rhododendrons. Some folks gold-pan here. Though primitive, the camp is ideal for a quiet getaway weekend.

Location: On Quartzville Creek; map D2, grid b4.

Campsites, facilities: There are 21 sites for tents, trailers, or RVs up to 28 feet, 10 are drive-through. Picnic tables, garbage bins, and fire grills are provided. Drinking water and vault toilets are available. Firewood is available for purchase. Some facilities are wheelchair accessible. Leashed pets are permitted. There is a camp host.

Reservations, fees: No reservations. Sites are $8 per night, with a 14-day stay limit, $5 per night for an additional vehicle. Open mid-May to late September.

Directions: From Albany drive east on U.S. 20 for 26 miles to Sweet Home and Quartzville Road. Turn left (northeast) on Quartzville Road and drive 24 miles to the campground on the left.

Contact: Bureau of Land Management, Salem District, 1717 Fabry Road SE, Salem, OR 97306; tel. (503) 375-5646; fax (503) 375-5622.

14 Cascadia State Park   7

The highlight of this 258-acre park is Soda Creek Falls, with a fun three-quarter mile hike to reach it. The park is set along the banks of the Santiam River. A newer trail ushers you through Douglas fir trees along the river, a good place to fish and swim. It's a great spot for a more intimate getaway.

Location: On the Santiam River; map D2, grid b4.

Campsites, facilities: There are 25 primitive sites for tents, trailers, or self-contained RVs up to 35 feet long, and two group areas for tents. Picnic tables, garbage bins, and fire grills are provided. Drinking water, vault toilets, and firewood are available. A store is located within one mile. Some facilities are wheelchair accessible. Leashed pets are permitted.

Reservations, fees: Reservations accepted for group areas only; phone (503) 854-3406. Sites are $7-12 per night, $5 per night for an additional vehicle. Major credit cards accepted. Open March through October, weather permitting.

Directions: From Albany drive east on U.S. 20 for 40 miles to the park on the left (14 miles east of the town of Sweet Home).

Contact: Cascadia State Park, P.O. Box 736, Cascadia, OR 97329; tel. (800) 551-6949 or (541) 367-6021.

15 Riverside   7

This campground is set at an elevation of 2,400 feet, along the banks of the Santiam River, where the fishing can be good. A point of interest is the Marion Forks Fish Hatchery and interpretive site, located 2.5 miles south. The Mount Jefferson Wilderness is directly to the east in Willamette National Forest, and Minto Mountain Trail is three miles to the east.

Location: On the Santiam River in Willamette National Forest; map D2, grid b6.

Campsites, facilities: There are 37 sites for tents, trailers, or RVs up to 21 feet long. Picnic tables and fire grills are provided. Drinking water and pit toilets are available. Leashed pets are permitted.

Reservations, fees: No reservations. Sites are $8 per night, $5 per night for an additional vehicle. Open late April to late September; a gate prevents access during the off season.

Directions: From Salem drive east on Highway 22 for 50 miles to Detroit. Continue southeast on Highway 22 for 14 miles to the campground on the right.

Contact: Willamette National Forest, Detroit Ranger District, HC 73, Box 320, Mill City, OR 97360; tel. (503) 854-3366; fax (503) 854-4239.

16 Marion Forks   8

This campground is along Marion Creek, adjacent to the Marion Forks Fish Hatchery. A U.S. Forest Service guard station and a restaurant are across Highway 22. There are some quality hiking trails in the area; the nearest is Independence Trail, one-quarter mile north of the campground.

Location: On the Santiam River in Willamette National Forest; map D2, grid b7.

Campsites, facilities: There are 15 sites for tents, trailers, or RVs up to 22 feet long. Picnic tables, fire grills, and garbage containers are provided. Pit toilets and drinking water are available. Leashed pets are permitted.

Reservations, fees: No reservations. Sites are $8 per night, $5 per night for an additional vehicle. Open year-round, weather permitting, with no winter services.

Directions: From Salem drive east on Highway 22 for 50 miles to Detroit. Continue southeast on Highway 22 for 16 miles to the campground on the left.

Contact: Willamette National Forest, Detroit Ranger District, HC 73, Box 320, Mill City, OR 97360; tel. (503) 854-3366; fax (503) 854-4239.

17 Big Meadows Horse Camp   10

Built by the U.S. Forest Service with the support of a horse club, this camp is used heavily by equestrians riding into the Big Meadows area and the adjacent Mount Jefferson Wilderness. If you're not a horse lover, you may want to stick with Riverside or Marion Forks.

Location: Near Mount Jefferson Wilderness in Willamette National Forest; map D2, grid b7.

Campsites, facilities: There nine sites for tents, trailers, or RVs. Picnic tables, garbage service, fire grills, and enclosed four-horse corrals are provided at each site. Drinking water and vault toilets are available. Leashed pets are permitted.

Reservations, fees: No reservations. Sites are $9 per night, $5 per night for an additional vehicle. Open mid-April to mid-September, weather permitting.

Directions: From Salem drive east on Highway 22 for 50 miles to Detroit. Continue southeast on Highway 22 for 27 miles to Big Meadows Road (Forest Road 2267). Turn left and drive one mile to Forest Road 2257. Turn left and drive one-half mile to the campground on the left.

Contact: Willamette National Forest, Detroit Ranger District, HC 73, Box 320, Mill City, OR 97360; tel. (503) 854-3366; fax (503) 854-4239.

18 Jack Creek   5

A more primitive option to the other camps in the area, this campground is set along the banks of Jack Creek in an open setting among ponderosa pine. In order to protect the bull trout habitat, no fishing is permitted here.

Location: Near Mount Jefferson Wilderness in Deschutes National Forest; map D2, grid b8.

Campsites, facilities: There is an area for dispersed tent, trailer, or RV camping with access to some picnic tables and fire grills. Vault toilets are available. There is no drinking water, and all garbage must be packed out. Leashed pets are permitted.

Reservations, fees: No reservations; no fee. Open mid-April to mid-October.

Directions: From Albany drive east on U.S. 20 for 87 miles to the sign for Jack Lake (located one mile east of Suttle Lake) and Suttle-Sherman Road. Turn left on Forest Road 12 and drive five miles to Forest Road 1230. Turn left and drive three-quarters of a mile to Forest Road 1232. Turn left and drive one-quarter mile to the campground on the left.

Contact: Deschutes National Forest, Sisters Ranger District, P.O. Box 249, Sisters, OR 97759; tel. (541) 549-2111; fax (541) 549-7746.

19 Sheep Springs Horse Camp   7

This well-shaded equestrian camp with privacy screening between sites is located near the trailhead for the Metolius-Windigo Horse Trail, which heads northeast into the Mount Jefferson Wilderness and south to Black Butte. Contact the U.S. Forest Service for details and maps of the backcountry. The camp is set at an elevation of 3,200 feet.

Location: Near the Mount Jefferson Wilderness in Deschutes National Forest; map D2, grid b8.

Campsites, facilities: There are 11 sites for tents, trailers, or RVs up to 30 feet long. Drinking water and fire grills are provided. Vault toilets and box stalls for horses are available.

Reservations, fees: Reservations required; phone (877) 444-6777 or access the website: www.reserveusa.com ($8.65 reservation fee). Sites are $10 per night, $5 per night for an additional vehicle. Open late May to mid-October.

Directions: From Albany drive east on U.S. 20 for 87 miles to the sign for Jack Lake (located one mile east of Suttle Lake) and Suttle-Sherman Road. Turn left on Forest Road 12 and drive eight miles to Forest Road 1260. Turn left and drive 1.5 miles to Forest Road 1260-200. Turn right and drive 1.5 miles to the campground on the right.

Contact: Deschutes National Forest, Sisters Ranger District, P.O. Box 249, Sisters, OR 97759; tel. (541) 549-2111; fax (541) 549-7746.

20 Diamond Hill RV Park   6

This private campground is located in the center of the Willamette Valley, just off the highway. It's a great layover spot if you're cruising up or down Interstate 5. Eugene Kamping World, 10 miles south, is the closest camp.

Location: In the Willamette Valley; map D2, grid c0.

Campsites, facilities: There are 10 tent sites and 52 sites for trailers or RVs of any length. Electricity, drinking water, sewer hookups, and picnic tables are provided. Flush toilets, bottled gas, sanitary services, showers, a store, a laundry room, ice, a playground, and a swimming pool are available. A cafe is located within one mile. Small, leashed pets and motorbikes are permitted.

Reservations, fees: Reservations accepted. Sites are $17-19 per night. Open year-round.

Directions: From Eugene drive north on Interstate 5 for 15 miles to Exit 209 and Diamond Hill Drive. Take that exit and drive west on Diamond Hill Drive for one block to the park.

Contact: Diamond Hill RV Park, 32917 Diamond Hill Drive, Harrisburg, OR 97446; tel. (541) 995-9279.

21 Trout Creek   8

This campground is set along the banks of the South Santiam River, about seven miles east of Cascadia. Fishing and swimming are some of the possibilities here. The Trout Creek Trail, located just across the highway, is routed into the Menagerie Wilderness. The Long Ranch Elk Viewing Area is immediately west of the campground, and at the Trout Creek Trailhead you'll also find a short trail leading to an elk-viewing platform. Nearby is the old Santium Wagon Road.

Location: On the South Santiam River in Willamette National Forest; map D2, grid c4.

Campsites, facilities: There are 24 sites for tents, trailers, or RVs up to 22 feet long. Six of the sites will accommodate RVs up to 36 feet long. Picnic tables, garbage bins, and fire grills are provided. Drinking water and vault toilets are available. Some facilities are wheelchair accessible. Leashed pets are permitted.

Reservations, fees: No reservations. Sites are $8 per night, plus $5 for each additional vehicle. Open May through October.

Directions: From Albany drive east on U.S. 20 for 45 miles (19 miles past Sweet Home) to the campground entrance on the right.

Contact: Willamette National Forest, Sweet Home Ranger District, 3225 Highway 20, Sweet Home, OR 97386; tel. (541) 367-5168; fax (541) 367-5506.

22 Yukwah   7

Yukwah campground is located in a second-growth Douglas fir forest on the banks of the Santiam River. The camp is a quarter of a mile east of Trout Creek Campground and offers the same recreation possibilities. There is a half-mile-long, compacted surface interpretive trail at the camp that's barrier-free.

Location: On the Santiam River in Willamette National Forest; map D2, grid c4.

Campsites, facilities: There are 19 sites for tents, trailers, or RVs up to 28 feet long. Picnic tables, garbage bins, and fire grills are provided. Drinking water, vault toilets, a large picnic area, and a fishing platform are available. Some facilities are wheelchair accessible. Leashed pets are permitted.

Reservations, fees: No reservations. Sites are $8 per night, plus $5 for each additional vehicle. Open May through October.

Directions: From Albany drive east on U.S. 20 for 45 miles (19 miles past Sweet Home) to the campground.

Contact: Willamette National Forest, Sweet Home Ranger District, 3225 Highway 20, Sweet Home, OR 97386; tel. (541) 367-5168; fax (541) 367-5506.

23 Fernview   7

This campground is set high above the confluence of Boulder Creek and the Santiam River just south of the Menagerie Wilderness. Just across U.S. 20 lies the Rooster Rock Trail, which leads to—where else?—Rooster Rock, the site of an old lookout tower. The Old Santiam Wagon Road runs through the back of the campground. The camp is better suited for tent and small RV camping; the sites are small.

Location: On the Santiam River in Willamette National Forest; map D2, grid c5.

Campsites, facilities: There are 11 sites for tents, trailers, or RVs up to 22 feet long. Picnic tables garbage bins, and fire grills are provided. Drinking water and vault toilets are available. Some facilities are wheelchair accessible. Leashed pets are permitted.

Reservations, fees: No reservations. Sites are $8 per night, plus $5 for each additional vehicle. Open May through September.

Directions: From Albany drive east on U.S. 20 for 49 miles (23 miles past Sweet Home) to the campground entrance on the right.

Contact: Willamette National Forest, Sweet Home Ranger District, 3225 Highway 20, Sweet Home, OR 97386; tel. (541) 367-5168; fax (541) 367-5506.

24 House Rock   8

This campground is set at the confluence of Sheep Creek and the South Santiam River. Trout fishing can be good, particularly during summer evenings. The camp is located in the midst of an old-growth forest and is surrounded by huge, majestic evergreens. History buffs should explore the short loop trail out of camp, which passes by House Rock, a historic shelter for Native Americans, and continues to the historic Old Santiam Wagon Road.

Location: On the Santiam River in Willamette National Forest; map D2, grid c5.

Campsites, facilities: There are 17 sites for tents, trailers, or RVs up to 22 feet long. Picnic tables, garbage bins, and fire grills are provided. Vault toilets and drinking water are available. Some facilities are wheelchair accessible. Leashed pets are permitted.

Reservations, fees: No reservations. Sites are $8 per night, plus $5 for each additional vehicle. Open May through October.

Directions: From Albany drive east on U.S. 20 for 52.5 miles (26.5 miles past Sweet Home) to Squaw Creek Road (Forest Road 2044). Turn right and drive a short distance to the campground.

Contact: Willamette National Forest, Sweet Home Ranger District, 3225 Highway 20, Sweet Home, OR 97386; tel. (541) 367-5168; fax (541) 367-5506.

25 Mona   8

This forested campground is along the shore of Blue River Reservoir, close to where the Blue River joins it. A boat ramp is located across the river from the campground. After launching a boat, campers can ground it near the campsite. This camp is extremely popular when the reservoir is full. Lookout Campground (located next to the boat launch at Blue River Reservoir) is another option if this camp is full.

Location: Near Blue River Reservoir in Willamette National Forest; map D2, grid c5.

Campsites, facilities: There are 23 sites for tents, trailers, or RVs up to 21 feet long. Picnic tables, garbage bins, and fire grills are provided. Drinking water and flush toilets are available. Some facilities are wheelchair accessible. Leashed pets are permitted.

Reservations, fees: No reservations. Sites are $12-20 per night. Open mid-April to late September.

Directions: From Eugene drive east on Highway 126 for 37 miles to Blue River. Continue east on Highway 126 for three miles to Forest Road 15. Turn north and drive three miles to the campground.

Contact: Willamette National Forest, Blue River Ranger District, P.O. Box 199, Blue River, OR 97413; tel. (541) 822-3317; fax (541) 822-1255.

26 Lost Prairie   7

This campground is set along the banks of Hackleman Creek at 3,200 feet in an area of fir, spruce, and Douglas fir. Three excellent hiking trails can be found within five miles of the camp: Hackleman Old-Growth Grove, Cone Peak, and Iron Mountain. The latter two offer spectacular wildflower viewing in the late spring and early summer. This camp is an alternative to nearby Fish Lake.

Location: On Hackleman Creek in Willamette National Forest; map D2, grid c6.

Campsites, facilities: There are two tent sites and two sites for trailers or RVs up to 22 feet long. Picnic tables, garbage bins, and fire grills are provided. Drinking water and vault toilets are available. Some facilities are wheelchair accessible. Leashed pets are permitted.

Reservations, fees: No reservations. Sites are $8 per night, $4 per night for an additional vehicle. Open mid-May through October, weather permitting.

Directions: From Albany drive east on U.S. 20 for 63 miles to the camp on the right.

Contact: Willamette National Forest, Sweet Home Ranger District, 3225 Highway 20, Sweet Home, OR 97386; tel. (541) 367-5168; fax (541) 367-5506.

27 Olallie   7

This campground (2,000 feet elevation) along the banks of the McKenzie River offers opportunities for boating, fishing, and hiking. Other bonuses include easy access from Highway 126. Fishing for rainbow trout usually is good. The campground is two miles southwest of Trailbridge Reservoir off of Highway 26.

Location: On the McKenzie River in Willamette National Forest; map D2, grid c5.

Campsites, facilities: There are 17 sites for tents, trailers, or RVs up to 30 feet long. Picnic tables, garbage service, and fire grills are provided. Vault toilets and drinking water are available. A boat launch is nearby (non-motorized boats only). Leashed pets are permitted.

Reservations, fees: Reservations accepted; phone (877) 444-6777 or access the website: www.reserveusa.com ($8.65 reservation fee). Sites are $8 per night, plus $4 for each additional vehicle. Open mid-April through September, weather permitting.

Directions: From Eugene drive east on Highway 126 for 47 miles to the town of McKenzie Bridge. Continue on Highway 126 for 11 miles to the campground on the left.

Contact: Willamette National Forest, McKenzie Ranger District, 57600 McKenzie Highway, McKenzie Bridge, OR 97413; tel. (541) 822-3381; fax (541) 822-3854.

28 Trailbridge   6

This campground is set along the shore of Trailbridge Reservoir, where boating, fishing, and hiking are recreation options. It's an exceptional spot for car campers. Highway 126 east of McKenzie Bridge is a designated scenic route, providing a pleasant trip to the camp. A good side trip is to take the beautiful 40-minute drive east to the little town of Sisters. From this camp there is access to the McKenzie River National Recreation Trail.

Location: On Trailbridge Reservoir in Willamette National Forest; map D2, grid c5.

Campsites, facilities: There are 20 sites for tents and 21 sites for trailers or RVs up to 45 feet long. Picnic tables, garbage service, and fire grills are provided. Drinking water, and vault and flush toilets are available. Boat ramps are nearby. Leashed pets are permitted.

Reservations, fees: No reservations. Sites are $6 per night, plus $3 for each additional vehicle. Open late April to late September.

Directions: From Eugene drive east on Highway 126 for 47 miles to the town of McKenzie Bridge. Continue on Highway 126 for 13 miles to the signed turnoff for Trailbridge Reservoir. Turn left on Forest Road 1477 and drive a short distance; then bear left and continue one-quarter mile to the campground.

Contact: Willamette National Forest, McKenzie Ranger District, 57600 McKenzie Highway, McKenzie Bridge, OR 97413; tel. (541) 822-3381; fax (541) 822-3854.

29 Lakes End Boat-In   9

This secluded boat-in campground is set along the shore of the headwaters of Smith Reservoir, a long narrow lake. You'll find no cars and no traffic. The trout fishing in this reservoir can be exceptional, and there's a 10-mph speed limit. The campground is split into two areas, providing camping opportunities on Smith Creek or on the reservoir.

Location: On Smith Reservoir in Willamette National Forest; map D2, grid c6.

Campsites, facilities: There are 17 boat-in tent sites. Picnic tables and fire grills are provided. Pit toilets are available, but there is no drinking water, and all garbage must be packed out. Boat docks are nearby. Leashed pets are permitted.

Reservations, fees: No reservations; no fee. Open late April to late September.

Directions: From Eugene drive east on Highway 126 for 47 miles to the town of McKenzie Bridge. Continue on Highway 126 for 13 miles to the signed turnoff for Lakes End at the north end of Trailbridge Reservoir. Turn left on Forest Road 1477 and drive a short distance; then bear left and continue (past Trailbridge Campground) for one-half mile to Forest Road 730 (Smith Reservoir Road). Continue three miles to the boat launch.

Contact: Willamette National Forest, McKenzie Ranger District, 57600 McKenzie Highway, McKenzie Bridge, OR 97413; tel. (541) 822-3381; fax (541) 822-3854.

30 Ice Cap   9

This campground (3,000 feet elevation) is set on a hill above Carmen Reservoir, which was created by a dam on the McKenzie River. The McKenzie River National Recreation Trail passes by the camp, and Koosah Falls and Sahalie Falls are nearby. Clear Lake, a popular local vacation destination, is two miles away.

Location: On Carmen Reservoir in Willamette National Forest; map D2, grid c6.

Campsites, facilities: There are 11 tent sites and 11 sites for tents, trailers, or RVs up to 16 feet long. Picnic tables, garbage service, and fire grills are provided. Drinking water and flush toilets, boat launching facilities, and boat rentals are about two miles away at Clear Lake Resort. Only non-motorized boats are allowed on Carmen Reservoir. Leashed pets are permitted.

Reservations, fees: No reservations. Sites are $10 per night, plus $5 for each additional vehicle. Open mid-May to mid-September.

Directions: From Eugene drive east on Highway 126 for 47 miles to the town of McKenzie Bridge. Continue on Highway 126 for 19 miles to the campground entrance road on the left. Turn left and drive 200 yards to the campground.

Contact: Willamette National Forest, McKenzie Ranger District, 57600 McKenzie Highway, McKenzie Bridge, OR 97413; tel. (541) 822-3381; fax (541) 822-3854.

31 Coldwater Cove   10

This campground (3,000 feet elevation) is on the south shore of Clear Lake, a spring-fed lake formed by a natural lava dam and the source of the McKenzie River. No motors are permitted on the lake, making it ideal for anglers in rowboats or canoes. The northern section of the McKenzie River National Recreation Trail passes by the camp.

Location: On Clear Lake in Willamette National Forest; map D2, grid c6.

Campsites, facilities: There are 35 sites for tents, trailers, or RVs up to 30 feet long. Picnic tables, garbage service, and fire grills are provided. Drinking water and vault toilets are available. Some facilities are wheelchair accessible. Boat docks, launching facilities, rowboats, a store, a cafe, and cabin rentals are available nearby at Clear Lake Resort. Leashed pets are permitted.

Reservations, fees: Reservations accepted; phone (877) 444-6777 or access the website: www.reserveusa.com ($8.65 reservation fee). Sites are $10 per night, plus $5 for each additional vehicle. Open late May to early October.

Directions: From Eugene drive east on Highway 126 for 47 miles to the town of McKenzie Bridge. Continue on Highway 126 for 14 miles to Forest Road 770. Turn right (east) and drive to the campground.

Contact: Willamette National Forest, McKenzie Ranger District, 57600 McKenzie Highway, McKenzie Bridge, OR 97413; tel. (541) 822-3381; fax (541) 822-3854.

32 Fish Lake   7

This campground (3,200 feet elevation) is on the shore of Fish Lake, though the "lake" usually dries up by the middle of the summer. Interpretive information is set up at the guard station nearby. Across the road is a trail that follows the Old Santiam Wagon Road and the northern trailhead for the McKenzie River National Recreation Trail. The Clear Lake picnic area is two miles south off Highway 126.

Location: Near Clear Lake in Willamette National Forest; map D2, grid c6.

Campsites, facilities: There are eight sites for tents, trailers, or RVs up to 16 feet long. Picnic tables, garbage service, and fire grills are provided. Drinking water and vault toilets are available. Leashed pets are permitted.

Reservations, fees: No reservations. Sites are $6 per night, plus $3 for each additional vehicle. Open late May to early September.

Directions: From Eugene drive east on Highway 126 for 47 miles to the town of McKenzie Bridge. Continue on Highway 126 for 23 miles to the campground entrance road on the left. Turn left and drive 100 yards to the campground.

Contact: Willamette National Forest, McKenzie Ranger District, 57600 McKenzie Highway, McKenzie Bridge, OR 97413; tel. (541) 822-3381; fax (541) 822-3854.

33 Scott Lake Walk-In   10

This campground offers hike-in sites (only about an eighth of a mile from the road) set around Scott Lake at an elevation of 4,680 feet. Only non-motorized boats are allowed on the lake. Trails leading out from camp provide access to several small lakes in the Mount Washington Wilderness. There are great views of the Three Sisters Mountains from this camp. Mosquitoes are heavy during the spring and early summer.

Location: On Scott Lake in Willamette National Forest; map D2, grid c7.

Campsites, facilities: There are 12 walk-in tent sites. Picnic tables are provided. Pit toilets are available, but there is no drinking water, and garbage must be packed out. Leashed pets are permitted.

Reservations, fees: No reservations; no fee. Open late June to early October.

Directions: From Eugene drive east on Highway 126 and drive 54 miles to the junction with Highway 242 (part of the Santiam Scenic Byway). Turn right (east) on Highway 242 and drive 14.5 miles to Forest Road 260. Turn left and drive to the campground. (Highway 242 is spectacularly scenic, but it's also very narrow, winding, and steep; not recommended for trailers. The maximum vehicle length is 35 feet.)

Contact: Willamette National Forest, McKenzie Ranger District, 57600 McKenzie Highway, McKenzie Bridge, OR 97413; tel. (541) 822-3381; fax (541) 822-3854.

34 Big Lake   9

This jewel of a spot on the north shore of Big Lake at 4,650 feet offers a host of activities, including fishing, swimming, waterskiing, and hiking. Big Lake has heavy motorized boat use. One of the better hikes is the five-mile wilderness loop trail (Patjens Lakes Trail) that heads out from the south shore of the lake and cuts past a few small lakes before returning. There's a great view of Mt. Washington from the lake. The Pacific Crest Trail is only one-half mile away.

Location: On Big Lake in Willamette National Forest; map D2, grid c7.

Campsites, facilities: There are 49 sites for tents, trailers, or RVs up to 16 feet long. Picnic tables, garbage service, and fire grills are provided. Drinking water, and vault and flush toilets are available. Boat ramps and launching facilities are nearby. Leashed pets are permitted.

Reservations, fees: Reservations accepted; phone (877) 444-6777 or access the website:www.reserveusa.com ($8.65 reservation fee). Sites are $12 per night, plus $6 for each additional vehicle. Open late May to early October.

Directions: From Eugene drive east on Highway 126 for 47 miles to the town of McKenzie Bridge. Continue northeast on Highway 126 for 40 miles to Big Lake Road (Forest Road 2690). Turn right and drive three miles to the campground on the left.

Contact: Willamette National Forest, McKenzie Ranger District, 57600 McKenzie Highway, McKenzie Bridge, OR 97413; tel. (541) 822-3381; fax (541) 822-3854.

35 Big Lake West Walk-In   9

This spot at an elevation of 4,650 feet, west of the Big Lake Campground, has many of the same attractions, but the walk-in sites offer some seclusion and quiet. The Mount Washington Wilderness and Patjens Lake access trails can be reached from here. See the description of Big Lake Campground.

Location: On Big Lake in Willamette National Forest; map D2, grid c7.

Campsites, facilities: There are 11 walk-in sites (only 200 feet from the road). Fire pits, garbage service, and picnic tables are provided. Drinking water and vault toilets are available. Leashed pets permitted.

Reservations, fees: No reservations. Sites are $12 per night, plus $6 for each additional vehicle. Open late May to early October.

Directions: From Eugene drive east on Highway 126 for 47 miles to the town of McKenzie Bridge. Continue northeast on Highway 126 for 40 miles to Big Lake Road (Forest Road 2690). Turn right and drive four miles to the campground entrance on the left.

Contact: Willamette National Forest, McKenzie Ranger District, 57600 McKenzie Highway, McKenzie Bridge, OR 97413; tel. (541) 822-3381; fax (541) 822-3854.

36 Scout Lake   5

This campground with a mix of sunny or shady sites is about half a mile from Suttle Lake and is a good spot for swimming and hiking. The camp is available for groups of up to 100 campers, but reservations need to be made. Call the ranger district for details.

Location: On Scout Lake in Deschutes National Forest; map D2, grid c7.

Campsites, facilities: There are 13 sites for tents, trailers, or RVs up to 40 feet long. Picnic tables, garbage service, and fire grills are provided. Vault toilets and drinking water are available. Also available are a picnic shelter, volleyball court, and horseshoe pits. Leashed pets are permitted in the campground only (not in the day-use area).

Reservations, fees: Reservations accepted; phone (877) 444-6777 or access the website:www.reserveusa.com ($8.65 reservation fee). Sites are $11-25 per night, $5 per night for an additional vehicle. Open mid-April to mid-September.

Directions: From Eugene drive east on Highway 126 for 74 miles to the junction of Highway 20 and 126. Continue east on Highway 126 for 12 miles to Forest Road 2070 (Suttle Lake). Turn right and drive to Forest Road 2066. Turn left and drive less than one mile to the campground.

Contact: Deschutes National Forest, Sisters Ranger District, P.O. Box 249, Sisters, OR 97759; tel. (541) 549-2111; fax (541) 549-7746.

37 South Shore   6

This campground is located at 3,700 feet on the south shore of Suttle Lake, where waterskiing is permitted. A hiking trail winds around the lake, and a stable and horseback riding rentals are nearby. Fishing and windsurfing are other popular activities. The camp often fills up on weekends and holidays; reserve early. Quite a few dead trees have recently been removed, so the campground is now more open and spacious.

Location: On Suttle Lake in Deschutes National Forest; map D2, grid c7.

Campsites, facilities: There are 38 sites for tents, trailers, or RVs up to 40 feet long. Picnic tables, garbage service, and fire grills are provided. Drinking water and vault toilets are available. A fish cleaning station, boat docks, launching facilities, and rentals are nearby. Leashed pets are permitted.

Reservations, fees: Reservations accepted; phone (877) 444-6777 or access the website:www.reserveusa.com ($8.65 reservation fee). Sites are $10-12 per night, $6 per night for an additional vehicle. Open mid-April to late September.

Directions: From Eugene drive east on Highway 126 for 74 miles to the junction of Highway 20 and 126. Continue east on Highway 126 for 12 miles to Forest Road 2070 (Suttle Lake). Turn right and drive to Forest Road 2066. Turn right and proceed a short distance to the campground.

Contact: Deschutes National Forest, Sisters Ranger District, P.O. Box 249, Sisters, OR 97759; tel. (541) 549-2111; fax (541) 549-7746.

38 Link Creek   6

This campground (elevation 3,450 feet) is set at the west end of Suttle Lake. It's popular with water-skiers; the high-speed boating area is on this end of the lake. See the description of South Shore for recreation details.

Location: On Suttle Lake in Deschutes National Forest; map D2, grid c7.

Campsites, facilities: There are 33 sites for tents, trailers, or RVs up to 40 feet long. Picnic tables, garbage service, and fire grills are provided. Drinking water and vault toilets are available. Boat docks, launching facilities, and rentals are nearby. Leashed pets are permitted.

Reservations, fees: Reservations accepted; phone (877) 444-6777 or access the website:www.reserveusa.com ($8.65 reservation fee). Sites are $12 per night, $6 per night for an additional vehicle. Open mid-April to late September.

Directions: From Albany drive east on U.S. 20 for 74 miles to the junction of Highway 20 and 126. Continue east on Highway 126 for 12 miles to Forest Road 2070 (Suttle Lake). Turn right and drive a short distance to the campground.

Contact: Deschutes National Forest, Sisters Ranger District, P.O. Box 249, Sisters, OR 97759; tel. (541) 549-2111; fax (541) 549-7746.

39 Blue Bay   7

This campground is set along the south shore of Suttle Lake, the low- speed end of the lake. It's a quieter campground, with more tree cover than South Shore or Link Creek. See the description of South Shore for recreation details.

Location: On Suttle Lake in Deschutes National Forest; map D2, grid c7.

Campsites, facilities: There are 25 sites for tents, trailers, or RVs up to 30 feet long. Picnic tables, garbage service, and fire grills are provided. Drinking water and vault toilets are available. A fish cleaning station, boat docks, launching facilities, and rentals are nearby. Leashed pets are permitted.

Reservations, fees: Reservations accepted; phone (877) 444-6777 or access the website:www.reserveusa.com ($8.65 reservation fee). Sites are $12 per night, $6 per night for an additional vehicle. Open mid-April to late September.

Directions: From Albany drive east on U.S. 20 for 74 miles to the junction of Highway 20 and 126. Continue east on Highway 126 for 12 miles to Forest Road 2070 (Suttle Lake). Turn right and drive a short distance to the campground.

Contact: Deschutes National Forest, Sisters Ranger District, P.O. Box 249, Sisters, OR 97759; tel. (541) 549-2111; fax (541) 549-7746.

40 KOA Sisters   7

This park is located amid wooded mountains outside of Sisters at an elevation of 3,200 feet. Branchwater Lake offers swimming and good trout fishing. See the description of Belknap Springs Lodge for information about the surrounding area.

Location: On Branchwater Lake; map D2, grid c9.

Campsites, facilities: There are 64 sites for tents, trailers, or RVs. Drinking water, air-conditioning, electric heat, cable TV, rest rooms, showers, a sanitary dump, security, a public phone, a laundry room, limited groceries, ice, snacks, RV supplies, LP gas, and a barbecue are available. Recreational facilities include a sports field, a playground, a game room, horseshoes, a spa, and a heated swimming pool. Some facilities are wheelchair accessible. Leashed pets are permitted.

Reservations, fees: Reservations recommended. Sites are $22-25 per night. Open year-round.

Directions: From Eugene drive east on Highway 126 to its junction with Highway 20. Turn east and drive 26 miles to Sisters. Continue southeast for four miles to the park on the right side of the highway.

Contact: KOA Sisters, 67667 Highway 20 West, Bend, OR 97701; tel. (541) 549-3021; fax (541) 549-8144; website: www.koa.com

41 Belknap Springs Lodge

 9

This beautiful park has been featured on at least one magazine cover. It's located in a wooded, mountainous area on the McKenzie River. Trout fishing can be excellent here. If you're looking for hiking opportunities, check out the Three Sisters and Mount Washington Wilderness Areas, both accessible by driving west of Sisters on Highway 242. These are exceptionally scenic and pristine expanses of forest and well worth exploring. The Pacific Crest Trail runs north and south through both wilderness areas.

Location: On the McKenzie River; map D2, grid c9.

Campsites, facilities: There are 15 sites for tents and 42 sites for trailers or RVs with electrical and water hookups. There is also a lodge with 12 rooms, and six cabins are also available. Drinking water, rest rooms, showers, a sanitary dump, and a public phone are provided. Recreational facilities include a hotspring fed swimming pool, a recreation field, and a recreation hall. Some facilities are wheelchair accessible. Leashed pets are permitted, except in the lodge or the cabins.

Reservations, fees: Reservations are recommended. Sites are $17-18 per night, lodge rooms are $70-100 per night and cabins are $45-175 per night. Open year-round.

Directions: From Eugene drive east on Highway 126 for 56 miles to Belknap Spring Road. Turn left and drive a half mile. The road dead-ends at the lodge.

Contact: Belknap Springs Lodge, P.O. Box 2001, McKenzie Bridge, OR 97413; tel. (541) 822-3512; fax (541) 822-3327.

42 Riverside   7

This campground is set 100 yards back from the banks of the Metolius River, less than a mile from Metolius Springs at the base of Black Butte. Because it's a tent-only campground and just far enough off the highway to be missed by most other people, it's very quiet; you'll find plenty of solitude here.

Location: On the Metolius River in Deschutes National Forest; map D2, grid c9.

Campsites, facilities: There are 16 tent sites. Picnic tables and fire grills are provided. Vault toilets, garbage service, and drinking water are available. Leashed pets are permitted.

Reservations, fees: No reservations. Sites are $8 per night, $4 per night for an additional vehicle. Open mid-April through September.

Directions: From Albany drive east on U.S. 20 for 87 miles to the sign for Camp Sherman and Forest Road 14. Turn left and drive five miles to Forest road 800. Turn left and drive a short distance to the campground.

Contact: Deschutes National Forest, Sisters Ranger District, P.O. Box 249, Sisters, OR 97759; tel. (541) 549-2111; fax (541) 549-7746.

43 Indian Ford   4

This campground is on the banks of Indian Ford Creek at an elevation of 3,250 feet. There's a lot of traffic noise from U.S. 20. The camp is used primarily by overnighters on their way to the town of Sisters. The campground is sprinkled with aspen trees, and great bird-watching opportunities are available.

Location: On Indian Ford Creek in Deschutes National Forest; map D2, grid c9.

Campsites, facilities: There are 25 sites for tents, trailers, or RVs up to 40 feet long. Picnic tables, garbage service, and fire grills are provided. Vault toilets and drinking water are available. Leashed pets are permitted.

Reservations, fees: No reservations. Sites are $10 per night, $5 per night for an additional vehicle. Open May through September.

Directions: From Eugene drive east on Highway 126 to its junction with Highway 20. Turn east and drive 21 miles to the campground on the left (five miles west of Sisters).

Contact: Deschutes National Forest, Sisters Ranger District, P.O. Box 249, Sisters, OR 97759; tel. (541) 549-2111; fax (541) 549-7746.

44 Cold Springs   7

This wooded campground is located at 3,400 feet, set along the source of a small creek. It's just far enough off the main drag to be missed by many campers. Spring and early summer are the times for great bird-watching in the area's abundant aspen.

Location: In Deschutes National Forest; map D2, grid c9.

Campsites, facilities: There are 23 sites for tents, trailers, or RVs up to 40 feet long. Picnic tables, fire grills, and garbage service are provided. Vault toilets and drinking water are available. Leashed pets are permitted.

Reservations, fees: No reservations. Sites are $9 per night, plus $5 for each additional vehicle. Open May through September.

Directions: From Eugene drive east on Highway 126 to its junction with Highway 20. Turn east and drive 26 miles to Sisters and Highway 242. Turn right and drive 4.2 miles to the campground on the right.

Contact: Deschutes National Forest, Sisters Ranger District, P.O. Box 249, Sisters, OR 97759; tel. (541) 549-2111; fax (541) 549-7746.

45 Circle 5 RV Park   5

This RV park is just outside Sisters, within walking distance of the town. The sites are cool and shady. Nearby recreation options include a riding stable and tennis courts.

Location: Near Sisters; map D2, grid c9.

Campsites, facilities: There are 10 tent sites and 22 drive-through sites for trailers or RVs of any length. Electricity, drinking water, sewer hookups, cable TV, and picnic tables are provided. Flush toilets, bottled gas, sanitary services, showers, and a laundry room are available. A store, a cafe, and ice are located within one mile. Leashed pets are permitted.

Reservations, fees: Reservations accepted. Sites are $12-19 per night. Open year-round.

Directions: From Eugene drive east on Highway 126 to its junction with Highway 20. Turn east and drive 26 miles to Sisters. Continue southeast on U.S. 20 for one-half mile to the park entrance on the left.

Contact: Circle 5 RV Park, 68656 Highway 20 West, Bend, OR 97701; tel. (541) 549-3861.

46 Eugene Kamping World   5

Eugene is one of Oregon's major cities, but it offers many riverside parks and hiking opportunities. Both the Willamette and McKenzie Rivers run right through town. The McKenzie, in particular, provides good trout fishing. Recreation options near this campground include a golf course and tennis courts.

Location: Near the Willamette River; map D2, grid d0.

Campsites, facilities: There are 30 tent sites and 114 drive-through sites for trailers or RVs of any length. Electricity, drinking water, sewer hookups, and picnic tables are provided. Flush toilets, bottled gas, sanitary services, showers, a recreation hall, cable TV, a miniature golf course, a store, a laundry room, ice, and a playground are available. A cafe is located within one mile. Small leashed pets are permitted.

Reservations, fees: Reservations accepted. Sites are $16-21 per night. Open year-round.

Directions: From Eugene drive north on Interstate 5 for seven miles to Coburg and Exit 199. Take that exit and drive west for a quarter mile to the campground access road. Turn left and drive up the driveway.

Contact: Eugene Kamping World, 90932 South Stuartway, Coburg, OR 97408; tel. (541) 343-4832; fax (541) 343-3008.

47 Eugene Mobile Village   5

This RV park is in Eugene, a mile away from the Willamette River. (See the description of Eugene Kamping World, for more information.) The camp is wooded but close to many attractions. Nearby recreation options include a golf course, bike paths, a full-service marina, and tennis courts.

Location: Near the Willamette River; map D2, grid d0.

Campsites, facilities: There are 30 drive-through sites for trailers or RVs of any length. Electricity, drinking water, and sewer hookups are provided. Flush toilets, sanitary services, showers, and a laundry room are available. Bottled gas, a store, a cafe, and ice are located within one mile. Leashed pets are permitted.

Reservations, fees: Reservations accepted. Sites are $20 per night. Open year-round.

Directions: In Eugene on Interstate 5 take Exit 189 to Franklin Boulevard (no signs for Franklin). Turn left on Franklin Boulevard and drive one mile to the park on the left (park signs are posted along route).

Contact: Eugene Mobile Village, 4750 Franklin Boulevard, Eugene, OR 97403; tel. (541) 747-2257.

48 Vida-Lea Mobile Lodge   6

This private resort is on the banks of the scenic McKenzie River, with pleasant grassy sites among walnut and fig trees. Ben and Kay Dorris State Park, which is open for day use, is about six miles east of the campground on Highway 126 and is also set along the McKenzie River. Nearby recreation options include a golf course, hiking trails, and bike paths.

Location: On the McKenzie River; map D2, grid d2.

Campsites, facilities: There are 13 sites for trailers or RVs of any length in this adult-only campground, five are drive-through. Electricity, drinking water, cable TV, and sewer hookups are provided. Flush toilets, sanitary services, showers, and a laundry room are available. Boat docks and launching facilities are nearby. Leashed pets (one per unit) and motorbikes are permitted.

Reservations, fees: Reservations accepted. Sites are $16 per night. Open year-round.

Directions: From Eugene drive east on Highway 126 for 16 miles to Leaburg. Continue east on Highway 126 for three miles to the park.

Contact: Vida-Lea Mobile Lodge, 44221 McKenzie Highway, Leaburg, OR 97489; tel. (541) 896-3898.

49 Lazy Days   9

This beautiful RV park is set along the banks of the McKenzie River with a view of the Cascade Mountains, not far from Blue River Reservoir. Covering about 1,400 acres, the lake offers opportunities for fishing, swimming, and waterskiing. A golf course and several restaurants are nearby.

Location: On the McKenzie River; map D2, grid d4.

Campsites, facilities: There are 20 sites for trailers or RVs of any length, five are drive-through sites. Electricity, drinking water, sewer hookups, and picnic tables are provided. Flush toilets, a pay phone, showers, cable TV, and a laundry room are available. Boat launching facilities are nearby. Leashed pets are permitted.

Reservations, fees: Reservations accepted. Sites are $15 per night for a maximum of four campers per site. Open year-round.

Directions: From Eugene drive east on Highway 126 for 37 miles to the town of Blue River. Continue east on Highway 126 for 1.5 miles to the park on the left.

Contact: Lazy Days, 52511 McKenzie Highway, Unit 1, Blue River, OR 97413; tel. (541) 822-3889.

50 Patio RV Park   7

This RV park is near the banks of the South Fork of the McKenzie River, not far from Cougar Lake, which offers opportunities for fishing, swimming, and water-skiing. Nearby recreation options include a golf course, hiking trails, and bike paths.

Location: Near the South Fork of the McKenzie River; map D2, grid d4.

Campsites, facilities: There are 60 sites for trailers or RVs of any length in this adult-only RV park. Electricity, drinking water, sewer hookups, and picnic tables are provided. Flush toilets, ice, showers, firewood, a recreation hall, video rentals, full group kitchen facilities, cable TV, and a laundry room are available. A store and a cafe are within two miles. Leashed pets are permitted.

Reservations, fees: Reservations accepted. Sites are $18-20 per night. Open year-round, weather permitting.

Directions: From Eugene drive east on Highway 126 for 37 miles to the town of Blue River. Continue east on Highway 126 for six miles to McKenzie River Drive. Turn east and drive two miles to the park on the right.

Contact: Patio RV Park, 55636 McKenzie, Blue River, OR 97413; tel. (541) 822-3596; fax (541) 822-8292.

51 Delta   8

This popular, heavily forested campground is along the banks of the McKenzie River in a stand of old-growth Douglas fir. The Delta Old Growth Nature Trail, a half-mile wheelchair-accessible interpretive trail, is routed through the campground. There is an amphitheater in the camp as well. Blue River and Cougar Reservoirs are nearby, (seven and five miles away, respectively) both of which offer trout fishing, waterskiing, and swimming.

Location: On the McKenzie River in Willamette National Forest; map D2, grid d5.

Campsites, facilities: There are 38 sites for tents, trailers, or RVs up to 21 feet long. Picnic tables, garbage bins, and fire grills are provided. Drinking water and vault toilets are available. Some facilities are wheelchair accessible. Leashed pets are permitted.

Reservations, fees: No reservations. Sites are $10-19 per night. Open mid-May to late September.

Directions: From Eugene drive east on Highway 126 for 37 miles to the town of Blue River. Continue east on Highway 126 for five miles to Forest Road 19 (Aufderheide Scenic Byway). Turn south (right) and drive one-quarter mile to Forest Road 400. Turn right and drive one mile to the campground.

Contact: Willamette National Forest, Blue River Ranger District, P.O. Box 199, Blue River, OR 97413; tel. (541) 822-3317; fax (541) 822-1255.

52 Slide Creek   6

This campground sits on a hillside overlooking Cougar Reservoir, which covers about 1,300 acres, has a paved boat landing, and offers opportunities for fishing, swimming, and waterskiing. The pretty lakeside camp is quite popular, so plan to arrive early on weekends. If this camp is full, Cougar Crossing (off of Road 19) and Sunnyside (off of Road 500) are nearby options.

Location: On Cougar Reservoir in Willamette National Forest; map D2, grid d5.

Campsites, facilities: There are 16 sites for tents, trailers, or RVs. Picnic tables, garbage bins, and fire grills are provided. Drinking water and vault toilets are available. A boat ramp is available. Leashed pets are permitted.

Reservations, fees: No reservations. Sites are $12-20 per night. Open mid-May to mid-September.

Directions: From Eugene drive east on Highway 126 for 37 miles to the town of Blue River. Continue east on Highway 126 for five miles to Aufderheide Scenic Byway. Turn south (right) and drive 11 miles (along the west shore of Cougar Reservoir, crossing the reservoir bridge) to Eastside Road (Forest Road 500). Turn left and drive 1.5 miles northeast to the campground set on the southeast shore of the lake.

Contact: Willamette National Forest, Blue River Ranger District, P.O. Box 199, Blue River, OR 97413; tel. (541) 822-3317; fax (541) 822-1255.

53 French Pete   8

This quiet, wooded campground is on the banks of the South Fork of the McKenzie River and French Pete Creek. Fishing is catch-and-release only. A trail across the road from the campground provides access to the Three Sisters Wilderness. French Pete is only two miles from Cougar Reservoir, and the camp attracts campers wanting to use Cougar Reservoir facilities. Two more primitive camps (Homestead and Frissell Crossing) are a few miles southeast on the same road.

Location: On the South Fork of the McKenzie River in Willamette National Forest; map D2, grid d5.

Campsites, facilities: There are 17 sites for tents, trailers, or RVs. Picnic tables, garbage containers, and fire grills are provided. Drinking water and vault toilets are available. Some facilities are wheelchair accessible. Leashed pets are permitted.

Reservations, fees: No reservations. Sites are $10-19 per night. Open mid-May to mid-September.

Directions: From Eugene drive east on Highway 126 for 37 miles to the town of Blue River. Continue east on Highway 126 for five miles to Forest Road 19 (Aufderheide Scenic Byway). Turn south (right) and drive 12 miles to the campground.

Contact: Willamette National Forest, Blue River Ranger District, P.O. Box 199, Blue River, OR 97413; tel. (541) 822-3317; fax (541) 822-1255.

54 McKenzie Bridge   8

This campground (1,400 feet elevation) is set along the banks of the McKenzie River, one mile from the town of McKenzie Bridge. There is good evening fly-fishing for trout during summer on this stretch of river.

Location: On the McKenzie River in Willamette National Forest; map D2, grid d5.

Campsites, facilities: There are 20 sites for tents, trailers, or RVs up to 35 feet long. Picnic tables, garbage service, and fire rings are provided. Vault toilets and drinking water are available. A grocery store, gasoline, restaurants, and a pay phone are available within one mile. Leashed pets are permitted. Only non-motorized boats are permitted.

Reservations, fees: Reservations accepted; phone (877) 444-6777 or access the website:www.reserveusa.com ($8.65 reservation fee). Sites are $10 per night, plus $5 for each additional vehicle. Open late April to early September.

Directions: From Eugene drive east on Highway 126 for 46 miles to the campground entrance on the right (one mile west of the town of McKenzie Bridge).

Contact: Willamette National Forest, McKenzie Ranger District, 57600 McKenzie Highway, McKenzie Bridge, OR 97413; tel. (541) 822-3381; fax (541) 822-3854.

55 Horse Creek Group Camp   9

This campground (1,400 feet elevation) reserved for groups is on the banks of Horse Creek, near the town of McKenzie Bridge. In spite of the name, no horse camping is permitted, and fishing is catch-and-release only.

Location: On Horse Creek in Willamette National Forest; map D2, grid d5.

Campsites, facilities: There are 21 sites for tents or trailers, or RVs up to 35 feet long. Picnic tables, garbage service, and fire grills are provided. Drinking water and vault toilets are available. Leashed pets are permitted.

Reservations, fees: Reservations accepted; phone (877) 444-6777 or access the website:www.reserveusa.com ($8.65 reservation fee). Group sites are $40-60 per night. Open late April through October.

Directions: From Eugene drive east on Highway 126 for 47 miles to the town of McKenzie Bridge and Horse Creek Road. Turn right (south) on Horse Creek Road and drive three miles to the campground on the left.

Contact: Willamette National Forest, McKenzie Ranger District, 57600 McKenzie Highway, McKenzie Bridge, OR 97413; tel. (541) 822-3381; fax (541) 822-3854.

56 Paradise   9

This campground (1,600 feet elevation) along the banks of the McKenzie River may be right off the highway, but it's in a rustic, streamside setting with access to the McKenzie River National Recreation Trail. Trout fishing can be good here. See the description of McKenzie Bridge for other options.

Location: On the McKenzie River in Willamette National Forest; map D2, grid d5.

Campsites, facilities: There are 64 sites for tents, trailers, or RVs up to 40 feet long. Picnic tables, garbage service, and fire rings are provided. Flush, vault, and pit toilets; drinking water, a boat ramp, and firewood are available. Leashed pets are permitted.

Reservations, fees: Reservations accepted; phone (877) 444-6777 or access the website:www.reserveusa.com ($8.65 reservation fee). Sites are $12 per night, plus $6 for each additional vehicle. Open late April to mid-October.

Directions: From Eugene drive east on Highway 126 for 47 miles to the town of McKenzie Bridge. Continue east on Highway 126 for 3.5 miles to the campground on the left.

Contact: Willamette National Forest, McKenzie Ranger District, 57600 McKenzie Highway, McKenzie Bridge, OR 97413; tel. (541) 822-3381; fax (541) 822-3854.

Limberlost  9

This secluded campground is set at 1,800 feet of elevation along Lost Creek about two miles from where it empties into the McKenzie River. It's relatively unknown and gets light use; it's a good base camp for a trout fishing trip.

Location: On Lost Creek in Willamette National Forest; map D2, grid d6.

Campsites, facilities: There are two sites for tents only and 10 sites for tents or small trailers up to 16 feet long. Picnic tables, garbage service, and fire grills are provided. Vault toilets are available, but there is no drinking water. Leashed pets are permitted.

Reservations, fees: No reservations. Sites are $6 per night, plus $3 for each additional vehicle. Open mid-April to mid-September.

Directions: From Eugene drive east on Highway 126 for 47 miles to the town of McKenzie Bridge. Continue east on Highway 126 for five miles to Highway 242. Turn right (east) and drive 1.5 miles on Highway 242 to the camp. Note: Highway 242 is spectacularly scenic, but also very narrow, winding, and steep. RVs and trailers are discouraged (a 35-foot length limit is in effect).

Contact: Willamette National Forest, McKenzie Ranger District, 57600 McKenzie Highway, McKenzie Bridge, OR 97413; tel. (541) 822-3381; fax (541) 822-3854.

Alder Springs   7

Good hiking possibilities are a highlight of this remote campground at elevation 3,600 feet. There's hiking access to the Linton Lake Trail, and fishing is available at Linton Lake, a three-mile hike. The Three Sisters Wilderness is located just south of the highway.

Location: In Willamette National Forest; map D2, grid d6.

Campsites, facilities: There are six tent sites. No drinking water is available, and all garbage must be packed out. Picnic tables and fire grills are provided. Vault toilets are available. Leashed pets are permitted.

Reservations, fees: No reservations; no fee. Open late May to late September, weather permitting.

Directions: From Eugene drive east on Highway 126 for 47 miles to the town of McKenzie Bridge. Continue east on Highway 126 for five miles to Highway 242. Turn right (east) and drive 10 miles on Highway 242 to the campground on the left. Note: Highway 242 is spectacularly scenic, but also very narrow, winding, and steep. RVs and trailers are discouraged (a 35-foot length limit is in effect).

Contact: Willamette National Forest, McKenzie Ranger District, 57600 McKenzie Highway, McKenzie Bridge, OR 97413; tel. (541) 822-3381; fax (541) 822-3854.

Lava Camp Lake   4

This campground is set at 5,200 feet among subalpine fir in the McKenzie Pass, not far from the Pacific Crest Trail. Other trails provide hiking possibilities as well. A map of Deschutes National Forest details back roads, trails, and streams. Fishing is allowed, but don't expect to catch anything. Perhaps that is why this campground gets such light use.

Location: Near the Pacific Crest Trail in Deschutes National Forest; map D2, grid d7.

Campsites, facilities: There are 10 sites for tents, trailers, or RVs up to 22 feet long. Picnic tables and fire grills are provided. Pit toilets are available. There is no drinking water, and all garbage must be packed out. Leashed pets are permitted.

Reservations, fees: No reservations; no fee. Open June through September, weather permitting.

Directions: From Eugene drive east on Highway 126 for 47 miles to the town of McKenzie Bridge. Continue east on Highway 126 for five miles to Highway 242. Turn right (east) and drive 14.6 miles on Highway 242 to the campground entrance. Note: Highway 242 is spectacularly scenic, but also very narrow, winding, and steep. RVs and trailers are discouraged (a 35-foot length limit is in effect).

Contact: Deschutes National Forest, Sisters Ranger District, P.O. Box 249, Sisters, OR 97759; tel. (541) 549-2111; fax (541) 549-7746.

60 Whispering Pine Horse Camp   5

This wooded campground (elevation 4,400 feet) near Trout Creek Swamp is pretty, isolated, and private. Be sure to bring your own water. It's primarily set up as a horse camp with corrals. Although generally not crowded, the camp is gaining in popularity, and groups of horse users occasionally fill it up. Hikers, beware; you'll be sharing the trails with horses.

Location: Near the Trout Creek Swamp in Deschutes National Forest; map D2, grid d8.

Campsites, facilities: There are nine primitive sites for tents, trailers, or RVs. Picnic tables, garbage service, and fire grills are provided. Pit toilets are available. There is no drinking water. Leashed pets are permitted.

Reservations, fees: No reservations. Sites are $8 per night, $4 per night for an additional vehicle. Open June to September.

Directions: From Eugene drive east on Highway 126 for 47 miles to the town of McKenzie Bridge. Continue east on Highway 126 for five miles to Highway 242. Turn right (east) and drive six miles on Highway 242 to Forest Road 1018. Turn right and drive four miles to the campground entrance. Note: Highway 242 is spectacularly scenic, but also very narrow, winding, and steep. RVs and trailers are discouraged (a 35-foot length limit is in effect).

Contact: Deschutes National Forest, Sisters Ranger District, P.O. Box 249, Sisters, OR 97759; tel. (541) 549-2111; fax (541) 549-7746.

61 Todd Lake Hike-In   8

This is one of numerous camps in the area that offer a pristine mountain experience, yet can be reached by car. Small Todd Lake Campground is one-half mile from the shore of an alpine lake at 6,200 feet. It's popular for canoeing and offers great views. No bikes or horses are allowed on the trail around the lake.

Location: Near Todd Lake in Deschutes National Forest; map D2, grid d8.

Campsites, facilities: There are five hike-in tent sites. Picnic tables and fire grills are provided. Vault toilets are available. There is no drinking water, and all garbage must be packed out. Leashed pets are permitted.

Reservations, fees: No reservations. There is no camping fee, but a $25 annual pass or $3 per day parking fee is required. Open July to October, weather permitting.

Directions: From Bend drive southwest on Cascades Lakes Highway (also called Century Drive Highway and County Road 46) for 24 miles to Forest Road 370. Turn north (right) and drive one-half mile to the parking area. Hike one-half mile to the campground.

Contact: Deschutes National Forest, Bend-Fort Rock Ranger District, 1230 NE Third Street, Bend, OR 97701; tel. (541) 388-5664; fax (541) 383-4700.

62 Quinn Meadow Horse Camp   8

This scenic campground is open only to horse camping and gets high use. The Elk-Devil's Trail or Wickiup Plains Trail access the Three Sisters Wilderness. There's also a horse route via Katsuk Trail to Devil's Lake.

Location: near Quinn Creek in the Deschutes National Forest; map D2, grid d8.

Campsites, facilities: There are 24 sites for tents, trailers or RVs up to 30 feet long. Picnic tables, fire rings, and horse corrals are provided. Drinking water, vault toilets and garbage bins are available. Toilets are wheelchair accessible. Leashed pets are permitted.

Reservations, fees: Reservations required. Two-horse corral sites are $10, four-horse sites are $12. Open late June through September, weather permitting.

Directions: From Bend drive southwest on Cascades Lakes Highway (also called Century Drive Highway and County Road 46) for 31.2 miles to the campground entrance.

Contact: Deschutes National Forest, Bend-Fort Rock Ranger District, 1230 NE Third Street, Bend, OR 97701; tel. (541) 388-5664; fax (541) 383-4700.

63 Devil's Lake Walk-In   8

This walk-in campground is set along the shore of a scenic alpine lake with aqua-jade water and fishing access. Devil's Lake is a popular rafting and canoeing spot, and there are several trailheads that lead from the lake into the wilderness. The Elk-Devil's Trail or Wickiup Plains Trail accesses the Three Sisters Wilderness. There's also a horse route via Katsuk Trail to Quinn Meadow Horse Camp.

Location: On Devil's Lake in Deschutes National Forest; map D2, grid d8.

Campsites, facilities: There are nine walk-in tent sites. Picnic tables and fire grills are provided. Vault toilets are available. There is no drinking water, and all garbage must be packed out. Leashed pets are permitted.

Reservations, fees: No reservations. There is no camping fee, but a $25 annual pass or $3 per day parking fee is required. Open July through September, weather permitting.

Directions: From Bend drive southwest on Cascades Lakes Highway (which becomes County Road 46) for 28.7 miles to the parking area. Walk 200 yards to the campground

Contact: Deschutes National Forest, Bend-Fort Rock Ranger District, 1230 N.E. Third Street, Bend, OR 97701; tel. (541) 388-5664; fax (541) 383-4700.

64 Soda Creek   5

This campground is located on the road to Sparks Lake, nestled between two meadows in a pastoral setting at 5,450 feet elevation. Boating—particularly canoeing—is ideal at Sparks Lake, about a two-mile drive away. Also at Sparks Lake is a trail which loops the lake; about one-half mile of it is paved and barrier-free. Only fly-fishing is permitted.

Location: Near Sparks Lake in Deschutes National Forest; map D2, grid d8.

Campsites, facilities: There are four tent sites and eight sites for tents, trailers, or RVs up to 22 feet long. Picnic tables and fire grills are provided. Vault toilets are available. There is no drinking water and all garbage must be packed out. Leashed pets are permitted.

Reservations, fees: No reservations. There is no camping fee, but a $25 annual pass or $3 per day parking fee is required. Open July through October, weather permitting.

Directions: From Bend drive southwest on Cascades Lakes Highway (also called Century Drive Highway and County Road 46) for 26.2 miles to Forest Road 400 (at sign for Sparks Lake). Turn east (left) and drive 100 yards to the campground.

Contact: Deschutes National Forest, Bend-Fort Rock Ranger District, 1230 NE Third Street, Bend, OR 97701; tel. (541) 388-5664; fax (541) 383-4700.

65 Three Creeks Lake   8

This wooded campground is set along the south shore of Three Creeks Lake in a pretty spot at 6,600 feet in elevation. Fishing, swimming, hiking, and non-motorized boating are the highlights. Also see the description of Driftwood.

Location: On Three Creeks Lake in Deschutes National Forest; map D2, grid d9.

Campsites, facilities: There are 10 sites for tents, trailers, or RVs up to 30 feet long. Picnic tables, garbage service, and fire grills are provided. Vault toilets are available. There is no drinking water. Boat docks, launching facilities, and rentals are nearby. Boats with motors are not allowed. Leashed pets are permitted.

Reservations, fees: No reservations. Sites are $6 per night, plus $3 for each additional vehicle. Open mid-June to mid-September, weather permitting.

Directions: From Eugene drive east on Highway 126 to its junction with Highway 20. Turn east and drive 26 miles to Sisters and Forest Road 16. Turn right and drive 17 miles to the campground.

Contact: Deschutes National Forest, Sisters Ranger District, P.O. Box 249, Sisters, OR 97759; tel. (541) 549-2111; fax (541) 549-7746.

66 Driftwood   9

This wooded campground at an elevation of 6,600 feet is often blocked by snowdrifts until July 4. At this high elevation, the views of Tam McArthur Rim are spectacular. Although it's on the lakeshore hidden from outsiders, the area can get very crowded. The campground is full most weekends from July 4 to Labor Day. Fishing, swimming, hiking, and non-motorized boating are some of the recreation options.

Location: On Three Creeks Lake in Deschutes National Forest; map D2, grid d9.

Campsites, facilities: There are 17 tent sites and five sites for tents, trailers, or RVs up to 16 feet long. Picnic tables, garbage service, and fire grills are provided. Pit toilets are available. There is no drinking water. Boat docks, launching facilities, and rentals are nearby. Boats with motors are not allowed. Leashed pets are permitted.

Reservations, fees: No reservations. Sites are $6 per night, plus $3 for each additional vehicle. Open mid-June to mid-September, weather permitting.

Directions: From Eugene drive east on Highway 126 to its junction with Highway 20. Turn east and drive 26 miles to Sisters and Forest Road 16. Turn right and drive 16.4 miles to the campground.

Contact: Deschutes National Forest, Sisters Ranger District, P.O. Box 249, Sisters, OR 97759; tel. (541) 549-2111; fax (541) 549-7746.

67 Schwarz Park   7

This large campground is set below Dorena Lake on the Row River, where fishing, swimming, boating, and waterskiing are among the recreation options. The Row River Trail parallels Dorena Lake's north shoreline for 6.2 miles. This paved trail is excellent for walking, bike riding, and shoreline access.

Location: On Dorena Lake; map D2, grid e0.

Campsites, facilities: There are 72 sites for trailers or RVs of any length, and six group sites. Drinking water, garbage bins, picnic tables and fire rings are provided. Flush toilets, a sanitary disposal station, and showers are available. A mini-market is within one mile. Boat launching facilities are located on the lake, about two miles upstream. Three sites are wheelchair accessible. Leashed pets and street-legal motorbikes are permitted.

Reservations, fees: Reservations accepted; phone (877) 444-6777 or access the website: www.reserveusa.com ($8.65 reservation fee). Sites are $10 per night, group sties are $90 per night; an additional vehicle is $4 per night. Open late April to late September.

Directions: From Eugene drive south on Interstate 5 for 22 miles to Cottage Grove and Exit 174. Take that exit to Row Road and drive four miles east to the campground entrance.

Contact: U.S. Army Corps of Engineers, Recreation Information, Cottage Grove, OR 97424; tel. (541) 942-5631, (541) 942-1418; website: www.usace.army.mil.

68 Dolly Varden   6

This pretty campground is adjacent to Fall Creek and is at the lower trailhead for the scenic, 13.7-mile Fall Creek National Recreation Trail, which follows the creek and ranges between 960 and 1,385 feet in elevation. This campground gets moderate to heavy use. It is set on the inlet stream for Fall Creek Reservoir.

Location: On Fall Creek in Willamette National Forest; map D2, grid e1.

Campsites, facilities: There are three sites for tents and two sites for tents, trailers, or RVs up to 16 feet long. Picnic tables, garbage service, and fire grills are provided. Flush toilets are available. There is no drinking water. Leashed pets are permitted.

Reservations, fees: No reservations. Sites are $9 per night, $3 per night for an additional vehicle. Open May to mid-September.

Directions: From south Eugene on Interstate 5, take Exit 188 to Highway 58. Drive 11 miles south to Lowell and Pioneer Street (at the covered bridge). Turn left and drive less than a quarter mile to West Boundary Road. Turn left and drive one block to Lowell Jasper Road. Turn right and drive 1.5 miles to Unity and Place Road. Turn right and drive about one mile to a fork with North Shore Road. Bear left onto North Shore Road (Big Fall Creek Road) and drive about 10 miles (road becomes Forest Road 18) to the campground on the left.

Contact: Willamette National Forest, Lowell Service Center, 60 Pioneer Street, Lowell, OR 97452; tel. (541) 937-2129; fax (541) 937-2032.

69 Dexter Shores Motorhome and RV Park   7

If you're driving on Interstate 5, this RV park is well worth the 15-minute drive out of Springfield. It's across the street from Dexter Point Reservoir, where fishing and boating are permitted, and within walking distance of Lookout Point. Swimming, sailing, windsurfing, ad waterskiing are allowed on nearby Dexter and Fall Creek Lakes.

Location: Near Lookout Point Reservoir; map D2, grid e1.

Campsites, facilities: There are five tent sites and 56 sites for trailers or Rvs up to 40 feet in length. Electricity, drinking water, sewer, cable TV, and telephone hookups, and picnic tables are provided. Flush toilets, sanitary services, showers, firewood, a laundry room, and a playground are available. Bottled gas, a cafe, a restaurant, and ice are within one mile. Boat docks and launching facilities are nearby. Leashed pets and motorbikes permitted.

Reservations, fees: Reservations accepted. Sites are $18-22 per night. Pet fee is $1 per pet per night. Open year-round.

Directions: From south Eugene on Interstate 5, take Exit 188 to Highway 58. Take Highway 58 east and drive 11.5 miles to Lost Creek Road. Turn south and drive to Dexter Road. Turn left and drive east for one-half block to the park on the right.

Contact: Dexter Shores Motorhome and RV Park, P.O. Box 70, Dexter, OR 97431; tel. (541) 937-3711; fax (541) 937-1724.

70 Baker Bay County Park
          6

This campground is along the shore of Dorena Lake, where fishing, sailing, waterskiing, canoeing, swimming, and boating are among the recreation options. Row River Trail follows around part of the lake for a hike or bike ride, and there are covered bridges in the area. Golf can be pursued in Cottage Grove.

Location: On Dorena Lake; map D2, grid e1.

Campsites, facilities: There are 49 sites for tents, trailers, or self-contained RVs up to 35 feet long, plus two group sites for up to 25 people per group. Picnic tables and fire grills are provided. Drinking water, flush toilets, coin-operated showers, firewood, garbage bins, and a dump station are available. Some facilities are wheelchair accessible. A concession stand with ice is in the park. A store is located within two miles. Boat docks and launching facilities are nearby, with seasonal on shore facilities for catamarans. Leashed pets are permitted.

Reservations, fees: Reservations accepted for group sites only, with a $40 deposit. Call (541) 942-7669. Single sites are $11 per night, with an additional fee of $5 for the third vehicle, and group sites are $40 per night. Open mid-April through mid-October.

Directions: From Eugene drive south on Interstate 5 for 22 miles to Cottage Grove and Exit 174 (Dorena Lake exit). Take that exit to Row Road and drive east for 4.4 miles (the road becomes Government Road). Bear right and drive 2.8 miles to the campground entrance on the left.

Contact: Baker Bay, 356 Government Road, Dorena, OR 97434; tel. (541) 942-7669.

71 Winberry   6

This campground is located on Winberry Creek, in a tree-shaded area. The closest hiking option is Station Butte Trail, just downstream from the campground on Forest Road 1802-150. Be cautious—there is poison oak at the top of the butte.

Location: On Winberry Creek in Willamette National Forest; map D2, grid e2.

Campsites, facilities: There are five sites for tents and two sites for trailers or RVs up to 16 feet long. Picnic tables, garbage service, and fire grills are provided. Drinking water, vault toilets, and A-frame shelters are available. Leashed pets are permitted.

Reservations, fees: No reservations. Sites are $8-10 per night, plus $3 for each additional vehicle. Open late May to mid-September.

Directions: From south Eugene on Interstate 5, take Exit 188 to Highway 58. Drive 11 miles south to Lowell and Pioneer Street (at the covered bridge). Turn left and drive less than a quarter mile to West Boundary Road. Turn left and drive one block to Lowell Jasper Road. Turn right and drive 1.5 miles to Unity and Place Road. Turn right and drive about one mile to a fork with Winberry Road. Bear right and drive six miles (the road becomes Forest Road 1802). Continue 3.5 miles to the campground.

Contact: Willamette National Forest, Lowell Service Center, 60 Pioneer Street, Lowell, OR 97452; tel. (541) 937-2129; fax (541) 937-2032.

72 Cascara Campground   7

Campsites are set back and across the road from the reservoir, but you still get a lake view. Most sites have Douglas fir and white fir tree cover. These are spacious campsites. Water recreation is the primary activity here. Personal watercraft and water skiing are allowed. Lake level drops in August. Water temperature is ideal for summer swimming.

Location: Fall Creek Reservoir State Recreation Area; map D2, grid e2.

Campsites, facilities: There are five walk-in sites for tents and 42 sites for trailers or RVs; no pull-through sites. Picnic tables, garbage service, and fire grills are provided. Drinking water, vault toilets, pay phone, firewood for sale, wheelchair facilities, and a camp host are available. A boat launch, dock and swimming area are also available. Leashed pets are permitted.

Reservations, fees: No reservations. Sites are $11 per night, plus $5 for each additional vehicle. Major credit cards accepted. Open May through September.

Directions: From south Eugene on Interstate 5, take Exit 188 to Highway 58. Drive 11 miles south to Lowell and Pioneer Street (at the covered bridge). Turn left and drive less than a quarter mile to West Boundary Road. Turn left and drive one block to Lowell Jasper Road. Turn right and drive 1.5 miles to Unity and Place Road. Turn right and drive about one mile to a fork with North Shore Road (Big Fall Creek Road). Bear left onto Big Fall Creek Road and drive about eight miles to the head of Fall Creek Reservoir and Peninsula Road (Forest Road 6250). Turn right and drive a half mile to the campground.

Contact: Fall Creek Reservoir State Recreation Area, P.O. Box 511, Lowell, OR 97452; tel. (541) 937-1173; Oregon Parks and Recreation Department, Portland, OR, tel. (800) 551-6949.

73 Big Pool   6

This campground along Fall Creek at about 1,000 feet is quiet, secluded, and primitive. The scenic Fall Creek National Recreation Trail passes the camp on the other side of the creek. See the description of Dolly Varden for more details on the area.

Location: On Fall Creek in Willamette National Forest; map D2, grid e2.

Campsites, facilities: There are three tent sites and two sites for tents, trailers, or RVs up to 16 feet long. Picnic tables, garbage containers, and fire grills are provided. Vault toilets are available. There is no drinking water. Leashed pets are permitted.

Reservations, fees: No reservations. Sites are $8 per night, plus $5 for each additional vehicle. Open May to mid-September.

Directions: From south Eugene on Interstate 5, take Exit 188 to Highway 58. Drive 11 miles south to Lowell and Pioneer Street (at the covered bridge). Turn left and drive less than a quarter mile to West Boundary Road. Turn left and drive one block to Lowell Jasper Road. Turn right and drive 1.5 miles to Unity and Place Road. Turn right and drive about one mile to a fork with North Shore Road. Bear left onto North Shore Road (Big Fall Creek Road) and drive about 12 miles (road becomes Forest Road 18) to the campground on the right.

Contact: Willamette National Forest, Lowell Service Center, 60 Pioneer Street, Lowell, OR 97452; tel. (541) 937-2129; fax (541) 937-2032.

74 Black Canyon   7

This campground is along the banks of the Middle Fork of the Willamette River, not far above Lookout Point Reservoir, where fishing and boating are available. The camp is pretty and wooded, with comfortable sites. Within the camp is a one-mile-long nature trail with interpretive signs. Weekend programs are offered in the amphitheater in July and August. You will hear train noise from the other side of the river.

Location: On the Middle Fork of the Willamette River in Willamette National Forest; map D2, grid e2.

Campsites, facilities: There are 72 sites for tents, trailers, or RVs up to 22 feet long. Picnic tables, garbage service, and fire grills are provided. Drinking water, vault toilets, and firewood are available. Sanitary services, a cafe, and a coin laundry are within six miles. Some of the facilities are wheelchair accessible. Launching facilities are nearby at the south end of Lookout Point Reservoir. Leashed pets are permitted.

Reservations, fees: No reservations. Sites are $10-12 per night, plus $5 for each additional vehicle. Open May to late October.

Directions: From south Eugene on Interstate 5, take Exit 188 to Highway 58. Drive southeast on Highway 58 for 30 miles to the camp on the left (six miles west of Oakridge).

Contact: Willamette National Forest, Lowell Service Center, 60 Pioneer Street, Lowell, OR 97452; tel. (541) 937-2129; fax (541) 937-2032.

75 Bedrock    6

This campground along the banks of Fall Creek is one of the access points for the scenic Fall Creek National Recreation Trail, which accesses Jones Trail, a six-mile uphill climb. See the description of Dolly Varden for trail information. The campground is also adjacent to the Jones Trail, which heads north for about six miles before joining a forest road.

Location: On Fall Creek in Willamette National Forest; map D2, grid e3.

Campsites, facilities: There are 20 sites for tents, trailers, or RVs up to 22 feet long. Picnic tables, garbage service, and fire grills are provided. Vault toilets and drinking water are available. Leashed pets are permitted.

Reservations, fees: No reservations. Sites are $9-11 per night, plus $3 for each additional vehicle. Open May to late October.

Directions: From south Eugene on Interstate 5, take Exit 188 to Highway 58. Drive 11 miles south to Lowell and Pioneer Street (at the covered bridge). Turn left and drive less than a quarter mile to West Boundary Road. Turn left and drive one block to Lowell Jasper Road. Turn right and drive 1.5 miles to Unity and Place Road. Turn right and drive about one mile to a fork with North Shore Road. Bear left onto North Shore Road (Big Fall Creek Road) and drive about 14 miles (the road becomes Forest Road 18) to the campground on the left.

Contact: Willamette National Forest, Lowell Service Center, 60 Pioneer Street, Lowell, OR 97452; tel. (541) 937-2129; fax (541) 937-2032.

76 Puma Creek   6

This campground is set along the banks of Fall Creek, across from the Fall Creek National Recreation Trail. It's one of four camps in the immediate area. See the description of Dolly Varden for more information.

Location: On Fall Creek in Willamette National Forest; map D2, grid e3.

Campsites, facilities: There are 11 sites for tents, trailers, or RVs up to 16 feet long. Picnic tables, garbage containers, and fire grills are provided. Vault toilets and drinking water are available. Leashed pets are permitted.

Reservations, fees: No reservations. Sites are $9 per night, plus $4 for each additional vehicle. Open May to late October.

Directions: From Interstate 5 south of Eugene, take Exit 188 to Highway 58. Drive about 11 miles to Lowell. Turn left at Pioneer Street (at the covered bridge), drive 0.2 mile and turn left on West Boundary Road. Drive one block and turn right at Lowell Jasper Road. Drive 1.5 miles to Place Road and turn right. Drive about one mile to a fork and bear left onto North Shore Road (Big Fall Creek Road). Drive about 16 miles (road becomes Forest Road 18) to the campground on the left.

Contact: Willamette National Forest, Lowell Service Center, 60 Pioneer Street, Lowell, OR 97452; tel. (541) 937-2129; fax (541) 937-2032.

77 Shady Dell Group Camp   5

This campground is on the banks of the Middle Fork of the Willamette River, across from Lookout Point Reservoir, a long, narrow lake adjacent to Highway 58. Noteworthy here is a stand of old-growth cedars.

Location: On the Middle Fork of the Willamette River in Willamette National Forest; map D2, grid e3.

Campsites, facilities: There are group sites only for tents, trailers, or RVs up to 15 feet long. Picnic tables, garbage service, and fire grills are provided. Drinking water and vault toilets are available. Sanitary services, a cafe, and a coin laundry are available within five miles. Some of the facilities are wheelchair accessible. Leashed pets are permitted.

Reservations, fees: Reservations. Group sites are $40 per night. Open May to late October.

Directions: From south Eugene on Interstate 5, take Exit 188 to Highway 58. Drive southeast on Highway 58 for 32 miles (five miles west of Oakridge) to the camp on the right.

Contact: Willamette National Forest, Lowell Service Center, 60 Pioneer Street, Lowell, OR 97452; tel. (541) 937-2129; fax (541) 937-2032.

78 Salmon Creek Falls   8

This pretty campground is located in a lush, old-growth forest, right along Salmon Creek. The rocky gorge area creates two small beautiful waterfalls and several deep pools in the clear, blue-green waters. Springtime brings a full range of wildflowers and wild thimbleberries; hazelnuts abound in the summer. This area is a popular recreation spot.

Location: On Salmon Creek in Willamette National Forest; map D2, grid e3.

Campsites, facilities: There are 14 sites for tents, trailers, or RVs up to 24 feet long. Picnic tables, garbage bins, and fire grills are provided. Drinking water and vault toilets are available. A store, a cafe, a coin laundry, and ice are available within five miles. Leashed pets are permitted.

Reservations, fees: No reservations. Sites are $10-12 per night, plus $4 for each additional vehicle. Open late April through September.

Directions: From south Eugene on Interstate 5, take Exit 188 to Highway 58. Drive southeast on Highway 58 for 35 miles to Oakridge and the signal light for downtown. Turn left on Crestview Street and drive one-fourth mile to First Street. Turn right and drive six miles (the road becomes Forest Road 24, Salmon Creek Road) to the campground entrance on the right.

Contact: Willamette National Forest, Middle Fork Ranger District, 49098 Salmon Creek Road, Oakridge, OR 97463; tel. (541) 782-2283; fax (541) 782-5306.

79 Kiahanie   5

We almost hate to reveal it, but this is one heck of a spot for fly-fishing (the only kind allowed). This remote campground is set at 2,200 feet of elevation, along the North Fork of the Willamette River, a designated Wild and Scenic River. If you want beauty and quiet, among enormous Douglas fir trees, you came to the right place. An even more remote campground is farther north on Forest Road 19 at Box Canyon Horse Camp.

Location: On the West Fork of the Willamette River in Willamette National Forest; map D2, grid e4.

Campsites, facilities: There are 19 sites for tents, trailers, or RVs up to 24 feet long. Picnic tables, garbage bins, a recycle center, and fire rings are provided. Drinking water and vault toilets are available. Leashed pets are permitted.

Reservations, fees: No reservations. Sites are $8 per night, plus $4 for each additional vehicle. Open late May through October.

Directions: From south Eugene on Interstate 5, take Exit 188 to Highway 58. Drive 35 miles southeast on Highway 58 to Oakridge. Take the Westfir exit and drive two miles to Westfir and the junction with Aufderheide Drive (Forest Road 19). Bear left (northeast) and drive 19 miles to the campground.

Contact: Willamette National Forest, Middle Fork Ranger District, 49098 Salmon Creek Road, Oakridge, OR 97463; tel. (541) 782-2283; fax (541) 782-5306.

80 Homestead   8

This quiet little campground is set among the trees along the banks of the South Fork of the McKenzie River. It's primitive, little known, and free. Frissell is nearby and has water available from a hand pump.

Location: On the South Fork of the McKenzie River in Willamette National Forest; map D2, grid e4.

Campsites, facilities: There are eight sites for tents, trailers, or RVs. Picnic tables and fire grills are provided. Vault toilets are available, but there is no drinking water. All garbage must be packed out. Leashed pets are permitted.

Reservations, fees: No reservations; no fee. Open year-round.

Directions: From Eugene drive east on Highway 126 for 37 miles to Blue River. Continue east on Highway 126 for five miles to Forest Road 19 (Aufderheide Scenic Byway). Turn south on Forest Road 19 and drive 17 miles to the camp.

Contact: Willamette National Forest, Blue River Ranger District, P.O. Box 199, Blue River, OR 97413; tel. (541) 822-3317; fax (541) 822-1255.

81 Frissell Crossing   8

This campground (elevation 2,800 feet) is on the banks of the South Fork of the McKenzie River, adjacent to a trailhead that provides access to the backcountry of the Three Sisters Wilderness. This is the only camp in the immediate area that has drinking water. If you're looking for solitude, this should be heaven to you. Homestead provides a free, primitive alternative.

Location: Near the Three Sisters Wilderness in Willamette National Forest; map D2, grid e4.

Campsites, facilities: There are 12 sites for tents, trailers, or RVs. Picnic tables, garbage bins, and fire grills are provided. Drinking water and vault toilets are available. Leashed pets are permitted.

Reservations, fees: No reservations. Sites are $8-14 per night. Open mid-May to mid-September.

Directions: From Eugene drive east on Highway 126 for 37 miles to Blue River. Continue east on Highway 126 for five miles to Forest Road 19 (Aufderheide Scenic Byway). Turn south and drive 23 miles to the camp.

Contact: Willamette National Forest, Blue River Ranger District, P.O. Box 199, Blue River, OR 97413; tel. (541) 822-3317; fax (541) 822-1255.

82 Blair Lake Walk-In   6

If you're looking for a pristine alpine, lakeside setting, you'll find it here. The lake is small (only 35 acres) and shallow (20 feet). It supports a population of brook and rainbow trout and is stocked regularly. The surrounding meadows and woods are well known for their wide range of wildflowers and huckleberries.

Location: On Blair Lake in Willamette National Forest; map D2, grid e4.

Campsites, facilities: There are seven walk-in tent sites. Picnic tables and garbage bins are provided. Drinking water, fire rings, and a pit toilet are available. Leashed pets are permitted.

Reservations, fees: No reservations. Sites are $5 per night, plus $5 for each additional vehicle. Open June to mid-October, weather permitting.

Directions: From south Eugene on Interstate 5, take Exit 188 to Highway 58. Drive 35 miles southeast on Highway 58 to Oakridge. Turn left at the signal to downtown and Salmon Creek Road. Turn east and drive nine miles (it becomes Forest Road 24) to Forest Road 1934. Turn left and drive eight miles to Forest Road 733. Turn right and continue for less than one mile to the campground.

Contact: Willamette National Forest, Middle Fork Ranger District, 49098 Salmon Creek Road, Oakridge, OR 97463; tel. (541) 782-2283; fax (541) 782-5306.

83 Box Canyon Horse Camp   4

Only 80 miles from Eugene, this secluded campground with sparse tree cover offers trails into several wilderness areas, including the Chucksney Mountain Trail, Crossing-Way Trail, and Grasshopper Trail. It's a good base camp for a backpacking trip.

Location: Near Chucksney Mountain in Willamette National Forest; map D2, grid e5.

Campsites, facilities: There are 11 sites for tents, trailers, or RVs that allow horse and rider to camp close together. Picnic tables, fire grills, stock water, and corrals are provided. A manure disposal site and vault toilets are available. There is no drinking water and all garbage must be packed out. Leashed pets are permitted.

Reservations, fees: No reservations; no fee. Open year-round, weather permitting.

Directions: From Eugene drive east on Highway 126 for 37 miles to Blue River. Continue east on Highway 126 for five miles to Forest Road 19 (Aufderheide Scenic Byway). Turn south and drive 30 miles to the camp.

Contact: Willamette National Forest, Blue River Ranger District, P.O. Box 199, Blue River, OR 97413; tel. (541) 822-3317; fax (541) 822-1255.

84 West Cultus Hike-In/Boat-In

      5

This campground set at 4,700 feet along the west shore of Cultus Lake is accessible by boat or trail only. It's about three miles by trail from the parking area to the campground. This is a good spot for waterskiing, fishing, and swimming. Trails branch out from the campground and provide access to numerous small backcountry lakes. Drinking water and boat launching facilities are available at Cultus Lake campground.

Location: On Cultus Lake in Deschutes National Forest; map D2, grid e6.

Campsites, facilities: There are 12 boat-in or hike-in tent sites. Picnic tables and fire grills are provided. Vault toilets are available. There is no drinking water and all garbage must be packed out. Boat docks are available on-site; boat rentals are located at Cultus Lake Resort. Leashed pets are permitted.

Reservations, fees: No reservations. There is no camping fee, but a $25 annual trail pass or $5 per day parking fee is required. Open June to late September, weather permitting.

Directions: From Bend drive southwest on Cascades Lakes Highway (Highway 372, which becomes County Road 46) and drive 46 miles to Forest Road 4635. Turn west (right) and drive two miles to the parking area. Boat in or hike in about three miles to the west end of the lake.

Contact: Deschutes National Forest, Bend-Fort Rock Ranger District, 1230 N.E. Third Street, Bend, OR 97701; tel. (541) 388-5664; fax (541) 383-4700.

85 Irish and Taylor

   7

Little known and beautiful, this remote campground is set between two small lakes at 5,550 feet, about a mile from the Pacific Crest Trail. Other nearby trails provide access into the Three Sisters Wilderness.

Location: Near Irish and Taylor Lakes in Deschutes National Forest; map D2, grid e6.

Campsites, facilities: There are six tent sites. Picnic tables and fire grills are provided. Pit toilets are available. There is no drinking water. Leashed pets are permitted.

Reservations, fees: No reservations; no camping fee, but a $3 per day parking pass is required. Open mid-June to mid-September.

Directions: From Bend drive southwest on Cascades Lakes Highway (Century Drive Highway, which becomes County Road 46) and drive 46 miles to Forest Road 4635. Turn west (right) on Forest Road 4635 and drive a short distance to Forest Road 4630. Turn south and drive 1.7 miles to Forest Road 4636. Turn west and drive 6.4 miles to the campground. A high-clearance vehicle is needed for the last four miles.

Contact: Deschutes National Forest, Bend-Fort Rock Ranger District, 1230 N.E. Third Street, Bend, OR 97701; tel. (541) 388-5664; fax (541) 383-4700.

86 Point   8

This campground is along the shore of Elk Lake, where fishing for kokanee salmon, rainbow trout and brown trout, and hiking can be good. Swimming and water sports are popular during warm weather.

Location: On Elk Lake in Deschutes National Forest; map D2, grid e7.

Campsites, facilities: There are eight sites for tents, trailers, or RVs up to 22 feet long. Picnic tables, garbage service, and fire grills are provided. Vault toilets and drinking water are available. Boat docks and launching facilities are on-site. Boat rentals, a store, a restaurant, gas, and propane are located at Elk Lake Resort, one mile away. Leashed pets are permitted.

Reservations, fees: No reservations. Sites are $10 per night, plus $5 per additional vehicle. Open late May to late September, weather permitting.

Directions: From Bend drive southwest on Cascades Lakes Highway (Century Drive Highway, which becomes County Road 46) for 34 miles to the campground on the left.

Contact: Deschutes National Forest, Bend-Fort Rock Ranger District, 1230 N.E. Third Street, Bend, OR 97701; tel. (541) 388-5664; fax (541) 383-4700.

87 Elk Lake   8

This campground is on the shore of Elk Lake, adjacent to Elk Lake Resort, which has boat rentals, a store, a restaurant, gas, and propane. Elk Lake is popular for windsurfing and sailing. See the description of Point Campground for recreation options.

Location: On Elk Lake in Deschutes National Forest; map D2, grid e7.

Campsites, facilities: There are 23 sites for tents, trailers, or RVs up to 22 feet long. Picnic tables, garbage service, and fire grills are provided. Vault toilets and drinking water are available. Boat launching facilities are on-site. Boat rentals can be obtained nearby. Leashed pets are permitted.

Reservations, fees: No reservations. Sites are $10 per night, plus $5 per additional vehicle. Open June through September, weather permitting.

Directions: From Bend drive southwest on Cascades Lakes Highway (County Road 46) and drive 33.1 miles to the campground at the north end of Elk Lake.

Contact: Deschutes National Forest, Bend-Fort Rock Ranger District, 1230 N.E. Third Street, Bend, OR 97701; tel. (541) 388-5664; fax (541) 383-4700.

88 Cultus Lake 7

This camp along the east shore of Cultus Lake is a popular spot for windsurfing, waterskiing, swimming, fishing, and hiking. It fills up early on weekends and holidays.

Location: On Cultus Lake in Deschutes National Forest; map D2, grid e7.

Campsites, facilities: There are 54 sites for tents, trailers, or RVs up to 30 feet long. Picnic tables, garbage service, and fire grills are provided. Drinking water and vault toilets are available. Boat docks and launching facilities are on-site. Boat rentals are nearby. A restaurant, gasoline, and cabins are available at Cultus Lake Resort, nearby. Leashed pets are permitted.

Reservations, fees: No reservations. Sites are $10 per night, plus $5 per additional vehicle. Open June to October.

Directions: From Bend drive southwest on Cascades Lakes Highway (Century Drive Highway, which becomes County Road 46) and drive 46 miles to Forest Road 4635. Turn west (right) and drive two miles to the campground.

Contact: Deschutes National Forest, Bend-Fort Rock Ranger District, 1230 N.E. Third Street, Bend, OR 97701; tel. (541) 388-5664; fax (541) 383-4700.

89 Little Cultus Lake 7

This campground, set at an elevation of 4,800, is situated along the shore of Little Cultus Lake. It's a popular spot for swimming, fishing, boating (10 mph speed limit), and hiking. Nearby trails access numerous backcountry lakes, and the Pacific Crest Trail passes about six miles west of the camp.

Location: On Little Cultus Lake in Deschutes National Forest; map D2, grid e7.

Campsites, facilities: There are 23 sites for tents, trailers, or RVs up to 22 feet long. Picnic tables, garbage service, and fire grills are provided. Drinking water, vault toilets, and a boat launch are available. Leashed pets are permitted.

Reservations, fees: No reservations. Sites are $5 per night. Open late May to late September, weather permitting.

Directions: From Bend drive southwest on Cascades Lakes Highway (Century Drive Highway, which becomes County Road 46) and drive 46 miles to Forest Road 4635. Turn west (right) and drive two miles to Forest Road 4630. Turn south (left) and drive 1.7 miles to Forest Road 4636. Turn west (right) and drive one mile to the campground.

Contact: Deschutes National Forest, Bend-Fort Rock Ranger District, 1230 N.E. Third Street, Bend, OR 97701; tel. (541) 388-5664; fax (541) 383-4700.

90 Lava Lake 10

This well-designed campground is on the shore of pretty Lava Lake. Mount Bachelor and the Three Sisters are in the background, making a classic picture. Boating and fishing are popular here. A bonus is nearby Lava Lake Resort, which has showers, laundry facilities, a sanitary disposal station, a store, gasoline, and propane.

Location: On Lava Lake in Deschutes National Forest; map D2, grid e7.

Campsites, facilities: There are 43 sites for tents, trailers, or RVs up to 28 feet

long. Picnic tables, garbage service, and fire grills are provided. Vault toilets, drinking water, and a fish cleaning station are available. Boat docks and launching facilities are on-site. Boat rentals are nearby. Leashed pets are permitted.

Reservations, fees: No reservations. Sites are $10 per night, plus $5 per additional vehicle. Open mid-April through October, weather permitting.

Directions: From Bend drive southwest on Cascades Lakes Highway (Century Drive Highway, which becomes County Road 46) and drive 38.4 miles to Forest Road 4600-500. Turn east (left) and drive one mile to the campground.

Contact: Deschutes National Forest, Bend-Fort Rock Ranger District, 1230 N.E. Third Street, Bend, OR 97701; tel. (541) 388-5664; fax (541) 383-4700.

91 Cultus Corral Horse Camp   3

This campground is at 4,450 feet elevation, about one mile from Cultus Lake, in a stand of lodgepole pine. Many trees have been removed because of disease. The camp is near many trails that provide access to backcountry lakes. This is a good overflow campground for Quinn Meadow Horse Camp.

Location: Near Cultus Lake in Deschutes National Forest; map D2, grid e7.

Campsites, facilities: There are 11 sites for tents, trailers, or RVs of any length. Picnic tables, garbage service, fire grills, and four-horse corrals are provided. Drinking water and vault toilets are available. Leashed pets are permitted.

Reservations, fees: No reservations. Sites are $5 per night, per vehicle. Open June to October.

Directions: From Bend drive southwest on Cascades Lakes Highway (Century Drive Highway, which becomes County Road 46) and drive 44.7 miles to Forest Road 4630. Turn west (right) and drive 0.4 mile to the campground entrance.

Contact: Deschutes National Forest, Bend-Fort Rock Ranger District, 1230 N.E. Third Street, Bend, OR 97701; tel. (541) 388-5664; fax (541) 383-4700.

92 Cow Meadow   6

This campground is set near the north end of Crane Prairie Reservoir and near the Deschutes River. It's a pretty spot and the price is right. This is a great spot for fly-fishing and bird-watching.

Location: On Crane Prairie Reservoir in Deschutes National Forest; map D2, grid e7.

Campsites, facilities: There are 20 sites for tents, trailers, or RVs up to 22 feet long. Picnic tables, garbage service, and fire grills are provided. Vault toilets are available. There is no drinking water. Leashed pets are permitted.

Reservations, fees: No reservations. Sites are $5 per night, per vehicle. Open May to mid-October.

Directions: From Bend drive southwest on Cascades Lakes Highway (Century Drive Highway, which becomes County Road 46) and drive 44.7 miles to Forest Road 40. Turn east (left) and drive 0.4 mile to Forest Road 4000-970. Turn south (right) and drive two miles to the campground on the right.

Contact: Deschutes National Forest, Bend-Fort Rock Ranger District, 1230 N.E. Third Street, Bend, OR 97701; tel. (541) 388-5664; fax (541) 383-4700.

93 Crane Prairie   5

This campground along the north shore of Crane Prairie Reservoir is a good spot for fishing and boating. This reservoir is world-renowned for rainbow trout fishing and is also popular for bass fishing.

Location: On Crane Prairie Reservoir in Deschutes National Forest; map D2, grid e7.

Campsites, facilities: There are 146 sites for tents, trailers, or RVs. Picnic tables. garbage service, and fire grills are provided. Drinking water and vault toilets are available. Boat docks, launching facilities, and a fish cleaning station are available on-site. Boat rentals, showers, gas, and laundry facilities are located nearby. Leashed pets are permitted.

Reservations, fees: No reservations. Sites are $10-12 per night, plus $5 per additional vehicle. Open April 20 through October, weather permitting.

Directions: From Bend drive south on U.S. 97 for 26.8 miles to Wickiup Junction and County Road 43. Turn west (right) on County Road 43 and drive 11 miles to Forest Road 42. Continue west on Forest Road 42 for 5.4 miles to Forest Road 4270. Turn north (right) and drive 4.2 miles to the campground on the left.

Contact: Deschutes National Forest, Bend-Fort Rock Ranger District, 1230 N.E. Third Street, Bend, OR 97701; tel. (541) 388-5664; fax (541) 383-4700.

94 Crane Prairie Resort   6

This resort is set along the north shore of popular Crane Prairie Reservoir, a good spot for canoeing and fishing. No waterskiing is permitted.

Location: On Crane Prairie Reservoir; map D2, grid e7.

Campsites, facilities: There are 20 sites for trailers or RVs. Electricity, drinking water, sewer hookups, and picnic tables are provided. Bottled gas, firewood, a store, and ice are available. Boat docks, launching facilities, and rentals are nearby. Leashed pets are permitted.

Reservations, fees: Reservations accepted. Sites are $10-15 per night. Open late April to mid-October.

Directions: From Bend drive south on U.S. 97 for 26.8 miles to Wickiup Junction and County Road 43. Turn west (right) on County Road 43 and drive 11 miles to Forest Road 42. Continue west on Forest Road 42 for 5.4 miles to Forest Road 4270. Turn north (right) and drive seven miles to the resort entrance.

Contact: Crane Prairie Resort, P.O. Box 322, LaPine, OR 97739; tel. (541) 385-2173.

95 Little Fawn   5

Choose between sites on the water's edge or nestled nearby in the forest at this campground along the eastern shore of Elk Lake at 4,900 feet elevation. A play area for children can be found at one of the lake's inlets. See the description of Point Campground for recreation options. Little Fawn Group Camp is just beyond Little Fawn Campground.

Location: On Elk Lake in Deschutes National Forest; map D2, grid e8.

Campsites, facilities: There are 18 sites for tents, trailers, or RVs up to 22 feet long, and one group site that can accommodate up to 60 campers. Picnic tables, garbage service, drinking water, and fire grills are provided. Vault toilets are available. Boat launching facilities and rentals are on-site. Leashed pets are permitted.

Reservations, fees: Reservations required for the group sites. Sites are $8 per night; the group site is $70 per night; there is a fee of $5 per night for an additional vehicle. Open June through September, weather permitting.

Directions: From Bend drive southwest on Cascades Lakes Highway (Century Drive Highway, which becomes County Road 46) and drive 35.5 miles to Forest Road 4625. Turn east (left) and drive 1.7 miles to the campground.

Contact: Deschutes National Forest, Bend-Fort Rock Ranger District, 1230 N.E. Third Street, Bend, OR 97701; tel. (541) 388-5664; fax (541) 383-4700.

96 Mallard Marsh   8

This quiet campground is on the shore of Hosmer Lake, which is stocked with brown trout and Atlantic salmon and reserved for catch-and-release fly-fishing only. The lake is ideal for canoeing. You'll get a pristine, quality fishing experience. Non-motorized boats only.

Location: On Hosmer Lake in Deschutes National Forest; map D2, grid e7.

Campsites, facilities: There are 15 sites for tents, trailers, or RVs up to 22 feet long. Picnic tables, garbage service, vault toilets, No drinking water is available. Boat launching facilities are nearby. Leashed pets are permitted.

Reservations, fees: No reservations. Sites are $5 per night, per vehicle. Open late May to late September.

Directions: From Bend drive southwest on Cascades Lakes Highway (Century Drive Highway, which becomes County Road 46) and drive 35.5 miles to Forest Road 4625. Turn left (southeast) and drive two miles to the camp.

Contact: Deschutes National Forest, Bend-Fort Rock Ranger District, 1230 N.E. Third Street, Bend, OR 97701; tel. (541) 388-5664; fax (541) 383-4700.

97 South   8

This campground is along the shore of Hosmer Lake, adjacent to Mallard Marsh Campground. See the description of Mallard Marsh for recreation details.

Location: On Hosmer Lake in Deschutes National Forest; map D2, grid e8.

Campsites, facilities: There are 23 sites for tents, trailers, or RVs up to 22 feet long. Picnic tables, garbage service, and fire grills are provided. Vault toilets and boat launch facilities are available. No drinking water is provided. Leashed pets are permitted.

Reservations, fees: No reservations. Sites are $5 per night per vehicle. Open late May to late September, weather permitting.

Directions: From Bend drive southwest on Cascades Lakes Highway (Century Drive Highway, which becomes County Road 46) and drive 35.5 miles to Forest Road 4625. Turn left (east) and drive 1.2 miles to the campground on the right.

Contact: Deschutes National Forest, Bend-Fort Rock Ranger District, 1230 N.E. Third Street, Bend, OR 97701; tel. (541) 388-5664; fax (541) 383-4700.

98 Little Lava Lake   8

Boating, fishing, swimming, and hiking are some of the recreation options. This lake feeds into the Deschutes River. Some sites are lakeside and some are along the river.
Location: On Little Lava Lake in Deschutes National Forest; map D2, grid e8.
Campsites, facilities: There are 10 sites for tents, trailers, or RVs up to 22 feet long. Picnic tables, garbage service, and fire grills are provided. Vault toilets and drinking water are available. Boat docks and rentals are nearby. Launching facilities are on-site. Leashed pets are permitted.
Reservations, fees: No reservations. Sites are $5 per night, per vehicle. Open May to late September, weather permitting.
Directions: From Bend drive southwest on Cascades Lakes Highway (Century Drive Highway, which becomes County Road 46) and drive 38.4 miles to Forest Road 4600-500. Turn east (left) and drive 0.7 mile to Forest Road 4600-520. Continue east for 0.4 mile to the campground.
Contact: Deschutes National Forest, Bend-Fort Rock Ranger District, 1230 N.E. Third Street, Bend, OR 97701; tel. (541) 388-5664; fax (541) 383-4700.

99 Deschutes Bridge   4

This wooded campground is on the banks of the Deschutes River in a beautiful, lush green spot. It's set at 4,650 feet. Fishing prospects are typically poor here and only artificials (lures and flies) are allowed.
Location: On the Upper Deschutes River in the Deschutes National Forest; map D2, grid e8.
Campsites, facilities: There are 12 sites for tents, trailers, or RVs up to 22 feet long. Picnic tables, garbage service, and fire grills are provided. Drinking water and vault toilets are available. Leashed pets are permitted.
Reservations, fees: No reservations. Sites are $5 per night per vehicle. The entire camp is $50 per night, with a two-night minimum on weekends and a three-night minimum on holidays. Open June to October.
Directions: From Bend drive southwest on Cascades Lakes Highway (Century Drive Highway, which becomes County Road 46) and drive 41.1 miles to the campground on the left (just past the Deschutes River Bridge).
Contact: Deschutes National Forest, Bend-Fort Rock Ranger District, 1230 N.E. Third Street, Bend, OR 97701; tel. (541) 388-5664; fax (541) 383-4700.

100 Sharps Creek   5

Like the nearby Rujada site, this camp on the banks of Sharps Creek is just far enough off the beaten path to be missed by most campers. It's quiet, primitive, and remote, and fishing, swimming, and gold-panning are popular activities in the day-use area.
Location: On Sharps Creek; map D2, grid f1.
Campsites, facilities: There are 10 sites for tents, trailers, or RVs up to 30 feet long. Picnic tables and fire pits are provided. Drinking water, vault toilets, and

firewood are available. A camp host is available in summer months. Some facilities are wheelchair accessible. Leashed pets are permitted.

Reservations, fees: No reservations. Sites are $5 per night, with a 14-day stay limit, plus $3 for each additional vehicle. Open mid-May to mid-October, weather permitting.

Directions: From Eugene drive south on Interstate 5 to Cottage Grove and Exit 174. Take that exit and drive east on Row River Road for 18 miles to Sharps Creek Road. Turn south and drive four miles to the campground.

Contact: Bureau of Land Management, Eugene District, P.O. Box 10226, Eugene, OR 97440-2226; tel. (541) 683-6600; fax (541) 683-6981.

101 Rujada   7

This campground is situated on a river terrace on the banks of Layng Creek, right at the national forest border. The Swordfern Trail follows along Layng Creek through a beautiful forest within a lush fern grotto. There's a good swimming spot about two miles upstream from its confluence with the Row River, and those with time and patience can fish in the creek. By continuing east on Forest Road 17, you can access a trailhead that leads one-half mile to beautiful Spirit Falls, a spectacular 60-foot waterfall. A bit farther east is another easy trail to Moon Falls, even more awe-inspiring at 125 feet. Another campground option is Cedar Creek, located about six miles southeast on Brice Creek Road (County Road 2470).

Location: On Layng Creek in Umpqua National Forest; map D2, grid f1.

Campsites, facilities: There are 10 sites for tents, trailers, or RVs up to 22 feet long. Picnic tables, garbage bins, and fire pits are provided. Flush toilets, drinking water, and a softball field are available. Some facilities are wheelchair accessible. Leashed pets are permitted.

Reservations, fees: No reservations. Sites are $7 per night, $3 per night for an additional vehicle. Open late May to late September.

Directions: From Eugene drive south on Interstate 5 to Cottage Grove and Exit 174. Take that exit and drive east on Row River Road for 19 miles to Layng Creek Road (Forest Road 17). Turn left and drive two miles to the campground on the right.

Contact: Umpqua National Forest, Cottage Grove Ranger District, 78405 Cedar Park Road, Cottage Grove, OR 97424; tel. (541) 942-5591.

102 Sand Prairie   6

Located at 1,600 feet in a mixed stand of Douglas fir, western hemlock, cedar, dogwood, and hazelnut, this campground is within easy access to the Middle Fork of the Willamette River. There's an access road to the south (upstream) end of the Hills Creek Reservoir. The 27-mile Middle Fork Trail begins at the south end of the campground. Fishing is good here, where you can expect to catch large-scale suckers, rainbows, and cutthroat trout in the Middle Fork.

Location: On the Willamette River in Willamette National Forest; map D2, grid f3.

Campsites, facilities: There are 20 sites for tents, trailers, or RVs up to 22 feet long. Picnic tables, garbage bins, a recycle center, and fire rings are provided.

Vault and flush toilets, a group picnic area, and drinking water are available. Some of the facilities are wheelchair accessible. A boat launch is nearby on Hills Creek Reservoir. Leashed pets are permitted.

Reservations, fees: No reservations. Sites are $10 per night, plus $4 per additional vehicle. Open May through September.

Directions: From Eugene drive south on Interstate 5 for four miles to Exit 188 and Highway 58. Turn southeast and drive 35 miles to Oakridge. Continue east on Highway 58 for two miles to Kitson Springs Road. Turn right and drive one-half mile to Forest Road 21. Turn right and continue 11 miles to the campground.

Contact: Willamette National Forest, Middle Fork Ranger District, 49098 Salmon Creek Road, Oakridge, OR 97463; tel. (541) 782-2283; fax (541) 782-5306.

103 Packard Creek   6

Situated on a large flat beside Hills Creek Reservoir, this campground is extremely popular with families and fills up on weekends and holidays. There is a mix of vegetation in the campground, which includes an abundance of poison oak. The speed limit around the swimming area and boat ramp is 5 mph.

Location: On Hills Creek Reservoir in Willamette National Forest; map D2, grid f3.

Campsites, facilities: There are 33 sites for tents, trailers, or RVs up to 30 feet long. Picnic tables, garbage bins, and fire rings are provided. Drinking water, vault toilets, and firewood are available. Some facilities are wheelchair accessible. Fishing and boat docks, boat launching facilities, a roped swimming area, a picnic shelter, and an amphitheater are available. Some sites have their own docks. Leashed pets are permitted.

Reservations, fees: No reservations. Sites are $10-12 per night, plus $4 per additional vehicle. Open mid-April to mid-September.

Directions: From Eugene drive south on Interstate 5 for four miles to Exit 188 and Highway 58. Turn southeast and drive 35 miles to Oakridge. Continue east on Highway 58 for two miles to Kitson Springs Road. Turn right and drive one-half mile to Forest Road 21. Turn right and continue six miles to the campground.

Contact: Willamette National Forest, Middle Fork Ranger District, 49098 Salmon Creek Road, Oakridge, OR 97463; tel. (541) 782-2283; fax (541) 782-5306.

104 Blue Pool   4

This campground is situated in an old-growth forest alongside Salt Creek at 1,900 feet elevation. There is a large picnic area along the creek with picnic tables, a large grassy area, and fire stoves built in the 1930's by the Civilian Conservation Corps. One-half mile east of the campground on Highway 58 is McCredie Hot Springs. This spot is undeveloped, without any facilities. Caution should be exercised when using the hot springs; they can be very hot.

Location: On Salt Creek in Willamette National Forest; map D2, grid f3.

Campsites, facilities: There are 24 sites for tents, trailers, or RVs up to 18 feet long. Picnic tables, garbage bins, a recycle center, and fire rings are provided. There is no potable water, but pit and flush toilets are available. Leashed pets are permitted.

Reservations, fees: No reservations. Sites are $8 per night, plus $4 per additional vehicle. Open mid-May to mid-September.

Directions: From Eugene drive south on Interstate 5 for four miles to Exit 188 and Highway 58. Turn southeast and drive 35 miles to Oakridge. Continue east on Highway 58 for 10 miles to the campground.

Contact: Willamette National Forest, Middle Fork Ranger District, 49098 Salmon Creek Road, Oakridge, OR 97463; tel. (541) 782-2283; fax (541) 782-5306.

105 Sacandaga   5

At 2,400 feet elevation, this campground is along the Middle Fork of the Willamette River where a segment of the historic Oregon Central Military Wagon Road can be seen. The Willamette River is accessible by two trails from the campground, and the Middle Fork Trail is in close proximity. There is also a short trail leading to a viewpoint with a bench for a short break. This campground gets low use and the sites are well separated by vegetation. Count on solitude here.

Location: On the Willamette River in Willamette National Forest; map D2, grid f4.

Campsites, facilities: There are 16 sites for tents, trailers, or RVs up to 24 feet long. Picnic tables and fire rings are provided, and vault toilets and firewood are available. There is no drinking water. Leashed pets are permitted.

Reservations, fees: No reservations. Sites are $5 per night, $3 per night for an additional vehicle. Open mid-May to mid-November, weather permitting.

Directions: From Eugene drive south on Interstate 5 for four miles to Exit 188 and Highway 58. Turn southeast and drive 35 miles to Oakridge. Continue east on Highway 58 for two miles to Kitson Springs Road. Turn right and drive one-half mile to Forest Road 21. Turn right and drive 24 miles to the campground.

Contact: Willamette National Forest, Middle Fork Ranger District, 49098 Salmon Creek Road, Oakridge, OR 97463; tel. (541) 782-2283; fax (541) 782-5306.

106 Skookum Creek   7

This is a popular starting point for backcountry fishing, hiking, or horse use. The Erma Bell Lakes Trail begins here and is a portal into the Three Sisters Wilderness. This trail is maintained to be accessible for wheelchair users, though it is challenging.

Location: Near the Three Sisters Wilderness in Willamette National Forest; map D2, grid f5.

Campsites, facilities: There are eight walk-in tent sites, two of which are wheelchair accessible. Picnic tables and fire rings are provided. Drinking water, hitching rails, and pit toilets are available. All garbage must be packed out. Leashed pets are permitted.

Reservations, fees: No reservations. Sites are $5 per night, plus $3 for each additional vehicle. Open mid-May through September, weather permitting.

Directions: From Eugene drive east on Highway 126 for 37 miles to Blue River. Continue east for five miles to Forest Road 19 (Aufderheide Scenic Byway). Turn right and drive 35 miles south to Forest Road 1957. Turn left (south) and drive four miles to the campground.

Contact: Willamette National Forest, Middle Fork Ranger District, 49098 Salmon Creek Road, Oakridge, OR 97463; tel. (541) 782-2283; fax (541) 782-5306.

107 Shadow Bay   10

This campground is located on a large bay at the south end of Waldo Lake. It is a considerably wetter environment than either North Waldo or Islet Campgrounds, supporting a more diverse and prolific ground cover as well as more mosquitoes. The use rate is considerably lighter than North Waldo. You can access the Shore Line Trail and then the Waldo Lake Trail from here. The boating speed limit is 10 mph for all of Waldo Lake.

Location: On Waldo Lake in Willamette National Forest; map D2, grid f6.

Campsites, facilities: There are 92 sites for tents, trailers, or RVs up to 24 feet long. Picnic tables, garbage bins, a recycle center, and fire grills are provided. Drinking water, a sanitary disposal station, and pit and flush toilets are available. Boat launching facilities are nearby. Leashed pets are permitted.

Reservations, fees: No reservations. Sites are $10-12 per night, plus $5 for each additional vehicle. Open July through September, weather permitting.

Directions: From Eugene drive south on Interstate 5 for four miles to Exit 188 and Highway 58. Turn southeast and drive about 60 miles southeast to Waldo Lake Road (Forest Road 5897). Turn left on Waldo Lake Road and drive north for 6.5 miles to the Shadow Bay turnoff. Turn left and drive on Forest Road 5896 to the campground at the south end of Waldo Lake.

Contact: Willamette National Forest, Middle Fork Ranger District, 49098 Salmon Creek Road, Oakridge, OR 97463; tel. (541) 782-2283; fax (541) 782-5306.

108 North Waldo   10

This camp, at an elevation of 5,400 feet, is the most popular of the Waldo Lake campgrounds. The drier environment supports fewer mosquitoes, but they are still plentiful in season. Amphitheater programs are presented on weekends from late July to Labor Day. The boat launch is deeper than the others on the lake, making it more accommodating for large sailboats. North Waldo is also a popular starting point for many wilderness trails and lakes, most notably the Rigdon, Wahanna, and Torrey Lakes. Waldo Lake has the special distinction of being one of the three purest lakes in the world. Of those three lakes, two are in Oregon (the other is Crater Lake), and the third is in Siberia.

Location: On Waldo Lake in Willamette National Forest; map D2, grid f6.

Campsites, facilities: There are 58 sites for tents, trailers, or RVs up to 30 feet long. Picnic tables, garbage bins, a recycle center, and fire rings are provided. Drinking water, pit and flush toilets, a swimming area, and an amphitheater are available. A sanitary disposal station is nearby. Boat launching facilities are available. Leashed pets are permitted.

Reservations, fees: No reservations. Sites are $10-12 per night, plus $5 for each additional vehicle. Open July through September, weather permitting.

Directions: From Eugene drive south on Interstate 5 for four miles to Exit 188 and Highway 58. Turn southeast and drive about 60 miles southeast to Waldo

Lake Road (Forest Road 5897). Turn left and drive north on Waldo Lake Road for 14 miles to Forest Road 5898. Turn left and drive about two miles to the campground at the northeast end of Waldo Lake.

Contact: Willamette National Forest, Middle Fork Ranger District, 49098 Salmon Creek Road, Oakridge, OR 97463; tel. (541) 782-2283; fax (541) 782-5306.

109 Islet   10

You'll find sandy beaches and an interpretive sign at this campground which is located at the north end of Waldo Lake. The winds blow consistently every afternoon. A picnic table placed strategically on the rock jetty is a great spot to enjoy a sunset. There's a one-mile shoreline trail between Islet and North Waldo Campground. Bring your mosquito repellent from June to August; you'll need it. For more information, see North Waldo.

Location: On Waldo Lake in Willamette National Forest; map D2, grid f6.

Campsites, facilities: There are 55 sites for tents, trailers, or RVs up to 30 feet long. Picnic tables, garbage bins, a recycle center, and fire rings are provided. Drinking water, flush toilets, garbage bins, and a recycle center are available. A sanitary disposal station is nearby. Boat launching facilities are available. Leashed pets are permitted.

Reservations, fees: No reservations. Sites are $10-12 per night, plus $5 for each additional vehicle. Group sites are $20 per night. Open July through September, weather permitting.

Directions: From Eugene drive south on Interstate 5 for four miles to Exit 188 and Highway 58. Turn southeast and drive about 60 miles southeast to Waldo Lake Road (Forest Road 5897). Turn left and drive north on Waldo Lake Road for 14 miles to Forest Road 5898. Turn left and continue 1.5 miles to the campground at the northeast end of Waldo Lake.

Contact: Willamette National Forest, Middle Fork Ranger District, 49098 Salmon Creek Road, Oakridge, OR 97463;

110 North Davis Creek   4

This remote, secluded campground is set along a western channel that feeds into Wickiup Reservoir and receives little use. It can be used as an overflow camp if campsites are filled at Wickiup. In late summer, the reservoir level tends to drop. Fishing for brown and rainbow trout as well as kokanee salmon is good here.

Location: On North Davis Creek in Deschutes National Forest; map D2, grid f6.

Campsites, facilities: There are 17 sites for tents, trailers, or RVs up to 22 feet long. Picnic tables, garbage service, and fire grills are provided. Drinking water and vault toilets are available. Boat launching facilities are on-site. Leashed pets are permitted.

Reservations, fees: No reservations. Sites are $5 per night, per vehicle. Open May to late October.

Directions: From Bend drive south on U.S. 97 for 26.8 miles to Wickiup Junction at Crescent and County Road 61. Drive west on County Road 61 for nine miles to Forest Road 46. Turn north on Forest Road 46 and drive 14 miles to the campground.

Contact: Deschutes National Forest, Bend-Fort Rock Ranger District, 1230 N.E. Third Street, Bend, OR 97701; tel. (541) 388-5664; fax (541) 383-4700.

111 Quinn River   5

This campground is set along the western shore of Crane Prairie Reservoir, a popular spot for anglers. A separate, large parking lot is available for boats and trailers. Boat speed is limited to 10 mph here.
Location: On Crane Prairie Reservoir in Deschutes National Forest; map D2, grid f7.
Campsites, facilities: There are 41 sites for tents, trailers, or RVs up to 30 feet long. Picnic tables, garbage service, and fire grills are provided. Drinking water and vault toilets are available. Boat launch facilities are available. Leashed pets are permitted.
Reservations, fees: No reservations. Sites are $9 per night, plus $5 per additional vehicle. Open late April to mid-October.
Directions: From Bend drive southwest on Cascade Lakes Highway (Century Drive Highway, which becomes County Road 46) and drive 48 miles to the campground.
Contact: Deschutes National Forest, Bend-Fort Rock Ranger District, 1230 N.E. Third Street, Bend, OR 97701; tel. (541) 388-5664; fax (541) 383-4700.

112 Rock Creek   5

This campground is set along the west shore of Crane Prairie Reservoir. See the description of Quinn River Campground.
Location: On Crane Prairie Reservoir in Deschutes National Forest; map D2, grid f7.
Campsites, facilities: There are 32 sites for tents, trailers, or RVs up to 22 feet long. Picnic tables, garbage service, and fire grills are provided. Drinking water, a fish cleaning station, and vault toilets are available. Boat docks and launching facilities are on-site. Leashed pets are permitted.
Reservations, fees: No reservations. Sites are $10 per night, plus $5 per additional vehicle. Open mid-April through October, weather permitting.
Directions: From Bend drive southwest on Cascade Lakes Highway (Century Drive Highway, which becomes County Road 46) and drive 48 miles to the campground.
Contact: Deschutes National Forest, Bend-Fort Rock Ranger District, 1230 N.E. Third Street, Bend, OR 97701; tel. (541) 388-5664; fax (541) 383-4700.

113 North Twin Lake   6

This campground on the shore of North Twin Lake is a popular weekend spot for families. It's small and fairly primitive, but has lake access and a pretty setting. Only non-motorized boats are permitted.
Location: On North Twin Lake in Deschutes National Forest; map D2, grid f7.
Campsites, facilities: There are 10 sites for tents, trailers, or RVs up to 22 feet long. Picnic tables and fire grills are provided. Vault toilets are available. There is no drinking water. Boat launching facilities are on-site. Leashed pets are permitted.

Reservations, fees: No reservations. Sites are $5 per night, per vehicle. Open June to late September, weather permitting.

Directions: From Bend drive southwest on Cascade Lakes Highway (County Road 46) and drive past Crane Prairie Reservoir to Forest Road 42. Turn east and drive four miles to Forest Road 4260. Turn right (south) and drive a quarter-mile to the campground.

Contact: Deschutes National Forest, Bend-Fort Rock Ranger District, 1230 N.E. Third Street, Bend, OR 97701; tel. (541) 388-5664; fax (541) 383-4700.

114 Lava Flow   8

This campground is set in old-growth forest, along the northeast shore of Davis Lake, a very shallow lake formed by lava flow. The water level fluctuates here, and this campground can sometimes be closed in summer months. There's good duck hunting during the fall. Fishing can be decent, but only fly fishing is allowed. Boat speed is limited to 10 mph.

Location: On Davis Lake in Deschutes National Forest; map D2, grid f7.

Campsites, facilities: There is a dispersed camping area for 12 tents, trailers, or RVs up to 22 feet long. Picnic tables and fire grills are provided. Vault toilets and firewood (to be gathered from the surrounding area) are available. There is no drinking water, and all garbage must be packed out. A boat launch is nearby. Leashed pets are permitted.

Reservations, fees: No reservations; no fee. Open September through December, weather permitting.

Directions: From Eugene drive south on Interstate 5 for five miles to Exit 188 and Highway 58. Turn east on Highway 58 and drive 86 miles to County Road 61. Turn left and drive three miles to Forest Road 46. Turn left and drive 7.7 miles to Forest Road 850. Turn left and drive 1.8 miles to the campground.

Contact: Deschutes National Forest, Crescent Ranger District, P.O. Box 208, Crescent, OR 97733; tel. (541) 433-2234; fax (541) 433-3224.

115 West South Twin   4

This camp is set on South Twin Lake adjacent to Wickiup Reservoir, and a major access point to the Wickiup Reservoir. It's a popular angling spot with very good kokanee salmon fishing. Twin Lakes Resort is adjacent to West South Twin.

Location: On South Twin Lake in Deschutes National Forest; map D2, grid f7.

Campsites, facilities: There are 24 sites for trailers or RVs up to 22 feet long. Picnic tables, garbage service, and fire grills are provided. Drinking water and flush toilets are available. Boat launching facilities are on-site, and boat rentals, a restaurant, showers, coin-operated laundry, gas, propane, cabins, and a store are nearby. Leashed pets are permitted.

Reservations, fees: No reservations. Sites are $10 per night, plus $5 per additional vehicle. Open mid-May to mid-October, weather permitting.

Directions: From Bend drive southwest on Cascade Lakes Highway (County Road 46) past Crane Prairie Reservoir to Forest Road 42. Turn east and drive four miles to Forest Road 4260. Turn right (south) and drive a quarter-mile to the campground.

Contact: Deschutes National Forest, Bend-Fort Rock Ranger District, 1230 N.E. Third Street, Bend, OR 97701; tel. (541) 388-5664; fax (541) 383-4700.

116 Gull Point   5

This campground is in an open ponderosa stand on the north shore of Wickiup Reservoir. You'll find good fishing for kokanee salmon here. It's about two miles from West South Twin Campground. This is the most popular campground on Wickiup Reservoir.

Location: On Wickiup Reservoir in Deschutes National Forest; map D2, grid f7.

Campsites, facilities: There are 79 sites for tents, trailers, or RVs up to 30 feet long. There are also two sites available for groups of up to 25 people. Picnic tables, garbage service, and fire grills are provided. Drinking water, a sanitary dump station, and flush and vault toilets are available. Boat launching facilities and fish cleaning stations are on-site. Leashed pets are permitted.

Reservations, fees: Reservations accepted only for group sites. Individual sites are $10-12 per night, and group sites are $40 per night, plus $5 per additional vehicle. Open mid-April through October, weather permitting.

Directions: From Bend drive south on U.S. 97 for about 25 miles to County Road 43 (three miles north of LaPine). Turn west on County Road 43 and drive 12 miles to Forest Road 42. Turn west on Forest Road 42 and drive 4.6 miles to Forest Road 4260. Turn south (left) and drive three miles to the campground on the right.

Contact: Deschutes National Forest, Bend-Fort Rock Ranger District, 1230 N.E. Third Street, Bend, OR 97701; tel. (541) 388-5664; fax (541) 383-4700.

117 Twin Lakes Resort

        8

This resort is a popular family vacation destination, with a full-service marina and all the amenities, including beach areas. Recreational activities range from hiking to fishing, swimming, and boating on Wickiup Reservoir. Nearby South Twin Lake is popular with paddleboaters and kayakers. It's stocked with rainbow trout. See the description of West South Twin and South Twin Lake.

Location: On Twin Lakes; map D2, grid f7.

Campsites, facilities: There are 22 full-hookup sites for trailers and RVs of any length. There are also 14 cabins. Rest rooms, showers, a sanitary dump, a private tel., a laundry room, a store, a full-service restaurant, ice, snacks, some RV supplies, LP gas, gasoline, and a barbecue are available. A boat ramp, rentals, and a dock are provided; no motors are permitted on South Twin Lake. Leashed pets are permitted.

Reservations, fees: Reservations are recommended. Sites are $25 per night, and cabins are $85-125 per night. Open late April to mid-October.

Directions: From Bend drive south on U.S. 97 for 26.8 miles to Wickiup Junction. Turn west (right) on County Road 43 and drive 11 miles to Forest Road 42. Continue 4.6 miles west on Forest Road 42 to Forest Road 4260. Turn south (left) and drive two miles to the resort.

Contact: Twin Lakes Resort, P.O. Box 3550, Sun River, OR 97707; tel. (541) 593-6526; fax (541) 410-4688.

118 Sheep Bridge   3

This campground is set along the north Deschutes River Channel of Wickiup Reservoir in an open, treeless area that has minimal privacy and is dusty in summer. Dispersed sites here are popular with group campers.

Location: Near Wickiup Reservoir in Deschutes National Forest; map D2, grid f7.

Campsites, facilities: There are 18 sites for tents, trailers, or RVs of any length. Picnic tables, garbage service, and fire grills are provided. Drinking water, vault toilets, boat launching facilities, and a picnic area are available. Leashed pets are permitted.

Reservations, fees: No reservations. Sites are $5 per night, per vehicle. Open April through October, weather permitting.

Directions: From Bend drive south on U.S. 97 for 26.8 miles to Wickiup Junction. Turn west (right) on County Road 43 and drive 11 miles to Forest Road 42. Continue 4.6 miles west on Forest Road 42 to Forest Road 4260. Turn south (left) and drive three-quarters of a mile to the campground on the right.

Contact: Deschutes National Forest, Bend-Fort Rock Ranger District, 1230 N.E. Third Street, Bend, OR 97701; tel. (541) 388-5664; fax (541) 383-4700.

119 South Twin Lake   6

This campground is on the shore of South Twin Lake, a popular spot for swimming, fishing, and boating (non-motorized only). See the description of West South Twin Campground.

Location: On South Twin Lake in Deschutes National Forest; map D2, grid f7.

Campsites, facilities: There are 24 sites for tents, trailers, or RVs up to 22 feet long. Picnic tables, garbage service, and fire grills are provided. Drinking water, vault and flush toilets are available. Boat launching facilities (small boats only), boat rentals, showers, and laundry facilities are nearby. Leashed pets are permitted.

Reservations, fees: No reservations. Sites are $12 per night, plus $5 per additional vehicle. Open mid-April through October, weather permitting.

Directions: From Bend drive south on U.S. 97 for 26.8 miles to Wickiup Junction. Turn west (right) on County Road 43 and drive 11 miles to Forest Road 42. Continue west on Forest Road 42 for 4.6 miles to Forest Road 4260. Turn left (south) and drive two miles to the campground on the left.

Contact: Deschutes National Forest, Bend-Fort Rock Ranger District, 1230 N.E. Third Street, Bend, OR 97701; tel. (541) 388-5664; fax (541) 383-4700.

120 Reservoir   4

This campground is set along the south shore of Wickiup Reservoir, where the kokanee salmon fishing is good. The camp is best in early summer, before the lake level drops. This campground gets little use, so you won't find crowds here.

Location: On Wickiup Reservoir in Deschutes National Forest; map D2, grid f7.

Campsites, facilities: There are 28 sites for tents, trailers, or RVs up to 22 feet long. Picnic tables, garbage service, and fire grills are provided. Boat launching facilities and vault toilets are available, but there is no drinking water. Leashed pets are permitted.

Reservations, fees: No reservations. Sites are $5 per night per vehicle. Open May to late October, weather permitting.

Directions: From Bend drive southwest on Cascade Lakes Highway (County Road 46) and drive 57.8 miles to Forest Road 44. Turn left (east) and drive 1.7 miles to the campground.

Contact: Deschutes National Forest, Bend-Fort Rock Ranger District, 1230 N.E. Third Street, Bend, OR 97701; tel. (541) 388-5664; fax (541) 383-4700.

121 Fall River   5

This campground is on the Fall River, where fishing is restricted to fly-fishing only. Check the regulations for other restrictions. Fall River is beautiful, crystal clear, and cold. Fall River Trail meanders along the river for 3.5 miles and is open for bicycling.

Location: On the Fall River in Deschutes National Forest; map D2, grid f8.

Campsites, facilities: There are 12 sites for tents, trailers, or RVs up to 22 feet long. Picnic tables, garbage service, and fire grills are provided. Vault toilets are available. There is no drinking water. Leashed pets are permitted.

Reservations, fees: No reservations. Sites are $5 per night, per vehicle. Open mid-April through October, weather permitting.

Directions: From Bend drive south on U.S. 97 for 17.3 miles to Forest Road 42. Turn southwest (right) and drive 12.2 miles to the campground.

Contact: Deschutes National Forest, Bend-Fort Rock Ranger District, 1230 N.E. Third Street, Bend, OR 97701; tel. (541) 388-5664; fax (541) 383-4700.

122 Pringle Falls   4

This campground is set along the Deschutes River and is less than a mile from Pringle Falls. The camp gets light use and is pretty and serene.

Location: On the Deschutes River in Deschutes National Forest; map D2, grid f8.

Campsites, facilities: There are seven sites for tents, trailers, or RVs up to 22 feet long. Picnic tables, garbage service, and fire grills are provided. Vault toilets are available. There is no drinking water. Leashed pets are permitted.

Reservations, fees: No reservations. Sites are $5 per night, per vehicle. Open April through September, weather permitting.

Directions: From Bend drive south on U.S. 97 for 26.8 miles to Wickiup Junction. Turn west (right) on County Road 43 and drive 7.4 miles to Forest Road 4330-500. Turn right (north) and drive one mile to the campground.

Contact: Deschutes National Forest, Bend-Fort Rock Ranger District, 1230 N.E. Third Street, Bend, OR 97701; tel. (541) 388-5664; fax (541) 383-4700.

123 Wickiup Butte   4

This campground is set along the southeast shore of Wickiup Reservoir at 4,350 feet, where kokanee salmon fishing is good during the early summer. Wickiup Butte is more remote than the other campgrounds on Wickiup Reservoir.

Location: On Wickiup Reservoir in Deschutes National Forest; map D2, grid f8.

Campsites, facilities: There are 12 sites for tents, trailers, or RVs up to 22 feet long. Picnic tables, garbage service, and fire grills are provided. Vault toilets are available. There is no drinking water. Boat launching facilities are nearby. Leashed pets are permitted.

Reservations, fees: No reservations. Sites are $5 per night, per vehicle. Open May to late October, weather permitting.

Directions: From Bend drive south on U.S. 97 for 26.8 miles to Wickiup Junction. Turn west (right) on County Road 43 and drive 10.4 miles to Forest Road 4380. Turn south (left) and drive 3.6 miles to Forest Road 4260. Turn east (left) and drive three miles to the campground.

Contact: Deschutes National Forest, Bend-Fort Rock Ranger District, 1230 N.E. Third Street, Bend, OR 97701; tel. (541) 388-5664; fax (541) 383-4700.

124 Riverview Trailer Park   8

This grassy campground is set along the bank of the Little Deschutes River, which offers excellent trout fishing. It's missed by a lot of highway travelers; they just plain don't know about it.

Location: On the Little Deschutes River; map D2, grid f8.

Campsites, facilities: There are 15 tent sites and 19 sites for trailers or RVs of any length. Electricity, cable TV, well water, sewer hookups, and picnic tables are provided. Flush toilets, showers, a recreation hall, and a laundry room are available. Small leashed pets are permitted.

Reservations, fees: Reservations accepted. Sites are $11-18 per night. Open year-round.

Directions: From Eugene drive south on Interstate 5 for five miles to Exit 188 and Highway 58. Turn east and drive 86 miles to U.S. 97. Turn north on U.S. 97 and drive 26 miles to LaPine. Continue 2.5 miles northeast on U.S. 97 County Road 43 (Burgess Road). Turn left and drive one mile to Huntington Road. Turn left and drive one mile to the park on the left.

Contact: Riverview Trailer Park, 52731 Huntington Road, LaPine, OR 97739; tel. (541) 536-2382.

125 Hidden Pines RV Park

       7

So you think you've come far enough, eh? If you want a spot in a privately run RV park two miles from the bank of the Little Deschutes River, you've found it. Within a 30-minute drive are two reservoirs, four lakes, and a golf course. The nearby town of LaPine is the gateway to the Newberry National Volcanic Monument.

Location: Near the Little Deschutes River; map D2, grid f8.

Campsites, facilities: There are six tent sites and 25 sites for RVs up to 40 feet; 16 are pull-through sites. Electricity, drinking water, cable TV, and sewer hookups (19 sites only), and picnic tables are provided. Flush toilets, sanitary services, showers, a laundry room, RV supplies, LP gas, a community fire ring with firewood, and ice are available. The full-service community of LaPine is about five miles away. No pets are allowed.

Reservations, fees: Reservations accepted. Sites are $14-19 per night. Open from mid-April to mid-October.

Directions: From Bend drive south on U.S. 97 for 27 miles to Wickiup Junction. Turn left on Pringle Falls Loop Road and drive 2.5 miles to Pine Forest Road. Turn south and drive one-half mile to Wright Avenue. Turn east and drive 400 yards to the campground.

Contact: Hidden Pines RV Park, 52158 Elderberry Lane, LaPine, OR 97739; tel. (541) 536-2265; e-mail: hdnpnsrvpk@aol.com.

126 Bull Bend   5

This campground is on the inside of a major bend in the Deschutes River at 4,300 feet. A mini float trip can be made by starting at the upstream end of camp, floating around the bend, and then taking out at the downstream end of camp. This is a low-use getaway spot.

Location: On the Deschutes River in Deschutes National Forest; map D2, grid f8.

Campsites, facilities: There are 12 sites for tents, trailers, or RVs. Picnic tables, garbage service, fire grills, vault toilets, and boat launching facilities are available. There is no drinking water. Leashed pets are permitted.

Reservations, fees: No reservations. Sites are $5 per night, per vehicle. Open April through September, weather permitting.

Directions: From Bend drive south on U.S. 97 for 26.8 miles to Wickiup Junction. Turn west (right) on County Road 43 and drive eight miles to Forest Road 4370. Turn south (left) and drive 1.5 miles to the campground.

Contact: Deschutes National Forest, Bend-Fort Rock Ranger District, 1230 N.E. Third Street, Bend, OR 97701; tel. (541) 388-5664; fax (541) 383-4700.

127 Big River   4

This is a good spot between the banks of the Deschutes River and the road. Rafting, fishing, and motorized boating are permitted. Access is easy. This is a popular overnight spot.

Location: On the Deschutes River in Deschutes National Forest; map D2, grid f9.

Campsites, facilities: There are two tent sites and nine sites for tents, trailers, or RVs up to 22 feet long. There is also one group site that can accommodate up to 60 people. Picnic tables, garbage service, and fire grills are provided. Vault toilets are available. There is no drinking water. Boat launching facilities are onsite. Leashed pets are permitted.

Reservations, fees: No reservations. Individual sites are $5 per night per vehicle. Open April through September.

Directions: From Bend drive south on U.S. 97 for 17.3 miles to Forest Road 42. Turn west (right) and drive 4.7 miles to the campground.

Contact: Deschutes National Forest, Bend-Fort Rock Ranger District, 1230 N.E. Third Street, Bend, OR 97701; tel. (541) 388-5664; fax (541) 383-4700.

128 LaPine State Park   7

Here is a clean, quiet campground next to a twisting, cold river brimming with trout and a nearby legendary fly-fishing spot. Set in a subalpine pine forest, you just might see an eagle or red-tailed hawk grabbing breakfast right in front of you. Many high mountain lakes are in proximity, as is snow-skiing in the winter months.

Location: On the Deschutes River; map D2, grid f9.

Campsites, facilities: There are 137 sites with full or partial hookups for trailers or RVs up to 85 feet long; 87 have full hookups. There are also five cabins and three yurts. Picnic tables and fire grills are provided. Drinking water, rest rooms with flush toilets and showers, garbage bins, a dump station, and firewood are available. Leashed pets are permitted.

Reservations, fees: Contact Reservations Northwest at (800) 452-5687 ($6 reservation fee). Sites are $12-15 per night, with an additional charge of $7 per additional vehicle. Yurts are $27 per night, and cabins are $35 per night. Major credit cards accepted. Open year-round.

Directions: From Bend turn south on U.S. 97 and drive 23 miles to State Recreation Road. Turn right and drive four miles to the park.

Contact: LaPine State Park, Oregon State Parks, 15800 State Recreation Road, Alpine, OR 97739; tel. (800) 551-6949 or (541) 536-2071.

129 Highlander Motel and Trailer Park 5

This campground is near the Little Deschutes River. A golf course and tennis courts are close by.

Location: Near the Little Deschutes River; map D2, grid f9.

Campsites, facilities: There are 30 sites for trailers or RVs up to 35 feet long; 16 are drive-through sites. Electricity, drinking water, and sewer hookups are provided. Flush toilets, bottled gas, sanitary services, showers, a store, a cafe, and ice are available. A coin laundry is located within one mile. Leashed pets are permitted.

Reservations, fees: Reservations accepted. Sites are $14 per night. Open year-round.

Directions: From Interstate 5 south of Eugene, take Exit 188 and turn east on Highway 58. Drive 86 miles east to U.S. 97. Turn north on U.S. 97 and drive 26 miles to LaPine. The campground is located at the north edge of town.

Contact: Highlander Motel and Trailer Park, P.O. Box 322, LaPine, OR 97739; tel. (541) 536-2131; fax (541) 536-5246.

130 Prairie   4

Here's another good overnight campground that it is quiet and private. This camp along the banks of Paulina Creek is about one-half mile from the trailhead for the

Peter Skene Ogden National Recreation Trail.

Location: On Paulina Creek in Deschutes National Forest; map D2, grid f9.

Campsites, facilities: There are 16 sites for tents, trailers, or RVs up to 30 feet long. Picnic tables, garbage service, and fire grills are provided. Drinking water, firewood, and vault toilets are available. Leashed pets are permitted.

Reservations, fees: No reservations. Sites are $10 per night, $5 per additional vehicle. Open mid-May through October, weather permitting.

Directions: From Bend drive south on U.S. 97 for 23.5 miles to County Road 21 (Paulina/East Lake Road). Turn east (left) and drive 3.1 miles to the campground.

Contact: Deschutes National Forest, Bend-Fort Rock Ranger District, 1230 N.E. Third Street, Bend, OR 97701; tel. (541) 388-5664; fax (541) 383-4700.

131 McKay Crossing   6

This pleasant little campground is set along the banks of Paulina Creek. The nearby Peter Skene Ogden National Recreation Trail travels east for six miles to Paulina Lake (also reachable by car). This is the gateway to Newberry National Volcanic Monument, about 10 miles east on County Road 21.

Location: On Paulina Creek in Deschutes National Forest; map D2, grid f9.

Campsites, facilities: There are 10 sites for tents, trailers, or RVs up to 22 feet long. Picnic tables, garbage service, and fire grills are provided. Vault toilets are available. There is no drinking water. Leashed pets are permitted.

Reservations, fees: No reservations. Sites are $5 per night, per vehicle. Open June to late October.

Directions: From Bend drive south on U.S. 97 for 23.5 miles to County Road 21 (Paulina/East Lake Road). Turn east (left) and drive 3.2 miles to Forest Road 2120. Continue east for 2.7 miles to the campground.

Contact: Deschutes National Forest, Bend-Fort Rock Ranger District, 1230 N.E. Third Street, Bend, OR 97701; tel. (541) 388-5664; fax (541) 383-4700.

132 Rock Creek   8

This campground on the banks of Rock Creek in a relatively obscure spot is sparse and primitive, but supplies all the necessities at a reasonable price. It's not well known, either, so you're likely to have privacy as a bonus. No fishing is allowed in Rock Creek.

Location: On Rock Creek; map D2, grid g0.

Campsites, facilities: There are 17 sites for tents, trailers, or RVs up to 30 feet long. Picnic tables and fire grills are provided. Vault toilets, drinking water, a camp host, a pavilion, and firewood are available. Leashed pets are permitted.

Reservations, fees: No reservations. Sites are $8 per night, with a 14-day stay limit, plus $3 for each additional vehicle. Open mid-May to mid-October.

Directions: From Roseburg drive east on Highway 138 for 22 miles to Rock Creek Road. Turn right (north) and drive seven miles to the campground.

Contact: Bureau of Land Management, Roseburg District, 777 N.W. Garden Valley Boulevard, Roseburg, OR 97470; tel. (541) 440-4930; fax (541) 440-4948.

133 Millpond   8

Rock Creek flows past Millpond and empties into the North Umpqua River five miles downstream. Just above this confluence is the Rock Creek Fish Hatchery, which is open year-round to visitors, with free access. This campground along the banks of Rock Creek is the first camp you'll see along Rock Creek Road, which accounts for its relative popularity in this area. Like Rock Creek Campground, it's primitive and remote. No fishing is allowed in Rock Creek.

Location: On Rock Creek; map D2, grid g0.

Campsites, facilities: There are 12 sites for tents, trailers, or RVs up to 30 feet long. Picnic tables. garbage service, and fire grills are provided. Flush and vault toilets, drinking water, a camp host, firewood, a ball field, a playground, and a pavilion (with 24 picnic tables, sinks, electricity, and fireplaces), are available. Some facilities are wheelchair accessible. Leashed pets are permitted.

Reservations, fees: No reservations. Sites are $8 per night, with a 14-day stay limit, plus $3 for each additional vehicle. Open mid-May to mid-October.

Directions: From Roseburg drive east on Highway 138 for 22 miles to Rock Creek Road. Turn right (north) and drive five miles to the campground.

Contact: Bureau of Land Management, Roseburg District, 777 N.W. Garden Valley Boulevard, Roseburg, OR 97470; tel. (541) 440-4930; fax (541) 440-4948.

134 Susan Creek   9

This popular and pretty campground is set along the banks of the North Umpqua Wild and Scenic River. The setting is pretty, with lots of trees and river access. Highlights include two barrier-free trails, one traveling one-half mile to the day-use area. From there a hike of about three-quarters of a mile leads to the 50-foot Susan Creek Falls. Another 0.4 mile up the trail are the Susan Creek Indian Mounds. The moss-covered rocks are believed to be a spiritual site visited by Native Americans in search of guardian spirit visions.

Location: On the North Umpqua River; map D2, grid g0.

Campsites, facilities: There are 31 sites for trailers or RVs up to 35 feet long. Picnic tables, garbage service, and fire grills are provided. Flush toilets, drinking water, showers, a camp host, and firewood are available. Some facilities and trails are wheelchair accessible. Leashed pets are permitted.

Reservations, fees: No reservations. Sites are $10 per night, with a 14-day stay limit, plus $3 for each additional vehicle. Open early May to late October.

Directions: From Roseburg drive east on Highway 138 for 29.5 miles to the campground.

Contact: Bureau of Land Management, Roseburg District, N.W. 777 Garden Valley Boulevard, Roseburg, OR 97470; tel. (541) 440-4930; fax (541) 440-4948.

135 Scaredman   6

This small campground along the banks of Canton Creek is virtually unknown to out-of-towners. Set in an old-growth forest, it offers a chance to swim in the creek and it's also private and secluded. Even though fishing is closed on Canton Creek and all Steamboat drainages, the North Umpqua River 3.5 miles downstream offers fly-fishing for steelhead or salmon.

Location: On Canton Creek; map D2, grid g1.

Campsites, facilities: There are nine sites for tents, trailers, or RVs up to 25 feet long. Picnic tables, garbage service, and fire grills are provided. Vault toilets and camp hosts are available. There is no drinking water. Leashed pets are permitted.

Reservations, fees: No reservations; no fee. The stay limit is 14 days. Open year-round.

Directions: From Roseburg drive east on Highway 138 for 40 miles to Steamboat Creek Road. Turn north (left) and drive one-half mile to Canton Creek Road. Turn left (north) and drive three miles to the campground.

Contact: Bureau of Land Management, Roseburg District, 777 N.W. Garden Valley Boulevard, Roseburg, OR 97470; tel. (541) 440-4930; fax (541) 440-4948.

136 Island   8

This scenic campground is set along the banks of the Umpqua River at a spot popular for both rafting and steelhead fishing (fly-fishing only and with a 20-inch minimum size limit). A hiking trail that leads east and west along the river is accessible by driving a short distance west. See a U.S. Forest Service map for details.

Location: On the Umpqua River in Umpqua National Forest; map D2, grid g1.

Campsites, facilities: There are seven sites for tents, trailers, or RVs up to 24 feet long. Picnic tables, garbage bins, and fire grills are provided. Barrier-free vault toilets are available. There is no drinking water. Leashed pets are permitted.

Reservations, fees: No reservations. Sites are $5 per night, $2 per night for an additional vehicle. Open year-round.

Directions: From Roseburg drive east on Highway 138 for 40 miles (just past Steamboat). The campground is located along the highway.

Contact: Umpqua National Forest, North Umpqua Ranger District, 18782 North Umpqua Highway, Glide, OR 97443; tel. (541) 496-3532; fax (541) 496-3534.

137 Canton Creek   8

This campground (1,195 feet elevation) at the confluence of Canton and Steamboat Creeks less than a mile from the North Umpqua River gets little overnight use, but there are lots of day swimmers in July and August. No fishing is permitted on Steamboat or Canton Creeks because they are spawning areas for steelhead and salmon. Steamboat Falls is six miles north on Forest Road 38. See the description of Steamboat Falls for other area details.

Location: Near the Umpqua River in Umpqua National Forest; map D2, grid g2.

Campsites, facilities: There are five sites for tents, trailers, or RVs up to 22 feet long. Picnic tables, garbage bins, and fire grills are provided. Drinking water, a covered picnic gazebo, and flush toilets are available. Leashed pets are permitted.

Reservations, fees: No reservations. Sites are $7 per night, $2 per night for an additional vehicle. Open mid-May to mid-October.

Directions: From Roseburg drive east on Highway 138 for 39 miles to Steamboat and Forest Road 38 (Steamboat Creek Road). Turn left and drive a quarter mile to the campground.

Contact: Umpqua National Forest, North Umpqua Ranger District, 18782 North Umpqua Highway, Glide, OR 97443; tel. (541) 496-3532; fax (541) 496-3534.

138 Steamboat Falls   8

There is excellent scenery at this campground on the banks of Steamboat Creek, at beautiful Steamboat Falls, which features a fish ladder that provides passage for steelhead and salmon on their upstream migration. No fishing is permitted in Steamboat Creek. Other camping options are Island and Canton Creek.

Location: On Steamboat Creek in Umpqua National Forest; map D2, grid g2.

Campsites, facilities: There are 10 sites for tents, trailers, or RVs up to 24 feet long. Picnic tables, garbage bins, vault toilets, and fire grills are provided. There is no drinking water. Leashed pets are permitted.

Reservations, fees: No reservations. Sites are $5 per night, $2 per night for an additional vehicle. Open year-round, with no fee from November through late May.

Directions: From Roseburg on Interstate 5, take Exit 120 to Highway 138. Drive east on Highway 138 to Steamboat and Forest Road 38. Turn left on Forest Road 38 (Steamboat Creek Road) and drive six miles to a fork with Forest Road 3810. Bear right and drive one mile to the campground.

Contact: Umpqua National Forest, North Umpqua Ranger District, 18782 North Umpqua Highway, Glide, OR 97443; tel. (541) 496-3532; fax (541) 496-3534.

139 Boulder Flat   8

This campground is set along the banks of the North Umpqua River at the confluence of Boulder Creek. There's good trout fishing here (fly-angling only) and outstanding scenery. The camp is adjacent to a major whitewater rafting launching point. Across the river from the campground a trail follows Boulder Creek north for 10.5 miles through the Boulder Creek Wilderness, a climb in elevation from 2,000 to 5,400 feet. Access to the trail is at Soda Springs Dam, two miles east of the camp. It's a good thumper for backpackers. A little over a mile to the east are some huge, dramatic pillars of volcanic rock, colored with lichen.

Location: On the North Umpqua River in Umpqua National Forest; map D2, grid g2.

Campsites, facilities: There are 11 sites for tents, trailers, or RVs up to 24 feet long. Picnic tables, garbage bins, and fire grills are provided. Vault toilets are available. There is no drinking water. A store, propane, and ice are located within five miles. A raft launch is on-site. Leashed pets are permitted.

Reservations, fees: No reservations. Sites are $5 per night, $2 per night for an additional vehicle. Open year-round.

Directions: From Roseburg drive east on Highway 138 for 54 miles to the campground on the left.

Contact: Umpqua National Forest, North Umpqua Ranger District, 18782 North Umpqua Highway, Glide, OR 97443; tel. (541) 496-3532; fax (541) 496-3534.

140 Campers Flat   5

This pretty, but small campground is on a small flat adjacent to the Middle Fork of the Willamette River. The river drowns out the sound of traffic from the road right next to the campground. There is an interpretive sign about the Oregon Central Military Wagon Road in the campground. Fishing is good with easy access to the water's edge. Young's Rock Trailhead is across the road from the campground entrance and is very popular with mountain bikers.

Location: On the Willamette River in Willamette National Forest; map D2, grid g3.

Campsites, facilities: There are five sites for tents, trailers, or RVs up to 21 feet long. Picnic tables, garbage bins, and fire grills are provided. Drinking water, vault toilets, and firewood are available. Leashed pets are permitted.

Reservations, fees: No reservations. Sites are $8 per night, plus $4 for each additional vehicle. Open mid-April through September.

Directions: From Eugene drive south on Interstate 5 for five miles to Exit 188 and Highway 58. Turn east and drive 35 miles to the town of Oakridge. From Oakridge continue east on Highway 58 about two miles to Kitson Springs Road. Turn right and drive one-half mile to Forest Road 21. Turn right and drive 19 miles to the campground.

Contact: Willamette National Forest, Middle Fork Ranger District, 49098 Salmon Creek Road, Oakridge, OR 97463; tel. (541) 782-2283; fax (541) 782-5306.

141 Secret   5

This small campground, set on the Middle Fork of the Willamette River, gets regular use from local know-hows. The tree cover is scant, but there is adequate vegetation to buffer the campsites from the nearby road noise. Fishing the Middle Fork Willamette is generally fair.

Location: On the Willamette River in Willamette National Forest; map D2, grid g3.

Campsites, facilities: There are six sites for tents, trailers, or RVs up to 15 feet long. Picnic tables, garbage bins, and fire rings are provided. Vault toilets are available, but there is no drinking water. Leashed pets are permitted.

Reservations, fees: No reservations. Sites are $6 per night, plus $4 for each additional vehicle. Open mid-April through September.

Directions: From Eugene drive south on Interstate 5 for five miles to Exit 188 and Highway 58. Turn east and drive 35 miles to the town of Oakridge. From Oakridge continue east on Highway 58 about two miles to Kitson Springs Road. Turn right and drive one-half mile to Forest Road 21. Turn right and drive 19 miles to the campground.

Contact: Willamette National Forest, Middle Fork Ranger District, 49098 Salmon Creek Road, Oakridge, OR 97463; tel. (541) 782-2283; fax (541) 782-5306.

142 Toketee Lake   7

This campground is just north of Toketee Lake, set at an elevation of 3,600 feet. The North Umpqua River Trail passes near camp and continues north along the river for many miles. Diehard hikers can also take it west, where it meanders for a while before heading north into the Boulder Creek Wilderness. Toketee Lake is an 80-acre reservoir offering a good population of brown and rainbow trout and many recreation options. A worthwhile point of interest is Toketee Falls, located just west of the lake turnoff. Another is Umpqua Hot Springs, a few miles northeast of the camp. There's a wide variety of wildlife in the area. You might see otter, beaver, great blue heron, kingfishers, a variety of ducks and geese, and bald eagles in fall and winter.

Location: On Toketee Lake in Umpqua National Forest; map D2, grid g3.

Campsites, facilities: There are 33 sites for tents, trailers, or RVs up to 22 feet long, and one group site. Picnic tables, garbage bins, and fire grills are provided. Vault toilets are available, but there is no drinking water. Boat docks and launching facilities are nearby. Leashed pets are permitted.

Reservations, fees: Reservations required for the group site only; call (877) 444-6777 or access the website: www.reserveusa.com ($8.65 reservation fee). Sites are $5 per night. $15 per night for the group site; $2 per night for an additional vehicle Open mid-April to late October.

Directions: From Roseburg drive east on Highway 138 for 60 miles to Forest Road 34. Turn north and drive one mile, and at the bottom of a hill, cross a concrete bridge on the right. Continue for 1.5 miles to the campground on the left.

Contact: Umpqua National Forest, Diamond Lake Ranger District, 2020 Toketee Ranger Station Road, Idleyld Park, OR 97447; tel. (541) 498-2531; fax (541) 498-2515.

143 Indigo Springs   5

This is a small, semi-open campground at 2,800 feet elevation in a stand of old-growth Douglas fir. Nearby is a 250-foot walk to the origin of this cold water spring. A remnant of the historic Oregon Central Military Wagon Road passes near the campground, with an interpretive sign explaining it.

Location: Near the Willamette River in Willamette National Forest; map D2, grid g4.

Campsites, facilities: There are three sites for tents, trailers, or RVs up to 16 feet long. Picnic tables and fire grills are provided. Vault toilets and firewood are available. There is no drinking water. Leashed pets are permitted.

Reservations, fees: No reservations; no fee. Open mid-April to mid-November, weather permitting.

Directions: From Eugene drive south on Interstate 5 for five miles to Exit 188 and Highway 58. Turn east and drive 35 miles to the town of Oakridge. From Oakridge continue east on Highway 58 about two miles to Kitson Springs Road. Turn right and drive one-half mile to Forest Road 21. Turn right and drive 27 miles to the campground.

Contact: Willamette National Forest, Middle Fork Ranger District, 49098 Salmon Creek Road, Oakridge, OR 97463; tel. (541) 782-2283; fax (541) 782-5306.

144 East Lemolo   8

This campground is on the southeastern shore of Lemolo Lake, where boating and fishing are some of the recreation possibilities. Boats with motors are allowed.

The North Umpqua River and its adjacent trail are just beyond the north shore of the lake. If you hike for two miles northwest of the lake, you can reach spectacular Lemolo Falls. Large German brown trout, a wild, native fish, can be taken on troll and fly. Lemolo Lake also provides fishing for kokanee, brook trout, and a sprinkling of rainbow trout.

Location: On Lemolo Lake in Umpqua National Forest; map D2, grid g5.

Campsites, facilities: There are 15 sites for tents or small RVs up to 22 feet long. No drinking water is available. Picnic tables, garbage bins, and fire rings are provided. Vault toilets are available. Boat docks, launching facilities, and rentals are nearby. Leashed pets are permitted.

Reservations, fees: No reservations. Sites are $5 per night, $2 per night for an additional vehicle. Open mid-May to late October.

Directions: From Roseburg drive east on Highway 138 for 72 miles to Forest Road 2610 (three miles east of Clearwater Falls). Turn north and drive three miles to Forest Road 2614. Turn right and drive two miles to Forest Road 2610-430. Turn left and drive a short distance to campground at the end of the road.

Contact: Umpqua National Forest, Diamond Lake Ranger District, 2020 Toketee Ranger Station Road, Idleyld Park, OR 97447; tel. (541) 498-2531; fax (541) 498-2515.

145 Poole Creek 8

This campground on the western shore of Lemolo Lake isn't far from Lemolo Lake Resort, which is open for recreation year-round. The camp is located just south of the mouth of Poole Creek in a lodgepole pine, mountain hemlock, and Shasta red fir forest. This is by far the most popular U.S. Forest Service camp at the lake, especially with water-skiers, who are allowed to ski in designated areas of the lake. See the description of East Lemolo for more information.

Location: On Lemolo Lake in Umpqua National Forest; map D2, grid g5.

Campsites, facilities: There are 59 sites for tents, trailers, or RVs up to 30 feet long. Picnic tables and fire grills are provided. Drinking water and vault toilets are available. A grocery store, restaurant, lounge, boat docks, launching facilities, and rentals are nearby. Leashed pets are permitted.

Reservations, fees: Reserve the group sites by calling (877) 444-6777 or access the website: www.reserveusa.com ($8.65 reservation fee). Sites are $9-12 per night, $3 per night for an additional vehicle. Open late April to late October.

Directions: From Roseburg drive east on Highway 138 for 72 miles to Forest Road 2610 (Bird's Point Road). Turn north and drive four miles. Continue another four miles and turn right at the sign for the campground entrance.

Contact: Umpqua National Forest, Diamond Lake Ranger District, 2020 Toketee Ranger Station Road, Idleyld Park, OR 97447; tel. (541) 498-2531; fax (541) 498-2515.

146 Lemolo Lake Resort

 9

This resort is on the western shore of Lemolo Lake and offers recreation opportunities year-round. See the description of East Lemolo for more details.

Location: On Lemolo Lake; map D2, grid g5.

Campsites, facilities: There are three tent sites and 32 sites for trailers or RVs of any length; 27 are drive-through sites. There are also 10 cabins. Electricity, drinking water, sewer hookups, and picnic tables are provided. Flush toilets, a gas station, sanitary disposal services, showers, a convenience store, a cafe, a laundry room, a lounge, boat docks, boat rentals, launching facilities, and ice are available. Leashed pets and motorbikes are permitted.

Reservations, fees: Reservations accepted. Sites are $10-17 per night. Open March through October, weather permitting.

Directions: From Roseburg drive east on Highway 138 for 80 miles to Lemolo Lake Road. Turn north and drive five miles to the resort.

Contact: Lemolo Lake Resort, 2610 Birds Point Road, Idleyld Park, OR 97447; tel. (541) 793-3300.

147 Trapper Creek   8

The west end of Odell Lake is the setting for this camp. Boat docks and rentals are nearby at the Shelter Cove Resort. The lake is one of the prime fisheries in Oregon for kokanee salmon and mackinaw (lake trout). There are also some huge brown trout in this lake.

Location: On Odell Lake in Deschutes National Forest; map D2, grid f6.

Campsites, facilities: There are 32 sites for tents, trailers, or RVs up to 22 feet long. Picnic tables, garbage service, and fire grills are provided. Drinking water, vault toilets, and a boat launch are available. Firewood may be gathered from the surrounding area. A store, a coin laundry, and ice are within one mile. Leashed pets are permitted.

Reservations, fees: No reservations. Sites are $10-12 per night, $5 per night for an additional vehicle. Open June through September, weather permitting.

Directions: From Eugene drive south on Interstate 5 for five miles to Exit 188 and Highway 58. Turn east and drive 61 miles to the turnoff for Odell Lake and Forest Road 5810. Turn right on Forest Road 5810 and drive 1.9 miles to the campground on the left.

Contact: Deschutes National Forest, Crescent Ranger District, P.O. Box 208, Crescent, OR 97733; tel. (541) 433-2234; fax (541) 433-3224.

148 Shelter Cove Resort
   9

This private resort along the north shore of Odell Lake is at the base of the Diamond Peak Wilderness and offers opportunities for hiking, fishing, and swimming. The cabins are right on the lakefront. A general store and tackle shop are available.

Location: On Odell Lake; map D2, grid g6.

Campsites, facilities: There are 11 tent sites and 42 drive-through sites for trailers or RVs up to 30 feet long, plus eight cabins. Electricity and picnic tables are provided. Drinking water, flush toilets, showers, a store, a cafe, laundry facilities, and ice are available. Boat docks, launching facilities, and boat rentals are on-site. Leashed pets are permitted.

Reservations, fees: Reservations are recommended. Sites are $9-14 per night, and cabins are $65-155 per night. Open year-round.

Directions: From Eugene drive south on Interstate 5 for five miles to Exit 188 and Highway 58. Turn east and drive 61 miles to the turnoff for Odell Lake and West Odell Lake Road. Take that road and drive south for 1.8 miles to the camp.

Contact: Shelter Cove Resort, West Odell Lake Road, Highway 58, Cascade Summit, OR 97425; tel. (541) 433-2548.

149 Simax Group Camp   8

This camp is set at an elevation of 4,850 feet on Crescent Lake with trails to day-use beaches. Fishing is variable year to year and is usually better earlier in the season. A boat launch is available at Crescent Lake, about two miles away. See neighboring Crescent Lake for more details.

Location: On Crescent Lake in Deschutes National Forest; map D2, grid g6.

Campsites, facilities: There are three group campsites for 30 to 40 campers each. Drinking water, tent pads, flush toilets, showers, picnic tables, garbage service, fireplaces, and a group shelter (with an electrical outlet) that accommodates 50 campers are available. Tents must be placed on tent pads. Facilities are wheelchair accessible. Leashed pets are permitted.

Reservations, fees: Reservations required; phone (877) 444-6777 or access the website: www.reserveusa.com ($8.65 reservation fee). Rates are $65 per night for Site A (the most accessible) and $85 per night for Sites B and C. Site B is the most difficult to access and only tents are advised; Site C is best for RVs. The group shelter fee is $25 per day. The campground is generally open from Memorial Day through Labor Day, weather permitting.

Directions: From Eugene drive south on Interstate 5 for five miles to Exit 188 and Highway 58. Turn east and drive 70 miles to Crescent Lake Highway (Forest Road 50). Turn right and drive two miles to Forest Road 6005. Turn left and drive one mile to the campground on the right.

Contact: Deschutes National Forest, Crescent Ranger District, P.O. Box 208, Crescent, OR 97733; tel. (541) 433-2234; fax (541) 433-3224.

150 Crescent Lake   8

This campground is set along the north shore of Crescent Lake, and it is often windy here in the afternoon. Boat docks, launching facilities, and rentals are also nearby at Crescent Lake Resort, adjacent to the campground. A trail from camp heads into the Diamond Peak Wilderness and also branches north to Odell Lake.

Location: On Crescent Lake in Deschutes National Forest; map D2, grid g6.

Campsites, facilities: There are 47 sites for tents, trailers, or RVs up to 35 feet long. Picnic tables, garbage service, and fire grills are provided. Drinking water, vault toilets, and boat launching facilities are available. Firewood may be gathered from the surrounding area. Leashed pets are permitted.

Reservations, fees: No reservations. Sites are $10-12 per night, plus $5 for each additional vehicle. Open mid-May to late October, weather permitting.

Directions: From Eugene drive south on Interstate 5 for five miles to Exit 188 and Highway 58. Turn east and drive 70 miles to the town of Crescent Lake Highway (Forest Road 60). Turn right (west) and drive 2.2 miles southwest. Bear right to remain on Forest Road 60, and drive another one-quarter mile to the campground on the left.

Contact: Deschutes National Forest, Crescent Ranger District, P.O. Box 208, Crescent, OR 97733; tel. (541) 433-2234; fax (541) 433-3224.

151 Whitefish Horse Camp   5

   This just might be the best horse camp in the state. Horse camping only is allowed here, and manure removal is required. High lines are not allowed; horses must be kept in stalls. Located on Whitefish Creek at the west end of Crescent Lake, this campground is set in lodgepole pine with shaded sites. It's across the road from the lake in a flat area with no lake view from the campground. Moderately to heavily used, at 4,850 feet elevation, it has access to about 100 miles of trail, including Diamond Peak Wilderness, the Oregon Cascades Recreation Area, many high mountain lakes, and the Metolius-Windigo National Recreation Trail.

Location: On Whitefish Creek in Deschutes National Forest; map D2, grid g6.

Campsites, facilities: There are 17 sites for tents, trailers, or RVs up to 40 feet long. Picnic tables, horse corrals, and fire rings are provided. Drinking water and garbage bins are available in the summer season only. Vault toilets are available. Firewood may be gathered from the surrounding area. Leashed pets are permitted.

Reservations, fees: Reservations recommended. Call (877) 444-6777, or access the website at www.reserveusa.com. There is an $8.65 reservation fee. Sites are $8 per night for two stalls, and $9 per night for four stalls, plus $5 for each additional vehicle. Open May through November, weather permitting.

Directions: From Eugene drive south on Interstate 5 for five miles to Exit 188 and Highway 58. Turn east and drive 70 miles Crescent Lake Highway (Forest Road 60). Turn right (west) and drive 2.2 miles southwest. Stay to the right to remain on Forest Road 60, and drive six miles to the campground on the right.

Contact: Deschutes National Forest, Crescent Ranger District, P.O. Box 208, Crescent, OR 97733; tel. (541) 433-2234; fax (541) 433-3224.

152 Odell Creek   9

   You can fish, swim, and hike at this campground (4,800 foot elevation) along the east shore of Odell Lake. A trail from the nearby Crater Buttes trailhead heads southwest into the Diamond Peak Wilderness and provides access to several small lakes in the backcountry. Another trail follows the north shore of the lake. Boat docks, launching facilities, and rentals are nearby at the Odell Lake Lodge and Resort, adjacent to the campground. Windy afternoons are common here.

Location: On Odell Lake in Deschutes National Forest; map D2, grid g6.

Campsites, facilities: There are 22 sites for tents, trailers, or RVs up to 22 feet long. Picnic tables, garbage service, and fire grills are provided. Vault toilets are available, but there is no drinking water. Firewood may be gathered from the surrounding area. Leashed pets are permitted.

Reservations, fees: No reservations. Sites are $5 per night, plus $3 for each additional vehicle. Open mid-May to late September, weather permitting.

Directions: From Eugene drive south on Interstate 5 for five miles to Exit 188 and Highway 58. Turn east and drive 68 miles to Odell Lake and Forest Road 680 (at the east end of the lake). Turn right on Forest Road 680 and drive 400 yards to the campground on the right.

Contact: Deschutes National Forest, Crescent Ranger District, P.O. Box 208, Crescent, OR 97733; tel. (541) 433-2234; fax (541) 433-3224.

153 Sunset Cove   8

This campground is on the northeast shore of Odell Lake. Boat docks and rentals are available nearby at Odell Lake Lodge and Resort. Campsites are surrounded by large Douglas fir and some white pine. The camp backs up to the highway; expect to hear the noise.

Location: On Odell Lake in Deschutes National Forest; map D2, grid g6.

Campsites, facilities: There are 21 sites for tents, trailers, or RVs up to 22 feet long. Picnic tables and fire grills are provided. Drinking water, vault toilets, a barrier-free boat launch and day-use area, and fish cleaning facilities are available. Firewood may be gathered from the surrounding area. Leashed pets are permitted.

Reservations, fees: No reservations. Sites are $10 per night, plus $5 for each additional vehicle. Open mid-May to mid-October, weather permitting.

Directions: From Eugene drive south on Interstate 5 for five miles to Exit 188 and Highway 58. Turn east and drive 67 miles to the campground on the right.

Contact: Deschutes National Forest, Crescent Ranger District, P.O. Box 208, Crescent, OR 97733; tel. (541) 433-2234; fax (541) 433-3224.

154 Princess Creek   9

This wooded campground is on the northeast shore of Odell Lake, but it backs up to the highway; expect traffic noise. See the description of Odell Creek for recreation details. Boat docks and rentals are available nearby at the Shelter Cove Resort.

Location: On Odell Lake in Deschutes National Forest; map D2, grid g6.

Campsites, facilities: There are 46 sites for tents, trailers, or RVs up to 22 feet long. Picnic tables and fire grills are provided. Drinking water, vault toilets, and boat launching facilities are available. Firewood may be gathered from the surrounding area. Showers, a store, coin-operated laundry facilities, and ice are within five miles. Leashed pets are permitted.

Reservations, fees: No reservations. Sites are $10-12 per night, plus $5 for each additional vehicle. Open mid-May through September, weather permitting.

Directions: From Eugene drive south on Interstate 5 for five miles to Exit 188 and Highway 58. Turn east and drive 64 miles to the campground on the right.

Contact: Deschutes National Forest, Crescent Ranger District, P.O. Box 208, Crescent, OR 97733; tel. (541) 433-2234; fax (541) 433-3224.

155 Gold Lake   8

This campground wins the popularity contest for high use. Although motors are not allowed on this small lake (100 acres, 25 feet deep), rafts and rowboats provide excellent fishing access. A primitive log shelter built in the early 1940s provides a dry picnic area. In the spring and summer, this area abounds with wild flowers and huckleberries. The Gold Lake Bog is another special attraction where one can often see deer, elk, and other smaller wildlife.

Location: On Gold Lake in Willamette National Forest; map D2, grid g7.

Campsites, facilities: There are 25 sites for tents, trailers, or RVs up to 22 feet long. Picnic tables, garbage bins, and fire grills are provided. Drinking water and vault toilets are available. Boat docks and launching facilities are nearby. Leashed pets are permitted.

Reservations, fees: No reservations. Sites are $10 per night, plus $5 for each additional vehicle. Open June through September, weather permitting.

Directions: From Eugene drive south on Interstate 5 for five miles to Exit 188 and Highway 58. Turn east and drive 35 miles to the town of Oakridge. From Oakridge, continue east on Highway 58 for 28 miles to Gold Lake Road (Forest Road 500). Turn left (north) and drive two miles to the campground on the right.

Contact: Willamette National Forest, Middle Fork Ranger District, 49098 Salmon Creek Road, Oakridge, OR 97463; tel. (541) 782-2283; fax (541) 782-5306.

156 Inlet   5

This campground is on the eastern inlet of Lemolo Lake, hidden in the deep, green and quiet forest, where the North Umpqua River rushes into Lemolo Reservoir. The lake exceeds 100 feet in depth in some spots. The camp is just across the road from the North Umpqua River Trail, which is routed east into the Oregon Cascades Recreation Area and the Mount Thielsen Wilderness. See the description of East Lemolo for more recreation details.

Location: On Lemolo Lake in Umpqua National Forest; map D2, grid g6.

Campsites, facilities: There are 14 sites for tents, trailers, or RVs up to 22 feet long. Vault toilets are available, but there is no drinking water. Picnic tables, garbage bins, and fire grills are provided. Boat docks, launching facilities, rentals, a restaurant, lounge, groceries, and gas station are available nearby. Leashed pets are permitted.

Reservations, fees: No reservations accepted. Sites are $5 per night, $2 per night for an additional vehicle. Open mid-May to late October.

Directions: From Roseburg drive east on Highway 138 for 74 miles to Forest Road 2610. Turn north and drive three miles to Forest Road 2666. Turn east and drive three miles to the campground.

Contact: Umpqua National Forest, Diamond Lake Ranger District, 2020 Toketee Ranger Station Road, Idleyld Park, OR 97447; tel. (541) 498-2531; fax (541) 498-2515.

157 Timpanogas   8

At 5,200 elevation, this campground is situated in a stand of silver, grand, and noble fir. Timpanogas Lake is the headwaters of the Middle Fork Willamette River. Only non-motorized boating is permitted. Fishing in the lake if often very good for cutthroat and brook trout. The Timpanogas Basin offers 23 miles of hiking trails, with a bonus of excellent views of Diamond Peak, Sawtooth, and Cowhorn Mountains. Warning: Time it wrong and the mosquitoes will eat you alive if you forget your insect repellent.
Location: On Timpanogas Lake in Willamette National Forest; map D2, grid g6.
Campsites, facilities: There are 11 sites for tents, trailers, or RVs up to 24 feet long. Picnic tables, garbage bins, and fire rings are provided. Drinking water, vault toilets, and firewood are available. Boat docks are nearby, but no boats with motors are allowed. Leashed pets are permitted.
Reservations, fees: No reservations. Sites are $6 per night, plus $3 for each additional vehicle. Open mid-June to mid-October, weather permitting.
Directions: From Eugene drive south on Interstate 5 for five miles to Exit 188 and Highway 58. Turn east and drive 35 miles to the town of Oakridge. Continue east on Highway 58 for two miles to Kitson Springs Road. Turn right and drive one-half mile to Forest Road 21. Turn right and drive 32 miles to Forest Road 2154. Turn left and drive about 10 miles to the campground.
Contact: Willamette National Forest, Middle Fork Ranger District, 49098 Salmon Creek Road, Oakridge, OR 97463; tel. (541) 782-2283; fax (541) 782-5306.

158 Spring   8

This campground is on the southern shore of Crescent Lake at an elevation of 4,850 feet. Located in a lodgepole pine forest, sites are open and some are on the lake with Diamond Peak views. See Contorta Point (below) for more information.
Location: On Crescent Lake in Deschutes National Forest; map D2, grid g6.
Campsites, facilities: There are 68 sites for tents, trailers, or RVs up to 22 feet long. Picnic tables, garbage service, and fire grills are provided. Drinking water, vault toilets, boat launching facilities, and firewood (to be gathered from the surrounding area) are available. Leashed pets are permitted.
Reservations, fees: No reservations. Sites are $10-12 per night, plus $5 for each additional vehicle. Open June through September, weather permitting.
Directions: From Eugene drive south on Interstate 5 for five miles to Exit 188 and Highway 58. Turn east and drive 70 miles to Crescent Lake Highway (Forest Road 60). Turn right and drive eight miles west to the campground entrance road on the left. Turn left and drive one mile to the campground.
Contact: Deschutes National Forest, Crescent Ranger District, P.O. Box 208, Crescent, OR 97733; tel. (541) 433-2234; fax (541) 433-3224.

159 Contorta Point

 8

This campground at 4,850 feet elevation is on the southern shore of Crescent Lake, where swimming, boating, and waterskiing are among the summer pastimes. A number of trails from the nearby Windy-Oldenburg Trailhead provide access to lakes in the Oregon Cascades Recreation Area. Motorized vehicles are restricted to open roads only.

Location: On Crescent Lake in Deschutes National Forest; map D2, grid g6.

Campsites, facilities: There are about 15 sites in an area for dispersed camping for tents, trailers, or RVs up to 22 feet long. There is no drinking water, and all garbage must be packed out. Picnic tables and vault toilets are provided. Boat docks and launching facilities are located three miles away at Spring Campground. Leashed pets are permitted.

Reservations, fees: No reservations. There is no fee. Open May to late October, weather permitting.

Directions: From Eugene drive south on Interstate 5 for five miles to Exit 188 and Highway 58. Turn east and drive 70 miles to Crescent Lake Highway (Forest Road 60). Turn right and drive 9.9 miles to Forest Road 280. Turn left and drive one mile to the campground.

Contact: Deschutes National Forest, Crescent Ranger District, P.O. Box 208, Crescent, OR 97733; tel. (541) 433-2234; fax (541) 433-3224.

160 East Davis Lake 9

This campground is nestled in the lodgepole pines along the south shore of Davis Lake. Recreation options include fly-fishing, boating (speed limit is 10 mph), and hiking. Leeches prevent swimming here. Bald eagles and sandhill cranes are frequently seen.

Location: On Davis Lake in Deschutes National Forest; map D2, grid g7.

Campsites, facilities: There are 33 sites for tents, trailers, or RVs up to 22 feet long. Picnic tables, garbage service, fire grills, drinking water, and vault toilets are provided. Firewood may be gathered from the surrounding area. Primitive boat launching facilities are available on-site. Leashed pets are permitted.

Reservations, fees: No reservations. Sites are $8 per night, plus $4 for each additional vehicle. Open May to late October, weather permitting.

Directions: From Eugene drive south on Interstate 5 for five miles to Exit 188 and Highway 58. Turn east and drive 73 miles to County Road 61. Turn left (east) and drive three miles to Forest Road 46. Turn left and drive 7.7 miles to Forest Road 850. Turn left and drive one-quarter mile to Forest Road 855. Turn left and drive two miles to the campground.

Contact: Deschutes National Forest, Crescent Ranger District, P.O. Box 208, Crescent, OR 97733; tel. (541) 433-2234; fax (541) 433-3224.

161 West Davis Lake   9

Spacious sites and easy access to the water are highlights of this campground on the south shore of Davis Lake. Only fly-fishing is permitted, and the boat speed limit is 10 mph. See notes for East Davis Lake.

Location: On Davis Lake in Deschutes National Forest; map D2, grid g7.

Campsites, facilities: There are 25 sites for tents, trailers, or RVs up to 22 feet long. Picnic tables, garbage service, and fire grills are provided. Drinking water, vault toilets, and firewood (to be gathered from the surrounding area) are available. A boat launch is on-site. Leashed pets are permitted.

Reservations, fees: No reservations. Sites are $8 per night, plus $4 for each additional vehicle. Open May to late October, weather permitting.

Directions: From Eugene drive south on Interstate 5 for five miles to Exit 188 and Highway 58. Turn east and drive 73 miles to County Road 61. Turn left (east) and drive three miles to Forest Road 46. Turn left and drive three miles north to Forest Road 4660. Turn left and drive three miles to Forest Road 4669. Turn right and drive 1.5 miles to the campground.

Contact: Deschutes National Forest, Crescent Ranger District, P.O. Box 208, Crescent, OR 97733; tel. (541) 433-2234; fax (541) 433-3224.

162 Crescent Creek   7

This is one of the Cascade's classic hidden campgrounds, set along the banks of Crescent Creek at 4,500 feet. The buzzwords here are pretty, developed, and private. What use it gets is light, and that primarily from hunters in the fall. There's some highway noise here; and even if you can't hear it, traffic is visible from some sites.

Location: On Crescent Creek in Deschutes National Forest; map D2, grid g7.

Campsites, facilities: There are 10 sites for tents, trailers, or RVs up to 22 feet long. Picnic tables, garbage service, and fire grills are provided. Drinking water and vault toilets are available. Firewood may be gathered from the surrounding area. Leashed pets are permitted.

Reservations, fees: No reservations. Sites are $8 per night, plus $4 for each additional vehicle. Open May to late October, weather permitting.

Directions: From Eugene drive south on Interstate 5 for five miles to Exit 188 and Highway 58. Turn east and drive 73 miles to County Road 61. Turn left (east) and drive three miles to the campground on the right.

Contact: Deschutes National Forest, Crescent Ranger District, P.O. Box 208, Crescent, OR 97733; tel. (541) 433-2234; fax (541) 433-3224.

VISITORS

MAP D3

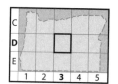

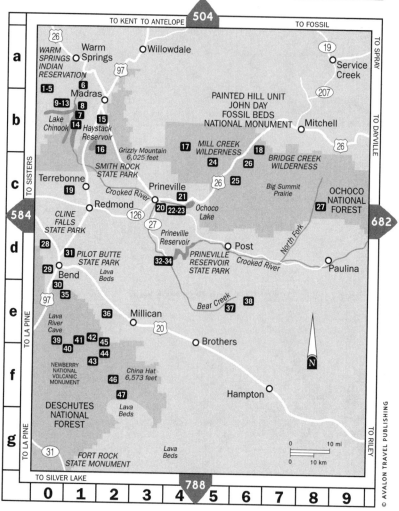

TO KENT   TO ANTELOPE   **504**   TO FOSSIL

a

WARM SPRINGS INDIAN RESERVATION
Warm Springs
Willowdale
19
Service Creek

26
97
207

b

1-5
6 Madras
9-13
8
7
14 15
Lake Chinook
Haystack Reservoir
16
Grizzly Mountain 6,025 feet
SMITH ROCK STATE PARK
17 MILL CREEK WILDERNESS
18 BRIDGE CREEK WILDERNESS
Mitchell
26

PAINTED HILL UNIT JOHN DAY FOSSIL BEDS NATIONAL MONUMENT

TO SISTERS
TO SPRAY
TO DAYVILLE

c

Terrebonne
19
Crooked River
Prineville
21
24 26
26 25
Big Summit Prairie
27 OCHOCO NATIONAL FOREST

584
Redmond
126
20 22-23
Ochoco Lake
27
682

d

CLINE FALLS STATE PARK
PILOT BUTTE STATE PARK
28
31
29
32-34
Prineville Reservoir
27
PRINEVILLE RESERVOIR STATE PARK
Crooked River
North Fork
Post
Paulina

e

Bend
30
35
97
Lava Beds
Lava River Cave
36 Millican
20
Bear Creek
37 38
N

f

39 41 42 45
40 44
43
NEWBERRY NATIONAL VOLCANIC MONUMENT
46 China Hat 6,573 feet
47 Lava Beds
Brothers
Hampton

g

DESCHUTES NATIONAL FOREST
31 FORT ROCK STATE MONUMENT
Lava Beds

TO LA PINE
TO LA PINE
TO RILEY

0   10 mi
0   10 km

TO SILVER LAKE   **788**

0 1 2 3 4 5 6 7 8 9

© AVALON TRAVEL PUBLISHING

CHAPTER D3

1 Black Butte Motel and RV Park   6

This RV park offers a choice of graveled or grassy sites in a clean, scenic environment. See the description of Camp Sherman for more area information.

Location: Near the Metolius River; map D3, grid a0.

Campsites, facilities: There are 19 sites with full hookups and 12 sites with partial hookups for trailers or RVs of any length. Electricity, drinking water, sewer hookups, and picnic tables are provided. Flush toilets, showers, firewood, and a laundry room are available. Bottled gas, sanitary services, a store, a cafe, and ice are located within one block. Leashed pets and motorbikes are permitted.

Reservations, fees: Reservations accepted. Sites are $18-20 per night. Open year-round.

Directions: From Albany drive east on U.S. 20 for 87 miles (near Black Butte) to the sign for Camp Sherman. Turn north and drive about five miles to Forest Road 1419. Turn east on Forest Road 1419 and drive one-quarter mile to the park on the right.

Contact: Black Butte Motel and RV Park, 25635 S.W. Forest Road 1419, Camp Sherman, OR 97730; tel. (877) 595-6514; fax (541) 595-5971; e-mail: cdog@outlawnet.com.

2 Cold Springs Resort and RV Park

   7

This pretty, wooded RV park on the Metolius River with an acre of riverfront lawn is world famous for its fly-fishing. Nearby recreation options include a golf course, swimming, boating, waterskiing, windsurfing, hiking and biking trails, a riding stable, and tennis courts. Winter activities range from alpine and Nordic skiing to sledding, snowmobiling, and winter camping. There is a private bridge from the resort to Camp Sherman, and the towns of Sisters and Bend are nearby (15 miles and 35 miles, respectively).

Location: On the Metolius River; map D3, grid a0.

Campsites, facilities: There are 45 sites with full hookups for trailers or RVs of any length, plus two cabins on the river. Fire pits, picnic tables, and patios are provided. Rest rooms, showers, laundry facilities, firewood, and a riverfront picnic facility are available. Bottled gas, a store with groceries, fishing and sport supplies, a cafe, a coin-operated laundry, a post office, and ice are located within one-quarter mile. Leashed pets are permitted.

Reservations, fees: Reservations accepted. Sites are $18-20 per night; cabins are $88-129 per night, depending on the season and the number of people. Open year-round.

Directions: From Albany drive east on U.S. 20 for 87 miles (near Black Butte) to the sign for Camp Sherman. Turn north and drive about five miles to the stop sign. Turn right at the stop sign and drive about 300 feet to Cold Springs Resort Lane. Turn right and drive through the forest and the meadow, crossing Cold Springs Creek, to the resort.

Contact: Cold Springs Resort and RV Park, 25615 Cold Springs Resort Lane, Camp Sherman, OR 97730; tel. (541) 595-6271; fax (541) 595-1400.

3 Allen Springs   7

This shady campground is located in a conifer forest along the banks of the Metolius River, where fishing and hiking can be good. For an interesting side trip, head to the Wizard Falls Fish Hatchery about a mile away.

Location: On the Metolius River in Deschutes National Forest; map D3, grid a0.

Campsites, facilities: There are three tent sites and 12 sites for tents, trailers, or RVs up to 22 feet long. Picnic tables, garbage service, and fire grills are provided. Vault toilets and drinking water are available. A store, a cafe, a coin-operated laundry, and ice are located within five miles. Leashed pets are permitted.

Reservations, fees: No reservations. Sites are $12 per night, $6 per night for an additional vehicle. Open May through September; there is no fee from October through April, when no water is available.

Directions: From Albany drive east on U.S. 20 for 87 miles (near Black Butte) to the sign for Camp Sherman and Forest Road 14. Turn left on Forest Road 14 and drive about nine miles to the campground on the left.

Contact: Deschutes National Forest, Sisters Ranger District, P.O. Box 249, Sisters, OR 97759; tel. (541) 549-2111; fax (541) 549-7746.

4 Pioneer Ford   7

This quiet and serene, wooded campground with grassy sites is along the banks of the Metolius River. See the description of Camp Sherman for recreation options.

Location: On the Metolius River in Deschutes National Forest; map D3, grid a0.

Campsites, facilities: There are two tent sites and 18 sites for tents, trailers, or RVs up to 40 feet long. Drinking water, garbage service, and fire grills are provided. Vault toilets, a barrier-free picnic shelter, and firewood are available. Leashed pets are permitted.

Reservations, fees: No reservations. Sites are $12 per night, $6 per night for an additional vehicle. Open April through September.

Directions: From Albany drive east on U.S. 20 for 87 miles (near Black Butte) to the sign for Camp Sherman and Forest Road 14. Turn left on Forest Road 14 and drive 11 miles to the campground on the left.

Contact: Deschutes National Forest, Sisters Ranger District, P.O. Box 249, Sisters, OR 97759; tel. (541) 549-2111; fax (541) 549-7746.

5 Lower Bridge   6

This campground is set along the banks of the Metolius River. See the description of Camp Sherman for details about the area. This camp is similar to Pioneer Ford, but with less vegetation.

Location: On the Metolius River in Deschutes National Forest; map D3, grid a0.

Campsites, facilities: There are 12 sites for tents, trailers, or RVs up to 22 feet long. Picnic tables, garbage service, and fire grills are provided. Vault toilets and drinking water are available. Leashed pets are permitted.

Reservations, fees: No reservations. Sites are $12 per night, $6 per night for an additional vehicle. Open year-round, with limited services and no fee in the off-season (October through March).

Directions: From Albany drive east on U.S. 20 for 87 miles (near Black Butte) to the sign for Camp Sherman and Forest Road 14. Turn left on Forest Road 14 and drive 12 miles to the campground on the left.

Contact: Deschutes National Forest, Sisters Ranger District, P.O. Box 249, Sisters, OR 97759; tel. (541) 549-2111; fax (541) 549-7746.

6 Pelton   8

This campground claims one-half mile of shoreline along the north side of Lake Simtustus. Campsites here are shaded with juniper, in an area of rolling hills and sagebrush. One section of the lake is accessible for waterskiing and jet skiing. It's a trophy fishing lake for kokanee and rainbow, brown, and bull trout. Cove Palisades State Park is located about 15 miles south, providing additional recreational opportunities. Watch for osprey, bald and golden eagles.

Location: On Lake Simtustus in Deschutes National Forest; map D3, grid a1.

Campsites, facilities: There are 75 sites for tents, trailers, or RVs up to 40 feet long, 30 with partial hook-up, and one group site which can accommodate up to 50 campers. Drinking water, picnic tables, garbage service, and fire grills are provided. Rest rooms, a restaurant, snack bar, mini-mart, gasoline, and a picnic shelter with sinks and electric stoves are available. Also a full-service marina with boat rentals, a boat launch, boat dock, fishing pier, swimming beach, volleyball courts, horseshoe pits, and a playground are available. Leashed pets are permitted.

Reservations, fees: Reservations recommended; phone (503) 464-8515. Sites are $14.50-20 per night; the group site is $65 per night. Major credit cards accepted. Open mid-April through October.

Directions: From Portland drive south on U.S. 26 for 108 miles to the town of Warm Springs. Continue south two miles to Pelton Dam Road. Turn right and drive three miles to the campground on the right.

Contact: Portland General Electric, 121 S.W. Salmon Street, Portland, OR 97204; tel. (503) 464-8515; fax (503) 464-2944; website: www.pge-online.com.

7 Perry South   6

This campground is set near the shore of the Metolius arm of Lake Billy Chinook. The lake can get very crowded and noisy; it attracts the powerboat/water-ski enthusiasts. See the description of KOA Madras/ Culver and Crooked River Ranch RV Park for recreation details. The lake borders the Warm Springs Indian Reservation.

Location: On Lake Billy Chinook in Deschutes National Forest; map D3, grid b1.

Campsites, facilities: There are four tent sites and 59 sites for tents, trailers, or RVs up to 40 feet long. Picnic tables, garbage service, and fire grills are provided. Drinking water, barrier-free vault toilets, fish cleaning station, boat docks, and launching facilities are available. Leashed pets are permitted.

Reservations, fees: No reservations. Sites are $12 per night, plus $6 for each additional vehicle. Open May through September.

Directions: From Bend drive north on U.S. 97 to Redmond, then continue north for 15 miles to the Culver Highway. Take the Culver Highway north to Culver, and continue two miles to Gem Lane. Turn left and drive two miles to Frazier Drive. Turn left and drive a short distance to Peck Road. Turn right and drive through Cove Palisades State Park to Jordan Road at the shore of Lake Billy Chinook. Turn left on Jordan Road and drive about 10 miles (over the bridge) to County Road 64. Turn left and drive about eight miles to the campground entrance on the right (on the upper end of the Metolius Fork of Lake Billy Chinook).

Contact: Deschutes National Forest, Sisters Ranger District, P.O. Box 249, Sisters, OR 97759; tel. (541) 549-2111; fax (541) 549-7746.

8 Monty   5

Trout fishing can be good at this remote campground along the banks of the Metolius River near where it empties into Lake Billy Chinook. It gets light use. Warm Springs Indian Reservation is across the river.

Location: On the Metolius River in Deschutes National Forest; map D3, grid b1.

Campsites, facilities: There are 20 sites for tents, trailers, or RVs up to 22 feet long. Picnic tables, garbage service, and fire grills are provided. Firewood and vault toilets are available. There is no drinking water. Boat docks and launching facilities are nearby at Perry South. Leashed pets are permitted.

Reservations, fees: No reservations. Sites are $6 per night, $3 per night for an additional vehicle. Open May through September.

Directions: From Bend drive north on U.S. 97 to Redmond and continue north for 15 miles to the Culver Highway. Take the Culver Highway north to Culver and continue two miles to Gem Lane. Turn left and drive two miles to Frazier Drive. Turn left and drive a short distance to Peck Road. Turn right and drive through Cove Palisades State Park to Jordan Road at the shore of Lake Billy Chinook. Turn left on Jordan Road and drive about 10 miles (over the bridge) to County Road 64. Turn left and drive about 13 miles to the campground entrance (on the Metolius River above the headwaters of Lake Billy Chinook). The last five miles are very rough.

Contact: Deschutes National Forest, Sisters Ranger District, P.O. Box 249, Sisters, OR 97759; tel. (541) 549-2111; fax (541) 549-7746.

9 Camp Sherman   6

Camp Sherman is set at an elevation of 2,950 feet along the banks of the Metolius River, where you can fish for wild trout. This place is for expert fly anglers seeking a quality fishing experience. It's advisable to obtain a map of the Deschutes National Forest that details back roads, trails, and streams. This is one of five camps in the immediate area.

Location: On the Metolius River in Deschutes National Forest; map D3, grid b1.

Campsites, facilities: There are 15 sites for tents, trailers, or RVs up to 40 feet

long. Picnic tables, garbage service, and fire grills are provided. Vault toilets, a picnic shelter, and drinking water are available. Leashed pets are permitted.

Reservations, fees: No reservations. Sites are $12 per night, $6 per night for an additional vehicle. Open year-round, with limited services and no fee in the off-season (October through March).

Directions: From Albany drive east on U.S. 20 for 87 miles (near Black Butte) to the sign for Camp Sherman and Forest Road 14. Turn left on Forest Road 14 and drive five miles to Camp Sherman, the store and Forest Road 900. Turn left on Forest Road 900 and drive one-half mile to the campground on the left.

Contact: Deschutes National Forest, Sisters Ranger District, P.O. Box 249, Sisters, OR 97759; tel. (541) 549-2111; fax (541) 549-7746.

🔟 Allingham   5

This campground along the banks of the Metolius River is one of five camps in the immediate area. See the description of Camp Sherman for area details.

Location: On the Metolius River in Deschutes National Forest; map D3, grid b1.

Campsites, facilities: There are 10 sites for tents, trailers, or RVs up to 40 feet long. Picnic tables, garbage service, and fire grills are provided. Vault toilets and drinking water are available. A sanitary disposal station is nearby. Leashed pets are permitted.

Reservations, fees: No reservations. Sites are $12 per night, $6 per night for an additional vehicle. Open April through September.

Directions: From Albany drive east on U.S. 20 for 87 miles (near Black Butte) to the sign for Camp Sherman and Forest Road 14. Turn left on Forest Road 14 and drive five miles to Camp Sherman, the store, and Forest Road 900. Turn left on Forest Road 900 and drive one mile to the campground on the left.

Contact: Deschutes National Forest, Sisters Ranger District, P.O. Box 249, Sisters, OR 97759; tel. (541) 549-2111; fax (541) 549-7746.

1️⃣1️⃣ Smiling River   5

Here's another camp along the banks of the Metolius River. It's set at an elevation of 2,900 feet. See the description of Camp Sherman for more details.

Location: On the Metolius River in Deschutes National Forest; map D3, grid b1.

Campsites, facilities: There are 37 sites for tents, trailers, or RVs up to 30 feet long. A few sites can accommodate RVs up to 40 feet in length. Picnic tables, garbage service, and fire grills are provided. Vault toilets and drinking water are available. Leashed pets are permitted.

Reservations, fees: No reservations. Sites are $12 per night, $6 per night for an additional vehicle. Open May through September.

Directions: From Albany drive east on U.S. 20 for 87 miles (near Black Butte) to the sign for Camp Sherman and Forest Road 14. Turn left on Forest Road 14 and drive five miles to Camp Sherman, the store, and Forest Road 900. Turn left on Forest Road 900 and drive one mile to the campground on the left.

Contact: Deschutes National Forest, Sisters Ranger District, P.O. Box 249, Sisters, OR 97759; tel. (541) 549-2111; fax (541) 549-7746.

12 Pine Rest   5

This campground is set at an elevation of 2,900 feet, along the banks of the Metolius River. See the description of Camp Sherman for more information.

Location: On the Metolius River in Deschutes National Forest; map D3, grid b1.

Campsites, facilities: There are eight tent sites. Picnic tables, garbage service, and fire grills are provided. Vault toilets, a picnic shelter, and drinking water are available. Leashed pets are permitted.

Reservations, fees: No reservations. Sites are $12 per night, $6 per night for an additional vehicle. Open April through September.

Directions: From Albany drive east on U.S. 20 for 87 miles (near Black Butte) to the sign for Camp Sherman and Forest Road 14. Turn left on Forest Road 14 and drive five miles to Camp Sherman, the store, and Forest Road 900. Turn left on Forest Road 900 and drive two miles to the campground on the left.

Contact: Deschutes National Forest, Sisters Ranger District, P.O. Box 249, Sisters, OR 97759; tel. (541) 549-2111; fax (541) 549-7746.

13 Gorge   5

Here is another of the camps set along the banks of the Metolius River. This campground is more open with less vegetation than many of the others, and is set at an elevation of 2,900 feet. See the description of Camp Sherman for more details.

Location: On the Metolius River in Deschutes National Forest; map D3, grid b1.

Campsites, facilities: There are 18 sites for tents, trailers, or RVs up to 22 feet long. A few of the sites can accommodate RVs up to 40 feet long. Picnic tables, garbage service, and fire grills are provided. Vault toilets and drinking water are available. Leashed pets are permitted.

Reservations, fees: No reservations. Sites are $10 per night, plus $5 for each additional vehicle. Open April through September.

Directions: From Albany drive east on U.S. 20 for 87 miles (near Black Butte) to the sign for Camp Sherman and Forest Road 14. Turn left on Forest Road 14 and drive five miles to Camp Sherman, the store, and Forest Road 900. Turn left on Forest Road 900 and drive 2.5 miles to the campground on the left.

Contact: Deschutes National Forest, Sisters Ranger District, P.O. Box 249, Sisters, OR 97759; tel. (541) 549-2111; fax (541) 549-7746.

14 The Cove Palisades State Park
 7

This park is a mile away from the shore of Lake Billy Chinook, where some lakeshore cabins are available. Located in Oregon's high desert region, the weather is sunny and warm in the summer months and chilly but generally mild in the winter. Towering cliffs surround the lake and there are about 10 miles of hiking trails. Two popular special events are held here annually: Lake Billy Chinook Day in September and the Eagle Watch in February. Houseboats are available in the nearby marina.

Location: On Lake Billy Chinook; map D3, grid b1.

Campsites, facilities: There are 94 tent sites and 178 sites with full or partial hookups for trailers or RVs up to 60 feet long, plus three cabins, and a group area. Picnic tables and fire grills are provided. Drinking water, garbage bins, flush toilets, sanitary disposal station, showers, firewood, a store, a restaurant, and ice are available. Some facilities are wheelchair accessible. Boat docks, launching facilities, a marina and boat rentals are nearby. Leashed pets are permitted.

Reservations, fees: Reservations accepted; phone (800) 452-5687 ($6 reservation fee). Sites are $13-20 per night; cabins are $45-65 per night, the group area is $60 per night; there is a fee of $7 per night for an additional vehicle. Major credit cards accepted. Open year-round.

Directions: From Bend drive north on U.S. 97 to Redmond and continue north for 15 miles to the Culver Highway. Take the Culver Highway north to Culver and continue two miles to Gem Lane. Turn left and drive two miles to Frazier Drive. Turn left and drive a short distance to Peck Road. Turn right and drive to the park entrance.

Contact: The Cove Palisades State Park, Route 1, P.O. Box 60 CP, Culver, OR 97734; tel. (800) 551-6949, (541) 546-3412.

🔢 KOA Madras/Culver   6

This campground has a relaxing atmosphere, with some mountain views, and is about three miles from Lake Billy Chinook, a steep-sided reservoir formed where the Crooked River, Metolius River, Deschutes River, and Squaw Creek all merge. Like much of the country east of the Cascades, this is a high desert area.

Location: Near Lake Billy Chinook; map D3, grid b2.

Campsites, facilities: There are 31 tent sites and 68 drive-through sites for trailers or RVs of any length. Electricity, drinking water, sewer hookups, and picnic tables are provided. Flush toilets, bottled gas, sanitary services, showers, firewood, a recreation hall, a store, a laundry room, ice, a playground, and a swimming pool are available. Boat docks and launching facilities are nearby. Leashed pets and motorbikes are permitted.

Reservations, fees: Reservations accepted; phone (800) 563-1992. Sites are $16-21 per night. Open year-round.

Directions: From Madras drive south on U.S. 97 for nine miles to Jericho Lane. Turn east and drive a half mile to the campground.

Contact: KOA Madras/Culver, S.W. Jericho Lane, Culver, OR 97734; tel. (541) 546-3046 2435.

🔢 Haystack Reservoir   5

This campground can be found in the high desert along the shore of Haystack Reservoir, where waterskiing, swimming, and fishing are some of the recreation options. There's lots of sheltering between sites, and a view of Jefferson Mountain. The camping and fishing crowds are relatively light.

Location: On Haystack Reservoir in Crooked River National Grassland; map D3, grid b2.

Campsites, facilities: There are 24 sites for tents, trailers, or RVs up to 22 feet long. Picnic tables and fire grills are provided. Flush toilets and drinking water are available. All garbage must be packed out. Firewood is available for purchase. A store, a cafe, and ice are located within five miles. Boat docks, launching facilities, and rentals are nearby. Leashed pets are permitted.

Reservations, fees: No reservations. Sites are $8 per night, plus $3 for each additional vehicle. Open mid-May through September.

Directions: From Madras drive south on U.S. 97 for nine miles to County Road 100. Turn southeast and drive three miles to Forest Road 96. Turn north and drive one-half mile to the campground.

Contact: Crooked River National Grassland, 813 S.W. Highway 92, Madras, OR 97741; tel. (541) 416-6640; fax (514) 416-6694; website: www.fs.fed.us/r6/ochoco.

17 Whistler   7

This is a trailhead camp for the Wildcat Trail heading into the Mill Creek Wilderness. The area is extremely popular with rock hounds, who search for thunder eggs, jasper, and agates (digging is forbidden in wilderness areas, however). Though primitive, this is a pretty camp in a conifer forest that guarantees quiet and privacy.

Location: In Ochoco National Forest; map D3, grid b4.

Campsites, facilities: There is a large area for dispersed tent camping. A picnic table and a vault toilet are provided. There is no drinking water, and garbage must be packed out. Horses are welcome. Leashed pets are permitted.

Reservations, fees: No reservations; no fee. Open late May to late October.

Directions: From Prineville drive east on U.S. 26 to Forest Road 27 (just east of Bandit Spring State Rest Area, near Ochoco Pass). Turn left on Forest Road 27 and drive nine miles to the campground entrance on the left.

Contact: Ochoco National Forest, Prineville Ranger District, P.O. Box 490, Prineville, OR 97754; tel. (541) 416-6500.

18 Ochoco Divide   5

This camp is set at an elevation of 2,600 feet amid an old-growth stand of ponderosa pine just off of scenic U.S. 26. An unused forest road on the far side of the campground provides an easy stretch walk after a long day of driving. Most visitors arrive late in the day and leave early in the morning, so the area is normally quiet during the day. Marks Creek is nearby and the Bandit Springs Rest Stop one mile west is the jumping off point for a network of trails.

Location: In Ochoco National Forest; map D3, grid b6.

Campsites, facilities: There are 28 sites for tents, trailers, or RVs up to 30 feet long, with a separate area with walk-in and bike-in sites. Picnic tables and fire pits are provided. Drinking water, garbage bins, and vault toilets are available. Some facilities are wheelchair accessible. Leashed pets are permitted.

Reservations, fees: No reservations. Sites are $8 per night, $3 per night for an additional vehicle. Open late May to mid-November, weather permitting.

Directions: From Prineville drive east on U.S. 26 for 30 miles to the campground at the summit of Ochoco Pass.

Contact: Ochoco National Forest, Big Summit Ranger District, 348855 Ochoco Ranger District, Prineville, OR 97754-9612; tel. (541) 416-6645.

19 Crooked River Ranch RV Park   6

This campground is a short distance from Smith Rock State Park, which contains unusual, colorful volcanic formations overlooking the Crooked River Canyon. Lake Billy Chinook to the north is a good spot for waterskiing and fishing for bass and panfish. The park has a basketball court and a softball field; nearby recreation options include a golf course and tennis courts.

Location: Near Smith Rock State Park; map D3, grid c0.

Campsites, facilities: There are 21 tent sites and 88 sites for trailers or RVs of any length; 15 are drive-through sites. Electricity, drinking water, and sewer hookups are provided. Flush toilets, sanitary services, cable TV, showers, a store, a cafe, laundry facilities, ice, a playground, and a swimming pool are available. Leashed pets are permitted.

Reservations, fees: Reservations accepted. Sites are $12-21 per night. Open April through October.

Directions: From Redmond drive north on U.S. 97 for six miles to Lower Bridge Road. Turn west on Lower Bridge Road at Terrebonne and drive to 43rd Street. Turn right and drive seven miles (the road names changes to Chinook, then to Clubhouse Road) to Hays Lane. Turn right on Hays Lane and drive one-quarter mile to the park.

Contact: Crooked River Ranch RV Park, P.O. Box 1448, Crooked River Ranch, OR 97760; tel. (800) 841-0563, (541) 923-1441; fax (541) 548-0278.

20 Crook County RV Park   6

This campground is set among old oaks in a landscaped and grassy area next to the Crooked River, where fly-fishing is popular. In season, the nearby fairgrounds offers horse races, rodeos, and various expositions.

Location: Near the Crooked River; map D3, grid c3.

Campsites, facilities: There are 81 sites for tents, trailers, or RVs up to 70 feet long, all with full hookups. There are also two cabins. Electricity, drinking water, sewer hookups, and picnic tables are provided. Flush toilets, sanitary services, cable TV, vending machines, and showers are available. A mini-mart, restaurant, laundry facilities, ice, and propane are available within one mile. Some facilities are wheelchair accessible. Leashed pets are permitted.

Reservations, fees: Reservations accepted; phone (800) 609-2599 or fax (541) 416-9022. Sites are $9-19.50 per night. Weekly and monthly rates are available. Open year-round.

Directions: From Redmond drive east on Highway 126 for 18 miles to Prineville (Highway 126 becomes Third Street). Turn east on Third Street and drive to Main Street. Turn right on Main Street and drive about one-half mile south to the campground on the left, next to the fairgrounds.

Contact: Crook County RV Park, 1040 South Main Street, Prineville, OR 97754; tel. (541) 447-2599; fax (541) 416-9022; website: www.rvcampground.com/or/crookco /.

21 Crystal Corral RV Park

     5

This RV park isn't far from Ochoco Lake State Park, where boating and fishing are among the activities. There's a golf course within two miles and there are hiking trails within five miles.

Location: Near Ochoco Lake State Park; map D3, grid c4.

Campsites, facilities: There are 20 tent sites and 22 sites for trailers or RVs of any length and another two sites that can accommodate trailers or RVs up to 40 feet. Electricity, drinking water, sewer hookups, flush toilets, bottled gas, showers, a store, a cafe, a laundry room, and ice are available. Boat docks, launching facilities, and rentals are nearby. Leashed pets (one per site) and motorbikes are permitted.

Reservations, fees: Reservations accepted. Sites are $8-16 per night. Open year-round.

Directions: From Prineville drive east on U.S. 26 for eight miles to the park on the left.

Contact: Crystal Corral RV Park, 11777 N.E. Ochoco Highway, Prineville, OR 97754; tel. (541) 447-5932.

22 Ochoco Lake County Park   6

This is one of the nicer camps along U.S. 26 in eastern Oregon. The state park is on the shore adjacent to Ochoco Lake, where boating and fishing are popular pastimes. Some quality hiking trails can be found in the area.

Location: On Ochoco Lake; map D3, grid c4.

Campsites, facilities: There are 22 primitive sites for tents, trailers, or self-contained RVs up to 30 feet long, and a special area for hikers and bicyclists. Picnic tables, garbage bins, and fire grills are provided. Drinking water, firewood, hot showers, and flush toilets are available. Boat launching facilities are nearby. Leashed pets are permitted.

Reservations, fees: No reservations. Sites are $12 per night, and $4 for hikers/bikers. Open April through October, weather permitting.

Directions: From Prineville drive east on U.S. 26 for seven miles to the park entrance.

Contact: Crook County Parks & Recreation, 398 N.E. Fairview Street, Prineville, OR 97754; tel. (541) 447-1209; fax (541) 447-9894.

23 Lakeshore RV Park and Store

       5

Set on grassy hills on beautiful Ochoco Lake, this park offers many recreational opportunities, including hunting, year-round fishing, swimming, and boating. It's a more developed option to the nearby county park campground.

Location: On Ochoco Lake; map D3, grid c4.

Campsites, facilities: There are 19 sites for tents and 43 sites for trailers or RVs up to 45 feet long. Air-conditioning, electric heat, cable TV, rest rooms, showers, a sanitary dump, a public phone, limited groceries, ice, and RV supplies are available. Recreational facilities include a recreation hall, a marina, a boat dock, and a ramp. Some facilities are wheelchair accessible. Small leashed pets are permitted.

Reservations, fees: Reservations recommended. Sites are $18 per night. Open year-round.

Directions: From Prineville drive east on U.S. 26 for eight miles to the park on the left.

Contact: Lakeshore RV Park and Store, 12333 N.E. Ochoco Highway, Prineville, OR 97754; tel. (541) 447-6059; fax (541) 447-6059.

24 Wildcat   4

This quiet, cool campground is set at an elevation of 3,799 feet in conifer forest and in a canyon. Situated along the East Fork of Mill Creek, the camp is near the Twin Pillars Trailhead that provides access into the Mill Creek Wilderness. Stein's Pillar and Twin Pillars, popular rock climbing spots, are nearby. Ochoco Lake and Ochoco Lake State Park to the south provide side trip possibilities.

Location: On the East Fork of Mill Creek in Ochoco National Forest; map D3, grid c5.

Campsites, facilities: There are 17 sites for tents, trailers, or RVs up to 30 feet long. Picnic tables and fire grills are provided. Drinking water and vault toilets are available, but garbage must be packed out. Leashed pets are permitted.

Reservations, fees: No reservations. Sites are $8 per night, plus $3 for each additional vehicle. Open mid-April to late October.

Directions: From Prineville drive east on U.S. 26 for nine miles to Mill Creek Road (Forest Road 33). Turn left on Mill Creek Road and drive about 10 miles to the campground

Contact: Ochoco National Forest, Prineville Ranger District, P.O. Box 490, Prineville, OR 97754; tel. (541) 416-6500.

25 Ochoco Forest Camp   4

Campsites here are set at an elevation of 4,000 feet, along Ochoco Creek in a lush setting of ponderosa pine and aspen. Fishing for rainbow trout is fair. A large, group picnic area with a beautiful log shelter is available for reservation. It's a perfect setting for weddings, family reunions, and other group events. The nearby Lookout Mountain Trail accesses the Lookout Mountain Recreation Area of 15,000 acres without roads. But hey, the truth is: Don't expect privacy and solitude at this campground.

Location: In Ochoco National Forest; map D3, grid c6.

Campsites, facilities: There are six sites for tents, trailers, or RVs up to 24 feet long. Picnic tables and fire rings are provided. Drinking water, garbage bins, and vault toilets are available. Some facilities are wheelchair accessible. Boat launching facilities are nearby (only electric motors are allowed). Leashed pets are permitted.

Reservations, fees: No reservations. Sites are $8 per night, $3 per night for an additional vehicle. Open mid-May through November, weather permitting.

Directions: From Prineville drive east on U.S. 26 for 16.5 miles to County Road 23. Turn on County Road 23 and drive nine miles to the campground, across from the Ochoco Ranger Station.

Contact: Ochoco National Forest, Big Summit Ranger District, 348855 Ochoco Ranger District, Prineville, OR 97754-9612; tel. (541) 416-6645.

26 Walton Lake   7

This campground is along the shore of small Walton Lake, among old growth ponderosa pine and mountain meadows, where fishing and swimming are popular; only non-motorized boats or those with electric motors are allowed. Hikers can explore a nearby trail that leads south to Round Mountain. The lake is stocked with rainbow trout and the fishing can range from middle-of-the-road fair right up to downright excellent.

Location: On Walton Lake in Ochoco National Forest; map D3, grid c6.

Campsites, facilities: There are 30 sites for tents, trailers, or RVs up to 31 feet long, and one group site. Picnic tables, garbage bins, and fire grills are provided. Drinking water and vault toilets are available. Some facilities are wheelchair accessible. Boat launching facilities are nearby (only electric motors are allowed). Leashed pets are permitted.

Reservations, fees: Reservations required for the group site only; phone (877) 444-6777 or access the website: www.reserveusa.com ($8.65 reservation fee). Sites are $10 per night, $27 per night for the group site, $3 per night for an additional vehicle. Open June to late September.

Directions: From Prineville drive east on U.S. 26 for 16.5 miles to County Route 123. Turn northeast and drive 14 miles to Forest Road 23. Turn north on Forest Road 23 and drive to the Ochoco Ranger Station; then continue seven miles to the campground.

Contact: Ochoco National Forest, Big Summit Ranger District, 348855 Ochoco Ranger District, Prineville, OR 97754-9612; tel. (541) 416-6645.

27 Deep Creek   5

This small camp is on the edge of high desert and gets little use, but it's in a nice spot—the confluence of Deep Creek and the North Fork of the Crooked River. Highlights include pretty, shady sites and river access. Fishing is possible here.

Location: On the North Fork of the Crooked River in Ochoco National Forest; map D3, grid c8.

Campsites, facilities: There are six sites for tents, trailers, or RVs up to 22 feet long. Picnic tables and fire grills are provided. Vault toilets are available, but there is no drinking water, and all garbage must be packed out. Leashed pets are permitted.

Reservations, fees: No reservations; no fee. Open June to mid-October.

Directions: From Prineville drive east on U.S. 26 for 16.5 miles to County Route 23. Turn right (northeast) and drive 8.5 miles (becomes Forest Road 42). Continue east on Forest Road 42 for 23.5 miles to the campground.

Contact: Ochoco National Forest, Big Summit Ranger District, 348855 Ochoco Ranger District, Prineville, OR 97754-9612; tel. (541) 416-6645.

28 Tumalo State Park

 7

Trout fishing can be good at this camp along the banks of the Deschutes River, just five miles from Bend. Mount Bachelor is just up the road with plenty of winter recreation. The swimming area is safe and ideal for school children, and boating is also an option here. See the description of Bend Keystone RV Park for more recreation information.

Location: On the Deschutes River; map D3, grid d0.

Campsites, facilities: There are 61 sites for tents, 21 sites with full hookups for trailers or RVs up to 44 feet long, a special camping area for hikers and bicyclists, four yurts, a group area, and two tepees. Electricity, drinking water, sewer hookups, fire grills, and picnic tables are provided. Flush toilets, showers, firewood, and a playground are available. A store, a cafe, and ice are located within one mile. Leashed pets are permitted.

Reservations, fees: Reservations accepted; phone (800) 452-5687 ($6 reservation fee). Sites are $13-19 per night, $4 per night for hikers/bikers, $29 per night for yurts and teepees, $60 per night for the group area, and $7 per night for an additional vehicle. Major credit cards accepted. Open year-round.

Directions: From Bend drive north on U.S. 97 for two miles to U.S. 20. Turn northwest and drive five miles to Tumalo Junction. Turn left at Tumalo Junction on to Cook Avenue, and drive on miles to the campground.

Contact: High Desert Management Unit, 62976 O.B. Riley Road, Bend, OR 97701; tel. (800) 551-6949 or (541) 388-6055.

29 Scandia RV and Mobile Park

 5

This park near the Deschutes River is close to a golf course, a stable, bike paths, and tennis courts. See the description of Bend Keystone RV Park for additional recreation information.

Location: Near the Deschutes River; map D3, grid d0.

Campsites, facilities: There are 60 sites for tents, trailers, or RVs of any length; seven are drive-through sites. Electricity, drinking water, picnic tables, cable TV, and sewer hookups are provided. Flush toilets, showers, and a laundry room are available. Bottled gas, sanitary services, a store, a cafe, and ice are located within one mile. Leashed pets are permitted.

Reservations, fees: Reservations accepted. Sites are $20 per night. Open year-round.

Directions: In Bend drive south on U.S. 97 for a half mile to the park entrance.

Contact: Scandia RV and Mobile Park, 61415 South Highway 97, Bend, OR 97702; tel. (541) 382-6206; fax (541) 382-4087.

30 Bend Keystone RV Park 5

This park is right off the highway in Bend, a popular spot to use as a home base. The 100-mile Deschutes Forest Highway Loop connects here. Several state parks are within an hour's drive, and several city-managed parks provide access to the Deschutes River. Good side trips include the Oregon High Desert Museum, just six miles south of Bend on U.S. 97. A few miles farther is the Lava River Cave and the Lava Butte Geological Area.

Location: Near the Deschutes River; map D3, grid e0.

Campsites, facilities: There are 29 sites for trailers or RVs of any length. Electricity, cable TV, drinking water, and sewer hookups are provided. Flush toilets, showers, and a laundry room are available. Bottled gas, sanitary services, a store, a cafe, and ice are located within one mile. Cats are permitted.

Reservations, fees: Reservations accepted. Sites are $16 per night. Open year-round.

Directions: In Bend drive south on U.S. 97 for a half mile to the park entrance road.

Contact: Bend Keystone RV Park. 305 N.E. Burnside, Bend, OR 97701; (tel. 541) 382-2335.

31 Bend Kampground   5

Recreation options near this camp include a golf course, hiking trails, bike paths, and tennis courts. See the description of Bend Keystone RV Park for additional recreation information.

Location: Near Bend; map D3, grid d1.

Campsites, facilities: There are 40 tent sites and 74 sites for trailers or RVs of any length; 40 are drive-through sites. Drinking water and picnic tables are provided. Electricity, sewer hookups, flush toilets, showers, a laundry room, a store, a deli, ice, firewood, a playground, a swimming pool, a recreation room, bottled gas, and a sanitary disposal station are available. Leashed pets are permitted.

Reservations, fees: Reservations accepted. Sites are $18-24 per night. Open year-round.

Directions: In Bend drive north on U.S. 97 for two miles to the park entrance road.

Contact: Bend Kampground, 63615 North Highway 97, Bend, OR 97701; tel. (541) 382-7738.

32 Chimney Rock   6

This well-spaced campground is a favorite for picnicking and wildlife viewing. The Chimney Rock Trailhead, located just across the highway, is the jump-off point for the 1.7-mile, moderately difficult hike to Chimney Rock. There are numerous scenic overlooks along the trail, and wildlife sightings are common. The elevation here is 3,000 feet. Chimney Rock Campground is one of eight BLM camps located along a six-mile stretch of Highway 27.

Location: On the Crooked River; map D3, grid d3.

Campsites, facilities: There are 20 sites for tents, trailers or RVs of any length. Drinking water and picnic tables are provided. Flush toilets and garbage bins are available. Also available are wheelchair-accessible toilets, tables, a fishing dock, and a boat ramp. Leashed pets are permitted.

Reservations, fees: No reservations. Sites are $5 per night, $2 per night for an additional vehicle. Open year-round.

Directions: In Prineville drive south on Highway 27 for 16.4 miles to the campground.

Contact: Bureau of Land Management, Prineville District, P.O. Box 550, Prineville, OR 97754; tel. (541) 416-6700; fax (541) 416-6798; website: www.or.blm.gov.

33 Prineville Reservoir Resort   6

This resort is on the shore of Prineville Reservoir in the high desert, a good spot for water sports and fishing. The mostly shaded sites are a combination of dirt and gravel, and there is easy access to the reservoir. There are some colorful rock formations to check out.

Location: On Prineville Reservoir; map D3, grid d4.

Campsites, facilities: There are 70 sites for trailers or RVs of any length; four are drive-through sites. Electricity, drinking water, fire pits, and picnic tables are provided. Flush toilets, bottled gas, sanitary disposal services, showers, firewood, a store, a cafe, a laundry room, and ice are available. A full-service marina, boat ramp, and boat rentals are on-site. Leashed pets are permitted.

Reservations, fees: Reservations accepted. Sites are $11-17 per night. Open mid-March to mid-October, weather permitting.

Directions: From Prineville drive east on U.S. 26 for one mile to Combs Flat Road. Turn south and drive one mile to Juniper Canyon Road. Turn south and drive 18 miles to the campground.

Contact: tel. (541) 447-7468 19600 S.E. Juniper Canyon Road, Prineville, OR 97754.

34 Prineville Reservoir State Park   7

This state park is set along the shore of Prineville Reservoir, formed by damming the Crooked River. Swimming, boating, fishing, and waterskiing are among the activities here. The nearby boat docks and ramp are a bonus. The reservoir supports rainbow and cutthroat trout, small- and largemouth bass, catfish, and crappie. You can even ice fish in the winter. This is one of two campgrounds on the lake; the other is Prineville Reservoir Resort (RVs only).

Location: On Prineville Reservoir; map D3, grid d4.

Campsites, facilities: There are 25 tent sites and 75 sites with partial hookups for trailers or RVs up to 40 feet long. There are also three camper cabins. Electricity, drinking water, sewer hookups, garbage bins, and picnic tables are provided. Flush toilets, showers, and firewood are available. Boat docks and launching facilities are nearby. Pets are permitted.

Reservations, fees: Reservations accepted. Sites are $10-20 per night. Major credit cards accepted. Open year-round.

Directions: From Prineville drive east on U.S. 26 for 14 miles to the park entrance.

Contact: Prineville Reservoir State Park, 19300 S. Junipers Canyon Road, Prineville, OR 97754; tel. (800) 452-5687, (541) 447-4363.

35 Crown Villa RV Park   6

This RV park offers large and landscaped, grassy sites. Nearby recreation options include horseback riding and golf. See the description of Bend Keystone RV Park for additional recreation information.

Location: Near Bend; map D3, grid e0.

Campsites, facilities: There are 124 sites for trailers or RVs of any length; 106 have full hookups, and 24 have partial hookups. Electricity, drinking water, sewer hookups, picnic tables, flush toilets, showers, cable TV, a laundry room, bottled gas, ice, a sanitary disposal station, and a playground are available. A store and a cafe are located within one mile. Leashed pets are permitted.

Reservations, fees: Reservations accepted. Sites are $17-32 per night. Open year-round.

Directions: From Bend drive south on U.S. 97 for two miles to Brosterhous Road. Turn east and drive to the park.

Contact: Crown Villa RV Park, 60801 Brosterhous Road, Bend, OR 97702; tel. (541) 388-1131.

36 Swamp Wells Horse Camp   3

After looking at the map, this campground may appear to be quite remote, but it's actually in an area that is less than 30 minutes from Bend. This is a good place for horseback riding, and trails heading south reenter the forested areas. The system of lava tubes nearby at the Arnold Ice Caves is fun to explore. A U.S. Forest Service map details trail options. Non-horse campers are welcome.

Location: Near the Arnold Ice Caves in Deschutes National Forest; map D3, grid e2.

Campsites, facilities: There are six primitive sites for tents, trailers, or RVs up to 22 feet long. Picnic tables and fire grills are provided. There are vault toilets, but no drinking water, and all garbage must be packed out. Leashed pets are permitted.

Reservations, fees: No reservations; no fee. Open April to late November.

Directions: From Bend drive south on U.S. 97 for four miles to Forest Road 18. Turn southeast and drive 5.4 miles to Forest Road 1810. Turn south (right) and drive 5.8 miles to Forest Road 1816. Turn east (left) and drive three miles to the campground.

Contact: Deschutes National Forest, Bend-Fort Rock Ranger District, 1230 N.E. Third Street, Bend, OR 97701; tel. (541) 388-5664; fax (541) 383-4700.

37 Antelope Flat Reservoir   6

This pretty spot is set along the west shore of Antelope Flat Reservoir. The campground is amid ponderosa pine and juniper, on the edge of the high desert at an elevation of 4,600 feet. It has wide sites and easy access to the lake. Trout fishing can be good in the spring, and boating with motors is permitted. This is also a good lake for canoes.

Location: On Antelope Flat Reservoir in Ochoco National Forest; map D3, grid e5.

Campsites, facilities: There are 25 sites for tents, trailers, or RVs up to 30 feet long. Picnic tables and fire grills are provided. Drinking water and vault toilets are available, but all garbage must be packed out. Boat launching facilities are nearby. Leashed pets are permitted.

Reservations, fees: No reservations. Sites are $8 per night, plus $3 for each additional vehicle. Open early May to late October.

Directions: From Prineville drive southeast on Highway 380 for 30 miles to Forest Road 17 (Antelope Reservoir Junction). Turn right on Forest Road 17 and drive three miles to Forest Road 1700-600. Drive a quarter mile on Forest Road 1700-600 to the campground.

Contact: Ochoco National Forest, Prineville Ranger District, P.O. Box 490, Prineville, OR 97754; tel. (541) 416-6500.

38 Wiley Flat   3

This campground is set along Wiley Creek in a nice, hidden spot with minimal crowds and is popular with hunters. A map of Ochoco National Forest details nearby access roads. A good gut-thumping hike is the trip to Tower Point Lookout. It's one mile north of the camp-and a 1,000-foot climb straight up. Double Cabin and Elkhorn provide nearby alternatives.

Location: On Wiley Creek in Ochoco National Forest; map D3, grid e6.

Campsites, facilities: There are five sites for tents, trailers, or RVs up to 30 feet long. Picnic tables and fire grills are provided. Vault toilets are available, but there is no drinking water, and all garbage must be packed out. Leashed pets are permitted.

Reservations, fees: No reservations; no fee. Open mid-June to late October.

Directions: From Prineville drive southeast on Highway 380 for 34 miles to Forest Road 16. Turn southeast and drive 10 miles to Forest Road 1600-400. Turn west and drive one mile to the camp.

Contact: Ochoco National Forest, Prineville Ranger District, P.O. Box 490, Prineville, OR 97754; tel. (541) 416-6500.

39 Paulina Lake   8

This campground is set along the south shore of Paulina Lake at 6,300 feet and located within the Newberry National Volcanic Monument. The lake itself sits in a volcanic crater. Nearby trails provide access to the remains of volcanic activity, including craters and obsidian flows. The state's record brown trout was caught here by my longtime friend Guy Carl, right after I'd written a story about his unique method of using giant bass lures for giant browns. The boat speed limit is 10 mph. The camp is adjacent to Paulina Lake Resort. The recreation options here include boating, sailing, fishing, and hiking.

Location: On Paulina Lake in Deschutes National Forest; map D3, grid f0.

Campsites, facilities: There are 69 sites for trailers or RVs up to 30 feet long. Picnic tables, garbage service, and fire grills are provided. Flush and vault toilets, showers, and a coin-operated laundry are located within five miles. Drinking water is available. Boat docks, launching facilities, boat rentals, a small store, restaurant, cabins, gas, and propane are located within five miles. Leashed pets are permitted.

Reservations, fees: No reservations. Sites are $10-12 per night, $5 for each additional vehicle. Open late May to late October.

Directions: From Bend drive south on U.S. 97 for 23.5 miles to County Road 21 (Paulina/East Lake Road). Turn east (left) and drive 12.9 miles to the campground.

Contact: Deschutes National Forest, Bend-Fort Rock Ranger District, 1230 N.E. Third Street, Bend, OR 97701; tel. (541) 388-5664; fax (541) 383-4700.

🔟 Chief Paulina Horse Camp   4

This campground is about one-quarter mile from the south shore of Paulina Lake. Horse trails and a vista point are close by. See the description of Paulina Lake Campground for additional recreation information.

Location: On Paulina Lake in Deschutes National Forest; map D3, grid f1.

Campsites, facilities: There are 14 sites for tents, trailers, or RVs up to 30 feet long. Picnic tables, garbage service, and fire grills are provided. Vault toilets are available, but there is no drinking water. Boat docks and rentals are nearby. Leashed pets are permitted.

Reservations, fees: No reservations. Sites are $12 per night, $5 per additional vehicle. The entire camp can be reserved for $45 a night. Open late May to late October, weather permitting.

Directions: From Bend drive south on U.S. 97 for 23.5 miles to County Road 21 (Paulina/East Lake Road). Turn east (left) and drive 14 miles to the campground.

Contact: Deschutes National Forest, Bend-Fort Rock Ranger District, 1230 N.E. Third Street, Bend, OR 97701; tel. (541) 388-5664; fax (541) 383-4700.

4️⃣1️⃣ Little Crater   8

This campground is near the east shore of Paulina Lake in Newberry National Volcanic Monument, a caldera. This camp is very popular. See the description of Paulina Lake for more information.

Location: Near Paulina Lake in Deschutes National Forest; map D3, grid f1.

Campsites, facilities: There are 50 sites for tents, trailers, or RVs up to 30 feet long. Picnic tables, garbage service, and fire grills are provided. Drinking water and vault toilets are available. Boat docks and launching facilities are on site, and boat rentals are nearby. Leashed pets are permitted.

Reservations, fees: No reservations. Sites are $14 per night, plus $5 per additional vehicle. Open late May to late October.

Directions: From Bend drive south on U.S. 97 for 23.5 miles to County Road 21 (Paulina/East Lake Road). Turn east (left) and drive 14.5 miles to Forest Road 2110. Turn north (left) and drive one-half mile to the campground.

Contact: Deschutes National Forest, Bend-Fort Rock Ranger District, 1230 N.E. Third Street, Bend, OR 97701; tel. (541) 388-5664; fax (541) 383-4700.

42 Cinder Hill   7

Located within the Newberry National Volcanic Monument, this is a good base camp for area activities. The campground is situated along the northeast shore of East Lake at an elevation of 6,400 feet. Boating, fishing, and hiking are among the recreation options here. Boat speed is limited to 10 mph.

Location: On East Lake in Deschutes National Forest; map D3, grid f1.

Campsites, facilities: There are 110 sites for tents, trailers, or RVs up to 30 feet long. Picnic tables, garbage service, and fire grills are provided. Drinking water and flush and vault toilets are available. Boat docks and launching facilities are on-site, and boat rentals, a store, restaurant, showers, coin-operated laundry, and cabins are nearby at East Lake Resort. Leashed pets are permitted.

Reservations, fees: No reservations. Sites are $10-12 per night, plus $5 per additional vehicle. Open late May to late October.

Directions: From Bend drive south on U.S. 97 for 23.5 miles to County Road 21 (Paulina/East Lake Road). Turn east (left) and drive 17.6 miles to Forest Road 2110-700. Turn north (left) and drive one-half mile to the campground.

Contact: Deschutes National Forest, Bend-Fort Rock Ranger District, 1230 N.E. Third Street, Bend, OR 97701; tel. (541) 388-5664; fax (541) 383-4700.

43 East Lake   8

This campground is set along the south shore of East Lake. Boating and fishing are popular here, and hiking trails provide access to signs of former volcanic activity in the area. East Lake Campground is similar to Cinder Hill, but smaller. Boat speed is limited to 10 mph.

Location: On East Lake in Deschutes National Forest; map D3, grid f1.

Campsites, facilities: There are 29 sites for tents, trailers, or RVs up to 30 feet long. Picnic tables, garbage service, and fire grills are provided. Drinking water and flush and vault toilets are available. Boat docks, launching facilities, and rentals are nearby. Leashed pets are permitted.

Reservations, fees: No reservations. Sites are $10 per night, plus $5 per additional vehicle. Open late May to late October.

Directions: From Bend drive south on U.S. 97 for 23.5 miles to County Road 21 (Paulina/East Lake Road). Turn east (left) and drive 16.6 miles to the campground.

Contact: Deschutes National Forest, Bend-Fort Rock Ranger District, 1230 N.E. Third Street, Bend, OR 97701; tel. (541) 388-5664; fax (541) 383-4700.

44 Hot Springs   5

This campground lies across the road from East Lake. It's a good tent camping spot if you want to be near East Lake, but farther away from RVs. See the description of East Lake for additional recreation information.

Location: Near East Lake in Deschutes National Forest; map D3, grid f2.

Campsites, facilities: There are 42 sites for tents, trailers, or RVs up to 30 feet long. Picnic tables, garbage service, and fire grills are provided. Drinking water and vault toilets are available. Boat docks, launching facilities, and rentals are nearby. Leashed pets are permitted.

Reservations, fees: No reservations. Sites are $8 per night, plus $5 per additional vehicle. Open late May to late October.

Directions: From Bend drive south on U.S. 97 for 23.5 miles to County Road 21 (Paulina/East Lake Road). Turn east (left) and drive 17.2 miles to the campground.

Contact: Deschutes National Forest, Bend-Fort Rock Ranger District, 1230 N.E. Third Street, Bend, OR 97701; tel. (541) 388-5664; fax (541) 383-4700.

45 East Lake
Resort and RV Park   7

This resort is in a wooded, mountainous setting with shaded sites on the east shore of East Lake. Opportunities for fishing, boating, and swimming abound.

Location: On East Lake; map D3, grid f2.

Campsites, facilities: There are 38 sites for tents, trailers, or RVs up to 36 feet in length. Electricity, drinking water, and picnic tables are provided. Flush toilets, bottled gas, showers, barbecues, cabins, firewood, a store, a cafe, a laundry room, ice, boat launching facilities, boat rentals, and a playground are available. A dump station is nearby. Leashed pets are permitted.

Reservations, fees: Reservations accepted. Sites are $15 per night. Open mid-May to mid-October, weather permitting.

Directions: From Bend drive south on U.S. 97 for 23.5 miles to County Road 21 (Paulina/East Lake Road). Turn east (left) and drive 18 miles to the campground at the end of the road.

Contact: East Lake Resort and RV Park, P.O. Box 95, La Pine, OR 97739; tel. (541) 536-2230.

46 China Hat   3

This remote campground is set at 5,100 feet in a rugged, primitive area. Hunters use it as a base camp in the fall. Hiking and bird-watching opportunities are a highlight.

Location: In Deschutes National Forest; map D3, grid f2.

Campsites, facilities: There are 14 sites for tents, trailers, or RVs up to 30 feet long. Picnic tables and fire grills are provided. Vault toilets are available. There is no drinking water, and all garbage must be packed out. Leashed pets are permitted.

Reservations, fees: No reservations; no fee. Open May to late October, weather permitting.

Directions: From Bend drive south on U.S. 97 for 29.6 miles to Forest Road 22. Turn east (left) and drive 26.4 miles to Forest Road 18. Turn north (left) and drive 5.9 miles to the campground on the left.

Contact: Deschutes National Forest, Bend-Fort Rock Ranger District, 1230 N.E. Third Street, Bend, OR 97701; tel. (541) 388-5664; fax (541) 383-4700.

47 Cabin Lake   3

This remote campground set at 4,500 feet is adjacent to an over-80-year-old bird blind—a great place to watch birds. The spot is primitive and secluded, with sparse tree cover and receiving little use even in the busy summer months.

Location: In Deschutes National Forest; map D3, grid f2.

Campsites, facilities: There are 14 sites for tents, trailers, or RVs up to 30 feet long. Picnic tables and fire grills are provided. Vault toilets and drinking water are available. All garbage must be packed out. Leashed pets are permitted.

Reservations, fees: No reservations; no fee. Open mid-May to late October.

Directions: From Bend drive south on U.S. 97 for 29.6 miles to Forest Road 22. Turn east (left) and drive 26.4 miles to Forest Road 18. Turn north (left) and drive six miles to the campground on the left.

Contact: Deschutes National Forest, Bend-Fort Rock Ranger District, 1230 N.E. Third Street, Bend, OR 97701; tel. (541) 388-5664; fax (541) 383-4700.

A NICE, FLAT SPOT

MAP D4

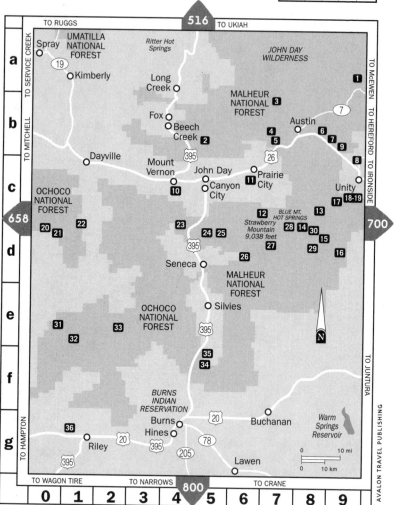

TO RUGGS 516 TO UKIAH

a

TO SERVICE CREEK
TO MITCHELL

Spray
UMATILLA
NATIONAL
FOREST
19
Kimberly

Ritter Hot
Springs

JOHN DAY
WILDERNESS

1

Long
Creek

MALHEUR
NATIONAL
FOREST 3

Austin 7

b

Fox
Beech
Creek 2

395

4
5

26

6
7
9

8

Dayville

Mount
Vernon
10

John Day
Canyon
City

Prairie
City 11

Unity
18-19
17

c

TO McEWEN TO HEREFORD TO IRONSIDE

OCHOCO
NATIONAL
FOREST

22

20
21

23

24 25

12 BLUE MT.
HOT SPRINGS
Strawberry
Mountain
9,038 feet
27

13
28 14
30
29

15
16

658

700

d

26

Seneca

MALHEUR
NATIONAL
FOREST

N

e

31

OCHOCO
NATIONAL
FOREST

33

32

Silvies

395

f

35
34

BURNS
INDIAN
RESERVATION

TO JUNTURA

TO HAMPTON

g

36

Burns
Hines
20
Riley
20
395
205
78

20 Buchanan

Lawen

Warm
Springs
Reservoir

0   10 mi
0   10 km

TO WAGON TIRE TO NARROWS 800 TO CRANE

0 1 2 3 4 5 6 7 8 9

© AVALON TRAVEL PUBLISHING

CHAPTER D4

■ McCully Forks   5

Here's an easy-access campground at 4,600 elevation along the banks of McCully Creek that's tiny, free, and primitive. This tiny camp, wedged in between highway and mountains, gets moderately heavy use and is often full on weekends, and highway noise can be audible. Sites are wooded with alder and cottonwood.

Location: On McCully Creek in Wallowa-Whitman National Forest; map D4, grid a9.

Campsites, facilities: There are six tent sites. Picnic tables and fire grills are provided. Vault toilets are available. There is no drinking water and all garbage must be packed out. Leashed pets are permitted.

Reservations, fees: No reservations. There is no fee. Open late May to late October.

Directions: From Baker City drive southwest on Highway 7 for 29 miles (bear west at Salisbury) to Sumpter. Continue three miles past Sumpter (the road becomes Forest Road 24) to the campground.

Contact: Wallowa-Whitman National Forest, Baker Ranger District, 3165 10th Street, Baker City, OR 97814; tel. (541) 523-1932; fax (541) 523-1965.

■ Magone Lake   8

This campground is set along the shore of little Magone Lake at an elevation of 5,100 feet. A 1.8-mile trail rings the lake, and the portion extending from the beach area to the campground (about a quarter mile) is barrier-free. A half-mile trail is routed to Magone Slide, an unusual geological formation. Swimming, fishing, sailing, and canoeing are some of the popular activities at this lake. Easy-access bike trails can be found within a quarter mile of the campground.

Location: On Magone Lake in Malheur National Forest; map D4, grid b5.

Campsites, facilities: There are three sites for tents and 18 sites for trailers or RVs up to 40 feet long; four are drive-through sites. There is a separate group camping site designed for 10 families and a picnic shelter that can accommodate 50 to 100 people. Some facilities are wheelchair accessible, including two of the campsites. Picnic tables and fire grills are provided. Drinking water, composting toilets, a boat ramp, and a beach area are available. Boat docks and launching facilities are nearby. Leashed pets are permitted.

Reservations, fees: No reservations required, except for the group site and picnic shelter. Sites are $5 per night, $2.50 per night for an additional vehicle. Open May through November, weather permitting.

Directions: From John Day drive east on U.S. 26 for eight miles to County Road 18. Turn north and drive 10 miles to Forest Road 3620. Turn west (left) on Forest Road 3620 and drive 1.5 miles to Forest Road 3618. Turn right (northwest) and drive 1.5 miles to the campground.

Contact: Malheur National Forest, Long Creek Ranger District, P.O. Box 849, John Day, OR 97845; tel. (541) 575-3000; fax (541) 575-3001.

3 Olive Lake   9

This campground is set at 6,100 feet along the shore of Olive Lake, located between two sections of the North Fork John Day Wilderness. Dammed to hold an increased volume of water, the glacial lake is a beautiful tint of blue. Motorized boats are allowed, but waterskiing is prohibited. Fishing is fair for Kokanee, cutthroat, rainbow and brook trout. Portions of the old wooden pipeline for the historical Fremont Powerhouse can still be seen. Nearby trails provide access to the wilderness. Motorbikes and mountain bikes are not permitted there. The old mining town of Granite is 12 miles west of camp.

Location: On Olive Lake in Umatilla National Forest; map D4, grid b7.

Campsites, facilities: There are 28 sites for tents, trailers, or RVs up to 31 feet long (four can handle up to 45 feet). Vault toilets are available, but there is no drinking water and garbage must be packed out. Picnic tables and fire grills are provided. Boat docks, launching facilities, and two picnic areas are available. Leashed pets are permitted.

Reservations, fees: No reservations accepted. Sites are $5 per night, with a 14-day stay limit. Open June to mid-October, weather permitting.

Directions: From Pendleton drive south on U.S. 395 for 62 miles to Forest Road 55 (one mile north of Dale). Turn right and drive one-half mile to Forest Road 10. Turn right on Forest Road 10 and drive 26 miles to the campground on the right.

Contact: Umatilla National Forest, North Fork John Day Ranger District, P.O. Box 158, Ukiah, OR 97880; tel. (541) 427-3231; fax (541) 276-5026.

4 Middle Fork   6

Scattered along the banks of the Middle Fork of the John Day River at 4,100 feet elevation, this rustic spot is easy to reach off a paved road. Besides wildlife-watching and berry picking, the main activity at this camp is fishing, so bring along your fly rod, and pinch down your barbs for catch-and-release. The John Day is a state scenic waterway.

Location: On the Middle Fork of the John Day River in Malheur National Forest; map D4, grid b7.

Campsites, facilities: There are 10 sites for tents, trailers, or RVs up to 30 feet long. Picnic tables and fire grills are provided. Vault toilets are available. There is no drinking water, and all garbage must be packed out. Some facilities are wheelchair accessible. Leashed pets are permitted.

Reservations, fees: No reservations. Sites are $5 per night, $2.50 per night for an additional vehicle. Open May through November, weather permitting.

Directions: From John Day drive northeast on U.S. 26 for 28 miles to Highway 7. Turn left (north) and drive one mile to County Road 20. Turn left and drive five miles to the campground on the left.

Contact: Malheur National Forest, Long Creek Ranger District, P.O. Box 849, John Day, OR 97845; tel. (541) 575-3000; fax (541) 575-3001.

5 Dixie   5

This campground is set at Dixie Summit (elevation 5,300 feet) near Bridge Creek, where you can toss in a fishing line. The camp is just off U.S. 26, close enough to provide easy access. It draws overnighters, but otherwise gets light use. The Sumpter Valley Railroad interpretive site is one mile west on U.S. 26.

Location: Near Dixie Summit in Malheur National Forest; map D4, grid b7.

Campsites, facilities: There are 11 sites for tents, trailers, or RVs up to 30 feet long. Picnic tables, vault toilets, and fire grills are provided. Drinking water is available, but all garbage must be packed out. A store, a cafe, gas, and ice are available within six miles. Some facilities are wheelchair accessible. Leashed pets are permitted.

Reservations, fees: No reservations. Sites are $5 per night, $2.50 per night for an additional vehicle. Open May through November, weather permitting.

Directions: From John Day drive northeast on U.S. 26 for 24 miles to Forest Road 365. Turn left and drive one-quarter mile to the campground.

Contact: Malheur National Forest, Long Creek Ranger District, P.O. Box 849, John Day, OR 97845; tel. (541) 575-3000; fax (541) 575-3001.

6 Oregon   6

This campground at 4,880 elevation, is just off U.S. 26 and is a staging site for ATV trails. The camp is surrounded by hillside, Douglas fir, white fir, and tamarack. Bald eagles nest in the area.

Location: Near Austin Junction in Wallowa-Whitman National Forest; map D4, grid b8.

Campsites, facilities: There are 11 sites for tents, trailers, or RVs up to 28 feet long. Picnic tables and fire grills are provided. Drinking water and vault toilets are available, but garbage must be packed out. Pets are permitted.

Reservations, fees: No reservations. Sites are $5 per night. Open May to mid-September.

Directions: From John Day drive east on U.S. 26 for 29 miles to Austin Junction. Continue east for 20 miles to the campground.

Contact: Wallowa-Whitman National Forest, Unity Ranger District, P.O. Box 38, Unity, OR 97884; tel. (541) 446-3351; fax (541) 523-1479.

7 Yellow Pine   7

Highlights of this camp include easy access and good recreation potential, including hiking trails. One half-mile-long, wheelchair-accessible trail connects to the Wetmore Campground. This is similar to Oregon Campground, but larger. Keep an eye out for bald eagles in this area.

Location: On Road Creek in Wallowa-Whitman National Forest; map D4, grid b8.

Campsites, facilities: There are 21 sites for tents, trailers, or RVs up to 28 feet long. Picnic tables and fire grills are provided. Drinking water, a waste disposal station, and vault toilets are available, but all garbage must be packed out. Pets are permitted.

Reservations, fees: No reservations. Sites are $8 per night. Open late May to mid-September.

Directions: From John Day drive east on U.S. 26 for 29 miles to Austin Junction. Continue east for 21 miles to the campground.

Contact: Wallowa-Whitman National Forest, Unity Ranger District, P.O. Box 38, Unity, OR 97884; tel. (541) 446-3351; fax (541) 523-1479.

🔟 Unity Lake State Recreation Site   7

This camp is set along the east shore of Unity Reservoir and is a popular spot when the weather is good. Campers can choose from hiking, swimming, boating, fishing, picnicking, or enjoying the scenic views. Set in the high desert, the grassy park is a contrast to the sagebrush and cheat grass of the bordering land.

Location: On Unity Reservoir; map D4, grid b9.

Campsites, facilities: There are 21 sites with water and electrical hookups for tents or RVs up to 40 feet long, and a separate area for hikers and bicyclists, and two tepees. Picnic tables, garbage bins, and fire grills are provided. Drinking water, flush toilets, showers, a sanitary disposal station, and firewood are available. Some facilities are wheelchair accessible. Boat docks and launching facilities are nearby. Leashed pets are permitted.

Reservations, fees: No reservations accepted. Sites are $13-15 per night, $4 per night for hikers/bikers, $27 per night for tepees. and $7 per night for an additional vehicle. Open mid-April to late October.

Directions: From John Day drive east on U.S. 26 for 62 miles to Highway 245. Turn north (left) on Highway 245 and drive three miles to the park on the left.

Contact: Unity Lake State Recreation Site, P.O. Box 9 Canyon City, OR 97820; tel. (800) 551-6949 or (541) 932-4453.

🔟 Wetmore   7

This campground set at an elevation of 4,320 feet near the Middle Fork of the Burnt River is a nice base camp for a fishing or hiking trip. The stream can provide good trout fishing. Trails are detailed on a map of Wallowa-Whitman National Forest. In addition, an excellent half-mile, wheelchair-accessible trail passes through old-growth forest. Watch for bald eagles.

Location: On the Middle Fork of the Burnt River in Wallowa-Whitman National Forest; map D4, grid b9.

Campsites, facilities: There are 16 sites for tents, trailers, or RVs up to 28 feet long. Picnic tables and fire grills are provided. Drinking water, firewood, and vault toilets are available, but all garbage must be packed out. Some facilities are wheelchair accessible. Leashed pets are permitted.

Reservations, fees: No reservations. Sites are $8 per night. Open late May to mid-September.

Directions: From John Day drive east on U.S. 26 for 29 miles to Austin Junction. Continue east on U.S. 26 for 10 miles to the campground.

Contact: Wallowa-Whitman National Forest, Unity Ranger District, P.O. Box 38, Unity, OR 97884; tel. (541) 446-3351; fax (541) 523-1479.

🔟 Clyde Holliday State Recreation Site   7

Think of this campground as an oasis. Its tall, willowy cottonwood trees provide shade and serenity, giving you that private, secluded feeling. Bordering the John Day River, you're as likely to have wildlife neighbors as human ones; Rocky Mountain elk and mule deer are frequent visitors. You might also see steelhead rushing upriver to spawn.

Location: Near the John Day River; map D4, grid c4.

Campsites, facilities: There are 30 sites for trailers or RVs up to 60 feet long, a hiker/biker area, and two tepees. Electricity, picnic tables, and fire grills are provided. Drinking water, firewood, sanitary disposal services, showers, and flush toilets are available. Leashed pets are permitted.

Reservations, fees: No reservations accepted. Sites are $10-15 per night, $4 per night for hiker/bikers, $28 per night for tepees, and $7 per night for an additional vehicle. The campground is open March through November, weather permitting.

Directions: From John Day drive west on U.S. 26 for eight miles to the park on the left.

Contact: Clyde Holliday State Recreation Site, P.O. Box 10, Mt. Vernon, OR 97865; tel. (800) 551-6949, (541) 932-4453.

1️⃣1️⃣ Depot Park   6

This urban park on grassy flatlands has access to the John Day River, a good trout fishing spot. The camp is a more developed alternative to the many U.S. Forest Service campgrounds in the area. A historic rail depot is in the camp, with a related museum. Nearby attractions include the Strawberry Mountain Wilderness (prime hiking trails) and Clyde Holliday State Recreation Site.

Location: On the John Day River; map D4, grid c6.

Campsites, facilities: There are 20 sites for tents, trailers, or RVs up to 35 feet. Rest rooms, showers, a sanitary dump, gazebo, picnic area, and a public phone are provided. Leashed pets are permitted.

Reservations, fees: No reservations accepted. Sites are $13 per night. Open May through November, weather permitting.

Directions: From John Day drive east on U.S. 26 for 13 miles to Prairie City and the junction of U.S. 26 and Main Street. Turn south on Main Street and drive one-half mile to the park (well signed).

Contact: Prairie City Hall, P.O. Box 370, Prairie City, OR 97869; tel. (541) 820-3605.

1️⃣2️⃣ Strawberry   7

This campground is set along the banks of Strawberry Creek at 5,700 feet in elevation. Nearby trails provide access to the Strawberry Mountain Wilderness, Strawberry Lake, and Strawberry Falls. It's a pretty area with hiking and hunting options. Fishing in Strawberry Creek is another possibility.

Location: On Strawberry Creek in Malheur National Forest; map D4, grid c7.

Campsites, facilities: There are 11 sites for tents. Picnic tables and fire grills are provided. Drinking water and wheelchair-accessible vault toilets are available. Leashed pets are permitted. Pack out all garbage.

Reservations, fees: No reservations. Sites are $6 per night, $3 per night for an additional vehicle. Open June to mid-October.

Directions: From John Day drive east on U.S. 26 for 13 miles to County Road 62. Turn right (southeast and drive one-half mile to County Road 60. Turn right and drive south on County Road 60 for 8.5 miles (County Road 60 becomes Forest Road 6001). Continue 2.5 miles to the campground.

Contact: Malheur National Forest, Prairie City Ranger District, P.O. Box 337, Prairie City, OR 97869; tel. (541) 820-3311; fax (541) 820-3838.

13 Elk Creek  8

This tiny, pretty camp at the confluence of the North and South Forks of Elk Creek (elevation 5,000 feet) has lots of hunting and fishing opportunities. This camp gets light use, except during the hunting season. North Fork Malheur is an alternate camp in the area.

Location: On Elk Creek in Malheur National Forest; map D4, grid c8.

Campsites, facilities: There are five tent sites. Picnic tables and fire grills are provided. Wheelchair-accessible vault toilets are available. There is no drinking water and all garbage must be packed out. Leashed pets are permitted.

Reservations, fees: No reservations accepted. There is no fee. Open mid-May to mid-November.

Directions: From John Day drive east on U.S. 26 for 13 miles to Prairie City and County Road 62. Turn right (southeast) on County Road 62 and drive 8.5 miles to Forest Road 13. Turn left and drive 16 miles to Forest Road 16. Turn right and drive 1.5 miles south to the campground.

Contact: Malheur National Forest, Prairie City Ranger District, P.O. Box 337, Prairie City, OR 97869; tel. (541) 820-3311; fax (541) 820-3838.

14 Mammoth Springs 4

The South Fork of the Burnt River is a nice trout creek with, according to the local ranger, "good evening bites for anglers who know how to sneak-fish." The camp is private and scenic. Popular with hunters in the fall, the camp is set in brush and Douglas firs. By the way, the hot springs consist of a spot the size of a washtub, not large enough for human use. Maybe a Lemurian could fit in.

Location: On the South Fork of the Burnt River in Wallowa-Whitman National Forest; map D4, grid c8.

Campsites, facilities: There is a dispersed camping area for tents, trailers, or RVs up to 28 feet long. Picnic tables and fire grills are provided. Vault toilets are available. Leashed pets are permitted. Pack out all garbage.

Reservations, fees: No reservations accepted. There is no fee. Open May to mid-September.

Directions: From John Day drive east on U.S. 26 and drive 29 miles to Austin Junction. Continue east on U.S. 26 and drive 23 miles to Unity and Highway 600. Turn west on Highway 600 and drive to Forest Road 6005. Turn west and drive to Forest Road 2640. Turn west again and drive to the camp. (The camp is nine miles from Unity.)
Contact: Wallowa-Whitman National Forest, Unity Ranger District, P.O. Box 38, Unity, OR 97884; tel. (541) 446-3351; fax (541) 523-1479.

ⓕ Long Creek   4

This small, little-known campground set at 4,430 feet elevation, boasts good trout fishing in Long Creek Reservoir. Several nearby campgrounds are similar in surroundings and facilities: Mammoth Springs, Long Creek, Eldorado and Elk Creek No. 2.
Location: On Long Creek Reservoir in Wallowa-Whitman National Forest; map D4, grid d8.
Campsites, facilities: There is one group site for tents, trailers, or RVs up to 28 feet long. Picnic tables and fire grills are provided. A vault toilet is available, but there is no drinking water, and all garbage must be packed out. Leashed pets are permitted.
Reservations, fees: No reservations accepted. There is no fee. Open May to mid-September.
Directions: From John Day drive east on U.S. 26 and drive 29 miles to Austin Junction. Continue east on U.S. 26 and drive 23 miles to Unity. Drive through Unity to Forest Road 1680. Turn south and drive nine miles to the campground on the left.
Contact: Wallowa-Whitman National Forest, Unity Ranger District, P.O. Box 38, Unity, OR 97884; tel. (541) 446-3351; fax (541) 523-1479.

ⓖ Eldorado    5

Trout fishing in spring and early summer at East Camp Creek is a draw here. The campground is also convenient for fishing at Murray Reservoir. It is set at an elevation of 4,600 feet.
Location: On East Camp Creek in Wallowa-Whitman National Forest; map D4, grid d9.
Campsites, facilities: There are six sites for tents, trailers, or RVs up to 28 feet long. Picnic tables and fire grills are provided. Vault toilets are available, but there is no drinking water, and all garbage must be packed out. Leashed pets are permitted.
Reservations, fees: No reservations accepted. There is no fee. Open May to mid-September.
Directions: From John Day drive east on U.S. 26 and drive 52 miles to Unity. Drive through Unity and continue another 10 miles to Forest Road 16 (well signed). Turn south and drive three miles to the campground.
Contact: Wallowa-Whitman National Forest, Unity Ranger District, P.O. Box 38, Unity, OR 97884; tel. (541) 446-3351; fax (541) 523-1479.

17 Elk Creek No. 2   5

This small, obscure camp is set at an elevation of 4,520 feet, along the banks of the South Fork of the Burnt River, and is a good base for fishing and hiking.

Location: On the South Fork of the Burnt River in Wallowa-Whitman National Forest; map D4, grid c8.

Campsites, facilities: There is one group area for up to six tents, trailers, or RVs up to 28 feet long. Picnic tables and fire grills are provided. Vault toilets are available. There is no drinking water. Leashed pets are permitted. Garbage must be packed out.

Reservations, fees: No reservations accepted. There is no fee. Open late May to mid-September.

Directions: From John Day drive east on U.S. 26 and drive 52 miles to Unity and County Road 600. Turn right and drive eight miles (the road becomes Forest Road 6005, South Fork Road) to the campground on the left.

Contact: Wallowa-Whitman National Forest, Unity Ranger District, P.O. Box 38, Unity, OR 97884; tel. (541) 446-3351; fax (541) 523-1479.

18 South Fork   5

This campground is set at an elevation of 4,400 feet along the banks of the South Fork of the Burnt River, a nice trout creek with good evening bites for anglers who know how to sneak-fish. It's a gem of a spot, with drinking water, privacy, and scenery-all for free.

Location: On the South Fork of the Burnt River in Wallowa-Whitman National Forest; map D4, grid c9.

Campsites, facilities: There are 14 sites for tents, trailers, or RVs up to 28 feet long. Picnic tables and fire grills are provided. Drinking water and vault toilets are available, but all garbage must be packed out. Pets are permitted.

Reservations, fees: No reservations accepted. There is no fee. Open late May to mid-September.

Directions: From John Day drive east on U.S. 26 and drive 52 miles to Unity and County Road 600. Turn right and drive six miles (the road becomes Forest Road 6005, South Fork Road) to the campground on the left.

Contact: Wallowa-Whitman National Forest, Unity Ranger District, P.O. Box 38, Unity, OR 97884; tel. (541) 446-3351; fax (541) 523-1479.

19 Stevens Creek   5

This campground along the banks of the South Fork of the Burnt River is an option to the other small camps along the river. It is set at an elevation of 4,480 feet. The trout fishing is often good here. See the description of South Fork for more information.

Location: On the South Fork of the Burnt River in Wallowa-Whitman National Forest; map D4, grid c9.

Campsites, facilities: There is one group area for up to six tents, trailers, or RVs of any length. Picnic tables and fire grills are provided, but there is no drinking water, and all garbage must be packed out. Vault toilets are available. Pets are permitted.

Reservations, fees: No reservations accepted. There is no fee. Open late May to mid-September.

Directions: From John Day drive east on U.S. 26 and drive 52 miles to Unity and County Road 600. Turn right and drive seven miles (the road becomes Forest Road 6005, South Fork Road) to the campground on the left.

Contact: Wallowa-Whitman National Forest, Unity Ranger District, P.O. Box 38, Unity, OR 97884; tel. (541) 446-3351; fax (541) 523-1479.

20 Wolf Creek   5

This campground is set along the banks of Wolf Creek, a nice trout stream that runs through Ochoco National Forest. It's a quality spot. Some excellent hiking trails can be found to the northeast in the Black Canyon Wilderness.

Location: On Wolf Creek in Ochoco National Forest; map D4, grid d0.

Campsites, facilities: There are 11 sites for tents, trailers, or RVs up to 22 feet long. Picnic tables and fire grills are provided, but there is no drinking water, and all garbage must be packed out. Vault toilets are available. Leashed pets are permitted.

Reservations, fees: No reservations accepted. Sites are $5 per night, with a 14-day stay limit, and $3 per night for an additional vehicle. Open May to early November.

Directions: From Prineville drive southeast on Highway 380 for 55 miles to Paulina. Continue east on County Road 380 for 3.5 miles to County Road 113. Turn north and drive 6.5 miles to Forest Road 42. Turn north and drive 1.5 miles to the campground.

Contact: Ochoco National Forest, Paulina Ranger District, 71500 Beaver Creek Road, Paulina, OR 97751; tel. (541) 416-6679; fax (541) 416-6679.

21 Sugar Creek   6

This campground is on the banks of Sugar Creek, small, quiet, and remote. It is set at an elevation of 4,000 feet. A three-quarter mile trail is available that loops along Sugar Creek. There is also a covered group shelter in the new day-use area and a wheelchair-accessible trail. Due to the presence of bald eagles, there may be seasonal closures on land access in the area. Be sure to check posted notices.

Location: On Sugar Creek in Ochoco National Forest; map D4, grid d0.

Campsites, facilities: There are 17 sites for tents, trailers, or RVs up to 21 feet long. Picnic tables, garbage bins, and fire grills are provided. Drinking water, a picnic shelter, and vault toilets are available. Some facilities are wheelchair accessible. Leashed pets are permitted.

Reservations, fees: No reservations accepted. Sites are $8 per night, with a 14-day stay limit, and $4 per night for an additional vehicle. Open June to early November.

Directions: From Prineville drive southeast on Highway 380 for 55 miles to Paulina. Continue east and drive 3.5 miles to a fork with County Road 113. Bear left at the fork to County Road 113 and drive 7.5 miles to Forest Road 58. Continue on Forest Road 58 for 2.25 miles to the campground on the right.

Contact: Ochoco National Forest, Paulina Ranger District, 71500 Beaver Creek Road, Paulina, OR 97751; tel. (541) 416-6679; fax (541) 416-6679.

22 Frazier   4

This small, remote, and little-used camp in a meadow setting, is located at an elevation of 4,300 feet. Some dirt roads adjacent to the camp are good for mountain biking in summer and cross-country skiing and snowmobiling in winter. The camp is popular for reunions during the holidays. This campground is set in an open, grassy area sprinkled with a few large trees.

Location: On Frazier Creek in Ochoco National Forest; map D4, grid d1.

Campsites, facilities: There are six sites for tents, trailers, or RVs up to 21 feet long. Picnic tables and fire grills are provided. Vault toilets are available. There is no drinking water and all garbage must be packed out. Leashed pets are permitted.

Reservations, fees: No reservations accepted. There is no fee. The stay-limit is 14 days. Open June to early November.

Directions: From Prineville drive southeast on Highway 380 for 55 miles to Paulina. Continue east and drive 3.5 miles to a fork with County Road 113. Bear left at the fork to County Road 113 and drive 2.5 miles to County Road 135. Turn east and drive 10 miles to Forest Road 58. Continue for six miles to Forest Road 58-500, and continue two miles to the campground.

Contact: Ochoco National Forest, Paulina Ranger District, 71500 Beaver Creek Road, Paulina, OR 97751; tel. (541) 416-6679; fax (541) 416-6679.

23 Starr   4

This good layover spot (5,100 elevation) for travelers on U.S. 395, happens to be adjacent to Starr Ski Bowl, which is popular in winter for skiing and sledding. The camp itself doesn't offer much in the way of recreation, but to the northeast is the Strawberry Mountain Wilderness, which has a number of trails, lakes, and streams.

Location: On Starr Ridge in Malheur National Forest; map D4, grid d4.

Campsites, facilities: There are eight sites for tents, trailers, or RVs up to 25 feet long; one site is wheelchair accessible. Picnic tables and fire grills are provided. Vault toilets are available. There is no drinking water, and all garbage must be packed out. Leashed pets are permitted.

Reservations, fees: No reservations. Sites are $4 per night, $2 per night for an additional vehicle. Open early May to November.

Directions: From John Day drive south on U.S. 395 for 15 miles to the campground.

Contact: Malheur National Forest, Bear Valley Ranger District, P.O. Box 849, John Day, OR 97845; tel. (541) 575-3000; fax (541) 575-3001.

24 Wickiup   5

This campground is along the forks of Wickiup Creek and Canyon Creek at a historic site, with many original Civilian Conservation Corps structures still in place. There is limited fishing in the creek. To the north are many trails that are routed into the Strawberry Mountain Wilderness.

Location: On Wickiup Creek in Malheur National Forest; map D4, grid d5.

Campsites, facilities: There are eight sites for tents, trailers, or RVs up to 25 feet long. Picnic tables and fire grills are provided. Drinking water, vault toilets, and horse corrals are available, but all garbage must be packed out. Leashed pets are permitted.

Reservations, fees: No reservation; no fee. Open early May to November.

Directions: From John Day drive south on U.S. 395 for 10 miles to Forest Road 15. Turn southeast and drive eight miles to the campground.

Contact: Malheur National Forest, Bear Valley Ranger District, P.O. Box 849, John Day, OR 97845; tel. (541) 575-3000; fax (541) 575-3001.

25 Canyon Meadows   5

This campground is on the shore of Canyon Meadows Reservoir, where non-motorized boating, plus swimming, sailing, fishing, and hiking, are recreation options. However, this reservoir dries up by the fourth of July, due to a leak in the dam. There are several hiking trails nearby that lead north into the Strawberry Mountain Wilderness.

Location: On Canyon Meadows Reservoir in Malheur National Forest; map D4, grid d5.

Campsites, facilities: There are 14 sites for tents, trailers, or RVs up to 25 feet long. Picnic tables and fire grills are provided. Drinking water and vault toilets are available, but all garbage must be packed out. Leashed pets are permitted. Some facilities are wheelchair accessible.

Reservations, fees: No reservations accepted. There is no fee. Open mid-May to late October.

Directions: From John Day drive south on U.S. 395 for 10 miles to Forest Road 15. Turn left and drive nine miles southeast to Forest Road 1520. Turn left and drive five miles to the campground.

Contact: Malheur National Forest, Bear Valley Ranger District, P.O. Box 849, John Day, OR 97845; tel. (541) 575-3000; fax (541) 575-3001.

26 Parish Cabin   6

This campground along the banks of Little Bear Creek at an elevation of 4,900 feet is in a pretty spot that's not heavily used. Limited fishing is available in the creek. The road is paved all the way to the campground. This campground is popular with groups of families and hunters in season.

Location: On Little Bear Creek in Malheur National Forest; map D4, grid d6.

Campsites, facilities: There are 16 sites for tents, trailers, or RVs up to 32 feet long. Picnic tables and fire grills are provided. Drinking water, vault toilets, and horse facilities are available. One toilet is barrier-free. Leashed pets are permitted. All garbage must be packed out.

Reservations, fees: No reservations. Sites are $6 per night. Open mid-May to late November.

Directions: From John Day drive south on U.S. 395 for 10 miles to Forest Road 15. Turn left and drive 16 miles southeast to Forest Road 16. Turn right onto Forest

Road 16 and drive a short distance to the campground on the right.
Contact: Malheur National Forest, Bear Valley Ranger District, P.O. Box 849, John Day, OR 97845; tel. (541) 575-3000; fax (541) 575-3001.

27 Big Creek   6

This campground is set at an elevation of 5,100 feet along the banks of Big Creek. Nearby forest roads provide access into the Strawberry Mountain Wilderness. Fishing and mountain biking are other recreational options. In the appropriate seasons, elk, bear, coyote, and deer are hunted here.
Location: Near the Strawberry Mountain Wilderness in Malheur National Forest; map D4, grid d7.
Campsites, facilities: There are 15 sites for tents, trailers, or RVs up to 16 feet long. Picnic tables and fire grills are provided. Drinking water and vault toilets are available, but all garbage must be packed out. Leashed pets are permitted.
Reservations, fees: No reservations. Sites are $5 per night, $2.50 per night for an additional vehicle. Open mid-May to mid-November.
Directions: From John Day drive east on U.S. 26 for 13 miles to Prairie City and County Road 62. Turn right and drive 24 miles to Forest Road 16. Turn right and drive six miles to Forest Road 815. Turn right and drive one-half mile to the campground on the right.
Contact: Malheur National Forest, Prairie City Ranger District, P.O. Box 337, Prairie City, OR 97869; tel. (541) 820-3311; fax (541) 820-3838.

28 Trout Farm   6

This campground (4,900 feet elevation) is on the Upper John Day River, which provides good trout fishing with easy access for people who don't wish to travel off paved roads. A picnic shelter is available for family picnics, and a small pond at the campground has a wheelchair-accessible trail.
Location: Near Prairie City in Malheur National Forest; map D4, grid d7.
Campsites, facilities: There are six sites for tents, trailers, or RVs up to 21 feet long. Picnic tables and fire grills are provided. Drinking water and vault toilets are available, but all garbage must be packed out. Leashed pets are permitted.
Reservations, fees: No reservations. Sites are $5 per night. Open June to mid-October.
Directions: From John Day drive east on U.S. 26 for 13 miles to Prairie City and County Road 62. Turn right and drive 15 miles to the campground entrance on the right.
Contact: Malheur National Forest, Prairie City Ranger District, P.O. Box 337, Prairie City, OR 97869; tel. (541) 820-3311; fax (541) 820-3838.

29 North Fork Malheur   7

This secluded campground is set at an elevation of 4,700 feet, along the banks of the North Fork of the Malheur River, a designated Wild and Scenic River. Hiking trails and dirt roads provide additional access to the river and backcountry streams.

It's essential to obtain a U.S. Forest Service map. Good fishing, hunting, and mountain biking opportunities abound in the area.

Location: On the North Fork of the Malheur River in Malheur National Forest; map D4, grid d8.

Campsites, facilities: There are five tent or trailer sites. Picnic tables and fire grills are provided. Vault toilets are available. There is no drinking water, and all garbage must be packed out. Leashed pets are permitted.

Reservations, fees: No reservations accepted. There is no fee. Open mid-May to mid-November.

Directions: From John Day drive east on U.S. 26 for 13 miles to Prairie City and County Road 62. Turn right and drive 8.5 miles to Forest Road 13. Turn left and drive 16 miles to Forest Road 16. Turn right and drive two miles south to a fork with Forest Road 1675. Take the left fork to Forest Road 1675 and drive two miles to the camp on the right.

Contact: Malheur National Forest, Prairie City Ranger District, P.O. Box 337, Prairie City, OR 97869; tel. (541) 820-3311; fax (541) 820-3838.

30 Little Crane   5

Small, primitive, quiet, and private all describe this camp along the banks of Little Crane Creek at an elevation of 5,500 feet. The stream is good for trout fishing (only artificial bait and lures are allowed). There are also some nice hiking trails in the area, the closest one at the North Fork of the Malheur River, about 10 miles away.

Location: On Little Crane Creek in Malheur National Forest; map D4, grid d8.

Campsites, facilities: There are four tent and trailer sites. Picnic tables and fire grills are provided. Vault toilets are available. There is no drinking water, and all garbage must be packed out. Leashed pets are permitted.

Reservations, fees: No reservations accepted. There is no fee. Open June to mid-November.

Directions: From John Day drive east on U.S. 26 for 13 miles to Prairie City and County Road 62. Turn right and drive 8.5 miles to Forest Road 13. Turn left and drive 16 miles to Forest Road 16. Turn right and drive 5.5 miles south to the campground.

Contact: Malheur National Forest, Prairie City Ranger District, P.O. Box 337, Prairie City, OR 97869; tel. (541) 820-3311; fax (541) 820-3838.

31 Delintment Lake   7

Not many people know about this very pretty, forested camp set along the shore of Delintment Lake, originally a beaver pond which was gradually developed into a lake covering 57 acres. The large, blue lake is stocked with trout, providing good bank and boat fishing. The fishing dock is barrier-free. Here's a secret: rainbow trout here average 12 to 18 inches.

Location: On Delintment Lake in Ochoco National Forest; map D4, grid e0.

Campsites, facilities: There are 29 sites for tents, trailers, or RVs up to 30 feet long. Picnic tables and fire grills are provided. Drinking water, a group picnic area on the lake with tables and grills, and vault toilets are available. All garbage must be packed out. Wheelchair-accessible facilities include five sites, three toilets, and a fishing dock. Launching facilities are located in the campground. Leashed pets are permitted.

Reservations, fees: No reservations accepted. Sites are $8 per night, $3 per night for an additional vehicle. Open May through October.

Directions: From Burns drive southwest on U.S. 20 for three miles to County Road 127. Turn northwest and drive 12 miles to Forest Road 41. Turn left and continue for 26.5 miles to a junction. Turn left and drive five miles to the campground.

Contact: Ochoco National Forest, Snow Mountain Ranger District, HC 74, P.O. Box 12870, Hines, OR 97738; tel. (541) 573-4300; fax (541) 573-4398.

32 Emigrant Creek   4

You'll get peace and quiet here because this spot is usually uncrowded. One of three camps in the immediate area, it is set at an elevation of 5,200 feet on the border of Ochoco and Malheur National Forests, in a meadow near Emigrant Creek. There's good fly-fishing here in the spring and early summer. Several nearby backcountry dirt roads are good for mountain biking. See a U.S. Forest Service map for details.

Location: Near Emigrant Creek in Ochoco National Forest; map D4, grid e1.

Campsites, facilities: There are seven sites for tents, trailers, or RVs up to 30 feet long. Picnic tables and fire grills are provided, but there is no drinking water, and all garbage must be packed out. Vault toilets are available. Some facilities are wheelchair accessible. Leashed pets are permitted.

Reservations, fees: No reservations accepted. Sites are $5 per night, $3 per night for an additional vehicle. Open May through October.

Directions: From Burns drive southwest on U.S. 20 for three miles to County Road 127. Turn northwest and drive 25 miles to Forest Road 43 and the junction for Allison Guard Station, Delintment Lake and Paulina. Turn left on Forest Road 43 and drive 9.75 miles to Forest Road 4340. Turn left and drive on Forest Road 4340-050 to the campground.

Contact: Ochoco National Forest, Snow Mountain Ranger District, HC 74, P.O. Box 12870, Hines, OR 97738; tel. (541) 573-4300; fax (541) 573-4398.

33 Yellowjacket   8

This campground (elevation 4,800 feet) in the ponderosa pines, is set along the shore of Yellowjacket Lake, where fishing for rainbow trout can be very good in the summer. Boats without motors are encouraged. The camp is quiet and uncrowded.

Location: On Yellowjacket Lake in Malheur National Forest; map D4, grid e2.

Campsites, facilities: There are 20 sites for tents, trailers, or RVs up to 22 feet long. Picnic tables, drinking water, and pit or vault toilets are available, but all garbage must be packed out. A boat launch is nearby. Leashed pets are permitted.

Reservations, fees: No reservations. Sites are $6-9 per night, $3 per night for an additional vehicle. Open late May through October, weather permitting.

Directions: From Burns drive southwest on U.S. 395 for one mile to Forest Road 47. Turn northwest and drive 32 miles to Forest Road 37. Turn right and drive three miles to Forest Road 3745. Turn right and drive one mile to the campground on the right.

Contact: Malheur National Forest, Burns Ranger District, HC 74, P.O. Box 12870, Hines, OR 97738; tel. (541) 573-4300; fax (541) 573-4398.

34 Idlewild   8

This campground is set, at an elevation of 5,300 feet in Divine Canyon, a designated sno-park in the winter that's popular with locals for snowmobiling and cross-country skiing. Several hiking and biking trailheads start here, including the Divine Summit Interpretive Loop Trail and the Idlewild Loop Trail. It's also a popular spot for visitors traveling up U.S. 395 and in need of a stopover, since it provides easy access and a pretty setting. Bird-watching for white-headed woodpeckers and goshawks is popular. Expect to hear some highway noise.

Location: In Divine Canyon in Malheur National Forest; map D4, grid f5.

Campsites, facilities: There are 26 sites for tents, trailers, or RVs up to 30 feet long. Picnic tables, fire grills, and picnic areas are provided. Drinking water, a group shelter, and vault toilets are available. All garbage must be packed out. Some facilities are wheelchair accessible. Leashed pets are permitted.

Reservations, fees: No reservations. Sites are $6 per night, $3 per night for an additional vehicle. Open late May to mid-October.

Directions: From Burns drive north on U.S. 395 for 17 miles to the campground on the right.

Contact: Malheur National Forest, Burns Ranger District, HC 74, P.O. 12870, Hines, OR 97738; tel. (541) 573-4300; fax (541) 573-4398.

35 Joaquin Miller Horse Camp   5

Campsites are spread out and there's a fair amount of privacy here among mature ponderosa pine and adjacent to a meadow. Expect some highway noise. Lots of old logging roads are available for walking, biking, and horseback riding. The camp gets low use, but even though it caters to horse campers, all are welcome.

Location: In Malheur National Forest; map D4, grid f5.

Campsites, facilities: There are 18 sites for tents, trailers, or RVs up to 28 feet long. Picnic tables and fire rings are provided. Drinking water and vault toilets are available. All garbage must be packed out. Stock facilities include four corrals and hitching rails. Leashed pets are permitted.

Reservations, fees: No reservations; no fee. Open mid-May through November, weather permitting.

Directions: From Burns drive north on U.S. 395 for 19 miles to the campground on the right.

Contact: Malheur National Forest, Burns Ranger District, HC 74, P.O. 12870, Hines, OR 97738; tel. (541) 573-4300; fax (541) 573-4398.

36 Chickahominy Reservoir   4

This is a good spot for group camping, but it's in the high desert with no shade. Weather conditions can be extreme, so come prepared. The camp is used primarily as an overnight stop for travelers driving through the area. Boats with motors are allowed on the reservoir. The nearest services are eight miles east (via U.S. 20) in Riley.

Location: On Chickahominy Reservoir; map D4, grid g1.

Campsites, facilities: There are 28 sites for tents, trailers, or RVs up to 35 feet long. Picnic tables, garbage bins, and fire grills are provided. Drinking water and vault toilets are available. Some facilities are wheelchair accessible. Leashed pets are permitted.

Reservations, fees: No reservations. Sites are $6 per night per vehicle, with a stay limit of 14 days. Open April through October, weather permitting.

Directions: From Burns drive west on U.S. 20 for 30 miles to the campground on the right.

Contact: Bureau of Land Management, Burns District, HC 74-12533 Highway 20 West, Hines, OR 97738; tel. (541) 573-4400; fax (541) 573-4411; website: www.or.blm.gov.

MAP D5

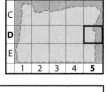

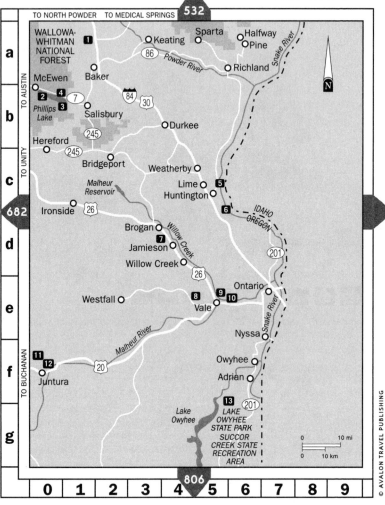

© AVALON TRAVEL PUBLISHING

CHAPTER D5

■ Mountain View Trav-L Park   6

This shaded, grassy campground is "the gateway to camping on the Oregon Trail," complete with an Oregon Trail Interpretive Center for those with a historical bent. The park is clean and cool, with spacious sites and many recreation options nearby.

Location: In Baker City; map D5, grid a2.

Campsites, facilities: There are 11 tent sites and 69 full-hookup sites for trailers or RVs of any length; most are pull-through sites. Electricity, drinking water, sewer hookups, cable TV hookups, and picnic tables are provided. Flush toilets, sanitary disposal services, showers, a laundry room, ice, a playground, a meeting room, a convenience store, and a swimming pool are available. Bottled gas and a cafe are located within one mile. Leashed pets and motorbikes are permitted.

Reservations, fees: Reservations accepted; phone (800) 806-4824. Sites are $15.05-20.19 per night. Open year-round, with limited winter facilities.

Directions: In Baker City on U.S. 84, take exit 304 to Campbell Street. Drive west on Campbell Street for 1.5 miles to 10th Street. Turn right and drive one mile north to Hughes Lane. Turn east and drive one block.

Contact: Mountain View Trav-L Park, 2845 Hughes Lane, Baker City, OR 97814; tel. (800) 806-4824, (541) 523-4824.

■ Southwest Shore
      7

This campground is set at 4,120 feet elevation along the south shore of Phillips Lake, a four-mile-long reservoir created by the Mason Dam on the Powder River. It's one of two primitive camps on the lake. The boat ramp is usable only when water is high in the reservoir. An old narrow-gauge railroad runs out of McEwen Depot. See the description of Union Creek Campground.

Location: On Phillips Lake in Wallowa-Whitman National Forest; map D5, grid b0.

Campsites, facilities: There are 18 sites for tents, trailers, or RVs up to 24 feet long. Fire grills and vault toilets are available. There is no drinking water, and all garbage must be packed out. A boat ramp is located adjacent to the campground. Pets are permitted.

Reservations, fees: No reservations accepted. There is no fee. Open from May to mid-November.

Directions: From Baker City drive southwest on Highway 7 for 24 miles (just past Phillips Lake) to Hudspeth Lane (County Road 667). Turn south on Hudspeth Lane and drive two miles to Forest Road 2220. Turn southeast and drive 2.5 miles to the campground.

Contact: Wallowa-Whitman National Forest, Baker Ranger District, 3165 10th Street, Baker City, OR 97814; tel. (541) 523-1932; fax (541) 523-1965.

3 Millers Lane   7

This small campground is situated at an elevation of 4,120 feet along the south shore of Phillips Lake, a long, narrow reservoir that's the largest in the region. Millers Lane is one of two primitive camps on the lake. An old narrow-gauge railroad runs out of McEwen Depot. See the description of Union Creek Campground.

Location: On Phillips Lake in Wallowa-Whitman National Forest; map D5, grid b1.

Campsites, facilities: There are seven sites for tents, trailers, or RVs up to 20 feet long. Picnic tables and fire grills are provided. Firewood and vault toilets are available. There is no drinking water, and all garbage must be packed out. A boat ramp is located at Southwest Shore Campground. Leashed pets are permitted.

Reservations, fees: No reservations. There is no fee. Open from May to mid-November.

Directions: From Baker City, drive southwest on Highway 7 for 24 miles (just past Phillips Lake) to Hudspeth Lane (County Road 667). Turn south on Hudspeth Lane and drive two miles to Forest Road 2220. Turn southeast and drive 3.5 miles to the campground.

Contact: Wallowa-Whitman National Forest, Baker Ranger District, 3165 10th Street, Baker City, OR 97814; tel. (541) 523-1932; fax (541) 523-1965.

4 Union Creek   8

This campground along the north shore of Phillips Lake is easy to reach, yet missed by most travelers on Interstate 84. It's the largest of three camps on the lake and the only one with drinking water. An old narrow-gauge railroad has been restored and runs up the valley from McEwen Depot (six miles from the campground) to Sumpter (10 miles from the camp). An old dredge can be seen in Sumpter.

Location: On Phillips Lake in Wallowa-Whitman National Forest; map D5, grid b1.

Campsites, facilities: There are 58 sites for tents, trailers, or RVs up to 32 feet long. Electricity, drinking water, sewer hookups, garbage bins (summer only), and picnic tables are provided. Flush toilets, a sanitary disposal station, firewood, and ice are available. There is a small concession stand for packaged goods and fishing tackle. Some facilities are wheelchair accessible. Boat docks and launching facilities are adjacent to the campground. Leashed pets are permitted.

Reservations, fees: No reservations. Sites are $10-16 per night, $12 per night for an additional vehicle. Open from mid-April to mid-September.

Directions: From Baker City drive southwest on Highway 7 for 20 miles to the campground.

Contact: Wallowa-Whitman National Forest, Baker Ranger District, 3165 10th Street, Baker City, OR 97814; tel. (541) 523-1932; fax (541) 523-1965.

5 Farewell Bend
    State Recreation Area   7

This campground offers a desert experience on the banks of the Snake River's Brownlee Reservoir. Situated along the Oregon Trail, there are historic interpretive displays and an evening interpretive program at the amphitheater. Among the amenities are horseshoe pits, basketball hoops, and a sand volleyball court.

Location: On the Snake River; map D5, grid c5.

Campsites, facilities: There are 45 primitive tent sites and 91 sites with partial hookups for trailers or RVs up to 56 feet long. There are also four tepees, two cabins, three covered camper wagons, and two group tent areas. Drinking water, garbage bins, barbecues, and picnic tables are provided. Flush toilets, sanitary disposal services, showers, and firewood are available. Boat launching facilities are nearby. Leashed pets are permitted.

Reservations, fees: Reservations accepted; phone (800) 452-5687 ($6 reservation fee). Sites are $10-16 per night, tepees or covered wagons are $27 a night, and cabins are $35 per night; there is a $7 per night fee for an additional vehicle. Major credit cards accepted. Open year-round, with limited winter facilities.

Directions: From Ontario (near the Oregon/Idaho border), drive northwest on Interstate 84 for 21 miles to the park entrance on the right side of the road.

Contact: Farewell Bend State Recreation Area, 23751 Old Highway 30, Huntington, OR 97907; tel. (800) 551-6949 or (541) 869-2365.

6 Spring   5

This campground along the banks of the Snake River Reservoir is one of two camps in or near Huntington. A more developed alternative is Farewell Bend State Recreation Area, which offers showers and all the other luxuries a camper could want. Fishing is popular at this reservoir.

Location: On the Snake River; map D5, grid c5.

Campsites, facilities: There are 35 sites for tents, trailers, or RVs. Picnic tables. garbage service, and fire grills are provided. Drinking water (summer only), sanitary disposal services, and vault toilets are available. Boat launching facilities and a fish cleaning station are on-site. Leashed pets are permitted.

Reservations, fees: No reservations accepted. Sites are $4 per night per vehicle, with a 14-day stay limit. Open from March through October and some off-season weekends.

Directions: From Ontario (near the Oregon/Idaho border), drive northwest on Interstate 84 for 28 to Huntington and Snake River Road. Turn northeast on Snake River Road and drive five miles to the campground.

Contact: Bureau of Land Management, Bakersfield Office, 3165 10th Street, Baker City, OR 97814; tel. (541) 523-1256; fax (541) 523-1285.

7 Brogan Trailer Park and Camp   5

This rural campground is on the inner edge of the West's Great Basin, a high-desert area that extends to Idaho. Nearby side trips include Willow Creek, which runs along U.S. 26, and Malheur Reservoir, northwest of Brogan.

Location: Near Willow Creek; map D5, grid d3.

Campsites, facilities: There are four tent sites and 24 drive-through sites for trailers or RVs of any length. Electricity, drinking water, sewer hookups, and picnic tables are provided. Flush toilets, showers, laundry facilities, and ice are available. Bottled gas, a store, and a cafe are located within one mile. Leashed pets are permitted.

Reservations, fees: Reservations accepted. Sites are $6-10 per night. Open from April through December.

Directions: From Ontario (near the Oregon/Idaho border), drive west on U.S. 20/26 for 12 miles to Vale and U.S. 26. Turn northwest on U.S. 26 and drive 24 miles to Brogan. Continue into town to the campground on the left (Brogan is a very small town that consists of a few stores and this park on U.S. 26).

Contact: Brogan Trailer Park and Camp, 3029 Sixth Street, Brogan, OR 97903; tel. (541) 473-3062.

8 Bully Creek Park   7

The reservoir is in a kind of high desert area, with sagebrush and poplar trees for shade. People swim, boat, water-ski, and fish in it, mostly for warm water fish like crappie and large- and smallmouth bass. You can bike on the gravel roads. It's beautiful if you like the desert, and the sunsets are worth the trip. It's primitive with deer, jackrabbits, squirrels, and many birds around. The elevation is 2,300 feet.

Location: On Bully Creek Reservoir; map D5, grid e4.

Campsites, facilities: There are 33 double sites for tents, trailers, or RVs up to 30 of any length. There are also three group sites. Electricity, picnic tables and fire pits are provided. Drinking water, flush toilets, showers, ice, garbage bins, a dump station, and a boat ramp and dock are available. A restaurant, cafe, grocery, mini-mart, gasoline, bottled gas, charcoal, and coin-operated laundry are located within ten miles. Bring your own firewood. Leashed pets are permitted.

Reservations, fees: Reservations are recommended. Call (541) 473-2969 or fax (541) 473-9462. Reservations require a $10 deposit. Sites are $10 per sleeping unit per night. Open April through mid-November, weather permitting.

Directions: From Ontario (near the Oregon/Idaho border), drive west on U.S. 20/26 for 12 miles to Vale and Graham Boulevard. Turn northwest on Graham Boulevard and drive five miles to Bully Creek Road. Turn west (left) and drive three miles to Bully Creek Park.

Contact: Bully Creek Park, 2475 Bully Creek Road, Vale, OR 97918; tel. (541) 473-2969.

9 Prospector Travel Trailer Park   5

This is one of two camps (Westerner Trailer Park is the other) for travelers in the Vale area. This one is more comfortable for tents, with a specifically designated wooded and grassy area. It claims to be a fishing and hunting paradise, and it even has a game bird cleaning room. It is set on the historical Oregon Trail.

Location: In Vale; map D5, grid e5.

Campsites, facilities: There are 10 tent sites and 28 drive-through sites for trailers or RVs of any length, plus a separate area for tents. Picnic tables are provided. Flush toilets, bottled gas, sanitary disposal services, showers, a laundry room, and ice are available. A store and a cafe are located within one mile. Leashed pets and motorbikes are permitted.

Reservations, fees: Reservations accepted. Sites are $5 per person and $16-20 per RV a night. Open year-round.

Directions: From Ontario (near the Oregon/Idaho border) drive west on U.S. 20/26 for 12 miles to Vale and U.S. 26. Turn north on U.S. 26 and drive one-half mile to Hope Street. Turn east and drive one block east to park on the left.

Contact: Prospector Travel Trailer Park, 511 North 11th Street East, Vale, OR 97918; tel. (541) 473-3879; fax (541) 473-2338.

🔟 Westerner Trailer Park   5

This campground on the banks of Willow Creek is a good layover spot for travelers heading to or from Idaho on U.S. 20. See the description of Prospector Travel Trailer Park for more information.

Location: On Willow Creek; map D5, grid e6.

Campsites, facilities: There are 10 sites for tents, trailers, or RVs of any length. Electricity, drinking water, cable TV, sewer hookups, and picnic tables are provided. Flush toilets, showers, a laundry room, and ice are available. Bottled gas, a store, a cafe, and a swimming pool are located within two blocks. Leashed pets and motorbikes are permitted.

Reservations, fees: Reservations accepted. Sites are $10 per night. Open year-round.

Directions: From Ontario (near the Oregon/Idaho border) drive west on U.S. 20/26 for 12 miles to Vale and to the junction of U.S. 26. The campground is located on the left at the junction of U.S. 20 and U.S. 26.

Contact: Westerner Trailer Park, 317 A Street East, Vale, OR 97918; tel. (541) 473-3947.

1️⃣1️⃣ Chukar Park   7

This campground is set along the banks of the North Fork of the Malheur River. The area in general provides habitat for chukar, an upland game bird species. Hunting can be good in season during the fall, but requires much hiking in rugged terrain. Trout fishing is also a popular activity here. The camp is often filled from May through October.

Location: Near the North Fork of the Malheur River; map D5, grid f0.

Campsites, facilities: There are 18 sites for tents, trailers, or RVs up to 28 feet long. Picnic tables, fire grills and garbage services are provided. Drinking water (May through October only) and vault toilets are available. Leashed pets are permitted.

Reservations, fees: No reservations. Sites are $5 per night per vehicle, with a 14-day stay limit. Open year-round, with limited winter facilities.

Directions: From Burns drive north on U.S. 395 for three miles to U.S. 20. Turn east and drive 55 miles to Juntura and Beulah Reservoir Road. Turn northwest and drive six miles to the campground.

Contact: Bureau of Land Management, Vale District, 100 Oregon Street, Vale, OR 97918-9630; tel. (541) 473-3144; fax (541) 473-6213.

12 Oasis RV Park   6

One of the only camps in the area, this well-maintained RV park is close to Chukar State Park. See the description of Chukar Park for more details.
Location: In Juntura; map D5, grid f0.
Campsites, facilities: There are 22 sites for trailers or RVs of any length; eight are drive-through. Electricity, drinking water, and sewer hookups are provided. Flush toilets, showers, a cafe, and ice are available. Leashed pets are permitted.
Reservations, fees: No reservations accepted. Sites are $12 per night. Open year-round.
Directions: From Burns, drive north on U.S. 395 for three miles to U.S. 20. Turn east and drive 55 miles to Juntura. The park is located in Juntura (a very small town) along U.S. 20.
Contact: Oasis RV Park, P.O. Box 277, Juntura, OR 97911; tel. (541) 277-3605.

13 Lake Owyhee State Park   7

This state park is set along the shore of 53-mile long Owyhee Lake, a good lake for waterskiing in the day and fishing for warm-water species in the morning and evening. Owyhee is famous for its superb bass fishing. Other highlights include views of unusual geological formations and huge rock pinnacles from the park. Bighorn sheep, pronghorn antelope, golden eagles, coyotes, mule deer, wild horses, and mountain lions live around here.
Location: On Owyhee Lake; map D5, grid f5.
Campsites, facilities: There are seven sites for tents or self-contained RVs, and 33 sites with water and electrical hookups for trailers or RVs up to 55 feet long. There are also two tepees. Drinking water, garbage bins, picnic tables and fire grills are provided. Flush toilets, a sanitary disposal station, and showers are available. Boat docks and launching facilities are available nearby. Leashed pets are permitted.
Reservations, fees: Reservations required for tepees; phone (800) 452-5687 ($6 reservation fee). Sites are $12-19 per night, tepees are $27 per night; $7 per night for an additional vehicle. Open from mid-April through October.
Directions: From Ontario (near the Oregon/Idaho border), drive south on U.S. 20/U.S. 26 for six miles to a highway junction and the Nyssa exit. Turn south and drive eight miles to Nyssa and Highway 201. Turn southeast on Highway 201 and drive eight miles to Owyhee. Turn east and drive about 20 miles to road's end and the entrance to the park.
Contact: Lake Owyhee State Park, 3012 Island Avenue, LaGrande, OR 97850; tel. (800) 551-6949.

THE DISTINCTIVE BRIDGE AT GOLD BEACH

BOB RACE

MAP E1

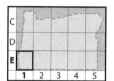

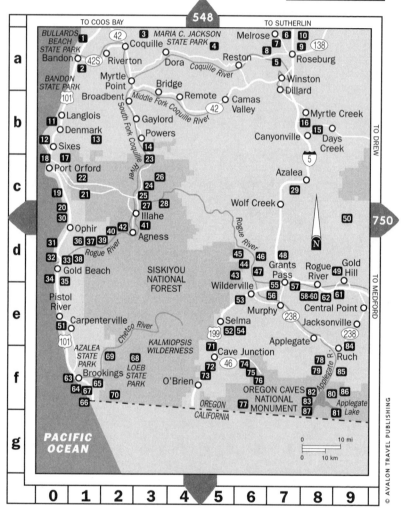

CHAPTER E1

■ Bullards Beach State Park

 7

The Coquille River is the centerpiece of this park, which has good fishing in season for both boaters and crabbers, with four miles of shore access. If fishing is not your thing, the park also has several hiking trails. The Coquille River Lighthouse is at the end of the road that wanders through the park. During the summer there are tours to the tower. Equestrians can explore the seven-mile horse trail.

Location: On the Coquille River; map E1, grid a1.

Campsites, facilities: There are 185 sites with full or partial hookups for trailers or RVs up to 64 feet long; 13 yurts are also available, one of which is wheelchair accessible. Each yurt can sleep five people. Other options include a special area for horses, as well as an area reserved for hikers and bicyclists. Drinking water, garbage bins, picnic tables, and fire grills are provided. Flush toilets, a sanitary disposal station, showers, firewood, a yurt meeting hall, and a loading ramp for horses are available. Some facilities are wheelchair accessible. Boat docks and launching facilities are located in the park on the Coquille River. Leashed pets are permitted.

Reservations, fees: Reservations accepted; phone (800) 452-5687 ($6 reservation fee). Sites are $10-19 per night; yurts are $27-30 per night; and sites for hikers/bicyclists are $4 per night; additional vehicles are $7 per night. Horse camping is $10-14 per night and $1.50 per night per horse. Major credit cards accepted. The campground is open year-round.

Directions: In Coos Bay drive south on U.S. 101 for about 22 miles to the park on the right (located two miles north of Bandon).

Contact: Bullards Beach State Park, P.O. Box 569, Bandon, OR 97411; tel. (800) 452-5687 or (541) 347-2209.

■ Bandon RV Park

 7

This in-town RV park is a good base for many adventures. Rock hounds will enjoy combing for agates and other semiprecious stones hidden along the beaches, while kids can explore the West Coast Game Park Walk-Through Safari petting zoo seven miles south of town. Bandon State Park, four miles south of town, has a nice wading spot in the creek at the north end of the park. Nearby recreation opportunities include two 18-hole golf courses, a riding stable, and tennis courts. Bullards State Beach is located about 2.5 miles north.

Location: Near Bullards State Park; map E1, grid a1.

Campsites, facilities: There are 40 sites for trailers or RVs of any length; some are drive-through sites. Electricity, drinking water, cable TV, and sewer hookups are provided. Flush toilets, sanitary services, showers, and a laundry room are available. Bottled gas and a store are located within two blocks. Boat docks and launching facilities are nearby. Leashed pets are permitted.

Reservations, fees: Reservations accepted; phone (800) 393-4122. Sites are $17-19 per night. Major credit cards accepted. Open year-round.

Directions: From Coos Bay drive south on U.S. 101 for 26 miles to Bandon and the Highway 42S junction. Continue south on U.S. 101 for one block to the park.

Contact: Bandon RV Park, 935 Second Street SE Bandon, OR 97411; tel. (541) 347-4122.

3 Laverne County Park

 9

This beautiful park is on the river with a small falls and many trees including a myrtlewood grove and old-growth Douglas fir. Mountain bikers can take an old wagon road, and golfers can enjoy any of several courses. There are a few hiking trails and a very popular swimming hole. Fishing includes salmon, steelhead, and trout, and the wildlife includes deer, elk, bear, raccoons, and cougar. Side trips include the museums at Myrtle Point and Coos Bay, local Indian items, and an old stage-coach house in Dora.

Location: in Fairview on North Fork of the Coquille River; map E1, grid a3.

Campsites, facilities: There are 76 sites for tents, trailers, or RVs of any size. There is also a large group site at West Laverne B for up to 22 people. Drinking water, electricity, picnic tables, and fire pits are provided. Rest rooms with flush toilets and showers (two barrier-free), garbage bins, dump station, playground, four cooking shelters with barbecue, a swimming hole with lifeguards, horse-shoe pits, and volleyball and baseball areas are available. Ice and a restaurant are within 1.5 miles. Propane, bottled gas, a store, and gasoline are within five miles. Leashed pets are permitted, and there is a pet area.

Reservations, fees: No reservations accepted. Call about group site information. Family sites are $9-13 per night, with an additional charge of $5 per each additional vehicle. Open year-round.

Directions: From Coos Bay drive south on U.S. 101 for six miles to the junction with Highway 42. Turn east and drive 11 miles to Coquille and West Central. Turn left and drive a half mile to Fairview McKinley Road. Turn right and drive 13 miles (past Fairview store) to Laverne Park.

Contact: Laverne County Park, Coos County, HC83 Box 3890, Coquille, OR 97423; tel. (541) 396-2344; website: www.cooscountyparks.com.

4 Park Creek 7

Want to be by yourself? You came to the right place. This pretty little campground offers peaceful, shady campsites under an old-growth canopy of Douglas fir, western hemlock, red cedar, and myrtlewood. Relax and enjoy nearby Park Creek and Middle Creeks.

Location: Near Coquille; map E1, grid a5.

Campsites, facilities: There are 15 sites for tents, small trailers, or camping vans. Picnic tables and fire grills are provided. Vault toilets are available. There is no drinking water, and all garbage must be packed out. Leashed pets are permitted.

Reservations, fees: No reservations accepted. There is no fee, but the stay limit is 14 days. Open year-round.

Directions: From Coos Bay drive south on U.S. 101 for six miles to the junction with Highway 42. Turn east and drive 11 miles to Coquille and Coquille Fairview Road. Turn east on Coquille Fairview Road and drive 7.5 miles to Fairview and Coos Bay Wagon Road. Turn right and drive four miles to Middle Creek Access Road. Turn east (left) and drive nine miles to the campground.

Contact: Bureau of Land Management, Coos Bay District, 1300 Airport Lane, North Bend, OR 97459; tel. (541) 756-0100; fax (541) 751-4303.

5 Wildlife Safari RV Park   6

This park is part of the Wildlife Safari Park in Winston (near Roseburg), which offers a walk-through petting zoo. Nearby recreation options include an 18-hole golf course, hiking trails, and marked bike trails.

Location: Near Roseburg; map E1, grid a7.

Campsites, facilities: There are 18 drive-through sites for self-contained trailers or RVs. Electricity, a gift shop, and a cafe are available. There is no drinking water. Leashed pets and motorbikes are permitted.

Reservations, fees: No reservations accepted. Sites are $11.95 per night. The campground is closed in the winter.

Directions: From Roseburg drive south on Interstate 5 for five miles to Exit 119 and Highway 42. Take Highway 42 southwest for three miles to Looking Glass Road (just before reaching Winston). Turn right and drive one block to Safari Road. Turn right and enter the park.

Contact: Wildlife Safari RV Park, P.O. Box 1600, Winston, OR 97496; tel. (541) 679-6761; fax (541) 679-9210; e-mail: maserith.com/safari.

6 John P. Amacher County Park

 6

This prime layover spot for Interstate 5 RV cruisers is in a wooded county park along the banks of the North Umpqua River, just far enough off the beaten track to be missed by most out-of-towners. An 18-hole golf course and tennis courts are close by. Riding stables are within a 20-minute drive, and Winchester Dam is within one-quarter mile.

Location: On the Umpqua River; map E1, grid a7.

Campsites, facilities: There are 10 sites for tents and 20 sites with full or partial hookups for trailers or RVs up to 30 feet long; 11 are drive-through sites. Electricity, drinking water, sewer hookups, and picnic tables are provided. Flush toilets, showers, a gazebo, and a playground are available. Bottled gas, a store, a cafe, a coin laundry, and ice are located within one mile. Boat launching facilities are available. Some facilities are wheelchair accessible. Leashed pets and motorbikes are permitted.

Reservations, fees: No reservations accepted. Sites are $11-14 per night. Open year-round, but subject to closure for renovation. phone for current status; phone (541) 440-4500.

Directions: From Roseburg drive five miles north on Interstate 5 to Exit 129. Take that exit and drive south on Old Highway 99 for one-quarter mile to the park on the right (just across Winchester Bridge).

Contact: tel. (541) 672-4901; fax (541) 440-6248, P.O. Box 800, Winchester, OR 97495.

7 Twin Rivers Vacation Park

      6

This wooded campground near the Umpqua River is the only camp in Roseburg with tent as well as RV sites. There are large shaded pull-through sites and over 100 different kinds of trees on the property. Nearby recreation options include a golf course, a county park, and bike paths.

Location: Near the Umpqua River; map E1, grid a7.

Campsites, facilities: There are 5 tent sites and 72 sites for trailers or RVs of any length; 35 are drive-through with full hookups. Electricity, drinking water, cable TV, sewer hookups, and picnic tables are provided. Flush toilets, bottled gas, showers, firewood, a store, a laundry room, ice, and a playground are available. Boat launching facilities are nearby. Leashed pets and motorbikes are permitted.

Reservations, fees: Reservations accepted. Sites are $15-28 per night. The campground is open year-round.

Directions: In Roseburg on Interstate 5, take Exit 125. Take that exit to Garden Valley Road and drive west for five miles (over the river) to Old Garden Valley Road. Turn left and drive 1.5 mile to River Forks Road. Turn left and drive to the entrance to the park.

Contact: tel. (541) 673-3811 433 River Forks Park, Roseburg, OR 97470.

8 Douglas County Fairgrounds RV Park

       8

This county park is very easily accessible off the highway, and covers 74 acres. It is also is near the Umpqua River, one of Oregon's prettiest rivers. There is often good fishing in season. A golf course, bike paths, and tennis courts are nearby. Horse stalls and a boat ramp are available at the nearby fairgrounds. The campground fills up the third weekend in March during the annual fiddler's convention.

Location: On the South Umpqua River; map E1, grid a6.

Campsites, facilities: There are 50 sites for tents, trailers, or RVs of any length with partial hookups. Tent camping is limited to two nights. Electricity, drinking water, and picnic tables are provided. Flush toilets, sanitary services, showers, and a dump station are available. A store, a cafe, a coin-operated laundry, and ice are located within one mile. Some facilities are wheelchair accessible. Leashed pets are permitted.

Reservations, fees: No reservations accepted. Sites are $15 per night, with a 14-day stay limit, $1 per night for an additional tent. Open year-round, except one

week in August during the county fair. phone ahead to confirm current status.
Directions: From Interstate 5 in Roseburg, take Exit 123 and drive south under the freeway to Fair Street. Turn right and enter the park.
Contact: tel. (541) 957-7010; fax (541) 440-6023, 2110 Southwest Frear Street, Roseburg, OR 97470.

9 Alameda Avenue Trailer Park 3

Alameda Avenue Trailer Park, one of four parks in Roseburg, is near the Umpqua River and located within walking distance to grocery stores and restaurants. A golf course, bike paths, and tennis courts are among the recreation possibilities in the area.
Location: Near the Umpqua River; map E1, grid a7.
Campsites, facilities: There are 35 sites for trailers or RVs up to 30 feet long. Electricity, drinking water, and sewer hookups are provided. Flush toilets, sanitary services, showers, and a laundry room are available. Bottled gas, a store, a cafe, and ice are located within one mile. Leashed pets are permitted.
Reservations, fees: Reservations accepted. Sites are $15 per night. The campground is open year-round.
Directions: In Roseburg on Interstate 5, take the Garden Valley exit. Drive east on Garden Valley Road to Business Route 99. Turn north and drive one-quarter mile north to Northeast Alameda Avenue. The park is on the left.
Contact: tel. (541) 672-2348 581 N.E. Alameda Avenue #36 Roseburg, OR 97470.

10 Mount Nebo Trailer Park   5

This is an option for RVers stopping in Roseburg. The park is near the Umpqua River and close to a golf course, bike paths, and tennis courts.
Location: Near the Umpqua River; map E1, grid a7.
Campsites, facilities: There are 26 sites for trailers or RVs up to 45 feet long; four are drive-through sites. Electricity, drinking water, and sewer hookups are provided. Flush toilets, sanitary services, showers, and a laundry room are available. Bottled gas, a store, and a cafe are within one mile. Leashed pets are permitted.
Reservations, fees: Reservations accepted. Sites are $17 per night. The campground is open year-round.
Directions: From Roseburg on Interstate 5, take Exit 125 to Garden Valley Road. Drive east on Garden Valley Road for three-quarters mile to Stephens Street. Turn left and drive less than a mile to the park on the right.
Contact: tel. (541) 673-4108 2071 N.E. Stephens Street, Roseburg, OR 97470.

11 KOA Bandon-Port Orford   7

This spot is considered to be just a layover camp, but it offers large, secluded sites nestled among big trees and coastal ferns. A pool and spa will be opening in summer 2000. The Elk and Sixes Rivers, where the fishing can be good, are minutes away, and Cape Blanco State Park is just a few miles down the road.
Location: Near the Elk River; map E1, grid b0.

Campsites, facilities: There are 46 tent sites and 26 drive-through sites for trailers or RVs of any length. Cabins are also available. Picnic tables are provided. Flush toilets, bottled gas, sanitary services, showers, firewood, a recreation hall, a store, a laundry room, ice, a playground, electricity, drinking water, and sewer hookups are available. Pets and motorbikes are permitted.

Reservations, fees: Reservations accepted. Sites are $18-25 per night; cabins are $36 per night. The park is open year-round.

Directions: From Coos Bay drive south on U.S. 101 for 50 miles to the campground at milepost 286 near Langlois, on the west side of highway.

Contact: tel. (541) 348-2358 46612 Highway 101, Langlois, OR 97450.

12 Cape Blanco State Park

       8

This large park is named for the white ("blanco") chalk appearance of the sea cliffs, which rise 200 feet above the ocean. Sea lions inhabit the offshore rocks, and trails and a road lead to the black sand beach below the cliffs. Another highlight is the good access to the Sixes River, which runs for more than two miles through the meadows and forests of the park. Trails for horseback riding are also available and there are more than eight miles of trails with many spectacular ocean vistas, woodland and wetland settings. Lighthouse and historic Hughes House tours are nearby.

Location: Between the Sixes and Elk Rivers; map E1, grid b0.

Campsites, facilities: There are 54 sites with water and electrical hookups for tents, trailers, or RVs up to 65 feet long. Other options are a special camp for horses, a camping area reserved for hikers and bicyclists, four cabins and one primitive group site that can accommodate 25 people. Garbage bins, Picnic tables, drinking water, electrical hookups, and fire grills are provided. Firewood, flush toilets, showers, and a sanitary disposal station are available. Some facilities are wheelchair accessible. Leashed pets are permitted.

Reservations, fees: Reservations accepted; phone (800) 452-5687 ($6 reservation fee). Sites are $7-18 per night; cabins are $35 per night; and sites for hikers/bicyclists are $4 per night. $7 per night for all additional vehicles. Horse camping is $11 per night, plus $1.50 per horse per night. Major credit cards accepted. The campground is open year-round.

Directions: From Coos Bay, turn south on U.S. 101 and drive approximately 46 miles (south of Sixes; nine miles north of Port Orford) to Cape Blanco Road. Turn right (northwest) and drive five miles to the campground on the left.

Contact: Humbug Mountain State Park, P.O. Box 1345, Port Orford, OR 97465; tel. (541) 332-6774.

13 Sixes River   6

Set along the banks of the Sixes River at an elevation of 4,303 feet, this site is a favorite of miners, fishermen, and nature lovers. There are opportunities to pan or sluice for gold year-round or through a special limited permit. Dredging is permitted from July 15 through September. The camp roads are paved.

Location: On the Sixes River; map E1, grid b1.

Campsites, facilities: There are 11 sites for tents, trailers, or RVs up to 30 feet long. Picnic tables, garbage service, and fire grills are provided. Vault toilets are available. There is no drinking water. Leashed pets are permitted.

Reservations, fees: No reservations accepted. Sites are $5 per night, plus $3 for each additional vehicle, with a 14-day stay limit. Open year-round.

Directions: From Coos Bay drive south on U.S. 101 for 40 miles to Sixes and Sixes River Road. Turn left (east) on Sixes River Road and drive 13.5 miles to the campground. The last half mile is an unpaved road.

Contact: Bureau of Land Management, Coos Bay District, 1300 Airport Lane, North Bend, OR 97459; tel. (541) 756-0100; fax (541) 751-4303.

14 Powers County Park

        9

This private and secluded public park in a wooded, mountainous area is a great stop for travelers going between Interstate 5 and the coast. A small lake at the park provides a spot for visitors to boat, swim, and fish for trout. Only non-motorized boats allowed. On display at the park are an old steam donkey and a hand-carved totem pole. This park is reputed to have the biggest cedar tree in Oregon.

Location: Near the South Fork of the Coquille River; map E1, grid b3.

Campsites, facilities: There are 40 sites for tents, trailers, or RVs. Drinking water, rest rooms, showers, a sanitary dump, and a public phone are provided. Other facilities include a boat ramp, horseshoes, a playground, three large picnic shelters, tennis courts, and a recreation field. Supplies are available within one mile. Some facilities are wheelchair accessible. Leashed pets are permitted.

Reservations, fees: No reservations for sites. Picnic shelters may be reserved by phoning (541) 396-3121. Sites are $9-13 per night. Open year-round.

Directions: From Coos Bay drive south on U.S. 101 for six miles to the junction with Highway 42. Turn east and drive 20 miles to Myrtle Point. Continue on Highway 42 to the Powers Highway exit. Turn southwest (right) and drive 19 miles to the park on the right.

Contact: Coos County Parks, Coos County Courthouse, 250 North Baxter Street, Coquille, OR 97423; tel. (541) 439-2791.

15 Charles V. Stanton Park   7

This campground set along the banks of the South Umpqua River is an all-season spot with a nice beach for swimming in the summer, good steelhead fishing in the winter, and wild grape picking in the fall.

Location: On the South Umpqua River; map E1, grid b8.

Campsites, facilities: There are 20 tent sites and 20 sites for trailers or RVs up to 30 feet long. Electricity, sewer hookups, and picnic tables are provided. Drinking water, flush toilets, showers, a dump station, a pavilion, and a playground are available. Bottled gas, a store, a cafe, a coin laundry, and ice are located within one mile. Leashed pets and motorbikes are permitted.

Reservations, fees: No reservations accepted for sites. For pavilion reservations, phone (541) 440-4500. Sites are $11-14 per night. Open year-round.

Directions: Note: Depending on your heading on Interstate 5, there are two routes to reach this campground. In Canyonville northbound on Interstate 5, take Exit 99 and drive one mile north on the frontage road to the campground on the right. Otherwise: In Canyonville southbound on Interstate 5, take Exit 101 and drive one mile south on the frontage road to the campground on the left.

Contact: Charles V. Stanton Park, 1540 Stanton Park Road, Canyonville, OR 97417; tel. (541) 839-4483.

16 Surprise Valley RV Park   7

This RV park is near the South Umpqua River about two miles from a gambling casino. If you desire a more remote setting, the following sites are the answer: Dumont Creek, Boulder Creek, and Camp Comfort (in Chapter E2). This is a nice park with new rest rooms, gravel on the roads, and grass at all sites.

Location: On the South Umpqua River; map E1, grid b8.

Campsites, facilities: There are 15 tent sites and four drive-through sites for trailers or RVs of any length. Electricity, drinking water, sewer hookups, and picnic tables are provided. Flush toilets, showers, and a laundry room are available. Leashed pets are permitted.

Reservations, fees: No reservations accepted. Sites are $10-15 per night. The campground is open year-round.

Directions: In Canyonville drive north on Interstate 5 for three miles to Exit 102. Take that exit and drive east on Gazley Road for one miles to the campground.

Contact: Surprise Valley RV Park, P.O. Box 909, Canyonville, OR 97417; tel. (541) 839-6634.

17 Elk River Campground   7

This quiet and restful camp is an excellent base for fall and winter fishing on the Elk River, which is known for its premier salmon fishing. A one-mile private access road goes to the river, so guests get their own personal fishing hole.

Location: Near the Elk River; map E1, grid c0.

Campsites, facilities: There are 50 sites for tents, trailers, or RVs up to 40 feet long, all with full hookups. Drinking water, rest rooms, showers, a sanitary dump, a public phone, picnic tables, cable TV, and a laundry room are available. Recreational facilities include a sports field, horseshoes, a recreation hall, and a boat ramp. Some facilities are wheelchair accessible. Leashed pets are permitted.

Reservations, fees: Reservations recommended. Sites are $14 per night. Weekly and monthly rates are available. Open year-round.

Directions: From Port Orford drive north on U.S. 101 for 1.5 miles to Elk River Road (milepost 297). Turn right (east) on Elk River Road and drive 1.8 miles to the campground on the left.

Contact: Elk River Campground, 93363 Elk River Road, Port Orford, OR 97465; tel. (541) 332-2255; fax (541) 332-6033.

18 Port Orford Trailer Village

 5

The hosts make you feel at home at this friendly mom-and-pop campground in Port Orford. An informal group campfire and happy hour is scheduled each evening. Other nice touches include a small gazebo where you can get coffee each morning and a patio where you can sit. Fishing is good during the fall and winter on the nearby Elk and Sixes Rivers, and the campground has a smokehouse, a freezer, and a cleaning table.

Location: Near the Elk and Sixes Rivers; map E1, grid c0.

Campsites, facilities: There are seven tent sites and 49 sites for trailers or RVs of any length; two are drive-through sites. Electricity, drinking water, sewer hookups, and picnic tables are provided. Flush toilets, bottled gas, sanitary services, showers, a recreation hall and a laundry room are available. Boat docks and launching facilities are nearby. Lake, river and ocean are all within 1.5 miles. Pets and motorbikes are permitted.

Reservations, fees: Reservations accepted. Sites are $17 per night. The campground is open year-round.

Directions: In Port Orford on U.S. 101, drive to Madrona Avenue. Turn east and drive one block to Port Orford Loop. Turn north and drive one-half mile to the camp on the left side.

Contact: Port Orford Trailer Village, P.O. Box 697, Port Orford, OR 97465; tel. (541) 332-1041.

19 Humbug Mountain State Park   7

The park and campground are dominated by Humbug Mountain (1,756 elevation) and surrounded by forested hills. The campground enjoys some of the warmest weather on the Oregon coast. Windsurfing and scuba diving are popular, as is hiking the three-mile trail to Humbug Peak. Both ocean and freshwater fishing are accessible nearby.

Location: Near the Pacific Ocean; map E1, grid c0.

Campsites, facilities: There are 78 tent sites and 30 sites with full hookups for trailers or RVs up to 55 feet long. A special camping area is provided for hikers and bicyclists. Fire grills and picnic tables, garbage bins and drinking water are provided. Flush toilets, showers, and firewood are available. Leashed pets are permitted.

Reservations, fees: No reservations. Sites are $11-18 per night; $7 per night for all additional vehicles. The camping area for hikers/bicyclists is $4 per night. The campground is open year-round.

Directions: From Port Orford drive south on U.S. 101 for six miles to the park entrance on the left.

Contact: Humbug Mountain State Park, P.O. Box 1345, Port Orford, OR 97465; tel. (541) 332-6774.

20 Arizona Beach Campground

 6

This pleasant campground offers grassy, tree-lined sites along half a mile of ocean beach frontage. A creek runs through the campground, and you can swim at the mouth of it in the summer. Elk and deer roam nearby. An 11-unit motel is available for campers who need some cleanup time.

Location: Near Gold Beach; map E1, grid c0.

Campsites, facilities: There are 48 tent sites and 78 sites for trailers or RVs of any length; seven are drive-through sites. There is also a motel on the grounds. Electricity, drinking water, sewer hookups, and picnic tables are provided. Flush toilets, bottled gas, sanitary services, showers, firewood, a store, a laundry room, and a playground are available. Leashed pets and motorbikes are permitted.

Reservations, fees: Reservations accepted. Sites are $14-22 per night, and the motel is $39-99 per night. The campground is open year-round.

Directions: From Gold Beach drive north on U.S. 101 for 14 miles to the campground on the right.

Contact: Arizona Beach Campground, 36939 Highway 101, Gold Beach, OR 97444; tel. (541) 332-6491.

21 Laird Lake 8

This secluded campground is set at 1,600 feet elevation, along the shore of pretty Laird Lake (six feet at its deepest point) in a very private and scenic spot. Some old-growth cedar logs are in the lake. Most campers have no idea such a place exists in the area. This can be just what you're looking for if you're tired of fighting the crowds for the more developed camps along U.S. 101.

Location: On Laird Lake in Siskiyou National Forest; map E1, grid c1.

Campsites, facilities: There are undeveloped, dispersed tent sites, with no designated spaces. There is no drinking water, and all garbage must be packed out. Leashed pets are permitted.

Reservations, fees: No reservations; no fee. Open year-round.

Directions: From Port Orford drive north on U.S. 101 for three miles to County Road 208. Turn right and drive 7.5 miles southeast to Forest Road 5325. Turn southeast and drive 15.5 miles to the campground. The road is paved for 11 miles and rock surfaced for the last 4.5 miles to the campground.

Contact: Siskiyou National Forest, Powers Ranger District, Powers, OR 97466; tel. (541) 439-3011; fax (541) 439-7704.

22 Butler Bar 6

This campground at an elevation of 800 feet is set back from the shore of the Elk River and surrounded by old-growth, hardwood forest, with some reforested areas nearby. Across the river is the Grassy Knob Wilderness, but it has no trails and is generally too rugged to hike. For fishing enthusiasts, the Elk River has native trout and steelhead in the winter.

Location: On the Elk River in Siskiyou National Forest; map E1, grid c1.

Campsites, facilities: There are nine sites for tents, trailers, or RVs up to 16 feet long. Picnic tables and fire grills are provided. Drinking water and pit toilets are available, but all garbage must be packed out. Leashed pets are permitted.

Reservations, fees: No reservations; no fee. Open year-round.

Directions: From Port Orford drive north on U.S. 101 for three miles to County Road 208. Turn right and drive 7.5 miles southeast to Forest Road 5325. Turn southeast and drive 11 miles to the campground. The road is paved.

Contact: Siskiyou National Forest, Powers Ranger District, Powers, OR 97466; tel. (541) 439-3011; fax (541) 439-7704.

23 Myrtle Grove   6

   This U.S. Forest Service campground is located along the South Fork of the Coquille River, a little downstream from Daphne Grove Campground, at an elevation of 500 feet. No fishing is allowed. Campsites are set under a canopy of big leaf maple and Douglas fir, in a narrow, steep canyon. The Big Tree Recreation Site, home to a huge Port Orford cedar, is a few miles away. A prime hike can be made on the trail that runs adjacent to Elk Creek. (The road to Big Tree may be closed due to slides, so be sure to check with the ranger district in advance.)

Location: On the South Fork of the Coquille River in Siskiyou National Forest; map E1, grid c3.

Campsites, facilities: There are five tent sites. Picnic tables and fire grills are provided. Pit toilets are available. There is no drinking water, and all garbage must be packed out. Leashed pets are permitted.

Reservations, fees: No reservations; no fee. Open year-round.

Directions: From Coos Bay drive south on U.S. 101 for six miles to the junction with Highway 42. Turn east and drive 20 miles to Myrtle Point. Continue on Highway 42 to Powers Highway (Highway 242). Turn southwest (right) and drive 18 miles to Powers and County Road 90. Turn south and drive 4.3 miles to Forest Road 33. Turn south to the camp. The road is paved all the way to the camp.

Contact: Siskiyou National Forest, Powers Ranger District, Powers, OR 97466; tel. (541) 439-3011; fax (541) 439-7704.

24 Daphne Grove   7

   This prime spot (at 1,000 feet of elevation) along the South Fork of the Coquille River, surrounded by old-growth Douglas fir, cedar, and maple, is far enough out of the way to attract little attention. No fishing is allowed. The road is paved all the way to, as well as in, the campground, a plus for RVs and "city cars."

Location: On the South Fork of the Coquille River in Siskiyou National Forest; map E1, grid c3.

Campsites, facilities: There are 15 sites for tents, trailers, or RVs up to 35 feet long. There is one group site that can accommodate up to 25 people. Picnic tables, garbage bins, and fire grills are provided. Vault toilets and drinking water are available. Some facilities are wheelchair accessible. Leashed pets are permitted.

Reservations, fees: No reservations accepted. Sites are $6 per night from late May to late September and free the rest of the year. Phone the Powers Ranger District for current group rates. Open year-round, with limited winter facilities.

Directions: From Coos Bay drive south on U.S. 101 for six miles to the junction with Highway 42. Turn east and drive 20 miles to Myrtle Point. Continue on Highway 42 to Powers Highway (Highway 242). Turn southwest (right) and drive 18 miles to Powers and County Road 90. Turn south and drive 4.3 miles to Forest Road 33. Turn south and drive 10.5 miles to the campground entrance.

Contact: Siskiyou National Forest, Powers Ranger District, Powers, OR 97466; tel. (541) 439-3011; fax (541) 439-7704.

25 Rock Creek   6

This little-known camp (elevation 1,400 feet) in a tree-shaded canyon is surrounded by old-growth forest and some reforested areas. It is set near Rock Creek, just upstream from its confluence with the South Fork of the Coquille River. No fishing is allowed. A good side trip here is the one-mile climb to Azalea Lake, which is stocked with trout. There are some hike-in campsites at the lake, but they have no piped drinking water. In July the azaleas are spectacular.

Location: Near the South Fork of the Coquille River in Siskiyou National Forest; map E1, grid c3.

Campsites, facilities: There are seven sites for tents, trailers, or RVs. Picnic tables, drinking water, and fire grills are provided; all garbage must be packed out. Vault toilets and firewood are available. Leashed pets are permitted.

Reservations, fees: No reservations accepted. Sites are $5 per night from late May to late September and free the rest of the year. Open year-round, with limited winter facilities.

Directions: From Coos Bay drive south on U.S. 101 for six miles to the junction with Highway 42. Turn east and drive 20 miles to Myrtle Point. Continue on Highway 42 to Powers Highway (Highway 242). Turn southwest (right) and drive 18 miles to Powers and County Road 90. Turn south and drive 4.3 miles to Forest Road 33. Turn south and drive for 13 miles to Forest Road 3347. Turn southwest and drive 1.5 miles to the campground. The road is paved all the way.

Contact: Siskiyou National Forest, Powers Ranger District, Powers, OR 97466; tel. (541) 439-3011; fax (541) 439-7704.

26 Squaw Lake   8

This campground (at 2,200 feet elevation) along the shore of one-acre Squaw Lake is set in rich, old-growth forest. Squaw is more of a pond than a lake, but it is stocked with trout in the spring. Get there early; the fish are generally gone by mid-summer. The trailheads for the Panther Ridge Trail and Coquille River Falls Trail are a 10-minute drive from the campground. It's strongly advised that you obtain a U.S. Forest Service map detailing the backcountry roads and trails.

Location: On Squaw Lake in Siskiyou National Forest; map E1, grid c3.

Campsites, facilities: There are seven partially developed sites for tents, trailers, or RVs up to 21 feet. Pit toilets are available. There is no drinking water, and all garbage must be packed out. Leashed pets are permitted.

Reservations, fees: No reservations; no fee. Open year-round.

Directions: From Coos Bay drive south on U.S. 101 for six miles to the junction with Highway 42. Turn east and drive 20 miles to Myrtle Point. Continue on Highway 42 to Powers Highway (Highway 242). Turn southwest (right) and drive 18 miles to Powers and County Road 90. Turn south and drive 4.3 miles to Forest Road 33. Turn south and drive 12.5 miles to Forest Road 3348. Turn southeast and drive 4.5 miles to Forest Road 3342. Turn east and drive one mile to the campground. The road is paved for all but the last half mile.

Contact: Siskiyou National Forest, Powers Ranger District, Powers, OR 97466; tel. (541) 439-3011; fax (541) 439-7704.

27 Illahe   7

This quiet and isolated camping area has great hiking opportunities, beginning at the nearby Upper Rogue River Trail. Boating and fishing are just a mile away at Foster Bar Campground. It's a pretty spot with privacy between sites and hidden from the majority of tourists. Deer are in abundance here.

Location: On the Rogue River in Siskiyou National Forest; map E1, grid c3.

Campsites, facilities: There are 14 sites for tents, trailers, or RVs up to 21 feet long. Drinking water, fire rings, garbage bins, and picnic tables are provided. Flush toilets are available. A store is located within five miles. Boat docks are nearby. Leashed pets are permitted.

Reservations, fees: No reservations accepted. Sites are $5 per night, plus $3 for each additional vehicle. Open mid-May to mid-October.

Directions: From Gold Beach on U.S. 101, turn east on County Road 595. Drive east for 35 miles (it becomes Forest Road 33) to a junction for Illahe, Illahe Campground, and Foster Bar. Turn right on County Road 375 and drive five miles to the campground.

Contact: Siskiyou National Forest, Gold Beach Ranger District, 29279 Ellensburg Avenue, Gold Beach, OR 97444; tel. (541) 247-3600; fax (541) 247-3617.

28 Tucker Flat   7

Located above the clear waters of Mule Creek, this campground borders the Wild Rogue Wilderness. Mosquitoes can be a problem, and bears occasionally wander through. The historic Rogue River Ranch is just one-quarter mile away, and the museum and other buildings are open during the summer. This campground can also be reached by hiking the Rogue River Trail or by floating the Rogue River and hiking up past the Rogue River Ranch.

Location: On the Rogue River; map E1, grid c4.

Campsites, facilities: There are eight primitive tent sites. Picnic tables and fire grills are provided. Vault toilets and bear-proof trash cans are available. There is no drinking water, and all garbage must be packed out. Leashed pets are permitted.

Reservations, fees: No reservations; no fee. Open May to late October, weather permitting.

Directions: From Grants Pass drive one mile north on Interstate 5 to Exit 61. Take that exit and drive west on Merlin-Galice Access Road for 20 miles to the Grave Creek Bridge (the second bridge over the Rogue River). Cross the bridge and drive short distance to BLM Road 34-8-1. Turn left and drive 16 miles to BLM Road 32-8-31. Turn left and drive seven miles to BLM Road 32-9-14.2. Turn left and drive 15 miles to the campground (located around the bend from the Rogue River Ranch).

Contact: Bureau of Land Management, Medford District, 3040 Biddle Road, Medford, OR 97504; tel. (541) 770-2200; fax (541) 770-2400.

Meadow Wood RV Resort and Camp

      6

This is a good option for RVers looking for a camping spot along Interstate 5. There are 80 wooded acres. All the amenities are available. Nearby attractions include an old ghost town, gold panning, and Wolf Creek Tavern.

Location: In Glendale; map E1, grid c7.

Campsites, facilities: There are 25 tent sites and 34 drive-through sites for trailers or RVs of any length; 23 sites have full hookups. Electricity, drinking water, and picnic tables are provided. Flush toilets, bottled gas, sanitary disposal services, showers, firewood, a store, a laundry room, ice, a playground, and a heated swimming pool are available. Leashed pets are permitted.

Reservations, fees: Reservations accepted. Sites are $12-20 per night. The campground is open year-round.

Directions: Note: Depending on your heading on Interstate 5, there are two routes to reach this campground. From Roseburg drive south on Interstate 5 to Exit 86 (near Glendale). Take that exit and drive south on the frontage road for three miles to Barton Road. Turn east and drive a quarter mile to Autumn Lane. Turn south on Autumn Lane and drive three-quarters of a mile to the park. From Grants Pass drive north on Interstate 5 to Exit 83 (near Glendale) and drive east for a quarter mile to Autumn Lane. Turn south on Autumn Lane and drive three-quarters of a mile to the camp.

Contact: Meadow Wood RV Resort and Camp, 869 Autumn Lane, Glendale, OR 97442; tel. (800) 606-1279, (541) 832-3114; fax (541) 832-2454.

Honeybear Campground

      10

This campground offers wooded sites with ocean views. The owners have built a huge, authentic chalet that contains a German deli, a recreation area, and a big dance floor. On summer nights they hold dances with live music.

Location: Near Gold Beach; map E1, grid d0.

Campsites, facilities: There are 20 tent sites and 65 sites for trailers or RVs of any length; 30 are drive-through sites with partial hookups, 15 with patios. Picnic tables are provided. Flush toilets, electricity, drinking water, cable TV, sanitary services, showers, firewood, a recreation hall, a restaurant, a store, a laundry room, ice, and a playground are available. Leashed pets and motorbikes are permitted.

Reservations, fees: Reservations accepted. Sites are $14.95-22.95 per night. The campground is open year-round, weather permitting.

Directions: From Gold Beach drive north on U.S. 101 for nine miles to Ophir Road near milepost 321. Turn north and drive two miles to the campground on the right side of the road.

Contact: Honeybear Campground, P.O. Box 97, Ophir, OR 97464; tel. (541) 247-2765, (800) 822-4444.

31 Nesika Beach Trailer Park   7

This campground next to Nesika Beach is a good layover spot for U.S. 101 cruisers. An 18-hole golf course is close by.

Location: Near Gold Beach; map E1, grid d0.

Campsites, facilities: There are six tent sites and 32 sites for trailers or RVs of any length. Electricity, drinking water, cable TV, sewer hookups, and picnic tables are provided. Flush toilets, sanitary services, showers, a store, a laundry room, and ice are available. Pets and motorbikes are permitted.

Reservations, fees: Reservations accepted. Sites are $12-15 per night. The campground is open year-round.

Directions: From Gold Beach drive north on U.S. 101 for six miles to Nesika Road. Turn left and drive one-half mile west to the campground on the right.

Contact: Nesika Beach Trailer Park, 32887 Nesika Road, Gold Beach, OR 97444; tel. (541) 247-6077.

32 Ireland's Ocean View RV Park   8

One of the newest RV parks in the area, this spot is on the beach in the quaint little town of Gold Beach, only one mile from the famous Rogue River. This park is very clean with blacktop roads and grass beside each site. Recreation options include beachcombing, fishing, and boating. Great ocean views are possible from the observatory/lighthouse.

Location: On the Pacific Ocean; map E1, grid d0.

Campsites, facilities: There are 32 sites for trailers or RVs up to 40 feet. Tent camping is permitted only in combination with an RV. Cable TV, phones, showers, rest rooms, a laundry room, a recreation room, horseshoe pits, and picnic areas are available. Leashed pets are permitted.

Reservations, fees: Reservations recommended. Sites are $14-20 per night. The campground is open year-round.

Directions: In Gold Beach drive on U.S. 101 and look for the camp across from the U.S. Forest Service office on U.S. 101 (Ellensburg Avenue).

Contact: Ireland's Ocean View RV Park, 29272 Ellensburg Avenue, P.O. Box 727, Gold Beach, OR 97444; tel. (541) 247-0148.

33 Indian Creek Recreation Park   7

This campground is along the Rogue River on the outskirts of the town of Gold Beach. Nearby recreation options include a riding stable, riding trails, and boat trips on the Rogue.

Location: On the Rogue River; map E1, grid d0.

Campsites, facilities: There are 25 tent sites and 100 sites for trailers or RVs of any length. Electricity, drinking water, sewer and cable TV hookups, and picnic tables are provided. Flush toilets, showers, firewood, a recreation hall, a store, a sauna, a cafe, a laundry room, ice, and a playground are available. Bottled gas is located within two miles. Boat docks, launching facilities, and rentals are nearby. Leashed pets and motorbikes are permitted.

Reservations, fees: Reservations accepted. Sites are $15-22 per night. The campground is open year-round.

Directions: In the town of Gold Beach, drive on U.S. 101 to Jerry's Flat Road. Turn east and drive one-half mile to the campground.

Contact: Indian Creek Recreation Park, 94680 Jerry's Flat Road, Gold Beach, OR 97444; tel. (541) 247-7704.

34 Oceanside RV Park   5

Set 100 yards from the ocean, this park is close to beachcombing terrain, marked bike trails, and boating facilities. The park is also adjacent to the mouth of the Rogue River, in the Port of Gold Beach.

Location: On the Pacific Ocean; map E1, grid d0.

Campsites, facilities: There are 90 sites for trailers or RVs of any length; 20 are drive-through sites. Electricity, drinking water, sewer hookups, and picnic tables are provided. Flush toilets, showers, a coin-operated laundry, cable TV, a small store, and ice are available. Bottled gas, sanitary services, a store, and a cafe are located within two miles. Boat docks, launching facilities, and rentals are nearby. Leashed pets and motorbikes are permitted.

Reservations, fees: Reservations recommended in the summer. Sites are $10-15 for camping per night, $13-20 for partial hookups, and $15-22 for full hookups. The campground is open year-round.

Directions: In Gold Beach on U.S. 101, drive to Moore Street. Turn west and drive to Airport Way. Turn right and drive to South Jetty Road. Turn left and look for the park on left.

Contact: Oceanside RV Park, tel. P.O. Box 1107, Gold Beach, OR 97444; tel. (541) 247-2301.

35 Hunter Creek RV Park

       7

This camp set amid wooded mountains on a small stream in the town of Gold Beach is preferred by tent campers over the other camps in town since it's a bit more private and secluded. For anglers, steelhead fishing can be excellent from January through March.

Location: On Hunter Creek; map E1, grid d0.

Campsites, facilities: There are 60 sites for tents, trailers, or RVs. Rest rooms, showers, drinking water, a public phone, a laundry room, limited groceries, RV supplies, LP gas, a playground, and a game room are available.

Reservations, fees: Reservations recommended. Sites are $13-16 per night. The campground is open year-round.

Directions: In Gold Beach drive on U.S. 101 to the southern end of town to Hunter Creek Road. Turn east and drive three-quarters of a mile to the campground on the left side of the road.

Contact: Hunter Creek RV Park, P.O. Box 1227, 28555 Hunter Creek Loop, Gold Beach, OR 97444; tel. (541) 247-2322; fax (541) 247-0578.

36 Kimball Creek Bend   6

This campground on the scenic Rogue River is just far enough from the coast to provide quiet and its own distinct character. Nearby recreation options include an 18-hole golf course, hiking trails, and boating facilities.

Location: On the Rogue River; map E1, grid d1.

Campsites, facilities: There are 13 tent sites and 56 sites for trailers or RVs of any length; 18 are drive-through sites. Electricity, drinking water, sewer hookups, and picnic tables are provided. Flush toilets, bottled gas, sanitary services, showers, a recreation hall, a store, a laundry room, ice, and a playground are available. Boat docks and launching facilities are nearby. Leashed pets are permitted.

Reservations, fees: Reservations accepted; phone (888) 814-0633. Sites are $17-25.50 per night. The campground is open year-round.

Directions: From Gold Beach drive north on U.S. 101 for one mile (on the north side of the Rogue River) to Rogue River Road. Turn east and drive about eight miles to the campground.

Contact: Kimball Creek Bend, 97136 North Bank Rogue, Gold Beach, OR 97444; tel. (541) 247-7580.

37 Lucky Lodge RV Park

 6

This is a good layover spot for U.S. 101 travelers who want to get off the highway circuit. It is set on the shore of the river and offers opportunities for fishing, boating, and swimming. Most sites have a view of the river. Nearby recreation options include hiking trails.

Location: On the Rogue River; map E1, grid d1.

Campsites, facilities: There are four tent sites and 32 full-hookup sites for trailers or RVs of any length; most are drive-through sites. Electricity, drinking water, sewer hookups, and picnic tables are provided. Flush toilets, bottled gas, sanitary services, showers, firewood, a recreation hall, and a laundry room are available. Boat docks and rentals are located within eight miles. Leashed pets are permitted.

Reservations, fees: Reservations accepted. Sites are $17 per night. The campground is open year-round.

Directions: From Gold Beach drive north on U.S. 101 for one mile (on the north side of the Rogue River) to Rogue River Road. Turn east and drive 7.5 miles to the campground.

Contact: Lucky Lodge RV Park, 32040 Watson Lane, Gold Beach, OR 97444; tel. (541) 247-7618.

38 Anglers Trailer Village   6

This is one of seven campgrounds on the lower Rogue River near Gold Beach. It is best used as an overnight layover.

Location: On the Rogue River; map E1, grid d1.

Campsites, facilities: There are 36 sites with full hookups for trailers or RVs of any length and an area that can accommodate about three tents. Electricity, drinking water, cable TV, and sewer hookups are provided. Flush toilets, showers, a recreation hall, and a laundry room are available. Leashed pets are permitted.

Reservations, fees: Reservations accepted. Sites are $15 per night. The campground is open year-round.

Directions: In Gold Beach drive on U.S. 101 to the southern end of the Rogue River Bridge and Jerry's Flat Road. Turn east on Jerry's Flat Road and drive 3.5 miles to the campground.

Contact: Anglers Trailer Village, 95706 Jerry's Flat Road, Gold Beach, OR 97444; tel. (541) 247-7922.

39 Lobster Creek   6

This small campground on a river bar along the Rogue River about a 15-minute drive from Gold Beach, makes a good base for a fishing trip. It's heavily forested with myrtles and Douglas fir and the Shrader Old-Growth Trail and Myrtle Tree Trail are nearby.

Location: On the Rogue River in Siskiyou National Forest; map E1, grid d2.

Campsites, facilities: There are six sites for tents, trailers, or RVs up to 21 feet long. Fire rings and picnic tables are provided. Flush toilets are available, but there is no drinking water and all garbage must be packed out. A boat launch is also available. Leashed pets are permitted.

Reservations, fees: No reservations accepted. Sites are $6 per night, plus $2 for each additional vehicle. Camping is also permitted on a gravel bar area for $3 per night. Open mid-May to mid-October.

Directions: In Gold Beach drive on U.S. 101 to County Road 595. Turn east and drive 10 miles (it becomes Forest Road 33) to the campground on the left.

Contact: Siskiyou National Forest, Gold Beach Ranger District, 29279 Ellensburg Avenue, Gold Beach, OR 97444; tel. (541) 247-3600; fax (541) 247-3617.

40 Quosatana   6

This campground is set along the banks of the Rogue River upstream from the much smaller Lobster Creek Campground. In the campground are a large, grassy area, and a barrier-free trail with interpretive signs. Ocean access is just a short drive away, and the quaint town of Gold Beach offers a decent side trip. Nearby Otter Point State Park (day use only) has further recreation options. The Shrader Old-Growth Trail and Myrtle Tree Trail are nearby hiking opportunities. This is a good base camp for a hiking or fishing trip

Location: On the Rogue River in Siskiyou National Forest; map E1, grid d2.

Campsites, facilities: There are 42 sites for tents, trailers, or RVs up to 32 feet long. Drinking water, fire grills, garbage bins, and picnic tables are provided. Flush toilets, a sanitary disposal station, a fish cleaning station, and a boat ramp are available. Some facilities are wheelchair accessible. Leashed pets are permitted.

Reservations, fees: No reservations accepted. Sites are $8 per night, plus $3 for each additional vehicle. Open year-round.

Directions: In Gold Beach drive on U.S. 101 to County Road 595. Turn east and drive 13 miles (it becomes Forest Road 33) to the campground on the left.

Contact: Siskiyou National Forest, Gold Beach Ranger District, 29279 Ellensburg Avenue, Gold Beach, OR 97444; tel. (541) 247-3600; fax (541) 247-3617.

41 Foster Bar   5

This camping area is located on the banks of the Rogue River. At the nearby Rogue River Tail, there's a take-out point for rafters. Hiking opportunities are good and you can also fish from the river bar. Illahe Campground and Agness RV Park provide nearby camping options.

Location: On the Rogue River in Siskiyou National Forest; map E1, grid d3.

Campsites, facilities: There are several dispersed sites for tents, trailers, or RVs up to 16 feet long, though access is difficult for RVs and trailers. Flush toilets, garbage bins, and boat launching facilities are available, but there is no drinking water. Leashed pets are permitted.

Reservations, fees: No reservations; no fee. Open year-round.

Directions: In Gold Beach drive on U.S. 101 to County Road 595. Turn east and drive 35 miles (it becomes Forest Road 33) to the junction for Illahe, Illahe Campground, and Foster Bar. Turn right on County Road 375 and drive five miles to the campground.

Contact: Siskiyou National Forest, Gold Beach Ranger District, 29279 Ellensburg Avenue, Gold Beach, OR 97444; tel. (541) 247-3600; fax (541) 247-3617.

42 Agness RV Park   7

This is a destination campground on the scenic Rogue River in the middle of the Siskiyou National Forest. Fishing is the main focus here. Boating is sharply limited because the nearest pullout is 12 miles downstream. It's advisable to obtain a U.S.

Forest Service map detailing the backcountry.

Location: On the Rogue River; map E1, grid d2.

Campsites, facilities: There are 81 sites for trailers or RVs of any length; 43 are drive-through sites. Electricity, drinking water, sewer hookups and picnic tables are provided. Flush toilets, sanitary services, showers, and a laundry room are available. A store, a cafe, bottled gas, and ice are located within 100 yards. Boat launching facilities are nearby. Pets are permitted.

Reservations, fees: Reservations accepted. Sites are $17 per night. The RV park is open year-round.

Directions: In Gold Beach drive on U.S. 101 to the southern end of the Rogue River Bridge and Jerry's Flat Road. Turn east on Jerry's Flat Road and you'll see the entrance to the campground on the left.

Contact: Agness RV Park, 4215 Agness Road, Agness, OR 97406; tel. (541) 247-2813.

43 Sam Brown and Sam Brown Horse Camp   8

This campground is located in an isolated area near Grants Pass along Briggs Creek in a valley of pine and Douglas fir. It is set at an elevation of 2,500 feet. Many sites lie in the shade of trees, and a creek runs along one side of the campground. Taylor Creek Trail, Briggs Creek Trail, and Dutchy Creek Trail are nearby and popular for hiking and horseback riding. An amphitheater is available for small group presentations.

Location: Near Grants Pass in Siskiyou National Forest; map E1, grid d5.

Campsites, facilities: There are 37 sites for tents, trailers, or RVs of any length at Sam Brown and seven equestrian tent sites with small corrals across the road at Sam Brown Horse Camp. At Sam Brown, picnic tables, fire rings or grills, drinking water, and vault toilets are provided. A picnic shelter and an amphitheater are available. Many sites are wheelchair accessible.

Reservations, fees: No reservations accepted. Sites are $5 per night. There is a $2 charge for each additional vehicle at both camps. Open late May to mid-October.

Directions: From Grants Pass drive north on Interstate 5 for 3.5 miles to Exit 61 (Merlin-Galice Road). Take that exit and drive northwest for 12.5 miles to Forest Road 26. Turn left on Forest Road 25 and head southwest for 13.5 miles to the campground.

Contact: Siskiyou National Forest, Galice Ranger District, 200 N.E. Greenfield Road, Grants Pass, OR 97526; tel. (541) 471-6500; fax (541) 471-6514.

44 Big Pine   8

This little campground (elevation of 2,400 feet) is near the banks of Myers Creek in a valley of large pine and Douglas fir. Many sites are right on the creek, and all are shaded. One of the world's tallest ponderosa pine trees is located near the campground. A 1.1-mile barrier-free, interpretive trail starts at the campground and a day-use area is available.

Location: On Myers Creek in Siskiyou National Forest; map E1, grid d6.

Campsites, facilities: There are 14 tent sites. Picnic tables and fire grills are provided. Vault toilets, drinking water, garbage bins, and firewood are available. The facilities are wheelchair accessible. Leashed pets are permitted.

Reservations, fees: No reservations accepted. Sites are $5 per night, $2 per night for an additional vehicle. Open late May to mid-October.

Directions: From Grants Pass drive north on Interstate 5 for 3.5 miles to Exit 61 (Merlin-Galice Road). Take that exit and drive northwest for 12.5 miles for Forest Road 26. Turn left on Forest Road 25 and head southwest for 12.8 miles to the campground on the right.

Contact: Siskiyou National Forest, Galice Ranger District, 200 N.E. Greenfield Road, Grants Pass, OR 97526; tel. (541) 471-6500; fax (541) 471-6514.

45 Bend O' the River RV Park   7

This campground is set along the banks of the Rogue River. It's a pretty spot far enough out of Grants Pass to have its own unique feel.

Location: On the Rogue River; map E1, grid d6.

Campsites, facilities: There are no tent sites and 25 sites for trailers or RVs of any length. Electricity, drinking water, sewer hookups, and picnic tables are provided. Flush toilets, sanitary disposal services, showers, firewood, a store, a laundry room, and ice are available. Leashed pets are permitted.

Reservations, fees: Reservations accepted. Sites are $7-15 per night. The campground is open year-round.

Directions: In Grants Pass on Interstate 5, take Exit 58 to Sixth Street. Drive south on Sixth Street to G Street. Turn west and drive 7.5 miles (the road becomes Upper River Road, then Lower River Road) to the park.

Contact: Bend O' the River RV Park, 7501 Lower River Road, Grants Pass, OR 97526; tel. (541) 479-2547.

46 Indian Mary Park   9

This park is the crown jewel of the Josephine County parks. Set right on the Rogue River at an elevation of 900-1,000 feet, the park sports hiking trails, a picnic shelter for 150 people, swimming (unsupervised), fishing, disc golf, and an historic mining town nearby. Rogue River is famous for its rafting, which can be done commercially or on your own.

Location: on the Rogue River; map E1, grid d6.

Campsites, facilities: There are 34 sites for tents and 68 sites for trailers or RVs of up to 40 feet; 44 are full hookup, and 14 are partial. There is also a group site of six sites together. Picnic tables and fire pits are provided. Drinking water, rest rooms with flush toilets and coin-operated showers, a barrier-free campsite and rest room, garbage bins, dump station, boat ramp, playground, ice and firewood are available. A store and cafe are seven miles away, and a laundry is 16 miles away. Leashed pets are permitted.

Reservations, fees: Reservations recommended; phone (541) 474-5285; fax (541) 474-5288, or access the website: www.jocopark@magick.net. Family sites are $12-18 per night, $5 for a third vehicle. Call for group rates. Open year-round.

Directions: From Grants Pass drive north on Interstate 5 for 3.5 miles to Exit 61 (Merlin-Galice Road). Take that exit and drive northwest for 10 miles to Indian Mary Park on the right.

Contact: Josephine County Parks, 125 Ringuette Street, Grants Pass, OR 97527; tel. (541) 474-5285; fax (541) 474-5288.

47 White Horse   9

This pleasant county park on the banks of the Rogue River is one of several parks in the Grants Pass area that provide opportunities for trout fishing, hiking, and boating. Take your pick. Possible side trips include Oregon Caves, Kerby Museum, and Crater Lake National Monument (two hours away).

Location: On the Rogue River; map E1, grid d6.

Campsites, facilities: There are 42 sites for tents, trailers, or RVs; eight have full hookups. Drinking water and picnic tables are provided. Rest rooms, coin-operated showers, a public phone, fire grills, horseshoes, a reservable picnic shelter, and a playground are available. Leashed pets are permitted.

Reservations, fees: Reservations accepted. Sites are $12-19 per night, plus $5 for each additional vehicle. Major credit cards accepted. Open year-round, but only to self-contained RVs in the winter.

Directions: In Grants Pass on Interstate 5, take Exit 58 to Sixth Street. Drive south on Sixth Street to G Street. Turn west and drive seven miles (the road becomes Upper River Road, then Lower River Road). The park is on the left at 7600 Lower River Road.

Contact: Josephine County Parks, 125 Ringuette Street, Grants Pass, OR 97527; tel. (541) 474-5285; fax (541) 474-5288.

47 Grants Pass Overniters   7

This wooded park is set in a rural area just outside Grants Pass and is mostly shaded. There are several other campgrounds in the area.

Location: Near Grants Pass; map E1, grid d7.

Campsites, facilities: There are eight tent sites and 26 drive-through sites for trailers or RVs of any length. Electricity, drinking water, sewer hookups, and picnic tables are provided. Flush toilets, showers, a laundry room, ice, and a swimming pool are available. A store is located within one mile. Leashed pets are permitted.

Reservations, fees: Reservations accepted. Sites are $12-16 per night. The campground is open year-round.

Directions: From Grants Pass drive north on Interstate 5 for three miles to Exit 61 (and bear right) to a stop sign and Highland Avenue. Turn left and drive a very short distance to the campground on the right.

Contact: Grants Pass Overniters, 5941 Highland Avenue, Grants Pass, OR 97526; tel. (541) 479-7289.

49 Lazy Acres RV

 6

This wooded campground on the Rogue River may be a bit less scenic than KOA Medford-Gold Hill, but there are evergreen, maple and birch trees which still make this a beautiful spot. It also offers the same recreation options.

Location: On the Rogue River; map E1, grid d9.

Campsites, facilities: There are 60 sites with full hookups for trailers or RVs of any length and 15 dry tent camping sites. Electricity, drinking water, sewer hookups, and picnic tables are provided. Flush toilets, bottled gas, cable TV, a dump station, a playground, and a laundry room are available. Boat docks are nearby. Leashed pets are permitted.

Reservations, fees: No reservations accepted. Sites are $18 per night. The campground is open year-round.

Directions: From Medford drive north on Interstate 5 for 18 miles to the South Gold Hill exit. Take that exit and drive one-quarter mile north to Second Avenue. Turn west and drive 1.2 miles to the campground on the left.

Contact: Lazy Acres RV, 1550 Second Avenue, Gold Hill, OR 97525; tel. (541) 855-7000.

50 Elderberry Flat 7

Virtually unknown, this campground on the banks of Evans Creek is only about a 30-minute drive from Interstate 5. It's small and primitive, and swimming holes are located along the creek. ATV/motorcycle trails originate from this area. No fishing is allowed in the creek.

Location: On West Fork Evans Creek; map E1, grid d9.

Campsites, facilities: There are nine primitive tent sites. Picnic tables and fire grills are provided. Vault toilets and garbage service are available, but there is no drinking water. Some facilities are wheelchair accessible. Leashed pets are permitted.

Reservations, fees: No reservations; no fee. There is a 14-day stay limit. Open mid-April to mid-November.

Directions: From Grants Pass drive south on Interstate 5 for 10 miles to Rogue River exit. Take that exit and turn right on Depot Street and drive to Pine Street. Turn left and drive 18 miles (it becomes East Evans Creek Road) to West Fork Evans Creek Road. Turn left and drive nine miles to the campground.

Contact: Bureau of Land Management, Medford District, 3040 Biddle Road, Medford, OR 97504; tel. (541) 770-2200; fax (541) 770-2400.

51 Whaleshead Beach Resort 7

This resort, about a quarter of a mile from the beach, is set in a forested area with a small stream nearby. Activities at and around the camp include ocean and river fishing, jet boat trips, whale-watching excursions, and a golf course (30 minutes away). Each campsite has a deck, and all cabins have an ocean view. What makes this camp unique is a tunnel that connects the campground to a trail to the beach.

Location: Near the Pacific Ocean; map E1, grid e0.

Campsites, facilities: There are 115 sites for tents, trailers, or RVs of any length. Ten cabins are also available. Cable TV, rest rooms, showers, drinking water, a public phone, a laundry room, limited groceries, ice, snacks, RV supplies, and LP gas are available. There is a sanitary dump station six miles away. Recreational facilities include horseshoe pits, a restaurant and a game room. Some facilities are wheelchair accessible. Leashed pets are permitted.

Reservations, fees: Reservations recommended. Sites are $15-25 per night. Cabins are $65-130 per night. The campground is open year-round.

Directions: From Brookings drive nine miles north on U.S. 101 to Milepost 349.5 and look for the park on the right.

Contact: Whaleshead Beach Resort, 19921 Whaleshead Road, Brookings, OR 97415; tel. (541) 469-7446; fax (541) 469-7447.

52 Lake Selmac   9

Nestled in a wooded, mountainous area, this 300-acre park offers swimming, hiking, boating, sailing, and good trout fishing on beautiful Lake Selmac.

Location: On Lake Selmac; map E1, grid e5.

Campsites, facilities: There are 81 sites for tents, trailers, or RVs up to 32 feet long. Drinking water and picnic tables are provided. Facilities include rest rooms, coin-operated showers, a sanitary dump, a public phone, snacks, a barbecue, horseshoes, a playground, a recreation field, and two boat ramps and dock. Facilities are wheelchair accessible. Leashed pets are permitted.

Reservations, fees: Reservations recommended. Sites are $12-18 per night, plus $5 for each additional vehicle. Major credit cards accepted. Open year-round, with limited winter service.

Directions: In Grants Pass on Interstate 5, take the U.S. 199 exit. Turn southwest on U.S. 199 and drive for 23 miles to Selma and the Lake Selmac exit (Lakeshore Drive). Turn left (east) and drive two miles to the lake and the campground entrance.

Contact: Josephine County Parks, 125 Ringuette Street, Grants Pass, OR 97527; tel. (541) 474-5285; fax (541) 474-5288.

53 Grants Pass/Redwood KOA   8

This KOA campground along a stream in the hills outside of Grants Pass is popular with bird-watchers. It's a perfect layover spot for travelers who want to get away from the highway for a while. For an interesting side trip, drive south down scenic U.S. 199 to Cave Junction or Illinois River State Park.

Location: Near Grants Pass; map E1, grid e6.

Campsites, facilities: There are 40 sites for tents, trailers, or RVs. Rest rooms, showers, drinking water, a sanitary dump, security, a public phone, a laundry room, limited groceries, ice, RV supplies, LP gas, and a barbecue are available. There is also a recreation hall, a playground, and a recreation field. Leashed pets are permitted.

Reservations, fees: Reservations recommended. Sites are $17-22 per night. The campground is open year-round.

Directions: In Grants Pass on Interstate 5, take the U.S. 199 exit. Turn southwest on U.S. 199 and drive for 14.5 miles to the campground on the right (at milepost 14.5).
Contact: Grants Pass/ Redwood KOA, 13370 Redwood Highway, Wilderville, OR 97543; tel. (541) 476-6508.

54 Flying W   7

This resort is along the shore of Lake Selmac. About 30 miles away is Oregon Caves National Monument. Fishing is great for largemouth bass (Lake Selmac has won the state record three times). Trout, crappie, bluegill, and catfish are also available here. There is a 5-mile-per-hour speed limit on the lake. A trail circles the lake, and hikers, bikers, and horses are welcome. A golf course is about six miles away.
Location: On Lake Selmac; map E1, grid e6.
Campsites, facilities: There are 18 tent sites and 25 sites for trailers or RVs of any length. Electricity, drinking water, sewer hookups, fire rings, and picnic tables are provided. Flush toilets, bottled gas, sanitary services, showers, firewood, a store, a cafe, a laundry room, ice, and a playground are available. Boat docks and launching facilities are nearby, and rentals are on-site. Horseback riding trails are available in the summer. Leashed pets and motorbikes are permitted. Corrals are available for horse campers.
Reservations, fees: Reservations accepted. Tent sites are $10 per night, RV sites are $12-14 per night. The campground is open year-round, with limited winter facilities.
Directions: In Grants Pass on Interstate 5, take the U.S. 199 exit. Turn southwest on U.S. 199 and drive for 23 miles to Selma and the Lake Selmac exit (Lakeshore Drive). Turn left (east) and drive two miles to the lake and the resort on the left.
Contact: Flying W, 2700 Lakeshore Drive, Selma, OR 97538; tel. (541) 597-2277.

55 Rogue Valley Overniters

         5

This park is just off the freeway in Grants Pass, the jumping-off point for trips down the Rogue River. The summer heat in this part of Oregon can surprise visitors in late June and early July. This is a nice comfortable park with shade trees.
Location: Near the Rogue River; map E1, grid e7.
Campsites, facilities: There are 110 sites for tents, trailers, and RVs; 26 are drive-through sites. Electricity, drinking water, cable TV, and sewer hookups are provided. Flush toilets, sanitary disposal services, showers, and a laundry room are available. Bottled gas, a store, a cafe, and ice are available within one mile. Leashed pets are permitted.
Reservations, fees: Reservations accepted. Sites are $19-20 per night. The campground is open year-round.
Directions: In Grants Pass on Interstate 5, take Exit 58 to Sixth Street. Drive south on Sixth Street for a quarter-mile to the park.
Contact: Rogue Valley Overniters, 1806 Northwest Sixth Street, Grants Pass, OR 97526; tel. (541) 479-2208.

56 Schroeder

 9

Trout fishing, swimming, and boating are among the possibilities at this camp along the Rogue River. Just a short jog off the highway, it makes an excellent layover for Interstate 5 travelers. It's not a highly publicized camp, so many tourists pass by it in favor of the more commercial camps in the area. Tennis courts are located close by, and horse rentals are available within a 10- minute drive.

Location: On the Rogue River; map E1, grid e7.

Campsites, facilities: There are 22 tent sites and 28 sites for trailers and RVs; three are partial hookups. Rest rooms, coin-operated showers, and a public phone are available. Recreational facilities include horseshoes, a recreation field, a barbecue, a playground, and a boat ramp. Some facilities are wheelchair accessible. Leashed pets are permitted.

Reservations, fees: Reservations accepted. Sites are $12-18 per night. Major credit cards accepted. Open year-round.

Directions: In Grants Pass on Interstate 5, take Exit 58 to U.S. 199. Drive west on U.S. 199 for four miles to the campground.

Contact: Josephine County Parks, 125 Ringuette Street, Grants Pass, OR 97527; tel. (541) 474-5285; fax (541) 474-5288.

57 River Park RV Resort

 6

This park has a quiet, serene riverfront setting, yet is close to all the conveniences of a small city. Highlights here include 700 feet of Rogue River frontage for trout fishing and swimming. It's one of several parks in the immediate area.

Location: On the Rogue River; map E1, grid e7.

Campsites, facilities: There are three tent sites and 47 sites for trailers or RVs. Cable TV, rest rooms, showers, a sanitary dump, a public phone, laundry facilities, and ice are available. Leashed pets are permitted.

Reservations, fees: Reservations recommended. Sites are $18-20 per night. The campground is open year-round.

Directions: In Grants Pass on Interstate 5, take Exit 55 to Sixth Street. Drive on Sixth Street across the Rogue River to Parkdale. Turn left on Parkdale and drive one block to Highway 99. Turn left on Highway 99 and drive two miles to the park on the left.

Contact: River Park RV Resort, 2956 Rogue River Highway, Grants Pass, OR 97527; tel. (800) 677-8857 or (541) 479-0046; fax (541) 471-1448.

58 Circle W Campground

 6

This campground along the Rogue River is close to chartered boat trips down the Rogue, a golf course, and tennis courts. Fishing and swimming access are available from the campground.

Location: On the Rogue River; map E1, grid e8.

Campsites, facilities: There are 25 sites for trailers or RVs of any length; four are drive-through sites. Electricity, drinking water, sewer hookups, and picnic tables are provided. Flush toilets, sanitary disposal services, showers, a laundry room, and ice are available. A cafe and a boat dock are located nearby. Leashed pets are permitted.

Reservations, fees: Reservations accepted. Sites are $17-22 per night. The campground is open year-round.

Directions: From Grants Pass drive south on Interstate 5 for 10 miles to Exit 48 at Rogue River. Take that exit to Highway 99 and drive west for one mile to the campground.

Contact: Circle W Campground, 8110 Rogue River Highway, Grants Pass, OR 97527; tel. (541) 582-1686.

59 Have a Nice Day Campground   6

This campground with grassy, shaded sites is set along the Rogue River, where fishing, swimming, and boating are options. This camp has nice river views.

Location: On the Rogue River; map E1, grid e8.

Campsites, facilities: There are 22 sites for tents, trailers, or RVs and 18 for trailers or RVs only. Three are drive-through sites. Electricity, drinking water, sewer hookups, and picnic tables are provided. Flush toilets, sanitary disposal services, showers, a laundry room, and a playground are available. A store and a cafe are located within two miles. Boat docks and launching facilities are nearby. Leashed pets and motorbikes are permitted.

Reservations, fees: Reservations accepted. Sites are $17 per night. The campground is open year-round, with limited winter facilities.

Directions: From Grants Pass drive south on Interstate 5 for 10 miles to Exit 48 at Rogue River. Take that exit and drive west over the bridge to Highway 99. Turn right (downriver) drive west for 2.5 miles to the campground (on both sides of the road).

Contact: Have a Nice Day Campground, 7275 Rogue River Highway, Grants Pass, OR 97527; tel. (541) 582-1421.

60 Riverfront Trailer Park   6

This spot is convenient to good fishing, swimming, and boating on the Rogue River. Many of these large sites face the river. This park features a round driveway, so there is no backing up.

Location: On the Rogue River; map E1, grid e8.

Campsites, facilities: There are 22 sites for trailers or RVs of any length; 19 have full and three have partial hookups. Electricity, drinking water, sewer and cable TV hookups, and picnic tables are provided. Flush toilets, sanitary disposal services, showers, a laundry room, and ice are available. Bottled gas, a store, and a cafe are located within two miles. Fishing docks, boat docks, and launching facilities are nearby. Small leashed pets are permitted.

Reservations, fees: Reservations accepted. Sites are $20 per night. The campground is open year-round.

Directions: From Interstate 5 south of Grants Pass, turn west at Exit 48 and drive two miles on Highway 99 to the park.

Contact: Riverfront Trailer Park, 7060 Rogue River, Grants Pass, OR 97527; tel. (541) 582-0985.

61 Valley of the Rogue State Park   7

With easy highway access, this popular spot along the banks of the Rogue River is often filled to near capacity during the summer months. Recreation options include fishing, swimming, and boating. This is a good base camp for taking in the Rogue Valley and surrounding attractions: Crater Lake National Park, Oregon Caves National Monument, historic Jacksonville, Ashland's Shakespearean Festival, or the Britt Music Festival.

Location: On the Rogue River; map E1, grid e8.

Campsites, facilities: There are 21 sites for tents or self-contained RVs and 146 sites with full or partial hookups for trailers or RVs up to 75 feet long. Three group tent areas, and six yurts are available. Picnic tables and fire grills are provided. Flush toilets, drinking water, garbage bins, sanitary disposal station, showers, firewood, a laundry room, a meeting hall, and playgrounds are available. A restaurant is nearby. Some facilities are wheelchair accessible. Boat launching facilities are nearby. Leashed pets are permitted.

Reservations, fees: Reservations accepted; phone (800) 452-5687 ($6 reservation fee). Sites are $13-18 per night. (Weekly and monthly rates are available in the winter months.) Group areas are $60 per area, yurts are $27 per night, and additional vehicles are $7 per night. The campground is open year-round, with limited winter facilities. Major credit cards accepted.

Directions: From Grants Pass drive south on Interstate 5 for 12 miles to Exit 45B. Take that exit to the Rogue River Highway. Turn and drive one mile to the park on the right.

Contact: Valley of the Rogue State Park, 3792 North River Road, Gold Hill, OR 97525; tel. (541) 582-1118.

62 KOA Gold 'n' Rogue   6

This campground along the banks of the Rogue River is near a golf course, bike paths, tennis courts, and the Oregon Vortex. It's one of the many camps located between Gold Hill and Grants Pass. The access road was paved for the first time in 1999.

Location: On the Rogue River; map E1, grid e8.

Campsites, facilities: There are 12 tent sites and 53 sites for trailers or RVs of any length; 27 are drive-through sites. Electricity, drinking water, sewer hookups, and picnic tables are provided. Flush toilets, bottled gas, sanitary disposal services, showers, firewood, a store, a laundry room, ice, a playground, and a swimming pool are available. A cafe is located within one mile, and boat launching facilities are within five miles. Leashed pets and motorbikes are permitted.

Reservations, fees: Reservations accepted. Sites are $15-20 per night. Major credit cards accepted. The campground is open year-round.

Directions: From Medford drive north on Interstate 5 for 18 miles to South Gold Hill and Exit 40. Take that exit and drive a quarter-mile to Blackwell Road. Turn right (on a paved road) and drive a quarter-mile to the park.

Contact: KOA Gold 'n' Rogue, P.O. Box 320, Gold Hill, OR 97525; tel. (541) 855-7710.

63 Harris Beach State Park   8

The park boasts the largest island off the Oregon coast. Bird Island (also called Goat Island) is a breeding site for such rare birds as the tufted puffin. This park has sandy beaches interspersed with eroded sea stacks. The park's beauty changes with the seasons. Wildlife viewing opportunities are abundant (gray whales, harbor seals and sea lions). In the fall and winter the nearby Chetco River attracts good runs of salmon and steelhead, respectively.

Location: On the Pacific Ocean; map E1, grid f1.

Campsites, facilities: There are 63 sites for tents or self-contained RVs, and 86 sites with full or partial hookups for trailers or RVs up to 50 feet long. There are four yurts, each accommodating five people, and a special camping area for hikers and bicyclists. Picnic tables, garbage bins, and fire grills are provided. Electricity, drinking water, sewer and cable TV hookups, flush toilets, sanitary services, showers, and firewood are available. Some facilities are wheelchair accessible. Leashed pets are permitted.

Reservations, fees: Reservations accepted; phone (800) 452-5687 ($6 reservation fee). Sites are $13-19 per night; yurts are $27 per night, and all additional vehicles are $7 per night; sites for hikers/bikers are $4 per night;. Major credit cards accepted. The campground is open year-round.

Directions: From Brookings drive north on U.S. 101 for two miles to the park entrance on the left.

Contact: Harris Beach State Park, 1655 Highway 101, Brookings, OR 97415; tel. (800) 452-5687 or (541) 469-2021.

64 Port of Brookings Harbor Beachfront RV Park

 8

This park is a great layover spot located just past the Oregon/California border on the Pacific Ocean. Oceanfront sites are available, and recreational activities include boating, fishing, and swimming. Nearby Harris Beach State Park makes a good side trip, with beach access and hiking trails.

Location: On the Pacific Ocean; map E1, grid f1.

Campsites, facilities: There are 25 tent sites and 138 spaces for trailers or RVs of any length. Rest rooms, showers, a sanitary dump, a public phone, a laundry room, ice, and a marina with a boat ramp, a boat dock, and snacks are available nearby. The facilities are wheelchair accessible. Leashed pets are permitted.

Reservations, fees: Reservations recommended. Sites are $13-21 per night. The campground is open year-round.

Directions: From Brookings drive south on U.S. 101 for 2.5 miles to Benham Lane. Turn west on Benham Lane and drive a half mile (it becomes Lower Harbor Road) to Boat Basin Road. Turn left and drive two blocks to the park on the right.

Contact: Port of Brookings Harbor Beachfront RV Park, 16035 Boat Basin Road, Brookings, OR 97415; tel. (541) 469-5867, or (800) 441-0856 in Oregon.

65 At Rivers Edge RV Resort

 7

This campground along the banks of the Chetco River offers complete fishing services, including guided salmon and steelhead trips on the Chetco in the fall and winter. Deep-sea trips for salmon or rockfish are available in the summer. Other amenities include bait, tackle, and a free fishing class for campers, plus a beach for sunbathing and swimming. This resort looks like the Rhine Valley in Germany. A pretty canyon between the trees and the river.

Location: On the Chetco River; map E1, grid f1.

Campsites, facilities: There are 110 sites for trailers or RVs of any length; 15 are drive-through sites. Electricity, drinking water, and sewer hookups are provided. Two cabins will be available in the spring of 2000. Flush toilets, bottled gas, sanitary services, showers, a recreation hall with exercise equipment, a laundry room, a small boat launch, and cable TV are available. Leashed pets are permitted.

Reservations, fees: Reservations accepted. Sites are $20-25 per night. The campground is open year-round.

Directions: In Brookings drive on U.S. 101 to South Bank Chetco River Road. Turn east on South Bank Chetco River Road and drive 1.5 miles to the park entrance (well signed).

Contact: At Rivers Edge RV Resort, 98203 South Bank Chetco Road, Brookings, OR 97415; tel. (541) 469-3356.

66 Chetco RV Park   7

This park is near both the Chetco River, known for its winter steelhead run, and the beach. Whale watching is good from January through May. The nature trails located a short drive up the river road are a nice side trip.

Location: Near the Chetco River; map E1, grid f1.

Campsites, facilities: There are 117 drive-through sites for trailers or RVs of any length. Electricity, drinking water, sewer hookups, and picnic tables are provided. Flush toilets, sanitary services, showers, a recreation hall, a laundry room, and ice are available. Boat docks, launching facilities, and rentals are nearby. Small pets are permitted.

Reservations, fees: Reservations accepted. Sites are $15-18 per night. The campground is open year-round.

Directions: In Brookings drive on U.S. 101 to the Chetco River Bridge. Drive one mile south on U.S. 101 to the park entrance on the east side of the road.

Contact: Chetco RV Park, 16117 Highway 101 South, Brookings, OR 97415; tel. (541) 469-3863; fax (541) 469-4025.

67 Sea Bird RV   5

This is one of several campgrounds set along the beach here. Nearby recreation options include marked bike trails, a full-service marina, and tennis courts. This park has paved roads and granite sites. It is a nice, neat park.

Location: On the Pacific Ocean; map E1, grid f1.

Campsites, facilities: There are 60 sites for trailers or RVs of any length; nine are drive-through sites. Electricity, drinking water, sewer hookups, and picnic tables are provided. Flush toilets, sanitary services, showers, a recreation hall, and a laundry room are available. Boat docks, launching facilities, and rentals are nearby. Leashed pets and motorbikes are permitted.

Reservations, fees: Reservations accepted. Sites are $16 per night. The campground is open year-round.

Directions: In Brookings drive on U.S. 101 to the Chetco River Bridge. Drive one-quarter mile south on U.S. 101 to the park entrance.

Contact: Sea Bird RV, P.O. Box 1026, Brookings, OR 97415; tel. (541) 469-3512.

68 Little Redwood   7

This campground is set among old-growth fir trees near the banks of the Chetco River. This is an official put-in spot for rafting and river boats. The camp is also on the main western access route to the Kalmiopsis Wilderness, which is about 20 miles away. Campsites are fairly private, though close together.

Location: On the Chetco River in Siskiyou National Forest; map E1, grid f2.

Campsites, facilities: There are 12 sites for tents, trailers, or RVs up to 16 feet long. Picnic tables, garbage containers, and fire grills are provided. Drinking water and vault toilets are available. Leashed pets are permitted.

Reservations, fees: No reservations accepted. Sites are $8 per night, plus $2 for each additional non-towed vehicle. Open late May to mid-September.

Directions: In Brookings drive on U.S. 101 to North Bank Chetco River Road (County Road 784). Turn northeast on North Bank Chetco River Road and drive 13.5 miles (the road becomes Forest Road 1376) to the campground.

Contact: Siskiyou National Forest, Chetco Ranger District, 555 Fifth Street, Brookings, OR 97415; tel. (541) 469-2196; fax (541) 469-2196.

69 Loeb State Park   8

This park is located in a canyon formed by the Chetco River. The campsites are nestled in a beautiful old myrtlewood grove. The northernmost Redwood grove in the U.S. can be reached by a three-quarter mile self-guided River View Trail adjacent to Chetco River. Nature programs and interpretive tours are available.

Location: Near the Chetco River; map E1, grid f2.

Campsites, facilities: There are 50 sites with water and electrical hookups for trailers or RVs up to 50 feet long. Picnic tables, drinking water, garbage bins and fire grills are provided. Flush toilets and firewood are available. Leashed pets are permitted.

Reservations, fees: No reservations accepted. Sites are $12-16 per night, $7 per night for all additional vehicles. (Weekly and monthly rates are available from November through March.) The campground is open year-round.

Directions: In Brookings drive on U.S. 101 to County Road 784 (North Bank Chetco River Road). Turn northeast and drive ten miles northeast on North Bank Road to the park entrance on the right.

Contact: Harris Beach State Park, 1655 Highway 101, Brookings, OR 97415; tel. (541) 469-2021 or (800) 551-6949.

70 Winchuck   6

This forested campground is on the banks of the Winchuck River, an out-of-the-way stream that out-of-towners don't know exists. It's quiet, remote, and not that far from the coast, although it feels like an inland spot. If full, Ludlum Campground is about two miles away on Forest Road 1108.

Location: On the Winchuck River in Siskiyou National Forest; map E1, grid f2.

Campsites, facilities: There are 15 sites for tents, trailers, or RVs of any length. Picnic tables, garbage bins, and fire grills are provided. Vault toilets and drinking water are available. Leashed pets are permitted.

Reservations, fees: No reservations accepted. Sites are $8 per night, plus $2 for each additional non-towed vehicle. Open late May to mid-September.

Directions: From Brookings drive south on U.S. 101 for 5.5 miles to County Road 896. Turn east and drive six miles to Forest Road 1107. Turn east and drive one mile to the campground.

Contact: Siskiyou National Forest, Chetco Ranger District, 555 Fifth Street, Brookings, OR 97415; tel. (541) 469-2196; fax (541) 469-2196.

71 Kerby Trailer Park and Campground   5

This small campground is near the Illinois River, a good stream during the summer for swimming. Lake Selmac provides a nearby side trip. Other recreation options include an 18-hole golf course, hiking trails, and tennis courts.

Location: Near the Illinois River; map E1, grid f5.

Campsites, facilities: There are 13 sites for trailers and RVs; five have full and nine have partial hookups. Electricity, drinking water, sewer hookups, and picnic tables are provided. Flush toilets, showers, and a laundry room are available. A store and ice are located within 1.5 miles. One pet per site and motorbikes are permitted.

Reservations, fees: Reservations accepted. Sites are $12-13 per night. The campground is open from May through late October.

Directions: In Grants Pass drive south on U.S. 199 for 26 miles to Kerby. Continue south on U.S. 199 for a quarter mile to the campground.

Contact: tel. (541) 592-2897 P.O. Box 256, Kerby, OR 97531.

72 Shady Acres   7

This park is in a forested area near the banks of the Illinois River. Lake Selmac and Oregon Caves National Monument provide nearby side-trip options.

Location: On the Illinois River; map E1, grid f5.

Campsites, facilities: There are six tent sites and 28 sites for trailers or RVs of any length; four are drive-through sites. Electricity, drinking water, sewer hookups, and picnic tables are provided. Cable TV can be obtained for a fee. Flush toilets, bottled gas, sanitary services, showers, and a laundry room are available. A store, a cafe, and ice are within one mile. Small leashed pets are permitted.

Reservations, fees: Reservations accepted. Sites are $12-14.95 per night. The campground is open year-round.

Directions: In Grants Pass drive south on U.S. 199 for 30 miles to Cave Junction. Continue south on U.S. 199 for one mile to the campground entrance.

Contact: Shady Acres, 27550 Redwood Highway, Cave Junction, OR 97523 tel. (541) 592-3702.

73 Town and Country RV Park   7

This park on the Illinois River provides good opportunities for swimming, fishing, and boating (no motors are permitted). Nearby side trips include Oregon Caves National Monument (21 miles) and Grants Pass (31 miles). Crescent City is located 50 miles away.

Location: On the Illinois River; map E1, grid f5.

Campsites, facilities: There are 51 sites for tents, trailers, or RVs. Cable TV, showers, rest rooms, a sanitary dump, a public phone, a laundry room, and ice are available. Horseshoe pits, a clubhouse, and a playground are also provided. Leashed pets are permitted.

Reservations, fees: Reservations recommended. Sites are $16 per night. The campground is open year-round.

Directions: In Grants Pass drive south on U.S. 199 for 30 miles to Cave Junction. Continue south on U.S. 199 for two miles to the campground on the right.

Contact: Town and Country RV Park, 28288 Redwood Highway, Cave Junction, OR 97523; tel. (541) 592-2656.

74 Country Hills Resort   7

Lots of sites at this wooded camp border Sucker Creek, a popular spot for swimming. Lake Selmac and Oregon Caves National Monument provide nearby side-trip options.

Location: Near Oregon Caves National Monument; map E1, grid f6.

Campsites, facilities: There are 12 tent sites and 20 sites for trailers or RVs of any length; two are drive-through sites. There are also six cabins. Picnic tables are provided. Flush toilets, showers, drinking water electricity, firewood, a small store, a laundry room, motel, and ice are available. Leashed pets are permitted.

Reservations, fees: Reservations accepted. Tent sites are $12-17 per night; RV sites are $17 per night, cabins are $48-59 per night. The campground is open year-round.

Directions: In Grants Pass drive south on U.S. 199 for 30 miles to Cave Junction and Highway 46. Turn east on Highway 46 and drive eight miles to the campground.

Contact: Country Hills Resort, 7901 Caves Highway, Cave Junction, OR 97523; tel. (541) 592-3406; fax (541) 592-3406.

75 Grayback   7

This wooded campground at an elevation of 2,000 feet along the banks of Sucker Creek has sites with ample shade and is a good choice if you're planning to visit Oregon Caves National Monument, which is about 10 miles away. The camp is in a grove of old-growth firs and is a prime place for bird-watching. A half-mile barrier-free trail cuts through the camp.

Location: Near Oregon Caves National Monument in Siskiyou National Forest; map E1, grid f6.

Campsites, facilities: There are 37 sites for tents, trailers, or RVs up to 22 feet long; one site has a full hookup. Picnic tables, garbage bins, and fire grills are provided. Flush toilets and drinking water are available. Some facilities are wheelchair accessible. Leashed pets are permitted.

Reservations, fees: Some sites can be reserved by calling (541) 591-3400 ($8.65 reservation fee). Sites are $12 per night. Open May through October.

Directions: In Grants Pass drive south on U.S. 199 for 30 miles to Cave Junction and Highway 46. Turn east on Highway 46 and drive 12 miles to the campground.

Contact: Siskiyou National Forest, Illinois Valley Ranger District, P.O. Box 389, Cave Junction, OR 97523; tel. (541) 592-2166; fax (541) 592-6545.

76 Cave Creek   7

No campground is closer to Oregon Caves National Monument than this U.S. Forest Service camp, a mere four miles away. There is even a two-mile trail out of camp that leads directly to the caves. The camp, at an elevation of 2,500 feet, lies in a grove of old-growth timber along the banks of Cave Creek, a small stream with some trout fishing opportunities (catch-and-release only). The sites are shaded, and an abundance of wildlife can be spotted in the area. Hiking opportunities abound.

Location: Near Oregon Caves National Monument in Siskiyou National Forest; map E1, grid f6.

Campsites, facilities: There are 18 tent sites. Drinking water, garbage bins, vault toilets, and picnic tables are provided. Showers are located within eight miles. Leashed pets are permitted.

Reservations, fees: No reservations. Sites are $8 per night. Open mid-May to mid-September.

Directions: In Grants Pass drive south on U.S. 199 for 30 miles to Cave Junction and Highway 46. Turn east on Highway 46 and drive 16 miles to Forest Road 4032. Turn right and drive south for one mile to the campground.

Contact: Siskiyou National Forest, Illinois Valley Ranger District, P.O. Box 389, Cave Junction, OR 97523; tel. (541) 592-2166; fax (541) 592-6545.

77 Bolan Lake   9

Very few out-of-towners know about this camp set at an elevation of 5,500 feet, with pretty, shaded sites along the shore of 15-acre Bolan Lake. The lake is stocked with trout. Only non-motorized boats are allowed. A trail from the lake leads up to a fire lookout and ties into miles of other trails, including the Bolan Lake Trail. This spot is truly a bird-watcher's paradise, with a variety of species to view. The fishing can be good here as well.

Location: On Bolan Lake in Siskiyou National Forest; map E1, grid f6.

Campsites, facilities: There are 12 sites for tents, trailers, or RVs up to 16 feet long. Picnic tables and fire grills are provided. Vault toilets and firewood are available, but there is no drinking water, and all garbage must be packed out. Leashed pets are permitted.

Reservations, fees: No reservations. Site are $5 per night. Open July through October.

Directions: In Grants Pass drive south on U.S. 199 for 30 miles to Cave Junction and County Road 5560. Turn southeast and drive eight miles to County Road 5828. Turn southeast and drive 14 miles to Forest Road 4812. Turn east and drive four miles to Forest Road 4812-040. Turn south and drive two miles to the campground. This road is very narrow and rough. Large trailers or RVs are not advised.

Contact: Siskiyou National Forest, Illinois Valley Ranger District, P.O. Box 389, Cave Junction, OR 97523; tel. (541) 592-2166; fax (541) 592-6545.

78 Jackson   7

This camp is located at 1,700 feet elevation nestled in an old mining area. It's between the Applegate River and the road, in a canopy of ponderosa pine, with a swimming hole and good trout fishing. Mining tailings can be seen from the camp.

Location: On the Applegate River in Rogue River National Forest; map E1, grid f8.

Campsites, facilities: There are 10 sites for tents, trailers, or RVs up to 20 feet long. Drinking water (summer only), garbage service (summer only), and flush toilets are available. Firewood is available for purchase. Leashed pets are permitted. Some facilities are wheelchair accessible.

Reservations, fees: No reservations accepted. Sites are $10 per night, plus $5 for each additional vehicle. Open year-round, with limited winter services.

Directions: In Medford on Interstate 5, take the Jacksonville exit to the Jacksonville Highway. Drive west on the Jacksonville Highway (Highway 238) for seven miles to Jacksonsville. Bear left on Highway 238 and drive eight miles to the town of Ruch and Upper Applegate Road (County Road 10). Turn left and drive nine miles to the campground on the right (this camp is directly across from Flumet Flat Campground).

Contact: Rogue River National Forest, Applegate Ranger District, 6941 Upper Applegate Road, Jacksonville, OR 97530; tel. (541) 899-1812; fax (541) 858-2401.

79 Flumet Flat   7

This campground is set at an elevation of 1,700 feet along the banks of the Applegate River about six miles north of Applegate Reservoir. The Gin-Lin National Recreation Trail, named for the Chinese miner who struck it rich in local gold mines, is nearby. The camp has a large park-like lawn area with a lot of willow and cottonwood trees. Four of the sites require a short walk in and are secluded.

Location: On the Applegate River in Rogue River National Forest; map E1, grid f8.

Campsites, facilities: There are 34 sites for tents, trailers, or RVs up to 40 feet long. Picnic tables, garbage bins (summer only) and fire grills are provided. Drinking water (summer only) and flush toilets are available. Showers, a store, a cafe, a laundry room, and ice are available nearby at McKee Bridge. Firewood is available for purchase in the summer. Leashed pets are permitted.

Reservations, fees: Reservations available for groups only. Sites are $10 per night, plus $5 for each additional vehicle. Open year-round.

Directions: In Medford on Interstate 5, take the Jacksonville exit to the Jacksonville Highway. Drive west on the Jacksonville Highway (Highway 238) for seven miles to Jacksonsville. Bear left on Highway 238 and drive eight miles to the town of Ruch and Upper Applegate Road (County Road 10). Turn left and drive nine miles to Forest Road 1095. Continue one mile to the campground.

Contact: Rogue River National Forest, Applegate Ranger District, 6941 Upper Applegate Road, Jacksonville, OR 97530; tel. (541) 899-1812; fax (541) 858-2401.

80 French Gulch Walk-In   5

This campground along the shore of Applegate Reservoir at an elevation of 2,000 feet is a popular summer fishing spot for anglers. It's also a good boat-in campground when the lake level allows. A seasonal launch ramp is not far from the camp. A 10-mph speed limit is in effect for boats. Mountain biking is available around the lake. See the description of Watkins and Carberry Campgrounds.

Location: On Applegate Reservoir in Rogue River National Forest; map E1, grid f8.

Campsites, facilities: There are nine walk-in sites for tents. Picnic tables and fire grills are provided. Drinking water and vault toilets are available, and firewood is for sale. Boat launching facilities are within one-half mile. Leashed pets are permitted.

Reservations, fees: No reservations accepted. Sites are $10 per night, plus $5 for each additional vehicle. Open May through October.

Directions: In Medford on Interstate 5, take the Jacksonville exit to the Jacksonville Highway. Drive west on the Jacksonville Highway (Highway 238) for seven miles to Jacksonsville. Bear left on Highway 238 and drive eight miles to the town of Ruch and Upper Applegate Road (County Road 10). Turn left and drive 14 miles to Forest Road 1075. Turn right and drive 1.5 miles to the parking area. A short walk is required.

Contact: Rogue River National Forest, Applegate Ranger District, 6941 Upper Applegate Road, Jacksonville, OR 97530; tel. (541) 899-1812; fax (541) 858-2401.

81 Latgawa Cove Boat-In   5

The elevation of this lake is 2,000 feet. Latgawa Cove has semi-primitive lakeshore campsites with tree cover providing shade. A mountain bike trail runs through the campground. The water level fluctuates, sometimes preventing boat access. Several boat launches can be used to access this campground and the other boat-in campgrounds on Applegate Lake: Harr Point and Typsu Tyee, both with similar amenities as Latgawa and within three miles of each other by boat.

Location: On Applegate Reservoir, Rogue River National Forest; map E1, grid g8.

Campsites, facilities: There are 5 boat-in sites. No drinking water is available, but picnic tables and fire rings are provided. Pit toilets are available. Pack out all garbage. Leashed pets are permitted.

Reservations, fees: No reservations accepted. No fee. Open year-round.

Directions: In Medford on Interstate 5, take the Jacksonville exit to the Jacksonville Highway. Drive west on Jacksonville Highway (Highway 238) for seven miles to Jacksonville. Bear left on Highway 238 and drive eight miles to the town of Ruch and Upper Applegate Road (County Road 10). Turn left and drive 14 miles to Forest Road 1075. Turn right and drive 1.5 miles to the parking area for French Gulch Campground and the boat ramp. Drive by boat to Latgawa Cove Campground.

Contact: Rogue River National Forest, Applegate Ranger District, 6941 Upper Applegate Road, Jacksonville, OR 97530; tel. (541) 899-1812; fax (541) 858-2401.

82 Hart-tish
Recreation Area Walk-In   7

This concessionaire-managed campground located on Applegate Lake has a great view of the lake and shaded sites. Bald eagles and osprey nest in the area, and it's a treat to watch them fish. A nearby boat launch and boat rentals are available. The walk-in sites are only 200 yards from the parking area.

Location: on Applegate Reservoir, Rogue River National Forest; map E1, grid f8.

Campsites, facilities: There are four walk-in tent sites, and eight RV parking lot sites. Picnic tables and fire pits are provided. Drinking water, flush toilets, garbage bins, firewood, a mini-mart, and wheelchair facilities (rest room, one site, and a barrier-free boat ramp) are available. Leashed pets are permitted.

Reservations, fees: No reservations accepted, except for groups. Sites are $10 per night. There is an additional charge of $5 per each additional vehicle. Open Memorial Day through September.

Directions: In Medford on Interstate 5, take the Jacksonville exit to the Jacksonville Highway. Drive west on the Jacksonville Highway (Highway 238) for seven miles to Jacksonville. Bear left on Highway 238 and drive eight miles to the town of Ruch and Upper Applegate Road (County Road 10). Turn south (left) and drive 15.5 miles to the campground.

Contact: Rogue River National Forest, Applegate Ranger District, 6941 Upper Applegate Road, Jacksonville, OR 97530; tel. (541) 899-1812; fax (541) 858-2401.

83 Watkins   6

Located on the southwest shore of Applegate Reservoir at an elevation of 2,000 feet, this campground, like Carberry and French Gulch, is small and quite primitive, but it's pretty and offers all the same recreation options. Few campers know about this spot, so it usually doesn't fill up quickly. There are good views of the lake and the surrounding Siskiyou Mountains.

Location: On Applegate Reservoir in Rogue River National Forest; map E1, grid f8.

Campsites, facilities: There are 14 walk-in sites for tents. Picnic tables, drinking water, garbage bins, and fire grills are provided. Vault toilets and firewood are available. Boat docks and launching facilities are within two miles. Some facilities are wheelchair accessible. Leashed pets are permitted.

Reservations, fees: No reservations accepted. Sites are $10 per night, plus $5 for each additional vehicle. Open May through September.

Directions: In Medford on Interstate 5, take the Jacksonville exit to the Jacksonville Highway. Drive west on the Jacksonville Highway (Highway 238) for seven miles to Jacksonsville. Bear left on Highway 238 and drive eight miles to the town of Ruch and Upper Applegate Road (County Road 10). Turn south (left) and drive 17 miles to the campground.

Contact: Rogue River National Forest, Applegate Ranger District, 6941 Upper Applegate Road, Jacksonville, OR 97530; tel. (541) 899-1812; fax (541) 858-2401.

84 Cantrall-Buckley Park   8

This county park outside of Medford offers pleasant, shady sites in a wooded setting. The Applegate River, which has good trout fishing, runs nearby.

Location: On the Applegate River; map E1, grid f9.

Campsites, facilities: There are 25 sites for tents, trailers, and RVs up to 25 feet long. Drinking water, rest rooms, showers, and a public phone are provided. Recreational facilities include horseshoes, a playground, a recreation field, and a barbecue. Leashed pets are permitted.

Reservations, fees: Group reservations accepted. Sites are $10 per night. Major credit cards accepted with reservations only. Open year-round.

Directions: In Medford on Interstate 5, take the Jacksonville exit to the Jacksonville Highway. Drive west on the Jacksonville Highway (Highway 238) for seven miles to Jacksonsville. Bear left on Highway 238 and drive to Hamilton Road. Turn south on Hamilton Road and drive one mile to the campground.

Contact: Jackson County Parks, 400 Antelope Road, White City, OR 97503; tel. (541) 774-8183; fax (541) 826-8360.

85 Beaver Sulphur   7

Tiny and hidden, this camp is set at an elevation of 2,100 feet and situated in an area with mixed tree cover, including maple, live oak, and tall Douglas fir. Located along the banks of Beaver Creek, the camp is about nine miles from Applegate Reservoir, has pretty, shaded sites, and offers easy access to the creek. Fishing is a possibility. Some recreational mining is done here; a permit can be obtained at the ranger station.

Location: On Beaver Creek in Rogue River National Forest; map E1, grid f9.

Campsites, facilities: There are 10 sites for tents. Picnic tables and fire grills are provided. One site is barrier-free, but there are no wheelchair-accessible toilets. Vault toilets, garbage bins (summer only), and drinking water are available. Leashed pets are permitted.

Reservations, fees: No reservations accepted. Sites are $4 per night, plus $2 per extra vehicle. Open May through November.

Directions: In Medford on Interstate 5, take the Jacksonville exit to the Jacksonville Highway. Drive west on the Jacksonville Highway (Highway 238) for seven miles to Jacksonsville. Bear left on Highway 238 and drive eight miles to the town of Ruch and Upper Applegate Road (County Road 10). Turn south (left) and drive 9.5 miles to Forest Road 20. Continue three miles to the campground.

Contact: Rogue River National Forest, Applegate Ranger District, 6941 Upper Applegate Road, Jacksonville, OR 97530; tel. (541) 899-1812; fax (541) 858-2401.

86 Squaw Lake Hike-In   10

"Paradise Found" should be the name here. Numerous trails crisscross the area around this camp (3,000 feet elevation) on the shore of spectacular Squaw Lake. The setting is more intimate than the larger Applegate Reservoir to the west. This spot has a mix of developed and primitive sites and is also more popular. It's the only campground in the district that requires reservations. This area attracts the canoe/kayak crowd. Be sure to call ahead for a space. Campers with disabilities are welcome, but arrangements should me made in advance with the local U.S. Forest Service office.

Location: On Squaw Lake in Rogue River National Forest; map E1, grid f9.

Campsites, facilities: There are 17 walk-in sites for tents and two family group sites that can accommodate up to 10 people each. Picnic tables, garbage bins (summer only), and fire grills are provided. Vault toilets are available. Drinking water is available at one end of the camp during the summer only. Two sites are barrier-free. Leashed pets are permitted.

Reservations, fees: Reservations required; phone (541) 899-1812. Sites are $5 per night, group sites are $10 per night. Open year-round, with limited winter services.

Directions: In Medford on Interstate 5, take the Jacksonville exit to the Jacksonville Highway. Drive west on the Jacksonville Highway (Highway 238) for seven miles to Jacksonsville. Bear left on Highway 238 and drive eight miles to the town of Ruch and Upper Applegate Road (County Road 10). Turn south (left) and drive 15 miles to Forest Road 1075. Continue eight miles to the campground. Hike from one mile to the campsites.

Contact: Rogue River National Forest, Applegate Ranger District, 6941 Upper Applegate Road, Jacksonville, OR 97530; tel. (541) 899-1812; fax (541) 858-2401.

87 Carberry Walk-In   5

You'll find recreational opportunities aplenty at this campground on Cougar Creek near the southwest shore of Applegate Reservoir, including fishing, boating, hiking, mountain biking, and swimming. Dense forest covers the campsites providing much-needed shade. This camp is similar to French Gulch and Watkins Campgrounds.

Location: Near Applegate Reservoir in Rogue River National Forest; map E1, grid g8.

Campsites, facilities: There are 10 walk-in sites for tents. Space is available in the parking lot for trailers or RVs. Picnic tables and fire grills are provided. Vault toilets and drinking water are available. Boat docks and launching facilities are within two miles. Leashed pets are permitted. Some facilities are accessible for wheelchairs.

Reservations, fees: No reservations accepted. Sites are $10 per night, plus $5 for each additional vehicle. Open May through September.

Directions: In Medford on Interstate 5, take the Jacksonville exit to the Jacksonville Highway. Drive west on the Jacksonville Highway (Highway 238) for seven miles to Jacksonville. Bear left on Highway 238 and drive eight miles to the town of Ruch and Upper Applegate Road (County Road 10). Turn south (left) and drive 18 miles to the campground parking area. A short walk is required.

Contact: Rogue River National Forest, Applegate Ranger District, 6941 Upper Applegate Road, Jacksonville, OR 97530; tel. (541) 899-1812; fax (541) 858-2401.

BEAUTIFUL CRATER LAKE

TAULK TOURS

MAP E2

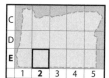

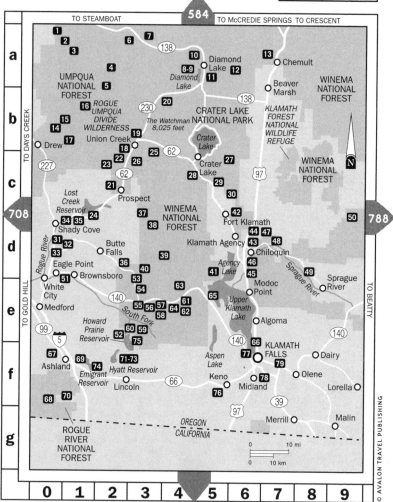

TO STEAMBOAT　　　584　　TO McCREDIE SPRINGS　TO CRESCENT

a

1
2
3
6 **7**
(138)
10
Diamond **13** Chemult
8-9 Lake
Diamond **12**
4 Lake **11**

UMPQUA
NATIONAL Beaver WINEMA
FOREST **5** Marsh NATIONAL
FOREST
16 ROGUE (138)
UMPQUA **20** KLAMATH
DIVIDE (230) FOREST
b **15** WILDERNESS CRATER LAKE NATIONAL
14 The Watchman NATIONAL PARK WILDLIFE
17 Drew 8,025 feet REFUGE
Union Creek **19** Crater WINEMA
18 Lake NATIONAL
22 **25** (62) **27** FOREST
23 **26** Crater
c **21** **28** Lake
Prospect **29**
30
Lost
Creek **42**
Reservoir **37** Fort Klamath **50**
34 **35** **24** **44** **47**
Shady Cove **38** Klamath Agency **43** **48**
d **31** **32** Chiloquin
33 Butte **39** **46**
Falls **36** Agency **45** **49**
Eagle Point **40** Lake Sprague
51 Brownsboro **53** **41** Modoc River
White **54** **63** Point
City **55** **57** **61** **65** Upper Algoma
e Medford **56** **64** **62** Klamath
(140) **58** Lake
60 **59** (140) **66** KLAMATH
Howard **52** **75** **77** FALLS Dairy
Prairie **79**
Reservoir Aspen **78** Olene
67 **69** **71-73** Lake Keno
f Ashland **74** Hyatt Reservoir Midland Lorella
Emigrant (66) **76** (39)
Reservoir Lincoln (97)
68 **70** Merrill Malin
OREGON
CALIFORNIA
ROGUE 0   10 mi
g RIVER 0   10 km
NATIONAL
FOREST

0 1 2 3 4 5 6 7 8 9

© AVALON TRAVEL PUBLISHING

CHAPTER E2

1 Wolf Creek   6

Close to civilization with easy access, this pretty camp is located at the entrance to the national forest along the banks of the Little River near the Wolf Creek Civilian Conservation Center. It is set at an elevation of 1,100 feet. This camp has abundant wildflowers in the spring. If you want to get deeper into the interior of the Cascades, Hemlock Lake and Lake of the Woods are about 21 and 15 miles east, respectively.

Location: On the Little River in Umpqua National Forest; map E2, grid a0.

Campsites, facilities: There are eight sites for tents, trailers, or RVs up to 30 feet long and one group site. A covered pavilion for groups, 14 tables and stone fireplaces are available. Picnic tables, fire grills, garbage bins, horseshoe pits, softball field and volleyball court are provided. Flush toilets and drinking water are available. Some facilities are wheelchair accessible. Leashed pets are permitted.

Reservations, fees: Reservations required for groups. Individual sites are $7 per night, the group site is $70 per night; $2 per night for an additional vehicle. Open from mid-May through September.

Directions: From Roseburg on Interstate 5, take Exit 120. Drive east on Highway 138 for 18 miles to Glide and County Road 17. Turn southeast and drive 12 miles southeast (the road becomes Little River Road) to the campground.

Contact: Umpqua National Forest, North Umpqua Ranger District, 18782 North Umpqua Highway, Glide, OR 97443; tel. (541) 496-3532; fax (541) 496-3534.

2 Coolwater   6

This campground along the banks of the Little River gets moderate use. It is set at 1,300 feet elevation and is in a pretty forest setting with some scenic hiking trails nearby. Overhang Trail is within one-half mile of the campground. Fishing and swimming are also options here. Scenic Grotto Falls can be reached by traveling north on Forest Road 2703 (across the road from the camp). Near the falls is Emile Grove, home of a thicket of old-growth Douglas firs and the huge "Bill Taft Tree," named after the former president.

Location: On the Little River in Umpqua National Forest; map E2, grid a0.

Campsites, facilities: There are seven sites for tents, trailers, or RVs up to 24 feet long. Picnic tables and fire grills are provided. Vault toilets and drinking water are available. Leashed pets are permitted.

Reservations, fees: No reservations. Sites are $5 per night (with no fee from November to May 20); $2 per night for an additional vehicle. Open year-round.

Directions: From Roseburg on Interstate 5, take Exit 120. Drive east on Highway 138 for 18 miles to Glide and County Road 17. Turn southeast and drive 15.5 miles southeast (the road becomes Little River Road) to the campground on the right.

Contact: Umpqua National Forest, North Umpqua Ranger District, 18782 North Umpqua Highway, Glide, OR 97443; tel. (541) 496-3532; fax (541) 496-3534.

3 White Creek   6

Hiking and fishing are two of the recreation options at this campground set at the confluence of White Creek and the Little River. There is a sandy beach on shallow Little River. See the description of Coolwater for other details about the area.

Location: On the Little River in Umpqua National Forest; map E2, grid a1.

Campsites, facilities: There are four sites for tents, trailers, or RVs up to 31 feet long. Picnic tables, fire grills and garbage bins are provided. Vault toilets and drinking water are available. Leashed pets are permitted.

Reservations, fees: No reservations. Sites are $5 per night (with no fee from November through May 20), $2 per night for an additional vehicle. Open year-round.

Directions: From Roseburg on Interstate 5, take Exit 120. Drive east on Highway 138 for 18 miles to Glide and County Road 17. Turn southeast and drive 17 miles southeast (the road becomes Little River Road) to Forest Road 2792 (Red Butte Road). Bear right and drive one-quarter mile to the campground on the left.

Contact: Umpqua National Forest, North Umpqua Ranger District, 18782 North Umpqua Highway, Glide, OR 97443; tel. (541) 496-3532; fax (541) 496-3534.

4 Hemlock Lake   8

This is a little-known jewel of a spot. For starters, it's set along the shore of Hemlock Lake at 4,400 feet elevation. There is a 28-acre, man-made reservoir that is 33 feet at its deepest point. An eight-mile loop trail called the Yellow Jacket Loop is just south of the campground. For finishers, another trail leaves camp and heads north for about three miles to the Lake of the Woods Campground. From there, it's just a short hike to either Hemlock Falls or Yakso Falls, both spectacularly scenic.

Location: On Hemlock Lake in Umpqua National Forest; map E2, grid a2.

Campsites, facilities: There are 13 sites for tents, trailers, or RVs up to 35 feet long. Picnic tables, fire grills, and garbage bins are provided. Vault toilets are available, but there is no drinking water. Boat docks and launching facilities are nearby. No motors are allowed on the lake. Leashed pets are permitted.

Reservations, fees: No reservations. Sites are $5 per night (with no fee from November through May 20), $2 per night for an additional vehicle. Open year-round.

Directions: From Roseburg on Interstate 5, take Exit 120. Drive east on Highway 138 for 18 miles to Glide and County Road 17. Turn southeast and drive 32 miles to the campground.

Contact: Umpqua National Forest, North Umpqua Ranger District, 18782 North Umpqua Highway, Glide, OR 97443; tel. (541) 496-3532; fax (541) 496-3534.

5 Lake in the Woods   7

The shore of little Lake of the Woods is the setting of this camp, which makes a nice home base for several good hikes. One of them leaves the camp and heads south for about three miles to the Hemlock Lake Campground. Two other nearby trails provide short, scenic hikes to either Hemlock Falls or Yakso Falls. The campground is set at 3,200 feet elevation. There is a man-made, four-acre lake, eight feet at its deepest point. Boats without motors are allowed.

Location: On Lake of the Woods in Umpqua National Forest; map E2, grid b2.

Campsites, facilities: There are 11 sites for tents, trailers, or RVs up to 35 feet long. Picnic tables, fire grills and garbage bins are provided. Flush toilets and drinking water are available. Leashed pets are permitted.

Reservations, fees: No reservations. Sites are $7 per night, $2 per night for an additional vehicle. Open from June to late October.

Directions: From Roseburg on Interstate 5, take Exit 120. Drive east on Highway 138 for 18 miles to Glide and County Road 17. Turn southeast and drive 16.5 miles southeast (the road becomes Little River Road) to Forest Road 27. Turn east and drive 11 miles to the campground. The last seven miles are gravel.

Contact: Umpqua National Forest, North Umpqua Ranger District, 18782 North Umpqua Highway, Glide, OR 97443; tel. (541) 496-3532; fax (541) 496-3534.

6 Horseshoe Bend   8

This campground is in the middle of a big bend in the North Umpqua River, set at an elevation of 1,300 feet. This is a major launching point for whitewater rafting. Fly-fishing is popular here.

Location: On the Umpqua River in Umpqua National Forest; map E2, grid a2.

Campsites, facilities: There are 24 sites for tents, trailers, or RVs up to 35 feet long and one group site. Picnic tables, fire grills, garbage bins, drinking water and flush toilets are provided. A coin-operated laundry, a store, gas, and propane are available one mile east. Some facilities are wheelchair accessible. Raft launching facilities are nearby. Leashed pets are permitted.

Reservations, fees: Reservations accepted for the group site only. Individual sites are $10 per night, and the group site is $60 per night; $3 per night for an additional vehicle. Open from mid-May to late September.

Directions: From Roseburg on Interstate 5, take Exit 120. Drive east on Highway 138 for 47 miles to Forest Road 4750. Turn right and drive south a short distance to the campground.

Contact: Umpqua National Forest, North Umpqua Ranger District, 18782 North Umpqua Highway, Glide, OR 97443; tel. (541) 496-3532; fax (541) 496-3534.

7 Whitehorse Falls   8

This campground is along the Clearwater River, one of the coldest streams in Umpqua National Forest. Even though the camp is adjacent to the highway, the setting is primitive. It is shaded by old-growth Douglas fir and is set at an elevation of 3,790 feet. This camp is a major launching point for whitewater rafting. Pretty Clearwater Falls, a few miles east, is a good side trip option. Fishing, hiking, rafting, and swimming are among the other recreation possibilities.

Location: On the Clearwater River in Umpqua National Forest; map E2, grid a3.

Campsites, facilities: There are five tent sites. Picnic tables, fire grills and garbage bins are provided. Vault toilets are available, but there is no drinking water. Leashed pets are permitted.

Reservations, fees: Reservations accepted. Sites are $5 per night, $2 per night for an additional vehicle. Open from June to late October.

Directions: From Roseburg on Interstate 5, take Exit 120. Drive east on Highway 138 for 67 miles (before reaching the Lemolo Lake turnoff) to the campground.

Contact: Umpqua National Forest, Diamond Lake Ranger District, 2020 Toketee Ranger Station Road, Idleyld Park, OR 97447; tel. (541) 498-2531; fax (541) 498-2515.

8 Broken Arrow   6

This campground is set at 5,190 feet near the south shore of Diamond Lake, the largest natural lake in Umpqua National Forest. It is set back from the lake and surrounded by lodgepole pine with views of Mount Bailey and Mount Thielsen. Boating, fishing, swimming, hiking, and bicycling keep visitors busy here. Concerns over the size of the trout have reduced visitor numbers, but plans are in effect to solve that problem and regain the lake's status as a preeminent fishery. Diamond Lake is adjacent to the Mount Thielsen Wilderness, Crater Lake National Park, and Mount Bailey, all of which offer a variety of recreation opportunities year-round. Diamond Lake is quite popular with anglers because of its good trout trolling, particularly in early summer.

Location: On Diamond Lake in Umpqua National Forest; map E2, grid a4.

Campsites, facilities: There are 148 sites for tents, trailers, or RVs up to 35 feet long. Picnic tables, fire grills, and garbage bins are provided. Flush toilets, showers, a sanitary disposal station, and drinking water are available. Some facilities are wheelchair accessible. Boat docks, launching facilities, and rentals are nearby. Leashed pets are permitted.

Reservations, fees: Reservations accepted for groups only; call (877) 444-6777 ($8.65 reservation fee). Individual sites are $9-12 per night and $3 per night for an additional vehicle. Open from late May to mid-September.

Directions: From Roseburg on Interstate 5, take Exit 120. Drive east on Highway 138 for 80 miles to Diamond Lake Loop (Forest Road 4795). Turn right and drive a short distance to the junction with loop road. Turn south and drive four miles (along the east shore) to the campground at the southern end of the lake.

Contact: Umpqua National Forest, Diamond Lake Ranger District, 2020 Toketee Ranger Station Road, Idleyld Park, OR 97447; tel. (541) 498-2531 or (541) 498-2515.

9 Thielsen View   7

This campground is along the west shore of Diamond Lake, in the shadow of majestic Mt. Bailey. There is a beautiful view of Mount Thielsen from here. See the description of Broken Arrow for information on recreation opportunities.

Location: On Diamond Lake in Umpqua National Forest; map E2, grid a4.

Campsites, facilities: There are 60 sites for tents, trailers, or RVs up to 30 feet long. Picnic tables, fire grills, and garbage bins are provided. Drinking water and vault toilets are available. Some facilities are wheelchair accessible. Boat docks, launching facilities, and rentals are nearby. Leashed pets are permitted.

Reservations, fees: No reservations. Sites are $9-12 per night; $3 per night for an additional vehicle. Open from late May to late September.

Directions: From Roseburg on Interstate 5, take Exit 120. Drive east on Highway 138 for 80 miles to Diamond Lake Loop (Forest Road 4795). Turn right and drive a short distance to the junction with loop road. Continue straight on Loop Road and drive four miles to the campground on the left.

Contact: Umpqua National Forest, Diamond Lake Ranger District, 2020 Toketee Ranger Station Road, Idleyld Park, OR 97447; tel. (541) 498-2531 or (541) 498-2515.

🔟 Clearwater Falls   8

The main attraction at this campground along the banks of the Clearwater River is the cascading section of stream called Clearwater Falls. It is set at an elevation of 4,100 feet. See the description of Whitehorse Falls for area details. There is another camping area two miles away within Clearwater Falls with eight more sites that include picnic tables and fire rings.

Location: On the Clearwater River in Umpqua National Forest; map E2, grid a4.

Campsites, facilities: There are nine sites for tents or RVs up to 25 ft. long. Picnic tables, fire grills and garbage bins are provided. Vault toilets are available, but there is no drinking water. Leashed pets are permitted.

Reservations, fees: No reservations. Sites are $5 per night, $3 per night for an additional vehicle. Open from mid-May to late October.

Directions: From Roseburg on Interstate 5, take Exit 120. Drive east on Highway 138 for 70 miles to Forest Road 4785 (10 miles before Diamond Lake Loop). Turn right and drive one mile to the campground.

Contact: Umpqua National Forest, Diamond Lake Ranger District, 2020 Toketee Ranger Station Road, Idleyld Park, OR 97447; tel. (541) 498-2531 or (541) 498-2515.

1️⃣1️⃣ Diamond Lake   9

This extremely popular camp along the east shore of Diamond Lake has all the luxuries: flush toilets, showers, and drinking water. See the description of Broken Arrow for recreation information.

Location: On Diamond Lake in Umpqua National Forest; map E2, grid a5.

Campsites, facilities: There are 238 sites for tents, trailers, or RVs up to 45 feet long. Picnic tables, garbage bins, and fire grills are provided. Flush toilets, showers, drinking water, sanitary disposal station, firewood, and an amphitheater are available. Boat docks, launching facilities, rentals and fish cleaning station are nearby. Leashed pets are permitted.

Reservations, fees: Some sites can be reserved by calling (877) 444-6777 ($8.65 reservation fee). Sites are $10-20 per night; $5 per night for an additional vehicle. Open from late April to late October.

Directions: From Roseburg on Interstate 5, take Exit 120. Drive east on Highway 138 for 80 miles to Diamond Lake Loop (Forest Road 4795). Turn right and drive a short distance to the junction with a loop road. Turn south and drive two miles (along the east shore) to the campground on the right.

Contact: Umpqua National Forest, Diamond Lake Ranger District, 2020 Toketee Ranger Station Road, Idleyld Park, OR 97447; tel. (541) 498-2531 or (541) 498-2515.

12 Digit Point   7

This campground set in lodgepole forest at 5,600 feet, on the shore of Miller Lake, a popular spot for boating, fishing, and swimming. Nearby trails provide access to the Mount Thielsen Wilderness and the Pacific Crest Trail.

Location: On Miller Lake in Winema National Forest; map E2, grid a6.

Campsites, facilities: There are 64 sites for tents, trailers, or RVs up to 30 feet long. Picnic tables, garbage bins, and fire grills are provided. Drinking water, a sanitary disposal station, and flush toilets are available. Boat docks and launching facilities are nearby. Leashed pets are permitted.

Reservations, fees: No reservations. Sites are $8 per night, $4 per night for an additional vehicle. Open from Memorial Day to mid-October.

Directions: From Eugene drive southeast on Highway 58 for 86 miles to U.S. 97. Turn south and drive seven miles to Forest Road 9772 (one mile north of Chemult). Turn right and drive 12 miles west to the campground.

Contact: Winema National Forest, Chemult Ranger District, P.O. Box 150, Chemult, OR 97731; tel. (541) 365-7001; fax (541) 365-7019.

13 Corral Spring   4

This flat campground with no water source is next to Corral Spring at 4,900 feet elevation. The main attraction is solitude; it's primitive, remote, and quiet.

Location: In Winema National Forest; map E2, grid a7.

Campsites, facilities: There are six sites for tents, trailers, or RVs up to 22 feet long. Picnic tables, garbage bins, and fire grills are provided. Vault toilets are available, but there is no drinking water. A store, a cafe, a coin-operated laundry, and ice are located within five miles. Leashed pets are permitted.

Reservations, fees: No reservations; no fee. Open mid-May to late October.

Directions: From Eugene drive southeast on Highway 58 for 86 miles to U.S. 97. Turn south and drive 6.5 miles to Forest Road 9774 (2.5 miles north of Chemult). Turn right and drive two miles west to the campground.

Contact: Winema National Forest, Chemult Ranger District, P.O. Box 150, Chemult, OR 97731; tel. (541) 365-7001; fax (541) 365-7019.

14 Dumont Creek   4

This campground set at 1,300 feet elevation along the banks of the South Umpqua River just above the mouth of Dumont Creek is quiet, primitive, and remote. It gets moderate to heavy use. A short trail leads to a small beach on the river. No fishing is allowed at this camp, and there is no trailer turn around here. Boulder Creek, just a few miles east, provides a camping option. A good side trip is nearby South Umpqua Falls, a beautiful, wide waterfall featuring a fish ladder and a platform so you can watch the fish struggle upstream.

Location: On the South Umpqua River in Umpqua National Forest; map E2, grid b0.

Campsites, facilities: There are five sites for tents, trailers, or RVs up to 16 feet long. Picnic tables, fire grills, and garbage bins are provided. Vault toilets are available, but there is no drinking water. Leashed pets are permitted.

Reservations, fees: No reservations; no fee. Open all year.

Directions: At Canyonville on Interstate 5, take Exit 99 to County Road 1. Drive east on County Road 1 for 25 miles to Tiller and County Road 46. Turn left and drive six miles northeast (County Road 46 turns into South Umpqua Road/Forest Road 28). Continue northeast and drive 5.5 miles to the camp.

Contact: Umpqua National Forest, Tiller Ranger District, 27812 Tiller Trail Highway, Tiller, OR 97484; tel. (541) 825-3201; fax (541) 825-3259.

15 Boulder Creek   4

This campground is on the banks of the South Umpqua River near Boulder Creek. No fishing is allowed here. It is set at 1,400 feet elevation See the description of Dumont Creek for information on the area.

Location: On the South Umpqua River in Umpqua National Forest; map E2, grid b1.

Campsites, facilities: There are 12 sites for tents, trailers, or RVs up to 25 feet long. Picnic tables, fire grills and garbage bins are provided. Vault toilets are available, but there is no drinking water. Leashed pets are permitted.

Reservations, fees: No reservations; no fee. Open from late May to late October.

Directions: At Canyonville on Interstate 5, take Exit 99 to County Road 1. Drive east on County Road 1 for 25 miles to Tiller and County Road 46. Turn left and drive six miles northeast (County Road 46 turns into South Umpqua Road/Forest Road 28). Continue northeast and drive seven miles to the camp.

Contact: Umpqua National Forest, Tiller Ranger District, 27812 Tiller Trail Highway, Tiller, OR 97484; tel. (541) 825-3201; fax (541) 825-3259.

16 Camp Comfort   6

This campground is near the upper South Umpqua River, deep in the Umpqua National Forest, at an elevation of 2,000 feet. No fishing is permitted. Campsites are shaded by large old-growth cedar and first, and a restored shelter is part of one site. Trailheads providing access to the Rogue-Umpqua Divide Wilderness can be found at the ends of the Forest Roads west of the camp. A good side trip is South Umpqua Falls, which you pass on the road to the camp.

Location: On the South Umpqua River in Umpqua National Forest; map E2, grid b1.

Campsites, facilities: There are five sites for tents, trailers, or RVs up to 22 feet long. Picnic tables, fire grills and garbage bins are provided. Vault toilets are available, but there is no drinking water. Leashed pets are permitted.

Reservations, fees: No reservations; no fee. Open year round.

Directions: At Canyonville on Interstate 5, take Exit 99 to County Road 1. Drive east on County Road 1 for 25 miles to Tiller and County Road 46. Turn left and drive six miles northeast (County Road 46 turns into South Umpqua Road/Forest Road 28). Continue northeast and drive 18 miles to the camp on the right.

Contact: Umpqua National Forest, Tiller Ranger District, 27812 Tiller Trail Highway, Tiller, OR 97484; tel. (541) 825-3201; fax (541) 825-3259.

17 Cover   4

If you want quiet, this camp set at 1,700 feet elevation along the banks of Jackson Creek is the right place, since hardly anyone knows about it. It gets light use during the summer. During the fall hunting season, however, it is known to fill. If you head east to Forest Road 30 and follow it south, you can access a major trail into the Rogue-Umpqua Divide Wilderness. Be sure not to miss the world's largest sugar pine tree, a few miles west of camp. No fishing is allowed here.

Location: On Jackson Creek in Umpqua National Forest; map E2, grid b1.

Campsites, facilities: There are seven sites for tents, trailers, or RVs up to 22 feet long. Picnic tables, fire grills and garbage bins are provided. Vault toilets are available, but there is no drinking water. Leashed pets are permitted.

Reservations, fees: No reservations; no fee. Open year round.

Directions: At Canyonville on Interstate 5, take Exit 99 to County Road 1. Drive east on County Road 1 for 25 miles to Tiller and County Road 46. Turn left and drive five miles to Forest Road 29 (Jackson Creek Road). Turn right and drive east for 12 miles to the campground on the right.

Contact: Umpqua National Forest, Tiller Ranger District, 27812 Tiller Trail Highway, Tiller, OR 97484; tel. (541) 825-3201; fax (541) 825-3259.

18 Union Creek   8

One of the most popular camps in the district, this spot is more developed than the nearby camps of Mill Creek, River Bridge, and Natural Bridge. It's set along the banks of Union Creek at 3,200 feet elevation, where it joins the Upper Rogue River. The Upper Rogue River Trail passes near camp. Interpretive programs are offered in the summer, and a convenience store and a restaurant are within walking distance. A private riding stable is located less than one mile away.

Location: Near the Upper Rogue River in Rogue River National Forest; map E2, grid b2.

Campsites, facilities: There are 75 sites for tents, trailers, or RVs up to 30 feet long. Picnic tables, garbage service, and fire grills are provided. Drinking water and vault toilets are available. Firewood can be purchased. A store and a restaurant are within walking distance. At least one toilet and one site are wheelchair accessible. Leashed pets are permitted.

Reservations, fees: Group reservations accepted; phone (800) 416-6992. Sites are $10 per night, plus $4 per second vehicle a night. Open mid-May to mid-October.

Directions: From Medford drive northeast on Highway 62 for 56 miles (near Union Creek) to the campground on the left.

Contact: Rogue Recreation, 2990 North Pacific Highway, Medford, OR 97501; tel. (541) 770-5146 or (541) 560-3400, or fax (541) 865-2795.

19 Farewell Bend   7

This extremely popular campground is set at an elevation of 3,400 feet along the banks of the Upper Rogue River near the Rogue River Gorge. A quarter-mile barrier-free trail leads from camp to the Rogue Gorge Viewpoint and is definitely worth the trip. The Upper Rogue River Trail passes near camp. It attracts a lot of the campers who also visit Crater Lake. See description of Union Creek Campground.

Location: On the Upper Rogue River in Rogue River National Forest; map E2, grid b3.

Campsites, facilities: There are 61 sites for tents, trailers, or RVs up to 40 feet long. Picnic tables, fire grills, and fire rings are provided. Drinking water, firewood for purchase, and flush toilets are available. Some facilities are wheelchair accessible. Leashed pets are permitted.

Reservations, fees: No reservations. Sites are $12 per night, plus $5 per extra vehicle a night. Open late May to late October.

Directions: From Medford drive northeast on Highway 62 for 59 miles (near Union Creek) to the campground on the left.

Contact: Rogue Recreation, 2990 North Pacific Highway, Medford, OR 97501; tel. (541) 770-5146 or (541) 560-3400, or fax (541) 865-2795.

20 Hamaker   8

Set at 4,000 feet near the Upper Rogue River, this is a beautiful little spot high in a mountain meadow. Wildflowers and wildlife abound in the spring and early summer. This is one of the least-used camps in the area, and a prime camp for Crater Lake visitors.

Location: Near the Upper Rogue River in Rogue River National Forest; map E2, grid b4.

Campsites, facilities: There are 10 sites for tents, trailers, or RVs up to 30 feet long. Picnic tables, fire grills, garbage service, and stoves are provided. Drinking water and vault toilets are available. Firewood can be purchased. Leashed pets are permitted.

Reservations, fees: No reservations. Sites are $8 per night, plus $4 per extra vehicle a night. Open late May to late October.

Directions: From Medford drive northeast on Highway 62 for 57 miles (just past Union Creek) to Highway 230. Turn left (north) and drive 11 miles to a junction with Forest Road 6530. Continue on Forest Road 6530 for a half mile to Forest Road 6530-900. Turn right and drive one-half mile to the campground on the right.

Contact: Rogue Recreation, 2990 North Pacific Highway, Medford, OR 97501; tel. (541) 770-5146 or (541) 560-3400, or fax (541) 865-2795.

21 River Bridge   7

This campground situated at 2,900 feet elevation along the banks of the Upper Rogue River is particularly scenic, with secluded sites and river views. This is a calmer part of the Wild and Scenic Upper Rogue, though no swimming or rafting is recommended. The Upper Rogue River Trail passes by the camp and follows the river for many miles to the Pacific Crest Trail in Crater Lake National Park.

Location: On the Upper Rogue River in Rogue River National Forest; map E2, grid c2.

Campsites, facilities: There are six sites for tents, trailers, and RVs up to 30 feet long. Picnic tables, garbage service, and fireplaces are provided. Vault toilets are available. There is no drinking water. Leashed pets are permitted.

Reservations, fees: No reservations. Sites are $3 per night, $1.50 per night for an additional vehicle. Open April to November.

Directions: From Medford drive northeast on Highway 62 for 42 miles (before reaching Union Creek) to Forest Road 6210. Turn left and drive one mile north to the campground on the left.

Contact: Rogue River National Forest, Prospect Ranger District, 47201 Highway 62, Prospect, OR 97536; tel. (541) 560-3400; fax (541) 560-3444.

22 Natural Bridge   8

Expect lots of company in the midsummer months at this popular camp, which is located at an elevation of 3,200 feet, where the Upper Rogue River runs underground. The Upper Rogue River Trail passes by the camp and follows the river for many miles to the Pacific Crest Trail in Crater Lake National Park. There is an interpretive area and a spectacular geological viewpoint adjacent to the camp. A quarter-mile, barrier-free trail is also available.

Location: On the Upper Rogue River Trail in Rogue River National Forest; map E2, grid c2.

Campsites, facilities: There are 17 sites for tents, trailers, or RVs up to 30 feet long. Picnic tables, garbage service, and fire grills are provided. Vault toilets are available, but there is no drinking water. One toilet and one site are wheelchair accessible. Leashed pets are permitted.

Reservations, fees: No reservations. Sites are $3 per night, $1.50 per night for an additional vehicle. Open early May to early November.

Directions: From Medford drive northeast on Highway 62 for 54 miles (near Union Creek) to Forest Road 300. Turn left and drive one mile west to the campground on the right.

Contact: Rogue River National Forest, Prospect Ranger District, 47201 Highway 62, Prospect, OR 97536; tel. (541) 560-3400; fax (541) 560-3444.

23 Abbott Creek   8

Set at an elevation of 3,100 feet, at the confluence of Abbott and Woodruff Creeks about two miles from the Upper Rogue River, this is a better camp for visitors with children than some of the others along the Rogue River. Abbott Creek is small and tame compared to the roaring Rogue. The kids probably still won't be tempted to dip their toes, however, because the water usually runs at a body-numbing 42 degrees, even in the summer.

Location: On Abbott and Woodruff Creeks in Rogue River National Forest; map E2, grid c2.

Campsites, facilities: There are 25 sites for tents, trailers, or RVs up to 20 feet long. Picnic tables, garbage service, and fire grills are provided. Drinking water and vault toilets are available. Firewood can be purchased. Leashed pets are permitted.

Reservations, fees: Reservations accepted; phone (800) 416-6972. Sites are $8 per night, plus $4 per extra vehicle a night. Open late May to late October.

Directions: From Medford drive northeast on Highway 62 for 47 miles (near Union Creek) to Forest Road 68. Turn left and drive 3.5 miles west to the campground on the left.

Contact: Rogue Recreation, 2990 North Pacific Highway, Medford, OR 97501; tel. (541) 770-5146 or (541) 560-3400, or fax (541) 865-2795.

24 Joseph H. Stewart State Park

      7

This state park is on the shore of Lost Creek Reservoir, a lake with a marina, a beach, and boat rentals. The park is home to eight miles of hiking and biking trails. The park is about 40 miles from Crater Lake National Park, and makes an excellent jumping-off point for an exploration of southern Oregon.

Location: On Lost Creek Reservoir; map E2, grid d1.

Campsites, facilities: There are 50 sites for tents or self-contained RVs and 151 sites with water and electrical hookups for trailers or RVs up to 80 feet long and two group tent areas. Picnic tables and fire grills are provided. Flush toilets, garbage bins, drinking water, sanitary disposal services, showers, firewood, and a playground are available. Boat rentals and launching facilities are nearby. Leashed pets are permitted.

Reservations, fees: No reservations. Sites are $10-15 per night, $7 per night for an additional vehicle. Group camping is $60 per area. Open from mid-April to late October.

Directions: From Medford drive northeast on Highway 62 for 34 miles to the Lost Creek Reservoir and the campground on the left.

Contact: Joseph H. Stewart State Park, 35251 Highway 62, Trail, OR 97524; tel. (800) 551-6949 or (541) 560-3334.

25 Huckleberry Mountain   6

Here's a hideaway for Crater Lake visitors. Set at an elevation of 5,400 feet, this camp, about 15 miles from the entrance to Crater Lake National Park, really does get overlooked by highway travelers, so you have a good shot at privacy. The camp is located at the site of an old 1930s Civilian Conservation Corps camp, and an ATV trail runs through and next to the campground.

Location: Near Crater Lake National Park in Rogue River National Forest; map E2, grid c3.

Campsites, facilities: There are 26 primitive sites for tents, trailers, or RVs up to 26 feet long. Picnic tables and fireplaces are provided. Drinking water and vault toilets are available, but all garbage must be packed out. Leashed pets are permitted.

Reservations, fees: No reservations; no fee. Open June to late October.

Directions: From Medford drive north on Highway 62 for 52 miles (near Union Creek) to Forest Road 60. Turn south and drive four miles to the campground on the right. Note: The access road is quite rough; trailers are not recommended.

Contact: Rogue River National Forest, Prospect Ranger District, 47201 Highway 62, Prospect, OR 97536; tel. (541) 560-3400; fax (541) 560-3444.

26 Mill Creek   7

This campground along the banks of Mill Creek at an elevation of 2,800 feet, about two miles from the Upper Rogue River, has beautiful, private sites and is heavily vegetated. It's one in a series of remote, primitive camps near Highway 62 missed by out-of-towners and is an excellent choice for tenters.

Location: Near the Upper Rogue River in Rogue River National Forest; map E2, grid c3.

Campsites, facilities: There are eight sites for tents, trailers, or RVs up to 25 feet long. Picnic tables, garbage service, and fire grills are provided. Vault toilets are available, but there is no drinking water. Leashed pets are permitted.

Reservations, fees: No reservations. Sites are $3 per night, $1.50 per night for an additional vehicle. Open April to November.

Directions: From Medford drive north on Highway 62 for 47 miles (near Union Creek) to Forest Road 30. Turn right (southeast) and drive one mile to the campground on the right.

Contact: Rogue River National Forest, Prospect Ranger District, 47201 Highway 62, Prospect, OR 97536; tel. (541) 560-3400; fax (541) 560-3444.

27 Lost Creek   6

In good weather this is a prime spot in Crater Lake National Park; you avoid most of the crowd driving the Rim Drive. This campground is set near little Lost Creek and the Pinnacles, a series of spires. The only trail access down to Crater Lake is at Cleetwood Cove. This campground is set in a lodgepole pine forest and is more private than Mazama Campground. There are paved roads in the campground and there is a possibility (hint, hint) that a black bear could visit your campsite. Follow all bear precautions described in the "Camping Tips" chapter of this book.

Location: Near the Crater Lake Pinnacles in Crater Lake National Park; map E2, grid c5.

Campsites, facilities: There are 16 sites for tents. Picnic tables and fire grills are provided. Drinking water, flush toilets, and garbage bins are available. Leashed pets and motorbikes are permitted on paved roads only.

Reservations, fees: Reservations are not accepted. Sites are $10 for two campers and $3 per night for each additional camper. Open from mid-July to mid-September, weather permitting.

Directions: From Interstate 5 at Medford, turn east on Highway 62 and drive 72 miles into Crater Lake National Park and to Annie Springs junction. Turn left and drive to the junction with Rim Drive. Turn right and drive east on Rim Drive to Pinnacles Road Junction. Turn right on Pinnacles Road and drive five miles to the campground.

Contact: Crater Lake National Park, P.O. Box 7, Crater Lake, OR 97604; tel. (541) 594-2211.

28 Mazama   6

This is one of two campgrounds at Crater Lake; the other is Lost Creek. This one is set at 6,000 feet, known for cold nights, even in late June and early September; I once got caught buried in a snowstorm here at the opening in mid-June. A nearby store is a great convenience. The Pacific Crest Trail passes near the camp, but the only trail access down to Crater Lake is at Cleetwood Cove. Note that winter access to the park is available only from the west on Highway 62 to Rim Village.

Location: Near the Pacific Crest Trail in Crater Lake National Park; map E2, grid c5.

Campsites, facilities: There are 213 sites for tents, trailers, or RVs up to 32 feet long. Picnic tables, fire grills, and garbage bins are provided. Drinking water, flush toilets, sanitary disposal services, coin-operated showers, a laundry room, gas pumps, a mini-mart, firewood, and ice are available. Some facilities are wheelchair accessible. Leashed pets and motorbikes are permitted on paved roads only.

Reservations, fees: No reservations. Sites are $15-18 for two campers and $3 per night for each additional person. Open from late-June to early October.

Directions: From Interstate 5 at Medford, turn east on Highway 62 and drive 72 miles into Crater Lake National Park and to Annie Springs junction. Turn left and drive to the national park entrance kiosk. Just beyond the kiosk, turn right to the campground and Mazama store entrance.

Contact: Mazama Campground, P.O. Box 2704, White City, OR 97503; tel. (541) 830-8700; fax (541) 830-8514.

29 Crater Lake Camp and RV Park   6

This campground is located near the south entrance to Crater Lake National Park, the nearest private park in the area. Traffic is heavy during the summer months, but this can be a good option to the packed national park camps. The campground features a tepee and a trout pond for fishing, as well as a swimming pond. There is a separate group picnic area and group functions are welcome.

Location: Near Crater Lake National Park; map E2, grid c5.

Campsites, facilities: There is an area for dispersed tent camping and 24 sites for trailers or RVs of any length. Two sites are drive-through; eight sites have full hookups and the remaining 16 have partial hookups. There are two cabins and one tepee. Electricity, drinking water, sewer hookups, and picnic tables are provided. Flush toilets, showers, garbage bins, dump station, firewood, store with limited supplies, laundry room, ice, swimming pond, volleyball, tether ball and horseshoe pits are available. Leashed pets and motorbikes are permitted.

Reservations, fees: Reservations accepted. Sites are $12-20 per night for two people, $2.50 per each additional person; cabins are $35 and the tepee is $25 per night. Open from mid-May through October.

Directions: From Klamath Falls drive north on U.S. 97 for 21 miles to Highway 62. Turn northwest on Highway 62 and drive 13 miles to Fort Klamath. Continue northeast for four miles to the campground (near Milepost 85).

Contact: Crater Lake Camp and RV Park, P.O. Box 490, Fort Klamath, OR 97626; tel. (541) 381-2275.

30 Jackson F. Kimball State Park   7

This primitive state campground located at the headwaters of the Wood River is another nice spot just far enough off the main drag to remain a secret. Wood River offers fine fishing that can be accessed from the park by canoe. A walking trail leads from the campground to a clear spring bubbling from a rocky hillside.

Location: On the Wood River; map E2, grid c6.

Campsites, facilities: There are ten primitive sites for tents, trailers, or self-contained RVs up to 45 feet long. Picnic tables, fire grills and garbage bins are provided. Firewood and vault toilets are available, but there is no drinking water. Leashed pets are permitted.

Reservations, fees: No reservations. Sites are $7 per night, $7 per night for an additional vehicle. Open from mid-April to late October.

Directions: From Klamath Falls drive north on U.S. 97 for 21 miles to Highway 62. Turn northwest on Highway 62 and drive 10 miles to Highway 232 (near Fort Klamath). Turn north and drive three miles to the campground.

Contact: Jackson F. Kimball State Park, 63030 O.B. Riley Road, Suite A, Bend, OR 97701; tel. (800) 551-6949 or (541) 783-2471.

31 Fly-Casters RV Park   6

This spot along the banks of the Rogue River is a good base camp for RVers who want to fish or hike. The county park in Shady Cove offers picnic facilities and a boat ramp. Lost Creek Lake is about a 15-minute drive northeast.

Location: On the Rogue River; map E2, grid d0.

Campsites, facilities: There are 47 sites for trailers or RVs of any length; two are drive-through sites. Electricity, drinking water, sewer hookups, and picnic tables are provided. Flush toilets, bottled gas, showers, cable, a clubhouse, and a laundry room are available. A store, a cafe, and ice are located within one mile. Boat launching facilities are nearby. Leashed pets are permitted.

Reservations, fees: Reservations accepted. Sites are $14-29 per night. Open year-round.

Directions: From Medford drive northeast on Highway 62 for 23 miles to the campground on the right (it is located 2.7 miles south of the junction of Highways 62 and 227).

Contact: Fly-Casters RV Park, P.O. Box 699, Shady Cove, OR 97539; tel. (541) 878-2749; fax (541) 878-2742.

32 Shady Trails RV Park and Camp   7

This grassy park is set along the banks of the Rogue River in a wooded, mountainous area, with many shaded sites. Recreation options include fishing on the Rogue River or exploring Casey State Park.

Location: On the Rogue River; map E2, grid d0.

Campsites, facilities: There are 10 tent sites and 40 sites for trailers or RVs of any length. Electricity, drinking water, sewer hookups, and picnic tables are provided. Flush toilets, cable TV, bottled gas, sanitary disposal services, showers, a store, ice, and a playground are available. A cafe is located within one mile. Boat launching facilities are nearby. Pets and motorbikes are permitted.

Reservations, fees: Reservations accepted. Sites are $18-22 per night. Open year-round.

Directions: From Interstate 5 at Medford, drive northeast on Highway 62 for 23 miles to the campground.

Contact: Shady Trails RV Park and Camp, 1 Meadow Lane, Shady Cove, OR 97539; tel. (541) 878-2206.

33 Rogue River RV Park

 8

This resort provides access to mountain lakes, the surrounding wilderness, and the Rogue River. The beautiful setting is lush and heavily wooded. Activities on the river include riverbank fishing, rafting, and guided trips. Hunting facilities and winter sports are also available at the resort.

Location: On the Rogue River; map E2, grid d0.

Campsites, facilities: There are 70 sites for trailers or RVs up to 60 feet long. Free cable TV, rest rooms, showers, security, a public phone, laundry facilities, limited groceries, ice, and RV supplies are available. Other facilities include a barbecue pavilion, green lawns, horseshoe pits, nearby restaurants, and a boat ramp. The facilities are wheelchair accessible. Leashed pets under 35 pounds are permitted.

Reservations, fees: Reservations are recommended. Sites are $18-25 per night. Open year-round.

Directions: From Medford drive northeast on Highway 62 for 20 miles to the park on the right.

Contact: Rogue River RV Park, 21800 Crater Lake Highway 62, Shady Cove, OR 97539; tel. (800) 775-0367 or (541) 878-2404.

34 Bear Mountain RV Park 7

This campground is in an open, grassy area on the Rogue River about six miles from Lost Creek Lake, where boat ramps and picnic areas are available for day use. The campsites are spacious and shaded.

Location: On the Rogue River; map E2, grid d1.

Campsites, facilities: There are some tent sites and 37 drive-through sites for trailers or RVs of any length; 30 have full hookups and seven have partial hookups. Electricity, drinking water, sewer hookups, and picnic tables are provided. Flush toilets, bottled gas, sanitary disposal services, showers, a laundry room, ice, and a playground are available. A store and a cafe are located within one mile. Boat docks and launching facilities are nearby. Leashed pets and motorbikes are permitted.

Reservations, fees: Reservations accepted. Sites are $14-18 per night. Open year-round.

Directions: From Medford drive northeast on Highway 62 to the junction with Highway 227. Continue east on Highway 62 for 2.5 more miles to the campground.
Contact: Bear Mountain RV Park, 27301 Highway 62, Trail, OR 97541; tel. (541) 878-2400.

35 Rogue Elk Campground

        8

Set right on the Rogue River at an elevation of 1,476 feet, the park has biking and hiking trails, creek swimming (unsupervised), fishing, a Douglas fir tree forest, and wildlife. The forest is very beautiful here, set on the north flank of Bear Mountain. It is only a four-mile drive east to Lost Creek Lake.

Location: on the Rogue River east of the city of Trail; map E2, grid d1.

Campsites, facilities: There are 37 sites for tents, trailers, or RVs of up to 25 feet; 15 are partial hookup. Picnic tables and fire pits are provided. Drinking water, restrooms with flush toilets and coin-operated showers, a barrier-free campsite and rest room, garbage bins, dump station, soft drink machine, boat ramp and playground are available. A cafe, mini-mart, ice, laundry facilities, and firewood are available within three miles. Leashed pets are permitted.

Reservations, fees: No reservations. Family sites are $14-15 per night, $6 for a third vehicle. There is a pet fee of $1. Open mid-April through mid-October, weather permitting.

Directions: From Medford, take the exit for the Crater Lake Highway (Highway 62) and drive northeast on Highway 62 for 29 miles to the park entrance (well signed).

Contact: Jackson County Parks, 400 Antelope Road, White City, OR 97503; tel. (541) 774-8183; fax (541) 826-8360.

36 Whiskey Springs

  9

This campground at Whiskey Springs, near Fourbit Creek, is one of the larger, more developed backwoods U.S. Forest Service camps in the area. A one-mile, wheelchair-accessible nature trail is nearby. You can see beaver dams and wood-peckers here. The camp is set at 3,200 feet.

Location: Near Willow Lake in Rogue River National Forest; map E2, grid d2.

Campsites, facilities: There are 33 sites for tents, trailers, or RVs up to 30 feet long. Picnic tables, garbage service, and fire grills are provided. Drinking water and vault toilets are available. Firewood can be purchased. Boat docks, launching facilities, and rentals are within 1.5 miles. Some facilities are wheelchair accessible. Leashed pets are permitted.

Reservations, fees: No reservations. Sites are $8 per night, plus $4 per extra vehicle a night. Open late May through September.

Directions: From Medford drive northeast on Highway 62 for 16 miles to the Butte Falls Highway. Turn right and drive east for 16 miles to the town of Butte Falls. Continue southeast on Butte Falls Highway for nine miles to Forest Road 3065. Turn left on Forest Road 3065 and drive 300 yards to the campground on the left.

Contact: Rogue Recreation, 2990 North Pacific Highway, Medford, OR 97501; tel. (541) 770-5146 or (541) 560-3400, or fax (541) 865-2795.

37 Imnaha 7

This campground along Imnaha Creek at an elevation of 3,800 feet is a good base camp for a wilderness trip. Trailheads at the ends of the nearby Forest Roads lead east into the Sky Lakes Wilderness and there are two, shorter interpretive trails.

Location: Near the Sky Lakes Wilderness in Rogue River National Forest; map E2, grid d3.

Campsites, facilities: There are four sites for tents. Picnic tables, garbage service, and fire grills are provided. Vault toilets are available, but there is no drinking water. Leashed pets are permitted.

Reservations, fees: No reservations. Sites are $3 per night, $1.50 per night for an additional vehicle. Open mid-June to mid-November.

Directions: From Medford drive northeast on Highway 62 for about 35 miles to Prospect and Mill Creek Drive. Turn right and drive one mile to County Road 992/Butte Falls Prospect Highway. Turn right and drive 2.5 miles to Forest Road 37. Turn left and drive 10 miles east to the campground.

Contact: Rogue River National Forest, Butte Falls Ranger District, P.O. Box 227, Butte Falls, OR 97522; tel. (541) 865-2700; fax (541) 865-2795.

38 South Fork   7

This campground is set at an elevation of 4,000 feet along the South Rogue River. To the east, trails at the ends of the nearby forest roads provide access to the Sky Lakes Wilderness. The Southfork Trail is across the road from the campground and has a good biking trail in one direction and hiking trail in the other. A map of Rogue River National Forest details all back roads, trails, and waters.

Location: On the South Rogue River in Rogue River National Forest; map E2, grid d3.

Campsites, facilities: There are six sites for tents, trailers, or RVs up to 15 feet long. Picnic tables, drinking water, garbage service, and fire grills are provided. Vault toilets are available. Leashed pets are permitted.

Reservations, fees: No reservations. Sites are $3 per night, $1.50 per night for an additional vehicle. Open mid-June to mid-November.

Directions: From Medford drive northeast on Highway 62 for 16 miles to Butte Falls Highway. Turn right and drive 16 miles east to the town of Butte Falls. Continue one mile past Butte Falls to County Road 992 (Butte Falls Prospect Highway). Turn left and drive nine miles to Forest Road 34. Turn right and drive 8.5 miles to the campground on the right.

Contact: Rogue River National Forest, Butte Falls Ranger District, P.O. Box 227, Butte Falls, OR 97522; tel. (541) 865-2700; fax (541) 865-2795.

39 Parker Meadows   7

Fantastic views of nearby Mount McLoughlin are among the highlights of this rustic camp set at 5,000 feet in a beautiful meadow. Trailheads at the ends of the forest roads lead into the Sky Lakes Wilderness. This is a nice spot, complete with water and lots of privacy between sites.

Location: On Parker Meadow in Rogue River National Forest; map E2, grid d3.

Campsites, facilities: There are eight sites for tents, trailers, or RVs up to 15 feet long. Picnic tables, garbage service, and fire grills are provided. Drinking water and vault toilets are available. Leashed pets are permitted.

Reservations, fees: No reservations. Sites are $3 per night, $1.50 per night for an additional vehicle. Open mid-June to late October.

Directions: From Medford drive northeast on Highway 62 for 16 miles to Butte Falls Highway. Turn right and drive 16 miles east to the town of Butte Falls and County Road 821. Turn left and drive 10 miles southeast to Forest Road 37. Turn left and drive 11 miles to the campground on the left.

Contact: Rogue River National Forest, Butte Falls Ranger District, P.O. Box 227, Butte Falls, OR 97522; tel. (541) 865-2700; fax (541) 865-2795.

40 Fourbit Ford   6

This campground set at an elevation of 3,200 feet elevation along Fourbit Creek is one in a series of hidden spots tucked away near County Road 821. This campground tends to be full and noisy. Fishing here is catch-and-release only.

Location: On Fourbit Creek in Rogue River National Forest; map E2, grid d3.

Campsites, facilities: There are seven sites for tents. Picnic tables, garbage service, and fire grills are provided. Drinking water and vault toilets are available. A store, a cafe, and ice are located within five miles. Boat docks, launching facilities, and rentals are nearby. Leashed pets are permitted.

Reservations, fees: No reservations. Sites are $8 per night, plus $4 per extra vehicle per night. Open late May to late September.

Directions: From Medford drive northeast on Highway 62 for 16 miles to Butte Falls Highway. Turn right and drive 16 miles east to the town of Butte Falls and County Road 821. Turn left and drive nine miles southeast to Forest Road 3065. Turn left and drive one mile to the campground on the left.

Contact: Rogue Recreation, 2990 North Pacific Highway, Medford, OR 97501; tel. (541) 770-5146 or (541) 560-3400; fax (541) 865-2795.

41 Rocky Point Resort   7

Rocky Point Resort is located at the Upper Klamath Wildlife Refuge with 10 miles of canoe trails, with opportunities for fishing, boating, and canoeing. See the description of Harriman Springs Resort and Marina for more details about the area.

Location: On Upper Klamath Lake; map E2, grid d5.

Campsites, facilities: There are four tent sites and 28 sites for RVs, some pull-through, some waterfront sites. All RV sites have electricity, drinking water, and picnic tables are provided. Some sewer hookups are available. Flush toilets, showers, firewood, a store, a laundry room, ice and marina with boat gas, boat and canoe rentals are available. There is a free boat launch and game area. A restaurant and lounge overlook the lake. Leashed pets are permitted.

Reservations, fees: Reservations accepted. Sites are $14-18 per night. Open April through December.

Directions: From Klamath Falls drive northeast on Highway 140 for about 25 miles to Rocky Point Road. Turn north and drive three miles to the campground. **Contact:** Rocky Point Resort, 28121 Rocky Point Road, Klamath Falls, OR 97601; tel. (541) 356-2287; fax (541) 356-2222; email rvoregon@aol.com.

42 Crater Lake Resort

        6

This campground set among huge pine trees is on the banks of the beautiful, crystal-clear Wood River, just outside Fort Klamath, the site of numerous military campaigns against the Modoc Indians in the late 1800s.

Location: On the Wood River; map E2, grid d6.

Campsites, facilities: There are some tent sites and 23 sites for trailers or RVs of any length; 11 have full hookups and 12 have partial hookups. Electricity, drinking water, sewer hookups, and picnic tables are provided. Flush toilets, showers, a recreation hall, a laundry room, and a trout pool are available. Bottled gas, a store, a cafe, and ice are within one mile. Leashed pets and motorbikes are permitted.

Reservations, fees: Reservations accepted. Sites are $16-22 per night. Open from mid-April to mid-October.

Directions: From Klamath Falls drive north on U.S. 97 for 21 miles to Highway 62. Bear left on Highway 62 and drive 12.5 miles north to the campground (just before reaching Fort Klamath).

Contact: Crater Lake Resort, P.O. Box 457, Fort Klamath, OR 97626; tel. (541) 381-2349; e-mail: crtrlkrst@aol.com.

43 Walt's Cozy Camp

        7

This heavily treed campground along the banks of the Williamson River near Collier Memorial State Park is one of three camps in the immediate area. For a more remote setting, Potter's Trailer Park and Head of the River Campgrounds are to the east.

Location: On the Williamson River; map E2, grid d6.

Campsites, facilities: There are 20 tent sites and 34 sites for trailers or RVs of any length; six are drive-through sites. Electricity, drinking water, sewer hookups, and picnic tables are provided. Flush toilets, showers, firewood, a store, a cafe, a laundry room, and ice are available. Leashed pets and motorbikes are permitted.

Reservations, fees: Reservations accepted. Sites are $12 per night. Open from April to mid-October.

Directions: From Klamath Falls drive north on U.S. 97 for 21 miles to Highway 62. Continue north on U.S. 97 for three miles to the campground (adjacent to the Chiloquin Ranger Station) on the west side of the road.

Contact: Walt's Cozy Camp, P.O. Box 243, Chiloquin, OR 97624; tel. (541) 783-2537.

44 Collier Memorial State Park

     7

This campground is set at the confluence of Spring Creek and the Williamson River, both of which are superior trout streams. A nature trail is also available. The park features a pioneer village and one of the state's finer logging museums. Movies about old-time logging and other activities are shown on weekend nights during the summer.

Location: On the Williamson River; map E2, grid d6.

Campsites, facilities: There are 18 sites for tents or self-contained RVs and 50 sites with full hookups for trailers or RVs up to 60 feet long. Picnic tables, fire grills, garbage bins, and drinking water are provided. Flush toilets, sanitary disposal services, showers, firewood, a laundry room, a playground, and a day-use hitching area are available. Some facilities are wheelchair accessible. Leashed pets are permitted.

Reservations, fees: No reservations. Sites are $10-17 per night, $7 per night for an additional vehicle. Open from April to late October, weather permitting.

Directions: From Klamath Falls drive north on U.S. 97 for 21 miles to Highway 62. Continue north on U.S. 97 for five miles (three miles north of the Chiloquin turnoff) to the park on the left.

Contact: Collier Memorial State Park, 63030 O. B. Riley Road, Suite A, Bend, OR 97701; tel. (800) 551-6949 or (541) 783-2471.

45 Agency Lake Resort

 5

This campground is on Upper Klamath Lake in an open, grassy area with some shaded sites. It has over 700 feet of lakefront property, with world-class trout fishing. Look across the lake and watch the sun set on the Cascades. See the description of Rocky Point Resort for more information.

Location: On Upper Klamath Lake; map E2, grid e6.

Campsites, facilities: There are 15 tent sites and 25 sites for trailers or RVs of any length, plus four cabins. Electricity, drinking water, sewer hookups, and picnic tables are provided. Flush toilets, showers, a general store, ice, boat docks, launching facilities, and marine gas are available. Leashed pets and motorbikes are permitted.

Reservations, fees: Reservations accepted. Sites are $8-16 per night, and cabins start at $45 per night. Open year-round.

Directions: From Klamath Falls drive north on U.S. 97 for 17 miles to Modoc Point. Continue north for four miles to Milepost 4 and the campground on the left.

Contact: Agency Lake Resort, 37000 Modoc Point Road, Chiloquin, OR 97624; tel. (541) 783-2489; e-mail: agncylke@kfalls.net.

46 Waterwheel Camp and RV Park

 6

This rural campground right on the Williamson River is close to hiking trails. Fishing can be excellent here, with a boat ramp and fishing tackle right at the camp.

Location: On the Williamson River; map E2, grid d6.

Campsites, facilities: There are six tent sites and 28 sites for trailers or RVs of any length; 22 are drive-through sites. Electricity, drinking water, sewer hookups, and picnic tables are provided. Flush toilets, bottled gas, sanitary disposal services, showers, firewood, a store, a laundry room, ice, and a playground are available. A cafe is located within one mile. Boat docks and launching facilities are nearby. Leashed pets and motorbikes are permitted.

Reservations, fees: Reservations accepted. Sites are $15-19 per night. Open year-round, weather permitting.

Directions: From Klamath Falls drive north on U.S. 97 for 20 miles to the campground (a quarter-mile south of the junction of U.S. 97 and Highway 62.

Contact: Waterwheel Camp and RV Park, 200 Williamson River Drive, Chiloquin, OR 97624; tel. (541) 783-2738.

47 Williamson River   6

Another great little spot is discovered, this one at 4,200 feet elevation, with excellent trout fishing along the banks of the Williamson River. It's a world-famous fly-fishing river, but the camp does not get high use. Mosquitoes are numerous in spring and early summer, and that can drive people away. A map of Winema National Forest details the back roads and trails. Collier Memorial State Park provides a nearby side trip option.

Location: Near Collier Memorial State Park in Winema National Forest; map E2, grid d7.

Campsites, facilities: There are three tent sites and seven sites for trailers or RVs up to 30 feet long. Picnic tables, garbage bins, and fire grills are provided. Drinking water and vault toilets are available. Some facilities are wheelchair accessible. A restaurant is located within five miles. Leashed pets are permitted.

Reservations, fees: No reservations. Sites are $5 per night, plus $2 for each additional vehicle. Open from May 15 to November 25, weather permitting.

Directions: From Klamath Falls drive north on U.S. 97 for 30 miles to Chiloquin. Continue north on U.S. 97 for 5.5 miles to Forest Road 9730 on the right. Turn northeast and drive one mile to the campground.

Contact: Winema National Forest, Klamath Ranger District, 1936 California Avenue, Klamath Falls, OR 97601; tel. (541) 885-3400; fax (541) 885-3452.

48 Williamson River Resort   6

This little RV park is along the banks of the Williamson River. The Williamson is one of Oregon's famous fishing streams, attracting anglers from many miles away, and can be fished by drift boat or by shore.

Location: On the Williamson River; map E2, grid d7.

Campsites, facilities: There are eight sites for trailers or RVs of any length. Electricity, drinking water, and picnic tables are provided. A dump station, a store, and ice are available. Boat docks, launching facilities, and rentals are on site. Leashed pets are permitted.

Reservations, fees: Reservations accepted. Sites are $10 per night; Open year-round.

Directions: From Klamath Falls drive north on U.S. 97 for 22 miles Modoc Point Road (the first turnoff north of Klamath Lake). Turn left on Modoc Point Road and drive 3.5 miles to the park.

Contact: Williamson River Resort, 31900 Modoc Point Road, Chiloquin, OR 97624; tel. (541) 783-2071.

49 Potter's Trailer Park   6

This park on a bluff overlooking the river is in woods and bordered by the Sprague River and the Winema National Forest. For the most part the area east of Klamath Lake doesn't get much attention. But if you want to check out a relatively close spot that's out in remote country, try Head of the River Campground.

Location: On the Sprague River; map E2, grid d8.

Campsites, facilities: There are 17 tent sites and 23 full-hookup sites for trailers or RVs of any length. Electricity, drinking water, sewer hookups, and picnic tables are provided. Flush toilets, showers, firewood, convenience store, cafe, tavern, laundry room, telephone, and ice are available. Pets and motorbikes are permitted.

Reservations, fees: Reservations accepted. Sites are $15 per night. Open year-round, with limited winter facilities.

Directions: From Klamath Falls drive north on U.S. 97 for 30 miles to Chiloquin and Sprague River Highway. Turn east on Sprague River Highway and drive 12 miles to the resort.

Contact: Potter's Trailer Park, 11700 Sprague River Road, Chiloquin, OR 97624; tel. (541) 783-2253.

50 Head of the River   8

Almost nobody knows about this small, extremely remote spot on the edge of meadow in the lodgepole and ponderosa pine, though hunters make use of it in the fall. The only camp for miles around, it's set at 4,500 feet elevation, along the Williamson River headwaters, where you can actually see the beginning of the river bubbling-up from underground springs. The trout fishing can be excellent.

Location: On the Williamson River in Winema National Forest; map E2, grid d9.

Campsites, facilities: There are five sites for tents, trailers, or RVs up to 30 feet long. Picnic tables, garbage bins, and fire pits are provided. Vault toilets are available. There is no drinking water. Leashed pets are permitted.

Reservations, fees: No reservations; no fee. Open from Memorial Day through late November.

Directions: From Klamath Falls drive north on U.S. 97 for 30 miles to Chiloquin and Sprague River Highway. Turn east on Sprague River Highway and drive five miles to Williamson River Road. Turn northeast and drive 20 miles to Forest Road 4648. Turn north on Forest Road 4648 and drive one-half mile to the campground.

Contact: Winema National Forest, Klamath Ranger District, 1936 California Avenue, Klamath Falls, OR 97601; tel. (541) 885-3400; fax (541) 885-3452.

51 Medford Oaks Campark   6

This park is in a quiet, rural setting among the trees. Just a short hop off Interstate 5, it's an excellent choice for travelers heading south to California. The campground is located along the shore of a pond that provides good fishing.

Location: Near Eagle Point; map E2, grid e1.

Campsites, facilities: There are 60 sites for tents, trailers, or RVs of any length. Cabins are also available. Rest rooms, showers, a sanitary dump, a public phone, a laundry room, limited groceries, ice, RV supplies, and LP gas are available. Recreational facilities include a seasonal, heated swimming pool, movies, horseshoe pits, table tennis, a recreation field for baseball and volleyball, and a playground. Call for pet policy.

Reservations, fees: Reservations are recommended. Sites are $8-11 per night. Group rates are available. Call for cabin information. Open year-round.

Directions: From Medford drive northeast on Highway 62 for five miles to Exit 30 and Highway 140. Turn east on Highway 140 and drive 6.8 miles to the campground on the left.

Contact: Medford Oaks Campark, 7049 Highway 140, Eagle Point, OR 97524; tel. (541) 826-5103; fax (541) 826-5984.

52 Lily Glen Campground

          6

Set along the shore of Howard Prairie Lake, this horse camp is a secluded, primitive getaway. Trout fishing is available. Tubb Springs Wayside State Park and the nearby Rogue River National Forest are possible side trips.

Location: Near Howard Prairie Lake; map E2, grid e2.

Campsites, facilities: There are 20 sites for tents, trailers, or RVs, with no hookups. Picnic tables, drinking water, vault toilets, individual corrals, and a large barn are available. Leashed pets are permitted.

Reservations, fees: Only reservations for groups are accepted. Sites are $12 per night. Major credit cards accepted for reservations. Open year-round, with limited winter services.

Directions: In Ashland on Interstate 5, take Exit 14 to Highway 66. Drive east for less than a mile to Dead Indian Memorial Road. Turn left (east) and drive 21 miles to the campground.

Contact: Jackson County Parks, 400 Antelope Road, White City, OR 97503; tel. (541) 774-8183; fax (541) 826-8360.

53 Willow Lake Resort   9

This campground is on the shore of Willow Lake. There is a hiking trail that starts near camp.

Location: On Willow Lake; map E2, grid e3.

Campsites, facilities: There are 37 tent sites and 45 drive-through sites for tents, trailers or RVs up to 30 feet long. There are also four cabins for up to six people each. Picnic tables are provided. Electricity, drinking water and sewer hookups are available. Flush toilets, sanitary disposal services, coin-operated showers, and firewood are available. Leashed pets are permitted.

Reservations, fees: Reservations accepted for groups and cabins only; phone (541) 774-8183. Sites are $12-16 per night. Major credit cards accepted with reservations only. Open year-round.

Directions: From Medford drive northeast on Highway 62 for 15 miles to Butte Falls Highway. Turn east and drive 25 miles to Willow Lake Road. Turn southeast and drive two miles to the campground.

Contact: Jackson County Parks, 400 Antelope Road, White City, OR 97503; tel. (541) 774-8183; fax (541) 826-8360.

54 Willow Prairie   7

This spot near the origin of the west branch of Willow Creek has riding trails nearby and is primarily used as a horse camp. A map of Rogue River National Forest details the back roads and can help you get here. Fish Lake is four miles south.

Location: Near Fish Lake in Rogue River National Forest; map E2, grid e3.

Campsites, facilities: There are 10 sites for tents, trailers, or RVs up to 15 feet long. Picnic tables, garbage service, horse corrals, and fire grills are provided. Drinking water, two stock water troughs, and vault toilets are available. A store, a cafe, and ice are located within five miles. Boat docks, launching facilities, and rentals are nearby. Leashed pets are permitted.

Reservations, fees: Reservations required during the summer months. Sites are $6 per night, $3 per night for an additional vehicle. Open late May to late October.

Directions: From Medford drive northeast on Highway 62 for five miles to Exit 30 and Highway 140. Turn east on Highway 140 and drive 31.5 miles to Forest Road 37. Turn left and drive north 1.5 miles to Forest Road 3738. Turn left and drive one mile west to Forest Road 3735. Turn left and drive 100 yards to the campground.

Contact: Rogue River National Forest, Butte Falls Ranger District, P.O. Box 227, Butte Falls, OR 97522; tel. (541) 865-2700; fax (541) 865-2795.

55 North Fork   7

Here is a small, pretty campground with easy access from the highway and proximity to Fish Lake. It is situated on the North Fork of Little Butte Creek at an elevation of 4,500 feet. It's fairly popular, so reserve your spot early. Excellent fly-fishing can be found along the Fish Lake Trail, which leads directly out of camp.

Location: Near Fish Lake in Rogue River National Forest; map E2, grid e3.

Campsites, facilities: There are six tent sites and three sites for trailers or RVs up to 24 feet long. Picnic tables and fire grills are provided. All garbage must be packed out. Vault toilets and drinking water are available. Boat docks, launching facilities, and rentals are nearby. Some facilities are wheelchair accessible, including a barrier-free vault toilet. Leashed pets are permitted.

Reservations, fees: No reservations. There is no fee, but donations are accepted. Open from early May to mid-November.

Directions: From Medford drive northeast on Highway 62 for five miles to Exit 30 and Highway 140. Turn east on Highway 140 and drive 31.5 miles to Forest Road 37. Turn south and drive a half mile to the campground.

Contact: Rogue River National Forest, Ashland Ranger District, 645 Washington Street, Ashland, OR 97520; tel. (541) 482-3333; fax (541) 858-2402.

56 Fish Lake   8

Boating, fishing, hiking, and bicycling are among the recreation options at this campground on the north shore of Fish Lake. Easy one-mile access to the Pacific Crest Trail is also available. If this campground is full, Doe Point and Fish Lake Resort are nearby.

Location: On Fish Lake in Rogue River National Forest; map E2, grid e3.

Campsites, facilities: There are 19 sites for tents, trailers, or RVs up to 32 feet long. There is one wheelchair-accessible site. Picnic tables, fire grills and garbage bins are provided. Drinking water, showers, flush toilets, sanitary disposal station, a wheelchair-accessible picnic shelter, a store, a cafe, and ice are available. Firewood can be purchased. Boat docks, launching facilities, and rentals are nearby. Leashed pets are permitted.

Reservations, fees: Group reservations only; phone (800) 416-6992. Sites are $12 per night, plus $5 per extra vehicle a night. Boat ramp parking is $2. Open from mid-May to mid-October, weather permitting.

Directions: From Medford drive northeast on Highway 62 for five miles to Exit 30 and Highway 140. Turn east on Highway 140 and drive 30 miles to the campground on the right.

Contact: Rogue River National Forest, Ashland Ranger District, 645 Washington Street, Ashland, OR 97520; tel. (541) 482-3333; fax (541) 858-2402.

57 Doe Point   8

This campground (at 4,600 feet elevation) is along the north shore of Fish Lake, nearly adjacent to Fish Lake Campground. Doe Point is slightly preferable because it's densely vegetated, offering shaded, quiet, well-screened sites. Privacy, rare at many campgrounds, can be found here. Recreation options include boating, fishing, hiking, and biking, plus an easy one-mile access trail to the Pacific Crest Trail.

Location: On Fish Lake in Rogue River National Forest; map E2, grid e3.

Campsites, facilities: There are five walk-in tent sites and 25 sites for tents, trailers, or RVs up to 32 feet long. Picnic tables and fire grills are provided. Drinking water, garbage service, flush toilets, a store, a cafe, and ice are available. Firewood can be purchased. Boat docks, launching facilities, boat rentals, showers, and a sanitary disposal station are nearby. Leashed pets are permitted.

Reservations, fees: No reservations. Sites are $12 per night, plus $5 per extra vehicle a night. Open mid-May to late September.

Directions: From Medford drive northeast on Highway 62 for five miles to Exit 30 and Highway 140. Turn east on Highway 140 and drive 30 miles to the campground on the right.

Contact: Rogue River National Forest, Ashland Ranger District, 645 Washington Street, Ashland, OR 97520; tel. (541) 482-3333; fax (541) 858-2402.

58 Fish Lake Resort   7

This campground along Fish Lake is privately operated under permit by the U.S. Forest Service and offers a resort-type feel, catering primarily to families. Hiking, bicycling, fishing, and boating are some of the activities here. This is the largest and most developed of the three camps at Fish Lake. Cozy cabins are available for rental, and the resort is quite active in winter, with opportunities for cross-country skiing, ice fishing, and snowmobiling. Boat speed on the lake is limited to 10 mph.
Location: On Fish Lake; map E2, grid e3.
Campsites, facilities: There are six tent sites and 45 sites for trailers or RVs up to 30 feet long, plus 11 cabins. Electricity, drinking water, sewer hookups, garbage bins, and picnic tables are provided. Flush toilets, bottled gas, sanitary disposal services, showers, a recreation hall, a store, a cafe, a laundry room, ice, boat docks, boat rentals, and launching facilities are available. Leashed pets and motorbikes are permitted.
Reservations, fees: Reservations accepted. Sites are $15-20 per night; cabins are $45-155 per night. Open May through October, weather permitting.
Directions: From Medford drive northeast on Highway 62 for five miles to Exit 30 and Highway 140. Turn east on Highway 140 and drive 30 miles to Fish Lake Road. Turn right (south) and drive half a mile to the campground on the left.
Contact: Fish Lake Resort, P.O. Box 990, Gayle Point, OR 97524; tel. (541) 949-8500.

59 Daley Creek   6

This campground (at 4,500 feet elevation) along the banks of Daley Creek among old-growth Douglas and white fir is a primitive and free alternative to some of the more developed spots in the area. The camp is near the confluence of Beaver Dam and Daley Creeks. The Beaver Dam Trail heads right out of camp, leading along the creek. Fishing can be decent downstream from here.
Location: On Daley Creek in Rogue River National Forest; map E2, grid e3.
Campsites, facilities: There are three tent sites and three sites for trailers or RVs up to 18 feet long. Picnic tables, garbage bins, and fire grills are provided, but there is no drinking water. Some facilities are wheelchair accessible, including two campsites and a barrier-free vault toilet. Leashed pets are permitted.
Reservations, fees: No reservations. There is no fee, but donations are accepted. Open early May to mid-November.
Directions: In Ashland on Interstate 5, take Exit 14 to Highway 66. Drive east for less than a mile to Dead Indian Memorial Road. Turn left (east) and drive 22 miles to Forest Road 37. Turn north and drive 1.5 miles to the campground.
Contact: Rogue River National Forest, Ashland Ranger District, 645 Washington Street, Ashland, OR 97520; tel. (541) 482-3333; fax (541) 858-2402.

60 Beaver Dam   5

This campground sits at an elevation of 4,500 feet along Beaver Dam Creek. Look for beaver dams. There's not much screening between sites, but it's a pretty, rustic, and quiet spot, with unusual vegetation along the creek for botany fans. The trailhead for the Beaver Dam Trail is also here. The camp is adjacent to Daley Creek Campground.

Location: On Beaver Dam Creek in Rogue River National Forest; map E2, grid e3.

Campsites, facilities: There are two primitive tent sites and two sites for trailers or RVs up to 16 feet long. Picnic tables, garbage bins, and fire grills are provided. Vault toilets are available, but there is no drinking water. Leashed pets are permitted.

Reservations, fees: No reservations. There is no fee, but donations are accepted. Open early May to early November.

Directions: In Medford on Interstate 5, take Exit 14 to Highway 66. Drive east for less than a mile to Dead Indian Memorial Road. Turn left (east) and drive 22 miles to Forest Road 37. Turn left (north) and drive 1.5 miles to the campground.

Contact: Rogue River National Forest, Ashland Ranger District, 645 Washington Street, Ashland, OR 97520; tel. (541) 482-3333; fax (541) 858-2402.

61 Aspen Point   8

This campground (at 5,000 feet elevation) is near the north shore of Lake of the Woods, adjacent to Lake of the Woods Resort. It's heavily timbered with old growth fir and has a great view of Mount McLoughlin (9,495 feet). A hiking trail just north of camp leads north for several miles, wandering around Fourmile Lake and extending into the Sky Lakes Wilderness. Other trails nearby head into the Mountain Lakes Wilderness. Fishing, swimming, boating, and waterskiing are among the activities here.

Location: On Lake of the Woods in Winema National Forest; map E2, grid e4.

Campsites, facilities: There are 60 sites for tents, trailers, or RVs up to 55 feet long. Picnic tables, garbage bins, and fire grills are provided. Drinking water, a sanitary disposal station, and flush toilets are available. Boat docks, launching facilities, and rentals are nearby. Leashed pets are permitted.

Reservations, fees: Reservations accepted for groups only; phone (877) 444-6777 or access the website: www.reserveusa.com ($8.65 reservation fee). Sites are $12 per night, $6 per night for an additional vehicle. Open from late May to late September.

Directions: In Medford on Interstate 5, take Exit 14 to Highway 66. Drive east for less than a mile to Dead Indian Memorial Road. Turn left (east) and drive 40 miles to Lake of the Woods. Continue along the east shore to the campground turnoff on the left.

Contact: Winema National Forest, Klamath Ranger District, 136 California Avenue, Klamath Falls, OR 97601; tel. (541) 885-3400; fax (541) 885-3452.

62 Sunset   8

This campground at 5,000 feet elevation near the eastern shore of Lake of the Woods is fully developed and offers a myriad of recreation options. It's popular for both fishing and rafting.

Location: Near Lake of the Woods in Winema National Forest; map E2, grid e4.

Campsites, facilities: There are 67 sites for tents, trailers, or RVs up to 55 feet

long. Picnic tables, garbage bins, and fire grills are provided. Drinking water and flush toilets are available. Some facilities are wheelchair accessible. Boat docks, launching facilities, and rentals are nearby. Leashed pets are permitted.

Reservations, fees: Reservations accepted; phone (877) 444-6777 or access the website: www.reserveusa.com ($8.65 reservation fee). Sites are $12 per night, $6 per night for an additional vehicle. Open from June to mid-September.

Directions: In Medford on Interstate 5, take Exit 14 to Highway 66. Drive east for less than a mile to Dead Indian Memorial Road. Turn left (east) and drive 40 miles to Lake of the Woods. Continue along the east shore to Forest Road 3738. Turn west and drive a one-half mile to the camp.

Contact: Winema National Forest, Klamath Ranger District, 136 California Avenue, Klamath Falls, OR 97601; tel. (541) 885-3400; fax (541) 885-3452.

63 Fourmile Lake   8

This beautiful spot is the only camp on the shore of Fourmile Lake. Several nearby trails provide access to the Sky Lakes Wilderness. The Pacific Crest Trail passes about two miles from camp. This campground is near the foot of Mount McLoughlin (9,495 feet). More primitive and with lots of solitude, it attracts a calm and quiet crowd. Afternoon winds can be a problem, and in the evening, if the wind isn't blowing, the mosquitoes often arrive. There is no view of Mount McLoughlin from the campground, but there is a good view from the lake.

Location: At Fourmile Lake in Winema National Forest; map E2, grid e4.

Campsites, facilities: There are 25 sites for tents, trailers, or RVs up to 22 feet long. Picnic tables, garbage bins, and fire grills are provided. Drinking water and vault toilets are available. Leashed pets are permitted.

Reservations, fees: No reservations. Sites are $9 per night, $4 per night for an additional vehicle. Open from June to late September.

Directions: From Medford drive northeast on Highway 62 for five miles to Exit 30 and Highway 140. Turn east on Highway 140 and drive approximately 40 miles to Forest Road 3661. Turn north and drive six miles to the campground.

Contact: Winema National Forest, Klamath Ranger District, 136 California Avenue, Klamath Falls, OR 97601; tel. (541) 885-3400; fax (541) 885-3452.

64 Lake of the Woods Resort

   9

Located on beautiful Lake of the Woods, this resort offers fishing (four kinds of trout, catfish, and bass) and boating in a secluded forest setting. It's on one of the most beautiful lakes in the Cascade mountains, surrounded by tall pine trees. It's a family-oriented campground with all the amenities. In the winter, snowmobiling and cross-country skiing are popular (you can rent equipment at the resort). Attractions in the area include the Mountain Lakes Wilderness and the Pacific Crest Trail.

Location: On Lake of the Woods; map E2 grid e4.

Campsites, facilities: There are 27 sites for tents, trailers, or RVs up to 35 feet long, plus eight cabins that can accommodate from one to six people. Rest rooms, showers, a sanitary dump, a public phone, a laundry room, ice, snacks, a restaurant, a lounge, and LP gas bottles are available. There is also a boat ramp, dock, marina, boat and mountain bike rentals, and a barbecue. Leashed pets are permitted.

Reservations, fees: Reservations recommended. Sites are $14-20 per night, and cabins are $45-249 per night. Open year-round, weather permitting.

Directions: In Medford on Interstate 5, take Exit 14 to Highway 66. Drive east for less than a mile to Dead Indian Memorial Road. Turn left (east) and drive 40 miles to Lake of the Woods Road. Turn north and drive to the resort.

Contact: Lake of the Woods Resort, 950 Harriman Route, Klamath Falls, OR 97601; tel. (541) 949-8300.

65 Odessa   4

This campground is set at an elevation of 4,100 feet, along Odessa Creek, near the shore of Upper Klamath Lake. The lake is the main attraction, with fishing the main activity. Campsites are in among scattered mixed conifers and native brush. Boating is allowed, but not waterskiing. The lake can provide excellent fishing for rainbow trout on both flies and Rapalas.

Location: Near Klamath Lake in Winema National Forest; map E2, grid e5.

Campsites, facilities: There are five tent sites. Picnic tables, garbage bins, and fire grills are provided. Vault toilets are available, but there is no drinking water. Leashed pets are permitted.

Reservations, fees: No reservations; no fee. Open year-round, weather permitting.

Directions: From Klamath Falls drive north on Highway 140 about 18 miles to Forest Road 3639. Turn northeast and drive one miles to the campground.

Contact: Winema National Forest, Klamath Ranger District, 136 California Avenue, Klamath Falls, OR 97601; tel. (541) 885-3400; fax (541) 885-3452.

66 Oregon 8 RV Park

       6

This campground, surrounded by mountains, big rocks, and trees, is near Hanks Marsh on the southeast shore of Upper Klamath Lake, within 50 miles of Crater Lake. Nearby recreation options include a golf course, bike paths, and a marina.

Location: On Upper Klamath Lake; map E2, grid e6.

Campsites, facilities: There are 10 tent sites and 29 drive-through sites for trailers or RVs of any length. Electricity, drinking water, cable TV, sewer hookups, and picnic tables are provided. Flush toilets, showers, a recreation hall, a laundry room, ice, and a swimming pool are available. Bottled gas, a store, and a cafe are located within one mile. Leashed pets and motorbikes are permitted.

Reservations, fees: Reservations accepted. Sites are $10-17 per night. Open year-round, with limited winter facilities.

Directions: From Klamath Falls drive north on U.S. 97 for 3.5 miles to the campground.

Contact: Oregon 8 RV Park, 5225 Highway 97 North, Klamath Falls, OR 97601; tel. (541) 882-0482.

67 Jackson Hot Springs

 5

This wooded campground has mineral hot springs that empty into a swimming pool, not a hot pool (76 degrees). Hot mineral baths are available in private rooms. This is an old Indian birthing ground. Nearby recreation options include a golf course, hiking trails, bike path, and tennis courts. Boating, fishing, and waterskiing are within ten miles.

Location: Near Ashland; map E2, grid f0.

Campsites, facilities: There are 30 tent sites and 20 drive-through sites for trailers or RVs of any length. Electricity, drinking water, sewer hookups, and picnic tables are provided. Flush toilets, showers, a cafe, a laundry room, ice, and a swimming pool are available. Bottled gas is located within one mile. Pets are permitted with deposit.

Reservations, fees: No reservations. Sites are $13-20 per night. Open year-round.

Directons: From Ashland drive north on Interstate 5 to Exit 19. Take that exit and drive west for one-quarter mile to the stoplight at Highway 99. Turn right and drive 500 feet to the campground.

Contact: Jackson Hot Springs, 2253 Highway 99 North, Ashland, OR 97520; tel. (541) 482-3776.

68 Wrangle   10

This campground is set at the headwaters of Glade Creek in the Siskiyou Mountains at an elevation of 6,400 feet. The Pacific Crest Trail passes near camp. Dutchman Peak Lookout, built in the late 1920s and featured in the National Historic Register, is located within five miles. This is a lovely campground, in a beautiful, high country setting, with huge Shasta red firs and views of the Siskiyou Mountains. Wrangle is along the Scenic Siskiyou Loop driving tour.

Location: Near the Pacific Crest Trail in Rogue River National Forest; map E2, grid f0.

Campsites, facilities: There are five sites for tents. Picnic tables and fire grills are provided. The availability of drinking water is intermittent. All garbage must be packed out. Vault toilets and a community kitchen are available. Leashed pets are permitted.

Reservations, fees: No reservations; no fee. Open early June to late October, weather permitting.

Directions: In Ashland on Interstate 5, take the Jacksonville exit. Drive east on the Jacksonville Highway to Jacksonville and Highway 238. Bear left on Highway 238 and drive eight miles to the town of Ruch and County Road 10 (Upper Applegate Road). Turn left and drive 9.5 miles to Forest Road 20. Turn left and drive 21 miles to Forest Road 2030. Continue one mile on Forest Road 2030 to the campground.

Contact: Rogue River National Forest, Applegate District, 6941 Upper Applegate Road, Jacksonville, OR 97530; (41) 899-1812 or fax (541) 858-2401.

69 Glenyan Campground of Ashland   7

This campground within seven miles of Ashland offers shady sites near Emigrant Lake. Recreation options in the area include a golf course, hiking trails, bike path, and tennis courts. It's an easy jump from Interstate 5 at Ashland.

Location: Near Emigrant Lake; map E2, grid f1.

Campsites, facilities: There are 68 sites for tents, trailers, or RVs of any length; 12 have full and 38 have partial hookups. Electricity, drinking water, sewer hookups, and picnic tables are provided. Flush toilets, bottled gas, sanitary disposal services, showers, firewood, a recreation hall, a store, a laundry room, ice, a playground, and a swimming pool are available. Leashed pets are permitted.

Reservations, fees: Reservations accepted. Sites are $17.50-22 per night. Open year-round.

Directions: From Ashland drive east on Highway 66 for 3.5 miles to the campground on the right.

Contact: Glenyan Campground of Ashland, 5310 Highway 66, Ashland, OR 97520; tel. (541) 488-1785.

70 Mount Ashland   8

Set at 6,600 feet along the Pacific Crest Trail, this beautiful site is heavily wooded and has abundant wildlife. On clear days there are great lookouts nearby from Siskiyou Peak, particularly to the south, where California's 14,162-foot Mount Shasta is an awesome sight. Mt. Ashland Ski Resort is one mile west of the campground.

Location: On the Pacific Crest Trail in Klamath National Forest; map E2, grid f1.

Campsites, facilities: There are nine sites for tents, trailers, or RVs up to 15 feet long. Picnic tables and fire grills are provided. All garbage must be packed out. Vault toilets are available, but there is no drinking water. Leashed pets are permitted.

Reservations, fees: No reservations; no fee. Open from May to late October.

Directions: From Ashland drive south on Interstate 5 for 12 miles to Mount Ashland Ski Park Road (County Road 993). Turn west and drive 10 miles (the road becomes Forest Road 20) to the campground.

Contact: Klamath National Forest, Scott River Ranger District, 11263 N. Highway 3, Fort Jones, CA 96032; tel. (530) 468-5351; fax (530) 468-1290.

71 Hyatt Lake   8

This campground is on the south end of Hyatt Reservoir, which has six miles of shoreline. Fishing is good for brook and rainbow trout and smallmouth bass. Another campground option is Wildcat, about two miles north, with 12 semi-primitive sites. Boat speed limit here is 10 mph.

Location: On Hyatt Lake; map E2, grid f2.

Campsites, facilities: There are 47 sites for tents, trailers, or RVs up to 40 feet in length, one horse campsite, one group site, and a few walk-in, tent sites. Picnic tables and fire grills are provided. Drinking water, garbage service, showers, flush toilets, a sanitary disposal station, a fish cleaning station, a day-use area, athletic fields, a playground, horseshoe pits, and two boat ramps are available. Some sites and facilities are wheelchair accessible. Leased pets are permitted.

Reservations, fees: No reservations. Sites are $10 per night, with a 14-day stay limit. Open late April through October, weather permitting.

Directions: From Ashland drive east on Highway 66 for 17 miles to East Hyatt Lake Road. Turn north and drive three miles to the campground entrance on the left.

Contact: Bureau of Land Management, Medford District, 3040 Biddle Road, Medford, OR 97504; tel. (541) 770-2200; fax (541) 770-2400.

72 Hyatt Lake Resort   7

This campground is set along the shore of Hyatt Lake, just west of the dam, where hiking and fishing are some of the recreation options. This is a scaled-down option to the resort at adjacent Howard Prairie Lake. The Pacific Crest Trail is just half a mile away.

Location: On Hyatt Lake; map E2, grid f2.

Campsites, facilities: There are 13 no-hookup and 22 full-hookup sites for trailers or RVs of any length; three are drive-through sites. There are also four cabins with no kitchen facilities; each sleeps four. Electricity (10 sites have 50 amp), drinking water, sewer hookups, and picnic tables are provided. Flush toilets, sanitary disposal services, showers, a store, a laundry room, ice, and boat rentals are available. Boat docks and launching facilities are on the resort property. Leashed pets and motorbikes are permitted.

Reservations, fees: Reservations accepted. Sites are $14-20 per night; call for cabin fees (monthly rates are available). Open from April through October.

Directions: From Ashland drive east on Highway 66 for 17 miles to East Hyatt Lake Road. Turn north and drive three miles to Hyatt Prairie Road. Turn and drive one mile to the resort.

Contact: Hyatt Lake Resort, 7979 Hyatt Prairie Road, Ashland, OR 97520; tel. (541) 482-3331.

73 Camper's Cove   7

This campground is along the shore of Hyatt Lake, with the Pacific Crest Trail passing about a mile away. It is located in a cove east of the dam.

Location: On Hyatt Lake; map E2, grid f2.

Campsites, facilities: There are 23 sites for trailers or RVs up to 30 feet long; seven are drive-through sites. Electricity, drinking water, sewer hookups, and picnic tables are provided. Flush toilets, showers, firewood, a store, a cafe, and ice are available. Boat docks are nearby. Leashed pets are permitted.

Reservations, fees: Reservations accepted. Sites are $15 per night. Open year-round.

Directions: From Ashland drive east on Highway 66 for 17 miles to East Hyatt Lake Road. Turn north and drive three miles to Hyatt Dam Road. Turn right and drive 2.5 miles (over the dam) to the resort.

Contact: Camper's Cove, 7900 Hyatt Prairie Road, Ashland, OR 97520; tel. (541) 482-1201.

7.4 Emigrant Campground

 8

In this campground nestled among the trees along Emigrant Lake, you're just about guaranteed a site. Emigrant Lake is a well-known recreational area, and activities at this park include swimming, hiking, boating, waterskiing, and fishing. There are also two super water slides. The park has its own swimming cove. Side trip possibilities include exploring nearby Mount Ashland, where a ski area operates in the winter, and visiting the world-renowned Shakespeare Festival in Ashland.

Location: On Emigrant Lake; map E2, grid f2.

Campsites, facilities: There are at least 42 sites for tents, trailers, and self-contained RVs, plus an overflow area. Two group camp areas, the picnic and barbecue areas can be reserved. Rest rooms, coin-operated showers, a sanitary dump, a public phone, snacks in summer, and a barbecue are available. Recreational facilities include horseshoe pits, and a recreation field. Two boat ramps are provided. Some facilities are wheelchair accessible. Laundry and food facilities are located within six miles. Pets are permitted in designated areas only.

Reservations, fees: Reservations accepted only for the group camps and picnic areas. Sites are $14 per night. Children 15 and under are free, and pets are $1 per night. Open from mid-March to mid-October.

Directions: From Ashland drive east on Highway 66 for five miles to the campground.

Contact: Jackson County Parks, 400 Antelope Road, White City, OR 97503; (41) 774-8183 or fax (541) 826-8360.

7.5 Howard Prairie Lake Resort   7

This wooded campground is along the shore of Howard Prairie Lake, where hiking, swimming, fishing, and boating are among the recreation options. This is one of the largest campgrounds in more than a hundred miles.

Location: On Howard Prairie Lake; map 2, grid f3.

Campsites, facilities: There are 300 sites for tents, trailers, or RVs of any length. Electricity, drinking water, sewer hookups, 24-hour security, and picnic tables are provided. Flush toilets, bottled gas, sanitary disposal services, showers, firewood, a store, a cafe, a laundry room, boat docks, boat rentals, moorage, and launching facilities are available. Leashed pets are permitted.

Reservations, fees: No reservations. Sites are $12-17 per night. Open from mid-April through October.

Directions: In Ashland on Interstate 5, take Exit 14 to Highway 66. Drive east for less than a mile to Dead Indian Memorial Road. Turn left (east) and drive 19 miles to Howard Prairie Road. Turn south and drive five miles to the reservoir.

Contact: Howard Prairie Lake Resort, 3249 Hyatt Prairie Road, Ashland, OR 97520; tel. (541) 482-1979; fax (541) 773-3130.

76 Topsy   7

This campground is on the Upper Klamath River, which is a good spot for trout fishing and a top river for rafters (experts only, or non-experts with professional licensed guides). There is Class IV and V white water about four miles southwest at Caldera, Satan's Gate, Hell's Corner, and Three Rocks. I flipped at Caldera and up swimming for it, finally getting out at an eddy. Luckily, I was wearing a dry suit and the best lifejacket available, perfect fitting, which saved my bacon. The area is good for mountain biking, too.

Location: On the Upper Klamath River; map E2, grid f5.

Campsites, facilities: There are 15 sites for trailers or RVs up to 40 feet long. Picnic tables, garbage service, and fire grills are provided. Pit toilets, a sanitary disposal station, and drinking water are available. Facilities are wheelchair accessible. Boat launching facilities are nearby. Leashed pets are permitted.

Reservations, fees: No reservations. Sites are $7 per night, $4 per night for an additional vehicle, with a 14-day stay limit. Open mid-May through Labor Day.

Directions: From Klamath Falls drive west on Highway 66 for 14.5 miles to Topsy Road. Turn south on Topsy Road and drive 1.5 miles to the campground on the right.

Contact: Bureau of Land Management, Klamath Falls Resource Area, 2795 Anderson Avenue, Building 25, Klamath Falls, OR 97603; tel. (541) 883-6916; fax (541) 884-2097.

77 KOA Klamath Falls   6

This wooded and grassy campground with a creek running through is along the shore of Upper Klamath Lake, near the marina. Hiking trails and tennis courts are nearby. This is a good base camp if you plan to explore the Crater Lake area.

Location: On Upper Klamath Lake; map E2, grid f6.

Campsites, facilities: There are 18 tent sites and 73 sites for trailers or RVs of any length; 37 are drive-through sites. Electricity, drinking water, sewer hookups, and picnic tables are provided. Flush toilets, bottled gas, sanitary disposal services, showers, a recreation hall, a store, a laundry room, ice, a playground, and a swimming pool are available. A cafe is located within one mile. Boat docks and launching facilities are nearby. Leashed pets and motorbikes are permitted.

Reservations, fees: Reservations accepted; call (800) 562-9036. Sites are $17-22 per night. Open year-round, with limited winter facilities.

Directions: From Klamath Falls drive northwest on U.S. 97 for 1.5 miles to Shasta Way. Turn west and drive one block to the park.

Contact: KOA Klamath Falls, 3435 Shasta Way, Klamath Falls, OR 97603; tel. (541) 884-4644; website: www.koa.com.

78 Tingley Lake Estates   6

This privately operated RV park provides a layover for travelers crossing the Oregon border on U.S. 97. You can see Mt. Shasta from this park right on the lake. All sites have a view of the lake. Tingley Lake has opportunities for bass fishing, boating, and swimming.

Location: On Tingley Lake; map E2, grid f6.

Campsites, facilities: There are six tent sites and 10 sites for trailers or RVs of any length; three have full and seven have partial hookups. Electricity, drinking water, sewer hookups, and picnic tables are provided. Telephone and cable TV hookups, flush toilets, sanitary disposal services, showers, boat docks, and a playground are available. A store, a cafe, and ice are located within two miles. Leashed pets are permitted.

Reservations, fees: Reservations accepted. Sites are $14-16 per night. Open year-round, weather permitting, with limited winter services.

Directions: From Klamath Falls drive southwest on U.S. 97 for seven miles to Old Midland Road. Turn east and drive two miles to Tingley Lane. Turn south and drive a half mile to the park.

Contact: Tingley Lake Estates, 11800 Tingley Lane, Klamath Falls, OR 97603 tel. (541) 882-8386.

79 Wiseman's Mobile Court and RV   5

This is a suburban RV park with the barest essentials, including trees and lawn. It's a decent layover spot if you need a quick place to stay. You can find golf within two miles.

Location: Near Upper Klamath Lake; map E2, grid f7.

Campsites, facilities: There are 17 sites for trailers or RVs of any length. Electricity, drinking water, and sewer hookups are provided. Flush toilets, sanitary disposal services, showers, and laundry facilities are available. Bottled gas is located within one block. Leashed pets are permitted.

Reservations, fees: Reservations accepted. Sites are $16 per night. Open year-round.

Directions: From Klamath Falls drive east on Highway 140 for 4.5 miles to the park.

Contact: Wiseman's Mobile Court and RV, 6800 S. Sixth Street, Klamath Falls, OR 97603; tel. (541) 884-4327.

MAP E3

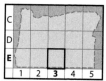

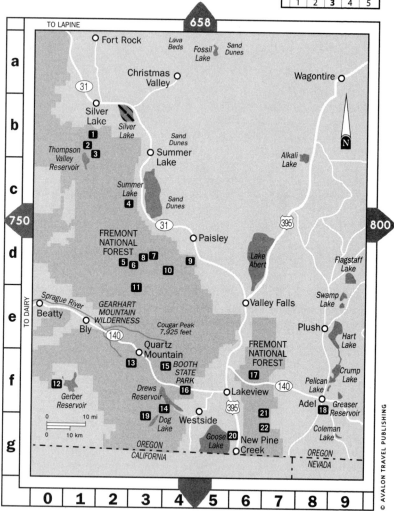

TO LAPINE

658

Fort Rock

Lava Beds

Fossil Lake

Sand Dunes

a

Christmas Valley

Wagontire

31

N

b

Silver Lake

1

Silver Lake

Sand Dunes

2

3

Thompson Valley Reservoir

Summer Lake

Alkali Lake

c

Summer Lake

Sand Dunes

4

750

31

Paisley

395

800

FREMONT NATIONAL FOREST

Lake Abert

Flagstaff Lake

d

5 **6** **8** **7**

9

10

Swamp Lake

11

Sprague River

GEARHART MOUNTAIN WILDERNESS

Valley Falls

e

TO DAIRY

Beatty

Bly

Cougar Peak 7,925 feet

Plush

Hart Lake

140

Quartz Mountain

FREMONT NATIONAL FOREST

Crump Lake

f

13

15 BOOTH STATE PARK

17

Pelican Lake

12

Gerber Reservoir

Drews Reservoir

16

Lakeview

Adel

18 Greaser Reservoir

0   10 mi

0   10 km

19

14

Dog Lake

Westside

395

21

22

Coleman Lake

140

g

OREGON CALIFORNIA

Goose Lake

20

New Pine Creek

OREGON NEVADA

© AVALON TRAVEL PUBLISHING

0   1   2   3   4   5   6   7   8   9

CHAPTER E3

■ Silver Creek Marsh   4

A trailhead and terminus for segments of the National Recreational Trail are located at this small, quiet, and primitive camp that gets little attention. It's a short walk to the creek, a popular fishing spot.

Location: Near Silver Creek in Fremont National Forest; map E3, grid b1.

Campsites, facilities: There are 17 tent sites. Picnic tables and fire grills are provided. Drinking water, firewood, vault toilets, and hitching rails and corrals for horses are available. All garbage must be packed out. Leashed pets are permitted.

Reservations, fees: No reservations; no fee. Open May to mid-November.

Directions: From Bend drive south on U.S. 97 for 32 miles to Highway 31. Turn southeast on Highway 31 and drive 48 miles to County Road 4-11 (one mile west of the town of Silver Lake). Turn right and drive six miles (the road becomes Forest Road 27) and continue south for five miles to the campground entrance road on the left.

Contact: Fremont National Forest, Silver Lake Ranger District, P.O. Box 129, Silver Lake, OR 97638; tel. (541) 576-2107; fax (541) 576-7587.

■ Thompson Reservoir   3

Located on the north shore of Thompson Reservoir among black bark ponderosa pine the height of telephone poles, this camp is simple and pretty, with shaded sites close to the water. Fishing and boating are permitted. See description of East Bay Campground. Water in the reservoir fluctuates and sometimes dries up altogether in late summer. This is a popular fishing and boating area.

Location: On Thompson Reservoir in Fremont National Forest; map E3, grid b1.

Campsites, facilities: There are 19 sites for tents, trailers, or RVs up to 22 feet long, plus a separate group camping area. Picnic tables and fire grills are provided. Drinking water and vault toilets are available, but all garbage must be packed out. Boat launching facilities are nearby. Leashed pets are permitted.

Reservations, fees: No reservations; no fee. Open May to mid-November.

Directions: From Bend drive south on U.S. 97 for 32 miles to Highway 31. Turn southeast on Highway 31 and drive 48 miles to County Road 4-11 (one mile west of the town of Silver Lake). Turn right and drive six miles (the road becomes Forest Road 27) and continue south for nine miles to the campground entrance road. Turn left and drive one mile to the camp.

Contact: Fremont National Forest, Silver Lake Ranger District, P.O. Box 129, Silver Lake, OR 97638; tel. (541) 576-2107; fax (541) 576-7587.

■ East Bay   3

This campground on the east shore of Thompson Reservoir has paved roads, but it's still a long way from home, so be sure to bring all of your supplies with you. A day-use area is adjacent to the camp. Silver Creek Marsh Campground is an even more primitive setting along a stream.

Location: On Thompson Reservoir in Fremont National Forest; map E3, grid c1.

Campsites, facilities: There are 17 sites for tents, trailers, or RVs. Picnic tables, garbage bins, and fire grills are provided. Drinking water, vault toilets, and a fishing pier are available. The facilities are wheelchair accessible. Boat launching facilities are nearby. Leashed pets are permitted.

Reservations, fees: No reservations accepted. Sites are $6 per night. Open May to mid-November.

Directions: From Bend drive south on U.S. 97 for 32 miles to Highway 31. Turn southeast on Highway 31 and drive 50 miles to Silver Lake. Continue east a short distance on Highway 31 to Forest Road 28. Turn right on Forest Road 28 and drive 13 miles to Forest Road 014. Turn right on Forest Road 014 and drive two miles to the campground.

Contact: Fremont National Forest, Silver Lake Ranger District, P.O. Box 129, Silver Lake, OR 97638; tel. (541) 576-2107; fax (541) 576-7587.

4 Dairy Point   6

This campground, elevation 5,200 feet, is located next to the Dairy Creek Bridge, in a stand of ponderosa pine and white fir at the edge of a large and open meadow. The setting is beautiful and peaceful, with a towering backdrop of mountains. Fishing and inner tubing are popular activities at Dairy Creek. Warning: This campground is suitable for large groups and is often full on holidays and most weekends.

Location: On Dairy Creek in Fremont National Forest; map E3, grid c3.

Campsites, facilities: There are four sites for tents or trailers. Picnic tables, fire grills, a vault toilet, and drinking water are provided. All garbage must be packed out. Leashed pets are permitted.

Reservations, fees: No reservations; no fee. Open mid-May through October.

Directions: From Lakeview drive north on U.S. 395 for 18 miles to Highway 31. Turn northwest and drive 22 miles to Paisley. Continue one Highway 31 for one-half mile to Mill Street. Turn west on Mill Street and drive 20 miles (the road becomes Forest Road 33) and continue to the T intersection with Forest Road 28. Turn left and drive two miles (crossing the Dairy Creek Bridge) to Forest Road 3428. Turn left and drive to the campground (located just past the intersection on the left).

Contact: Fremont National Forest, Paisley Ranger District, P.O. Box 67, Paisley, OR 97636; tel. (541) 943-3114; fax (541) 943-4479.

5 Sandhill Crossing   6

If you're looking for a combination of beauty and solitude, you've found it. This camp is located at 6,306 feet on the banks of the designated Wild and Scenic North Fork Sprague River, where fishing is superior. This is a low-use camp, but it is popular with anglers and hunters in the fall.

Location: On the North Fork of the Sprague River in Fremont National Forest; map E3, grid d2.

Campsites, facilities: There are five sites for tents, trailers, or RVs; some are drive-through sites. Picnic tables, fire grills, vault toilets, and drinking water are provided. All garbage must be packed out. Leashed pets are permitted.

Reservations, fees: No reservations; no fee. Open June through October.

Directions: From Lakeview drive north on U.S. 395 for 18 miles to Highway 31. Turn northwest and drive 22 miles to Paisley. Continue one Highway 31 for one-half mile to Mill Street. Turn west on Mill Street and drive 20 miles (the road becomes Forest Road 33) and continue to the T intersection with Forest Road 28. Turn right and drive 11 miles to Forest Road 3411. Turn left and drive eight miles to the campground.

Contact: Fremont National Forest, Paisley Ranger District, P.O. Box 67, Paisley, OR 97636; tel. (541) 943-3114; fax (541) 943-4479.

6 Lee Thomas   6

Nestled along the North Fork of the Sprague River in the interior of Fremont National Forest, this small, cozy camp is a genuine hideaway, with all the necessities provided. It is set at an elevation of 6,306 feet. Like Sandhill Crossing Campground, two miles downstream, this camp is popular with fishermen and hunters in the fall. Lee Thomas is located two miles upstream from Sandhill Crossing and is set in a meadow.

Location: Near the North Fork of the Sprague River in Fremont National Forest; map E3, grid d3.

Campsites, facilities: There are eight sites for tents, trailers, or RVs up to 16 feet long. Picnic tables and fire grills are provided. Drinking water and vault toilets are available. All garbage must be packed out. Leashed pets are permitted.

Reservations, fees: No reservations; no fee. Open June to late October.

Directions: From Lakeview drive north on U.S. 395 for 18 miles to Highway 31. Turn northwest and drive 22 miles to Paisley. Continue on Highway 31 for one-half mile to Mill Street. Turn west on Mill Street and drive 20 miles (the road becomes Forest Road 33) and continue to the T intersection with Forest Road 28. Turn right and drive 11 miles to Forest Road 3411. Turn left and drive five miles to the campground.

Contact: Fremont National Forest, Paisley Ranger District, P.O. Box 67, Paisley, OR 97636; tel. (541) 943-3114; fax (541) 943-4479.

7 Campbell Lake   9

This campground on the pebbled shore of Campbell Lake is near Dead Horse Lake Campground. These high-elevation, crystal-clear lakes were formed during the glacier period. Both camps are very busy and are full most weekends in July and August. No boats with gas motors are permitted on Campbell Lake. Good side trips are available in Fremont National Forest. A U.S. Forest Service map details the back roads.

Location: On Campbell Lake in Fremont National Forest; map E3, grid d3.

Campsites, facilities: There are 18 sites for tents, trailers, or RVs up to 16 feet long. Picnic tables and fire grills are provided. Drinking water and vault toilets are available. A boat launch is adjacent to the camp. Boats with electric motors are permitted, but gas motors are prohibited. All garbage must be packed out. Leashed pets are permitted.

Reservations, fees: No reservations; no fee. Open July to late October.

Directions: From Lakeview drive north on U.S. 395 for 18 miles to Highway 31. Turn northwest and drive 22 miles to Paisley. Continue one Highway 31 for one-half mile to Mill Street. Turn west on Mill Street and drive 20 miles (the road becomes Forest Road 33) and continue to the T intersection with Forest Road 28. Turn right and drive eight miles to Forest Road 033. Turn left and drive two miles to the campground.

Contact: Fremont National Forest, Paisley Ranger District, P.O. Box 67, Paisley, OR 97636; tel. (541) 943-3114; fax (541) 943-4479.

8 Dead Horse Lake   9

The shore of Dead Horse Lake is home to this camp (at 7,372 feet elevation). A hiking trail winds around the perimeter of the lake, hooking up with other trails along the way. One original Civilian Conservation Corps canoe is left in the lake, a relic of the 1930s. Good side trips are nearby in Fremont National Forest. See description of Campbell Lake Campground.

Location: On Dead Horse Lake in Fremont National Forest; map E3, grid d3.

Campsites, facilities: There are nine sites, 10 sites for tents, trailers, or RVs up to 16 feet long, and a separate area for group camping. Picnic tables and fire grills are provided. Drinking water and vault toilets are available, but all garbage must be packed out. A boat launch is nearby. Boats with electric motors are permitted, but gas motors are prohibited. All garbage must be packed out. Leashed pets are permitted.

Reservations, fees: No reservations; no fee. Open July through October.

Directions: From Lakeview drive north on U.S. 395 for 18 miles to Highway 31. Turn northwest and drive 22 miles to Paisley. Continue one Highway 31 for one-half mile to Mill Street. Turn west on Mill Street and drive 20 miles (the road becomes Forest Road 33) and continue to the T intersection with Forest Road 28. Turn right and drive 11 miles (watch for the turn to Campbell-Dead Horse Lakes) to Forest Road 033. Turn left and drive three miles (gravel road) to the campground.

Contact: Fremont National Forest, Paisley Ranger District, P.O. Box 67, Paisley, OR 97636; tel. (541) 943-3114; fax (541) 943-4479.

9 Marster Spring   6

This pretty campground is set at an elevation of 4,845 feet on the banks of the Chewaucan River, a good fishing area. It's right on the river among ponderosa pine trees, yet close to the town of Paisley. It's the largest of several popular camps in this river corridor.

Location: On the Chewaucan River in Fremont National Forest; map E3, grid d4.

Campsites, facilities: There are 11 sites for tents, trailers, or RVs up to 22 feet long. Picnic tables and fire grills are provided. Drinking water and vault toilets are available. Leashed pets are permitted.

Reservations, fees: No reservations; no fee. Open May to October.

Directions: From Lakeview drive north on U.S. 395 for 18 miles to Highway 31.

Turn northwest and drive 22 miles to Paisley. Continue one Highway 31 for one-half mile to Mill Street. Turn west on Mill Street and drive 20 miles (the road becomes Forest Road 33) and continue to the T intersection with Forest Road 28. Turn left (still Forest Road 33) and drive seven miles to the campground on the left.

Contact: Fremont National Forest, Paisley Ranger District, P.O. Box 67, Paisley, OR 97636; tel. (541) 943-3114; fax (541) 943-4479.

10 Happy Camp   6

Here's a pleasant spot at 5,289 feet elevation, with open sites along Dairy Creek, though only one site is close to the water. The camp houses some old Depression-era Civilian Conservation Corps shelters, preserved in their original state. Horseshoe pits are provided. Fishing is available here for stocked rainbow trout.

Location: On Dairy Creek in Fremont National Forest; map E3, grid d4.

Campsites, facilities: There are nine sites for tents, trailers, or RVs up to 16 feet long. Picnic tables and fire grills are provided. Vault toilets are available, but there is no drinking water. All garbage must be packed out. Leashed pets are permitted.

Reservations, fees: No reservations; no fee. Open mid-May to late October.

Directions: From Lakeview drive north on U.S. 395 for 18 miles to Highway 31. Turn northwest and drive 22 miles to Paisley. Continue on Highway 31 for one-half mile to Mill Street. Turn west on Mill Street and drive 20 miles (the road becomes Forest Road 33) and continue to the T intersection with Forest Road 28. Turn right and drive two miles (just before Dairy Creek) to Forest Road 047. Turn left and drive two miles to the campground on the left.

Contact: Fremont National Forest, Paisley Ranger District, P.O. Box 67, Paisley, OR 97636; tel. (541) 943-3114; fax (541) 943-4479.

11 Corral Creek   4

Set along Corral Creek, this camp is adjacent to a trailhead that provides access into the Gearhart Mountain Wilderness, making it a prime base camp for a backpacking trip. Access is also available from camp to the Palisade Rocks, a worthwhile side trip. Another option is Quartz Mountain Snowpark, which is located 14 miles east of the campground.

Location: Near the Gearhart Mountain Wilderness in Fremont National Forest; map E3, grid e3.

Campsites, facilities: There are six sites for tents, trailers, or RVs up to 16 feet long. Picnic tables and fire grills are provided. Vault toilets are available. There is no drinking water, and all garbage must be packed out. Stock facilities include hitching posts, stalls, and corrals. Leashed pets are permitted.

Reservations, fees: No reservations; no fee. Open mid-May to late October.

Directions: From Klamath Falls drive east on Highway 140 for 53 miles to the town of Bly. Continue east on Highway 140 for another 13 miles to Forest Road 3660. Turn left and drive 13 miles to Forest Road 34. Turn right and drive about one-eighth mile to Forest Road 012 and continue to the campground.,

Contact: Fremont National Forest, Bly Ranger District, P.O. Box 25, Bly, OR 97622; tel. (541) 353-2427.

12 Gerber Reservoir 6

This camp can be found at an elevation of 4,800 feet alongside the west shore of Gerber Reservoir (10-mph boat speed limit). Almost nobody has heard of Gerber because it's out in the middle of nowhere. And that's just how we like it, right? Recreation options include swimming, fishing, boating, and hiking.

Location: On Gerber Reservoir; map E3, grid f0.

Campsites, facilities: There are 50 sites for tents, trailers, or RVs up to 30 feet long. Picnic tables and fire grills are provided. Drinking water, firewood, a sanitary dump station, wheelchair-accessible vault toilets, a boat ramp, a boat dock, launching facilities, and a fish cleaning station are available. Leashed pets are permitted.

Reservations, fees: No reservations accepted. Sites are $7 per night, $4 per night for an additional vehicle. Open May to mid-October.

Directions: From Klamath Falls drive east on Highway 140 for 16 miles to Dairy and Highway 70. Turn south on Highway 70 and drive seven miles to Bonanza and East Langell Valley Road. Turn east on East Langell Valley Road and drive for 11 miles to Gerber Road. Turn left on Gerber Road and drive eight miles to the campground on the right.

Contact: Bureau of Land Management, Klamath Falls Resource Area, 2795 Anderson Avenue, Building 25, Klamath Falls, OR 97603; tel. (541) 883-6916; fax (541) 884-2097.

13 Lofton Reservoir 6

This remote campground is on the shore of Lofton Reservoir, the biggest lake in the area. Other lakes are nearby and are accessible by forest roads. This area marks the beginning of the Great Basin, a high-desert area that extends to Idaho. A large fire burned much of the surround forest about 20 years ago, creating an oasis of sorts at this campground.

Location: On Lofton Reservoir in Fremont National Forest; map E3, grid f2.

Campsites, facilities: There are 26 sites for tents, trailers, or RVs up to 22 feet long. Picnic tables and fire grills are provided. Drinking water and vault toilets are available. Boat docks and launching facilities are nearby. Leashed pets are permitted.

Reservations, fees: No reservations; no fee. Open mid-May to late October.

Directions: From Klamath Falls drive east on Highway 140 for 54 miles to Bly. Continue east on Highway 140 for 13 miles to Forest Road 3715. Turn right and drive seven miles to Forest Road 013. Turn left on Forest Road 013 and drive one mile to the campground.

Contact: Fremont National Forest, Bly Ranger District, P.O. Box 25, Bly, OR 97622; tel. (541) 353-2427.

14 Drews Creek 9

This is an exceptionally beautiful campground, set along Drews Creek at 4,900 feet. Wild roses grow near the creek, and there are several unmarked trails that lead to nearby hills where campers can enjoy scenic views. The wild roses are often gorgeous. This is a great spot for a family trip and is also popular with group campers, with horseshoe pits, an area for baseball, and a large group barbecue. Fishing is available in nearby Dog Lake, which also provides facilities for boating. Waterskiing is another option at Drews Reservoir, two miles to the west.

Location: Near Lakeview in Fremont National Forest; map E3, grid f4.

Campsites, facilities: There are five sites for tents, trailers, or RVs. Picnic tables, fire grills, vault toilets, and drinking water are provided. All garbage must be packed out. Leashed pets are permitted.

Reservations, fees: No reservations; no fee. Open early June to mid-October.

Directions: From Lakeview drive west on Highway 140 for 10 miles to County Road 1-13. Turn left and drive four miles to County Road 1-11D. Turn right and drive six miles (the road will become Forest Road 4017) to the bridge provides access to the campground.

Contact: Fremont National Forest, Lakeview Ranger District, HC 64, Box 60, Lakeview, OR 97630; tel. (541) 947-3334; fax (541) 947-6375.

15 Cottonwood Recreation Area   6

This campground along the shore of Cottonwood Meadow Lake is one of the better spots in the vicinity for fishing and hiking. Boats with electric motors are allowed on the lake, but gas motors are prohibited. Three hiking trails wind around the lake, and facilities for horses include hitching posts, feeders, water, and corrals. It is set at an elevation of 6,150 feet.

Location: On Cottonwood Meadow Lake in Fremont National Forest; map E3, grid f4.

Campsites, facilities: There are 21 sites for tents, small trailers, or RVs. Picnic tables and fire grills are provided. Drinking water and vault toilets are available, but all garbage must be packed out. Boat docks are nearby. Electric motors are allowed, but gasoline motors are prohibited on the lake. The boating speed limit is 5 mph. Leashed pets are permitted.

Reservations, fees: No reservations; no fee. Open early June to late October.

Directions: From Lakeview drive west on Highway 140 for 24 miles to Forest Road 3870. Turn right and drive eight miles to the campground.

Contact: Fremont National Forest, Lakeview Ranger District, HC 64, Box 60, Lakeview, OR 97630; tel. (541) 947-3334; fax (541) 947-6375.

16 Junipers Reservoir RV Resort   6

This resort on an 8,000-acre cattle ranch is in a designated Oregon Wildlife Viewing Area, and campers may catch glimpses of seldom-seen species. There are many nature walking trails at the park, and driving tours are offered for guests. Fishing for catfish is good in the vicinity (though not at the reservoir), and the summer climate is mild and pleasant. Antelope and elk can be spotted in this area.

Location: On Junipers Reservoir; map E3, grid f4.

Campsites, facilities: There are 15 tent sites and 40 sites for trailers or RVs.

Drinking water, rest rooms, showers, a sanitary dump station, a public phone, modem access, a laundry room, and ice are available. Recreational facilities include a recreation hall, a volleyball court, and horseshoe pits. Some of the facilities are wheelchair accessible. Leashed pets are permitted.

Reservations, fees: Reservations are recommended. Sites are $18-24 per night. Open May to mid-October.

Directions: From Lakeview drive west on Highway 140 for 10 miles to the resort (at milepost 86.5) on the right.

Contact: Junipers Reservoir RV Resort, HC 60, Box 1994A, Lakeview, OR 97630; tel. (541) 947-2050.

17 Mud Creek   4

This remote and quiet camp (at 6,600 feet) is in an isolated stand of lodgepole pines along the banks of Mud Creek. Drake Peak (8,405 feet) is nearby. There are no other camps in the immediate vicinity. Fishing in Mud Creek is surprisingly good.

Location: On Mud Creek in Fremont National Forest; map E3, grid f6.

Campsites, facilities: There are seven sites for tents, trailers, or RVs up to 16 feet long. Drinking water, picnic tables, fire grills, and vault toilets are available. Leashed pets are permitted.

Reservations, fees: No reservations; no fee. Open June to mid-October.

Directions: From Lakeview drive five miles north on U.S. 395 to Highway 140. Turn right on Highway 140 and drive eight miles to Forest 3615. Turn left and drive seven miles to the campground

Contact: Fremont National Forest, Lakeview Ranger District, HC 64, Box 60, Lakeview, OR 97630; tel. (541) 947-3334; fax (541) 947-6375.

18 Adel Store and Park   5

This remote park is the only game in town, so you'd better grab it while you can. Recreation options in the area include hang gliding, rockhounding, or visiting Hart Mountain National Antelope Refuge, 40 miles north of Adel.

Location: In Adel; map E3, grid f8.

Campsites, facilities: There are eight sites for trailers or RVs of any length. Electricity, drinking water, and sewer hookups are provided. A store, a cafe, and ice are available. Leashed pets and motorbikes are permitted.

Reservations, fees: No reservations accepted. Sites are $15 per night. Open April through October, weather permitting.

Directions: From Lakeview drive five miles north on U.S. 395 to Highway 140. Turn right (east) on Highway 140 and drive 28 miles to Adel (a very small town). The RV park is in town along Highway 140.

Contact: Adel Store and Park, P.O. Box 58, Adel, OR 97620; tel. (541) 947-3850.

19 Dog Lake   5

This campground is on the west shore of Dog Lake at an elevation of 6,375 feet. Fishing and boats with motors are permitted, though limited to a speed of 5 mph. Dog

Lake provides a popular fishery for bass, perch and crappie. It was named by Native Americans for the lake's resemblance in shape to the hind leg of a dog. Prospects for seeing waterfowl and eagles are good, too.

Location: On Dog Lake in Fremont National Forest; map E3, grid g3.

Campsites, facilities: There are eight sites for tents, trailers, or RVs up to 16 feet long. Drinking water, picnic tables, and fire grills are provided. Vault toilets are available. A boat launch is nearby. Leashed pets are permitted.

Reservations, fees: No reservations; no fee. Open mid-April to mid-October.

Directions: From Lakeview drive west on Highway 140 for seven miles to County Road 1-13. Turn left on County Road 1-13 and drive four miles to County Road 1-11D (Dog Lake Road). Turn right and drive four miles (the road becomes Forest Road 4017) into national forest. Continue on Forest Road 4017 for 12 miles (two miles past Drew Reservoir), then to Dog Lake and the campground entrance on the left.

Contact: Fremont National Forest, Lakeview Ranger District, HC 64, Box 60, Lakeview, OR 97630; tel. (541) 947-3334; fax (541) 947-6375.

20 Goose Lake State Park   7

This park is on the east shore of unusual Goose Lake, which lies half in Oregon and half in California. Waterfowl from the Pacific flyway frequent this out-of-the-way spot. It is home to many species of birds and other wildlife including a large herd of mule deer which spend much of the time in the campground. Boating is popular here.

Location: On Goose Lake; map E3, grid g6.

Campsites, facilities: There are 48 sites with water and electrical hookups for trailers or RVs up to 50 feet long. Picnic tables, fire grills, garbage bins and drinking water are provided. Flush toilets, showers, a sanitary disposal station, telephone, and firewood are available. Boat launching facilities are nearby. Leashed pets are permitted.

Reservations, fees: No reservations. Sites are $11-16 per night, $5 per night for an additional vehicle. Open from mid-April to late October.

Directions: From Lakeview drive south on U.S. 395 for 14 miles to the park entrance road on the right. Turn right (west) and drive one mile to the campground.

Contact: Goose Lake State Park, P.O. Box 207, New Pine Creek, OR 97635; tel. (800) 551-6949 or (541) 947-3111.

21 Willow Creek   4

This campground (at 5,800 feet elevation) is situated among tall pines and quaking aspen, not far from the banks of Willow Creek, near a dirt road that heads north to Burnt Creek. Among the secluded campsites wild flowers bloom in the spring. The campground is set in a canyon, with campsites along the creek. A hiking trail accesses the Crane Mountain Trail. Pick up a U.S. Forest Service map that details the back roads.

Location: Near Willow Creek in Fremont National Forest; map E3, grid g7.

Campsites, facilities: There are eight sites for tents, trailers, or RVs up to 22 feet long. Picnic tables and fire grills are provided. There is no drinking water, and all garbage must be packed out. Vault toilets are available. Leashed pets are permitted.

Reservations, fees: No reservations; no fee. Open June to mid-October.

Directions: From Lakeview drive five miles north on U.S. 395 to Highway 140. Turn right (east) on Highway 140 and drive seven miles to Forest Road 3915. Turn right and drive nine miles to Forest Road 4011. Turn right and drive one mile to the campground

Contact: Fremont National Forest, Lakeview Ranger District, HC 64, Box 60, Lakeview, OR 97630; tel. (541) 947-3334; fax (541) 947-6375.

22 Deep Creek   8

Shaded by huge ponderosa pine and cottonwoods, this pretty, little-used campground at an elevation of 5,600 feet on the banks of Deep Creek is the place if you're after privacy. Magnificent spring wildflowers are a highlight here.

Location: On Deep Creek in Fremont National Forest; map E3, grid g7.

Campsites, facilities: There are two sites for tents and four sites for trailers or RVs up to 22 feet long. Picnic tables and fire grills are provided. Vault toilets are available. There is no drinking water, and all garbage must be packed out. Leashed pets are permitted.

Reservations, fees: No reservations; no fee. Open June to mid-October.

Directions: From Lakeview drive five miles north on U.S. 395 to Highway 140. Turn right (east) on Highway 140 and drive six miles to Forest Road 3915. Turn right on Forest Road 3915 and drive 14 miles to Deep Creek and the campground entrance road on the right (Forest Road 4015). Turn right and drive one mile to the campground

Contact: Fremont National Forest, Lakeview Ranger District, HC 64, Box 60, Lakeview, OR 97630; tel. (541) 947-3334; fax (541) 947-6375.

WHY CAMPERS SHOULD HANG
THEIR FOOD IN TREES

TOM FURRER

MAP E4

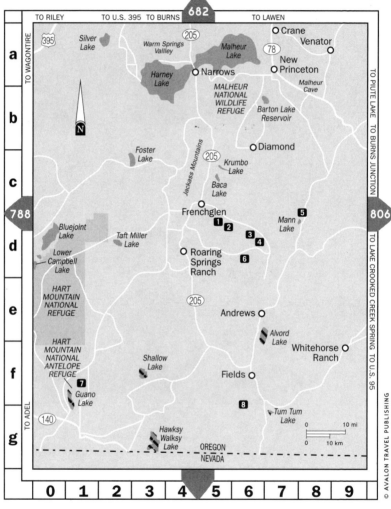

TO RILEY   TO U.S. 395   TO BURNS   TO LAWEN

682

TO WAGONTIRE

395

Silver Lake

Warm Springs Vallley

Malheur Lake

Crane

Venator

78

New Princeton

Harney Lake

Narrows

MALHEUR NATIONAL WILDLIFE REFUGE

Malheur Cave

Barton Lake Reservoir

N

Foster Lake

Jackass Mountains

205

Krumbo Lake

Diamond

Baca Lake

788

Frenchglen

1
2

3
4

Mann Lake

5

806

Bluejoint Lake

Taft Miller Lake

Roaring Springs Ranch

6

TO PIUTE LAKE   TO BURNS JUNCTION   TO LAKE CROOKED CREEK SPRING   TO U.S. 95

Lower Campbell Lake

HART MOUNTAIN NATIONAL REFUGE

205

Andrews

HART MOUNTAIN NATIONAL ANTELOPE REFUGE

Alvord Lake

Whitehorse Ranch

Shallow Lake

Fields

TO ADEL

140

7

Guano Lake

8

Tum Tum Lake

0   10 mi
0   10 km

Hawksy Walksy Lake

OREGON
NEVADA

0   1   2   3   4   5   6   7   8   9

© AVALON TRAVEL PUBLISHING

CHAPTER E4

🔢 Steens Mountain Resort

 9

The self-proclaimed "gateway to the Steens Mountains," this resort is bordered by the Malheur National Wildlife Refuge on three sides, and has great views. The mile-high mountain and surrounding gorges make an excellent photo opportunity. Hiking and hunting are other possibilities in the area. Fishing is available on the Blitzen River, with easy access from the camp.

Location: On the Blitzen River; map E4, grid d5.

Campsites, facilities: There are 99 sites for tents, trailers, or RVs, plus five cabins. Drinking water, rest rooms, showers, a sanitary dump station, a public phone, laundry facilities, and ice are available. Leashed pets are permitted.

Reservations, fees: Reservations recommended. Sites are $10-18 per night; cabins are $55 per night. Open year-round.

Directions: From Burns drive east on Highway 78 for two miles to Highway 205. Turn south on Highway 205 and drive 60 miles to Frenchglen and Steens Mountain Road. Turn east and drive three miles to the resort.

Contact: Steens Mountain Resort, North Loop Road, Frenchglen, OR 97738; tel. (541) 493-2415.

🔢 Page Springs   7

This campground is adjacent to Page Springs and the Malheur National Wildlife Refuge. The Frenchglen Hotel (2.5 miles away) is administered by the state parks department and offers overnight accommodations and meals. Activities include hiking on the trails in the area, plus bird-watching, fishing, hunting, and sight-seeing.

Location: Near Malheur National Wildlife Refuge; map E4, grid d5.

Campsites, facilities: There are 36 sites for tents, trailers, or RVs up to 35 feet long. Picnic tables, garbage service, and fire grills are provided. Drinking water, firewood, and vault toilets are available. Some facilities are wheelchair accessible. Leashed pets are permitted.

Reservations, fees: No reservations accepted. Sites are $6 per vehicle per night, with a 14-day stay limit. Open year-round.

Directions: From Burns drive east on Highway 78 for two miles to Highway 205. Turn south on Highway 205 and drive 60 miles to Frenchglen and Steens Mountain Loop Road. Turn east and drive three miles to the campground.

Contact: Bureau of Land Management, Burns District, HC 74-12533, Highway 20 West, Hines, OR 97738; tel. (541) 573-4400; fax (541) 573-4411; website: www.or.blm.gov/.

❸ Fish Lake   8

The shore of Fish Lake is the setting for this primitive but pretty camp among the aspens, elevation 7,400 feet. Not known to many, it can make an excellent weekend-getaway spot for backpacking and sight-seeing. Trout fishing is an option, made easier by the boat ramp near camp.

Location: On Fish Lake; map E4, grid d6.

Campsites, facilities: There are 23 sites for tents, trailers, or RVs up to 35 feet long. Picnic tables, garbage bins, and fire grills are provided. Drinking water, firewood, and vault toilets are available. Boat launching facilities are nearby (non-motorized boats only). Some facilities are wheelchair accessible. Leashed pets are permitted.

Reservations, fees: No reservations accepted. Sites are $6 per vehicle a night, with a 14-day stay limit. Open from June through October, weather permitting.

Directions: From Burns drive east on Highway 78 for two miles to Highway 205. Turn south on Highway 205 and drive 60 miles to Frenchglen and Steens Mountain Loop Road. Turn east and drive 20 miles to the campground.

Contact: Bureau of Land Management, Burns District, HC 74-12533, Highway 20 West, Hines, OR 97738; tel. (541) 573-4400; fax (541) 573-4411; website: www.or.blm.gov/.

❹ Jackman Park   8

Set at 8,100 feet in the eastern Oregon desert, this is one of four camps in the area. Fish Lake is 2.5 miles away. This scenic campground has aspen and willow trees. It's often used as an overflow camp for Fish Lake.

Location: Near Malheur National Wildlife Refuge; map E4, grid d7.

Campsites, facilities: There are six primitive sites for tents, trailers, or RVs up to 35 feet long. Picnic tables are provided. Firewood, drinking water, and pit toilets are available. Leashed pets are permitted.

Reservations, fees: No reservations accepted. Sites are $6 per vehicle a night, with a 14-day stay limit. Open from July to late October, weather permitting.

Directions: From Burns drive east on Highway 78 for two miles to Highway 205. Turn south on Highway 205 and drive 60 miles to Frenchglen and Steens Mountain Loop Road. Turn east and drive 22 miles to the campground

Contact: Bureau of Land Management, Hines District, 74-12533 Highway 20 West, Hines, OR 97738; tel. (541) 573-4400; fax (541) 573-4411, website: www.or.blm.gov/.

❺ Mann Lake   8

There are two small boat ramps, and a 10 horsepower limit on motors. Fishing, including wintertime ice fishing, and wildlife viewing are popular here. Weather can be extreme. The campground sits at the base of Steens Mountains, and is open, with sagebrush and no trees. The scenic, high desert camp is mainly used as a fishing camp. Fishing can be very good for cutthroat trout.

Location: on Mann Lake; map E4, grid c8.

Campsites, facilities: There are dispersed sites for tents, trailers, or RVs of up to 35 feet; open areas on each side of the lake. No drinking water is available, but vault toilets, with wheelchair access and boat ramps are. Pack out all garbage. Leashed pets are permitted.

Reservations, fees: No reservations accepted. There is a no fee. Open year-round.

Directions: From Burns drive southeast on Highway 78 for 65 miles to Fields/Denio Road (Harney County Road 201). Turn south (right) and drive 22 miles to the campground at Mann Lake.

Contact: Bureau of Land Management, Hines District, HC 74-12533 Highway 20 West, Hines, OR 97738; tel. (541) 573-4400; fax (541) 573-4411.

6 South Steens   6

Redband trout fishing is a mile away at Donner und Blitzen River and its tributaries. This campground caters to horse campers. Riding and hiking trails can be accessed from the campground. Campground is set up so that horse campers are in a separate area from the other campers.

Location: near Donner und Blitzen River; map E4, grid d6.

Campsites, facilities: There are 36 sites for tents, trailers, or RVs of up to 35 feet; 15 of the sites are designated for horse campers. Picnic tables, hitching posts, and fire grills are provided. Drinking water, wheelchair-accessible vault toilets, two wheelchair-accessible sites, and garbage bins are available. Leashed pets are permitted.

Reservations, fees: No reservations accepted. There is a 14-day stay limit. Sites are $6 per vehicle per night. Open May through October, weather permitting.

Directions: From Burns drive east on Highway 78 for two miles to Highway 205. Turn south on Highway 205 and drive 60 miles to Frenchglen. Continue south on Highway 205 for 10 miles to Steens South Loop Road. Turn left (east) and drive 18 miles to the campground on the right.

Contact: Bureau of Land Management, Burns District, HC 74-12533 Highway 20 West, Hines, OR 97738; tel. (541) 573-4400; fax (541) 573-4411.

7 Hart Antelope Refuge

         6

This unusual refuge offers canyons and hot springs in a high desert area. There is no drinking water at the campground, but it can be obtained at the headquarters, which you pass on the way in. Some of Oregon's largest antelope herds roam this large area. The nearest place for supplies is in the town of Adel.

Location: Near Adel; map E4, grid f1.

Campsites, facilities: There are 12 primitive sites for tents, trailers, or RVs up to 20 feet long. Pit toilets are provided, but there is no drinking water. Leashed pets are permitted.

Reservations, fees: No reservations accepted. There is no fee. Open from May to November, with limited facilities in the winter.

Directions: From Lakeview drive north on U.S. 395 for five miles to Highway 140. Turn east on Highway 140 and drive 28 miles to Adel and the Plush-Hart Mountain Cutoff. Turn left (signed for Hart Antelope Refuge) and drive north for 43 miles (first paved, then gravel) to the refuge headquarters. Continue four miles to the campground (the road is often impassable in the winter).

Contact: Hart Antelope Refuge, P.O. Box 111, Lakeview, OR 97630; (541) 947-3315; fax (541) 947-4414.

🔢 Willow Creek Hot Springs   7

This campground can be difficult to find, and only the adventurous should attempt this trip. A very small campground with no privacy, the campsites are about 100 feet from the hot springs, which are two connected smaller pools. Despite its being out of the way, travelers from far and away find their way here. The surrounding scenery is rocky hills, not a flat expanse.

Location: near Whitehorse Butte; map E4, grid f6.

Campsites, facilities: There are four sites for tents, small trailers, or RVs. Fire rings are provided. Vault toilets are available. No drinking water is available, and all garbage must be packed out. Leashed pets are permitted.

Reservations, fees: No reservations. There is a no fee. Open year-round, weather permitting.

Directions: From Burns drive southeast on Highway 78 for 105 miles to Burns Junction and U.S. 95. Turn right (south) on U.S. 95 and drive 20 miles to Whitehorse Road. Turn right (southwest) and drive 21 miles (passing Whitehorse Ranch) and continue for 2.5 miles to a fork. Bear left and drive two miles to the campground.

Contact: Bureau of Land Management, Vale District, 100 Oregon Street, Vale, OR 97918-9630; tel. (541) 473-3144; fax (541) 473-6213.

MAP E5

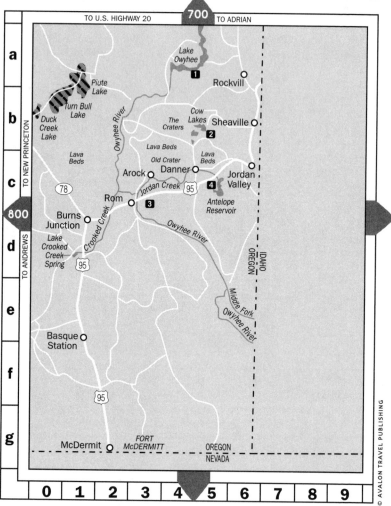

TO U.S. HIGHWAY 20   **700**   TO ADRIAN

TO NEW PRINCETON

TO ANDREWS

Lake Owyhee

Rockvill

Piute Lake

Turn Bull Lake

Duck Creek Lake

Owyhee River

The Craters

Cow Lakes

Sheaville

Lava Beds

Lava Beds

Old Crater

Lava Beds

78

Arock

Danner

Jordan Valley

Rom

Jordan Creek

95

Antelope Reservoir

Burns Junction

800

Lake Crooked Creek Spring

95

Crooked Creek

Owyhee River

IDAHO

OREGON

Middle Fork Owyhee River

Basque Station

95

McDermit

FORT McDERMITT

OREGON

NEVADA

© AVALON TRAVEL PUBLISHING

CHAPTER E5

1 Leslie Gulch-Slocum Creek   6

This campground is on the eastern shore of Owyhee Lake, not far from the Oregon/Idaho border. Warm-water fishing, waterskiing, and hiking are among the recreation options in this high desert area. Lake Owyhee State Park provides the other nearby recreation destination. There are no other campgrounds located within a one-hour drive.

Location: On Owyhee Lake; map E5, grid a4.

Campsites, facilities: There are 10 undeveloped sites for tents, trailers, or RVs up to 20 feet long. Picnic tables and garbage service are provided. Vault toilets are available. There is no drinking water. Boat launching facilities are available on site. Leashed pets are permitted.

Reservations, fees: No reservations accepted. There is no fee. The campground is open from mid-March to mid-November.

Directions: From U.S. 95 where it crosses the Idaho/Oregon border, drive south for five miles to McBride Creek Road. Turn northwest and drive one mile to Leslie Gulch Road. Turn left (west) and drive 15 miles to the campground.

Contact: Bureau of Land Management, Vale District, 100 Oregon Street, Vale, OR 97918-9630; tel. (541) 473-3144, fax (541) 473-6213.

2 Cow Lakes   6

This little used campground is adjacent to an old lava flow. The lake is shallow and murky, which makes fishing popular here. The campsites are open and treeless, and the road is rutted and rough in places.

Location: adjacent to Cow Lakes; map E5, grid b5.

Campsites, facilities: There are 10 sites for tents, small trailers, or RVs. Picnic tables and fire rings are provided. Vault toilets and a boat ramp are available. No drinking water is available, and all garbage must be packed out. Leashed pets are permitted.

Reservations, fees: No reservations. No fee. Open year-round, weather permitting.

Directions: From Burns drive east on U.S. 95 for 30 miles to Danner Loop Road. Turn left (north) and drive 14 miles (past Danner) to Cow Lakes and the campground.

Contact: Bureau of Land Management, Vale District, 100 Oregon Street, Vale, OR 97918-9630; tel. (541) 473-3144; fax (541) 473-6213.

3 Rome Launch   6

This campground is used mainly for people rafting the Owyhee River and overnighters passing through. A few cottonwood trees and sagebrush live in this campground. There are a few farms and ranches in the area. Campsites are adjacent to the Owyhee River. This is a good wildlife viewing area; mountain lions and bobcats have been spotted. The Owyhee Canyon itself is quite dramatic, like a miniature Grand Canyon; I once canoed from its headwaters in Nevada through Idaho and out to Oregon.

Location: on the Owyhee River; map E5, grid c3.

Campsites, facilities: There are five sites for tents, small trailers, or RVs. Picnic tables and fire rings are provided. Drinking water, vault toilets and a boat launch are available. No firewood is available, and all garbage must be packed out. Leashed pets are permitted.

Reservations, fees: No reservations; no fee. Open March through November, weather permitting.

Directions: From Burns drive east on U.S. 95 for 46 miles to Jordan Valley and the signed turnoff for Owyhee River and BLM-Rome boat launch. Turn south and drive one-quarter mile to the campground.

Contact: Bureau of Land Management, Vale District, 100 Oregon Street, Vale, OR 97918-9630; tel. (541) 473-3144; fax (541) 473-6213.

◢ Antelope Reservoir   3

The lake level fluctuates at this shallow lake and it can dry up. There is no tree cover in this open area on a slope above the reservoir. Be prepared for extreme weather. The campground gets little use except during the hunting season.

Location: on the Antelope Reservoir; map E5, grid c5.

Campsites, facilities: There are four sites for tents, small trailers, or RVs. Picnic tables and fire rings are provided. Vault toilets and boat access are available. No drinking water is available and all garbage must be packed out. Leashed pets are permitted.

Reservations, fees: No reservations; no fee. Open year-round, weather permitting.

Directions: From Burns drive east on U.S. 95 for 36 miles to the signed turnoff for Antelope Reservoir. Turn south and drive one mile to the campground on the left.

Contact: Bureau of Land Management, Vale District, 100 Oregon Street, Vale, OR 97918-9630; tel. (541) 473-3144; fax (541) 473-6213.

INDEX

BIRDWATCHING

CANOES/KAYAKS/ ROWBOATS/RAFTING

HORSEBACK RIDING/HORSE FACILITIES

MUSEUMS

OFF-ROAD VEHICLE (ORV) AREAS

SCUBA DIVING

TRAILS/TRAILHEADS

WINTER SPORTS

Tom Stienstra

Tom Stienstra has made it his life's work to explore the West, traveling 200 days a year camping, hiking, fishing, and boating, always searching for the best of the outdoors and writing about it. To complete this edition of *Pacific Northwest Camping,* he worked closely with Senior Research Editor Stephani Cruickshank and explored Washington and Oregon to find hidden spots. They also networked with three research editors and more than 250 field scouts across the Pacific Northwest.

Tom Stienstra is the nation's top-selling author of outdoor guidebooks. *The Oregonian,* Portland's daily newspaper, has twice named *Pacific Northwest Camping* as No. 1 on its bestseller list, and in 1999 Amazon.com honored his book *California Camping* as the No. 1 outdoor book in the nation. In the 1990s, Stienstra was twice named national Outdoor Writer of the Year, newspaper division, by the Outdoor Writers Association of America. His newspaper column is distributed weekly on the New York Times News Service and is accessible on the Internet at www.SFGate.com. He lives with his wife and two sons in the Pacific Northwest in the "state of Jefferson."

He can be reached directly on the internet at www.TomStienstra.com, where signed copies of his books with Foghorn Outdoors (listed below) are available.

Epic Trips of the West
California Wildlife (with illustrator Paul Johnson)
California Camping
California Hiking (with Ann Marie Brown)
California Fishing
California Recreational Lakes & Rivers
Tom Stienstra's Outdoor Getaway Guide: Northern California
Easy Camping in Northern California
Sunshine Jobs: Careeer Opportunities Working Outdoors

" When you're 90 percent done with a book, it means you only have 50 percent to go."

FOGHORN ✹ OUTDOORS

Founded in 1985, Foghorn Press has quickly become one of the country's premier publishers of outdoor recreation guidebooks. Foghorn Press books are available throughout the United States in bookstores and some outdoor retailers.

101 Great Hikes of the San Francisco Bay Area, 1st ed.	1-57354-068-4	$15.95
Alaska Fishing, 2nd ed.	0-935701-51-6	$20.95
America's Wilderness, 1st ed.	0-935701-47-8	$19.95
Arizona and New Mexico Camping, 3rd ed.	1-57354-044-7	$18.95
Atlanta Dog Lover's Companion, 1st ed.	1-57354-008-0	$17.95
Baja Camping, 3rd ed.	1-57354-069-2	$14.95
Bay Area Dog Lover's Companion, 3rd ed.	1-57354-039-0	$17.95
Boston Dog Lover's Companion, 2nd ed.	1-57354-074-9	$17.95
California Beaches, 2nd ed.	1-57354-060-9	$19.95
California Camping, 11th ed.	1-57354-053-6	$20.95
California Dog Lover's Companion, 3rd ed.	1-57354-046-3	$20.95
California Fishing, 5th ed.	1-57354-052-8	$20.95
California Golf, 9th ed.	1-57354-091-9	$24.95
California Hiking, 4th ed.	1-57354-056-0	$20.95
California Recreational Lakes and Rivers, 2nd ed.	1-57354-065-x	$19.95
California Waterfalls, 2nd ed.	1-57354-070-6	$17.95
California Wildlife: The Complete Guide, 1st ed.	1-57354-087-0	$16.95
Camper's Companion, 3rd ed.	1-57354-000-5	$15.95
Colorado Camping, 2nd ed.	1-57354-085-4	$18.95
Day-Hiking California's National Parks, 1st ed.	1-57354-055-2	$18.95
Easy Biking in Northern California, 2nd ed.	1-57354-061-7	$12.95
Easy Camping in Northern California, 2nd ed.	1-57354-064-1	$12.95
Easy Camping in Southern California, 1st ed.	1-57354-004-8	$12.95
Easy Hiking in Northern California, 2nd ed.	1-57354-062-5	$12.95
Easy Hiking in Southern California, 1st ed.	1-57354-006-4	$12.95
Florida Beaches, 1st ed.	1-57354-054-4	$19.95
Florida Camping, 1st ed.	1-57354-018-8	$20.95
Florida Dog Lover's Companion, 2nd ed.	1-57354-042-0	$20.95
Montana, Wyoming and Idaho Camping, 1st ed.	1-57354-086-2	$18.95
New England Camping, 2nd ed.	1-57354-058-7	$19.95
New England Hiking, 2nd ed.	1-57354-057-9	$18.95
Outdoor Getaway Guide: Southern CA, 1st ed.	1-57354-011-0	$14.95
Pacific Northwest Camping, 7th ed.	1-57354-080-3	$19.95
Pacific Northwest Hiking, 3rd ed.	1-57354-059-5	$20.95
Seattle Dog Lover's Companion, 1st ed.	1-57354-002-1	$17.95
Tahoe, 2nd ed.	1-57354-024-2	$20.95
Texas Dog Lover's Companion, 1st ed.	1-57354-045-5	$20.95
Texas Handbook, 4th ed.	1-56691-112-5	$18.95
Tom Stienstra's Outdoor Getaway Guide: No. CA, 3rd ed.	1-57354-038-2	$18.95
Utah and Nevada Camping, 1st ed.	1-57354-012-9	$18.95
Utah Hiking, 1st ed.	1-57354-043-9	$15.95
Washington Boating and Water Sports, 1st ed.	1-57354-071-4	$19.95
Washington Fishing, 3rd ed.	1-57354-084-6	$18.95
Washington, DC-Baltimore Dog Lover's Companion, 1st ed.	1-57354-041-2	$17.95

For more information, call 1-800-FOGHORN
email: info@travelmatters.com
or write to: Avalon Travel Publishing, Foghorn Outdoors
5855 Beaudry St., Emeryville, CA 94608

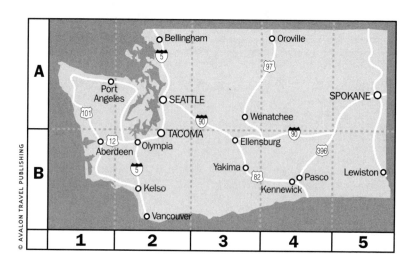

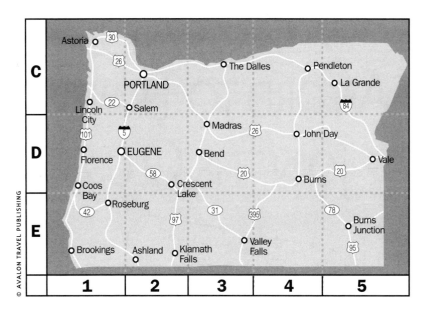

IF YOU CAN'T AFFORD TO TRAVEL, JOIN THE CLUB

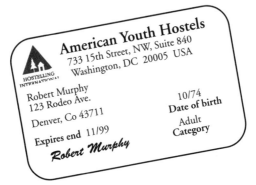